PEARSON ALWAYS LEARNING

Roger LeRoy Miller • Mushtaq Ahmad • Sam Fefferman
Lia Rizzo • George Sroka • Terry Sulyma

# Economics Today
## The Micro View

Updated Fourth Custom Edition

Taken from:
*Economics Today: The Macro View*, Fifth Canadian Edition
by Roger LeRoy Miller, Brenda Abbott, Sam Fefferman,
Ronald K. Kessler, and Terrence Sulyma

Cover Art: Courtesy of Faraways, Sai Yeung Chan, Fedor A. Sidorov, Twonix Studio/Shutterstock

Taken/Excerpts from:

*Economics Today: The Macro View*, Fifth Canadian Edition
by Roger LeRoy Miller, Brenda Abbott, Sam Fefferman, Ronald K. Kessler, and Terrence Sulyma


Pearson Learning Solutions, 330 Hudson Street, New York, New York 10013
A Pearson Education Company
www.pearsoned.com

Printed in the United States of America

1 17

000200010272128552

ES

PEARSON

ISBN 10: 1-323-81794-8
ISBN 13: 978-1-323-81794-0

*To my parents Abdullah & Mehraj, and brother Abbas, for their love and guidance. To Safia, Imran and Omar for their love and support.*

M.A.

*I would like to dedicate this book to Brenda, Tara, Amy, Shane, Brad, Kaitlyn, and Cohen. I am very fortunate to have the support of such a loving family.*

—S.F.

*To John and Mary Sulyma, for instilling in me a thirst for knowledge and love of learning. To Andrea, Drew, and Vanya for their love and support.*

—T.S.

# Brief Contents


| | | | |
|---|---|---|---|
| | | Preface | xix |
| | | Acknowledgments | xxiii |
| **Part 1** | | **Introduction** | **1** |
| | 1 | The Nature of Economics | 1 |
| | | APPENDIX A Reading and Working with Graphs | 21 |
| | 2 | Production Possibilities and Economic Systems | 29 |
| | | APPENDIX B The Production Possibilities Curve and Comparative Advantage | 56 |
| | 3 | Demand and Supply | 61 |
| **Part 2** | | **Dimensions of Microeconomics** | **92** |
| | 4 | Elasticity | 92 |
| | 5 | Market Efficiency and Market Failure | 112 |
| | 6 | Extensions of Demand, Supply, and Elasticity | 132 |
| | | APPENDIX C The Deadweight Loss Due to Government Market Intervention | 160 |
| | 7 | Consumer Choice | 164 |
| | | APPENDIX D More Advanced Consumer Choice Theory | 179 |
| | 8 | The Firm: Cost and Output Determination | 188 |
| **Part 3** | | **Market Structure and Resource Allocation** | **212** |
| | 9 | Perfect Competition | 212 |
| | 10 | Monopoly | 244 |
| | | APPENDIX E The Deadweight Loss Due to Monopoly | 274 |
| | 11 | Monopolistic Competition and Oligopoly | 279 |
| | 12 | Regulation and Competition Policy | 312 |
| **Part 4** | | **Productive Factors, Poverty, the Environment, and the Public Sector** | **336** |
| | 13 | Labour Demand and Supply | 336 |
| | 14 | Income and Poverty | 362 |
| | 15 | Environmental Economics | 378 |
| | 16 | The Public Sector | 396 |
| | | Answers to Odd-Numbered Problems | 417 |
| | | Answers to Business Applications | 432 |
| | | Answers to "For Critical Analysis" Questions | 435 |
| | | Glossary | 454 |
| | | Index | 460 |
| | | Credits | 474 |
| | | APPENDIX F ECON1110 NAIT-1 Microeconomics Problems, Reviews, and Sample Exams | 475 |
| | | Appendix F Provided by the Faculty at NAIT | |

# Contents


Preface xix
Acknowledgments xxiii

## Part 1 Introduction 1

### 1 The Nature of Economics 1

1.1 Scarcity 2
Scarcity and Wants 2
Scarcity and Resources 2
1.2 Defining Economics 3
EXAMPLE 1–1 **The Economics of Web Page Design** 3
Microeconomics versus Macroeconomics 4
The Power of Economic Analysis 4
1.3 Rational Decision Making 5
The Rationality Assumption 5
Opportunity Cost 5
EXAMPLE 1–2 **Is the Opportunity Cost of Finding a Mate Lower on the Internet?** 6
Making Decisions at the Margin 7
EXAMPLE 1–3 **What Does a Year at College Really Cost?** 7
Responding to Incentives 7
POLICY EXAMPLE 1–1 **International Smuggling and Counterfeiting** 8
Defining Self-Interest 9
EXAMPLE 1–4 **Nice Guys Can Finish First** 9
1.4 The Scientific Method 9
Models and Realism 10
Assumptions 10
EXAMPLE 1–5 **The Science behind COLD-fX** 11
Testing Models 11
Models of Behaviour, Not Thought Processes 12
EXAMPLE 1–6 **An Economic Model of Crime** 12
1.5 Positive versus Normative Economics 13
A Warning: Recognize Normative Analysis 13
1.6 Economic Policy and Socioeconomic Goals 14
Theory and Policy 14
ISSUES AND APPLICATIONS **Bottled Water: The Hummer of Beverages?** 15

APPENDIX A **Reading and Working with Graphs** 21
Direct and Inverse Relationships 21
Constructing a Graph 22
A Number Line 22
Combining Vertical and Horizontal Number Lines 22
Graphing Numbers in a Table 23
The Slope of a Line (A Linear Curve) 24
Slopes of Nonlinear Curves 26

| | | |
|---|---|---|
| 2 | **Production Possibilities and Economic Systems** | **29** |
| 2.1 | The Production Possibilities Curve | 30 |
| | The Production Possibilities Curve: An Example | 30 |
| 2.2 | Applications of the Production Possibilities Curve | 31 |
| | The Production Possibilities Curve, Scarcity, and Trade-Offs | 31 |
| | EXAMPLE 2–1 **Beware of "Free" Lecture Podcasts** | 32 |
| | The Production Possibilities Curve and Unemployment | 32 |
| | The Production Possibilities Curve and Efficiency | 33 |
| | EXAMPLE 2–2 **One Laptop per Child** | 33 |
| | The Production Possibilities Curve and Opportunity Cost | 34 |
| | POLICY EXAMPLE 2–1 **The Multi-Billion Dollar Park** | 35 |
| | The Production Possibilities Curve and Economic Growth | 36 |
| 2.3 | Consumption Goods versus Capital Goods | 37 |
| | Why We Make Capital Goods | 37 |
| | Forgoing Current Consumption | 37 |
| | The Trade-Off between Consumption Goods and Capital Goods | 37 |
| | EXAMPLE 2–3 **Canadian Post-Secondary Education Pays Off Big Time!** | 39 |
| 2.4 | Specialization and Greater Productivity | 40 |
| | Absolute Advantage | 40 |
| | Comparative Advantage | 40 |
| | Scarcity, Self-Interest, and Specialization | 41 |
| | EXAMPLE 2–4 **Specializing in Providing Baggage-Free Business Trips** | 41 |
| | Comparative Advantage and Trade among Nations | 41 |
| | The Division of Labour | 42 |
| 2.5 | Economic Systems | 42 |
| | Pure Command Economy | 43 |
| | Pure Capitalist Economy | 43 |
| | Mixed Economic Systems | 43 |
| 2.6 | Capitalism in More Depth | 44 |
| | Features of Capitalism | 44 |
| | POLICY EXAMPLE 2–2 **Canadian Politics: Right, Left, and Centre** | 45 |
| | Capitalism and the Three Economic Questions | 45 |
| | EXAMPLE 2–5 **India Has More Cellphones Than Toilets** | 46 |
| | ISSUES AND APPLICATIONS **Private or Public Auto Insurance: What Is Best for Canada?** | 47 |
| | APPENDIX B **The Production Possibilities Curve and Comparative Advantage** | 56 |
| | Before Specialization and Trade | 56 |
| | After Specialization and before Trade | 57 |
| | Opportunity Costs Incurred by the Pulets | 57 |
| | Opportunity Costs Incurred by the Dowbys | 57 |
| | Comparative Advantage Principle | 57 |
| | After Specialization and after Trade | 58 |
| | The Terms of Trade Principle | 58 |
| 3 | **Demand and Supply** | **61** |
| 3.1 | The Law of Demand | 62 |
| | Relative Prices versus Money Prices | 62 |
| | The Demand Schedule | 63 |
| | The Demand Curve | 63 |

| | | |
|---|---|---|
| | Individual versus Market Demand Curves | 64 |
| | EXAMPLE 3–1 **Why RFID Tags Are Catching On Fast** | 66 |
| 3.2 | Shifts in Demand | 66 |
| | The Other Determinants of Demand | 66 |
| | EXAMPLE 3–2 **A Recession Tale of Two Macs** | 67 |
| | EXAMPLE 3–3 **Brunettes Now Have More Fun** | 68 |
| | Changes in Demand versus Changes in Quantity Demanded | 69 |
| | EXAMPLE 3–4 **Garth Brooks, Used CDs, and the Law of Demand** | 70 |
| 3.3 | The Law of Supply | 71 |
| | The Supply Schedule | 71 |
| | The Supply Curve | 71 |
| | The Market Supply Curve | 71 |
| 3.4 | Shifts in Supply | 73 |
| | The Other Determinants of Supply | 74 |
| | EXAMPLE 3–5 **Surge in Electronics Sales Follows Dramatic Drop in LCD Prices** | 74 |
| | Changes in Supply versus Changes in Quantity Supplied | 75 |
| 3.5 | Putting Demand and Supply Together | 75 |
| | Demand and Supply Schedules Combined | 76 |
| | Demand and Supply Curves Combined | 77 |
| | Shortages | 77 |
| | Surpluses | 77 |
| 3.6 | Changes in Equilibrium | 78 |
| | Shifts in Demand or Supply | 78 |
| | EXAMPLE 3–6 **Chocoholics Beware** | 79 |
| | When Both Demand and Supply Shift | 80 |
| | EXAMPLE 3–7 **Shale Natural Gas: A Game Changer for Alberta?** | 82 |
| | ISSUES AND APPLICATIONS **A Canadian Housing Bubble?** | 83 |
| **Part 2** | **Dimensions of Microeconomics** | **92** |
| **4** | **Elasticity** | **92** |
| 4.1 | Price Elasticity | 93 |
| | Price Elasticity of Demand | 93 |
| | EXAMPLE 4–1 **"If They Doubled the Price, We'd Still Drink Coffee"** | 94 |
| | Calculating Elasticity | 94 |
| | EXAMPLE 4–2 **The Price Elasticity of Demand for a Tablet Device** | 95 |
| 4.2 | Price Elasticity Ranges | 95 |
| | POLICY EXAMPLE 4–1 **Who Pays Higher Cigarette Taxes?** | 96 |
| | Extreme Elasticities | 97 |
| | Elasticity and Total Revenues | 97 |
| | Labelling Elasticity | 98 |
| 4.3 | Determinants of the Price Elasticity of Demand | 100 |
| | Existence of Substitutes | 100 |
| | Share of Budget | 100 |
| | Time for Adjustment | 101 |
| | EXAMPLE 4–3 **What Do Real-World Price Elasticities of Demand Look Like?** | 102 |
| 4.4 | Cross-Elasticity of Demand | 103 |
| | POLICY EXAMPLE 4–2 **Do People Substitute Wireless Phone Services for Wired Services?** | 103 |
| | Income Elasticity of Demand | 104 |
| | EXAMPLE 4–4 **Frequent Flyer Miles as Income** | 104 |

4.5 Elasticity of Supply 105
Classifying Supply Elasticities 105
Determinants of the Elasticity of Supply 105
ISSUES AND APPLICATIONS **To Combat Cigarette Consumption, Should the Government Raise Taxes on Beer?** 107

5 **Market Efficiency and Market Failure** **112**

5.1 Market Efficiency 113
Consumer Surplus 113
EXAMPLE 5–1 **Price Discrimination: Do All Discounts Benefit the Consumer?** 114
Producer Surplus 115
Market Equilibrium and Allocative Efficiency 116
Market Failure 117
5.2 Externalities 117
External Costs 118
EXAMPLE 5–2 **What's Wrong with Alberta's Oil Sands?** 119
External Benefits 120
POLICY EXAMPLE 5–1 **Why Should the Public Financially Support Higher Education?** 121
5.3 Asymmetric Information 121
Moral Hazard 121
5.4 Non-excludable Goods and Services 122
Public Goods 122
POLICY EXAMPLE 5–2 **Should Our Tax Dollars Pay for Own the Podium?** 123
Common Property Resources 123
POLICY EXAMPLE 5–3 **A Global Trade Ban on the Porsche of the Oceans?** 123
ISSUES AND APPLICATIONS **The Great Global Recession of 2009** 124

6 **Extensions of Demand, Supply, and Elasticity** **132**

6.1 The Price System 133
Exchange and Markets 133
Transaction Costs 133
The Role of the Intermediary 134
EXAMPLE 6–1 **Booking Your Airline Flight—An Agent? Or the Web?** 134
The Rationing Function of Prices 134
The Essential Role of Rationing 135
EXAMPLE 6–2 **Is Ticketmaster in Cahoots with Scalpers?** 136
6.2 Price Ceilings and Price Floors 137
Price Ceilings: Rent Controls 137
POLICY EXAMPLE 6–1 **Assisted Human Reproduction Not for Sale in Canada?** 140
Price Floors: Minimum Wage 140
POLICY EXAMPLE 6–2 **Do Minimum Wage Rates Benefit Canadian Workers?** 142
6.3 Price Supports: Offer to Purchase and Marketing Boards 142
Offer-to-Purchase Policy 143
Marketing Board Policy 143
POLICY EXAMPLE 6–3 **The Beginning of the End for the Canadian Wheat Board?** 145
6.4 Quantity Restrictions 146
POLICY EXAMPLE 6–4 **Could Legalizing Marijuana Reduce Mexican Drug Violence?** 146

| | | |
|---|---|---|
| 6.5 | Elasticity and Excise Taxes | 147 |
| | The Effects of a Per-Unit Tax on Market Supply | 147 |
| | Tax Incidence | 148 |
| | Elasticity and Tax Incidence | 148 |
| | Elasticity and Resource Allocation | 149 |
| | Elasticity and Government Tax Revenue | 150 |
| | POLICY EXAMPLE 6–5 **An Excise Tax on Music Piracy?** | 150 |
| | ISSUES AND APPLICATIONS **For-Profit Health Care in Canada?** | 151 |
| | APPENDIX C **The Deadweight Loss Due to Government Market Intervention** | 160 |
| | Market Equilibrium and Allocative Efficiency | 160 |
| | Price Ceiling Policies and Allocative Inefficiency | 161 |
| | Price Floor Policies and Allocative Inefficiency | 161 |
| **7** | **Consumer Choice** | **164** |
| 7.1 | Utility Theory | 165 |
| | Utility and Utils | 165 |
| | Total and Marginal Utility | 166 |
| | Applying Marginal Analysis to Utility | 166 |
| | Graphic Analysis | 166 |
| | Marginal Utility | 167 |
| 7.2 | Diminishing Marginal Utility | 168 |
| | EXAMPLE 7–1 **Newspaper Vending Machines versus Candy Vending Machines** | 168 |
| | Optimizing Consumption Choices | 169 |
| | A Little Math | 170 |
| | How a Price Change Affects Consumer Optimum | 171 |
| | The Demand Curve Revisited | 171 |
| | Marginal Utility, Total Utility, and the Diamond–Water Paradox | 172 |
| | EXAMPLE 7–2 **The Price of Water in Saudi Arabia** | 173 |
| | Behavioural Economics and Consumer Choice Theory | 173 |
| | ISSUES AND APPLICATIONS **Contingent Valuation: Pricing the "Priceless"** | 174 |
| | APPENDIX D **More Advanced Consumer Choice Theory** | 179 |
| | On Being Indifferent | 179 |
| | Properties of Indifference Curves | 180 |
| | Downward Slope | 180 |
| | Curvature | 180 |
| | The Marginal Rate of Substitution | 181 |
| | The Indifference Map | 182 |
| | The Budget Constraint | 183 |
| | Slope of the Budget Constraint | 183 |
| | Consumer Optimum Revisited | 184 |
| | Effects of Changes in Income | 184 |
| | The Price-Consumption Curve | 185 |
| | Deriving the Demand Curve | 186 |
| **8** | **The Firm: Cost and Output Determination** | **188** |
| 8.1 | The Profits of a Firm | 189 |
| | Opportunity Cost of Capital | 189 |
| | Opportunity Cost of Owner-Provided Labour and Capital | 190 |
| | POLICY EXAMPLE 8–1 **Nonprofit Firms Join in the Quest for Profits** | 190 |
| | Accounting Profits versus Economic Profits | 190 |
| | The Goal of the Firm: Profit Maximization | 191 |

8.2 Short Run versus Long Run 191
The Firm 191
The Relationship between Output and Inputs 192
EXAMPLE 8–1 **China's Increasing Labour Costs** 193
The Production Function: A Numerical Example 193
Average and Marginal Physical Product 195
Diminishing Marginal Returns 195
Measuring Diminishing Returns 195
An Example of the Law of Diminishing Returns 196
8.3 Short-Run Costs to the Firm 196
Total Fixed Costs 196
Total Variable Costs 197
Short-Run Average Cost Curves 197
Marginal Cost 199
The Relationship between Average and Marginal Costs 199
Minimum Cost Points 200
EXAMPLE 8–2 **The Cost of Driving a Car** 200
8.4 The Relationship between Diminishing Marginal Returns and Cost Curves 201
Breakeven Analysis 203
8.5 Long-Run Cost Curves 203
Long-Run Average Cost Curve 203
Why the Long-Run Average Cost Curve Is U-Shaped 204
Reasons for Economies of Scale 205
Why a Firm Might Experience Diseconomies of Scale 205
EXAMPLE 8–3 **Economies of Scale at Dell** 206
Minimum Efficient Scale 206
ISSUES AND APPLICATIONS **Businesses Look Toward Costs To Determine Viability** 207

## Part 3 Market Structure and Resource Allocation 212

### 9 Perfect Competition 212

9.1 The Characteristics of Perfect Competition 213
Four Market Structures 213
The Perfectly Competitive Market Structure 213
EXAMPLE 9–1 **When Blogging Becomes a Competitive Business** 214
The Demand Curve of the Perfect Competitor 215
9.2 Determining Output and Profit in the Short Run 215
Total Revenues 216
Comparing Total Costs with Total Revenues 217
Using Marginal Analysis to Determine the Profit-Maximizing Rate of Production 217
When Are Profits Maximized? 218
POLICY EXAMPLE 9–1 **Quelling Fears of "Mad Cow Disease" in Asia** 218
Short-Run Profits 219
Minimizing Losses 220
EXAMPLE 9–2 **High Sunk Costs Can Mean Deep Discounts** 221
Calculating the Short-Run Breakeven Price 222
Calculating the Short-Run Shutdown Price 222
The Meaning of Zero Economic Profits 223
9.3 Short-Run Supply and Equilibrium 224
The Short-Run Industry Supply Curve 224
Factors That Influence the Industry Supply Curve 225

| | | |
|---|---|---|
| | Short-Run Equilibrium | 226 |
| | Short-Run Equilibrium for the Industry | 226 |
| | Short-Run Equilibrium for the Firm | 226 |
| | EXAMPLE 9–3 **U.S. Recession Takes Its Toll on Canadian Lumber Firms** | 227 |
| 9.4 | Long-Run Equilibrium | 228 |
| | Adjustments to Long-Run Equilibrium | 228 |
| 9.5 | Long-Run Industry Supply Curves | 230 |
| | Constant-Cost Industries | 230 |
| | Increasing-Cost Industries | 230 |
| | Decreasing-Cost Industries | 230 |
| | EXAMPLE 9–4 **The Big Rush to Provide Digital Snaps in a Snap** | 231 |
| | Long-Run Adjustments to Technological Change | 232 |
| 9.6 | Social Evaluation of Perfect Competition | 233 |
| | Perfect Competition and Productive Efficiency | 233 |
| | Perfect Competition and Allocative Efficiency | 233 |
| | Perfect Competition and a Normal Profit | 234 |
| | Possible Shortcomings of Perfect Competition | 234 |
| | Perfect Competition and Innovation | 235 |
| | ISSUES AND APPLICATIONS **Does the PEI Potato Industry Have a Future?** | 235 |
| **10** | **Monopoly** | **244** |
| 10.1 | The Characteristics of Monopoly | 245 |
| | Barriers to Entry | 245 |
| | EXAMPLE 10–1 **Microsoft's Abuse of Monopoly** | 247 |
| | Price and Revenue Behaviour under Monopoly | 248 |
| | Elasticity and Monopoly | 249 |
| | POLICY EXAMPLE 10–1 **Should Canada Post Remain a Monopoly—Or Does It Matter?** | 250 |
| 10.2 | Determining Output, Price, and Profit in Monopoly | 251 |
| | The Total Revenues–Total Costs Approach | 251 |
| | The Marginal Revenue–Marginal Cost Approach | 251 |
| | What Price to Charge for Output? | 252 |
| | Calculating Monopoly Profit | 253 |
| 10.3 | On Making Higher Profits: Price Discrimination | 254 |
| | Different Prices for Different Units of the Same Product | 255 |
| | POLICY EXAMPLE 10–2 **Forcing Individuals to Reveal How Much They Are Willing to Pay** | 255 |
| | Different Prices for Different Groups of Buyers of the Same Product | 257 |
| | EXAMPLE 10–2 **Pricing Internet Service to Maximize Profit** | 257 |
| | Necessary Conditions for Price Discrimination | 258 |
| 10.4 | Social Evaluation of Monopoly | 258 |
| | Monopoly and Allocative Efficiency | 258 |
| | EXAMPLE 10–3 **The High Cost of Staying Alive** | 260 |
| | Monopoly and Productive Efficiency | 261 |
| | Monopoly and Long-Run Excess Profit | 261 |
| | POLICY EXAMPLE 10–3 **Monopolies are Milking Canadian Food Consumers** | 261 |
| | Should All Monopolies Be Eliminated? | 262 |
| | POLICY EXAMPLE 10–4 **Swapping Songs on the Internet: Is It Really Free?** | 263 |

| | | |
|---|---|---|
| 10.5 | The Regulation of a Natural Monopoly | 264 |
| | The Pricing and Output Decision of the Natural Monopolist | 264 |
| | Regulation Using Marginal Cost Pricing | 265 |
| | Regulation Using Average Cost Pricing | 265 |
| | ISSUES AND APPLICATIONS **Is It Fair to Practise Price Discrimination in Higher Education?** | 266 |
| | APPENDIX E **The Deadweight Loss Due to Monopoly** | 274 |
| | Consumer Surplus | 274 |
| | Producer Surplus | 275 |
| | Allocative Efficiency and Perfect Competition | 276 |
| | Allocative Inefficiency and Monopoly | 276 |
| **11** | **Monopolistic Competition and Oligopoly** | **279** |
| 11.1 | The Characteristics of Monopolistic Competition | 280 |
| | Number of Firms | 280 |
| | Easy Entry | 281 |
| | Product Differentiation | 281 |
| | EXAMPLE 11–1 **A Canadian Retail Success: Thirty Years Running** | 281 |
| 11.2 | Short-Run Price, Output, and Profit in Monopolistic Competition | 283 |
| | The Individual Firm's Demand and Cost Curves | 283 |
| | Short-Run Equilibrium | 283 |
| 11.3 | Long-Run Equilibrium in Monopolistic Competition | 283 |
| | Comparing Monopolistic Competition with Perfect Competition | 284 |
| 11.4 | The Characteristics of Oligopoly | 285 |
| | Small Number of Firms | 285 |
| | Interdependence | 285 |
| | Barriers to Entry | 286 |
| | Measuring Industry Concentration | 286 |
| 11.5 | Price Behaviour in Oligopoly | 287 |
| | Some Basic Notions about Game Theory | 287 |
| | Noncooperative Price Behaviour | 288 |
| | EXAMPLE 11–2 **The Prisoners' Dilemma** | 288 |
| | Cooperative Price Behaviour | 290 |
| | POLICY EXAMPLE 11–1 **Sweet Deal Between Canadian Chocolate Bar Makers?** | 291 |
| | EXAMPLE 11–3 **OPEC Continues to Rule the World Oil Market?** | 291 |
| | Factors Conducive to Cooperative Price Behaviour | 293 |
| | EXAMPLE 11–4 **De Beers Diamond Cartel: A Thing of The Past?** | 293 |
| | Pricing to Deter Entry into an Industry | 294 |
| | POLICY EXAMPLE 11–2 **Turbulence in the Canadian Airline Industry** | 294 |
| | Price Wars | 295 |
| | EXAMPLE 11–5 **Wind Blows Down Canadian Wireless Prices** | 296 |
| 11.6 | Nonprice Forms of Competition in Oligopoly | 296 |
| | Product Differentiation | 297 |
| | EXAMPLE 11–6 **Can Advertising Lead to Efficiency?** | 297 |
| | Mergers | 298 |
| | Exclusive Dealing | 298 |
| | EXAMPLE 11–7 **Intel Bags Record Fine** | 298 |

| | | |
|---|---|---|
| | Raising Customers' Switching Costs | 299 |
| | EXAMPLE 11–8 **High Switching Costs in the Credit World** | 299 |
| | Network Effects | 299 |
| | EXAMPLE 11–9 **Facebook Frenzy** | 300 |
| | Innovation | 301 |
| | EXAMPLE 11–10 **Apple's iMania** | 301 |
| 11.7 | Social Evaluation of Oligopoly | 302 |
| | ISSUES AND APPLICATIONS **Game Theory: Opening Up the Brewing Industry** | 303 |
| **12** | **Regulation and Competition Policy** | **312** |
| 12.1 | Types of Government Regulation | 313 |
| | Economic Regulation | 313 |
| | EXAMPLE 12–1 **Deregulation Hits Canadian Phone Markets** | 315 |
| | Social Regulation | 316 |
| | POLICY EXAMPLE 12–1 **Can the CRTC Effectively Regulate Cable TV?** | 317 |
| | Creative Response and Feedback Effects: Results of Regulation | 317 |
| | EXAMPLE 12–2 **The Effectiveness of Auto Safety Regulation** | 318 |
| 12.2 | Explaining Regulators' Behaviour | 318 |
| | The Capture Hypothesis | 318 |
| | Share the Gains, Share the Pains | 319 |
| | Deregulation | 319 |
| 12.3 | Short-Run versus Long-Run Effects of Deregulation | 320 |
| | POLICY EXAMPLE 12–2 **Ontario's Feeble Attempt at Energy Deregulation** | 320 |
| | Deregulation and Contestable Markets | 321 |
| | Rethinking Regulation Using Cost–Benefit Analysis | 322 |
| | EXAMPLE 12–3 **Cutting Through the Red Tape** | 322 |
| 12.4 | How Competition Policy Benefits the Consumer | 323 |
| | The History of Anticombines Legislation | 323 |
| | Anti-Competitive Behaviour Prohibited by Competition Policy | 325 |
| | EXAMPLE 12–4 **HMV Boycotts Rolling Stones Products** | 327 |
| | EXAMPLE 12–5 **Suzy Shier Pays $1 Million to Settle Misleading Advertising Dispute** | 328 |
| | ISSUES AND APPLICATIONS **Media Concentration in Canada: A Public Concern?** | 329 |
| **Part 4** | **Productive Factors, Poverty, the Environment, and the Public Sector** | **336** |
| **13** | **Labour Demand and Supply** | **336** |
| 13.1 | Demand for Labour | 337 |
| | Competition in the Product Market | 337 |
| | Marginal Physical Product | 337 |
| | Why the Decline in MPP? | 338 |
| | Marginal Revenue Product | 338 |
| | General Rule for Hiring | 338 |
| | The MRP Curve: Demand for Labour | 340 |
| | Derived Demand | 340 |
| | The Market Demand for Labour | 341 |

| | | |
|---|---|---|
| | Reasons for Labour Demand Curve Shifts | 342 |
| | EXAMPLE 13–1 **Does It Pay to Study?** | 342 |
| | Determinants of Demand Elasticity for Inputs | 343 |
| 13.2 | Supply of Labour and Equilibrium | 344 |
| | Supply of Labour | 344 |
| | Determinants of the Supply of Labour | 344 |
| | POLICY EXAMPLE 13–1 **Should the Minimum Wage Be Raised to Help Young People?** | 345 |
| 13.3 | Union Goals and Labour Unions | 346 |
| | The Current Status of Labour Unions | 346 |
| | Unions and Collective Bargaining Contracts | 347 |
| | Strike: The Ultimate Bargaining Tool | 347 |
| | EXAMPLE 13–2 **Strike Activity in Canada** | 347 |
| | Union Goals | 348 |
| | Union Strategies | 348 |
| | Limiting Entry over Time | 349 |
| | Altering the Demand for Union Labour | 349 |
| | Have Unions Raised Wages? | 350 |
| | Can Unions Increase Productivity? | 351 |
| | The Benefits of Labour Unions | 351 |
| 13.4 | Pricing and Employment in Various Market Conditions | 352 |
| | Monopsony: A Buyer's Monopoly | 352 |
| | EXAMPLE 13–3 **Monopsony in College Sports** | 352 |
| | Marginal Factor Cost | 353 |
| | Derivation of a Marginal Factor Cost Curve | 353 |
| | Employment and Wages under Monopsony | 353 |
| | ISSUES AND APPLICATIONS **Canadian Wheat Board: Monopoly or Monopsony** | 356 |
| **14** | **Income and Poverty** | **362** |
| 14.1 | The Distribution of Wealth and Income | 363 |
| | Income | 363 |
| | Measuring Income Distribution: The Lorenz Curve | 363 |
| | Income Distribution in Canada | 364 |
| | EXAMPLE 14–1 **Increasing Income Inequality and Working Spouses** | 365 |
| | The Distribution of Wealth | 365 |
| | EXAMPLE 14–2 **Are We Running to Stay in Place?** | 366 |
| 14.2 | Determinants of Income Differences | 366 |
| | Age | 367 |
| | Marginal Productivity | 368 |
| | EXAMPLE 14–3 **Economics, Aging, and Productivity** | 369 |
| | Inheritance | 370 |
| | Discrimination | 370 |
| | Theories of Desired Income Distribution | 370 |
| | Productivity | 370 |
| | Equality | 371 |
| 14.3 | Poverty and Federal Income Support Programs | 371 |
| | EXAMPLE 14–4 **Poverty Rates in the European Union** | 372 |
| | Defining Poverty | 372 |
| | Transfer Payments as Income | 372 |
| | Attacks on Poverty: Major Federal Income | 372 |
| | Reduction in Poverty Rates | 374 |
| | ISSUES AND APPLICATIONS **Eradicating Child Poverty** | 374 |

| | | |
|---|---|---|
| **15** | **Environmental Economics** | **378** |
| 15.1 | Private versus Social Costs | 379 |
| | The Costs of Polluted Air | 379 |
| | Externalities | 380 |
| | Correcting for Externalities | 380 |
| | The 4 Rs—Reduce, Reuse, Recycle, and Recover | 381 |
| | Market Incentives | 381 |
| | EXAMPLE 15–1 **Carbon Offset Projects: Real or Just Hot Air?** | 381 |
| | Is a Uniform Tax Appropriate? | 382 |
| 15.2 | Pollution | 383 |
| | The Optimal Quantity of Pollution | 383 |
| | POLICY EXAMPLE 15–1 **Canada Confronts a High Marginal Cost of Pollution Abatement** | 384 |
| 15.3 | Common Property | 385 |
| | EXAMPLE 15–2 **Wind as a Renewable Resource** | 385 |
| | Voluntary Agreements and Transactions Costs | 386 |
| | Changing Property Rights | 387 |
| | EXAMPLE 15–3 **Not In My Backyard (NIMBY)!** | 387 |
| | Are There Alternatives to Pollution-Causing Resource Use? | 387 |
| | Wild Species, Common Property, and Trade-Offs | 388 |
| | EXAMPLE 15–4 **Preventing Overfishing by Trading Quotas** | 388 |
| 15.4 | Recycling | 389 |
| | EXAMPLE 15–5 **Reducing Waste by Recycling** | 389 |
| | Recycling's Invisible Costs | 389 |
| | Landfills | 389 |
| | EXAMPLE 15–6 **Are We Running Out of Everything?** | 390 |
| | Should We Save Scarce Resources? | 390 |
| | ISSUES AND APPLICATIONS **Climate Change: What Can Canada Do?** | 391 |
| **16** | **The Public Sector** | **396** |
| 16.1 | Economic Functions of Government | 397 |
| | POLICY EXAMPLE 16–1 **Who Should Pay the High Cost of a Legal System?** | 397 |
| | EXAMPLE 16–1 **Are Lighthouses a Public Good?** | 399 |
| 16.2 | The Political Functions of Government | 400 |
| | Merit and Demerit Goods | 400 |
| | POLICY EXAMPLE 16–2 **Do Government-Funded Sports Stadiums Have a Net Positive Effect on Local Economies?** | 400 |
| | Income Redistribution | 401 |
| | Collective Decision Making: The Theory of Public Choice | 401 |
| | Similarities in Market and Public-Sector Decision Making | 401 |
| | Differences between Market and Collective Decision Making | 402 |
| | The Role of Bureaucrats | 403 |
| | Gauging Bureaucratic Performance | 403 |
| | Rational Ignorance | 404 |
| 16.3 | Tax Rates and the Canadian Tax System | 404 |
| | Marginal and Average Tax Rates | 405 |
| | Taxation Systems | 405 |

POLICY EXAMPLE 16–3 **Tax Freedom Day around the World** 406
The Most Important Federal Taxes 406
The Federal Personal Income Tax 406
The Treatment of Capital Gains 407
The Corporate Income Tax 407
Unemployment and Pension Taxes 408
EXAMPLE 16–2 **Employment Insurance** 408
The Goods and Services Tax 408
Spending, Government Size, and Tax Receipts 409
Government Receipts 409
ISSUES AND APPLICATIONS **Should We Switch to a Flat Tax?** 410

Answers to Odd-Numbered Problems 417
Answers to Business Applications 432
Answers to "For Critical Analysis" Questions 435
Glossary 454
Index 460
Credits 474
APPENDIX F ECON1110 NAIT-1 Microeconomics Problems, Reviews, and Sample Exams 475
Appendix F Provided by the Faculty at NAIT

# Preface

## From the Authors

In creating *Economics Today: The Micro View*, Fifth Canadian Edition, substantial revisions to the previous edition were made, based on the helpful suggestions and comments provided by adopters and reviewers. We were careful to ensure that any changes we made to the fifth edition would maintain the straightforward and approachable style that has made this book so popular in postsecondary institutions across Canada.

As instructors with extensive teaching experience in both college and university settings, we want to continue to present a text that students can relate to based on their personal, social, and career interests. We also hope that this book will encourage students to broaden their interests to include local, national, and global economic issues. Many of our students will not take subsequent economics courses; in that case, we want them to be ready for the world, and not just for intermediate economics courses.

The approach used in *Economics Today: The Micro View*, Fifth Canadian Edition, is based on the belief that students learn more when they are involved and engaged in the material they are studying. The presentation of issues and applications in a Canadian setting is a major strength of this text. Each chapter begins with an issue that introduces certain economic principles; those principles are presented throughout the chapter, and at the end of the chapter an Issues and Applications section explains how those principles can be applied to that issue. This section ends with For Critical Analysis questions, which help reinforce the theory at hand and encourage students to reflect on economics in the "real" world—their world.

In addition, each chapter contains numerous short Examples and Policy Examples that further illustrate the points being made in the text. Each of these examples is accompanied by For Critical Analysis questions, which encourage students to actively apply the economic principles presented in the chapter. Mindful of the importance of global events to Canada's economic well-being, we have used many examples and issues that connect Canada with the rest of the world. Suggested solutions to all of the For Critical Analysis questions are provided at the end of the text.

The text's emphasis on real world current socioeconomic issues provides for numerous engaging student assessment activities, including critical thinking exercises, Internet and paper-based research projects, student group debates, online discussions, blogs, and wikis. By encouraging each student to learn to analyze an issue from numerous viewpoints, the text helps develop critical analysis and advocacy skills that will prove invaluable in future employment situations.

For the Fifth Canadian Edition we have reorganized and consolidated chapter material, updated numerous Issues and Applications and Example boxes, included additional Canadian and international comparisons and examples, and added new end-of-chapter questions and exercises.

Below is a sample of some of the new issues and examples discussed in the Fifth Canadian Edition:

- Nice Guys Can Finish First (Example 1-4)
- Beware of "Free" Lecture Podcasts (Example 2-1)
- A Canadian Housing Bubble? (Chapter 3 Issues and Applications)
- The Great Global Recession of 2009 (Chapter 5 Issues and Applications)
- Is Ticketmaster in Cohoots with Scalpers? (Example 6-2)
- When Blogging Becomes a Competitive Business (Example 9-1)
- The High Cost of Staying Alive (Example 10-3)
- Wind Blows Down Canadian Wireless Prices (Example 11-5)

In addition, we have made several important changes to the chapter content.

As suggested by reviewers, we have removed the former Chapter 7, "Rents, Profit, and Financial Environment of Business," as this does not directly relate to the key microeconomic topics typically covered in a Principles of Microeconomics course.

The two labour chapters—Chapter 13 "Labour Demand and Supply" and Chapter 14 "Unions and Labour Market Monopoly Power"—have been combined into one chapter by streamlining the concepts covered.

A new chapter entitled "Market Efficiency and Market Failure" has been added, which follows the chapter covering elasticity. This new chapter introduces key concepts such as consumer surplus, producer surplus, and deadweight loss, which provides the option of more rigorously assessing the efficiency losses related to different types of market failure and government policies. In subsequent chapters new appendices have been added that apply these key concepts to situations of market failure and government policies covered in the main body of the chapter. **Those who wish to proceed to subsequent chapters without covering this new content can easily do so, without any loss of continuity.**

In the end, we believe that *Economics Today: The Micro View* and MyEconLab will provide students with a relevant and interesting resource—one that will present students with a "window to the world" that will help them in their personal lives as citizens and professionals. We hope that you will enjoy this book and begin to appreciate the many ways in which economics can be a part of your day-to-day activities.

# Economic Principles in Practice

**CHAPTER OPENING ISSUES.** Each opening issue motivates student interest in the key chapter concepts. The issue presented is revisited in the Issues and Applications section at the culmination of the chapter.

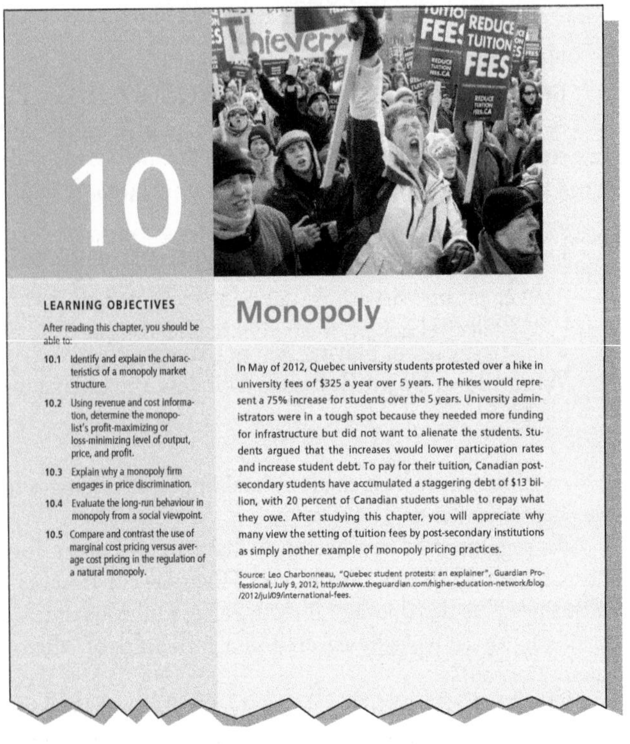

10

## Monopoly

LEARNING OBJECTIVES

After reading this chapter, you should be able to:

10.1 Identify and explain the characteristics of a monopoly market structure.

10.2 Using revenue and cost information, determine the monopolist's profit-maximizing or loss-minimizing level of output, price, and profit.

10.3 Explain why a monopoly firm engages in price discrimination.

10.4 Evaluate the long-run behaviour in monopoly from a social viewpoint.

10.5 Compare and contrast the use of marginal cost pricing versus average cost pricing in the regulation of a natural monopoly.

In May of 2012, Quebec university students protested over a hike in university fees of $325 a year over 5 years. The hikes would represent a 75% increase for students over the 5 years. University administrators were in a tough spot because they needed more funding for infrastructure but did not want to alienate the students. Students argued that the increases would lower participation rates and increase student debt. To pay for their tuition, Canadian post-secondary students have accumulated a staggering debt of $13 billion, with 20 percent of Canadian students unable to repay what they owe. After studying this chapter, you will appreciate why many view the setting of tuition fees by post-secondary institutions as simply another example of monopoly pricing practices.

Source: Leo Charbonneau, "Quebec student protests: an explainer", Guardian Professional, July 9, 2012, http://www.theguardian.com/higher-education-network/blog/2012/jul/09/international-fees.

**ISSUES AND APPLICATIONS.** The Issues and Applications feature is designed to encourage students not just to apply economic concepts, but also to think critically about them. Each begins with the concepts being applied and is followed by For Critical Analysis questions that could be used to prompt in-class discussions. Suggested answers to these questions are given at the back of the text, as well as in the Instructor's Manual at the end of the appropriate chapter.

ISSUES AND APPLICATIONS

## Media Concentration in Canada: A Public Concern?

Concepts Applied: Regulation, Competition Policy, Media Concentration and the Public Interest

CanWest Global's newspaper, the *National Post*, competes with Canada's only other major national newspaper, *The Globe and Mail*, owned by BCE. CanWest and BCE have substantial media holdings in Canada. Does media concentration threaten editorial diversity?

### A Decade of Mega-Takeovers and Mergers

Over the past decade, Canada has experienced a significant increase in concentration in its various media industries, as noted below.

In mid 1996, Conrad Black, publisher of almost 650 newspapers worldwide, approached the Competition Bureau for approval of his plan to acquire 50.7 percent of Southam Incorporated, publisher of 32 Canadian daily papers. After the Bureau gave its consent, Mr. Black's company, Hollinger Inc., became the largest newspaper publisher in Canada. Subsequent to the acquisition, Hollinger owned 59 of the 105 daily newspapers in Canada, including all the dailies in Saskatchewan, Prince Edward Island, and Newfoundland. Shortly after, Mr. Black purchased the *Financial Post* and incorporated it in his new national newspaper, the *National Post*, which debuted on October 27, 1998.

On November 3, 2000, The Competition Bureau announced that it would not challenge the $3.2 billion acquisition by CanWest Global of the majority of Hollinger's Canadian media interests. As a result, on November 15, 2000, CanWest became the largest daily newspaper publisher in Canada and one of the country's leading international multimedia news, information, and entertainment providers. Immediately after its Hollinger

In addition to its newspaper holdings, CanWest Global owns Canada's Global Television Network, which broadcasts over the air via 11 television stations, licensed in eight provinces, and reaches 94 percent of English-speaking Canada. CanWest also owns Canada.com, which is one of Canada's largest Internet news sites.

In December 2000, the CRTC allowed BCE to buy the CTV network, a decision that created Canada's largest communications company—Bell Globemedia, later known as CTV Globemedia (CTVgm). The CTV purchase closely followed BCE's acquisition of *The Globe and Mail*. In securing the ownership of CTV, BCE promised the CRTC that it would pump over $200 million into Canadian broadcasting during the next seven years. The CRTC has stipulated that $140 million of these monies should go into drama and documentary production created by independent Canadian writers and producers.

On July 5, 2001, the CRTC approved Quebecor Inc.'s purchase of the TVA television network, the dominant firm in the Quebec television broadcasting market. Prior to the CRTC decision, Quebecor had already accumulated significant Canadian media assets including Videotron, the largest cable TV producer in Quebec, and Sun Media, the second-largest newspaper group in Canada, with eight metropolitan dailies, eight community dailies, and 175 local weeklies and specialty publications. As in the

**POLICY EXAMPLES.** Many of the economic debates reported in the media involve important policy issues. Here, students are presented with various key policy questions on both the domestic and international fronts. Each Policy Example is followed by a For Critical Analysis question that encourages students to consider exactly what is involved in the discussion and what the further ramifications might be. Suggested solutions to these questions are provided at the back of the text and in the Instructor's Manual.

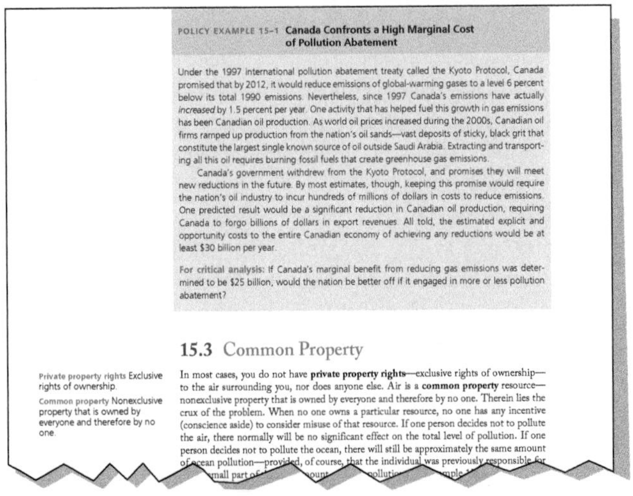

POLICY EXAMPLE 15-1 **Canada Confronts a High Marginal Cost of Pollution Abatement**

Under the 1997 international pollution abatement treaty called the Kyoto Protocol, Canada promised that by 2012, it would reduce emissions of global-warming gases to a level 6 percent below its total 1990 emissions. Nevertheless, since 1997 Canada's emissions have actually *increased* by 1.5 percent per year. One activity that has helped fuel this growth in gas emissions has been Canadian oil production. As world oil prices increased during the 2000s, Canadian oil firms ramped up production from the nation's oil sands—vast deposits of sticky, black grit that constitute the largest single known source of oil outside Saudi Arabia. Extracting and transporting all this oil requires burning fossil fuels that create greenhouse gas emissions.

Canada's government withdrew from the Kyoto Protocol, and promises they will meet new reductions in the future. By most estimates, though, keeping this promise would require the nation's oil industry to incur hundreds of millions of dollars in costs to reduce emissions. One predicted result would be a significant reduction in Canadian oil production, requiring Canada to forgo billions of dollars in export revenues. All told, the estimated explicit and opportunity costs to the entire Canadian economy of achieving any reductions would be at least $30 billion per year.

For critical analysis: If Canada's marginal benefit from reducing gas emissions was determined to be $25 billion, would the nation be better off if it engaged in more or less pollution abatement?

### 15.3 Common Property

Private property rights Exclusive rights of ownership.

Common property Nonexclusive property that is owned by everyone and therefore by no one.

In most cases, you do not have **private property rights**—exclusive rights of ownership—to the air surrounding you, nor does anyone else. Air is a **common property** resource—nonexclusive property that is owned by everyone and therefore by no one. Therein lies the crux of the problem. When no one owns a particular resource, no one has any incentive (conscience aside) to consider misuse of that resource. If one person decides not to pollute the air, there normally will be no significant effect on the total level of pollution. If one person decides not to pollute the ocean, there will still be approximately the same amount of ocean pollution—provided, of course, that the individual was previously responsible for

**EXAMPLES.** Many thought-provoking and relevant examples highlight Canadian, as well as international, events and demonstrate economic principles. The For Critical Analysis questions that follow encourage students to apply the knowledge and information gained from the example. Possible answers to the questions are provided at the back of the text and in the Instructor's Manual.

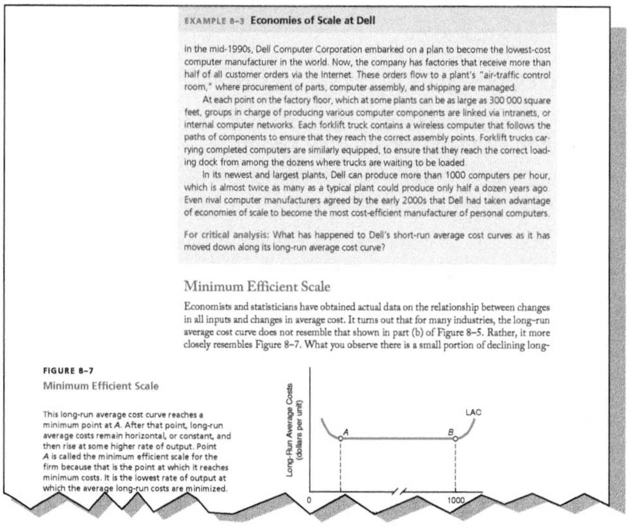
EXAMPLE 8–3 **Economies of Scale at Dell**

In the mid-1990s, Dell Computer Corporation embarked on a plan to become the lowest-cost computer manufacturer in the world. Now, the company has factories that receive more than half of all customer orders via the Internet. These orders flow to a plant's "air-traffic control room," where procurement of parts, computer assembly, and shipping are managed.

At each point on the factory floor, which at some plants can be as large as 300 000 square feet, groups in charge of producing various computer components are linked via intranets, or internal computer networks. Each forklift truck contains a wireless computer that follows the paths of components to ensure that they reach the correct assembly points. Forklift trucks carrying completed computers are similarly equipped, to ensure that they reach the correct loading dock from among the dozens where trucks are waiting to be loaded.

In its newest and largest plants, Dell can produce more than 1000 computers per hour, which is almost twice as many as a typical plant could produce only half a dozen years ago. Even rival computer manufacturers agreed by the early 2000s that Dell had taken advantage of economies of scale to become the most cost-efficient manufacturer of personal computers.

For critical analysis: What has happened to Dell's short-run average cost curves as it has moved down along its long-run average cost curve?

Minimum Efficient Scale

Economists and statisticians have obtained actual data on the relationship between changes in all inputs and changes in average cost. It turns out that for many industries, the long-run average cost curve does not resemble that shown in part (b) of Figure 8–5. Rather, it more closely resembles Figure 8–7. What you observe there is a small portion of declining long-

FIGURE 8–7
Minimum Efficient Scale

This long-run average cost curve reaches a minimum point at *A*. After that point, long-run average costs remain horizontal, or constant, and then rise at some higher rate of output. Point *A* is called the minimum efficient scale for the firm because that is the point at which it reaches minimum costs. It is the lowest rate of output at which the average long-run costs are minimized.



**BUSINESS APPLICATIONS.** New to the Fifth Canadian Edition, a comprehensive business-related problem is presented at the end of each chapter. This pedagogical activity has two major purposes. Each problem applies chapter concepts to relevant real-life business situations. After a student has worked through a number of these business applications, he or she will begin to appreciate the broad range of business careers that are available in the functional areas of accounting, finance, marketing, and management.

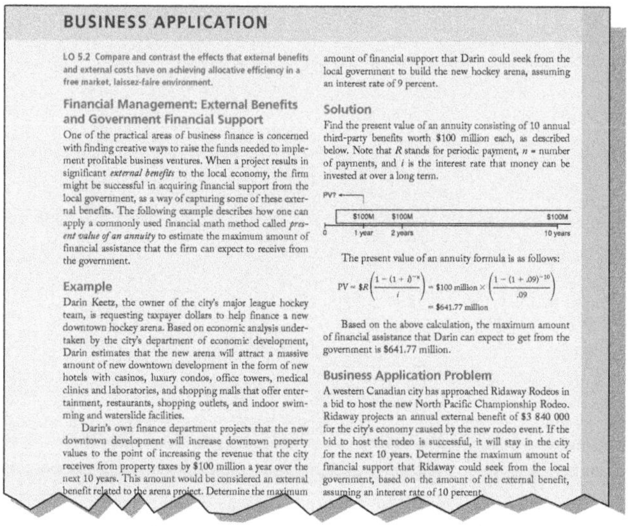
BUSINESS APPLICATION

LO 5.2 Compare and contrast the effects that external benefits and external costs have on achieving allocative efficiency in a free market, laissez-faire environment.

Financial Management: External Benefits and Government Financial Support

One of the practical areas of business finance is concerned with finding creative ways to raise the funds needed to implement profitable business ventures. When a project results in significant *external benefits* to the local economy, the firm might be successful in acquiring financial support from the local government, as a way of capturing some of these external benefits. The following example describes how one can apply a commonly used financial math method called *present value of an annuity* to estimate the maximum amount of financial assistance that the firm can expect to receive from the government.

Example

Darin Keetz, the owner of the city's major league hockey team, is requesting taxpayer dollars to help finance a new downtown hockey arena. Based on economic analysis undertaken by the city's department of economic development, Darin estimates that the new arena will attract a massive amount of new downtown development in the form of new hotels with casinos, luxury condos, office towers, medical clinics and laboratories, and shopping malls that offer entertainment, restaurants, shopping outlets, and indoor swimming and waterslide facilities.

Darin's own finance department projects that the new downtown development will increase downtown property values to the point of increasing the revenue that the city receives from property taxes by $100 million a year over the next 10 years. This amount would be considered an external benefit related to the arena project. Determine the maximum amount of financial support that Darin could seek from the local government to build the new hockey arena, assuming an interest rate of 9 percent.

Solution

Find the present value of an annuity consisting of 10 annual third-party benefits worth $100 million each, as described below. Note that *R* stands for periodic payment, *n* = number of payments, and *i* is the interest rate that money can be invested at over a long term.



The present value of an annuity formula is as follows:

$$PV = \$R\left(\frac{1-(1+i)^{-n}}{i}\right) = \$100 \text{ million} \times \left(\frac{1-(1+.09)^{-10}}{.09}\right) = \$641.77 \text{ million}$$

Based on the above calculation, the maximum amount of financial assistance that Darin can expect to get from the government is $641.77 million.

Business Application Problem

A western Canadian city has approached Ridaway Rodeos in a bid to host the new North Pacific Championship Rodeo. Ridaway projects an annual external benefit of $3 840 000 for the city's economy caused by the new rodeo event. If the bid to host the rodeo is successful, it will stay in the city for the next 10 years. Determine the maximum amount of financial support that Ridaway could seek from the local government, based on the amount of the external benefit, assuming an interest rate of 10 percent.

# Pedagogy With a Purpose: The *Micro View*

This Fifth Canadian Edition of *Economics Today: The Micro View* is loaded with the same highly regarded pedagogy of the previous edition. It helps students apply what they learn.

**FOR CRITICAL ANALYSIS.** At the end of each Example and Policy Example, students are asked to reflect on real-world problems by answering For Critical Analysis questions. The answers to the questions are found at the end of the student text and in the Instructor's Manual.

**DID YOU KNOW THAT . . . ?** Each chapter starts with a provocative question to engage students' interest and lead them into the content of the chapter.

**LEARNING OBJECTIVES.** On the first page of each chapter, several learning objectives are presented, giving purpose and focus to the chapter. These are then fully reviewed at the end of the chapter.

**GRAPHS.** Articulate and precise, the four-colour graphs illustrate key concepts.

**KEY TERMS.** Key terms are printed in **bold type** and are defined in the margin of the text the first time they appear. These terms are also reproduced alphabetically in the Glossary at the end of the text.

**MYECONLAB SUMMARY CHART.** Each chapter ends with a chart linking the learning objectives with the MyEconLab study plan. It identifies what students should know after reading each chapter and where to go when they need to practise.

**PROBLEMS.** A variety of problems support each chapter, with each problem linked to the appropriate learning objective in the chapter. Answers for all odd-numbered problems are provided at the back of the textbook. The complete set of problem answers (both even- and odd-numbered) appears in the Instructor's Manual.

# Teaching/Learning Package

## Instructor's Resource CD-ROM

This resource provides all of the following supplements in one convenient package.

- **Instructor's Manual.** The Instructor's Manual has been adapted for this Fifth Canadian Edition of *Economics Today: The Micro View*. This extensive manual includes chapter overviews, objectives, and outlines; points to emphasize, including more theoretical issues for those who wish to stress theory; suggested questions for further class discussion; answers to the For Critical Analysis questions and end-of-chapter problems from the text; and selected references.
- **Pearson Canada TestGen.** This software enables instructors to view and edit the existing test-bank questions, add new questions, and generate custom tests. It includes a minimum of 100 multiple-choice questions, 10 short-answer questions, and 5 essay questions per chapter.
- **PowerPoint Presentations.** PowerPoint Presentations are available for each chapter of the text to highlight and illustrate important ideas.

## MyEconLab

This text is fully integrated with MyEconLab, a robust online learning system featuring lots of practice exercises and study tools as well as a personalized study plan generated to suit your individual study needs. The site is available 24 hours a day so you can study where you want, how you want, and when you want.

MyEconLab is found at www.myeconlab.com. Follow the simple registration instructions on the Access Code card bound into every new copy of this text.

## CourseSmart

CourseSmart is a new way for instructors and students to access textbooks online anytime from anywhere. With thousands of titles across hundreds of courses, CourseSmart helps instructors choose the best textbook for their class and give their students a new option for buying the assigned textbook as a lower cost eTextbook. For more information, visit www.coursesmart.com.

**TECHNOLOGY SPECIALISTS.** Pearson's Technology Specialists work with faculty and campus course designers to ensure that Pearson technology products, assessment tools, and online course materials are tailored to meet your specific needs. This highly qualified team is dedicated to helping schools take full advantage of a wide range of educational resources by assisting in the integration of a variety of instructional materials and media formats. Your local Pearson Canada sales representative can provide you with more details on this service program.

# Acknowledgments

We could not have completed the Fifth Canadian Edition without the help of a terrific team of professionals at Pearson Canada. Thanks to Don Thompson, our Sponsoring Editor, for giving us this opportunity. Our Developmental Editor, Paul Donnelly, was a constant source of timely advice and encouragement. Avinash Chandra, Project Manager, and Leanne Rancourt, Production Editor, guided the book through the final stages with calm and sure hands. Our Copy Editor, Caroline Miller, juggled four authors and four different writing styles with great dexterity.

We would also like to thank the following professors who helped with the development of this text by offering us their insightful comments and constructive criticisms:

Sarah Arliss, Seneca College
Constantin Colonescu, Grant MacEwan University
Carl Graham, Assiniboine Community College
Moshe Lander, Northern Alberta Institute of Technology
Stephen Law, Mount Allison University
Joan McEachern, Kwantlen Polytechnic University
A. Gyasi Nimarko, Vanier College
John Pirrie, St. Lawrence College
Carl Weston, Mohawk College

In completing this work, we sincerely appreciate the support and patience we have received from each of our families.

Finally, we would like to thank our colleagues and students at Northern Alberta Institute of Technology and British Columbia Institute of Technology for their valuable advice and support during the writing of this book.

*Mushtaq Ahmad*
*Sam Fefferman*
*Lia Rizzo*
*George Sroka*
*Terrance Sulyma*

PART 1
INTRODUCTION

1

# The Nature of Economics

On March 16, 2016, thousands of students participated in events held at university and college campuses across the country to stage Canada's annual Bottled Water Free Day. Amid pledges to "kick the bottle" and get "back to the tap," the event organizers raised awareness regarding the wasteful and negative effects of consuming bottled water. To date in Canada, over 90 municipalities, 26 college and university campuses, 11 school boards, and countless businesses and organizations have implemented restrictions on bottled water.

Meanwhile, more than a billion people around the world are without safe drinking water. How are these events related? Why are they of interest to economists? Read on.

Sources: 'National Bottled Water Free Day". Niagara Sustainability Initiative. February 15, 2016 http://niagarasustainability.org/national-bottled-water-free-day/(Accessed Dec 21, 2016); "Bottled Water Free Day 2013." Water. Polaris Institute. March 18, 2013. Accessed Dec 22, 2013. http://www.polarisinstitute.org/water

myeconlab

MyEconLab helps you master each objective and study more efficiently. See end of chapter for details.

## LEARNING OBJECTIVES

After reading this chapter, you should be able to:

1.1 Explain the meaning of scarcity.

1.2 Define economics and distinguish between microeconomics and macroeconomics.

1.3 Describe how resource use decisions are affected by the rationality assumption, costs and benefits at the margin, and incentives.

1.4 Explain the three key processes involved in the scientific method.

1.5 Distinguish between positive and normative economics.

1.6 Describe the relationship among theories, policies, and socioeconomic goals.

# DID YOU KNOW THAT...?

Starting in 2010, Canadians reported that they spend more of their weekly leisure time using the Internet than watching TV. Overall, in 2016, 89 percent of Canadians have Internet access. The percentage of Canadians engaging in each of the following major online activities, listed in order of importance, is: emailing (92%), banking (68%), social networking (59%),reading news and current events (55%), general browsing and surfing (49%), shopping (46%), product researching (43%), looking for information related to hobbies/interests (41%) , researching travel (39%), movie and video watching (36%), instant messaging (32%), Looking for health/medical information (30%), music downloading (30%), and online gaming (25%).

In 2015 sixty-eight percent of Canadians own smartphones, representing a 24% increase over the previous year. The top three uses of smartphones in Canada are: instant messaging (86%), gaming (80%) and social media (69%) The world around us continues to change rapidly, and much of that change stems from the decreasing cost and increasing convenience associated with information technology. As you will learn from this chapter, the increasing importance of the online world can be explained in terms of rational behaviour, an important premise that underlies the study of economics.

Sources: CANADA'S INTERNET, DOMAIN INDUSTRY DATA AND CANADIAN INTERNET TRENDS, CIRA Internet Factbook 2016, pages 16-23, https://cira.ca/sites/default/files/public/CIRA-Internet-Factbook-2016-EN.pdf?utm_source=Factbook&utm_medium=PR (Accessed December 21, 2016) WITH GROWTH COMES CHANGE: THE EVOLVING MOBILE LANDSCAPE IN 2015, Catalyst, http://catalyst.ca/2015-canadian-smartphone-market/ (Accessed December 21, 2016)

## 1.1 Scarcity

You can't have it all! You were probably first exposed to this very important economics lesson when you were a toddler and your parents denied your request to buy you a new toy at the supermarket. You undoubtedly experienced this same lesson many times over by the time you enrolled in this course. After you graduate, you may face such choices as buying a brand new car, putting a down payment on a condo, travelling to faraway places, or getting married and starting a family. As a senior member of your community, you may have to choose between spending tax dollars on building a new hospital and improving the education system for the next generation.

Whenever individuals or communities cannot obtain everything they desire, choices occur. Choices occur because of the fundamental economic problem of *scarcity*. Scarcity is the most basic concept in all of economics.

**Scarcity** The condition that arises because wants always exceed what can be produced with limited resources.

**Scarcity refers to the condition that arises because wants always exceed what can be produced with limited resources.**

As a result of scarcity, we do not and cannot have enough income and wealth to satisfy our every desire.

Scarcity is not the same thing as poverty. Scarcity occurs among the rich as well as the poor. Even the richest person faces scarcity because available time is limited. Low income levels do not create more scarcity. High income levels do not create less scarcity.

### Scarcity and Wants

**Goods** The physical items that consumers are willing to pay for.

**Services** The tasks performed by others that consumers are willing to pay for.

Wants refer to the goods and services that we wish to consume as well as the goals that we seek to achieve. **Goods** are physical items that we as consumers are willing to pay for, such as meat, jeans, DVDs, and cars. **Services** are the tasks performed by others that we as consumers are willing to pay for, such as haircuts, education, and medical, dental, and legal services. The goals that we seek to achieve can be individual or social in nature. The important thing to note is that we are referring to goods, services, and goals that require the use of our limited resources.

### Scarcity and Resources

**Production** Any activity that results in the conversion of resources into goods and services.

The scarcity concept arises from the fact that resources are insufficient to satisfy our every desire. Resources are the inputs used in the production of the things that we want. **Production** can be defined as virtually any activity that results in the conversion of resources into goods and services. Production includes the manufacturing, wholesaling, and retailing of goods as well as the delivery of services. The resources used in production are called *factors of production,* and some economists use the terms *resources* and *factors of production* interchangeably. The total quantity of all resources that an economy has at any one time determines what that economy can produce.

Factors of production can be classified in many ways. Here is one such classification:

1. **Land** encompasses all the nonhuman gifts of nature, including timber, water, fish, minerals, and the original fertility of the land. It is often called the *natural resource.*
2. **Labour** is the human resource, which includes all productive contributions made by individuals who work, such as steelworkers, ballet dancers, and professional baseball players.
3. **Physical capital** consists of the factories and equipment used in production. It also includes improvements to natural resources, such as irrigation ditches.
4. **Human capital** is the economic characterization of the education and training of workers. How much the nation produces depends not only on how many hours people work but also on how productive they are, and that, in turn, depends in part on education and training. To become more educated, individuals have to devote time and resources, just as a business has to devote resources if it wants to increase its physical capital. Whenever a worker's skills increase, human capital has been improved.
5. **Entrepreneurship** is actually a subdivision of labour and involves human resources that perform the functions of risk taking, organizing, managing, and assembling the other factors of production to make business ventures. Entrepreneurship also encompasses taking risks that involve the possibility of losing large sums of wealth on new ventures. It includes new methods of doing common things, and generally experimenting with any type of new thinking that could lead to making more money income. Without entrepreneurship, virtually no business organization could operate.

Land Nonhuman gifts of nature.

Labour Productive contributions made by individuals who work.

Physical capital Factories and equipment used in production.

Human capital The education and training of workers.

Entrepreneurship Human resources that perform the functions of risk taking, organizing, managing, and assembling other factors of production to make business ventures.

When resources are used to produce goods and services, they earn income. The incomes earned by land, labour, capital, and entrepreneurship are referred to as **rent**, **wages**, **interest**, and **profit**, respectively.

Rent Income earned by land.

Wages Income earned by labour.

Interest Income earned by capital.

Profit Income earned by the entrepreneur.

## 1.2 Defining Economics

What is economics exactly? *Economics* is one of the social sciences and, as such, seeks explanations of real events. All social sciences analyze human behaviour. The physical sciences, on the other hand, generally analyze the behaviour of electrons, atoms, and other nonhuman phenomena.

**Economics is a social science that studies how people allocate their limited resources to satisfy their wants. That is, economics is concerned with how individuals, groups, and societies respond to the economic problem of scarcity.**

Economics A social science that studies how people allocate their limited resources to satisfy their wants.

Resources are limited relative to wants. Consumers, managers, business owners, citizens, and politicians must continually make choices among alternative courses of action. For example, as a consumer, you choose how to spend your limited income on a vast array of goods and services. If you own a business or manage a government department, you will have to decide what resources to hire in order to best promote the goals of your organization, while working within a limited budget. As a citizen and potential politician, you make decisions that affect how limited tax dollars are used for the betterment of society. Economics helps us study how such choices can be made.

As Example 1–1 suggests, even a web page designer, who prefers to engage in artistic endeavours, must practise economics on a regular basis.

### EXAMPLE 1–1 The Economics of Web Page Design

As noted in this chapter's Did You Know That . . . ? section, Canadians are spending more time on the Web than watching television. During a typical month, Canadians spent more than 45 billion minutes on the Internet.

*continued*

Companies that want to sell their products realize that the explosive growth in Internet use suggests that advertisements posted on the Web can potentially reach very large audiences, in Canada and worldwide. These companies also know that when people access the Internet, their home pages are typically those of their Internet service provider, a popular search engine such as Yahoo!, or their favourite media website. Consequently, many companies advertise on these web pages. During 2016, Canadian online advertising is predicted to balloon to a record $5.6 billion, up 21% over the previous year. In every year over the past decade, online advertising has increased at double digit annual rates, making it the fastest growing media in terms of advertising revenues. In 2015, online advertising increased its lead to +43% over television's $3.2 billion.

The owner of any web page that carries advertising faces the economic problem of scarcity. For example, advertisers widely consider the Yahoo! search engine home page "prime real estate" because so many people see it each day. But there is relatively little space on the computer screen to view the page without having to scroll farther down the screen. Thus, when Yahoo! allocates space to promote its own services and products, it gives up space that it could sell to advertisers. On the other hand, if Yahoo! fills up too much of its prime screen space with ads, some users will switch to a less cluttered search engine. Web designers try to minimize the space taken up by ads on prime screen space by using animations that cycle through a number of different ads in the same space on a web page. However, Net surfers are willing to spend only a limited amount of time viewing such animations. All these considerations make web design a crucial economic concern.

**For critical analysis:** What are the "unlimited wants" and "limited resources" that face a person in charge of designing a frequently visited web page?

Source: IAB Canada. *2012 Actual + 2013 Estimated Canadian Online Advertising Revenue Survey Detailed Report.* Ernst & Young. September 18, 2013. http://iabcanada.com/files/Canadian_Internet_Advertising_Revenue_Survey_2012-13English.pdf (Accessed December 24, 2013.) Annual Internet Advertising Revenue Reports.iab.Canada. http://iabcanada.com/annual-internet-advertising-revenue-reports/(Accessed January 3, 2016)

How does the economic problem of scarcity apply to a web designer?

## Microeconomics versus Macroeconomics

Economics is typically divided into two fields of study: *microeconomics* and *macroeconomics*.

**Microeconomics** The study of decision making undertaken by individuals and by firms in specific parts of the economy.

**Macroeconomics** The study of the behaviour of the economy as a whole.

**Microeconomics** studies decision making undertaken by individuals and by firms in specific parts of the economy. It is like looking through a microscope to focus on individual households, firms, industries, and occupations.

**Macroeconomics** studies the behaviour of the economy as a whole. It deals with economywide phenomena, such as changes in unemployment, the general price level, and national income.

Microeconomic analysis, for example, is concerned with the effects of changes in the price of natural gas relative to that of other energy sources. It examines the effects of new taxes on a specific product or industry. If price controls were to be reinstituted in Canada, how individual firms and consumers would react to them would be in the realm of microeconomics. The raising of wages by an effective union strike would also be analyzed using the tools of microeconomics.

By contrast, such issues as the rate of inflation, the amount of economywide unemployment, and the yearly growth in the output of goods and services in the nation all fall into the domain of macroeconomic analysis. In other words, macroeconomics deals with **aggregates**, or economywide measures, such as total output in an economy.

**Aggregates** Economywide measures.

## The Power of Economic Analysis

Knowing that an economic problem of scarcity exists every time you make a decision is not enough. As you study economics, you will be encouraged to develop a framework of analysis that will allow you to effectively analyze possible solutions to each economic problem—whether you are a student trying to decide how much studying time you should devote to a course, a consumer making the choice between renting and owning your next home, a business owner interested in setting the most profitable price for your product, or a government leader searching for the policy that would most effectively create jobs in your province.

The remainder of this chapter is concerned with introducing you to a powerful framework of analysis that includes the *economic way of thinking*, the *scientific approach*, and *policy analysis* based on valued economic goals.

Indeed, just as taking an art or literature appreciation class increases the pleasure you receive when you view paintings or read novels, taking an economics course will increase your understanding when viewing news clips on the Internet, watching the news on TV, listening to newscasts on the radio, or reading newspapers.

## 1.3 Rational Decision Making

The **economic way of thinking** assumes that the typical response to an economic problem of scarcity is rational behaviour. That is, individuals behave as if they compare the costs and benefits of different possible choices when they make resource use decisions. They behave in this manner in order to further their own self-interest.

**Economic way of thinking** Assumes that the typical response to an economic problem of scarcity is rational behaviour.

Economists presume that individuals act *as if* motivated by self-interest and respond predictably to opportunities for gain. This central insight of economics was first clearly articulated by Adam Smith in 1776. Smith wrote in his most famous book, *An Inquiry into the Nature and Causes of the Wealth of Nations*, that "it is not from the benevolence of the butcher, the brewer, or the baker that we expect our dinner, but from their regard to their own interest." Otherwise stated, the *typical* person about whom economists make behavioural predictions is assumed to look out for his or her own self-interest in a rational manner. The word *typical* is very important. Economists know that not all people respond in the same way when faced with the same circumstances. If offered a free trip to Hawaii for participating in a marketing experiment, for example, most people will take part. There inevitably will be some who do not want to go to Hawaii, perhaps because they do not like travelling, so they will not participate in the study. But, *on average*, the promised trip to Hawaii will be sufficient to attract participants because people behave in a predictably self-interested way.

### The Rationality Assumption

The **rationality assumption** of economics, simply stated, is as follows:

**An individual makes decisions based on maximizing his or her own self-interest.**

**Rationality assumption** An individual makes decisions based on maximizing his or her own self-interest.

The distinction here is between what people may think—the realm of psychology and psychiatry and perhaps sociology—and what they do. Economics does *not* involve itself in analyzing individual or group thought processes. Economics looks at what people actually do in life with their limited resources. It does little good to criticize the rationality assumption by stating, "Nobody thinks that way" or "I never think that way" or "How unrealistic! That's as irrational as anyone can get!"

Take the example of driving. When you consider passing another car on a two-lane highway with oncoming traffic, you have to make very quick decisions: you must estimate the speed of the car you are going to pass, the speed of the oncoming cars, the distance between your car and the oncoming cars, and your car's potential rate of acceleration. If we were to apply a model to your behaviour, we would use the laws of calculus. In fact, you and most other drivers in such a situation do not actually think of using the laws of calculus, but we could predict your behaviour *as if* you did.

In practical terms, the rationality assumption implies that an individual will adopt a course of action if the action's relevant benefits exceed its relevant costs. Let us proceed to examine what we mean by *relevant* costs and benefits.

### Opportunity Cost

The natural fact of scarcity implies that we must make choices. One of the most important results of this fact is that every choice made (or not made, for that matter) means that some opportunity had to be sacrificed. Every choice involves giving up another opportunity to do or use something else.

Consider a practical example. Every choice you make to study one more hour of economics requires that you give up the opportunity to do any of the following activities: study more of another subject, listen to music, sleep, browse at a local store, read a novel, or work out at the gym. Many more opportunities are forgone if you choose to study economics for an additional hour.

Because there were so many alternatives from which to choose, how could you determine the value of what you gave up to engage in that extra hour of studying economics? First of all, no one else can tell you the answer because only you can *subjectively* put a value on each alternative. Only you know the value of another hour of sleep or of an hour looking for the latest CDs. That means that only you can determine the highest-valued alternative that you had to sacrifice in order to study economics one more hour. It is you who must come up with the *subjective* estimate of the expected value of the best alternative.

**Opportunity cost** The value of the best alternative that must be given up because a choice was made.

The value of the best alternative that must be sacrificed to satisfy a want is called *opportunity cost*. The **opportunity cost** of any action is the value of what is given up—the highest-ranked alternative—because a choice was made. When you study one more hour, there may be many alternatives available for the use of that hour, but assume that you can do only one thing in that hour—your highest-ranked alternative. What is important is the choice that you would have made if you had not studied one more hour. Your opportunity cost is the *highest-ranked* alternative, not *all* alternatives.

**In economics, cost is a forgone opportunity.**

In this chapter's Issues and Applications we use the concept of *opportunity cost* to assess the value of allocating tens of billions of dollars a year of limited resources to the manufacture of bottled water products such as Aquafina and Dasani, which contribute to pollution and solid waste, despite the fact that we already have a much cheaper source of safe water flowing from our municipal water systems. The opportunity costs are that we forgo the option to have a healthier environment and we forgo allocating the invested resources to important causes such as providing drinking water to the more than one billion people around the world who don't have access to safe water.

In Example 1–2 we will examine how the relatively high opportunity cost of searching for a compatible romantic partner has helped create an industry based in cyberspace.

### EXAMPLE 1–2 Is the Opportunity Cost of Finding a Mate Lower on the Internet?

Why are individuals willing to pay for online dating services?

For many single people looking for a companion, the biggest difficulty is not necessarily a lack of potential mates. The problem is that the time spent dating in search of "Ms. Right" or "Mr. Right" could otherwise be devoted to alternative activities. The highest-valued of these alternative activities is the opportunity cost of the time spent on each date.

This provides a fundamental rationale for the existence of such Internet-based companies as Match.com. For about $42 per month, a person looking for "that special someone" with desired characteristics, similar interests, and so on can enter personal information into a database and be matched, by computer, with someone else. According to the company's "director of flirting and dating," its business is all "about numbers, and it's also about time." In short, it is about the high opportunity cost of finding a compatible partner. For the really picky people who face especially high opportunity costs of screening candidate mates for very specific characteristics, there are special Internet services available, albeit at higher prices. Goodgenes.com is open to graduates of Ivy League universities and a select group of other top-notch colleges and universities. For Jewish men and women, there is JDate.com, and Matrimony.org helps link Islamic singles.

**For critical analysis:** Why do the prices charged by websites specializing in people who share very specific characteristics tend to be higher than the prices charged by general dating services, such as Match.com?

## Making Decisions at the Margin

As you progress through this text, you will be reminded frequently that in order to rationally evaluate a possible course of action, you must compare the action's *marginal benefit* with its *marginal cost*. **Marginal benefit** refers to all the *extra* benefits that one receives in pursuing a course of action, while **marginal cost** refers to all the *extra* costs or sacrifices incurred. In order to ensure that you properly identify the marginal cost relevant to your decision at hand, you must be careful not to include *sunk costs*. **Sunk costs** refer to irreversible costs incurred prior to your decision.

**Marginal benefit** All the extra benefits that one receives in pursuing a course of action.

**Marginal cost** All the extra costs or sacrifices incurred.

**Sunk costs** Irreversible costs incurred prior to your decision.

As an example, suppose you are in the process of estimating the extra (marginal) transportation costs associated with a Nova Scotia vacation that you are planning to take. You own your car and you have paid the annual insurance and car licence fee long before contemplating this vacation. If you decide to use your own car for this trip, the annual licence fee and insurance are sunk costs that are not relevant to the decision of travelling to Nova Scotia. As such, you should not include these two costs in your estimate of the extra (marginal) transportation costs. To better understand the notion of marginal and sunk costs, we refer you to Example 1–3: "What Does a Year at College Really Cost?"

Making decisions at the margin will often reveal that there can be too much of a good thing! As an example, suppose that at a time when marijuana use is at an all-time low, one of the contenders for prime minister, in a federal election campaign, proposes a policy for eliminating all marijuana use in Canada. While this type of zero tolerance policy proposal can win votes, if implemented, it can result in the transfer of a massive amount of policing resources away from the prevention of serious violent crimes in order to achieve a very small reduction in marijuana use. In other words, the marginal cost of the zero tolerance policy far exceeds the marginal benefit!

### EXAMPLE 1–3 What Does a Year at College Really Cost?

Jane Sanders is currently earning $2000 per month working full time in Hamilton, Ontario. She lives in a one-bedroom apartment and pays $700 per month in rent. Her monthly food, personal care, and entertainment expenses are $500 per month. Since she does not own a vehicle, she pays $65 per month for a bus pass.

Jane is in the process of estimating the extra cost related to the decision to enroll full time in the first year of a business program at a college in the Hamilton area. If she enrolls, she will give up her full-time job for the eight-month period of the first-year program. If Jane goes to college, she plans to continue to live in her one-bedroom apartment, take the bus to the college campus, and maintain her current lifestyle. Jane estimates that her decision to enroll in college for the first year (eight-month period) will cost $13 720, estimated as follows:

**TABLE 1–1**

| | | |
|---|---|---|
| Rent | $700 × 8 = | $ 5 600 |
| Food, Personal Care, Entertainment | $500 × 8 = | $ 4 000 |
| Public Transportation | $ 65 × 8 = | $ 520 |
| Tuition, Books, College Fees | | $ 3 600 |
| **Total Cost** | | **$13 720** |

**For critical analysis:** Did Jane correctly determine the extra cost related to the decision to enroll in college full time for eight months? What else must Jane try to estimate in order to make a rational decision? Explain.

## Responding to Incentives

If it is reasonable to assume that individuals make decisions by comparing marginal costs and benefits, then we are in a position to better understand and predict how people respond to incentives. We define an **incentive** as an inducement to take a particular action. The inducement can be a reward, or a "carrot," which would take the form of an increase in

**Incentive** Inducement to take a particular action.

benefit or a decrease in cost. Alternatively, the inducement can be a punishment, or a "stick," in the form of an increase in cost or a decrease in benefit. To the extent that a change in incentives implies a change in the relation between the marginal costs and benefits associated with various choices, individual decisions will change.

Indeed, much of human behaviour can be explained in terms of how individuals respond to changing incentives over time. School students are motivated to do better by a variety of incentive systems, ranging from gold stars and certificates of achievement when they are young to better grades with accompanying promises of a "better life" as they get older. The rapid growth in Internet use noted in this chapter's Did You Know That . . . ? section can be explained in terms of increased incentives due to the decline in cost and increase in convenience associated with information technology.

In Policy Example 1–1, you are asked to help governments reduce incentives to engage in smuggling and counterfeiting activities by identifying policies that either increase the marginal costs or decrease the marginal benefits related to these illegal actions.

### POLICY EXAMPLE 1–1 International Smuggling and Counterfeiting

In order to develop a domestic, state-owned cigarette manufacturing monopoly industry, the Chinese government has pursued strategies to keep out foreign-made cigarettes. One such strategy is the imposition of tariffs (taxes) as high as 430 percent on cigarettes imported into China that are manufactured by large, multinational cigarette companies such as British American Tobacco (BAT). These high tax rates have encouraged the annual flow of tens of billions of dollars in contraband cigarettes.

One example of contraband is the smuggling of foreign-made cigarettes into China, which avoids the government-imposed tariffs. In 2006, it was discovered that BAT, one of the world's biggest tobacco companies, had restructured its operations to expand its own smuggling trade in China, where one-third of all the world's smokers reside.

A second example of contraband is the rapid growth in the Chinese manufacturing and trade of counterfeit brand-name cigarettes such as Marlboro and State Express 555. It is estimated that hundreds of illegal Chinese cigarette businesses manufacture approximately 400 billion fake brand-name cigarettes a year. These businesses operate illicit factories hidden in thickly forested mountain regions and in deep caves buried metres below ground. Over the past decade, the production of counterfeit cigarettes in China has increased eightfold!

In September 2013 a study published by Oxford Economics and the International Tax and Investment Centre (ITIC) indicated that there was still a significant amount of illegal consumption of cigarettes in Asian countries. As an example, in response to significant increases in taxes imposed on cigarettes, 35.9 percent of the cigarettes consumed in Hong Kong in 2012 were illicit and resulted in a loss of HK$3.3 billion in government revenues.

Closer to home, on April 13, 2010, the Canadian federal government levied fines totalling $225 million on two large multinational cigarette companies—JTI–Macdonald Corp. and R.J. Reynolds—for their roles in smuggling cigarettes into Canada. A Canadian study, published by the Macdonald Laurier Institute in March 2016, estimates Canada's contraband market in tobacco and cigarettes to be more than $1.3 billion, rivaling the illicit drug market. It is projected that Ontario alone sacrifices over $1 billion in tax revenue annually due to contraband tobacco and cigarettes. The smuggling of cheap cigarettes into Canada is attributed to the relatively high tax rates that federal and provincial governments impose on legal cigarettes manufactured and sold in Canada.

**For critical analysis:** What actions can governments in China and Canada take to increase the marginal cost related to illegal smuggling and counterfeiting activities? Can you identify other policy actions that decrease the marginal benefit related to these illegal activities?

Sources: "Research reveals tobacco company's role in China's cigarette smuggling crisis." Tuesday, July 18, 2006. London School of Hygiene and Tropical Medicine Press; Te-Ping Chen. "China's Marlboro Country." June 28, 2009. Tobacco Underground. Organized Crime and Corruption Reporting Project. http://www.reportingproject.net/underground/index.php?option=com_content&view=article&id=9&Itemid=22; Tibbetts, Janice. "Record fines for smuggled smokes." Canwest News Service. Ottawa. *Edmonton Journal*. April 14, 2010. P. A5; Asia-11 Illicit Tobacco Indicator 2012. Prepared by International Tax and Investment Center and Oxford Economics. September

2013. page 38. http://www.oxfordeconomics.com/Media/Default/ThoughtLeadership. "Smoking Gun: Strategic Containment of Contraband Tobacco and Cigarette Trafficking in Canada. "Christian Leuprecht. Macdonald Laurier Institute. March 2016. http://www.macdonaldlaurier.ca/files/pdf/MLILeuprechtContrabandPaper-03-16-WebReady.pdf (Accessed January 3, 2017).

## Defining Self-Interest

Self-interest does not always mean increasing one's wealth as measured in dollars and cents. We assume that individuals seek many goals, not just increased monetary wealth. Thus, the self-interest part of our economic-person assumption includes goals relating to prestige, friendship, love, power, helping others, creating works of art, and many other matters. As Example 1–4 illustrates, performing acts of kindness can go hand in hand with pursuing one's own self interest.

### EXAMPLE 1–4 Nice Guys Can Finish First

An academic study discredits the popular myth that people who exhibit altruistic or generous behaviour are typically less attractive to potential romantic partners compared to "bad boys" or "selfish people."

This research study examined heterosexual men's and women's attraction to opposite sex photographs, which were matched with descriptions (profiles) that varied in the level of generosity portrayed. The research participants, whose mean age ranged from 19.15 to 20.10 years, each received a package consisting of four photographs and four descriptions. Each research participant saw a "neutral person" and a "generous person," each seeking a short-term relationship. The same research participant observed a "neutral person" and a "generous person," each seeking a long-term relationship. After viewing each picture with its description, the research participants rated how willing they were to associate with the person in different ways, including as a short-term romantic partner, as a long term romantic partner, as a fellow worker, and as a platonic friend.

An example of a "neutral person" would be a picture of a person of the opposite sex accompanied by a profile that did not reference any tendencies for generous acts and behaviour. The corresponding example of a "generous person" would be a picture of a person of the opposite sex accompanied by a profile that did reference tendencies for generous acts and behaviour, such as "I enjoy helping people" or "One of my hobbies is volunteering at the food bank."

All photographs were downloaded from an Internet site where each picture had already been rated by the opposite sex in terms of physical attractiveness. The pictures chosen for this study had been given neutral physical attractiveness ratings. This was done so that physical traits such as "good looks" or "unattractive appearance" would not affect the results of the study.

The findings of this study can be briefly summarized as follows. Research participants of both sexes rated people with generous tendencies as desirable for long-term relationships. Female research participants preferred the males that exhibited generous behaviour for short-term romantic relationships. However, male research participants tended to rate altruistic females as less desireable for short-term relationships.

**For critical analysis:** Based on this Example, critically evaluate this statement: "When individuals consistently engage in generous acts and behaviour, this contradicts the rationality assumption described in this chapter."

Source: Pat Barclay. "Altruism as a courtship display: Some effects of third party generosity on audience perceptions." *British Journal of Psychology*, February 2010, 101(1), 123–135.

# 1.4 The Scientific Method

Economics is a social science that makes use of the same kinds of methods used in other sciences, such as biology, physics, and chemistry. Similar to these other sciences, economics engages in key processes that include making assumptions, forming models or theories, and testing these models with real-world facts. Economic **models or theories** are sim-

**Models or theories** Simplified representations of the real world used to understand and predict economic phenomena.

plified representations of the real world that we use to help us understand and predict economic phenomena in the real world. There are, of course, differences among the sciences. The social sciences, especially economics, make little use of laboratory methods in which changes in variables can be explained under controlled conditions. Rather, social scientists, and especially economists, usually have to examine what has already happened in the real world to test their models.

## Models and Realism

At the outset, it must be emphasized that no model in *any* science, and therefore no economic model, is complete in the sense that it captures *every* detail or interrelationship that exists. Indeed, a model, by definition, is an abstraction from reality. It is conceptually impossible to construct a perfectly complete, realistic model. For example, in physics, we cannot account for every molecule and its position, nor every atom and subparticle. Not only would such a model be prohibitively expensive to build, but also working with it would be impossibly complex.

The nature of scientific model building is such that the model should capture only the essential relationships that are sufficient to analyze the particular problem or answer the particular question with which we are concerned. *An economic model cannot be faulted as unrealistic simply because it does not represent every detail of the real world.* A map of a city that shows only major streets is not necessarily unrealistic if, in fact, all you need to know is how to navigate through the city using major streets. As long as a model is realistic in terms of shedding light on the *central* issue at hand or forces at work, it may be useful.

A map is a basic model. It is always a simplified representation, always unrealistic. But it is also useful in making (refutable) predictions about the world. If the model—the map—predicts that when you take Campus Avenue to the north, you always reach the campus, that is a (refutable) prediction. If our goal is to explain observed behaviour, the simplicity or complexity of the model we use is irrelevant. If a simple model can explain observed behaviour in repeated settings just as well as a complex one, the simple model has some value and is probably easier to use.

## Assumptions

Every model, or theory, is based on a set of assumptions. Assumptions define the conditions under which a model is meant to apply. By eliminating detail that is not considered to be essential to the economic phenomena under investigation, assumptions help simplify a model.

In the theory of the firm, we assume that, typically, firms attempt to maximize profits when deciding how much of a product to produce in an industry. This assumption leads to an economic model of the firm that provides numerous predictions about how the firm will react to various events and incentives. As an example, one prediction would be that if a firm can sell its product at a higher price, it will tend to produce more of this product. Another prediction would be that if a major cost of producing this product increases, such as energy costs, the firm will likely reduce the level of production of this product. Finally, this model would predict that if the government lowered the taxes imposed on the firms in this industry, this would entice firms to increase their supply of this product.

While the owners of the firms in the industry under investigation may well have a variety of other motives for producing the product, the profit-maximizing assumption model is valid to the extent that it consistently provides accurate predictions of real-world behaviour.

**THE CETERIS PARIBUS ASSUMPTION: ALL OTHER THINGS BEING EQUAL.** Constructing a model typically involves making generalizations of how variables in our environment relate to each other. It would be impossible to isolate the effects of changes in one variable on another variable if we always had to worry about the many additional variables that might also enter the analysis. As in other sciences, economics uses the **ceteris paribus assumption**, which is the assumption that nothing changes except the factor or factors being studied. *Ceteris paribus* means "other things being constant" or "other things being equal."

**Ceteris paribus [KAY-ter-us PEAR-uh-bus] assumption** The assumption that nothing changes except the factor or factors being studied; "other things being constant," or "other things being equal."

Consider an example taken from economics. One of the most important determinants of how much of a particular product a family buys is the price of that product relative to other products. We know that in addition to relative prices, other factors influence decisions about making purchases. Some of them have to do with income, others with tastes, and yet others with custom and religious beliefs. Whatever these other factors are, we hold them constant when we look at the relationship between changes in prices and changes in how much of a given product people will purchase. As Example 1–5 illustrates, Canadian researchers applied the *ceteris paribus* assumption in designing a scientific study to test the effectiveness of a popular anti-cold formulation created in Canada.

### EXAMPLE 1–5 The Science behind COLD-fX

On October 5, 2005, the *Canadian Medical Association Journal* published the results of a scientific study that showed COLD-fX, an anti-cold formulation, reduced the incidence and frequency of recurrent colds by more than half. COLD-fX also cut the duration of colds and significantly reduced their severity. Shortly after the research results were published, the stock price of CV Technologies, the company manufacturing COLD-fX, reached an all-time high of $4.74 per share, an increase of 166 percent over the previous year's stock price!

Research subjects for the COLD-fX study were required to be in good general health, to be between 18 and 65 years of age, and to have contracted at least two colds in the past year. Subjects were excluded if they had been vaccinated against influenza in the previous six months.

Volunteers who qualified for the study were randomly assigned to receive either the ginseng extract that makes up COLD-fX or a placebo, which was made to look exactly like the COLD-fX capsule except that the placebo did not contain any type of medication. All subjects were instructed to take two capsules per day for a period of six months following the onset of influenza season. They were instructed not to take any other cold medication while involved in the study. All observations and analyses were performed by a statistician under double-blind conditions. That is, the statistician did not know which subjects were actually taking COLD-fX or the placebo. Similarly, each subject did not know whether he or she was taking COLD-fX or the placebo.

More recent studies suggest that, if effective at all, Cold FX has a possible positive impact after being taken daily for prolonged periods of two-to-six months. As of April 2016, the makers of Cold FX are facing legal challenges from consumers regarding ads that suggest that the product provides "immediate relief of cold and flu" if taken over a three-day period at the first sign of cold and flu symptoms.

**For critical analysis:** The COLD-fX study is interested in examining the relationship between which two variables? Explain how the study attempts to apply the *ceteris paribus* assumption.

Sources: "Interactive charts. CV technologies." CTVGlobemedia. http://www.globeinvestor.com. (Accessed May 12, 2007.); Gerald N. Predy, Vinti Goel, Ray Lovlin, Allan Donner, Larry Stitt, and Tapan K. Basu. "Efficacy of an extract of North American ginseng containing poly-furanosyl-pyranosyl-saccharides for preventing upper respiratory tract infections: a randomized controlled trial." *CMAJ*, October 25, 2005, 173(9). doi:10.1503/cmaj.1041470. "Cold-fX makers misstated effectiveness and misled consumers, lawsuit alleges". Business. CBC News. April 11, 2016.http://www.cbc.ca/news/business/cold-fx-class-action-lawsuit-1.3519345. (Accessed January 6, 2016).

## Testing Models

We generally do not attempt to determine the usefulness, or "goodness," of a model merely by evaluating how realistic its assumptions are. Rather, we consider a model good if it yields usable predictions and implications for the real world. In other words, can we use the model to predict what will happen in the world around us?

Once we have determined that the model does predict real-world phenomena, the scientific approach to the analysis of the world around us requires that we consider evidence. Evidence is used to test the usefulness of a model. This is why we call economics an *empirical* science, **empirical** meaning using real-world data to test the usefulness of a model. Economists are often engaged in empirically testing their models.

**Empirical** Using real-world data to test the usefulness of a model.

Consider two competing models for the way students act when doing complicated probability problems to choose the best gambles. One model predicts that, on the basis of the assumption of rational self-interest, students who are paid more for better performance will, in fact, perform better on average during the experiment. A competing model might be that students whose last names start with the letters A through L will do better than students with last names starting with M through Z, irrespective of how much they are paid. The model that consistently predicts more accurately is the model that we would normally choose. In this example, the "alphabet" model did not work well; the first letter of the last name of the students who actually did the experiment was irrelevant in predicting how well they would perform the mathematical calculations necessary to choose the correct gambles. The model based on rational self-interest predicted well, in contrast.

## Models of Behaviour, Not Thought Processes

Take special note of the fact that economists' models do not relate to the way people *think*; they relate to the way people *act*, to what they do in life with their limited resources. Models tend to generalize human behaviour. Normally, the economist does not attempt to predict how people will think about a particular topic, such as a higher price of oil products, accelerated inflation, or higher taxes. Rather, the task at hand is to predict how people will act, which may be quite different from what they say they will do (much to the consternation of poll takers and market researchers). The people involved in examining thought processes are psychologists and psychiatrists, who are not usually economists.

Example 1–6 provides you with an economic model that is used to explain and predict criminal behaviour.

### EXAMPLE 1–6 **An Economic Model of Crime**

What marginal benefits and costs relate to car theft?

As you may suspect, numerous sociological, cultural, psychological, and physiological theories are used to explain criminal behaviour. Traits such as deviance, abnormality, depravity, insanity, and genetics are used to characterize those who break the law. In this Example, we will present an economic model of crime, based on the rationality assumption. That is, in an economic model of criminal behaviour, individuals compare the marginal costs and marginal benefits of engaging in an illegal act (as opposed to a legal act). If the marginal benefits of engaging in a crime exceed its marginal costs, the individual will commit the crime.

What might be included in the marginal benefits of engaging in a crime? For many crimes, such as property theft, identity theft, financial fraud, drug trafficking, and tax evasion, part of the marginal benefit would be the extra monies received. Other marginal benefits might prove to be psychological in nature, such as the thrill of danger, peer approval, retribution, the need to feed an addiction, or even a sense of accomplishment.

What about the marginal costs of committing an illegal act? The costs would include material costs (equipment, guns, vehicles), psychological costs (guilt, anxiety, fear, aversion to risk), expected punishment costs, and opportunity costs.

The expected punishment costs are a combination of the probability of being "caught" (arrested and convicted) and the severity of the penalty when convicted. If there is a high probability of being caught and/or there is a large penalty when convicted, this results in a relatively large marginal cost of committing a crime.

The opportunity cost of committing a crime consists of the net benefit of the legal activity that is forgone while planning, performing, and concealing the criminal act. The lower an individual's income from legal activity, the lower the opportunity cost of committing a crime.

As with any scientific model, the validity of the economic model of crime depends on testing the model's predictions with real-world evidence. Numerous studies have found a clear negative association between high costs of punishment and crime rates. These studies suggest that the probability of getting caught is a stronger deterrent to criminal action than

*continued*

the severity of the penalty when convicted. Studies also indicate that individuals are more apt to engage in crimes when they earn low incomes in an environment of significant income inequality. In other words, one is more apt to commit a crime when there is a lot to gain and little to lose.

**For critical analysis:** Based on the economic model of crime, predict how each of the following would affect the crime rate: an increase in the unemployment rate, a decrease in conviction rates.

Source: E. Eide (1999). "Economics of criminal behaviour." *Handbook of Law and Economics*, 8100, 345–389. (Adobe Acrobat document - 145Kb) http://www-staff.lboro.ac.uk/~ecrs3/Econ%20of%20Criminology/media/-Eide%20(1999).pdf.

The economic model of crime presented in Example 1–6 above can prove useful in identifying incentives that help to reduce specific crimes. As an example, the international cigarette smuggling and counterfeiting problem noted in Policy Example 1–1, could be reduced by decreasing the benefits derived from smuggling cigarettes. If the Chinese government reduced the taxes imposed on cigarettes legally sold in the country, this would reduce the price and profit that criminals would get from smuggling and counterfeiting cigarettes.

# 1.5 Positive versus Normative Economics

Economic theory uses *positive analysis*, a value-free approach to inquiry. No subjective or moral judgments enter into the analysis. Positive analysis relates to such statements as "If *A*, then *B*." For example, "If the price of gasoline goes up relative to all other prices, then the amount of it that people will buy will fall." That is a positive economic statement. It is a statement of *what is*, and its validity can be tested by observing the facts. It is not a statement of anyone's value judgment or subjective feelings. For many problems analyzed in the hard sciences, such as physics and chemistry, the analyses are considered to be virtually value-free. After all, how can someone's values enter into a theory of molecular behaviour? But economists face a different problem. They deal with the behaviour of individuals, not molecules. That makes it more difficult to stick to what we consider to be value-free or *positive economics* without reference to our feelings. **Positive economics** refers to analysis that can be tested by observing the facts.

**Positive economics** Analysis that can be tested by observing the facts.

When our values are interjected into the analysis, we enter the realm of *normative economics*, involving *normative analysis*. **Normative economics** refers to analysis based on value judgments made about what ought to be. A positive economic statement is, "If the price of gas rises, people will buy less." If we add to that analysis the statement, "so we should not allow the price to go up," we have entered the realm of normative economics—we have expressed a value judgment. In fact, any time you see the word *should*, you will know that values are entering into the discussion. Just remember that positive statements are concerned with *what is*, whereas normative statements are concerned with *what ought to be*.

**Normative economics** Analysis based on value judgments made about what ought to be.

In the last section of this chapter, we will introduce the important social and economic goals that governments try to achieve when they design economic policy. Normative analysis is often encountered when you examine the various goals that form the basis of policy. As an example, in this chapter's Issues and Applications, you will see that the proposal to tax bottled water is, in part, based on certain goals, such as "a pollution-free environment," which are normative in nature.

## A Warning: Recognize Normative Analysis

It is easy to define positive economics. It is quite another matter to catch all unlabelled normative statements in a textbook such as this one (or any other), even though the authors go over the manuscript many times before it is printed. Therefore, do not get the impression that a textbook's authors will be able to keep all personal values out of the book. They will slip through. In fact, the very choice of which topics to include in an introductory textbook involves normative economics. There is no value-free, or objective, way to decide which topics to include in a textbook. The authors' values ultimately make a difference when choices have to be made. But from your own standpoint, you might want to be able to recognize when you are engaging in normative, as opposed to positive, economic analysis. Reading this text will help equip you for that task.

# 1.6 Economic Policy and Socioeconomic Goals

As we noted above, economic models will enhance your ability to understand and predict behaviour. In the chapters to come, we will illustrate how these models prove useful in formulating, assessing, and reacting to government policies that affect you as a consumer, an employee, an investor, a business owner, and a concerned citizen.

**Policies** Action plans designed to achieve goals.

Most government economic **policies** are action plans designed to achieve commonly accepted socioeconomic goals. The goals that are most frequently considered, when forming and evaluating economic policies, are described below.

1. Full Employment: an economy in which people looking for work find jobs reasonably quickly.
2. Efficiency: an economy in which resources are allocated to the production of goods and services in a way that achieves maximum benefit for society.
3. Economic Growth: an economy with the ability to increase its rate of production over time to enhance society's well being.
4. Price Stability: an economy in which prices remain relatively stable over time.
5. Equity: an economy that moves closer toward some social consensus of fairness. An example often used as a basis of economic policy is the goal of a *more equitable distribution of income*, which aims to reduce the level of poverty in the economy.

## Theory and Policy

Economic theory plays a useful role in helping us understand how existing and proposed policies relate to major socioeconomic goals. As you progress through this text, you may be surprised at the frequency with which a proposed policy is shown to conflict with the very goals it is meant to promote, once you employ the relevant economic model.

For example, a local politician may propose a rent control policy aimed at reducing apartment rents in order to make housing more affordable to the poor. That is, the rent control policy is aimed at promoting a more equitable distribution of income. However, once you become familiar with the demand-and-supply model presented in Chapter 4, you will see that this policy will more likely conflict with the goal of an equitable distribution of income because of the resulting shortages in livable accommodation. Moreover, this same policy will also conflict with the goal of full employment to the extent that construction workers are laid off as fewer new apartments are being built.

We hope that you will enjoy the challenge of using economic models to formulate superior alternative policies. A superior policy refers to a plan of action that promotes as many socioeconomic goals as possible with minimal goal conflict. In the rent control example, you may find that relevant economic theory suggests that a policy of increasing competition in the apartment construction and rental industries may prove to be the superior policy. By increasing the supply of affordable, quality housing units, the goals of full employment and equitable distribution can both be promoted!

ISSUES AND APPLICATIONS

# Bottled Water: The Hummer of Beverages?

**Concepts Applied: Economics, Microeconomics versus Macroeconomics, Scarcity, Opportunity Cost, Economic Way of Thinking, Incentives, Policy Analysis**

In Canada, consumption of bottled water exceeds that of coffee, tea, apple juice, milk, and beer.

## The Rapid Growth of the Bottled Water Industry

Everyone knows that water is an essential resource. Yet, more than a billion people around the world don't have access to safe, clean water. The worldwide demand for water is doubling every 20 years, to the point that two-thirds of the people on this planet may be facing severe water shortages by the year 2025.

Despite the fact that clean and safe publicly owned and operated tap water is available in developed nations such as Canada and the U.S., the bottled water market has been exploding in North America. Today, close to one-fifth of the population relies exclusively on bottled water for their daily hydration. In Canada, bottled water consumption exceeds coffee, tea, apple juice, milk, and beer consumption.

The global bottled water industry is dominated by four companies: Coca-Cola (Dasani), Pepsi (Aquafina), Nestlé (Perrier), and Danone (Evian). In response to growing interest in healthier lifestyles and declining demand for soft drinks, these companies have been promoting bottled water as a more desirable option than tap water. North Americans spend more than US$11 billion per year drinking over 8 billion gallons of bottled water. Currently, bottled water is the fastest growing and most profitable segment of the beverage industry in North America. Within the next ten years, industry analysts project that bottled water could overtake soft drinks as the leading beverage.

Critics of the bottled water industry argue that its rapid growth is not due to informed individual consumer choices but rather is in response to the deceptive and non-competitive practices of the large beverage companies. Moreover, these critics point to the significant resource costs and environmental degradation related to the bottled water industry. The specific arguments are explained below.

## Concerns Related to the Bottled Water Industry

Consumers can be easily misled by the "pure," "crisp," "fresh," and "sparkling" glossy advertising of the leading brands of bottled water. The product has often been depicted as coming from pristine natural spring and glacier-like environments, when in fact the water comes from municipal water sources (the same as tap water) or from borehole ground water wells located near the bottling plants. In response to consumer demands, industry leader Aquafina (Pepsi) has agreed to print "Public Water Source" on Aquafina labels. To date, Coca-Cola (Dasani) has not followed suit, even though its water source is the same as tap water.

One might have legitimate health-related concerns over the fact that while cities such as Toronto test their water quality every few hours, bottled water plants are publicly inspected only once every three to six years. To date, companies such as Coca-Cola have refused to publicly report on the health and quality of their bottled water in ways required of public water systems.

Through the widespread use of exclusivity contracts with schools, colleges, and universities, Coca-Cola and Pepsi have conducted successful marketing campaigns aimed at weaning the younger generation off of tap water in favour of bottled water. The University of British Columbia (UBC) was the first university in Canada to sign an exclusivity contract with Coca-Cola in 1995. Under this contract, UBC was to receive $8.5 million dollars in return for giving Coca-Cola the exclusive right to sell its products on campus. This contract excluded all Coca-Cola competitors from selling their products at UBC. During the contract period it was reported that over 40 percent of water fountains were removed or disabled on the UBC campus. Needless to say, these exclusivity contracts set the stage for Coca-Cola to charge high prices for its bottled water products.

We must question whether the bottled water industry is squandering our limited resources in producing a product that is arguably no better than tap water, which is available at a much lower cost. A 1.5 litre bottle of Aquafina costs around $2.70, but the same amount of water taken from the Montreal municipal system costs 1/500th of a cent. The extra costs for the higher priced bottled water include what some might consider unnecessary "purifying" of already good quality water, creating plastic bottles, packaging, advertising, marketing, transportation, and a healthy profit. Globally, an estimated US$100 billion is spent every year on the purchase of bottled water. It is estimated that it would only take US$30 billion to halve the number of people who do not have ready access to clean, safe, drinking water, and achieve one of the Millennium Development Goals established by the United Nations (UN) in 2000.

Yet another concern has to do with bottled water's impact on the environment. The plastic bottles create carbon dioxide ($CO_2$) when they are made, trucked to the store, and later disposed of in a landfill or recycled. It is estimated that the energy required to manufacture a single plastic 1 litre bottle, fill it with water, truck it to a typical retail location, and then bury it in a landfill creates about .23 pounds of $CO_2$. That's equivalent to what an average car would emit in driving about half a kilometre.

## A Tax on Bottled Water?

What types of policies might the government employ in order to reduce the degree to which our limited resources are used to produce bottled water? If we apply the economic way of thinking to those who manufacture and sell bottled water, any policy which reduces the marginal benefit or increases the marginal cost of supplying this product will reduce its production.

Starting January 1, 2008, Chicago began levying a tax of 5 cents per litre of bottled water sold in its city, thereby increasing the marginal cost of selling this product. In the latter part of 2007, Toronto City Council was reviewing a proposal to impose a tax of 5 cents per litre on water bottled in Ontario and 10 cents per litre for water bottled outside of the province.

## The Industry Response to the Proposed Toronto Tax

The Canadian Bottled Water Association (CBWA), representing the major bottled water manufacturers, mounted a strong campaign opposing Toronto's proposed tax on the sale of bottled water. The CBWA argued that it is unfair and unwise to impose a discriminatory tax on a single grocery item, especially a healthy beverage alternative. The CBWA also noted that imposing a tax within Toronto would drive consumers to buy their food and beverage items outside the city limits, which could harm local businesses and create unemployment.

On November 27, 2007, Toronto City Council decided not to pursue a policy of taxing bottled water. Council members stated that this type of tax would be too costly to administer and that it may not even be legal.

## Other Policies Aimed at Slowing the Growth in the Bottled Water Industry

On April 23, 2009, Vancouver City Council voted to eliminate the use of bottled water at all municipal facilities over the following few years. The move was meant to reduce environmental costs, cut solid waste, and battle greenhouse-gas emissions. City staff were directed to find alternative sources of drinking water on city properties, such as the increased use of tap water and water fountains.

On October 17, 2016, the Ontario government proposed a policy that would impose a moratorium until 2019 on water taking permits for new or expanded operations for the purposes of bottling water. The government is also under mounting public pressure to significantly increase the price companies pay for the water they use in bottling operations, which is a laughable $3.71 for every million litres of water taken.

To date in Canada, over 90 municipalities, 26 college and university campuses, 11 school boards, and countless businesses and organizations have implemented restrictions on bottled water.

**For critical analysis:**

1. Explain how this issue relates to the concepts of scarcity, opportunity cost, and the meaning of economics.
2. This issue focuses on production and consumption related to one industry in Canada. Is this a microeconomic or macroeconomic focus? Explain.
3. How might the government affect the marginal benefit derived from supplying bottled water so as to reduce the amount of resources used in the production of bottled water?
4. How does this issue apply to policy analysis?

Sources: "November 21st campus day of action: update and results." *Inside the Bottle*. December 2, 2007. http://www.inside the bottle .org/november-21st-campus-day-action-update-and-results; Kelly Grant. "Toronto mulls bottled-water tax; several U.S. cities have adopted similar measure." *National Post*. November 21, 2007. pg A1; Polaris Institute. "Water royalties coming soon: Quebec eyes B.C. and Ontario models." November 27, 2007. http://www.polarisinstitute.org/water_royalties _coming_soon_quebec_eyes_b_c_and_ontario_models. Kelly Grant. "Bottled water tax will not be studied." *National Post*. National edition. November 27, 2007. Pg. A14; "Vancouver bans bottled water on city property." *CBC News*. Thursday, April 23, 2009. http://www.cbc.ca/canada /british-columbia/story/2009/04/23/bc-vancouver-bottled-water.html; "Nestle backs down in Canadian bottled water drought restriction fight." Mark Astley. *BeverageDaily.com*. October 14, 2013. (Accessed December 24, 2013). http://www.beveragedaily.com/Manufacturers/ Nestle-backs-down-in-Canadian-bottled-water-drought-restrictions-figh. "Ontario proposes two-year hold on new water-taking permits" KEITH LESLIE. Canadian Press. GlobeandMail. October 17, 2016. http://www. theglobeandmail.com/news/national/ontario-proposes-new-rules-for-bottled-water-companies/article32386149/ (Accessed on January 6, 2016)

# SUMMARY

Here is what you should know after reading this chapter. MyEconLab will help you identify what you know, and where to go when you need to practise. We suggest that as soon as you review one of the Learning Objective sections below, you then proceed to go through the related section in MyEconLab.

| LEARNING OBJECTIVES | KEY TERMS | MYECONLAB PRACTICE |
|---|---|---|
| **1.1 Scarcity.** Scarcity refers to the condition that arises because human wants in terms of goods, services, and goals always exceed what can be produced with the available limited resources—land, labour, entrepreneurship, and physical and human capital. Economics is a social science that studies how people allocate limited resources to satisfy unlimited wants. | scarcity, 2<br>goods, 2<br>services, 2<br>production, 2<br>land, 3<br>labour, 3<br>physical capital, 3<br>human capital, 3<br>entrepreneurship, 3<br>rent, 3<br>wages, 3<br>interest, 3<br>profit, 3 | • **MyEconLab** Study Plan 1.1 |
| **1.2 Defining Economics.** Economics is usually divided into microeconomics, which is the study of individual decision making by households and firms, and macroeconomics, which is the study of economywide phenomena such as inflation, unemployment, and national income. | economics, 3<br>microeconomics, 4<br>macroeconomics, 4<br>aggregates, 5 | • **MyEconLab** Study Plan 1.2 |
| **1.3 Rational Decision Making. Benefits at the Margin, Incentives, and Resource Use.** Under the rationality assumption, the individual will employ resources in uses where the marginal benefit exceeds the marginal cost so as to maximize his or her own self-interest. Marginal cost is measured in terms of opportunity cost, which is the highest-valued alternative that must be sacrificed to satisfy a want. A change in marginal cost or marginal benefit will change the incentives that an individual faces and will lead to a change in resource use decisions. | economic way of thinking, 5<br>rationality assumption, 6<br>opportunity cost, 6<br>marginal benefit, 7<br>marginal cost, 7<br>sunk costs, 7<br>incentive, 8 | • **MyEconLab** Study Plan 1.3 |
| **1.4 The Scientific Method.** In using the scientific method, one makes assumptions, constructs models or theories, and tests these models with the facts. Models are simplified representations of the real world that make predictions that can be tested by the facts. | models or theories, 10<br>ceteris paribus assumption, 11<br>empirical, 12 | • **MyEconLab** Study Plan 1.4 |

| LEARNING OBJECTIVES | KEY TERMS | MYECONLAB PRACTICE |
|---|---|---|
| **1.5 Positive versus Normative Economics.** Positive economics deals with *what is*, whereas normative economics deals with what *ought to be*. Positive statements are of the "if . . . then" nature and are testable by facts. By contrast, normative statements are based on subjective value judgments. | positive economics, 14<br>normative economics, 14 | • **MyEconLab** Study Plan 1.5 |
| **1.6 Economic Policy and Socioeconomic Goals.** Theories can help us identify how various policies affect socioeconomic goals, such as full employment, efficiency, economic growth, price stability, and equity. | policies, 15 | • **MyEconLab** Study Plan 1.6 |

# PROBLEMS

(Answers to the odd-numbered problems appear at the back of the book.)

**LO 1.1 Explain the meaning of scarcity.**

1. Identify the factor of production that best relates to each of the following:
   a. a degree in engineering
   b. underground oil reserves
   c. the factor that earns profit
   d. a newly constructed pulp and paper mill
   e. the factor that earns wages

**LO 1.2 Define economics and distinguish between microeconomics and macroeconomics.**

2. According to Example 1–1, "The Economics of Web Page Design," what aspects of web design make it an "economic concern"?
3. Categorize the following issues as either a microeconomic issue or a macroeconomic issue.
   a. The national unemployment rate increases.
   b. The wage increases of nurses do not keep up with the wage increases of doctors.
   c. The price of cigarettes increases due to a tax imposed on cigarette manufacturers.
   d. The Canadian annual inflation rate exceeds the average annual increase in Canadian wages.
   e. The nation's total annual rate of production declines.
   f. In response to strong competition, a Canadian retail corporation files for bankruptcy.

**LO 1.3 Describe how resource use decisions are affected by the rationality assumption, costs and benefits at the margin, and incentives.**

4. In order to spend a winter in Victoria, B.C., Paul Dafoe rents out his Montreal condo, as well as his car, to a married couple attending university. Paul estimates that the total cost associated with his decision to winter in Victoria for the eight-month period is $15 000. He calculates this total cost by adding the following costs: round trip airfare; eight months' rental fees for a Victoria condo; estimated total grocery, personal care, and entertainment expenses while staying in Victoria; and total rental car expenses incurred in Victoria. Is $15 000 the correct marginal cost associated with Paul's decision to winter in Victoria? Explain.
5. Jon Krechen is currently earning $3000 per month working full time as a computer technical support person for a college situated in Toronto. Jon lives in a one-bedroom apartment and pays $1000 per month in rent. Jon's monthly living expenses, including food, personal care, taxes, insurance, and entertainment amount to $1600 per month. Since Jon does not own a vehicle, he pays $75 per month for a bus pass.

Jon is in the process of estimating the marginal (extra) cost related to his decision to enroll full-time in an intensive two-month computer networking course in the Toronto area. While taking the computer course, Jon will be on a two-month leave without pay from the college where he works. Jon will continue to live in the same apartment and will travel by bus to the training centre offering the computer course. Jon estimates that his living expenses will be the same as if he were working. The tuition, books, and fees related to taking the computer course are $4500. Compute Jon's marginal cost of taking the two-month computer course.

6. Recent Canadian studies indicate that Canadians in the lower income brackets tend to donate more time, per year, to volunteer activities, compared to individuals who earn higher levels of income. Is this observation consistent with rational behaviour? Explain.
7. Your bank advertises that cash withdrawals from your bank machine are "free" if you always keep a minimum monthly balance of $5000 in your chequing account. In this case, are your cash withdrawals truly "free"? Explain.
8. According to Example 1–2, "The Opportunity Cost of Finding a Mate—Lower on the Internet?", what economic concept helps explain the popularity of online dating websites? Explain.
9. The mayor of a Canadian city justifies the construction of a beautiful new city hall on the basis of there being sufficient tax dollars available to pay for this project. Is the mayor's decision to construct the city hall a rational one? Explain.
10. Since health care is an essential service, all health-care services should be provided free of charge. Moreover, the government should continue to increase the resources to health care until all hospital waitlists across the nation disappear. Is this view consistent with making decisions at the margin? Explain.

**LO 1.4 Explain the three key processes involved in the scientific method.**

11. Give a refutable implication (one that can be tested by evidence from the real world) for each of the following models:
    a. The accident rate of drivers is inversely related to their age.
    b. The rate of inflation is directly related to the rate of change in the nation's money supply.
    c. The wages of professional basketball players are directly related to their high-school grade-point averages.
    d. The rate at which bank employees are promoted is inversely related to their frequency of absenteeism.
12. Consider the following statements on the basis of positive economic analysis that assumes ceteris paribus. List one other thing that might change and thus alter the outcome stated.
    a. Increased demand for laptop computers will drive up their price.
    b. Falling gasoline prices will result in additional vacation travel.
    c. A reduction in corporate income tax rates will result in more people working.

**LO 1.5 Distinguish between positive and normative economics.**

13. Identify which of the following statements use positive economic analysis and which use normative analysis.
    a. Increasing the minimum wage will reduce employment opportunities for young people.
    b. A teacher should earn a higher salary than a hockey player, since the teacher's job is far more valuable to society.
    c. Everyone should enjoy free access to dental care.
    d. If the price of admission to each NHL hockey game is reduced, there will be an increase in ticket sales for each NHL game.

**LO 1.6 Describe the relationship among theories, policies, and socioeconomic goals.**

14. Identify which socioeconomic goal(s) may be promoted and which goal(s) may be conflicted with, for each policy listed below.
    a. Policy: In order to provide free public-health services, the government severely taxes Canadian corporation profits.
    b. Policy: The government raises the rate of income tax on all employees. The extra tax dollars raised are used to compensate upper-income investors who were swindled by fraud schemes.
    c. Policy: The government increases the monthly benefits (payments) to those collecting welfare. These people immediately spend the extra income on new goods and services.
    d. Policy: The government levies a special tax on all luxury goods. The taxes collected are used to keep college and university tuition fees relatively low.

# BUSINESS APPLICATION

**LO 1.2 Define economics and distinguish between microeconomics and macroeconomics.**

## Finance: Fundamental Stock Investment Analysis

How might you go about determining whether to buy or sell a specific company stock?

Obviously, if you could predict the stock price, you would buy the stock if the price were predicted to increase in the near future, and possibly sell if the price were expected to fall. According to what is often called *fundamental stock analysis*, the single most important factor affecting a stock price is the expected profitability of the company that originally issued the stock. According to fundamental stock analysis, a company's stock price will increase if investors expect that the annual profit of this firm will increase significantly in the near future.

The expected profit of any corporation will be affected by both *macroeconomic* and *microeconomic* factors. Macroeconomic factors would include broad global and national events and trends. In formulating profit expectations, investors will also closely monitor microeconomic measures and trends at the specific industry and company level.

## Business Application Problem

For each event and hypothetical company listed below, answer the following questions:

i. Is it a macroeconomic event or a microeconomic event?
ii. Will it tend to increase or decrease the company's stock price? (Hint: predict how the event will affect the expected profit of the firm in question.)

a. *Event:* Due to the declining Canadian dollar (exchange rate), Canadian companies that export products to the U.S. experience a major increase in annual sales.
Company: Timber Corp., a Canadian lumber company that exports 80 percent of its products.

b. *Event:* Special taxes are imposed on Canadian firms that manufacture cigarettes.
Company: The Smoke Factory, a Canadian cigarette manufacturer.

c. *Event:* With global inflation escalating out of control, investors lose confidence in paper currency. As a result, there is a worldwide trend toward the purchase of items that investors feel will retain their value over time.
Company: Bre-Y Mining Corp., a large, multinational gold mining firm.

d. *Event:* As a result of new management, a department store is able to achieve the same annual sales as the previous year with much lower operating costs.
Company: Wardwoods, a Canadian department store.

e. *Event*: Due to an upward trend in Canadian interest rates, investors sell stocks in all the major Canadian industries in order to purchase Canadian bonds.
Company: Morgan Mutual Fund, a corporation that manages investor funds by buying blue chip stocks in a wide range of Canadian industries (on behalf of investors).

# Reading and Working with Graphs

# APPENDIX A

A graph is a visual representation of the relationship between variables. In this appendix, we will stick to just two variables: an **independent variable**, which can change freely in value, and a **dependent variable**, which changes only as a result of changes in the value of the independent variable. For example, if nothing else is changing in your life, your weight depends on the amount of food you eat. Food is the independent variable and weight the dependent variable.

**Independent variable** A variable whose value is determined independently of, or outside, the equation under study.

**Dependent variable** A variable whose value changes according to changes in the value of one or more independent variables.

A table is a list of numerical values showing the relationship between two (or more) variables. Any table can be converted into a graph, which is a visual representation of that list. Once you understand how a table can be converted to a graph, you will understand what graphs are and how to construct and use them.

Consider a practical example. A conservationist may try to convince you that driving at lower highway speeds will help you conserve gas. Table A–1 shows the relationship between speed—the independent variable—and the distance you can go on a litre of gas at that speed—the dependent variable. This table does show a pattern of sorts. As the data in the first column get larger in value, the data in the second column get smaller.

**TABLE A–1**
**Gas Consumption as a Function of Driving Speed**

| Kilometres per Hour | Kilometres per Litre |
|---|---|
| 70 | 11 |
| 80 | 10 |
| 90 | 9 |
| 100 | 8 |
| 110 | 7 |
| 120 | 6 |
| 130 | 5 |

Now, let us take a look at the different ways in which variables can be related.

## Direct and Inverse Relationships

Two variables can be related in different ways, some simple, others more complex. For example, a person's weight and height are often related. If we measured the height and weight of thousands of people, we would surely find that taller people tend to weigh more than shorter people. That is, we would discover that there is a **direct relationship** between height and weight. By this, we simply mean that an increase in one variable is usually associated with an increase in the related variable. This can easily be seen in part (a) of Figure A–1.

**Direct relationship** A relationship between two variables that is positive, meaning that an increase in one variable is associated with an increase in the other, and a decrease in one variable is associated with a decrease in the other.

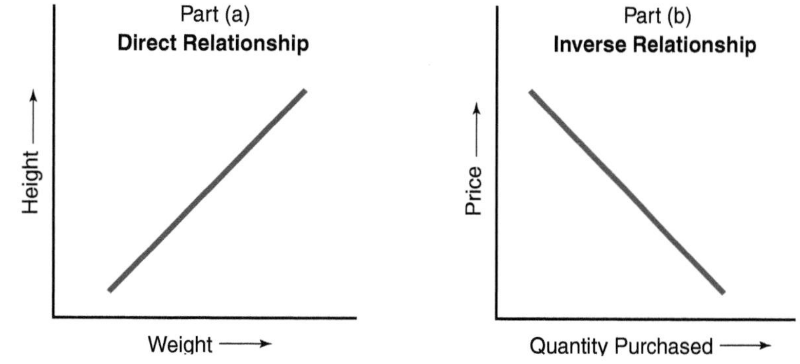


**FIGURE A–1**
**Relationships**

**Inverse relationship** A relationship between two variables that is negative, meaning that an increase in one variable is associated with a decrease in the other, and a decrease in one variable is associated with an increase in the other.

Let us look at another simple way in which two variables can be related. Much evidence indicates that as the price of a specific commodity rises, the amount purchased decreases—there is an **inverse relationship** between the variable's price per unit and quantity purchased. A table listing the data for this relationship would indicate that for higher and higher prices, smaller and smaller quantities would be purchased. We see this relationship in part (b) of Figure A–1.

# Constructing a Graph

Let us now examine how to construct a graph to illustrate a relationship between two variables.

## A Number Line

**Number line** A line that can be divided into segments of equal length, each associated with a number.

The first step is to become familiar with what is called a **number line**. One is shown in Figure A–2. There are two things that you should know about it.

1. The points on the line divide the line into equal segments.
2. The numbers associated with the points on the line increase in value from left to right; saying it the other way around, the numbers decrease in value from right to left. However you say it, what we are describing is formally called an *ordered set of points*.

**FIGURE A–2**
**Horizontal Number Line**

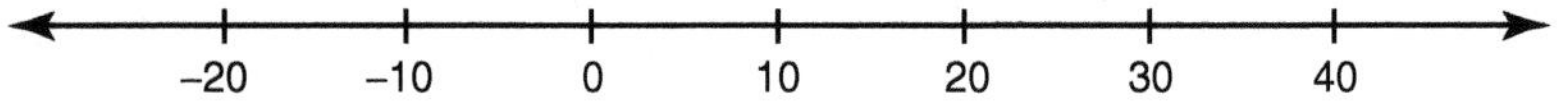


On the number line, we have shown the line segments—that is, the distance from 0 to 10 or the distance between 30 and 40. They all appear to be equal and, indeed, are equal to 13 mm. When we use a distance to represent a quantity, such as barrels of oil, graphically, we are scaling the number line. In the example shown, the distance between 0 and 10 might represent 10 barrels of oil, or the distance from 0 to 40 might represent 40 barrels. Of course, the scale may differ on different number lines. For example, a distance of 1 cm could represent 10 units on one number line but 5000 units on another. Note that on our number line, points to the left of 0 correspond to negative numbers and points to the right of 0 correspond to positive numbers.

Of course, we can also construct a vertical number line. Consider the one in Figure A–3. As we move up this vertical number line, the numbers increase in value; conversely, as we descend, they decrease in value. Below 0 the numbers are negative, and above 0 the numbers are positive. And as on the horizontal number line, all the line segments are equal. This line is divided into segments such that the distance between –2 and –1 is the same as the distance between 0 and 1.

## Combining Vertical and Horizontal Number Lines

By drawing the horizontal and vertical lines on the same sheet of paper, we are able to express the relationships between variables graphically. We do this in Figure A–4.

We draw them so that they intersect at each other's 0 point, and so that they are perpendicular to each other. The result is a set of coordinate axes, where each line is called an axis. When we have two axes, they span a plane.

**y-axis** The vertical axis in a graph.

**x-axis** The horizontal axis in a graph.

**Origin** The intersection of the y-axis and the x-axis in a graph.

For one number line, you need only one number to specify any point on the line; equivalently, when you see a point on the line, you know that it represents one number or one value. With a coordinate value system, you need two numbers to specify a single point in the plane; when you see a single point on a graph, you know that it represents two numbers or two values.

The basic things that you should know about a coordinate number system are that the vertical number line is referred to as the **y-axis**, the horizontal number line is referred to as the **x-axis**, and the point of intersection of the two lines is referred to as the **origin**.

Any point such as $A$ in Figure A–4 represents two numbers—a value of $x$ and a value of $y$. But we know more than that; we also know that point $A$ represents a positive value of $y$ because it is above the $x$-axis, and we know that it represents a positive value of $x$ because it is to the right of the $y$-axis.

Point $A$ represents a "paired observation" of the variables $x$ and $y$; in particular, in Figure A–4, $A$ represents an observation of the pair of values $x = 10$ and $y = 1$. Every point in the coordinate system corresponds to a paired observation of $x$ and $y$, which can be simply written $(x, y)$—the $x$-value is always specified first, then the $y$-value. When we give the values associated with the position of point $A$ in the coordinate number system, we are, in effect, giving the coordinates of that point. $A$'s coordinates are $x = 10$, $y = 1$, or $(10, 1)$.

**FIGURE A–3**
**Vertical Number Line**

## Graphing Numbers in a Table

Consider Table A–2. Column 1 shows different prices for T-shirts, and column 2 gives the number of T-shirts purchased per week at these prices. Note the pattern of these numbers. As the price of a T-shirt falls, the number of T-shirts purchased per week increases. Therefore, an inverse relationship exists between these two variables, and as soon as we represent it on a graph, you will be able to see the relationship. We can graph this relationship using a coordinate number system—a vertical and a horizontal number line for each of these two variables. Such a graph is shown in part (b) of Figure A–5.

In economics, it is conventional to put dollar values on the $y$-axis. We therefore construct a vertical number line for price and a horizontal number line, the $x$-axis, for quantity of T-shirts purchased per week. The resulting coordinate system allows the plotting of each of the paired observation points; in part (a), we repeat Table A–2, with a column added expressing these points in paired-data $(x, y)$ form. For example, point $J$ is the paired observation $(30, 9)$. It indicates that when the price of a T-shirt is $9, 30 will be purchased per week.

If it were possible to sell parts of a T-shirt (½ or 1/20 shirt), we would have observations at every possible price. That is, we would be able to connect our paired observations, represented as lettered points. Let us assume that we can make T-shirts perfectly divisible. We would then have a line that connects these points, as shown in the graph in Figure A–6.

In short, we have now represented the data from the table in the form of a graph. Note that an inverse relationship between two variables shows up on a graph as a line or curve that slopes downward from left to right. (You might as well get used to the idea that economists call a straight line a "curve," even though it may not curve at all. Much of economists' data turn out to be curves, so they refer to everything represented graphically, even straight lines, as curves.)

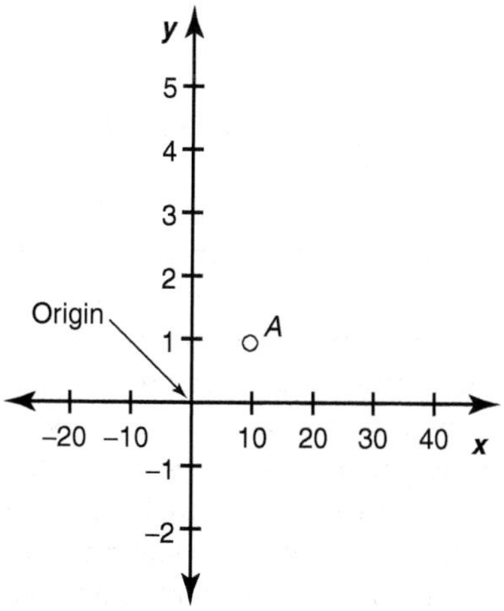


**FIGURE A–4**
**A Set of Coordinate Axes**

**TABLE A–2**
**T-Shirts Purchased**

| (1) Price per T-Shirt | (2) Number of T-Shirts Purchased per Week |
|---|---|
| $10 | 20 |
| 9 | 30 |
| 8 | 40 |
| 7 | 50 |
| 6 | 60 |
| 5 | 70 |

**FIGURE A–5**
**Graphing the Relationship between T-Shirts Purchased and Price**

Part (a)

| T-Shirts Purchased per Week | Price per T-Shirt | Point on Graph |
|---|---|---|
| 20 | $10 | *I* (20, 10) |
| 30 | 9 | *J* (30, 9) |
| 40 | 8 | *K* (40, 8) |
| 50 | 7 | *L* (50, 7) |
| 60 | 6 | *M* (60, 6) |
| 70 | 5 | *N* (70, 5) |

Part (b)

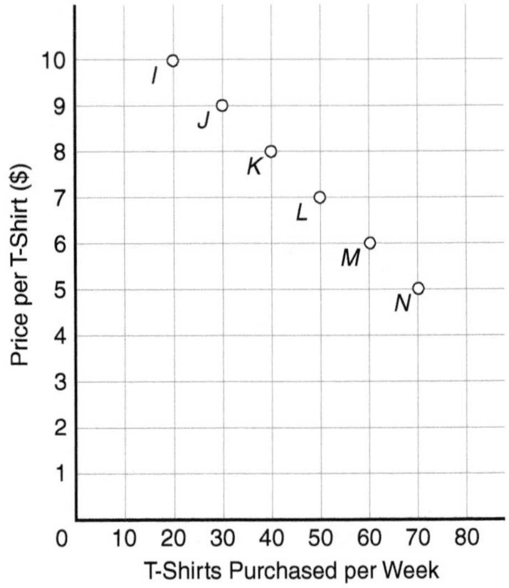


**FIGURE A–6**
**Connecting the Observation Points**

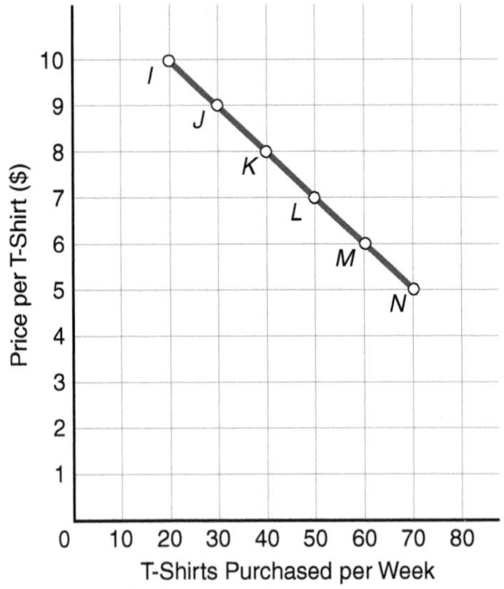


# The Slope of a Line (A Linear Curve)

An important property of a curve represented on a graph is its *slope*. Consider Figure A–7, which represents the quantities of shoes per week that a seller is willing to offer at different prices. Note that in part (a) of Figure A–7, as in Figure A–5, we have expressed the coordinates of the points in parentheses in paired-data form.

The *slope* of a line is defined as the change in the $y$-values divided by the corresponding change in the $x$-values as we move along the line. Let us move from point $E$ to point $D$ in part (b) of Figure A–7. As we move, we note that the change in the $y$-values, which is the

Part (a)

| Pairs of Shoes Offered per Week | Price per Pair | Point on Graph |
|---|---|---|
| 400 | $100 | A (400,100) |
| 320 | 80 | B (320, 80) |
| 240 | 60 | C (240, 60) |
| 160 | 40 | D (160, 40) |
| 80 | 20 | E (80, 20) |

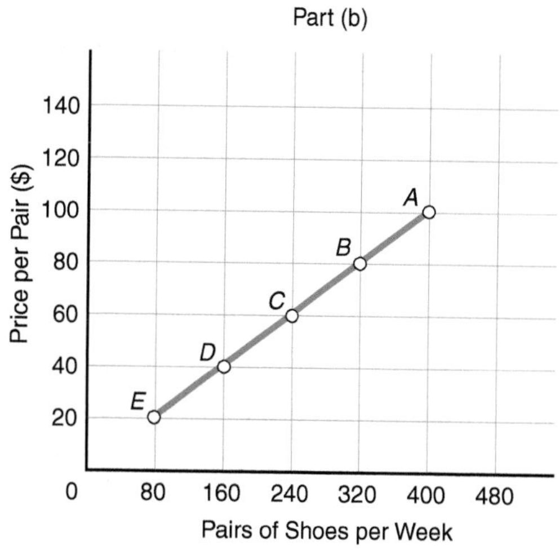


**FIGURE A–7**
**A Positively Sloped Curve**

change in price, is +$20 because we have moved from a price of $20 to a price of $40 per pair. As we move from *E* to *D*, the change in the *x*-values is +80; the number of pairs of shoes willingly offered per week rises from 80 to 160 pairs. The slope calculated as a change in the *y*-values divided by the change in the *x*-values is, therefore,

$$\frac{20}{80} = \frac{1}{4}$$

It may be helpful for you to think of slope as a "rise" (movement in the vertical direction) over a "run" (movement in the horizontal direction). We show this abstractly in Figure A–8. The slope is measured by the amount of rise divided by the amount of run. In the example in Figure A–8, and of course in Figure A–7, the amount of rise is positive and so is the amount of run. That is because it is a direct relationship. We show an inverse relationship in Figure A–9. The slope is still equal to the rise divided by the run, but in this case, the rise and the run have opposite signs because the curve slopes downward.

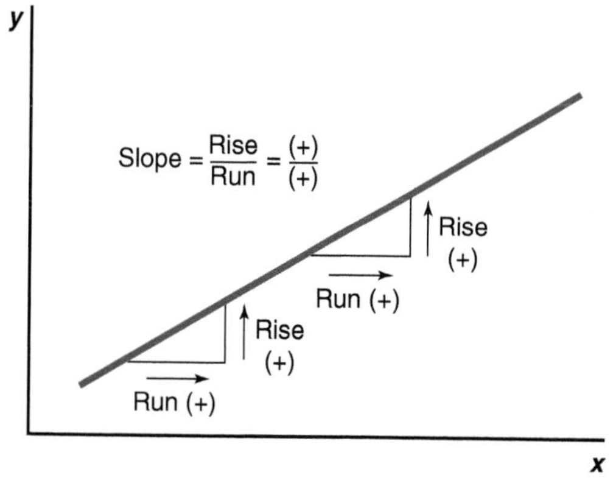


**FIGURE A–8**
**Figuring Positive Slope**

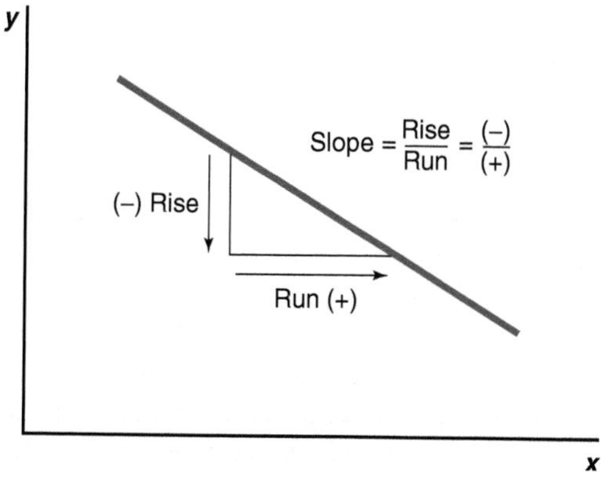


**FIGURE A–9**
**Figuring Negative Slope**

That means that the slope will have to be negative and that we are dealing with an inverse relationship.

Now, let us calculate the slope for a different part of the curve in part (b) of Figure A–7. We will find the slope as we move from point $B$ to point $A$. Again, we note that the slope, or rise over run, from $B$ to $A$ equals

$$\frac{20}{80} = \frac{1}{4}$$

A specific property of a straight line is that its slope is the same between any two points; in other words, the slope is constant at all points on a straight line in a graph.

We conclude that for our example in Figure A–7, the relationship between the price of a pair of shoes and the number of pairs of shoes willingly offered per week is linear, which simply means "in a straight line," and our calculations indicate a constant slope. Moreover, we calculate a direct relationship between these two variables, which turns out to be an upward-sloping (from left to right) curve. Upward-sloping curves have positive slopes—in this case, it is $+\frac{1}{4}$.

We know that an inverse relationship between two variables shows up as a downward-sloping curve—rise over run will be a negative slope because the rise and run have opposite signs as shown in Figure A–9. When we see a negative slope, we know that increases in one variable are associated with decreases in the other. Therefore, we say that downward-sloping curves have negative slopes. Can you verify that the slope of the graph representing the relationship between T-shirt prices and the quantity of T-shirts purchased per week in Figure A–6 is $-\frac{1}{10}$?

## Slopes of Nonlinear Curves

The graph presented in Figure A–10 indicates a *nonlinear* relationship between two variables—total profits and output per unit of time. Inspection of this graph indicates that at first, increases in output lead to increases in total profits; that is, total profits rise as output increases. But beyond some output level, further increases in output cause decreases in total profits.

Can you see how this curve rises at first, reaches a peak at point $C$, and then falls? This curve relating total profits to output levels appears mountain-shaped.

Considering that this curve is nonlinear (it is obviously not a straight line), should we expect a constant slope when we compute changes in $y$ divided by corresponding changes in $x$ in moving from one point to another? A quick inspection, even without specific numbers, should lead us to conclude that the slopes of lines joining different points in this curve, such as between $A$ and $B$, $B$ and $C$, or $C$ and $D$, will *not* be the same. The curve slopes upward (in a positive direction) for some values and downward (in a negative direction) for other values. In fact, the slope of the line between any two points on this curve will be different from the slope of the line between any two other points. Each slope will be different as we move along the curve.

**FIGURE A–10**

**The Slope of a Nonlinear Curve**

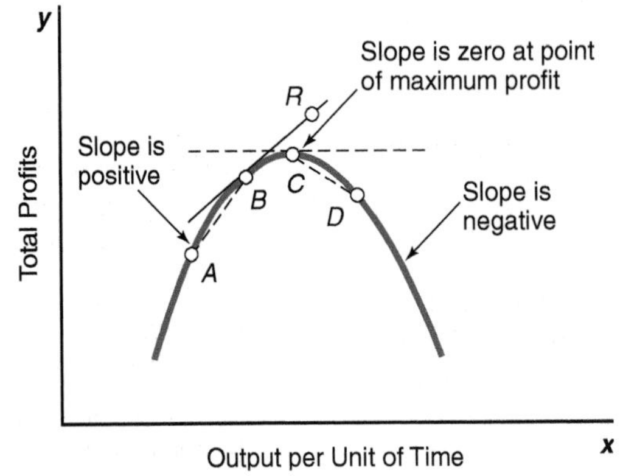

Instead of using a line between two points to discuss slope, mathematicians and economists prefer to discuss the slope *at a particular point*. The slope at a point on the curve, such as point *B* in the graph in Figure A–10, is the slope of a line *tangent* to that point. A tangent line is a straight line that touches a curve at only one point. For example, it might be helpful to think of the tangent at *B* as the straight line that just "kisses" the curve at point *B*.

To calculate the slope of a tangent line, you need to have some additional information besides the two values of the point of tangency. For example, in Figure A–10, if we knew that the point *R* also lay on the tangent line and we knew the two values of that point, we could calculate the slope of the tangent line. We could calculate rise over run between points *B* and *R*, and the result would be the slope of the line tangent to the one point *B* on the curve.

## APPENDIX SUMMARY

1. Direct relationships involve a dependent variable changing in the same direction as the change in the independent variable.
2. Inverse relationships involve the dependent variable changing in the opposite direction of the change in the independent variable.
3. When we draw a graph showing the relationship between two economic variables, we are holding all other things constant (the Latin term for which is *ceteris paribus*).
4. We obtain a set of coordinates by putting vertical and horizontal number lines together. The vertical line is called the $y$-axis; the horizontal line, the $x$-axis.
5. The slope of any linear (straight-line) curve is the change in the $y$-values divided by the corresponding change in the $x$-values as we move along the line. Otherwise stated, the slope is calculated as the amount of rise over the amount of run, where rise is movement in the vertical direction and run is movement in the horizontal direction.
6. The slope of a nonlinear curve changes; it is positive when the curve is rising and negative when the curve is falling. At a maximum or minimum point, the slope of the nonlinear curve is zero.

## APPENDIX PROBLEMS

(Answers to the odd-numbered problems appear at the back of the book.)

A-1. Explain which is the independent variable and which is the dependent variable in the following examples.

a. Once you determine the price of a notebook at your college bookstore, you will decide how many notebooks to buy.

b. You will decide how many credit hours to register for this semester once the university tells you how many work-study hours you will be assigned.

c. You are anxious to receive your Economics exam grade because you studied many hours in the weeks preceding the exam.

A-2. For the following items, state whether a direct or an indirect relationship exists.

a. the number of hours you study for an exam and your exam mark.

b. the price of pizza and the quantity purchased.

c. the number of games your college basketball team won last year and the number of season tickets sold this year.

A-3. Complete the table and plot the following function:

$y = 3x$

| $x$ | $y$ |
|---|---|
| 4 | |
| 3 | |
| 2 | |
| 1 | |
| 0 | |
| −1 | |
| −2 | |
| −3 | |
| −4 | |

A-4. Review Figure A–4, and then state whether the following paired observations are on, above, or below the $x$-axis and on, to the left of, or to the right of the $y$-axis.

a. (−10, 4)

b. (20, −2)

c. (10, 0)

A-5. Calculate the slope for the function you graphed in Problem A-3.

A-6. Complete the table and plot the following function:

$y = x^2$

| $x$ | $y$ |
|---|---|
| 4 | |
| 3 | |
| 2 | |
| 1 | |
| 0 | |
| −1 | |
| −2 | |
| −3 | |
| −4 | |

A-7. Indicate at each ordered pair whether the slope of the curve you plotted in Problem A-6 is positive, negative, or zero.

A-8. State whether the following functions imply a positive or negative relationship between $x$ and $y$.

a. $y = 5x$
b. $y = 3 + x$
c. $y = -3x$

2

# Production Possibilities and Economic Systems

Soaring Canadian car insurance rates created havoc for politicians and consumers alike in the first decade of the twenty-first century. The issue of skyrocketing auto insurance rates threatened the election campaigns of free-enterprise, conservative governments in New Brunswick, Ontario, and Alberta. In 2005, the Consumers' Association of Canada completed research involving 714 Canadian communities and close to 4 000 000 insurance quotes and found that car insurance rates tended to be lower in provinces where this service is provided by government, rather than the private sector. A follow-up Quebec study found that between 2001 to 2010, the lowest provincial car insurance rates were provided by government-run auto insurance organizations. More recently, in 2015, the Manitoba government Department of Finance compared average auto insurance premiums across Canada, and continued to find the lowest rates being offered in those provinces operating public auto insurance. The concepts presented in this chapter will help you understand both the public benefits and costs related to delivering services, such as auto insurance, under different economic systems.

Source: Brett J. Skinner. "Three of four provinces with government auto insurance monopolies have highest rates in Canada." News Releases. Fraser Institute. November 18, 2008. http://www.fraserinstitute.org/researchnews/news/display.aspx?id=12720 (Accessed August 27, 2010.); Comparison by Province. Statistics. Groupement des assureurs automobiles. https://www.gaa.qc.ca/en/comparison-province (Accessed Dec 28, 2013); "Annual Basic Utility Bundle Cost Comparison for the Year Ended March 31, 2015" Manitoba Finance. Manitoba Government. 2016. https://www.gov.mb.ca/finance/publications/pubs/utility_2015.pdf (Accessed January 7, 2016)

myeconlab

MyEconLab helps you master each objective and study more efficiently. See end of chapter for details.

## LEARNING OBJECTIVES

After reading this chapter, you should be able to:

2.1 Define the production possibilities curve and identify its assumptions.

2.2 Use the production possibilities curve to illustrate the concepts of scarcity, trade-offs, unemployment, productive efficiency, allocative efficiency, increasing opportunity cost, and economic growth.

2.3 Use the production possibilities curve to explain the trade-off between consumption goods and capital goods.

2.4 Distinguish between absolute advantage and comparative advantage and use these concepts to explain how specialization and trade can increase production and consumption.

2.5 Explain the differences between the pure capitalist, pure command, and mixed economic systems.

2.6 Describe the features of pure capitalism and explain how capitalism answers the three basic economic questions.

# DID YOU KNOW THAT...?

Identity theft is the fastest growing fraud in both Canada and the United States. In 2012, the total reported dollar loss by Canadian identity theft victims was $15.98 million. This amounts to an increase of 150 percent over the losses of $6.4 million reported in 2007 in Canada. During the two year period - 2012 to 2014 - the total number of Canadians victimized by identity theft increased by over 20%. However, this figure falls dramatically short of the number of cases of identity theft that are suspected to occur in Canada.

Identity thieves are looking for the following information: your signature; date of birth; Social Insurance Number; full address; username and password for online services; driver's license number; personal identification numbers (PIN); credit card information (numbers, expiry dates, and the last three digits printed on the signature panel); bank account and PIN numbers; passport number.

Criminals can use your stolen or reproduced personal or financial information to: access your bank accounts; open new bank accounts; transfer bank balances; apply for loans, credit cards, and other goods and services; make purchases; hide their criminal activities; obtain passports; or receive government benefits.

In economics, identity theft can be viewed as a form of capital investment undertaken by dishonest individuals, as explained in this chapter.

Sources: Canadian Anti-Fraud Centre Criminal Intelligence Analytical Unit. *Annual Statistical Report 2012: Mass Marketing Fraud and Identity Theft Activities.* Page 18. http://www.antifraudcentre-centre antifraude.ca/english/documents/annual%202012%20cafc.pdf (Accessed Dec 26, 2013); Identity Theft and Identity Fraud. Scams and Fraud. Royal Canadian Mounted Police. http://www.rcmp-grc.gc.ca /scams-fraudes/id-theft-vol-eng.htm (Accessed on Dec 26, 2013); "Mass Marketing Fraud & ID Theft Activities". Annual Statistical Report 2014. Canadian Ant-Fraud Centre. Government of Canada. March 11, 2015. http://www.antifraudcentre-centreantifraude.ca/reports-rapports/2014/ann-ann-eng.htm#a28 (Accessed January 8, 2017).

## 2.1 The Production Possibilities Curve

We begin this chapter by introducing an economic model called the production possibilities curve. We will use this model to sharpen your understanding of concepts discussed in Chapter 1, such as scarcity, choice, opportunity cost, efficiency, full employment, and economic growth. As well, we will illustrate how production possibilities can be expanded through specialization and trade. Finally, we will complete this chapter by examining the different economic systems that nations and industries can use to determine production possibilities.

**Production possibilities curve (PPC)** A curve that represents all possible production combinations of two goods that can be produced.

The **production possibilities curve (PPC)** is a curve representing all possible production combinations of two goods that can be produced under the following assumptions:

1. The nation's resources—land, labour, capital, and entrepreneurship—are fully and efficiently employed producing just these two goods (or services).
2. The production is measured over a specific period of time—for example, one year.
3. The quantity and quality of resources used to produce these two goods are fixed over this period of time.
4. The technology is fixed over this period of time.

**Technology** Society's pool of applied knowledge concerning how goods and services can be produced.

**Technology** is defined as society's pool of applied knowledge concerning how goods and services can be produced by managers, workers, engineers, scientists, and craftspeople, using land and capital. You can think of technology as the formula (or recipe) used to combine factors of production. When better formulas are developed, more production can be obtained from the same amount of resources. The level of technology sets the limit on the amount and types of goods and services that we can derive from any given amount of resources. The production possibilities curve is drawn under the assumption that we use the best technology that we currently have available and that this technology does not change over the time period under study.

### The Production Possibilities Curve: An Example

Figure 2–1 describes a production possibilities curve for Canada for two goods—automobiles and newsprint—for 2007 (the data in Figure 2–1 are hypothetical). We assume for the moment that automobiles and newsprint are the only two goods that can be produced in Canada.

Part (a) of Figure 2–1 shows the various production combinations of automobiles and newsprint, assuming full and efficient employment of resources and a fixed level of resources and technology. If all resources are devoted to automobile production (point *A*), 3 million autos can be produced per year. Instead, if Canada decides to devote all its resources to newsprint production (point *G*), 6 million tonnes of newsprint per year can be produced. In between are other alternative possible production combinations. All of these production combinations are plotted as points *A, B, C, D, E, F,*and *G* in part (b) of Figure 2–1. Once connecting these points with a smooth curve, constructs Canada's production possibilities.

Note that this production possibilities curve indicates the *maximum* quantity of one good that can be produced in 2007, given some quantity of the other good that is to be produced. Therefore, if we are given that 2 million autos are to be produced in 2007, then the maximum amount of newsprint that can be produced in 2007 is 4 million tonnes at point *E* on the curve.

Part (a)

| Combination | Newsprint (millions of tonnes per year) | Automobiles (millions of units per year) |
|---|---|---|
| *A* | 0 | 3.0 |
| *B* | 1 | 2.9 |
| *C* | 2 | 2.7 |
| *D* | 3 | 2.4 |
| *E* | 4 | 2.0 |
| *F* | 5 | 1.4 |
| *G* | 6 | 0 |

Part (b)

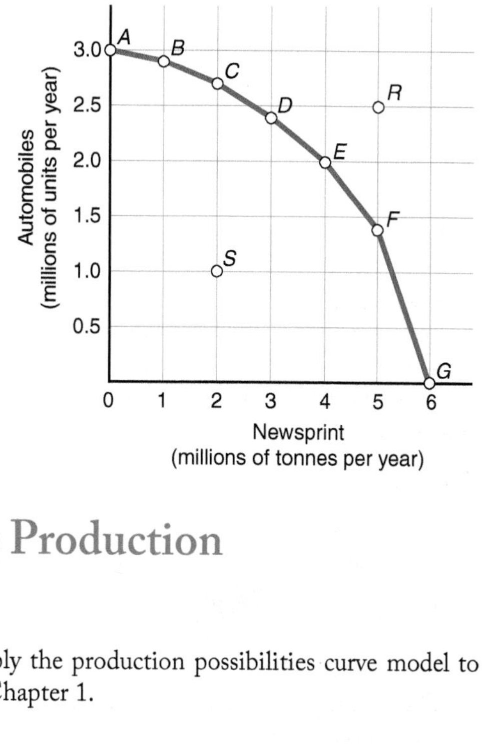


**FIGURE 2–1**

**A Society's Trade-Off between Automobiles and Newsprint**

The production of automobiles is measured in millions of units per year, while the production of newsprint is measured in millions of tonnes per year. The various combinations are given in part (a) and plotted in part (b). Connecting the points *A–G* with a relatively smooth line gives the production possibilities curve for automobiles and newsprint. Point *R* lies outside the production possibilities curve and is therefore unattainable at the point in time for which the graph is drawn. Point *S* lies inside the production possibilities curve and therefore represents an inefficient use of available resources or unemployment.

# 2.2 Applications of the Production Possibilities Curve

We now turn to examine how we can apply the production possibilities curve model to better understand concepts introduced in Chapter 1.

## The Production Possibilities Curve, Scarcity, and Trade-Offs

Recall from the previous chapter that *scarcity* refers to the condition that arises because wants always exceed what can be produced with limited resources. The production possibilities curve in Figure 2–1 can be viewed as a boundary that separates the attainable production combinations, on or inside the curve, from the unattainable points outside of the curve (such as point *R* in Figure 2–1). That is, even though we are assuming that the resources are being fully and efficiently employed using the most up-to-date technology, Canada faces a *limit*, in terms of what it can produce, as portrayed by the production possibilities curve. The existence of this boundary, in the face of unlimited wants, gives us a vision of the economic problem of scarcity.

The fact that the production possibilities curve slopes downward to the right suggests that due to scarcity, society is forced to make choices that involve trade-offs. In Figure 2–1, you can clearly see that if Canada is currently at point *E* in the current year, and chooses to move to point *F*, next year, when it can produce additional tonnes of newsprint, Canada has to trade off some automobile production. Note that trade-offs will occur anywhere *on* the production possibilities curve.

As a student, you face the scarcity problem of using a limited amount of time to achieve both your academic and personal goals. Every time you attend a class or a study group session you trade off the opportunity to spend that time learning in a different manner or engaging in a work- or leisure-related activity. As Example 2–1 illustrates, new technologies are changing the nature of the trade-offs students face when they consider whether they will attend their next class or choose the best alternative use of their time.

What is the opportunity cost of replacing a face-to-face lecture with a podcast lecture?

### EXAMPLE 2–1 Beware of "Free" Lecture Podcasts

At Simon Fraser University (SFU) in Vancouver, the class lectures for numerous university courses are recorded as podcasts that registered students can download to their computers or to portable devices such as iPods or iPhones. From 2008 to 2010, SFU created podcasts for 23 622 lectures in 1353 university courses. The lecture podcasts are available free of charge to students registered in the related courses. Each lecture podcast is made available to the student within 15 minutes after the class being taped. As of the start of 2017, the bank of online lectures covers about one-half of SFU classes, and includes audio, video and presentation recordings. In this Example, we critically assess the increasingly frequent practice of using these podcasts as a reason to skip the corresponding face-to-face class sessions.

Every student has his or her own subjective estimate of the expected value of the next-best alternative to attending class. For each student, the value of an hour spent in class depends in part on what time of the day the class meets. SFU's lecture podcasts permit students to reallocate their time. For example, if a particular student would rather work a few additional hours on a part-time job that starts in the mid-afternoon or enjoy a sunny afternoon on the beach, she can miss afternoon classes. She can then listen to the class lectures later that evening, when the opportunity cost of that learning activity is lower.

Of course, there is still an opportunity cost associated with skipping the actual face-to-face class meeting. The student misses out on the opportunity to ask questions of her professor during the lecture and to interact with other class members. The student may also score poorly on a class participation mark.

**For critical analysis:**

1. What opportunity costs (sacrifices) might you incur when you skip your classes?
2. In classes where group discussion or group work is an essential feature of the learning process, who bears some of the additional costs of higher absenteeism rates resulting from posting lectures on the Web?

Source: "Podcasting @ SFU." Simon Fraser University website. http://cgi.sfu.ca/~lectures/pub_html_podcasts/cgi-bin/index.php; Audio Lecture Recording. IT Services. Simon Fraser University. http://www.sfu.ca/itservices/technical/av_services/burnaby/lecture_recording/audio.html (Accessed on Dec 26, 2013); "Resources on lectures & note-taking for courses & classes". Learning and Studying. Student Learning Commons. SFU Library. http://www.lib.sfu.ca/about/branches-depts/slc/learning/lectures (Accessed on January 8, 2017).

## The Production Possibilities Curve and Unemployment

Recall that full employment is one of the important socioeconomic goals identified in Chapter 1. Our simple production possibilities model helps us better understand the importance of this goal. Suppose, looking at Figure 2–1, that Canada failed to achieve the goal of full employment. Where, roughly speaking, would Canada's production combination be located—inside, on, or outside of the production possibilities curve? The answer would be somewhere *inside* the production possibilities curve, such as point *S*. When Canada is inside its production possibilities curve, a major cost of unemployment is that society forgoes some production of goods and services. That is, unemployment leads to a lower standard of living for society as a whole. If Canada were to eliminate this unemployment and move from point *S* to point *E*, would this involve a trade-off? The answer is no, as the extra production would be derived from putting unemployed workers back to work, allowing more of both goods to be produced.

# The Production Possibilities Curve and Efficiency

The production possibilities curve can be used to define the notion of efficiency. Whenever the economy is operating on the PPC in Figure 2–1 at such points as *A*, *B*, *C*, or *D*, we say that its production is efficient. Such points as *S*, which lie below the production possibilities curve, are said to represent production situations that are not efficient.

**PRODUCTIVE EFFICIENCY.** Efficiency can mean many things to many people. Even within economics, there are different types of efficiency. Here, we are discussing efficiency in production, or **productive efficiency**, which occurs when a given output level is produced at minimal cost. Alternatively stated, productive efficiency occurs when a given level of inputs is used in a manner that produces the maximum output possible, given the level of technology.

**Productive efficiency** Occurs when a given output level is produced at minimal cost.

A simple, common-sense definition of productive efficiency is getting the most out of what we have as an economy. Clearly, we are not getting the most out of what we have if we are at point *S* in part (b) of Figure 2–1. We can move from point *S* to, say, point *C*, thereby increasing the total quantity of automobiles produced without any decrease in the total quantity of newsprint produced. We can move from point *S* to point *E*, for example, and have both more automobiles and more newsprint. Point *S* is called a **productively inefficient point**, which is defined as any point below the production possibilities curve, assuming resources are fully employed.

**Productively inefficient point** Any point below the production possibilities curve, assuming resources are fully employed.

Example 2–2 below describes a global initiative designed to educate children in the poorest regions of the world in a productively efficient (minimal cost) manner.

## EXAMPLE 2–2 One Laptop per Child

Most of the nearly 2 billion children in the developing world are inadequately educated or uneducated. One in three does not complete grade five. Children are resigned to poverty and isolation, never knowing what the light of learning could mean to their lives. At the same time, their governments struggle to compete in a very dynamic, social, and global information economy.

Attempting to enhance the education of children living in the developing (poorer) nations using traditional "bricks and mortar" educational resources—building schools, hiring teachers, buying textbooks—seems to be too expensive a task, and hence unrealistic. As an example, in Canada, it costs on average over US$7500 per year for every student in the traditional education system. Given the resources that poor countries can reasonably allocate to education—sometimes less than $20 per year per pupil—a worldwide nonprofit association called "One Laptop per Child (OLPC)" is seeking to bring education to children (and their parents) in poorer nations through the creation of a laptop costing less than $100. OLPC has currently developed the XO laptop, a machine designed for "learning learning."

What is the economic argument for using laptops to educate children in poorer nations?

The XO laptop has been designed to provide the most engaging wireless network available at a cost of $100 per unit. The laptops are connected to each other and to the Internet. The children in the neighbourhood are thus permanently connected to chat, share information on the Web, gather by videoconference, make music together, edit texts, read ebooks, and enjoy the use of collaborative games online. As the children grow and pursue new ideas, the software, content, resources, and tools should be able to grow with them. The battery of the laptop can work for many hours and can be charged in special gang chargers in the school or by mechanical or solar power, so there is no need to have electricity. The unique XO display allows the use of the laptop under a bright sun, enabling the user to work outside, if need be.

During the period 2010–2013 the pilot phase of Canada's first National One Laptop per Child program, OLPC Canada, was launched. OLPC Canada seeks to enhance the educational success of aboriginal youth by providing access to learning centered technology. To date, more than 3600 laptops have been distributed to Aboriginal youth 6–12 years of age in rural, remote, and urban communities in seven provinces and two territories.

Near the end of 2015, over 3 million laptops have been delivered to children in more than 50 countries around the world. As of 2016, OLPC Canada has successfully delivered the technology to more than 15,000 Indigenous youth in 70+ communities located in 9 provinces and 3 territories.

**For critical analysis:** Explain how the One Laptop per Child concept promotes productive efficiency.

*continued*

Sources: Peter Beaumont. "Rwanda's laptop revolution." *The Observer*. March 28, 2010. http://www.guardian.co.uk/technology/2010/mar/28/rwanda-laptop-revolution; "Mission." One Laptop per Child. http://www.laptop.org/en/vision/mission/index.shtml; "Laptop." Countries. About the Project. One Laptop Per Child. http://laptop.org/about/countries (Accessed Dec 26, 2013); "Annual expenditure on educational institutions per student for all services (2006). *Education at a Glance 2009: OECD Indicators.* September 2009. http://www.oecd.org/dataoecd/41/25/43636332.pdf. (Accessed Dec 26, 2013); "Technological tools for Indigenous students from coast to coast to coast. " About OLPC Canada. http://www.olpccanada.com/aboutolpccanada (Accessed January 8, 2016); "OLPC Announces Partnership with Zamora Teran Foundation"Sept 3, 2015. http://blog.laptop.org/2015/09/03/olpc-announces-partnership-with-zamora-teran-foundation/#.WHLSHvkrLa8 (Accessed January 8, 2016).

**Allocative efficiency** Producing the mix of goods and services most valued by consumers.

**ALLOCATIVE EFFICIENCY.** The concept of **allocative efficiency** is concerned with producing the mix of goods and services most valued by consumers. While all the points along the production possibilities curve in Figure 2–1 are productively efficient, only one production combination on this curve will be allocatively efficient. Suppose that point *E* in part (b) of Figure 2–1 is the most highly valued combination. If Canada ends up producing this combination, it is being allocatively efficient.

Stated in terms of the concepts learned in Chapter 1, if society were to move away from point *E*, in either direction, the marginal benefit derived from this move would be less than the marginal cost associated with this move. In other words, the extra value derived from producing a different combination of cars and newsprint would be less than the value given up by departing from point *E*. If the firms that produce these goods make decisions on the basis of society's marginal benefits and marginal costs, rational behaviour has the potential to lead us to this allocatively efficient production combination.

In this chapter's Issues and Applications, the merits of providing auto insurance via privately owned companies is compared with the merits of having the government administer auto insurance in Canada. One of the advantages of private auto insurance is that each injured individual can take the necessary legal action to ensure that the dollar value of the compensation resulting from an accident claim (marginal benefit) is sufficient to cover the full marginal cost related to the individual's injuries and losses sustained from the accident. In this way, private auto insurance promotes allocative efficiency.

In contrast, under public auto insurance, the government dictates the maximum insurance payouts to injured parties for claims, such as those relating to the pain and suffering incurred in an accident. Since these maximum payouts are often set in a manner that attempts to reduce the total cost of these claims, the public insurance system may tend to underallocate resources in the payment of claims to injured individuals.

## The Production Possibilities Curve and Opportunity Cost

We have re-created the curve in Figure 2–1 as Figure 2–2. Each combination, *A* through *G*, of automobiles and newsprint is represented on the production possibilities curve. Starting with the production of zero newsprint, Canada could produce 3 million automobiles with its available resources and technology. When we increase production of newsprint from zero to 1 million tonnes per year, we have to give up the automobile production represented by that first vertical arrow, *Aa*. From part (a) of Figure 2–1 you can see that this is 0.1 million autos a year (3.0 million – 2.9 million). Again, if we increase production of newsprint by 1 million tonnes per year, we go from *B* to *C*. In order to do so, we have to give up the vertical distance *Bb*, or 0.2 million automobiles a year. By the time we go from 5 million to 6 million tonnes of newsprint, to obtain that 1 million tonne increase we have to forgo the vertical distance *Ff*, or 1.4 million automobiles. In other words, the opportunity cost of the last 1 million tonnes of newsprint is 1.4 million autos, compared with 0.1 million autos, the opportunity cost for the first million tonnes of newsprint (starting at zero production).

**Law of increasing relative cost** When society takes more resources and applies them to the production of any specific good, the opportunity cost increases for each additional unit produced.

**LAW OF INCREASING RELATIVE COST.** What we are observing is called the **law of increasing relative cost**: when society takes more resources and applies them to the production of any specific good, the opportunity cost increases for each additional unit produced. The reason that, as a country, we face the law of increasing relative cost (which causes the production possibilities curve to bow outward) is that certain resources are better suited for

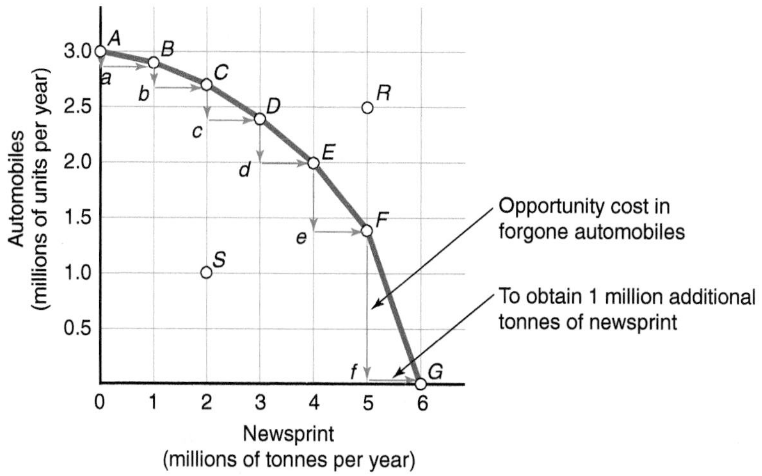


**FIGURE 2–2**

**The Law of Increasing Relative Cost**

Consider equal increments of newsprint production, as measured on the horizontal axis. All the horizontal arrows—*aB*, *bC*, and so on—are of equal length (1 million tonnes). The opportunity cost of going from 5 million tonnes of newsprint per year to 6 million *(Ff)* is much greater than going from zero tonnes to 1 million tonnes *(Aa)*. The opportunity cost of each additional equal increase in newsprint production rises.

producing some goods than they are for others. Resources are generally not *perfectly* adaptable for alternative uses. When increasing the output of a particular good, producers must use less adaptable resources than those already used in order to produce the additional output. Hence the cost of producing the additional units increases. In our hypothetical example here, at first, the mechanical technicians in the automobile industry would shift over to producing newsprint. After a while, though, upholstery specialists and windshield installers would also be asked to help. Clearly, they would be less effective in making newsprint.

As a rule of thumb, *the more specialized the resources, the more bowed the production possibilities curve.* At the other extreme, if all resources are equally suitable for newsprint production or automobile production, the curves in Figures 2–1 and 2–2 would approach a straight line representing a constant opportunity cost situation.

Policy Example 2–1 describes recent policy decisions made by the government of British Columbia that affect the production combination of two highly valued types of goods: natural-wilderness-area-related goods and energy-related goods (oil and gas). This example encourages you to apply the concepts of opportunity cost and allocative efficiency to evaluate policies that affect the way in which our resources are used.

## POLICY EXAMPLE 2–1 The Multi-Billion Dollar Park

In October 1997, the British Columbia New Democratic Party (NDP) government established the Muskwa-Kechika land-use area, a wilderness area larger than Switzerland, located in the northeast part of the province. In 2000, more land was added, bringing the total Muskwa-Kechika Management Area (M-KMA) to 6.3 million hectares, which made it the largest land-use decision of its kind in North America.

The management intent for the M-KMA is to maintain in perpetuity the wilderness quality, the diversity and abundance of wildlife, and the ecosystems on which the wildlife depends. One of the primary challenges is to be able to prevent corporate interests from exploiting the region's natural resources by engaging in logging, oil and gas drilling, and mining practices that would jeopardize the area's natural beauty and wildlife.

On June 25, 2003, the British Columbia Liberal government announced that it would allow exploration of extensive natural gas deposits, with a potential development value of $16 billion, in parts of the M-KMA.

According to the 2005–2006 M-KMA annual report to the premier and public, resource extraction for energy products such as oil and natural gas is permitted in 75 percent of the area, while 25 percent is designated under the provincial park system. This report noted that the intent is to use "best practices" to ensure that resource extraction occurs with minimal reduction in the quality of the natural wilderness area. For example, in extracting oil and gas for energy production, methods used to reduce negative impacts include building winter ice and snow roads that will be deactivated once the activity at well sites has been completed, and coordinating resource road development with other industry companies.

*continued*

On December 19, 2013, the Canadian National Energy Board (NEB) gave preliminary approval (subject to 209 conditions) to the Northern Gateway pipeline project that plans to transport 525,000 barrels of condensed bitumen (crude oil) per day from Alberta to Kitimat B.C., destined for Asian markets. Since the planned pipeline route is just south of the M-KMA, there are renewed concerns regarding the tradeoff between economic development and the preservation of the environment.

In a written decision on June 23, 2016, the Federal Court of Appeal, overturned the NEB preliminary approval of Northern Gateway, citing a failure to appropriately consult with First Nations in regards to the project. On November 29, 2016, the Trudeau government firmly rejected the Northern Gateway pipeline, on the basis of preserving the environment and local communities.

**For critical analysis:** Sketch the appropriate two-good production possibilities curve, assuming the law of increasing relative cost and illustrating the trade-off indicated in this example. On this production possibilities curve, sketch the allocatively efficient point *E*, which we assume is halfway down the curve you sketched. Sketch another point *F*, which is on the curve but in the direction of more energy products (oil and gas) when compared to point *E*. What is the opportunity cost of moving from point *E* to point *F*? If British Columbia's economy moved from point *E* to point *F*, how would the marginal benefit of such a move compare with the marginal cost of such a move? Explain.

Source: "Muskwa-Kechika, BC's working wilderness, 2005–2006, Report to the Premier and the public." Muskwa-Kechika Management Area. Muskwa-Kechika Advisory Board. http://www.muskwa-kechika.com/pdf/2005-2006_annual_report.pdf; Federal panel green-lights Northern Gateway pipeline, with 209 conditions. Bloomberg. Dec 19, 2013. The Province. http://www.theprovince.com/business/Federal+panel+green+lights+Northern+Gateway+pipeline+with+conditions/9307280/story.html (Accessed Dec 26, 2013); "Northern Gateway pipeline approval overturned". British Columbia. Canada. News. CBCnews. June 30, 2016. http://www.cbc.ca/news/canada/british-columbia/northern-gateway-pipeline-federal-court-of-appeal-1.3659561 (Accessed: January 8, 2016); "Trudeau cabinet approves Trans Mountain, Line 3 pipelines, rejects Northern Gateway". Politics. News. CBCnews. November 29, 2016. http://www.cbc.ca/news/politics/federal-cabinet-trudeau-pipeline-decisions-1.3872828 (Accessed: January 8, 2016)

## The Production Possibilities Curve and Economic Growth

During any particular time period, a society cannot be outside the production possibilities curve. Over time, however, it is possible to have more of everything. This occurs through economic growth. Figure 2–3 shows the production possibilities curve for automobiles and newsprint shifting outward. The two additional curves represent new choices open to an economy that has experienced economic growth. Such economic growth occurs because of many things, including increases in the quantity of resources available, increases in the productivity of existing resources, and changes in technology.

Scarcity still exists, however, no matter how much economic growth there is. At any point in time, we will always be on some production possibilities curve; thus, we will always face trade-offs. The more we want of one thing, the less we can have of others.

**FIGURE 2–3**

**Economic Growth Allows for More of Everything**

If the country experiences economic growth, the production possibilities curve between automobiles and newsprint will shift out, as shown. This takes time, however, and it does not occur automatically. This means, therefore, that we can have more automobiles and more newsprint only after a period of time during which we have experienced economic growth.

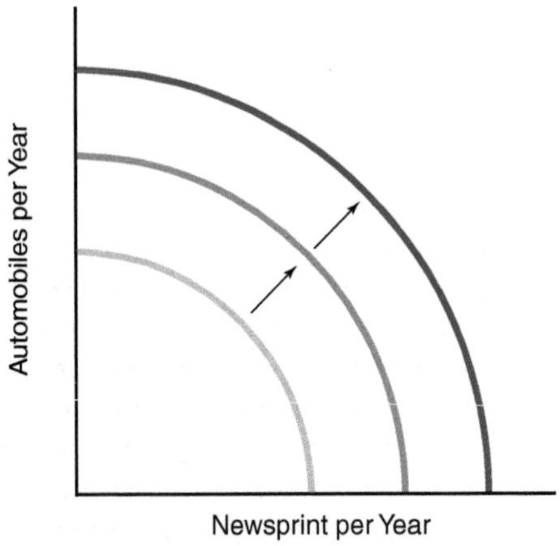

If a country experiences economic growth, the production possibilities curve between automobiles and newsprint will move outward, as is shown in Figure 2–3. This takes time and does not occur automatically. One reason it will occur involves the choice about how much to consume today.

# 2.3 Consumption Goods versus Capital Goods

The production possibilities curve and economic growth can be used to examine the trade-off between present consumption and future consumption. **Consumption** is the use of goods and services for direct personal satisfaction. These goods and services are what we call consumption or consumer goods—food, clothes, and entertainment, for example. And we have already defined physical capital as the manufactured goods, such as machines and factories, used to make other goods and services.

**Consumption** The use of goods and services for direct personal satisfaction.

## Why We Make Capital Goods

Why would we be willing to use productive resources to make things—capital goods—that we cannot consume directly? For one thing, capital goods enable us to produce larger quantities of consumer goods or to produce them less expensively than we otherwise could. Before fish are "produced" for the market, such equipment as fishing boats, nets, and poles are produced first. Imagine how expensive it would be to obtain fish for the market without using these capital goods. Catching fish with one's hands is not an easy task. The price per fish would be very high if capital goods were not used.

## Forgoing Current Consumption

Whenever we use productive resources to make capital goods, we are implicitly forgoing current consumption. We are waiting until some time in the future to consume the fruits that will be reaped from the use of capital goods. In effect, when we forgo current consumption to invest in capital goods, we are engaging in an economic activity that is forward looking—we do not get instant utility or satisfaction from our activity.

At the start of this chapter, in the Did You Know That . . . ? section, we noted the rapid growth of identity theft in Canada. Even an individual contemplating a theft faces a choice between increased current consumption versus increased capital accumulation. That is, instead of breaking into a home to steal a consumer item, such as a TV or stereo, the identity thief uses sophisticated electronic devices to steal the identity of others. While securing the identity of others does not, in itself, provide immediate self-gratification in terms of current consumption, it does allow the sophisticated thief the ability to enhance his or her future consumption through the fraudulent use of credit cards and debit cards. Just as a new machine can reduce the costs of a legitimate business, identity theft lowers the cost of engaging in illegal activity by reducing the probability of being "caught in the act." That is, identity thieves often acquire the personal data of others, without ever having any direct contact with the victims. Indeed, identity theft can be viewed as a form of capital investment undertaken by dishonest individuals.

## The Trade-Off between Consumption Goods and Capital Goods

To have more consumer goods in the future, we must accept fewer consumer goods today. In other words, an opportunity cost is involved here. Every time we make a choice for more goods today, we incur an opportunity cost of fewer goods tomorrow, and every time we make a choice of more goods in the future, we incur an opportunity cost of fewer goods today. With the resources that we do not use to produce consumer goods for today, we invest in capital goods that will produce more consumer goods for us later. The trade-off is shown in Figure 2–4. On the left in part (a), you can see this trade-off depicted as a production possibilities curve between capital goods and consumption goods.

**FIGURE 2–4**

## Capital Goods and Growth

In part (a), the nation chooses not to consume $1 billion, so it invests that amount in capital goods. In part (b), it chooses even more capital goods. The PPC moves even farther to the right on the right-hand diagram in part (b) as a result.

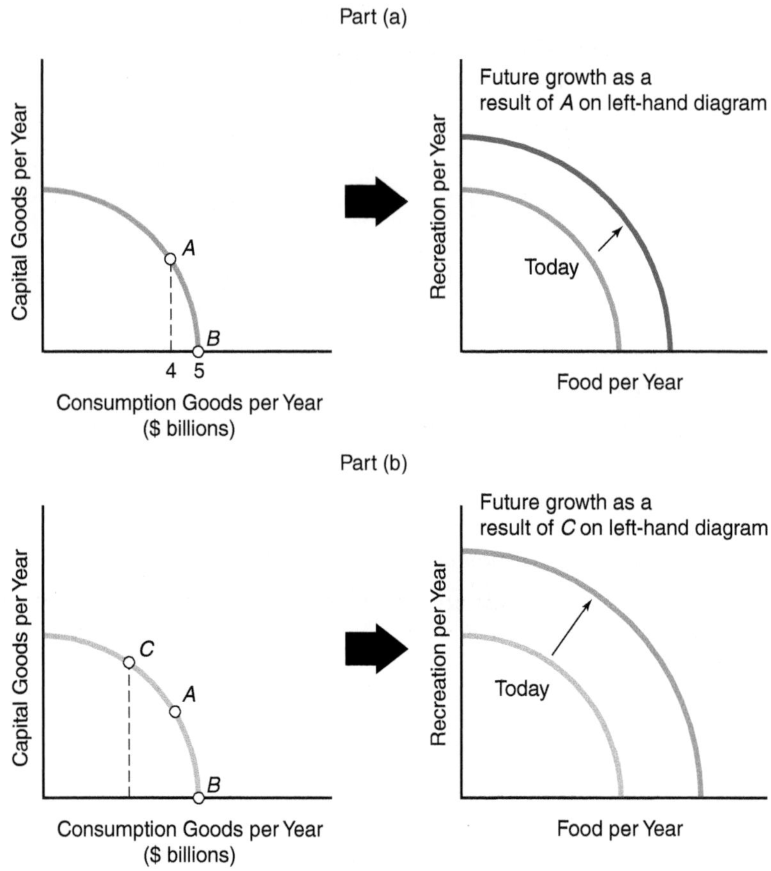


Assume that we are willing to give up $1 billion worth of consumption today. We will be at point *A* in the left-hand diagram of part (a). This will allow the economy to grow. We will have more future consumption because we invested in more capital goods today. In the right-hand diagram of part (a), we see two goods represented: food and recreation. The production possibilities curve will move outward if we collectively decide to restrict consumption each year and invest in capital goods.

In part (b), we show the results of our willingness to forgo more current consumption. We move to point *C*, where we have much fewer consumer goods today, but produce a lot more capital goods. This leads to more future growth in this simplified model, and thus, the production possibilities curve in the right-hand side of part (b) shifts outward more than it did in the right-hand side of part (a).

In other words, the more we give up today, the more we can have tomorrow, provided, of course, that the capital goods are productive in future periods and that society desires the consumer goods produced by this additional capital.

At the individual consumer's level, the decision to enroll full time in a post-secondary educational institution entails a trade-off between additional capital goods and additional consumer goods. As we noted in Chapter 1, the decision to enroll in a college or university on a full-time basis entails the extra costs of lost employment income for eight months per year, as well as additional out-of-pocket costs, such as tuition, fees, and textbooks. These additional educational costs mean that the individual full-time student sacrifices some current consumption goods when enrolled in a post-secondary institution.

So, what does an individual gain when he or she purchases additional years of postsecondary education? Since post-secondary education is a form of human capital, the student should be more productive upon graduation and therefore should earn a higher income in future years. This means that the college or university graduate will be able to consume a greater quantity of consumer goods in the future. Example 2–3 examines whether the facts support the view that Canadian post-secondary education is a productive form of human capital.

## EXAMPLE 2–3 Canadian Post-Secondary Education Pays Off Big Time!

Canadian college and university students can indeed look forward to a higher level of consumption upon graduation, and their future prospects continually improve as they accumulate even greater levels of post-secondary education, according to a report published by the C.D. Howe Institute in Canada.

Based on the C.D. Howe report, Table 2–1 presents annualized percentage rates of returns for Canadian males and females for each of the three Canadian post-secondary education achievement levels: bachelor's/undergraduate degree, master's degree, and Ph.D. degree. These rates of return are computed by utilizing a sophisticated compound interest formula to compare the extra annual income gained (marginal benefit) over one's lifetime with the extra annual costs (marginal cost), including the extra forgone income, tuition, fees, and textbook costs associated with each of the three levels of post-secondary education.

**TABLE 2–1**

**Private Rates of Return for University Graduates by Sex and Type of Degree**

| Highest Level of Education Achieved | Percentage Rate of Return for Male Graduates | Percentage Rate of Return for Female Graduates |
|---|---|---|
| Undergraduate/bachelor's degree | 11.5% | 14.1% |
| Master's degree | 2.9% | 5% |
| Ph.D. degree | <0 | 3.6% |

Source: Karim Moussaly-Sergieh and François Vaillancourt. *Extra Earning Power: The Financial Returns to University Education in Canada.* C.D. Howe Institute. May 14, 2009. http://www.cdhowe.org/pdf/ebrief_79.pdf; Labour force survey estimates, by immigrant status, educational attainment, sex and age group, Canada, 3-month moving average, unadjusted for seasonality, monthly CANSIM TABLE 2820105. CANSIM TIME SERIES. Statistics Canada available through CHASS. (accessed Dec 27, 2013). Five-in-One GIC. Investments. Personal Banking. RBC Royal Bank. http://www.rbcroyalbank.com/products/gic/5in1.html (Accessed April 13, 2014).

As you can see from Table 2–1, for Canadian males, the annual percentage rates of return are 11.5 percent, 2.9 percent, and a negative return for a bachelor's degree, a master's degree, and a Ph.D. degree, respectively. The corresponding rates of return for female graduates appear to be significantly larger at 14.1 percent, 5 percent, and 3.6 percent, respectively.

The fact that each rate of return is positive (except the Ph.D. for males) implies that for each level of post-secondary education, the marginal benefit exceeds the marginal cost, making the investment a productive one.

What is perhaps even more impressive is that the undergraduate/bachelor's degree rate of return compares very favourably with other alternative investments available. In April 2010, a five-year term deposit at a typical Canadian chartered bank earned a mere 3 percent a year in interest. Clearly, an investment in post-secondary education in Canada pays off big time!

It is important to note that those Canadians that have post secondary education have a much greater chance of finding a job, compared to those who do not. For the first eleven months in 2013, the average unemployment rate for each of the different levels of education attainment were: those without a certificate, diploma, or degree 14.8 percent; and those with a post secondary certificate, diploma or degree 5.6 percent.

**For critical analysis:** Sketch two identical production possibilities curves for 2011 for post-secondary education and current consumption goods. On the first production possibilities curve, show point A that describes the production combination chosen by a 2011 high-school graduate who decides not to enroll in post-secondary education. On the second production possibilities curve, show point B that describes the production combination chosen by a 2011 high-school graduate who decides to seek and obtain a bachelor's degree. For each of the two production possibilities curves, roughly sketch the appropriate 2030 production possibilities curve.

**Specialization** Working at a relatively well-defined, limited endeavour; individuals, regions, and nations producing a narrow range of products.

# 2.4 Specialization and Greater Productivity

Individuals and societies have sought to increase their production possibilities through specialization. **Specialization** involves working at a relatively well-defined, limited endeavour, such as accounting or teaching. Individuals, regions, and nations produce a narrow range of products. Most people, in fact, do specialize. For example, you could probably change the oil in your car if you wanted to. Typically, though, you would take your car to a garage and let the mechanic do it. You benefit by letting the garage mechanic specialize in changing the oil and in completing other repairs on your car. The specialist has all the proper equipment to do the work and will likely get the job finished sooner than you could. Specialization usually leads to greater productivity, not only for each individual but also for the country.

## Absolute Advantage

**Absolute advantage** The ability to perform a task using the fewest number of labour hours.

Specialization occurs because different individuals and different nations have different skills. Sometimes, it seems that some individuals are better at doing everything than anyone else and are said to have an **absolute advantage**, the ability to perform a task using the fewest number of labour hours. A president of a large company might be able to type better than any of the typists, file better than any of the file clerks, and wash windows better than any of the window washers. The president has an absolute advantage in all these endeavours—by using fewer labour hours for each task than anyone else in the company. The president does not, however, spend time doing those other activities. Why not? Because a president is paid the most for undertaking managerial duties and specializes in that one particular task despite having an absolute advantage in all tasks. Indeed, absolute advantage is irrelevant in predicting how the president's time is spent; only *comparative advantage* matters.

## Comparative Advantage

**Comparative advantage** The ability to perform an activity at the lowest opportunity cost.

**Comparative advantage** is the ability to perform an activity at the lowest opportunity cost. You have a comparative advantage in one activity whenever you have the lowest opportunity cost of performing that activity. Take the example of a lawyer and her secretary who can both review law cases and type legal opinions. Suppose the lawyer can review two law cases or type one legal opinion in one hour. At the same time, her secretary can review one law case or type one legal opinion in one hour. Here, the lawyer has an absolute advantage in reviewing law cases and seemingly is just as good as her secretary at typing legal opinions. Is there any reason for the lawyer and her secretary to "trade"? The answer is yes, because such trading will lead to higher output.

Consider the scenario of no trading. Assume that during each eight-hour day, the lawyer and her secretary devote half of their day to reviewing law cases and half to typing legal opinions. The lawyer would review eight law cases (4 hours $\times$ 2 per hour) and type four legal opinions (4 $\times$ 1). During that same period, the secretary would review four law cases (4 $\times$ 1) and type four legal opinions (4 $\times$ 1). Each day the combined output for the lawyer and her secretary would be 12 reviewed law cases and eight typed legal opinions.

If the lawyer specialized only in reviewing law cases and her secretary specialized only in typing legal opinions, their combined output would rise to 16 reviewed law cases (8 $\times$ 2) and eight typed legal opinions (8 $\times$ 1). Overall, production would increase by four law cases per day.

The lawyer has a comparative advantage in reviewing cases. In the time it takes her to review one case (one-half hour), she could have typed one-half of a legal opinion. Her opportunity cost of reviewing the law case is therefore one-half of a legal opinion. The secretary, however, gives up typing an entire legal opinion each time she reviews a case. Since the lawyer's opportunity cost of reviewing law cases is less than her secretary's, she has the comparative advantage in reviewing law cases. See if you can work out why the secretary has a comparative advantage in typing legal opinions.

You may be convinced that everybody can do everything better than you. In this extreme situation, do you still have a comparative advantage? The answer is yes. To discover your comparative advantage, you need to find a job in which your *disadvantage* relative to others is the smallest. You do not have to be a mathematical genius to figure this out. To determine your comparative advantage, simply find out which job maximizes your income.

The coaches of sports teams are constantly faced with determining each player's comparative advantage. Former Blue Jay Dave Winfield was originally one of the best pitchers in college baseball, winning the most valuable player award for pitching for the University of Minnesota Golden Bears in the 1973 College World Series. After he was drafted by the San Diego Padres, the coach decided to make him an outfielder, even though he was one of the best pitchers on the roster. The coach wanted Winfield to concentrate on his hitting. Good pitchers do not bring in as many fans as home-run kings. Dave Winfield's comparative advantage was clearly in hitting homers, rather than practising and developing his pitching game.

## Scarcity, Self-Interest, and Specialization

In Chapter 1, you learned about the assumption of rational self-interest. It says that for the purposes of our analyses, we assume that individuals are rational in that they will do what is in their own self-interest. They will not consciously carry out actions that will make them worse off. In this chapter, you learned that scarcity requires people to make choices. We assume that they make choices based on their self-interest and attempt to maximize benefits net of opportunity cost. In so doing, individuals recognize their comparative advantage and end up specializing. Ultimately, when people specialize, they increase the money they make and become richer, as illustrated by Example 2–4.

### EXAMPLE 2–4 Specializing in Providing Baggage-Free Business Trips

When Steve Zilinek was working as an investment adviser, he noticed something about travelling businesspeople. Although many of these individuals possess considerable financial resources, they must expend another key resource when they travel—namely, time that they could otherwise devote to other activities. Zilinek estimated that packing bags; waiting at airport check-in, security, and baggage stations; and laundering clothing takes about three hours per trip—time that could otherwise be devoted to alternative pursuits.

Zilinek decided that he might have a comparative advantage in providing baggage services to frequent travellers. He founded FlyLite, a company that specializes in storing, caring for, and shipping all the items that individuals desire to have with them on business trips, such as clothing and toiletries. FlyLite's customers send the items they regularly take on business trips to the company, which places them in storage. Before a trip, a client fills out and submits a Web form indicating which items she will require at her destination. FlyLite then arranges for the items to be shipped to her hotel. When her business trip concludes, the customer sends the items back to FlyLite, which dry cleans the clothing and then re-stores all items until her next trip. For FlyLite's clients, paying about $100 per trip for its services is the next-best alternative to devoting three hours to handling baggage on their own.

**For critical analysis:**

1. Use this example to explain how specialization based on comparative advantage increases the income for both the owner of FlyLite and the business traveller.
2. How do you suppose that an increase in the average amount of time that people must spend dealing with baggage at airports affects the number of people utilizing FlyLite's services?

## Comparative Advantage and Trade among Nations

Though most of our analysis of absolute advantage, comparative advantage, and specialization has dealt with individuals or firms, it is equally applicable to countries. First, consider Canada. The Prairie provinces have a comparative advantage in the production of grains and other agricultural goods. Ontario and Quebec in Central Canada tend to specialize in industrialized production, such as automobiles and newsprint. Not surprisingly, grains are shipped from the Prairies to Central Canada, and automobiles are shipped in the reverse direction. Such specialization and trade allow for higher incomes and standards of living. If the Prairies and Central Canada were politically defined as separate countries, the same analysis would still hold, but we would call it international trade. Indeed, Europe is smaller than Canada in area, but instead of one nation, Europe has 15. What we call *interprovincial trade* in Canada is called *international trade* in Europe. There is no difference, however, in the economic results—both yield greater economic efficiency and higher average incomes.

Political problems that do not normally arise within a particular nation often do between nations. For example, if Nova Scotia crab fishers develop a cheaper method of harvesting crabs than fishers in British Columbia, British Columbia fishers will lose out. They cannot do much about the situation, except try to lower their own costs of production. If crab fishers in Alaska, however, develop a cheaper method, both Nova Scotia and British Columbia fishers can (and likely will) try to raise political barriers to prevent Alaskan fishers from freely selling their product in Canada. Canadian crab fishers will use such arguments as "unfair" competition and loss of Canadian jobs. In so doing, they are only partly right: crab-fishing jobs may decline in Canada, but jobs will not necessarily decline overall. If the argument of Canadian crab fishers had any validity, every time a region in Canada developed a better way to produce a product manufactured somewhere else in the country, employment in Canada would decline. That has never happened and never will.

When countries specialize where they have a comparative advantage and then trade with the rest of the world, the average standard of living in the world rises. In effect, international trade allows the world to move from inside the global production possibilities curve toward the curve itself, thereby improving worldwide economic efficiency.

### The Division of Labour

**Division of labour** Individuals specializing in a subset of tasks related to a specific product.

In any firm that includes specialized human and nonhuman resources, there is a division of labour among those resources. **Division of labour** occurs when individuals specialize in a subset of tasks related to a specific product. The best-known example of all time comes from one of the earliest and perhaps most famous economists, Adam Smith, who, in his book *The Wealth of Nations* (1776), illustrated the benefits of a division of labour in the making of pins: "One man draws out the wire, another straightens it, a third cuts it, a fourth points it, a fifth grinds it at the top for receiving the head; to make the head requires two or three distinct operations; to put it on is a peculiar business, to whiten the pins is another; it is even a trade by itself to put them into the paper."

Making pins this way allowed 10 workers without very much skill to make almost 48 000 pins "of a middling size" in a day. One worker, toiling alone, could have made perhaps 20 pins a day; therefore, 10 workers could have produced 200. Division of labour allowed for an increase in the daily output of the pin factory from 200 to 48 000! (Smith did not attribute all of the gain to the division of labour according to talent but credited also the use of machinery and the fact that less time was spent shifting from task to task.)

What we are discussing here involves a division of the resource called labour into different kinds of labour. The different kinds of labour are organized in such a way as to increase the amount of output possible from the fixed resources available. We can, therefore, talk about an organized division of labour within a firm leading to increased output.

## 2.5 Economic Systems

In the remainder of this chapter, we will study some of the established social arrangements that various nations use in choosing their production possibilities that, realistically, can include millions of goods and services being produced to satisfy the wants of millions of consumers.

**Economic system** The social arrangements or institutional means through which resources are used to satisfy human wants.

At any point in time, every nation has its own **economic system**, which can be defined as the social arrangements or institutional means through which resources are used to satisfy human wants. No matter what institutional means—marketplace or government—a nation chooses to use, the following three basic economic questions must always be answered because of the economic problem of scarcity.

1. *What and how much will be produced?* Literally billions of different things could be produced with society's scarce resources, but not all at the same time. Some mechanism must exist that causes some things to be produced and others to remain as either inventors' pipe dreams or individuals' unfulfilled desires.
2. *How will it be produced?* There are many ways to produce a desired item. It is possible to use more labour and less capital or *vice versa*. It is possible to use more unskilled labour and fewer units of skilled labour. Somehow, in some way, a decision must be made as to the particular mix of inputs, the way they should be organized, and how they are brought together at a particular place.
3. *For whom will it be produced?* Once a commodity is produced, who should get it? In a modern economy, individuals and businesses purchase commodities with money income. The question then is what mechanism is there to distribute income, which then determines how commodities are distributed throughout the economy.

Not long ago, in response to the problem of scarcity, textbooks presented two extreme economic systems as possible polar alternatives for the industrialized nations to consider—the *pure command economy* versus the *pure capitalist economy*—in order to answer the three basic economic questions. Despite the fact that many countries have recently moved away from a command economy, it is appropriate to review both types of economic systems. This is because many informed citizens within Canada and other capitalist economies feel that elements of the command economy should prevail in the provision of important services, such as health care, education, and national security.

## Pure Command Economy

Public (government) ownership of all property resources characterizes a pure command economy. A **pure command economy** is an economic system characterized by public ownership of all property resources. The three basic economic questions—What, How, For Whom—are answered in a very centralized manner by government or the "state." Detailed five-year plans are formulated by the central authorities in order to respond to the three basic economic questions.

**Pure command economy** An economic system characterized by public ownership of all property resources.

Until recently, such nations as Russia and China used the pure command economy to make their resource-allocation decisions. In the past, this type of system has typically been associated with nations practising communism or socialism.

## Pure Capitalist Economy

In contrast to the pure command economy, a **pure capitalist economy** is an economic system characterized by private ownership of all property resources. Households and firms interacting through a system of markets answer the three basic economic questions—What, How, For Whom—in a decentralized manner. The pure capitalist economy goes by other names, such as *capitalism, market economy*, or *price system*.

**Pure capitalist economy** An economic system characterized by private ownership of all property resources.

## Mixed Economic Systems

The pure command and the pure capitalist systems are extreme economic systems. Real-world economies, which typically fall somewhere between these two extreme systems, are called mixed economies. In **mixed economies**, decisions about how resources are used are made partly by the private sector and partly by the public sector. As an example, Canada is referred to as a mixed capitalist system. This is because, while the majority of products are produced in the private sector, there are other goods and services provided by the government.

**Mixed economy** An economic system in which decisions about how resources are used are made partly by the private sector and partly by the public sector.

# 2.6 Capitalism in More Depth

Since there has been a global trend away from pure command economies toward capitalist economies, we will describe pure capitalism in more depth below.

## Features of Capitalism

In elaborating on the pure capitalist economy, we will periodically refer to the Circular Flow Model presented in Figure 2–5.

Key features of pure capitalism include:

1. *Private ownership of resources:* Individual households and individual firms own the productive resources in pure capitalism. As described in Figure 2–5, households have two essential roles in capitalism—they supply resources to firms, and they demand goods and services with the income received from supplying resources. Firms, in turn, demand or hire resources in order to supply goods and services to households.
2. *Self-interest:* The primary motive underlying decisions made by households and firms in pure capitalism is the pursuit of self-interest. More specifically, firms attempt to maximize their own profit, when deciding what resources to demand or hire and what products to supply. Similarly, households are assumed to attempt to maximize individual wealth and other personal goals when deciding on where to supply their resources. When demanding goods and services, households attempt to maximize self-satisfaction or utility.
3. *Consumer sovereignty:* The pure capitalist system is to serve the household in its consumer role. Operationally, this means that capitalism is to produce the mix of goods and services that consumers desire, at the lowest possible prices.
4. *Markets and prices:* The Circular Flow Diagram in Figure 2–5 indicates the two broad types of markets that exist in pure capitalism—product markets and factor (resource) markets. When consumer demand changes or resource availability changes, this sets off changes in relative prices in affected product and factor markets. These price changes ultimately reallocate resources in line with the change in consumer demand or resource availability. While we will examine how prices are determined in individual markets in the chapters that follow, we will provide a simple example below.

   Suppose that consumer demand for red wine increases and consumer demand for cigarettes decreases. Referring to the product markets in Figure 2–5, the price of red wine will increase, while the price of cigarettes will decrease. The higher price for red wine serves as a signal to firms that red wine is now relatively more profitable to produce than cigarettes.

   Driven by the profit motive, the red wine firms will increase their demand to hire resources, while the cigarette firms will decrease their demand for resources, to reduce their losses. Prices will now change in the factor markets in Figure 2–5. Prices (i.e., wages) of resources (i.e., employees) that engage in the production of red wine will increase relative to the prices offered to resources in the cigarette industry. Resources, guided by self-interest, will move out of cigarette production and into the production of red wine. Eventually, red wine production will increase. Note how this system of markets and prices operates to reallocate resources in line with changes in consumer demand, thus promoting consumer sovereignty.

**FIGURE 2–5**
**Circular Flow Model**

This model describes how households and firms interact through both product and factor markets in a pure capitalist economy. In the product markets, the households demand goods and services, while the firms supply the goods and services. In the factor markets, these roles are reversed. That is, households supply the resources, and the firms demand the resources.

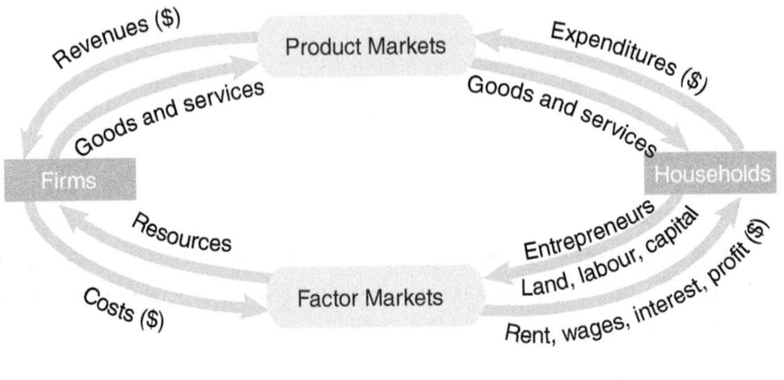

5. *Competition:* In order to ensure that the self-interests of firms and resources work to the best interests of consumers, it is necessary that many independent sellers and buyers compete in each market. This will be more fully explained in the subsequent chapters of this text.
6. *Limited government:* To the extent that competition exists in each market, the "invisible hand" of self-interest will serve to promote consumer sovereignty. Hence, allocating resources to meet changes in consumer demand does not require the "heavy hand" of government. The French have termed this feature of capitalism "**laissez-faire**," which means that the government should leave it (the economy) alone or "let it be."

**Laissez-faire** French term for "leave it alone"; the government should leave it (the economy) alone or "let it be."

One way to remember some of the important attributes of the market economy is by thinking of capitalism's **Three Ps**: Private property, Profits, and Prices.

**Three Ps** Private property, Profits, and Prices inherent in capitalism.

As Policy Example 2–2 outlines, political factors play a role in issues surrounding the use of alternate economic systems to allocate and distribute our limited economic resources, goods, and services.

### POLICY EXAMPLE 2–2 Canadian Politics: Right, Left, and Centre

Chapter 1 noted that Canadian government policies are, in part, based on economic theories applied to government efforts that attempt to achieve key socioeconomic goals. To more fully understand how policies are determined, it is important to recognize that political factors often play an important role. That is, policies are frequently guided by the principles of the political party of the government in power. In Canada, the three major political parties at both the federal and provincial levels are the Conservatives, the New Democrats, and the Liberals. The Conservative Party, often referred to as the right-wing party, seeks to move the economy more toward the pure capitalist model, with private ownership and competition, decentralized individual decision-making through free markets, and a laissez-faire approach to the economy. The New Democrats, who sit on the left side of the political landscape, place a high priority on serving the interests of labour and working families, promoting social justice, reducing poverty and inequality, protecting the rights of minorities, and ensuring public funding and provision of social programs and services. Often, the principles of the New Democrats tend to move various industries and services in the direction of a command system, with more government involvement. The Liberal Party, known as the centralists, supports a variety of policies from both the right and the left ends of the political spectrum, seemingly guided by public opinion as identified through political polls. The most recent federal Liberal Party platform highlights values such as: equality of opportunity; fiscal responsibility; sustainable universal public health care; and access to affordable post secondary education. Liberals typically favour mixed economic systems. Voters who wish to avoid extreme shifts in policies often vote for the Liberals.

**For critical analysis:** State whether each of the following policies is more consistent with the principles of the Conservatives or New Democrats. Policy A: Waiting time for surgeries is reduced through the expansion of government-funded surgical units located in government-run hospitals. Policy B: Waiting time for surgeries is reduced through the provision of new surgical services through privately owned health-care clinics.

Sources: Platform. Where We Stand. Conservative Party of Canada. http://www.conservative.ca/ (Accessed Dec 27, 2013); "Issues. NDP." The NDP Party of Canada. http://www.ndp.ca/ (Accessed Dec 27, 2013.); What We Stand For. Liberal Party of Canada. http://www.liberal.ca/what-we-stand-for/ (Accessed Dec 27, 2013).

## Capitalism and the Three Economic Questions

Now that we have reviewed the essential features of pure capitalism, we can proceed to examine how this economic system operates to answer the three basic economic questions—What, How, and For Whom.

**TABLE 2–2**

## Production Costs for 100 Units of Product X

Technique A or B can be used to produce the same output. Obviously, B will be used because its total cost is less than A's. Using production technique B will generate a $2 savings for every 100 units produced.

| Inputs | Input Unit Price | A Production Technique A (input units) | Cost | B Production Technique B (input units) | Cost |
|---|---|---|---|---|---|
| Labour | $10 | 5 | $50 | 4 | $40 |
| Capital | 8 | 4 | 32 | 5 | 40 |
| Total cost of 100 units | | | 82 | | 80 |

**WHAT AND HOW MUCH WILL BE PRODUCED?** Since firms can enhance profits by producing what consumers are willing to buy, we can see that consumer demand plays an important role in deciding what goods and services are produced. In more formal terms, the profit motive and competition lead firms to promote allocative efficiency—that is, firms will produce the mix of goods and services most wanted by society. However, we must keep in mind that if the highest price that consumers are willing to pay for a good is less than the lowest resource cost at which the good can be produced, no profit will result, and none of this good will be produced. In other words, resource availability also plays a role in determining what goods and services are produced.

**HOW WILL IT BE PRODUCED?** The question of how output will be produced in a pure capitalist system relates to the efficient use of scarce inputs. Consider the possibility of using only two types of resources: capital and labour. A firm may have the options given in Table 2–2. It can use various combinations of labour and capital to produce the same amount of output.

Two hypothetical combinations are given in Table 2–2. How then is it decided which combination will be used? Under pure capitalism, the least cost combination (technique B, in our example) will be chosen by firms because it will maximize profits. In other words, in pure capitalism, competition and the profit motive encourage firms to achieve productive efficiency.

**FOR WHOM WILL IT BE PRODUCED?** This last question involves how households share in the consumption of the goods and services produced. This, in turn, is based on the distribution of money incomes and wealth among households. Households with higher levels of income and wealth will get to purchase and consume a greater portion of the goods produced in the economy.

What determines the distribution of wealth and money income among different households? This distribution is based on the quantities, qualities, and types of the various human and nonhuman resources that different households own and supply to the marketplace. Households that own large quantities of resources that are highly in demand in the marketplace will earn high levels of income.

As Example 2–5 illustrates, the way in which a nation answers the economic question "For whom will it be produced?" will affect what and how much will be produced.

How can improved sanitation in India improve economic well being?

### EXAMPLE 2–5 India Has More Cellphones Than Toilets

Since the early 1990s, India, the most populous country in the world, has moved significantly closer to becoming a capitalist economy. According to a research study undertaken by the Pew Research Centre, released in 2015, India is now wealthy enough to have 77 percent of its population own a cellphone, yet only 40 percent of its population have access to safe and private toilets. In other words, over 700 million people in India do not have access to basic sanitation.

A United Nations University report points out that there would be a return of between $3 and $4 for every additional dollar spent on improved sanitation due to reduced health and poverty related costs, as well as higher productivity.

*continued*

Source: "Mobile telephones more common than toilets in India, UN report finds." UN News Centre. United Nations University. Tokyo. April 14, 2010. http://www.un.org/apps/news/story.asp?NewsID=34369&Cr=mdg&Cr1=; "SMARTPHONE OWNERSHIP RATES SKYROCKET IN MANY EMERGING ECONOMIES, BUT DIGITAL DIVIDE REMAINS". Global Attitudes and Trends. PewResearchCentre. Feb 19, 2016. http://www.pewglobal.org/2016/02/22/smartphone-ownership-rates-skyrocket-in-many-emerging-economies-but-digital-divide-remains/technology-report-03-06/ (Accessed: January 8, 2016); "India has 60.4 per cent people without access to toilet: Study". The Indian Express. November 19, 2015 http://indianex press.com/article/india/india-news-india/india-has-60-4-per-cent-people-without-access-to-toilet-study/(Accessed: January 8, 2016)

**For critical analysis:** Using this Example, explain the way India answers the economic question "For whom will it be produced?" has affected what and how much will be produced. Since total wealth in India is increasing rapidly, can you suggest a government policy that could improve basic sanitation conditions? How will this policy pay for itself in the long run?.

It should be noted that many current debates regarding economic systems apply to individual industries within a national economy. The central question posed in this chapter's Issues and Applications is, "What economic system should be used to best provide auto insurance in Canada?" As this Issues and Applications section points out, different economic systems are currently being used to provide auto insurance in Canada, depending on the province in which one resides.

## ISSUES AND APPLICATIONS

# Private or Public Auto Insurance: What Is Best for Canada?

### Concepts Applied: Capitalist, Command, and Mixed Systems; Productive Efficiency; Allocative Efficiency; and Equity

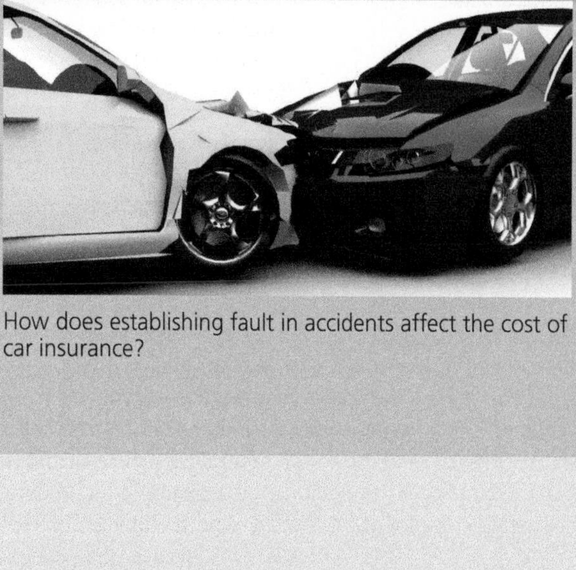

How does establishing fault in accidents affect the cost of car insurance?

In response to public outrage over skyrocketing car insurance premiums, the Consumers' Association of Canada completed a comprehensive report on auto insurance rates in Canada in September 2003. In presenting the report, the association noted that government-owned, or public, auto insurance systems offer the lowest premiums for Canadian drivers.

### Provincial Automobile Insurance Rates

Figure 2–6, taken from the report, compares the average annual auto insurance premiums among provinces, assuming the same insurance coverage, vehicle, driving record, and claims history. The average premiums are based on over 7000 rate quotes across Canada. All quotes assume an insurance coverage of $2 million liability, $500 collision deductible, and $300 comprehensive deductible. As you can see from this figure, the annual car insurance premiums are significantly lower in the provinces of British Columbia, Saskatchewan, Manitoba, and Quebec, where the mandatory insurance is provided by a government monopoly.

The Consumers' Association of Canada's report also noted the differences in the annual rate of increase in premiums between the private and public insurance systems in 2003. While premiums were escalating by up to 70 percent per year in the six provinces where privately owned insurance companies operate, Manitoba's publicly run auto insurance system was increasing annual premiums by only 7.2 percent.

FIGURE 2–6

**Comparison of Average Auto Insurance Rates by Province, 2003**

Source: *Review of Automobile Insurance Rates*. Consumers' Association of Canada. September 2003, pg. 11. http://www.consumer.ca/pdfs/030910_report.pdf. Copyright Consumers' Association of Canada. (Accessed November 11, 2003).

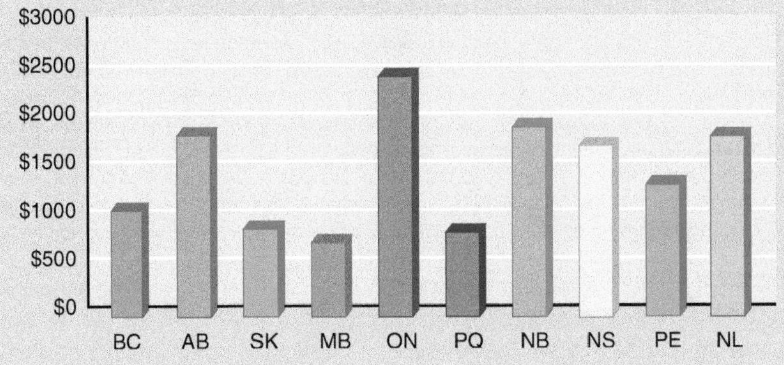


To add fuel to the fire, in provinces offering private insurance, individuals can pay significantly higher premiums based on such criteria as age, gender, and marital status, regardless of the driving record or type of vehicle being insured. In New Brunswick, in 2003, older drivers who drove newer, much more expensive cars, and who had driving convictions, paid up to $2000 less for auto insurance compared to young drivers with clean driving records. A 2002 Ford Taurus SE was more than $7000 cheaper for an 18-year-old male with a clean driving record to insure in Saskatoon's public insurance system than in Toronto or St John's, where private insurance companies operate. In provinces with public auto insurance, where rates were not based on age or gender, a young driver with a clean record paid a lower premium than an older driver with driving convictions.

## Follow-Up Studies

On October 15, 2005, the Consumers' Association of Canada published a follow-up study comparing the automobile insurance rates in different provinces, keeping factors constant such as the driver's vehicle, driving record, claims history, deductibles and liability, and other types of coverage. Similar to the 2003 study, the insurance rates continue to be significantly lower in British Columbia, Manitoba, and Saskatchewan, where the mandatory insurance is provided by a government monopoly.

A Quebec study examined car insurance premiums in the six provinces west of New Brunswick and found that in each of the ten years, 2001 to 2010, the lowest rates were found in the provinces with government-run auto insurance organizations.

More recently, in 2015, as Figure 2-7 indicates, the Manitoba government Department of Finance compared average auto insurance premiums across Canada, and continued to find the lowest rates being offered in those provinces operating public auto insurance.

## Providing Auto Insurance: Two Extreme Models

To better understand the significant differences in automobile premiums being charged across provinces and across customers within the same province, we will first contrast the two extreme economic systems that are possible in the provision of car insurance.

Under the pure capitalist or pure market model, privately owned, for-profit insurance companies sell the mandatory auto insurance policies, and the claims are paid out according to a decentralized tort-based or fault-based system.

In a fault-based system, the injured party must first prove that the other party is at fault, and then the injured party can bring legal action for recovery of damages against the person who caused the accident. The claim for recovery of damages will typically include monies to replace lost wages, out-of-pocket expenses, medical expenses, damages to the vehicle, and an amount to compensate for the pain and suffering related to injuries sustained as a result of the accident. If the injured party and the party at fault cannot agree on the amount of the total claim, the matter will eventually go to court. The fault-based system awards damages in a very decentralized manner, as the amount of each accident claim is assessed on the merits of each individual situation.

At the other extreme, auto insurance can be delivered in a manner resembling a pure command economic system. In this model, the one government-owned Crown corporation (public monopoly) provides all mandatory auto insurance for the entire province, and the claims are paid out on a pure no-fault basis.

In a pure no-fault system, one's own insurance company (or the government monopoly) pays for the damages that one incurs, regardless of fault. A comprehensive predetermined compensation schedule would dictate the maximum payment for specific types of losses, expenses, and injuries. In a pure no-fault system, one's individual right to sue for damages is eliminated.

## The Advantages of Using the Command Model

It is interesting to note that Manitoba, the province that charges the lowest average annual auto insurance premiums, according to the Consumers' Association of Canada's study, operates an insurance system that most closely resembles the pure command model. That is, Manitoba Public Insurance (MPI), a government-owned monopoly, provides the manda-

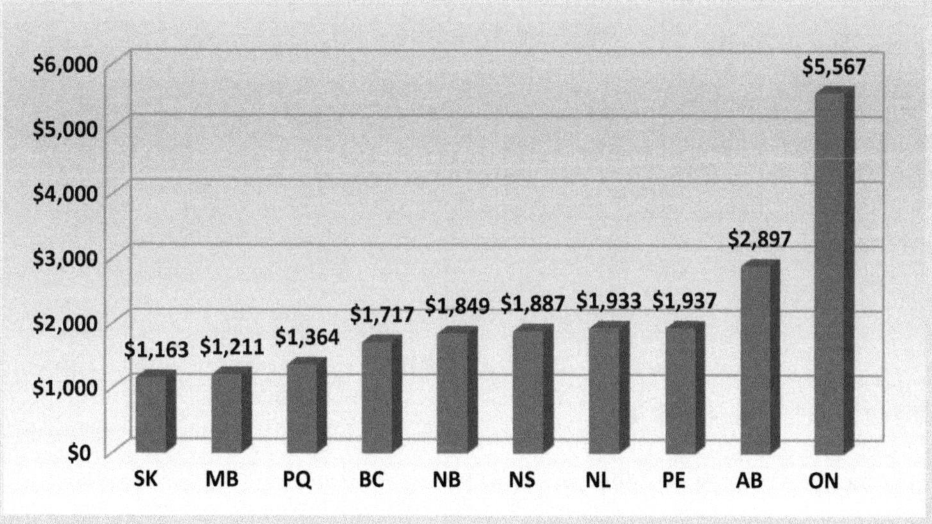


FIGURE 2-7

**Comparison of Average Annual Auto Insurance Rates by Province: 2015**

Source: "Annual Basic Utility Bundle Cost Comparison for the year ended 2015". Manitoba Finance. Manitoba Government. 2016. https://www.gov.mb.ca/finance/publications/pubs/utility_2015.pdf (Accessed January 7, 2016).

tory car insurance, and the claims are paid out on a no-fault basis.

So, how can a pure command system result in lower auto insurance premiums when compared with the pure capitalist model? First, there are factors inherent in the public system that make it more productively efficient. Due to its no-fault feature, the system does not have to employ the expensive legal and court-related resources to establish fault and to establish the extent of the legal damages experienced by each injured party in each accident. As well, the amount of benefits paid out per claim to compensate an injured party for pain and suffering is significantly lower in the public system.

Since the government is the sole organization providing mandatory car insurance in the province, it does not have to employ resources to market its services to the customer. Moreover, as the sole provider, the public insurance organization is able to avoid the duplication in administrative resources that typically occurs when numerous private car insurance companies compete with each other in the same province. Because the public system can offer the same insurance coverage with minimal use of resources, it is able to keep its costs down and, in turn, charge low premiums.

A public insurance organization, such as Manitoba Public, does not have to raise premiums to a point where profits have to be earned on its operations, as is the case with privately run companies. Unlike the provincially owned public insurance providers, multinational private insurance corporations face the added pressure of raising premiums in order to recoup losses incurred in past global disasters, such as the September 11 terrorist attacks in the United States.

## The Advantages of Using the Capitalist Model

In a series of recent studies, the Fraser Institute, a Canadian organization that promotes market-based policies, defends the use of the capitalist model in providing mandatory auto insurance. The Institute argues that a public auto insurance system results in more accidents and imposes greater burdens on the health-care system when compared with private insurance. After examining two private insurance provinces and three public insurance provinces, the Institute notes that the number of collisions and the number of collision related deaths, injuries, and hospital admissions is significantly higher, per 100 000 population or per vehicle kilometres travelled, in those provinces with public insurance. This difference is most pronounced for males between the ages of 16 and 25 years. The Institute suggests that since the public insurance system fails to charge higher premiums for certain high-risk classes, such as the younger male class, it encourages too many risky drivers to take to the road, and it shifts collision costs to other drivers—primarily female, safer, and older drivers. As well, the expensive lawsuits that accompany the fault system can provide incentives for safer driving.

Another benefit of the pure capitalist approach to auto insurance relates to the goal of allocative efficiency. A fault-based insurance system provides the opportunity for each injured individual to take the necessary legal action to ensure that the dollar value of the compensation resulting from an accident claim (marginal benefit) is sufficient to cover the full marginal cost related to the individual's injuries and losses sustained from the accident.

As an example, two individuals may suffer the same physical injury in an accident, but the pain and suffering experienced by one of the individuals would be significantly greater if that individual could no longer engage in his or her favourite hobby—playing the piano. The fault-based insurance system could enable the piano lover to receive a higher level of compensation based on the higher level of pain and suffering (i.e., the higher level of marginal cost). In contrast, the pure command model's no-fault system would likely pay out the same level of benefits to both injured individuals.

## Using a Mixed System

Despite the potential benefits of using a pure capitalist approach in the provision of auto insurance, Canadians residing in the private insurance jurisdictions are putting political pressure on their provincial governments to play an active role in the auto insurance industry. Many of the private insurance provinces are moving toward a mixed economic system of providing auto insurance. While privately owned corporations continue to provide the car insurance in these provinces, the provincial governments are proposing to fix the premium rates and set maximum dollar limits for the payout of certain types of claims, such as pain and suffering. These governments have a difficult task ahead of them as they attempt to strike an acceptable balance between affordable premiums, public safety, equity, and their own political party's commitment to promote a capitalist provincial economy.

### For critical analysis:

1. Explain how the pure command model of providing auto insurance can promote productive efficiency.
2. Explain how the pure capitalist model of providing auto insurance can promote the goals of public safety and allocative efficiency.
3. Explain what equity (fairness) trade-offs are involved when choosing the pure command model of providing auto insurance.
4. A provincial government freezes the premiums charged by private insurance companies but lets the fault system determine the payment of claims. What problems will likely occur with this mixed-system policy?

Sources: *Review of Automobile Insurance Rates. Consumers' Association of Canada*. September 2003, pg. 5. http://www.consumer.ca/pdfs/030910_report.pdf. (Accessed August 25, 2010.); *Auto Insurance Rate Comparison Study*—July 28, 2003. Consumers' Association of Canada. July 2003, pg. 3. http://www.cacbc.com/reports/July%2028,2003%20Report%20Auto%20NB.pdf. (Accessed November 11, 2003.); SGI 2003 Rate Comparison Profiles. http://www.sgi.sk.ca/sgi_internet/rates/2003_rate_profiles.html#. (Accessed November 11, 2003.); Mark, Mullins "Public auto insurance: a mortality warning for motorists." Fraser Institute, September 2003, pp. 1–4. http://www.fraserinstitute.org/research-news/display.aspx?id=13327. (Accessed August 25, 2010.) Comparison by Province. Statistics. Groupement des assureurs automobiles. https://www.gaa.qc.ca/en/comparison-province (Accessed Dec 28, 2013).

# SUMMARY

Here is what you should know after reading this chapter. MyEconLab will help you identify what you know, and where to go when you need to practise. We suggest that as soon as you review one of the Learning Objective sections below, you then proceed to go through the related section in MyEconLab.

| LEARNING OBJECTIVES | KEY TERMS | MYECONLAB PRACTICE |
|---|---|---|
| **2.1 The Production Possibilities Curve.** The production possibilities curve describes all possible combinations of two goods that can be produced, assuming full and efficient employment of resources, a fixed time period, fixed quantity and quality of resources, and fixed technology. | production possibilities curve, 30<br>technology, 30 | • **MyEconLab** Study Plan 2.1 |
| **2.2 Applications of the Production Possibilities Curve.** The production possibilities curve illustrates the scarcity problem by acting as a production boundary in the face of unlimited wants. Its downward slope implies a trade-off—more of one good means less of another. An increasing opportunity cost situation is shown by a "bowed out" production possibilities curve. Unemployment is reflected by a point inside the curve, signifying lost production. Any production combination on the curve is productively efficient and the one combination that society values the most is allocatively efficient. Economic growth shifts the production possibilities curve outward over time. | productive efficiency, 33<br>productively inefficient point, 33<br>allocative efficiency, 34<br>law of increasing relative cost, 34 | • **MyEconLab** Study Plan 2.2 |
| **2.3 Consumption Goods versus Capital Goods.** A production possibilities curve that involves capital goods and consumption goods illustrates that when we use more of our resources to produce capital goods that enhance future consumption, we must forgo present consumption goods. | consumption, 37 | • **MyEconLab** Study Plan 2.3 |
| **2.4 Specialization and Greater Productivity.** Absolute advantage refers to the ability to produce one unit of a product at a lower labour cost than another producer. Comparative advantage refers to producing a unit of a product at a lower opportunity cost than another producer. According to the comparative advantage principle, the combined production of two producers can be increased if each producer specializes according to comparative advantage. The terms of trade principle states that each producer will gain from | specialization, 39<br>absolute advantage, 40<br>comparative advantage, 40<br>division of labour, 42 | • **MyEconLab** Study Plan 2.4 |

myeconlab

| LEARNING OBJECTIVES | KEY TERMS | MYECONLAB PRACTICE |
|---|---|---|
| specialization and trade, if the terms of trade are between each producer's opportunity cost of production. | | |
| **2.5 Economic Systems.** In a pure command system, the government owns the resources and the three basic questions—What, How, For Whom—are answered in a centralized manner by government. In pure capitalism, resources are privately owned and the basic questions are answered in a decentralized manner by individual firms and households interacting in markets. In a mixed economic system, where there is both private and public ownership of resources, the basic questions are partly answered by government and partly by individual firms and households in markets. | economic system, 42<br>pure command economy, 43<br>pure capitalist economy, 43<br>mixed economy, 43 | • **MyEconLab** Study Plan 2.5 |
| **2.6 Capitalism in More Depth.** The key features of pure capitalism include private ownership of resources, self-interest motives, consumer sovereignty, markets and prices, competition, and limited government. Consumer demand and resource availability determine *what* goods and services will be produced; the least costly method will be chosen in deciding *how* the goods will be produced; the degree to which households own marketable resources will determine *for whom* goods are produced. | laissez-faire, 45<br>Three *P*s, 45 | • **MyEconLab** Study Plan 2.6 |

# PROBLEMS

(Answers to the odd-numbered problems appear at the back of the book.)

**LO 2.1, LO 2.2 Define the production possibilities curve and identify its assumptions; use the production possibilities curve to illustrate the concepts of scarcity, trade-offs, unemployment, productive efficiency, allocative efficiency, increasing opportunity cost, and economic growth.**

1. The production possibilities curve for the nation of Epica for the two goods—factories and yachts—for 2017 is described in the accompanying graph.

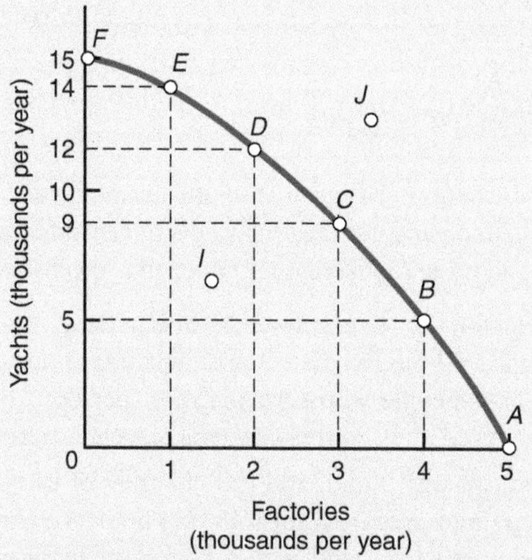


   a. If Epica produces 12 000 yachts in 2017, what is the maximum number of factories that can be produced in 2017?
   b. If Epica devotes all its resources to the production of factories, what is the maximum number of factories that can be produced in 2017?
   c. What factors prevent Epica from producing the combination at point *J* in 2017?
   d. If Epica is at point *I* in 2017, this situation could conflict with what two socioeconomic goals?
   e. What is the opportunity cost of producing an additional factory when moving: (i) from point *E* to *D*? (ii) from point *C* to *B*?
   f. What is the opportunity cost of producing an additional yacht when moving: (i) from point *A* to *B*? (ii) from point *E* to *F*?
   g. What economic law is illustrated by your answers to parts (e) and (f) above?
   h. If society values production combination *D* the most, but Epica is producing combination *C*, this situation conflicts with what socioeconomic goal?
   i. How will economic growth affect Epica's production possibilities curve over time?

2. The production possibilities curve for the nation of Fantasia for the two goods, TVs and business machines, for 2017 is described in the accompanying graph.

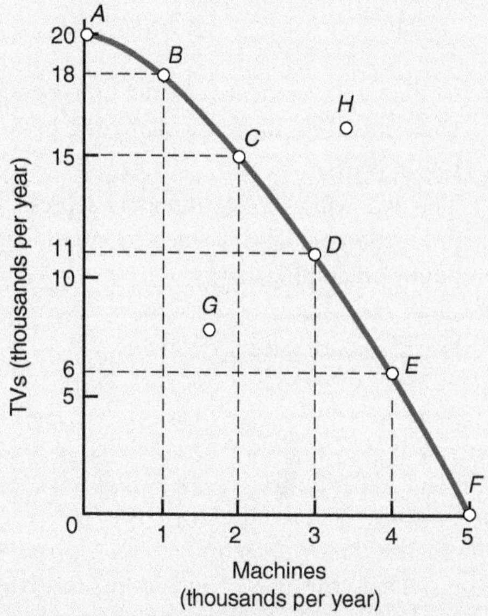


   a. If Fantasia produces 2000 machines in 2017, what is the maximum number of TVs that can be produced in 2017?
   b. What factors prevent Fantasia from producing the combination at point *H* in 2017?
   c. If Fantasia completely specializes in the production of TVs in 2017, what maximum number of TVs could it produce per year?
   d. If Fantasia is at point *G* in 2017, this situation could conflict with what two socioeconomic goals?
   e. What is the opportunity cost of producing an additional machine when moving from: (i) point *A* to point *B*? (ii) point *D* to point *E*?
   f. What economic law is illustrated by your answers to part (e) above?
   g. Which of the points *A, B, C, D, E, F, G,* and *H* are productively efficient?
   h. If society values the production combination at point *D* the most, but Fantasia is currently producing at point *C*, this situation conflicts with what socioeconomic goal?
   i. Which one of the two points *B* or *E* would lead to a greater rate of economic growth? Why? What important trade-off is illustrated here?
   j. How will economic growth affect Fantasia's production possibilities curve over time?

3. The table on page 54 illustrates the marks a student can earn on examinations in economics and biology if the student uses all available hours for study.

| Economics | Biology |
|---|---|
| 100 | 40 |
| 90 | 50 |
| 80 | 60 |
| 70 | 70 |
| 60 | 80 |
| 50 | 90 |
| 40 | 100 |

Plot this student's production possibilities curve. Does this PPC illustrate increasing or constant opportunity costs?

4. The following sets of numbers represent hypothetical production possibilities for a country in 2017. Plot these points on graph paper.

| Cheese | Apples |
|---|---|
| 4 | 0 |
| 3 | 1.6 |
| 2 | 2.4 |
| 1 | 2.8 |
| 0 | 3.0 |

Does the law of increasing relative cost seem to hold? Why? On the same graph, plot and draw the production possibilities curve that will represent 10 percent economic growth.

5. Construct a production possibilities curve for a country facing increasing opportunity costs for producing food and video games. Show how the PPC changes given the following events:
   a. A new and better fertilizer is developed.
   b. There is a surge in labour that can be employed in both the agriculture sector and the video game sector.
   c. A new programming language is invented that is less costly to code and is more memory-efficient, enabling the use of smaller games cartridges.
   d. A heat wave and drought result in a decrease of 10 percent in usable farmland.

**LO 2.3 Use the production possibilities curve to explain the trade-off between consumption goods and capital goods.**

6. Two countries, Workland and Playland, have similar populations and identical production possibilities curves but different preferences. The production possibilities combinations are as follows:

| Point | Capital Goods | Consumption Goods |
|---|---|---|
| A | 0 | 20 |
| B | 1 | 19 |
| C | 2 | 17 |
| D | 3 | 14 |
| E | 4 | 10 |
| F | 5 | 5 |

Playland is located at point *B* on the PPC, and Workland is located at point *E*. Assume that this situation continues into the future and that all other things remain the same.
   a. What is Workland's opportunity cost of capital goods in terms of consumption goods?
   b. What is Playland's opportunity cost of capital goods in terms of consumption goods?
   c. How would the PPCs of Workland and Playland be expected to compare with each other 50 years in the future?

7. If, by going to college, you give up the chance to work in your mother's business for 35 hours per week at $7 per hour, what would be your opportunity cost of earning a two-year college diploma? What incentives exist to make you incur that opportunity cost? What are you giving up today in order to have more in the future? Assume that you will need to spend 60 weeks in college to earn a diploma.

**LO 2.4 Distinguish between absolute advantage and comparative advantage and use these concepts to explain how specialization and trade can increase production and consumption.**

8. Referring to Example 2–4: Specializing in Providing Baggage-Free Business Trips, why might one expect the businesspeople who earn the most per hour to be most interested in using this new type of baggage-free service?

9. You can wash, fold, and iron a basket of laundry in two hours and prepare a meal in one hour. Your roommate can wash, fold, and iron a basket of laundry in three hours and prepare a meal in one hour. Should you and your roommate specialize in particular tasks? Why? And if so, who should specialize in which task? Calculate how much labour time you save if you choose to "trade" an appropriate task with your roommate, as opposed to doing it yourself.

**LO 2.5, 2.6 Explain the differences between the pure capitalist, pure command, and mixed economic systems; describe the features of pure capitalism and explain how capitalism answers the three basic economic questions.**

10. Noah and Nora are partners in a fast-food submarine sandwich shop. In one hour, Noah can prepare 10 sandwiches and 30 pasta salads. In the same hour, Nora can prepare 10 sandwiches and 20 pasta salads.
    a. Who has the absolute advantage in preparing pasta salads?
    b. Who has the comparative advantage in preparing sandwiches?
    c. For each hour spent on specializing in preparing the items in which each partner has a comparative advantage, what will be the net gain in production?

11. Toby and Tony are partners in their popular downtown Italian eatery. In one hour, Toby can produce 10 gourmet pizzas and five lasagne supremes. In the same hour,

Tony can prepare five gourmet pizzas and five lasagne supremes.

a. Who has the absolute advantage in producing pizzas?
b. Who has the comparative advantage in producing the lasagne?
c. For each hour spent on specializing in preparing the items in which each partner has a comparative advantage, what will be the net gain in production?

12. State whether each of the following policies is more consistent with the principles of the Conservative party or the New Democratic party.

*Policy A:* The Canadian government provides tax cuts to parents of young children that amount to $100 per child.

*Policy B:* The Canadian government expands day-care spaces through the expansion of government-owned and -operated day-care services.

13. What features of capitalism help explain how consumer sovereignty can be achieved with limited government involvement?

14. Briefly explain how capitalism answers the three basic economic questions.

15. The following table gives the production techniques and input prices for 100 units of product X.

| | | Production Technique | | |
|---|---|---|---|---|
| Input | Input Unit Price | A (units) | B (units) | C (units) |
| Labour | $10 | 6 | 5 | 4 |
| Capital | 8 | 5 | 6 | 7 |

a. In a market system, which techniques will be used to produce 100 units of product X?
b. If the market price of a unit of X is $1, which technique will lead to the greatest profit?
c. The output of X is still 100 units, but the price of labour and capital changes so that labour is $8 and capital is $10. Which production technique will be used?
d. Using the information in part (c), what is the potential profit of producing 100 units of X?

# BUSINESS APPLICATION

**LO 2.3 Use the production possibilities curve to explain the trade-off between consumption goods and capital goods.**

## Finance: Is Deficit Financing Always Undesirable?

Deficit financing refers to the practice of having to incur a new debt when purchasing a good. Understanding the difference between consumer and capital goods may shed some light on whether or not deficit financing is appropriate. In general, economists are more likely to suggest financing capital goods on a deficit basis than consumption goods. Since most of the benefits of a capital good accrue in future periods, it is rational to borrow funds and then gradually pay back the loan in the future when the benefits of the investment good accrue. This holds true for both private and public sector goods, as the following problem illustrates.

## Business Application Problem

For each pair of goods listed below, indicate which good is better suited to deficit financing.

a. Spending $30 000 on a "fully loaded" sports car or spending $30 000 obtaining a Bachelor of Commerce degree.
b. Constructing a civic convention centre or constructing community leisure pools with waterslides.
c. Constructing an exercise gym on a work site that is freely available to your employees or paying for trips to Mexico for your employees.
d. An insurance salesman purchasing a season's pass to a posh golf course or a college instructor purchasing a season's pass to a posh golf course.
e. Constructing an expensive, beautifully designed city hall or subsidizing the city's major-league sports team.

APPENDIX

B

# The Production Possibilities Curve and Comparative Advantage

The gains from specialization and trade can be effectively illustrated by the production possibilities curve model. Let us assume that two Canadian family farms, the Pulets and the Dowbys, can produce chicken and perogies on each of their farm operations. The Pulets can produce one kilogram of chicken per hour or one kilogram of perogies per hour. The Dowbys can produce two kilograms of chicken per hour or eight kilograms of perogies per hour. Armed with this productivity information, we can proceed to construct production possibilities for each family farm.

## Before Specialization and Trade

We will construct a daily production possibilities curve for the two products, chicken and perogies, for each family farm, by assuming that each family works an eight-hour day.

The Pulets' production possibilities curve in Figure B–1 part (a) shows that in a typical day, if they devote all eight hours to producing perogies, they can produce eight kilograms of perogies per day, which is at point *A*. Alternatively, if the Pulets devote all of the eight hours to producing chicken, they can produce eight kilograms of chicken per day, which is at point *B* in Figure B–1 part (a). Currently, the Pulets are not specializing and trading, and so they are producing and consuming six kilograms of perogies and two kilograms of chicken on a daily basis, which is at point *C* in Figure B–1 part (a).

The Dowbys' production possibilities curve in Figure B–1 part (b) shows that in a typical day, if they devote all eight hours to producing perogies, they can produce 64 kilograms of perogies per day, which is at point *A*. Alternatively, if the Dowbys devote all of the eight hours to producing chicken, they can produce 16 kilograms of chicken per day, which is at point *B* in Figure B–1 part (b). Currently, the Dowbys are not specializing and trading, and so they are producing and consuming 48 kilograms of perogies and four kilograms of chicken on a daily basis, which is at point *C* in Figure B–1 part (b).

You will notice that both production possibilities curves are assumed to be straight lines. This implies that the opportunity cost of production will stay constant as each farm

**FIGURE B–1**

**The Before-Specialization, Before-Trade Production Possibilities**

In part (a), the Pulets have chosen to produce and consume two kilograms of chicken and six kilograms of perogies. In part (b), the Dowbys have chosen to produce and consume four kilograms of chicken and 48 kilograms of perogies.

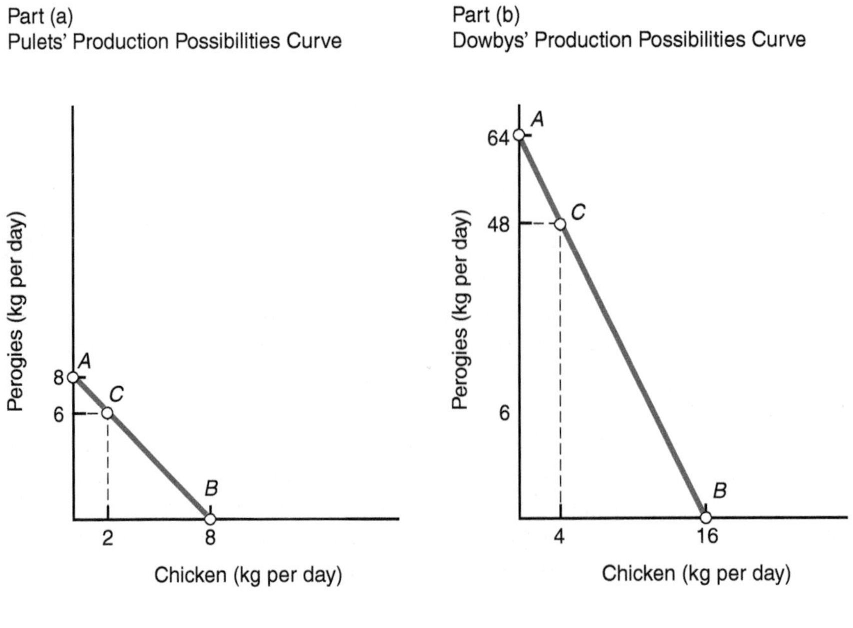

specializes in the production of one of its products. This assumption will simplify our production possibilities illustration of the gains from trade and specialization.

Figure B–1 illustrates that the Dowbys can produce more of both products, when compared to the Pulets, despite the fact that both family farms are employing the same level of total labour input on a daily basis. This implies that the Dowbys can produce a kilogram of each product at a lower labour cost than the Pulets. In other words, the Dowbys have the absolute advantage in the production of chicken and in the production of perogies.

Since the Dowbys have the absolute advantage in the production of each product, it may appear that there would be no incentive for the Dowbys to specialize and trade with the Pulets. However, as we will explain below, the Pulets do have the comparative advantage in the production of chicken, and therefore, the Dowbys can increase their consumption possibilities by specializing and trading with the Pulets.

# After Specialization and before Trade

As noted in Chapter 2, we can identify the family farm that has the comparative advantage in each product by computing opportunity costs.

## Opportunity Costs Incurred by the Pulets

According to Figure B–1 part (a), if the Pulets switch production possibilities from point *A* to point *B*, eight additional kilograms of chicken can be produced by giving up eight kilograms of perogies. Therefore, one additional kilogram of chicken has an opportunity cost or sacrifice of one kilogram of perogies on the Pulets' farm. If the Pulets switch production possibilities from point *B* to point *A* in Figure B–1 part (a), you can see that one additional kilogram of perogies has an opportunity cost of one kilogram of chicken. These opportunity costs are summarized in Table B–1.

## Opportunity Costs Incurred by the Dowbys

According to Figure B–1 part (b), if the Dowbys switched production possibilities from point *A* to point *B*, 16 additional kilograms of chicken can be produced by giving up 64 kilograms of perogies. Therefore, one additional kilogram of chicken has an opportunity cost of four kilograms of perogies. If the Dowbys were to switch production possibilities from point *B* to point *A* in Figure B–1 part (b), you can see that one additional kilogram of perogies has an opportunity cost of one-quarter of a kilogram of chicken. These opportunity costs are summarized in Table B–1.

**TABLE B–1**

**Opportunity Costs for Each Farm for Each Product**

The Pulets can produce a kilogram of chicken at a lower opportunity cost than the Dowbys. The Dowbys can produce a kilogram of perogies at a lower opportunity cost than the Pulets.

| | Opportunity cost of 1 kg of chicken: | Opportunity cost of 1 kg of perogies: |
|---|---|---|
| Pulets | 1 kg of perogies | 1 kg of chicken |
| Dowbys | 4 kg of perogies | 1/4 = 0.25 kg of chicken |

## Comparative Advantage Principle

Table B–1 indicates that the Pulets can produce an additional kilogram of chicken at a lower opportunity cost, one kilogram of perogies, than the Dowbys' opportunity cost of four kilograms of perogies. This implies that the Dowbys can produce an additional kilogram of the other product, perogies, at a lower opportunity cost than the Pulets (0.25 kilograms versus one kilogram of chicken). In other words, the Pulets have the comparative advantage in the production of chicken, and the Dowbys have the comparative advantage in the production of perogies.

The **Comparative Advantage Principle** states that the combined production of two producers can be enhanced if each producer specializes in the product in which it has the comparative advantage. According to this principle, the combined daily production of both family farms can be increased by having the Pulets specialize in the production of chicken and the Dowbys specialize in the production of perogies.

**Comparative Advantage Principle** States that the combined production of two producers can be enhanced if each producer specializes in the product in which it has the comparative advantage.

Figure B–1 part (a) reminds us that before specialization, the Pulets were producing two kilograms of chicken and six kilograms of perogies. Figure B–1 part (b) indicates that before specialization, the Dowbys were producing four kilograms of chicken and 48 kilograms of perogies. Therefore, the combined family farm production before specialization was 2 + 4 = 6 kilograms of chicken and was 6 + 48 = 54 kilograms of perogies.

According to Figure B–1 part (a), if the Pulets specialized in the production of chicken, they would switch production possibilities to point *B* and produce eight kilograms of chicken and zero kilograms of perogies per day. Figure B–1 part (b) indicates that if the Dowbys specialized in perogies, they would switch production possibilities to point *A* and produce 64 kilograms of perogies and zero kilograms of chicken per day. Note that by specializing according to comparative advantage, the combined family farm production of chicken has increased from six kilograms to eight kilograms per day. Similarly, the combined family farm production of perogies has increased from 54 kilograms to 64 kilograms per day.

# After Specialization and after Trade

With each family farm specializing according to comparative advantage, the need will arise to trade the surplus production between family farms. Under specialization, the only way the Pulets can obtain perogies is by trading off some chicken. Similarly, the Dowbys will have to trade some of their perogies in order to consume some chicken. In trading with each other, the question now becomes, how much of one product should each farm trade away in order to get an additional kilogram of the other product?

## The Terms of Trade Principle

**Terms of trade** The amount of one product that must be traded in order to obtain an additional unit of another product.

**Terms of Trade Principle** Each producer will gain from specialization and trade if the terms of trade is between the producers' opportunity costs of production.

The **terms of trade** for chicken is the amount of the other product, perogies, that must be traded in order to obtain one additional kilogram of chicken. The **Terms of Trade Principle** states that each producer will gain from specialization and trade if the terms of trade is between the producers' opportunity costs of production.

As an example, a mutually beneficial terms of trade for one kilogram of chicken would be anywhere between one kilogram of perogies (opportunity cost at the Pulets farm) and four kilograms of perogies (opportunity cost at the Dowbys farm). Thus, one acceptable terms of trade for one kilogram of chicken would be two kilograms of perogies. Assuming these terms of trade and assuming that the Pulets end up trading five kilograms of their chicken in exchange for 10 kilograms of perogies with the Dowbys, Table B–2 illustrates how both family farms can increase their consumption possibilities.

**THE PULETS' GAIN FROM TRADE.** According to Table B–2, if the Pulets specialize and produce eight kilograms of chicken and then trade away five kilograms of chicken for 10 kilograms of perogies, they end up consuming 8 − 5 = 3 kilograms of chicken and 0 + 10 = 10 kilograms of perogies, after specialization and after trade. On the basis of point *C* of Figure B–1, the Pulets produced and consumed only two kilograms of chicken and six kilograms of perogies, before specialization and trade. In other words, specialization and trade increased the Pulets' consumption of chicken and perogies by one kilogram and four kilograms per day, respectively.

Figure B–2 part (a) describes the Pulets' gain as a rightward shift from point *C* on the Pulets' production possibilities curve to point *C1* on the Pulets' new consumption possibilities curve. Note that the slope of the Pulets' new consumption possibilities curve is 2, which is based on the terms of trade for one kilogram of chicken.

**THE DOWBYS' GAIN FROM TRADE.** Table B–2 also describes how the Dowbys can enhance their consumption possibilities with the terms of trade of two kilograms of perogies for one kilogram of chicken. Before trade and specialization, the Dowbys produced and consumed four kilograms of chicken and 48 kilograms of perogies (point *C* in Figure B–1 part (b)). After trade and specialization, the Dowbys can consume five kilograms of chicken and 54 kilograms of perogies. Specialization and trade increased the Dowbys' consumption of chicken and perogies by one kilogram and six kilograms per day, respectively.

**TABLE B–2**

**Gains from Specialization and Trade**

After specialization and trade, the Pulets gain one kilogram of chicken and four kilograms of perogies. The Dowbys gain one kilogram of chicken and six kilograms of perogies.

| | (1) | (2) | (3) | (4) = (2) + (3) | (5) = (4) − (1) |
|---|---|---|---|---|---|
| **Farm** | **Production Before Specialization** | **Production After Specialization** | **Trade: Sells (−) Buys (+)** | **Consumption After Specialization and Trade** | **Gains from Specialization and Trade** |
| **Pulets** | | | | | |
| Chicken | 2 kg | 8 kg | −5 kg | 8 − 5 = 3 kg | 3 − 2 = +1 kg |
| Perogies | 6 kg | 0 kg | +10 kg | 0 + 10 = 10 kg | 10 − 6 = +4 kg |
| **Dowbys** | | | | | |
| Chicken | 4 kg | 0 kg | +5 kg | 0 + 5 = 5 kg | 5 − 4 = +1 kg |
| Perogies | 48 kg | 64 kg | −10 kg | 64 − 10 = 54 kg | 54 − 48 = +6 kg |

Figure B–2 part (b) describes the Dowbys' gain as a rightward shift from point *C* on the Dowbys' production possibilities curve to point *C1* on the Dowbys' new consumption possibilities curve. Again, note that the slope of the Dowbys' new consumption possibilities curve is 2, which is based on the terms of trade for one kilogram of chicken.

In summary, we have just shown how the Dowbys can benefit by specializing and trading with the Pulets, despite the fact that the Dowbys have the absolute advantage in both products. This is because the opportunity costs of production differ between both family farms. In other words, *the gains from specialization and trade are based on comparative advantage and not absolute advantage.*

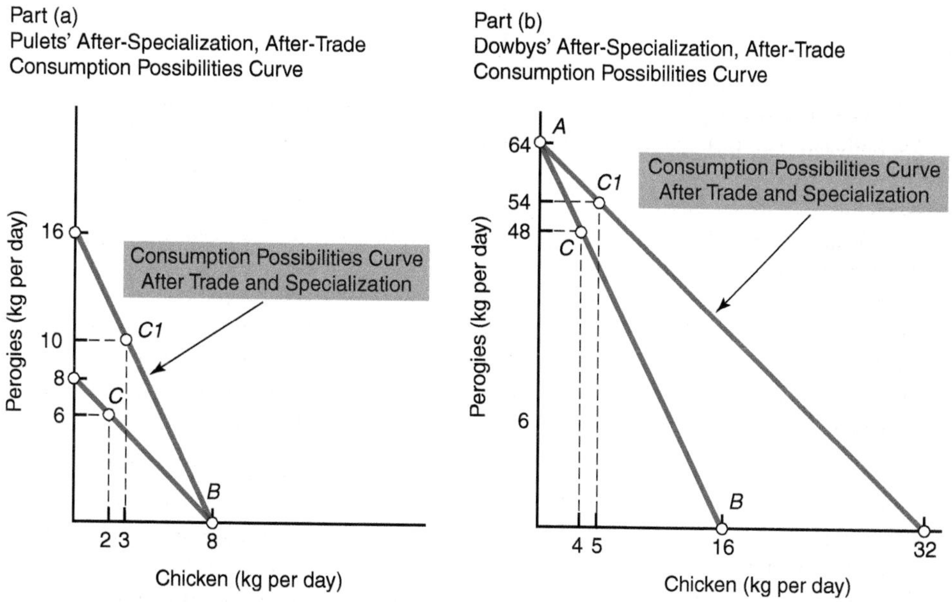


**FIGURE B–2**

**After-Specialization, After-Trade Consumption Possibilities**

In part (a) and part (b), specialization and trade allow both the Pulets and the Dowbys to increase their consumption possibilities beyond their production possibilities.

# APPENDIX SUMMARY

1. Absolute advantage refers to the ability to produce one unit of a product at a lower labour cost than another producer. Comparative advantage refers to the ability to produce a unit of a product at a lower opportunity cost than another producer.
2. According to the Comparative Advantage Principle, the combined production of two producers can be increased if each producer specializes according to comparative advantage. This principle applies even in those cases where one producer has the absolute advantage in both product areas.
3. The terms of trade for one product, *A,* is the amount of the other product, *B,* that must be traded in order to obtain one additional unit of *A.*
4. The Terms of Trade Principle states that each producer will gain from specialization and trade if the terms of trade is between the producers' opportunity costs of production. In this case, consumption possibilities can exceed production possibilities.

# APPENDIX PROBLEMS

(Answers to the odd-numbered problems appear at the back of the book.)

B-1. Answer each of the following questions on the basis of the before-specialization and trade production possibilities for the Martin and the Richard families described in the accompanying two graphs. Before specialization and trade, each family is producing and consuming production combination *C*.

a. Which family has the absolute advantage in the production of each product?

b. Compute the opportunity cost of producing one litre of beer for each family.

c. Which family has the comparative advantage in the production of each product?

d. Before specialization, each family is producing combination *C* on its respective production possibilities curve. Assuming that each family decides to specialize in its area of comparative advantage, compute the gains in total combined production for each product.

e. In order for both families to share the gains from specialization, the terms of trade for one litre of beer should be somewhere between ___ and ___ litres of wine.

B-2. Answer each of the following questions on the basis of the before-specialization and trade production possibilities for the nations of Mazland and Attica for the two products, cellphones and digital cameras, as shown in the accompanying graphs. Before specialization and trade, each nation is producing and consuming production combination *C*.

a. Which nation has the absolute advantage in the production of each product?

b. Compute the opportunity cost of producing one camera for each nation.

c. Which nation has the comparative advantage in the production of each product?

d. Before specialization, both nations are producing combination *C* on their respective production possibilities curve. Assuming that each nation decides to specialize in its area of comparative advantage, compute the gains in total combined production for each product.

e. In order for both nations to share the gains from specialization, the terms of trade for one camera should be somewhere between ___ and ___ phones.

**Martin's Production Possibilities**

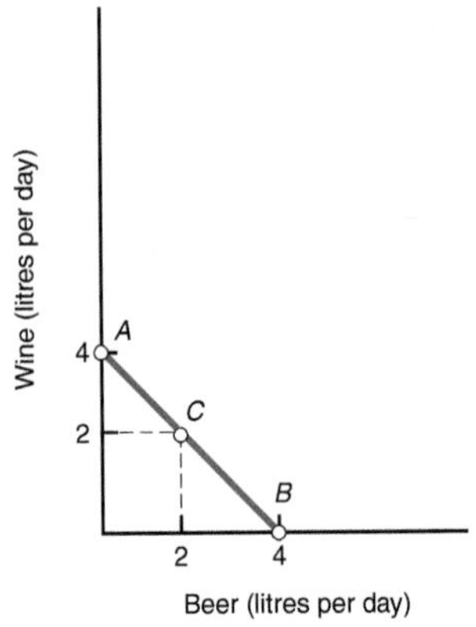


**Richard's Production Possibilities**

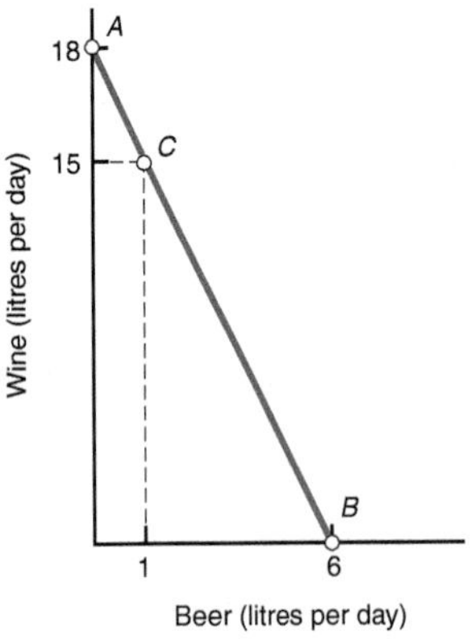


**Mazland's Production Possibilities**

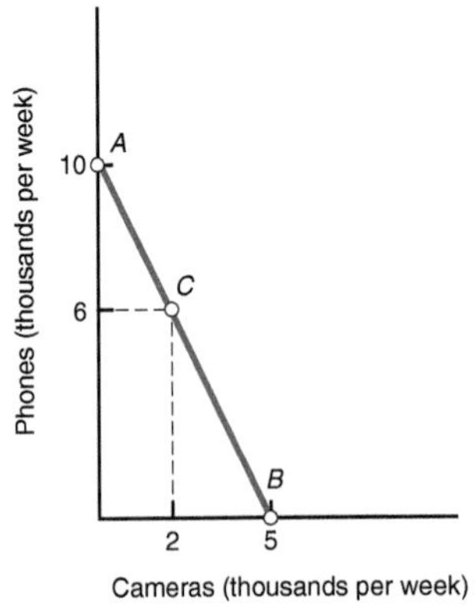


**Attica's Production Possibilities**

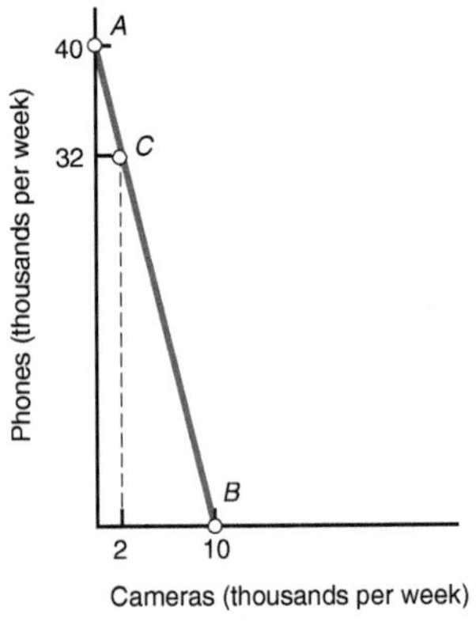

3

# Demand and Supply

While the average annual Canadian inflation rate rose only 1.5 percent in 2016, the average price of Canadian owner-occupied dwellings increased at an annual rate of 10.5 percent. During this same period, Canadian household debt as a percent of household income soared to an historic high of 167.6 percent. Canadian households are starting 2017 with a record home mortgage debt valued at approximately 1.29 trillion dollars.

Is Canada experiencing a housing bubble similar to the one recently experienced before the U.S. housing crash that preceded the 2008–2009 great recession? The theory in this chapter will provide you with the tools needed to predict the future direction of prices in any market, including the Canadian housing market.

Sources:"Quarterly Forecasts". Housing Market Stats. Canadian Real Estate Association. December 15, 2016. (Accessed January 26, 2017) http://www.crea.ca/housing-market-stats/quarterly-forecasts/(Accessed January 26, 2017); "Consumer Price Index by province".Summary Tables. Statistics Canada. January 20, 2017. http://www.statcan.gc.ca/tables-tableaux/sum-som/l01/cst01/cpis01a-eng.htm.(Accessed January 26, 2017); "Canadian key household debt ratio hits record high".Business. CBC News. September 15, 2016. http://www.cbc.ca/news/business/debt-income-ratio-record-1.3763343. (Accessed January 26, 2017); "Canada's household debt is now bigger than its GDP, for the first time". Economy. News. Financial Post. September 15, 2016. http://business.financialpost.com/news/economy/canadas-household-debt-is-now-bigger-than-its-gdp-for-the-first-time (Accessed on Jnauary 30, 2017).

myeconlab

MyEconLab helps you master each objective and study more efficiently. See end of chapter for details.

## LEARNING OBJECTIVES

After reading this chapter, you should be able to:

3.1 Explain the law of demand.

3.2 Distinguish between a change in quantity demanded and a change in demand.

3.3 Explain the law of supply.

3.4 Distinguish between a change in quantity supplied and a change in supply.

3.5 Explain how the forces of demand and supply interact to determine equilibrium price and quantity.

3.6 Describe how changes in demand and supply can change equilibrium price and quantity.

## DID YOU KNOW THAT...?

How do your household's spending habits compare to the typical household in Canada? According to Statistics Canada's Survey of Household Spending, released on February 12 2016, each Canadian household spends an average monthly amount of $1239 on income taxes; $1430 on shelter: rent or mortgage, utilities, supplies, equipment, and furnishings; $991 on transportation: auto-related and public transportation; $676 on food ($169 per week); $320 on recreation ($80 per week); $406 per month on personal insurance payments and pension contributions; $288 on health and personal care; $292 on clothing; $161 on gifts and charitable contributions; $1378 on tobacco, alcohol, and games of chance; $125 on education; $134 on miscellaneous items; and $12 on reading materials and printed matter. The contents of this chapter will help you identify the various factors that both explain and predict the composition of household consumer expenditures.

Source: "Survey of household spending." *The Daily*. Statistics Canada. February 2, 2016. http://www.statcan.gc.ca/daily-quotidien/160212/dq160212a-eng.htm. (Accessed January 26, 2017).

# 3.1 The Law of Demand

**Demand** The quantities of a specific good or service that individuals are willing to purchase at various possible prices, other things being constant.

**Law of demand** The observation that there is an inverse relationship between the price of any good and its quantity demanded, holding other factors equal.

**Demand** has a special meaning in economics. It refers to the quantities of specific goods or services that individuals, either singly or as a group, will purchase at various possible prices, other things being constant. We can, therefore, talk about the demand for microprocessor chips, french fries, CD players, and health care.

Associated with the concept of demand is the **law of demand**, which can be stated as follows:

**When the price of a good goes up, people buy less of it, other things being equal. When the price of a good goes down, people buy more of it, other things being equal.**

The law of demand tells us that the quantity demanded of any commodity is inversely related to its price, other things being equal. In an inverse relationship, one variable moves up in value when the other moves down. The law of demand states that a change in price causes the quantity demanded to change in the *opposite* direction.

Note that we tacked onto the end of the law of demand the statement "other things being equal." We referred to this in Chapter 1 as the *ceteris paribus* assumption. It means, for example, that when we predict that people will buy fewer CD players if their price goes up, we are holding constant the price of all other goods in the economy as well as people's incomes. Implicitly, therefore, if we are assuming that no other prices change when we examine the price behaviour of CD players, we are looking at the *relative* price of CD players.

The law of demand is supported by millions of observations of how people behave in the marketplace. Theoretically, it can be derived from an economic model based on rational behaviour, as was discussed in Chapter 1. Basically, if nothing else changes and the price of a good falls, the lower price induces us to buy more over a certain period of time. This is because we can enjoy additional net gains that were unavailable at the higher price. For the most part, if you examine your own purchasing behaviour, you will see that it generally follows the law of demand.

## Relative Prices versus Money Prices

**Relative price** Any commodity's price in terms of another commodity.

**Money price** The actual price that you pay in dollars and cents for any good or service at any point in time.

The **relative price** of any commodity is its price in terms of another commodity. The actual price that you pay in dollars and cents for any good or service at any point in time is called its **money price**. Consider an example that you might hear quite often around older friends or relatives. "When I bought my first new car, it cost only $1500." The implication, of course, is that the price of cars today is outrageously high because the average new car might cost $20 000. But that is not an accurate comparison. What was the price of the average house during that same year? Perhaps it was only $12 000. By comparison, then, given that houses today average about $200 000, the current price of a new car does not sound so far out of line, does it?

The point is that comparing money prices during different time periods does not tell you much. You have to find out relative prices. Consider the example of the price comparison of detached homes versus condo apartments between 2015 and 2016. In Table 3–1, we show the money prices of detached homes and condo apartments for two years during which time both have gone up. That means that we have to pay more for detached homes and more for condo apartments in 2016 dollars. If we look, though, at the relative prices of detached homes and condo apartments, we find that in 2015, detached homes were 2.18 times as expensive as condo apartments, whereas in 2016 they are 2.31 times as expensive. Conversely, if we compare condo apartments to detached homes, in 2015 they cost 0.46 times as much as detached homes , but in 2016 they cost only 43 percent as much. In the one-year period, though both prices have gone up in money terms, the relative price of apartment condos has fallen (and equivalently, the relative price of detached homes has risen).

When evaluating the effects of price changes, we must always compare prices per *constant-quality unit*. Sometimes, relative price changes occur because the quality of a product improves, thereby bringing about a decrease in the item's effective price per constant-quality unit.

**TABLE 3–1**

**Money Price versus Relative Price**

The money prices of both detached homes and condo apartments have risen. But the relative price of condo apartments has fallen (or conversely, the relative price of detached homes has risen).

| Greater Toronto | Home Type: Money Price (000's dollars) | | Home Type: Relative Price | |
|---|---|---|---|---|
| | 2015 | 2016 | 2015 | 2016 |
| Detached home | 825.46 | 1016.15 | 825.46/378.26=**2.18** | 1016.15/440.67 = **2.31** |
| Condo apartment | 378.26 | 440.67 | 378.26/825.46=**0.46** | 440.67/1016.15 = **0.43** |

Source: "Market Watch". Toronto Real Estate Board. December 2016. http://www.trebhome.com/market_news/market_watch/2016/mw1612.pdf (Accessed January 28, 2017).

## The Demand Schedule

Let us take a hypothetical demand situation to see how the inverse relationship between the price and the quantity demanded looks (holding other things equal). We will consider the quantity of rewriteable DVDs demanded *per year* by one person. Without stating the *time dimension*, we could not make sense out of this demand relationship because the numbers would be different if we were talking about the quantity demanded per month or the quantity demanded per decade.

In addition to implicitly or explicitly stating a time dimension for a demand relationship, we are also implicitly referring to constant-quality units of the good or service in question. Prices are always expressed in constant-quality units in order to avoid the problem of comparing commodities that are, in fact, not truly comparable.

In part (a) of Figure 3–1, we see that if the price were $1 per DVD, 50 of them would be bought each year by our representative individual, but if the price were $5 per DVD, only 10 would be bought each year. This reflects the law of demand. Part (a) is also simply called *demand*, or a *demand schedule*, because it gives a schedule of alternative quantities demanded per year at different possible prices.

## The Demand Curve

Tables expressing relationships between two variables can be represented in graphical terms. To do this, we need only construct a graph that has the price per constant-quality DVD on the vertical axis, and the quantity measured in constant-quality DVDs per year on the horizontal axis. All we have to do is take combinations *A* through *E* from part (a) of Figure 3–1 and plot those points in part (b). Now we connect the points with a smooth line,

**FIGURE 3–1**
**The Individual Demand Schedule and the Individual Demand Curve**

In part (a), we show combinations *A* through *E* of the quantities of DVDs demanded, measured in constant-quality units at prices ranging from $5 down to $1 per DVD. In part (b), we plot combinations *A* through *E* on a grid. The result is the individual demand curve for DVDs.

Part (a)

| Combination | Price per Constant-Quality DVD | Quantity of Constant-Quality DVDs per Year |
|---|---|---|
| *A* | $5 | 10 |
| *B* | 4 | 20 |
| *C* | 3 | 30 |
| *D* | 2 | 40 |
| *E* | 1 | 50 |

Part (b)

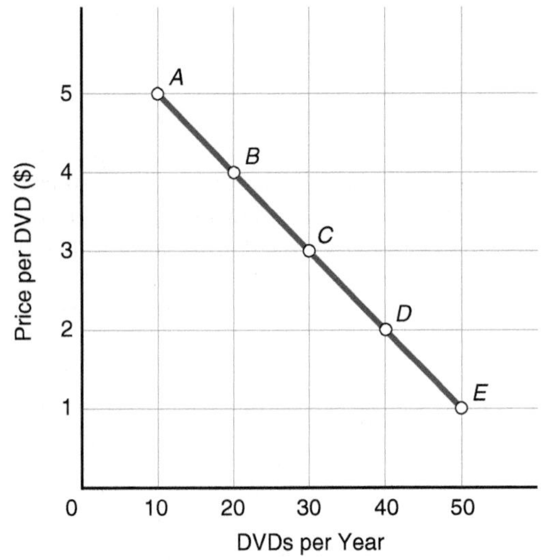


and *voila*, we have a *demand curve*.[1] It is downward-sloping (from left to right) to indicate the inverse relationship between the price of DVDs and the quantity demanded per year. Our presentation of demand schedules and curves applies equally well to all commodities, including toothpicks, hamburgers, textbooks, credit, and labour services. Remember, the **demand curve** is simply a graphical representation of the law of demand.

**Demand curve** A graphical representation of the law of demand.

## Individual versus Market Demand Curves

**Market** All of the arrangements that individuals have for exchanging with one another.

**Market demand** Determined by adding the individual demand at each price for all the consumers in the market.

The demand schedule shown in part (a) of Figure 3–1 and the resulting demand curve shown in part (b) are both given for one individual. As we shall see, determining price in the **market** (all of the arrangements that individuals have for exchanging with one another) depends on, among other things, the *market demand* for a particular commodity. The way in which we measure a **market demand** schedule and derive a market demand curve for DVDs or any other commodity is by adding the individual demand at each price for all consumers in the market. Suppose that the market for DVDs consists of only two buyers: buyer 1, for whom we have already shown the demand schedule in Figure 3–1, and buyer 2, whose demand schedule is displayed in Figure 3–2, part (a), column 3. Column 1 of Figure 3–2, part (a) shows the price, and column 2 gives the quantity demanded by buyer 1 (data taken directly from Figure 3–1). Column 4 states the total quantity demanded at each price, obtained by adding columns 2 and 3. Graphically, in part (d) of Figure 3–2, we add the demand curves of buyer 1 (part (b)) and buyer 2 (part (c)) to derive the market demand curve.

There are, of course, millions of potential consumers for DVDs. We will assume that the summation of all of the consumers in the market results in a demand schedule, given in part (a) of Figure 3–3, and a demand curve, given in part (b). The quantity demanded is now measured in millions of units per year. Remember, part (b) in Figure 3–3 shows the market demand curve for the millions of users of DVDs. The "market" demand curve that we derived in Figure 3–2 assumed that there were only two buyers in the entire market. This is why that demand curve is not a smooth line—whereas the true market demand curve in part (b) of Figure 3–3 is—and has no kinks.

You have likely heard about the increased interest in using technology such as radio frequency identification tags (RFID tags) to track items such as manufacturing, wholesale, and retail merchandise; precious jewellery and art; and library books at all times in their life cycle. As Example 3–1 implies, the increased use of RFID tags can be illustrated graphically as a downward movement along the demand curve for RFID tags.

[1]Even though we call them "curves," for the purposes of exposition, we often draw straight lines. In many real-world situations, demand and supply curves will, in fact, be lines that do curve. To connect the points in part (b) with a line, we assume that for all prices in between the ones shown, the quantities demanded will be found along that line.

## FIGURE 3–2

### The Horizontal Summation of Two Demand Schedules

Part (a) shows how to sum the demand schedule for one buyer with that of another buyer. Column 2 shows the quantity demanded by buyer 1, taken from part (a) of Figure 3–1. Column 4 is the sum of columns 2 and 3. We plot the demand curve for buyer 1 in part (b) and the demand curve for buyer 2 in part (c). When we add those two demand curves horizontally, we get the market demand curve for two buyers, shown in part (d).

Part (a)

| (1) Price per DVD | (2) Buyer 1 Quantity Demanded | (3) Buyer 2 Quantity Demanded | (4) = (2) + (3) Combined Quantity Demanded per Year |
|---|---|---|---|
| $5 | 10 | 10 | 20 |
| 4 | 20 | 20 | 40 |
| 3 | 30 | 40 | 70 |
| 2 | 40 | 50 | 90 |
| 1 | 50 | 60 | 110 |

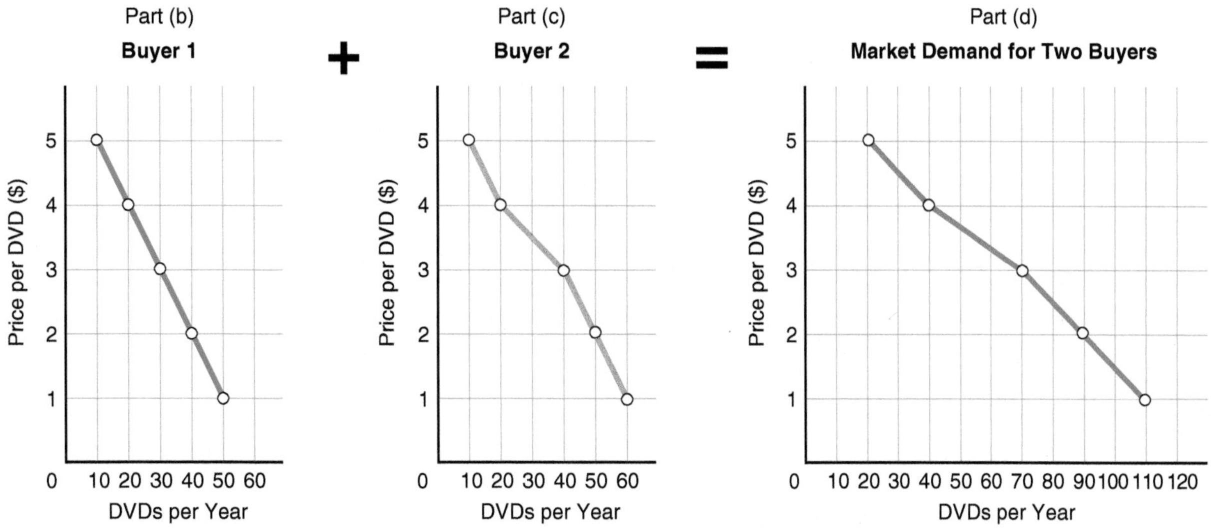


## FIGURE 3–3

### The Market Demand Schedule for DVDs

In part (a), we add up the millions of existing demand schedules for DVDs. In part (b), we plot the quantities from part (a) on a grid; connecting them produces the market demand curve for DVDs.

Part (a)

| Price per Constant-Quality DVD | Total Quantity Demanded of Constant-Quality DVDs per Year (millions) |
|---|---|
| $5 | 20 |
| 4 | 40 |
| 3 | 60 |
| 2 | 80 |
| 1 | 100 |

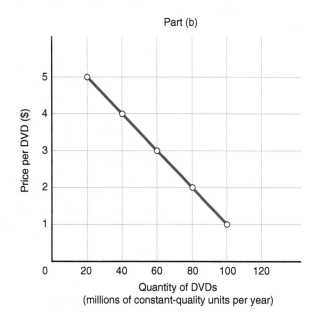

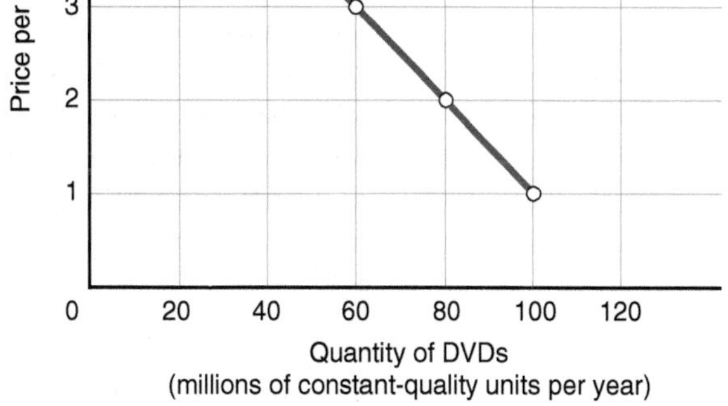

**EXAMPLE 3–1 Why RFID Tags Are Catching On Fast**

An RFID tag contains a tiny microchip and a radio antenna, and it emits a unique signal that a computer-operated reader can use to track any item to which the tag is attached. In principle, any tagged item can be tracked as it travels in planes, trucks, or ships through ports and warehouses, onto retailers shelves, through checkout lines, and into homes and offices.

Just a couple of years ago, the price of an RFID tag was about 30 cents. In 2017, it dropped to between 7 and 15 cents per tag, and in just a few more years the price is likely to decline to less than a nickel per tag. Given this trend in RFID prices, an increasing number of tags have been put to use by retailers, hospitals, trucking firms, airlines, railroads and shipping lines.

Staples Business Depot piloted RFID tagging with four suppliers and one retail location in Toronto. Suppliers placed RFID tags on pallets and cases bound for Staples, and when they were delivered, the company found that the time to process each pallet was reduced from nearly 18 minutes to less than three minutes, significantly reducing the cost of handling. It is estimated that Wal-Mart and other large retailers saved nearly $100 million by adopting RFID. The European Central Bank, which already embeds RFID tags in the largest denomination euro notes to help deter theft and counterfeiting, is now contemplating placing tags in smaller denomination notes.

As of January 2017 RFID tags have been utilized in a wide range of industries including: automotive, animals and livestock, electronics, education, financial, lumber and paper, manufacturing, medical and pharmaceutical, oil drilling, packaging, public sector, libraries, retail, supply chain, and transportation.

Sources: "Frequently asked questions: the cost of RFID equipment." *RFID Journal*. http://www.rfidjournal.com/faq/20; Ken Hunt. "Are you reading me?" *The Globe and Mail*. April 12, 2007. Pg. 28; Applications. RFID Canada. http://www.rfidcanada.com/applications/ (Accessed January 29, 2017).

**For critical analysis:** What economic principle (law) explains why there is an increase in the practice of RFID tagging?

# 3.2 Shifts in Demand

Assume that the federal government gives every student registered in a Canadian college, university, or technical school a personal computer that uses DVDs. The demand curve shown in part (b) of Figure 3–3 is no longer an accurate representation of the total market demand for DVDs. There will now be an increase in the number of DVDs demanded *at each and every possible price*. What we have to do is shift the curve outward, or to the right, to represent the rise in demand. The demand curve in Figure 3–4 will shift from $D_1$ to $D_2$. Take any price, say, $3 per DVD. Originally, before the federal government giveaway of personal computers, the amount demanded at $3 was 60 million DVDs per year. After the government giveaway, however, the quantity demanded at $3 is 100 million DVDs per year. What we have seen is a shift in the demand for DVDs.

The shift can also go in the opposite direction. What if colleges uniformly outlawed the use of personal computers by students? Such a regulation would cause a shift inward—to the left—of the demand curve for DVDs. In Figure 3–4, the demand curve would shift to $D_3$; the amount demanded would now be less at each and every possible price.

## The Other Determinants of Demand

The demand curve in part (b) of Figure 3–3 is drawn with other things held constant, specifically all of the other factors that determine how much will be bought. There are many such determinants. The major ones are income; tastes and preferences; the prices of related goods; expectations regarding future prices, future incomes, and future product availability; and population (market size). Let us examine each determinant more closely.

**INCOME.** For most goods, an increase in income will lead to an increase in demand. The phrase *increase in demand* always refers to a comparison between two different demand

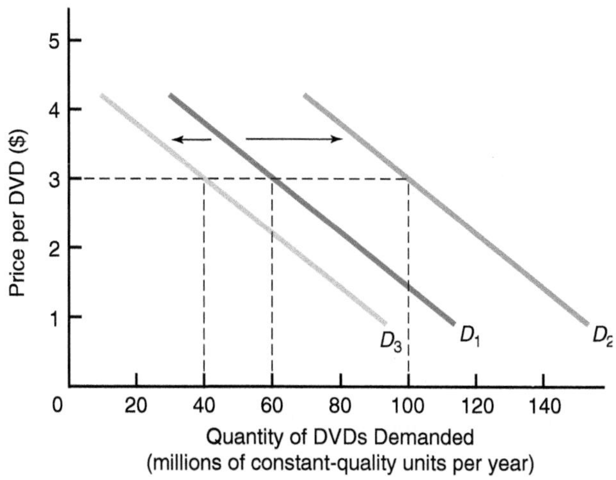


**FIGURE 3–4**

**A Shift in the Demand Curve**

If some factor other than price changes, the only way we can show its effect is by moving the entire demand curve, say, from $D_1$ to $D_2$. We have assumed in our example that the move was precipitated by the government's giving a free personal computer to every registered post-secondary student in Canada. That meant that at all prices, a larger number of DVDs would be demanded than before. Curve $D_3$ represents reduced demand compared to curve $D_1$, caused by a law prohibiting computers on campus.

curves. Thus, for most goods, an increase in income will lead to a rightward shift in the position of the demand curve from, say, $D_1$ to $D_2$ in Figure 3–4. You can avoid confusion about shifts in curves by always relating a rise in demand to a rightward shift in the demand curve and a fall in demand to a leftward shift in the demand curve.

Goods for which the demand rises when income rises are called **normal goods**. Most goods, such as shoes, computers, and CDs, are "normal goods." For some goods, however, demand *falls* as income rises. These are called **inferior goods**. Beans might be an example. As households get richer, they tend to spend less and less on beans and more and more on meat. (The terms *normal* and *inferior* are merely part of the economist's terminology; no value judgments are implied by or associated with them.)

**Normal goods** Goods for which demand rises as income rises.

**Inferior goods** Goods for which demand falls as income rises.

Remember, a shift to the left in the demand curve represents a fall, or decrease, in demand, and a shift to the right represents a rise, or increase, in demand.

Example 3–2 illustrates how an economic recession (downturn) can have quite different effects on consumer demand, depending on whether the product being consumed is a normal or an inferior good.

## EXAMPLE 3–2 A Recession Tale of Two Macs

During the 2008–2009 global recession, sales in Apple retail stores experienced significant declines. Between December 2008 and December 2009, the number of visitors per Apple retail outlet dropped 1.8 percent, while same-store sales dropped 17.4 percent. Overall, Mac computer shipments decreased an average of 17.5 percent.

The global recession appeared to be much kinder to the other "Mac"—the McDonald's fast-food chain. In February 2009, McDonald's Corp. recorded a whopping 7.1 percent rise in global January sales at restaurants open at least 13 months. McDonald's and other fast-food restaurants have benefited as declining household incomes have encouraged restaurant customers to seek lower-priced menus.

**For critical analysis:**

1. Based on the data provided in this example, would you classify Mac computers as a normal or an inferior good? Explain. Sketch a graph showing how the demand for Mac computers has been affected by the global recession.
2. Would you classify a meal from McDonald's as a normal or an inferior good? Sketch a graph showing how the demand for McDonald's meals has been affected by the global recession.

Sources: "Recession hitting Apple retail stores hard." Hot Stories. Macnn News. January 28, 2009. http://www.macnn.com/articles/09/01/28/needham.on.apple.stores/; "McDonald's thrives in downturn." Business Browser. *Edmonton Journal*. February 10, 2009. Pg. E2.

**TASTES AND PREFERENCES.** A change in consumer tastes in favour of a good can shift its demand curve outward to the right. When Frisbees became the rage, the demand curve for them shifted outward to the right; when the rage died out, the demand curve shifted inward to the left. Fashions depend to a large extent on people's tastes and preferences. Economists have little to say about the determination of tastes; they have no "good" theories of taste determination or why people buy one brand of a product rather than others. Advertisers, however, do have various theories that they use in trying to make consumers prefer their products to those of competitors.

Example 3–3 illustrates how taste-related factors have recently affected the demand for hair dye.

### EXAMPLE 3–3 Brunettes Now Have More Fun

In the 1960s, manufacturers of hair dye aired television and radio commercials claiming that "Blondes Have More Fun" and that "Gentlemen Prefer Blondes." For years thereafter, purchases of blonde hair colourings were a significantly higher share of total U.S. expenditures on hair dyes.

Women's tastes in hair colour began to change in the mid-2000s, however. More of the top female stars of stage and screen are brunettes, such as Sandra Bullock, Demi Moore, Penelope Cruz, and Rihanna. In addition, there has been an increase in U.S. populations of Hispanic, Asian, and Arabic women, whose natural hair shades tend to be brunette colours. Finally, greying women from the baby boom generation born between the mid-1940s and the late 1950s have found that darker shades better cover grey and require less maintenance.

**For critical analysis:** Explain how various taste-related factors have shifted the demand curve for brunette hair dyes.

**PRICES OF RELATED GOODS: SUBSTITUTES AND COMPLEMENTS.** Demand schedules are always drawn with the prices of all other commodities held constant. In other words, when deriving a given demand curve, we assume that only the price of the good under study changes. For example, when we draw the demand curve for butter, we assume that the price of margarine is held constant. When we draw the demand curve for stereo speakers, we assume that the price of stereo amplifiers is held constant. When we refer to *related goods*, we are talking about goods for which demand is interdependent. If a change in the price of one good shifts the demand for another good, those two goods are related. There are two types of related goods: *substitutes* and *complements*. We can define and distinguish between substitutes and complements in terms of how the change in price of one commodity affects the demand for its related commodity.

**Substitutes** Two goods are substitutes when either one can be used to satisfy a similar want.

Two goods are **substitutes** when either one can be used to satisfy a similar want. Butter and margarine are substitutes. Let us assume that each originally cost $4 per kilogram. If the price of butter remains the same and the price of margarine falls from $4 to $2 per kilogram, people will buy more margarine and less butter. The demand curve for butter will shift inward to the left. If, conversely, the price of margarine rises from $4 to $6 per kilogram, people will buy more butter and less margarine. The demand curve for butter will shift outward to the right. An increase in the price of margarine will lead to an increase in the demand for butter, and an increase in the price of butter will lead to an increase in the demand for margarine. For substitutes, a price change in the substitute will cause a change in demand *in the same direction*.

**Complements** Two goods are complements if both are used together for consumption or enjoyment.

Two goods are **complements** if both are used together for consumption or enjoyment. For complements, the situation is reversed. Consider stereo speakers and stereo amplifiers. We draw the demand curve for speakers with the price of amplifiers held constant. If the price per constant-quality unit of stereo amplifiers decreases from, say, $500 to $200, that will encourage more people to purchase component stereo systems. They will now buy more speakers than before at any given price. The demand curve for speakers will shift outward to the right. If, by contrast, the price of amplifiers increases from $200 to $500, fewer people will purchase component stereo systems. The demand curve for speakers will shift inward to the left. To summarize, a decrease in the price of amplifiers leads to an increase in the demand for speakers. An increase in the price of amplifiers leads to a decrease in the demand for speakers. Thus, for complements, a price change in a product will cause a change in demand *in the opposite direction*.

**EXPECTATIONS.** Consumers' expectations regarding future prices, future incomes, and future availability may prompt them to buy more or less of a particular good without a change in its current money price. For example, consumers getting wind of a scheduled 100 percent price increase in DVDs next month may buy more of them today at today's prices. Today's demand curve for DVDs will shift from $D_1$ to $D_2$ in Figure 3–4 on page 67. The opposite would occur if a decrease in the price of DVDs were scheduled for next month.

Expectations of a rise in income may cause consumers to want to purchase more of everything today at today's prices. Again, such a change in expectations of higher future income will cause a shift in the demand curve from $D_1$ to $D_2$ in Figure 3–4. Finally, expectations that goods will not be available at any price will induce consumers to stock up now, increasing current demand.

**POPULATION.** An increase in the population in an economy (holding per-capita income constant) often shifts the market demand outward for most products. This is because an increase in population means an increase in the number of buyers in the market. Conversely, a reduction in the population will shift most market demand curves inward because of the reduction in the number of buyers in the market.

The rapid growth of Canadian Internet pharmacies selling prescription drugs to American consumers can be explained in terms of some of the nonprice determinants mentioned above. That is, the higher prices of substitute products, such as prescription drugs sold by American pharmacies, have resulted in a significant increase in American consumer demand for the cheaper Canadian prescription drugs. As well, Internet and fax technology has made it very easy to promote and sell Canadian prescription drugs to virtually any location in the United States. This, in turn, has increased the population or number of American buyers wishing to purchase prescription drugs from Canadian online pharmacies. As a result of these changes in nonprice determinants, the market demand curve for prescription drugs sold by Canadian Internet pharmacies has been shifting to the right.

## Changes in Demand versus Changes in Quantity Demanded

We have made repeated references to demand and to quantity demanded. It is important to realize that there is a difference between a *change in demand* and a *change in quantity demanded.*

Demand refers to a schedule of planned rates of purchase and depends on a great many nonprice determinants. Whenever there is a change in a nonprice determinant, there will be a change in demand—a shift in the entire demand curve to the right or to the left.

Quantity demanded is a specific quantity at a specific price, represented by a single point on a demand curve. When price changes, quantity demanded changes according to the law of demand, and there will be a movement from one point to another along the same demand curve. Look at Figure 3–5. At a price of $3 per DVD, 60 million DVDs per year are demanded. If the price falls to $1, quantity demanded increases to 100 million per year. This movement occurs because the current market price for the product changes. In Figure 3–5, you can see the arrow pointing down the given demand curve $D$.

When you think of demand, think of the entire curve. Quantity demanded, in contrast, is represented by a single point on the demand curve.

**A change or shift in demand causes the *entire* curve to move. The *only* thing that can cause the entire curve to move is a change in a determinant *other than its own price.***

If the price of iPods goes down, what will happen to the demand for amplified speaker systems for iPods?

**FIGURE 3–5**

## Movement along a Given Demand Curve

A change in price changes the quantity of a good demanded. This can be represented as movement along a given demand schedule. If, in our example, the price of DVDs falls from $3 to $1 apiece, the quantity demanded will increase from 60 million to 100 million units per year.

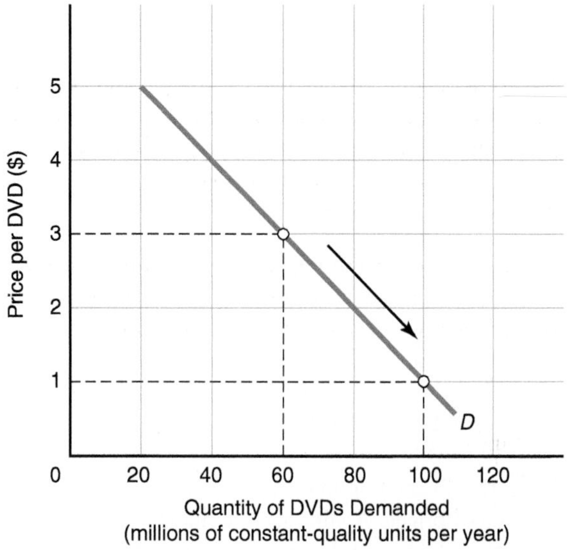


In economic analysis, we cannot emphasize too much the following distinction that must constantly be made:

> **A change in a good's own price leads to a change in quantity demanded, for any given demand curve, other things held constant. This is a movement *along* the curve.**

A change in any other determinant of demand leads to a change in demand. This causes a shift *of* the curve.

As Example 3–4 explains, knowing the difference between a change in quantity demanded and a change in demand will help you understand the effects that a used or secondary market has on the market for a new good.

### EXAMPLE 3–4 Garth Brooks, Used CDs, and the Law of Demand

A few years ago, country singer Garth Brooks tried to prevent his latest album from being sold to any retail chain or store that also sold used CDs. His argument was that the used-CD market deprived labels and artists of earnings. His announcement came after a giant American retailer started selling used CDs side by side with new releases, at half the price. Brooks, along with the distribution arms of Sony, Warner Music, Capitol-EMI, and MCA were trying to quash the used-CD market. This shows that none of these parties understood the law of demand.

Let us say the price of a new CD is $15. The existence of a secondary used-CD market means that to people who choose to resell their CDs for $5, the net cost of a new CD is, in fact, only $10. Because we know that quantity demanded is inversely related to price, more copies of a new CD will be sold at a price of $10 than of the same CD at a price of $15. Taking only this force into account, eliminating the used-CD market will reduce the sales of new CDs.

But there is another force at work here, too. Used CDs are substitutes for new CDs. If used CDs are not available, some people who would have purchased them will instead purchase new CDs. If this second effect outweighs the incentive to buy less because of the higher effective price, then Brooks' attempt to suppress the used-CD market is correct.

**For critical analysis:** Sketch a demand curve for the product "new music CDs." On this same graph, describe the various effects that the used-CD market has on the "quantity demanded" and the "demand" for "new music CDs."

# 3.3 The Law of Supply

The other side of the market for a product involves the quantities of goods and services that *firms* are prepared to *supply* to the market. The **supply** of any good or service is the amount that firms are willing to sell at various possible prices, other things being constant. The relationship between price and quantity supplied, called the **law of supply**, can be summarized as follows:

**At higher prices, a larger quantity will generally be supplied than at lower prices, all other things held constant. At lower prices, a smaller quantity will generally be supplied than at higher prices, all other things held constant.**

**Supply** The quantities of a specific good or service that firms are willing to sell at various possible prices, other things being constant.

**Law of supply** The observation that there is a direct relationship between the price of any good and its quantity supplied, holding other factors constant.

There is generally a direct relationship between quantity supplied and price. Producers are normally willing to produce and sell more of their product at a higher price than at a lower price, other things being constant. At $5 per DVD, 3M, Sony, Maxell, Fuji, and other manufacturers would almost certainly be willing to supply a larger quantity than at $1 per unit, assuming, of course, that no other prices in the economy had changed.

As with the law of demand, millions of instances in the real world have given us confidence in the law of supply. On a theoretical level, the law of supply is based on a model in which producers and sellers seek to make the most gain possible from their activities. For example, as a DVD manufacturer attempts to produce more and more DVDs over the same time period, it will eventually have to hire more workers and overutilize its machines. Only if offered a higher price per DVD will the manufacturer be willing to incur these extra costs. That is why the law of supply implies a direct relationship between price and quantity supplied.

## The Supply Schedule

Just as we were able to construct a demand schedule, we can construct a *supply schedule*, which is a table relating prices to the quantity supplied at each price. A supply schedule can also be referred to simply as *supply*. It is a set of planned production rates that depends on the price of the product. We show the individual supply schedule for a hypothetical producer in part (a) of Figure 3–6. At $1 per DVD, for example, this producer will supply 200 000 DVDs per year; at $5, it will supply 550 000 DVDs per year.

## The Supply Curve

We can convert the supply schedule in part (a) of Figure 3–6 into a *supply curve*, just as we created a demand curve in Figure 3–1. All we do is take the price–quantity combinations from part (a) of Figure 3–6 and plot them in part (b). We have labelled these combinations *F* through *J*. Connecting these points, we obtain the **supply curve**, an upward-sloping curve that shows the typically direct relationship between price and quantity supplied. Again, we have to remember that we are talking about quantity supplied *per year*, measured in constant-quality units.

**Supply curve** An upward-sloping curve that shows the typically direct relationship between price and quantity supplied.

## The Market Supply Curve

Just as we had to add the individual demand curves to get the market demand curve, we need to add the individual producers' supply curves to get the market supply curve. Look at Figure 3–7, in which we horizontally sum two typical DVD manufacturers' supply curves. Supplier 1's data are taken from Figure 3–6; supplier 2 is added. The numbers are presented in part (a). The graphical representation of supplier 1 is in part (b), of supplier 2 in part (c), and of the summation in part (d). The result, then, is the supply curve for DVDs for suppliers 1 and 2.

There are many more suppliers of DVDs, however. The total market supply schedule and total market supply curve for DVDs are represented in Figure 3–8, with the curve in part (b) obtained by adding all of the supply curves, such as those shown in parts (b) and (c) of Figure 3–7. Note the difference between the market supply curve with only two

**FIGURE 3-6**

## The Individual Producer's Supply Schedule and Supply Curve for DVDs

Part (a) shows that at higher prices, a hypothetical supplier will be willing to provide a greater quantity of DVDs. We plot the various price-quantity combinations in part (a) on the grid in part (b). When we connect these points, we find the individual supply curve for DVDs. It is positively sloped.

Part (a)

| Combination | Price per Constant-Quality DVD | Quantity of DVDs Supplied (thousands of constant-quality units per year) |
|---|---|---|
| *F* | $5 | 550 |
| *G* | 4 | 400 |
| *H* | 3 | 350 |
| *I* | 2 | 250 |
| *J* | 1 | 200 |

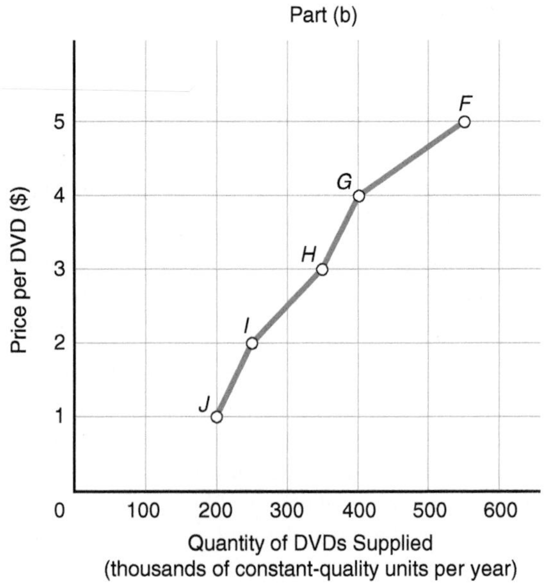


**FIGURE 3-7**

## Horizontal Summation of Supply Curves

In part (a), we show the data for two individual suppliers of DVDs. Adding how much each is willing to supply at different prices, we arrive at the combined quantities supplied in column 4. When we plot the values in columns 2 and 3 on grids in parts (b) and (c) and add them horizontally, we obtain the combined supply curve for the two suppliers in question, shown in part (d).

Part (a)

| (1) Price per DVD | (2) Supplier 1 Quantity Supplied (thousands) | (3) Supplier 2 Quantity Supplied (thousands) | (4) = (2) + (3) Combined Quantity Supplied per Year (thousands) |
|---|---|---|---|
| $5 | 550 | 350 | 900 |
| 4 | 400 | 300 | 700 |
| 3 | 350 | 200 | 550 |
| 2 | 250 | 150 | 400 |
| 1 | 200 | 100 | 300 |

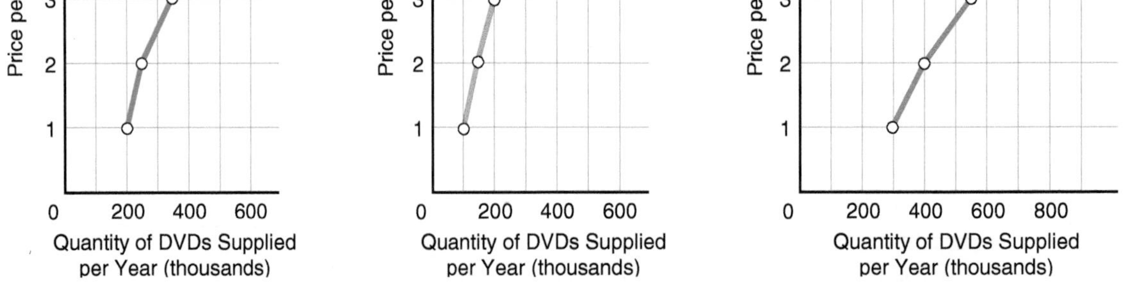

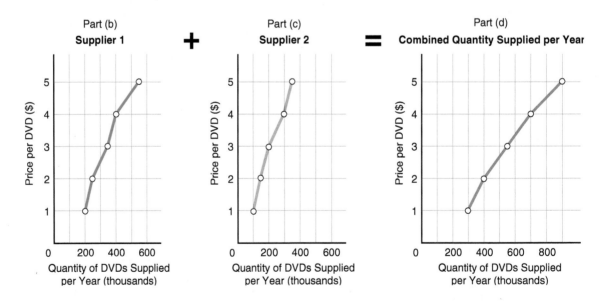


suppliers in Figure 3–7 and the one with a large number of suppliers—the entire true market—in part (b) of Figure 3–8. There are no kinks in the true total market supply curve because there are so many suppliers.

Observe what happens at the market level when price changes. If the price is $3, the quantity supplied is 60 million DVDs. If the price goes up to $4, the quantity supplied increases to 80 million per year. If the price falls to $2, the quantity supplied decreases to 40 million DVDs per year. Changes in quantity supplied are represented by movements along the supply curve in part (b) of Figure 3–8.

FIGURE 3–8

**The Market Supply Schedule and the Market Supply Curve for DVDs**

In part (a), we show the summation of all the individual producers' supply schedules; in part (b), we graph the resulting supply curve. It represents the market supply curve for DVDs and is upward sloping.

Part (a)

| Price per Constant-Quality DVD | Quantity of DVDs Supplied (millions of constant-quality units per year) |
|---|---|
| $5 | 100 |
| 4 | 80 |
| 3 | 60 |
| 2 | 40 |
| 1 | 20 |

Part (b)

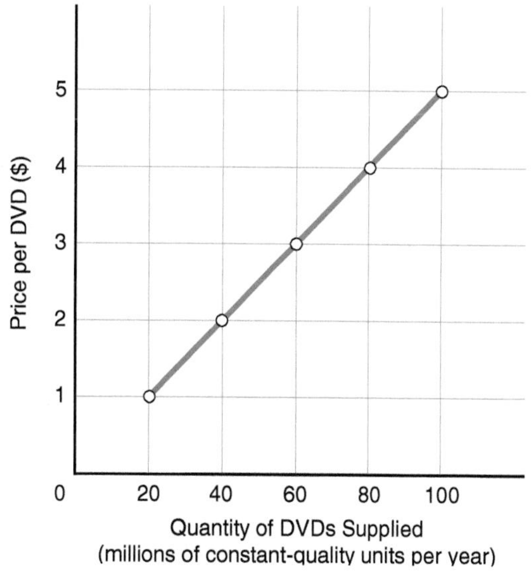


# 3.4 Shifts in Supply

When we looked at demand, we found out that any change in anything relevant other than the price of the good or service caused the demand curve to shift inward or outward. The same is true for the supply curve. If something relevant changes apart from the price of the product or service being supplied, we will see the entire supply curve shift.

Consider an example. A new method of putting magnetic material on DVDs has been invented. It reduces the cost of producing a DVD by 50 percent. In this situation, DVD producers will supply more of their product at all prices because their cost of so doing has fallen dramatically. Competition among DVD manufacturers to produce more at every price will shift the supply schedule of DVDs outward to the right from $S_1$ to $S_2$ in Figure 3–9. At a price of $3, the quantity supplied was originally 60 million DVDs per year, but now the quantity supplied (after the reduction in the costs of production) at $3 a DVD will be 90 million DVDs a year. (This is similar to what has happened to the supply curve of personal computers and fax machines in recent years as the price of the computer memory chip has fallen.)

Now, consider the opposite case. If the cost of the magnetic material needed for making DVDs doubles, the supply curve in Figure 3–9 will shift from $S_1$ to $S_3$. At each price, the number of DVDs supplied will fall due to the increase in the price of raw materials.

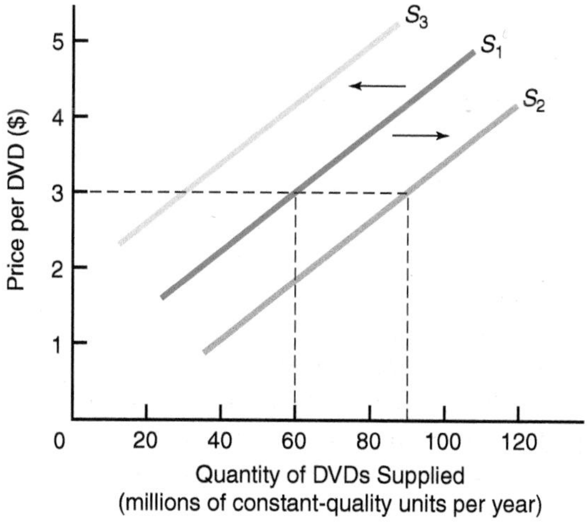


FIGURE 3–9

**A Shift in the Supply Curve**

If the cost of producing DVDs were to fall dramatically, the supply curve would shift rightward from $S_1$ to $S_2$ such that at all prices, a larger quantity would be forthcoming from suppliers. Conversely, if the cost of production rose, the supply curve would shift leftward to $S_3$.

## The Other Determinants of Supply

When supply curves are drawn, only the price of the good in question changes, and it is assumed that other things remain constant. The other things assumed constant are the costs of resources (inputs) used to produce the product, technology and productivity, taxes and subsidies, producers' price expectations, and the number of firms in the industry. These are the major nonprice determinants of supply. If any of them changes, there will be a shift in the supply curve.

**COST OF INPUTS USED TO PRODUCE THE PRODUCT.** If one or more input prices fall, the supply curve will shift outward to the right; that is, more will be supplied at each price. The opposite will be true if one or more inputs become more expensive. For example, when we draw the supply curve of new cars, we are holding the cost of steel (and other inputs) constant. If the price of steel decreases, the supply curve for new cars will shift *outward to the right.* When we draw the supply curve of blue jeans, we are holding the cost of cotton fixed. The supply curve for blue jeans will shift inward to the left if the price of cotton *increases.*

**TECHNOLOGY AND PRODUCTIVITY.** Supply curves are drawn by assuming a given technology, or "state of the art." When the available production techniques change, the supply curve will shift. For example, when a better, cheaper, production technique for DVDs becomes available, the supply curve will shift to the right. A larger quantity will be forthcoming at every price because the cost of production is lower.

**TAXES AND SUBSIDIES.** Certain taxes, such as a per-unit tax, are effectively an addition to production costs and therefore reduce the supply. If the supply curve were $S_1$ in Figure 3–9, a per-unit tax increase would shift it to $S_3$. A subsidy would do the opposite; it would shift the curve to $S_2$. Every producer would receive from the government a "gift" of a few cents for each unit produced.

**PRICE EXPECTATIONS.** A change in the expectation of a future relative price of a product can affect a producer's current willingness to supply, just as price expectations affect a consumer's current willingness to purchase. For example, DVD suppliers may withhold part of their current supply from the market if they anticipate higher prices in the future. The current amount supplied at all prices will decrease.

**NUMBER OF FIRMS IN THE INDUSTRY.** In the short run, when firms can only change the number of employees they use, we hold the number of firms in the industry constant. In the long run, the number of firms (or the size of some existing firms) may change. If the number of firms increases, the supply curve will shift outward to the right. If the number of firms decreases, it will shift inward to the left.

Example 3–5 describes how some of the determinants of supply, noted above, have affected the markets relating to popular electronic products. Indeed, the current trends in supply may help us predict whether Plasma or LCD will dominate the flat screen TV markets in the future.

### EXAMPLE 3–5 Surge in Electronics Sales Follows Dramatic Drop in LCD Prices

Why have sales of LCD TVs grown rapidly?

Beginning in 2004, the prices of liquid crystal displays (LCDs), which are key components in many electronic devices, plummeted. Worldwide, manufacturers of cellphones, computers, electronic hand-held gadgets, and flat screen TVs dramatically increased production—particularly for those brands made up of LCDs. Market research indicates that the average North American price of an LCD TV in the most popular 30- to 34-inch size averaged US$780 in the first quarter ending in March 2007, down 45.7 percent from US$1437 a year earlier.

Industry observers predicted that in 2007, LCD TV prices would fall by 30 percent or more, compared with a decline of 15 to 20 percent for plasma TVs, due to ample LCD panel supplies. They forecast that the plasma TV market would start shrinking in 2009 after hitting $24 billion in 2008, while they saw LCD TV demand reaching $75 billion in 2008 and $93 billion in 2010.

continued

Large corporations such as Sony and Taiwan's Chunghwa Picture Tubes have already made decisions to halt production of plasma TVs in order to increase their focus on LCD flat screens. About 80 percent of global flat screen research and development spending is being allocated to LCD panels, with the remaining 20 percent to plasma and some other technologies.

In 2009, new technology embodied in LCD TVs began to close the gap between the picture quality produced by LCD TVs and that produced by plasma sets. Major manufacturers started replacing LCD backlighting from cold cathode fluorescent lamps (CCFL) with light-emitting diodes (LEDs). With LED backlighting, LCD TVs can now independently turn off clusters of lights to create deeper black levels and produce a picture quality equal to, if not surpassing, plasma high-definition TVs (HDTVs).

In October 2013 Panasonic announced that it was exiting the plasma TV market, with new production halting in December 2013 and all related operations to cease by March 2014. In 2014 both Samsung and LG announced their plans to halt production of plasma TVs by the end of that year.

At the end of January 2017 Best Buy was selling brand name 43" LCD (LED) HD TV's for as low as $319.99 in Canada.

**For critical analysis:** With the aid of a diagram explain what has been happening to the market supply curve for LCD flat screen TVs and why. In a separate diagram, sketch the predicted effects on the supply curve for plasma TVs in 2009 and after.

Sources: Tom Katsiroubas. "LCD pic catches up with plasmas; with LED backlighting, black levels and colours on LCD sets are now comparable to plasmas." Toronto Star. November 26, 2009. Pg. L9.; Kiyoshi Takenaka. "Shift to big-screen TVs favours LCD over plasma: Quality rising as price gap narrows." Calgary Herald. Final edition. December 4, 2006. Pg. B7; "TV sales enhance Best Buy picture; same-store sales up 14% in Canada." Calgary Herald. Final edition. April 5, 2007. Pg. D10; Panasonic concedes plasma TV defeat, ends production. The Verge. http://www.theverge.com/2013/10/31/5050038/panasonic-plasma-tv-production-end. (Accessed January 19, 2014). "LG officially announces shutdown of plasma display business".Brad Bourque. Home Theatre. Digital Trends. October 29, 2014. http://www.digitaltrends.com/home-theater/lg-getting-out-plasma-game/ (Accessed January 30, 2017); "On Sale". TV and Home Theatre. Best Buy. Sale Ends Feb 2, 2017. http://www.bestbuy.ca/Search/(Accessed on January 30, 2017).

## Changes in Supply versus Changes in Quantity Supplied

We cannot overstress the importance of distinguishing between a movement along the supply curve—which occurs only when the product's price changes—and a shift in the supply curve—which occurs only with changes in other nonprice factors. A change in price always brings about a change in quantity supplied along a given supply curve. We move from one point to another along the same supply curve. This is specifically called a *change in quantity supplied.*

When you think of *supply,* think of the entire curve. Quantity supplied is represented by a single point on the curve.

> **A change in supply causes the entire curve to shift. The *only* thing that can cause the entire curve to shift is a change in a determinant *other than price.***
>
> Consequently,
>
> **A change in the price leads to a change in the quantity supplied, other things being constant. This is a *movement along* the curve.**
>
> **A change in any other determinant of supply leads to a change in supply. This causes a *shift of* the curve.**

# 3.5 Putting Demand and Supply Together

In the sections on supply and demand, we tried to confine each discussion to supply or demand only. But you have probably already realized that we cannot view the world just from the supply side or just from the demand side. There is an interaction between the two. In this section, we will discuss how they interact and how that interaction determines the prices that prevail in our economy. Understanding how demand and supply interact is essential to understanding how prices are determined in our economy and other economies in which the forces of supply and demand are allowed to work.

Let us first combine the demand and supply schedules and then combine the curves.

## Demand and Supply Schedules Combined

Let us place part (a) from Figure 3–3 (the market demand schedule) and part (a) from Figure 3–8 (the market supply schedule) together in part (a) of Figure 3–10. Column 1 shows the price; column 2, the quantity supplied per year at any given price; and column 3, the quantity demanded. Column 4 is merely the difference between columns 2 and 3, or the difference between the quantity supplied and the quantity demanded. In column 5, we label those differences as either excess quantity supplied (a **surplus**), or excess quantity demanded (a **shortage**). For example, at a price of $2, only 40 million DVDs would be supplied, but the quantity demanded would be 80 million. The difference is 40 million, which we label as excess quantity demanded (a shortage). At the other end of the scale, a price of $5 per DVD would elicit 100 million in quantity supplied, but quantity demanded would drop to 20 million. This leaves a difference of 80 million units, which we call excess quantity supplied (a surplus).

**Surplus** A situation in which quantity supplied is greater than quantity demanded at a price above the market clearing price.

**Shortage** A situation in which the quantity demanded exceeds the quantity supplied at a price below the market clearing price.

What do you notice about the price of $3? At that price, the quantity supplied and the quantity demanded per year are both 60 million. The difference, then, is zero. There is

Part (a)

| (1) Price per Constant-Quality DVD | (2) Quantity Supplied (DVDs per year) | (3) Quantity Demanded (DVDs per year) | (4) Difference (2) – (3) (DVDs per year) | (5) Condition |
|---|---|---|---|---|
| $5 | 100 million | 20 million | 80 million | Excess quantity supplied (surplus) |
| 4 | 80 million | 40 million | 40 million | Excess quantity supplied (surplus) |
| 3 | 60 million | 60 million | 0 | Market clearing price—equilibrium (no surplus, no shortage) |
| 2 | 40 million | 80 million | –40 million | Excess quantity demanded (shortage) |
| 1 | 20 million | 100 million | –80 million | Excess quantity demanded (shortage) |

Part (b)

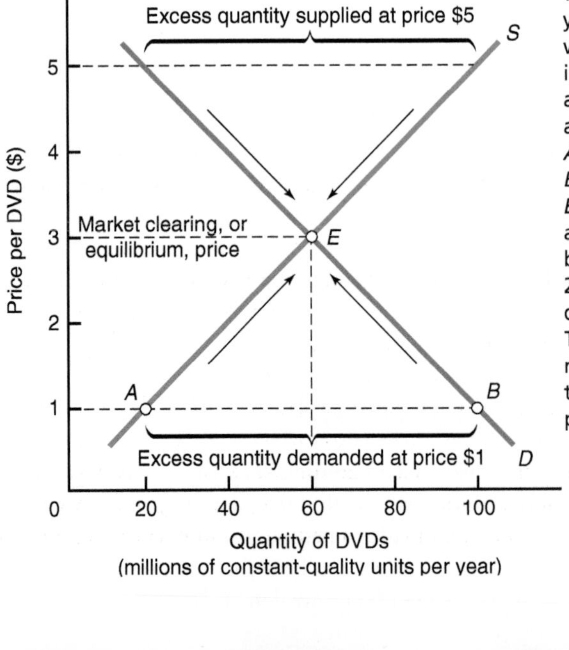


**FIGURE 3–10**

**Putting Demand and Supply Together**

In part (a), we see that at the price of $3, the quantity supplied and the quantity demanded are equal, resulting in neither an excess in the quantity demanded nor an excess in the quantity supplied. We call this price the equilibrium, or market clearing, price. In part (b), the intersection of the supply and demand curves is at *E*, at a price of $3 per constant-quality DVD and a quantity of 60 million per year. At point *E*, there is neither an excess in the quantity demanded nor an excess in the quantity supplied. At a price of $1, the quantity supplied will be only 20 million DVDs per year, but the quantity demanded will be 100 million. The difference is excess quantity demanded at a price of $1. The price will rise, and so we will move from point *A* up the supply curve and point *B* up the demand curve to point *E*. At the other extreme, $5 elicits a quantity supplied of 100 million but a quantity demanded of only 20 million. The difference is excess quantity supplied at a price of $5. The price will fall, and so we will move down the demand curve and the supply curve to the equilibrium price, $3 per DVD.

neither excess quantity demanded (shortage) nor excess quantity supplied (surplus). Hence the price of $3 is very special. It is called the **market clearing price** or **equilibrium price**—the price at which market quantity demanded equals market quantity supplied. The market clearing price of $3 clears the market of all excess supply or excess demand. We refer to this price as the equilibrium price, in the sense that this is the price at which there is no tendency for change. At this price, consumers are able to buy all that they wish to purchase and suppliers are able to sell all that they wish to supply.

**Market clearing price** or **equilibrium price** The price at which market quantity demanded equals market quantity supplied.

We can define **equilibrium** in general as a point from which there tends to be no movement unless demand or supply changes. Any movement away from this point will set in motion certain forces that will cause movement back to it. Therefore, equilibrium is a stable point. Any point that is not at equilibrium is unstable and cannot be maintained.

**Equilibrium** A point from which there tends to be no movement unless demand or supply changes.

## Demand and Supply Curves Combined

The equilibrium point occurs where supply and demand intersect. Part (b) from Figure 3–3 and part (b) from Figure 3–8 are combined as part (b) in Figure 3–10. The only difference now is that the horizontal axis measures both the quantity supplied and the quantity demanded per year. Everything else is the same. The demand curve is labelled *D*, the supply curve *S*. We have labelled the intersection of the two curves as point *E*, for equilibrium. That corresponds to a market clearing price of $3, at which both the quantity supplied and the quantity demanded are 60 million units per year. There is neither a surplus nor a shortage. Point *E*, the equilibrium point, always occurs at the intersection of the supply and demand curves. This is the price toward which the market price will automatically tend to gravitate.

## Shortages

The demand and supply curves in Figure 3–10 represent a situation of equilibrium. But a non–market-clearing, or disequilibrium, price will bring into play forces that cause the price to change and move toward the market clearing price. Then, equilibrium is again sustained. Look once more at part (b) in Figure 3–10. Suppose that instead of being at the market clearing price of $3 per DVD, for some reason the market price is $1 per DVD. At this price, the quantity demanded (100 million), exceeds the quantity supplied (20 million). We have a situation of excess quantity demanded at the price of $1. This is usually called a shortage. Consumers of DVDs would find that they could not buy all that they wished at $1 apiece. But forces will cause the price to rise: Competing consumers will bid up the price, and suppliers will raise the price and increase output, whether explicitly or implicitly. (Remember, some buyers would pay $5 or more, rather than do without DVDs. They do not want to be left out.) We would move from points *A* and *B* toward point *E*. The process would stop when the price again reached $3 per DVD.

## Surpluses

Now, let us repeat the experiment with the market price at $5 per DVD, rather than at the market clearing price of $3. Clearly, the quantity supplied will exceed the quantity demanded at that price. The result will be an excess quantity supplied at $5 per unit. This is often called a surplus, a situation in which quantity supplied is greater than quantity demanded at a price above the market clearing price. Given the curves in part (b) in Figure 3–10, however, there will be forces pushing the price back down toward $3 per DVD. Competing suppliers will attempt to reduce their inventories by cutting prices and reducing output, and consumers will offer to purchase more at lower prices. Suppliers will want to reduce inventories, which will be above their optimal level; that is, there will be an excess over what each seller believes to be the most profitable stock of DVDs. After all, inventories are costly to hold. But consumers may find out about such excess inventories and see the possibility of obtaining increased quantities of DVDs at a decreased price. It benefits consumers to attempt to obtain a good at a lower price, and they will therefore try to do so. If the two forces of supply and demand are unrestricted, they will bring the price back to $3 per DVD.

# 3.6 Changes in Equilibrium

## Shifts in Demand or Supply

When a nonprice determinant of demand or supply changes, this will result in a shift in the demand or the supply curve for the product under study. In turn, this will cause the product's equilibrium price and equilibrium quantity to change. In certain situations, it is possible to predict in which direction the equilibrium price and equilibrium quantity will change. Specifically, whenever one curve is stable while the other curve shifts, we can tell what will happen to price and quantity. Consider the four possibilities in Figure 3–11. Each possibility starts with the equilibrium price of DVDs equal to \$3 ($P_1$) and the equilibrium quantity equal to 60 million DVDs ($Q_1$).

**INCREASE IN DEMAND.** In Figure 3–11 part (a), the supply curve remains stable but *demand increases* from $D_1$ to $D_2$. Note that the result is both *an increase in the equilibrium price* of DVDs from $P_1$ to $P_2$ and an *increase in equilibrium quantity* from $Q_1$ to $Q_2$ ($Pe\uparrow$ $Qe\uparrow$).

Nonprice determinants that can cause an increase in demand include an increase in income with DVDs being a normal good; an increase in the price of a substitute good for DVDs; a decrease in the price of a complement good for DVDs; an increase in population or number of buyers; a change in tastes that favours DVDs; and expectations that DVD prices will increase in the future.

Example 3–6 shows how increased incomes in large nations such as China and taste factors such as the perceived health benefits of eating dark chocolate have caused an increase in demand for chocolate. According to Figure 3–11(a), this increase in demand helps to explain why chocolate prices increased in 2007.

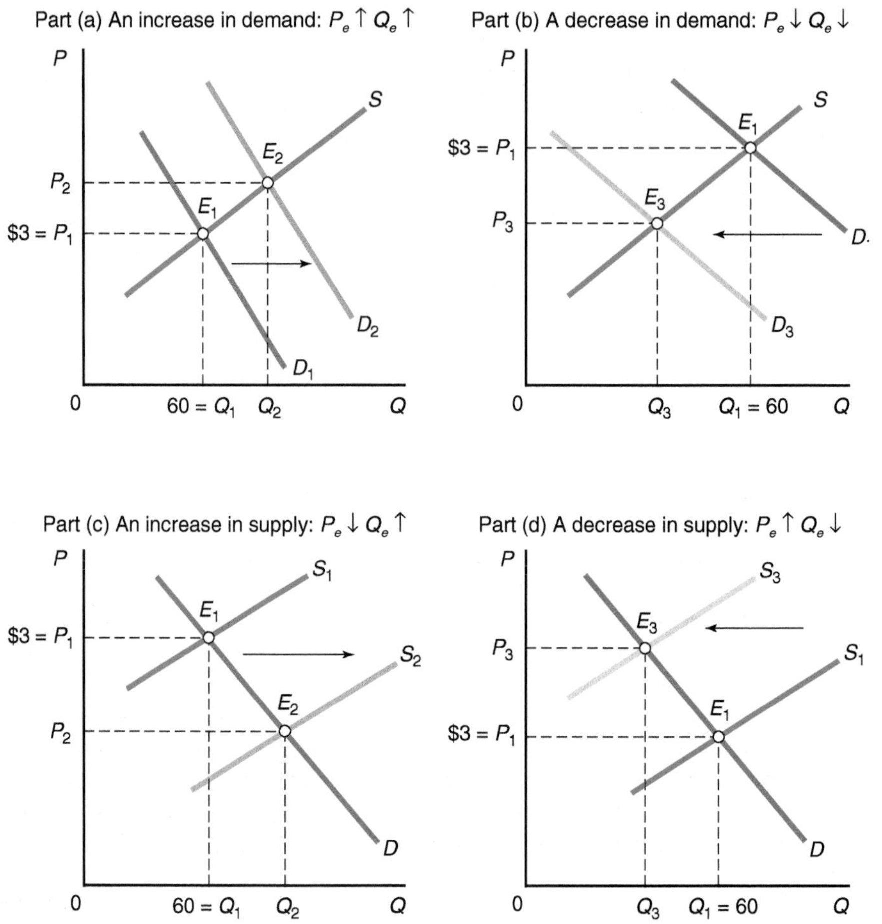


**FIGURE 3–11**

**Shifts in Demand or Supply**

In part (a), the supply curve is stable at $S$. The demand curve shifts outward, or increases, from $D_1$ to $D_2$. The equilibrium price $P_e$ increases from $P_1$ to $P_2$ and the equilibrium quantity $Q_e$ increases from $Q_1$ to $Q_2$. In part (b), with the supply curve stable, the demand curve shifts to the left or decreases. In this case, the equilibrium price decreases from $P_1$ to $P_3$, while the equilibrium quantity decreases from $Q_1$ to $Q_3$. In part (c), the demand curve is stable at $D$. Now the supply curve shifts to the right or increases. This results in a decrease in the equilibrium price from $P_1$ to $P_2$ but an increase in equilibrium quantity from $Q_1$ to $Q_2$. In part (d), with the demand curve stable at $D$, there is a leftward shift, or a decrease in the supply. While this causes the equilibrium price to increase from $P_1$ to $P_3$, the equilibrium quantity decreases from $Q_1$ to $Q_3$.

**DECREASE IN DEMAND.** In Figure 3–11 part (b), the supply curve remains stable but *demand decreases* from $D_1$ to $D_3$. Note that the result is both a *decrease in the equilibrium price* of DVDs from $P_1$ to $P_3$ and a *decrease in equilibrium quantity* from $Q_1$ to $Q_3$ ($P_e \downarrow Q_e \downarrow$).

**INCREASE IN SUPPLY.** In Figure 3–11 part (c), the demand curve remains stable but supply increases from $S_1$ to $S_2$. Note that the result is a decrease in the equilibrium price of DVDs from $P_1$ to $P_2$ and an increase in equilibrium quantity from $Q_1$ to $Q_2$ ($P_e \downarrow Q_e \uparrow$).

Nonprice determinants that can cause an increase in supply include a decline in the costs of inputs used to manufacture DVDs; a technological change increasing the productivity of manufacturing DVDs; a reduction in taxes imposed on DVD manufacturers; an increase in the subsidies enjoyed by DVD manufacturers; and an increase in the number of firms manufacturing DVDs.

Example 3–5 on pages 74–75 shows how the increase in supply of LCD flat screen TVs has increased significantly due to the decline in a key cost of input—LCD panels. Figure 3–11 part (c) explains how this increase in supply has led to a decline in the price of LCD flat screen TVs relative to comparable plasma TVs. Even though in 2007 the prices of LCD TVs were still typically higher than for the same size plasma TVs, the price gap had significantly narrowed.

**DECREASE IN SUPPLY.** In Figure 3–11 part (d), the demand curve remains stable but supply decreases from $S_1$ to $S_3$. Note that the result is both an increase in the equilibrium price of DVDs from $P_1$ to $P_3$ and a decrease in equilibrium quantity from $Q_1$ to $Q_3$ ($P_e \uparrow Q_e \downarrow$).

In addition to the demand factors noted above, supply shifts also help to explain the rising chocolate bar prices described in Example 3–6 "Chocoholics Beware." Government policies aimed at increasing the supply of the alternative, environment-friendly fuel source ethanol are driving up the prices of corn, sugar, cattle feed, and therefore milk. This rise is causing the costs of key inputs in the production of chocolate to increase. Figure 3–11 part (d) explains how this translates into higher chocolate prices by shifting the supply curve of chocolate to the left.

The principles of supply and demand presented above are powerful tools that will allow you to predict the future effects that current events will have on markets that affect you, as Example 3–6 illustrates. Presumably, you will be able to react to these predictions in a manner that promotes your self-interest.

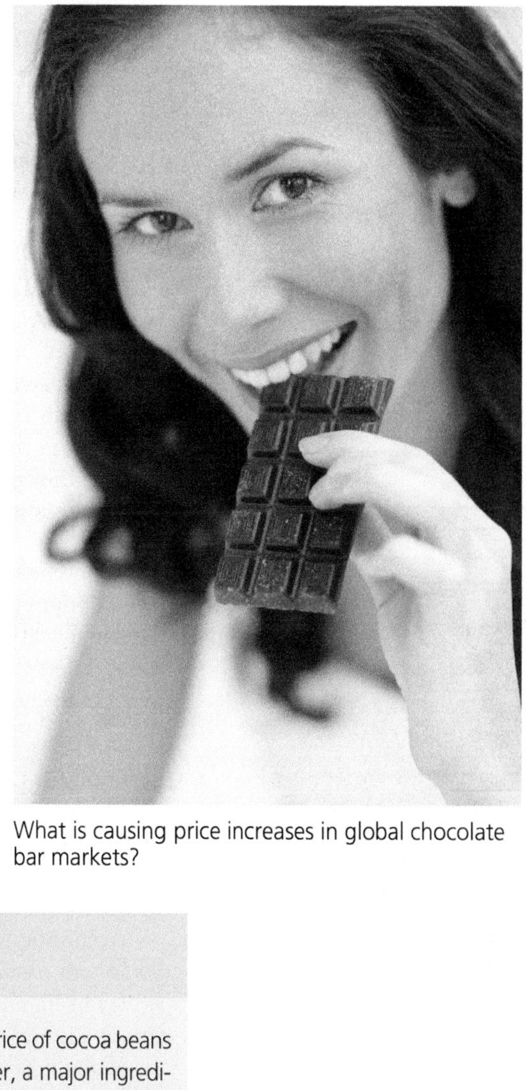

What is causing price increases in global chocolate bar markets?

EXAMPLE 3–6 **Chocoholics Beware**

During the ten year period between November 2005 and November 2015, the price of cocoa beans increased by a whopping 135%. Cocoa beans are used to produce cocoa butter, a major ingredient in the manufacture of chocolate bars. The West African region, including the Ivory Coast and Ghana, hosts the largest producers of cocoa beans. This region has been experiencing the following factors that have affected the production of cocoa butter: persistence of very dry weather conditions; social tensions; and a reduction in government fertilizer and pest control subsidies.

In addition Indonesia, the third largest global producer of cocoa, implemented an export tax on cocoa. This tax encourages more domestic processing of cocoa beans but reduces the amount of cocoa supplied to international chocolate manufacturers.

Higher incomes in developing countries like China and India, as well as the perceived cancer-fighting antioxidant health benefits of dark chocolate, are enhancing the long-term demand for chocolate bars. Chinese chocolate consumption has been increasing by a yearly average of 40 percent between 2009 and 2013, while Indian chocolate consumption is expected to grow at an annual rate of 21 percent between 2013 to 2018.

*continued*

Since the global increase in demand for cocoa is expected to significantly exceed the global growth in supply in future years, it is expected that the cocoa butter in the typical mass produced 100g chocolate bar will be increasingly replaced by cheaper substitute ingredients such as palm oil, nuts, and raisins. It may well be that "real chocolate" will become a luxury item destined for the wealthiest consumers.

**For critical analysis:** Identify two factors noted in this Example that are shifting the demand curve for chocolate bars. Sketch a graph to show how the demand curve for chocolate bars is shifting and how this affects the equilibrium price of chocolate bars.

Identify two factors noted in this Example that are shifting the supply curve for chocolate bars. Sketch a graph to show how the supply curve for chocolate bars is shifting and how this affects the equilibrium price of chocolate bars.

Sources: Dana Flavelle. "Cocoa finds its sweet spot; as prices for the flavourful beans soar on global markets, it may be time to stock up on chocolate." *Toronto Star*. Ontario edition. April 6, 2007. Pg. F1; "Cocoa supplies likely to be down on last year, report." Confectionary News. April 22, 2010. http://www.confectionerynews.com/The-Big-Picture/Cocoa-supplies-likely-to-be-down-on-last-year-report; Choc horror! Cocoa shortage, rising prices threaten chocolate bars. Alice Tidy Special to CNBC.com. Oct. 18, 2013.Business. NBC News. http://www.nbcnews.com/business/warning-cocoa-shortage-rising-prices-threaten-chocolate-bars-8C11418435 (Accessed January 26, 2014). "ICCO Monthly Averages of Daily Prices". Statistics. International Cocoa Organization. https://www.icco.org/statistics/cocoa-prices/ (Accessed January 30, 2017).

## When Both Demand and Supply Shift

Each example given in Figure 3–11 shows a predictable outcome for equilibrium price and quantity based on a shift in either the demand curve holding the supply curve constant or the supply curve holding the demand curve constant. Often, we want to predict the changes in equilibrium price and quantity in market situations where *multiple nonprice determinants* are changing at the same time, resulting in shifts in *both* demand and supply. As you will see below, unless you know the full extent of each individual shift in demand and supply, the overall outcome will be *indeterminate* for *either* equilibrium price *or* equilibrium quantity.

**INCREASE IN DEMAND AND INCREASE IN SUPPLY.** Suppose the price of CDs, a substitute for DVDs, significantly increases, causing an *increase in demand* for DVDs. At the same time, new technology reduces the cost of manufacturing DVDs, resulting in an *increase in supply* of DVDs. To predict the overall effect on the equilibrium price and quantity of DVDs, we suggest that you begin by analyzing the effect of *each individual shift* on equilibrium price and quantity using the appropriate part in Figure 3–11.

According to part (a) in Figure 3–11, an *increase in demand* for DVDs will cause the *equilibrium price to increase* and the *equilibrium quantity to increase* ($Pe\uparrow Qe\downarrow$). Similarly, part (c) in Figure 3.11 suggests that *an increase in supply* will cause *the equilibrium price to decrease* and the *equilibrium quantity to increase* ($P_e\downarrow Qe\uparrow$).

If you now combine the effects of both shifts, you can conclude that the *equilibrium quantity will certainly increase*, but the overall effect on equilibrium price is *indeterminate,* meaning that it could go up or down or stay the same, depending on the extent of the shift in both curves. Figure 3–12 describes a situation where the supply shifts by a larger amount than the demand shifts, resulting in an overall decrease in the equilibrium price of DVDs.

Consider another similar example. Cellphone prices have been declining despite the fact that the demand for cellphones has been significantly increasing worldwide. Now that you have been exposed to the tools of demand and supply, you are in a better position to understand these trends in the cellular phone industry.

The smaller computer chips that have been invented have reduced the size and increased the portability of cellphones, resulting in an increase in demand for these phones. As well, the concern for personal safety has increased the demand for cellphones. At the same time, new technology has significantly reduced the cost of the computer chips used in the manufacture of cellphones, and this has increased the supply of cellphones. Since you know that the price of cellphones has been declining, you can conclude that the increase in supply has

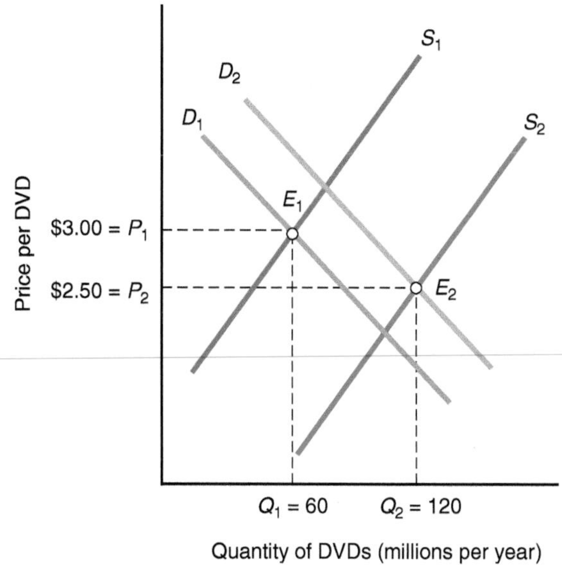


**FIGURE 3–12**

**An Increase in Demand and Supply**

The original equilibrium price is \$3.00 per DVD, and the original equilibrium quantity is 60 million DVDs, which is determined by the intersection of $D_1$ and $S_1$. With an increase in demand and supply, the new demand curve is $D_2$, and the new supply curve is $S_2$. The new equilibrium price and quantity, located at the intersection of $D_2$ and $S_2$, is \$2.50 and 120 million DVDs, respectively. The overall result is that the equilibrium price decreases and the equilibrium quantity increases significantly.

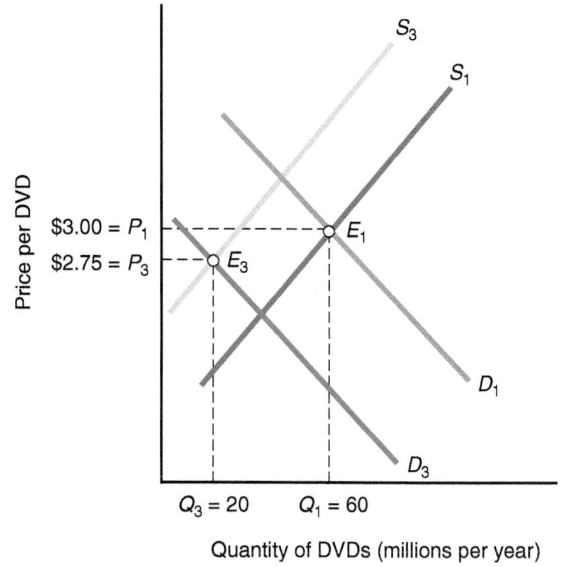


**FIGURE 3–13**

**A Decrease in Demand and Supply**

The original equilibrium price is \$3.00 per DVD, and the original equilibrium quantity is 60 million DVDs, which is determined by the intersection of $D_1$ and $S_1$. With a decrease in demand and supply, the new demand curve is $D_3$, and the new supply curve is $S_3$. The new equilibrium price and quantity, located at the intersection of $D_3$ and $S_3$, is \$2.75 and 20 million DVDs, respectively. The overall result is that the equilibrium price decreases and the equilibrium quantity decreases significantly.

exceeded the increase in demand in the cellphone industry. The graph describing the relative shifts in demand and supply for cellphones will look similar to Figure 3–12.

**DECREASE IN DEMAND AND DECREASE IN SUPPLY.** Suppose the average household income declines, causing a *decrease in demand* for DVDs. At the same time, the number of firms manufacturing DVDs declines, resulting in *a decrease in supply* of DVDs. On the basis of parts (b) and (d) of Figure 3–11, you can conclude that the *equilibrium quantity will certainly decrease,* but the overall *effect on equilibrium price is indeterminate.* If after further investigation, you determine that the decrease in demand (pulling the price down) far exceeds the decrease in supply (pushing the price up), you can predict that the equilibrium price will decline, as illustrated in Figure 3–13.

**INCREASE IN DEMAND AND DECREASE IN SUPPLY.** Suppose consumers, expecting the prices of DVDs to skyrocket in the future, increase their demand for DVDs in the current period. At the same time, the government imposes a new tax on DVD manufacturers, causing a *decrease in supply* of DVDs. On the basis of parts (a) and (d) of Figure 3–11, you can conclude that the *equilibrium price will certainly increase*, but the overall *effect on equilibrium quantity is indeterminate.*

**DECREASE IN DEMAND AND INCREASE IN SUPPLY.** Suppose the price of DVD players, a complement of DVDs, significantly increases, causing a decrease in demand for DVDs. At the same time, the government provides subsidies to Canadian DVD manufacturers, resulting in an increase in supply of DVDs. On the basis of parts (b) and (c) of Figure 3–11, you can conclude that the *equilibrium price will certainly decrease*, but the overall *effect on equilibrium quantity is indeterminate.*

As Example 3–7 explains, industry supply and demand trends can have a significant impact on the fortunes or misfortunes of Canadian provincial governments.

## EXAMPLE 3–7 Shale Natural Gas: A Game Changer for Alberta?

Canada, and particularly Alberta, has traditionally been a major producer (supplier) of natural gas in the continental North American market. Between Oct 2005 and October 2016, natural gas prices dropped significantly from $11.38 per gigajoule to $2.41 per gigajoule, an 80% decrease.

This decrease in natural gas prices was attributed to a number of factors. The global recession of 2008–2009 significantly reduced the level of global production, which has a negative impact on the demand for natural gas. As well, subsequent North American winters have been relatively mild (compared to previous winters), further reducing the need for natural gas for heating.

Recently, new shale technology has enhanced the efficiency of extracting natural gas from shale, a type of rock with low permeability. This new technology has been responsible for dramatic increases in U.S. natural gas production, which is considerably more cost efficient than the conventional processes used for extracting natural gas in Alberta. Thus, while North American supplies of natural gas have increased substantially, Canadian production has significantly declined.

The steep drop in natural gas prices, production, and drilling activity has significantly reduced the royalty revenue that the Alberta government collects from the natural gas industry. In the Alberta 2005–06 budget year, natural gas royalties accounted for over 70% of total non-renewable resource revenue, which, in turn accounted for 28% of total Alberta government revenue. In Budget 2016, the Alberta government projects that that natural gas royalties will account for only 11 percent of the province's non-renewable resource revenues, which, in turn, will account for a mere 3% of total Alberta government revenue. As a result, the once envied Alberta government annual budget surpluses, have given way to large budget deficits in recent years.

These budget deficits will make it more difficult to maintain valued government services in the future.

Sources: "Alberta Gas Reference Price History". Our Business. Alberta Energy. http://www.energy.alberta.ca/NaturalGas/1322.asp (Accessed January 30, 2017); "Revenue". 2005 -2008 Fiscal Plan. Budget 2005: Investing in the Next Alberta. (Accessed January 30, 2017); "Revenue". Budget. Alberta Government. https://www.alberta.ca/budget-revenue.aspx (Accessed January 30, 2017).

**For critical analysis:** Identify three factors noted in this example that contributed to the decrease in natural gas prices between 2005 and 2016. Sketch a graph of the North American natural gas market and show how demand and supply changed in that period.

ISSUES AND APPLICATIONS

# A Canadian Housing Bubble?

## Concepts Applied: Changes in Demand and Supply, Changes in Equilibrium Price, Opportunity Cost, Rational Decision Making, Consumption vs. Investment

Record-low interest rates increased the demand for home ownership since the 2008–2009 great recession.

Near the end of 2016, as Canadian household debt as a percent of Canadian income rose to a record high of of 167.6 percent, Canadian unemployment continued to hover at an above average rate. Despite this negative economic situation, Canadian home prices continued to increase at double digit rates, as indicated in Table 1 below.

**TABLE 1**

**Average Canadian Home Prices**

| Region | 2015 Price in Dollars | 2016 Price in Dollars | 2016 Annual % Change |
|---|---|---|---|
| Canada | 443,045 | 489,500 | 10.5 |
| British Columbia | 636,627 | 688,300 | 8.1 |
| Alberta | 393,138 | 393,700 | 0.1 |
| Saskatchewan | 297,487 | 295,600 | –0.6 |
| Manitoba | 270,375 | 276,900 | 2.4 |
| Ontario | 465,554 | 535,700 | 15.1 |
| Quebec | 275,302 | 282,100 | 2.5 |
| New Brunswick | 160,400 | 163,500 | 1.9 |
| Nova Scotia | 219,440 | 219,800 | .2 |
| PED | 161,175 | 179,800 | 11.6 |
| Newfoundland | 275,579 | 257,000 | –6.7 |

Source:" Quarterly Forecasts". Housing Market Stats. Canadian Real Estate Association. http://www.crea.ca/housing-market-stats/quarterly-forecasts/ (Accessed January 30, 2017).

Given that the one year increase in Canadian home prices (10.5 percent) significantly exceeded the annual rate of Canadian inflation (only 1.5 percent), a key question on the minds of Canadian households, investors, economists, and politicians has been, "Is Canada experiencing a housing bubble similar to the one experienced in the United States that preceded, and possibly caused, the great recession of 2008–2009?" In other words, are Canadian home prices going to sharply decline in the near future, causing a full blown Canadian recession? In order to address this question, we must first review some basic terms and concepts that relate to a homeowner's decision to purchase a home.

## Financing a Home Purchase

Given that a Canadian home can cost hundreds of thousands of dollars, most homeowners finance this large purchase by making an initial down payment and incurring a mortgage loan.

DOWN PAYMENT To purchase a home, the household must be able to put down a minimum cash down payment equal to 5 percent of the purchase price. Consider a detached home in Edmonton with a purchase price of $369,212. The minimum down payment required to buy this type of home would be .05 × $369,212 = $18,460.60. In cases where the down payment is less than 20 percent of the purchase price, the purchaser has to purchase mortgage insurance from the Canada Mortgage and Housing Corporation (CMHC), which typically increases the monthly mortgage payment.

MORTGAGE LOAN A home mortgage loan is a loan that one incurs to purchase the remainder owing on a property, where the loan is backed by the value of the home. Once the home is purchased with this type of loan, the purchaser has an obligation to make regular monthly payments over a period of time.

As an example, suppose that Cidnee Gerard, a resident of Edmonton. purchases a $369,212 home by putting down a 20 percent down payment equal to $73,842. She finances the remainder of the purchase price by incurring a mortgage loan with a principal amount equal to $369,212 - $73,842 = $295,370.

MONTHLY MORTGAGE PAYMENT The home purchaser must pay off the mortgage loan by making regular monthly or biweekly payments. A portion of each regular payment goes towards interest to the borrower and the remainder goes towards paying back the principal amount borrowed. Once the principal amount of the mortgage loan is paid off, the borrower owns the home outright and the regular payments come to an end.

The size of each regular payment depends on a number of factors, including the principal amount borrowed, the life or amortization period of the mortgage loan, the interest rate, and the interest rate term.

In our example, let us assume that Cidnee signed a mortgage loan with a principal amount of $295,370 with an amortization period of 25 years and a five-year fixed interest rate of 5.25 percent. The amortization period of 25 years means that Cidnee plans to pay off the entire principal amount in 25 years, at which time she will own the home outright and will cease making monthly payments. The five-year fixed interest rate of 5.25 percent means that the interest rate will stay fixed at 5.25 percent for the next five years, which will fix the monthly payments for the five-year period. In this example, the payments will be $1760.17 each month for the next five years. Note that you can easily calculate the monthly payment using a mortgage calculator at the one of the Canadian bank websites.

If Cidnee wanted to reduce her monthly payments on the same $295,370 loan, she could increase the amortization principal to, say, 35 years and she could choose a one-year fixed-rate mortgage at 3.14 percent. This means that she will take 35 years to pay off the mortgage loan, and her current monthly payment would be $1156.55. This monthly payment will only stay fixed for one year. After that, it could increase depending on the market rate of interest in the economy.

QUALIFYING FOR A MORTGAGE LOAN During the period 2008 to 2016, the Canadian government has implemented policies to tighten mortgage rules in order to try to avoid the bursting of a housing bubble. All borrowers must meet the standards for a five-year fixed-rate mortgage even if they choose a mortgage with a lower interest rate and shorter interest-rate term. The standards typically consist of two affordability rules imposed by the lending bank. The first affordability rule, called the Gross Debt Service (GDS) ratio, is that your monthly housing expenses—mortgage payment, property taxes, and heating costs—should not be more than 39 percent of your gross household monthly income. The second affordability rule, known as the Total Debt Service (TDS) ratio, is that your entire monthly debt expenses—including mortgage, car, and credit card payments—should not be more than 44 percent of your gross monthly income.

Other mortgage loan tightening changes include the following: increasing premiums (the amount a borrower must pay) for mortgage default insurance; reducing the maximum amortization period for insured mortgages from 40 years to 25 years; requiring banks to qualify all borrowers applying for an insured mortgage at the Bank of Canada's conventional five-year fixed posted mortgage rate, an interest rate that is typically higher than what they will actually be paying; requiring a down payment of at least five per cent of the home purchase price (a further 10 per cent must be added to the down payment for the portion of the house price between $500,000 and $999,999); limiting borrowing to a maximum of 80 per cent of the value of their homes when refinancing; and making government-backed mortgage insurance available only for homes with a purchase price of less than $1 million.

## Renting vs. Owning Your Home

MARGINAL COST OF HOME OWNERSHIP The decision to own rather than rent your home depends on both financial and non-financial considerations. Table 2 below compares the financial costs related to two alternatives facing Cidnee Gerard. In the first alternative, Cidnee rents a three-bedroom apartment in Edmonton and pays $1128 in rent per month. If Cidnee rents the apartment, she must put down a $1000 damage deposit, which she expects to get back when she leaves the apartment. Therefore the only sacrifice (opportunity cost) related to the damage deposit is the interest that the down payment could have earned if invested in a bank GIC earning 2.35 percent interest per year.

In the second alternative, Cidnee purchases a $369,212 home with a 20 percent down payment equal to $73,842 and a mortgage loan of $295,370 with the following terms: an amortization period of 25 years and a five-year fixed interest rate of 5.25 percent. The costs of owning the home include the down payment; the interest that the down payment could have earned if invested in a bank GIC earning 2.35 percent interest per year; property taxes; home insurance; closing and transaction costs, including inspection and appraisal fees and the legal costs of securing the home; and maintenance costs related to the upkeep of the home. When computing the costs over the three years between renting and owning a home, Cidnee assumes that the home price stays fixed at $369,212.

Note that monthly utility costs are not shown in Table 2 because these would be incurred in either alternative, so they have been cancelled out.

**TABLE 2**

### Costs of Renting vs. Owning a Home

| | Amount Per Year | Total Over Next 3 Years |
|---|---|---|
| *Cost of Renting* | | |
| Rent ($1128 per month) | $13 536 | $40 608 |
| Opportunity Cost of Damage Deposit: 2.35% × $1000 = $23.50 forgone interest each year | $23.50 | $70.50 |
| **Total Cost of Renting** | **$13 559.50** | **$40 678.50** |
| *Cost of Owning* | | |
| Mortgage Payment ($1760.17 per month) | $21 122.04 | $63 366.12 |
| Down Payment of $73 842 (incurred in the first year only) | $73 842 | $73 842 |
| Opportunity Cost of Down Payment: 2.35% × $73 842 = $1735.29 forgone interest each year | $1735.29 | $5205.86 |
| Property Taxes = $2500 per year | $2500 | $7500 |
| Home Insurance = $600 per year | $600 | $1800 |
| Transaction and Closing Costs (incurred in the first year only) | $3,500 | $3500 |
| Home Maintenance Expenses = $1500 per year | $1500 | $4500 |
| **Total Cost of Owning** | **$104,799.33** | **$159,713.98** |

Based on the financial considerations in Table 2, the marginal cost of owning a home (vs. renting) over a three year period equals $159,713.98 – $40,678.50 = $119,035.48. Depending on Cidnee's personal values, there may be additional sacrifices related to owning a home. If Cidnee rents a home, she can easily move to another location to quickly exploit a new opportunity. If Cidnee owns a home, she may not be able to sell the home at a desirable price in order to be able to move to another location quickly. As well, as a homeowner, Cidnee has the added responsibility of maintaining her home, which takes time and may be stressful.

MARGINAL BENEFIT OF HOME OWNERSHIP In making a rational decision to own rather than rent a home, one must compare the marginal benefit with the marginal cost of home ownership. In terms of financial considerations, one potential benefit of owning a home is the accumulation of personal equity (wealth). As you likely realize, if you rent a home, all your rent payments go to the landlord, and at the end of the day, you have nothing to show for incurring all those monthly rental expenses.

In Cidnee's example, if her home price stays the same over the next three years, she will accumulate equity equal to the $73,842 down payment she incurred in the first year as well as the portion of her monthly mortgage payments that paid off the principal amount borrowed, which equals $18,201.39. In total, she will accumulate $92,043.35, which would be part of the marginal benefit related to owning her home.

The marginal benefit of owning her home could be significantly higher if Cidnee's home increases in value over the three-year period under study. As an example, if Cidnee's original home value of $369,212 increases by 5 percent in each of the three years, the home will be valued at $427,409.04. This amounts to an additional capital (equity) gain of $58,197.04. In this situation, the marginal benefit associated with home ownership would be $92,043.35 + $58,197.04 = $150,240.39. The $150,240.39 marginal benefit exceeds the $$119,035.48 marginal cost, making the decision to become a homeowner a rational one.

It should be noted that the marginal benefit of owning a home (based on financial considerations) depends crucially on the future direction of home prices. If over the three-year period of study the value of Cidnee's home decreases, this will reduce the amount of personal equity accumulated and the marginal benefit of home ownership will be significantly less than its marginal cost.

Depending again on Cidnee's personal values, additional benefits related to owning a home may include privacy; pride of ownership; tenure of home ownership—nobody can ask her to leave once her home is paid for; freedom to have pets; and freedom to renovate and landscape to suit her own preferences.

## Factors Affecting Canadian Housing Prices

After reviewing home ownership fundamentals, we can now return to the question of whether the sharp increase in home prices witnessed in 2016 constitutes a Canadian housing bubble. If the factors that caused the increases in Canadian home prices are temporary, once they run their course, the bubble will burst and Canadian home prices would drastically decline, causing significant hardship to individual homeowners, as well as to the Canadian economy as a whole. In this section, we will examine key factors that typically affect Canadian home prices.

CANADIAN INTEREST RATES In order to stimulate the Canadian economy since the 2008–2009 recession, the Bank of Canada, a policy arm of the federal government, pursued policies that resulted in record low Canadian interest rates. This significantly reduced home mortgage interest rates, lowering the costs (monthly payments) related to purchasing homes.

TIGHTER MORTGAGE LENDING RULES As noted above, between 2008 and 2016, the Canadian government has implemented a number of policies aimed at tightening mortgage lending rules. These policies are aimed at making sure that mortgage lenders can afford to pay back their loans.

HIGH UNEMPLOYMENT RATES Since 2008, the Canadian unemployment rate has significantly increased above historic levels. High unemployment rates tend to reduce many households' willingness and ability to purchase homes. When job security is low, consumers are reluctant to make long-term purchase commitments involving hundreds of thousands of dollars.

AFFORDABILITY During the period 2008 to 2016, the average price of a Canadian home has increased at a greater rate than average Canadian wages. Put another way, the increase in average consumer income is significantly below the increase in Canadian home prices. This trend reduces the affordability of Canadian homes.

RECORD NUMBER OF RETIREES A key demographic trend expected to impact home prices is Canada's aging population, whereby a much greater portion of the population will consist of seniors and retirees. This trend is expected to favour the purchase of condos and leasing of rental units over owner-occupied single detached homes.

HIGH DEBT TO ASSET RATIO One key factor that affects the ability of Canadian households to purchase big-ticket items, such as homes and cars, is the household debt-to-asset ratio. Household assets refer to the total wealth, or assets or equity, of a household, which includes physical assets such as homes and financial assets such as stocks, bonds, and bank accounts. Household debt includes the value of mortgage loans, personal lines of credit, and credit card debt.

Some Canadian economists have suggested that the debt-to-income ratio can be a misleading indicator of the mortgage lenders ability to repay his/her loan. This ratio ignores accumulated wealth (assets). Trevor Tombe, an assistant professor of economics at the University of Calgary, notes that household debt is about 17 per cent of total assets, and that Canadian households have about $3 in financial assets per $1 of debt.

HOUSING STARTS Housing starts refer to the number of new homes constructed over a specified period of time. This adds to the stock or supply of homes. The seasonally adjusted annualized rate (SAAR) of Canadian housing starts increased by a mere 1.2 percent in December 2016 to 197,915 units, adding to the stability of home prices.

SALES TO NEW HOME LISTING RATIO While housing starts relate to newly built homes, new home listings is a better measure of all homes available for sale-both new and used. In general, a sales to new home listing ratio between 40% and 60% is considered to be a balanced market. Ratios below and above this range indicate buyers' and sellers' markets respectively. In December 2016, the sales to new home listings ratio was 63.5%.

## Owner-Occupied Homes: Investment or Consumption Goods?

For most Canadian households, an owner-occupied home can be considered both an investment and a consumption good. This implies that a decision to own a home can be rational, even if it appears to be an inferior investment. A recent study examined the annual compound rate of return on residential real estate in 12 Canadian cities over a 25-year period. Toronto provided the best rate of return at 5.75 percent per year. This rate of return fell significantly below the annual increase in the Toronto Stock Exchange (TSE) over the same 25-year period, which was 8.64 percent.

Even in situations where home prices "bubble to a boil," households can derive a significant amount of personal satisfaction from home ownership. As was already noted, there are many benefits to home ownership beyond the financial ones. Owning your own home can also enhance the enjoyment you derive from shopping for home-related items such as home furnishings, tools, and pictures.

Sources: Quarterly Forecasts". Housing Market Stats. Canadian Real Estate Association. December 15, 2016. (Accessed January 26, 2017) http://www.crea.ca/housing-market-stats/quarterly-forecasts/(Accessed January 26, 2017); "Consumer Price Index by province".Summary Tables. Statistics Canada. January 20, 2017. http://www.statcan.gc.ca/tables-tableaux/sum-som/l01/cst01/cpis01a-eng.htm.(Accessed January 26, 2017); "Canadian key household debt ratio hits record high". Business. CBC News. September 15, 2016. http://www.cbc.ca/news/business/debt-income-ratio-record-1.3763343. (Accessed January 26, 2017); "Canada's household debt is now bigger than its GDP, for the first time". Economy. News. Financial Post. September 15, 2016. http://business.financialpost.com/news/economy/canadas-household-debt-is-now-bigger-than-its-gdp-for-the-first-time (Accessed on January 30, 2017); "Revenue". Budget. Alberta Government. https://www.alberta.ca/budget-revenue.aspx (Accessed January 31, 2017); "Issue Brief: Changes to Canada's Mortgage Market" Research and Advocacy. Canadian Bankers Association. (Accessed January 31, 2017).

**For critical analysis:**

1. Identify one key factor noted in this Issues and Applications that contributed to an increase in demand (housing bubble) for Canadian homes in 2016. Sketch a demand and supply graph for Canadian owner-occupied homes, and show how these factors have affected the Canadian housing market as well as the equilibrium price of Canadian homes.
2. Identify three factors noted in this Issues and Applications that have the potential to burst the Canadian housing bubble by decreasing the demand for Canadian owner-occupied homes. Sketch a demand and supply graph for Canadian owner-occupied homes, and show how these factors have affected the Canadian housing market as well as the equilibrium price of Canadian homes.
3. Briefly explain how one's decision to purchase a home can be a rational decision even if the home turns out to be a poor investment.

# SUMMARY

Here is what you should know after reading this chapter. MyEconLab will help you identify what you know, and where to go when you need to practise. We suggest that as soon as you review one of the Learning Objective sections below, you then proceed to go through the related section in MyEconLab.

| LEARNING OBJECTIVES | KEY TERMS | MYECONLAB PRACTICE |
|---|---|---|
| **3.1 The Law of Demand.** According to the law of demand, other things being equal, households will purchase fewer units of a good at a higher price and more units of a good at a lower price. This law is described by a downward-sloping demand curve. | demand, 62<br>law of demand, 62<br>relative price, 62<br>money price, 63<br>demand curve, 64<br>market, 64<br>market demand, 64 | • **MyEconLab** Study Plan 3.1 |
| **3.2 Shifts in Demand.** A change in the good's own price causes a change in quantity demanded, which is a movement along the same demand curve. A change in demand is described as a shift in the entire demand curve caused by a change in a nonprice determinant, such as income, tastes, prices of related goods, expectations, and number of buyers. An increase in demand means that the demand curve shifts rightward, while a decrease in demand implies a leftward shift. | normal goods, 67<br>inferior goods, 67<br>substitutes, 68<br>complements, 68 | • **MyEconLab** Study Plan 3.2 |
| **3.3 The Law of Supply.** According to the law of supply, firms will produce and offer for sale more units of a good at a higher price and fewer units of a good at a lower price. This law is described by an upward-sloping supply curve. | supply, 71<br>law of supply, 71<br>supply curve, 71 | • **MyEconLab** Study Plan 3.3 |
| **3.4 Shifts in Supply.** A change in the good's own price causes a change in quantity supplied, which is a movement along the same supply curve. A change in supply is described as a shift in the entire supply curve caused by a change in a nonprice determinant such as input prices, technology and productivity, taxes and subsidies, price expectations, and number of sellers. An increase in supply means that the supply curve shifts rightward, while a decrease in supply implies a leftward shift. | | • **MyEconLab** Study Plan 3.4 |

| LEARNING OBJECTIVES | KEY TERMS | MYECONLAB PRACTICE |
|---|---|---|
| **3.5 Putting Demand and Supply Together.** The equilibrium price and equilibrium quantity occur where market demand equals market supply. Graphically, equilibrium occurs where the market demand curve intersects the market supply curve. At this point, the plans of sellers and buyers match, meaning that shortages and surpluses are eliminated. surplus, 76 | shortage, 76<br>market clearing price or equilibrium price, 76<br>equilibrium, 77 | • **MyEconLab** Study Plan 3.5 |
| **3.6 Changes in Equilibrium.** An increase in demand will cause equilibrium price and quantity to increase, whereas a decrease in demand will cause equilibrium price and quantity to decrease. An increase in supply will cause equilibrium price to decrease and equilibrium quantity to increase, while a decrease in supply will cause equilibrium price to increase and equilibrium quantity to decrease. When both demand and supply change in the same direction, the equilibrium quantity will also change in the same direction, but the equilibrium price might increase, decrease, or remain the same. When both demand and supply change in opposite directions, the equilibrium price will change in the same direction as demand, but the equilibrium quantity might increase, decrease, or remain the same. | | • **MyEconLab** Study Plan 3.6 |

# PROBLEMS

(Answers to the odd-numbered problems appear at the back of the book.)

**LO 3.1, 3.2 Explain the law of demand; distinguish between a change in quantity demanded and a change in demand.**

1. Examine the following table, and then answer the questions.

| | Price per Unit Last Year | Price per Unit Today |
|---|---|---|
| Heating oil | \$1.00 | \$2.00 |
| Natural gas | \$0.80 | \$3.20 |

What has happened to the absolute price of heating oil? Of natural gas? What has happened to the price of heating oil relative to the price of natural gas? What has happened to the relative price of natural gas? Will consumers, through time, change their relative purchases? If so, how?

2. Give an example of a complement and a substitute in consumption for each of the following items:
   a. bacon
   b. coffee
   c. automobiles

3. Consider the market for Canadian beef. Explain whether each of the following events would cause an increase in demand, a decrease in demand, an increase in quantity demanded, or a decrease in quantity demanded. Also describe how each event will affect the demand curve for Canadian beef.
   a. The price of chicken decreases.
   b. Household income increases, and beef is a normal good.
   c. The price of Canadian beef decreases.
   d. A Canadian cow is found to have mad cow disease.
   e. The Canadian government raises the price of Canadian beef.

**LO 3.3, 3.4 Explain the law of supply; distinguish between a change in quantity supplied and a change in supply.**

4. Consider the market for newly constructed bungalow homes in Canada. Explain whether each of the following events would cause an increase in supply, a decrease in supply, an increase in quantity supplied, or a decrease in quantity supplied. Also describe how each event will affect the supply curve for new Canadian bungalow homes.
   a. The price of lumber skyrockets in Canada.
   b. The Canadian government lowers the price of new bungalow homes in Canada.
   c. New technology is developed that significantly reduces the cost of building new bungalows.
   d. The Canadian government provides subsidies to builders of new Canadian bungalows.
   e. The price of Canadian bungalows increases.

**LO 3.5, 3.6 Explain how the forces of demand and supply interact to determine equilibrium price and quantity; describe how changes in demand and supply can change equilibrium price and quantity.**

5. Suppose that, in a recent market period, an industry-wide survey determined the following relationship between the price of rock music CDs and the quantity supplied and demanded.

| Price | Quantity Demanded | Quantity Supplied |
|---|---|---|
| $ 9 | 100 million | 40 million |
| $10 | 90 million | 60 million |
| $11 | 80 million | 80 million |
| $12 | 70 million | 100 million |
| $13 | 60 million | 120 million |

   a. What is the equilibrium price and equilibrium quantity?
   b. If the industry price is $13, is there a shortage or a surplus of CDs? How much is the shortage or surplus? Will the price stay at $13? Explain.
   c. If the industry price is $10, is there a shortage or a surplus of CDs? How much is the shortage or surplus? Will the price stay at $10? Explain.

6. Refer to Example 3–6, "Chocoholics Beware," and use a demand and supply diagram (for chocolate bars) to describe the changes in supply that have occurred in the chocolate bar market. Show graphically how these changes in supply will affect the equilibrium price of chocolate bars.

7. Suppose that a survey for a later market period indicates that the quantities supplied in the table in Problem 5 are unchanged. The quantity demanded, however, has increased by 30 million at each price. Construct the resulting demand curve in the illustration you made for Problem 5. Is this an increase or a decrease in demand? What is the new equilibrium quantity and the new market price? Give two examples that might cause such a change.

8. Example 3–7, "Shale Natural Gas: A Game Changer for Alberta" noted that concern over the environment will likely have some positive effects for the producers of natural gas in the long run. Identify and briefly explain specific factors related to the environment that will affect the market for natural gas. Sketch a demand and supply diagram, and explain how these factors will affect the graph and the equilibrium price for natural gas.

9. In the market for rock music CDs, explain whether the following events would cause an increase or decrease in demand or an increase or decrease in the quantity demanded. Also explain what happens to the equilibrium quantity and the equilibrium price.
   a. The price of CD packaging material declines.
   b. The price of CD players declines.
   c. The price of cassette tapes increases dramatically.
   d. A booming economy increases the income of the typical CD buyer.
   e. Many rock fans suddenly develop a fondness for country music.

10. Consider the market for laptop computers. Explain whether the following events would cause an increase or decrease in supply or an increase or decrease in the quantity supplied. Illustrate each, and show what would happen to the equilibrium market price, given a typical downward-sloping demand curve.
    a. The price of memory chips used in laptop computers declines.
    b. The price of memory chips used in desktop personal computers declines.
    c. The number of manufacturers of laptop computers increases.
    d. The prices of computer peripherals, printers, fax-modems, and scanners decrease.

11. The following diagram describes the hypothetical monthly demand and supply conditions for eggs in a small provincial market.
    a. If the price in the egg market above were initially at $1.40 per dozen, there would be a (surplus or shortage) equal to ___ thousands of dozens of eggs per week. Will the price stay at $1.40?

b. If the price in the egg market above were initially at $0.80 per dozen, there would be a (surplus or shortage) equal to ___ thousands of dozens of eggs per week. Will the price stay at $0.80?

c.

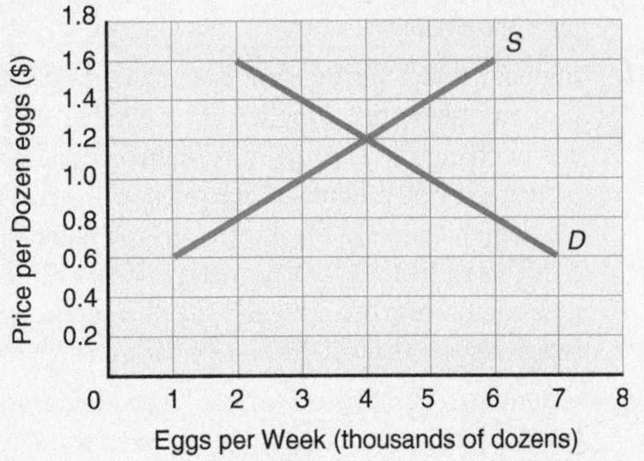


Determine the equilibrium price and equilibrium quantity in the egg market described above.

d. In the egg market described above, explain whether each of the following events would cause an increase or decrease in demand or supply. Also explain what happens to the equilibrium price and quantity.
   i. Studies show that daily use of eggs reduces the risk of getting serious diseases.
   ii. The cost of feeding chickens significantly increases.
   iii. Average consumer income increases, and eggs are an inferior good.
   iv. The government provides a subsidy to egg producers. A subsidy is a situation where the government pays the egg producers a set amount per dozen produced.

12. Airline routes are typically controlled by imposing a quota on the number of airline companies that may use the route and the number of flights on the route. Consequently, the government restricts the number of round-trip seats available on these flight routes. Suppose that the following table describes the daily demand and supply schedules for seats on round-trip flights between Toronto and Vancouver.

| Price per seat | Quantity Demanded (number of seats) | Quantity Supplied (number of seats) |
|---|---|---|
| ($)200 | 2000 | 1200 |
| 300 | 1800 | 1400 |
| 400 | 1600 | 1600 |
| 500 | 1400 | 1800 |
| 600 | 1200 | 2000 |

a. What is the equilibrium price and quantity for the Toronto-to-Vancouver airline seats? How much, in total dollars, do passengers spend on this route each day?

b. Suppose the government limits the daily number of round-trip seats to ensure that only 1200 seats can be made available on the Toronto-to-Vancouver route. What will be the new price per round-trip seat on this route? With the quota policy, do passengers end up spending more or less each day on this same route in total dollars? Can you think of how this quota policy might actually benefit the passengers (consumers) in the longer run?

13. The following diagram describes the hypothetical monthly demand and supply for one-bedroom apartments in a small college town.

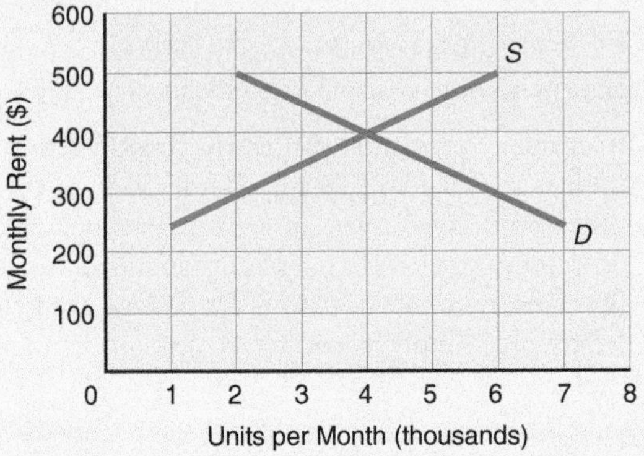


a. What is the equilibrium monthly rent (price) and equilibrium monthly quantity?

b. Suppose that the mayor of this town decides to make housing more affordable for the local college students by imposing a rent control that holds the price of a one-bedroom apartment to $300 per month.

   This rent control policy will result in a (shortage or surplus) of _____ units per month.

c. What will this rent control policy do to the market for two-bedroom apartments that are not regulated by the government? What will happen to the equilibrium price and quantity for the unregulated two-bedroom apartments?

14. In May 2000, the Canadian government imposed a tax on bicycles imported from Taiwan and China. Show how this tax affects the market for Taiwanese and Chinese bicycles, shifting the appropriate curve and indicating a new market equilibrium quantity and price. In a separate graph, show the effect of the tax on Canadian-made bicycles, shifting the appropriate curve and indicating the new market equilibrium and price.

15. The following diagram describes the market for Canadian red wine. Explain how each of the following sets of events will affect the equilibrium price and equilibrium quantity of Canadian red wine. Note that in some cases, your answer will be "indeterminate," meaning that with the given information, you cannot predict the direction of change.

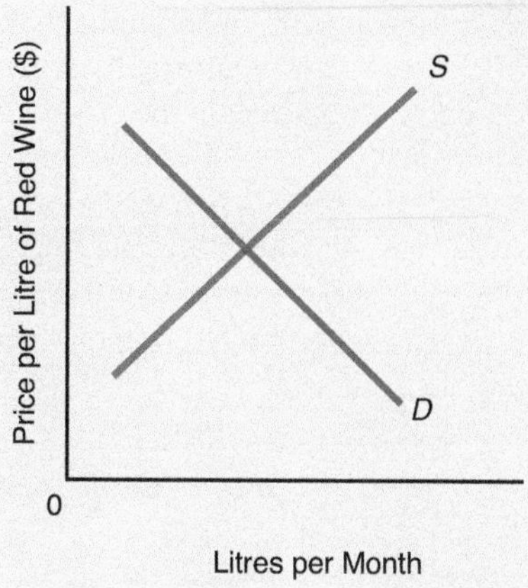


a. Studies indicate that Canadian red wine reduces the risk of heart disease. At the same time, the cost of the grapes used to produce red wine decreases.
b. Frost destroys a significant amount of the red grapes used to produce Canadian red wine. At the same time, the price of California red wine, a key substitute for Canadian red wine, increases.
c. New technology significantly lowers the cost of producing wine. At the same time, the price of Canadian white wine decreases.

# BUSINESS APPLICATION

**LO 3.2 Distinguish between a change in quantity demanded and a change in demand.**

## Marketing: Market Segmentation—The Aging Population

A typical first-year economics text tends to focus on a market at the product (or resource) level. However, in order to gain a better understanding of consumer demand, the marketing staff of a company will often segment (subdivide) a product market in order to identify a potentially profitable target market or market niche. In short, a market segment (target market) consists of a group of consumers who respond in a similar way to a given set of marketing efforts.

A very useful basis of market segmentation starting in the early 2000s was the age-related demographic trends in the Canadian population. Due to Canada's relatively low fertility rates and long life expectancy, Canada's population is aging.

The baby boom generation, born between 1946 and 1964, was aged between 46 and 64 in 2010 and is considered to be the consumer group with the most buying power. In 2010, the fastest growing age group (amongst the boomers) consisted of individuals aged 55 to 64, who are just starting to retire. As the baby boom generation begins to reach age 65 by 2011, we will experience a marked acceleration in the number and proportional population of seniors. Projections suggest that by 2021, there will be almost 7 million people over 65, who will make up 19 percent of the total population, and by 2041, seniors will represent approximately 25 percent of the population.

In the 1970s, for every person aged 55 to 64 years, there were 2.3 individuals in the 15- to 24-year-old age group. By 2010, this ratio had fallen to close to 1.0. Beginning in 2011, seniors will make up a greater percentage of the total population than dependent children.

Sources: "2006 Census: age and sex." *The Daily.* Statistics Canada. July 17, 2007. http://www.statcan.ca/Daily/English/070717/d070717a.htm; *Growing Up: The Social and Economic Implications of an Aging Population.* Certified General Accountants Association of Canada. January 26, 2005. pp. 17–20. http://www.cga-canada.org/en-ca/ResearchAndAdvocacy/AreasofInterest/AgingPopulation/Pages/ca_aging_report.aspx.

### Business Application Problem

Contrast the effects that the aging population will have on the demand for each of the following sets of items.

a. tennis vs. golf
b. Diet Coke vs. Pepsi
c. urban condominiums vs. suburban homes
d. minivans vs. recreational vehicles
e. red meat vs. chicken

PART 2 DIMENSIONS OF MICROECONOMICS

# 4

## LEARNING OBJECTIVES

After reading this chapter, you should be able to:

**4.1** Define price elasticity of demand and calculate it using two different methods.

**4.2** Define the three price elasticity ranges and explain their effects on total revenues.

**4.3** Discuss the three factors that determine the price elasticity of demand.

**4.4** Describe the effects of substitutes, complements, and income on elasticity of demand.

**4.5** Define price elasticity of supply and the four determinants of elasticity of supply.

# Elasticity

Cigarette smoking is unhealthy, which is one reason that governments tax cigarettes. Cigarette consumption is relatively insensitive to price changes, however, and so higher cigarette taxes only moderately reduce cigarette purchases. Beer consumption tends to be more responsive to price changes. Thus, if beer drinking and cigarette smoking are complementary activities, boosting taxes on beer might do more to reduce cigarette consumption. How can we measure the responsiveness of consumption to a change in price? How can we determine whether cigarettes and beer are complements? In this chapter, you will learn the answers to these questions.

myeconlab

EconLab helps you master each objective and study more efficiently. See end of chapter for details

# DID YOU KNOW THAT...?

A fall in the price of beer might lead to an increase in campus violence. The law of demand indicates that a decline in the price of beer increases consumption. Economists have found that a 10 percent reduction in the price of beer is associated with an increase in the incidence of campus violence of just over 3.5 percent.

College officials are not alone in having to worry about how individuals respond to lower prices. Businesses must constantly take into account consumer response to changing prices. If McDonald's lowers its prices by 10 percent, will fast-food consumers respond by buying so many more Big Macs that the company's revenues will rise? At the other end of the spectrum, can Rolls Royce dealers "get away with" a 2 percent increase in prices? In other words, will Rolls-Royce purchasers respond so little to the relatively small increase in price that the total revenues received for Rolls-Royce sales will not fall and may actually rise? The only way to answer these questions is to know how responsive people in the real world will be to changes in prices. Economists have a special name for price responsiveness—elasticity, which is the subject of this chapter.

## 4.1 Price Elasticity

To begin to understand what elasticity is all about, just keep in mind that it means "responsiveness" or "sensitivity." Here, we are concerned with the price elasticity of demand and the price elasticity of supply. We wish to know the extent to which a change in the price of, say, petroleum products will cause the quantity demanded and the quantity supplied to change, other things held constant. Let us restrict our discussion at first to the demand side.

### Price Elasticity of Demand

**Price elasticity of demand ($E_p$)** is the relative amount by which the quantity demanded will change in response to a change in the price of a particular good.

We will formally define price elasticity of demand, which we will label $E_p$, as follows:

What impact would a tax on beer have on consumption?

$$E_p = \frac{\text{Percentage change in quantity demanded}}{\text{Percentage change in price}}$$

**Price elasticity of demand ($E_p$)** The relative amount by which the quantity demanded will change in response to a change in the price of a particular good.

Consider an example in which a 10 percent rise in the price of oil leads to a reduction in quantity demanded of only 1 percent. Putting these numbers into the formula, we find that the price elasticity of demand for oil, in this case, equals the percentage change in quantity demanded divided by the percentage change in price, or

$$E_p = \frac{-1\%}{+10\%} = -0.1$$

An elasticity of –0.1 means that a 1 percent *increase* in the price would lead to a mere 0.1 percent *decrease* in the quantity demanded. If you were now told, in contrast, that the price elasticity of demand for oil was –2, you would know that a 1 percent increase in the price of oil would lead to a 2 percent decrease in the quantity demanded.

**RELATIVE QUANTITIES ONLY.** Note that in our elasticity formula, we talk about *percentage* changes in quantity demanded divided by *percentage* changes in price. We are, therefore, not interested in the absolute changes, only in relative amounts. This means that it does not matter if we measure price changes in terms of cents, dollars, or hundreds of dollars. It also does not matter whether we measure quantity changes in bushels, grams, or litres. The percentage change will be independent of the units chosen. So, a $1 increase in a cup of coffee has more of an impact than a $1 increase in the price of a car.

**ALWAYS NEGATIVE.** The law of demand states that quantity demanded is *inversely* related to the relative price. An increase in the price of a good leads to a decrease in the quantity demanded. If a decrease in the relative price of a good should occur, the quantity demanded would increase by a certain percentage. The point is that price elasticity of demand will always be negative. By convention, *we will ignore the minus sign in our discussion from this point on.*

Basically, the greater the *absolute* price elasticity of demand (disregarding sign), the greater is the demand responsiveness to relative price changes—a small change in price has a great impact on quantity demanded. The smaller the absolute price elasticity of demand, the smaller is the demand responsiveness to relative price changes—a large change in price has little effect on quantity demanded. See Example 4–1 for further insight.

**EXAMPLE 4–1 "If They Doubled the Price, We'd Still Drink Coffee"**

Every time there is frost in Brazil, the price of coffee beans rises, and everyone fears a big rise in the price of coffee. Members of the media interview coffee drinkers and ask how they will respond to the higher prices. Not surprisingly, even when coffee prices soared 150 percent a few years ago, some interviewees said they had to have their cup of coffee, no matter what. But if that were true for all coffee drinkers, why don't coffee prices rise as much as bean prices? If what coffee drinkers tell us were really true, their price elasticity of demand would be zero, and the retail price of coffee could skyrocket. But it never does. The truth is, interviewing coffee drinkers (or other consumers) about intentions tells us little. We need to examine the change in total market quantity demanded after an increase in price. The data make it clear: at least some people drink less coffee when the relative price goes up.

**For critical analysis:** Would the same be true for gas prices?

## Calculating Elasticity

To calculate the price elasticity of demand, we have to compute percentage changes in quantity demanded and in price. To find the percentage change in quantity demanded, we divide the change in the quantity demanded by the original quantity demanded:

$$\frac{\text{Change in quantity demanded}}{\text{Original quantity demanded}}$$

To find the percentage change in price, we divide the change in price by the original price:

$$\frac{\text{Change in price}}{\text{Original price}}$$

There is an arithmetic problem, though, when we calculate percentage changes in this manner. The percentage change, say, from 2 to 3—50 percent—is not the same as the percentage change from 3 to 2—33⅓ percent. In other words, you obtain a different value for the elasticity depending on whether you look at the change in demand when the price increased or when the price decreased.

To compute the average price elasticity of demand, we need to deal with the average change in quantity demanded caused by the average change in price. That means that we take the average of the two prices and the two quantities over the range we are considering and compare the change with these averages. For relatively small changes in price, the formula for computing the price elasticity of demand then becomes

$$E_p = \frac{\text{Change in quantity}}{\text{Sum of quantities/2}} \div \frac{\text{Change in price}}{\text{Sum of prices/2}}$$

We can rewrite this more simply if we do two things: (1) We can let $Q_1$ and $Q_2$ equal the two different quantities demanded before and after the price change and let $P_1$ and $P_2$ equal the two different prices. (2) Because we will be dividing a percentage by a percentage, we simply use the ratio, or the decimal form, of the percentages. Therefore,

$$E_p = \frac{\Delta Q}{(Q_1 + Q_2)/2} \div \frac{\Delta P}{(P_1 + P_2)/2}$$

where the Greek letter Δ stands for "change in." Example 4–2 provides a real-life example.

**EXAMPLE 4–2 The Price Elasticity of Demand for a Tablet Device**

During a two-month period, the price of Hewlett-Packard's TouchPad tablet device decreased from $499.99 to $99.99. As a consequence, during this two-month period the total quantity of tablet devices demanded increased from 25,000 per month to 425,000 per month.

Assuming other things were equal, we can calculate the price elasticity of demand for TouchPad tablets during this period:

$$E_p = \frac{\text{Change in } Q}{\text{Sum of quantities/2}} \div \frac{\text{Change in } P}{\text{Sum of prices/2}}$$

$$= \frac{425{,}000 - 25{,}000}{(425{,}000 + 25{,}000)/2} \div \frac{\$499.99 - \$99.99}{(\$499.99 + \$99.99)/2}$$

$$= \frac{400{,}000}{450{,}000/2} \div \frac{\$400.00}{\$599.98/2} = 1.33.$$

The price elasticity of 1.33 means that each 1 percent decrease in price generated a 1.33 percent increase in the quantity of TouchPad tablet devices demanded. Thus, the quantity of tablets demanded was relatively responsive to a reduction in the price of the devices.

**For critical analysis:** Would the estimated price elasticity of demand for TouchPad tablets have been different if we had *not* used the average-values formula? How?

# 4.2 Price Elasticity Ranges

We have names for the varying ranges of price elasticities, depending on whether a 1 percent change in price elicits more or less than a 1 percent change in the quantity demanded.

1. **Elastic demand** is a demand relationship in which a given percentage change in price will result in a larger percentage change in quantity demanded. We say that a good has an elastic demand whenever the price elasticity of demand is greater than 1. A 1 percent change in price causes a change of more than 1 percent in the quantity demanded.
2. **Unit elasticity of demand** is a demand relationship in which the quantity demanded changes exactly in proportion to the changes in price. In a situation of unit elasticity of demand, a 1 percent change in price causes a response of exactly a 1 percent change in the quantity demanded.

**Elastic demand** A demand relationship in which a given percentage change in price will result in a larger percentage change in quantity demanded.

**Unit elasticity of demand** A demand relationship in which the quantity demanded changes exactly in proportion to the changes in price.

**Inelastic demand** A demand relationship in which a given percentage change in price will result in a less than proportionate percentage change in the quantity demanded.

3. **Inelastic demand** is a demand relationship in which a given percentage change in price will result in a less than proportionate percentage change in the quantity demanded. In a situation of inelastic demand, a 1 percent change in price causes a response of less than a 1 percent change in the quantity demanded.

When we say a commodity's demand is elastic, we are indicating that consumers are relatively responsive to changes in price. When we say that a commodity's demand is inelastic, we are indicating that its consumers are relatively unresponsive to price changes. When economists say that demand is inelastic, it does not mean that quantity demanded is totally unresponsive to price changes. Remember, the law of demand suggests that there will be some responsiveness in quantity demanded to a price change. The question is how much. That is what elasticity attempts to determine. As you can see from Policy Example 4–1, who actually pays when a tax is imposed depends on whether the demand for the product is elastic or inelastic. So, if you are a smoker and a tax is imposed, are you going to pay most of that tax or will the producer absorb the tax?

### POLICY EXAMPLE 4–1 Who Pays Higher Cigarette Taxes?

Governments impose cigarette taxes, which are assessed as a flat amount per pack sold. These taxes are paid by sellers of cigarettes from the revenues they earn from their total sales. Thus, to receive the same effective price for selling a given quantity, a cigarette seller would have to receive a price that is higher by exactly the amount of the tax. As shown in part (a) of Figure 4–1, this means that imposing a cigarette tax shifts the supply curve upward by the amount of the tax. Sellers supply a given quantity of cigarettes at a price that is higher by the amount of the tax that they will transmit to the government.

Who *truly* pays the tax depends on the price elasticity of demand, however. Take a look at part (b) of Figure 4–1, which illustrates what would happen to the market price in the case of perfectly inelastic demand for cigarettes. In this instance, the market price rises by the full amount that the supply curve shifts upward. This amount, of course, is the amount of the tax. Consequently, if cigarette consumers were to have a perfectly inelastic demand for cigarettes, they would effectively pay the entire tax in the form of higher prices. Part (c) illustrates the opposite case, in which the demand for cigarettes happens to be perfectly elastic. In this situation, the

*continued*

**FIGURE 4–1**

**Price Elasticity and a Cigarette Tax**

Placing a per-pack tax on cigarettes causes the supply curve to shift upward by the amount of the tax, as illustrated in part (a), in order for sellers to receive the same effective price for any given quantity of cigarettes they sell. If the demand for cigarettes were perfectly inelastic, as depicted in part (b), imposing the tax would cause the market price of cigarettes to rise by the amount of the tax, so that cigarette consumers would effectively pay all the tax. Conversely, if the demand for cigarettes were perfectly elastic, as shown in part (c), the market price would not change, and sellers would pay all the tax. The quantity demanded would fall to $Q_2$.

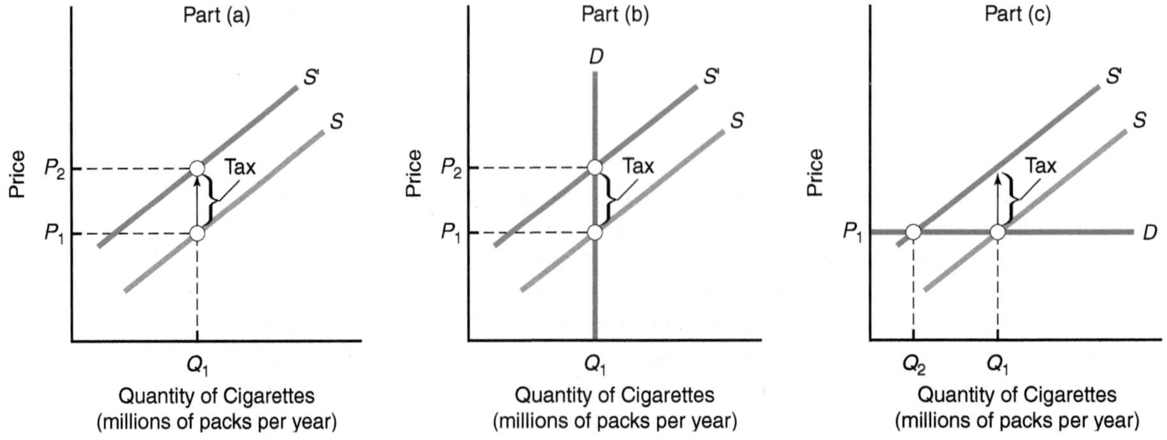

market price is unresponsive to a tax-induced shift in the supply curve, so sellers must pay all the tax.

Realistically, the price elasticity of demand for cigarettes is relatively low—most cigarette price elasticity estimates indicate values of 0.2 to 0.4. Thus, the burden of cigarette taxes falls mainly on cigarette consumers.

**For critical analysis:** Based on the information in this example, if taxes on cigarettes increase by 10 percent, by what range of percentages may desired cigarette purchases decline?

## Extreme Elasticities

There are two extremes in price elasticities of demand. One extreme represents total unresponsiveness of quantity demanded to price changes, which is referred to as **perfectly inelastic demand**, or zero elasticity—a demand that exhibits zero responsiveness to price changes. The other represents total responsiveness, which is referred to as infinitely elastic demand, or **perfectly elastic demand**—even the slightest increase in price will lead to zero quantity demanded.

**Perfectly inelastic demand** A demand that exhibits zero responsiveness to price changes.

**Perfectly elastic demand** A demand that has the characteristic that even the slightest increase in price will lead to zero quantity demanded.

We show perfect inelasticity in part (a) of Figure 4–2. Note that the quantity demanded per year is 8 million units, no matter what the price. Hence, for any percentage price change, the quantity demanded will remain the same, and thus, the change in the quantity demanded will be zero. Look back at our formula for computing elasticity. If the change in the quantity demanded is zero, the numerator is also zero, and a nonzero number divided into zero results in an answer of zero, too. Hence, there is perfect inelasticity.

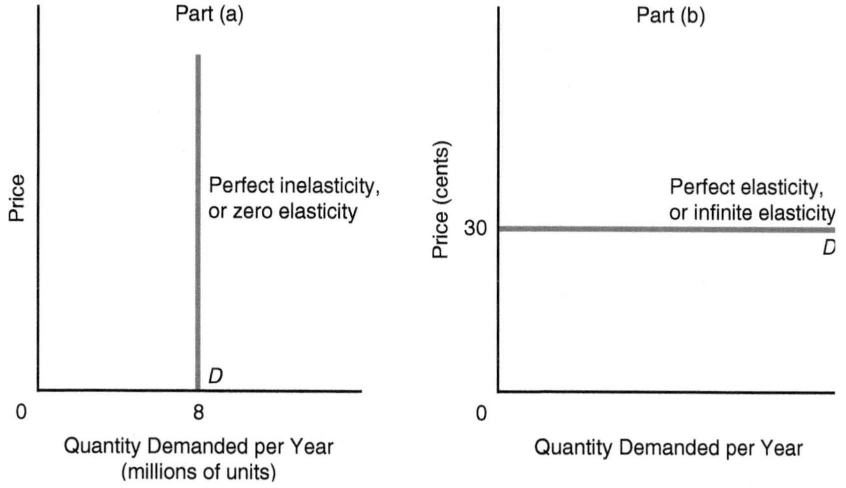


**FIGURE 4–2**

**Extreme Price Elasticities**

In part (a), we show complete price unresponsiveness. The demand curve is vertical at the quantity of 8 million units per year. This means that the price elasticity of demand is zero. In part (b), we show complete price responsiveness. At a price of 30 cents, in this example, consumers will demand an unlimited quantity of the particular good in question. This is a case of infinite price elasticity of demand.

At the opposite extreme is the situation depicted in part (b) of Figure 4–2. Here, we show that at a price of 30 cents, an unlimited quantity will be demanded. At a price that is only slightly above 30 cents, no quantity will be demanded. There is complete, or infinite, responsiveness here, and hence, we call the demand schedule in part (b) infinitely elastic or perfectly elastic.

## Elasticity and Total Revenues

Suppose that you are in charge of the pricing decision for a cellphone service company. How would you know when it is best to raise or not to raise prices? The answer depends, in part, on the effect of your pricing decision on total revenues, or the total receipts of your company. (The rest of the equation is, of course, your cost structure, a subject we examine later.) It is commonly thought that the way to increase total receipts is to increase price per unit. But is this always the case? Is it possible that a rise in price per unit could lead to a decrease in total revenues? The answers to these questions depend on the price elasticity of demand.

Let us look at Figure 4–3. In part (a), column 1 shows the price of cellphone service in dollars per minute, and column 2 represents billions of minutes demanded per year. In column 3, we multiply column 1 by column 2 to derive total revenue because total revenue is always equal to the number of units (quantity) sold times the price per unit. In column 4, we calculate values of elasticity. Note what happens to total revenues throughout the schedule. They rise steadily as the price rises from 10 cents to 50 cents per minute; but when the price rises further to 60 cents per minute, total revenues remain constant at $3 billion. At prices per minute higher than 60 cents, total revenues fall as price increases. Indeed, if prices are above 60 cents per minute, total revenues can be increased only by *cutting* prices, not by raising them.

## Labelling Elasticity

The relationship between price and quantity on the demand schedule is given in columns 1 and 2 of part (a) in Figure 4–3. Part (b) shows the demand curve, *D*, representing that schedule. Part (c) shows the total revenue curve representing the data in column 3. Note, first, the level of these curves at small quantities. The demand curve is at a maximum height, but total revenue is zero, which makes sense according to this demand schedule—at a price of $1.10 and above, no units will be purchased, and therefore, total revenue will be zero. As the price is lowered, we travel down the demand curve, and total revenues increase until the price is 60 cents per minute, remain constant from 60 cents to 50 cents per minute, and then fall at lower unit prices. Corresponding to those three sections, demand is elastic, unit-elastic, and inelastic. Hence, we have three relationships among the three types of price elasticity and total revenues.

1. *Elastic demand.* For some products, consumers are very price sensitive. If the price is lowered, total revenues will rise when the firm faces demand that is elastic, and if it raises the price, total revenues will fall. Consider another example. If the price of Diet Coke were raised by 25 percent and the price of all other soft drinks remained constant, the quantity demanded of Diet Coke would probably fall dramatically. The decrease in quantity demanded due to the increase in the price of Diet Coke would lead, in this example, to a reduction in the total revenues of the Coca-Cola Company. Therefore, if demand is elastic, price and total revenues will move in *opposite* directions.
2. *Unit-elastic demand.* When the firm is facing demand that is unit-elastic, if it increases the price, total revenues will not change. If it decreases the price, total revenues will not change either. If demand is unit-elastic, changes in price do not change total revenues.
3. *Inelastic demand.* For some products, consumers are not sensitive to price changes. When the firm is facing demand that is inelastic, if it raises the price, total revenues will go up; if it lowers the price, total revenues will fall. Consider another example. You have just invented a cure for the common cold, and the medication has been approved by Health Canada for sale to the public. You are not sure what price you should charge, and so you start out with a price of $1 per pill. You sell 20 million pills at that price over a year. The next year, you decide to raise the price by 25 percent, to $1.25. The number of pills you sell drops to 18 million per year. The price increase of 25 percent has led to a 10 percent decrease in quantity demanded. Your total revenues, however, will rise to $22.5 million because of the price increase. We therefore conclude that if demand is inelastic, price and total revenues move in the *same* direction.

The elastic, unit-elastic, and inelastic areas of the demand curve are shown in Figure 4–3. For prices from $1.10 per minute of cellphone time to 60 cents per minute, as the price decreases, total revenues rise from zero to $3 billion. Demand is price-elastic. When the price changes from 60 cents to 50 cents, however, total revenues remain constant at $3 billion; demand is unit-elastic. Finally, when the price falls from 50 cents to 10 cents, total revenues decrease from $3 billion to $1 billion; demand is inelastic. In parts (b) and (c) of Figure 4–3,

**FIGURE 4–3**

## The Relationship between Price Elasticity of Demand and Total Revenues for Cellphone Service

In part (a), we show the elastic, unit-elastic, and inelastic sections of the demand schedule according to whether a reduction in price increases total revenues, causes them to remain constant, or causes them to decrease, respectively. In part (b), we show these regions graphically on the demand curve. In part (c), we show them on the total revenue curve.

Part (a)

| (1) Price, $P$, per Minute of Cellphone Service | (2) Quantity Demanded, $D$ (billions of minutes) | (3) Total Revenue ($ billions) = (1) X (2) | (4) Elasticity, $E_p$ = $\frac{\text{Change in Q}}{(Q_1 + Q_2)/2} \div \frac{\text{Change in P}}{(P_1 + P_2)/2}$ | |
|---|---|---|---|---|
| $1.10 | 0 | 0 | | |
| | | | 21.000 | Elastic |
| 1.00 | 1 | 1.0 | | |
| | | | 6.330 | Elastic |
| 0.90 | 2 | 1.8 | | |
| | | | 3.400 | Elastic |
| 0.80 | 3 | 2.4 | | |
| | | | 2.143 | Elastic |
| 0.70 | 4 | 2.8 | | |
| | | | 1.444 | Elastic |
| 0.60 | 5 | 3.0 | | |
| | | | 1.000 | Unit-elastic |
| 0.50 | 6 | 3.0 | | |
| | | | 0.692 | Inelastic |
| 0.40 | 7 | 2.8 | | |
| | | | 0.467 | Inelastic |
| 0.30 | 8 | 2.4 | | |
| | | | 0.294 | Inelastic |
| 0.20 | 9 | 1.8 | | |
| | | | 0.158 | Inelastic |
| 0.10 | 10 | 1.0 | | |

Part (b)

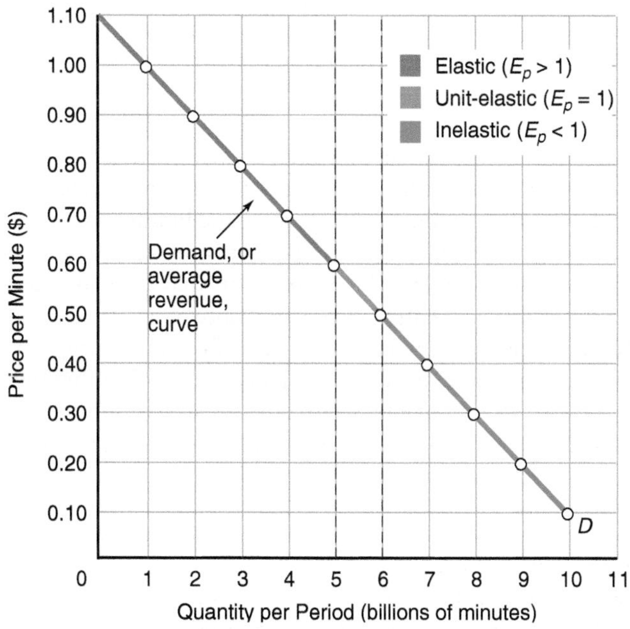


Part (c)

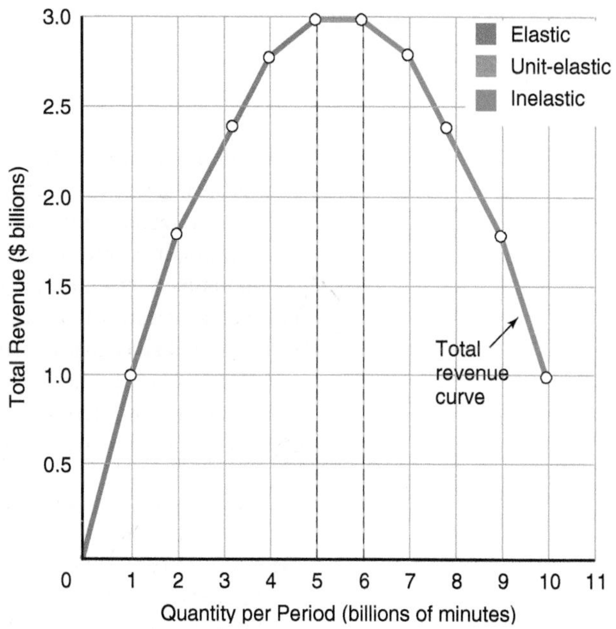

**TABLE 4–1**

**Relationship between Price Elasticity of Demand and Total Revenues**

| Price Elasticity of Demand | | Effect of Price Change on Total Revenues (TR) | |
|---|---|---|---|
| | | Price Decrease | Price Increase |
| Inelastic | ($E_p < 1$) | TR ↓ | TR ↑ |
| Unit-elastic | ($E_p = 1$) | No change in TR | No change in TR |
| Elastic | ($E_p > 1$) | TR ↑ | TR ↓ |

we have labelled the sections of the demand curve accordingly, and we have also shown how total revenues first rise, then remain constant, and finally fall.

The relationship between price elasticity of demand and total revenues brings together some important microeconomic concepts. Total revenues, as we have noted, are the product of price per unit times number of units sold. The law of demand states that along a given demand curve, price and quantity changes will move in opposite directions: One increases as the other decreases. Consequently, what happens to the product of price times quantity depends on which of the opposing changes exerts a greater force on total revenues. But this is just what price elasticity of demand is designed to measure—responsiveness of quantity demanded to a change in price. The relationship between price elasticity of demand and total revenues is summarized in Table 4–1.

# 4.3 Determinants of the Price Elasticity of Demand

We have learned how to calculate the price elasticity of demand. We know that, theoretically, it ranges numerically from zero (completely inelastic) to infinity (completely elastic). What we would like to do now is come up with a list of the determinants of the price elasticity of demand. The price elasticity of demand for a particular commodity at any price depends, at a minimum, on the following nonprice determinants:

1. the existence, number, and quality of substitutes
2. the percentage of a consumer's total budget devoted to purchases of that commodity
3. the length of time allowed for adjustment to changes in the price of the commodity

## Existence of Substitutes

The closer the substitutes for a particular commodity and the more substitutes there are, the greater will be its price elasticity of demand. At the limit, if there is a perfect substitute, the elasticity of demand for the commodity will be infinite. Thus, even the slightest increase in the commodity's price will cause an enormous reduction in the quantity demanded; quantity demanded will fall to zero. We are really talking about two goods that the consumer believes are exactly alike and equally desirable, like five-dollar bills whose only difference is serial numbers. When we talk about less extreme examples, we can only speak in terms of the number and the similarity of substitutes that are available. Thus, we will find that the more narrowly we define a good, the closer and greater will be the number of substitutes available. For example, the demand for Diet Coke may be highly elastic because consumers can switch to Diet Pepsi. The demand for diet drinks in general, however, is relatively less elastic because there are fewer substitutes.

## Share of Budget

We know that the greater the percentage of a person's total budget spent on a commodity, the greater that person's price elasticity of demand for that commodity. The demand for pepper is thought to be very inelastic merely because individuals spend so little on it relative to their total budgets. In contrast, the demand for such things as transportation and housing is thought to be far more elastic because they occupy a large part of people's budgets. Changes in their prices cannot be ignored so easily without sacrificing a lot of other alternative goods that could be purchased.

Consider a numerical example. A household earns \$40 000 per year. It spends \$4 on pepper per year and \$4000 on transportation services. Now, consider the spending power of this family when the price of pepper and the price of transportation both go up by 100 percent. If the household buys the same amount of pepper, it will now spend \$8. It will thus have to reduce other expenditures by \$4. This \$4 represents only 0.01 percent of the entire household budget. By contrast, a doubling of transportation costs requires that the family spend \$8000 on transportation, if it is to purchase the same quantity. That increased expenditure on transportation of \$4000 represents 10 percent of total expenditures that must be switched from other purchases. We would therefore predict that the household will react differently to the doubling of prices for pepper than it will for transportation. It will buy almost the same amount of pepper but will spend significantly less on transportation.

## Time for Adjustment

When the price of a commodity changes and that price change persists, more people will learn about it. Further, consumers will be better able to revise their consumption patterns when they have more time to do so. In fact, the longer they do take, the less costly it will be for them to engage in this revision of consumption patterns. Consider a price decrease. The longer the price decrease persists, the greater will be the number of new uses that consumers will discover for the particular commodity, and the greater will be the number of new users of that particular commodity.

**The longer any price change persists, the greater is the elasticity of demand, if other things hold constant. Elasticity of demand is greater in the long run than in the short run.**

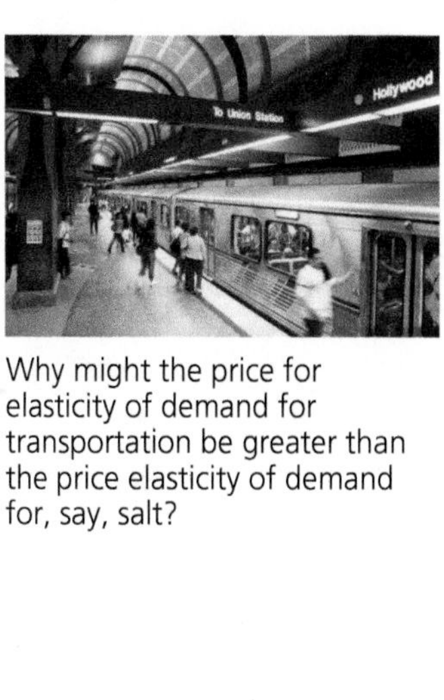


Why might the price for elasticity of demand for transportation be greater than the price elasticity of demand for, say, salt?

Let us take an example. Suppose that the price of electricity goes up by 50 percent. How do you adjust in the short run? You can turn the lights off more often, you can stop using the stereo as much as you do, and so on. Otherwise it is very difficult to cut back on your consumption of electricity. In the long run, though, you can devise methods to reduce your consumption. Instead of using electric heating, the next time you have a house built, you might install solar heating. Instead of using an electric stove, the next time you move, you might have a gas stove installed. You might purchase fluorescent bulbs because they use less electricity. The more time you have to think about it, the more ways you will find to cut your electricity consumption. We would expect, therefore, that the short-run demand curve for electricity would be relatively inelastic (in the price range around $P_e$), as demonstrated by $D_1$ in Figure 4–4. However, the long-run demand curve may exhibit

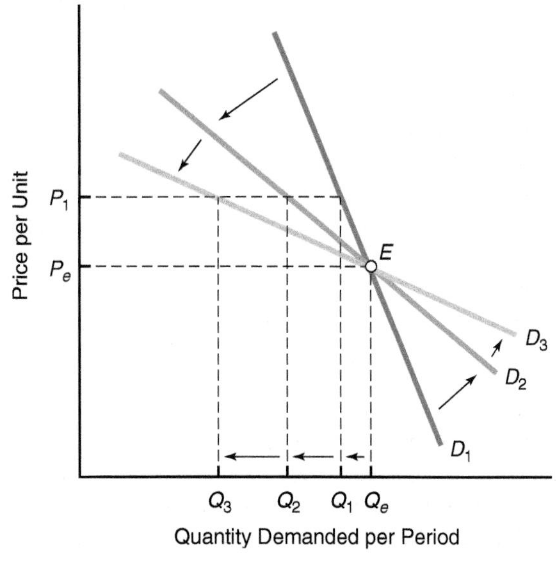


**FIGURE 4–4**

**Short-Run and Long-Run Price Elasticity of Demand**

Consider an equilibrium situation in which the market price is $P_e$ and the quantity demanded is $Q_e$. Then, there is a price increase to $P_1$. In the short run, as evidenced by the demand curve $D_1$, we move from equilibrium quantity demanded, $Q_e$, to $Q_1$. After more time is allowed for adjustment, the demand curve rotates at original price $P_e$ to $D_2$. Quantity demanded falls again, now to $Q_2$. After even more time is allowed for adjustment, the demand curve rotates at price $P_e$ to $D_3$. At the higher price $P_1$, in the long run, the quantity demanded falls all the way to $Q_3$.

much more elasticity (in the neighbourhood of $P_e$), as demonstrated by $D_3$. Indeed, we can think of an entire family of demand curves, such as those depicted in that figure. The short-run demand curve is for the period when there is no time for adjustment. As more time is allowed, the demand curve goes first to $D_2$ and then all the way to $D_3$. Thus, in the neighbourhood of $P_e$, elasticity differs for each of these curves. It is greater for the less steep curves (but slope alone does not measure elasticity for the entire curve).

Example 4–3 clearly shows that long-run price elasticities of demand tend to exceed the short-run elasticities.

Does the addition of solar panels to a newly built house represent a short-run or a long-run response to an increase in the price of electricity?

**HOW TO DEFINE THE SHORT RUN AND THE LONG RUN.** We have mentioned the short run and the long run. Is the short run one week, two weeks, one month, or two months? Is the long run three years, four years, or five years? The answer is that there is no single answer. What we mean by the long run is the period of time necessary for consumers to make a full adjustment to a given price change, all other things held constant. In the case of the demand for electricity, the long run will be however long it takes consumers to switch over to cheaper sources of heating, to buy houses that are more energy efficient, to purchase appliances that are more energy efficient, and so on. The long-run elasticity of demand for electricity, therefore, relates to a period of at least several years. The short run—by default—is any period less than the long run.

## EXAMPLE 4–3 What Do Real-World Price Elasticities of Demand Look Like?

In Table 4–2, we present demand elasticities for selected goods. None of them is zero, and the largest is 4.6. Remember that even though we are leaving off the negative sign, there is an inverse relationship between price and quantity demanded, and the minus sign is understood. Also remember that these elasticities represent averages over given price ranges. Choosing different price ranges could yield different elasticity estimates for these goods.

Economists have consistently found that estimated price elasticities of demand are greater in the long run than in the short run, as seen in Table 4–2. There you see that all available estimates indicate that the long-run price elasticity of demand for vacation air travel is 2.7, whereas the estimate for the short run is 1.1. Throughout the table, you see that all estimates of long-run price elasticities of demand exceed their short-run counterparts.

**TABLE 4–2**

### Price Elasticity of Demand for Selected Goods

Here are estimated demand elasticities for selected goods. All of them are negative, although we omit the minus sign. We have given some estimates of the long-run price elasticities of demand. The long run is associated with the time necessary for consumers to adjust fully to any given price change. (Note: "N.A." indicates that no estimate is available.)

| | Estimated Elasticity | |
|---|---|---|
| **Category** | **Short Run** | **Long Run** |
| Air travel (business) | 0.4 | 1.2 |
| Air travel (vacation) | 1.1 | 2.7 |
| Beef | 0.6 | N.A. |
| Cheese | 0.3 | N.A. |
| Electricity | 0.1 | 1.7 |
| Fresh tomatoes | 4.6 | N.A. |
| Gasoline | 0.2 | 0.5 |
| Intercity bus service | 0.6 | 2.2 |
| Private education | 1.1 | 1.9 |
| Restaurant meals | 2.3 | N.A. |
| Tires | 0.9 | 1.2 |

**For critical analysis:** Explain the intuitive reasoning behind the difference between long-run and short-run price elasticity of demand.

# 4.4 Cross-Elasticity of Demand

In an earlier chapter, we discussed the effect of a change in the price of one good on the demand for a related good. We defined substitutes and complements in terms of whether a reduction in the price of one caused a decrease or an increase in the demand for the other. If the price of compact discs (CDs) is held constant, the amount of CDs demanded (at any price) will certainly be influenced by the price of a close substitute, such as MP3 players. If the price of stereo speakers is held constant, the amount of stereo speakers demanded (at any price) will certainly be affected by changes in the price of stereo amplifiers.

What we now need to do is come up with a numerical measure of the price responsiveness of demand to the prices of related goods. This is called the **cross-elasticity of demand ($E_{xy}$)**, which is defined as the percentage change in the quantity demanded of one good (holding its price constant) divided by the percentage change in the price of the related good. In equation form, the cross-elasticity of demand for good X with respect to good Y is

**Cross-elasticity of demand ($E_{xy}$)** The percentage change in the quantity demanded of one good (holding its price constant) divided by the percentage change in the price of a related good.

$$E_{xy} = \frac{\text{Percentage change in quantity demanded of good X}}{\text{Percentage change in price of good Y}}$$

When two goods are substitutes, the cross-elasticity of demand will be positive. For example, when the price of margarine goes up, the demand for butter will rise as consumers shift away from the now relatively more expensive margarine to butter. A producer of margarine could benefit from a numerical estimate of the cross-elasticity of demand between butter and margarine. For example, if the price of butter went up by 10 percent and the margarine producer knew that the cross-elasticity of demand was 1, the margarine producer could estimate that the demand for margarine would also go up by 10 percent at any given price. Plans for increasing margarine production could then be made.

When two related goods are complements, the cross-elasticity of demand will be negative (and we will not disregard the minus sign). For example, when the price of stereo amplifiers goes up, the demand for stereo speakers will fall. This is because as prices of amplifiers increase, the quantity of amplifiers demanded will naturally decrease. Because amplifiers and stereo speakers are often used together, the demand for speakers is likely to fall. Any manufacturer of stereo speakers must take this into account in making production plans. In this chapter's Issues and Applications, we look at whether increasing taxes on beer would lead to a decrease in cigarette consumption. If beer and cigarettes are complements, then the cross-elasticity of demand will be negative, and when the price of beer goes up the demand for cigarettes will fall.

If goods are completely unrelated, their cross-elasticity of demand will be zero. Read Policy Example 4–2 for further discussion of cross-elasticity.

### POLICY EXAMPLE 4–2 Do People Substitute Wireless Phone Services for Wired Services?

If people regard cellphones as a form of communication that they use mainly on the go and traditional land-wired phone service as a means of communication from their homes, then the two types of services are not substitutes. In contrast, if people respond to higher prices of land-wired phone service by consuming more wireless phone services instead—and perhaps using only wireless services—then they are substitute services.

Recently, two economists, Allan Ingraham and J. Gregory Sidak, estimated that the cross-elasticity of demand between wireless and wired phone services is about 0.02. This estimate implies that a 10 percent increase in the price of land-wired phone services induces a 0.2 percent increase in the quantity of wireless phone services demanded. The two types of phone services are substitutes, but the degree of substitution is very slight.

**For critical analysis:** As younger people, who tend to use cellphones more than land-line phones, gradually replace their elders, what is likely to happen to the cross-elasticity of demand for the two types of telecommunications services?

## Income Elasticity of Demand

In Chapter 3, we discussed the determinants of demand. One of those determinants was income. Briefly, we can apply our understanding of elasticity to the relationship between changes in income and changes in demand. We measure the responsiveness of quantity demanded to income changes by the *income elasticity of demand* ($E_i$), holding relative price constant:

$$E_i = \frac{\text{Percentage change in quantity demanded}}{\text{Percentage change in income}}$$

**Income elasticity of demand**
A horizontal shift in the demand curve in response to changes in income.

**Price elasticity of demand**
A movement along the curve in response to price changes.

**Income elasticity of demand** refers to a *horizontal shift* in the demand curve in response to changes in income, whereas **price elasticity of demand** refers to a movement *along* the curve in response to price changes. Thus, income elasticity of demand is calculated at a given price, and price elasticity of demand is calculated at a given income.

A simple example will demonstrate how income elasticity of demand can be computed. Table 4–3 gives the relevant data. The product in question is DVDs. We assume that the price of DVDs remains constant relative to other prices. In period 1, six DVDs per month are purchased. Income per month is $400. In period 2, monthly income increases to $600, and the quantity of DVDs demanded per month increases to eight. Using the same mid-point formula that we used in computing the price elasticity of demand, we get:

$$E_i = \frac{(8-6)/7}{(600-400)/500} = \frac{2/7}{2/5} = \frac{5}{7} = 0.714$$

Note that the sign of the income elasticity of demand is positive. That is because as income rises, the quantity of DVDs demanded also increases. In Chapter 3, we defined this kind of good as a "normal" good—one that we want more of as our income increases. An "inferior" good is one that we want less of as our income increases. The sign of the income elasticity of demand for an inferior good will therefore be negative, since quantity demanded will decrease as income increases. It is important to retain the negative sign on the income elasticity of demand for an inferior good, since the sign tells us whether the good is, in fact, normal or inferior.

You have just been introduced to three types of elasticities. Two of them—the price elasticity of demand ($E_p$), and income elasticity ($E_i$)—are the two most important factors in influencing the quantity demanded for most goods. Reasonably accurate estimates of these can go a long way toward making accurate forecasts of demand for goods or services. For an illustration of income elasticity, see Example 4–4. Should Canadian Tire "Money" be considered income, just like frequent flyer points?

**TABLE 4–3**
**How Income Affects Quantity of DVDs Demanded**

| Period | Number of DVDs Demanded per Month | Income per Month |
|---|---|---|
| 1 | 6 | $400 |
| 2 | 8 | 600 |

### EXAMPLE 4–4 Frequent Flyer Miles as Income

For the past 20 years, airlines have been discovering that consumers measure their income in more than one way. Most airlines now offer frequent flyer points for air travel, and many are affiliated with other businesses as well. For example, Air Canada gives frequent flyer points for renting cars from Budget and for staying in any number of hotels. Travellers can also apply for a Visa card that gives them one frequent flyer mile for every dollar charged. Airlines have found the demand for their services is increasing. It appears that air travellers count their frequent flyer miles as part of their incomes and, thus, they demand more air travel as their incomes increase. As anyone who has ever shopped at Canadian Tire knows, Canadian Tire money can add up quickly. Some of the older Canadian Tire money is even traded on eBay.

*continued*

**For critical analysis:** The federal government has decided that the value of flights paid for with frequent flyer miles earned while travelling on business should be considered part of an individual's income—and thus subject to income tax. What effect will this have on the income elasticity of demand for air travel?

# 4.5 Elasticity of Supply

The **price elasticity of supply ($E_s$)** is defined similarly to the price elasticity of demand—the responsiveness of the quantity supplied of a commodity to a change in its price. Supply elasticities are generally positive. This is because at higher prices, larger quantities will generally be forthcoming from suppliers. The formula for the price elasticity of supply is as follows:

**Price elasticity of supply ($E_s$)** The responsiveness of the quantity supplied of a commodity to a change in its price.

$$E_s = \frac{\text{Percentage change in quantity supplied}}{\text{Percentage change in price}}$$

## Classifying Supply Elasticities

Just as with demand, there are different types of supply elasticities. They are similar to the types of demand elasticities.

If a 1 percent increase in price elicits a greater than 1 percent increase in the quantity supplied, we say that at the particular price in question on the supply schedule, *supply is elastic.* The most extreme elastic supply is called **perfectly elastic supply**—the slightest reduction in price will cause quantity supplied to fall to zero.

**Perfectly elastic supply** When the slightest reduction in price will cause quantity supplied to fall to zero.

If, conversely, a 1 percent increase in price elicits a less than 1 percent increase in the quantity supplied, we refer to that as an *inelastic supply.* The most extreme inelastic supply is called **perfectly inelastic supply**—no matter what the price, the quantity supplied remains the same.

**Perfectly inelastic supply** When no matter what the price, the quantity supplied remains the same.

If the percentage change in the quantity supplied is equal to the percentage change in the price, we call this *unit-elastic supply.*

We show in Figure 4–5 two supply schedules, *S* and *S'*. You can tell at a glance, without reading the labels, which one is perfectly elastic and which one is perfectly inelastic. As you might expect, most supply schedules exhibit elasticities that are somewhere between zero and infinity.

## Determinants of the Elasticity of Supply

**1. SHORT- AND LONG-RUN ELASTICITIES OF SUPPLY.** We pointed out earlier that the longer the time period allowed for adjustment, the greater the price elasticity of demand. It

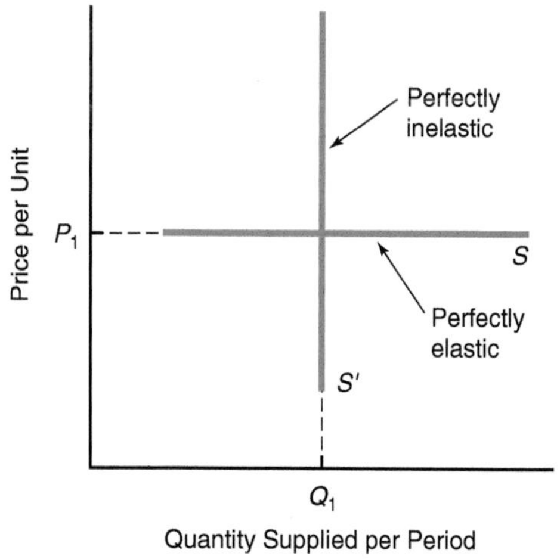


**FIGURE 4–5**

**The Extremes in Supply Curves**

Here, we have drawn two extremes of supply schedules: *S* is a perfectly elastic supply curve; *S'* is a perfectly inelastic one. In the former, an unlimited quantity will be supplied at price $P_1$. In the latter, no matter what the price, the quantity supplied will be $Q_1$. An example of *S'* might be the supply curve for fresh fish on the morning the boats come in.

turns out that the same proposition applies to supply. The longer the time for adjustment, the more elastic is the supply curve. Consider why this is true:

> **The longer the time allowed for adjustment, the more firms are able to figure out ways to increase (or decrease) production in an industry.**
>
> **The longer the time allowed for adjustment, the more resources can flow into (or out of) an industry through expansion (or contraction) of existing firms.**

We therefore talk about short-run and long-run price elasticities of supply. The short run is defined as the time period during which full adjustment has not yet taken place. The long run is the time period during which firms have been able to adjust fully to the change in price.

Consider an increase in the price of housing. In the very short run, when there is no time allowed for adjustment, the amount of housing offered for rent or for sale is relatively inelastic. However, as more time is allowed for adjustment, current owners of the housing stock can find ways to increase the amount of housing they will offer for rent from given buildings. The owner of a large house can decide, for example, to have two children move into one room so that a "new" extra bedroom can be rented out. This can also be done by the owner of a large house who decides to move into an apartment and rent each floor of the house to a separate family. Thus, the quantity of housing supplied will increase. With more time, landlords will find it profitable to build new rental units.

We can show a whole set of supply curves similar to the ones we generated for demand. As Figure 4–6 shows, when nothing can be done in the short run, the supply curve is vertical, $S_1$. As more time is allowed for adjustment, the supply curve rotates to $S_2$ and then to $S_3$, becoming more elastic as it rotates.

**2. AVAILABILITY OF RAW MATERIALS.** If the supply of raw materials, such as oil, is limited and non-renewable, a change in production may be hard for firms, making supply inelastic. If producers can increase their output without a rise in costs, then supply is elastic.

**3. COMPLEXITY OF PRODUCTION.** If the production process is relatively easy and labour is unskilled and mobile, supply is elastic. If the production process is more complex and not as mobile, supply is inelastic.

**4. EXCESS CAPACITY AND INVENTORIES.** If the supplier has excess capacity, it is easier to increase supply to the market. A producer who has a ready supply of the product can quickly increase its supply to the market.

**FIGURE 4–6**

**Short-Run and Long-Run Price Elasticity of Supply**

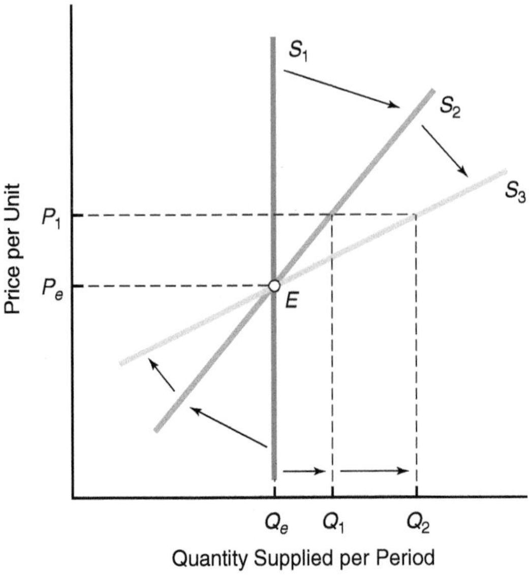


Consider a situation in which the price is $P_e$ and the quantity supplied is $Q_e$. In the short run, we hypothesize a vertical supply curve, $S_1$. With the price increase to $P_1$, therefore, there will be no change in the short run in quantity supplied; it will remain at $Q_e$. Given some time for adjustment, the supply curve will rotate to $S_2$. The new amount supplied will increase to $Q_1$. The long-run supply curve is shown by $S_3$. The amount supplied again increases to $Q_2$.

ISSUES AND APPLICATIONS

# To Combat Cigarette Consumption, Should the Government Raise Taxes on Beer?

**Concepts Applied: Price Elasticity of Demand, Cross-Elasticity of Demand**

Smoking and drinking seem to go hand in hand.

According to the Canadian Cancer Society, cancer is the leading cause of death in Canada and is responsible for 30% of all deaths. In 2016 it is estimated that, every day, on average, 555 Canadians will be diagnosed with cancer and 216 Canadians will die (daily). Smoking is responsible for 30% of all cancer deaths in Canada. Cigarette smoking contributes to the development of cancers of the lungs, head and neck, and throat. In addition, cigarette smoking contributes to cardiovascular disease and significantly raises the chance a heart attack. Smoking also poses problems for fetuses. Women who smoke during pregnancy are more likely to give birth to babies with below-average weights.

## The Price Elasticity of Demand for Cigarettes

Why do so many people continue to smoke? One reason is that the average price of a cigarette sold in Canada is not much more than 50 cents. Among bad habits that people can pick up, smoking remains one of the least expensive.

In addition, cigarettes contain nicotine, which is a very addictive substance. This undoubtedly helps explain why the price elasticity of cigarette demand is approximately 0.3. Because the demand for cigarettes is relatively inelastic, relatively large price increases would be required to bring about a significant decline in cigarette consumption.

## Taxation Policies to Combat Cigarette Consumption

Both the provincial and the federal governments levy taxes on cigarettes. Because the demand for cigarettes is inelastic, the market price of cigarettes reflects most of these taxes. Consequently, consumers pay the bulk of cigarette taxes, which account for about 70 percent of the average after-tax price of a pack of cigarettes.

Critics of the cigarette tax policy contend that in light of the relatively low price elasticity of demand for cigarettes, much higher taxes would be required to generate a significant drop in cigarette consumption. Canada raised taxes and found that teenage smoking fell from 42 percent to 16 percent, but smuggling of cigarettes increased.

## Reducing Cigarette Consumption via Taxation of Alcohol?

Recently, some economists have proposed raising taxes on alcohol as another means of discouraging cigarette consumption. Their idea originates from the observation that bars are often smoke filled, which suggests that many people who drink regard alcoholic beverages as complements to cigarette smoking. Heavier taxes on alcohol would push up the price of alcoholic beverages, thereby generating a reduction in cigarette consumption.

Estimates indicate that the cross-elasticity of demand for cigarettes is approximately −0.2; each 10 percent increase in the price of beer thereby reduces cigarette demand by about 2 percent, and so cigarette smokers do indeed regard beer as a complement to cigarette consumption. Significant increases in taxes on beer could potentially supplement the use of cigarette taxes as a means of discouraging cigarette consumption.

Higher alcohol taxes would also help discourage the excessive use of alcohol, which imposes its own public health costs. The price elasticity of the demand for beer is only slightly less than 1, meaning that the demand for beer is nearly unit-elastic. This implies that a significant percentage increase in the price of beer due to higher taxes on beer would generate a nearly equal percentage reduction in beer consumption. In principle, therefore, higher taxes on beer and other alcoholic beverages could contribute to improved public health by reducing consumption of both cigarettes and alcohol.

Sources: "Cancer statistics at a glance". Cancer Information. Canadian Cancer Society. http://www.cancer.ca/en/cancer-information/cancer-101/cancer-statistics-at-a-glance/?region=ab (Accessed February 1, 2017); "Smoking and tobacco". Prevention and Screening. Canadian Cancer Society. http://www.cancer.ca/en/prevention-and-screening/live-well/smoking-and-tobacco/?region=on (Accessed on February 1, 2017); "Federal and Provincial/Territorial Tobacco Tax Rates, February 2016; Per 200 cigarettes" Non-Smokers' Rights Association/Smoking and Health Action Foundation. https://www.nsra-adnf.ca/cms/file/files/160203_map_and_table.pdf. (Accessed February 1, 2017).

**For critical analysis:**

1. On the basis of the information given here, would you expect that beer consumers pay a higher portion of the total tax on each unit of beer, compared with the fraction of the total tax that cigarette consumers pay on each pack of cigarettes? Why?
2. If a beer producer and a cigarette producer both raise their prices, which is more likely to experience an increase in total revenues? Explain.

# SUMMARY

Here is what you should know after reading this chapter. MyEconLab will help you identify what you know, and where to go when you need to practise. We suggest that as soon as you review one of the Learning Objective sections below, you then proceed to go through the related section in MyEconLab.

| LEARNING OBJECTIVES | KEY TERMS | MYECONLAB PRACTICE |
|---|---|---|
| **4.1 Price Elasticity of Demand.** Price elasticity of demand is a measure of the percentage change in quantity demanded relative to the percentage change in price, given income, the prices of other goods, and time. Because of the law of demand, price elasticity of demand is always negative. | price elasticity of demand ($E_p$), 93 | • **MyEconLab** Study Plan 4.1 |
| **4.2 Price Elasticity Ranges.** We classify demand as *elastic* if a 1 percent change in price leads to a more than 1 percent change in quantity demanded, *unit-elastic* if it leads to exactly a 1 percent change in quantity demanded, and *inelastic* if it leads to less than a 1 percent change in quantity demanded.<br>When facing a perfectly elastic demand, the slightest increase in price leads to zero quantity demanded; when facing a perfectly inelastic demand, no matter what the price, the quantity demanded remains unchanged. Perfect inelasticity means absolutely no price responsiveness.<br>Price elasticity of demand falls as we move down a straight-line demand curve. It goes from infinity to zero. Elasticity and slope are not equivalent; for example, the slope of a straight-line curve is always constant, whereas elasticity changes as we move along a linear curve. A vertical demand curve is perfectly inelastic; a horizontal demand curve is perfectly elastic. | elastic demand, 95<br>unit elasticity of demand, 95<br>inelastic demand, 96<br>perfectly inelastic demand, 96<br>perfectly elastic demand, 96 | • **MyEconLab** Study Plan 4.2 |

myeconlab

| LEARNING OBJECTIVES | KEY TERMS | MYECONLAB PRACTICE |
|---|---|---|
| **4.3 Determinants of the Price Elasticity of Demand.** Price elasticity of demand depends on (a) the existence, number, and quality of substitutes, (b) the share of total budget accounted for by the commodity, and (c) the length of time allowed for adjustment to changes in the price of the commodity. | | • **MyEconLab** Study Plan 4.3 |
| **4.4 Cross-Elasticity of Demand.** Cross-elasticity of demand measures the responsiveness of the demand for one product, either a substitute or a complement, to changes in the price of another product. When the cross-elasticity of demand is negative, the two commodities under study are complements; when the cross-elasticity of demand is positive, they are substitutes.<br>Income elasticity of demand is given by the percentage change in quantity demanded divided by the percentage change in income, given the relative price. When the income elasticity of demand is positive, the good in question is a normal good; when the income elasticity of demand is negative, the good is an inferior good. | cross-elasticity of demand ($E_{xy}$), 103<br>income elasticity of demand, 104<br>price elasticity of demand, 104 | • **MyEconLab** Study Plan 4.4 |
| **4.5 Price Elasticity of Supply.** Price elasticity of supply is given by the percentage change in quantity supplied divided by the percentage change in price. The greater the time allowed for adjustment, the availability of raw materials, the complexity of production, and the inventories, the greater the price elasticity of supply. | price elasticity of supply ($E_S$), 105<br>perfectly elastic supply, 105<br>perfectly inelastic supply, 105 | • **MyEconLab** Study Plan 4.5 |

# PROBLEMS

(Answers to the odd-numbered problems appear at the back of the book.)

**LO 4.1 Define price elasticity of demand and calculate it using two different methods.**

1. Use the following hypothetical demand schedule for tea to answer the questions.

| Quantity Demanded per Week (kilograms) | Price per Kilogram | Elasticity |
|---|---|---|
| 1000 | $5 | |
| 800 | 10 | ______ |
| 600 | 15 | ______ |
| 400 | 20 | ______ |
| 200 | 25 | |

   a. Using the mid-point formula, determine the elasticity of demand for each price change. (Example: When price changes from $5 to $10, quantity demanded changes from 1000 to 800 kilograms, so the elasticity of demand, using average values, is ⅓ or 0.33.)
   b. Could coffee be considered a substitute for tea?
   c. Would you consider this commodity a luxury or a necessity?

2. Calculate the price elasticity of demand for the product in the table below using average values for the prices and quantities in your formula. Over the price range in question, is this demand schedule inelastic, unit-elastic, or elastic? Is total revenue greater at the lower price or the higher price?

| Price per Unit | Quantity Demanded |
|---|---|
| $4 | 22 |
| 6 | 18 |

3. A new mobile home park charges nothing for water used by its inhabitants. Consumption is 100 000 litres per month. The decision is then made to charge according to how much each mobile home owner uses, at a rate of $10 per 1000 litres. Consumption declines to 50 000 litres per month. What is the difficulty here in accurately estimating the price elasticity of the demand for water by these residents?

4. Suppose that the price of salt rises from 15 cents to 17 cents a kilogram. The quantity demanded decreases from 525 kilograms to 475 kilograms per month, and the quantity supplied increases from 525 kilograms to 600 kilograms per month. (Use averages in calculating elasticities.)
   a. Calculate the price elasticity of demand ($E_p$) for salt.
   b. Is the demand for salt price-elastic or price-inelastic?

5. Suppose that an automobile dealer cuts his car prices by 15 percent. He then finds that his car sales have increased by 20 percent.
   a. What can you say about the price elasticity of demand for cars?
   b. What will happen to the dealer's total revenue?

6. The diagram below depicts the demand curve for "mini-burgers" purchased from Joe's Campus Grill. Use the information in this diagram to answer the following questions.
   a. What is the price elasticity of demand along the range of the demand curve between a price of $0.20 per miniburger and a price of $0.40 per miniburger? Is demand elastic or inelastic over this range?
   b. What is the price elasticity of demand along the range of the demand curve between a price of $0.80 per miniburger and a price of $1.20 per miniburger? Is demand elastic or inelastic over this range?

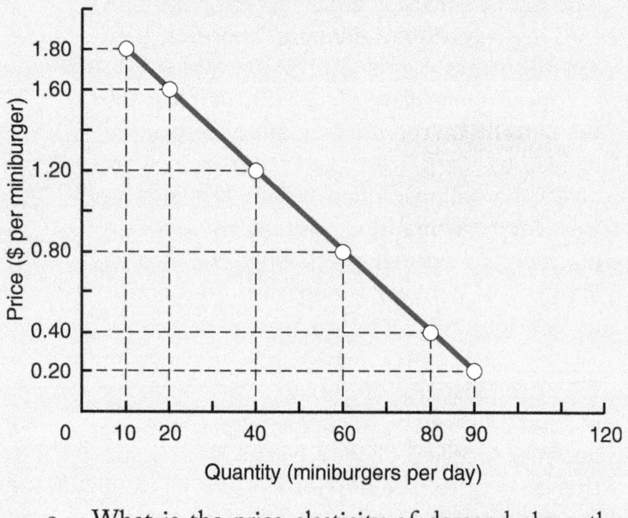


   c. What is the price elasticity of demand along the range of the demand curve between a price of $1.60 per miniburger and a price of $1.80 per miniburger? Is demand elastic or inelastic over this range?

**LO 4.2 Define the three price elasticity ranges and explain their effects on total revenues.**

7. Can any demand curve possibly be perfectly inelastic ($E_p = 0$)? Explain.

**LO 4.3 Discuss the three factors that determine the price elasticity of demand.**

8. Given each example, determine whether price elasticity will tend to be elastic or inelastic.
   a. a 45-cent box of salt you buy once a year
   b. a type of high-powered ski boat you can rent from any number of rental agencies
   c. a 75-cent guitar pick for the lead guitarist of a major rock band

For Example 4–3, "What Do Real-World Price Elasticities of Demand Look Like?", cheese has a price elasticity of demand of around 0.3. Does the quality of substitutes affect this elasticity?

**LO 4.4 Describe the effects of substitutes, complements, and income on elasticity of demand.**

9. Calculate the income elasticity of demand for the product in the following table, using average values for incomes and quantities.

| Quantity of DVD Players per Year | Per Capita Annual Group Income |
|---|---|
| 1000 | $15 000 |
| 2000 | 20 000 |

   a. Is the demand for this product income-elastic or income-inelastic?
   b. Would you consider this commodity a luxury or a necessity?

10. Which of the following cross-elasticities of demand would you expect to be positive and which to be negative?
    a. tennis balls and tennis racquets
    b. tennis balls and golf balls
    c. dental services and toothpaste
    d. dental services and candy
    e. soft drinks and ice cubes
    f. soft drinks and fruit juices

**LO 4.5 Define price elasticity of supply and describe the difference between the long-run and short-run supply schedules.**

11. Suppose that the price of salt rises from 15 cents to 17 cents a kilogram. The quantity demanded decreases from 525 kilograms to 475 kilograms per month, and the quantity supplied increases from 525 kilograms to 600 kilograms per month. (Use averages in calculating elasticities.)
    a. Calculate the elasticity of supply ($E_s$) for salt.
    b. Is the supply of salt price-elastic or price-inelastic?

12. From Issues and Applications, "To Combat Cigarette Consumption, Should the Government Raise Taxes on Beer?", we found out that smokers regard beer as a complement. If taxes are increased on beer, what will happen to cigarette consumption?

# BUSINESS APPLICATION

**LO 4.1 Define price elasticity of demand and calculate it using two different methods.**

## Finance: Why Have Pharmaceutical Companies Been Profitable Investments?

The following graph shows a comparison of stock index performance (annualized percent rate of return) for pharmaceutical companies and the Dow Jones industrials.

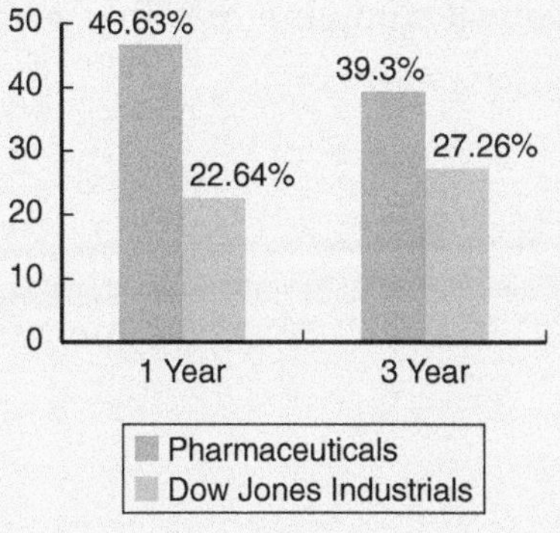


## Business Application Problem

Use the concept of *price elasticity of demand* to explain why pharmaceutical companies have been good stock investments compared to the performance of the stock market as a whole.

5

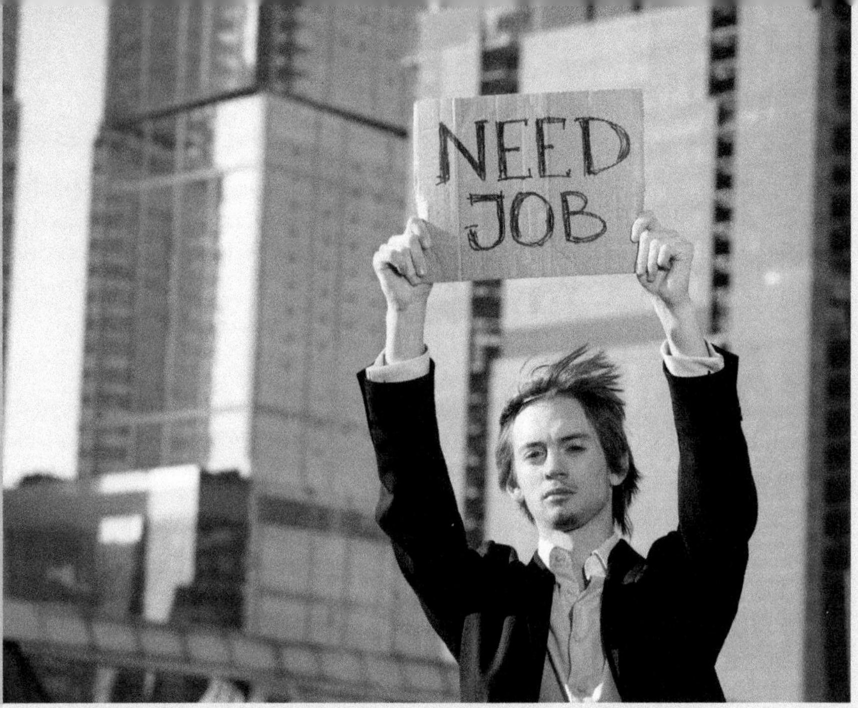


# Market Efficiency and Market Failure

## LEARNING OBJECTIVES

After reading this chapter, you should be able to:

**5.1** Use the concepts of consumer and producer surplus to explain how market equilibrium can promote allocative efficiency.

**5.2** Compare and contrast the effects that external benefits and external costs have on achieving allocative efficiency in a free market, laissez-faire environment.

**5.3** Explain how a type of asymmetric information called moral hazard can affect the efficient allocation of resources.

**5.4** Compare and contrast the effects that public goods and common property resources have on achieving allocative efficiency in a free market, laissez-faire environment.

Between 2006 and 2009, the global economy faced the largest financial and economic crisis in the post–world-war era. In the United States, average home prices declined 32 percent, with cities such as Las Vegas and Phoenix seeing their home values plunge 55.4 percent and 51.3 percent. The U.S., Canadian, German, and French stock markets plummeted 58 percent, 48 percent, 55 percent, and 57 percent, respectively. To prevent America's largest financial institutions from going bankrupt, the U.S. government approved a $700 billion bailout package. Of all the developed industrial countries, Canada was considered best able to weather this economic storm. In this chapter, we will study the role that market failure played in contributing to these events.

myeconlab

MyEconLab helps you master each objective and study more efficiently. See end of chapter for details.

# DID YOU KNOW THAT...?

In an investigation conducted by the Ontario Provincial Police, in 2016, it was noted that twice as many vehicle crash deaths were caused by distracted driving, when compared to impaired driving. In 2016 the Canadian Auto Association (CAA) reported that individuals who are engaged in text messaging while driving are 23 times more likely to be in a crash or near crash event compared with non-distracted drivers. Typing a typical text message results in the driver taking his or her eyes off the road for 4.6 seconds. This is equivalent to travelling the length of a football field at 92 kilometres per hour without looking at the road. Reaching for a moving object makes the risk of a crash or near crash 9 times as high as for non-distracted driving. When one is talking on a cell phone he or she is 4 to 5 times more likely to crash or near crash, compared to a non-distracted driver.

If the use of cellphones while driving does cause accidents, then this private activity intrudes on other individuals, resulting in extra social costs—pain or injury to other drivers and pedestrians and grief to their loved ones, insurance premium increases for the general public, and tax increases to pay for increased health-care costs. As this chapter explains, the social costs related to the use of cellphones while driving can be viewed as a form of market failure, which may require some type of government intervention.

Source: "Statistics". Distracted Driving. Canadian Auto Association. https://www.caa.ca/distracted-driving/ (Accessed February 2, 2017); "Distracted driving resulting in nearly twice as many deaths as impaired: OPP". Canada. CTV News. August 30, 2016. http://www.ctvnews.ca/canada/distracted-driving-resulting-in-nearly-twice-as-many-deaths-as-impaired-opp-1.3050230; "New data from Virginia Tech Transportation Institute provides insight into cellphone use and driving distraction." *Virginia Tech News*. July 29, 2009. http://www.vtnews.vt.edu/story.php?relyear=2009&itemno=571.

# 5.1 Market Efficiency

In Chapter 3, we studied how market equilibrium quantity is determined in a competitive market. In this section, we focus on how market equilibrium relates to the goal of allocative efficiency. You may recall from Chapter 2 that allocative efficiency is concerned with producing the appropriate mix or quantities of goods so as to maximize consumer value, given our limited resources. To understand how market equilibrium relates to efficiency, we must first examine the concepts of *consumer surplus* and *producer surplus*.

## Consumer Surplus

Think about what made you feel good about a recent purchase: it is likely that you ended up paying less than what you consider the true value of the product or service. In a specific market situation, **consumer surplus** refers to the difference between the maximum amount that consumers are willing to pay and the actual amount paid for all units of a product consumed.

**Consumer surplus** The difference between the maximum amount that consumers are willing to pay and the actual amount paid for all units of a product consumed.

**DEMAND CURVE AND MARGINAL BENEFIT.** The height of the demand curve reflects the maximum that consumers are willing to pay for a unit of quantity. This is also called the **marginal benefit** (MB), or extra value, of that unit of quantity. For example, Figure 5–1 describes the market for vegetarian sub sandwiches in a Canadian province. The maximum that consumers are willing to pay for the 6 millionth sub is $2, which equals the height of the demand curve at this quantity level. Stated another way, the marginal benefit or extra value of the 6 millionth sub is $2. In general, one can view the demand curve as the marginal benefit curve for the product being analyzed.

**Marginal benefit** The maximum amount that consumers are willing to pay for a specified unit of quantity. It is the height of the demand curve at the specified unit of quantity.

For any given market situation, the consumer surplus can be determined once the market demand curve and the equilibrium price and quantity re known. In Figure 5–1, the equilibrium market price and quantity for vegetarian subs will be $5 per sub and 3 million subs, respectively.

We can compute the consumer surplus in Figure 5–1 as follows. The maximum that a consumer is willing to pay for the first sub consumed is given by the height of the demand curve at a quantity of 1 sub, which is close to $8 (note that since the scale is in millions, the first sub is close to zero on the $x$-axis). Since the price actually paid for the first sub is $5, the consumer derives a "surplus" of $8 – $5 = $3. This $3 "surplus" is described by the vertical distance $AC$ in Figure 5–1. The consumer surplus for all 3 million subs consumed

**FIGURE 5–1**

## Consumer Surplus in the Vegetarian Sub Sandwich Market

Given the market price of \$5 per sub and the market quantity of 3 million subs, the consumer surplus is the area of the region below the demand curve and above the price for 3 million subs. This is the green shaded area of triangle *ABC*, which equals .5 × base × height, or .5 × 3 million subs × \$3 per sub = \$4.5 million.

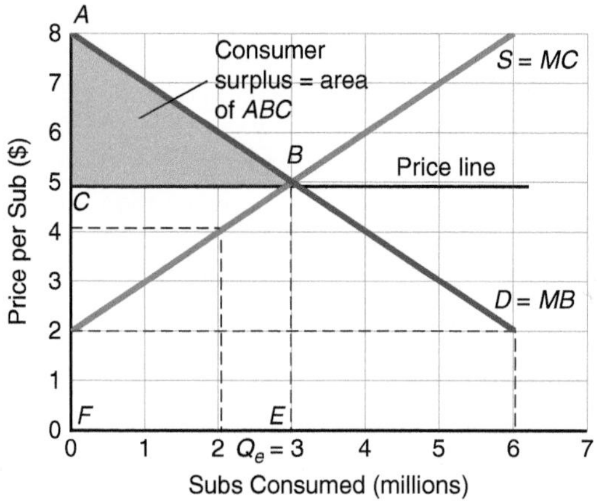


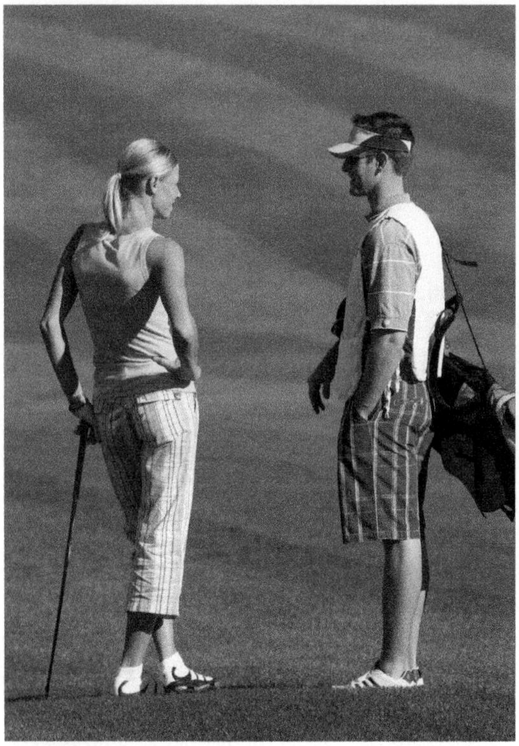

How can golf discounts reduce consumer well being?

would be equal to the area of the light green triangle *ABC* in Figure 5–1. Since the area of a triangle is .5 × base × height, the consumer surplus in this sub market is .5 × 3 million subs × \$3 per sub = \$4.5 million. In general, the consumer surplus is the area of the region below the demand curve and above the price line. This surplus stems from a negatively sloped demand curve, which implies that there exist different amounts of willingness to pay for different units of the same product.

Another way of determining the consumer surplus from Figure 5–1 is to subtract the total amount that consumers paid from the total consumer benefit or value derived from consuming the 3 million units of subs. The total consumer benefit or value equals the total area under the demand curve, over the 3 million subs quantity level, which equals the area of the region *ABEF*. The total amount paid by the consumers equals the area of region *BEFC*. The difference between the total consumer value (*ABEF*) and the total amount paid (*BEFC*) is the area of triangle *ABC*, which we now know is the consumer surplus. Viewed in this way, we can see that the \$3 million consumer surplus represents the additional consumer value or net benefit derived from consuming subs as opposed to alternate products. In this way, we can say that consumer surplus measures the net benefit (well being) to buyers when participating in a specific market.

### EXAMPLE 5–1 Price Discrimination: Do All Discounts Benefit the Consumer?

Pricing schemes such as "buy one, get one half-price" and "last minute discounts" are popular promotional strategies. In economics, these practices are called price discrimination. Price discrimination refers to the practice of selling different units of the same product at different prices, not justified by cost or supply differences. In other words, price discrimination is based on consumer differences in willingness to pay.

While price discrimination appears to benefit the consumer, it in fact reduces the amount of consumer surplus and enhances the firm's total revenue. In simpler terms, this "discount" price strategy adds to the profits of business firms at the expense of consumers, as the following hypothetical example will illustrate.

Figure 5–2 describes the daily demand and supply for weekday rounds of golf at Shady Meadows, a plush, 18-hole golf course that caters to retired couples. The supply curve is

*continued*

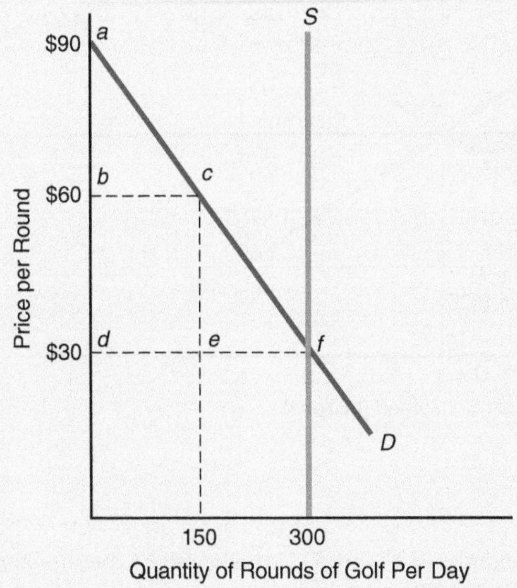


**FIGURE 5–2**
**Demand and Supply for 18-Hole Rounds of Golf at Shady Meadows**

perfectly inelastic, indicating that the number of rounds of golf available per day is *not* based on the price charged per round of golf, but instead is based on other factors such as the typical speed of play and the number of daylight hours.

**Single Price Policy:** If Shady Meadows wants to fully utilize the course (300 rounds per day) with a single price policy (no discrimination), then the price per round would have to be $30 to achieve an equilibrium quantity of 300 rounds per day. The consumer surplus under the single price policy is the area of triangle *adf*, which equals .5 × 300 rounds × $60 per round = $9000. The total revenue received by Shady Meadow would be $30 per round × 300 rounds per day = $9000 per day.

**Price Discrimination Policy:** Shady Meadows realizes that 150 golfers are willing to pay $60 or more to play a round each day. Therefore, instead of dropping the price of *all* rounds to $30 per day, Shady Meadows sells all rounds of golf per day to golf couples under the condition "buy one full round at $60, get the second one half-price." According to the demand curve, this implies that 150 golfers will end up paying $60 per round, and another 150 will pay $30 per round.

The total consumer surplus becomes the sum of the two triangular areas *abc* and *cef*, which equals (.5 × 150 rounds × $30 per round) + (.5 × 150 rounds × $30 per round) = $4500. This is $4500 less than the single price policy.

Where did this $4500 of value disappear? It has been transferred into the pockets of Shady Meadows, as its total revenue is now (150 rounds × $60 per round) + (150 rounds × $30 per round) = $9000 + $4500 = $13 500. Shady Meadows' total revenue is now $4500 more than the single price policy!

**For critical analysis:** Can you think of examples of "last-minute deals" or other discount schemes that can be explained by the price discrimination concept described in this example?

## Producer Surplus

We now turn to examine the well being of producers or suppliers in a specific market. **Producer surplus** refers to the difference between the actual amount that producers receive for a product and the lowest amount that they would be prepared to accept for it.

**Producer surplus** The difference between the actual amount that producers receive for a product and the lowest amount that they would be prepared to accept for it.

**Marginal cost** The minimum amount that firms must receive in order to supply a specified unit of quantity. It is the height of the supply curve at the specified unit of quantity.

**SUPPLY CURVE AND MARGINAL COST.** For any given unit of quantity, the height of the supply curve reflects the minimum amount (minimum price) that firms must receive in order to supply that unit of quantity. This is also called the **marginal cost** (MC) of that

**FIGURE 5–3**

**Producer Surplus in the Vegetarian Sub Sandwich Market**

Given the market price of \$5 per sub and the market quantity of 3 million subs, the producer surplus is the area of the region above the supply curve and below the price over the 3 million subs produced. This is the red shaded area of triangle *BCD* which equals .5 × base × height, which equals .5 × 3 million subs × \$3 per sub = \$ 4.5 million.

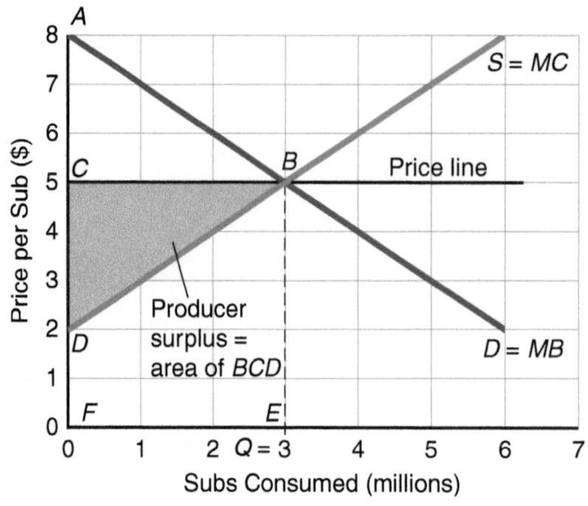


unit of quantity. For example, in Figure 5–1, the height of the supply curve at the quantity level of 2 million subs is \$4. This means that the firms must receive at least \$4 to entice them to cover the extra costs involved in reallocating resources from the next-best alternative so as to produce the 2 millionth sub. In other words, the marginal cost or opportunity cost of producing the 2 millionth sub is \$4, so the producers must receive at least this amount if they are to produce this unit of output. If producers receive less than \$4 for the 2 millionth sub, this will reduce the profit they receive. In general, the supply curve is the marginal cost curve for the product.

Thus, the producer surplus can be determined once the market supply curve and the market price and quantity is known. In the sub market in Figure 5–3, with the market price and quantity as \$5 per sub and 3 million subs, respectively, we can compute the producer surplus as follows.

To produce the first sub, the producer must receive a minimum amount equal to its marginal cost, which is \$2 (the height of the supply curve at a quantity of 1 sub). Since the price actually paid to a producer for the first sub is \$5, the producer derives a "surplus" of \$5 − \$2 = \$3. This \$3 "surplus" is described by the vertical distance between the supply curve and the \$5 price line at the quantity of 1 sub (the vertical distance *CD* in Figure 5–3). The producer surplus related to all 3 million units of subs produced would be equal to the area of the red triangle *BCD*. Since the area of a triangle is .5 × base × height, the producer surplus in this sub market is .5 × 3 million subs × \$3 per sub = \$4.5 million. In general, the producer surplus is the area of the region above the supply curve and below the price line. This surplus stems from a positively sloped supply curve, which implies that there exists a different marginal cost for different units of the same product. The producer surplus measures the benefit (well being) to producers of participating in a specific market.

## Market Equilibrium and Allocative Efficiency

As explained in Chapter 3, market equilibrium occurs where industry demand equals industry supply. This means that at equilibrium, the marginal benefit of the last unit purchased just equals the marginal cost of the last unit supplied. As Figure 5–4 illustrates, the sum of consumer and producer surplus is maximized at this equilibrium level, which is another way of saying that allocative efficiency occurs at this point.

> **Allocative efficiency occurs when the sum of consumer and producer surplus is maximized.**

Figure 5–4 describes the vegetarian sub sandwich market, where the equilibrium price is \$5 ($P_e$) and the equilibrium quantity is 3 million ($Q_e$). At this equilibrium, the sum of consumer and producer surplus is maximized at \$4.5 million + \$4.5 million = \$9 million. There is no better quantity of sub sales for maximizing both consumer and producer surplus. We will explain this further below.

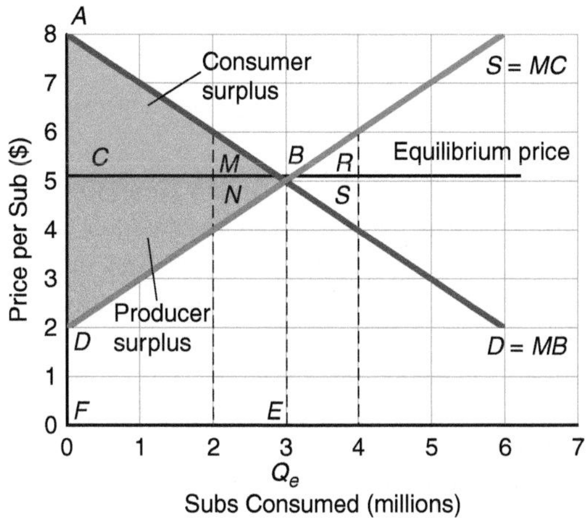


**FIGURE 5–4**

**Market Equilibrium and Allocative Efficiency**

In this sub industry example, the equilibrium price is $P_e = \$5$, and the equilibrium quantity is $Q_e = 3$ million subs. At this quantity, the sum of consumer and producer surplus is maximized, which implies allocative efficiency. If the quantity is reduced to 2 million subs, consumer surplus and producer surplus will be reduced by triangular areas *M* and *N*, respectively. If production is increased to 4 million subs, consumer and producer surplus will be reduced by triangular areas *S* and *R*, respectively.

**UNDERPRODUCTION SITUATION.** Figure 5–4 shows that if the quantity of sub sales is set at a level below 3 million—say, at 2 million subs—then the marginal cost of the next sub (2 million + 1) is approximately \$4 (the height of the supply curve); and the marginal benefit of the next sub is approximately \$6 (the height of the demand curve). The marginal cost of \$4 reflects the value of the output in the next-best product area (say, production of hamburgers), which the producer sacrifices (an opportunity cost) by using additional resources to produce the next (2 million + 1) sub. The marginal benefit of \$6 indicates that society places a \$6 value on the next (2 million + 1) sub produced.

This is an inefficient situation. As Figure 5–4 shows, if one more sub is produced, the extra \$6 value gained will exceed the \$4 value of lost production in the next-best product area (hamburgers). From society's view, there will be a net gain in value of approximately \$2 by allocating more resources to the sub sandwich industry and less to the hamburger industry. By not producing more than 2 million subs, this extra net gain in value (well being) is lost, and society is *underproducing* subs.

The total net loss of producing 2 million subs instead of the equilibrium quantity of 3 million subs is the loss in consumer and producer surplus, which is equal to the sum of the triangular areas *M* and *N* in Figure 5–4. This net loss is called **deadweight loss**, which is the decrease in consumer and producer surplus that results from a situation of allocative inefficiency.

**Deadweight Loss** The decrease in consumer and producer surplus that results from a situation of allocative inefficiency.

**OVERPRODUCTION SITUATION.** Figure 5–4 also shows that if the quantity of sub sales is set at a level above 3 million—say, at 4 million subs—then the marginal cost of the last sub (4 millionth sub) is approximately \$6 (the height of the supply curve); and the marginal benefit of the last sub is approximately \$4 (height of the demand curve). By allocating resources to produce the 4 millionth sub, the producer sacrifices \$6 of value in the hamburger industry to gain just \$4 worth of value in the sub industry. Overall, society is *overproducing subs*. By producing 4 million subs instead of the equilibrium quantity of 3 million subs, there is a deadweight loss equal to the sum of the triangular areas *R* and *S*.

## Market Failure

At this point, it is important to recognize that there are situations where laissez-faire market equilibrium does not achieve allocative efficiency. We call this type of situation **market failure**. The remainder of this chapter will examine types of market failure, including externalities, asymmetric information, public goods, and common property resources.

**Market failure** Situations where laissez-faire market equilibrium does not achieve allocative efficiency.

# 5.2 Externalities

**Externality** A situation in which the private costs or benefits related to the production or consumption of a good diverge from a social costs or benefits.

**Externalities** are situations where decisions made by the firms and households (who directly participate in a market) impose costs or confer benefits to outside third parties. In these situations, market equilibrium will either overproduce or underproduce the product or activity, resulting in a deadweight loss to society. There are two types of externalities: external costs and external benefits.

## External Costs

Consider pulp and paper firms operating in British Columbia that purchase wood chips and chemicals and hire labour in order to produce paper. In the manufacturing process, these firms discharge liquid effluent (waste) in nearby rivers, harming fish and other wildlife. As well, sludge waste is burned off, emitting cancer-causing and hormone-disrupting chemicals into the air.

Figure 5–5 illustrates the market for this paper. The supply curve, $S_1$, reflects the **private marginal costs**, which are the extra costs that the firms have to pay, such as the wood and labour costs. Based on $S_1$, the paper market, with no government intervention, would end up producing $Q_1$ tonnes of paper per year.

**Private marginal costs** The extra costs that the firms supplying the market must pay for.

But paper producers also impose additional costs on third parties in the form of water and air pollution. These costs are called **external costs**, and the producers do not account for them when deciding how much paper to produce.

**External costs** The additional costs that direct market participants impose on third parties.

**Social marginal costs** Private marginal costs plus external costs.

In Figure 5–5, the supply curve $S_2$ reflects the full **social marginal costs** of producing each unit of quantity of paper. The social marginal costs equal the private marginal costs plus the external costs related to each unit of quantity produced. Because of the external costs (extra pollution costs), the supply curve $S_2$ is higher than $S_1$ at each quantity level.

From society's view, the allocatively efficient quantity would be $Q_2$, where $S_2$ intersects the demand curve. Without government intervention, the firms end up producing $Q_1$, where $S_1$ intersects the demand curve. In other words, the laissez-faire market equilibrium will *overproduce* paper from society's viewpoint. By producing $Q_1$ tonnes instead of the socially optimum $Q_2$ tonnes, the paper industry will create a deadweight loss equal to the sum of the triangular areas $R$ and $S$ in Figure 5–5

**In general, where there are external costs, the private sector will tend to overproduce goods and services.**

One possible solution to this market failure problem is for the government to get involved in the paper market. For example, the government could impose a per tonne tax on the pulp and paper firms equal to the external costs per tonne of production. This would

**FIGURE 5–5**

**External Cost Situation in the Paper Industry**

With no government intervention, the private sector will make decisions based on the private costs and so will produce $Q_1$ tonnes of paper, where $S_1$ intersects $D$. Including the external costs, the full marginal social cost is reflected in the supply curve $S_2$. A laissez-faire market equilibrium will overproduce paper, with a deadweight loss equal to the sum of the triangular areas $R$ and $S$.

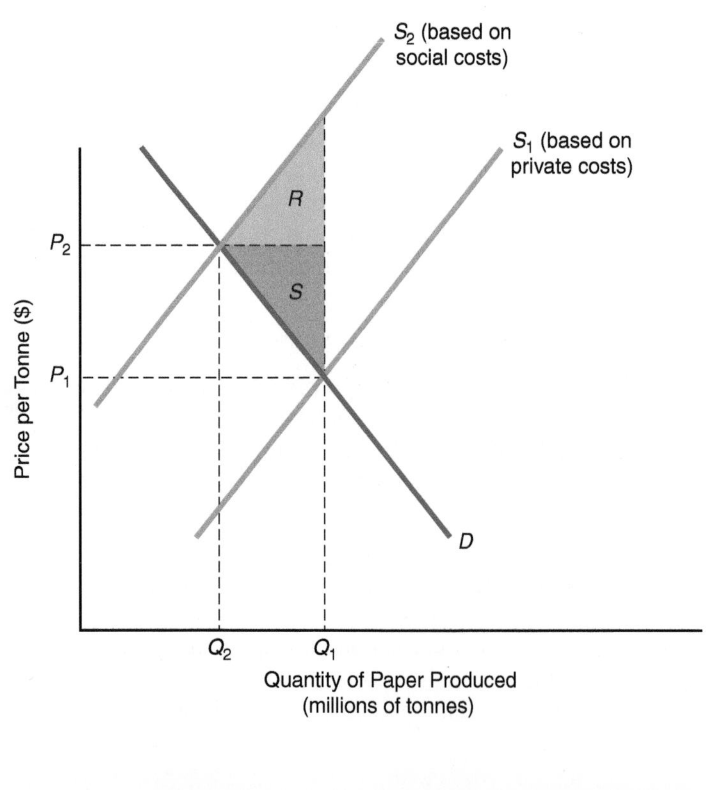

cause the firms to make their production decisions based on social marginal costs and therefore operate on the supply curve $S_2$. In turn, the firms would then produce $Q_2$, the allocatively efficient quantity.

As discussed in this chapter's Did You Know That . . . ? section, recent large-scale studies have found that cellphone use while driving can significantly increase the risk of vehicle crashes. This evidence implies that private activities such as dialling cellphones and texting while driving constitutes an external cost situation—creating risks for others. In the absence of government intervention, drivers will *overengage* in these dangerous activities, according to the theory just examined.

What external costs are associated with oil sands development?

### EXAMPLE 5-2 What's Wrong with Alberta's Oil Sands?

A former U.S. vice president once told Canadian journalists that "Gas from the tar sands [also known as oil sands] gives a Prius the same carbon footprint as a Hummer."

It is true that end products made from the oil sands, such as transportation fuels, are the same as those made from conventional oil. However, three times more greenhouse gas pollution (emissions of carbon dioxide) results from the production of a barrel of synthetic crude oil from the oil sands than for a barrel of pumped oil, making the oil sands a significant contributor to global warming. This is because the heat needed to extract bitumen from the tar sands and upgrade it to synthetic crude requires a huge amount of natural gas and coal.

In addition, depending on the depth of the extraction, between two and five barrels of fresh water is drawn from nearby rivers to produce one barrel of oil. Unfortunately, this water gets contaminated and ends up stored in vast "tailing ponds" that leak pollutants into the soil and nearby rivers, posing health risks to birds, water fowl, aquatic life, and possibly human life. On April 28, 2008, over 1600 ducks and geese died in an oil sands tailing pond the size of 640 football fields.

As of January 2013, oilsands mining operations have disturbed 715 square kilometres of boreal forest. The current area disturbed by oilsands mining is the same size as the urban area of the city of Calgary. In total, 4,700 square kilometres have been leased for oilsands surface mining operations as of January 2013. By 2022, it is expected that mining and in situ oilsands development will result in the daily clearing of 18.6 hectares of forest, or the equivalent of 34.5 football fields, every day. This deforestation further adds to the greenhouse gas impact, since forests are a source of carbon capture. The cleared forests can also no longer serve as a home to a wide variety of wildlife, such as woodland caribou and numerous species of birds and waterfowl.

An Environment Canada study published in 2016 found that Canadian oil sands is one of the largest sources of harmful air pollutants called secondary organic aerosols (SOAs). This type of air pollution is linked to respiratory problems such as asthma, as well as possible increased deaths caused by cardiovascular disease and lung cancer. The study reports that Alberta's oil sands generate 45 to 84 tonnes of SOAs a day, comparable to the daily output of this type of air pollution generated in the Greater Toronto Area.

**For critical analysis:** Sketch a demand and supply graph for the product "synthetic crude oil" produced from oil sands. Include a hypothetical demand curve, a supply curve reflecting the private costs of production, and another supply curve based on the social cost of production. Use this diagram to explain how production of synthetic crude oil under a laissez-faire policy contributes to market failure.

*continued*

Sources: Alberta Oil Sands. Oil Sands 101. Oilsands. Issue Areas. Pembina Institute. http://www.pembina.org/oil-sands/os101/alberta (accessed February 16, 2014); "Alberta's oil sands: black gold or black eye?" *CBC News*. Edmonton. March 3, 2010. http://www.cbc.ca/edmonton/features/dirtyoil/index.html; Oakland Ross. Oil sands threaten our survival Al Gore warns. Nov. 24, 2009. *Toronto Star*. http://www.thestar.com/news/sciencetech/environment/article/729836—oil-sands-threaten-our-survival-al-gore-warns?bn=1. Dan Woynillowicz. "The harm the tar sands will do." *The Tyee*. September 20, 2007. http://thetyee.ca/Views/2007/09/20/TarSands/; Alexandra Zabjek. "Industrial horror evoked." *Edmonton Journal*. March 2, 2010. FP; "Alberta's oil sands industry is a huge source of harmful air pollution, study says."Technology and Science. CBC News. Emily Chung. May 25, 2016. http://www.cbc.ca/news/technology/oilsands-soas-1.3599074. (Accessed on February 2, 2017).

## External Benefits

Externalities can also be positive in nature. For example, consider the Canadian market for flu vaccinations. Figure 5–6 describes the market for flu shots for a given flu season. At any unit of quantity, the height of the demand curve $D_1$ reflects the marginal benefit that the person receiving the flu shot receives. The demand curve shows the maximum amount that individuals would be willing to pay for the flu shot if the private sector supplied it. In other words, the demand curve $D_1$ reflects the **private marginal benefits** obtained by the individuals directly paying for and receiving the shot.

**Private marginal benefits** The marginal benefits that accrue to the direct consumers of the product or service.

With no government intervention, the private sector will make decisions based on the private marginal benefits, or $D_1$, and will supply and administer $Q_1$ flu shots over the flu season, where $D_1$ intersects $S$.

But for flu vaccinations, individuals who decided not to pay for the flu shot (third parties) still receive benefits from having others pay and get the flu shot, since the vaccinations could prevent a major flu epidemic. These benefits are called **external benefits**. The flu market producers and buyers do not account for these external benefits when deciding on how many flu shots to sell and buy.

**External benefits** The additional benefits that direct market participants confer on third parties.

**Social marginal benefits** Private marginal benefits plus external benefits.

In Figure 5–6, the demand curve $D_2$ reflects the full **social marginal benefits** of consuming each flu shot. The social marginal benefits equal the private marginal benefits plus the external benefits related to each vaccination. Because of the external benefits, the demand curve $D_2$ is higher than $D_1$ for each flu shot quantity level.

From society's point of view, the allocatively efficient quantity would be $Q_2$, where $D_2$ intersects the supply curve. Without government intervention, firms would produce $Q_1$, where $D_1$ intersects the supply curve. In other words, the laissez-faire market equilibrium

**FIGURE 5–6**

**External Benefit Situation: Flu Shots**

With no government intervention, the private sector will make decisions based on the private benefits and so will produce $Q_1$ flu shots, where $D_1$ intersects $S$. Including the external benefits, the full marginal social benefit is reflected in the demand curve $D_2$. A laissez-faire market equilibrium will underproduce flu shots, with a deadweight loss equal to the sum of the triangular areas $M$ and $N$.

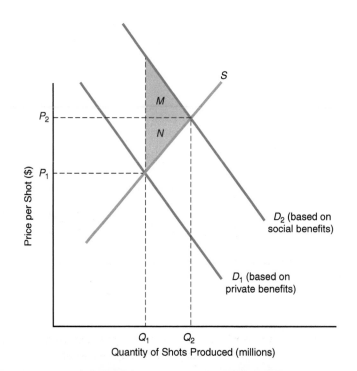

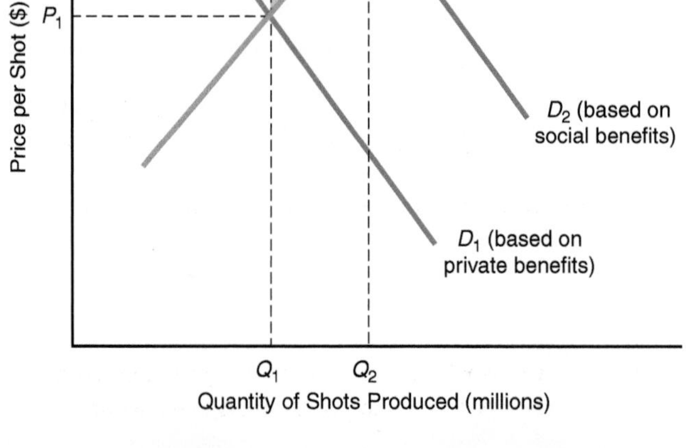

will *underproduce* vaccinations, due to the external benefits. By producing $Q_1$ instead of the socially optimum $Q_2$, the vaccination industry will creates a deadweight loss equal to the sum of the triangular areas $M$ and $N$ in Figure 5–6.

**In general, where there are external benefits, the private sector will tend to underproduce goods and services.**

As Policy Example 5–1 indicates, understanding the notion of external benefits sheds some light on matters relating to the funding of post-secondary education.

### POLICY EXAMPLE 5–1 Why Should the Public Financially Support Higher Education?

Between 1990 and 2012, the portion of funding that Canadian universities and colleges receive through government grants (i.e., from taxpayers) significantly declined, from 70 percent to 55 percent. As a result, universities and colleges are becoming increasingly dependent on private sector funding, high tuition fees, sales of university goods and services, and individual and corporate donations.

Yet the activities of universities and colleges result in external benefits to society, in addition to the private benefits to the paying student. A recent study entitled *The Economic Contribution of Canada's Colleges and Institutes* found that the training and knowledge that graduates receive from their post-secondary education adds over $123 billion of income to the Canadian economy, by providing industry with increased human capital. From the taxpayer's viewpoint, the increase in annual national income results in increased tax revenues, possibly reducing future tax rates. As well, the report suggests that those with higher education are less likely to smoke or abuse alcohol, draw welfare or unemployment benefits, or commit crimes. This translates into additional dollar savings to the taxpayer of approximately $215.1 million per year.

**For critical analysis:**

1. Sketch a demand and supply graph for the service higher education. Include a hypothetical supply curve, a demand curve reflecting the private benefits of higher education that accrue to students who pay and graduate, and another demand curve for the benefits to society. Use this diagram to explain how a policy requiring students to pay 100 percent of college and university operational costs (through tuition fees) would affect allocative efficiency.
2. Critically evaluate a policy requiring the government to pay 100 percent of college and university operational costs—a "free" tuition fee policy.

Sources: Funding for Post-Secondary Education. Fall 2013. Canadian Federation of Students. http://cfs-fcee.ca/wp-content/uploads/sites/2/2013/11/Fact-Sheet-Funding-2013-11-En.pdf (Accessed February 17, 2014). "Universities and colleges revenue and expenditures." Government Financial Statistics. Education, Training and Learning. Statistics Canada CANSIM Table 385-0007. http://www40.statcan.gc.ca/l01/cst01/govt31a-eng.htm; M. Henry Robison and Kjell A. Christopheren of EMSI. *The Economic Contribution of Canada's Colleges and Institutes*. Executive Summary. Association of Canadian Community Colleges. May 2008. http://www.accc.ca/ftp/pubs/studies/2008.econ.contrib/Canada_AGG_ES_2008_Final.pdf.

# 5.3 Asymmetric Information

Another source of market failures is exchange situations where one party possesses special knowledge that is not available to the other party. These are called situations of **asymmetric information**.

**Asymmetric information** Exchange situations where one party directly participating in the market possesses special knowledge that is not available to the other party.

The next section examines one important type of market failure due to asymmetric information—moral hazard.

## Moral Hazard

**Moral hazard** refers to situations where one party to a transaction has both the ability and incentive to shift costs to other parties. The private marginal cost of this party is less than

**Moral hazard** A situation where one party to a transaction has both the ability and incentive to shift costs to other parties.

the social marginal cost. As a result, moral hazard will tend to overallocate resources to certain market activities (overproduce) and result in allocative inefficiency.

For example, suppose that to prevent bank failures, the Canadian government implements a bank bailout policy of paying each bank monies equivalent to the amount of loss that the bank incurs on any loan made to the public. The government will always make a payout to the bank, regardless of the amount of loans made or the level of risk taken on each loan. Since banks can make a higher potential profit on riskier loans, this new bailout policy will encourage Canadian banks to create too many high risk loans, in essence misallocating depositors' funds and causing an excessive burden on taxpayers. The private marginal cost of creating additional risky loans is less than the social marginal cost, since the banks are able to shift loan default losses to taxpayers. In this case, the banks possess information relating to the degree of risk associated with its various loans that depositors and taxpayers are not aware of.

# 5.4 Non-excludable Goods and Services

**Private goods** Goods and services that are both excludable and rivalrous.

The above discussion of market equilibrium and allocative efficiency was based on private goods and services. **Private goods** are goods and services that are both excludable and rivalrous. A good is excludable if the owner can exclude non-payers from having it. For example, if you do not pay for a package of coffee at your local supermarket, you will not be able to take it out of the store and consume it. A good is rivalrous if one person's consumption reduces the amount available for other potential consumers. For example, if you purchase packages of coffee at the supermarket, this diminishes the amount of coffee available for others to purchase. But market failure can also arise with certain goods that are either non-excludable or non-rivalrous.

## Public Goods

**Public goods** Goods that are neither excludable nor rivalrous.

**Public goods** are goods that are neither excludable nor rivalrous. An example would be national defence. Once the government has created a powerful national defence system, it is not possible to exclude any of its citizens from benefiting from the security, regardless of whether they individually paid for it. Furthermore, when one citizen enjoys the benefits (feeling of security) derived from national defence, this does not diminish the amount of benefit that can accrue to a fellow citizen.

**FREE-RIDER PROBLEM.** The nature of public goods leads to the free-rider problem. A free rider is a person who takes advantage of the fact that others will shoulder the burden of paying for public goods, such as defence, while continuing to enjoy the benefits. Under these conditions, the free private market would most likely underproduce the public good from society's view, since many individuals who do not pay for the good still benefit from it. If we had to rely on the private sector to produce this public good, this would bring about an external benefit situation with a deadweight loss, as described in Figure 5–6. In

What type of market failure relates to the training of winning Olympic athletes?

general, if there are too many free riders, the private sector would not even bother to produce the public good, despite its value to society.

One solution to the public good problem is for the government to provide the public good through taxes collected from the general public. Examples of this solution include public defence and police and fire protection.

### POLICY EXAMPLE 5-2 Should Our Tax Dollars Pay for Own the Podium?

During the 2016-17 budget year, the Canadian federal government plans to spend over 57 million dollars on the "Own the Podium" program,which seeks to develop, train, and prepare high performance (elite) athletes for world class competition in the Olympics and Paralympics.

The Own the Podium program is a national effort begun in 2005 that was aimed at having Canada win the most medals at the Vancouver 2010 Winter Olympics. While the U.S. ended up winning the most medals at this Olympics, Canada did win the most gold medals ever won in a Winter Olympics. No doubt, this successful performance had a role to play in the Canadian government's decision to continue to use taxpayer dollars to help finance the Own the Podium program.

One economic argument supporting the use of taxpayer dollars for the Own the Podium program is that this program constitutes a public good that promotes national pride. Public funding eliminates the free rider problem—any Canadian could derive national pride from medals won by Canadian athletes, whether they paid for sports training or not. Moreover, one person's gain in national pride does not diminish another person's national pride, so rivalrous consumption does not occur.

**For critical analysis:**

1. Explain how the policy of using taxpayer dollars to "own the podium" may promote the goal of allocative efficiency.
2. What might be the opportunity cost of using tax payer dollars to support the Own the Podium program? Explain.

Sources: "Chapter 3.4: Supporting families and communities and standing up for those who helped build Canada." *Budget 2010*. Department of Finance Canada. March 4, 2010. http://www.budget.gc.ca/2010/plan/chap3d-eng.html; "About OTP." Own the Podium. The Vancouver Organizing Committee for the 2010 Olympic and Paralympic Games and Own the Podium 2010. http://www.ownthepodium2010.com/About/; "Funding." Own the Podium. http://www.ownthepodium.org/Funding. (Accessed on February 2017).

## Common Property Resources

**Common property resources** are goods or resources that are non-excludable but still rivalrous. For example, it is very difficult, if not impossible, to monitor and charge fishers for the fish they catch in a large ocean area. Yet as more fish are being caught by one fisher, fewer are available for others. Knowing this, each fisher has the incentive to catch as many fish as possible, as soon as possible, while fish stocks are available. This situation will lead to over-fishing (overproduction), with the looming danger of species extinction.

**Common property resources** Goods or resources that are non-excludable but are rivalrous.

To prevent the overuse of the fishing resources, governments typically intervene by requiring fishers to purchase licences and quotas. As well, governments have international agreements establishing national boundaries to limit fishing rights offshore. As Policy Example 5-3 suggests, an outright trade ban might be called upon to protect common property resources.

### POLICY EXAMPLE 5-3 A Global Trade Ban on the Porsche of the Oceans?

One hundred and seventy-five nations met in March, 2010, at the Convention on International Trade in Endangered Species (CITES) to vote on over 40 proposals for regulating trade in endangered species. One of these proposals includes a global ban on international trade involving the bluefin tuna.

*continued*

The bluefin tuna has often been called the "Porsche of the oceans," as each fish carries a $100 000-plus price tag. Bluefin tuna are also the size of a Porsche (3 metres long and weighing 680 kilograms) and as fast as a Porsche (accelerating from 0 to 96 km in 5 seconds).

Scientists have observed that the bluefin tuna stocks have fallen by more than 80 percent over the last 40 years, largely due to overfishing in vulnerable ocean waters. Between 1994 and 2006, the European Union (EU) bluefin tuna fishing industry received government subsidies totalling 34.5 million euros. It is suspected that more than one-third of these subsidies were provided to vessel owners recently convicted of illegal fishing activities. The vast majority of the subsidies were used for the construction and modernization of vessels, which worsened the over-fishing problem.

Japan opposes the proposed trade ban, which will only occur if supported by two-thirds of the 175 countries voting. Currently, 80 percent of the tuna catch is exported to Japan, where it is consumed by sushi lovers at a price of $200 to $300 per kilogram.

On March 18, 2010, at the Convention on International Trade in Endangered Species, the majority of the voting countries voted against the trade ban on bluefin tuna.

Research published in April 2016 indicates a catastrophic drop in bluefin tuna stocks in the North Pacific Ocean exceeding 97 percent. Ninety percent of tuna currently being fished are young fish that have not yet reproduced. The scarcity of the bluefin tuna is evidenced by an all time high price of 1 million British pounds that was paid for one bluefin tuna at the first auction of 2013 at Tsukiji fish market, in Tokyo, Japan.

**For critical analysis:**

1. What type of market failure is responsible for the significant reduction in the bluefin tuna stocks? How have European government policies contributed to this problem?
2. Explain how a global trade ban on bluefin tuna could contribute to a solution to this example of market failure.

Sources: "Bleak outlook for sushi favourite as bluefin tuna levels drop 97 per cent." News.The Telegraph. by Danielle Demetriou, Tokyo. April 22, 2016. http://www.telegraph.co.uk/news/2016/04/22/bleak-outlook-for-sushi-favourite-as-bluefin-tuna-levels-drop-97/ (Accessed February 2, 2017); "Overfishing takes toll on Bluefin tuna." Mongabay.com. August 5, 2007. http://news.mongabay.com/2007/0806-tuna.html; "EU confirms support for bluefin tuna trade ban." EurActiv with Reuters. March 11, 2010. http://www.euractiv.com/en/sustainability/eu-confirms-support-bluefin-tuna-trade-ban-news-329139; Doha. "Governments not ready for trade ban on bluefin tuna." Press Release. Convention on International Trade in Endangered Species of Wild Fauna and Flora. March 18, 2010. http://www.cites.org/eng/news/press/2010/20100318_tuna.shtml. (Accessed September 4, 2010.)

## ISSUES AND APPLICATIONS

# The Great Global Recession of 2009

### Concepts Applied: Rational Behaviour, Incentives, Demand and Supply, Moral Hazard, Allocative Inefficiency

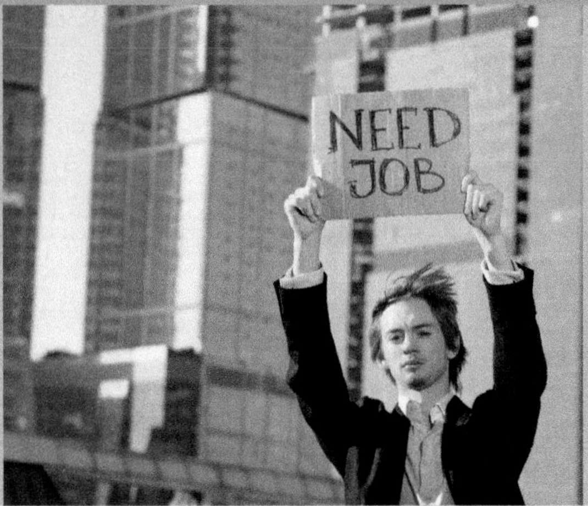

In 2010, one out of every 10 adults in the U.S. labour force was looking for work.

## The Financial Crisis

Between 2006 and 2009, the global economy faced the largest financial crisis and economic recession in the post–world-war era. The financial declines appeared to start in the U.S. housing markets, where home prices fell an average of 32 percent between the summer of 2006 and the first quarter of 2009. Through to October 2009, Las Vegas, Phoenix, and Miami saw home prices plummet 55.4 percent, 51.3 percent, and 46.9 percent from their 2006 peak. Total home equity in the United States, which was valued at $13 trillion in 2006, had dropped to $8.8 trillion by mid-2008 and was still falling in 2009.

As the U.S. housing bubble burst, stock markets crashed worldwide. Between October 6 and 10, 2008, the U.S. Dow Jones Industrial Average stock index plunged 18 percent, the largest one-week drop in the history of the index. During the period of October 2007 to the first quarter of 2009, the U.S., Canadian, German, and French stock markets dropped 58 percent, 48 percent, 55 percent, and 57 percent, respectively.

As housing and financial markets collapsed, large brand-name blue chip financial institutions were being pushed to the brink of disaster. On September 15, 2008, the once highly respected Lehman Brothers investment bank went bankrupt. One day later, the U.S. government provided an $85 billion loan to American International Group (AIG), the largest insurance company in the U.S. In October 2008, the U.S. government approved a $700 billion dollar plan to bail out other troubled financial institutions.

## The Economic Crisis

The financial crisis eventually led to a global economic recession. A recession is defined as six consecutive months of negative growth in Real Gross Domestic Product (Real GDP). During the period from 2008 Quarter 2 to 2009 Quarter 3, the Real GDP in Canada, the United States, the United Kingdom, Germany, and Japan declined by 3.5 percent, 3.8 percent, 6.2 percent, 6.7 percent, and 8.4 percent, respectively. As annual production plummeted, 2009 unemployment rates increased significantly. From 2000 to 2008, the unemployment rate averaged 6.9 percent in Canada and 5.1 percent in the United States. In 2009, the unemployment rate jumped to 8.3 percent in Canada and 9.1 percent in the United States. In 2010, the U.S. rate is expected to increase further to 9.9 percent. To prevent further unemployment, both the Canadian and U.S. governments have provided billions of dollars of bailout monies to large non-financial corporations, such as GM and Chrysler.

Of course, the one trillion dollar question is, "What caused the financial crisis, which in turn resulted in the economic recession?" While economic observers have identified numerous factors as being responsible for the crisis, we will explain the role that market failure and misguided incentives appear to have played. In order to do so, we must first examine the meaning of the following terms: non-recourse mortgage, mortgage foreclosure, traditional prime mortgage model, sub-prime mortgage securitization model, and housing bubble.

## Non-Recourse Mortgage

A non-recourse home mortgage is a loan to purchase a home, where the loan is backed by the value of the home. Once the home is purchased, the purchaser has an obligation to make regular monthly payments over a set period of time. A portion of each monthly payment goes toward interest to the lender, and the remainder goes toward paying back the principal amount borrowed. Once the principal amount of the mortgage loan is paid off, the borrower owns the home outright and the monthly payments come to an end.

## Mortgage Foreclosure

If the borrower fails to make the monthly payments on the mortgage (loan default), the lender (e.g., the bank) has the option of foreclosing: the lender can sell the home and use the proceeds to pay off the amount owing. If the proceeds from selling the home are not sufficient to pay back the full principal amount borrowed, the bank takes a financial loss or reduction in its equity, often called a "capital loss." If a lender has to deal with significant capital losses, it can go bankrupt.

## Traditional Prime Mortgage Model

Traditionally, commercial banks in the United States created mortgage loans based on the amount of deposits they had. The banks also held onto these loans until they matured, so they were responsible for capital losses if the borrower defaulted. To minimize their risks, the banks created only prime mortgage loans—loans to home purchasers who have good credit histories, who have significant down payments, and whose monthly mortgage loan payments comprise a small portion of their total monthly household income.

## Sub-prime Mortgage Securitization Model

In the run-up to the financial crisis, banks had loosened these rules. They created sub-prime mortgages—mortgage loans issued to borrowers with poor credit histories and weak documentation of income, who were shunned by the "prime" bank lenders. In a significant number of cases, these borrowers put down very little, if any, down payment. Sub-prime loans were often adjustable-rate mortgage (ARM) loans. ARM loans typically carry a very low initial interest rate called a "teaser rate" (say, for the first two years), but the interest rate is later adjusted to a significantly higher rate. In March 2007, it was estimated that U.S. financial institutions had issued $1.3 trillion worth of sub-prime mortgages.

Moreover, banks started the practice of reselling mortgages. Large pools of the sub-prime mortgage loans issued by commercial banks were resold, at a profit, to other financial institutions, such as investment banks that do activities similar to commercial banks, but are not as tightly regulated by the U.S. government. Investment banks do not have to hold as much capital (financial cushion) to cover possible losses as the commercial banks do. Examples of investment banks include Bear Stearns, J.P. Morgan, Lehman Brothers, and Goldman, Sachs & Co. These investment banks repackaged the mortgage loans into mortgage-backed securities (MBS) or bonds and then resold them to investors in global securities markets. This process of selling investors' shares in the monthly mortgage payments received from borrowers (home purchasers) has been commonly termed "securitization of mortgage loans." The value of these mortgage-backed securities—MBSs—depended on the ability of homeowners to pay their monthly mortgage payments.

Initially, investors were interested in purchasing these MBSs due to their relatively high rate of return and the fact that they were at least partially backed by real estate. As well, the reputable private sector bond rating firms, such as Moody's Investors Services and Standard & Poor's, gave high quality AAA ratings to MBSs. The investors who purchased these securities included various banks, insurance companies, pension funds, and investors all across the globe. Later, MBSs became known as "toxic assets" once their poor value became apparent.

## The U.S. Housing Bubble

Between 2000 and 2006, many regions in the United States encountered a housing boom, with record numbers of new housing starts and record home prices. This rise in housing prices has been termed the "U.S. housing bubble." By 2006, house prices soared to well over twice their normal ratio to rents. Between 1997 and 2006, the price of the typical American house increased by over 120 percent. Factors causing the bubble included low borrowing costs in the form of low interest rates; lax lending policies on the part of banks, which increased the number of eligible buyers; and low gains on stock markets, which encouraged investors to seek higher rates of return in real estate.

## The U.S. Housing Bubble Bursts

By the middle of 2006, U.S. home prices had risen to unaffordable and unsustainable levels, especially for those with sub-prime mortgages. Prior to 2001, the median home price ranged from 2.9 to 3.1 times median household income. By 2004, this ratio had risen to 4.0 in 2004, and to 4.6 by 2006.

Once the housing bubble burst, home prices in the United States declined significantly. By September 2008, average U.S. housing prices had declined by over 20 percent from their mid-2006 peak. This decline put many borrowers in a negative equity situation: their mortgage debt was higher than the market value of the home. As of March 2008, an estimated 8.8 million borrowers—10.8 percent of all homeowners—had negative equity in their homes.

Borrowers in this situation had an incentive to walk away from their mortgages and abandon their homes, which resulted in foreclosures. This was especially true for people with sub-prime mortgages who had made very small down payments. This large number of foreclosures, in turn, put too many houses on the market through bank sales, causing housing prices to fall even further, which caused yet another round of foreclosures, and so forth. With approximately 12 million U.S. households in negative equity in 2008, the U.S. mortgage market was in store for a record number of home foreclosures, which would result in very large financial losses for financial institutions and other investors in mortgage-backed securities.

As soon as it became publically known that brand-name, blue-chip investment banks were selling "toxic assets" in the form of MBSs that were backed by nonperforming sub-prime mortgages, and that these securities were embedded in global financial markets, potential investors withdrew from private security markets and fled to "safer" government bonds and treasury bills. This mass behaviour created the global stock market crashes in October 2008. Suddenly, less of the public's savings were available through security markets for ongoing business operations and expansions. As a result, there were mass layoffs. Many countries experienced significant declines in real GDP and increases in unemployment rates.

## Moral Hazard

Lax lending standards in the form of sub-prime mortgage loans significantly contributed to an increased demand for housing and therefore the housing bubble and its eventual burst. Economic observers have suggested that mortgage standards became lax because of market failure in the form of moral hazard. Each link in the sub-prime mortgage chain collected profits and at the same time passed on risk to other parties. The original lenders (commercial banks) did not concern themselves with the quality of the loans, as they quickly resold these loans at a profit to investment banks. Investment banks were eager to buy these "risky" mortgages because they could increase their profits by slicing them into mortgage-backed securities. It is interesting to note that the rating agencies were paid handsomely by the investment banks to give high ratings to these MBSs.

## Misguided Incentives

Wall Street executives working in the investment banks received extravagant bonuses based on the volume of the MBSs they could create and sell, not on the long-term related profits yielded by these new types of investments. Moreover, these bonuses were skewed toward cash payouts rather than stock options. Thus, if the MBSs did not perform well, these bonuses would not be affected. It is estimated that Wall Street executives took home MBS-related bonuses totalling $23.9 billion in 2006.

## The Canadian Situation

To date, Canada's financial institutions have been better able to cope with the global financial crisis compared to U.S. institutions. The fall in home prices, as well as the increase in unemployment, has been significantly lower in our country than in the United States.

The Canadian counterparts to the commercial banks in the United States are the large, national chartered banks, such as RBC, TD, Scotiabank, CIBC, and Bank of Montreal. These Canadian financial institutions have tended to favour the traditional mortgage lending model. Sub-prime mortgages make up a much smaller percentage of Canadian mortgages. As well, the practice of securitizing mortgages into mortgage-backed loans is less widespread in Canada than in the United States.

As well, the Canadian government, through the Bank of Canada, imposes higher capital requirements (larger financial cushions) and more cautious lending rules on the chartered banks than the U.S. government demands of American banks. By law, a Canadian mortgage loan that exceeds 80 percent of the value of the home must carry mortgage insurance. Approximately 67 percent of Canadian mortgage insurance is provided by the CMHC, which is backed by the Canadian government. Due to the more stringent mortgage insurance practices in Canada, it is more difficult for Canadians to obtain mortgage loans if they cannot afford to pay the monthly payments.

By the end of 2016, the Canadian government had further tightened mortgage lending in Canada by implementing the following policies: increasing premiums (the amount a borrower must pay) for mortgage default insurance; reducing the maximum amortization period for insured mortgages from 40 years to 25 years; requiring banks to qualify all borrowers applying for an insured mortgage at the Bank of Canada's conventional five-year fixed posted mortgage rate, an interest rate that is typically higher than what they will actually be paying; requiring a down payment of at least five per cent of the home purchase price (a further 10 per cent must be added to the down payment for the portion of the house price between $500,000 and $999,999); limiting borrowing to a maximum of 80 per cent of the value of their homes when refinancing; and making government-backed mortgage insurance available only for homes with a purchase price of less than $1 million.

Sources: *S&P/Case-Shiller Home Price Indices 2009, A Year In Review*. Standard & Poor's. January 2010. http://img.en25.com/Web/StandardandPoors/S&P_Case_Shiller_2009_Review.pdf; "Major indices." Financial Market Report. TheFinancials.com http://www.thefinancials.com; Glenn Hubbard and Anthony Patrick O'Brien. *Teaching Notes for the Current Financial Crisis*. Pearson Education. October 16, 2008; "Chart 2.6: Overall Contraction in Real GDP During the Recession." "Chapter 2: Recent Economic Developments and Prospects." *Budget 2010*. Department of Finance Canada. http://www.budget.gc.ca/2010/plan/chap2-eng.html; *Global Forecast Update*. Global Economic Research. Scotiabank Group. February 3, 2010. http://www.scotiacapital.com/English/bns_econ/forecast.pdf; Kimberly Amadeo. "The Auto Bailout." About.com. December 31, 2009. http://useconomy.about.com/od/criticalssues/a/auto_bailout.htm;"Canadian auto industry gets bailout too." CNN.com/world. December 20, 2008. http://www.cnn.com/2008/WORLD/americas/-12/20/canada.auto.bailout/index.html; "Will subprime mess ripple through economy?" Associated Press. March 13, 2007. http://www.msnbc.msn.com/id/17584725;http://www.economist.com/specialreports/displaystory.cfm?story_id=9972489. (Accessed February 1, 2009; Ben Steverman and David Bogoslaw. "The financial crisis blame game." *Bloomberg Businessweek*. October 18, 2008. http://www.businessweek.com/investor/content/oct2008/pi20081017_950382.htm?chan=top+news_top+news+index+-+temp_top+story. (Accessed February 1, 2009.); "A helping hand to homeowners" *The Financial Express*. October 28, 2008. http://www.financialexpress.com/news/a-helping-hand-to-homeowners/378549/#; Edmund L. Andrews and Louis Uchitelle. "Rescues for homeowners in debt weighed." *New York Times*. February 22, 2008. http://www.nytimes.com/2008/02/22/business/22homes.html?_r=1 (Accessed February 1, 2009); "Worldwide financial crisis largely bypasses Canada. *Washington Post*. October 16, 2008. http://www.washingtonpost.com/wp-dyn/content/article/2008/10/15/AR2008101503321.html. "Issue Brief: Changes to Canada's Mortgage Market" Research and Advocacy. Canadian Bankers Association. (Accessed January 31, 2017).

**For critical analysis:**

1. Sketch a graph that shows a market demand and supply curve and an initial equilibrium for U.S. homes. Based on the contents of this Issues and Applications, identify at least three separate factors that have contributed to the U.S. housing bubble. On your graph, indicate how the demand or supply curve shifted as a result of each separate factor identified.
2. Explain how moral hazard has affected allocative efficiency in the mortgage lending market.
3. Critically evaluate this statement: "The financial crisis is a result of irrational behaviour." Why is it important to know whether the behaviour witnessed is based on irrational or rational behaviour?
4. Due to the global recession, both the United States and Canada have spent billions of dollars bailing out both financial and non-financial corporations. What concept explored in this chapter suggests that these types of bailouts will be detrimental to the economy? Explain.

# SUMMARY

Here is what you should know after reading this chapter. MyEconLab will help you identify what you know, and where to go when you need to practise. We suggest that as soon as you review one of the Learning Objective sections below, you then proceed to go through the related section in MyEconLab.

myeconlab

| LEARNING OBJECTIVES | KEY TERMS | MYECONLAB PRACTICE |
|---|---|---|
| **5.1 Market Equilibrium and Allocative Efficiency.** Consumer surplus refers to the difference between the maximum amount that consumers are willing to pay and the actual amount paid for all units of a product consumed. This surplus measures the net benefits to buyers of participating in the market. Producer surplus refers to the difference between the actual amount that producers receive for | consumer surplus, 113<br>marginal benefit, 113<br>producer surplus, 115<br>marginal cost, 115<br>deadweight loss, 117<br>market failure, 117 | • **MyEconLab** Study Plan 5.1 |

| LEARNING OBJECTIVES | KEY TERMS | MYECONLAB PRACTICE |
|---|---|---|
| a product and the lowest amount that they would be prepared to accept for it. This surplus measures the net benefits to sellers of participating in the market. Market equilibrium promotes allocative efficiency by maximizing consumer and producer surplus. Market failure refers to situations where the free market equilibrium does not promote allocative efficiency, so dead-weight losses result. Examples of market failure include externalities, asymmetric information, public goods, and common property resources. | | |
| **5.2 External costs and benefits and allocative efficiency.** External costs refer to market situations where the social marginal cost of producing a good or service exceeds the private marginal cost. A laissez-faire free market equilibrium will tend to overproduce the good or service if external costs are involved. External benefits refer to market situations where the social marginal benefit of producing a good or service exceeds the private marginal benefit. A laissez-faire free market equilibrium will tend to underproduce the good or service if external benefits are involved. | private marginal costs, 118<br>external costs, 118<br>social marginal costs, 118<br>private marginal benefits, 120<br>external benefits, 120<br>social marginal benefits, 120 | • **MyEconLab** Study Plan 5.2 |
| **5.3 Moral hazard and allocative efficiency.** Moral hazard refers to a situation where one party to a transaction has both the ability and incentive to shift costs to other parties. In this type of situation, the private marginal cost related to market behaviour is less than the social marginal cost. As a result, moral hazard will tend to overallocate resources to certain market activities and, in this way, result in allocative inefficiency. | asymmetric information, 121<br>moral hazard, 121 | • **MyEconLab** Study Plan 5.3 |
| **5.4 Public goods and common property resources and allocative efficiency.** Public goods, such as national defence, are goods or services that are neither excludable nor rivalrous. The free market will underproduce public goods due to their non-rivalrous nature as well as the free-rider problem. Common property resources, such as fish stocks in oceans, are rivalrous and non-excludable. The free market will overuse common property resources to the point of possible extinction. | private goods, 122<br>public goods, 122<br>common property resources, 123 | • **MyEconLab** Study Plan 5.4 |

# PROBLEMS

(Answers to the odd-numbered problems appear at the back of the book)

**LO 5.1 Use the concepts of consumer and producer surplus to explain how market equilibrium can promote allocative efficiency.**

1. The following diagram describes the weekly market demand and supply for the popular sports drink PowerPlus in a mid-sized Canadian city.

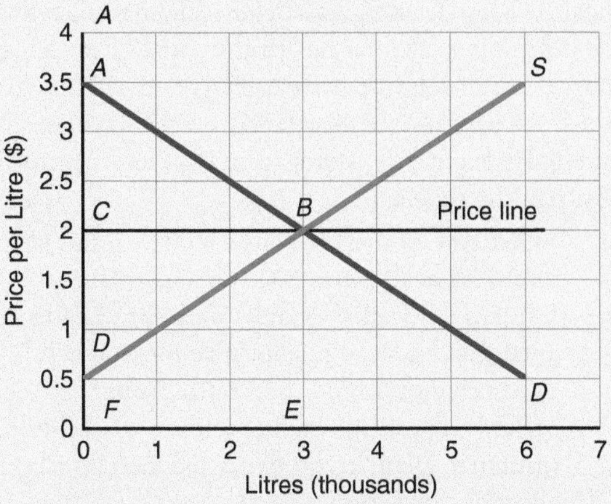


a. What is the maximum amount that consumers are willing to pay for the one thousandth litre of PowerPlus?
b. What is the marginal benefit of the two thousandth litre of PowerPlus?
c. What is the consumer surplus derived from consuming the two thousandth litre of PowerPlus at a price of $2?
d. What is the minimum amount that sellers of PowerPlus must receive in order supply the one thousandth litre of PowerPlus?
e. What is the marginal cost of the two thousandth litre of PowerPlus?
f. What amount of producer surplus is derived from supplying the one thousandth unit of PowerPlus at a price of $2?
g. What would be the allocatively efficient quantity level (litres per week)? Briefly explain.
h. What would be the maximum total amount of producer and consumer surplus (combined) that is possible in this sports drink market? Briefly explain.
i. If the government fixed the weekly quantity level at 2000 litres per week, what would be the total amount of deadweight loss?

2. The following diagram describes the daily market demand and supply for a large soya latte prepared and sold by Third Cup Coffee Bar, located at numerous outlets on the campus of a large university.

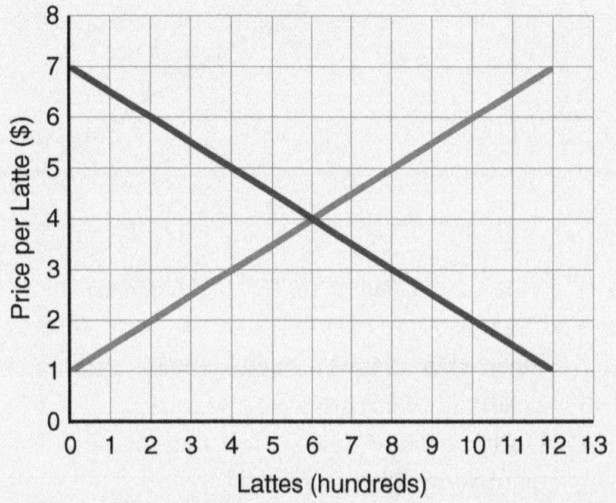


a. What is the maximum that consumers are willing to pay for the two hundredth latte?
b. What is the marginal benefit of the four hundredth latte?
c. What is the consumer surplus derived from consuming the four hundredth latte at a price of $4?
d. What is the minimum amount that sellers of the soya latte must receive in order to supply the two hundredth latte?
e. What is the marginal cost of the four hundredth latte?
f. What is the producer surplus derived from supplying the two hundredth latte at a price of $4?
g. What would be the allocatively efficient quantity level be (lattes per day)? Briefly explain.
h. What would be the maximum total amount of producer and consumer surplus (combined) that is possible in this soya latte market? Briefly explain.
i. If the government fixed the weekly quantity level at 800 lattes per day, what would be the total amount of deadweight loss?

**LO 5.2 Compare and contrast the effects that external benefits and external costs have on achieving allocative efficiency in a free market, laissez-faire environment.**

3. In the market diagram below, $D_1$ reflects the private marginal benefits derived by consumers, who directly

participate in this market. $D_2$ reflects the overall marginal social benefits related to each quantity produced.

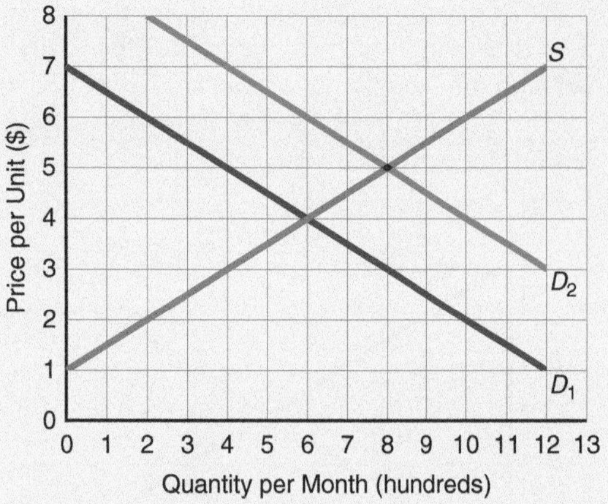


a. Does this diagram relate to an external cost or external benefit situation? Explain.
b. Under a laissez-faire free market situation, what quantity will be produced?
c. What will be the socially optimum (allocatively efficient) quantity level?
d. If the market produced the quantity identified in part b) above, compute the deadweight loss.

4. The diagram below describes the weekly market demand for a national coal market.

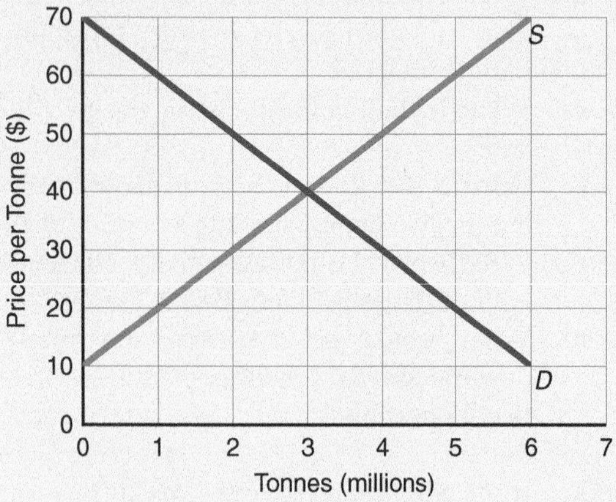


In addition to the private marginal costs indicated (i.e., supply curve, S), there are external air pollution costs of $20 per tonne at each quantity.

a. Sketch the marginal social costs curve in the diagram above.
b. What is the socially optimum (allocatively efficient) coal production level?
c. What is the amount of the deadweight loss associated with the laissez-faire free market equilibrium?

**LO 5.3 Explain how a type of asymmetric information called moral hazard can affect the efficient allocation of resources.**

5. Consider an individual who exercises regularly and rigorously adheres to a healthy diet during a period when she is not covered by any sickness/disability health insurance plan. The individual loses a day's pay for each workday she misses due to sickness. Based on her healthy lifestyle and perfect work attendance record, she qualifies for a lifelong health insurance plan that reimburses her one day's pay for each day missed due to sickness. As soon as she is covered by this insurance plan, she quits exercising, starts to smoke, and begins to eat less healthy foods.
   a. What type of market failure relates to this sickness/disability health insurance plan? Explain.
   b. Explain how this sickness/disability health insurance plan can lead to allocative inefficiency.
   c. What changes could the health insurance company make to the terms of the sickness/disability health insurance plan in order to reduce the degree of allocative inefficiency?

6. In bargaining with the provincial medical association, the provincial government agrees to implement a malpractice insurance plan where the government reimburses each surgeon the full amount of any malpractice lawsuit launched due to surgery errors and complications.
   a. What type of market failure may result from this new provincial malpractice insurance plan? Explain.
   b. Explain how this new provincial malpractice insurance plan could lead to allocative inefficiency.
   c. What changes could the health insurance company make to the terms of the malpractice insurance plan in order to reduce the degree of allocative inefficiency?

**LO 5.4 Compare and contrast the effects that public goods and common property resources have on achieving allocative efficiency in a free market, laissez-faire environment.**

7. Which of the following two situations will typically lead to the overproduction of a good or service—public good or common property resource? Explain.

# BUSINESS APPLICATION

**LO 5.2 Compare and contrast the effects that external benefits and external costs have on achieving allocative efficiency in a free market, laissez-faire environment.**

## Financial Management: External Benefits and Government Financial Support

One of the practical areas of business finance is concerned with finding creative ways to raise the funds needed to implement profitable business ventures. When a project results in significant *external benefits* to the local economy, the firm might be successful in acquiring financial support from the local government, as a way of capturing some of these external benefits. The following example describes how one can apply a commonly used financial math method called *present value of an annuity* to estimate the maximum amount of financial assistance that the firm can expect to receive from the government.

### Example

Darin Keetz, the owner of the city's major league hockey team, is requesting taxpayer dollars to help finance a new downtown hockey arena. Based on economic analysis undertaken by the city's department of economic development, Darin estimates that the new arena will attract a massive amount of new downtown development in the form of new hotels with casinos, luxury condos, office towers, medical clinics and laboratories, and shopping malls that offer entertainment, restaurants, shopping outlets, and indoor swimming and waterslide facilities.

Darin's own finance department projects that the new downtown development will increase downtown property values to the point of increasing the revenue that the city receives from property taxes by $100 million a year over the next 10 years. This amount would be considered an external benefit related to the arena project. Determine the maximum amount of financial support that Darin could seek from the local government to build the new hockey arena, assuming an interest rate of 9 percent.

### Solution

Find the present value of an annuity consisting of 10 annual third-party benefits worth $100 million each, as described below. Note that $R$ stands for periodic payment, $n$ = number of payments, and $i$ is the interest rate that money can be invested at over a long term.

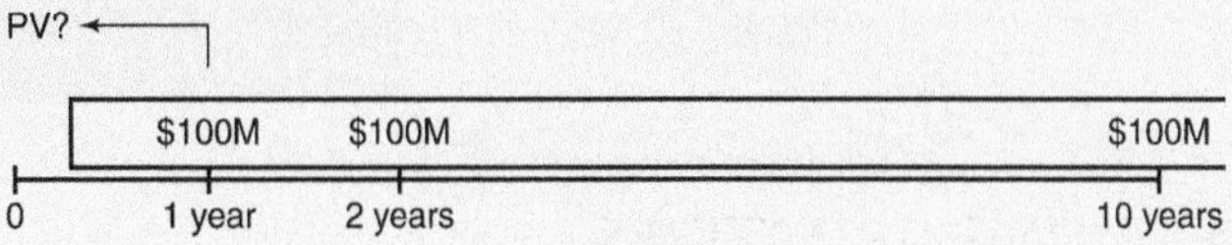


The present value of an annuity formula is as follows:

$$PV = \$R\left(\frac{1-(1+i)^{-n}}{i}\right) = \$100 \text{ million} \times \left(\frac{1-(1+.09)^{-10}}{.09}\right)$$
$$= \$641.77 \text{ million}$$

Based on the above calculation, the maximum amount of financial assistance that Darin can expect to get from the government is $641.77 million.

### Business Application Problem

A western Canadian city has approached Ridaway Rodeos in a bid to host the new North Pacific Championship Rodeo. Ridaway projects an annual external benefit of $3 840 000 for the city's economy caused by the new rodeo event. If the bid to host the rodeo is successful, it will stay in the city for the next 10 years. Determine the maximum amount of financial support that Ridaway could seek from the local government, based on the amount of the external benefit, assuming an interest rate of 10 percent.

# 6

## LEARNING OBJECTIVES

After reading this chapter, you should be able to:

**6.1** Explain the role of markets, intermediaries, and prices in the price system.

**6.2** Compare and contrast price ceiling and price floor policies.

**6.3** Compare and contrast the offer-to-purchase and the marketing board price support policies.

**6.4** Describe the various types of quantity restrictions that governments can impose on markets.

**6.5** Explain how price elasticity governs the effects that a per-unit excise tax has on tax incidence, resource allocation, and government tax revenue collected.

# Extensions of Demand, Supply, and Elasticity

Hospital and bed closures, crowded emergency rooms, health-care worker strikes, physician emigration to the United States, and growing waitlists for a variety of medical treatments have all become part of the daily news across Canada. Politicians, academics, and concerned citizens are debating the merits of using market incentives to address these reported problems. Michael Moore's blockbuster movie documentary *Sicko* urges a movement away from the practice of "for-profit" health care but some politicians consider privatization the best way to improve services.

The concepts presented in this chapter will enhance your ability to understand and evaluate the problems and proposed solutions relating to Canada's health-care system.

myeconlab

MyEconLab helps you master each objective and study more efficiently. See end of chapter for details.

# DID YOU KNOW THAT...?

In 2015 about 3.8 million Canadians, representing roughly 13 percent of the population aged 15 years and older, were smokers. Nine percent reported smoking daily, while 4 percent reported smoking occasionally. This is the lowest national smoking rate ever recorded. Approximately 15.6 percent of men aged 15 years and older were smokers, compared to 10.4 percent of women. Smokers consumed on average 14 cigarettes per day. In 2015 young adults aged 20–24 years reported the highest smoking rate, at 18.5 percent, compared to the 28 percent rate reported in 2008. In the 20–24 years age group, there was a significant decrease in the smoking rate among males; it fell to 23 percent from 32 percent in 2008. The current smoking rate among youth aged 15–19 years is 10 percent, the lowest rate on record since Health Canada first started reporting for this group. Many attribute the declining smoking rates to government policies such as excise taxes on cigarettes, a topic to be studied in this chapter.

Sources: Canadian Tobacco, Alcohol and Drugs Survey (CTADS) http://healthycanadians.gc.ca/science-research-sciences-recherches/data-donnees/ctads-ectad/tables-tableaux-2015-eng.php. (Accessed January 12, 2017).

# 6.1 The Price System

A **price system**, otherwise known as a *market system*, is one in which relative prices are constantly changing to reflect changes in supply and demand for different commodities. The prices of those commodities are the signals to everyone within the system as to what is relatively scarce and what is relatively abundant. Indeed, it is the *signalling* aspect of the price system that provides the information to buyers and sellers about what should be bought and what should be produced. In a price system, there is a clear-cut chain of events in which any changes in demand and supply cause changes in prices. Those price changes, in turn, affect the opportunities that businesses and individuals have for profit and personal gain. Such changes influence our use of resources.

**Price system** An economic system in which relative prices are constantly changing to reflect changes in supply and demand for different commodities.

## Exchange and Markets

The price system features **voluntary exchange**, acts of trading between individuals that make both parties to the trade subjectively better off. The **terms of exchange**—the prices we pay for the desired items—are determined by the interaction of the forces underlying supply and demand. In our economy, the majority of exchanges takes place voluntarily in markets. A market encompasses the exchange arrangements of both buyers and sellers that underlie the forces of supply and demand. Indeed, one definition of a market is a low-cost institution for facilitating exchange. A market in essence increases incomes by helping resources move to their highest-valued uses by means of prices. Prices are the providers of information.

**Voluntary exchange** Acts of trading between individuals that make both parties to the trade subjectively better off.

**Terms of exchange** The prices we pay for the desired items.

## Transaction Costs

Individuals turn to markets because markets reduce the cost of exchanges. These costs are sometimes referred to as **transaction costs**, which are broadly defined as the costs associated with finding out exactly what is being exchanged as well as the cost of enforcing contracts. If you were Robinson Crusoe and lived alone on an island, you would never incur a transaction cost. For everyone else, transaction costs are just as real as the costs of production. High-speed, large-scale computers have allowed us to reduce transaction costs by increasing our ability to process information and keep records.

**Transaction costs** The costs associated with finding out exactly what is being exchanged as well as the cost of enforcing contracts.

Consider some simple examples of transaction costs. The supermarket reduces transaction costs relative to your having to go to numerous specialty stores to obtain the items you desire. Organized stock exchanges, such as the Toronto Stock Exchange (TSX), have reduced transaction costs of buying and selling shares and bonds. In general, the more organized the market, the lower are the transaction costs. One group of individuals who constantly attempt to lower transaction costs are intermediaries.

## The Role of the Intermediary

As long as there are costs to bringing together buyers and sellers, there will be an incentive for intermediaries, often called middlemen, to lower those costs. This means that intermediaries specialize in lowering transaction costs. Whenever producers do not sell their products directly to the final consumer, there are, by definition, one or more intermediaries involved. Farmers typically sell their output to distributors, who are usually called wholesalers, who then sell those products to the retailers, or grocery stores.

Recently, technology has reduced the need, and hence the job prospects, for intermediaries in the travel agent business, as seen in Example 6–1.

### EXAMPLE 6–1 Booking Your Airline Flight—An Agent? Or the Web?

For decades, most airline travellers bought their tickets from an independent travel agent, not from the airline itself. On August 27, 2001, Air Canada announced plans to slash the maximum commission it paid to travel agents by half—from 10 percent to 5 percent. In 2002, Air Canada discontinued paying commissions to travel agents for tickets issued in Canada, claiming that this was necessary to remain competitive with other North American airlines, such as American, Continental, and Delta. The purpose of these moves by North American airlines was to encourage consumers to book their flights directly from the airlines' websites.

Topaz International, a leading provider of consultant and audit services to the corporate global travel industry, conducts yearly comparative studies of corporate travel airfares booked through travel agencies and various public Internet sites, including airline websites and travel sites such as Orbitz, Expedia, and Travelocity. Using the results from 2008, Topaz found that business travel itineraries booked through a designated corporate travel agency cost an average of $61 less than the same itinerary booked on an airline's website or other travel website. Moreover, for over 91 percent of the itineraries studied, the travel agency booking resulted in the same or lower fares. This was the eighth consecutive annual study conducted by Topaz International that has confirmed the cost savings that travellers realize when using the services of a professional travel agency.

Air Canada resumed paying commissions to travel agents in June 2009. As of January 2017, Topaz International on its corporate website, continues to claim that travel agency fares consistently beat rates displayed on the web.

**For critical analysis:** List a number of reasons why travellers might benefit from booking their air travel through travel agents rather than directly from the airline websites. Why might they have an even greater preference of booking through agents rather than through hotel websites when they are making accommodation plans?

Sources: CBC News Online Staff. "Travel agents sue over commission cuts." March 5, 2003; Buyers beat web fares, Topaz audits show." Topaz International. http://www.etopaz.com/assets/pdf/internet_audit.pdf; "Air Canada Resumes Paying Travel Agents." *Calgary Herald*. June 5, 2009. Pg. D1. Internet Travel Audits. Topaz International. http://www.etopaz.com/audits/internet. (Accessed January 12, 2017).

## The Rationing Function of Prices

A shortage creates a situation that forces price to rise toward a market clearing, or equilibrium, level. A surplus brings into play forces that cause the price of a product to fall toward its market clearing level. The synchronization of decisions by buyers and sellers that creates a situation of equilibrium is called the *rationing function of prices*. Prices are indicators of relative scarcity.

An equilibrium price clears the market. The plans of buyers and sellers, given the price, are not frustrated.[1] It is the free interaction of buyers and sellers that sets the price

[1]There is a difference between frustration and unhappiness. You may be unhappy because you cannot buy a Rolls-Royce, but if you had sufficient income, you would not be frustrated in your attempt to purchase one at the current market price. By contrast, you would be frustrated if you went to your local supermarket and could get only two cans of your favourite soft drink when you had wanted to purchase a dozen and had the necessary income.

that eventually clears the market. Price, in effect, rations a commodity to demanders who are willing and able to pay the highest price. Whenever the rationing function of prices is frustrated by government-enforced price ceilings that set prices below the market clearing level, a prolonged shortage situation is not allowed to be corrected by the upward adjustment of the price.

You should note that if prices are not allowed to ration goods, services, or resources, other forms of rationing will have to be used. Admission to universities and colleges is often rationed not by tuition (a dollars-and-cents-price) but by grade point average. The highest "bidders" for admission—those with the highest GPAs—are accepted.

There are other ways to ration goods. *First-come, first-served* is one method. *Political power* is another. *Physical force* is yet another. Cultural, religious, and physical differences have been and are used as rationing devices throughout the world.

Consider first-come, first-served as a rationing device. In countries that do not allow prices to reflect true relative scarcity, first-come, first-served has become a way of life. We call this *rationing by queues,* where *queue* means "line." Whoever is willing to wait in line the longest obtains meat that is being sold at less than the market clearing price. All who wait in line are paying a higher *total* price than the money price paid for the meat. Personal time has an opportunity cost. To calculate the total price of the meat, we must add up the money price plus the opportunity cost of the time spent waiting.

In this chapter's Issues and Applications, it is noted that Canada's current medicare system prohibits using prices to ration the services provided by doctors and hospitals. That is, patients are not allowed to pay a price or user fee to gain immediate access to the medical, diagnostic, or surgical services provided by specialist physicians. As a result, rationing by queues has become prevalent in the Canadian health-care system. Indeed, it is estimated that in 2009, Canadians waited an average of 26.1 weeks from the time they received a referral from their general practitioner to the time they received treatment from a medical specialist.

*Lotteries* are another way to ration goods. You may have been involved in a rationing-by-lottery scheme during your first year in college when you were assigned a parking pass for campus lots. Selling raffle tickets for popular college sweatshirts is also a method of rationing by lottery.

Rationing by *coupons* has also been used, particularly during wartime. In Canada, during World War II, families were allotted coupons that allowed them to purchase specified quantities of rationed goods, such as meat and gasoline. To purchase these goods, you had to pay a specified price *and* give up a coupon.

## The Essential Role of Rationing

In a world of scarcity, there is, by definition, competition for what is scarce. After all, any resources that are not scarce can be had by everyone at a zero price in as large a quantity as everyone wants, such as air to burn in internal combustion engines. Once scarcity arises, there has to be some method to ration the available resources, goods, and services. The price system is one form of rationing; the others that we mentioned are alternatives. Economists cannot say which system of rationing is the best. They can, however, say that rationing via the price system leads to the most efficient use of available resources. This means that generally in a price system, further trades could not occur without making somebody worse off. In other words, in a freely functioning price system, all of the gains from mutually beneficial trade will be exhausted.

**TICKET SCALPING.** The issue of using the price system to ration a limited good often arises when the media publicizes the practice of ticket scalping. If you have ever tried to purchase sold-out tickets to a major league playoff game or a superstar's rock concert, you probably know about the practice of ticket scalping.

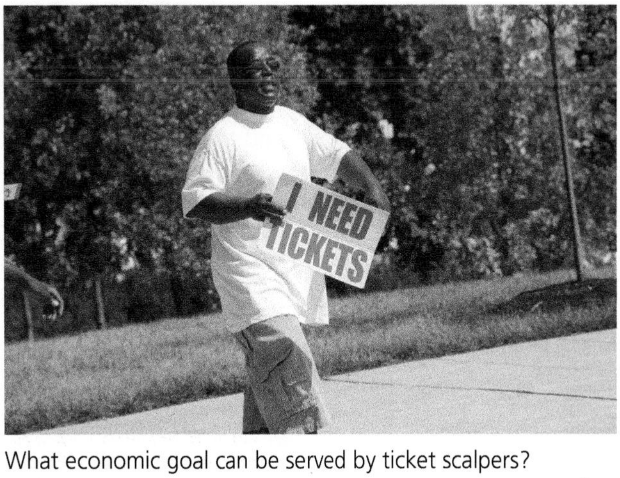

What economic goal can be served by ticket scalpers?

**FIGURE 6–1**

## Shortage of Tickets for the 2003 Heritage Classic Hockey Event

No matter what the ticket price, the available total quantity of tickets is at $Q_1$, which is the stadium capacity. The Heritage Classic tickets were originally offered for sale at the "face value" of $135. Just days before the event, the quantity demanded at the ticket price of $135 is $Q_2$. Without ticket scalpers, there would be a shortage ($Q_2 - Q_1$). If ticket scalping occurs, the ticket price can increase to the equilibrium price of $2500.

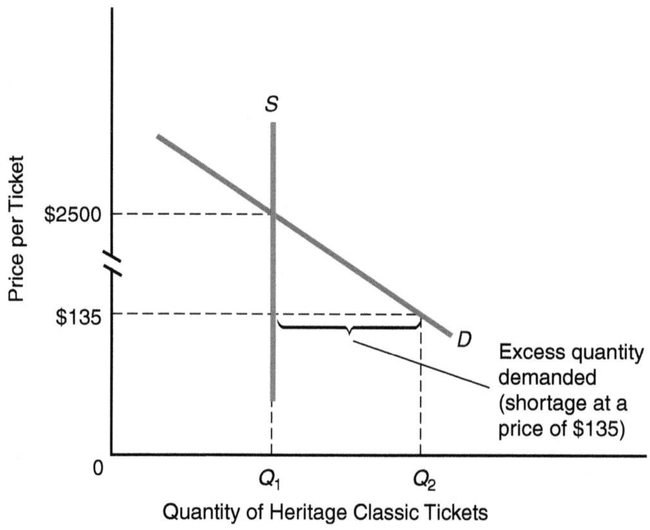


For many of these venues, ticket prices are initially set below the equilibrium price so that long lineups develop at ticket counters. These queues increase the media hype surrounding the event. As the day of the big event approaches, scalpers who paid the original price, or "face value," for the tickets end up selling those tickets at a much higher price, either online or just outside the gates, netting a handsome profit.

For example, when tickets were first issued for the 2003 Heritage Classic, the NHL's first outdoor game and star-studded hall-of-famers' match, good seats were selling for $135 each. At this price, the event planners reported that they could have sold 700 000 seats, more than 10 times the capacity of Edmonton's Commonwealth Stadium, where the games were to be played. Just days before the event, online scalpers were asking up to $2500 a ticket—almost 20 times the original price!

Figure 6–1 describes the market conditions for the Heritage Classic just before game day. If there had been no scalping of tickets, the price of each ticket would have remained at the face value of $135, with a shortage of tickets equal to ($Q_2 - Q_1$). However, according to Figure 6–1, there were potential ticket buyers who were willing to pay up to $2500 per ticket to be part of a moment that might come only once in a lifetime. Ticket scalpers were intermediaries who eliminated the shortage situation by getting the Heritage Classic tickets into the hands of consumers who tended to value the tickets the most (i.e., at a price of $2500).

### EXAMPLE 6–2 Is Ticketmaster in Cahoots with Scalpers?

In a number of Canadian provinces, ticket scalping is illegal. As result, in February 2009, Canadian ticket purchasers launched a $500-million class action against Ticketmaster. The suit alleges that the popular ticket seller is encouraging scalping of its tickets by limiting the original sale of tickets at face value on its main website and encouraging customers to buy scalped tickets at much higher prices at its subsidiary website, TicketsNow.com. For example, Ticketmaster came under fire for the way it handled ticket sales for Leonard Cohen's Canadian tour. On February 25, 2009, the tickets sold out the minute they officially went on sale at a face value of $99. However, some fans were able to buy these same tickets two days earlier via TicketsNow at the inflated price of $568 each.

In 2012 a court order directed Ticketmaster to pay an $850,000 settlement. The settlement requires Ticketmaster to pay $36 per ticket (less a minor amount for legal costs) to Canadians who purchased tickets from TicketsNow, depending on the time period and purchase location. Canadians began to receive cheques in early 2013.

*continued*

For many economists, anti-scalping laws seem unwarranted. The buying and selling of scalped tickets is purely voluntary. This implies that both the buyer and the seller expect to gain from the exchange, or it would not occur. In other words, ticket scalping is simply the price system's way of efficiently rationing a scarce commodity.

**For critical analysis:** Sketch a graph showing Leonard Cohen tickets that have a face value of $99 being scalped for $568.

Sources: Canadians get cheques in Ticketmaster class action. Arts & Entertainment. CBC News. January 31, 2013. http://www.cbc.ca/news/arts/canadians-get-cheques-in-ticketmaster-class-action-1.1406139 (Accessed February 17, 2014); "Ticketmaster facing $500-million class-action lawsuit." CanWest News. Don Mills, ON.: February 9, 2009; Linda Nguyen. "Ontario begins probe of *Ticketmaster* sales practices; Ticket outlet served with $500-million lawsuit in province." *Vancouver Sun*. March 3, 2009. Pg. C6.

# 6.2 Price Ceilings and Price Floors

The rationing function of prices is often not allowed to operate when governments impose price controls. **Price controls**—government-mandated minimum or maximum prices that may be charged for goods and services—typically involve setting a **price ceiling**—the maximum price that may be allowed in an exchange. The world has had a long history of price ceilings applied to some goods, wages, rents, and interest rates, among other things. Occasionally, a government will set a **price floor**—a minimum price below which a good or service may not be sold. These have most often been applied to wages and agricultural products. Let us consider price controls in terms of price ceilings.

**Price controls** Government-mandated minimum or maximum prices that may be charged for goods and services.

**Price ceiling** The maximum price that may be allowed in an exchange.

**Price floor** A minimum price below which a good or service may not be sold.

## Price Ceilings: Rent Controls

In order to understand and evaluate a price-ceiling situation, we will use the example of a rent control policy. **Rent control** refers to the placement of a price ceiling or maximum price on rents.

**Rent control** The placement of a price ceiling or maximum price on rents.

Figure 6–2 describes a hypothetical market situation relating to two-bedroom apartment units in a Canadian city. If there is no government intervention, the equilibrium monthly rental price of a two-bedroom unit is $800 per month. At this price, 60 000 quality two-bedroom units are being supplied and demanded for rental purposes each month.

In response to pressure due to public complaints that apartment rents are excessive, the provincial government decides to implement a price ceiling policy for two-bedroom apartment units. This rent control policy consists of legislating a maximum rental price of $650 per month. Any landlord who charges a monthly rent more than $650 for two-bedroom units would face large fines. The intent of the rent controls is to promote a

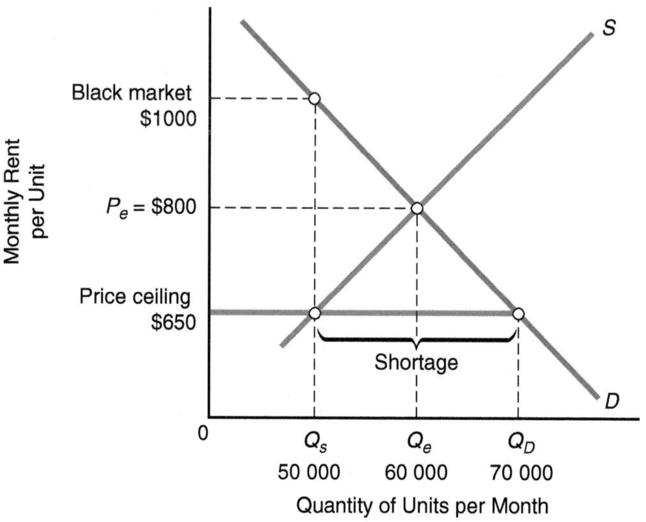


**FIGURE 6–2**

**Price Ceiling Policy: Rent Controls on Two-Bedroom Apartments**

If there is no government intervention in this apartment market, the equilibrium monthly rent will be $800 per month and the equilibrium quantity will be 60 000 units per month. Under rent controls, with a price ceiling of $650 per month, landlords will wish to supply only 50 000 quality two-bedroom rental units per month, while tenants will demand 70 000 units per month. A shortage of 20 000 units per month will eventually emerge. Moreover, once the quantity supplied is reduced to 50 000 units per month, according to the demand curve, there will be consumers who will pay a black market price up to $1000 per month.

more equitable distribution of income or simply "equity." That is, the government hopes to use the price ceiling policy as a means of ensuring that quality two-bedroom units remain affordable to lower-income families. By reducing the monthly rent charged, there will be a transfer of income from higher-income landlords to lower-income tenants (consumers).

What can we predict about the effects of the rent control policy, on the basis of the theory of supply and demand? In Figure 6–2, the price or rent of each two-bedroom unit is now set at $650 per month, which is below the equilibrium price. As is the case with any effective price ceiling policy, the maximum price will only replace the free market price if it is set below the equilibrium. As Figure 6–2 illustrates, at a monthly rent of $650 per month, 50 000 quality two-bedroom units will tend to be supplied per month (in the long run), while 70 000 apartment units would be demanded per month. A shortage of 20 000 units per month will result in the long run.

**Nonprice-rationing devices** Methods used to ration scarce goods that are price controlled.

The price ceiling policy leads to fewer exchanges and **nonprice-rationing devices**, which are methods used to ration scarce goods that are price controlled. With the rent controls imposed, the price system is no longer allowed to eliminate the shortage of apartment units. In other words, the available supply of apartment units is rationed according to nonprice criteria, such as first-come, first-served, or "rent only to friends," or "rent to desirable-looking people," and so forth. Typically, queuing or long line-ups develop, which means that many of those potential tenants wishing to rent two-bedroom apartments may have a lengthy wait before a rental unit becomes vacant.

**Black market** A market in which the price-controlled good is sold at an illegally high price through various under-the-table methods.

Typically, an effective price ceiling policy leads to a black market. A **black market** is a market in which the price-controlled good is sold at an illegally high price through various under-the-table methods. In our rental apartment example, landlords may charge "key money," which can be a relatively large lump-sum illegal cash payment that must be made before a tenant is allowed to obtain the keys for the apartment. If the illegal key money is included in determining the actual monthly rent, we would call this monthly amount the black market price. As the demand curve in Figure 6–2 indicates, after the rent controls are imposed and a reduced supply of 50 000 units occurs, there will be tenants who will be willing to pay a black market price of up to $1000 per month. In other words, the actual monthly rent that is being charged (with the key money included) is more than the free market price of $800 per month!

It should be noted that black market behaviour is not limited to apartment units. In any market where price ceilings are imposed, there is the potential for black markets. If, due to an energy crisis, the price of gasoline is controlled, a hidden cash payment to the gas attendant may be required to gas up one's car. If beef shortages develop due to ceiling prices on beef, the butcher may give special service to a customer who offers the butcher free tickets for great seats at an upcoming rock concert. Indeed, the number of ways in which the true, implicit price of a price-controlled good or service can be increased is infinite, limited only by the imagination.

**RENT CONTROLS AND EFFICIENCY.** Let us return to the example of rent controls in order to describe how a price ceiling policy can result in an inefficient allocation of scarce resources. In housing markets, equilibrium rental prices can promote allocative efficiency by serving three functions: (1) to promote the construction of new housing in response to increased consumer demand, (2) to promote the efficient maintenance of the existing supply of housing, and (3) to ration the current supply of housing to the highest-valued uses.

Rent controls have discouraged the construction of new rental units. Rents are the most important long-term determinant of profitability, and rent controls have artificially depressed them. Consider some examples. Halifax, with less than 15 percent of the population of Toronto, built proportionally more rental units than Toronto in 1995. This, in spite of a 7.2 percent vacancy rate in Halifax, compared with a 1.2 percent vacancy rate in Toronto. The major difference? There were no rent controls in Halifax, while rent increases were strictly controlled in Toronto. In the same year, Vancouver, with 70 percent of the population of Toronto, saw the construction of 11 000 rental units; only 4000 were built in Toronto. Again, the difference was that there were no rent controls in Vancouver.

Due to growing concerns over the negative impact that rent controls can have on the construction of new apartments, the Manitoba government changed its rent ceiling policy in 2004 so as to exempt newly constructed apartment buildings from the controls for a period of 15 years.

When rental rates are held below equilibrium levels, property owners cannot use higher rents to recover the cost of maintenance, repairs, and capital improvements. Hence, they curtail these activities. In the extreme situation, taxes, utilities, and the expenses of basic repairs exceed rental receipts. The result is abandoned and/or deteriorating buildings. In situations where landlords do maintain their apartment buildings, they often decide to sell these units as condominiums and recoup their investment that way. This has the effect of severely reducing the supply of rental housing, thus making the housing shortage even worse.

Like any other price, rents ration output: in this case, the allocation of apartments among prospective tenants. When the rent is held at an arbitrarily low level, the number of prospective tenants increases, and excess demand develops. Students, for example, who might otherwise live with their families, decide they can afford to live on their own. In this situation, rationing of the available supply of rental housing is achieved through nonprice mechanisms, such as queuing or making under-the-table payments to landlords.

**ATTEMPTS AT EVADING RENT CONTROLS.** The distortions produced by rent controls lead to efforts by both landlords and tenants to evade the rules. This, in turn, leads to the growth of expensive government bureaucracies whose job it is to make sure that those rules are, indeed, followed. In 1995, the Ontario government spent about $1.8 million administering its *Residential Rent Regulation Act*.

In the 1980s, Ontario landlords had an incentive to speculate on the real estate market. They bought and sold apartment buildings, driving up prices and financing costs. Then, they applied for rent increases to cover the rising costs. Tenants, for their part, routinely tried to sublet all or part of their rent-controlled apartments at fees substantially above the rent they paid to the owner. They pocketed the difference, perhaps to help pay for a more expensive apartment.

**RENT CONTROLS AND EQUITY.** The big losers from rent controls are clearly landlords. But there is another group of losers—low-income individuals, especially single mothers, trying to find their first apartment. Some observers now believe that rent controls have worsened the problem of homeless people in such cities as Toronto.

Poor individuals cannot afford a hefty key money payment, nor can they assure the landlord that they will pay their rents on time or even regularly. Because controlled rents are usually below market clearing levels, there is little incentive for apartment owners to take any risk on low-income individuals as tenants. As a result, economists question whether rent ceilings actually promote equity, especially in the long run.

Who benefits from rent control? Ample evidence indicates that upper-income professionals benefit the most. These are the people who can use their mastery of the bureaucracy and their large network of friends and connections to exploit the rent control system. These are also the people who can easily afford to pay key money or to pay an agency to locate an apartment for them.

Because the private sector was unwilling to finance construction of new rental units in an environment of rent controls, the Ontario government had to spend up to $3.5 billion per year subsidizing the building of nonprofit housing. Rents might have been controlled at lower-than-market levels, but renters and homeowners alike paid higher than necessary taxes to fund the government's subsidies.

Policy Example 6–1 provides an example of a price ceiling policy recently applied in Canada to the services of people engaged in assisted human reproduction.

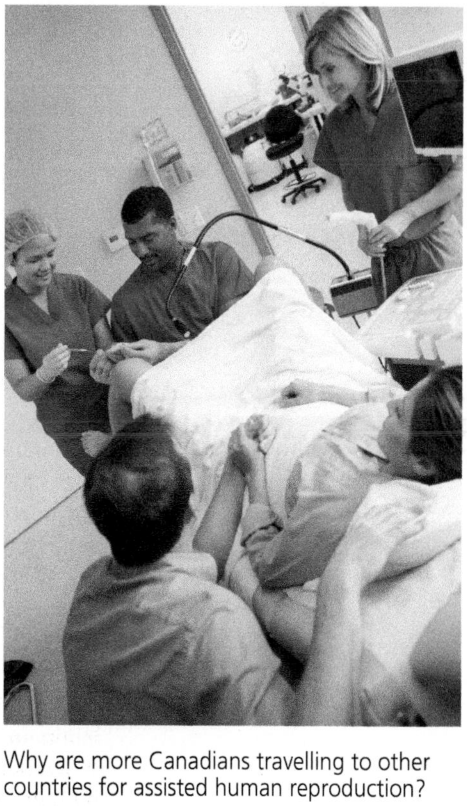

Why are more Canadians travelling to other countries for assisted human reproduction?

**POLICY EXAMPLE 6–1 Assisted Human Reproduction Not for Sale in Canada?**

In an attempt to regulate and control reproductive technologies, the Canadian government passed the *Assisted Human Reproduction Act* in 2004. Among other things, this legislation bans human cloning and prohibits Canadian infertility clinics from offering monetary payments to sperm and egg donors.

Critics of this act have warned that it will significantly reduce hope for numerous infertile couples residing in Canada, especially those who fall in the lower income brackets. Before the passage of this law, many U.S. companies were involved in matching U.S. women willing to sell their eggs with Canadian couples planning to undergo in vitro fertilization (IVF) at a cost of up to US$6000. These U.S. companies arranged for the donor to travel to a Canadian clinic, where her eggs were retrieved in a surgical procedure performed by a Canadian doctor. Under the *Assisted Human Reproduction Act,* this process becomes illegal, because the donor is getting paid. In economic terms, the act imposes a price ceiling of zero dollars for the act of donating eggs for fertilization within Canada.

Under this legislation, many Canadian couples have now found it much more expensive to undergo IVF because they must travel to the United States (or another country) to have the procedure done. In 2009, it was reported that Canadian couples were paying US$30 000 for egg donation and IVF in Seattle clinics. Since many Canadians cannot afford to complete an IVF treatment cycle in another country, these couples go "underground," finding donors online and paying them under the table. To date, there is much concern that this legislation threatens the health and welfare of Canadians because it encourages Canadian couples to find their own doctors, clinics, and donors underground or in an unregulated market in a foreign country.

In December 2013, a Canadian fertility consulting company pleaded guilty to the first-ever prosecution case under Canada's Assisted Human Reproduction Act. The Canadian firm was charging commercial rates for the services of egg and sperm donors and surrogate mothers. In addition, the company received tens of thousands of dollars for referring Canadian couples who ended up paying U.S. "brokers" as much as $150,000 for babies born to surrogates located in foreign countries.

**For critical analysis:** Sketch a graph of the demand and supply of the services of egg donors in Canada. Illustrate how the *Assisted Human Reproduction Act* affects this graph.

Sources: Canadian fertility consultant received $31K for unwittingly referring parents to U.S. 'baby-selling' ring. Tom Blackwell. December 15, 2013. Canada. News. National Post. http://news.nationalpost.com/2013/12/15/canadian-fertility-consultant-received-about-30000-for-unwittingly-referring-parents-to-u-s-baby-selling-ring/ (Accessed February 17, 2014); Heather Sokoloff. "Fertility tourists expected to flock to U.S. clinics." *National Post*. October 31, 2000; Kathryn Blaze Carlson. "Baby by stealth; Reproduction law forcing 'dangerous alternatives.'" *National Post*. March 13, 2010. Pg. A1.

## Price Floors: Minimum Wage

**Minimum wage** The lowest hourly wage rate that firms may legally pay their workers.

As we noted above, price controls can take the form of price floors, where a minimum price is fixed above the equilibrium price. An example of price floors currently in force in Canada are minimum wages set by provincial governments. The **minimum wage** is the lowest hourly wage rate that firms may legally pay their workers. Proponents want higher minimum wages to ensure low-income workers a "decent" standard of living. Opponents claim that higher minimum wages cause increased unemployment, particularly among unskilled teenagers.

Every province in Canada has a minimum wage. Figure 6–3 sets out the hourly minimum wage for each province in 2017.

What happens when the government passes legislation setting a floor on wages? The effects can be seen in Figure 6–4. We start off in equilibrium with the equilibrium wage rate of $W_e$ and the equilibrium quantity of labour demanded and supplied equal to $Q_e$. A minimum wage, $W_m$, higher than $W_e$, is imposed. At $W_m$, the quantity demanded for labour is reduced to $Q_d$, and some workers now become unemployed. Note that the reduction in employment from $Q_e$ to $Q_d$, or the distance from $B$ to $A$, is less than the excess quantity of labour supplied at wage rate $W_m$. This excess quantity supplied is the distance between

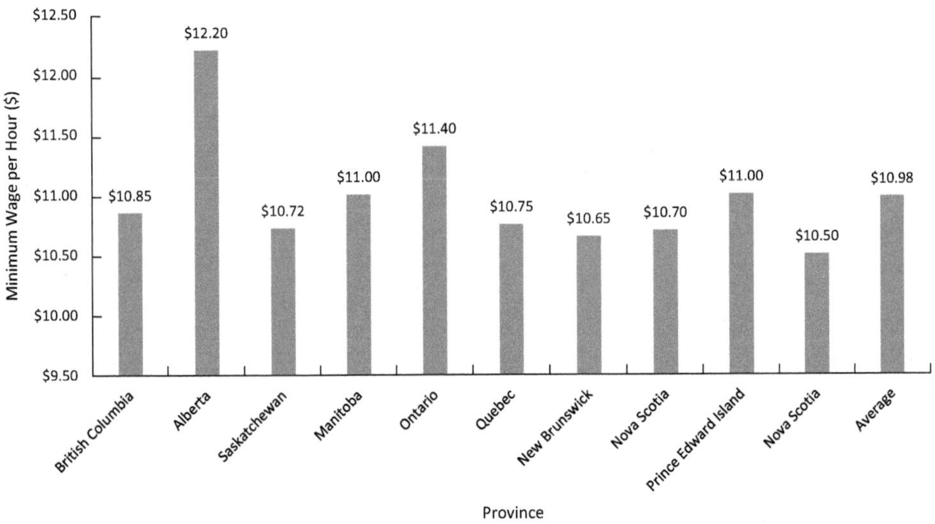


**FIGURE 6–3**

**Provincial Minimum Wage Rates per Hour 2017**

Every province in Canada legislates a minimum wage rate per hour. As of January 2017, the rate varied from $10.5 to $12.20 per hour. The average minimum wage was $10.98 per hour.

http://srv116.services.gc.ca/dimt-wid/sm-mw/rpt1.aspx (Accessed Janaury 16, 2017).

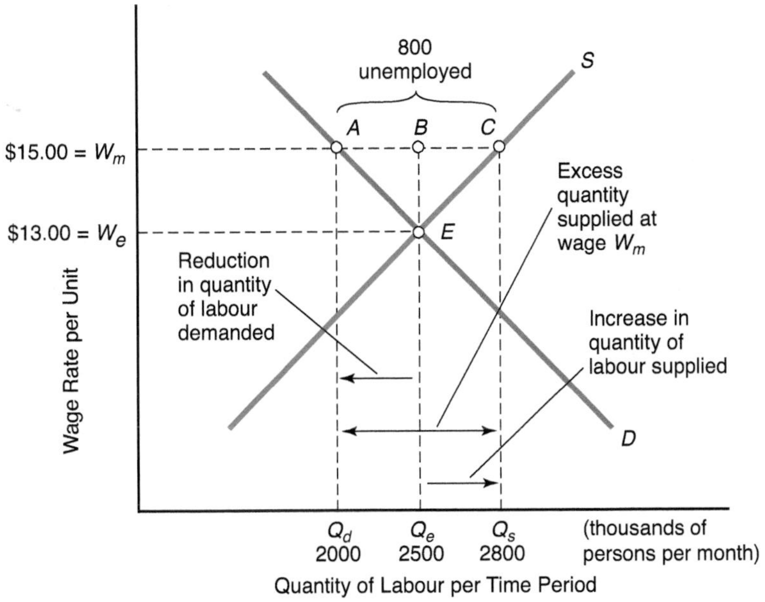


**FIGURE 6–4**

**The Effect of Minimum Wages**

The market clearing wage rate is $W_e = \$13.00$. The market clearing quantity of employment is $Q_e = 2500$, determined by the intersection of supply and demand at point *E*. A minimum wage equal to $W_m = \$15.00$ is established. The quantity of labour demanded is reduced to $Q_d = 2000$; the reduction in employment from $Q_e = 2500$ to $Q_d$ is equal to the distance between *B* and *A*. That distance is smaller than the excess quantity of labour supplied at wage rate $W_m$. The distance between *B* and *C* is the increase in the quantity of labour supplied that results from the higher minimum wage rate.

*A* and *C*, or the distance between $Q_d$ and $Q_s$. The reason the reduction in employment is smaller than the excess supply of labour at the minimum wage is that the latter also includes a second component, consisting of the additional workers who would like to work more hours at the new, higher minimum wage. Some workers may become unemployed as a result of the minimum wage, but others will move to sectors where minimum wage laws do not apply; wages will be pushed down in these uncovered sectors.

In the long run (a time period that is long enough to allow for adjustment by workers and firms), some of the reduction in labour demanded will result from a reduction in the number of firms, and some will result from changes in the number of workers employed by each firm. Economists estimate that a 10 percent increase in the real minimum wage decreases total employment of those affected by 3 to 20 percent.[2] Policy Example 6-2 questions whether minimum wage rates provide a net benefit to Canadian workers.

[2]Because we are referring to a long-run analysis here, the reduction in labour demanded would be demonstrated by an eventual shift inward to the left of the short-run demand curve, *D*, in Figure 6–4.

**POLICY EXAMPLE 6–2 Do Minimum Wage Rates Benefit Canadian Workers?**

Not that long ago, British Columbia consistently posted the highest minimum wage of all 10 provinces. Between 2004 and 2010, B.C. had not raised its minimum wage rate to the point of posting the lowest minimum wage in Canada of $8.00 per hour. In February 2014, B.C. implemented the second lowest minimum wage rate, just $.10 above the Alberta rate. Why has B.C. changed its view regarding the effectiveness of minimum wage policy, especially when it is being pressured by powerful union groups to raise the rate to $10 per hour?

Economic observers suggest that two key events help to explain B.C.'s stance on minimum wage rate policy. First, the left-leaning, pro-labour New Democrat government was replaced by a pro-business Liberal government. Second, the Fraser Institute, a right-wing economic think tank that has the ear of the B.C. Liberal government, published a labour market study entitled *The Economic Effects of Increasing British Columbia's Minimum Wage*. This report concluded that raising the minimum wage rate in B.C. would result in a greater marginal cost than marginal benefit.

In its study, the Fraser Institute assessed the marginal benefit of a higher minimum wage to discover how much this policy would reduce the poverty rate. Since only 3 to 4 percent of B.C. workers are currently earning a minimum wage, the policy of raising the rate would affect a very small pergentage of B.C. families. After examining the characteristics of those B.C. workers that would typically directly benefit from an increased minimum wage, the study found that the majority of these individuals (56 percent) were between 15 and 24 years of age, still going to school, and living at home with their parents.

Therefore, minimum wage increases would have a negligible effect on adults, generally, and those supporting families, specifically.

On the other hand, the study found significant marginal costs related to raising the minimum wage rate from $8 to $10 per hour. Based on other research conducted in Canada and the U.S., the Fraser Institute estimated that raising the minimum wage rate would result in the loss of between 10 898 and 52 200 jobs. Moreover, the research suggests that higher minimum wages have other negative effects, including fewer employee benefits and less training for workers.

**For critical analysis:** Sketch a demand and supply diagram for unskilled workers in B.C., assuming an equilibrium wage rate of $8 per hour and a minimum wage rate of $10 per hour. Use this diagram to explain the effects of a policy that would raise the B.C. minimum wage from $8 to $10 per hour.

Source: "Canada Minimum Wage Rates By Province. Canadian Minimum Wage." http://www.minimum-wage.ca/ (Accessed February 18, 2014); Keith Godin and Niels Veldhuis. *The Economic Effects of Increasing British Columbia's Minimum Wage*. Studies in the Labour Market. Fraser Institute. January 2009. Pg. 3–5. http://www.fraserinstitute.org/commerce.web/product_files/EconomicEffectsBCMinimumWage.pdf.

## 6.3 Price Supports: Offer to Purchase and Marketing Boards

Throughout the 20th century, governments around the world have implemented a variety of policies in support of farmers. Typically, the government initiatives have been in response to two well-publicized problems that plague the farm sector.

In the short run, on a year-to-year basis, a farmer's annual income can vary significantly due to uncontrollable supply factors, such as weather conditions and the uncoordinated production plans of the farmer's vast number of competitors. From a long-term viewpoint, due to high productivity and low income elasticity of demand, the increase in the supply of farm goods has significantly exceeded the increase in the demand for these same farm products, especially in the more developed nations. Therefore, the average annual income of farmers has lagged behind average incomes earned in nonfarm occupations. In response to the problems outlined above, governments have implemented policies in order to promote equity from the farmer's perspective.

In this section, we will apply the theory of demand, supply, and elasticity to understand and evaluate common types of farm **price support policies**, which aim to help the farmers by enhancing the prices they receive for the farm products they supply.

**Price support policies** Policies that aim to help the farmers by enhancing the prices they receive for the farm products they supply.

## Offer-to-Purchase Policy

One type of price support policy used to enhance farm income is the **offer-to-purchase policy**, which is a price floor policy reinforced by the purchase of surplus output by the government. Figure 6–5 describes a hypothetical market for apples in a Canadian province. Note that without government intervention, an equilibrium price of \$500 per tonne and an equilibrium of 15 000 tonnes (per year) would prevail. Annual total revenue for all the apple growers in the province would be \$500 × 15 000 = \$7 500 000.

**Offer-to-purchase policy** A price floor policy reinforced by the purchase of surplus output by the government.

In order to promote the goal of a more equitable distribution of income for the apple farmers, the provincial government sets a minimum price floor of \$700 per tonne. Since this price exceeds the equilibrium price, an annual surplus equal to (17 000 – 14 000) or 3000 tonnes results, as indicated in Figure 6–5. In order to maintain the price at \$700 per tonne, the government will also have to purchase this surplus at a total taxpayer cost of \$700 × 3000 tonnes = \$2 100 000. The apple growers' total revenue increases to \$700 × 17 000 tonnes = \$11 900 000. This means an increase in revenue of \$11 900 000 – \$7 500 000 = \$4 400 000 for the apple growers!

While the offer-to-purchase policy described above does increase the total revenues of the apple growers, it accomplishes this at the expense of the consumer and the taxpayer. The consumer pays a higher price of \$700 per tonne, compared with an equilibrium price of \$500 per tonne. As well, taxpayers pay a total of \$2 100 000 per year to purchase the surplus, which often rots in government storage bins. This policy results in allocative inefficiency due to the surplus output. Politically, the government becomes very unpopular if the voters find out that they are paying higher prices for apples that are rotting in storage. Finally, since the offer-to-purchase policy helps the farmers by securing a higher price per unit (per tonne), the largest, most affluent farms get the greatest benefit from the price supports.

## Marketing Board Policy

Due to some of the problems related to the offer-to-purchase policy, provincial governments in Canada have preferred to aid the farmers by allowing them to form producer **marketing boards**—a policy that allows producers to band together to restrict total quantity supplied by using quotas. Returning to the apple growers example, if the majority of the apple growers agree to form a marketing board, the board will typically use quotas

**Marketing boards** A policy that allows producers to band together to restrict total quantity supplied by using quotas.

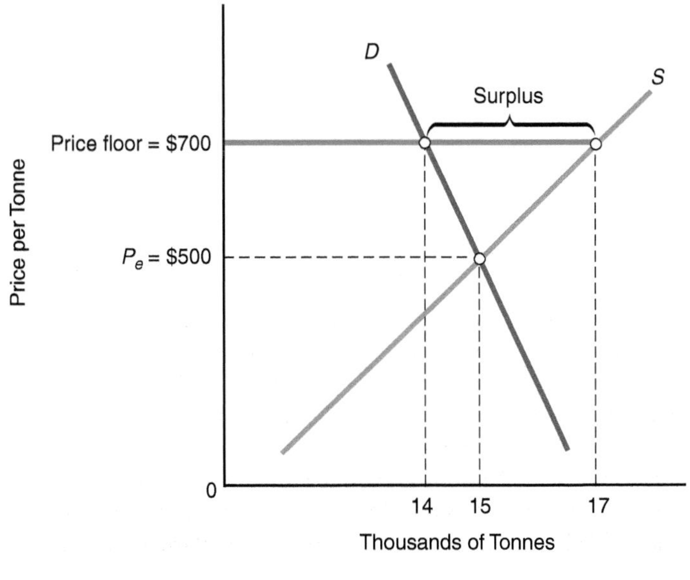


**FIGURE 6–5**

**The Offer-to-Purchase Price Support**

If the government does not intervene in the apple market, all the apple growers in the province will sell 15 000 tonnes a year at an equilibrium price of \$500 per tonne. In order to support the apple farmers' incomes, the government sets a price floor equal to \$700 per tonne. A surplus of (17 000 – 14 000) or 3000 tonnes per year will result. In order to keep the apple price at \$700 per tonne, the government will have to purchase the surplus of 3000 tonnes, paying \$700 per tonne of surplus.

to restrict the quantity of apples sold to a level below the equilibrium quantity. This, in turn, will increase the price per tonne above the equilibrium price. If demand for apples is inelastic, the higher price will result in an increase in total revenue.

Figure 6–6 describes how a marketing board can increase the apple growers' total revenue. We again note that without government intervention, the equilibrium price will be \$500 per tonne and the equilibrium quantity will be 15 000 tonnes. Under a laissez-faire policy, the apple growers' total revenue will be \$500 × 15 000 tonnes = \$7 500 000. The provincial government, not wanting to use taxpayer dollars to purchase surplus apples, decides to let the apple growers form a marketing board. The marketing board sets a quota on each of the apple growers, which results in a lower total quantity of 14 000 tonnes being sold to the consumer. Since the quantity sold is reduced, the price increases to \$700 per tonne. With the marketing board, the total revenue for the apple growers is now \$700 × 14 000 tonnes = \$9 800 000. Despite a reduced quantity sold, the farmers' total revenue increases because demand is inelastic!

Over one-half of Canadian farmers' total sales are regulated by agricultural marketing boards. Chickens, turkeys, eggs, milk, butter, tobacco, grapes, and mushrooms are all sold through marketing boards that restrict the supply of these products to the marketplace.

**WHO LOSES WHEN MARKETING BOARDS REGULATE SUPPLY?** The consumer pays more for the regulated goods than necessary and is therefore the biggest loser. One estimate suggests that the average Canadian family pays \$200 to \$400 per year more than it would if all farm produce were sold at unregulated prices.

Prospective farmers lose, too. When quotas were first established, they were given to existing producers. New producers, however, have to purchase quotas from other farmers or from the appropriate marketing board. Some quotas have become prohibitively expensive. A minimum-size quota for a chicken farm today would cost \$1 million; a minimum-size quota for a dairy farm in the Fraser Valley of British Columbia would cost \$3 million. And that is not counting the cost of the land and the livestock.

Another loser is the foreign farmer who would like to export farm products to Canada. The government restricts entry of foreign produce because the additional supply would reduce prices. Canada used to keep out foreign produce with import quotas, but the GATT (General Agreement on Tariffs and Trade) in its latest round of talks banned import quotas on agricultural goods. Thus, the federal government now uses import duties (i.e., taxes on imported produce) to restrict supply of foreign goods. The tariff on butter from the United States, for example, is 351 percent.

**WHO WINS WHEN MARKETING BOARDS REGULATE SUPPLY?** Existing farmers are clearly the major winners. The boards do stabilize their incomes, and so they can plan from one year to the next. To the extent that marketing boards restrict the supply of inelastic demand products, the total revenue of the existing farmers will increase. Supporters of

**FIGURE 6–6**

**Marketing Board Policy**

If there is no government policy, the equilibrium price of \$500 and the equilibrium quantity of 15 000 tonnes will prevail. The total farm revenue will be \$500 × 15 000 = \$7 500 000. If a marketing board is allowed to be established, the board will impose quotas on each of its apple grower members. As a result, the total quantity supplied will be fixed at 14 000 tonnes. At this quantity, the price per tonne will increase to \$700, and total farm revenue will increase to \$700 × 14 000 = \$9 800 000.

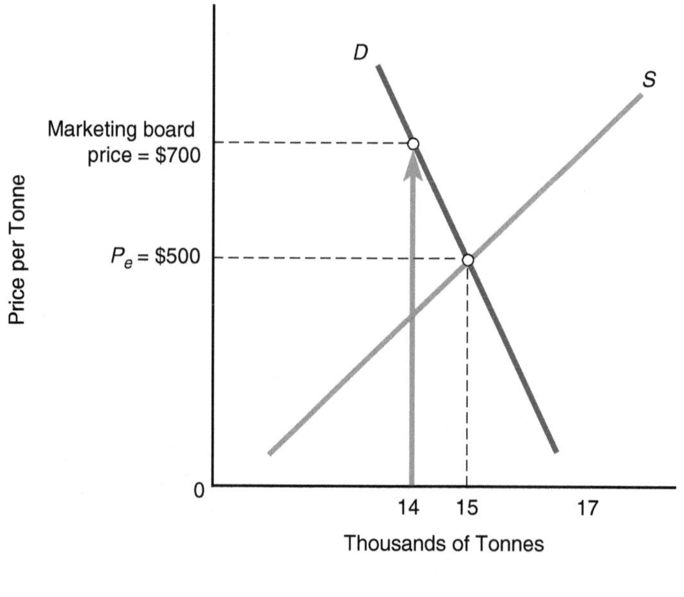

marketing boards also point out that by guaranteeing a living for Canadian farmers, we are providing ourselves with a made-at-home food supply—something much more valuable than the costs associated with supply management. In addition, we are helping preserve a way of life that is disappearing elsewhere—the family farm.

Some farmers object to being regulated by marketing boards. They believe that they, as entrepreneurs, will be better salespeople for their products than a government bureaucracy. This is happening most clearly in the wheat and barley industry, where a special form of marketing board exists. Policy Example 6–3 explains this policy.

### POLICY EXAMPLE 6–3 The Beginning of the End for the Canadian Wheat Board?

The Canadian government has been involved in guaranteeing prices for wheat farmers since World War I. In 1917, to regulate the supply of wheat to troops in Europe and to Canadians at home, and to guarantee grain farmers a reasonable living, the government set up the Board of Grain Supervisors. After the war, the Board's name was changed to the Canadian Wheat Board. It still operates today.

The Canadian Wheat Board buys all the wheat and barley a farmer produces and sells it on world markets. Farmers cannot sell their wheat and barley independently. The Board advances 75 percent of the expected price to farmers in the spring, and then settles up with them after the grain is sold in the fall. Farmers never receive less than the expected price, so if the world price is lower than predicted, the Wheat Board suffers a loss. But if the price is higher, farmers are paid more. This has the effect of reducing fluctuations in farm income by putting a floor under the price farmers receive.

Recently, some grain growers have been objecting to being forced to sell to the Wheat Board. They claim that by selling directly to the United States, they would earn $2 to $3 per bushel more, a significant price difference. But other farmers want the Wheat Board to remain. They fear that, as individual farmers, they would not have the leverage to stand up against major grain buyers and demand a high price. They fear that, in the end, their incomes would fall.

The federal Conservative government, consistent with its laissez-faire views, had set August 1, 2008, as the date when western Canadian farmers had the choice to bypass the Wheat Board and sell their barley on the open market. This date was delayed due to court battles between the Canadian Wheat Board and the federal government. On August 1, 2012, western farmers were permitted to bypass the Canadian Wheat Board and sell their grain to the buyer of their choice. If some farmers wish to do so, they can still sell their grain to the Wheat Board, but this is purely voluntary.

In Fall 2013, western grain farmers were facing significant delays in getting their crops shipped through rail to Canadian ports. Dozens of ships were lying idle waiting for the grain to arrive. Some observers have suggested that these severe delays would not have happened under a single-marketing operation like the one the Canadian Wheat Board used to manage. The Board would spread out the shipments over the different months of the year, so as to prevent a shortage of rail cars at any one time. In Fall 2015, some farmers established a class action lawsuit against the Canadian Wheat Board. The farmers are demanding accountability following Ottawa's seizure and dismantling of the Canadian Wheat Board in December 2011.

**For critical analysis:** Using a market demand and supply diagram for barley, describe how the price will change when more and more farmers bypass the Canadian Wheat Board (marketing board) to sell their barley. If demand for barley is inelastic, what will happen to the farmers' total revenue?

Sources: Monopoly ends, but Canadian Wheat Board stays confident. Jennifer Graham and Bob Weber. The Canadian Press. Jul. 31, 2012. Globe Investor. Globe and Mail. http://www.theglobeandmail.com/globe-investor/monopoly-ends-but-canadian-wheat-board-stays-confident/article4452731/ (Accessed February 19, 2014); Farmers call for fines on railways as grain backlog grows. Business. CBC News. Nov. 28, 2013. http://www.cbc.ca/news/business/farmers-call-for-fines-on-railways-as-grain-backlog-grows-1.2444179 (Accessed February 19, 2014); "Tories on iffy ground on wheat monopoly," *Leader-Post* (Regina). Final edition. June 23, 2007. Pg. D1.FRO.; "Ottawa eyes end to wheat board's monopoly on barley." *Dawson Creek Daily News* (Dawson Creek, B.C.). March 4, 2010. Pg. A3. http://www.cwbafacts.ca/constitutional-and-class-action/ (Accessed January 16, 2017).

## 6.4 Quantity Restrictions

Governments can impose quantity restrictions on a market. The most obvious restriction is an outright ban on the ownership or trading of a good. It is currently illegal to buy and sell human organs as well as certain psychoactive drugs such as cocaine and heroin. It is also illegal to open a new chartered bank without obtaining a government charter. This requirement effectively restricts the number of chartered banks in Canada. Policy Example 6–4 explains how an outright ban can create illegal markets that continue to supply the product.

### POLICY EXAMPLE 6–4 Could Legalizing Marijuana Reduce Mexican Drug Violence?

As evidenced in the media, Mexico has been plagued by a violent drug trade controlled by the Mexican drug mafia cartels. In 2009, there were 6500 drug-related killings, and as of mid-March 2010, more than 2000 people had died in drug-related homicides. That amounts to more than one death per hour. For three straight years ending January 2013, the number of drug- and organized crime-related homicides exceeded 1000 every month. The majority of the drugs peddled by the Mexican mafia are sold in the United States, where drugs such as marijuana are illegal to buy and sell, except for medicinal purposes.

How might the policy of legalizing marijuana in the U.S. promote the public's interest?

What these figures illustrate is that, while governments can enact laws that ban products such as marijuana, they cannot prevent the illegal demand and supply for marijuana in underground or black markets, often with ties to organized crime. Typically, the demand and supply curves differ when marijuana is banned compared to when it is legally available. The suppliers of the banned substance face higher costs due to the risk of getting caught and being convicted. Since the consumers also face the risk of being caught and convicted, demand decreases compared to the legal situation.

In 2014, Colorado and Washington became the first two states in the U.S. to legalize recreational marijuana. In the 2016 election, voters approved recreational pot laws in several states, including California. These legalization policies allow cities and counties to permit marijuana to be grown and sold locally, and for state and local governments to impose taxes on marijuana production and sales.

One reason for these legalization policies is to bring in new tax revenue to help reduce large state and local government deficits. As well, there would be a large decrease in demand for marijuana supplied by the Mexican drug lords, since millions of Americans will have access to the drug at lower prices, from legal, regulated, domestic producers. As the profits of the Mexican drug dealers are reduced, they will be less able to afford the military might that encourages the drug-related violence already witnessed.

A major concern related to the legalization of marijuana is that the increased supply of this substance may encourage greater drug abuse and addiction in California.

**For critical analysis:** Sketch a demand and supply diagram illustrating the equilibrium price and quantity of marijuana when it is banned (i.e., sold on the black market). In the same diagram, show what happens to demand and supply when marijuana is legalized, based on the contents of this Example. What will happen to the equilibrium price and quantity of marijuana when it is legalized? Explain.

Sources: Steve Chapman. "An unconventional cure for Mexico's drug violence." *Chicago Tribune*. March 28, 2010. http://articles.chicagotribune.com/2010-03-28/news/ct-oped-0328-chapman-md-20100328_1_drug-cartels-drug-related-killings-drug-trade; Will More States Follow Colorado and Washington in Marijuana Legalization? Fred Dews. January 2, 2014. Brookings. http://www.brookings.edu/blogs/brookings-now/posts/2014/01/will-more-states-follow-colorado-and-washington-in-marijuana-legalization (Accessed February 18, 2014); Where Will Marijuana Be Legal Next? This Map Points to 5 Specific States. Matt Essert. January 26, 2014. Live News. PolicyMic. http://www.policymic.com/articles/80099/where-will-marijuana-be-legal-next-this-map-points-to-5-specific-states (Accessed February 19, 2014); In Mexico, dozens fall to new violence across 4 troubled states. Cecilia Sanchez and Richard Fausset. July 22, 2013. *Los Angeles Times*. http://articles.latimes.com/2013/jul/22/world/la-fg-wn-mexico-violence-20130722. http://www.latimes.com/local/california/la-me-updates-best-year-review-marijuana-is-now-legal-in-more-than-1481749517-htmlstory.html (Accessed January 16, 2017).

Some of the most common quantity restrictions exist in the area of international trade. The Canadian government and many foreign governments impose import quotas on a variety of goods. An **import quota** is a supply restriction that prohibits the importation of more than a specified quantity of a particular good in a one-year period. Canada has had import quotas on cotton textiles, shoes, and immigrant labour. For many years, there were import quotas on dairy products coming into Canada from the United States. These quotas were recently removed and replaced by tariffs, but the effect is still to limit the amount of dairy products that we import. There are also "voluntary" import quotas on certain goods. Japanese car makers, for example, have agreed since 1981 "voluntarily" to restrict the number of cars they send to Canada.

**Import quota** A supply restriction that prohibits the importation of more than a specified quantity of a particular good in a one-year period.

In many cases, import quotas are designed to increase the total amount spent by Canadians on domestically produced goods. However, if the Canadian demand for the foreign good being restricted is price inelastic, Canadian consumers may end up spending more dollars on the foreign product, resulting in a decrease in demand for the made-in-Canada good.

# 6.5 Elasticity and Excise Taxes

Canadian governments at both the federal and provincial levels can levy various taxes in order to affect market outcomes. One example is the **excise tax**, which is a tax imposed on a particular commodity or service, such as cigarettes, alcohol, gasoline, CDs, MP3 players, or hotel services. In the following section, we will apply the theory of demand, supply, and elasticity to predict the effects of a per-unit tax imposed on the firms manufacturing and supplying cigarettes in a Canadian province.

**Excise tax** A tax imposed on a particular commodity or service.

## The Effects of a Per-Unit Tax on Market Supply

Suppose the federal government imposes an excise tax of $15 per carton of cigarettes on the firms manufacturing and supplying cigarettes in Ontario. To simplify the situation, we will assume that the manufacturers sell directly to cigarette consumers. In Figure 6–7, the pretax market supply and demand is $S_1$ and $D_1$.

Since the per-unit tax imposes an extra cost on the cigarette manufacturers at each price, this will cause a decrease in the supply of cigarettes.

**Graphically, the market supply curve will shift up vertically, at each quantity, by the amount of the per unit tax.**

In Figure 6–7, this means that the supply curve will shift upward by a vertical amount of $15 (the per-unit tax) to form $S_2$, the new after-tax supply curve. This shift can be explained as follows.

According to $S_1$, the pretax supply curve, the manufacturers will be willing to supply 5 million cartons per month if they receive $50 per carton. In order to supply 6 million cartons of cigarettes per month, the manufacturers will have to receive $55 per carton.

After a new tax of $15 per carton is imposed on the manufacturers, they will be willing to supply 5 million cartons per month only if the price charged to the consumers is now $65 per carton, which is based on the new supply curve, $S_2$. If the manufacturers charge the consumers $65, they will receive the $50 they require, after remitting to the government $15 for each carton sold.

Similarly, after the tax, the manufacturers will be willing to supply 6 million cartons per month only if the price charged to the consumers is now $70 (on $S_2$). By charging $70 per carton, the manufacturers will be able to receive the necessary $55, after paying to the government a tax of $15 per carton. On the basis of this example, we can conclude that for each possible quantity, the after-tax supply curve will shift upward by $15, the amount of the per-unit tax.

FIGURE 6–7

**The Effect of a Per-Unit Tax on Market Supply**

The before-tax supply curve, $S_1$, shows the dollar amount per carton that cigarette manufacturers must receive in order to be willing to supply each quantity. As an example, to be induced to supply 6 million cartons of cigarettes, the manufacturers must receive \$55 per carton. After the tax, the supply curve shifts up vertically by the amount of the tax, or by \$15, to $S_2$. After the tax, in order for the manufacturers to be willing to supply 6 million cartons of cigarettes, the price charged to the consumer must now be \$70, based on $S_2$. At a \$70 price, after paying the \$15 tax to the government, the sellers will receive \$55 per carton, which is the amount necessary to induce the 6 million carton supply.

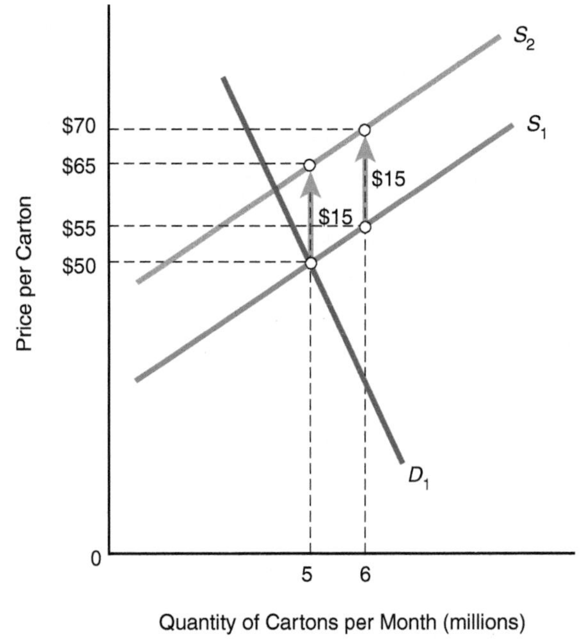


## Tax Incidence

**Tax incidence** The division of the burden of a tax between the buyer and the seller.

When the government imposes a per-unit excise tax, who bears the brunt of the tax—the buyer or the seller? This is a question relating to **tax incidence**, which is the division of the burden of a tax between the buyer and the seller. In our cigarette example above, the government imposes the tax on the manufacturers (sellers). However, the sellers can shift at least part of the tax to the buyers (consumers), to the extent that they can increase the equilibrium price charged for a carton of cigarettes.

**In general, the buyer's portion of the tax burden equals the increase in equilibrium price that results from the tax. The seller's portion of the tax burden equals the per-unit tax minus the buyer's tax burden.**

In Figure 6–8, the per-unit tax imposed on the cigarette manufacturers shifts the supply curve upward by \$15 (the tax per unit). This decrease in supply causes the equilibrium price to increase from \$50 per carton to \$62 per carton. The tax incidence can now be established as follows: The buyer's portion of the tax burden equals the increase in equilibrium price, which is \$62 – \$50 = \$12 per carton. The seller's tax burden is the difference between the per-unit tax and the buyer's tax burden, which is \$15 – \$12 = \$3 per carton.

The seller's tax burden of \$3 per carton can be further explained by referring to Figure 6–8. Before the tax, the sellers received the equilibrium price of \$50. After the tax, the sellers receive the new equilibrium price minus the per-unit tax that they have to remit to the government, which is \$62 – \$15 = \$47. The sellers end up receiving \$50 – \$47 = \$3 less per carton after the tax.

## Elasticity and Tax Incidence

Elasticity of demand and supply affects the degree to which the burden of an excise tax is shared between the buyers and the sellers of the product being taxed. If demand is relatively elastic, buyers can easily escape the burden of a tax imposed on product A, by switching their consumption to close substitutes for product A. In this situation, sellers will be careful not to increase the equilibrium price too much for fear of scaring away the consumers of their product. Therefore, when demand is elastic, sellers will bear a greater portion of the tax burden.

On the other hand, if demand for product A is relatively inelastic, sellers can shift a larger portion of the tax burden to consumers by significantly increasing the price, as the

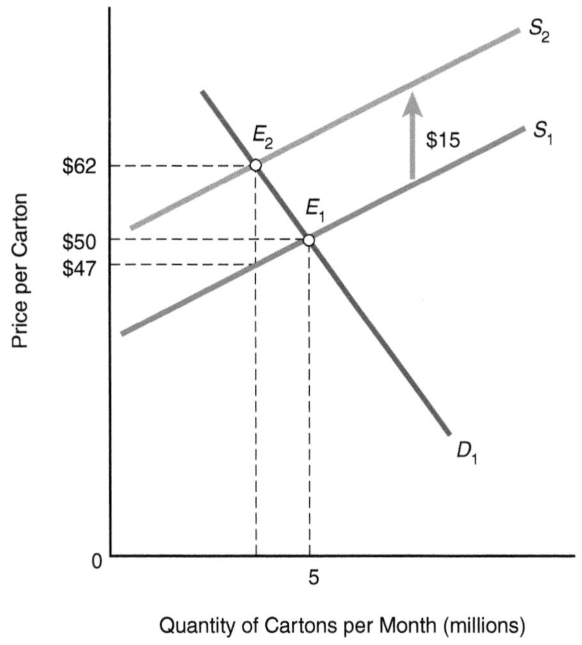


FIGURE 6–8

**The Tax Incidence Related to a $15 Per-Carton Excise Tax**

The before-tax equilibrium price equals $50 per carton, based on the intersection of $D_1$ and $S_1$. The $15 per-unit tax shifts the supply curve by $15 to $S_2$. The new after-tax equilibrium price is now $62 per carton, based on the intersection of $D_1$ and $S_2$. The buyer's portion of the tax burden equals the increase in equilibrium price, which is $62 − $50 = $12 per carton. The seller's portion of the tax burden is the per-unit tax minus the buyer's tax burden, which is $15 − $12 = $3 per carton. In other words, the seller receives $50 − $47 = $3 less for each carton sold, after the tax.

consumers have few alternative goods to switch to. In Figure 6–8, the demand for cigarettes is relatively inelastic, which explains why the consumer's tax burden of $12 significantly exceeds the seller's tax burden of $3 per carton.

Elasticity of supply can also affect tax incidence. If supply is relatively elastic, sellers can easily escape the burden of a tax imposed on product A, by switching their production and supply to alternative products that are not taxed. As many sellers leave the market for product A, the price of A will increase significantly, shifting a large portion of the tax burden to consumers of product A. Therefore, when supply is elastic, buyers will bear a greater portion of the tax burden.

If the supply for product A is relatively inelastic, this means that the sellers cannot easily switch to producing and supplying other nontaxed products. In this situation, sellers will continue to supply a significant amount of product A, even if faced with a large tax burden. In Figure 6–9, the supply of cigarettes is relatively inelastic. Under these market conditions, the same $15 per-carton tax causes the equilibrium price to go up to $54 per carton. The buyer's tax burden equals the increase in equilibrium price, which is $54 − $50 = $4 per carton. The seller's burden is the per-unit tax minus the buyer's burden, which is $15 − $4 = $11 per carton. You can see that when supply is relatively inelastic, the seller bears the greater portion of the tax burden.

**In general, the tax burden falls more heavily on the side of the market that is relatively more inelastic.**

## Elasticity and Resource Allocation

In many situations, an excise tax is imposed in order to discourage the production and consumption of a particular product that the government feels is detrimental to society. As an example, both the federal and provincial governments have imposed heavy excise taxes on cigarettes, which helps explain the significant decline in Canadian tobacco use noted in this chapter's Did You Know That . . . ? section. Under what elasticity conditions will the government be relatively successful in discouraging cigarette production and consumption?

**When demand and/or supply is relatively elastic, a per-unit excise tax will significantly reduce the equilibrium quantity of cigarettes, thereby effectively reducing the amount of resources being used to produce this undesirable product.**

**FIGURE 6–9**

**The Tax Incidence When Supply Is Inelastic**

The before-tax equilibrium price equals $50 per carton, based on the intersection of $D_1$ and $S_1$. The $15 per-unit tax shifts the supply curve up by $15 to $S_2$. The new after-tax equilibrium price is now $54 per carton, based on the intersection of $D_1$ and $S_2$. The buyer's portion of the tax burden equals the increase in equilibrium price, which is $54 − $50 = $4 per carton. The seller's portion of the tax burden is the per-unit tax minus the buyer's tax burden, which is $15 − $4 = $11 per carton. In other words, the seller receives $50 − $39 = $11 less for each carton sold, after the tax.

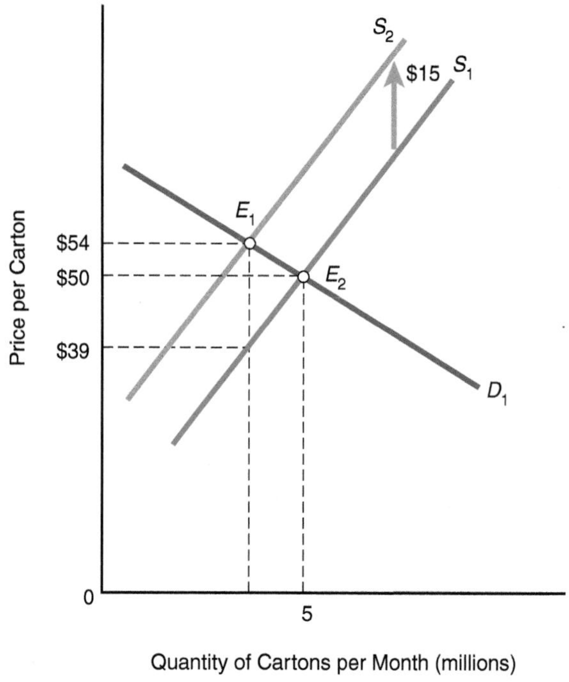


## Elasticity and Government Tax Revenue

Excise taxes provide tax revenues to both the federal and provincial governments in Canada. Elasticity affects the total amount of tax revenues that can be raised through these types of taxes.

> **A per-unit excise tax will generate greater total tax revenues when the demand and/or supply of the taxed product is relatively inelastic.**

In these situations, the equilibrium quantity of the taxed product will not significantly decrease in response to a per-unit tax. If the after-tax equilibrium quantity remains relatively large, the total tax revenue generated will also be relatively large.

Policy Example 6–5 describes the private copying levies that the Canadian government uses to discourage the widespread downloading of music from the Internet and through the burning of CDs. The proceeds from these levies are used to compensate the Canadian music industry for the piracy of copyrighted music. By viewing each levy as a per-unit excise tax, you can use the theory of elasticity to evaluate this government policy.

### POLICY EXAMPLE 6–5 An Excise Tax on Music Piracy?

Total Canadian album sales (CDs, CS, LP, digital) for 2016 were down 19 percent compared to 2015. Moreover, physical album sales also dropped a further 16 percent. This is consistent with the long-term decline in global music sales, which industry analysts attribute to widespread illegal Internet file-sharing and pre-recorded CD and DVD counterfeiting (copying).

In the December 17, 2016, *Supplement Canada Gazette*, The Copyright Board of Canada announced the tariffs to be imposed on the sale of blank audio recording media during 2014. The tariffs amount to per-unit taxes of $0.29 for each CD-R, CD-RW, CD-R Audio, or CD-RW Audio. These levies (taxes) represent the Canadian government's response to the flurry of free copying of copyrighted music through Internet downloads and CD burning. The proceeds from the levies on private copying are to be distributed to music performers, songwriters, and music producers, as partial compensation for the loss of sales due to piracy.

*continued*

**For critical analysis:** Explain how the price elasticity of demand and supply for blank media will affect the total amount collected from the levies on private copying. How will elasticity affect the degree to which these levies discourage the copying of copyrighted music? Under what circumstances would consumers be unfairly "taxed" by these private-copying levies?

Sources: Nielsen Releases 2016 Mid-year Canada Music Report http://www.nielsen.com/ca/en/press-room/2016/nielsen-releases-2016-mid-year-canada-music-report.html. July 7, 2016. Tariff of Levies to Be Collected by CPCC in 2017 on the Sale, in Canada, of Blank Audio Recording Media. Supplement Canada Gazette, Part I. December 17, 2016. Copyright Board of Canada. http://cb-cda.gc.ca/tariffs-tarifs/certified-homologues/2016/SUP-2016-12-17.pdf (Accessed January 16, 2017).

ISSUES AND APPLICATIONS

# For-Profit Health Care in Canada?

## Concepts Applied: Market versus Command Systems, Rationing Function of Prices, Price Ceilings, Allocative Efficiency, Productive Efficiency, and Equity

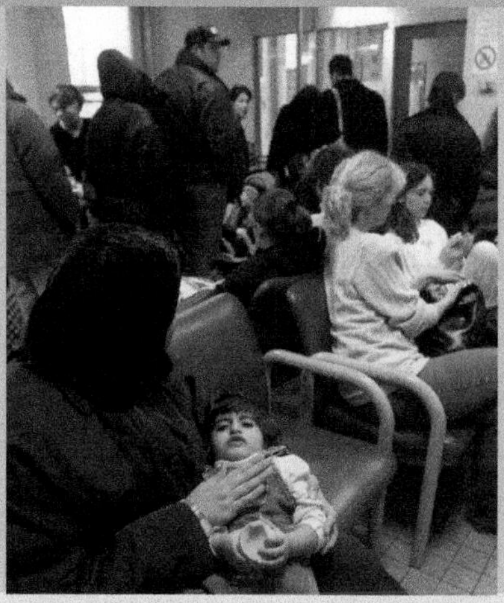

Is for-profit health care the way to reduce scenes like this?

In 2015 the Fraser Institute published its annual survey tracking the amount of time that Canadians typically wait to undergo a medical treatment or procedure performed by a medical specialist. Some of the results from this study are summarized in Table 6–1. When combining the wait-times for all types of procedures, Canadians waited an average of 18.3 weeks from the time they received a referral from their general practitioner to the time they received treatment from a medical specialist. This represents an increase of over 97 percent from 1993, when the typical waiting time was 9.3 weeks. In research involving 28 developed countries, published in October 2016 by the Fraser Institute, Canada ranked 24 out of 28 countries for number of physicians (2.59 per 1,000 people), and last for the number of acute care beds (1.77 per 1,000 people). Despite the apparent shortage of medical services in Canada, provincial governments have recently been spending an increasing portion of their budgets on health care.

These disturbing trends and statistics have renewed a debate over which type of system best suits the provision of health-care services—a market system or a command system. To appreciate the differing views, we will begin by examining Canada's existing system of providing health-care services.

### Canadian Medicare

Canada has a predominantly publicly financed, privately delivered health-care system that consists of 10 provincial (and three territorial) government health insurance plans. This mixed system of providing health-care services is frequently referred to as medicare.

The federal government's role in health care involves using financial incentives to ensure that each province provides equal access to universal, comprehensive coverage for medically necessary hospital, in-patient, and outpatient physician services.

**TABLE 6–1**

**Median Total Expected Waiting Time from Referral by GP to Treatment, by Specialty, 2015 (in weeks)**

| | BC | AB | SK | MB | ON | QC | NB | NS | PE | NL | CAN |
|---|---|---|---|---|---|---|---|---|---|---|---|
| Plastic Surgery | 52.5 | 29.5 | 46.2 | 26.7 | 12.3 | 15.1 | 25.5 | 17.1 | 15.9 | 17.8 | 22.8 |
| Gyneacology | 18.2 | 22.1 | 19.7 | 13.6 | 18.0 | 20.9 | 46.5 | 13.4 | — | 31.7 | 20.5 |
| Ophthalmology | 28.5 | 15.7 | 13.6 | 26.1 | 20.0 | 17.3 | 41.8 | 31.9 | 40.0 | 54.7 | 21.3 |
| Otolaryngolgy | 21.6 | 32.4 | 10.7 | 23.1 | 17.6 | 12.4 | 33.8 | 22.0 | 26.6 | — | 18.5 |
| General Surgery | 15.0 | 18.5 | 8.8 | 12.8 | 9.7 | 10.8 | 19.0 | 18.3 | — | 56.2 | 13.5 |
| Neurosurgery | 29.7 | 21.1 | 24.1 | — | 34.9 | 12.2 | 70.7 | 25.8 | — | — | 27.6 |
| Orthopaedic Surgery | 51.2 | 39.2 | 23.9 | 34.4 | 29.8 | 25.8 | 81.1 | 53.3 | 52.8 | 80.9 | 35.7 |
| Cardiovascular Surgery (Elective) | 11.9 | 9.6 | 4.9 | 16.5 | 8.5 | 9.6 | 17.8 | 8.2 | — | — | 9.9 |
| Urology | 11.6 | 16.3 | 6.0 | 19.1 | 9.6 | 19.6 | 62.2 | 40.1 | — | 17.9 | 13.9 |
| Internal Medicine | 21.4 | 19.7 | 10.0 | 15.5 | 8.2 | 23.6 | 13.4 | 14.6 | 29.8 | 23.1 | 14.5 |
| Radiation Oncology | 11.0 | 3.4 | 3.7 | 2.8 | 3.8 | 3.9 | 2.0 | 5.7 | — | 5.6 | 4.1 |
| Medical Oncology | 6.1 | — | — | 31.9 | 3.8 | 2.7 | — | 6.2 | — | — | 4.5 |
| Weighted Median | 22.4 | 21.2 | 13.6 | 19.4 | 14.2 | 16.4 | 42.8 | 26.1 | 43.1 | 42.7 | 18.3 |

Source: Table 2: Median Total Expected Waiting Time from Referral by GP to Treatment, by Specialty, 2015 (in weeks). Page 35. Waiting Your Turn. Wait Times for Health Care in Canada. 2015 Report by Bacchus Barua Fraser Institute. http://www.fraserinstitute.org/uploadedFiles/fraser-ca/Content/research-news/research/publications/waiting-your-turn-2015.pdf (Accessed January 16, 2017).

Typically, each province makes each of its working residents pay into the medicare insurance fund through compulsory taxation (or compulsory monthly premiums). When a Canadian consumer (patient) visits a physician (or hospital), monies from the medicare fund pay for the visit. This means that the patient does not incur any additional out-of-pocket expense each time he or she makes another visit to a physician or hospital.

In the Canadian medicare system, physicians typically operate their own private practices and are compensated from the medicare insurance fund on a fee-for-service basis. Since the majority of acute-care Canadian hospitals are operated by the public sector on a nonprofit basis, the only pressure to contain hospital costs is the annual hospital budget determined by government authorities.

## A Market-Oriented Health-Care Model?

Those who support market solutions for our health-care system criticize Canadian medicare for its price ceiling policy for medical services. Under this policy, the federal government commands that a maximum price of zero be charged for both doctor and hospital visits. Figure 6–10 illustrates this view.

According to the market supporters, medicare's zero price ceiling policy has caused shortages, resulting in Canadian patients waiting long periods before receiving treatment or surgery. A zero price encourages many individuals to frequently visit doctors and hospitals, and take diagnostic tests for the most trivial reasons, resulting in an excess demand for medical services. As a result, patients experiencing really serious health problems are forced to wait a long time before receiving the badly needed treatment.

A second problem with Canadian medicare, according to market advocates, is that it essentially results in government-owned monopolies providing health insurance and hospital services in each province. The lack of competition and the absence of the profit incentive helps contribute to medical shortages, productive inefficiency, and escalating health-care costs.

The market system supporters propose that Canada adopt a number of market incentives currently present in the American health-care system. In the United States, health-care services are predominantly provided in the for-profit private sector. As Table 6–2 indicates, public expenditures constitute a much smaller portion of total health expenditures in the United States compared with Canada.

**FIGURE 6–10**

**Zero Price Ceiling under Medicare**

Since there is no additional charge per visit, there is a zero price ceiling policy under medicare. This results in a shortage, where the quantity of visits demanded exceeds the quantity of visits supplied. The shortage is reflected in significant waiting times before Canadian patients receive health-care services.

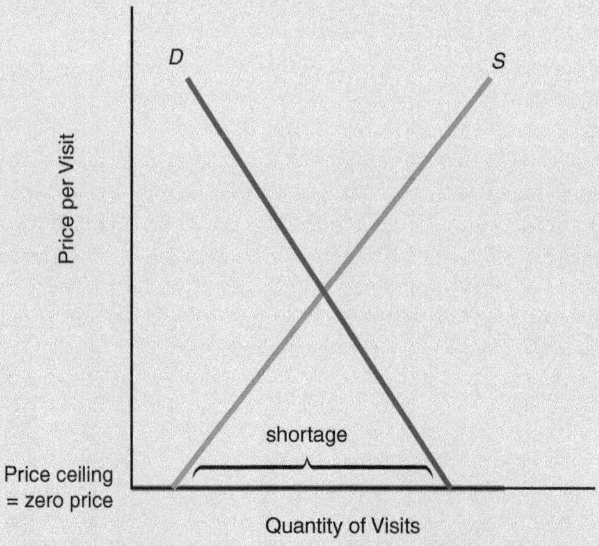

TABLE 6–2

**Annual Health Expenditures: Canada and the United States, 2008 and 2014**

| Expenditure as a Percentage | Canada 2008 | Canada 2014 | U.S. 2008 | U.S. 2014 |
|---|---|---|---|---|
| Total expenditure on health as a percentage of gross domestic product (GDP) | 10.03% | 10.45% | 16.02% | 17.14% |
| Public (government) expenditures on health as a percentage of total health expenditures | 70.41% | 70.93% | 48.98% | 48.3% |

Sources: Global Health Observatory Data Repository. By Country. World Health Organization. http://apps.who.int/gho/data/view.main.HEALTHEXPRATIOCAN and http://apps.who.int/gho/data/view.main.HEALTHEXPRATIOUSA?lang=en (Accessed January 20, 2017).

In order to finance their health-care costs, many American consumers voluntarily pay monthly premiums to private health insurance companies. In addition, consumers may have to pay a co-payment or user fee each time they visit a physician or hospital. Some private insurance plans may involve an experience rating, which is a situation where those who make more frequent visits to physicians may end up paying higher insurance premiums. According to market supporters, the user fees and experience ratings help eliminate waiting periods and ensure that those patients who value the medical services the most will be the ones visiting the health-care providers. The user fee will discourage frivolous use of scarce medical resources.

In the United States, large, private, for-profit health maintenance organizations (HMOs) operate hospitals, run diagnostic services, and hire physicians and nurses. In theory, one would expect to see a given quality of health care provided with minimal resource use in the United States, as it is in the interests of HMOs to contain the costs of providing health care, in order to enhance profits and stave off competition.

## Evaluation of the Market-Based Solutions

Those who defend Canadian medicare argue that one cannot use the market model to analyze health care, which many consumers view as an extreme-necessity (highly inelastic) good. Consumers of health care (patients) lack the knowledge necessary to evaluate whether a contemplated visit to the doctor is trivial or not. Moreover, after the first visit to the general practitioner, it is typically the doctor who makes the decision, on behalf of the patient, to consume additional health-care resources. In this situation, it is meaningless to suggest that user fees paid by the patients will ensure a more efficient use of medical resources. Indeed, user fees and experience ratings will unfairly penalize the poor and the chronically ill.

The view that private for-profit corporations will be more efficient than the government in providing health-care services can be challenged by comparing recent Canadian and American statistics. The data presented in Tables 6–2 and 6–3 indicate that although Canada spends a smaller percentage of GDP (national income) on health care than the United States, Canada manages to achieve a higher level of health achievement in terms of life expectancy, life expectancy adjusted for time spent in poor health, and infant mortality rates. It seems that a much larger portion of every dollar spent on health care in the United States is spent on activities not directly related to patient health care, such as administration, marketing, and earning corporate profits.

In November 2002, the Romanow Report, the last federal government commission on the future of Canadian health care, presented their findings and recommendations. The Commission rejected the notion of using additional market incentives to improve Canada's health-care system. The Commission attributes the recent shortcomings of various health-care services in Canada to a number of factors not related to medicare—a long-term decline in federal government cash transfers to the provinces for health-care spending; provincial budget cutbacks made during the early 1990s; the aging population; and the high income elasticity of demand for health care in Canada. The Commission recommended that Canada's health-care system be improved through an expanded public health sector financed by substantial increases in federal government cash transfers to the provinces.

The federal government funding of Canadian health care was changed in the 2014 budget. Under the new 10 year Canadian Health Transfer (CHT) plan, cash transfers to the provincial governments are predicted to increase at a decreased rate, putting greater financial pressures on the provinces. As well, the federal conservative government have been reluctant to present any type of coordinated national health care plan aimed at enforcing the principles of Canadian Medicare.

TABLE 6–3

**Health Achievement Levels: Canada and the United States, 2008 and 2015**

| Health Achievement | Canada 2008 | Canada 2015 | U.S. 2008 | U.S. 2015 |
|---|---|---|---|---|
| Life expectancy at birth—females | 83 | 84 | 81 | 82 |
| Life expectancy at birth—males | 79 | 80 | 76 | 77 |
| Healthy life expectancy at birth—life expectancy at birth adjusted for time spent in poor health | 73 | 72 | 70 | 69 |
| Probability of dying (per 1000 live births) under five years of age (under-five mortality rate) | 6 | 5 | 8 | 7 |

Sources: Global Health Observatory Data Repository. By Topic. World Health Organization. http://apps.who.int/gho/data/node.main (Accessed February 20, 2014) and http://www.who.int/gho/publications/world_health_statistics/2016/en/ (Accessed January 20, 2017).

**For critical analysis:**

1. According to those who promote market solutions in health care, what aspects of Canadian medicare encourage allocative inefficiency? Explain briefly.
2. According to those who promote market solutions in health care, what features of the American health-care system promote (a) allocative efficiency, and (b) productive efficiency?
3. According to the medicare supporters, why will user fees fail to promote allocative efficiency?
4. Explain how user fees for health-care services can conflict with equity.
5. Explain why it appears that the Canadian health-care system is more productively efficient than the American system.

Sources: Canadian patients wait longest to see family doctors. Health. CBC News. January 20, 2014. http://www.cbc.ca/news/health/canadian-patients-wait-longest-to-see-family-doctors-1.2501468 (Accessed February 19, 2014); Major Federal Transfers to Provinces and Territories. Chapter 4.2: Fiscal Outlook. Budget 2014. Government of Canada. http://www.budget.gc.ca/2014/docs/plan/ch4-2-eng.html (Accessed February 20, 2014); Nadeem Esmail and Michael Walker. "How good is Canadian health care?" August 2002. Fraser Institute. http://www.fraserinstitute.ca/shared/readmore.asp?sNav=pb&id=394. (Accessed December 27, 2003.); Nadeem Esmail and Michael Walker. "*Waiting Your Turn: Hospital Waiting Lists In Canada*." 13th Edition. October 2003. Fraser Institute. http://www.fraserinstitute.ca/shared/readmore.asp?sNav=pb&id=587. (Accessed December 27, 2003.); Roy Romanow, Commissioner. "Building on values: the future of health care in Canada." November 2002. pp. 100–106. http://www.hc-sc.gc.ca/english/pdf/care/romanow_e.pdf. (Accessed December 28, 2003.); Nadeem Esmail and Michael Walker. *Waiting Your Turn*, 16th Edition. October 2006. The Fraser Institute. http://www.fraserinstitute.ca/shared/readmore.asp?sNav=pb&id=863; Nadeem Esmail and Michael Walker. "How good is canadian health care? 2006 report: an international comparison of health care systems." December 2006. The Fraser Institute.http://www.fraserinstitute.ca/shared/readmore.asp?sNav=pb&id=877; "Practising physicians" OECD iLibrary. October 2013. http://www.oecd-ilibrary.org/social-issues-migration-health/practising-physicians-doctors_20758480-table4.

# SUMMARY

Here is what you should know after reading this chapter. MyEconLab will help you identify what you know, and where to go when you need to practise. We suggest that as soon as you review one of the Learning Objectives sections below, you then proceed to go through the related section in MyEconLab.

| LEARNING OBJECTIVES | KEY TERMS | MYECONLAB PRACTICE |
|---|---|---|
| **6.1 The Price System.** Markets and intermediaries reduce the costs of mutually beneficial exchanges between buyers and sellers. Equilibrium prices ensure that resources and goods are allocated to the highest-valued uses, and all the gains from mutually beneficial trades are exhausted. | price system, 133<br>voluntary exchange, 133<br>terms of exchange, 133<br>transaction costs, 133 | • **MyEconLab** Study Plan 6.1 |
| **6.2 Price Ceilings and Price Floors.** Price ceilings, such as rent controls, set a maximum legal price below the equilibrium price. Ceilings lead to shortages, inefficient nonprice-rationing devices, and black markets. Price floors, such as minimum wages, set a minimum legal price above the equilibrium price that results in surpluses. | price controls, 137<br>price ceiling, 137<br>price floor, 137<br>rent control, 137<br>nonprice-rationing devices, 137<br>black market, 138<br>minimum wage, 140 | • **MyEconLab** Study Plan 6.2 |

| LEARNING OBJECTIVES | KEY TERMS | MYECONLAB PRACTICE |
|---|---|---|
| **6.3 Price Supports: Offer to Purchase and Marketing Boards.** Offer-to-purchase and marketing board policies provide support to low and unstable farm incomes by establishing farm product prices at levels that exceed equilibrium prices. The offer-to-purchase policy is a floor price policy in which the resulting surpluses are purchased by the government. The policy provides the greatest support to the largest farm operators at the expense of consumers and taxpayers. Marketing boards typically restrict the quantity supplied of farm products in order to support farm prices. When demand is inelastic, this strategy will increase total farm revenues at the expense of consumers and prospective farmers. | price support policies, 143<br>offer-to-purchase policy, 143<br>marketing boards, 143 | • **MyEconLab** Study Plan 6.3 |
| **6.4 Quantity Restrictions.** Examples of quantity restrictions include direct government bans, licensing restrictions, and quotas. Consumers may end up spending more dollars on the restricted goods if demand is price inelastic. | import quota, 147 | • **MyEconLab** Study Plan 6.4 |
| **6.5 Elasticity and Excise Taxes.** A per-unit excise tax typically increases the equilibrium price and decreases the equilibrium quantity of the taxed good or service. In terms of tax incidence, the buyer's portion of the tax burden equals the equilibrium price increase, while the seller's portion equals the per-unit tax minus the buyer's portion of the tax burden. The excise tax burden falls more heavily on the side of the market that is relatively more inelastic. The resource allocation effects of an excise tax, in terms of a reduction in the quantity produced, will be greatest when demand and/or supply is relatively price elastic. The government will collect a larger amount of tax revenue when the demand and/or supply of the taxed product is relatively price inelastic. | excise tax, 147<br>tax incidence, 148 | • **MyEconLab** Study Plan 6.5 |

# PROBLEMS

(Answers to the odd-numbered problems appear at the back of the book.)

**LO 6.1 Explain the role of markets, intermediaries, and prices in the price system.**

1. Based on Example 6-2, "Is Ticketmaster in Cahoots with Scalpers," explain the economic role that ticket scalpers play in the market for a sold-out event.
2. Under Canadian medicare, how are the diagnostic, medical, and surgical services of specialist physicians being rationed?

**LO 6.2 Compare and contrast price ceiling and price floor policies.**

3. Below is the market demand-and-supply schedule for lettuce in a Canadian city.

| Price per Crate | Quantity Demanded (crates per year) | Quantity Supplied (crates per year) |
|---|---|---|
| $1 | 10 million | 0 million |
| 2 | 9 | 1 |
| 3 | 8 | 4 |
| 4 | 7 | 7 |
| 5 | 6 | 8 |
| 6 | 4 | 9 |

   a. Assuming no government intervention, what price and quantity would result in the lettuce market?
   b. Suppose that the price of lettuce in part (a) was considered excessive. Consequently, the government legislated a maximum price of $3 per crate. At this maximum price, a (shortage or surplus) of ____ million crates would develop. This policy is an example of a (price ceiling or price floor) policy.
   c. Assuming the policy in part (b) above, what would be the maximum black market price?
   d. Suppose that the price of lettuce in part (a) above was considered to be too low for lettuce farmers to make a decent living. Consequently, the government legislated a minimum price of $5 per crate. At this minimum price, a (shortage or surplus) of ____ million crates would develop. This policy is an example of a (price ceiling or price floor) policy.
4. Policy Example 6-1, "Assisted Human Reproduction Not for Sale in Canada" noted that under the *Assisted Human Reproduction Act*, couples go underground, where they turn to donors they find online and pay under the table. Based on the theory of demand and supply and price ceilings, would the amount paid under the table to an egg donor be the same or more than the equilibrium price? Explain.
5. This is a graph of the monthly demand for and supply of milk in a Canadian province.

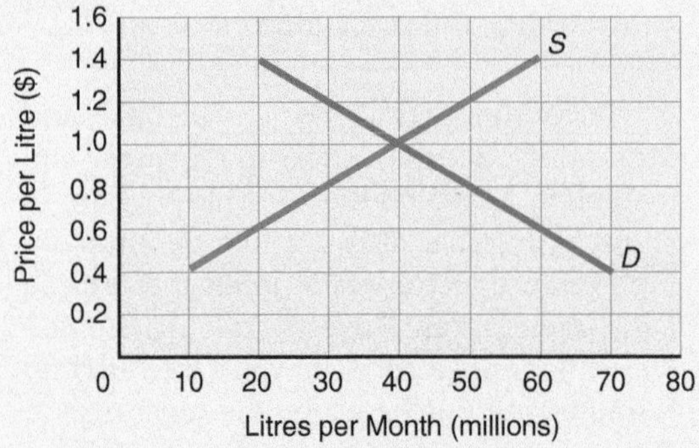


   a. If the government did not intervene in the milk market, what price and quantity would result?
   b. If the government imposed a maximum price policy of $0.80 per litre, this would result in a (shortage or surplus) of ____ millions of litres of milk per month. This would be called a (price floor or price ceiling) policy.
   c. For the policy described in part (b) above, what would be the black market price?
   d. If the government imposed a minimum price policy of $1.40 per litre, this would result in a (shortage or surplus) of ____ millions of litres of milk per month. This would be called a (price floor or price ceiling) policy.
6. "It is questionable whether a policy of rent controls promotes equity, despite leading to an inefficient allocation of resources." Fully explain the previous statement.

**LO 6.3 Compare and contrast the offer-to-purchase and the marketing board price support policies.**

7. For this problem, refer to the demand and supply schedules for lettuce provided in Problem 3 above.
   a. Assuming that the market sets the price and quantity for lettuce, compute the total revenue received by the lettuce farmers.
   b. If the government were to implement an offer-to-purchase policy to support the price of lettuce at $5 per crate, there would be a (shortage or surplus) equal to ____ million crates per year. Compute the total revenue received by the lettuce farmers under this policy. What would be the total taxpayer cost associated with this policy?
   c. Suppose that the government decided to support the price of lettuce by allowing a marketing board to develop and restrict the quantity of lettuce supplied to 6 million crates per year. What price per crate would develop? Compute the total revenue received by the lettuce farmers under this policy. Is the price elasticity of demand elastic or inelastic in the $4 to $5 price range? Explain.

8. Identify and explain both the short-run and long-run problems facing Canadian farmers.

9. For this problem, refer to the demand and supply curves for milk provided in Problem 5.

   a. Assuming that the market sets the price and quantity for milk, compute the total revenue received by the milk farmers.

   b. If the government were to implement an offer-to-purchase policy to support the price of milk at $1.20 per litre, there would be a (shortage or surplus) equal to ____ million litres per month. Compute the total revenue received by the milk farmers under this policy. What would be the total taxpayer cost associated with this policy?

   c. Suppose that the government decided to support the price of milk by allowing a marketing board to develop and restrict the quantity of milk supplied to 30 million litres per month. What price per litre would develop? What would be the total revenue received by the milk farmers under this marketing board policy? Is the price elasticity of demand elastic or inelastic in the $1.00 to $1.20 per litre price range? Explain.

**LO 6.4 Describe the various types of quantity restrictions that governments can impose on markets.**

10. Suppose the Canadian government imposes an import quota on California wines, with the goal of increasing the total dollar amount that Canadian consumers spend on Canadian wines. Sketch a demand and supply graph for California wines and use this graph to illustrate an import quota policy. (Hint: assume that this policy operates in the same way as a marketing board crop-restriction, policy.)

11. If the Canadian demand for California wines is inelastic, will the quota policy in question 10 increase or decrease the total dollar amount that Canadians spend on California wines? Explain.

12. The Canadian Liberal Party has introduced legislation a number of times to legalize the practice of possessing small amounts of marijuana. In the same proposed legislation, the policy increases the penalty for those caught trafficking or producing marijuana. Using a demand and supply graph for marijuana, show how this type of proposed legislation would affect the market demand, supply, and equilibrium price of marijuana. Under what conditions would the equilibrium quantity bought and sold increase, as a result of this legislation?

**LO 6.5 Explain how price elasticity governs the effects that a per-unit excise tax has on tax incidence, resource allocation, and government tax revenue collected.**

13. The market demand and the before-tax market supply for gasoline sold in a Canadian province are described in the following table.

| Price (per litre) | Market Demand (millions of litres per day) | Before-Tax Market Supply (millions of litres per day) | After-Tax Market Supply (millions of litres per day) |
|---|---|---|---|
| $0.70 | 20 | 80 | |
| 0.60 | 30 | 70 | |
| 0.50 | 40 | 60 | |
| 0.40 | 50 | 50 | |
| 0.30 | 60 | 40 | |
| 0.20 | 70 | 30 | |

If the government imposes an excise tax of $0.20 per litre on the suppliers of gasoline in this market, answer the following:

   a. In the above table, fill in the after-tax market supply, at each price per litre.

   b. Determine the after-tax equilibrium gas price and quantity.

   c. Determine the tax incidence related to this $0.20 per litre excise tax.

   d. Determine the total daily tax revenue that the government will receive from this gas excise tax.

   e. Under what conditions will the tax revenue computed in part (d) increase—when the demand for gasoline becomes more elastic or less elastic? Explain.

   f. Under what conditions will the excise tax more effectively reduce gas consumption—when the demand for gasoline becomes more elastic or less elastic?

14. Suppose the government imposes a per-litre excise tax on all the firms supplying vodka in Canada. For each of the following, pick the market conditions that would tend to increase the buyer's portion of the tax burden:

   a. Buyers have very few vodka substitutes available versus lots of good vodka substitutes available.

   b. Vodka makes up a large portion of each buyer's total monthly expenditures versus it makes up a very small portion of each buyer's total monthly expenditures.

   c. Buyers consider vodka to be a necessity item versus a luxury item.

   d. The firms supplying vodka can easily switch to supplying other products versus they cannot easily switch to supplying other products.

15. In order to raise funds for Canadian musicians, the Canadian government imposes a per-unit excise tax on all firms supplying blank recordable CDs in Canada. The accompanying graph describes the market demand, before-tax market supply, and after-tax market supply curves for the blank recordable CD market in Canada.

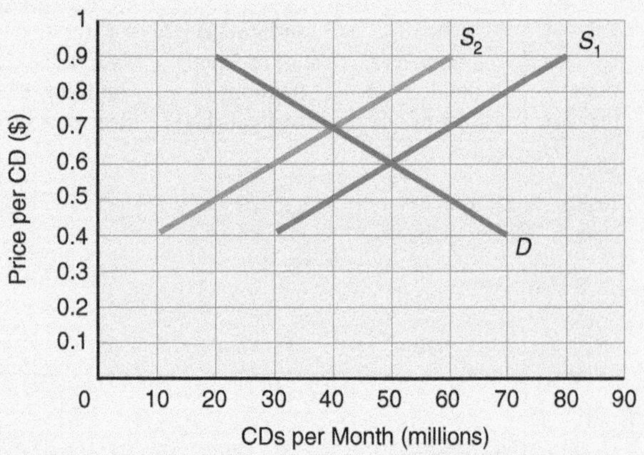


Use the above graph to answer each of the following:

a. What is the before-tax equilibrium price and quantity?
b. What is the amount of the CD excise tax on a per-CD basis?
c. What is the after-tax equilibrium price and quantity?
d. Determine the tax incidence.
e. Determine the total monthly tax revenue that the Canadian government will receive from this CD excise tax.
f. Under what conditions will the tax revenue computed in part (e) increase—when the supply for CDs becomes more elastic or less elastic? Explain.
g. Under what conditions will the CD excise tax more effectively discourage the use of CDs for illegal music downloads—when the supply for CDs becomes more elastic or less elastic?

16. Suppose a provincial government imposes an excise tax on all firms supplying beer in the province. Determine the tax incidence, under each of the following market conditions:
    a. The demand for beer is perfectly elastic.
    b. The demand for beer is perfectly inelastic.
    c. The supply of beer is perfectly elastic.
    d. The supply of beer is perfectly inelastic.

# BUSINESS APPLICATION

**LO 6.4** Describe the various types of quantity restrictions that governments can impose on markets.

## Concepts: Policies Aimed at Affecting Demand and Supply: Quantity Restriction Policies

**Small Business/Management: Industry Outlook and Strategies**

Demand and supply trends can be applied to develop an industry outlook, which is invaluable to a small business owner or upper-level corporate manager making strategic decisions about expansion plans or marketing strategies. One such strategy is a quantity restriction policy. To illustrate this application, consider the following hypothetical graph, which focuses on the market for dentist services.

**Market for Dentist Services**

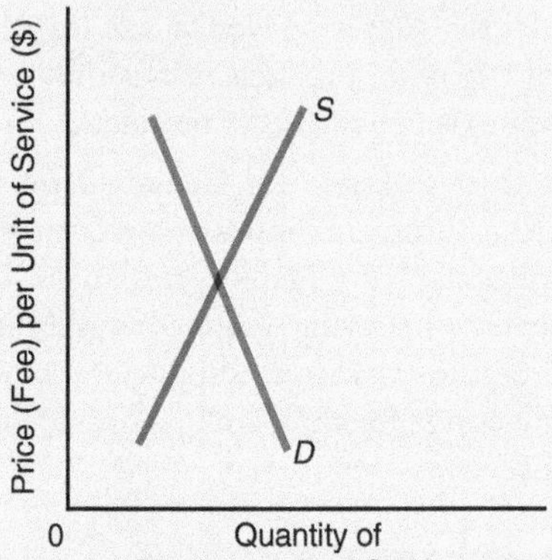


## Business Application Problems

1. For each of the following events, determine whether the event will increase or decrease the demand or the supply of dentist services. Also, for each event, predict whether the event will tend to cause an increase or decrease in the fee (price) that dentists can charge per unit of service.
   a. **EVENT:** The widespread use of fluorides has reduced tooth decay.
   b. **EVENT:** There has been a significant trend toward preventative practices, such as flossing and regular teeth cleaning.
   c. **EVENT:** More para-professionals, such as dental nurses, are performing standard dental procedures, such as fillings.
   d. **EVENT:** Compared to previous years, now fillings, crowns, and bridges are being made with more durable, longer-lasting materials.
   e. **EVENT:** Schools of dentistry across the nation are producing graduates at a much faster rate than the growth in the population.
2. From an existing dentist's point of view, do the trends in demand and supply (described in part (a), above) suggest a positive or negative industry outlook?
3. One advantage of trying to predict the industry outlook is that the business owner and/or corporate manager may be able to change that outlook, through strategies to change the industry demand and/or supply. For each of the following business strategies, determine whether the strategy will increase or decrease the demand or the

supply of dentist services. Also, for each event, predict whether the event will tend to cause an increase or decrease in the fee (price) that dentists can charge per unit of service.

a. **STRATEGY:** The National Association of Dentists requires a higher grade for a student to qualify for dental school.
b. **STRATEGY:** The National Association of Dentists increases the standards that foreign dentists must meet in order to practice dentistry in the country.
c. **STRATEGY:** The National Association of Dentists successfully lobbies the government to provide subsidized dental care to seniors and those on welfare.
d. **STRATEGY:** Through anaesthetics, "laughing gas," and hypnosis, dentists are increasingly making the visit to the dentist chair more relaxed and virtually pain free.
e. **STRATEGY:** Dental secretaries contact patients to remind them to attend their regular six-month checkup.

4. As president of your provincial dental association, you are examining the possibility of implementing a quantity restriction policy similar to that used by farmer marketing boards. You have just conducted statistical analysis on the nature of supply and demand for key services provided by dentists in your province. As an example, the graph below describes the current state of market demand and supply for crowns in your province.
   a. If you pursue a laissez-faire policy and let the current market conditions prevail, what will be the equilibrium price per crown?
   b. Under the laissez-faire policy, what will be the annual total revenue collected by the dentists from the provision of crowns in your province?

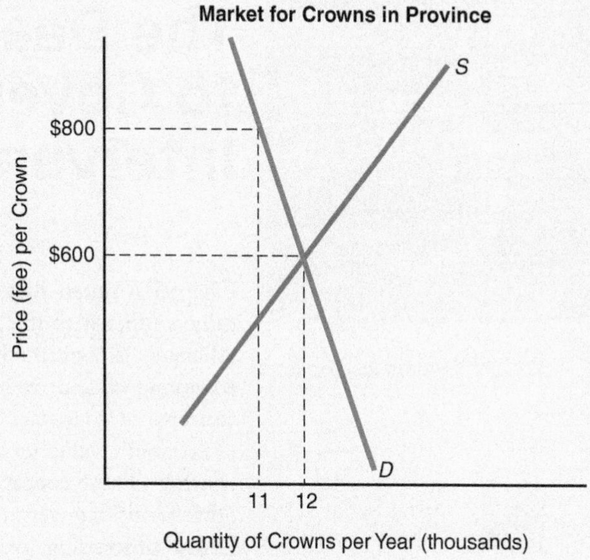


   c. Suppose you decide to convince your fellow dentists to pursue a marketing-board–type policy where the annual supply of crowns would be fixed at 11 000. This would be, in part, achieved by restricting the degree to which foreign dentists could practice in your province, as well as increasing the passing averages in your school of dentistry. Under this marketing board policy, what will be the annual total revenue collected by the dentists from the provision of crowns in your province?
   d. Is the demand for the crown services elastic or inelastic in the $600 to $800 price range? Explain.

# APPENDIX C

# The Deadweight Loss Due to Government Market Intervention

Chapter 6 noted that government policies such as price ceilings and price floors typically conflict with the goal of allocative efficiency. As noted in earlier chapters, allocative efficiency is concerned with producing the right mix or quantities of goods to maximize economic value or well being, given limited resources. This Appendix illustrates how the concepts of consumer and producer surplus can be used to estimate the total dollar loss in economic value resulting from government market intervention policies, such as price controls. These concepts can similarly be applied to estimate the efficiency loss related to other forms of government market intervention, such as marketing boards and excise taxes. Before proceeding, we will briefly review how a laissez-faire policy promotes allocative efficiency, as illustrated in Chapter 5.

## Market Equilibrium and Allocative Efficiency

In a laissez-faire (unregulated) market situation, production and consumption takes place to the point where market demand equals market supply, or where the marginal benefit received from the last unit consumed equals its marginal cost. At this market equilibrium, the sum of consumer and producer surplus is maximized, which means that allocative efficiency is achieved. This assumes that there are no forms of market failure present.

For example, consider Figure C-1, which describes the market for two-bedroom apartments in a Canadian city. Under a laissez-faire policy, the equilibrium price of $600 per unit and the equilibrium quantity of 60 000 units will prevail, where the marginal benefit of the last rental unit consumed ($600) just equals its marginal cost of production ($600). At this equilibrium point, the sum of consumer and producer surplus is maximized. For the equilibrium quantity of 60 000 units, the consumer surplus is the area under the demand curve and over the $600 price line, which equals the area of the blue triangle: .5 × base × height = .5 × 60 000 units × $700 per unit = $21 000 000. The producer surplus is the area above the supply curve and under the $600 price line, which

**FIGURE C–1**

**Allocative Efficiency in an Apartment Rental Market**

Allocative efficiency is achieved at the market equilibrium price of $600 per unit and quantity of 60 000 units. This is because the sum of consumer and producer surplus is maximized at this equilibrium point. For the equilibrium quantity of 60 000 units, the consumer surplus is the area under the demand curve and over the $600 price line, which equals the area of the blue triangle: .5 × base × height = .5 × 60 000 units × $700 per unit = $21 000 000. The producer surplus is the area above the supply curve and under the $600 price line, which equals the area of the red triangle: .5 × base × height = .5 × 60 000 units × $600 per unit = $18 000 000.

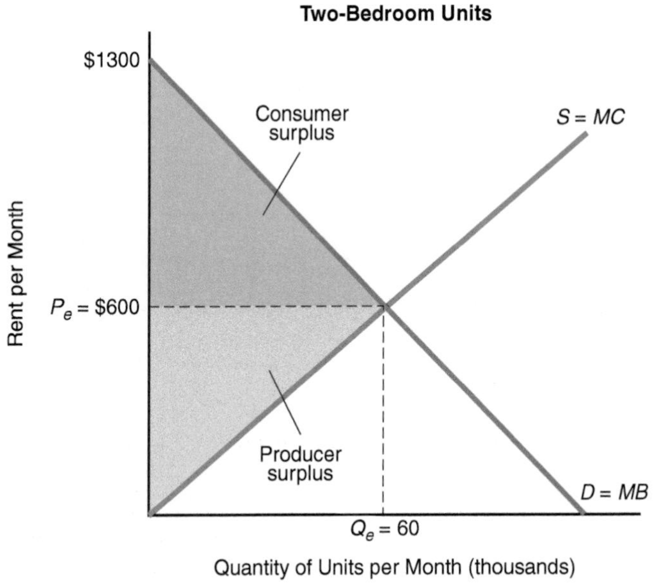

equals the area of the red triangle: .5 × base × height = .5 × 60 000 units × \$600 per unit = \$18 000 000. In this two-bedroom rental market, the maximum consumer and producer surplus that is possible occurs at the market equilibrium and equals \$21 000 000 + \$18 000 000 = \$39 000 000. This \$39 million represents the net benefit (net value) that buyers and sellers derive from participating in this apartment rental market and is maximized at this equilibrium point.

# Price Ceiling Policies and Allocative Inefficiency

In Chapter 6 we studied a price ceiling policy where, in a specific market, the government sets the price below the equilibrium price. We saw how this policy causes a shortage for the product that is being price controlled.

Figure C–2 describes a price ceiling policy that is being imposed on a two-bedroom apartment rental market. The ceiling price, $P_c$, of \$400 per unit is below the equilibrium price, $P_e$, of \$600 per unit. At the ceiling price, the number of rental units supplied will eventually decrease from 60 000 units per month at $Q_e$ to 40 000 units per month at $Q_c$. At $Q_e$ = 40 000 units, the consumer surplus and producer surplus will be reduced by triangular areas *M* and *N*, respectively, indicating a situation of allocative inefficiency.

At the ceiling policy quantity of 40 000 units, the marginal cost of supplying the next rental unit is approximately \$400 (height of the supply curve at $Q_c$ = 40 000), while the marginal benefit of the next rental unit is approximately \$850 (height of the demand curve at $Q_c$ = 40,000).

If one more rental unit is supplied, the extra \$850 value gained will exceed the \$400 value of lost production in the next-best product area. From society's view, there will be a net gain in value of approximately \$450 by renting out this additional two-bedroom unit. By not producing more than 40 000 rental units, this extra net gain in value is lost, and society is *underproducing* two-bedroom rental units.

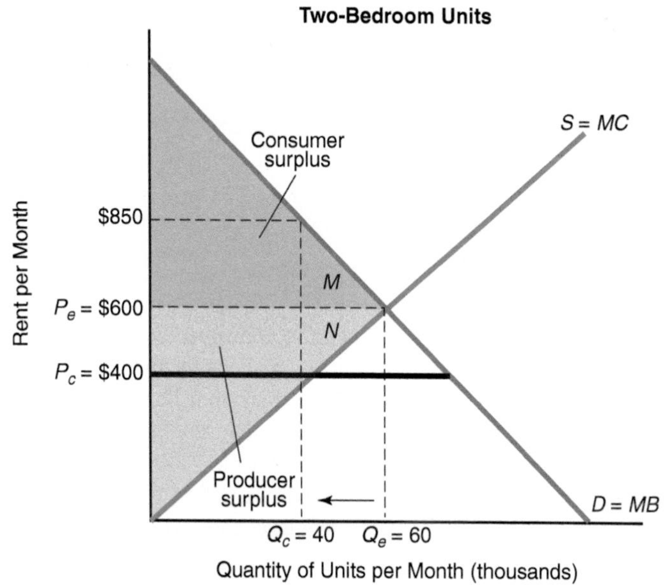


**FIGURE C–2**

**Rent Ceiling Policy and Allocative Inefficiency**

With the price ceiling set at \$400 per unit, the quantity supplied will decrease from 60 000 units to 40 000 units. This reduces the consumer and producer surpluses by the triangular areas of *M* and *N*, respectively, resulting in allocative inefficiency.

# Price Floor Policies and Allocative Inefficiency

In Chapter 6, we studied a price floor policy where, in a specific market, the government sets the price above the equilibrium price. We saw how this policy causes a surplus for the product that is being price controlled.

Figure C–3 describes a price floor policy being implemented in the wheat market. The floor price, $P_f$, of \$6 per bushel is above the equilibrium price, $P_e$, of \$5 per bushel. At the floor price, the quantity of wheat supplied will eventually increase from 3 million bushels per month at $Q_e$ to 4 million bushels per month at $Q_f$. At $Q_f = 4$ million bushels, the consumer surplus and producer surplus will be reduced by triangular areas $S$ and $R$, respectively, indicating a situation of allocative inefficiency.

At the floor policy quantity of 4 million bushels, the marginal cost of supplying the last bushel of wheat is approximately \$6 (height of the supply curve at $Q_f = 4$ million), while the marginal benefit of the last bushel of wheat is approximately \$4 (height of the demand curve at $Q_f = 4$ million).

If one fewer bushel of wheat is supplied, the \$4 value lost to wheat consumers (marginal benefit) will be less than \$6 value (marginal cost) gained by reallocating resources to the next-best product area (say, barley). From society's view, there will be a net gain in value of approximately \$2 by producing one fewer bushel of wheat and one more bushel of another product (barley). In other words, a price floor policy results in society *overproducing* the price-controlled good.

**FIGURE C–3**

**Price Floor Policy and Allocative Inefficiency**

With the price floor set at \$6 per bushel, the quantity supplied will increase from 3 million bushels to 4 million bushels. This reduces the consumer and producer surpluses by the triangular areas of *S* and *R*, respectively, resulting in allocative inefficiency.

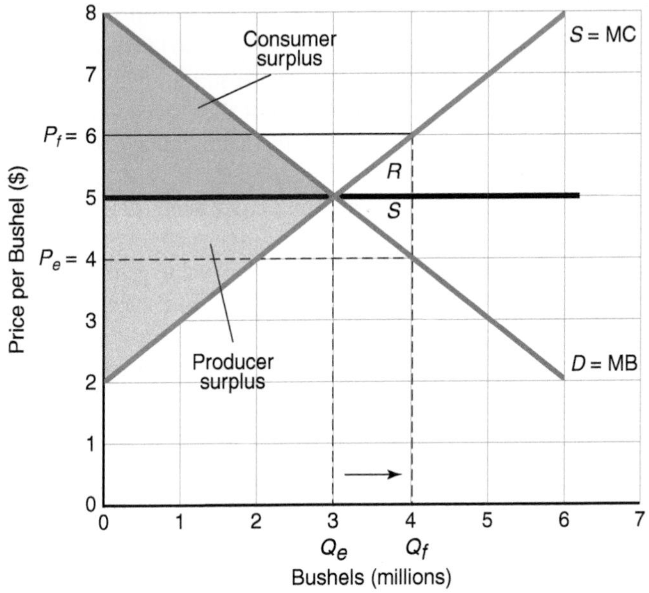


# APPENDIX SUMMARY

1. Allocative efficiency is concerned with producing the appropriate mix or quantities of goods so as to maximize economic value or well being, given our limited resources. In a laissez-faire (unregulated) market situation, production and consumption take place to the point where market demand equals market supply or where the marginal benefit received from the last unit consumed equals its marginal cost. At this market equilibrium, the sum of consumer and producer surplus is maximized, which means that allocative efficiency is achieved.
2. Under a price ceiling policy, the quantity supplied will be reduced to a level below equilibrium quantity. This will reduce the combined consumer and producer surplus, resulting in allocative inefficiency. For the last unit produced, the marginal benefit exceeds the marginal cost, indicating that the price-controlled product is being underproduced.
3. Under a price floor policy, the quantity supplied will be increased to a level above the equilibrium quantity. This will reduce the combined consumer and producer surplus, resulting in allocative inefficiency. For the last unit produced, the marginal benefit will be less than the marginal cost, indicating that the price controlled product is being overproduced.

## APPENDIX PROBLEMS

C-1. Refer to Figure C-4, which describes the regular gasoline market for a large Canadian city.

a. Under a laissez-faire market policy, calculate the sum of the consumer and producer surplus.
b. Suppose the government imposed a price ceiling of $.90 per litre. Calculate the change in consumer and producer surplus due to this policy. How does this policy affect the goal of allocative efficiency?
c. Does this price ceiling policy result in an over-production or under-production of regular gasoline? Explain.

C-2. Refer to Figure C-4, which describes the regular gasoline market for a large Canadian city.

a. Suppose the government imposed a price floor of $1.60 per litre. Calculate the change in consumer and producer surplus due to this policy. How does this policy affect the goal of allocative efficiency?
b. Does this price floor policy result in an over-production or underproduction of regular gasoline? Explain.

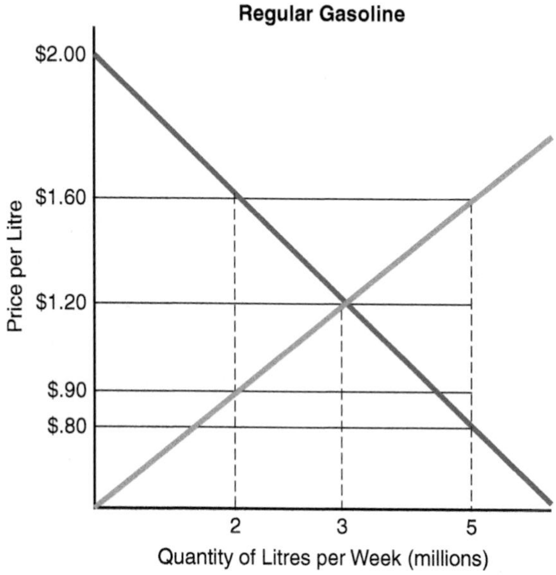


FIGURE C-4
Market for Regular Gasoline

# 7

## LEARNING OBJECTIVES

After reading this chapter, you should be able to:

**7.1** Describe the utility theory and how it impacts the decisions of consumers.

**7.2** Define the law of diminishing marginal utility and how it relates to consumer optimum.

# Consumer Choice

In Canada, even if you live in a city, you can surely appreciate the existence of Banff National Park, the Rocky Mountains, and the great wilderness areas in the North and other parts of the country. And even if you have never seen a whale, you may receive some satisfaction from knowing that whales have not been made extinct. Therefore, you may feel a certain loss when an environmental disaster, such as a huge oil spill, occurs. Should your feelings of loss be taken into account when government officials attempt to determine the policy response to environmental damage? To answer this question, you need to know how consumers make choices and what values they place on those choices.

myeconlab

MyEconLab helps you master each objective and study more efficiently. See end of chapter for details.

# DID YOU KNOW THAT...?

In a typical year, a Canadian family spends about 15 percent of its income on food and about the same on housing. Within individual families, however, these relative percentages may be quite different. Some families devote a much higher percentage of their income to housing than do others. What determines how much each family spends on different items in its budget? One explanation is, simply, individual tastes—the values that family members place on different items on which they can spend their income. The saying "you can't argue with tastes" suggests that individuals have different preferences about how to allocate their limited incomes. Although there is no real theory about what determines people's tastes, we can examine some of the behaviour that underlies how consumers react to changes in the prices of the goods and services that they purchase. Recall that people generally purchase less at higher prices than at lower prices. This is called the law of demand.

Because the law of demand is important, its derivation is useful as it allows us to arrange the relevant variables, such as price, income, and tastes, in a way that lets us understand the real world better and even perhaps generate predictions about it. One way of deriving the law of demand involves an analysis of the logic of consumer choice in a world of limited resources. In this chapter, therefore, we discuss what is called utility analysis.

## 7.1 Utility Theory

When you buy something, you do so because of the satisfaction you expect to receive from having and using that good. For everything that you like to have, the more you have of it, the higher the level of satisfaction you receive. Another term that can be used for satisfaction is **utility**, or want-satisfying power of a good or service. This property is common to all goods that are desired. The concept of utility is purely subjective, however. There is no way that we can measure the amount of utility that a consumer might be able to obtain from a particular good, for utility does not imply "useful" or "utilitarian" or "practical." For this reason, there can be no accurate, scientific assessment of the utility that someone might receive by consuming a frozen dinner or viewing a movie relative to the utility that another person might receive from that same good or service. Nevertheless, we can infer whether a person receives more utility from consuming one good versus another by that person's behaviour. For example, if an individual buys more coffee than tea (when both tea and coffee are priced equally), we are able to say that the individual receives more utility from consuming coffee than from consuming tea.

**Utility** The want-satisfying power of a good or service.

What are some of the determinants of this consumer's decision to buy a new cellphone?

The utility that individuals receive from consuming a good depends on their tastes and preferences. These tastes and preferences are normally assumed to be given and stable for a particular individual. It is tastes that determine how much utility that individual derives from consuming a good, and this, in turn, determines how that individual allocates income. People spend a greater proportion of their incomes on goods they like. But we cannot explain why tastes are different among individuals. For example, we cannot explain why some people like yogurt but others do not.

We can analyze in terms of utility the way consumers decide what to buy, just as physicists have analyzed some of their questions about what they call "force." No physicist has ever seen a unit of force, and no economist has ever seen a unit of utility. In both cases, however, these concepts have proven useful for analysis.

Throughout this chapter, we will be discussing **utility analysis**, which is the analysis of consumer decision making based on utility maximization.

**Utility analysis** The analysis of consumer decision making based on utility maximization.

### Utility and Utils

Economists once believed that utility could be measured. In fact, there is a school of thought based on utility theory called *utilitarianism*, developed by the English philosopher Jeremy Bentham (1748–1832). Bentham held that society should seek the greatest happiness for the greatest number. He sought to apply an arithmetic formula for

**Util** A representative unit by which utility is measured.

measuring happiness. He and his followers developed the notion of measurable utility and invented the **util** to measure it. For the moment, we will also assume that we can measure satisfaction using this representative unit. Our assumption will allow us to quantify the way we examine consumer behaviour.[1] Thus, the first chocolate bar that you eat might yield you four utils of satisfaction; the first peanut cluster, six utils; and so on. Today, no one really believes that we can actually measure utils, but the ideas forthcoming from such analysis will prove useful in our understanding of the way in which consumers choose among alternatives.

## Total and Marginal Utility

Consider the satisfaction, or utility, that you receive each time that you rent and watch a video. To make the example straightforward, let us say that there are hundreds of videos to choose from each year and that each of them is of the same quality. Let us say that you normally rent one video per week. You could, of course, rent two, or three, or four per week. Presumably, each time you rent another video per week, you will get additional satisfaction, or utility. The question, though, that we must ask is, given that you are already renting one per week, will the next one rented that week give you the same amount of additional utility?

**Marginal utility** The change in total utility divided by the change in the number of units consumed.

That additional, or incremental, utility is called **marginal utility**, the change in total utility divided by the change in the number of units consumed, where *marginal,* as before, means "incremental" or "additional." (Marginal changes also refer to decreases, in which cases we talk about *decremental* changes.) The concept of marginality is important in economics because we make decisions at the margin. At any particular point, we compare additional (marginal) benefits with additional (marginal) costs.

## Applying Marginal Analysis to Utility

The specific example presented in Figure 7–1 will clarify the distinction between total utility and marginal utility. The table in part (a) shows the total utility and the marginal utility of watching videos each week. Marginal utility is the difference between total utility derived from one level of consumption and total utility derived from another level of consumption. A simple formula for marginal utility is this:

$$\text{Marginal utility} = \frac{\text{Change in total utility}}{\text{Change in number of units consumed}}$$

In our example, when a person has already watched two videos in one week and then watches another, total utility increases from 16 utils to 19. Therefore, the marginal utility (of watching one more video after already having watched two in one week) is equal to three utils.

## Graphic Analysis

We can transfer the information in part (a) of Figure 7–1 onto a graph, as we do in parts (b) and (c). Total utility, which is represented in column 2 of part (a), is transferred to part (b).

[1]What follows is typically called *cardinal utility analysis* by economists. It requires cardinal measurement. Numbers such as 1, 2, and 3 are cardinal numbers. We know that 2 is exactly twice as many as 1 and that 3 is exactly three times as many as 1. You will see in Appendix D at the end of this chapter a type of consumer behaviour analysis that requires only *ordinal* measurement of utility, meaning ranked or ordered. *First, second,* and *third* are ordinal numbers; nothing can be said about their exact size relationships. We can only talk about their importance relative to each other. Temperature, for example, is an ordinal ranking. One hundred degrees Celsius is not twice as warm as 50 degrees Celsius. All we can say is that 100 degrees Celsius is warmer than 50 degrees Celsius.

**FIGURE 7–1**

## Total and Marginal Utility of Watching Videos

If we were able to assign specific values to the utility derived from watching videos each week, we could obtain a marginal utility schedule similar in pattern to the one shown in part (a). In column 1 is the number of videos watched per week; in column 2, the total utility derived from each quantity; and in column 3, the marginal utility derived from each additional quantity, which is defined as the change in total utility due to a change of one unit of watching videos per week. Total utility from part (a) is plotted in part (b). Marginal utility is plotted in part (c), where you see that it reaches zero where total utility hits its maximum at between four and five units.

Part (a)

| (1) Number of Videos Watched per Week | (2) Total Utility (utils per week) | (3) Marginal Utility (utils per week) |
|---|---|---|
| 0 | 0 | |
| 1 | 10 | 10 (10 – 0) |
| 2 | 16 | 6 (16 – 10) |
| 3 | 19 | 3 (19 – 16) |
| 4 | 20 | 1 (20 – 19) |
| 5 | 20 | 0 (20 – 20) |
| 6 | 18 | –2 (18 – 20) |

Part (b)

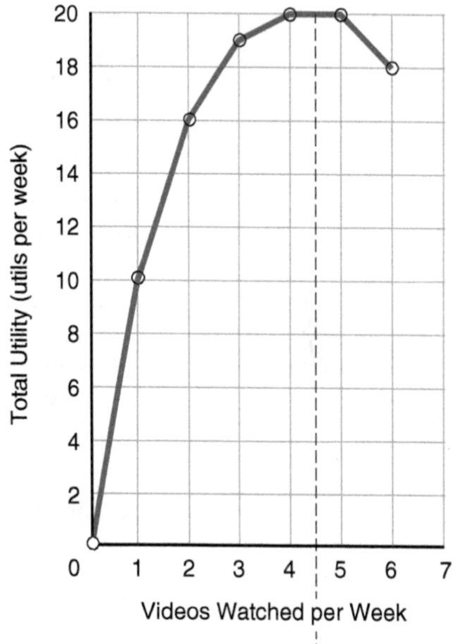


Part (c)

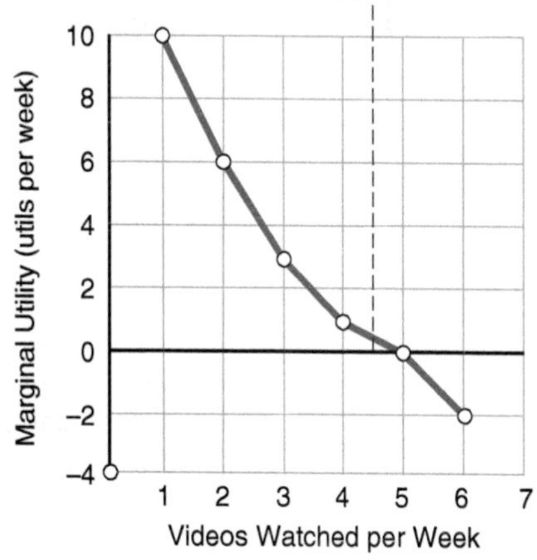


Total utility continues to rise until four videos are watched per week. This measure of utility remains at 20 utils through the fifth video, and at the sixth video per week it falls to 18 utils; we assume that at some quantity consumed per unit time period, boredom sets in. This is shown in part (b).

## Marginal Utility

If you look carefully at parts (b) and (c) of Figure 7–1, the notion of marginal utility becomes very clear. In economics, the term *marginal* always refers to a change in the total. The marginal utility of watching three videos per week instead of two videos per week is the increment in total utility and is equal to three utils per week. All of the points in part (c) are taken from column 3 of the table in part (a). Note that marginal utility falls throughout the

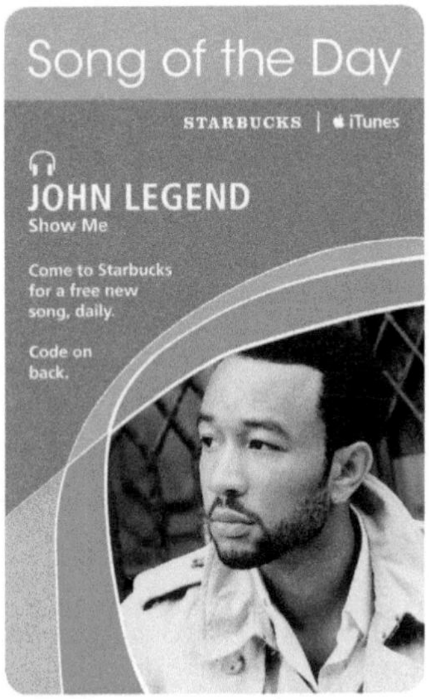


How does marginal utility derived from a music download influence the quantity of music downloads consumed?

graph. A special point occurs after four videos are watched per week because the total utility curve in part (b) is unchanged after the consumption of the fourth video. That means that the consumer receives no additional (marginal) utility from watching the fifth video. This is shown in part (c) as *zero* marginal utility. After that point, marginal utility becomes negative.

In our example, when marginal utility becomes negative, it means that the consumer is fed up with watching videos and would require some form of compensation to watch any more. When marginal utility is negative, an additional unit consumed actually lowers total utility by becoming a nuisance. Rarely does a consumer face a situation of negative marginal utility. Whenever this point is reached, goods become, in effect, "bads." A rational consumer will stop consuming at the point at which marginal utility becomes negative, even if the good is free.

## 7.2 Diminishing Marginal Utility

**Diminishing marginal utility** The principle that as an individual consumes more of a particular commodity, the total level of utility, or satisfaction, derived from that consumption usually increases. Eventually, however, the rate at which it increases diminishes as more is consumed.

Note that in part (c) of Figure 7–1, marginal utility is continuously declining. This property has been named *the principle of diminishing marginal utility*. It is not a concept that can be proven, but economists and others have believed in it for years and it has even been called a law. This supposed law concerns a psychological, or subjective, utility that you receive as you consume more and more of a particular good. Stated formally, the law of **diminishing marginal utility** is as follows:

> **As an individual consumes more of a particular commodity, the total level of utility, or satisfaction, derived from that consumption usually increases. Eventually, however, the rate at which it increases diminishes as more is consumed.**

Take a hungry individual at a dinner table. The first serving is greatly appreciated, and the individual derives a substantial amount of utility from it. The second serving does not have quite as much impact as the first one, and the third serving is likely to be even less satisfying. This individual experiences diminishing marginal utility of food and stops eating. This is true for most people. All-you-can-eat restaurants count on this fact; a second helping of ribs may provide some marginal utility, but the third helping would have only a little or even negative marginal utility. The fall in the marginal utility of other goods is even more dramatic. See, for instance, Example 7–1. Why are candy vending machines different from newspaper vending machines?

### EXAMPLE 7–1 Newspaper Vending Machines versus Candy Vending Machines

In the past, newspapers could be purchased from a newspaper vending machine. Newspaper vending machines where nearly everywhere in Canada and would allow you to put in the correct change—the cost of one newspaper—lift up the door, and take as many newspapers as you want? Contrast this type of vending machine with candy machines. They are completely locked at all times. You must designate the candy that you wish, normally by using some type of keypad. The candy then drops down to a place where you reach to retrieve it but from which you cannot grab any other candy. The difference between these two types of vending machines is explained by diminishing marginal utility. Newspaper companies dispense newspapers from coin-operated boxes that allow dishonest people to take more copies than they pay for. What would a dishonest person do with more than one copy of a newspaper, however? The marginal utility of a second newspaper is normally zero. The benefit of storing excessive newspapers is usually nil because yesterday's news has no value. But the same analysis does not hold for candy. The marginal utility of a second candy bar is certainly less than the first, but it is normally not zero. Moreover, one can store candy for relatively long periods of time at relatively low cost. Consequently, food vending machine companies have to worry about dishonest users of their machines and must make their machines much more theft-proof than newspaper companies do.

**For critical analysis:** Can you think of a circumstance under which there would be no diminished marginal utility to newspaper purchasers so that they might be inclined to take more than one newspaper out of a vending machine?

Consider for a moment the opposite possibility—increasing marginal utility. Under such a situation, the marginal utility after consuming, say, one hamburger would increase. The second hamburger would be more valuable to you, and the third would be even more valuable yet. If increasing marginal utility existed, each of us would consume only one good or service! Rather than observing that "variety is the spice of life," we would see that monotony in consumption was preferred. We do not observe this, and therefore, we have great confidence in the concept of diminishing marginal utility.

## Optimizing Consumption Choices

Every consumer has a limited income. Choices must be made. When a consumer has made all choices about what to buy and in what quantities, and when the total level of satisfaction, or utility, from that set of choices is as great as it can be, we say that the consumer has *optimized.* When the consumer has attained an optimum consumption set of goods and services, we say that this individual has reached **consumer optimum.**[2]

**Consumer optimum** Reached when the consumer has attained an optimum consumption set of goods and services.

Consider a simple two-good example. The consumer has to choose between spending income on the rental of videos at $5 each and on purchasing deluxe hamburgers at $3 each. Let us say that the last dollar spent on hamburgers yields three utils of utility, but the last dollar spent on video rentals yields 10 utils. Wouldn't this consumer increase total utility if some dollars were taken away from hamburger consumption and allocated to video rentals? The answer is yes. Given diminishing marginal utility, more dollars spent on video rentals will reduce marginal utility per last dollar spent, whereas fewer dollars spent on hamburger consumption will increase marginal utility per last dollar spent. The optimum—where total utility is maximized—might occur when the satisfaction per last dollar spent on both hamburgers and video rentals per week is equal for the two goods. Thus, the amount of goods consumed depends on the prices of the goods, the income of the consumers, and the marginal utility derived from each good.

Table 7–1 presents information on utility derived from consuming various quantities of videos and hamburgers. Columns 4 and 8 show the marginal utility per dollar spent on videos and hamburgers, respectively. If the prices of both goods are zero, individuals will consume each as long as their respective marginal utility is positive (at least five units of each and probably much more). It is also true that a consumer with infinite income will continue consuming goods until the marginal utility of each is equal to zero. When the price is zero or the consumer's income is infinite, there is no effective constraint on consumption.

Consumer optimum is attained when the marginal utility of the last dollar spent on each good is the same and income is completely exhausted. The individual's income is $26. From columns 4 and 8 of Table 7–1, maximum equal marginal utilities per dollar occur at the consumption level of four videos and two hamburgers (the marginal utility per dollar spent equals 7.3). Note that the marginal utility per dollar spent for both goods is also (approximately) equal at the consumption level of three videos and one hamburger, but here, total income is not completely exhausted. Likewise, the marginal utility per dollar spent is (approximately) equal at five videos and three hamburgers, but the expenditures necessary for that level of consumption exceed the individual's income.

Table 7–2 shows the steps taken to arrive at consumer optimum. The first video would yield a marginal utility per dollar of 10.0, while the first hamburger would yield a marginal utility of only 8.3 per dollar. Because it yields the higher marginal utility per dollar, the video is purchased. This leaves $21 of income. The second video yields a higher marginal utility per dollar (9.0, versus 8.3 for hamburgers), and so it is also purchased, leaving an unspent income of $16. At the third purchase, the first hamburger now yields a higher marginal utility per dollar than the next video (8.3 versus 8.0), and so the first hamburger is purchased. This leaves income of $13 to spend. The process continues until all income is exhausted and the marginal utility per dollar spent is equal for both goods.

[2]Optimization typically refers to individual decision-making processes. When we deal with many individuals interacting in the marketplace, we talk in terms of an equilibrium in the marketplace. Generally speaking, equilibrium is a property of markets rather than of individual decision making.

**TABLE 7–1**

## Total and Marginal Utility from Consuming Videos and Hamburgers on an Income of $26

| (1) Videos per Period | (2) Total Utility of Videos per Period (utils) | (3) Marginal Utility (utils) $MU_v$ | (4) Marginal Utility per Dollar Spent ($MU_v/P_v$) (price = $5) | (5) Hamburgers per Period | (6) Total Utility of Hamburgers per Period (utils) | (7) Marginal Utility (utils) $MU_h$ | (8) Marginal Utility per Dollar Spent ($MU_h/P_h$) (price = $3) |
|---|---|---|---|---|---|---|---|
| 0 | 0.0 | – | – | 0 | 0 | – | – |
| 1 | 50.0 | 50.0 | 10.0 | 1 | 25 | 25 | 8.3 |
| 2 | 95.0 | 45.0 | 9.0 | 2 | 47 | 22 | 7.3 |
| 3 | 135.0 | 40.0 | 8.0 | 3 | 65 | 18 | 6.0 |
| 4 | 171.5 | 36.5 | 7.3 | 4 | 80 | 15 | 5.0 |
| 5 | 200.0 | 28.5 | 5.7 | 5 | 89 | 9 | 3.0 |

**TABLE 7–2**

## Steps to Consumer Optimum

In each purchase situation described here, the consumer always purchases the good with the higher marginal utility per dollar spent ($MU/P$). For example, at the time of the third purchase, the marginal utility per last dollar spent on videos is 8.0, but it is 8.3 for hamburgers, and $16 of income remains, and so the next purchase will be a hamburger. Here, $P_v = \$5$ and $P_h = \$3$.

| | Choices | | | | | |
|---|---|---|---|---|---|---|
| | Videos | | Hamburgers | | | |
| Purchase | Unit | ($MU_v/P_v$) | Unit | ($MU_h/P_h$) | Buying Decision | Remaining Income |
| 1 | First | 10.0 | First | 8.3 | First video | $26 – $5 = $21 |
| 2 | Second | 9.0 | First | 8.3 | Second video | $21 – $5 = $16 |
| 3 | Third | 8.0 | First | 8.3 | First hamburger | $16 – $3 = $13 |
| 4 | Third | 8.0 | Second | 7.3 | Third video | $13 – $5 = $ 8 |
| 5 | Fourth | 7.3 | Second | 7.3 | Fourth video and second hamburger | $ 8 – $5 = $ 3<br>$ 3 – $3 = $ 0 |

To restate, consumer optimum requires the following:

**A consumer's money income should be allocated so that the last dollar spent on each good purchased yields the same amount of marginal utility (when all income is spent).**

## A Little Math

We can state the rule of consumer optimum in algebraic terms by examining the ratio of marginal utilities and prices of individual products. This is sometimes called the *utility maximization rule.*

The rule simply states that a consumer maximizes personal satisfaction when allocating money income in such a way that the last dollars spent on good A, good B, good C, and so on, yield equal amounts of marginal utility. Marginal utility (*MU*) from good A is indicated by *MU* of good A. For good B, it is *MU* of good B.

Our algebraic formulation of this rule, therefore, becomes

$$\frac{MU \text{ of good A}}{\text{Price of good A}} = \frac{MU \text{ of good B}}{\text{Price of good B}} = \cdots = \frac{MU \text{ of good Z}}{\text{Price of good Z}}$$

The letters A, B, . . . , Z indicate the various goods and services that the consumer might purchase.

We know, then, that the marginal utility of good A divided by the price of good A must equal the marginal utility of any other good divided by its price in order for the consumer to maximize utility. Note, though, that the application of the utility maximization rule is not an explicit or conscious act on the part of consumers. Rather, this is a model of consumer optimum.

## How a Price Change Affects Consumer Optimum

Consumption decisions are summarized in the law of demand, which states that the amount purchased is inversely related to price. We can now see why by using the law of diminishing marginal utility.

Purchase decisions are made such that the value of the marginal utility of the last unit purchased and consumed is just equal to the price that had to be paid. No consumer will, when optimizing, buy 10 units of a good per time period when the personal valuation placed on the tenth unit is less than the price of the tenth unit.

If we start out at consumer optimum and then observe a price decrease, we can predict that consumers will respond to the price decrease by consuming more. Now, with a lower price, it is possible to consume more than before and still not have the marginal utility be less than the price because the price has fallen. If the law of diminishing marginal utility holds, the purchase and consumption of additional units will cause marginal utility to fall. Eventually it will fall to the point at which it is equal to the price of the final good consumed. The limit to this increase in consumption is given by the law of diminishing marginal utility.

A hypothetical demand curve for video rentals per week for a typical consumer is presented in Figure 7–2. Because of the law of diminishing marginal utility, with the consumption of more videos, the marginal utility of the last unit of these additional videos is lower. What has happened is that at a lower price, the number of video rentals per week increased from two to three; marginal utility must have fallen. At a higher consumption rate, the marginal utility falls to meet the lower price for video rentals per week.

## The Demand Curve Revisited

Linking the "law" of diminishing marginal utility and the utility maximization rule gives us a negative relationship between the quantity demanded of a good or service and its price. As the relative price of video rentals goes up, for example, the quantity demanded will fall; and as the relative price of video rentals goes down, the quantity demanded will rise. Figure 7–2 shows this demand curve for video rentals. As the price

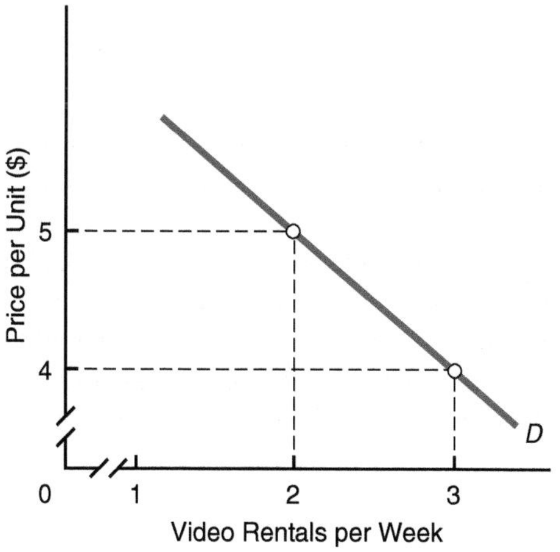


**FIGURE 7–2**

**Video Rental Prices and Marginal Utility**

A reduction in price from $5 to $4 per video rental causes consumers to increase consumption until marginal utility falls (because of the law of diminishing marginal utility).

of video rentals falls, the consumer can maximize total utility only by renting more videos and vice versa. In other words, the relationship between price and quantity desired is simply a downward-sloping demand curve. Note, though, that this downward-sloping demand curve (the law of demand) is derived under the assumption of constant tastes and incomes. You must remember that we are keeping these important determining variables constant when we simply look at the relationship between price and quantity demanded.

## Marginal Utility, Total Utility, and the Diamond–Water Paradox

Even though water is essential to life and diamonds are not, water is cheap and diamonds are dear. The economist Adam Smith in 1776 called this the "diamond–water paradox." The paradox is easily understood when we realize that the supply of water is abundant relative to demand and therefore carries a low price. Diamonds, however, are scarce relative to demand and therefore carry a high price. To better understand this, we must make the distinction between total utility and marginal utility. The total utility of water greatly exceeds the total utility derived from diamonds. What determines the price, though, is what happens on the margin. We have relatively few diamonds, and so the marginal utility of the last diamond consumed is high. The opposite is true for water. Total utility does not determine what people are willing to pay for a unit of a particular commodity; marginal utility does. Look at the situation presented graphically in Figure 7–3. We show the demand curve for diamonds, labelled $D_{\text{diamonds}}$. The demand curve for water is labelled $D_{\text{water}}$. We plot quantity in terms of kilograms per unit time period on the horizontal axis. On the vertical axis, we plot price in dollars per kilogram. We use kilograms as our common unit of measurement for water and for diamonds. We could just as well have used gallons, acre-feet, or litres.

Note that the demand for water is many, many times the demand for diamonds. We draw the supply curve of water as $S_1$ at a quantity of $Q_{\text{water}}$. The supply curve for diamonds is given as $S_2$ at quantity $Q_{\text{diamonds}}$. At the intersection of the supply curve of water with the demand curve of water, the price per kilogram is $P_{\text{water}}$. The intersection of the supply curve of diamonds with the demand curve of diamonds is at $P_{\text{diamonds}}$. Note that $P_{\text{diamonds}}$ exceeds $P_{\text{water}}$. Diamonds sell at a higher price than water. See Example 7–2 for an illustration of the diamond–water paradox.

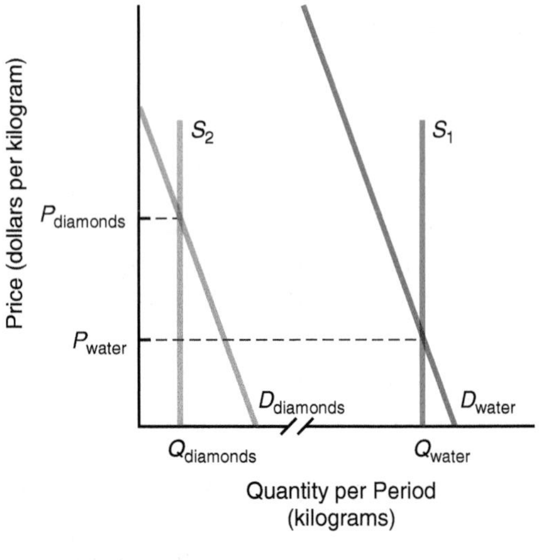


**FIGURE 7–3**

**The Diamond–Water Paradox**

We pick kilograms as a common unit of measurement for both water and diamonds. To demonstrate that the demand for and supply of water are immense, we have put a break in the horizontal quantity axis. Although the demand for water is much greater than the demand for diamonds, the marginal valuation of water is given by the marginal value placed on the last unit of water consumed. To find that, we must know the supply of water, which is given as $S_1$. At that supply, the price of water is $P_{\text{water}}$. But the supply for diamonds is given by $S_2$. At that supply, the price of diamonds is $P_{\text{diamonds}}$. The total valuation that consumers place on water is tremendous relative to the total valuation consumers place on diamonds. What is important for price determination, however, is the marginal valuation, or the marginal utility received.

**EXAMPLE 7–2 The Price of Water in Saudi Arabia**

The diamond–water paradox deals with the situation in which water, although necessary for life, may be much cheaper than some luxury items. In Saudi Arabia, as you might expect, the contrary can be true. A litre of water costs five times as much as a litre of gasoline, whereas a pair of custom-made British wool dress pants costs only $25. These relative prices are quite different from what we are used to seeing in Canada. Water costs next to nothing, a litre of gas costs about $1.10, and custom-made wool pants cost at least $200. To understand what has happened in Saudi Arabia, simply substitute gasoline for water and water for diamonds in Figure 7–3.

**For critical analysis:** List some of the effects on human behaviour that such a high relative price of water would cause.

## Behavioural Economics and Consumer Choice Theory

Utility analysis has long been appealing to economists because it makes clear predictions about how individuals will adjust their consumption of different goods and services based on the prices of those items and their incomes. Traditionally, another attraction of utility analysis to many economists has been its reliance on the assumption that consumers behave *rationally*, or that they do not intentionally make decisions that would leave them worse off. As we discussed in Chapter 1, proponents of behavioural economics have doubts about the rationality assumption, which causes them to question the utility-based theory of consumer choice.

**DOES BEHAVIOURAL ECONOMICS BETTER PREDICT CONSUMER CHOICES?** Advocates of behavioural economics question whether utility theory is supported by the facts, which they argue are better explained by applying the assumption of *bounded rationality*. Recall from Chapter 1 that this assumption states that human limitations prevent people from examining every possible choice available to them and thereby thwart their efforts to effectively pursue long-term personal interests.

For evidence supporting the bounded rationality assumption, proponents of behavioural economics point to real-world examples that they claim violate rationality-based utility theory. For instance, economists have found that when purchasing electric appliances such as refrigerators, people sometimes buy the lowest-priced, energy-inefficient models, even though the initial savings often fail to compensate for higher future energy costs. There is also evidence that people who live in earthquake- or flood-prone regions commonly fail to purchase sufficient insurance against these events. In addition, experiments have shown that when people are placed in situations in which strong emotions come into play, they may be willing to pay different amounts for items than they would pay in calmer settings.

These and other observed behaviours, behavioural economists suggest, indicate that consumers do not behave rationally. If the rationality assumption does not apply to actual behaviour, they argue, it follows that utility-based consumer choice theory cannot either.

Can behavioural economics explain why people who enjoy shopping for its own sake might later regret the purchases they make?

Do people behave rationally when making purchases?

**CONSUMER CHOICE THEORY REMAINS ALIVE AND WELL.** In spite of the doubts expressed by proponents of behavioural economics, most economists continue to apply the assumption that people behave *as if* they act rationally with an aim to maximize utility. These economists continue to apply utility theory because of a fundamental strength of this approach: it yields clear-cut predictions regarding consumer choices.

In contrast, if the rationality assumption is rejected, any number of possible human behaviours might be considered. To proponents of behavioural economics, ambiguities about actual outcomes make the bounded rationality approach to consumer choice more realistic than utility-based consumer choice theory. Nevertheless, a major drawback is that no clearly testable predictions emerge from the many alternative behaviours that people might exhibit if they fail to behave *as if* they are rational.

Certainly, arguments among economists about the "reasonableness" of rational consumers maximizing utility are likely to continue. So far, however, the use of utility-based consumer choice theory has allowed economists to make a wide array of predictions about how consumers respond to changes in prices, incomes, and other factors. By and large, these key predictions continue to be supported by the actual choices that consumers make.

ISSUES AND APPLICATIONS

# Contingent Valuation: Pricing the "Priceless"

**Concepts Applied: Utility, Total Utility, Demand Curve**

How much are we willing to pay to keep our national parks clean?

It is difficult to estimate the dollar amount an average citizen is willing to pay to keep Banff National Park's air clean. One way economists attempt to derive the demand for pristine wilderness is to use contingent valuation.

Obviously, not everything has a price. That is because not everything is bought and sold in the marketplace. Much of what occurs in the environment is outside the marketplace. A wilderness area so remote that hardly anyone visits it certainly has a value, but what is it? The fact that few people visit does not mean it has little worth. If the wilderness were privately owned and the owner received virtually no income from occasional visitors, that does not mean that it would have virtually no value.

## When Disaster Occurs

When the wilderness area with few visitors is harmed by some disaster of human origin, such as an oil spill, what has been lost? If your house is burned down, you can get a pretty accurate idea of what the insurance company will give you by looking at the housing market for an alternative. Such is not the case with an oil-blighted wilderness area in the far reaches of the North. Even though the BP oil spill in April 2010 occurred far out in the Gulf of Mexico, the oil still made it onto the beaches and affected the wildlife both in the ocean and on land.

## Nonuse Values

Even people who never use the wilderness area may place a value on it. They may place a value on the opportunity to preserve the wilderness for their grandchildren and on the mere knowledge that such a pristine wilderness area exists. The question, then, is how do we get an accurate valuation of these nonuse values?

## Contingent Valuation

Some economists believe that they can obtain an estimate of the demand curve for a wilderness area, for example, that includes nonuse values by conducting opinion polls. In this technique, called *contingent valuation*, people are asked what they are willing to pay for a particular benefit or what they would accept as compensation for its loss. This technique was used in developing multibillion-dollar damage claims against Exxon after its oil tanker, the *Exxon Valdez*, ran aground in Alaska in 1989. In essence, these contingent valuation surveys asked people *not* living in Alaska to place a value on the utility they lost by virtue of the fact that a part of Alaska's pristine beauty was harmed.

## Criticisms of Opinion Data

Many economists are critical of opinion surveys conducted to estimate utility. They point out that such estimates of supposed willingness to pay are without strong meaning if individuals do not actually have to make the payments. One opinion survey estimated the average individual's willingness to pay to prevent the extinction of the whooping crane at $200 per year. That comes to almost $3 billion per year for all Canadian adults. Given that there are fewer than 170 whooping cranes in existence, this total represents about $23.6 million per bird *per year*. There are literally thousands of species that might be protected. Even if households' average willingness to pay is only $10 per year per endangered species, summing that amount over all environmental "goods" would exceed the average family's yearly income many times.

The way in which opinion survey questions are phrased also reveals their weaknesses. In one study, the people interviewed said they would be willing to pay $90 a year to preserve clean air in Banff National Park. In a follow-up survey, when they were asked about paying for competing claims of cleaner air in Toronto and in the eastern provinces as well, they were willing to spend only $16 a year to preserve clean air in Banff National Park.

Finally, when people are asked about their willingness to accept money in exchange for a harm to a resource, rather than their willingness to pay to prevent that very same harm, the dollar values they cite are substantially higher.

**For critical analysis:**

1. Why can't opinion polls be used effectively to estimate demand curves?
2. How do individuals normally express their perceived level of satisfaction for a good or a service in the marketplace?

# SUMMARY

Here is what you should know after reading this chapter. MyEconLab will help you identify what you know and where to go when you need to practise. We suggest that as soon as you review one of the Learning Objective sections below, you then proceed to go through the related section in MyEconLab.

| LEARNING OBJECTIVES | KEY TERMS | MYECONLAB PRACTICE |
|---|---|---|
| **7.1 Utility Theory.** As an individual consumes more of a particular commodity, the total level of utility, or satisfaction, derived from that consumption increases. However, the rate at which it increases diminishes as more is consumed. This is known as the law of diminishing marginal utility. | utility, 165<br>utility analysis, 165<br>util, 166<br>marginal utility, 166 | • **MyEconLab** Study Plan 7.1 |
| **7.2 Diminishing Marginal Utility.** An individual reaches consumer optimum when the marginal utility per last dollar spent on each commodity consumed is equal to the marginal utility per dollar spent on every other good.<br>When the price of a particular commodity goes up, to get back into an optimum position, the consumer must reduce consumption of the now relatively more expensive commodity. As this consumer moves back up the marginal utility curve, marginal utility increases.<br>It is possible to derive a downward-sloping demand curve by using the principle of diminishing marginal utility. | diminishing marginal utility, 168<br>consumer optimum, 169 | • **MyEconLab** Study Plan 7.2 |

# PROBLEMS

(Answers to the odd-numbered problems appear at the back of the book.)

**LO 7.1 Describe the utility theory and how it impacts the decisions of consumers.**

1. Suppose that you are standing in the checkout line of a grocery store. You have 5 kilograms of oranges and three ears of corn. A kilogram of oranges costs 30 cents; so does an ear of corn. You have $2.40 to spend. You are satisfied that you have reached the highest level of satisfaction, or total utility. A friend comes along and tries to convince you that you have to put some of the corn back and replace it with oranges. From what you know about utility analysis, how would you explain this disagreement?
2. The campus pizzeria sells a single pizza for $12. If you order a second pizza, however, its price is only $5. Explain how this relates to marginal utility.
3. Assume that Alice Warfield's marginal utility is 100 utils for the last hamburger she consumed. If the price of hamburgers is $1 apiece, what is Warfield's marginal utility per dollar's worth of hamburger? What is her marginal utility per dollar's worth if the price is 50 cents per hamburger? If the price is $2? How do we calculate marginal utility per dollar's worth of specific commodities?
4. Where possible, complete the missing cells in the following table.

| Number of Cheese-burgers | Total Utility of Cheese-burgers | Marginal Utility of Cheese-burgers | Boxes of French Fries | Total Utility of French Fries | Marginal Utility of French Fries |
|---|---|---|---|---|---|
| 0 | 0 | — | 0 | 0 | — |
| 1 | 20 | — | 1 | — | 10 |
| 2 | 36 | — | 2 | — | 8 |
| 3 | — | 12 | 3 | — | 2 |
| 4 | — | 8 | 4 | 21 | — |
| 5 | — | 4 | 5 | 21 | — |

5. From the data in Problem 4, if the price of a cheeseburger is $2, the price of a box of fries is $1, and you have $6 to spend (and you spend all of it), what is the utility-maximizing combination of cheeseburgers and fries?
6. Return to Problem 5. Suppose that the price of cheeseburgers falls to $1. Determine the new utility-maximizing combination of cheeseburgers and french fries.

**LO 7.2 Define the law of diminishing marginal utility and how it relates to consumer optimum.**

7. A fall in the price of one good leads to more of that good being consumed, other things remaining constant. How might this increase in consumption be broken down?
8. Consider the table at the bottom of this page. Following the utility maximization rule, how much of each good will be consumed?
9. If total utility is increasing as more is consumed, what is happening to marginal utility?
10. Yesterday, you were consuming four eggs and two strips of bacon. Today, you are consuming three eggs and three strips of bacon. Your tastes did not change overnight. What might have caused this change? Are you better or worse off?
11. Complete the missing cells in the table below.

| Number of Cheese-burgers | Total Utility of Cheese-burgers | Marginal Utility of Cheese-burgers | Boxes of French Fries | Total Utility of French Fries | Marginal Utility of French Fries |
|---|---|---|---|---|---|
| 0 | 0 | — | 0 | 0 | — |
| 1 | 20 | — | 1 | — | 8 |
| 2 | 36 | — | 2 | — | 6 |
| 3 | — | 12 | 3 | — | 4 |
| 4 | — | 8 | 4 | 20 | — |
| 5 | — | 4 | 5 | 20 | — |

12. From the data in Problem 11, if the price of a cheeseburger is $2 and the price of a box of french fries is $1, and you have $6 to spend (and you spend all of it), what is the utility-maximizing combination of cheeseburgers and french fries?
13. In Example 7–1, "Newspaper Vending Machines versus Candy Vending Machines," newspaper vendors allow people to access more than one paper at a time. Similarly, in Prince Edward Island, you will see potatoes left by the roadside for people to buy, on their honour. Farmers say they more than come out ahead at the end of the day. What does this say about the diminishing marginal utility of potatoes?

| Quantity of Good A | Marginal Utility of Good A | Price of Good A | Quantity of Good B | Marginal Utility of Good B | Price of Good B |
|---|---|---|---|---|---|
| 100 | 15 | $4.51 | 9 | 7 | $1.69 |
| 101 | 12 | 4.51 | 10 | 5 | 1.69 |
| 102 | 8 | 4.51 | 11 | 3 | 1.69 |
| 103 | 6 | 4.51 | 12 | 2 | 1.69 |

# BUSINESS APPLICATION

**LO 7.1 and 7.2 Describe the utility theory and how it impacts the decisions of consumers; define the law of diminishing marginal utility and how it relates to consumer optimum.**

## Management: The Equi-Marginal Principle and Managing Resources Efficiently

Recall that a rational consumer will maximize utility (a goal) if the last dollar spent on each good consumed yields the same marginal utility. Similarly, the rational manager (or administrator) will maximize the achievement of the organization's goal(s) if the last budget dollar spent on hiring each resource yields the same marginal contribution to the organization's goal(s).

## Business Application Problem

The general manager of a municipal police force has just been presented with an economic study showing that for the budget year just completed,

- Marginal dollar reduction in theft for the last dollar spent on hiring new beat police officers = $5
- Marginal dollar reduction in theft for the last dollar spent on renting new police cars = $9

Theoretically speaking, if next year's budget stays the same, should the general manager consider re-allocating resources in order to maximize the dollar reduction in theft?

# More Advanced Consumer Choice Theory

APPENDIX

D

It is possible to analyze consumer choice verbally, as we did for the most part in Chapter 7. The theory of diminishing marginal utility can be fairly well accepted on intuitive grounds and by introspection. If we want to be more formal and perhaps more elegant in our theorizing, however, we can translate our discussion into a graphic analysis with what we call indifference curves and the budget constraint. Here, we discuss these terms and their relationship and demonstrate consumer equilibrium in geometric form.

## On Being Indifferent

What does it mean to be indifferent? It usually means that you do not care one way or the other about something—you are equally disposed to either of two alternatives. With this interpretation in mind, we will turn to two choices, video rentals and restaurant meals. In part (a) of Figure D–1, we show several combinations of video rentals and restaurant meals per week that a representative consumer considers equally satisfactory. That is to say, for each combination, *A, B, C,* and *D,* this consumer will have exactly the same level of total utility.

Part (a)

| Combination | Video Rentals per Week | Restaurant Meals per Week |
|---|---|---|
| *A* | 1 | 7 |
| *B* | 2 | 4 |
| *C* | 3 | 2 |
| *D* | 4 | 1 |

Part (b)

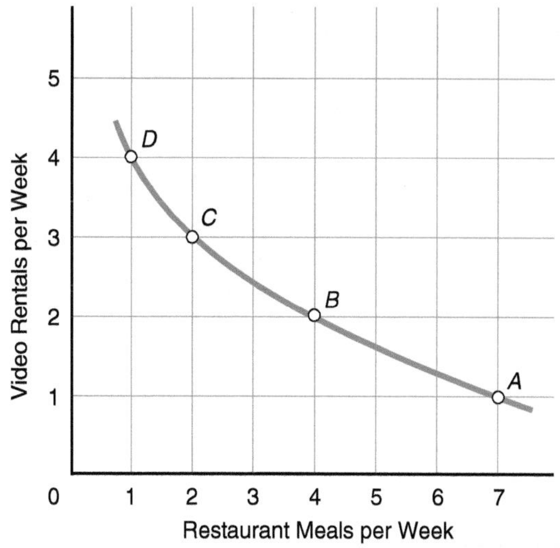


**FIGURE D–1**

**Combinations That Yield Equal Levels of Satisfaction**

*A, B, C,* and *D* represent combinations of video rentals and restaurant meals per week that give an equal level of satisfaction to this consumer. In other words, the consumer is indifferent among these four combinations.

The simple numerical example that we have used happens to concern video rentals and restaurant meals per week. This example is used to illustrate general features of indifference curves and related analytical tools that are necessary for deriving the demand curve. Obviously, we could have used any two commodities. Just remember that we are using a *specific* example to illustrate a *general* analysis.

We can plot these combinations graphically in part (b) of Figure D–1, with restaurant meals per week on the horizontal axis and video rentals per week on the vertical axis. These are our consumer's indifference combinations—the consumer finds each combination as acceptable as the others. When we connect these combinations with a smooth curve, we obtain what is called the consumer's *indifference curve.* Along the **indifference curve**, every combination of the two goods in question yields the same level of satisfaction. Every point along the indifference curve is equally desirable to the consumer. For

**Indifference curve** A curve where every combination of the two goods in question yields the same level of satisfaction.

example, four video rentals per week and one restaurant meal per week will give our representative consumer exactly the same total satisfaction as two video rentals per week and four restaurant meals per week.

## Properties of Indifference Curves

Indifference curves have special properties relating to their slope and shape.

### Downward Slope

The indifference curve shown in part (b) of Figure D–1 slopes downward; that is, it has a negative slope. Now, consider Figure D–2. Here, we show two points, *A* and *B*. Point *A* represents four video rentals per week and two restaurant meals per week. Point *B* represents five video rentals per week and six restaurant meals per week. Clearly, *B* is always preferred to *A* because *B* represents more of everything. If *B* is always preferred to *A*, it is impossible for points *A* and *B* to be on the same indifference curve because the definition of the indifference curve is a set of combinations of two goods that are equally preferred.

### Curvature

The indifference curve that we have drawn in part (b) of Figure D–1 is special. Note that it is curved. Why didn't we just draw a straight line, as we have usually done for a demand curve? To find out why we do not posit straight-line indifference curves, consider the implications. We show such a straight-line indifference curve in Figure D–3. Start at point *A*. The consumer has no restaurant meals and five video rentals per week. Now the consumer wishes to go to point *B*. He or she is willing to give up only one video rental in order to get one restaurant meal. Now, let us assume that the consumer is at point *C*, consuming one video rental and four restaurant meals per week. If the consumer wants to go to point *D*, he or she is again willing to give up one video rental in order to get one more restaurant meal per week.

In other words, no matter how many videos the consumer rents, he or she is willing to give up one video rental to get one restaurant meal per week—which does not seem plausible. Doesn't it make sense to hypothesize that the more videos the consumer rents per week, the less he or she will value an *additional* video rental? Presumably, when the consumer has five video rentals and no restaurant meals per week, he or she should be willing to give up more than one video rental in order to get one restaurant meal. Therefore, a straight-line indifference curve as shown in Figure D–3 no longer seems plausible.

**FIGURE D–2**

**Indifference Curves: Impossibility of an Upward Slope**

Point *B* represents a consumption of more video rentals per week and more restaurant meals per week than point *A*. *B* is always preferred to *A*. Therefore, *A* and *B* cannot be on the same indifference curve, which is positively sloped, because an indifference curve shows equally preferred combinations of the two goods.

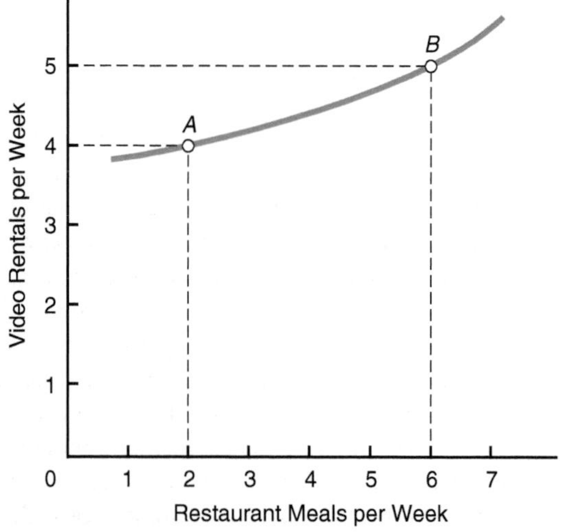

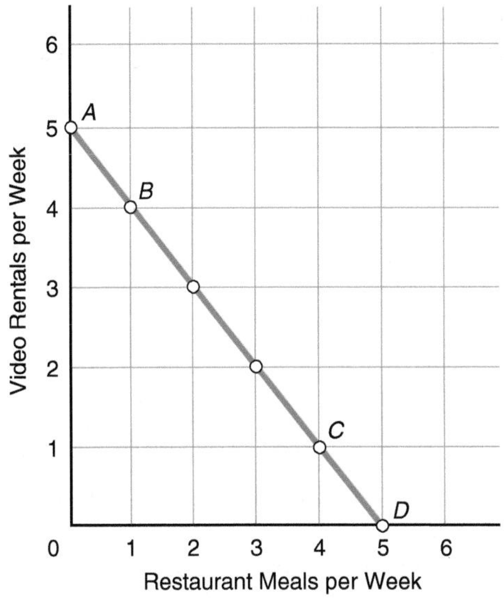


**FIGURE D–3**

**Implications of a Straight-Line Indifference Curve**

If the indifference curve is a straight line, the consumer will be willing to give up the same number of video rentals (one for one in this simple example) to get one more restaurant meal per week, whether the consumer has no restaurant meals or a lot of restaurant meals per week. For example, the consumer at point *A* has five video rentals and no restaurant meals per week. He or she is willing to give up one video rental in order to get one restaurant meal per week. At point *C*, however, the consumer has only one video rental and four restaurant meals per week. Because of the straight-line indifference curve, this consumer is willing to give up the last video rental in order to get one more restaurant meal per week, even though he or she already has four.

In mathematical language, an indifference curve is convex with respect to the origin. Let us look at this in part (a) of Figure D–1. Starting with combination *A*, the consumer has one video rental but seven restaurant meals per week. To remain indifferent, the consumer would have to be willing to give up three restaurant meals to obtain one more video rental (as shown in combination *B*). However, to go from combination *C* to combination *D*, note that the consumer would have to be willing to give up only one restaurant meal for an additional video rental per week. The quantity of the substitute considered acceptable changes as the rate of consumption of the original item changes.

Consequently, the indifference curve in part (b) of Figure D–1 will be convex when viewed from the origin.

# The Marginal Rate of Substitution

Instead of using marginal utility, we can talk in terms of the marginal rate of substitution between restaurant meals and video rentals per week. We can formally define the consumer's marginal rate of substitution as follows:

> **The marginal rate of substitution is equal to the change in the quantity of one good that just offsets a one-unit change in the consumption of another good, such that total satisfaction remains constant.**

We can see numerically what happens to the marginal rate of substitution in our example if we rearrange part (a) of Figure D–1 into Table D–1. Here, we show restaurant meals in the second column and video rentals in the third. Now we ask the question "What change in the consumption of video rentals per week will just compensate for a three-unit change in the consumption of restaurant meals per week and leave the consumer's total utility constant?" The movement from *A* to *B* increases video rental consumption by 1. Here, the marginal rate of substitution is 3:1—a three-unit decrease in restaurant meals requires an increase of one video rental to leave the consumer's total utility unaltered. Thus, the consumer values the three restaurant meals as the equivalent of one video rental. We do this for the rest of the table and find that as restaurant meals decrease further, the marginal rate of substitution goes from 3:1 to 1:1. The marginal rate of substitution of restaurant meals for video rentals per week falls as the consumer obtains more video rentals. That is, the consumer values successive units of video rentals less and less in terms of restaurant meals. The first video rental is valued at three restaurant meals; the last (fourth) video

**TABLE D–1**

## Calculating the Marginal Rate of Substitution

As we move from combination *A* to combination *B*, we are still on the same indifference curve. To stay on that curve, the number of restaurant meals decreases by three and the number of video rentals increases by one. The marginal rate of substitution is 3:1. A three-unit decrease in restaurant meals requires an increase of one video rental to leave the consumer's total utility unaltered.

| (1) Combination | (2) Restaurant Meals per Week | (3) Video Rentals per Week | (4) Marginal Rate of Substitution of Restaurant Meals for Video Rentals |
|---|---|---|---|
| *A* | 7 | 1 | |
| *B* | 4 | 2 | 3:1 |
| *C* | 2 | 3 | 2:1 |
| *D* | 1 | 4 | 1:1 |

rental is valued at only one restaurant meal. The fact that the marginal rate of substitution falls is sometimes called the *law of substitution.*

In geometric language, the slope of the consumer's indifference curve (actually, the negative of the slope) measures the consumer's marginal rate of substitution. Note that this marginal rate of substitution is purely subjective or psychological.

# The Indifference Map

Let us now consider the possibility of having both more video rentals *and* more restaurant meals per week. When we do this, we can no longer stay on the same indifference curve that we drew in Figure D–1. That indifference curve was drawn for equally satisfying combinations of video rentals and restaurant meals per week. If the individual can now attain more of both, a new indifference curve will have to be drawn, above and to the right of the one shown in part (b) of Figure D–1. Alternatively, if the individual faces the possibility of having less of both video rentals and restaurant meals per week, an indifference curve will have to be drawn below and to the left of the one in part (b) of Figure D–1. We can map out a whole set of indifference curves corresponding to these possibilities.

Figure D–4 shows three possible indifference curves. Indifference curves that are higher than others necessarily imply that for every given quantity of one good, more of the other good can be obtained on a higher indifference curve. Looked at another way, if one goes from curve $I_1$ to $I_2$, it is possible to consume the same number of restaurant meals *and* be able to rent more videos per week. This is shown as a movement from point *A* to point *B* in Figure D–4. We could do it the other way. When we move from a lower to a higher indifference curve, it is possible to rent the same number of videos *and* to consume more restaurant meals per week. Thus, the higher a consumer is on the indifference map, the greater is that consumer's total level of satisfaction.

**FIGURE D–4**

## A Set of Indifference Curves

An infinite number of indifference curves can be drawn. We show three possible ones. Realize that a higher indifference curve represents the possibility of higher rates of consumption of both goods. Hence, a higher indifference curve is preferred to a lower one because more is preferred to less. Look at points *A* and *B*. Point *B* represents more video rentals than point *A*; therefore, bundles on indifference curve $I_2$ have to be preferred over bundles on $I_1$ because the number of restaurant meals per week is the same at points *A* and *B*.

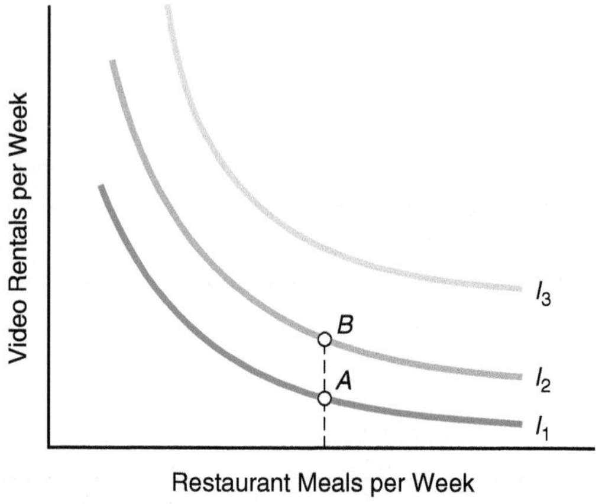

# The Budget Constraint

Our problem here is to find out how to maximize consumer satisfaction. To do so, we must consult not only our *preferences*—given by indifference curves—but also our *market opportunities*—given by our available income and prices, called our **budget constraint** (all of the possible combinations of goods that can be purchased [at fixed prices] with a specific budget). We might want more of everything, but for any given budget constraint, we have to make choices, or trade-offs, among possible goods. Everyone has a budget constraint; that is, everyone faces a limited consumption potential. How do we show this graphically? We must find the prices of the goods in question and determine the maximum consumption of each allowed by our budget. For example, let us assume that videos rent for $10 apiece and restaurant meals cost $20. Let us also assume that our representative consumer has a total budget of $60 per week. What is the maximum number of videos the consumer can rent? Six. And the maximum number of restaurant meals per week he or she can consume? Three. So, now, as shown in Figure D–5, we have two points on our budget line, which is sometimes called the *consumption possibilities curve.* These anchor points of the budget line are obtained by dividing money income by the price of each product. The first point is at *b* on the vertical axis; the second, at *b′* on the horizontal axis. The budget line is linear because prices are given.

**Budget constraint** All of the possible combinations of goods that can be purchased (at fixed prices) with a specific budget.

Any combination along line *bb′* is possible; in fact, any combination in the coloured area is possible. We will assume, however, that the individual consumer completely uses up the available budget, and we will consider as possible only those points along *bb′*.

## Slope of the Budget Constraint

The budget constraint is a line that slopes downward from left to right. The slope of that line has a special meaning. Look carefully at the budget line in Figure D–5. Remember in the discussion of graphs in Appendix A that we measure a negative slope by the ratio of the fall in *Y* over the run in *X*. In this case, *Y* is video rentals per week and *X* is restaurant meals per week. In Figure D–5, the fall in *Y* is –2 video rentals per week (a drop from 4 to 2) for a run in *X* of one restaurant meal per week (an increase from 1 to 2); therefore, the slope of the budget constraint is $-\frac{2}{1}$ or –2. This slope of the budget constraint represents the rate of exchange between video rentals and restaurant meals; it is the realistic rate of exchange, given their prices.

Now we are ready to determine how the consumer achieves the optimum consumption rate.

Consumers will try to attain the highest level of total utility possible, given their budget constraints. How can this be shown graphically? We draw a set of indifference

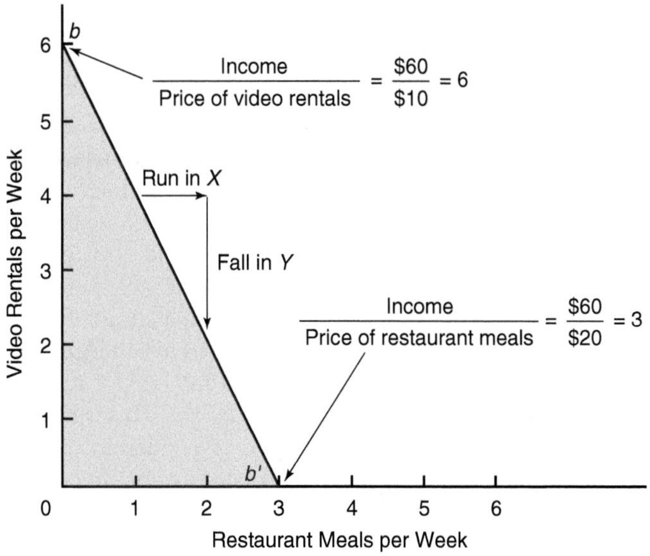


**FIGURE D–5**

**The Budget Constraint**

The line *bb′* represents this individual's budget constraint. Assuming that video rentals cost $10 each, restaurant meals cost $20 each, and the individual has a budget of $60 per week, a maximum of six video rentals or three restaurant meals can be bought each week. These two extreme points are connected to form the budget constraint. All combinations within the coloured area and on the budget constraint line are feasible.

curves similar to those in Figure D–4, and we bring in reality—the budget constraint $bb'$. Both are drawn in Figure D–6. Because a higher level of total satisfaction is represented by a higher indifference curve, we know that the consumer will strive to be on the highest indifference curve possible. However, the consumer cannot get to indifference curve $I_3$ because the budget will be exhausted before any combination of video rentals and restaurant meals represented on indifference curve $I_3$ is attained. This consumer can maximize total utility, subject to the budget constraint, only by being at point $E$ on indifference curve $I_2$ because here the consumer's income is just being exhausted. Mathematically, point $E$ is called the tangency point of the curve $I_2$ to the straight line $bb'$.

**FIGURE D–6**

**Consumer Optimum**

A consumer reaches an optimum when he or she ends up on the highest indifference curve possible, given a limited budget. This occurs at the tangency between an indifference curve and the budget constraint. In this diagram, the tangency is at *E*.

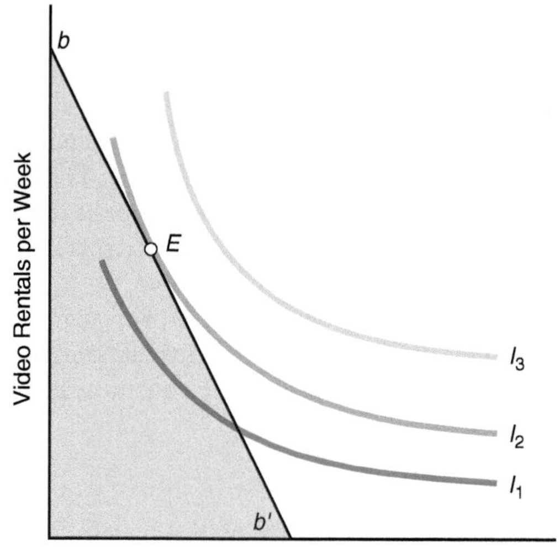


# Consumer Optimum Revisited

Consumer optimum is achieved when the marginal rate of substitution (which is subjective) is just equal to the feasible, or realistic, rate of exchange between video rentals and restaurant meals. This realistic rate is the ratio of the two prices of the goods involved. It is represented by the absolute value of the slope of the budget constraint. At point $E$, the point of tangency between indifference curve $I_2$ and budget constraint $bb'$, the rate at which the consumer wishes to substitute video rentals for restaurant meals (the numerical value of slope of the indifference curve) is just equal to the rate at which the consumer *can* substitute video rentals for restaurant meals (the slope of the budget line).

# Effects of Changes in Income

A change in income will shift the budget constraint $bb'$ in Figure D–6. Consider only increases in income, not changes in price. The budget constraint will shift outward. Each new budget line will be parallel to the original one because we are not allowing a change in the relative prices of video rentals and restaurant meals. We would now like to find out how an individual consumer responds to successive increases in income when relative prices remain constant. We do this in Figure D–7, using the example of fast-food meals and movie tickets. We start out with an income that is represented by a budget line $bb'$. Consumer optimum is at point $E$, where the consumer attains the highest indifference curve $I_1$, given the budget constraint $bb'$. Now we let income increase. This is shown by a shift outward in the budget line to $cc'$. The consumer attains a new optimum at point $E'$. That is where a higher indifference curve, $I_2$, is reached. Again the consumer's income is increased so that the new budget line is $dd'$. The new optimum now moves to $E''$. This is where indifference curve $I_3$ is reached. If we connect the three consumer optimum points, $E$, $E'$, and $E''$, we have what is called an income-consumption curve. The **income-consumption curve** shows the optimum consumption points that would occur if income for that consumer were increased continuously, holding the prices of fast-food meals and movie tickets constant.

**Income-consumption curve** The set of optimal consumption points that would occur if income were increased, relative prices remaining constant.

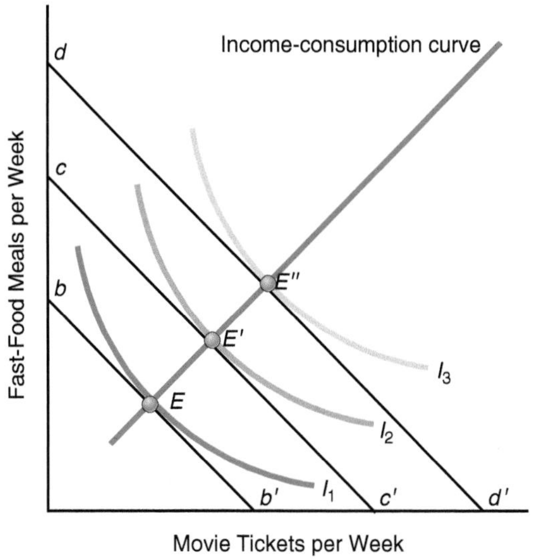


**FIGURE D-7**

**Income-Consumption Curve**

We start off with income sufficient to yield budget constraint *bb'*. The highest attainable indifference curve is $I_1$, which is just tangent to *bb'* at *E*. Next we increase income. The budget line moves outward to *cc'*, which is parallel to *bb'*. The new highest indifference curve is $I_2$, which is just tangent to *cc'* at *E'*. We increase income again, which is represented by a shift in the budget line to *dd'*. The new tangency point of the highest indifference curve, $I_3$, with *dd'* is at point *E''*. When we connect these three points, we obtain the income-consumption curve.

# The Price-Consumption Curve

In Figure D–8, we hold income and the price of fast-food meals constant while we lower the price of tickets to movies. As we keep lowering the price of movie tickets, the quantity of tickets that could be purchased if all income were spent on viewing movies increases; thus, the extreme points for the budget constraint keep moving outward to the right as the price of movie tickets falls. In other words, the budget line rotates outward from *bb'* to *bb''* and *bb''*. Each time the price of movie tickets falls, a new budget line is formed. There has to be a new optimum point. We find it by locating on each new budget line the highest attainable indifference curve. This is shown at points $E$, $E'$, and $E''$. We see that as price decreases for movie tickets, the consumer views more movies per week. We call the line connecting points $E$, $E'$, and $E''$ the **price-consumption curve** in Figure D-8. It connects the tangency points of the budget constraints and indifference curves, thus showing the amounts of two goods that a consumer will buy when money income and the price of one commodity are held constant while the price of the remaining good changes.

**Price-consumption curve** The set of consumer-optimum combinations of two goods that the consumer would choose as the price of one good changes while money income and the price of the other good remain constant.

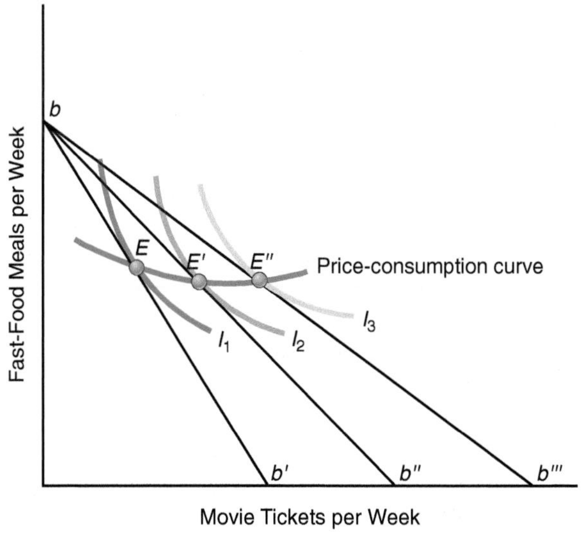


**FIGURE D-8**

**Price-Consumption Curve**

As we lower the price of movie tickets, income measured in terms of movie tickets per week increases. We show this by rotating the budget constraint from *bb'* to *bb''*and finally to *bb'''*. We then find the highest indifference curve that is attainable for each successive budget constraint. For budget constraint *bb'*, the highest indifference curve is $I_1$, which is tangent to *bb'* at point *E*. We do this for the next two budget constraints. When we connect the optimum points, *E*, *E'*, and *E''* we derive the price-consumption curve, which shows the combinations of the two commodities that a consumer will purchase when money income and the price of one commodity remain constant while the other commodity's price changes.

# Deriving the Demand Curve

We are now in a position to derive the demand curve using indifference curve analysis. In panel (a) of Figure D–9, we show what happens when the price of tickets to movies decreases, holding both the price of meals at fast-food restaurants and income constant. If the price of movie tickets decreases, the budget line rotates from *bb′* to *bb″*. The two optimum points are given by the tangency at the highest indifference curve that just touches those two budget lines. This is at *E* and *E′*. But those two points give us two price-quantity pairs. At point *E*, the price of movie tickets is $10; the quantity demanded is 2. Thus, we have one point that we can transfer to panel (b) of Figure D–9. At point *E′*, we have another price-quantity pair. The price has fallen to $5; the quantity demanded has increased to 5. We therefore transfer this other point to panel (b). When we connect these two points (and all the others in between), we derive the demand curve for tickets to movies, which slopes downward.

**FIGURE D–9**

**Deriving the Demand Curve**

In panel (a), we show the effects of a decrease in the price of movie tickets from $10 to $5. At $10, the highest indifference curve touches the budget line *bb′* at point *E*. The number of movies viewed is two. We transfer this combination—price, $10; quantity demanded, 2—down to panel (b). Next we decrease the price of movie tickets to $5. This generates a new budget line, or constraint, which is *bb″*. Consumer optimum is now at *E′*. The optimum quantity of movie tickets demanded at a price of $5 is five. We transfer this point—price, $5; quantity demanded, 5—down to panel (b). When we connect these two points, we have a demand curve, *D*, for tickets to movies.

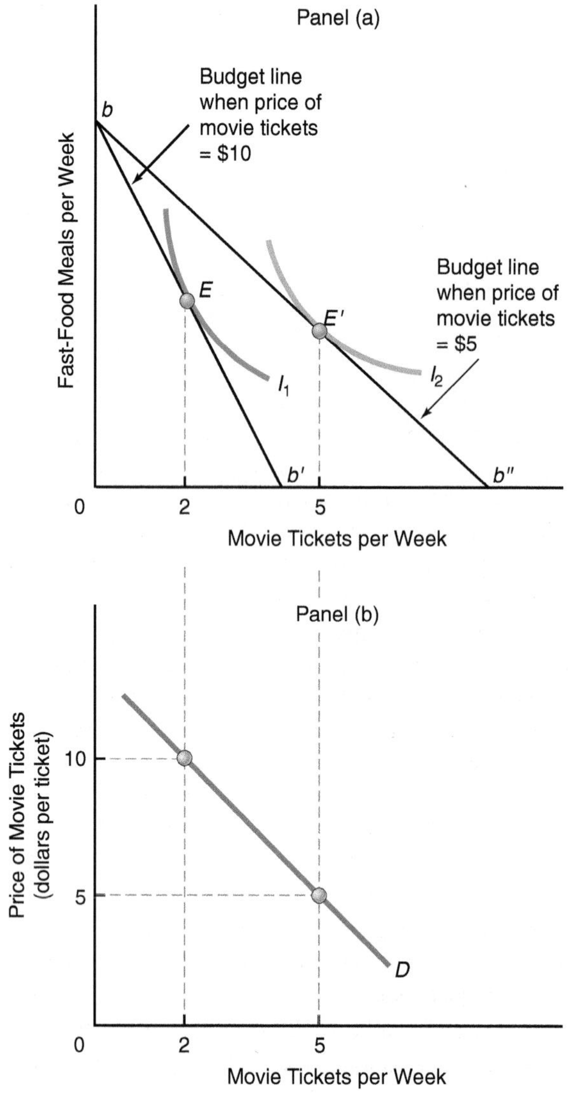

# APPENDIX SUMMARY

1. Along an indifference curve, the consumer experiences equal levels of satisfaction. That is to say, along any indifference curve, every combination of the two goods in question yields exactly the same level of satisfaction.
2. Indifference curves typically slope downward and are usually convex to the origin.
3. To measure the marginal rate of substitution, we find out how much of one good has to be given up in order to allow the consumer to consume one more unit of the other good while still remaining on the same indifference curve. The marginal rate of substitution falls as one moves down an indifference curve.
4. Indifference curves represent preferences. A budget constraint represents opportunities—how much can be purchased with a given level of income. Consumer optimum is obtained when the highest feasible indifference curve is just tangent to the budget constraint line; at that point, the consumer reaches the highest feasible indifference curve.
5. An increase in income will shift the budget constraints outward.
6. The price-consumption curve connects the tangency points of the budget constraints and indifference curves, thus showing the amounts of two goods that a consumer will buy when money income and the price of one commodity are held constant while the price of the remaining good changes.

# APPENDIX PROBLEMS

(Answers to the odd-numbered problems appear at the back of the book.)

D-1. Suppose that a consumer prefers *A* to *B* and *B* to *C* but insists that she also prefers *C* to *A*. Explain the logical problem here.

D-2. Suppose that you are indifferent among the following three combinations of food ($f$) and drink ($d$): 1$f$ and 10$d$, 2$f$ and 7$d$, 3$f$ and 2$d$. Calculate the marginal rate of substitution in consumption between the two goods. Does the substitution of the third $f$ imply a greater sacrifice of $d$ than the second did?

D-3. Construct a budget line from the following information: nominal income of \$100 per week; price of beef, $P_b$, \$2 per pound; price of shelter, $P_s$, \$20 per week; all income is spent on beef and shelter. Suppose that your money income remains constant, the price of beef doubles to \$4 per pound, and the price of shelter falls to \$10 per week. Draw the new budget line. Are you now better off or worse off? What do you need to know before deciding?

D-4. Given the following three combinations of goods, $A = 3x + 4y$, $B = 4x + 6y$, and $C = 5x + 4y$, answer the following questions:

a. Is any one bundle preferred to the other two?

b. Could a consumer possibly find *B* and *C* to be equally acceptable? How about *A* and *C*?

D-5. Calculate the marginal rate of substitution of burritos for yogurt for the following consumer's indifference schedule:

| Servings of Yogurt per Week | Burritos per Week |
|---|---|
| 10 | 1 |
| 6 | 2 |
| 3 | 3 |
| 1 | 4 |

D-6. Assume that you are consuming only yogurt ($Y$) and gymnasium exercise ($G$). Each serving of yogurt costs \$4, and each visit to the gym costs \$8. Given your food and exercise budget, you consume 15 servings of yogurt and five visits to the gym each week. One day, the price of yogurt falls to \$3 per serving and the price of gym visits increases to \$10. Now you buy 20 servings of yogurt and four gym visits per week.

a. Draw the old and new budget constraints, and show the two equilibrium bundles of yogurt servings and visits to the gym.

b. What is your weekly budget for food and exercise?

D-7. Explain why each of the following statements is or is not consistent with our assumptions about consumer preferences:

a. I cannot decide whether to go abroad this summer or to stay at home.

b. That is mine. You cannot have it. There is nothing you can do to make me change my mind.

c. I love hot pretzels with mustard at football games. If I had my way, I would never stop eating them.

8

## LEARNING OBJECTIVES

After reading this chapter, you should be able to:

**8.1** Distinguish between accounting profits and economic profits.

**8.2** Understand the short-run production function and diminishing marginal returns.

**8.3** Calculate the various costs for the firm in the short run.

**8.4** Explain the important relationships of the cost curves.

**8.5** Understand the long-run cost curve.

# The Firm: Cost and Output Determination

You drive to work by the same route every day and wonder why that one restaurant changes every six months. It has gone from a Chinese restaurant to a vegetarian one, and has now morphed into an Irish pub. Other businesses in the area seem to be stable, but that one does not appear to be a good investment.

What could all of those previous owners have done wrong? This chapter will start you thinking about how knowledge of supply and demand needs to be supplemented with knowledge about the costs of doing business.

myeconlab

MyEconLab helps you master each objective and study more efficiently. See end of chapter for details.

# DID YOU KNOW THAT...?

There are more than 25 steps in the process of manufacturing a simple lead pencil. In the production of an automobile, there are thousands. At each step, the manufacturer can have the job done by workers or machines or some combination of the two. The manufacturer must also figure out how much to produce each month. Should a new machine that can replace 10 workers be bought? Should more workers be hired, or should the existing workers be paid overtime? If the price of aluminum is rising, should the company try to make do with plastic? What you will learn about in this chapter is how producers can select the best combination of inputs for any given output that is desired.

## 8.1 The Profits of a Firm

Most people think of a firm's profit as the difference between the amount of revenues the firm takes in and the amount it spends for wages, materials, and so on. In a bookkeeping sense, the following formula could be used:

$$\text{Accounting profit} = \text{Total revenue} - \text{Explicit costs}$$

where **explicit costs** are expenses that business managers must take account of because they must actually be paid out by the firm. This definition of profit is known as **accounting profit**, total revenue minus total explicit costs. It is appropriate when used by accountants to determine a firm's taxable income. Economists are more interested in how firm managers react not just to changes in explicit costs but also to changes in **implicit costs**, defined as expenses that business managers do not have to pay out of pocket but are costs to the firm nonetheless because they represent an opportunity cost. They do not involve any direct cash outlay by the firm and must therefore be measured by the *alternative cost principle*. That is to say, they are measured by what the resources (land, capital) currently used in producing a particular good or service could earn in other uses. Economists use the full opportunity cost of all resources (including both explicit and implicit costs) as the figure to subtract from revenues to obtain a definition of profit. Another definition of implicit cost is therefore the opportunity cost of using factors that a producer does not buy or hire but already owns.

How can the manufacturing process for pencils be made more efficient?

**Explicit costs** Expenses that business managers must take account of because they must actually be paid out by the firm.

**Accounting profit** Total revenue minus total explicit costs.

**Implicit costs** Expenses that business managers do not have to pay out of pocket.

### Opportunity Cost of Capital

Firms enter or remain in an industry if they earn, at minimum, a **normal rate of return**—the amount that must be paid to an investor to induce investment in a business. People will not invest their wealth in a business unless they obtain a positive normal (competitive) rate of return—that is, unless their invested wealth pays off. Any business wishing to attract capital must expect to pay at least the same rate of return on that capital as all other businesses (of similar risk) are willing to pay. Put another way, when a firm requires the use of a resource in producing a particular product, it must bid against alternative users of that resource. Thus, the firm must offer a price that is at least as much as other potential users are offering to pay. For example, if individuals can invest their wealth in almost any publishing firm and get a rate of return of 10 percent per year, each firm in the publishing industry must *expect* to pay 10 percent as the normal rate of return to present and future investors. This 10 percent is a *cost to the firm*, the opportunity cost of capital. The **opportunity cost of capital** is the amount of income, or yield, that could have been earned by investing in the next-best alternative. Capital will not stay in firms or industries in which the expected rate of return falls below its opportunity cost, that is, what could be earned elsewhere. If a firm owns some capital equipment, it can either use it or lease it and earn a return. If the firm uses the equipment for production, part of the cost of using that equipment is the forgone revenue that the firm could have earned had it leased out that equipment.

**Normal rate of return** The amount that must be paid to an investor to induce investment in a business.

**Opportunity cost of capital** The amount of income, or yield, that could have been earned by investing in the next-best alternative.

## Opportunity Cost of Owner-Provided Labour and Capital

Single-owner proprietorships often grossly exaggerate their profit rates because they understate the opportunity cost of the labour that the proprietor provides to the business. Here, we are referring to the opportunity cost of labour. Take, for example, people who run a small grocery store. These people will sit down at the end of the year and figure out what their "profits" are. They will add up all their sales and subtract what they had to pay to other workers, to their suppliers, in taxes, and so on. The end result they will call "profit." They normally will not, however, have figured into their costs the salary that they could have made if they had worked for somebody else in a similar type of job. By working for themselves, they become residual claimants—they receive what is left after all explicit costs have been accounted for. Part of the costs, however, should include the salary the owner-operator could have received working for someone else.

Consider a simple example of a skilled auto mechanic working 14 hours a day at his own service station, six days a week. Compare this situation with how much he could earn as a trucking company mechanic working 84 hours a week. This self-employed auto mechanic might have an opportunity cost of about \$20 an hour. For his 84-hour week in his own service station, he is forfeiting \$1680. Unless his service station shows accounting profits of more than that per week, he is incurring losses in an economic sense.

Another way of looking at the opportunity cost of running a business is that opportunity cost consists of all explicit and implicit costs. Accountants only take account of explicit costs. Therefore, accounting profit ends up being the residual after only explicit costs are subtracted from total revenues.

This same analysis can apply to owner-provided capital, such as land or buildings. The fact that the owner owns the building or the land with which he or she operates a business does not mean that it is "free." Rather, use of the building and land still has an opportunity cost—the value of the next-best alternative use for those assets.

Some firms are nonprofit enterprises. Nevertheless, they face the same incentive to generate sufficient revenues or, in some cases, sufficient donations, to cover the opportunity cost of equipment and other capital resources.

### POLICY EXAMPLE 8–1 Nonprofit Firms Join in the Quest for Profits

The American Medical Association and other leading medical societies are nonprofit organizations. This entitles them to special exemptions from taxes faced by for-profit companies.

The National Geographic Society now operates National Geographic Ventures, Inc., a for-profit firm that produces video documentaries, operates a mapping service, and manages retail outlets. The American Cancer Society earns millions of dollars each year in royalties from for-profit companies that it grants the right to use its name in for-profit marketing.

Profits earned by nonprofit organizations allow them to enlarge and facilitate their streams of cash inflows. This helps ensure that they cover the opportunity cost of capital. Nevertheless, profit-earning activities by nonprofit organizations are raising red flags. Are some of these organizations "nonprofit" only in name?

**For critical analysis:** Must nonprofit firms earn a normal rate of return?

## Accounting Profits versus Economic Profits

The term "profits" in economics means the income that entrepreneurs earn, over and above all costs including their own opportunity cost of time, plus the opportunity cost of the capital they have invested in their business. Profits can be regarded as total revenues minus total costs—which is how accountants think of them—but we must now include *all* costs. Our definition of **economic profits** will be the following:

Economic profits = Total revenues − Total opportunity cost of all inputs used

or

Economic profits = Total revenues − (Explicit + Implicit costs)

Remember that implicit costs include a normal rate of return on invested capital. We show this relationship in Figure 8–1.

**Economic profits** Total revenues minus total opportunity costs of all inputs used, or total revenues minus the total of all implicit and explicit costs.

## The Goal of the Firm: Profit Maximization

When we examined the theory of consumer demand, utility (or satisfaction) maximization by the individual provided the basis for the analysis. In the theory of the firm and production, *profit maximization* is the underlying hypothesis of our predictive theory. The goal of the firm is to maximize economic profits, and the firm is expected to try to make the positive difference between total revenues and total costs as large as it can.

Our justification for assuming profit maximization by firms is similar to our belief in utility maximization by individuals. To obtain labour, capital, and other resources required to produce commodities, firms must first obtain financing from investors. In general, investors are indifferent about the details of how a firm uses the funds they provide. They are most interested in the earnings on these funds and the risk of obtaining lower returns or losing the funds they have invested. Firms that can provide relatively higher risk-corrected returns will therefore have an advantage in obtaining the financing needed to continue or expand production. Over time, we would expect a policy of profit maximization to become the dominant mode of behaviour for firms that survive.

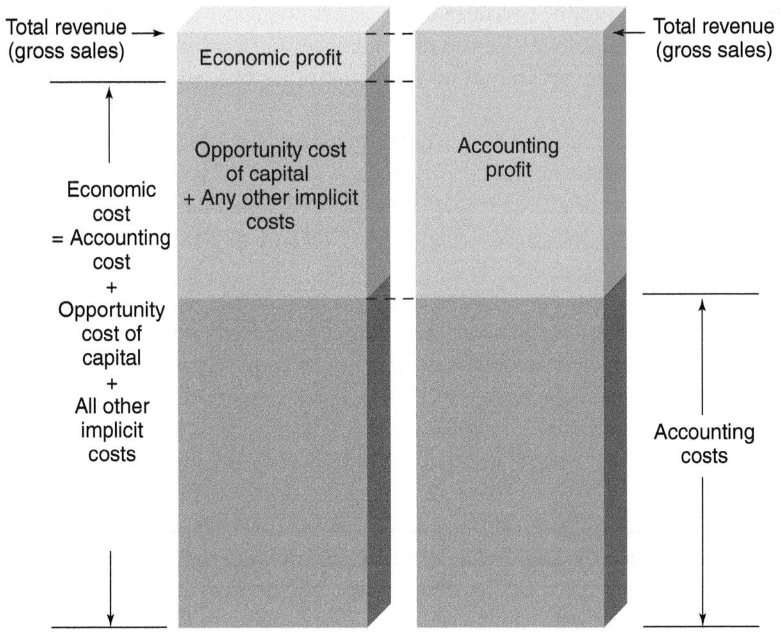


**FIGURE 8–1**
**Simplified View of Economic and Accounting Profit**

We see in the right column that accounting profit is the difference between total revenues and total explicit accounting costs. Conversely, we see in the left column that economic profit is equal to total revenues minus economic costs. Economic costs equal explicit accounting costs plus all implicit costs, including a normal rate of return on invested capital.

# 8.2 Short Run versus Long Run

## The Firm

We define a business, or **firm**, as follows:

**A firm is an organization that brings together factors of production—labour, land, physical capital, human capital, and entrepreneurial skill—to produce a product or service that it hopes can be sold at a profit.**

**Firm** An organization that brings together factors of production—labour, land, physical capital, human capital, and entrepreneurial skill—to produce a product or service that it hopes can be sold at a profit.

A typical firm will have an organizational structure consisting of an entrepreneur, managers, and workers. The entrepreneur is the person who takes the risks, mainly of losing personal wealth. In compensation, the entrepreneur will get any profits that are made. Entrepreneurs take the initiative in combining land, labour, and capital to produce a good or a service. Entrepreneurs are the ones who innovate in the form of new production and new products. The entrepreneur also decides whom to hire to manage the firm. Some economists maintain that the true quality of an entrepreneur becomes evident through the selection of managers. Managers, in turn, decide who should be hired or fired and how the business generally should be set up. The workers ultimately use the other inputs to produce the products or services that are being sold by the firm. Workers and managers are paid contractual wages. They receive a specified amount of income for a specified time period. Entrepreneurs are not paid contractual wages. They receive no reward specified in advance. The entrepreneurs make profits, if there are any, for profits accrue to those who are willing to take risks. Because the entrepreneur gets only what is left over after all expenses are paid, that individual is often referred to as a *residual claimant.* The entrepreneur lays claim to the residual—whatever is left.

We have discussed short-run and long-run price elasticities of supply and demand. For consumers, the long run meant the time period during which all adjustments to a change in price could be made, and anything shorter than that was considered the short run. For suppliers, the long run was the time in which all adjustments could be made, and anything shorter than that was the short run.

Now that we are discussing firms only, we will maintain a similar distinction between the short and the long run, but we will be more specific. In the theory of the firm, the **short run** is defined as any time period that is so short that there is at least one input, such as current **plant size** (the physical size of the factories that a firm owns and operates to produce its output), that the firm cannot alter.[1] In other words, during the short run, a firm makes do with whatever big machines and factory size it already has, no matter how much more it wants to produce because of increased demand for its product. We consider the plant and heavy equipment, the size or amount of which cannot be varied in the short run, as fixed resources. In agriculture and in some other businesses, land may be a fixed resource.

**Short run** Any time period that is so short that there is at least one input that the firm cannot alter.

**Plant size** The physical size of the factories that a firm owns and operates to produce its output.

There are, of course, variable resources that the firm can alter when it wants to change its rate of production. These are called *variable inputs* or *variable factors of production.* Typically, the variable inputs of a firm are its labour and its purchases of raw materials. In the short run, in response to changes in demand, the firm can, by definition, vary only its variable inputs.

The **long run** can now be considered the period of time in which *all* inputs can be varied. Specifically, in the long run, the firm can alter its plant size. How long is the long run? That depends on each individual industry. For Wendy's or McDonald's, the long run may be four or five months because that is the time it takes to add new franchises. For a steel company, the long run may be several years because that is how long it takes to plan and build a new plant. An electric utility might need over a decade to build a new dam, for example.

**Long run** The period of time in which all inputs can be varied.

*Short run* and *long run* in our discussion are, in fact, management planning terms that apply to decisions made by managers. The firm can operate only in the short run in the sense that decisions must be made in the present. The same analysis applies to your own behaviour. You may have many long-run plans about graduate school, vacations, and the like, but you always operate in the short run—you make decisions every day about what you do every day.

## The Relationship between Output and Inputs

A firm takes numerous inputs, combines them using a technological production process, and ends up with an output. There are, of course, a great many factors of production, or

[1]There can be many short runs but only one long run. For ease of analysis, in this section we simplify the case to one short run and talk about short-run costs.

inputs. We classify production inputs in two broad categories (ignoring land)—labour and capital. The relationship between output and these two inputs is as follows:

Output per time period = Some function of capital and labour inputs

Mathematically, the production relationship can be written $Q = f(K, L)$, where $Q$ = Output per time period, $K$ = Capital, and $L$ = Labour. What mix of capital and labour is used for production depends on many factors, as you can see from Example 8–1.

### EXAMPLE 8–1 China's Increasing Labour Costs

China has seen its labour costs increase as more companies build factories there. International companies are moving their factories to China to take advantage of the lower labour costs, but as more factories are built, the demand for skilled workers is exceeding the supply, thereby increasing wages.

Since 2001, hourly manufacturing wages in China have risen by an average of 12% a year. Many Chinese companies pay their employees just above the minimum wage ($270 a month). Companies are seeing a decline in profits because of the rising costs. For an emerging economy like China, a balance between capital investments and worker training is necessary so they can maintain their economic advantage over countries in Europe and North America.

**For critical analysis:** Should a company only consider labour costs when determining where to build a new factory?

Source: "A Tightening Grip." The Economist. http://www.economist.com/news/briefing/21646180-rising-chinese-wages-will-only-strengthen-asias-hold-manufacturing-tightening-grip.

Can China continue to keep labour costs low?

We have used the word *production* but have not defined it. **Production** is any process by which resources are transformed into goods or services. Production includes not only making things, but also transporting them, retailing, repackaging them, and so on. Note that if we know that production occurs, we do not necessarily know the value of the output. The production relationship tells nothing about the worth or value of the inputs or the output.

**Production** Any process by which resources are transformed into goods or services.

## The Production Function: A Numerical Example

The relationship between the amount of physical output the firm can produce and the quantity of capital and labour used to produce it can be called a **production function**. The production function specifies the maximum possible output that can be produced with a given amount of inputs. It also specifies the minimum amount of inputs necessary to produce a given level of output. Firms that are inefficient or wasteful in their use of capital and labour will obtain less output than the production function in theory will show.

**Production function** The relationship between the amount of physical output the firm can produce and the quantity of capital and labour used to produce it.

However, no firm can obtain more output than the production function shows. Since the production function is a technological relationship between inputs and output, it follows that an improvement in technology that allows the firm to produce more output with the same amount of inputs (or the same output with fewer inputs) results in a new production function.

Look at part (a) of Figure 8–2. It shows a production function relating the total output of pocket calculators in column 2 to the quantity of labour measured in workers in column 1. When there are zero workers, there is zero output. When there are five workers per hour of input (given the capital stock), there is a total output of 62 calculators per hour. (Ignore for the moment the rest of that part.) Part (b) of Figure 8–2 shows this particular production function graphically. Note again that it relates to the short run and that it is for an individual firm.

FIGURE 8–2

## Diminishing Returns, the Production Function, and Marginal Product: A Hypothetical Case of Pocket Calculator Production

Marginal product is the addition to the total product that results when one additional worker is hired. Thus, the marginal product of the fourth worker is 13 pocket calculators. With four workers, 52 calculators are produced, but with three workers, only 39 are produced; the difference is 13. In part (b), we plot the numbers from columns 1 and 2 of part (a). In part (c), we plot the numbers from columns 1 and 4 of part (a). When we go from zero workers to one, marginal product is eight. When we go from one worker to two, marginal product increases to 16. After two workers, marginal product declines, but it is still positive. Total product (output) reaches its peak at seven workers, so after seven workers marginal product becomes –5 calculators per hour.

Part (a)

| (1) Labour (number of workers per hour) | (2) Total Product (output in number of calculators per hour) | (3) Average Physical Product (Total product ÷ Number of workers per hour) (calculators per hour) | (4) Marginal Physical Product (Change in total product ÷ Change in number of workers) (calculators per hour) |
|---|---|---|---|
| 0 | 0 | — | |
| 1 | 8 | 8.0 | 8 |
| 2 | 24 | 12.0 | 16 |
| 3 | 39 | 13.0 | 15 |
| 4 | 52 | 13.0 | 13 |
| 5 | 62 | 12.4 | 10 |
| 6 | 68 | 11.3 | 6 |
| 7 | 69 | 9.9 | 1 |
| 8 | 64 | 8.0 | –5 |

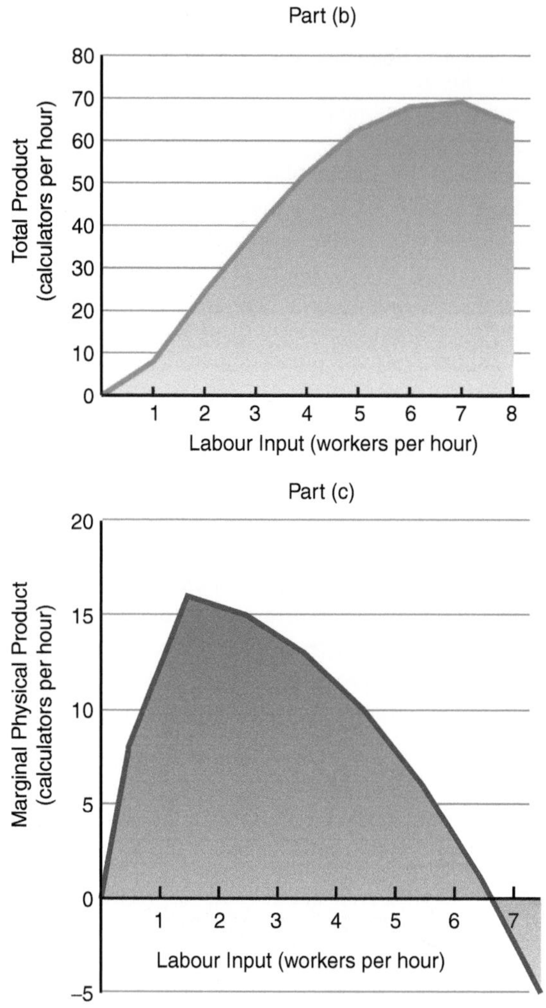


**Law of diminishing (marginal) returns** The observation that after some point, successive equal-sized increases in a variable factor of production, such as labour, added to fixed factors of production, will result in smaller increases in output.

Part (b) shows a total physical product curve, or the maximum amount of physical output that is possible when we add successive equal-sized units of labour while holding all other inputs constant. The graph of the production function in part (b) is not a straight line. In fact, it peaks at seven workers per hour and then starts to go down. To understand why it starts to go down with an individual firm in the short run, we have to analyze in detail the **law of diminishing (marginal) returns**—the observation that after some point, successive equal-sized increases in a variable factor of production, such as labour, added to fixed factors of production, will result in smaller increases in output.

But before that, let us examine the meaning of columns 3 and 4 of part (a) of Figure 8–2—that is, average and marginal physical product.

## Average and Marginal Physical Product

The **average physical product** of labour is the total product divided by the number of workers expressed in output per hour. You can see in column 3 of part (a) of Figure 8–2 that the average physical product of labour first rises and then steadily falls after four workers are hired.

**Average physical product** The total product divided by the number of workers expressed in output per hour.

Remember that *marginal* means "additional." Hence, the *marginal physical product* of labour (column 4 of part (a)) is the change in total product that occurs when a worker joins an existing production process. (The term *physical* here emphasizes the fact that we are measuring in terms of physical units of production, not in dollar terms.) It is also the *change* in total product that occurs when that worker quits or is laid off an existing production process. The **marginal physical product** of labour therefore refers to the *change in output caused by a one-unit change in the labour input*. (Marginal physical product is also referred to as *marginal productivity* and *marginal return*.)

**Marginal physical product** The change in output caused by a one-unit change in the labour input.

## Diminishing Marginal Returns

The concept of diminishing marginal returns—also known as diminishing marginal product—applies to many situations. If you put a seat belt across your lap, a certain amount of safety is obtained. If you add another seat belt over your shoulder, some additional safety is obtained, but less than when the first belt was secured. When you add a third seat belt over the other shoulder, the amount of *additional* safety obtained is even smaller.

The same analysis holds for firms in their use of productive inputs. When the returns from hiring more workers are diminishing, it does not necessarily mean that more workers will not be hired. In fact, workers will be hired until the returns, in terms of the *value* of the *extra* output produced, are equal to the additional wages that have to be paid for those workers to produce the extra output. Before we get into that decision-making process, let us demonstrate that diminishing returns can be represented graphically and can be used in our analysis of the firm.

## Measuring Diminishing Returns

How do we measure diminishing returns? First, we limit the analysis to only one variable factor of production (or input)—let us say the factor is labour. Every other factor of production, such as machines, must be held constant. Only in this way can we calculate the marginal returns from using more workers and know when we reach the point of diminishing marginal returns.

The marginal productivity of labour may increase rapidly at the very beginning. A firm starts with no workers, only machines. The firm then hires one worker, who finds it difficult to get the work started. But when the firm hires more workers, each is able to specialize, and the marginal productivity of those additional workers may actually be greater than it was with the previous few workers. Beyond some point, however, diminishing returns must set in, not because new workers are less qualified, but because each worker has (on average) fewer machines to work with (remember, all other inputs are fixed). In fact, eventually the firm will become so crowded that workers will start to get in each other's way. At that point, total production declines and marginal physical product becomes negative.

Using these ideas, we can define the law of diminishing returns as follows:

> **As successive equal increases in a variable factor of production are added to fixed factors of production, there will be a point beyond which the extra, or marginal, product that can be attributed to each additional unit of the variable factor of production will decline.**

Note that the law of diminishing returns is a statement about the *physical* relationships between inputs and outputs that we have observed in many firms. If the law of diminishing returns were not a fairly accurate statement about the world, what would stop firms from hiring additional workers forever?

## An Example of the Law of Diminishing Returns

Look again at Figure 8–2. The numbers in part (a) illustrate the law of diminishing marginal returns and are presented graphically in part (c). Marginal productivity (returns from adding more workers) first increases, then decreases, and finally becomes negative.

When one worker is hired, total output goes from 0 to 8. Thus, marginal physical product is eight calculators per hour. When the second worker is hired, total product goes from 8 to 24 calculators per hour. Marginal physical product therefore increases to 16 calculators per hour. When a third worker is hired, total product again increases, from 24 to 39 calculators per hour. This represents a marginal physical product of only 15 calculators per hour. Therefore, the point of diminishing marginal returns occurs after two workers are hired.

Note that after seven workers per hour, marginal physical product becomes negative. That means that the hiring of an eighth worker would create a situation that reduces total product. Sometimes, this is called the *point of saturation*, indicating that given the amount of fixed inputs, there is no further positive use for more of the variable input. We have entered the region of negative marginal returns.

# 8.3 Short-Run Costs to the Firm

You will see that costs are the extension of the production ideas just presented. Let us consider the costs the firm faces in the short run. To keep our example simple, assume that there are only two factors of production—capital and labour. Our definition of the short run will be the time during which capital is fixed but labour is variable.

**Total costs** The sum of all costs incurred.

In the short run, a firm incurs certain types of costs. We label the sum of all costs incurred **total costs**. Then, we break total costs down into total fixed costs and total variable costs, which we will explain shortly. Therefore,

Total costs (TC) = Total fixed costs (TFC) + Total variable costs (TVC)

Remember that these total costs include both explicit and implicit costs, including the normal rate of return on investment.

After we have looked at the elements of total costs, we will find out how to compute average and marginal costs.

## Total Fixed Costs

Let us look at an ongoing business, such as Chrysler Canada Inc. The decision makers in that corporate giant can look around and see big machines, thousands of parts, huge buildings, and a multitude of other components of plant and equipment that have already been bought and are in place. Chrysler Canada has to take into account the technological obsolescence of this equipment, no matter how many vehicles it produces. The payments on the loans taken out to buy the equipment will all be exactly the same. The opportunity costs of any land that Chrysler Canada owns will all be exactly the same. These costs are more or less the same for the auto manufacturer, no matter how many automobiles it produces.

The opportunity cost (or normal rate of return) of capital must be included along with other costs. Remember that we are dealing in the short run, during which capital is fixed. If investors in Chrysler Canada Inc. have already put $100 million into a new factory addition, the opportunity cost of that capital invested is now, in essence, a *fixed cost*. Why? Because in the short run, nothing can be done about that cost; the investment has already been made. This leads us to a very straightforward definition of fixed costs: All costs that do not vary—that is, all costs that do not depend on the rate of production—are called **fixed costs**.

**Fixed costs** All costs that do not vary—that is, all costs that do not depend on the rate of production.

Let us now take as an example the fixed costs incurred by our producer of pocket calculators. This firm's total fixed costs will equal the cost of the rent on its equipment and the insurance it has to pay. We see in part (a) of Figure 8–3 that total fixed costs per hour are $10.

In part (b), these total fixed costs are represented by the horizontal line at $10 per hour. They are invariant to changes in the output of calculators per hour—no matter how many are produced, fixed costs will remain at $10 per hour.

## Total Variable Costs

Total **variable costs** are costs whose magnitude varies with the rate of production. One obvious variable cost is wages. The more the firm produces, the more labour it has to hire; therefore, the more wages it has to pay. Another variable cost is parts. In the assembly of calculators, for example, microchips must be bought. The more calculators that are made, the more chips must be bought. Part of the rate of depreciation (the rate of wear and tear) on machines that are used in the assembly process can also be considered a variable cost if depreciation depends partly on how long and how intensively the machines are used. Total variable costs are given in part (a) of Figure 8–3 in column 3. These costs are translated into the total variable cost curve in part (b). Note that the total variable cost curve lies below the total cost curve by the vertical distance of $10. This vertical distance represents, of course, total fixed costs.

**Variable costs** Costs whose magnitude varies with the rate of production.

## Short-Run Average Cost Curves

In part (b) of Figure 8–3, we see total costs, total variable costs, and total fixed costs. Now we want to look at average cost. The average cost concept is one in which we are measuring cost per unit of output. It is a matter of arithmetic to figure the averages of these three cost concepts. We can define them as follows:

$$\text{Average total costs (ATC)} = \frac{\text{Total costs (TC)}}{\text{Output }(Q)}$$

$$\text{Average variable costs (AVC)} = \frac{\text{Total variable costs (TVC)}}{\text{Output }(Q)}$$

$$\text{Average fixed costs (AFC)} = \frac{\text{Total fixed costs (TFC)}}{\text{Output }(Q)}$$

The arithmetic is done in columns 5, 6, and 7 in part (a) of Figure 8–3. The numerical results are translated into a graphical format in part (c). Because total costs (TC) equal variable costs (TVC) plus fixed costs (TFC), the difference between average total costs (ATC) and average variable costs (AVC) will always be identical to average fixed costs (AFC). That means that average total costs and average variable costs move together as output expands.

Now let us see what we can observe about the three average cost curves in Figure 8–3.

**AVERAGE FIXED COSTS (AFC).** **Average fixed costs**—total fixed costs divided by the number of units produced—continue to fall throughout the output range. In fact, if we were to continue the diagram farther to the right, we would find that average fixed costs would get closer and closer to the horizontal axis. That is because total fixed costs remain constant. As we divide this fixed number by a larger and larger number of units of output, the resulting AFC has to become smaller and smaller. In business, this is called "spreading the overhead."

**Average fixed costs** Total fixed costs divided by the number of units produced.

**AVERAGE VARIABLE COSTS (AVC).** The **average variable cost**—total variable costs divided by the number of units produced—curve takes a form that is U-shaped: first it falls; then it starts to rise. It is possible for the AVC curve to take other shapes in the long run.

**Average variable costs** Total variable costs divided by the number of units produced.

**AVERAGE TOTAL COSTS (ATC).** **Average total costs** are total costs divided by the number of units produced; sometimes called per-unit total costs. This curve has a shape similar to that of the AVC curve. However, it falls even more dramatically in the beginning and rises more slowly after it has reached a minimum point. It falls and then rises because average total costs are the summation of the AFC curve and the AVC curve. Thus, when AFC and AVC are both falling, ATC must fall, too. At some point, however, AVC starts to increase, while AFC continues to fall. Once the increase in the AVC curve outweighs the decrease in the AFC curve, the ATC curve will start to increase and will develop its familiar U-shape.

**Average total costs** Total costs divided by the number of units produced; sometimes called per-unit total costs.

**FIGURE 8–3**

## Costs of Production: A Hypothetical Case of Pocket Calculator Production

In part (a), the derivation of columns 4 through 9 are given in parentheses in each column heading. For example, column 6, average variable costs, is derived by dividing column 3, total variable costs, by column 1, total output per hour. Note that marginal cost (MC) in part (c) intersects average variable costs (AVC) at the latter's minimum point. Also, MC intersects average total costs (ATC) at the latter's minimum point.

Part (a)

| (1) Total Output (Q/hour) | (2) Total Fixed Costs (TFC) | (3) Total Variable Costs (TVC) | (4) Total Costs (TC) (4) = (2) + (3) | (5) Average Fixed Costs (AFC) (5) = (2) ÷ (1) | (6) Average Variable Costs (AVC) (6) = (3) ÷ (1) | (7) Average Total Costs (ATC) (7) = (4) ÷ (1) | (8) Total Costs (TC) (4) | (9) Marginal Costs (MC) (9) = Change in (8) / Change in (1) |
|---|---|---|---|---|---|---|---|---|
| 0 | $10 | $ 0 | $10 | — | — | — | $10 | |
| 1 | 10 | 5 | 15 | $10.00 | $5.00 | $15.00 | 15 | $5 |
| 2 | 10 | 8 | 18 | 5.00 | 4.00 | 9.00 | 18 | 3 |
| 3 | 10 | 10 | 20 | 3.33 | 3.33 | 6.67 | 20 | 2 |
| 4 | 10 | 11 | 21 | 2.50 | 2.75 | 5.25 | 21 | 1 |
| 5 | 10 | 13 | 23 | 2.00 | 2.60 | 4.60 | 23 | 2 |
| 6 | 10 | 16 | 26 | 1.67 | 2.67 | 4.33 | 26 | 3 |
| 7 | 10 | 20 | 30 | 1.43 | 2.86 | 4.28 | 30 | 4 |
| 8 | 10 | 25 | 35 | 1.25 | 3.13 | 4.38 | 35 | 5 |
| 9 | 10 | 31 | 41 | 1.11 | 3.44 | 4.56 | 41 | 6 |
| 10 | 10 | 38 | 48 | 1.00 | 3.80 | 4.80 | 48 | 7 |
| 11 | 10 | 46 | 56 | 0.91 | 4.18 | 5.09 | 56 | 8 |

Part (b)

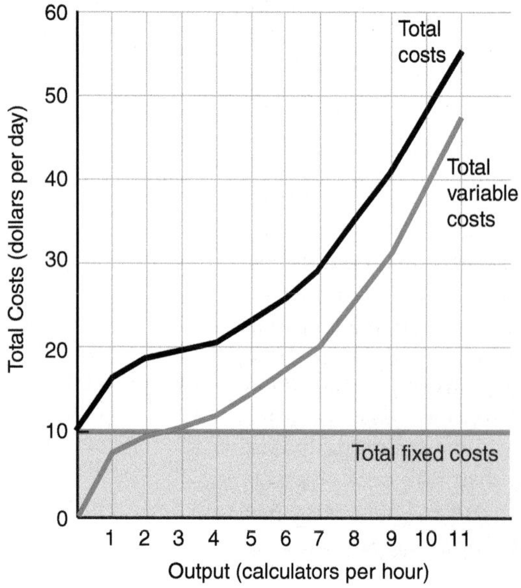


Part (c)

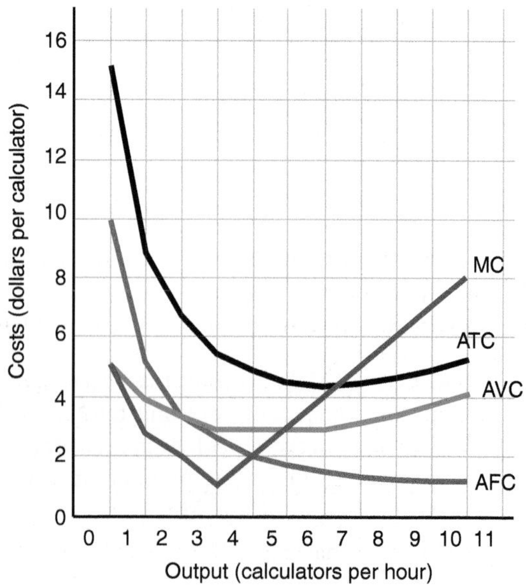

## Marginal Cost

We have stated repeatedly that the basis of decisions is always on the margin—decisions in economics are determined at the margin. This dictum also holds true within the firm. Firms, according to the analysis we use to predict their behaviour, are very interested in their *marginal costs*. Because the term *marginal* means "additional" or "incremental" (or "decremental") here, **marginal costs** refer to costs that result from a one-unit change in the production rate. For example, if the production of 10 calculators per hour costs a firm $48, and the production of 11 calculators costs it $56 per hour, the marginal cost of producing the eleventh calculator is $8.

**Marginal costs** Costs that result from a one-unit change in the production rate.

$$\text{Marginal cost} = \frac{\text{Change in total cost}}{\text{Change in output}}$$

We show the marginal costs of calculator production per hour in column 9 of part (a) in Figure 8–3, calculated according to the formula just given. A good example of the different costs is illustrated in Example 8–2 on page 200.

This marginal cost schedule is shown graphically in part (c) of Figure 8–3. Just like average variable costs and average total costs, marginal costs first fall and then rise. The U-shape of the marginal cost curve is a result of increasing and then diminishing marginal returns. At lower levels of output, the marginal cost curve declines. The reasoning is that as marginal physical product increases with each addition of output, the marginal cost of this last unit of output must fall. Conversely, when diminishing marginal returns set in, marginal physical product decreases (and eventually becomes negative); it follows that the marginal cost of the last unit must rise. These relationships are clearly reflected in the geometry of parts (b) and (c) of Figure 8–3.

In summary:

**As long as marginal physical product rises, marginal cost will fall, and when marginal physical product starts to fall (after reaching the point of diminishing marginal returns), marginal cost will begin to rise.**

Can the marginal cost of computer printers decline forever?

## The Relationship between Average and Marginal Costs

Let us now look at the relationship between average costs and marginal costs. There is always a definite relationship between averages and marginals. Consider your grade point average (GPA). Say your GPA is currently a B. If you take an economics course and earn an A, what will happen to your GPA? It must increase. When your grade in a marginal course (the economics course) is higher than (above) your GPA, it pulls your average up. If you subsequently take an accounting course and earn a C, your GPA will fall.

There is a similar relationship between average variable costs and marginal costs. When marginal costs are less than average costs, the latter must fall. Conversely, when marginal costs are greater than average costs, the latter must rise. When you think about it, the relationship makes sense. The only way for average variable costs to fall is for the extra cost of the marginal unit produced to be less than the average variable cost of all the preceding units. For example, if the average variable cost for two calculators is $4, the only way the average variable cost of three calculators can be less than that of two is for the variable costs attributable to the last calculator—the marginal cost—to be less than the average of the previously produced calculators. In this particular case, if average variable cost falls to $3.33 per calculator, total variable cost for the three calculators would be 3 × $3.33, or almost exactly $10. Total variable costs for two calculators is 2 × $4, or $8. The marginal cost is therefore $10 – $8 = $2, which is less than the average variable cost of $3.33.

A similar type of computation can be carried out for rising average variable costs. The only way for average variable costs to rise is for the cost of additional units to be more than that for units already produced. But the incremental cost is the marginal cost. In this particular case, the marginal costs have to be higher than the average variable costs.

There is also a relationship between marginal costs and average total costs. Remember that average total cost is equal to total cost divided by the number of units produced. Remember also that marginal cost does not include any fixed costs. Fixed costs are, by definition, fixed and cannot influence marginal costs. Our example can therefore be repeated substituting average total cost for average variable cost.

These rising and falling relationships can be seen in Figure 8–3 part (c), where MC intersects AVC and ATC at their respective minimum points.

## Minimum Cost Points

At what rate of output of calculators per hour does our producer experience the minimum average total costs? Column 7 in part (a) of Figure 8–3 shows that the minimum average total cost is $4.28, which occurs at an output rate of seven calculators per hour. We can also find this minimum cost by finding the point in part (c) of Figure 8–3 at which the marginal cost curve intersects the average total cost curve. This should not be surprising. When marginal cost is below average total cost, average total cost falls. When marginal cost is above average total cost, average total cost rises. At the point where average total cost is neither falling nor rising, marginal cost must then be equal to average total cost. When we represent this graphically, the marginal cost curve will intersect the average total cost curve at the latter's minimum.

The same analysis applies to the intersection of the marginal cost curve and the average variable cost curve. When are average variable costs at a minimum? According to part (a) of Figure 8–3, average variable costs are at a minimum of $2.60 at an output rate of five calculators per hour. This is where the marginal cost curve intersects the average variable cost curve in part (c) of Figure 8–3. A good example of the relationship of costs is shown in Example 8–2.

### EXAMPLE 8–2 The Cost of Driving a Car

The Canadian Automobile Association provides a "Driving Costs Calculator" on numerous types of vehicles from compact to full-sized vehicles. The calculator provided the costs of running a compact car in Alberta as follows:

**Costs per kilometre**
Fuel: $0.08 cents (based on $0.97 per liter)
Maintenance: 0.012 cents
Tires: 0.0125 cents
**Annual costs**
Insurance: $1,684
Licence and registration: $101
Financing charges: $593
Depreciation: $3,864

On the basis of an average annual driving distance of 20,000 kilometres, total costs amounted to $8492 per year.

**For critical analysis:** Which costs are total fixed costs, total variable costs, average total costs per kilometre, and marginal costs?

# 8.4 The Relationship between Diminishing Marginal Returns and Cost Curves

There is a unique relationship between output and the shape of the various cost curves we have drawn. Let us consider specifically the relationship between marginal cost and the example of diminishing marginal physical returns in part (a) of Figure 8–4. It turns out that if wage rates are constant, the shape of the marginal cost curve in part (d) of Figure 8–4 is both a reflection of and a consequence of the law of diminishing returns. Let us assume that each unit of labour can be purchased at a constant price. Further assume that labour is the only variable input. We see that as more workers are hired, marginal physical product first rises and then falls after the point at which diminishing returns are encountered. Thus, the marginal cost of each extra unit of output will first fall as long as marginal physical product is rising, and then it will rise as long as marginal physical product is falling. Recall that marginal cost is defined as:

$$\text{MC} = \frac{\text{Change in total cost}}{\text{Change in output}}$$

Because the price of labour is assumed to be constant, the change in total cost is simply the constant price of labour, *W* (we are increasing labour by only one unit). The change in output is simply the marginal physical product (MPP) of the one-unit increase in labour. Therefore, we see that:

$$\text{Marginal cost} = \frac{W}{\text{MPP}}$$

This means that initially, when there are increasing returns, marginal cost falls (we are dividing *W* by increasingly larger numbers), and later, when diminishing returns set in and marginal physical product is falling, marginal cost must increase (we are dividing *W* by smaller numbers). As marginal physical product increases, marginal cost decreases, and as marginal physical product decreases, marginal cost must increase. Thus, when marginal physical product reaches its maximum, marginal cost necessarily reaches its minimum. To illustrate this, let us return to Figure 8–4. Assume that a worker at our pocket calculator factory is paid \$5 per hour. When we go from zero labour input to one unit, output increases by eight calculators. Each of those eight calculators has a marginal cost of 63 cents. Now, the second unit of labour is hired, and it too costs \$5 per hour. Output increases by 16. Thus, the marginal cost is \$5 ÷ 16 = 31 cents. We continue the experiment. We see that the next unit of labour yields only 15 additional calculators, and so marginal cost starts to rise to 33 cents. The following unit of labour increases marginal physical product by only 13, so marginal cost becomes \$5 ÷ 13 = 38 cents.

All of the foregoing can be restated in relatively straightforward terms:

**Firms' short-run cost curves are a reflection of the law of diminishing marginal returns. Given any constant price of the variable input, marginal costs decline as long as the marginal product of the variable resource is rising. At the point at which diminishing marginal returns begin, marginal costs begin to rise as the marginal product of the variable input begins to decline.**

The result is a marginal cost curve that slopes down, hits a minimum, and then slopes up. The average total cost curve and average variable cost curve are of course affected. They will have their familiar U-shape in the short run. Again, to see this, recall that:

$$\text{AVC} = \frac{\text{Total variable costs}}{\text{Total output}}$$

As we move from zero labour input to one unit in part (a) of Figure 8–4, output increases from zero to eight calculators. The total variable costs are the price per worker,

**FIGURE 8–4**

## The Relationship between Physical Output and Costs

As the number of workers increases, the total number of calculators produced rises, as shown in parts (a) and (b). In part (c), marginal product (MPP) first rises and then falls. Average physical product (APP) follows. The mirror image of part (c) is shown in part (d), in which MC and AVC first fall and then rise.

Part (a)

| (1) Labour | (2) Total Product (number of calculators per hour) | (3) Average Physical Product (calculators per worker per hour) (3) = (2) ÷ (1) | (4) Marginal Physical Product (4) = Change in (2) ÷Change in (1) | (5) Average Variable Cost (5) = (W = \$5) ÷ (3) | (6) Marginal Cost (6) = (W = \$5) ÷ (4) |
|---|---|---|---|---|---|
| 0 | 0 | — | — | — | — |
| 1 | 8 | 8.0 | 8 | \$0.63 | \$0.63 |
| 2 | 24 | 12.0 | 16 | 0.42 | 0.31 |
| 3 | 39 | 13.0 | 15 | 0.38 | 0.33 |
| 4 | 52 | 13.0 | 13 | 0.38 | 0.38 |
| 5 | 62 | 12.4 | 10 | 0.40 | 0.50 |
| 6 | 68 | 11.3 | 6 | 0.44 | 0.83 |
| 7 | 69 | 9.9 | 1 | 0.55 | 5.00 |

Part (b)

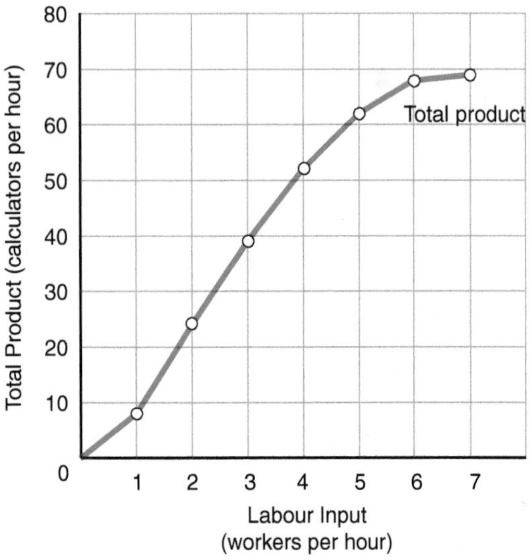


Part (c)

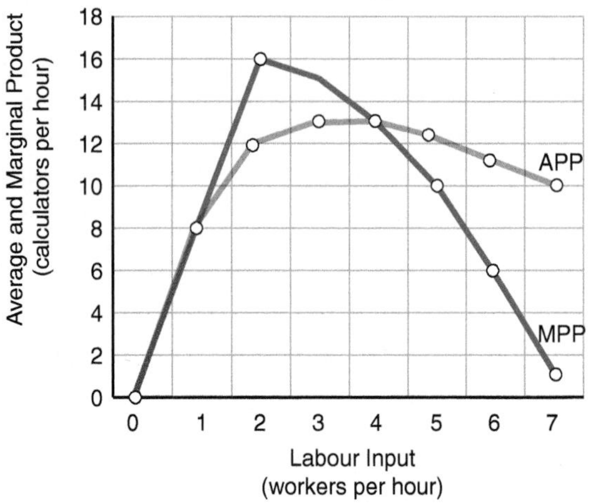


Part (d)

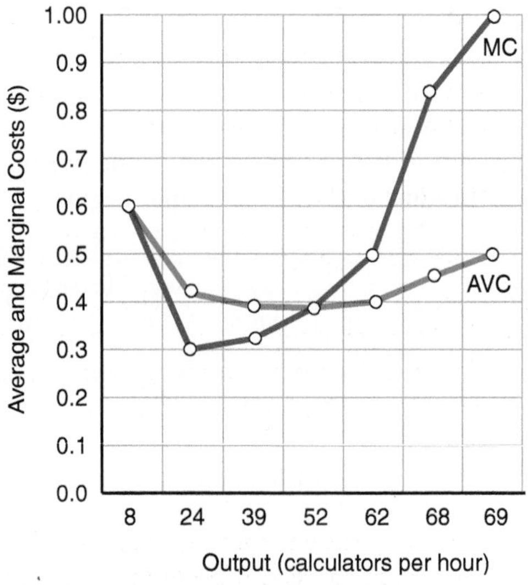

$W$($5), times the number of workers (1). Because the average product of one worker (column 3) is eight, we can write the total product, eight, as the average product, eight, times the number of workers, one. Thus we see that:

$$\text{AVC} = \frac{\$5 \times 1}{8 \times 1} = \frac{\$5}{8} = \frac{\text{W}}{\text{APP}}$$

From column 3 in part (a) of Figure 8–4, we see that the average product increases, reaches a maximum, and then declines. Because AVC = $W$/APP, average variable cost decreases as average product increases and increases as average product decreases. AVC reaches its minimum when average product reaches its maximum. Furthermore, because ATC = AVC + AFC, the average total cost curve inherits the relationship between the average variable cost and diminishing returns.

## Breakeven Analysis

A very useful analysis that firms use is **breakeven**, the output that a firm must produce to reach the point where its profits are zero. The breakeven point will cover all fixed and variable costs. It helps managers make better decisions about what quantity has to be produced so that profits can be realized. Breakeven quantity (BQ) is the total fixed costs divided by the selling price minus the average variable costs.

**Breakeven** The output that a firm must produce to reach the point where its profits are zero.

$$\text{BQ} = \frac{\text{TFC}}{\text{Selling price} - \text{AVC}}$$

If a firm wants a specific profit, it can add the desired profit to the total fixed cost and then divide by the selling price minus the average variable costs.

# 8.5 Long-Run Cost Curves

The long run is defined as a time period during which full adjustment can be made to any change in the economic environment. Long-run curves are sometimes called *planning curves,* and the long run, during which all inputs are variable, is sometimes called the **planning horizon**. We start out our analysis of long-run cost curves by considering a single firm contemplating the construction of a single plant. The firm has three alternative plant sizes from which to choose on the planning horizon. Each particular plant size generates its own short-run average total cost curve. Now that we are talking about the difference between long-run and short-run cost curves, we will label all short-run curves with an *S* and long-run curves with an *L;* short-run average (total) costs will be labelled SAC, and long-run average cost curves will be labelled LAC.

**Planning horizon** The long run, during which all inputs are variable.

Part (a) of Figure 8–5 shows three short-run average cost curves for three successively larger plants. Which is the optimal size to build? That depends on the anticipated normal, sustained (permanent) rate of output per time period. Assume for a moment that the anticipated normal, sustained rate is $Q_1$. If a plant of size 1 is built, the average costs will be $C_1$. If a plant of size 2 is built, we see on $\text{SAC}_2$ that the average costs will be $C_2$, which is greater than $C_1$. Thus, if the anticipated rate of output is $Q_1$, the appropriate plant size is the one from which $\text{SAC}_1$ was derived.

However, if the anticipated permanent rate of output per time period goes from $Q_1$ to $Q_2$ and a plant of size 1 had been decided on, average costs would be $C_4$. If a plant of size 2 had been decided on, average costs would be $C_3$, which is clearly less than $C_4$.

In choosing the appropriate plant size for a single-plant firm during the planning horizon, the firm will pick the size whose short-run average cost curve generates an average cost that is lowest for the expected rate of output.

## Long-Run Average Cost Curve

If we now assume that the entrepreneur faces an infinite number of choices of plant sizes in the long run, we can conceive of an infinite number of SAC curves similar to the three

**FIGURE 8–5**

**Preferable Plant Size and the Long-Run Average Cost Curve**

If the anticipated permanent rate of output per unit time period is $Q_1$, the optimal plant to build would be the one corresponding to $SAC_1$ in part (a) because average costs are lower. However, if the permanent rate of output increases to $Q_2$, it will be more profitable to have a plant size corresponding to $SAC_2$. Unit costs fall to $C_3$.

If we draw all the possible short-run average cost curves that correspond to different plant sizes and then draw the envelope (a curve tangent to each member of a set of curves) to these various curves, $SAC_1$ to $SAC_8$, we obtain the long-run average cost curve, or the planning curve, as shown in part (b).

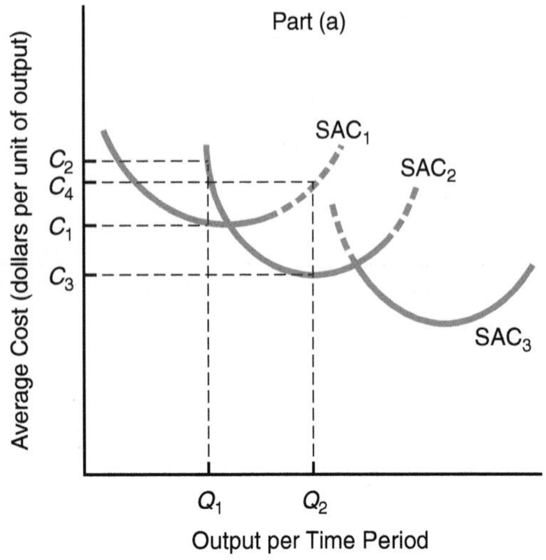


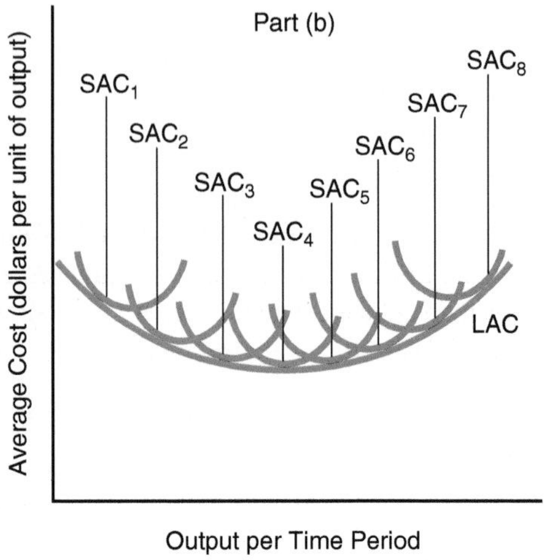


in part (a) of Figure 8–5. We are not able, of course, to draw an infinite number; we have drawn quite a few, however, in part (b) of Figure 8–5. We then draw the "envelope" to all these various short-run average cost curves. The resulting envelope is the **long-run average cost curve**, which is the locus (path) of points representing the minimum unit cost of producing any given rate of output, given current technology and resource prices. This long-run average cost curve is sometimes called the **planning curve**, for it represents the various average costs attainable at the planning stage of the firm's decision making. It represents the locus of points giving the least unit cost of producing any given rate of output. Note that the LAC curve is *not* tangent to each individual SAC curve at the latter's minimum points. This is true only at the minimum point of the LAC curve. Then and only then are minimum long-run average costs equal to minimum short-run average costs.

**Long-run average cost curve** The locus (path) of points representing the minimum unit cost of producing any given rate of output, given current technology and resource prices.

**Planning curve** The curve that represents the various average costs attainable at the planning stage of the firm's decision making.

## Why the Long-Run Average Cost Curve Is U-Shaped

Note that the long-run average cost curve, LAC in part (b) of Figure 8–5, is U-shaped, similar to the U-shape of the short-run average cost curve developed earlier in this chapter. The reason behind the U-shape of the two curves is not the same, however. The short-run average cost curve is U-shaped because of the law of diminishing marginal returns. But the law cannot apply to the long run because in the long run, all factors of production are variable; there is no point of diminishing marginal returns because there is no fixed factor of production. Why, then, do we see the U-shape in the long-run average cost curve? The reason has to do with **economies of scale** (decreases in long-run average costs resulting from increases in output), **constant returns to scale** (no change in long-run average costs when output increases), and **diseconomies of scale** (increases in long-run average costs that occur as output increases). When the firm is experiencing economies of scale, the long-run average cost curve slopes downward—an increase in scale and production leads to a fall in unit costs. When the firm is experiencing constant returns to scale, the long-run average cost curve is at its minimum point such that an increase in scale and production does not change unit costs. When the firm is experiencing diseconomies of scale, the long-run average cost curve slopes upward—an increase in scale and production increases

**Economies of scale** Decreases in long-run average costs resulting from increases in output.

**Constant returns to scale** No change in long-run average costs when output increases.

**Diseconomies of scale** Increases in long-run average costs that occur as output increases.

**FIGURE 8–6**

**Economies of Scale, Constant Returns to Scale, and Diseconomies of Scale Shown with the Long-Run Average Cost Curve**

Long-run average cost curves will fall when there are economies of scale, as shown in part (a). They will be constant (flat) when the firm is experiencing constant returns to scale, as shown in part (b). They will rise when the firm is experiencing diseconomies of scale, as shown in part (c).

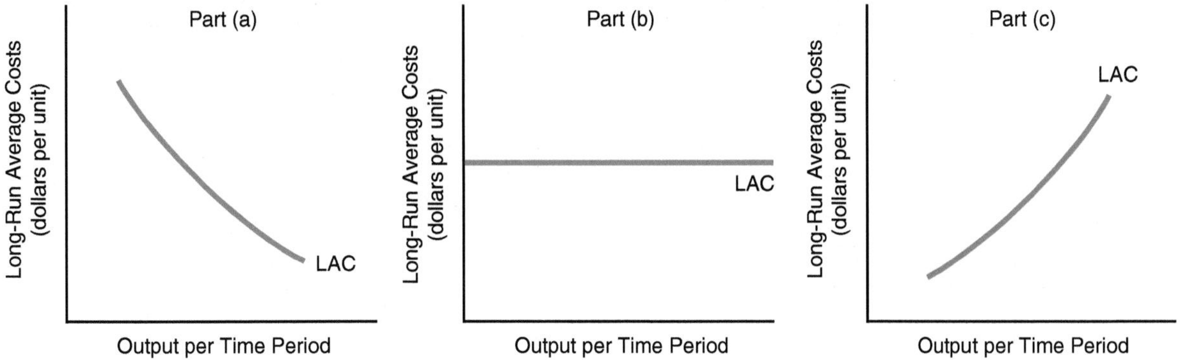


unit costs. These three sections of the long-run average cost curves are broken up into parts (a), (b), and (c) in Figure 8–6.

## Reasons for Economies of Scale

We shall examine three of the many reasons a firm might be expected to experience economies of scale: specialization, the dimensional factor, and improved productive equipment.

**SPECIALIZATION.** As a firm's scale of operation increases, the opportunities for specialization in the use of resource inputs also increase. This is sometimes called *increased division of tasks* or *operations.* Gains from such division of labour or increased specialization are well known. When we consider managerial staff, we also find that larger enterprises may be able to put together more highly specialized staff.

**DIMENSIONAL FACTOR.** Large-scale firms often require proportionately less input per unit of output simply because certain inputs do not have to be physically doubled in order to double the output. Consider the cost of storage of oil. The cost of storage is basically related to the cost of steel that goes into building the storage container; however, the amount of steel required goes up less than in proportion to the volume (storage capacity) of the container (because the volume of a container increases more than proportionately with its surface area).

**IMPROVED PRODUCTIVE EQUIPMENT.** The larger the scale of the enterprise, the more the firm is able to take advantage of larger-volume (output capacity) types of machinery. Small-scale operations may not be able profitably to use large-volume machines that can be more efficient per unit of output. Also, smaller firms often cannot use technologically more advanced machinery because they are unable to spread out the high cost of such sophisticated equipment over a large output.

For any of these reasons, the firm may experience economies of scale, which means that equal percentage increases in output result in a decrease in average cost. Thus, output can double, but total costs will less than double; hence average cost falls. Note that the factors listed for causing economies of scale are all *internal* to the firm; they do not depend on what other firms are doing or what is happening in the economy.

## Why a Firm Might Experience Diseconomies of Scale

One of the basic reasons a firm can expect to run into diseconomies of scale is that there are limits to the efficient functioning of management. Moreover, as more workers are hired, a more than proportionate increase in managers and staff people may be needed, and this could cause increased costs per unit. This is so because larger levels of output imply successively larger *plant* size, which, in turn, implies successively larger *firm* size. Thus, as the level of output increases, more people must be hired, and the firm gets bigger. However, as this happens, the support, supervisory and administrative staff, and the general paperwork of the firm, increase. As the layers of supervision grow, the costs of information and communication grow more than proportionately; hence the average unit cost will start to increase.

Some observers of corporate giants claim that many of them are experiencing some diseconomies of scale today. Witness the problems that General Motors and IBM had in the 2000s. Some analysts say that the financial problems that they have experienced are at least partly a function of their size relative to their smaller, more flexible competitors, who can make decisions faster and then take more rapid advantage of changing market conditions. This seems to be particularly true with IBM. It apparently adapted very slowly to the fact that the large mainframe computer business was declining as micro- and mini-computers became more and more powerful. Such companies as Dell, Oracle, and eBay all enjoy economies of scale because of standardized products. Example 8–3 is a great example of how Dell accomplished economies of scale.

### EXAMPLE 8–3 Economies of Scale at Dell

In the mid-1990s, Dell Computer Corporation embarked on a plan to become the lowest-cost computer manufacturer in the world. Now, the company has factories that receive more than half of all customer orders via the Internet. These orders flow to a plant's "air-traffic control room," where procurement of parts, computer assembly, and shipping are managed.

At each point on the factory floor, which at some plants can be as large as 300 000 square feet, groups in charge of producing various computer components are linked via intranets, or internal computer networks. Each forklift truck contains a wireless computer that follows the paths of components to ensure that they reach the correct assembly points. Forklift trucks carrying completed computers are similarly equipped, to ensure that they reach the correct loading dock from among the dozens where trucks are waiting to be loaded.

In its newest and largest plants, Dell can produce more than 1000 computers per hour, which is almost twice as many as a typical plant could produce only half a dozen years ago. Even rival computer manufacturers agreed by the early 2000s that Dell had taken advantage of economies of scale to become the most cost-efficient manufacturer of personal computers.

**For critical analysis:** What has happened to Dell's short-run average cost curves as it has moved down along its long-run average cost curve?

## Minimum Efficient Scale

Economists and statisticians have obtained actual data on the relationship between changes in all inputs and changes in average cost. It turns out that for many industries, the long-run average cost curve does not resemble that shown in part (b) of Figure 8–5. Rather, it more closely resembles Figure 8–7. What you observe there is a small portion of declining long-

**FIGURE 8–7**

**Minimum Efficient Scale**

This long-run average cost curve reaches a minimum point at *A*. After that point, long-run average costs remain horizontal, or constant, and then rise at some higher rate of output. Point *A* is called the minimum efficient scale for the firm because that is the point at which it reaches minimum costs. It is the lowest rate of output at which the average long-run costs are minimized.

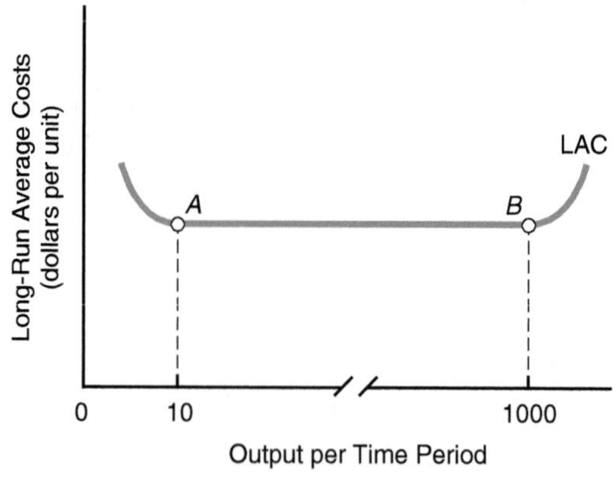

run average costs (economies of scale) and then a wide range of outputs over which the firm experiences relatively constant economies of scale. At the output rate when economies of scale end and constant economies of scale start, the **minimum efficient scale (MES)** for the firm is encountered. It occurs at point *A*. (The point is, of course, approximate. The more smoothly the curve declines into its flat portion, the more approximate will be our estimate of the MES.) The minimum efficient scale will always be the lowest rate of output at which long-run average costs are minimized. In any industry with a long-run average cost curve similar to the one in Figure 8–7, larger firms will have no cost-saving advantage over smaller firms as long as the smaller firms have at least obtained the minimum efficient scale at point *A*.

**Minimum efficient scale (MES)** The output rate when economies of scale end and constant economies of scale start.

Among its uses, the minimum efficient scale gives us a rough measure of the degree of competition in an industry. If the MES is small relative to industry demand, the degree of competition in that industry is likely to be high because there is room for many efficiently sized plants. Conversely, when the MES is large relative to industry demand, the degree of competition is likely to be small because there is room for a relatively small number of efficiently sized plants or firms. Looked at another way, if it takes a very large scale of plant to obtain minimum long-run average cost, the output of just a few of these very large firms can fully satisfy total market demand. This means that there is no room for a large number of smaller plants if maximum efficiency is to be obtained in the industry.

## ISSUES AND APPLICATIONS

# Businesses Look Toward Costs To Determine Viability

### Concepts Applied: Economic vs. Accounting Costs, Variable Costs, Fixed Costs, Long Run

Overproduction of books is a common practice since the marginal cost of printing additional copies is relatively low.

The reason that corner restaurant is constantly changing ownership could be because few small businesses take *all* costs into consideration when starting a business. As you can see from this chapter, there are many types of costs that need to be considered.

One of the first costs that a person must consider before opening up a business is the lost wages that he or she will suffer. Giving up a job that pays $50 000 per year to open up a business is an economic cost, not an accounting cost, but it will affect that person's ability to open up a business.

Next, if the person requests a loan, the bank will want to know what the fixed costs, such as rent, will be so it can take them into consideration. Variable costs are much harder to determine, especially in the long run. In a restaurant, for example, how much produce will be thrown out each week because it is not used? What are the average costs per plate of spaghetti? What are the yearly costs of having staff available when few customers are coming into the restaurant?

A restaurant owner will also have to know how many plates of spaghetti he or she needs to sell every week to just break even. Too many small business owners start a business thinking they will succeed just because they have a unique product to offer, only to fail because they miscalculated the costs of production.

**For critical analysis:**

Why should a business owner calculate his or her costs per unit? If you were starting a business, would you look at the economic costs associated with your business, or just the accounting costs?

# SUMMARY

Here is what you should know after reading this chapter. MyEconLab will help you identify what you know, and where to go when you need to practise. We suggest that as soon as you review one of the Learning Objective sections below, you then proceed to go through the related section in MyEconLab.

| LEARNING OBJECTIVES | KEY TERMS | MYECONLAB PRACTICE |
|---|---|---|
| **8.1 The Profits of a Firm.** Accounting profits differ from economic profits. Economic profits are defined as total revenues minus total costs, where costs include the full opportunity cost of all factors of production plus all other implicit costs.<br>The full opportunity cost of capital invested in a business is generally not included as a cost when accounting profits often overstate economic profits. We assume throughout that the goal of the firm is to maximize profits. | explicit costs, 189<br>accounting profit, 189<br>implicit costs, 189<br>normal rate of return, 189<br>opportunity cost of capital, 189<br>economic profits, 191 | • **MyEconLab** Study Plan 8.1 |
| **8.2 Short Run versus Long Run.** The short run for the firm is defined as the period during which plant size cannot be altered. The long run is the period during which all factors of production can be varied. | firm, 191<br>short run, 192<br>plant size, 192<br>long run, 192<br>production, 193<br>production function, 193<br>law of diminishing (marginal) returns, 194<br>average physical product, 195<br>marginal physical product, 195 | • **MyEconLab** Study Plan 8.2 |
| **8.3 Short-Run Costs to the Firm.** Fixed costs are costs that cannot be altered in the short run. Fixed costs are associated with assets that the firm owns that cannot be profitably transferred to another use. Variable costs are associated with input costs that vary as the rate of output varies. There are definitional relationships among average, total, and marginal costs. Total costs equal total fixed costs plus total variable costs. Fixed costs do not vary with the rate of production. Variable costs do vary with the rate of production. Average total cost equals total cost divided by quantity. Average variable cost equals total variable cost divided by quantity. Average fixed cost equals total fixed cost divided by quantity. | total costs, 196<br>fixed costs, 196<br>variable costs, 197<br>average fixed costs, 197<br>average variable costs, 197<br>average total costs, 197<br>marginal costs, 199 | • **MyEconLab** Study Plan 8.3 |

myeconlab

| LEARNING OBJECTIVES | KEY TERMS | MYECONLAB PRACTICE |
|---|---|---|
| **8.4 The Relationship between Diminishing Marginal Returns and Cost Curves.** Marginal cost equals the change in total cost divided by the change in quantity. Firms are also interested in how much they need to produce to break even. Breakeven quantity equals the total fixed cost divided by selling price minus average variable cost. | breakeven, 203 | • **MyEconLab** Study Plan 8.4 |
| **8.5 Long-Run Cost Curves.** Average total cost (ATC) equals the sum of average fixed cost (AFC) and average variable cost (AVC). The AFC curve continuously drops; the AVC curve falls during the early output stages but eventually AVC rises. So, ATC initially falls and then rises after the point of diminishing marginal returns, causing the long run ATC to appear to be U-shaped. | planning horizon, 203<br>long-run average cost curve, 204<br>planning curve, 204<br>economies of scale, 204<br>constant returns to scale, 204<br>diseconomies of scale, 204<br>minimum efficient scale (MES), 207 | • **MyEconLab** Study Plan 8.5 |

# PROBLEMS

(Answers to the odd-numbered problems appear at the back of the book.)

**LO 8.1 Distinguish between accounting profits and economic profits.**

1. After graduation, you face a choice. One option is to work for a multinational consulting firm and earn a starting salary (benefits included) of \$40 000. The other option is to use \$5000 in savings to start your own consulting firm. You could have earned an interest return of 5 percent on your savings. You choose to start your own consulting firm. At the end of the first year, you add up all of your expenses and revenues. Your total includes \$12 000 in rent, \$1000 in office supplies, \$20 000 for office staff, and \$4000 in telephone expenses. What are your total explicit costs and total implicit costs?
2. Suppose, as in Problem 1, that you choose to start your own consulting firm upon graduation. At the end of the first year, your total revenues are \$77 250. On the basis of the information in Problem 1, what is the accounting profit, and what is your economic profit?
3. An individual leaves a college faculty, where she was earning \$40 000 a year, to begin a new venture. She invests her savings of \$10 000, which were earning 10 percent annually. She then spends \$20 000 on office equipment, hires two students at \$30 000 a year each, rents office space for \$12 000, and has other variable expenses of \$40 000. At the end of the year, her revenues are \$200 000. What are her accounting profit and her economic profit for the year?

**LO 8.2 Understand the short-run production function and diminishing marginal returns.**

4. The short-run production function for a manufacturer of DVD drives is as follows:

| Input of Labour (workers per week) | Total Output of DVD Drives |
|---|---|
| 0 | 0 |
| 1 | 25 |
| 2 | 60 |
| 3 | 85 |
| 4 | 105 |
| 5 | 115 |
| 6 | 120 |

On the basis of this information, calculate the average physical product at each quantity of labour.

5. Using the information provided in Problem 4, calculate the marginal physical product of labour at each quantity of labour.

6. Define long-run average total cost. In light of the fact that businesses are operated day to day in the short run, of what use is the concept of long-run average total cost to the entrepreneur?

**LO 8.3 Calculate the various costs for the firm in the short run.**

7. Your school's basketball team had a foul-shooting average of 0.800 (80 out of 100) before last night's game, during which they shot 5 for 10 at the foul line.
   a. What was their marginal performance last night?
   b. What happened to the team's foul-shooting average?
   c. Suppose that their foul shooting in the next game is 6 for 10. What is happening to their marginal performance? Now what is the team average foul-shooting percentage?

8. The cost structure of a manufacturer of cable modems is described in the following table:

| Output (units) | Average Fixed Cost | Total Cost |
|---|---|---|
| 0 | — | $200 |
| 5 | $40 | 300 |
| 10 | 20 | 380 |
| 20 | 10 | 420 |
| 40 | 5 | 520 |

   a. Find the average variable cost at each level of production.
   b. What is the marginal cost of increasing output from 10 to 20 units? From 20 to 40 units?
   c. Find the average total cost at each level of production.

9. At the end of the year, a firm produced 10 000 laptop computers. Its total costs were $5 million, and its fixed costs were $2 million. What are the average variable costs of this firm?

10. The cost structure of a manufacturer of microchips is described in the following table. The firm's fixed costs equal $10 000 per day. Calculate the average variable cost, average fixed cost, and average total cost at each output level.

| Output (microchips per day) | Total Cost of Output ($ thousands) |
|---|---|
| 0 | 10 |
| 25 | 60 |
| 50 | 95 |
| 75 | 150 |
| 100 | 220 |
| 125 | 325 |
| 150 | 465 |

11. A watch manufacturer finds that at 1000 units of output, its marginal costs are below average total costs. If it produces an additional watch, will its average total costs rise, fall, or stay the same?

12. At its current short-run level of production, a firm's average variable costs equal $20 per unit, and its average fixed costs equal $30 per unit. Its total costs at this production level equal $2500.
   a. What is the firm's current output level?
   b. What are its total variable costs at this output level?
   c. What are its total fixed costs?

**LO 8.4 Explain the important relationships of the cost curves.**

13. You are given the following graph:

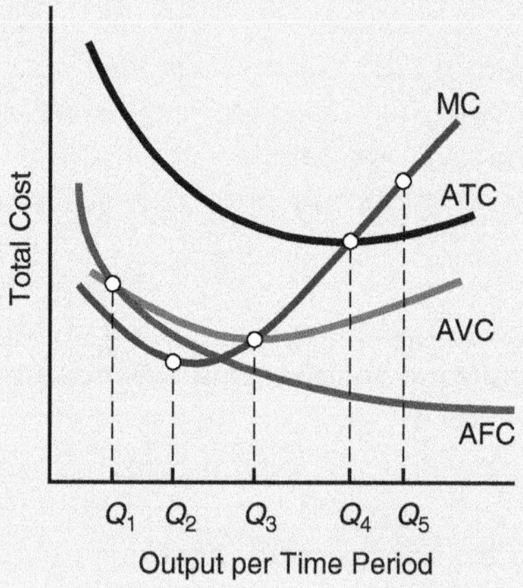


   a. At what output level is AVC at a minimum?
   b. At what output level is ATC at a minimum?
   c. At what output level is MC at a minimum?
   d. At what output level do the AVC and MC curves intersect?
   e. At what output level do the ATC and MC curves intersect?

14. The diagram below displays short-run cost curves for a facility that produces LCD screens for cellphones:

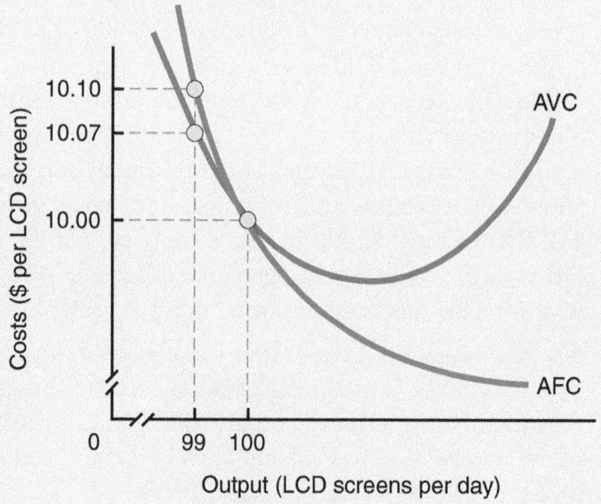


   a. What are the daily total fixed costs of producing LCD screens?

b. What are the total variable costs of producing 100 LCD screens per day?
c. What are the total costs of producing 100 LCD screens per day?
d. What is the marginal cost of producing the hundredth LCD screen? (Hint: To answer this question, you must first determine the total costs—or, alternatively, the total variable costs—of producing 99 LCD screens.)

**LO 8.5 Understand the long-run cost curve.**

15. A manufacturing firm with a single plant is contemplating changing its plant size. It must choose from among seven alternative plant sizes. In the following table plant size A is the smallest it might build, and size G is the largest. Currently, the firm's plant size is B.

| Plant Size | Average Total Cost |
|---|---|
| A (smallest) | $5000 |
| B | 4000 |
| C | 3500 |
| D | 3100 |
| E | 3000 |
| F | 3250 |
| G (largest) | 4100 |

a. Is this firm currently experiencing economies of scale or diseconomies of scale?
b. What is the firm's minimum efficient scale?

# BUSINESS APPLICATION

**LO 8.1 and 8.3 Distinguish between accounting profits and economic profits; calculate the various costs for the firm in the short run.**

## Cost Accounting and Management: How Much Should Management Reimburse Employees for Use of Their Personal Car for Work Purposes?

Copy Corporation is currently embroiled in a labour dispute over the appropriate level of compensation for a union employee who used his personal vehicle to travel 500 kilometres on company business. Copy Corporation reimbursed the employee an amount that covered just the total gas cost of the trip.

Both the union and the employer agreed that the employee had made his car purchase decision prior to working for Copy Corporation. The union and the employer also agreed to use the following set of cost figures published by the Canadian Automobile Association (CAA) to settle the dispute. Note that the following costs are based on travelling 18 000 km per year (a typical year of driving).

| Variable Costs | | Annual Fixed Costs | |
|---|---|---|---|
| Fuel (and Oil) | $1074.60 | Insurance | $1183.00 |
| Maintenance | $437.40 | Licence and Registration | $120.48 |
| Tires | $216.00 | Depreciation | $3729.13 |
| | | Finance Expense (Loan) | $709.00 |

Source: *1998 Driving Costs*, Canadian Automobile Association, 1998

### Business Application Problem

Based on CAA's cost figures above, answer the following questions.

a. Find the average fuel cost (per kilometre). Calculate the employee's reimbursement for the 500 km business trip based on the average fuel cost.
b. Find the average variable cost (per kilometre). Calculate the employee's reimbursement for the 500 km business trip based on the average variable cost.
c. Find the average total cost (per kilometre) Calculate the employee's reimbursement for the 500 km business trip based on the average total cost.
d. Based on the situation outlined above, which cost criteria would be most appropriate as a basis for reimbursement: average gas cost, average variable cost, or average total cost? Why?

PART 3
MARKET STRUCTURE AND RESOURCE ALLOCATION

9

# Perfect Competition

## LEARNING OBJECTIVES

After reading this chapter, you should be able to:

**9.1** Identify and explain the characteristics of a perfectly competitive market structure.

**9.2** Using revenue and cost information, determine the firm's short-run profit-maximizing or loss-minimizing level of output and profit.

**9.3** Derive the firm's short-run supply curve and explain how the short-run equilibrium price is determined in a perfectly competitive market.

**9.4** Explain the features and long-run adjustments associated with long-run equilibrium in perfect competition.

**9.5** Explain the three different long-run industry supply curve situations that are possible in perfect competition.

**9.6** From a social viewpoint, evaluate the long-run behaviour in perfect competition.

A potato is just a potato right? Tell that to the PEI potato farmers who market their potatoes worldwide and they certainly will not agree with you. As you drive around the countryside in PEI, you will see potato stands set up, with potatoes just sitting there and no one is around to sell them. The potato farmers use the honour system and rely on the consumer to pay the going rate. This works well at home, but how does a potato farmer from PEI convince a consumer in Quebec that their potato is superior to say, an Idaho potato? An understanding of the model of perfect competition will help you appreciate the nature of the potato industry.

myeconlab

MyEconLab helps you master each objective and study more efficiently. See end of chapter for details.

# DID YOU KNOW THAT...?

According to a major study entitled "Competitive Alternatives 2016," Canada ranks second as the least costly place to locate a business in ten of the most industrialized nations in the world. The study compared set-up and operating costs—26 cost components in all—of firms competing in 17 industries. In 2016, on average, Canadian businesses enjoyed a 14.6 percent cost advantage over similar firms in the United States. For each of the regions examined, the study identified the following as cities where businesses can operate at lowest unit cost: for the New England/Atlantic Canada region: Fredericton and Moncton, New Brunswick; for the Northeast U.S./Canada region: Quebec City, Quebec; for the Midwest U.S./Western Canada region: Winnipeg, Manitoba; and for the Pacific U.S./Canada region: Kelowna B.C.

As this chapter explains, for industries that resemble perfect competition, low costs become the primary factor contributing to business success, if not survival.

Source: "Competitive alternatives—highlights." 2016. KPMG. http://www.competitivealternatives.com/highlights/default.aspx

# 9.1 The Characteristics of Perfect Competition

## Four Market Structures

In order to better understand and predict the behaviour of firms in our economy, we need to study the types of industry environments or market structures that businesses typically operate within. **Market structure** refers to characteristics of an industry—such as the number of sellers, the ease of entry of new firms, each firm's ability to set the price, and the degree to which each firm's product differs from its competitor's.

**Market structure** Characteristics of an industry—such as the number of sellers, the ease of entry of new firms, each firm's ability to set the price, and the degree to which each firm's product differs from its competitor's.

In the next three chapters, we will study four distinct market structures—perfect competition, monopoly, monopolistic competition, and oligopoly. The vast majority of Canadian industries can be classified as one of these four types of market structures. As you will see, market structure affects a firm's market behaviour—price, profit, and nonprice competitive behaviour. In turn, for each of the four market structures studied, we will examine how the firm's market behaviour affects public interest, which we call the firm's market performance.

Table 9–1 provides an overview of the four types of market structures we will study in the next three chapters.

## The Perfectly Competitive Market Structure

In this chapter, we are interested in studying how a firm acting within a perfectly competitive market structure makes decisions about how much to produce. In a situation of **perfect competition**, each firm is such a small part of the industry that it cannot affect the price of the product in question. That means that each perfectly competitive firm in

**Perfect competition** A market structure in which each firm is such a small part of the industry that it cannot affect the price of the product in question.

**TABLE 9–1**

**Comparing Market Structures**

| Market Structure | Number of Sellers | Unrestricted Entry and Exit | Ability to Set Price | Long-Run Economic Profits Possible | Product Differentiation | Nonprice Competition | Examples |
|---|---|---|---|---|---|---|---|
| Perfect competition | Numerous | Yes | None | No | None | None | Agriculture, coal |
| Monopolistic competition | Many | Yes | Some | Not for most | Considerable | Yes | Restaurants, motels, retail trade |
| Oligopoly | Few | Partial | Some | Yes | Frequent | Yes | Cigarettes, steel, banks |
| Pure monopoly | One | No (for entry) | Considerable | Yes | None (product is unique) | Yes | Electric company, provincial telephone company, medicare |

**Price taker** A competitive firm that takes price as a given, something determined outside the individual firm.

the industry is a **price taker**—the firm takes price as a given, something determined *outside* the individual firm.

This definition of a competitive firm is obviously idealized, for in one sense, the individual firm *has* to set prices. How can we ever have a situation in which firms regard prices as set by forces outside their control? The answer is that even though every firm sets its own prices, a firm in a perfectly competitive situation will find that it will eventually have no customers at all if it sets its price above the competitive price. The best example is in agriculture. Although the individual farmer can set any price for a bushel of carrots, if that price does not coincide with the market price of a bushel of similar-quality carrots, no one will purchase the carrots at a higher price; nor would the farmer be inclined to reduce revenues by selling below the market price.

The following characteristics of perfect competition help us understand why a perfectly competitive firm is a price taker.

1. *Large numbers.* There must be a large number of buyers and sellers. When this is the case, no one buyer or one seller has any influence on price.
2. *Homogeneous product.* The product sold by each firm in the industry must be a perfect substitute for the product sold by another firm. Buyers must be able to choose from a large number of sellers of a product that the buyers believe to be the same.
3. *Easy entry and exit.* Firms in a competitive industry cannot be hampered in their ability to get resources or relocate resources. They move labour and capital in pursuit of profit-making opportunities to whatever business venture gives them their highest expected rate of return on their investment. New firms can easily enter the industry.
4. *Perfect market information.* Consumers are able to find out about lower prices charged by competing firms. Firms are able to find out about cost-saving innovations in order to lower production costs and prices, and they are able to learn about profitable opportunities in other industries.

In this chapter's Issues and Applications, it is noted that the Canadian potato industry closely resembles perfect competition. It is relatively easy for a firm to enter or exit this industry. As Example 9–1 illustrates, blogging has provided novel ways to start up competitive businesses supplying online advertising space.

What features of perfect competition apply to a blogging business?

## EXAMPLE 9–1 When Blogging Becomes a Competitive Business

There are an estimated 152 million weblogs (blogs) in existence. Most of them are personal diaries that happen to be online, have tiny audiences, and earn not a single penny in revenues. Nevertheless, a few blogs have emerged as essentially niche magazines run as businesses and published in an online format by companies such as Gawker Media; Weblogs, Inc.; and Engadget. Increasingly, others are also entering the blogging business. With today's low-cost computers and software in hand, bloggers face one main impediment to entering the blogging market: the opportunity cost of the time they devote to their blogs. Once bloggers attract a sufficient readership, they sell online ad space and begin generating revenues. Many, such as Heather Armstrong, author of a blog called Dooce, are now earning sufficient profits to account for the bulk of their family incomes. Effectively, Armstrong and other bloggers who have entered this market operate small proprietorships.

Surveys indicate that about 7 percent of bloggers post their blogs in hope of earning revenues. With some 152 million bloggers on the Web, this implies that more than 11 million people are competing to operate blogs as profitable businesses.

**For critical analysis:** Why is entry into the blogging market not entirely "free"?

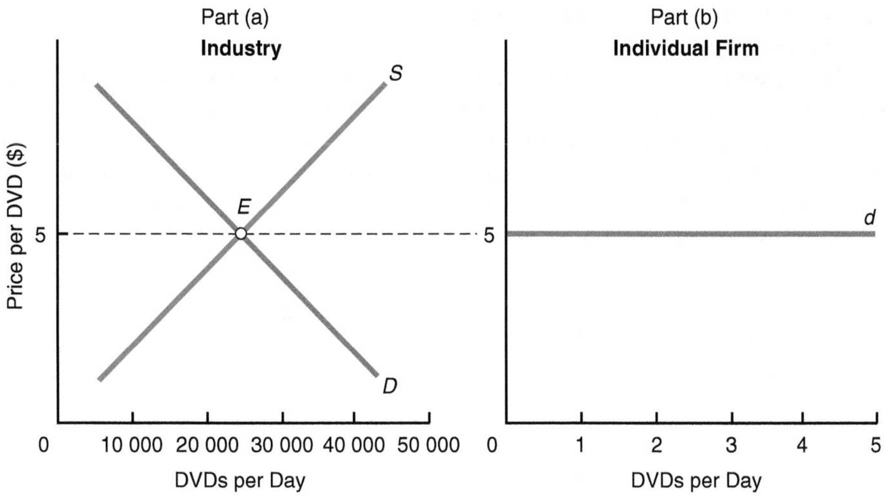


**FIGURE 9–1**

**The Demand Curve for a DVD Producer**

At \$5—where market demand, *D*, and market supply, *S*, intersect—the individual firm faces a perfectly elastic demand curve, *d*. If it raises its price even one penny, it will sell no DVDs at all. Note the difference in the quantities of DVDs represented on the horizontal axes of parts (a) and (b).

## The Demand Curve of the Perfect Competitor

When we discussed substitutes in Chapter 4, we pointed out that the more substitutes there were and the more similar they were to the commodity in question, the greater was the price elasticity of demand. Here, we assume for the perfectly competitive firm that it is producing a commodity that has perfect substitutes. That means that if the individual firm raises its price by one penny, it will lose all of its business. This, then, is how we characterize the demand schedule for a perfectly competitive firm: it is the going market price as determined by the forces of market supply and market demand—that is, where the market demand curve intersects the market supply curve. The single-firm demand curve in a perfectly competitive industry is perfectly elastic at the going market price. Remember that with a perfectly elastic demand curve, any increase in price leads to zero quantity demanded.

We show the market demand and supply curves in part (a) of Figure 9–1. Their intersection occurs at the price of \$5. The commodity in question is recordable DVDs, and we assume for the purposes of this exposition that all DVDs are perfect substitutes for all others. At the going market price of \$5 apiece, a hypothetical individual demand curve for a DVD producer who sells a very, very small part of total industry production is shown in part (b). At the market price, this firm can sell all the output it wants. At the market price of \$5 each, which is where the demand curve for the individual producer lies, consumer demand for the DVDs of that one producer is perfectly elastic. This can be seen by noting that if the firm raises its price, consumers, who are assumed to know that this supplier is charging more than other producers, will buy elsewhere, and the producer in question will have no sales at all. Thus, the demand curve for that producer is perfectly elastic. We label the individual producer's demand curve *d*, whereas the *market* demand curve is always labelled *D*.

# 9.2 Determining Output and Profit in the Short Run

As we have shown, a perfect competitor has to accept the price of the product as a "given." If the firm raises its price, it sells nothing; if it lowers its price, it makes less money per unit sold than it otherwise could. The firm has one decision left: How much should it produce? We will apply our model of the firm to this question to come up with an answer. We will use the *profit-maximization model,* which assumes that firms attempt to maximize their total profits—the positive difference between total revenues and total costs.

## Total Revenues

**Total revenues** The quantity sold multiplied by the price.

Every firm has to consider its *total revenues*, or TR. **Total revenues** are defined as the quantity sold multiplied by the price. (They are the same as total receipts from the sale of output.) The perfect competitor must take the price as a given.

Look at Figure 9–2. Columns 1 and 2 show total output and sales per day and the total cost of producing that output. Column 3 is the market price, *P*, of $5 per DVD, which is also equal to average revenue (AR) because:

$$AR = \frac{TR}{Q} = \frac{PQ}{Q} = P$$

**FIGURE 9–2**

**Profit Maximization**

Given the firm's costs and the market price of $5, the daily quantity that results in the largest profit is seven DVDs per day. In the table in part (a), the profit-maximizing quantity (rate of production) occurs where (TR − TC) = $5.53, which is the maximum profit. Theoretically, this profit-maximizing quantity occurs where MR = MC. In part (b), we find the maximum profit at the quantity level, where the TR curve exceeds the TC curve by the largest vertical amount, at seven DVDs per day. In part (c), we find the maximum profit at the quantity level, where the MR curve intersects the MC curve, at seven DVDs per day.

Part (a)

| (1) Total Output per Day (*Q*) | (2) Total Costs (TC) | (3) Market Price (*P*) | (4) Total Revenues (TR) = (3) × (1) | (5) Total Profit (TR − TC) = (4) − (2) | (6) Average Total Cost (ATC) = (2) ÷ (1) | (7) Average Variable Cost (AVC) | (8) Marginal Cost (MC) = Change (2) / Change (1) | (9) Marginal Revenue (MR) = Change (4) / Change (1) |
|---|---|---|---|---|---|---|---|---|
| 0 | $10.00 | $5 | $ 0 | −$10.00 | | | | |
| 1 | 14.00 | 5 | 5 | −9.00 | $14.00 | $4.00 | $ 4.00 | $5.00 |
| 2 | 17.00 | 5 | 10 | −7.00 | 8.50 | 3.50 | 3.00 | 5.00 |
| 3 | 19.00 | 5 | 15 | −4.00 | 6.33 | 3.00 | 2.00 | 5.00 |
| 4 | 20.00 | 5 | 20 | 0.00 | 5.00 | 2.50 | 1.00 | 5.00 |
| 5 | 21.50 | 5 | 25 | 3.50 | 4.30 | 2.30 | 1.50 | 5.00 |
| 6 | 24.48 | 5 | 30 | 5.52 | 4.08 | 2.41 | 2.98 | 5.00 |
| 7 | 29.47 | 5 | 35 | 5.53 | 4.21 | 2.78 | 4.99 | 5.00 |
| 8 | 37.47 | 5 | 40 | 2.53 | 4.68 | 3.43 | 8.00 | 5.00 |
| 9 | 49.47 | 5 | 45 | −4.47 | 5.50 | 4.39 | 12.00 | 5.00 |
| 10 | 66.47 | 5 | 50 | −16.47 | 6.65 | 5.65 | 17.00 | 5.00 |

Part (b)

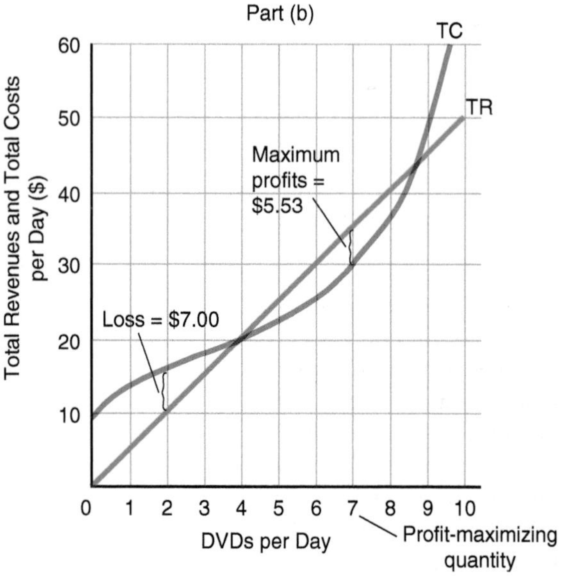


Part (c)

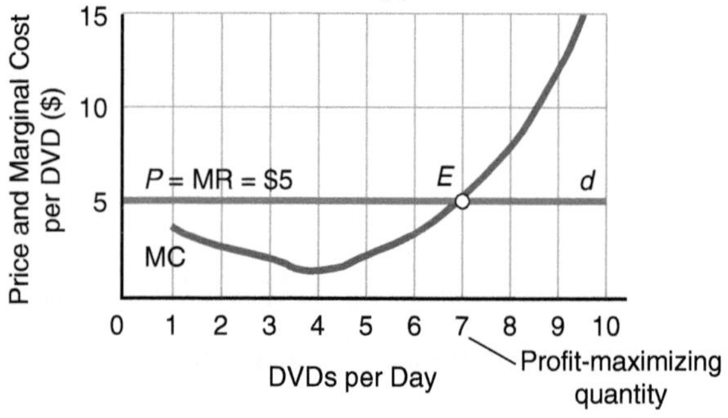

where $Q$ stands for quantity. If we assume that all units sell for the same price, it becomes apparent that another name for the demand curve is the *average revenue curve* (this is true regardless of the type of market structure under consideration).

Column 4 shows the total revenues, or TR, as equal to the market price, $P$, times the total output in sales per day, or $Q$. Thus, TR = $PQ$. We are assuming that the market supply and demand schedules intersect at a price of $5 and that this price holds for all the firm's production. We are also assuming that because our DVD maker is a small part of the market, it can sell all that it produces at that price. Thus, part (b) of Figure 9–2 shows the total revenue curve as a straight line. For every unit of sales, total revenue is increased by $5.

## Comparing Total Costs with Total Revenues

Total costs are also plotted in part (b). Remember, the firm's costs always include a normal rate of return on investment. So, whenever we refer to total costs, we are not talking about accounting costs but about economic costs. When the total cost curve is above the total revenue curve, the firm is experiencing economic losses. When it is below the total revenue curve, the firm is making economic profits.

By comparing total costs with total revenues, we can calculate the number of DVDs the individual competitive firm should produce per day. Our analysis rests on the assumption that the firm will attempt to maximize total profits. In part (a) of Figure 9–2, we see that total profits reach a maximum of $5.53 at a production rate of seven DVDs per day. We can see this graphically in part (b) of the figure. The firm will maximize profits where the total revenue curve exceeds the total cost curve by the greatest amount. That occurs at a rate of output and sales of seven DVDs per day; this rate is called the **profit-maximizing rate of production**—the rate of production that maximizes total profits, or the difference between total revenues and total costs; also, the rate of production at which marginal revenue equals marginal cost.

**Profit-maximizing rate of production** The rate of production that maximizes total profits, or the difference between total revenues and total costs; also, the rate of production at which marginal revenue equals marginal cost.

We can also find this profit-maximizing rate of production for the individual competitive firm by looking at marginal revenues and marginal costs.

## Using Marginal Analysis to Determine the Profit-Maximizing Rate of Production

It is possible—indeed, preferable—to use marginal analysis to determine the profit-maximizing rate of production. We end up with the same results derived in a different manner, one that focuses more on where decisions are really made—on the margin. Managers examine changes in costs and relate them to changes in revenues. In fact, we almost always compare changes in cost with changes in benefits, where change is occurring at the margin, whether it be with respect to how much more or less to produce, how many more workers to hire or fire, or how much more to study or not study.

**Marginal revenue** represents the change in total revenues attributable to changing production by one unit of the product in question. Hence, a more formal definition of marginal revenue is:

**Marginal revenue** The change in total revenues attributable to changing production by one unit of the product in question.

$$\text{Marginal revenue} = \frac{\text{Change in total revenues}}{\text{Change in output}}$$

In a perfectly competitive market, the marginal revenue curve is exactly equivalent to the price line or the individual firm's demand curve, because the firm can sell all of its output (production) at the market price. Thus, in Figure 9–1, the demand curve, $d$, for the individual producer is at a price of $5—the price line is coincident with the demand curve. But so is the marginal revenue curve, for marginal revenue, in this case, also equals $5.

The marginal revenue curve for our competitive DVD producer is shown as a line at $5 in part (c) of Figure 9–2. Note, again, that the marginal revenue curve is equal to the price line, which is equal to the individual firm's demand, or average revenue, curve, $d$.

## When Are Profits Maximized?

Now, we add the marginal cost curve, MC, taken from column 8 in part (a) of Figure 9–2. As shown in part (c) of that figure, the marginal cost curve first falls and then starts to rise because of the law of diminishing returns, eventually intersecting the marginal revenue curve and then rising above it. Note that column 8 in part (a) of Figure 9–2 indicates that the marginal cost of the first unit of output is $4; the second unit of output is $3; and so forth.

In part (c), the marginal cost curve intersects the marginal revenue curve at seven DVDs per day. The firm has an incentive to produce and sell until the amount of the additional revenue received from selling one more DVD just equals the additional costs incurred for producing and selling that DVD. This is how the firm maximizes profit. Whenever marginal cost is less than marginal revenue, the firm will always make more profit by increasing production.

Now, consider the possibility of producing at an output rate of eight DVDs per day. The marginal cost curve at that output rate is higher than the marginal revenue curve (or *d*). The firm would be spending more to produce that additional output than it would be receiving in revenues; it would be foolish to continue producing at this rate.

But how much should it produce? It should produce at point *E* in Figure 9–2 part (c), where the marginal cost curve intersects the marginal revenue curve from below.[1] The firm should continue production until the cost of increasing output by one more unit is just equal to the revenues obtainable from that extra unit. This is a fundamental rule in economics:

**Profit maximization normally occurs at the rate of output at which marginal revenue equals marginal cost.**

For a perfectly competitive firm, this is at the intersection of the demand schedule, *d*, and the marginal cost curve, MC. When MR exceeds MC, each additional unit of output adds more to total revenues than to total costs, causing losses to decrease or profits to increase. When MC is greater than MR, each unit produced adds more to total cost than to total revenues, causing profits to decrease or losses to increase. Therefore, profit maximization occurs when MC equals MR. In our particular example, our profit-maximizing, perfectly competitive DVD producer will produce at a rate of seven DVDs a day.

In the mid-2000s, the Canadian government faced significant public pressure to implement policies that would restore international confidence in Canadian beef, due to the discovery of "mad cow disease" in Canada. Policy Example 9–1 encourages you to use marginal analysis to evaluate a policy proposal that would have every cow destined for Asia tested for "mad cow disease."

### POLICY EXAMPLE 9–1 Quelling Fears of "Mad Cow Disease" in Asia

The Canada Beef Export Federation (CBEF) is an independent, nonprofit organization committed to improving export results for the perfectly competitive Canadian cattle and beef industry. In the year ending 2002, according to the CBEF, the three key export markets for Canadian beef were the United States, Mexico, and East Asia—purchasing 72 percent, 15 percent, and 10 percent, respectively, of all Canadian beef exports.

On the basis of current market and profit trends, the CBEF has established a marketing plan that would significantly increase Canadian beef exports to East Asia. According to this plan, East Asia will purchase over 30 percent of Canadian beef exports, the United States 45 percent, with the remaining 25 percent going to Mexico and other nations. East Asia is an attractive market to target because its consumers eat nonprime beef cuts, such as tripe, that North Americans generally shun. That means that a carcass processed for Asia is worth up to $200 more than one killed for the North American market.

*continued*

[1]The marginal cost curve, MC, also cuts the marginal revenue curve, *d*, from above at an output rate of less than 1 in this example. This intersection should be ignored because it is irrelevant to the firm's decisions.

When two cases of bovine spongiform encephalopathy (BSE) or "mad cow disease" were discovered in cows raised in Canada in 2003, many nations around the world closed their borders to Canadian beef and cattle. As of the first quarter of 2009, two major Asian countries—South Korea and Mainland China—still prohibited the import of Canadian beef. According to statistics collected by the CBEF, in 2009, only 8.5 percent of Canadian beef exports were sold to Asian markets. This is far short of the federation's previous marketing plan.

Canada's 19th case of BSE was reported in 2015. The Asian market including China quickly closed their borders to Canadian beef.

In the past, Asian nations have suggested that if Canada were to test all cattle slaughtered for BSE, they would reconsider importing Canadian beef. Canada has so far resisted this demand, but some industry observers have suggested a policy of testing all animals destined for Asian consumption.

Source: "Canadian beef and veal product exports." Trade Statistics. Canada Beef Export Federation. http://www.cbef.com/PDF/Stats_1990-2010.pdf. (Accessed February 22, 2004); "Trade statistics 1990–2015." Newsletters and Statistics. Canadian Beef Export Federation. http://www.cbef.com. (Accessed May 29, 2010.) "Latest BSE case in Alberta a setback for beef export strategy." CBC news. http://www.cbc.ca/news/politics/latest-bse-case-in-alberta-a-setback-for-beef-export-strategy-1.2982649.

**For critical analysis:** What maximum amount, per animal slaughtered, would Canadian beef producers be willing to pay, to ensure that all animals destined for the Asian markets are tested for BSE? Explain.

## Short-Run Profits

To find what our competitive individual DVD producer is making in terms of profits in the short run, we have to add the average total cost curve to part (c) of Figure 9–2. That is, we take the information from column 6 in part (a) of Figure 9–2 and add it to part (c) of Figure 9–2 to get Figure 9–3.

In Figure 9–3, assuming a price of $5 per DVD, the profit-maximizing rate of output is seven DVDs per day, where marginal revenue equals marginal cost. At this output of seven DVDs, total revenue will equal price multiplied by quantity, which is $5 × 7 or $35 per day. Total cost, at an output level of seven DVDs, will be average total cost multiplied by the profit-maximizing rate of output, which is $4.21 × 7 = $29.47 per day. Total profit will then be total revenue minus total cost, or $35 − $29.47 = $5.53 per day.

As Figure 9–3 illustrates, the maximum total profit of $5.53 per day can be shown geometrically as the area of the shaded rectangle *abcd*. Recall that the area of a rectangle is the height multiplied by the length of the rectangle. The height of rectangle *abcd* equals the distance *dc*, which is the difference between the price ($5) and the average total

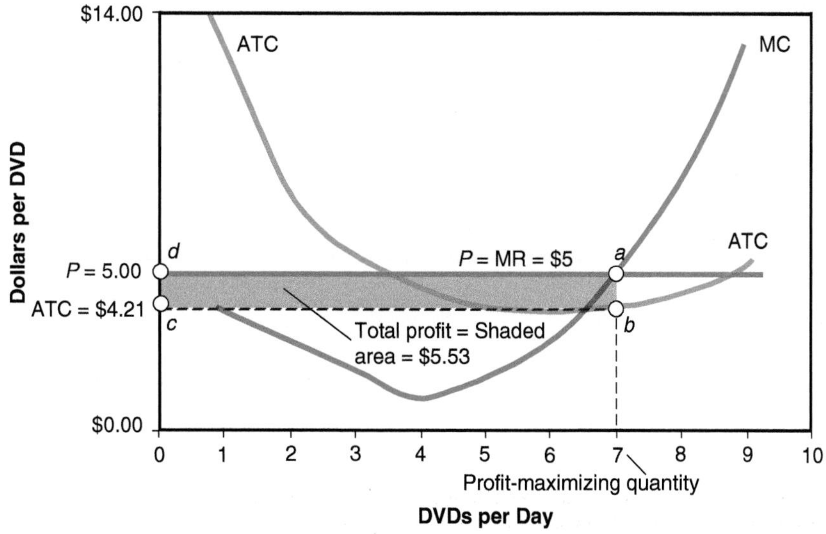


**FIGURE 9–3**

**Measuring Total Short-Run Profits**

To determine the profits graphically, first find the profit-maximizing quantity = $Q$ = 7 DVDs per day. This is where MR = MC. The maximum total profit = ($P$ – ATC) × $Q$, where $Q$ = 7 DVDs, $P$ = given price = $5 and ATC = $4.21 at $Q$ = 7 DVDs. Therefore, maximum total profit = ($5 – $4.21) × (7) = $5.53 = shaded area of rectangle *abcd*.

cost ($4.21). That is, the height of the shaded rectangle *abcd* is $5 – $4.21 = $0.79, which represents the *profit per unit* earned by the profit-maximizing firm. The length of rectangle *abcd* equals the profit-maximizing quantity of seven DVDs per day. Therefore, the area of the shaded rectangle, *abcd*, is the height multiplied by the length, or the profit per unit ($0.79) multiplied by the number of units sold (seven DVDs), which equals the total profit of $5.53 a day. Note that we are talking about an *economic profit* of $5.53 per day because a normal rate of return on investment is included in the average total cost curve, ATC.

## Minimizing Losses

It is certainly possible for the competitive firm to incur losses in the short run. We give an example in Figure 9–4, where the going market price has fallen from $5 to $3 per DVD because of changes in market demand or supply conditions (or both). The firm will always do the best it can by producing where marginal revenue equals marginal cost, assuming it continues to operate (a point explained below).

We see in part (b) of Figure 9–4 that the marginal revenue curve is intersected (from below) by the marginal cost curve at an output rate of six DVDs per day. The firm is no longer making an economic profit as its average total cost of $4.08 per DVD exceeds the $3 price it can charge. The firm's minimum loss is equal to the loss per unit of $1.08 ($4.08 – $3) multiplied by the quantity of six DVDs, which equals a total loss of $6.48 per day.

Part (a)

| (1) Total Output per Day (*Q*) | (2) Total Costs (TC) | (3) Market Price (*P*) | (4) Total Revenues (TR) = (3) × (1) | (5) Total Profit (TR – TC) = (4) – (2) | (6) Average Total Cost (ATC) = (2) ÷ (1) | (7) Average Variable Cost (AVC) | (8) Marginal Cost (MC) = Change (2) / Change (1) | (9) Marginal Revenue (MR) = Change (4) / Change (1) |
|---|---|---|---|---|---|---|---|---|
| 0 | $10.00 | $3 | $ 0 | –$10.00 | | | | |
| 1 | 14.00 | 3 | 3 | –11.00 | $14.00 | $4.00 | $4.00 | $3 |
| 2 | 17.00 | 3 | 6 | –11.00 | 8.50 | 3.50 | 3.00 | 3 |
| 3 | 19.00 | 3 | 9 | –10.00 | 6.33 | 3.00 | 2.00 | 3 |
| 4 | 20.00 | 3 | 12 | –8.00 | 5.00 | 2.50 | 1.00 | 3 |
| 5 | 21.50 | 3 | 15 | –6.50 | 4.30 | 2.30 | 1.50 | 3 |
| 6 | 24.48 | 3 | 18 | –6.48 | 4.08 | 2.41 | 2.98 | 3 |
| 7 | 29.47 | 3 | 21 | –8.47 | 4.21 | 2.78 | 4.99 | 3 |
| 8 | 37.47 | 3 | 24 | –13.47 | 4.68 | 3.43 | 8.00 | 3 |
| 9 | 49.47 | 3 | 27 | –22.47 | 5.50 | 4.39 | 12.00 | 3 |
| 10 | 66.47 | 3 | 30 | –36.47 | 6.65 | 5.65 | 17.00 | 3 |

Part (b)

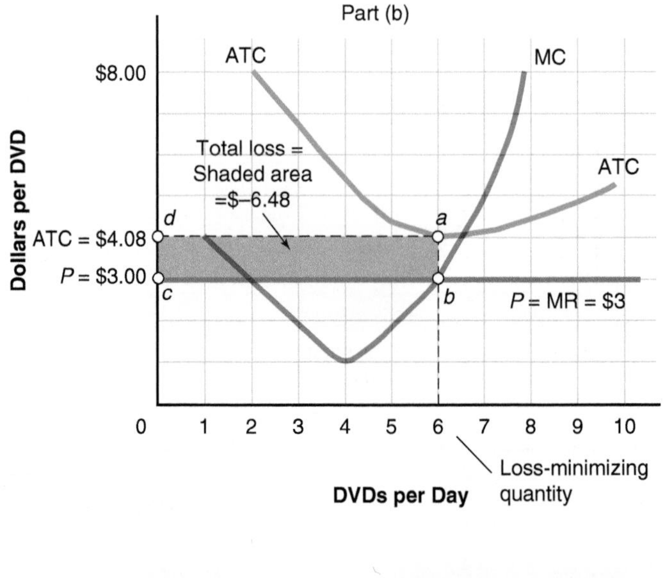


**FIGURE 9–4**
**Minimization of Short-Run Losses**

To determine the losses graphically, first find the loss-minimizing quantity = *Q* = 6 DVDs per day. This is where MR = MC. The maximum total profit = (*P* – ATC) × *Q*, where *Q* = 6 DVDs, *P* = given price = $3 and ATC = $4.08 at Q = 6 DVDs. Therefore, total profit = ($3 – $4.08) × 6 = $–6.48. This minimum total loss of $6.48 equals the shaded area of rectangle abcd.

Should this firm go out of business when it faces a loss of $6.48 per day? At this point, we should note that we are assuming a short-run situation, where the firm is stuck with meeting some of its fixed obligations, such as paying its monthly rent due to a lease agreement, or monthly interest on funds already borrowed from the bank. Also, in the short run, the firm is optimistic that the price will increase in the near future so that an economic profit can be earned during some of the days of the month. Therefore, we are assuming that the firm intends to stay in business in the short run.

Should this firm opt for a *shutdown*, with a loss of $6.48 per day? By **shutdown** we mean that the firm stays in business but temporarily produces at a zero quantity level. If the firm were to shut down, it avoids incurring variable costs, but it would still have to pay for its total fixed costs. According to column 2 in part (a) of Figure 9–4, if the firm operates at a zero quantity level, it will still incur a total cost of $10 per day. This means that its total fixed costs are $10 per day. If the firm were to shut down in the short run, its total revenue would equal zero and its total costs would equal $10, leaving a total loss of $10 per day.

**Shutdown** A short-run situation where the firm stays in business but temporarily produces at a zero quantity level.

If, instead, the firm operates at an output rate of six DVDs per day, it minimizes its losses at $6.48 per day, as described in Figure 9–4. As you can see, at a price of $3 per DVD, this firm should not shut down.

In general, how do we know when it is best *not* to shut down in the face of economic losses? A firm should operate at a positive quantity level whenever the extra revenue it gets exceeds the extra costs incurred when operating at a positive quantity level, which are its *variable* costs. On a per-unit basis, as long as it is possible for the price of the product to exceed the firm's average variable cost, the firm should operate at a positive quantity level.

In the DVD example, at a quantity level of six DVDs per day, we can see that the price of $3 per DVD exceeds the average variable cost of $2.41 per DVD. By selling six DVDs per day, the firm gets a positive contribution toward recovering some of its fixed costs. Therefore, the firm should not shut down.

**As long as the price per unit sold exceeds the average variable cost per unit produced, the firm will be recovering part of the opportunity cost of its investment in the business—that is, part of its fixed costs.**

Once you appreciate the importance of having price exceed average variable cost in the short run, you can appreciate why big discounts are frequently offered in businesses that face a large amount of fixed costs, as Example 9–2 explains.

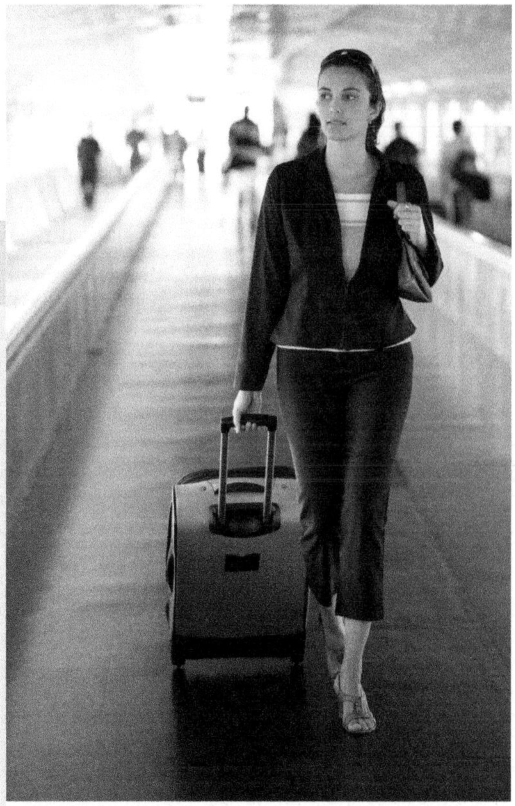

Why do airlines provide discounts for last minute bookings?

### EXAMPLE 9–2 High Sunk Costs Can Mean Deep Discounts

Have you ever wondered why airline "standby" rates are so cheap? Or why you can pay half price to stay at a three-star hotel off-season? Or why restaurants frequently offer two-for-one entrees? Or why golf courses offer cheaper green fees during the quiet times of day or week? The answer to all of these questions is the same.

Whenever the production or sale of a product or service entails high sunk (fixed) costs and low variable costs, the marginal cost of supplying additional units of the service is very close to zero. This being the case, the firm can get some contribution toward its sunk costs by selling its service at deep discounts, as long as the discounted price more than covers the variable cost per unit. In other words, the firm will continue to provide units of the service as long as the marginal revenue exceeds the marginal cost. In this way, the firm can minimize its losses in the short run. Remember, if the firm shuts down in the short run, it is stuck with paying those large fixed monthly costs, which is why they are called sunk costs.

*continued*

Consider the operation of a three-star hotel in a popular ski resort area during the off-season. Most of the costs incurred by the hotel's owners relate to the fixed monthly mortgage payment associated with the hotel's land, building, fixtures, and facilities. As well, the costs of furnishing each hotel room and bathroom are fixed. The variable costs of renting out additional rooms would include such expenses as paying additional staff to clean the rooms and the extra laundry, which would result in a relatively low variable cost per room. In the off-season, when room vacancies become more common, the hotel owners can attract hotel guests by offering deep discounts, as long as the discounted daily room charge more than covers the relatively low variable cost per room.

**For critical analysis:** Suppose there is available seating on a popular jet flight between Vancouver and Toronto, moments before take-off. What is the marginal cost of allowing a passenger to fill one of these vacant seats? How large a discount can the airline give to this passenger? Explain.

## Calculating the Short-Run Breakeven Price

**Short-run breakeven price** The price at which a firm's total revenues equal its total costs.

Look at demand curve $d_1$ in Figure 9–5. It just touches the minimum point of the average total cost curve, which is exactly where the marginal cost curve intersects the average total cost curve. At that price, which is about \$4, the firm will be making exactly zero short-run economic profits. That price, the **short-run breakeven price**, is the price at which a firm's total revenues equal its total costs. At the breakeven price, the firm is just making a normal rate of return on its capital investment. (It is covering its explicit and implicit costs.) Point $E_1$, therefore, occurs at the short-run breakeven price for a competitive firm. It is the point at which marginal revenue, marginal cost, and average total cost are all equal (that is, at which $P = \text{MC}$ and $P = \text{ATC}$). The breakeven price is the one that yields zero short-run economic profits or losses.

## Calculating the Short-Run Shutdown Price

**Short-run shutdown price** The price that just equals minimum average variable cost.

To calculate the firm's shutdown price, we must introduce the average variable cost (AVC) to our graph. In Figure 9–5, we have plotted the AVC values from column 7 in part (a) of Figure 9–2. For the moment, consider two possible demand curves, $d_1$ and $d_2$, which are also the firm's respective marginal revenue curves. Therefore, if demand is $d_1$, the firm will produce at $E_1$, where that curve intersects the marginal cost curve. If demand falls to $d_2$, the firm will produce at $E_2$. The special feature of the hypothetical demand curve, $d_2$, is that it just touches the average variable cost curve at the latter's minimum point, which is also where the marginal cost curve intersects it. This price is the **short-run shutdown price**, which just equals minimum average variable cost. Why? Below this price, the firm would be

**FIGURE 9–5**

**Short-Run Breakeven Point versus Short-Run Shutdown Point**

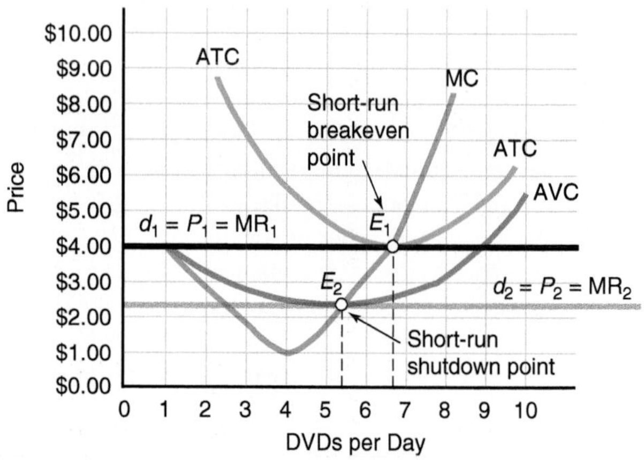


The short-run breakeven point occurs when the price ($P_1$) just equals minimum average total cost. Graphically, this occurs where the Price line is just tangent to the ATC curve at point $E_1$. At this point, the best the firm can do is "break even," which means that it earns "zero economic profit" or "normal profits." The short-run shutdown point occurs when the price ($P_2$) just equals minimum average variable cost. Graphically, this occurs where the Price line is just tangent to the AVC curve at point $E_2$. If the price goes below $P_2$, the firm is better off shutting down in the short run.

paying out more in variable costs than it is receiving in revenues from the sale of its product. Each unit it sold would add to its losses. Clearly, the way to avoid incurring these additional losses, if price falls below the shutdown point, is, in fact, to shut down operations.

As an example, suppose the price per DVD dropped to $2. As Table 9–2 indicates, the price is now below the average variable cost at every quantity. This indicates that the firm is better off shutting down in the short run. With this decision, the firm's total loss equals its total fixed costs of $10, which is the minimum loss displayed in Table 9–2. If, alternatively, the firm was to produce one DVD per day, the price of $2 would be $2 less than the average variable cost of $4 per DVD. In addition to the fixed costs of $10, the firm would lose an extra $2. Therefore, total losses would be $12 at an output of one DVD per day.

## The Meaning of Zero Economic Profits

The fact that we labelled point $E_1$ in Figure 9–5 the breakeven point may have puzzled you. At point $E_1$, price is just equal to average total cost. If this is the case, why would a firm continue to produce if it were making no profits whatsoever? If we again make the distinction between accounting profits and economic profits, then at that price the firm has zero economic profits but positive accounting profits. Recall that accounting profits are total revenues minus total explicit costs. What is ignored in such accounting is the reward offered to investors—the opportunity cost of capital—plus all other implicit costs.

In economic analysis, the average total cost curve includes the full opportunity cost of capital. Indeed, the average total cost curve includes the opportunity cost of *all* factors of production used in the production process. At the short-run breakeven price, economic profits are, by definition, zero. Accounting profits at that price are not, however, equal to zero; they are positive. Consider an example. A clock manufacturer sells clocks at some price. The owners of the firm have supplied all the funds in the business. They have borrowed no money from anyone else, and they explicitly pay the full opportunity cost to all factors of production, including any managerial labour that they themselves contribute to the business. Their salaries show up as a cost in the books and are equal to what they could have earned in the best alternative occupation. At the end of the year, the owners find that after they subtract all explicit costs from total revenues, they have earned $100 000. Let us say that their investment was $1 million. Thus, the rate of return on that investment is 10 percent per year. We will assume that this turns out to be equal to the rate of return that, on average, all other clock manufacturers make in the industry.

This $100 000, or 10 percent rate of return, is actually, then, a competitive, or normal, rate of return on invested capital in that industry or in other industries with similar risks. If the owners had made only $50 000, or 5 percent on their investment, they would have been

**TABLE 9–2**

**Short-Run Shutdown Example: Price = $2.00, or Below Minimum Average Variable Cost**

| (1) Total Output per Day (Q) | (2) Total Costs (TC) | (3) Market Price (P) | (4) Total Revenues (TR) = (3) × (1) | (5) Total Profit (TR – TC) = (4) – (2) | (6) Average Total Cost (ATC) = (2) ÷ (1) | (7) Average Variable Cost (AVC) | (8) Marginal Cost (MC) = Change (2) / Change (1) | (9) Marginal Revenue (MR) = Change (4) / Change (1) |
|---|---|---|---|---|---|---|---|---|
| 0 | $10.00 | $2 | $ 0 | –$10.00 | | | | |
| 1 | 14.00 | 2 | 2 | –12.00 | $14.00 | $4.00 | $ 4.00 | $2.00 |
| 2 | 17.00 | 2 | 4 | –13.00 | 8.50 | 3.50 | 3.00 | 2.00 |
| 3 | 19.00 | 2 | 6 | –13.00 | 6.33 | 3.00 | 2.00 | 2.00 |
| 4 | 20.00 | 2 | 8 | –12.00 | 5.00 | 2.50 | 1.00 | 2.00 |
| 5 | 21.50 | 2 | 10 | –11.50 | 4.30 | 2.30 | 1.50 | 2.00 |
| 6 | 24.48 | 2 | 12 | –12.48 | 4.08 | 2.41 | 2.98 | 2.00 |
| 7 | 29.47 | 2 | 14 | –15.47 | 4.21 | 2.78 | 4.99 | 2.00 |
| 8 | 37.47 | 2 | 16 | –21.47 | 4.68 | 3.43 | 8.00 | 2.00 |
| 9 | 49.47 | 2 | 18 | –31.47 | 5.50 | 4.39 | 12.00 | 2.00 |
| 10 | 66.47 | 2 | 20 | –46.47 | 6.65 | 5.65 | 17.00 | 2.00 |

able to make higher profits by leaving the industry. The 10 percent rate of return is the opportunity cost of capital. Accountants show it as a profit; economists call it a cost. We include that cost in the average total cost curve, similar to the one shown in Figure 9–5. At the short-run breakeven price, average total cost, including this opportunity cost of capital, will just equal that price. The firm will be making zero economic profits or a 10 percent *accounting* rate of return called "normal profits."

# 9.3 Short-Run Supply and Equilibrium

What does the supply curve for the individual firm in perfect competition look like? Actually, we have been looking at it all along. We know that when the price of DVDs is $5, the firm will supply seven of them per day. If the price falls to $3, the firm will supply six DVDs per day. And if the price falls to $2, the firm will shut down in the short run. Hence, in Figure 9–6, the firm's supply curve is the marginal cost curve above the short-run shutdown point. This is shown as the solid part of the marginal cost curve.

**The definition, then, of the individual firm's supply curve in a competitive industry is its marginal cost curve equal to and above minimum average variable cost.**

## The Short-Run Industry Supply Curve

In Chapter 3, we indicated that the market supply curve was the summation of individual supply curves. At the beginning of this chapter, we drew a market supply curve in Figure 9–1. Now, we want to derive more precisely a market, or industry, supply curve to reflect individual producer behaviour in that industry. First, we must ask: "What is an industry?" It is merely a collection of firms producing a particular product. Therefore, we have a way to figure out the total supply curve of any industry: We add the quantities that each firm will supply at every possible price. In other words, we sum the individual supply curves of all the competitive firms *horizontally*. The individual supply curves, as we just saw, are simply the marginal cost curves of each firm.

Consider doing this for a hypothetical world in which there are only two DVD producers in the industry, firm A and firm B. These two firms' marginal cost curves are given in parts (a) and (b) of Figure 9–7. The marginal cost curves for the two separate firms are presented as $MC_A$ in part (a) and $MC_B$ in part (b). Those two marginal cost curves are drawn only for prices above the minimum average variable cost for each firm. Hence, we are not including any of the marginal cost curves below minimum average variable cost. In part (a), for firm A, at $5, the quantity supplied would be seven. At $10, the quantity supplied would be nine. In part (b), we see the two different quantities that would be

**FIGURE 9–6**

**Individual Firm's Short-Run Supply Curve**

In general, the firm's supply curve indicates what quantity the firm will supply at different prices. In this figure, we can see that at different possible prices, the firm will supply that quantity that maximizes profit or minimizes losses. That is, when the price is above minimum average variable cost, the firm will supply that quantity where P = MC or MR = MC. Therefore, the firm's supply curve is the portion of its marginal cost curve that is above minimum average variable cost.

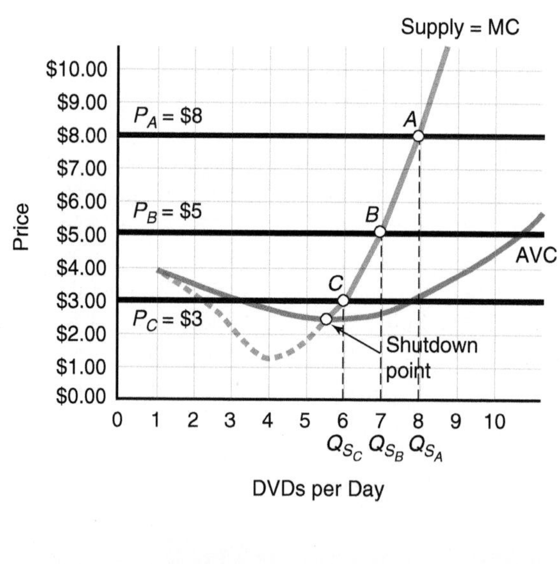

**FIGURE 9–7**

**Deriving the Industry Supply Curve**

Marginal cost curves above minimum average variable cost are presented in parts (a) and (b) for firms A and B. We horizontally sum the two quantities supplied, 7 and 10, at \$5. This gives us point *F* in part (c). We do the same thing for the quantities at \$10. This gives us point *G*. When we connect those points, we have the industry supply curve, *S*, which is the horizontal summation of the firms' marginal cost curves above their respective minimum average variable costs.

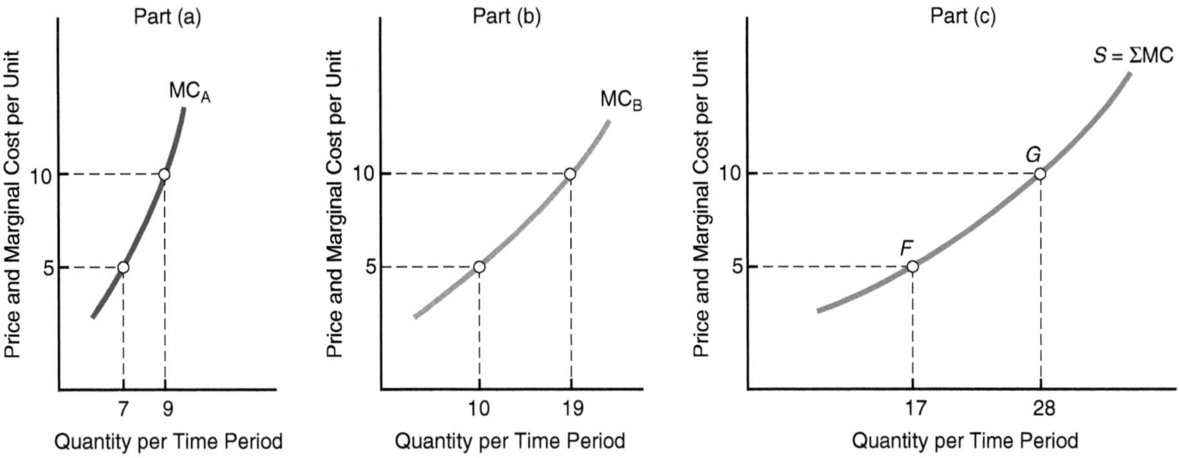


supplied by firm B corresponding to those two prices. In part (c), for the \$5 price, we add horizontally the quantities 7 and 10. This gives us one point, *F*, for our short-run **industry supply curve**, *S*—the locus of points showing the minimum prices at which given quantities will be forthcoming from the industry; also called the market supply curve. We obtain the other point, *G*, by doing the same horizontal adding of quantities at \$10. When we connect points *F* and *G*, we obtain industry supply curve *S*, which is also marked ΣMC, indicating that it is the horizontal summation of the marginal cost curves (above the respective minimum average variable cost of each firm).[2]

**Industry supply curve** The locus of points showing the minimum prices at which given quantities will be forthcoming from the industry; also called the market supply curve.

> **Because the law of diminishing returns makes marginal cost curves rise, the short-run supply curve of a perfectly competitive industry must be upward sloping.**

# Factors That Influence the Industry Supply Curve

As you have just seen, the industry supply curve is the horizontal summation of all of the individual firms' marginal cost curves above their respective minimum average variable cost points. This means that anything that affects the marginal cost curves of the firm will influence the industry supply curve. Therefore, the individual factors that will influence the supply schedule in a competitive industry can be summarized as the factors that cause the *variable costs* of production to change. These are factors that affect the individual marginal cost curves, such as changes in the individual firm's productivity, in factor costs (wages paid to labour, prices of raw materials, and so on), in taxes, and in anything else that would influence the individual firm's marginal cost curve.

All of these are *ceteris paribus* conditions of supply. Because they affect the position of the marginal cost curve for the individual firm, they affec-ion of the industry supply curve. A change in any of these will shift the market supply curve.

[2]The capital Greek sigma, Σ, is the symbol for summation.

## Short-Run Equilibrium

How is the market, or "going," price established in the short run in perfect competition? The short-run equilibrium price will occur where the short-run industry or market supply just equals the industry or market demand. We have just seen how the industry supply curve is the horizontal sum of the individual firms' marginal cost curves, assuming that firms maximize profits or minimize losses. This suggests that although no one single firm can affect the price, the supply plans of all the firms, combined, does play an important role in determining the industry price.

## Short-Run Equilibrium for the Industry

Table 9–3 illustrates the process by which the competitive industry price is determined for the DVD market, on the basis of the following assumptions. The DVD industry comprises 100 identical perfectly competitive firms. Each firm has the total and per-units costs described in Figure 9–2. The industry or market demand schedule is given in column 4 in Table 9–3. While we will not attempt to derive the industry demand schedule, you may recall that it is the "horizontal sum" of all individual demand schedules for DVDs. Each individual demand schedule is based on the assumption that the consumer maximizes his or her utility when responding to price.

To determine the short-run industry equilibrium price in Table 9–3, we must first determine the individual firm's quantity supplied in column 2 of Table 9–3. To do this, we compare each price in column 1 of Table 9–3 with the marginal costs described in Figure 9–2. For example, at the price of $12 per DVD, the firm will maximize its profits if it supplies nine DVDs per day, where the marginal revenue of $12 just equals the marginal cost of $12. If the price falls to $8 per DVD, the firm will instead supply eight DVDs per day, where marginal revenue equals marginal cost.

After determining the individual firm's quantity supplied for all of the prices in Table 9–3, you are ready to derive the short-run industry supply schedule in column 3 of Table 9–3. At each price, the industry supply is simply 100 multiplied by the individual firm's quantity supplied at that same price. Once the industry supply schedule is determined for all prices in Table 9–3, you can see that the industry quantity supplied equals the industry quantity demanded at $5 per DVD. In other words, the short-run equilibrium industry price is $5 per DVD, and the short-run equilibrium industry quantity is 700 DVDs per day.

Part (a) of Figure 9–8 provides a sketch of the graph of the short-run equilibrium in the DVD industry, on the basis of the industry demand in Table 9–3, and assuming that the industry comprises 100 identical firms. Each firm faces the total and per-unit costs described in Figure 9–2. Note that part (a) in Figure 9–8 shows how the short-run industry supply, made up of the horizontal sum of 100 identical marginal cost curves, interacts with the industry demand curve to establish an equilibrium price of $5 per DVD and an equilibrium industry quantity of 700 DVDs per day.

## Short-Run Equilibrium for the Firm

Where will each individual DVD firm settle at in the short run? The individual firm's *equilibrium quantity* will be the quantity that maximizes profits or minimizes losses, given the industry equilibrium price. As part (b) of Figure 9–8 illustrates, the firm will maximize its profit at an output level of seven DVDs per day, where the industry equilibrium

**TABLE 9–3**

**Short-Run Equilibrium in the DVD Industry**

| (1) Price per DVD | (2) Quantity Supplied by Individual Firms | (3) Quantity Supplied by Industry (100 Firms) | (4) Quantity Demanded of Industry (all consumers) |
|---|---|---|---|
| $12 | 9 | 900 | 200 |
| 8 | 8 | 800 | 500 |
| 5 | 7 | 700 | 700 |
| 3 | 6 | 600 | 800 |

**FIGURE 9–8**

**Short-Run Equilibrium for the DVD Industry and Firm**

In part (a), the horizontal sum of the 100 identical firm marginal cost curves determines the short-run industry supply curve. This short-run industry supply curve interacts with the industry demand curve, *D*, to establish an equilibrium industry price of $5 per DVD and an industry equilibrium quantity of 700 DVDs. In part (b), at the industry price of $5, each individual firm's equilibrium quantity will be seven DVDs per day with an economic profit of $5.53, which is equal to the shaded area.

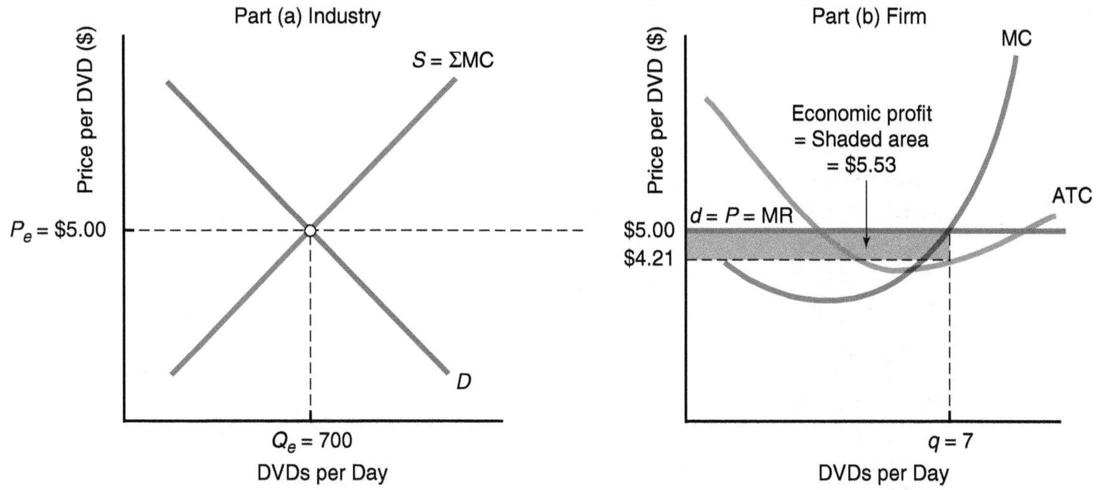


price of $5 per DVD is equal to the firm's marginal cost. Therefore, with an equilibrium industry price of $5 per DVD, the firm's equilibrium quantity is seven DVDs per day. As Figure 9–8 reveals, the firm's short-run total economic profit will be equal to its price minus average total cost multiplied by its equilibrium quantity, which equals ($5 – $4.21) × 7 = $5.53 per day.

In Figure 9–8, each firm earns a positive economic profit because at the firm's short-run equilibrium output level, price exceeds average total cost. If the industry demand for DVDs decreases so that the equilibrium price falls to a level equal to each firm's minimum average total cost, as described by point $E_1$ in Figure 9–5, then zero economic profits will prevail in short-run equilibrium. Further declines in industry demand will reduce the DVD price level below each firm's minimum average total cost. In these situations, each firm will operate at a loss or shut down with a loss, depending on whether price is above or below minimum average variable costs, as explained in Figures 9–4 and 9–5.

Canadian lumber firms manufacturing two-by-fours compete with lumber firms in the United States, South America, and Russia in a global market resembling perfect competition. Example 9–3 illustrates the importance that the U.S. economy and U.S. government policy have on the financial success of the Canadian lumber industry.

## EXAMPLE 9–3 U.S. Recession Takes Its Toll on Canadian Lumber Firms

On May 29, 2009, Canfor Corporation, a Canadian lumber company, announced that it was going to indefinitely shut down three sawmills in the B.C. Interior, laying off 570 workers at mills in the towns of Vavenby, Radium, and Prince George. Canfor had already shut down sawmills at Mackenzie and Chetwynd and cut back shifts at others to reduce its lumber capacity. The shutdowns that took place during the summer of 2009 reduced Canfor's lumber production to about 2.5 billion board feet a year, half the company's estimated capacity.

Between January 2006 and March 2009, lumber prices plummeted from US$365 to US$140 per 1000 board feet of two-by-four spruce (which is below the breakeven point).

*continued*

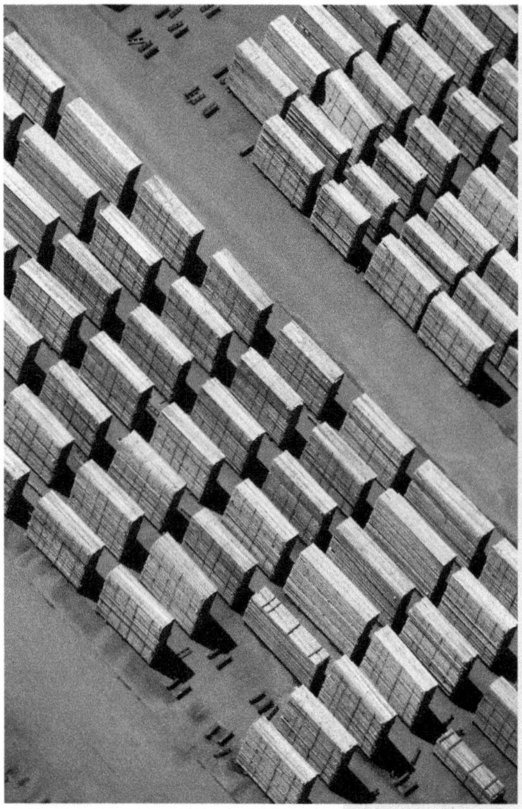

Why are Canadian lumber mills shutting down?

For the year ending December 31, 2009, the company's net loss was \$70.5 million (\$0.50 per share), compared to a net loss of \$345.2 million (\$2.42 per share) reported for 2008. Canfor responded to this loss by putting pressure on suppliers and unions to reduce material and labour costs.

The Canadian lumber firms' woes can be explained by a number of demand and supply factors in the global lumber market. There was a serious slowdown in U.S. housing starts due to the sub-prime mortgage crisis and the great global recession. The increasing interest rates and very high unemployment levels in the U.S. economy meant that a significant number of homeowners were unable to meet their monthly mortgage payments, resulting in an estimated record 4 million home mortgage foreclosure filings in the U.S. in 2009.

In November 2016, the U.S. Lumber Coalition filed a petition and started a new round of litigation between the two countries. In the past, international bodies have sided with Canadian lumber producers and workers. Talks between Canadian and American officials continue.

**For critical analysis:** Assuming perfect competition, construct both an industry and individual firm diagram relating to the Canadian lumber industry. In the industry diagram, describe the recent demand and supply shifts that have affected Canadian lumber prices. In the related firm diagram, sketch the price (US\$140), marginal cost, and average total cost curves of the typical Canfor sawmill that has been shut down, assuming that the firm is maximizing its profits (or minimizing its losses). In the firm diagram, illustrate Canfor's total profits or losses.

Sources: Gordon Hamilton. "Canfor shuts three sawmills, laying off 570 workers; Vavenby, Radium and Prince George lose out." Vancouver Sun. May 29, 2009. pg. C1; "Lumber." Quotes and News. Wikinvest. May 28, 2010. http://www.wikinvest.com/commodity/Lumber; "Canfor reports net loss of \$17.0 million for last quarter of 2009: Q4 lumber markets were weak, pulp markets continued to improve." News Release. Canfor. http://www.canfor.ca/_resources/news/2010/NR100210_Canfor_Reports_Net_Loss_of_\$17_Million_for_Q4_2009.pdf; Adler, Lynn. "Foreclosures at record high in first half 2009 despite aid." Reuters (New York). July 16, 2009. http://www.reuters.com/article/idUSTRE56F0XK20090716. Janyce McGregor. "U.S. Lumber Coalition files petition, restarting Canada-US. softwood lumber hostilities." CBC News. November 25, 2016. http://www.cbc.ca/news/politics/softwood-lumber-canada-united-states-filing-friday-1.3868117.

# 9.4 Long-Run Equilibrium

We have just seen that a competitive firm can be in short-run equilibrium earning positive economic profits, or negative economic profits, or just breaking even, depending on the price. Only *one* situation, the breakeven, is possible in the long run, after sufficient time has passed to allow firms to change plant sizes and enter or exit the industry. This one situation is called *long-run equilibrium* and is explained below, using our DVD industry example.

Long-run equilibrium, as described in Figure 9–9, refers to the best situation that a competitive firm can look forward to in the long run. That is, in the long run, the industry supply, $S_2$, in conjunction with the industry demand, $D$, sets a price of $P_2 = \$3$ per DVD in part (a) of Figure 9–9. At this price, the firm's profit-maximizing quantity is $q_2$, where price equals marginal cost, in part (b) of Figure 9–9. At $q_2$, the typical firm is operating at minimum short-run and long-run average total cost, earning zero economic profits, as price equals average total cost.

## Adjustments to Long-Run Equilibrium

Why does the typical firm in perfect competition end up in long-run equilibrium, as described in Figure 9–9? Suppose the initial industry supply is $S_1$ in part (a) of Figure 9–9,

**FIGURE 9–9**

## Long-Run Equilibrium in Perfect Competition

In general, long-run equilibrium occurs when the industry equilibrium price just equals the typical firm's minimum long-run average total cost. This occurs when the industry supply curve is $S_2$ and the equilibrium price is \$3 per DVD in part (a). At the \$3 price, the typical firm in part (b) will maximize profit at $q_2$, where marginal revenue equals marginal cost. At $q_2$, the typical firm is operating at minimum short-run and long-run average total cost, earning zero economic profits, as price just equals average total cost.

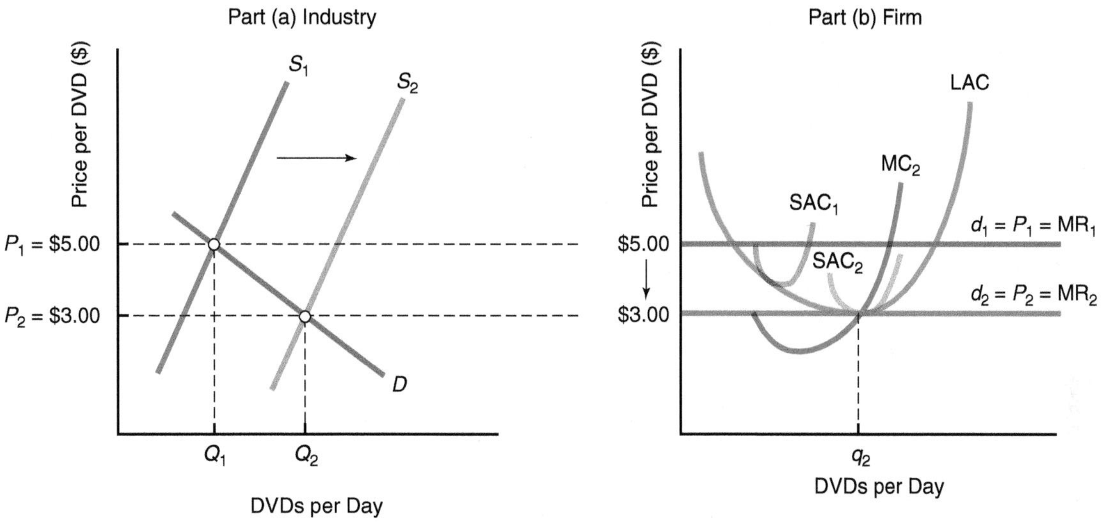


and the typical firm's plant size has a short-run average total cost equal to $SAC_1$ in part (b) of Figure 9–9. With the industry demand, *D*, the initial equilibrium price is \$5. At the price of \$5, the typical firm will be making positive economic profits, in short-run equilibrium (where the \$5 price will exceed $SAC_1$).

Due to the competitive characteristics of easy entry, large number of firms, and homogeneous product, the industry will not stay at the \$5 price in the long run. The positive economic profits earned by the typical competitive firm at the \$5 price will attract new firms to the DVD industry. As new firms enter, the short-run industry supply curve will increase or shift from $S_1$ toward $S_2$ in part (a) of Figure 9–9. As the industry supply increases, the industry price will decrease.

How do existing firms react to the increased competitive pressures stemming from the new entrants? Since their product is homogeneous, they cannot differentiate their product from their competitors'. Therefore, existing firms must attempt to lower costs per unit by adopting more efficient plant sizes. In part (b) of Figure 9–9, the existing firms are able to lower unit costs by changing the typical plant size from one with unit costs of $SAC_1$ to the larger plant size associated with $SAC_2$. As plant sizes expand, the short-run industry supply will continue to increase, leading to further declines in industry price. The price will continue to decrease until each firm earns zero economic profit (a normal profit) and each firm can no longer gain efficiencies by changing plant sizes. This occurs in long-run equilibrium, when the industry price falls to a level equal to the typical firm's minimum long-run average total cost, which is \$3 in Figure 9–9.

Note that our explanation of long-run equilibrium began with the typical firm earning positive economic profit in the short run. What if, in the short run, the typical firm was facing economic losses? In this case, some firms will leave the industry in the long run, causing a decrease in short-run industry supply. As a result, the industry price will increase to a level where the price will just equal minimum long-run average total cost. That is, the same long-run equilibrium situation will result.

It should be evident that perfectly competitive firms have no choice but to seek the most cost-efficient methods of operation in the long run. They do not have the luxury of controlling prices or differentiating their product. This implies that in the long run, competitive firms will seek to locate in geographical areas that minimize their production costs per unit. According to the Did You Know That . . . ? section of this chapter, this may result in a more rapid rate of economic growth for Canada in the future. In 2010, Canada was found to be the least costly place to locate a business, when one compares the setup and operating costs of firms competing in 17 major industrial sectors in nine of the most industrialized nations in the world. On average, Canadian businesses enjoyed a 5 percent cost advantage over similar firms situated in the United States.

## 9.5 Long-Run Industry Supply Curves

In part (a) of Figure 9–8, we drew the summation of all the portions of the individual firms' marginal cost curves, above each firm's respective minimum average variable costs, as the upward-sloping short-run supply curve for the competitive industry. We should be aware that a relatively steep upward-sloping supply curve might be appropriate only in the short run. In the long run, in perfect competition, further adjustments in quantity supplied will result, as firms adjust their plant size and enter or exit the industry.

**Long-run industry supply curve**
A market supply curve showing the relationship between quantities supplied by the entire industry and prices, after sufficient time has passed to allow firms to change plant sizes and enter or exit the industry.

The **long-run industry supply curve** is a market supply curve showing the relationship between quantities supplied by the entire industry and prices, after sufficient time has passed to allow firms to change plant sizes and enter or exit the industry. In other words, the long-run supply curve describes the industry response to a change in prices, after long-run equilibrium has been re-established.

The long-run industry supply curve can take one of three shapes, depending on whether the input costs stay constant, increase, or decrease, as the size of the industry changes.

### Constant-Cost Industries

**Constant-cost industry**
An industry that can increase its output in the long run, without affecting input prices.

In principle, there are small enough industries that use such a small percentage of the total supply of inputs necessary for their production that the industry can expand without affecting input prices. In such a situation, we are dealing with a **constant-cost industry**. Since long-run per-unit costs stay constant, as the industry expands, the long-run industry supply curve is horizontal and is represented by $S_L$ in part (a) of Figure 9–10.

We can work through the case in which constant costs prevail. We start out in part (a) with demand curve $D_1$ and supply curve $S_1$. The equilibrium price is $P_1$. Market demand shifts rightward to $D_2$. In the short run, the equilibrium price rises to $P_2$. This generates positive economic profits for existing firms in the industry. Such economic profits induce resources to flow into the industry. The existing firms expand and/or new firms enter. The short-run supply curve shifts outward to $S_2$. The new intersection with the new demand curve is at $E_3$. The new equilibrium price is again $P_1$. The long-run supply curve is obtained by connecting the intersections of the corresponding pairs of demand and supply curves, $E_1$ and $E_3$. Labelled $S_L$, it is horizontal; its slope is zero. In a constant-cost industry, long-run supply is perfectly elastic. Any shift in demand is eventually met by an equal shift in supply so that the long-run price is constant at $P_1$.

Retail trade is often given as an example of such an industry because output can be expanded or contracted without affecting input prices.

### Increasing-Cost Industries

**Increasing-cost industry**
A situation where input prices increase as the industry expands in the long run.

In an **increasing-cost industry**, expansion by existing firms and the addition of new firms cause the price of inputs specialized within that industry to be bid up. As costs of production rise, the ATC curve and the firms' MC curve shift upward, causing short-run supply curves (each firm's marginal cost curve) to shift upward. The result is a long-run industry supply curve that slopes upward, as represented by $S_L$ in part (b) of Figure 9–10. Examples are residential construction and coal mining—both use specialized inputs that cannot be obtained in ever-increasing quantities without causing their prices to rise.

### Decreasing-Cost Industries

**Decreasing-cost industry**
A situation where input prices decrease as the industry expands in the long run.

In a **decreasing-cost industry**, an expansion in the number of firms in an industry can lead to a reduction in input prices and a downward shift in the ATC and MC curves. When this occurs, the long-run industry supply curve will slope downward. This is described in part (c) of Figure 9–10. Examples are computers and long-distance phone service.

**FIGURE 9–10**

## Constant Cost, Increasing Cost, and Decreasing Cost Industries

In part (a), we show a situation in which the demand curve shifts from $D_1$ to $D_2$. Price increases from $P_1$ to $P_2$; however, in time, the short-run supply curve shifts outward because positive profits are being earned, and the equilibrium shifts from $E_2$ to $E_3$. The market clearing price is again $P_1$. If we connect such points as $E_1$ and $E_3$, we come up with the long-run supply curve $S_L$. This is a constant-cost industry. In part (b), unit costs are increasing for the industry, and therefore, the long-run supply curve slopes upward and long-run prices rise from $P_1$ to $P_2$. In part (c), unit costs are decreasing for the industry as it expands, and therefore, the long-run supply curve slopes downward such that long-run prices decline from $P_1$ to $P_2$.

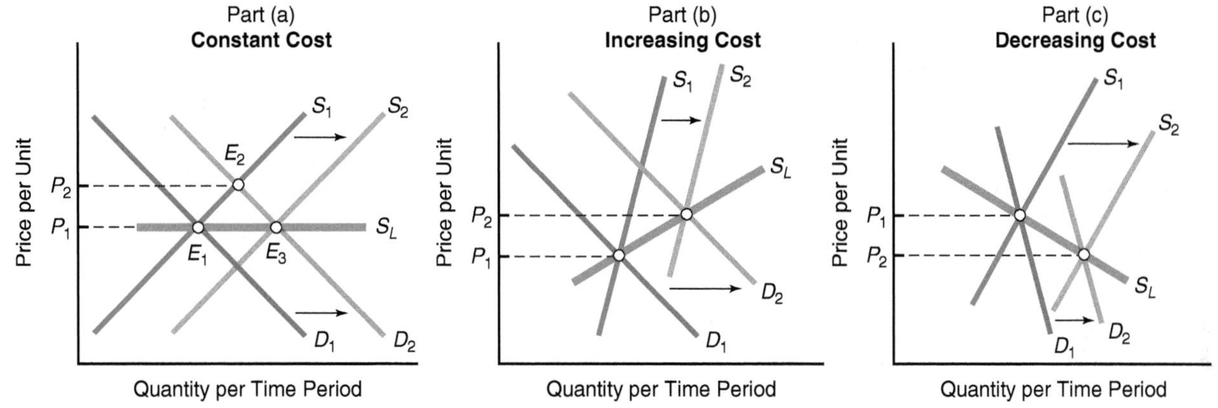


According to this chapter's Issues and Applications, the home-video movie industry is a good example of a decreasing-cost industry. As this industry has grown, the widespread use of DVDs has lowered the cost per unit of supplying these movies. Looking into the near future, the cost of supplying this product will continue to decrease, as the practice of downloading movies from the Internet becomes acceptable.

Not long ago, firms that provided digital photo printing services, such as discount department stores and pharmacies, charged as much as 50 cents per printed photo. Today, many consumers pay little more than a dime to have digital photos printed. Example 9–4 explains how this significant decrease in price can be explained by the long-run behaviour in a competitive industry.

### EXAMPLE 9–4 The Big Rush to Provide Digital Snaps in a Snap

The North American digital photographic sector brings in over $85 billion in revenues each year. Since 2000, the majority of those revenues have been earned from the sale of digital cameras and related digital photography products and services. A rapidly growing segment of this sector has been the market for digital photo printing services. The growth of this market can be explained in terms of both short-run and long-run adjustments.

Early entrants in the digital photo printing industry were retailers who for years had provided developing and printing services for old-style photography that utilized film instead of digital imaging technologies. Part (a) of the accompanying figure depicts the short-run adjustments that occurred as the demand for photo printing services increased. The movement from $E_1$ to $E_2$ represents the increase in quantity supplied by the existing firms in the industry as they begin to earn positive economic profits.

In the long run, new firms entered the photo printing industry, attracted by the positive economic profits. Entrepreneurs quickly determined that the only impediment to entry into the business of printing digital photos was the few thousand dollars required to purchase a small booth, called a kiosk, with photo printing software and hardware. These kiosks were located in shopping malls, hospitals, and college campuses. Within a few more months, large corporations including Sony, Eastman Kodak, Fuji Photo Film, Staples, Best Buy, and Future Shop started to offer in-store and online digital photo printing services. In part (b) of Figure 9–11,

*continued*

the relatively large shift in supply from $S_1$ to $S_2$ reflects the long-run adjustment that has taken place as a result of the explosion of new entrants into the market. In the long run, the typical price per photo print has decreased from \$0.15 to \$0.12 per print.

**FIGURE 9–11**

**Short-Run and Long-Run Adjustments in the Digital Photo Printing Industry**

Part (a) shows that when the demand for digital photo printing services increased in the early 2000s, the market clearing price rose from about 15 cents per photo at point $E_1$ to about 19 cents per photo at point $E_2$. The equilibrium quantity of services also increased. Part (b) displays the long-run adjustments that took place as numerous firms entered the industry, causing market supply to increase. The equilibrium quantity of digital photo printing services continued to rise, but the market clearing price declined, from 19 cents per photo at point $E_2$ to about 12 cents per photo at point $E_3$.

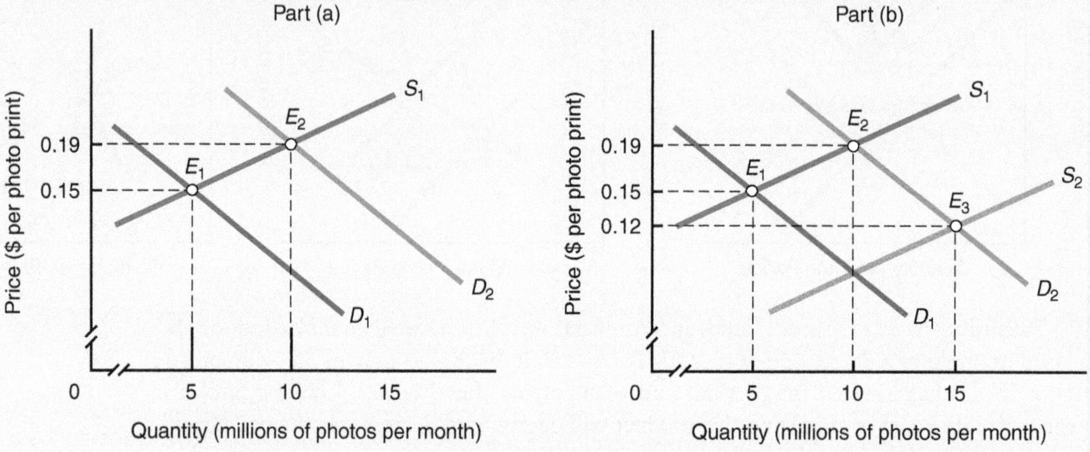


**For critical analysis:** Sketch part (b) and create the long-run supply curve based on your sketch. According to your sketch, is the digital photo printing industry a constant cost, increasing cost, or decreasing cost industry? What is happening to each firm's average total cost curve as the industry expands?

## Long-Run Adjustments to Technological Change

In the previous section, we examined how perfect competition responds to changes in demand and prices in the long run. We now turn to examine the long-run adjustments that a competitive industry will incur, when faced with a cost-saving technological change.

Suppose new technology that lowers the per-unit cost of producing DVDs has just been discovered. In order to benefit from the new technology, new plants must be constructed, which implies a long-run response on the part of the DVD firms. As soon as some firms complete this new construction, their short-run and long-run average cost and marginal cost curves will shift downward and to the right. This implies that at the same DVD price, these firms can now supply a larger rate of output. Firms that adopt this new technology will make short-run positive economic profits, as average total cost slips below the industry price. These economic profits will induce new firms to enter the DVD industry.

As the new technology spreads throughout the DVD industry, the short-run market supply curve will increase, causing the industry price to decline. Eventually, the industry will reach a new long-run equilibrium, when the industry price falls to a level equal to the reduced minimum long-run average total cost curve. While the DVD firms will no longer enjoy positive economic profits, consumers will derive a long-term benefit in the form of lower DVD prices.

# 9.6 Social Evaluation of Perfect Competition

As we shall study in a subsequent chapter, the Canadian government has passed laws that encourage various industries to adopt a market structure and behaviour that more closely resemble perfect competition. This suggests that perfect competition must promote important socioeconomic goals. This is particularly the case when we focus on perfect competition in long-run equilibrium.

## Perfect Competition and Productive Efficiency

Look again at Figure 9–9 part (b). In long-run equilibrium, the perfectly competitive firm finds itself producing at output rate $q_2$. At that rate of output, the price is just equal to the minimum long-run average cost as well as the minimum short-run average cost. In this sense, perfect competition results in the production of goods and services using the least costly combination of resources. This is called *productive efficiency*. This is an important attribute of a perfectly competitive long-run equilibrium, particularly when we wish to compare perfect competition with other market structures. We will examine these other market structures in later chapters.

## Perfect Competition and Allocative Efficiency

You may recall that allocative efficiency is concerned with producing the mix of goods and services that maximizes consumer satisfaction. Due to scarcity, it is crucial that economic resources are allocated to those uses that are most highly valued by consumers. In this section, we will explain how perfect competition promotes the goal of allocative efficiency.

We have seen that, in perfect competition, production takes place to the point where price just equals marginal cost. This is called **marginal cost pricing**, which is a system where the price charged to the consumer is equal to the opportunity cost to society of producing the last unit of the good in question. As we will explain below, marginal cost pricing promotes allocative efficiency.

Marginal cost pricing A system where the price charged to the consumer is equal to the opportunity cost to society of producing the last unit of the good in question.

**ALLOCATIVE EFFICIENCY: A GRAPHIC ILLUSTRATION.** In Figure 9–12, we illustrate how marginal cost pricing in the DVD industry promotes allocative efficiency. In this figure, we assume that the competitive industry is in long-run equilibrium with an equilibrium price of \$3 per DVD and an equilibrium output of 800 DVDs per day.

At this point, it is appropriate to focus on the useful information that an industry demand curve provides us with. At any given quantity level, the height of the industry demand curve describes the maximum price that consumers are willing to pay for the last unit of output. As an example, in Figure 9–12, consumers are willing to pay a maximum

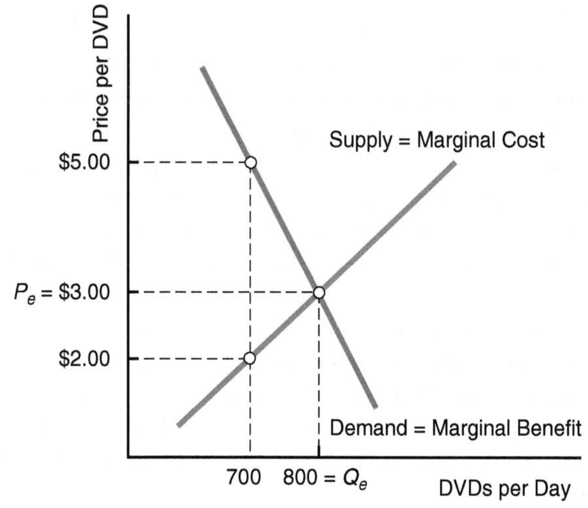


**FIGURE 9–12**

**Allocative Efficiency in the DVD Industry**

In perfect competition, production takes place at the equilibrium level of 800 DVDs per day. At this equilibrium level, allocative efficiency is achieved as the marginal benefit of the last DVD (800th DVD) produced, \$3, just equals the marginal cost of the last DVD produced. If, instead, 700 DVDs were produced per day, resources would be underallocated to the DVD industry as the marginal benefit of the 700th DVD produced, \$5, exceeds its marginal cost of \$2.

price of $3 for the 800th DVD produced, as this is the height of the demand curve at the 800 DVD output level. This suggests that the marginal benefit or extra value that the household derives from consuming the 800th DVD is also $3. Once we appreciate that the demand curve provides us with price and marginal benefit information, we can proceed to examine how a perfectly competitive industry promotes allocative efficiency. As Figure 9–12 illustrates, the competitive DVD industry will end up at an equilibrium quantity of 800 DVDs per day. At this output, we have industry demand equal to industry supply. But industry demand reflects price and marginal benefit, and industry supply reflects marginal cost. Therefore, we can see that in a competitive industry, production takes place to the point where *price just equals marginal cost or, more significantly, marginal benefit just equals marginal cost*.

In our DVD example, this means that just the "right" quantity of DVDs is being produced, from society's viewpoint. The consumer value for the last DVD produced, $3, just equals the extra cost to society of producing this last DVD (800th DVD). This extra cost, or marginal cost, reflects the value of the output in other industries that is sacrificed (opportunity cost), when additional resources are used to produce the 800th DVD.

**ALLOCATIVE INEFFICIENCY: A GRAPHIC ILLUSTRATION.** To better explain how a competitive equilibrium situation promotes allocative efficiency, we will use Figure 9–12 to illustrate why an alternative situation results in allocative inefficiency.

Suppose the competitive industry produces 700 DVDs per day, which is not an equilibrium situation, according to Figure 9–12. At this quantity, the marginal benefit of the 700th DVD is $5 (height of the demand curve), while its marginal cost to society is $2 per DVD (height of the supply curve). This represents a situation where there is an underallocation of resources to the production of DVDs and an overallocation of resources to other industries, as far as society is concerned. If resources are taken away from producing goods in other industries and used to produce one additional DVD, the extra $5 value gained by the DVD consumer (marginal benefit) will exceed the $2 value of lost production in the other industries (marginal cost). From society's view, there will be a net gain in value of $3 by allocating more resources to the DVD industry. Clearly, allocative efficiency is not achieved when 700 DVDs are produced.

## Perfect Competition and a Normal Profit

In long-run equilibrium, each firm operates at a quantity level where price equals average total cost. In other words, perfectly competitive firms earn zero economic or "normal" profits in the long run. This is due to the easy-entry feature of this market structure. One could look at this normal profit result as promoting an equitable distribution of income to the extent that corporate share ownership is concentrated in the hands of upper-income individuals. In other words, the shareholders are earning a rate of profit that is just necessary to maintain the current level of investment and output—no more and no less.

## Possible Shortcomings of Perfect Competition

**PERFECT COMPETITION AND MARKET FAILURE.** Situations arise when competitive markets either overallocate or underallocate resources to a good or service. These situations are instances of **market failure**. One example is when the production of a product entails external costs.

**Market failure** A situation in which perfect competition either overallocates or underallocates resources to a good or service.

**External costs** Situations where the marginal social costs of producing a product exceed the marginal private costs of production.

**External costs** refer to situations where the marginal social costs of producing a product exceed the marginal private costs of production. In these cases, some of the costs resulting from the production of the product spill over to affect third parties. Third parties refer to individuals or organizations other than the buyer and seller of the product.

An example of an external cost situation would be when the production of DVDs results in air pollution that causes health problems for those individuals who are not directly involved as buyers or sellers of DVDs. The firms who manufacture the DVDs typically do not have to pay for these extra spillover costs. In this situation, the DVD firms' marginal cost curves do not include the extra spillover pollution costs borne by others. In fact, the true marginal social cost curves would be somewhat higher than the private marginal cost curves that govern the actual maximum profit production levels. Perfectly competitive firms would tend to overproduce DVDs relative to the socially desired production level.

Sometimes the production of a product results in **external benefits**, where the marginal social benefits from producing a product exceed the marginal private benefits. The production of the product results in spillover benefits to third parties. An example would be the discovery and production of a vaccine that prevents the spread of a contagious disease. The price that is charged to the consumers of this product does not reflect the extra spillover benefits. In this case, competitive marginal cost pricing will tend to underallocate resources to the product, from society's viewpoint.

**External benefits** A situation where the marginal social benefits from producing a product exceed the marginal private benefits.

## Perfect Competition and Innovation

The rate of innovation and technological advance undertaken by perfectly competitive firms may prove to be socially sub-optimal. Activities related to such innovation as research and development are very expensive and entail significant risk. Since, in the long run, perfectly competitive firms can expect only normal profits, these firms may lack both the incentive and the level of funds necessary to engage in a socially desirable level of innovation.

## ISSUES AND APPLICATIONS

# Does the PEI Potato Industry Have a Future?

**Concepts Applied: Characteristics of Perfect Competition, Breakeven, Shutdown Price, Long-Run Equilibrium, Long-Run Supply Curve**

Rich soil of PEI grows world-class potatoes.

### The PEI Potato Market

The rich red soil in PEI has been known for generations to grow some of the best potatoes in the world. The PEI market accounts for a quarter of all potatoes grown in Canada, and is worth more than $1 billion annually to PEI's economy. Once primarily a fresh potato market, it has lately been changing into an industry where the potatoes are used mainly for processing. This trend is because of people's changing lifestyles. More people want faster meals that are lower in carbohydrates. In the last decade as many as 30 percent of PEI potato farmers have left the market because they were selling fresh potatoes at below cost.

### Competition from Other Commodities

With the trend towards healthier eating and no real demand in the emerging Asian markets, other commodities are replacing the traditional use of the potato. Rice, lentils, and beans are being added to many households' pantries and dinner menus. PEI potato farmers are turning away from the fresh potato market towards the processing industry. Farmers can now negotiate prices before they have even planted their crops, increasing the security of the market. Prices have fallen at least 40 percent in a year, so a contract with a food processor helps to make sure that farmers are getting at least a breakeven price for their product.

## Long-run Expectations for the Industry

With farms being abandoned and production falling, is there a future for the PEI potato industry? In the short run, prices were falling because of a glut on the market not only in Canada, but in the U.S. as well, meaning that supply exceeded demand. McCain Foods has a processing plant in PEI and they are leading the change towards more premium products such as sweet potatoes and red potatoes. In the long run this will help the industry survive, as long as the potato farmers are able to get a price that will allow them to break even.

**For critical analysis:**

1. What characteristics of perfect competition relate to the potato industry?
2. Does having signed contracts for the product before it is even planted distort the market?
3. What does long-run breakeven mean for the farmers?

Source: Tavia Grant and Jane Taber, "Even in PEI, potato farming is on the decline," The Globe and Mail, Jan 14, 2014. http://www.theglobeandmail.com/report-on-business/even-in-pei-potato-farming-is-on-the-decline/article12214393/Laura Chapin, "Fewer spuds grown across Canada good for P.E.I. potato farmers," CBC News, August 1, 2016. http://www.cbc.ca/news/canada/prince-edward-island/potato-acreage-canada-price-1.3703018.

# SUMMARY

Here is what you should know after reading this chapter. MyEconLab will help you identify what you know, and where to go when you need to practise. We suggest that as soon as you review one of the Learning Objectives sections below, you then proceed to go through the related section in MyEconLab.

| LEARNING OBJECTIVES | KEY TERMS | MYECONLAB PRACTICE |
|---|---|---|
| **9.1 The Characteristics of Perfect Competition.** The four fundamental characteristics of perfect competition are: (1) a large number of buyers and sellers, (2) a homogeneous product, (3) easy exit from and entry into the industry, and (4) perfect market information in the hands of both buyers and sellers. A perfectly competitive firm is a price taker, meaning that the firm takes the price as given and outside of its control. The individual firm's demand curve is perfectly elastic (horizontal), which implies that the firm can sell all it wants at the given industry price, so price equals marginal revenue. | market structure, 213<br>perfect competition, 213<br>price taker, 213 | • **MyEconLab** Study Plan 9.1 |
| **9.2 Determining Output and Profit in the Short Run.** Profit is maximized at the rate of output where the positive difference between total revenue and total cost is the greatest. Losses are minimized where the negative difference between total revenue and total cost is the smallest. We assume that each firm chooses that rate of output that maximizes profits or minimizes losses. This rate of output is called the firm's short-run equilibrium output level. | total revenues, 216<br>profit-maximizing rate of production, 217<br>marginal revenue, 217<br>shutdown, 221<br>short-run breakeven price, 222<br>short-run shutdown price, 222 | • **MyEconLab** Study Plan 9.2 |

| LEARNING OBJECTIVES | KEY TERMS | MYECONLAB PRACTICE |
|---|---|---|
| If the industry price is below the firm's minimum average variable cost, the firm will minimize its losses by shutting down, and will earn a negative economic profit (loss) equal to its total fixed costs. Graphically, the firm's shutdown point is where the price line is tangent to the minimum point on the average variable cost curve. When the industry price exceeds the firm's minimum average variable cost, the firm will maximize profits (minimize losses) by operating at the rate of output where marginal revenue or price equals marginal cost. The total amount of economic profit earned will depend on the following relation between price and average total cost at this rate of output: Total Profit = (P − ATC) × Q. If price exceeds average total cost, the firm will earn a positive economic profit. If price is less than average total cost, the firm will earn a negative economic profit. If the price just equals average total cost, the firm will earn a zero economic profit (break even). Graphically, the firm's breakeven point is where the price line is tangent to the minimum point of the average total cost curve. total revenues, 216 | | |
| **9.3 Short-Run Supply and Equilibrium.** The firm's short-run supply curve is the portion of its marginal cost curve at and above its minimum average variable cost. The industry short-run supply curve, which is the horizontal sum of the individual firms' supply curves, interacts with the industry demand curve to set the industry equilibrium price. | industry supply curve, 225 | • **MyEconLab** Study Plan 9.3 |

myeconlab

| LEARNING OBJECTIVES | KEY TERMS | MYECONLAB PRACTICE |
| --- | --- | --- |
| **9.4 Long-Run Equilibrium.** In long-run equilibrium, the industry supply adjusts to a level that sets an equilibrium price just equal to each firm's minimum long-run and short-run average total cost. Each firm produces an output level where the equilibrium price equals marginal cost and earns a zero economic profit.<br>Long-run adjustments, such as changes in plant size and entry and exit of firms, bring about long-run equilibrium. If the typical firm is earning short-run economic profits, new firms will enter, driving the price down to equal minimum average total cost (normal profit). If the typical firm is earning short-run economic losses, existing firms will leave, driving the price up to equal minimum average total cost. | | • **MyEconLab** Study Plan 9.4 |
| **9.5 Long-Run Industry Supply Curves.** The three different long-run supply situations are constant cost, increasing cost, and decreasing cost. In a constant cost industry, the long-run supply curve is horizontal (perfectly elastic) because input prices do not change as the industry expands. In an increasing cost industry, the long-run supply curve is upward sloping because input prices increase as the industry expands. In a decreasing cost industry, the long-run supply curve is downward sloping because input costs decrease as the industry expands. | long-run industry supply curve, 230<br>constant-cost industry, 230<br>increasing-cost industry, 230<br>decreasing-cost industry, 230 | • **MyEconLab** Study Plan 9.5 |

| LEARNING OBJECTIVES | KEY TERMS | MYECONLAB PRACTICE |
|---|---|---|
| **9.6 Social Evaluation of Perfect Competition.** In long-run equilibrium, perfect competition promotes the socioeconomic goals of productive efficiency (minimum ATC), allocative efficiency (P = MC), and an equitable distribution of income (normal economic profit). Possible shortcomings of perfect competition include market failure and a sub-optimal rate of innovation. | marginal cost pricing, 233<br>market failure, 234<br>external costs, 234<br>external benefits, 235 | • **MyEconLab** Study Plan 9.6 |

# PROBLEMS

(Answers to the odd-numbered problems appear at the back of the book.)

**LO 9.1 Identify and explain the characteristics of a perfectly competitive market structure.**

1. Explain why each of the following examples is not a perfectly competitive industry:
   a. The industry consists of one large firm and thousands of smaller firms, each selling an identical product. The large firm sets the price, and the remaining firms take this price as a given. Firms can easily enter or exit the industry.
   b. There are many buyers and sellers in the industry. Consumers and firms have perfect information about the prices of each competitor's product, which differ in quality from firm to firm.
   c. There are many independently owned taxicabs that compete in a city. The city's government requires all taxicabs to provide identical service. All taxicabs operate the identical automobile model, with identical options. All drivers must wear a designated uniform. Through licensing, the government limits the number of taxicab companies that can operate within the city's boundaries.
2. Refer to Example 9-1, "When Blogging Becomes a Competitive Business." Suppose you have established a blog that generates 100 000 visits (hits) per month. You currently charge advertisers $50 per month for each 125 pixel × 125 pixel button in the sidebar of your blog. You estimate that if you raise the price above $50, even by a penny, you will lose all your advertiser customers. Sketch the demand curve for hosting a 125 pixel × 125 pixel button placed on the sidebar of your blog. Are you a price taker? Briefly explain.
3. Answer the following:
   a. Sketch a graph of both the industry and the firm to illustrate the following situations in the market for video rentals, which is perfectly competitive. The industry supply and demand sets an equilibrium price of $4 per video rental per day. Illustrate the demand curve that a single independent video rental store faces, assuming the $4 price. Illustrate how a decrease in industry demand for video rentals results in a new equilibrium price of $3 and a new demand curve for the firm.
   b. In general, explain the difference between the industry's demand curve and the firm's demand curve in perfect competition.

**LO 9.2 Using revenue and cost information, determine the firm's short-run profit-maximizing or loss-minimizing level of output and profit.**

4. Refer to the video rental example in Problem 3 above. Fill in the daily total, average, and marginal revenue table, below, assuming a price of $3 per video.

| Daily Quantity (# of videos) | 1 | 2 | 3 | 4 | 5 |
|---|---|---|---|---|---|
| Total revenue | ____ | ____ | ____ | ____ | ____ |
| Average revenue | ____ | ____ | ____ | ____ | ____ |
| Marginal revenue | ____ | ____ | ____ | ____ | ____ |

5. The accompanying table represents the hourly output and cost structure for a local pizza outlet, which operates in perfect competition. Total fixed costs are $3 per hour.

| Hourly Quantity (# pizzas) | 0 | 1 | 2 | 3 | 4 | 5 | 6 | 7 | 8 | 9 | 10 |
|---|---|---|---|---|---|---|---|---|---|---|---|
| Total Variable Costs per Hour ($) | 0 | 6 | 8 | 9 | 11 | 15 | 21 | 29 | 40 | 54 | 71 |
| Total Costs per Hour ($) | 3 | 9 | 11 | 12 | 14 | 18 | 24 | 32 | 43 | 57 | 74 |

   a. If the price is $10 per pizza, compute the hourly total profit for each of the quantity levels in the accompanying table. What is the profit-maximizing (or loss-minimizing) quantity level? What is the maximum profit or minimum loss?
   b. Rework part (a) above assuming that the price drops to $3 per pizza.
   c. Rework part (a) above assuming that the price drops to $2 per pizza.
6. Refer to Example 9–2, "High Sunk Costs Can Mean Deep Discounts." Suppose that you own a restaurant that currently offers meals in the evening. If you decide to open your restaurant during lunch hours, identify the relevant fixed and variable costs. If you offered two-for-one lunch coupons, you would have to ensure that the average price per meal exceeded what amount?
7. In the accompanying table, we list the per-unit costs for a perfectly competitive firm manufacturing and selling a standard-sized bookcase unit.

| Output (units per hour) | Average Fixed Cost (AFC) | Average Variable Cost (AVC) | Average Total Cost (ATC) | Marginal Cost (MC) |
|---|---|---|---|---|
| 1 | $102.00 | $40 | $142.00 | |
| 2 | 51.00 | 35 | 86.00 | $30 |
| 3 | 34.00 | 40 | 74.00 | 50 |
| 4 | 25.50 | 45 | 70.50 | 60 |
| 5 | 20.40 | 50 | 70.40 | 70 |
| 6 | 17.00 | 55 | 72.00 | 80 |
| 7 | 14.57 | 60 | 74.57 | 90 |

a. If the price per unit is $81, determine the profit-maximizing quantity level and the maximum profit.
b. If the price per unit is $61, determine the profit-maximizing quantity level and the maximum profit. Should the firm shut down at this price, in the short run?
c. If the price per unit is $31, determine the profit-maximizing quantity level and the maximum profit.
d. The short-run breakeven point occurs at approximately what price?
e. The short-run shutdown point occurs at approximately what price?

8. Consider the accompanying graph. Then answer the questions.

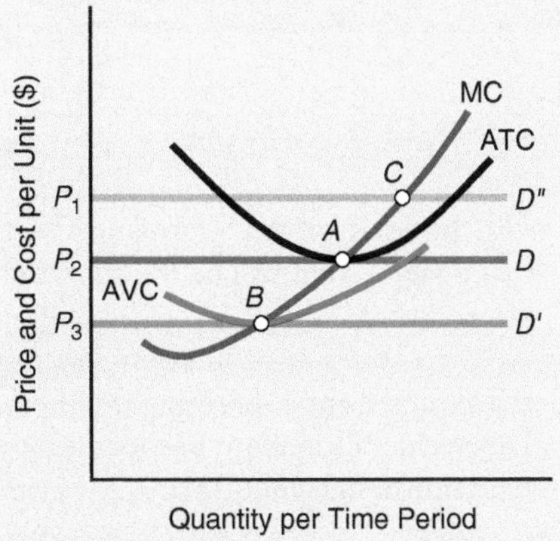


a. Which demand curve indicates that the firm is earning normal profits?
b. Which demand curve indicates that the firm is earning abnormal profits?
c. Which demand curve indicates that the firm is indifferent between shutting down and producing?
d. Which curve is the firm's supply curve?
e. Below which price will the firm shut down?

9. The accompanying graph is for firm J. Study it, then answer the questions.

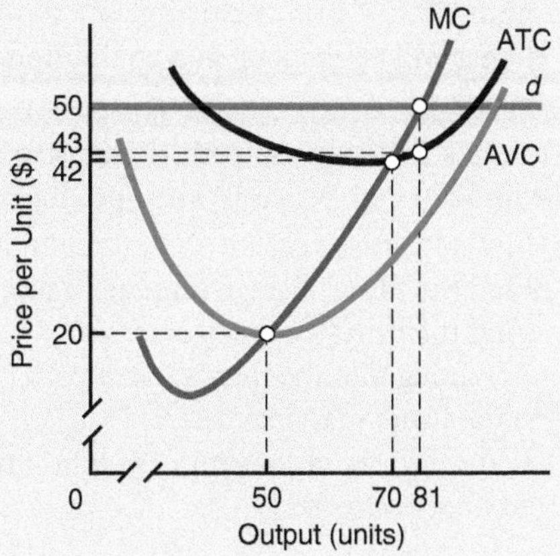


a. How many units will firm J sell in order to maximize profits?
b. What is firm J's total profit from selling the amount of output in part (a)?
c. At what price will firm J shut down in the short run?
d. If the cost curves shown represent production at the optimal long-run plant size, predict the long-run price.

10. Consider the following diagram. It applies to a perfectly competitive firm, which at present faces a market clearing price of $20 per unit and produces 10 000 units of output per week.

a. What is the firm's current average revenue per unit?
b. What are the present economic profits of this firm? Is the firm maximizing economic profits? Explain.
c. If the market clearing price drops to $12.50 per unit, should this firm continue to produce in the short run if it wishes to maximize its economic profits (or minimize its economic losses)? Explain.
d. If the market clearing price drops to $7.50 per unit, should this firm continue to produce in the short run if it wishes to maximize its economic profits (or minimize its economic losses)? Explain.

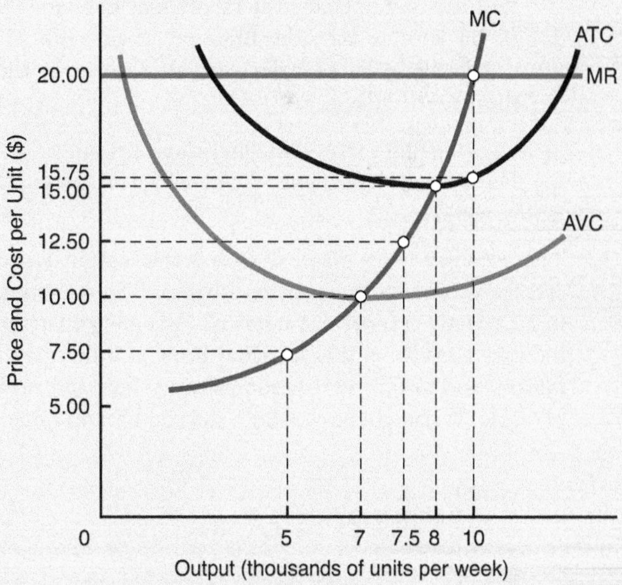

11. The accompanying diagram describes the short-run per-unit costs of Patio Pete's, which is a perfectly competitive firm manufacturing a standard white plastic patio chair.

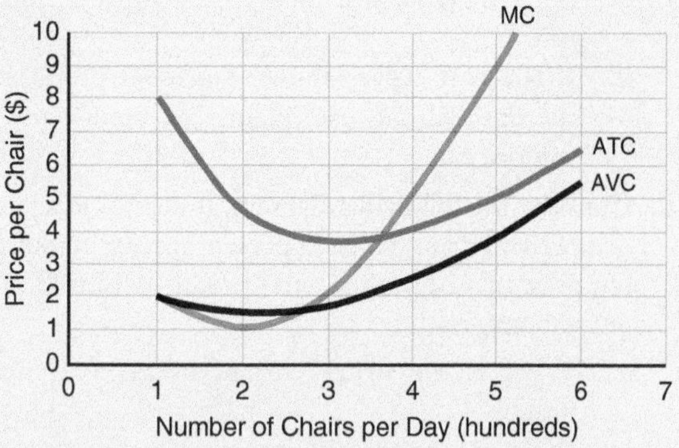


a. Suppose that the market sets the price at $5 per chair. What would be Patio Pete's daily profit-maximizing quantity? Find the firm's maximum daily total profit at this price.
b. Suppose, on another day, the price changed to $3 per chair. At this price, at best, would Patio Pete's be earning a positive or a negative economic profit? Explain.
c. Referring to question b above, should Patio Pete shut down or operate in the short run? Explain.
d. If, on another day, the price per chair were $1, should Patio Pete's operate or shut down in the short run? Explain.

**LO 9.3 Derive the firm's short-run supply curve and explain how the short-run equilibrium price is determined in a perfectly competitive market.**

12. The accompanying graph describes the marginal and average variable cost curves for a typical firm operating in a perfectly competitive industry. Assuming that the industry consists of 100 identical firms, use the graph information to fill in the accompanying short-run supply table. What will be the short-run equilibrium price?

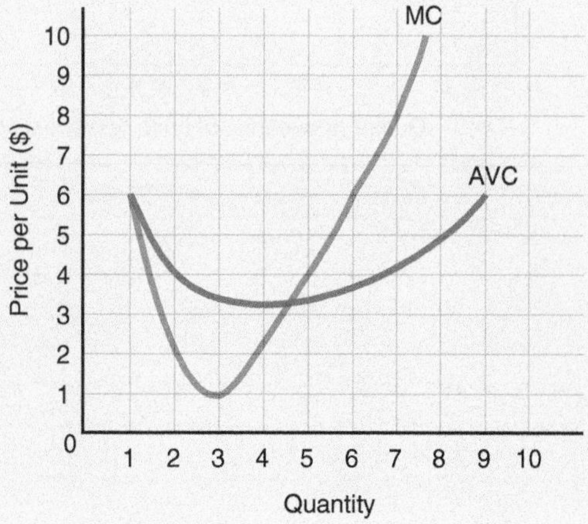


| Price per Unit | Individual Quantity Supplied | Industry Supply | Industry Demand |
|---|---|---|---|
| $8 | ——— | ——— | 400 |
| 6 | ——— | ——— | 600 |
| 4 | ——— | ——— | 800 |
| 2 | ——— | ——— | 1000 |

13. Use the perfectly competitive firm's per-unit cost data in Problem 7 to fill in the accompanying short-run supply table. Assume that the industry consists of 1000 firms identical to the firm in Problem 7.

| Price per Unit | Individual Quantity Supplied | Industry Supply (1000 firms) | Industry Demand |
|---|---|---|---|
| $91 | ——— | ——— | 5000 |
| 81 | ——— | ——— | 6000 |
| 51 | ——— | ——— | 8000 |
| 31 | ——— | ——— | 9000 |

a. On the basis of the information in the accompanying table, what will be the short-run equilibrium price?
b. At the short-run equilibrium price, what will be the typical firm's short-run equilibrium quantity? Determine the amount of total profit earned by the typical firm in equilibrium.

**LO 9.4 Explain the features and long-run adjustments associated with long-run equilibrium in perfect competition.**

14. Refer to the per-unit cost curves in Problem 9. Suppose that these costs relate to each firm's optimum long-run plant size. What will be the long-run equilibrium price in this industry?

15. Refer to the per-unit costs in Problem 7. Suppose that these costs relate to each firm's optimum long-run plant size.
a. Suppose the current price is $81 per unit. Will this be the long-run equilibrium price? Why, or why not?
b. What will be the long-run equilibrium price in this industry?

16. A firm in a perfectly competitive industry has total revenue of $200 000 per year, when producing 2000 units of output per year.
a. Find the firm's average revenue or price.
b. Find the firm's marginal revenue.
c. Assuming that the firm is maximizing profits, what is the firm's marginal cost?
d. If the firm is at long-run equilibrium, what is its average total cost?

**LO 9.5 Explain the three different long-run industry supply curve situations that are possible in perfect competition.**

17. What long-run supply situation best relates to each of the following? For each of the following situations, what will the long-run supply curve look like?
    a. As the number of active oil drilling rigs doubles, the extraction cost per barrel of oil increases.
    b. As the cellphone industry explodes in size, the per-unit cost of manufacturing cellphones decreases.

**LO 9.6 From a social viewpoint, evaluate the long-run behaviour in perfect competition.**

18. Explain the social benefits associated with each of the following long-run equilibrium conditions:
    a. The typical firm operates at a quantity level where price equals average total cost.
    b. Production takes place to the point where price equals marginal cost.
    c. The typical firm operates at minimum average total cost.
19. For each of the following, explain whether a competitive industry in long-run equilibrium will tend to overallocate or underallocate resources to the product it produces.
    a. Competitive research firms discover and supply a new drug that prevents the spread of a serious type of influenza.
    b. Competitive pulp producers pollute rivers and lakes, which increases the water treatment costs of nearby communities.
20. Identify and explain two reasons why a perfectly competitive industry environment may not foster innovation and technological advances.

# BUSINESS APPLICATION

**LO 9.2 Using revenue and cost information, determine the firm's short-run profit-maximizing or loss-minimizing level of output and profit.**

## Accounting: Short Run Analysis: Tools of a Cost Accountant

Monique's is a purely competitive firm that manufactures pulp in Quebec. The price of pulp is determined on a worldwide market in response to demand and supply forces.

At the end of every month, Ted Baxter, the cost accountant at Monique's, compares the projected pulp price with the company's short-run unit costs in order to determine the optimum production level for the next month. Once the optimum production schedule is determined, other important decisions can be made, such as the number of shifts to operate, hours of labour to employ, and the amount of raw materials to purchase. As well, the monthly profit or loss can be projected, which is important from a cash flow point of view.

Given the current plant facility and related commitments, the total monthly fixed cost is $250 000. The other relevant costs depend on the monthly production level and are described in the table below. Note that in the table below, the full capacity of the plant is 6000 tonnes per month.

| Monthly Production Rate in tonnes (Q) | Total Variable Cost (TVC) | Average Variable Cost (AVC) | Marginal Cost per tonne (MC) | Average Total Cost (ATC) |
|---|---|---|---|---|
| 0 | $0 | | | |
| 1000 | $124 000 | | | |
| 2000 | $240 000 | | | |
| 3000 | $375 000 | | | |
| 4000 | $540 000 | | | |
| 5000 | $750 000 | | | |
| 6000 | $1 020 000 | | | |

## Business Application Problem

1. a. Complete the accompanying table
   b. Due to a major union strike at competitive plants in the U.S., Ted projects that the price of pulp will increase to $230 per tonne in September. Based on this projection and the cost information provided, determine the profit maximizing (or loss minimizing) level of production and the total monthly profit in dollars.
   c. In October, the U.S. labour dispute was settled. As well, new competitive pulp plants started operation. As a result, the projected October price for pulp is only $140 per tonne. Based on this projected price and the cost information provided, determine the profit-maximizing (or loss-minimizing) October production rate, in tonnes. At this production rate, calculate the total monthly profit (or loss) in dollars.
   d. In November, the Asian economies—major buyers of Monique's pulp—went into a recession. As a result, the November price dropped to $118 per tonne. Based on the $118 price and the cost information provided, determine the profit-maximizing (or loss-minimizing) November production rate in tonnes. At this production rate, calculate the total monthly profit (or loss) in dollars.
   e. In general, in the short run, is the best production rate always going to be where Monique's achieves the lowest cost per tonne of pulp? Explain.
   f. In general, in the short run, should Ted always shut down the plant when he projects a loss? Explain.

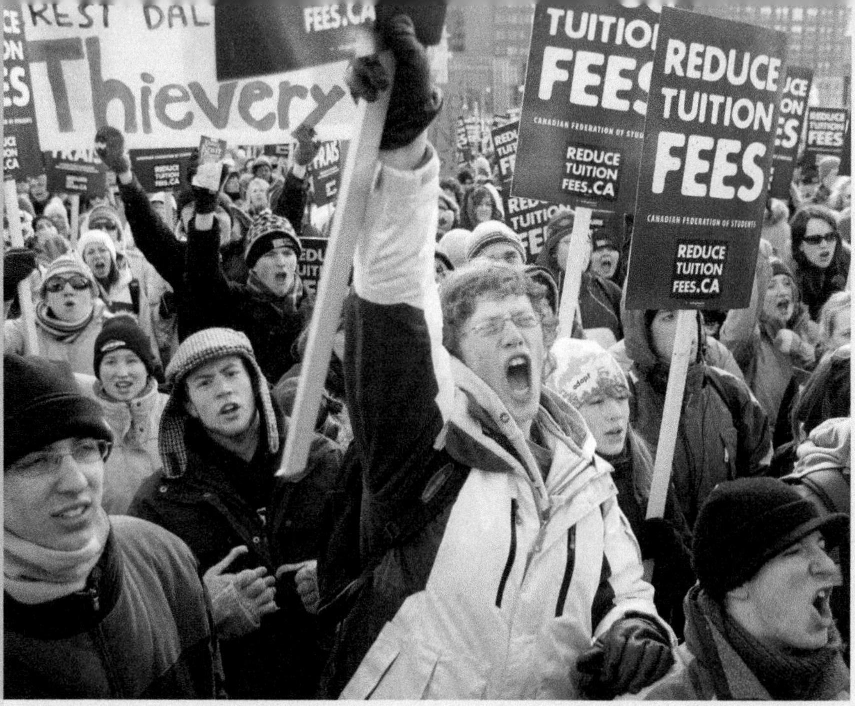


# 10

## LEARNING OBJECTIVES

After reading this chapter, you should be able to:

**10.1** Identify and explain the characteristics of a monopoly market structure.

**10.2** Using revenue and cost information, determine the monopolist's profit-maximizing or loss-minimizing level of output, price, and profit.

**10.3** Explain why a monopoly firm engages in price discrimination.

**10.4** Evaluate the long-run behaviour in monopoly from a social viewpoint.

**10.5** Compare and contrast the use of marginal cost pricing versus average cost pricing in the regulation of a natural monopoly.

# Monopoly

In 2015 just three years later, Quebec students are back on the streets protesting Quebec government's budget cuts and possible increases in tuition.

In May of 2012, Quebec university students protested over a hike in university fees of $325 a year over 5 years. The hikes would represent a 75 percent increase for students over the 5 years. University administrators were in a tough spot because they needed more funding for infrastructure but did not want to alienate the students. Students argued that the increases would lower participation rates and increase student debt. To pay for their tuition, Canadian post-secondary students have accumulated a staggering debt of $13 billion, with 20 percent of Canadian students unable to repay what they owe. After studying this chapter, you will appreciate why many view the setting of tuition fees by post-secondary institutions as simply another example of monopoly pricing practices.

Source: Leo Charbonneau, "Quebec student protests: an explainer", Guardian Professional, July 9, 2012, http://www.theguardian.com/higher-education-network/blog/2012/jul/09/international-fees; Benjamin Shingler. "Quebec student protests: What you need to know." CBC News. April 02, 2015. http://www.cbc.ca/news/canada/montreal/quebec-student-protests-what-you-need-to-know-1.3018153.

myeconlab

MyEconLab helps you master each objective and study more efficiently. See end of chapter for details.

## DID YOU KNOW THAT...?

Single sellers of goods and services exist all around you. The company that equips your labs with new computers has probably been granted the exclusive right to do so by your college or university. The ski resort that offers you food at the top of the mountain does not allow anyone else to open a restaurant next to it. Just one drug manufacturer will typically supply the new prescription drug that you are eager to buy. If you book your wedding reception at a popular hotel ballroom, you will likely have to promise to use the hotel's expensive menu and wine list for this momentous occasion. No doubt, you will pay a high price if you want to enjoy your favourite beverage and snack while watching your home team play at the local stadium. In this chapter, you will learn more about situations where competition is restricted to one supplier. We call such situations *monopoly*.

# 10.1 The Characteristics of Monopoly

The word *monopoly* probably brings to mind notions of large, corrupt business organizations that gouge the consumer. But if we are to succeed in analyzing and predicting the behaviour of a firm operating in a monopoly environment, we must be more objective in our description of this type of market structure. Whether applied to large or small businesses, monopoly situations typically have the following characteristics in common.

1. *A monopoly firm is a single seller.* That is, we can define a **monopolist** as the single supplier of a good or service for which there are no close substitutes.
2. *A monopolist is a price searcher.* A **price searcher** is a firm that must determine the price–output combination that maximizes profit because it faces a downward-sloping demand curve. In a monopoly market structure, the firm and the industry are one and the same. Therefore, the firm's demand curve, *d*, is the same as the industry demand curve, *D*. Since the typical industry demand curve is downward sloping, the monopolist's demand curve is also downward sloping. When the monopoly firm increases its output sold per time period, this will decrease the price of the product. In contrast to perfect competition, where the price is given, in a monopoly the firm must "search" or determine the profit-maximizing price and output combination.
3. *Barriers to entry must exist in monopoly.* Since new businesses are started daily in Canada, there must be some reason why new firms are not successful in entering a monopoly industry. The types of barriers to entry may include exclusive ownership of resources; problems in raising adequate capital; economies of scale; legal or government restrictions; and, possibly, predatory tactics of the monopolist.

**Monopolist** A single supplier of a good or service for which there are no close substitutes.

**Price searcher** A firm that must determine the price–output combination that maximizes profit because it faces a downward-sloping demand curve.

What are some common examples of monopoly industries? In many large cities, there is often just one firm supplying all the natural gas, one utility firm selling electricity, and one firm providing local phone service. If one resides in a small city, one may regularly read the city's only daily newspaper, travel on the one available airline carrier to the nearest provincial capital, or stay at home and enjoy frequent visits to a local ski resort or a golf course owned by a monopolist.

## Barriers to Entry

For any amount of monopoly power to continue to exist in the long run, the market must be closed to entry in some way. Either legal means or certain aspects of the industry's technical or cost structure may prevent entry. We will discuss several of the barriers to entry that have allowed firms to reap monopoly profits in the long run.

**OWNERSHIP OF RESOURCES WITHOUT CLOSE SUBSTITUTES.** Preventing a newcomer from entering an industry is often difficult. Indeed, some economists contend that no monopoly acting without government support has been able to prevent entry into the industry unless that monopoly has had the control of some essential natural resource. Consider the possibility of one firm's owning the entire supply of a raw material input that is essential to the production of a particular commodity. The exclusive ownership of such a vital resource serves as a barrier to entry until an alternative source of the raw material input is found or an alternative technology not requiring the raw material in question is developed. A good example of control over a vital input is the Aluminum Company of America, a firm that prior to World War II controlled the world's bauxite, which is the essential raw material in the production of aluminum. Such a situation is rare, though, and is usually temporary.

**PROBLEMS IN RAISING ADEQUATE CAPITAL.** Businesses in certain industries require a large initial capital investment. The firms already in the industry can, according to some economists, obtain monopoly profits in the long run because no competitors can raise the large amount of capital needed to enter the industry. This is called the "imperfect" capital market argument and is used to explain long-run, relatively high rates of return in certain industries. These industries are generally ones in which large fixed costs must be incurred merely to start production. Their fixed costs are generally for expensive machines necessary to the production process. Examples include industries that supply electricity, natural gas heating, cable TV, and local phone service using phone lines.

**ECONOMIES OF SCALE.** Sometimes it is not profitable for more than one firm to exist in an industry. This is so if, in order to realize lower unit costs, one firm would have to produce such a large quantity that there would be insufficient demand to warrant a second producer of the same product. Such a situation may arise because of a phenomenon we discussed in Chapter 8, economies of scale. When economies of scale exist, total costs increase less than proportionately to the increase in output. That is, proportional increases in output yield proportionately smaller increases in total costs, and per-unit costs drop. The advantage in economies of scale lies in the fact that larger firms (with larger output) have lower per-unit costs that enable them to charge lower prices, and that drives smaller firms out of business.

Natural monopoly The firm that first takes advantage of economies of scale in order to establish a monopoly position.

When long-run average costs decline as the scale of operation increases, a *natural monopoly* may develop. The **natural monopoly** is the firm that first takes advantage of economies of scale in order to establish a monopoly position. The natural monopolist is able to underprice its competitors and eventually force all of them out of the market.

In Figure 10–1, we have drawn a downward sloping long-run average cost curve (LAC). Recall that when average costs are falling, marginal costs are less than average costs. We can apply the same analysis in the long run. When the long-run average cost curve (LAC) is falling, the long-run marginal cost curve (LMC) will be below the LAC.

In our example, long-run average costs are falling over such a large range of production rates that we would expect only one firm to survive in such an industry. That firm would be the natural monopolist. It would be the first one to take advantage of the decreasing average costs; that is, it would construct the large-scale facilities first. As its average costs fell, it would lower prices and get an increasingly larger share of the market. Once that firm had driven all other firms out of the industry, it would set its price to maximize profits.

**FIGURE 10–1**

**The Cost Curves That Might Lead to a Natural Monopoly: The Case of Electricity**

Whenever long-run average costs are falling, so, too, will be long-run marginal costs. Also, long-run marginal costs (LMC) will always be below long-run average costs (LAC). A natural monopoly might arise in such a situation. The first firm to establish the low unit-cost capacity would be able to take advantage of the lower average total cost curve. This firm would drive out all rivals by charging a lower price than the others could sustain at their higher average costs.

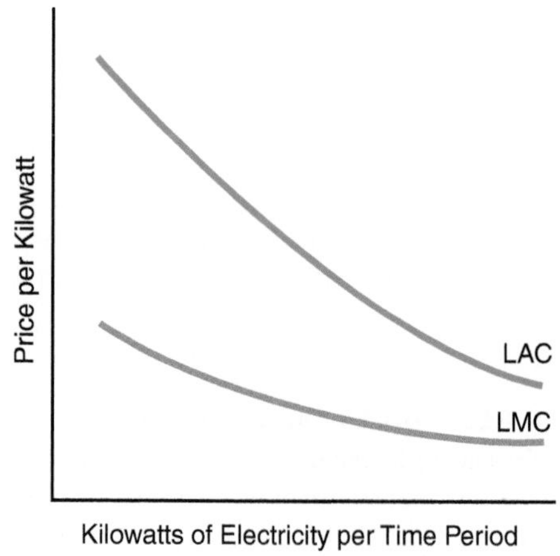

**PREDATORY BEHAVIOUR.** It should be noted that a firm may establish a monopoly position in a market by engaging in behaviour that has already eliminated its competition and/or that has the effect of deterring new entrants to its industry. In some countries, such behaviour is considered to be illegal. For example, a criminal sanction against predatory pricing has been part of Canada's competition law for over 50 years.

The concept of predatory pricing is best illustrated by a dominant firm in a market setting its prices so low, over a long enough period of time, that it may drive one or more of its competitors from the market, deter other companies from entering the market, or both. Following the exit of competitors from the market, the predator is expected to raise prices significantly in an attempt to recover the profit lost during the period of predatory pricing. Example 10–1 provides examples of how Microsoft has gained near-monopoly positions in a number of different markets by engaging in predatory behaviour.

### EXAMPLE 10–1 Microsoft's Abuse of Monopoly

On November 12, 2002, the U.S. Court of Appeals for the District of Columbia Circuit found Microsoft guilty of engaging in a series of exclusionary, anticompetitive, and predatory acts to maintain its monopoly power in the operating system software industry. At the time of the court decision, Microsoft's share of the worldwide market for Intel-compatible PC operating systems exceeded 90 percent.

On the basis of the dominance of its Windows operating system, Microsoft was in a position to unfairly dominate other industries, such as the Web browser market. In the early 1990s, Netscape Navigator controlled 70 percent of the Web browser market. Threatened by Netscape's dominance of the Internet, Microsoft created Internet Explorer and gave this new software away for free to Internet service providers and computer makers. Microsoft "packaged" Explorer as an integral part of Windows, which prevented computer manufacturers from modifying or deleting this browser software. Microsoft entered into agreements with computer manufacturers and Internet providers that restricted the distribution of competing software. Partly as a result of this predatory behaviour, the use of Internet Explorer has grown to the point of dominating the Web browser market worldwide.

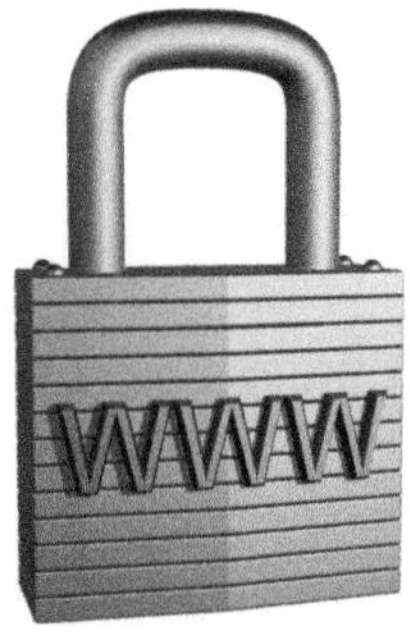

How has Microsoft attempted to "lock in" a large share of the internet browser market?

Despite the fact that the Court of Appeals ruling in November 2002 prohibits Microsoft from engaging in predatory behaviour, it appears that it continues to employ similar tactics in other markets. On March 25, 2004, the European Union (EU) fined Microsoft $606 million for using its near monopoly in operating systems to dominate the markets for Internet media software, server software, and the software that will run next generation computing devices. As an example, the EU's investigations support the view that Microsoft's Media Player has been bundled and sold with Windows in a way that has unfairly restricted the growth of rival software, such as RealNetworks Inc.'s Real Player and Apple Computer's QuickTime player. On March 1, 2007, the EU threatened Microsoft with a $4 million daily fine. It accused Microsoft of protecting its own interests by setting excessive prices for the documentation that competitors need to build products that interoperate with Windows PCs and servers.

In January 2009, the European Commission filed more charges against Microsoft. It claimed that company's plans to install Internet Explorer as part of the new Windows 7 operating system would severely reduce competition in the Internet browser market and give Microsoft an unfair, monopoly-like advantage in this industry. In December 2009, in order to prevent additional fines, Microsoft announced that it would create a version of Windows 7 for the European market that would, at the startup/installation stage, display a pop-up screen asking customers to pick one or more of 12 web browsers to download and install. Déjà vu!

**For critical analysis:** Using this example, explain the various ways that Microsoft has engaged in predatory behaviour.

Sources: "United States of America, plaintiff, v. Microsoft Corporation, defendant. United States District Court for the District of Columbia. November 12, 2002. United States Department of Justice. http://www.microsoft-antitrust.gov/pdf/Nov1202981232FinalJudgment.pdf; David Lawsky. "Microsoft ordered to strip Windows." *Financial Post*. March 25, 2004. Pg. FP4; "EU threatens Microsoft with new penalties." *Calgary Herald*. March 2, 2007. Pg. E8; Aoife White. "Microsoft, EU end current antitrust fight with deal to give European users more browser choice." The Canadian Press. Toronto. December 16, 2009.

**LEGAL OR GOVERNMENTAL RESTRICTIONS.** The federal and provincial governments can also erect barriers to entry. These include public franchises, licences, patents, tariffs, and specific regulations that tend to limit entry.

In many industries, it is illegal to enter without a government *licence*. For example, you could not start a medical practice in Canada without first obtaining a licence from the Canadian College of Physicians and Surgeons. Standards are closely monitored by the government to protect the health and safety of consumers. By restricting entry to the profession and by agreeing to a common fee structure, doctors maintain a relatively high earnings level.

A *public franchise* is necessary to enter some markets, such as in the provision of cable television service. The Canadian Radio-television and Telecommunications Commission (CRTC) must approve all applications for entry and, in many cases, grants local, or geographical, monopolies to cable TV providers. Because these franchises are restricted, long-run monopoly profits might be earned by such firms as Rogers Cablesystems, which are already in the industry.

In some cases, government might license itself to be the sole provider of some product or service. In some Canadian provinces, liquor is sold only through government-owned retail outlets.

A *patent* is issued to an inventor to provide protection from having the invention copied or stolen for a period of 20 years. Suppose that engineers working for Northern Telecom (Nortel) discover a way to build fibre-optic cable that requires half the amount of inputs of regular cable, and transmits data twice as fast. If Nortel is successful in obtaining a patent on this discovery, it can (in principle) prevent others from copying it. The patent holder has a monopoly.

**Tariffs** Special taxes that are imposed on certain imported goods.

**Tariffs** are special taxes that are imposed on certain imported goods. They have the effect of making imports relatively more expensive than their domestic counterparts so that consumers switch to the relatively cheaper domestically made products. If the tariffs are high enough, imports become overpriced, and domestic producers gain monopoly advantage as the sole suppliers. Many countries have tried this protectionist strategy by using high tariffs to shut out foreign competitors.

## Price and Revenue Behaviour under Monopoly

In this section, we will examine how price and revenue typically behave as a monopoly firm expands its production or quantity sold per time period. This will give you a better understanding of how the monopolist determines its profit-maximizing output level.

**THE MONOPOLIST'S MARGINAL REVENUE: LESS THAN PRICE.** A monopolist is the sole supplier of one product, good, or service. This means that the monopoly firm faces the same demand curve as the overall industry demand curve. As the industry demand curve, $D$, is typically downward sloping, we can deduce that the monopoly firm's demand curve, $d$, is also downward sloping. In order for the monopoly firm to increase its quantity sold per time period, the firm will have to decrease the price of its product.

How is marginal revenue related to price under a monopoly situation? Consider an egg farmer who is the sole supplier of eggs to an entire city. If on Monday the monopoly farmer decides to hold back daily output sold to just seven dozen eggs, the farmer can command a high price of, say, \$10 per dozen. Monday's total revenue will be \$10 × 7 dozen eggs = \$70. If the monopolist farmer wishes to increase the daily quantity sold on Tuesday to eight dozen eggs, the farmer will have to lower the price of each dozen sold on Tuesday to \$9 per dozen. This means that Tuesday's total revenue is \$9 × 8 = \$72. What is the marginal revenue of the eighth or last dozen of eggs sold on Tuesday? We will compute this marginal revenue in two different ways.

First, the marginal revenue refers to the change in total revenue in selling one more unit. If we compare Monday's with Tuesday's total revenue, we can see that the eighth unit (dozen) sold changes total revenue from \$70 to \$72. The marginal revenue of the last or eighth dozen of eggs sold on Tuesday is \$72 − \$70 = \$2. Note that while the price of the last or eighth unit (dozen) sold is \$9, the marginal revenue of this last unit is only \$2. Marginal revenue is less than the price for the eighth unit sold. In fact, if the same egg farmer were to reduce the price of the eggs even further on Wednesday, we would again

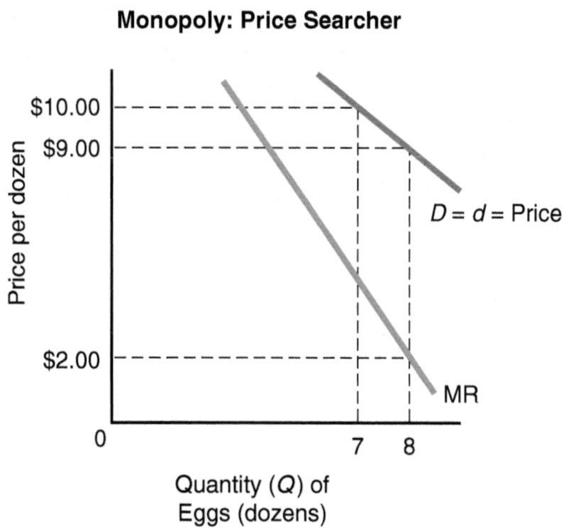


**FIGURE 10–2**

**Demand and Marginal Revenue Curves: Monopoly**

For the monopolist, marginal revenue is less than price at each quantity level.

find that the marginal revenue of the last dozen sold on Wednesday would again be lower than Wednesday's price.

Figure 10–2 graphs the behaviour of price and marginal revenue for the monopoly egg farmer at different daily quantities sold. Note that in general, at each possible output level, marginal revenue is less than price.

Why is marginal revenue less than price in monopoly? Let us examine another way of computing the marginal revenue the monopoly farmer received from selling the last unit (eighth dozen eggs) on Tuesday. When the price per dozen was reduced from $10 on Monday to $9 on Tuesday, the farmer gained an extra $9 from selling one more dozen eggs (eighth dozen) when compared with Monday. However, in comparing both days, the farmer sold each of the first seven dozen eggs on Tuesday at $9 (compared to $10 on Monday). Therefore, on Tuesday, the farmer received $1 less for each of the first seven dozen eggs sold, or $7 less. If we combine the $9 gain from selling the eighth unit of eggs with the $7 loss incurred on the first seven dozen eggs sold, we also arrive at a marginal revenue of $9 − $7 = $2 for the eighth unit sold on Tuesday. Figure 10–3 uses a graph to illustrate this second way of determining the marginal revenue of the eighth unit of eggs sold.

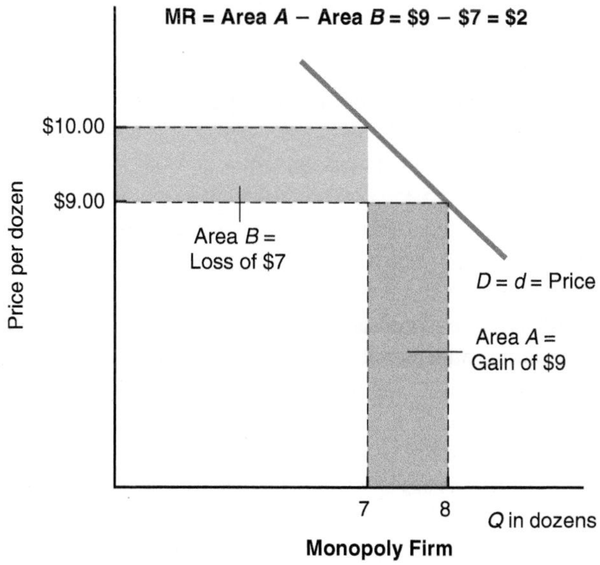


**FIGURE 10–3**

**Marginal Revenue Less Than Price**

In going from selling seven to eight units per day, the firm incurs a gain and a loss. The gain from selling the eighth unit equals $9 × 1 = $9 = Area *A*. The loss equals the loss of $1 on each of the first seven units = $1 × 7 = $7 = Area *B*. The net gain equals the marginal revenue of selling the eighth unit which equals Area *A* − Area *B* = 9 − 7 = $2. The marginal revenue of $2 is less than $9, which is the price of the eighth unit sold.

## Elasticity and Monopoly

The monopolist faces a downward-sloping demand curve (its average revenue curve). That means that it cannot charge just *any* price it wishes (a common misconception) because, depending on the price charged, a different quantity will be demanded.

Earlier we defined a monopolist as the single seller of a well-defined good or service with no *close* substitute. This does not mean, however, that the demand curve for a monopoly is vertical or exhibits zero price elasticity of demand. After all, consumers have limited incomes and alternative wants. The downward slope of a monopolist's demand curve occurs because individuals compare the marginal satisfaction they will receive with the cost of the commodity to be purchased. Take the example of telephone service. Even if there were absolutely no substitute whatsoever for telephone service, the market demand curve would still slope downward. At lower prices, people will add more phones and separate lines for different family members.

Furthermore, the demand curve for telephone service slopes downward because there are at least several *imperfect* substitutes, such as e-mail, letters, telegrams, in-person conversations, and CB and VHF-FM radios. Thus, even though we defined a monopolist as a single seller of a commodity with no *close* substitute, we can talk about the range of *imperfect* substitutes. The more such imperfect substitutes there are, the more elastic will be the monopolist's demand curve, all other things held constant.

Over time, the price elasticity of demand for the services provided by Canada Post, a legal monopoly, has changed, as explained by Policy Example 10–1.

## POLICY EXAMPLE 10–1 Should Canada Post Remain a Monopoly—Or Does it Matter?

The *Canada Post Corporation Act*, created by the federal government, confers an exclusive monopoly on Canada Post in terms of the delivery within Canada of "letters" not weighing more than 500 grams. One reason that Canada Post has a legal monopoly is that it is subject to a Universal Service Obligation (USO), which typically requires Canada Post to provide mail service at uniform rates and minimal quality standards to all regions of Canada.

The rationale for a USO is to promote economic development by reducing one of the costs of settling in remote or underdeveloped areas of the country and promoting national unity by enhancing social communication and cohesiveness. Granting a monopoly allows Canada Post to make enough profit in the highly populated regions to finance the losses that occur in providing postal services in the remote rural areas.

Any monopoly power that Canada Post once had with respect to parcel delivery, however, has been whittled away by the growth of private couriers, such as United Parcel Service (UPS), Federal Express (FedEx), and Purolator. Over the last decade, technology has rendered the most fatal blow to Canada Post's position. Typically, an email, a scanned document, an electronic signiture or a fax machine is faster than mailing a letter domestically or internationally. The use of the Internet and e-mail have provided numerous alternatives to mailing a letter or snail mail. The Canadian Radio-television and Telecommunications (CRTC) announced Internet service as essential. Currently, 18 percent of households do not have access to the Internet. The Federal government intends to fund high-speed Internet to allow all Canadians access by 2030. The most frequent Internet activities included e-mailing and social networking, cheap substitutes for mailing a letter anywhere in the world.

**For critical analysis:**

1. According to this example, what has happened to the price elasticity of demand for services provided by Canada Post, such as letter services and parcel deliveries? Explain. In what ways might Canada Post attempt to slow down the erosion of its monopoly position?
2. What would likely happen to postal service in the remote rural areas of Canada if Canada Post were to lose its legal monopoly?

Sources: E. Iacobucci, M. Trebilcock, and Tracey D. Epps. "Rerouting the mail: why Canada Post is due for reform." C.D. Howe Institute. http://www.cdhowe.org. February 2007; Matthew Kupler."CRTC declares broadband internet access a basic service." December 21, 2016. http://www.cbc.ca/news/politics/crtc-internet-essential-service-1.3906664.

# 10.2 Determining Output, Price, and Profit in Monopoly

To find out the rate of output at which the perfect competitor would maximize profits, we had to add cost data. We will do the same thing now for the monopolist. We assume that profit maximization is the goal of the pure monopolist, just as for the perfect competitor. The perfect competitor, however, has only to decide on the profit-maximizing rate of output because price was given. The competitor is a price taker. For the pure monopolist, we must seek a profit-maximizing *price–output combination* because the monopolist is a price searcher. We can determine this profit-maximizing price–output combination with either of two equivalent approaches—by looking at total revenues and total costs or by looking at marginal revenues and marginal costs. We shall examine both approaches.

## The Total Revenues–Total Costs Approach

We show hypothetical demand (rate of output and price per unit), revenues, costs, and other data in part (a) of Figure 10–4. In column 3, we see total revenues for our hypothetical monopolist, and in column 4, we see total costs. We can transfer these two columns to part (b). The difference between the total revenue and total cost diagram in part (b) and the one we showed for a perfect competitor in Chapter 9 is that the total revenue line is no longer straight. Rather, it curves. For any given demand curve, in order to sell more, the monopolist must lower the price. Thus, the basic difference between a monopolist and a perfect competitor has to do with the demand curve for the two types of firms. Monopoly market power is derived from facing a downward-sloping demand curve.

Profit maximization involves maximizing the positive difference between total revenues and total costs. This occurs at an output rate of nine units where the maximum profit equals $12.50.

## The Marginal Revenue–Marginal Cost Approach

Profit maximization will also occur where marginal revenue equals marginal cost. This is as true for a monopolist as it is for a perfect competitor (but the monopolist will charge a higher price). When we transfer marginal cost and marginal revenue information from columns 6 and 7 in part (a) of Figure 10–4 to part (c), we see that marginal revenue approximately equals marginal cost at an output rate of nine units. Remember that a marginal cost of $3.70 refers to the extra cost of producing the ninth unit of output; a marginal revenue of $3.75 refers to the extra revenue earned by selling the ninth unit of output. Therefore, the monopolist will continue to add to profit by producing the ninth unit. Profit maximization occurs at nine units of output, which is the same output as in part (b).

**WHY PRODUCE WHERE MARGINAL REVENUE EQUALS MARGINAL COST?** If the monopolist goes past the point where marginal revenue equals marginal cost, marginal cost will exceed marginal revenue. That is, the incremental cost of producing any more units will exceed the incremental revenue. It just would not be worthwhile, as was true also in perfect competition. But if the monopolist produces less than that, it is also not making maximum profits. Look at an output rate of seven units in Figure 10–4. Here, the monopolist's marginal revenue is $4.75, but marginal cost is only $2.90. The monopolist would be foolish to stop at seven units of output because if output is expanded, marginal revenue will still exceed marginal cost, and therefore, total profits will rise. In fact, the profit-maximizing monopolist will continue to expand output and sales until marginal revenue approximately equals marginal cost, which is at nine units of output.

The monopolist will not produce at an output rate of 10 because here, as we see, marginal cost is $4.20 and marginal revenue is $3.25. The difference of $0.95 represents the *reduction* in total profits from producing the tenth unit. Total profits will rise as the monopolist reduces its rate of output back toward nine units of output.

**FIGURE 10–4**

## Monopoly Costs, Revenues, and Profits

In part (a), we give hypothetical demand (rate of output and price per unit), revenues, and costs. As shown in part (b), the monopolist's maximum profit of $12.50 is where the positive difference between TR and TC is the greatest, at nine units. As part (c) indicates, this maximum profit occurs where MR = MC with a price of $5.75 per unit.

Part (a)

| (1) Output (units) | (2) Price per Unit | (3) Total Revenues (TR) = (2) × (1) | (4) Total Costs (TC) | (5) Total Profit (TR – TC) = (3) – (4) | (6) Marginal Cost (MC) | (7) Marginal Revenue (MR) = Change in (3) / Change in (1) | (8) Average Total Cost (ATC) = (4) ÷ (1) |
|---|---|---|---|---|---|---|---|
| 0 | $8.00 | $ 0.00 | $10.00 | –$10.00 | | | |
| 1 | 7.75 | 7.75 | 14.00 | –6.25 | $ 4.00 | $7.75 | $14.00 |
| 2 | 7.50 | 15.00 | 17.50 | –2.50 | 3.50 | 7.25 | 8.75 |
| 3 | 7.25 | 21.75 | 20.75 | 1.00 | 3.25 | 6.75 | 6.92 |
| 4 | 7.00 | 28.00 | 23.80 | 4.20 | 3.05 | 6.25 | 5.95 |
| 5 | 6.75 | 33.75 | 26.70 | 7.05 | 2.90 | 5.75 | 5.34 |
| 6 | 6.50 | 39.00 | 29.50 | 9.50 | 2.80 | 5.25 | 4.92 |
| 7 | 6.25 | 43.75 | 32.40 | 11.35 | 2.90 | 4.75 | 4.63 |
| 8 | 6.00 | 48.00 | 35.55 | 12.45 | 3.15 | 4.25 | 4.44 |
| 9 | 5.75 | 51.75 | 39.25 | 12.50 | 3.70 | 3.75 | 4.36 |
| 10 | 5.50 | 55.00 | 43.45 | 11.55 | 4.20 | 3.25 | 4.35 |
| 11 | 5.25 | 57.75 | 48.55 | 9.20 | 5.10 | 2.75 | 4.41 |
| 12 | 5.00 | 60.00 | 54.85 | 5.15 | 6.30 | 2.25 | 4.57 |
| 13 | 4.75 | 61.75 | 62.65 | –0.90 | 7.80 | 1.75 | 4.82 |
| 14 | 4.50 | 63.00 | 72.25 | –9.25 | 9.60 | 1.25 | 5.16 |
| 15 | 4.25 | 63.75 | 83.95 | –20.20 | 11.70 | 0.75 | 5.60 |

Part (b)

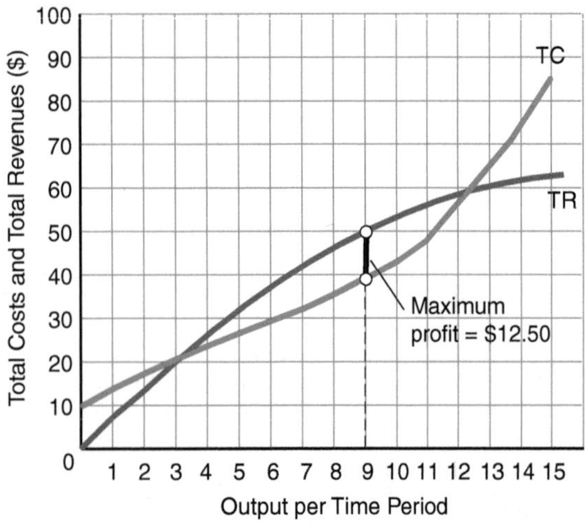


Part (c)

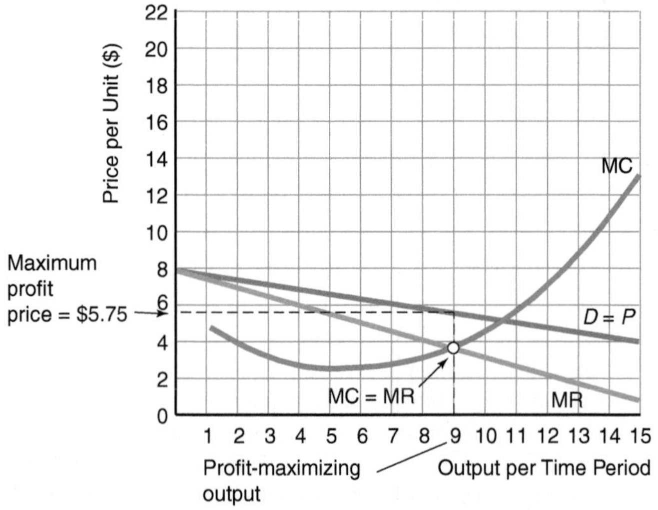


## What Price to Charge for Output?

How does the monopolist set prices? We know the quantity is set at the point at which marginal revenue equals marginal cost. The monopolist then finds out how much can be charged—how much the market will bear—for that particular quantity. We know that the demand curve is defined as showing the *maximum* price for which a given quantity can be sold. That means that our monopolist knows that to sell nine units, it can charge only $5.75 because that is the price at which that specific quantity is demanded according to Figure 10–4 part (c). This price is found by drawing a vertical line from the quantity to the market demand curve. Where that line hits the market demand curve, the price is determined. We find that price by drawing a horizontal line from the demand curve over to the price axis; that gives us the profit-maximizing price of $5.75, as described in Figure 10–4 part (c).

The basic procedure for finding the profit-maximizing short-run price–quantity combination for the monopolist is first to determine the profit-maximizing rate of output, by either the total revenue–total cost method or the marginal revenue–marginal cost method, and then to determine by use of the demand curve, *D*, the maximum price that can be charged to sell that output.

Do not get the impression that just because we are able to draw an exact demand curve in Figure 10–4, real-world monopolists have such perfect information. The process of price searching by a less than perfect competitor is just that—a process. A monopolist can only estimate the actual demand curve and therefore can only make an educated guess when it sets its profit-maximizing price. This is not a problem for the perfect competitor because price is given already by the intersection of market demand and market supply. The monopolist, in contrast, reaches the profit-maximizing output–price combination by trial and error.

## Calculating Monopoly Profit

We have talked about the monopolist's profit, but we have yet to indicate how much profit the monopolist makes. We have actually shown total profits in column 5 of part (a) in Figure 10–4. We can also find total profits by adding an average total cost curve to part (c) of that figure. We do that in Figure 10–5. When we add the average total cost curve, we find that the profit that a monopolist makes is equal to the shaded area, which is $(P_m - \text{ATC}_m) \times Q_m$ or ($5.75 − $4.36) × 9 = $12.51. Given the demand curve and a uniform pricing system (i.e., all units sold at the same price), there is no way for a monopolist to make greater profits than those shown by the shaded area.

It is possible for a monopoly firm to make positive economic profits in the long run. This is due to the existence of barriers to entry that prevents new firms from entering and eroding the monopolist's "excess" profit. The monopolist earns these positive economic profits by charging "excessive" prices—prices that exceed average total cost in the long run.

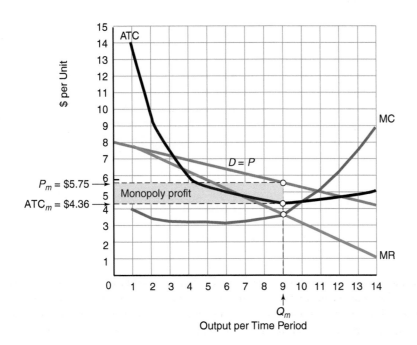

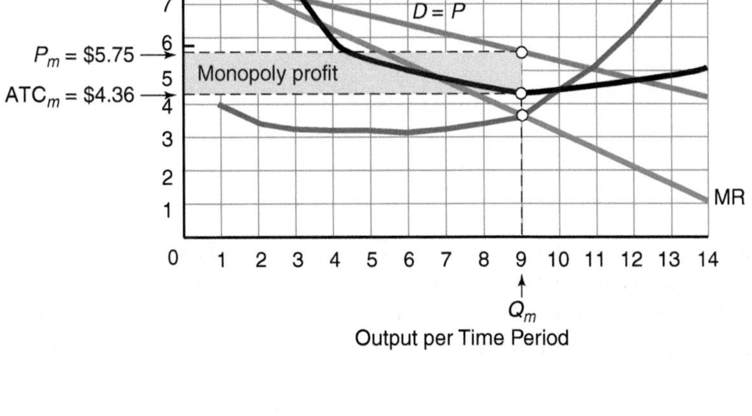


**FIGURE 10–5**

**Monopoly Profit**

In this figure, with per-unit dollar amounts measured on the vertical axis, we determine the maximum profit of a monopolist as follows. We first find the profit maximum quantity at $Q_m = 9$; the demand curve shows that the price $= P_m =$ $5.75 per unit. The average total cost curve shows that $\text{ATC}_m =$ $4.36 at $Q = 9$ units. Total profit is given as: $(P_m - \text{ATC}_m) \times Q_m$, which is ($5.75 − $4.36) × 9 units = $12.51 = Shaded area.

The Did You Know That . . . ? section of this chapter provides examples of monopoly situations where one can expect to pay relatively high prices. Suppose a large computer manufacturer donates funds toward the construction of a new building on campus on the basis of an agreement that the university will purchase all of its computer equipment from this one manufacturer. In this situation, the university can expect to pay "top dollar" for all the computer equipment it purchases, as it faces a monopoly situation. Similarly, in order for you to book your wedding reception at your favourite hotel ballroom, you will likely have to promise to use the hotel's menu and wine list for this joyous event. Since you face a monopoly in terms of planning for the food and beverages for your wedding, you will pay high prices for these refreshments.

**NO GUARANTEE OF PROFITS.** The term *monopoly* conjures up the notion of a greedy firm ripping off the public and making exorbitant profits. However, the mere existence of a monopoly does not guarantee high profits. Numerous monopolies have gone bankrupt. Figure 10–6 shows the monopolist's demand curve as *D* and the resultant marginal revenue curve as MR. It does not matter at what rate of output this particular monopolist operates; total costs cannot be covered. Look at the position of the average total cost curve. It lies everywhere above *D* (the average revenue curve). Thus, there is no price–output combination that will allow the monopolist even to cover costs, much less earn profits. This monopolist will, in the short run, suffer economic losses as shown by the shaded area. The graph in Figure 10–6 depicts a situation for millions of typical monopolies that exist; they are called inventions. The owner of a patented invention or discovery has a pure legal monopoly, but the demand and cost curves may be such that production is not profitable. Every year at inventors' conventions, one can see many inventions that have never been put into production because they were deemed "uneconomic" by potential producers and users.

**FIGURE 10–6**

**Monopolies: Not Always Profitable**

Some monopolists face the situation shown here. The average total cost curve, ATC, is everywhere above the average revenue, or demand, curve, *D*. In the short run, the monopolist will produce where MC = MR at point *E*. Output $Q_m$ will be sold at price $P_m$, but cost per unit is $C_1$. Losses are the shaded rectangle. Eventually, the monopolist will go out of business.

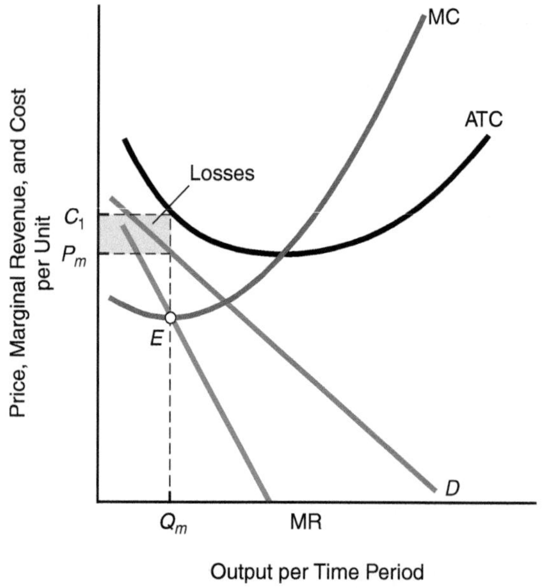


# 10.3 On Making Higher Profits: Price Discrimination

In a perfectly competitive market, each buyer is charged the same price for every unit of the particular commodity (corrected for differential transportation charges). Because the product is homogeneous and we also assume full knowledge on the part of the buyers, a difference in price cannot exist. Any seller of the product who tried to charge a price higher than the going market price would find that no one would purchase it from that seller.

In this chapter we have assumed until now that the monopolist charged all consumers the same price for all units. A monopolist, however, may be able to charge different people different prices or different prices for successive units sought by a given buyer. **Price discrimination** refers to the practice of charging different prices for units of the same product, not justified by cost differences. A firm will engage in price discrimination whenever feasible to increase profits.

**Price discrimination** The practice of charging different prices for units of the same product, not justified by cost differences.

## Different Prices for Different Units of the Same Product

A negatively sloped demand curve suggests that consumers are willing to pay different amounts for different units of the same product. If a monopoly firm is able to charge the maximum amount that consumers are willing to pay for different units of the same product, the firm will enjoy a higher level of profit. Returning to Figure 10–4, you will recall that when our hypothetical monopolist charges a single price of $5.75 per unit, the firm earns an economic profit of $12.50. What amount of profit could be earned if this monopoly firm were to price discriminate?

A price-discriminating monopolist would, in the extreme, charge a different price for each unit of output according to the demand for its product. Thus, it would sell the first unit for $7.75, the second for $7.50, the third for $7.25 and so on, until the price it could charge for the next unit of output just equalled the marginal cost of producing it. In our example, therefore, the price discriminator would sell 11 units of output, with the eleventh unit selling for $5.25, just equal to its marginal cost. How much extra profit would it make? Total revenue would be $71.50—the sum of all of the prices charged for the 11 units sold ($7.75 + $7.50 + $7.25 + $7 + $6.75 + $6.50 + $6.25 + $6 + $5.75 + $5.50 + $5.25). Total cost would be unchanged at $48.55, and the resulting profit would be $22.95. Figure 10–7 reproduces Figure 10–4 and highlights the extra revenues that accrue to the price-discriminating monopolist. Distributing units of a product by auction, based on sealed bids, is one way to approximate the practice of perfect price discrimination, as described in Policy Example 10–2.

### POLICY EXAMPLE 10–2 Forcing Individuals to Reveal How Much They Are Willing to Pay

Shanghai is a bustling city of more than 24 million people that is growing rapidly. Nevertheless, the city government strictly limits the number of available auto licence plates according to a mathematical formula that takes into account the number of recently scrapped cars and recent auto sales. In a typical month, this means that only 8,000 new permanent licence plates will be available for purchase, leaving 96% of applicants without plates. To determine how much people are willing to pay for the restricted number of plates, the government conducts a monthly sealed auction. Those willing to pay the most for a licence plate often pay amounts exceeding the equivalent of $16,000 to obtain the right to drive. In this way, Shanghai's government seeks to make economic profits from its control over licence plates.

**For critical analysis:**

1. As a monopoly provider of vehicle licence plates, what type of pricing practice is the Shanghai government pursuing and why?
2. Can you think of any benefits accruing to the citizens of Shanghai as a result of this type of licence plate pricing policy?

Source: Zhou Wenting. "Shanghai toughens rule on auto plates." China Daily News. December 04, 2016. http://usa.chinadaily.com.cn/china/2016-04/12/content_24457844.htm.

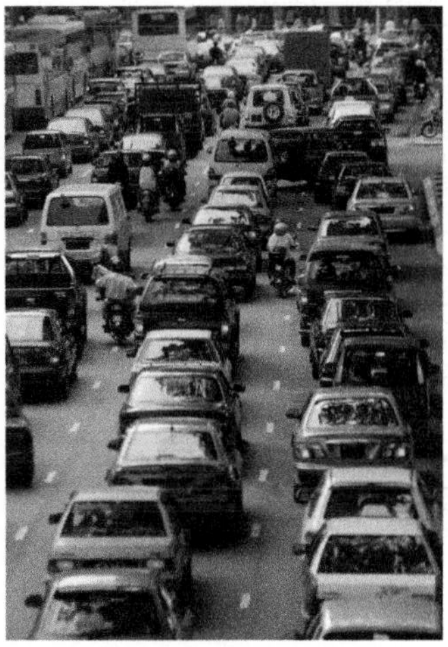

How is Shanghai attempting to reduce traffic jams?

**FIGURE 10–7**

## Additional Profits from Perfect Price Discrimination: Part (a)

Under perfect price discrimination, the firm charges the maximum that consumers are willing to pay for each unit sold. This increases total revenue at each output level. Put differently, marginal revenue is now equal to price under discrimination. The maximum profit quantity is now equal to 11 units, where price is just about equal to MC. The total maximum profit is now $22.95. This is higher than the total profit of $12.50 under the single-price monopoly.

| (1) Output (units) | (2) Price per Unit (P) | (3) Total Revenue: Perfect Discrimination (TRd) | (4) Total Costs (TC) | (5) Total Profit: Perfect Discrimination | (6) Marginal Cost (MC) | (7) Marginal Revenue with Perfect Discrimination P = MR |
|---|---|---|---|---|---|---|
| 0 | $8.00 | $ 0.00 | $10.00 | –$10.00 | | |
| 1 | 7.75 | 7.75 | 14.00 | –6.25 | $ 4.00 | $7.75 |
| 2 | 7.50 | 15.25 | 17.50 | –2.25 | 3.50 | 7.50 |
| 3 | 7.25 | 22.50 | 20.75 | 1.75 | 3.25 | 7.25 |
| 4 | 7.00 | 29.50 | 23.80 | 5.70 | 3.05 | 7.00 |
| 5 | 6.75 | 36.25 | 26.70 | 9.55 | 2.90 | 6.75 |
| 6 | 6.50 | 42.75 | 29.50 | 13.25 | 2.80 | 6.50 |
| 7 | 6.25 | 49.00 | 32.40 | 16.60 | 2.90 | 6.25 |
| 8 | 6.00 | 55.00 | 35.55 | 19.45 | 3.15 | 6.00 |
| 9 | 5.75 | 60.75 | 39.25 | 21.50 | 3.70 | 5.75 |
| 10 | 5.50 | 66.25 | 43.45 | 22.80 | 4.20 | 5.50 |
| 11 | 5.25 | 71.50 | 48.55 | 22.95 | 5.10 | 5.25 |
| 12 | 5.00 | 76.50 | 54.85 | 21.65 | 6.30 | 5.00 |
| 13 | 4.75 | 81.25 | 62.65 | 18.60 | 7.80 | 4.75 |
| 14 | 4.50 | 85.75 | 72.25 | 13.50 | 9.60 | 4.50 |
| 15 | 4.25 | 90.00 | 83.95 | 6.05 | 11.70 | 4.25 |

## Part (b)

The single-price monopoly will sell $Q_s = 9$ units of output at a price of $5.75 per unit. The single-price monopoly has a total revenue of $5.75 × 9 = $51.75 = light shaded area. The price discriminating monopoly will sell $Q_d = 11$ units and will charge the maximum price for each of these units. Under price discrimination, the total revenue will be equal to the total revenue of the single-price monopolist (light shaded area + dark shaded areas). Hence, for any cost structure, the price discriminator will earn a higher total revenue than the single-price monopoly.

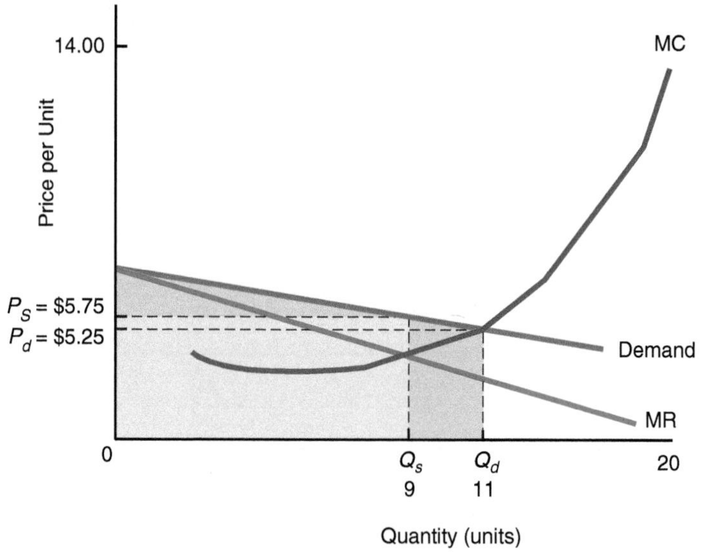


It is interesting to note that a monopolist that can price discriminate will usually produce a greater amount of output than a single-price monopoly. In fact, if the monopolist can perfectly price discriminate as in the above example, it will produce where price equals marginal cost—the perfectly competitive output.

Most monopolies, however, cannot charge a separate price for each unit of output. Instead, they sell blocks of output for different prices. For example, in some jurisdictions, electricity utility companies charge more for the first block of electricity consumed than for subsequent blocks used in the same month. For many years, when monopoly firms provided long-distance telephone service, consumers were charged a higher rate for the first minute of a long-distance telephone conversation compared with that for subsequent minutes. These practices reflect the fact that consumers typically place a higher marginal benefit on the first block of output than on subsequent blocks of output.

## Different Prices for Different Groups of Buyers of the Same Product

Price discrimination is often found in situations where the consumers of a product (or service) can be separated into subgroups that exhibit different price elasticities of demand. In general, the monopoly firm can increase its profit by charging a higher price in the more inelastic market(s) and a lower price in the more elastic market(s).

For example, higher airfares are frequently charged to business travellers who, out of necessity, have to book a specific return flight. In contrast, leisure travellers, who do not have to travel on any specific flight, pay a lower airfare by agreeing to stay over a Saturday night before returning home. In this case, the business traveller constitutes an inelastic demand situation, while the leisure traveller is more price elastic.

People who go to see movie matinees are very price conscious (elastic demand) and therefore enjoy lower admission fees than those who go to the movies in the evenings. Similarly, people who carry around coupons will pay a lower rate per litre of gas compared with those consumers who never use coupons (inelastic users).

Example 10–2 illustrates how Shaw Communications sets different prices for its high-speed Internet service for different groups of customers.

### EXAMPLE 10–2 Pricing Internet Service to Maximize Profit

In many Canadian cities and towns, high-speed Internet service is provided under a monopoly or close to a monopoly situation. In these cases, you will typically find that the Internet provider charges different prices to personal versus business users. This is because the elasticity of demand for high-speed Internet differs between personal and business users. The following table compares the rates that Shaw Communications charged to personal and business users for the same Internet service in a Canadian city in 2017.

**TABLE 10–1**

**Personal vs. Business High-Speed Internet Rates**

| Features of Service | High-Speed: Personal User | High-Speed: Business User |
|---|---|---|
| Price per month | $49.90 | $119.95 |
| Connection speed | 150 Mbps download | 150 Mbps download |

One of the graphs in Figure 10–8 describes the high-speed Internet market for the personal user, while the other graph describes the business market. For simplicity, we assume that the marginal cost of serving each additional user is constant.

**FIGURE 10–8**

**The High-Speed Internet Market**

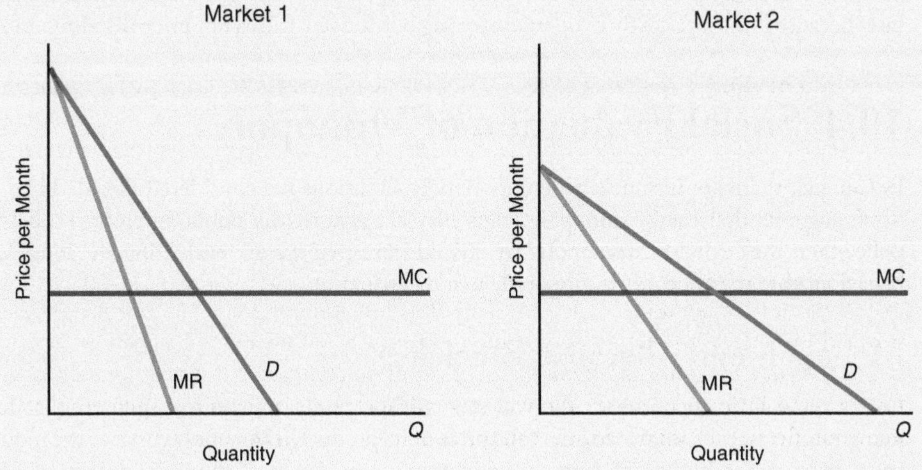


*continued*

**For critical analysis:**

1. Which market is the business market, and why?
2. What factors explain why the elasticity of demand for the business market differs from the personal market?
3. Why does the price charged to business users exceed the price charged to personal users?

Sources: High-Speed [Internet] Package. Business Products and Services. Shaw Communications. http://shop.shaw.ca/business/businessinternet/?semid=cab-bus-acq-goog-br_shaw-bint-sea-nat-c-shaw%20business%20internet-campaignid=612737707&adgroupid=9784510175&keyword=shaw%20business%20internet&matchtype=e&device=c&devicemodel=&adposition=1t1&gclid=Cj0KEQiA5bvEBRCM6vypnc7QgMkBEiQAUZftQCAUbzZcWfv6rF9le7BMYx8HIDv5OlHypCY7QpKxQxMaApvp8P8HAQ; High Speed Internet. Internet. Products and Services. Shaw Communications. https://shop.shaw.ca/test/new-internet-150_01-24?SegmentationLinkClicked=true. (Accessed on January 30, 2017.)

## Necessary Conditions for Price Discrimination

Four conditions are necessary for price discrimination to exist:

1. *The firm must face a downward-sloping demand curve.* In order to charge different consumers different prices, the firm must have some control over price setting.
2. *The firm must be able to separate markets at a reasonable cost.* The monopoly must be able to determine in a relatively simple manner which consumers are willing to pay high prices and which are not. If the cost of segregating the market is high, it will offset the extra profit gained from price discrimination.
3. *The buyers in the various markets must have different price elasticities of demand.* Buyers who are willing to pay high prices typically have fewer substitutes to choose from; hence, their demand is relatively price inelastic. Consumers with more elastic demands usually are less willing to pay high prices for goods and services.
4. *The firm must be able to prevent resale of the product or service.* If the purchaser of the monopoly's product can resell it to a higher-price buyer, then the low-price purchaser, and not the firm, captures the profit that accrues from price discrimination.

For example, charging students a lower price for a movie can be done relatively easily. The cost of checking student IDs is apparently not significant. Also, it is fairly easy to make sure that students do not resell their tickets to nonstudents.

As noted in this chapter's Issues and Applications, "Is it Fair to Practise Price Discrimination in Higher Education?", the practice of price discrimination may promote certain goals such as equity and allocative efficiency. That is, charging richer students higher tuition fees provides funds to help lower-income students attend top quality universities.

It must be made clear at the outset that charging different prices to different people or for different units that reflect differences in the cost of service to those particular people does not amount to price discrimination. If bus fares in the evening are higher than daytime fares because it is more costly to operate evening bus service, this is not price discrimination.

# 10.4 Social Evaluation of Monopoly

In Canada, there are instances where monopoly situations are considered illegal. This, in itself, suggests that many monopoly firms may act against the public interest. To better understand the "evils" of monopoly, we should note that we are evaluating the long-run behaviour that may occur in a monopoly market structure.

## Monopoly and Allocative Efficiency

Let us run a little experiment. We will start with a purely competitive industry that has numerous firms, each unable to affect the price of its product. The supply curve of the industry is equal to the horizontal sum of the marginal cost curves of the individual producers

**FIGURE 10–9**

## The Effects of Monopolizing an Industry

In part (a), we show a competitive situation in which equilibrium is established at the intersection of *D* and *S* at point *E*. The equilibrium price would be $P_e$, and the equilibrium quantity would be $Q_e$. Each individual competitive producer faces a demand curve that is a horizontal line at the market clearing price, $P_e$. What happens if the industry is suddenly monopolized? We assume that the costs stay the same; the only thing that changes is that the monopolist now faces the entire downward-sloping demand curve. In part (b), we draw the marginal revenue curve. Marginal cost is *S* because that is the horizontal summation of all the individual marginal cost curves. The monopolist therefore produces at $Q_m$ and charges price $P_m$. $P_m$ in part (b) is higher than $P_e$ in part (a), and $Q_m$ is less than $Q_e$. We see, then, that a monopolist charges a higher price and produces less than an industry in a competitive situation.

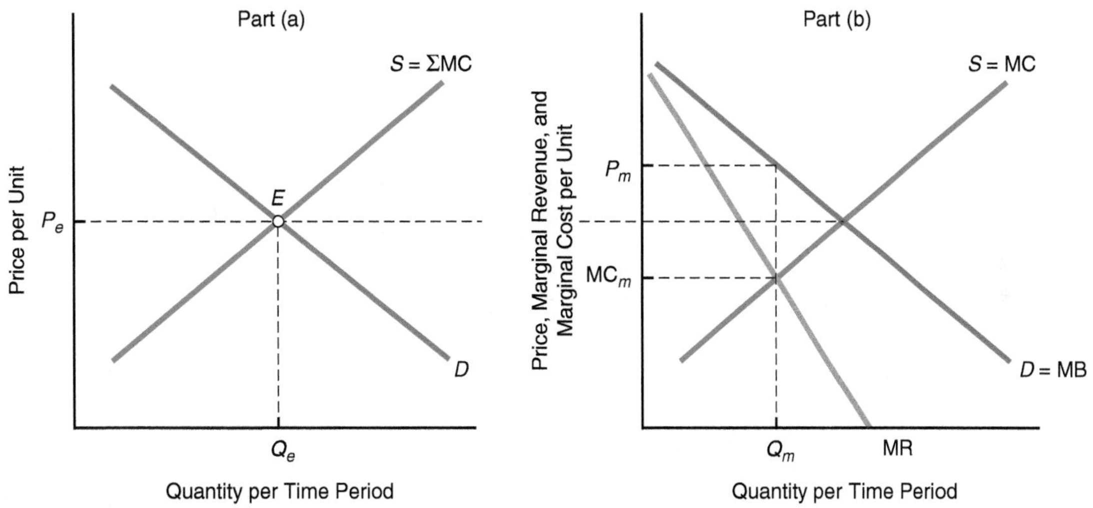


above their respective minimum average variable costs. In part (a) of Figure 10–9, we show the market demand curve and the market supply curve in a perfectly competitive situation. The competitive price in equilibrium is equal to $P_e$, and the equilibrium quantity at that price is equal to $Q_e$. Each individual competitor faces a demand curve (not shown) that is coincident with the price line $P_e$. No individual supplier faces the market demand curve, *D*.

Now, let us assume that a monopolist comes in and buys up every single competitor in the industry. In so doing, we will assume that the monopolist does not affect any of the marginal cost curves or demand. We can therefore redraw *D* and *S* in part (b) of Figure 10–9 exactly the same as in part (a).

How does this monopolist decide how much to charge and how much to produce? If the monopolist is maximizing profit, it is going to look at the marginal revenue curve and produce at the output where marginal revenue equals marginal cost. But what is the marginal cost curve in part (b) of Figure 10–9? It is merely *S* because we said that *S* was equal to the horizontal summation of the portions of the individual marginal cost curves above each firm's respective minimum average variable cost. The monopolist therefore produces quantity $Q_m$ and sells it at price $P_m$. Note that $Q_m$ is less than $Q_e$ and that $P_m$ is greater than $P_e$. A monopolist therefore produces a smaller quantity and sells it at a higher price. This is the reason usually given when economists criticize monopolists. Monopolists raise the price and restrict production compared with a competitive situation. For a monopolist's product, consumers are forced to pay a price that exceeds the marginal cost of production. Resources are misallocated in such a situation—too few resources are being used in the monopolist's industry and too many are used elsewhere.

Note from Figure 10–9 that by setting MR = MC, the monopolist produces at a rate of output, $Q_m$, where the price exceeds marginal cost (compare $P_m$ with $MC_m$). Suppose that $Q_m = 700$ units, $P_m = \$5$ per unit, and $MC_m = \$2$ per unit. The marginal cost of $2 per unit reflects the value of the output in other industries that is sacrificed (opportunity cost), when additional resources are used to produce the last unit or 700th unit in this monopoly industry. Price, by contrast, represents the marginal benefit that buyers derive from the last unit produced. Thus, society places a \$5 value on the last unit (700th unit) produced in this monopoly industry.

The monopoly outcome of $P > MC$ means that the value to society of the last unit produced is greater than its additional cost; hence not enough of the good is produced. In our example, if one more unit of the monopoly good is produced, the extra \$5 value gained in the monopoly industry will exceed the \$2 value of lost production in other industries (marginal cost). From society's point of view, there will be a net gain in value of approximately \$3 by allocating more resources to the monopoly industry. Clearly, monopoly conflicts with allocative efficiency, which is concerned with producing the mix of goods and services most valued by society.

As Example 10–3 indicates, the competitive price can sometimes be a very small fraction of the monopoly price.

### EXAMPLE 10–3 The High Cost of Staying Alive

Thalidomide is perhaps best known as a drug with a notorious past. In the 1950s and 1960s, it was given to pregnant women to treat nausea but tragically caused birth defects: thousands of children were born without arms or legs. The drug was ultimately banned around the world.

Remarkably, research findings published in the *New England Journal of Medicine* (*NEJM*) in 1999 indicated that thalidomide effectively treats diseases such as leprosy, childhood leukemia, and multiple myeloma (a life-threatening cancer). Subsequently, Celgene, a pharmaceutical company, was granted a new patent for thalidomide and was allowed to sell the drug to government-approved patients. Between 1999 and 2005, Celgene raised the price of thalidomide from \$400 for a month's supply to \$3600—a 900 percent increase! This compares to a monthly cost of \$108 in Mexico and \$168 in India, as posted in 2008.

In 2009, an Ontario resident was diagnosed with multiple myeloma. This person was successfully treated and the cancer went into remission. To prevent a relapse, his doctor prescribed thalidomide. Unfortunately, the man could not afford to pay the approximate cost of \$4000 per month and so, to date, he is not able to take this drug. Celgene defends the high price as being necessary to cover the very high risks and costs associated with drug's research and development expenses. Celgene's claim appears to be backed by the president of the association that represents pharmaceutical companies in Canada, who estimates that it costs over a billion dollars to discover and develop a typical pharmaceutical drug.

Recent evidence suggests that multinational drug companies grossly overstate the true costs of developing pharmaceuticals. One study undertaken at the University of Medicine and Dentistry of New Jersey School concluded that 84 percent of drug research money around the world comes from public and charitable sources, not from the pockets of private drug companies. Dr. Marcia Angell, the former Editor in Chief of the prestigious *NEJM* estimates that the research and development costs per new drug are closer to \$100 million, implying that the high drug prices charged by pharmaceutical companies result in excess profits. According to recently published data, the top pharmaceutical companies enjoy an average profit margin of 20 percent, compared to the 8 percent mean return earned by the 2000 companies studied. It is interesting to note that Celgene's profit margin rose from 16 percent in 2007 to 29 percent in 2009. In 2014, Mylan one of the largest generics pharmaceutical companies in the world filed a lawsuit accusing Celgene of blocking the generic manufacturing of Thalidomide. The verdict of the lawsuit is yet to be determined.

**For critical analysis:** Explain how Celgene's behaviour, as described in this example, is consistent with the theory of monopoly. In your answer, comment on how the nature of the price elasticity of demand for thalidomide affects Celgene's pricing behaviour.

Source: W5 Staff. "W5 investigates: pills, patients and profits." CTV News Video. W5. March 27, 2010. http://www.ctv.ca/servlet/ArticleNews/story/CTVNews/20100326/w5_pills_100326/20100327?s_name=W5; Fiona Barry. "Judge rules Mylan monopoly suit against Celgene can continue." in-Pharma. January 12, 2015. http://www.in-pharmatechnologist.com/Regulatory-Safety/Judge-rules-Mylan-monopoly-suit-against-Celgene-can-continue.

## Monopoly and Productive Efficiency

In theory, in long-run equilibrium, a perfectly competitive firm operates at minimum long-run average total cost. Being a price taker under intense competition, the perfectly competitive firm can survive only by being productively efficient.

Since a monopolist produces a product for which there is no close substitute, the firm can survive without having to operate at minimum average total cost. In cases where a monopolist is a very large corporation, the managers may pursue goals other than cost minimization. A manager may seek to enlarge the resources employed in his or her department as a way of obtaining a higher level of status and salary.

## Monopoly and Long-Run Excess Profit

Due to barriers to entry, a monopoly firm can earn annual profits in excess of a normal profit. The excessive monopoly prices charged can be viewed as a "tax" on poorer consumers. To the extent that the shares of these monopoly firm(s) are concentrated in the hands of upper-income individuals, the proceeds of this "tax" are shared among affluent shareholders. In short, the existence of monopoly firms can result in a more inequitable distribution of income in our society.

One key area of the Canadian economy plagued by monopoly industries is the food sector. You may recall from a previous chapter how the Canadian federal and provincial governments have supported farm incomes by allowing various farming groups to form marketing boards that determine the quantity and price of their products. Each marketing board can be viewed as a monopoly supplier of the product it sells.

When a group of farmers supplying a specific product in a Canadian province decides to switch from competing independently to forming a marketing board, farm incomes are enhanced (as illustrated in Figure 10–9). Essentially, the marketing board imposes production quotas on each farmer to restrict quantity to $Q_m$ (see Part (b)), and the price rises to $P_m$, so as to maximize profits. In order to keep the quantity sold in the province at the restricted level, trade barriers must be imposed to keep out similar products that are produced out of province and out of country.

The social costs of allowing legal monopolies in the form of farm marketing boards is discussed in Policy Example 10–3.

### POLICY EXAMPLE 10–3 Monopolies are Milking Canadian Food Consumers

In April 2010, the C.D. Howe Institute, an economic think tank, published a study entitled *Freeing Up Food: The Ongoing Cost, and Potential Reform, of Supply Management*. In this study, "supply management" essentially refers to the policy of allowing marketing boards (monopolies) to control or manage the supply (sale) of specific agricultural products. The report authors estimate that Canadian marketing boards that operate in just the three areas—eggs, dairy, and poultry products—are responsible for about 20 percent of annual agricultural sales.

Between 1995 and 2009, while the Canadian consumer price index increased by 32 percent, the prices for poultry, dairy, and eggs rose 61 percent, 51 percent, and 54 percent, respectively. Canadian milk prices are more than twice as high as in the U.S. The high food prices have a negative effect on consumers as well as on other industries, such as food processors and restaurants, which are forced to restrain the production of their products and services (due to the higher costs).

According to the C.D. Howe Institute study, the aggregated value of all the production quotas in the Canadian egg, dairy, and poultry industries is approximately $28 billion. This translates to above-normal profits somewhere between $1.1 billion and $1.6 billion a year being earned by producers in these three industries.

Under these policies, the marketing board farmers are protected from competition from outside of the province and country. Resources are "wasted" on unproductive activities such as lobbying to maintain the marketing boards, as well enforcement of trade barriers that keep products from being imported from other provinces or countries. These unproductive activities unnecessarily raise the cost of producing the farm products and divert efforts to make farm operations more efficient.

*continued*

A major conclusion of the C.D. Howe Report is that Canadian supply management policies are hindering entrepreneurship and economic growth in the Canadian food sector. Since marketing boards tend to restrict the entry of new farmers, innovative business that produce products such as raw milk, free-range eggs, and uncaged chickens are slow to expand. Canada will not be allowed to join international trade treaties such as the Trans-Pacific Partnership unless the supply management policies are abandoned. These treaties are considered important in terms of gaining access to the fast-growing Asian and Pacific markets. The Nielsen research firm conducted a study on the dairy Canadian supply management and concluded Canada's milk prices are comparable to those in other countries. Others may argue this conclusion but phasing out supply management would require some form of subsidy.

**For critical analysis:** Based on the C.D. Howe Report, identify and explain the various social costs related to permitting monopolies in the form of farm marketing boards.

Sources: William B.P. Robson and Colin Busby. *Freeing up Food: The Ongoing Cost, and Potential Reform, of Supply Management*. Backgrounder. C.D. Howe Institute. April 2010. Pg. 1–6. http://www.cdhowe.org/pdf/backgrounder_128.pdf; "Another reason to take on Big Milk" *National Post*. April 16, 2010. Pg. A14; Lucas Powers. Does supply management really mean Canadians pay more for milk? CBC News. June 3, 2016. http://www.cbc.ca/news/business/milk-dairy-cost-supply-management-1.3612834.

## Should All Monopolies Be Eliminated?

Before we leave the topic of the social cost of monopoly, we should recognize that some monopoly situations may benefit society as a whole. If large economies of scale exist in the monopoly industry, the monopolist can promote productive efficiency. If the government were to intervene to break up this one large efficient company into many smaller firms, average cost per unit may rise. Indeed, the consumers may end up paying more for the product under a more competitive structure! If the government were to try to eliminate a monopoly cable TV station in a small city by encouraging a second cable company to serve the city, think of the duplication of costs that could occur. As a start, two sets of cables would have to be laid throughout the city!

Monopolies created by patents may be socially desirable, to the extent that the promise of a monopoly encourages valuable inventions. Multinational drug companies have consistently argued that the lure of long-run "excess" profits, based on patent protection, serves as an excellent incentive to develop new and better prescription drugs.

As indicated in Policy Example 10–3 "The High Cost of Staying Alive," recent evidence suggests that the multinational drug companies may be grossly overstating the true cost of the research and development costs that they actually incur, so that a large portion of the excessive profits earned end up as profits for the shareholders of pharmaceutical corporations. As well, it appears that a significant portion of drug research money around the world comes from public and charitable sources, not from the pockets of private drug companies.

Governments around the world bestow monopoly rights called *copyright* to those who originate, create, or produce various works, performances, and broadcasts. From an economics viewpoint, copyright means that authors, artists, and musicians have the right to collect royalties (monies) from any form of reproduction and sale of their works. Because a monopoly is granted to the originators, they are able to restrict the distribution of their works in order to exact a higher price and maximize profits. In this way, copyright serves as an incentive to create high-quality literary, dramatic, artistic, and musical works that contribute to the enrichment and diversity of our culture, our freedom of expression, and our overall personal well-being. In Canada, the monopoly right related to copyright is bestowed for a term of the life of the originator and 50 years following his or her death.

Under copyright law, it is illegal for any person to reproduce the works of others, without the consent of the owner of the copyright. This type of illegal behaviour constitutes an *infringement of copyright*. As Policy Example 10–4 notes, the widespread practice of freely downloading music through the Internet is a form of copyright infringement that threatens the livelihoods of many artists and companies that record and distribute music.

## POLICY EXAMPLE 10-4 Swapping Songs on the Internet: Is It Really Free?

What are the social costs related to the practice of downloading songs for free?

The practice of music file sharing has presented significant challenges to the music industry globally, as well as to the economies of many nations. The Recording Industry Association of America (RIAA) estimates that in the U.S. alone, global music piracy costs $12.5 billion of economic losses every year, 71 060 U.S. jobs, $2.7 billion in workers' earnings, and $422 million in tax revenues. On its website, the Canadian Recording Industry Association (CRIA) reported that retail music sales in Canada have declined by more than half since the advent of widespread online music downloading just over a decade ago. Recorded music sales in Canada saw one of the sharpest drops among the world's top 10 music markets due to piracy. The remainder of this Policy Example provides a brief history of key events that have occurred over the past decade that have shaped government policy regarding music piracy.

On December 19, 2003, the Dutch Supreme Court ruled that companies like Kazaa cannot be prosecuted for copyright infringement of music and movies downloaded using its software. The file-sharing software makers (Kazaa, Grokster, and StreamCast Networks) have used two key arguments in their defence. The first is the Betamax doctrine, which states that products and services used for piracy are deemed legal if they are capable of substantial non-infringing uses.

The second source of defence for the software makers is that file-sharing software, such as Kazaa, Grokster, and Morpheus (different from Napster), does not require a central company server. It is peer-to-peer software that allows users to search each other's hard drives for files they want. The files are downloaded right from each user's hard drive. This second line of defence prompted the Canadian Recording Industry Association (CRIA) to go to court to try to force Canadian Internet service providers to turn over the names of 29 large-volume file sharers. On March 31, 2004, a Canadian federal court denied the CRIA's request, stating that the actions of file sharers were no different from that of libraries that place copying machines in a room full of copyrighted books. It is expected that the court ruling will be appealed.

On June 25, 2005, the U.S. Supreme Court ruled that companies that build businesses with the active intent of encouraging copyright infringement should be held liable for their customers' illegal actions. This ruling gave the recording industry the ammunition to file lawsuits against companies creating file-sharing software as well as individuals freely swapping music on the Internet.

On July 27, 2006, Kazaa agreed to pay a substantial sum in compensation to the record companies for the illegal swapping of music. In 2007, the RIAA sent pre-litigation letters to 36 American universities to warn them of forthcoming lawsuits against students and staff for illegal music downloading. Prior to this action, RIAA had successfully sued almost 1000 students for damages ranging anywhere from $750 to $150 000.

On May 12, 2010, a U.S. Federal Court ruled that LimeWire, one of the largest remaining peer-to-peer service providers, will be liable for encouraging widespread copyright theft (music piracy). The Court found that LimeWire had intentionally encouraged direct infringements by its users, as 93 percent of the files available through LimeWire are protected by copyright. On October 26, 2010, a U.S. federal court judge granted the music industry's request to shut down LimeWire.

**For critical analysis:** Who really "pays" for the actions of those who freely upload music files over the Internet?

Sources: "The free music myth." The Canadian Recording Industry Association. http://www.cria.ca/fmm.html. (Accessed March 20, 2004); CBC News Online. "Canadian recording industry to imitate U.S. file-sharing lawsuits." December 16, 2003. http://www.cbc.ca/arts/stories/CRIAtosue161203. (Accessed March 20 2004); "Dutch court throws out Kazaa case." December 19, 2003. Associated Press Wired News. http://www.wired.com/news/digiwood/0,1412,61672,00.html. (Accessed March 21, 2004); Janet McFarland. "Ruling deals blow to music industry." *The Globe and Mail*. April 1, 2004, Pg. B3; John Borland, "Supreme Court rules against file swapping," CNET News.com. June 27, 2005. http://news.com.com/; "IFPI Press Release: Kazaa settles with record industry and goes legitimate." July 27, 2006. http://www.cria.ca/news/270706_n.php; Macleans.ca staff. "Students at 36 US colleges sued for illegal downloading." April 4, 2007. http://www.macleans.ca/ education/universities/article.jsp?content=20070404_101813_11500; "Piracy: online and on the Street." Recording Industry Association of America. http://www.riaa.com/physicalpiracy.php; "Copyright bill introduction applauded by Canadian record labels." Press Release. Canadian Recording Industry Association. June 2, 2010. http://www.cria.ca/news.php/; "Canada's recording industry welcomes US federal court ruling against LimeWire." Press Release. Canadian Recording Industry Association. May 13, 2010. http://www.cria.ca/news.php; RIAA. The True Cost of Sound Recording Piracy to the U.S. Economy. https://www.riaa.com/reports/the-true-cost-of-sound-recording-piracy-to-the-u-s-economy/. (Accessed February 13, 2017).

# 10.5 The Regulation of a Natural Monopoly

You will recall from our discussion of barriers to entry that whenever a single firm has the ability to produce all of the industry's output at a lower per-unit cost than other firms attempting to produce less than total industry output, a natural monopoly arises. Natural gas and electric utilities are examples. Long-run average costs for those firms typically fall as output increases. In a natural monopoly, economies of large-scale production dominate, leading to a single-firm industry.

## The Pricing and Output Decision of the Natural Monopolist

We show data for a hypothetical natural monopoly in part (a) of Figure 10–10. Demand data is in columns 1 and 2, with marginal revenue in column 3. Total cost is in column 4. Notice that marginal cost in column 5 is constant over the range of demand provided. This might be typical of a hydroelectric utility—once the necessary dams are constructed, electricity can be produced at a relatively constant cost. Average total cost is in column 6.

**FIGURE 10–10**

**Profit Maximization and Regulation Through Marginal Cost Pricing**

The profit-maximizing monopolist here would produce at the point in part (b) where marginal cost equals marginal revenue, which means production of 5000 units of output. The price charged would be $8. If a regulatory commission attempted to regulate natural monopolies so that price equalled long-run marginal cost, the commission would make the monopolist set production at the point where the marginal cost curve intersects the demand curve. This is shown in part (c). The quantity produced would be 9000 units, and the price would be $4. However, average costs at 9000 units are equal to $5.56. Losses would ensue, equal to the shaded area. It would be self-defeating for a regulatory commission to force a natural monopoly to produce at an output rate at which MC = *P* without subsidizing some of its costs because losses would eventually drive the natural monopolist out of business.

Part (a)

| (1) Output (units) | (2) Price per Unit | (3) Marginal Revenue (MR) | (4) Long-Run Total Cost (TC) | (5) Long-Run Marginal Cost (MC) | (6) Long-Run Average Cost (ATC) |
|---|---|---|---|---|---|
| 0 | $13.00 | | $14 000 | | — |
| 1 000 | 12.00 | $12.00 | 18 000 | $4.00 | $18.00 |
| 2 000 | 11.00 | 10.00 | 22 000 | 4.00 | 11.00 |
| 3 000 | 10.00 | 8.00 | 26 000 | 4.00 | 8.67 |
| 4 000 | 9.00 | 6.00 | 30 000 | 4.00 | 7.50 |
| 5 000 | 8.00 | 4.00 | 34 000 | 4.00 | 6.80 |
| 6 000 | 7.00 | 2.00 | 38 000 | 4.00 | 6.33 |
| 7 000 | 6.00 | 0 | 42 000 | 4.00 | 6.00 |
| 8 000 | 5.00 | −2.00 | 46 000 | 4.00 | 5.75 |
| 9 000 | 4.00 | −4.00 | 50 000 | 4.00 | 5.56 |
| 10 000 | 3.00 | −6.00 | 54 000 | 4.00 | 5.40 |
| 11 000 | 2.00 | −8.00 | 58 000 | 4.00 | 5.27 |
| 12 000 | 1.00 | −10.00 | 62 000 | 4.00 | 5.17 |

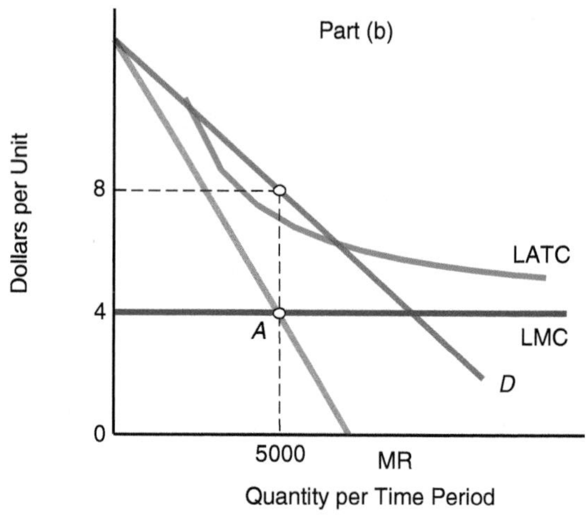


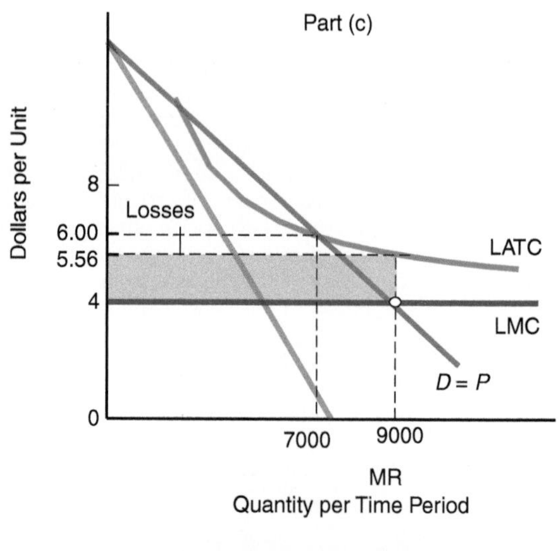

Columns 1, 2, 3, 5, and 6 are graphed in part (b). The intersection of MR and MC is at $4. The monopolist will, therefore, produce 5000 units and charge a price of $8 per unit.

What do we know about a monopolist's solution to the price–quantity question? When compared with a competitive situation, we know that consumers end up paying more for the product, and consequently they purchase less of it than they would purchase under competition. The monopoly solution is economically inefficient from society's point of view; the price charged for the product is higher than the opportunity cost to society, and consequently there is a misallocation of resources. That is, the price does not equal the true marginal cost of producing the good because the true marginal cost is at the intersection *A,* not at $8.

## Regulation Using Marginal Cost Pricing

Assume that the government wants the natural monopolist to produce at an output at which price equals marginal cost, so that the value of the satisfaction that individuals receive from the marginal unit purchased is just equal to the marginal cost to society. **Marginal cost pricing** occurs when the monopoly firm is forced to set price equal to marginal cost. Where is that solution in part (c) of Figure 10–10? It is at the intersection of the marginal cost curve and the demand curve, where price equals $4. If a regulatory commission forces the natural monopolist to engage in *marginal cost pricing,* and hence to produce 9000 units to sell for $4 each, how large will the monopolist's profits be? Profits, of course, are the *positive* difference between total revenues and total costs. Total revenues equal price times output, and total costs equal average costs times output. At 9000 units, average cost is equal to $5.56, higher than the price that the regulatory commission forces our natural monopolist to charge. Profits turn out to be losses and are equal to the shaded area in part (c) of Figure 10–10. Thus, regulation that forces a natural monopolist to produce and price as if it were in a competitive situation would also force that monopolist into negative profits, or losses. Obviously, the monopolist would rather go out of business than be subject to such regulation.

**Marginal cost pricing** Pricing that occurs when the monopoly firm is forced to set price equal to marginal cost.

## Regulation Using Average Cost Pricing

As a practical matter, then, regulators cannot force a natural monopolist to engage in marginal cost pricing. Consequently, regulation of natural monopolies has often taken the form of allowing the regulated natural monopolist to set price where LAC intersects *D,* at 7000 units of output, in part (c) of Figure 10–10. This is called **average cost pricing**—when the monopoly firm is forced to set price equal to average total cost. Average cost includes what the regulators deem a "fair" rate of return on investment.

**Average cost pricing** Pricing that occurs when the monopoly firm is forced to set price equal to average total cost.

While average cost pricing is not socially optimal—at 7000 units of output, price is still $2 above marginal cost—it does result in more output being produced at a lower cost to consumers. Regulators must beware, however, of problems associated with average cost pricing. Unless there are safeguards in place to ensure that the monopoly is cost efficient, the firm has no incentive to keep average costs low. It is easier for the firm to condone inefficiencies in the form of very generous fringe benefits and large expense accounts for executives, all of which inflate average costs. In the extreme, the monopoly could allow its average costs, and hence its regulated price, to rise to the profit-maximizing level of $8.

ISSUES AND APPLICATIONS

# Is It Fair to Practise Price Discrimination in Higher Education?

**Concepts Applied: Price Discrimination, Elasticity, Allocative Inefficiency, Equity**

Students from across Ontario protest the ever-increasing costs of post-secondary tuition fees.

In 2015 just three years later, Quebec students are back on the streets protesting Quebec government's budget cuts and possible increases in tuition. In May of 2012, Quebec university students protested over a hike in university fees of $325 a year over 5 years. The hikes would represent a 75 percent increase for students over the 5 years. University administrators were in a tough spot because they needed more funding for infrastructure but did not want to alienate the students. Students argued that the increases would lower participation rates and increase student debt. Despite the protests, and what appeared to initially be a win for the students, the tuition fees have still increased year over year.

To pay for their tuition, Canadian post-secondary students have accumulated a staggering debt of $13 billion, with 20 percent of Canadian students unable to repay what they owe. In other words, one in five college-bound students begins his or her adult career bankrupt!

## Tuition Fees: Selected Canadian Universities

Table 10–2 describes the annual tuition and fees for the 2016–2017 academic year for selected universities and programs for different groups of students.

## Tuition Fee Structure and Monopoly Pricing Practices

Recall that price discrimination refers to the practice of pricing different amounts of the same product based on differences in "willingness to pay," not on cost differences. Table 10–2

**TABLE 10–2**

**Tuition and Fees Combined: Programs at Selected Canadian Universities**

| University/Program | In-Province Students | Out-of-Province Canadian Students | International Students |
|---|---|---|---|
| **McGill (Quebec)** | | | |
| Undergraduate Arts | $ 4,141 | $ 9,040 | $ 18,603 |
| Medicine (year 1) | $ 7,059 | $ 17,348 | $ 40,414 |
| **University of Toronto** | | | |
| Undergraduate Arts | $ 6,400 | $ 6,400 | $ 41,920 |
| Medicine (year 1) | $ 23,280 | $ 23,280 | $ 69,370 |
| **University of Alberta** | | | |
| Undergraduate Arts | $ 6,880 | $ 6,880 | $ 21,954 |
| Medicine (year 1) | $ 13,603 | $ 13,603 | N/A |
| **University of B.C.** | | | |
| Undergraduate Arts | $ 6,084 | $ 6,084 | $ 35,843 |
| Medicine (year 1) | $ 18,434 | $ 18,434 | N/A |

Sources: https://www.mcgill.ca/student-accounts/tuition-charges/fallwinter-term-tuition-and-fees/undergraduate-fees
http://www.provost.utoronto.ca/link/students/fees17
http://apps.admissions.ualberta.ca/costcalculator/static/public/index.html#
https://students.ubc.ca/enrolment/finances/tuition-fees/undergraduate-tuition-fees

suggests that price discrimination exists in the setting of various tuition fees by any one of the three universities examined. As an example, at McGill University in Quebec, in-province, out-of-province, and out-of-country (international) students pay different tuition fees for the same university program. To study in the first year of McGill's Arts program costs $4,141, $9,040, and $18,603, respectively, for a Quebec student, an out-of-province Canadian student, and an international student.

It is reasonable to explain the price discrimination noted above in terms of the fact that the elasticity of demand for the same education program likely differs among the different groups of students. The international students who attend Canadian universities typically come from wealthy families who can afford to send their children to other countries to study. This implies that the demand for the same educational program is more inelastic for international students when compared to typical Canadian students.

To the extent that the higher fees charged to study in medical programs are not fully explained by the higher costs of offering medical education compared to an arts education, this fee differential (between programs) constitutes another example of price discrimination in the tuition fee structure. In this case, one can hypothesize that a Canadian student's demand for the medical program is more inelastic than the Canadian student's demand for an Arts program. One reason for this would be that the medical graduate can expect to earn a significantly higher income over his or her lifetime than the typical arts graduate. Another reason might be that the Canadian medical student is more apt to come from a wealthier family than the typical Canadian arts student.

## Evaluation of Price Discrimination in the Setting of Tuition Fees

At first glance, one might conclude that the significantly higher tuition fees paid by out-of-province or out-of-country students is a gross inequity and smacks of discrimination against "outsiders." However, one has to remember that tuition fees typically cover less than half the cost of a university student's education in Canada. The provincial taxpayer pays a significant amount of this education. Under this situation, many would argue that it would be inequitable to charge the same tuition fee to both the in-province student and the international student. This would result in a situation where the provincial taxpayer would pay for a significant portion of the education of a wealthy student coming from another country.

Why are taxpayers subsidizing university education? Why not charge all students the same higher tuition fee that covers the full cost of a university education? To the extent that a university education contributes to the economic growth of the province, the provincial community as a whole benefits and so should be willing to pay for some of the student's education. As well, if there were no subsidy, then tuition fees would increase significantly, reducing the ability of lower-income individuals to obtain a university degree. The provincial community as a whole would be losers to the extent that many of these lower-income individuals have the ability to be top performers in fields such as education, law, medicine, engineering, and business. A conflict with allocative efficiency occurs when limited educational resources are allocated to richer students as opposed to the students with the greatest ability and potential. This conflict may already be present, considering the high tuition fees for professional programs such as medicine.

**For critical analysis:**

1. How does the price discrimination practice noted in the tuition fee structure affect the university's total tuition revenue collected? Briefly explain with the aid of the appropriate diagrams.
2. Would one expect to see a larger or smaller degree of price discrimination in prestigious universities that have a very high level of global recognition? How might this type of pricing policy promote equity?
3. What would be the advantages and disadvantages of a government policy that eliminated tuition fees so that all university costs were paid by the taxpayer?

Source: Leo Charbonneau, "Quebec student protests: an explainer", Guardian Professional, July 9, 2012, http://www.theguardian.com/higher-education-network/blog/2012/jul/09/international-fees; Benjamin Shingler. "Quebec student protests: What you need to know." CBC News. April 02, 2015. http://www.cbc.ca/news/canada/montreal/quebec-student-protests-what-you-need-to-know-1.3018153

# SUMMARY

Here is what you should know after reading this chapter. MyEconLab will help you identify what you know, and where to go when you need to practise. We suggest that as soon as you review one of the Learning Objective sections below, you then proceed to go through the related section in MyEconLab.

| LEARNING OBJECTIVES | KEY TERMS | MYECONLAB PRACTICE |
|---|---|---|
| **10.1 The Characteristics of Monopoly.** A monopolist is a single seller of a product or a service for which there is no close substitute. To maintain a monopoly, there must be barriers to entry, which may include: (1) ownership of resources needed to enter the industry, (2) large capital outlays required for entry into the industry, (3) economies of scale, (4) legally required licences and public franchises, (5) patents, (6) tariffs, (7) safety and quality regulations, and (8) predatory behaviour. The monopoly firm is a price searcher, which means that it faces a downward-sloping demand curve, where marginal revenue is below the price, at each quantity level. | monopolist, 245<br>price searcher, 245<br>natural monopoly, 246<br>tariffs, 248 | • **MyEconLab** Study Plan 10.1 |
| **10.2 Determining Output, Price, and Profit in Monopoly.** The monopolist chooses the profit-maximizing price–output combination—the output at which marginal revenue equals marginal cost, and the highest price possible at this output level, as determined by the demand curve. Total maximum profit equals the monopolist's maximum profit quantity level multiplied by the difference between the firm's price and its average total cost, at the maximum profit quantity level. If, at the quantity where marginal revenue equals marginal cost, price is below average total cost, the firm will incur an economic loss. | | • **MyEconLab** Study Plan 10.2 |
| **10.3 On Making Higher Profits: Price Discrimination.** Price discrimination refers to the sale of the same product at different prices based on differences in willingness to pay. By price discriminating, the monopolist can increase its revenue and profit. Under perfect price discrimination, the firm charges the maximum amount that consumers are willing to pay for each unit sold. In this case, the demand or price curve equals the marginal revenue curve. The monopoly firm can increase its profit by charging a higher price in the market segment that is price inelastic | price discrimination, 255 | • **MyEconLab** Study Plan 10.3 |

| LEARNING OBJECTIVES | KEY TERMS | MYECONLAB PRACTICE |
|---|---|---|
| and a lower price in the market segment that is price elastic. Four conditions are necessary for price discrimination: (1) The firm faces a downward-sloping demand curve. (2) The firm must be able to separate different units sold or different customer groups at a reasonable cost. (3) Different groups of customers exhibit differing price elasticities of demand. (4) The resale of the product or service must be preventable. | | |
| **10.4 Social Evaluation of Monopoly.** The social costs of monopoly include: (1) The firm is allocatively inefficient, to the extent that price exceeds marginal cost. (2) Due to the lack of competition, the monopoly firm may be productively inefficient to the extent that it does not produce at minimum long-run average total cost. (3) Due to barriers to entry, monopoly firms can charge excessive prices so as to enjoy positive economic profits in the long run. This can conflict with an equitable distribution of income to the extent that the excessive prices transfer real income from poorer consumers to already rich shareholders. The social benefits of monopoly may include: (1) In natural monopoly situations, a monopoly firm can be more productively efficient than a competitive firm. (2) The lure of long-run excess profits under monopoly may provide the incentive to invent or develop new products or services. | | • **MyEconLab** Study Plan 10.4 |
| **10.5 The Regulation of a Natural Monopoly.** Under marginal cost pricing, the monopoly firm is forced to produce at the output level where price just equals marginal cost. While this promotes allocative efficiency, this will result in perpetual losses in a natural monopoly situation, as marginal cost is below average total cost. With average cost pricing, the monopoly firm is forced to operate at a quantity level where price just equals average total cost. Compared to unregulated monopoly, average cost pricing will result in a lower price to consumers. As well, average cost pricing promotes an equitable distribution of income as the monopolist just earns a normal profit. | marginal cost pricing, 265<br>average cost pricing, 265 | • **MyEconLab** Study Plan 10.5 |

# PROBLEMS

(Answers to the odd-numbered problems appear at the back of the book.)

**LO 10.1 Identify and explain the characteristics of a monopoly market structure.**

1. For each of the following monopoly situations, state whether the barrier to entry is due to *economies of scale*, *predatory behaviour*, or *legal (government) restrictions*.
   a. A large supermarket maintains its monopoly position in a city subdivision by temporarily reducing prices every time a new competitor attempts to enter this market.
   b. A multinational drug company patents one of its new prescription drugs.
   c. The first company to bring cable television to a Canadian community eventually establishes itself as a natural monopoly in this market area.
2. Suppose that a monopolist faces the following demand schedule. Compute marginal revenue.

| Price | Quantity Demanded | Marginal Revenue |
|---|---|---|
| $1000 | 1 | $_______ |
| 920 | 2 | $_______ |
| 840 | 3 | $_______ |
| 760 | 4 | $_______ |
| 680 | 5 | $_______ |
| 600 | 6 | $_______ |
| 520 | 7 | $_______ |
| 440 | 8 | $_______ |
| 350 | 9 | $_______ |
| 260 | 10 | $_______ |

In general, at each quantity level marginal revenue is ________ than price.

3. Explain the differences in the price elasticity of demand for an individual firm in a perfectly competitive industry as compared with a monopolist. Explain why the price elasticities differ.
4. A monopoly firm, being the sole supplier of its product, can charge any price it wants for the quantity level it decides to sell. Critically evaluate this statement.

**LO 10.2 Using revenue and cost information, determine the monopolist's profit-maximizing or loss-minimizing level of output, price, and profit.**

5. Use the graph to answer the questions.
   a. Suppose that a monopolist faces $ATC_1$. Define the rectangle that shows the monopolist's total costs at output rate *Q*. Also define the rectangle showing total revenue. Is the monopolist showing an economic loss, breakeven (normal profit), or an economic profit? What is the significance of the MC = MR output?

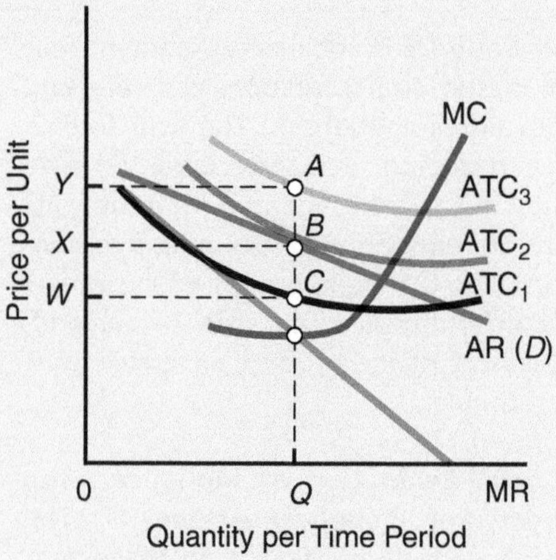


   b. Suppose that the monopolist faces $ATC_2$. Define the rectangle that shows the monopolist's total costs at output rate Q. Also define the rectangle showing total revenue. Is the monopolist showing an economic loss, breakeven (normal profit), or an economic profit? What is the significance of the MC = MR output?
   c. Suppose that the monopolist faces $ATC_3$. Define the rectangle that shows the monopolist's total costs at output rate *Q*. Also define the rectangle showing total revenue. Is the monopolist showing an economic loss, breakeven (normal profit), or an economic profit? What is the significance of the MC = MR output?
6. In the text, we indicated that a monopolist will produce at the rate of output at which MR = MC and will then charge the highest price consistent with that output level. What conditions would exist if the monopolist charged a lower price? A higher price?
7. Examine the revenue and cost figures for a monopoly firm in the table below. For parts (a), (b), (c), and (d), assume a single-price monopoly.

| Price | Quantity Demanded | Total Revenue | Marginal Revenue | Average Total Cost | Marginal Cost |
|---|---|---|---|---|---|
| $20 | 0 | $_______ | | | |
| 16 | 1 | $_______ | $_______ | $ 8.00 | $ 5.00 |
| 12 | 2 | $_______ | $_______ | 7.50 | 7.00 |
| 10 | 3 | $_______ | $_______ | 8.00 | 9.00 |
| 7 | 4 | $_______ | $_______ | 9.25 | 13.00 |
| 4 | 5 | $_______ | $_______ | 11.00 | 18.00 |
| 0 | 6 | $_______ | $_______ | 13.16 | 24.00 |

a. Fill in all the blank columns in the table.
b. At what rate of output would the firm maximize profits?
c. What will be the profit-maximizing price?
d. What would be the amount of the maximum profits?

8. Explain why a monopolist will never set a price (and produce the corresponding output) at which the demand is price-inelastic.

9. Answer the questions based on the accompanying graph for a monopolist.

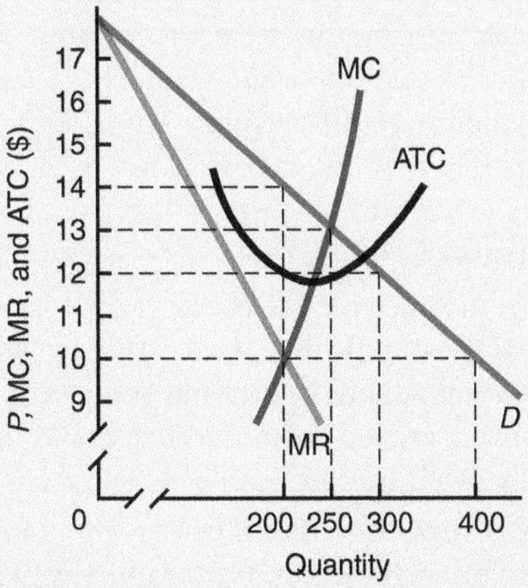


a. If this firm is a profit maximizer, how much output will it produce?
b. At what price will the firm sell its output?
c. How much profit or loss will this firm realize?

10. Pro-Golf Inc. has a monopoly over the manufacture and sale of the very popular Umph golf ball. The graph below describes Pro-Golf's per unit (per ball) daily costs and daily revenues in manufacturing the Umph golf ball.

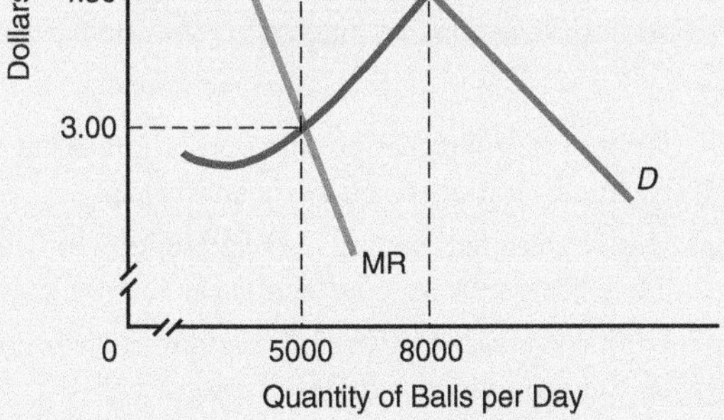

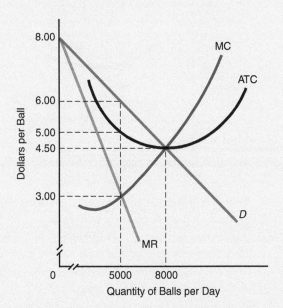


a. How many balls per day should Pro-Golf manufacture in order to maximize its profits?
b. At the profit-maximizing level, what price will be charged per ball sold?
c. At the profit-maximizing level, what is the average total cost per ball?
d. At the profit-maximizing level, what is the daily profit per unit (per ball)?
e. At the profit-maximizing level, what is the daily total profits earned?

11. Due to a patent, RX Med Inc. has a monopoly on the manufacture and sale of the new anti-cold drug called Colds-Away. The graph below describes the per-unit (per bottle) monthly costs and monthly revenues in manufacturing Colds-Away.

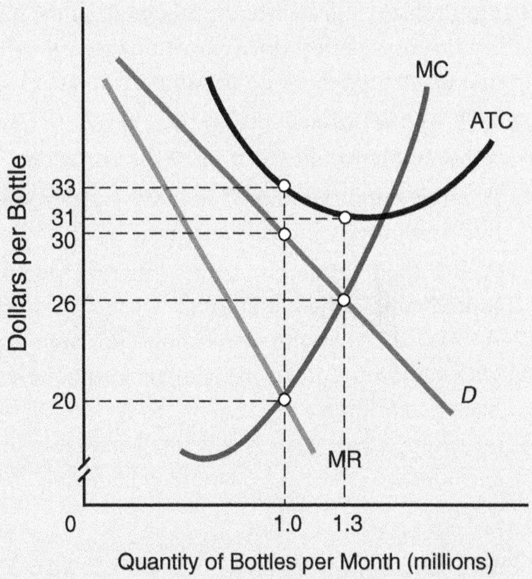


a. What is the profit-maximizing (or loss-minimizing) monthly production level?
b. What is the total dollar amount of the monthly maximum profits (or minimum losses)?

**LO 10.3 Explain why a monopoly firm engages in price discrimination.**

12. State the necessary conditions for price discrimination. Then, discuss how they might apply to the medical services of a doctor.

13. The accompanying table depicts the daily output, price, and costs of the only dry cleaner located near the campus of a small college town in a remote location. How much additional maximum profit can the monopoly dry cleaning firm earn by practising perfect price discrimination as opposed to charging a single price?

| Output (suits cleaned) | Price per Suit | Total Cost | Marginal Cost |
|---|---|---|---|
| 0 | $8.00 | $3.00 | |
| 1 | 7.50 | 6.00 | $3.00 |
| 2 | 7.00 | 8.50 | 2.50 |
| 3 | 6.50 | 10.50 | 2.00 |
| 4 | 6.00 | 11.50 | 1.00 |
| 5 | 5.50 | 13.50 | 2.00 |
| 6 | 5.00 | 16.00 | 2.50 |
| 7 | 4.50 | 19.00 | 3.00 |
| 8 | 4.00 | 23.00 | 4.00 |

14. Explain how the four conditions necessary for price discrimination apply to Example 10–2, "Pricing Internet Service to Maximize Profit."
15. Refer to Problem 7 to answer the following:
    a. If the monopoly firm practises perfect price discrimination, the new marginal revenue column would be the same as the ________ column.
    b. Under perfect price discrimination, what rate of output would maximize profits?
    c. What would be the amount of the maximum profit under perfect price discrimination?
16. Refer to Problem 9 to answer the following. If the monopoly firm practises perfect price discrimination, what rate of output and what price would maximize profits?
17. For each of the following examples, explain how and why a monopoly would try to price discriminate:
    a. A large hotel supplies the same hotel rooms for business purposes and leisure purposes.
    b. A fast-food restaurant serves business people and retired people the same menu.
    c. A theatre shows the same movie to large families with children and to individuals and couples who have no children.

**LO 10.4 Evaluate the long-run behaviour in monopoly from a social viewpoint.**

18. Refer to Problem 9 to answer the following. Assume that the monopoly firm does not price discriminate.
    a. At the profit-maximizing output level, is the firm being productively efficient? Explain.
    b. At the profit-maximizing output level, is the firm being allocatively efficient? Explain.
    c. Explain how the profit behaviour of this monopoly firm can conflict with the goal of promoting a more equitable distribution of income.
19. What type of monopoly situation can
    a. promote productive efficiency?
    b. promote allocative efficiency?
20. Refer to Policy Example 10-4, "Swapping Songs on the Internet: Is It Really Free?" When is the practice of using the Internet to freely share files considered illegal? Who seems to be legally responsible for this practice? Explain how copyright can benefit society at large.

**LO 10.5 Compare and contrast the use of marginal cost pricing versus average cost pricing in the regulation of a natural monopoly.**

21. Unwired, Inc., has just obtained a patent on a satellite dish it invented that transmits TV programs and Internet services to homeowners. The table below describes the daily price and cost data for the satellite dishes it supplies, as a monopolist, to homeowners in the city of Digiton.

| Quantity # dishes per day | Price per dish | Daily Total Revenue | Daily Marginal Revenue | Average Total Cost (per dish) | Marginal Cost (per dish) |
|---|---|---|---|---|---|
| 1 | $500 | | ______ | $500 | ______ |
| 2 | 450 | | | 350 | $200 |
| 3 | 395 | | | 300 | 200 |
| 4 | 350 | | | 275 | 200 |
| 5 | 300 | | | 260 | 200 |
| 6 | 250 | | | 250 | 200 |
| 7 | 200 | | | 243 | 200 |

    a. Assuming that Unwired, Inc., supplies the satellite dishes to Digiton residents without any government regulation, what would be Unwired's daily maximum profit quantity level? What would be Unwired's profit-maximizing price, assuming a single price monopoly? What would be the daily maximum profit?
    b. If Unwired were forced by regulators to use marginal cost pricing, what daily quantity would Unwired supply to Digiton residents? What price would Unwired charge? What would be Unwired's daily profit (or loss) under marginal cost pricing?
    c. If Unwired were forced by regulators to use average cost pricing, what daily quantity would Unwired supply to Digiton residents? What price would Unwired charge? What would be Unwired's daily profit (or loss) under average cost pricing?
    d. From a social viewpoint, identify two reasons why average cost regulation would be preferred over unregulated monopoly.
22. The accompanying graph depicts a situation for a monopolist.

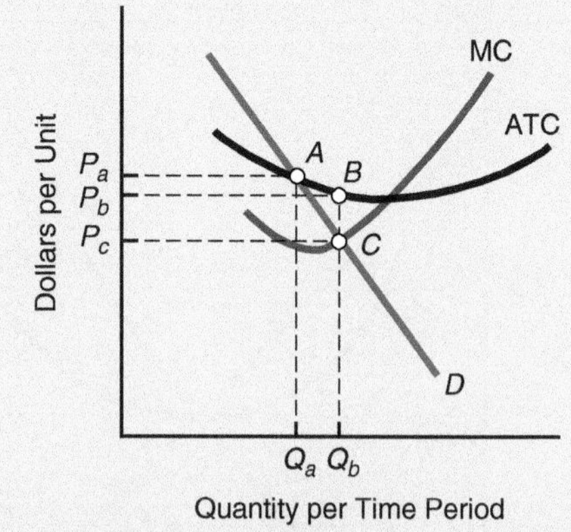


    a. Under marginal cost pricing regulation, what would be the monopolist's quantity and price?
    b. Under marginal cost pricing regulation, which rectangle in the graph would describe the firm's total losses?
    c. Under average cost pricing regulation, what would be the monopolist's quantity and price?
    d. What amount of profit (or loss) would the monopolist earn under average cost pricing?
    e. In general, does average cost pricing encourage productive efficiency? Explain.

# BUSINESS APPLICATION

**LO 10.3 and 10.5 Explain why a monopoly firm engages in price discrimination; compare and contrast the use of marginal cost pricing versus average cost pricing in the regulation of a natural monopoly.**

## Accounting: Production, Pricing, and Profit Under Different Monopoly Situations

By obtaining a patent on a new acupuncture treatment that provides long-lasting relief for back pain, Dr. Kildare has achieved a monopoly situation. The following table describes the demand and cost behaviour associated with providing this treatment. The quantity in the first column of the table refers to the number of treatments provided per day. The $300 marginal cost showing in the table refers to the extra cost of providing the first treatment of the day. Since the doctor finds each treatment physically demanding, there is a point where diminishing returns set in and thus marginal cost eventually increases.

| Quantity: # treatments per day | Price per treatment ($) | Total Revenue ($) | Marginal Revenue ($) | Average Total Cost ($) | Marginal Cost ($) |
|---|---|---|---|---|---|
| 0 | | | | | |
| 1 | 720 | | | 420 | 300 |
| 2 | 660 | | | 350 | 280 |
| 3 | 580 | | | 300 | 200 |
| 4 | 500 | | | 350 | 500 |
| 5 | 420 | | | 420 | 700 |
| 6 | 340 | | | 510 | 960 |
| 7 | 260 | | | 620 | 1280 |
| 8 | 180 | | | 750 | 1660 |

## Business Application Problems

1. Complete the Total Revenue and Marginal Revenue columns in the table.
2. Assume that the monopoly firm (Dr. Kildare) is not regulated and does not price discriminate.
   a. Find the profit-maximizing quantity level. Explain.
   b. Calculate the total dollar profit earned at the profit-maximizing level.
3. Assume that the monopoly firm practices perfect price discrimination.
   a. Determine the profit-maximizing quantity level.
   b. Calculate the total daily dollar profit at the profit-maximizing level.
4. Assume that the monopoly firm is regulated so as to receive a "fair profit."
   a. Find the "fair profit" quantity (imposed by the government). Explain.
   b. What would be the amount of economic profit earned under the "fair profit" form of regulation? Briefly explain.

# APPENDIX E

# The Deadweight Loss Due to Monopoly

We have just studied how a monopoly situation can conflict with the goal of allocative efficiency. That is, when compared with perfect competition, monopoly misallocates society's resources by restricting output. In this appendix, we examine some concepts that will allow us to estimate the total loss in economic well-being resulting from the allocative inefficiency that occurs in a monopoly industry.

## Consumer Surplus

**Consumer surplus** The difference between the maximum amount that consumers are willing to pay and the actual amount paid for all units of a product consumed.

If you think about what made you feel good about a recent purchase, it is likely that you ended up paying less than the price at which you valued the product or service. When considering a specific market situation, **consumer surplus** refers to the difference between the maximum amount that consumers are willing to pay and the actual amount paid for all units of a product consumed.

For any given market situation, the consumer surplus can be determined once the market demand curve and the market price and quantity are known. For example, Figure E–1 describes the market for frying chickens in a Canadian province. If we assume that this is a perfectly competitive market, the market price and quantity will be $5 per kilogram and 3 million kilograms, respectively.

We can compute the consumer surplus in Figure E–1, as follows. The maximum that a consumer is willing to pay for the very first unit of chicken consumed is given by the height of the demand curve at a quantity of one kilogram, which is close to $8 (note that since the scale is in millions, the very first kilogram is close to zero kilograms on the *x*-axis). Since the price actually paid for the first kilogram is $5, the consumer derives a "surplus" of $8 − $5 = $3. This $3 "surplus" is described by the vertical distance between the demand curve and the $5 price line at the quantity of one kilogram (the height of the line *AC* in Figure E–1). The consumer surplus for all 3 million kilograms of chicken consumed would be equal to the area of the triangle *ABC* in Figure E–1. Since the area of a triangle is (1/2 × base × height) the consumer surplus in this chicken market is (1/2 × 3 × $3) = $4.5 million. In general, the consumer surplus is the area of the region below the demand curve and above the price line. This surplus stems from a negatively sloped demand curve, which implies that there exists different willingness to pay for different units of the same product.

**FIGURE E–1**

**Consumer Surplus in the Chicken Market**

Given the market price of $5 per kilogram. and the market quantity of 3 million kilograms, the consumer surplus is the area of the region below the demand curve and above the price over the 3 million kilograms consumed. This is the shaded area of triangle ABC, which equals (½ × base × height), which equals (½ × 3 × 3) = $ 4.5 million.

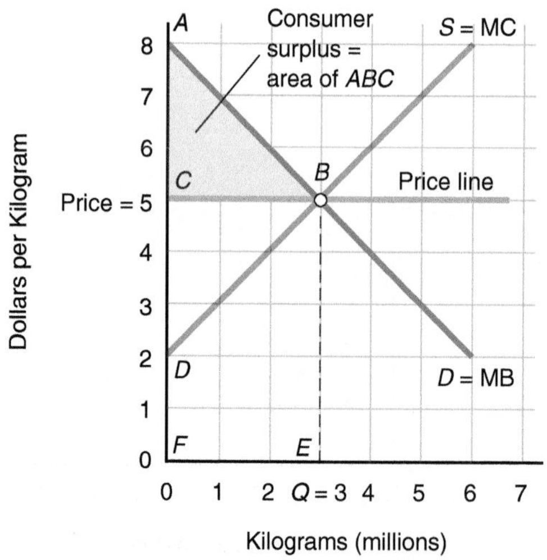

Another way of determining the consumer surplus from Figure E–1 is to subtract the total amount that consumers paid from the total consumer value derived from consuming the 3 million kilograms of chicken. The total consumer value equals the total area under the demand curve, over the 3 million kilogram quantity level, which equals the area of the region *ABEF*. The total amount paid by the consumers equals the area of region *BEFC*. The difference between the total consumer value (*ABEF*) and the total amount paid (*BEFC*) is the area of triangle ABC, which we now know is the consumer surplus.

Viewed in this way, we can see that the $4.5 million consumer surplus represents the additional consumer value or net benefit derived from consuming chicken as opposed to alternative products. In this way, we can say that consumer surplus measures the net benefit (well being) to buyers of participating in a specific market.

# Producer Surplus

We now turn to examine the well-being of producers or suppliers in a specific market. **Producer surplus** refers to the difference between the actual amount that producers receive for a product and the lowest amount that they would be prepared to accept for it, which is equal to the marginal cost.

**Producer surplus** The difference between the actual amount that producers receive for a product and the lowest amount that they would be prepared to accept for it.

For any given market situation, the producer surplus can be determined once the market supply curve and the market price and quantity are known. In the chicken market, in Figure E-2, with the market price and quantity being $5 per kilogram and 3 million kilograms, respectively, we can compute the producer surplus as follows.

In order to produce the first kilogram of chicken, a producer must receive a minimum amount equal to its marginal cost, which is $2 (the height of the supply curve at a quantity of one kilogram). Since the price actually paid to a supplier for the first kilogram is $5, the supplier derives a "surplus" of $5 − $2 = $3. This $3 "surplus" is described by the vertical distance between the supply curve and the $5 price line at the quantity of one kilogram. The producer surplus related to all 3 million kilograms of chicken produced would be equal to the area of the triangle *BCD* in Figure E–2. Since the area of a triangle is (½ × base × height), the producer surplus in this chicken market is (½ × 3 × $3) = $4.5 million. In general, the producer surplus is the area of the region above the supply curve and below the price line. This surplus stems from a positively sloped supply curve, which implies that there exists a different marginal cost for different units of the same product. The producer surplus measures the benefit (well-being) to suppliers of participating in a specific market.

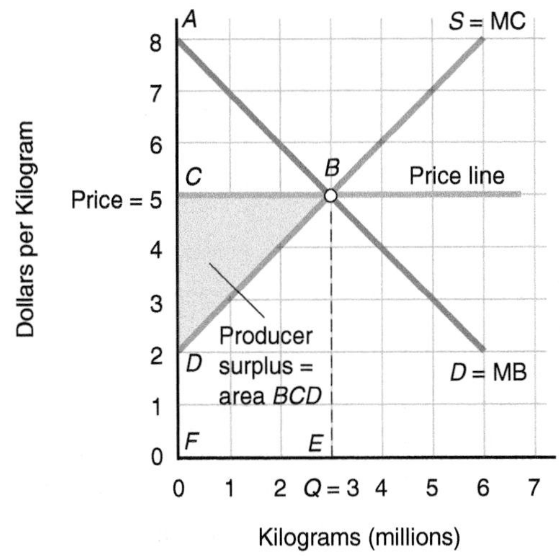


**FIGURE E–2**

**Producer Surplus in the Chicken Market**

Given the market price of $5 per kilogram, and the market quantity of 3 million kilograms, the producer surplus is the area of the region above the supply curve and below the price over the 3 million kilograms produced. This is the shaded area of triangle *BCD*, which equals (1/2 × base × height), which equals (1/2 × 3 × 3) = $ 4.5 million.

# Allocative Efficiency and Perfect Competition

As was noted in Chapter 9, perfect competition establishes an equilibrium price and quantity where industry demand equals industry supply. This means that perfect competition promotes *allocative efficiency* as production takes place to the point where the marginal benefit of the last unit produced equals its marginal cost. At this allocatively efficient quantity, it can be shown that the sum of consumer and producer surpluses is maximized.

**Allocative efficiency occurs when the sum of consumer and producer surpluses is maximized.**

Figure E–3 describes a perfectly competitive chicken market, where the equilibrium price is \$5 ($P_{pc}$) and the equilibrium quantity is 3 million ($Q_{pc}$). At this equilibrium, the sum of consumer and producer surplus is maximized at (\$4.5 million + \$4.5 million) = \$9 million. Try as you might, you will not find a better quantity, in terms of maximizing consumer and producer surpluses. As you can see from Figure E–3, if the quantity is set at a level below 3 million kilograms, say, at 2 million kilograms, consumer surplus and producer surplus will be reduced by areas *M* and *N*, respectively. Similarly, if production is increased beyond 3 million kilograms, say, to 4 million, consumer and producer surpluses will be reduced by areas *S* and *R*, respectively.

# Allocative Inefficiency and Monopoly

Suppose that all of the chicken producers in the province decide to form a marketing board that establishes a monopoly in terms of the sale of chicken. While marginal costs (the supply curve) stay the same, the monopoly's marginal revenue now lies below the demand curve, as shown in Figure E–4. In order to maximize profits, the chicken monopoly produces where marginal revenue equals marginal cost, which is at a quantity level of 2 million kilograms ($Q_m$) and at a price of \$6 per kilogram (*Pm*). Note that the monopoly quantity level is 1 million kilograms less than in perfect competition, and the monopoly price is \$1 higher than the competitive price.

**FIGURE E–3**

**Perfect Competition and Allocative Efficiency**

In this perfectly competitive chicken industry, the equilibrium price is $P_{pc}$ = \$5 and the equilibrium quantity = $Q_{pc}$ = 3 million kilograms. At this quantity, the sum of consumer and producer surpluses is maximized, which implies allocative efficiency. If the quantity is reduced to 2 million kilograms, consumer surplus and producer surpluses will be reduced by areas *M* and *N*, respectively. If production is increased to 4 million kilograms, consumer and producer surplus will be reduced by areas *S* and *R*, respectively.

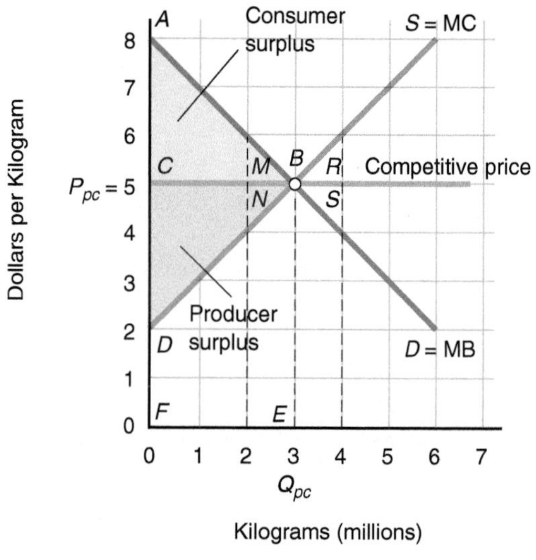


The allocative efficiency loss due to monopoly is the loss in consumer and producer surpluses due to the reduction in quantity from 3 million to 2 million kilograms. The consumer surplus lost due to this reduction in quantity is the area of the triangle *M*, which equals ½ × 1 × 1 = \$0.5 million. Similarly, the loss in producer surplus due to the

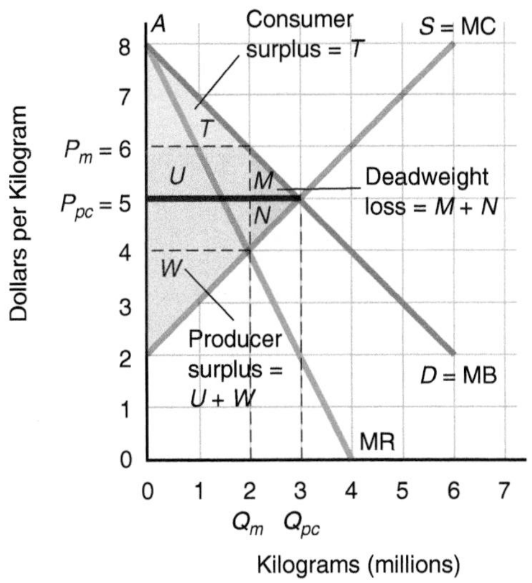


**FIGURE E–4**

**Monopoly and Allocative Inefficiency**

When the chicken industry is monopolized, the quantity drops from 3 million to 2 million kilograms and the price increases from \$5 to \$6 per kilogram. The reduction in quantity causes a reduction in consumer and producer surplus equal to the area of regions *M* and *N* combined, which equals ($\frac{1}{2} \times 2 \times 1$) = \$1 million. This is the deadweight loss due to allocative inefficiency in monopoly. The increase in price, under monopoly, results in a transfer in surplus from consumers to producers equal to the area of rectangle *U*, which equals \$2 million.

reduction in quantity is the area of the triangle *N*, which equals $\frac{1}{2} \times 1 \times 1 = \$0.5$ million. The allocative efficiency loss resulting from this monopoly equals the combined loss in consumer and producer surplus, which equals \$0.5 + \$0.5 = \$1 million (area of regions *M* and *N*). We call this loss the **deadweight loss**—the combined loss in producer and consumer surplus resulting from the reduction in quantity under monopoly. The deadweight loss of \$1 million is not recouped elsewhere in the economy, and so it is a loss to society as a whole.

**Deadweight loss** The combined loss in producer and consumer surplus resulting from the reduction in quantity under monopoly.

If you carefully examine Figure E–4, you will notice that under monopoly there is a loss in consumer surplus, in addition to the area of region *M*. The additional loss in consumer surplus is the area of rectangle *U*, which equals (height × length) = $1 \times 2 = \$2$ million. This \$2 million loss is due to the higher price charged, which translates to a \$2 million gain for the monopolist in the form of additional producer surplus. Note that this \$2 million loss in consumer surplus is not a deadweight loss, as it is recouped by another group in the economy—the chicken producers.

## APPENDIX SUMMARY

1. Consumer surplus refers to the difference between the maximum amount that consumers are willing to pay and the actual amount paid for all units of a product consumed. It is described as the area under the demand curve and above the price line over the quantity of the product consumed. It exists due to a negatively sloped demand curve, which reflects the differences in willingness to pay for different units of the same product. Consumer surplus refers to the net benefit that consumers get in participating in a market—a benefit that they do not pay for.
2. Producer surplus refers to the difference between the actual amount that producers receive for a product and the lowest amount that they would be prepared to accept for it. It is described as the area over the supply curve and below the price line over the quantity of the product produced. It exists due to a positively sloped supply curve, which reflects the differences in marginal cost incurred when producing different units of the same product. Producer surplus refers to the net benefit that suppliers get in participating in a market—a benefit that they do not pay for.
3. A perfectly competitive industry is allocatively efficient as it sets a price and quantity that maximizes the sum of consumer and producer surplus.
4. A monopoly industry restricts quantity and charges a higher price, when compared with perfect competition. The deadweight loss refers to the loss in producer and consumer surplus resulting from the reduction in quantity supplied, under monopoly. This deadweight loss is used to measure the cost of allocative inefficiency in monopoly.
5. The higher price in monopoly causes a transfer in surplus from consumers to producers.

# APPENDIX PROBLEMS

E-1. Refer to the data in Figure 10–4 in Chapter 10 on page 252. Assume that the monopoly firm in Figure 10–4 operates at the profit-maximizing output level, and charges a single price for all units sold.

a. Compute the total consumer surplus.

b. Compute the total producer surplus.

c. Is this monopoly firm maximizing the sum of producer and consumer surpluses? Explain.

E-2. What happens to the consumer surplus in a market where a monopoly firm practises perfect price discrimination? Explain.

E-3. The following diagram describes the whole-wheat bagel market in a mid-size Canadian city.

a. If the whole-wheat bagels are supplied under perfect competition, compute the sum of the consumer and producer surpluses.

b. If the whole-wheat bagels are supplied under monopoly, compute the total dollar loss due to allocative inefficiency.

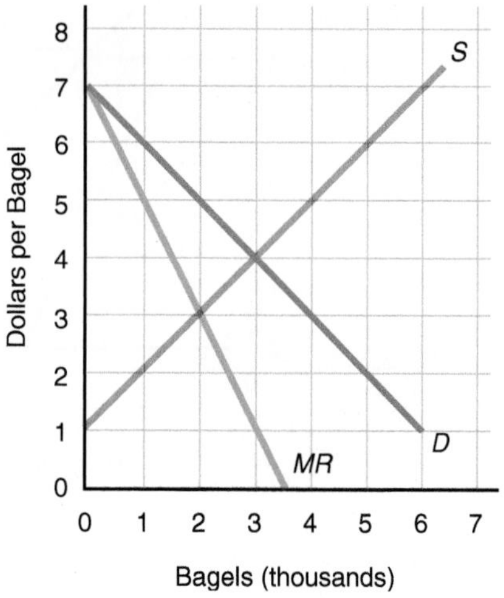

11

# Monopolistic Competition and Oligopoly

For most of this century, two firms have dominated the Canadian market for beer—John Labatt Ltd. and Molson Brewing Co. Ltd. Labatt, Canada's largest brewer, contributed to 28 percent of all Canadian beer sales in 2016. The two companies combined accounted for 53 percent of national beer sales. Labatt Blue is the best-selling Canadian beer in the world. Over the past two decades, the big two breweries have increasingly been challenged by imported beers, and by the entry of small microbreweries offering high-quality "craft" beers. Labatt and Molson appear to have decided not to fight the entry of these competitors. To understand this strategic behaviour, you need to learn more about markets that are not perfectly competitive but, at the same time, are not pure monopolies.

myeconlab

MyEconLab helps you master each objective and study more efficiently. See end of chapter for details.

## LEARNING OBJECTIVES

After reading this chapter, you should be able to:

**11.1** Identify and explain the characteristics of monopolistic competition.

**11.2** Using revenue and cost information, determine the price, output, and profit for a firm in monopolistic competition in the short run.

**11.3** Describe long-run equilibrium in monopolistic competition.

**11.4** Identify and explain the characteristics of oligopoly.

**11.5** Identify and explain the types of pricing behaviour that can occur in oligopoly.

**11.6** Identify, explain, and evaluate the various nonprice forms of competition in oligopoly.

**11.7** Evaluate the behaviour in oligopoly from a social viewpoint.

# DID YOU KNOW THAT...?

The so-called father of the modern department store, John Wanamaker, once said, "Half the money I spend on advertising is wasted. The trouble is, I don't know which half." Obviously, Canadian businesses do not know either, for they continue to advertise more each year. Total annual advertising expenditures in Canada amount to billions of dollars. The number of ads popping up on the Internet shows that Canadian businesses will leave no stone unturned in their quest to let people know about their existence, what they have to sell, how they sell it, where it can be bought, and at what price.

Advertising did not show up in our analysis of perfect competition and monopoly. Nonetheless, it plays a large role in industries that lie somewhere between these two extreme types of market structures. A combination of consumers' preferences for variety and competition among producers has led to similar but differentiated products in the marketplace. This situation has been described as monopolistic competition, the subject of the first part of this chapter. In the second part of the chapter, we look at how firms in industries with a few major competitors make strategic decisions. Such decisions do not exist for pure monopolists, who do not have to worry about actual competitors. And clearly, perfect competitors cannot make any strategic decisions, for they must take the market price as given. We call firms that have the ability to make strategic decisions oligopolies, which we will define more formally later in this chapter.

## 11.1 The Characteristics of Monopolistic Competition

In the 1920s and 1930s, economists became increasingly aware that there were many industries for which both the perfectly competitive model and the pure monopoly model did not apply and did not seem to yield very accurate predictions. Theoretical and empirical research was instituted to develop some sort of middle ground. Two separately developed models of *monopolistic competition* resulted. American economist Edward Chamberlin published *The Theory of Monopolistic Competition* in 1933. The same year, Britain's Joan Robinson published *The Economics of Imperfect Competition*. In this chapter, we will outline the theory as presented by Chamberlin.

**Monopolistic competition** A market structure in which there is a relatively large number of firms offering similar but differentiated products.

Chamberlin defined **monopolistic competition** as a market structure in which there is a relatively large number of firms offering similar but differentiated products. Monopolistic competition, therefore, has the following features:

1. Large numbers of sellers in a highly competitive market
2. Easy entry of new firms in the long run
3. Product differentiation

Even a cursory look at the Canadian economy leads to the conclusion that monopolistic competition is the dominant form of market structure in Canada. Indeed, that is true of all developed economies.

### Number of Firms

In a perfectly competitive situation, there is an extremely large number of firms; in pure monopoly, there is only one. In monopolistic competition, there is a large number of firms, but not as many as in perfect competition. This fact has several important implications for a monopolistically competitive industry.

1. *Small share of market.* With so many firms, each firm has a relatively small share of the total market. Thus, it has only a very small amount of control over the market clearing price.
2. *Lack of collusion.* With so many firms, it is very difficult for all of them to get together to collude—to cooperate in setting a pure monopoly price (and output). Price fixing in a monopolistically competitive industry is virtually impossible. Also, barriers to entry are minor, and the flow of new firms into the industry makes collusive agreements less likely. The large number of firms makes the monitoring and detection of cheating very costly and extremely difficult. This difficulty is compounded by differentiated products and high rates of innovation; collusive agreements are easier for a homogeneous product than for heterogeneous ones.

3. *Independence.* Because there are so many firms, each one acts independently of the others. No firm attempts to take into account the reaction of all of its rival firms—that would be impossible with so many rivals. Rivals' reactions to output and price changes are largely ignored.

## Easy Entry

For any current monopolistic competitor, potential competitors are always lurking in the background. Substantial barriers to entry, such as economies of scale, patents, and large initial capital costs, do not exist in monopolistic competition.

## Product Differentiation

Perhaps the most important feature of monopolistic competition is **product differentiation,** which refers to the ways that the firm distinguishes its product, in a positive manner, from similar products or services offered by competitors. The firm's product can be positively distinguished by consumers on the basis of its physical attributes; the bundle of services offered with the product; the product's superior location or accessibility; sales promotion and advertising; and by other qualities associated with the product, real or imagined.

**Product differentiation** The ways that the firm distinguishes its product, in a positive manner, from similar products or services offered by competitors.

Product differentiation means that the firm has some control over the price it charges. Unlike the perfectly competitive firm, the monopolistic competitive firm faces a downward-sloping demand curve, as shown in Figure 11–1. This means that the monopolistically competitive firm can increase the price of its product and still manage to attract loyal customers, due to product differentiation. For example, suppose that the typical daily rate charged to stay in a motel in a Canadian city is $75. One motel owner may decide to charge $100 per day. While this firm may end up renting fewer rooms per day than its competitors, some customers will still stay at this motel due to the motel's superior fitness facilities, convenient parking, and central location.

The elasticity of the monopolistically competitive firm's demand curve will depend on the degree to which the firm can positively differentiate its product in the eyes of the consumers in the industry. If the firm is very successful in establishing customer loyalty based on nonprice factors, then the firm's demand curve will be less elastic. Keep in mind, however, that the demand curve of the monopolistically competitive firm will still be relatively elastic compared with a monopoly situation, due to the presence of close substitutes.

A good example of a monopolistically competitive industry is the restaurant industry (excluding fast-food restaurants) in a Canadian city. Many small firms compete in the restaurant industry. Since the initial capital investment is not significant, it is relatively easy to enter this type of industry. Product differentiation in the restaurant industry can be established in a variety of ways. Any firm may choose to establish customer loyalty on the basis of the ethnic origin of the menu offerings, the superior service offered to patrons, the consistency of the quality of the meal established, the ease of parking at a convenient location, and the type of clientele attracted by the firm's advertising and brand image.

Monopolistically competitive industries are commonly found in the following sectors of the economy: retail apparel and gifts, personal services, entertainment and amusements, and hospitality. Example 11–1 describes a popular Canadian retail firm operating under conditions of monopolistic competition.

### EXAMPLE 11–1 A Canadian Retail Success: Thirty Years Running

Did you know that John Stanton, the founder of our nation's renowned Running Room Canada Inc., used to be an overweight food industry executive who smoked two packs of cigarettes a day? After struggling through a 3-kilometre fun run with his sons in 1981, Stanton realized that he had to change his lifestyle. He started to run secretly before dawn so his neighbours did not notice just how out of shape he was. Recognizing the need to sell quality running shoes by staff knowledgeable about running, in 1984 Stanton opened a store and meeting place for runners in an old house in Edmonton. Initially, he shared this location with a hairdresser shop.

*continued*

What types of product differentiation is The Running Room focusing on?

As of March 2015, the Running Room operated 120 stores in Canada and the U.S. The family-owned company is reported to be the largest specialty running and walking products business in Canada.

In the Montreal area, the Yellow Pages list hundreds of separately owned stores selling retail footwear and related products and services. Some of these stores are small, independent retailers that target a specific market niche, such as work-related footwear, children's shoes, golf shoes, western footwear, and shoes for customers with specific foot problems. Others are focused on providing footwear at a discounted price, such as Payless Shoes and Shoe Warehouse. Yet others are in the form of shoe departments in conveniently located department stores that offer brand name shoes at regular as well as discounted prices. Sporting goods stores have also become popular sellers of all sorts of sport-related footwear.

Running Room has successfully focused on providing high-quality products and services for customers who want a healthy and fit lifestyle that includes running and walking routines. Based on knowledgeable staff, all of whom are runners and fitness walkers, Running Room provides top brand-name footwear that meets the individual needs of customers in terms of gender, level of running/walking experience, and foot strike. To complement its products, the company offers a variety of services, which include clinics in Fitness Walking, Learn to Run, Marathon,

*continued*

**FIGURE 11–1**

## Short-Run and Long-Run Equilibrium with Monopolistic Competition

In part (a), the typical monopolistic competitor is shown making economic profits. If that were the situation, there would be entry into the industry, forcing the demand curve for the individual firm to decrease and shift leftward. Eventually, firms would find themselves in the situation depicted in part (c), where zero economic profits are being made. In part (b), the typical firm is in a monopolistically competitive industry making economic losses. If that were the case, firms would leave the industry. Each remaining firm's demand curve would shift outward to the right. Eventually, the typical firm would find itself in the situation depicted in part (c).

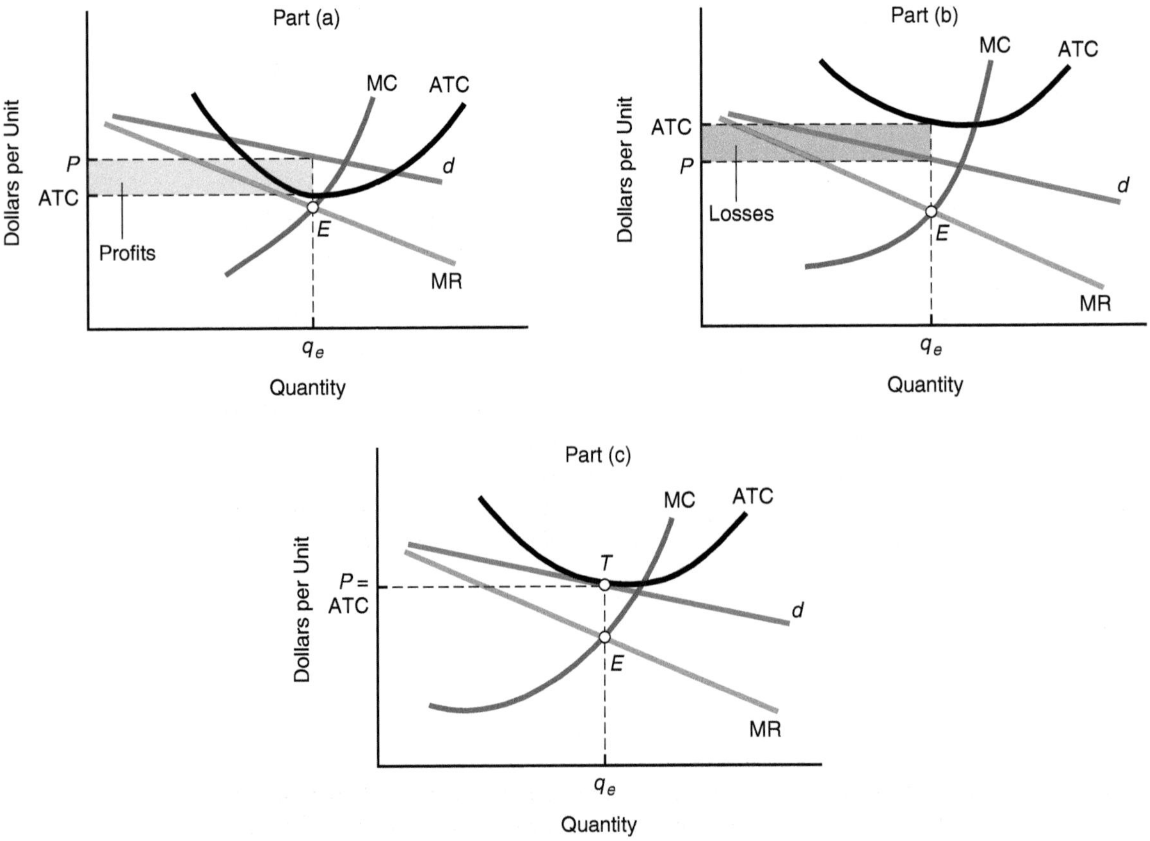

Half Marathon, 10K Training, Personal Best, and For Women Only Running, and a free Running Room Club, which encourages runners of all levels to run in a group twice weekly. Each year, the Running Room sponsors, organizes, and promotes numerous walks, runs, and charity events.

**For critical analysis:** Based on this example, would the Canadian retail footwear industry be classified as perfect competition or monopolistic competition? Explain.

Sources: "Running Room opens eighth store in Quebec." The Gazette (Montreal). May 6, 2010. Pg. B3; "Our history." Running Room. http://www.runningroom.com. Government of Canada. Company Profile. http://www.ic.gc.ca/app/ccc/srch/nvgt.do;jsessionid=0001U7FtCcl7RJpL3X-hq4Ljhlc:-44DMJN?lang=eng&prtl=1&sbPrtl=&estblmntNo=123456227465&profile=cmpltPrfl&profileId=1921&app=sold&searchNav=F. (Accessed February 13, 2017).

# 11.2 Short-Run Price, Output, and Profit in Monopolistic Competition

Now that we are aware of the assumptions underlying the monopolistic competition model, we can analyze the price and output behaviour of each firm in a monopolistically competitive industry. We assume in the analysis that follows that the desired product type and quality have been chosen. We further assume that the budget and the type of promotional activity have already been chosen and do not change.

## The Individual Firm's Demand and Cost Curves

Because the individual firm is not a perfect competitor, its demand curve slopes downward, as is shown in all three parts of Figure 11–1. Hence, it faces a marginal revenue curve that is also downward sloping and below the demand curve. To find the profit-maximizing rate of output and the profit-maximizing price, we go to the output where the marginal cost curve intersects the marginal revenue curve from below. That gives us the profit-maximizing output rate. Then, we draw a vertical line up to the demand curve. That gives us the price that can be charged to sell exactly that quantity produced. This is what we have done in Figure 11–1. In each part, a marginal cost curve intersects the marginal revenue curve at *E*. The profit-maximizing rate of output is $q_e$, and the profit-maximizing price is *P*.

## Short-Run Equilibrium

In the short run, it is possible for a monopolistic competitor to make economic profits—profits over and above the normal rate of return or beyond what is necessary to keep that firm in that industry. We show such a situation in part (a) of Figure 11–1. The average total cost curve is drawn in below the demand curve, *d*, at the profit-maximizing rate of output, $q_e$. Economic profits are shown by the shaded rectangle in that part.

Losses in the short run are clearly also possible. They are presented in part (b) of Figure 11–1. Here, the average total cost curve lies everywhere above the individual firm's demand curve, *d*. The losses are marked as the shaded rectangle.

Just as with any market structure or any firm, in the short run, it is possible to observe either economic profits or economic losses. In either case, the price does not equal marginal cost but, rather, is above it. Therefore, there is some misallocation of resources, a topic that we will discuss later in this chapter.

# 11.3 Long-Run Equilibrium in Monopolistic Competition

What can we expect of the typical firm in monopolistic competition in the long run? Economic profits will be reduced to zero—either through the entry of new firms that see a chance to make a higher rate of return than elsewhere, or by changes in the product quality and advertising outlays of existing firms in the industry. (Profitable products will be imitated by other firms.) As for economic losses in the short run, they will disappear in the long run because the firms that suffer them will leave the industry. They will go into another business where the expected rate of return is at least normal. Parts (a) and (b) of Figure 11–1, therefore, represent only short-run situations for a monopolistically competitive firm. In the long run, the average total cost curve will just touch the individual firm's demand curve *d* at the particular price that is profit-maximizing for that particular firm. This is shown in part (c) of Figure 11–1. This situation is called long-run equilibrium in monopolistic competition.

A word of warning: This is an idealized, long-run equilibrium situation for each firm in the industry. It does not mean that even in the long run we will observe every single firm in a monopolistically competitive industry making exactly zero economic profits or just a normal rate of return. We live in a dynamic world. All we are saying is that if this model is correct, the rate of return will tend toward normal—economic profits will tend toward zero.

## Comparing Monopolistic Competition with Perfect Competition

In the long run, there are similarities and differences between perfect competition and monopolistic competition.

**LONG-RUN PROFITS?** Due to easy entry, the typical firm operating in either perfect competition or monopolistic competition can expect to earn zero economic profit or just a normal profit. In Figure 11–2, we can see that at the profit-maximizing output level for both perfect competition and monopolistic competition, price equals average total cost. Some economists would view these normal profits as being consistent with the goal of an equitable distribution of income.

**FIGURE 11–2**

**Comparison of the Perfect Competitor with the Monopolistic Competitor**

In part (a), the perfectly competitive firm has zero economic profits in the long run. The price is set equal to marginal cost, and the price is $P_1$. The firm's demand curve is just tangent to the minimum point on its average total cost curve, which means that the firm is operating at an optimum rate of production. With the monopolistically competitive firm in part (b), there are also zero economic profits in the long run. The price is greater than marginal cost; the monopolistically competitive firm does not find itself at the minimum point on its average total cost curve. It is operating at a rate of output to the left of the minimum point on the ATC curve.

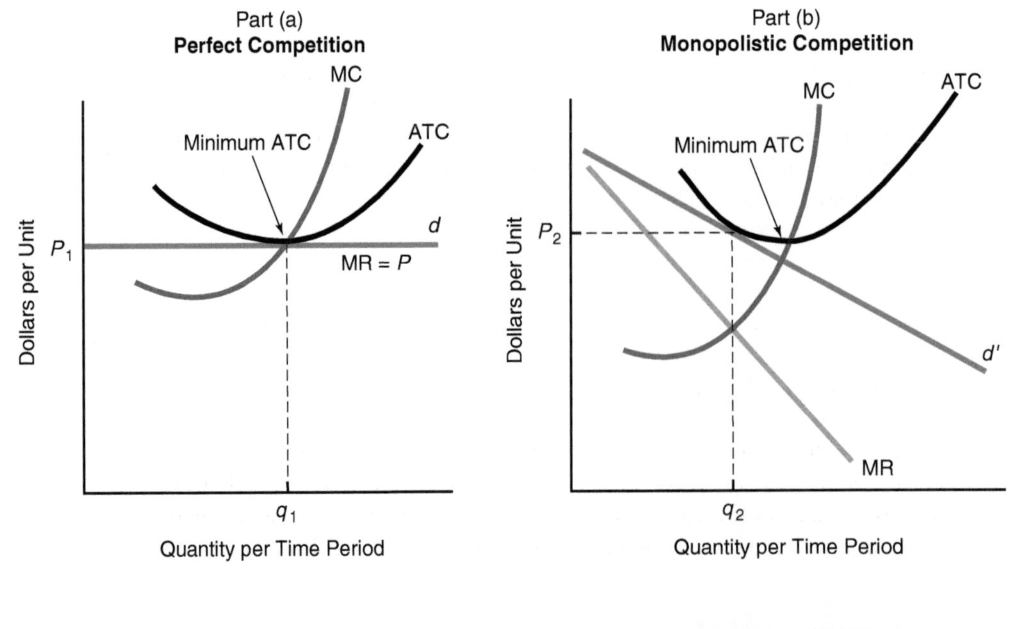

**PRODUCTIVE EFFICIENCY?** Figure 11–2 part (a) reminds us that, at the profit-maximizing level of output, $q_1$, the typical perfectly competitive firm operates at minimum average total cost. That is, productive efficiency is being achieved in perfect competition, assuming the absence of economies of scale.

An examination of Figure 11–2 part (b) shows that at the profit-maximizing output level, $q_2$, the monopolistically competitive firm is operating at a quantity level that is less than the productively efficient level. Figure 11–2 part (b) should help you understand that because the demand curve is downward sloping in monopolistic competition, the long-run normal profit situation must occur to the left of the quantity where average total cost is at a minimum. This situation is one of **excess capacity**—a situation where the firm is operating at an output level below that required to achieve minimum average total cost. Such characteristics as easy entry and product differentiation result in a long-run situation where there are too many competitors, each saddled with excess capacity. As an example, the typical motel will have vacancy signs at frequent times of the year or the typical restaurant will have empty tables during many hours of each day. In other words, society's limited resources are being wasted!

**Excess capacity** A situation where the firm is operating at an output level below that required to achieve minimum average total cost.

**CONSUMER CHOICE?** Chamberlin contended that the higher average total cost typical in monopolistic competition, when compared with the perfectly competitive firm, represents what he called the cost of producing "differentness." Chamberlin argued that it is rational for consumers to be willing to pay more for a product in an industry that offers a variety of close, but not identical, substitutes. Put differently, a range of consumer choices adds value to consumers.

# 11.4 The Characteristics of Oligopoly

There is another important market structure that we have yet to discuss. It involves a situation in which a few large firms dominate an entire industry. They are not competitive in the sense that we have used the term; they are not even monopolistically competitive. And because there are a few of them, a pure monopoly does not exist. We call such a situation an **oligopoly**, which consists of a small number of interdependent sellers. Each firm in the industry knows that other firms will react to its changes in prices, quantities, and qualities. An oligopoly market structure can exist for either a homogeneous or a differentiated product.

**Oligopoly** A market situation that consists of a small number of interdependent sellers.

## Small Number of Firms

How many is "a small number of firms"? More than two but less than 100? The question is not easy to answer. Basically, though, oligopoly exists when a handful of firms dominate the industry enough to set prices. The top few firms in the industry account for an overwhelming percentage of total industry output.

Oligopolies usually involve three to five big companies dominating the industry. The Canadian banking industry is dominated by five large firms: the Royal Bank of Canada (RBC), TD Canada Trust, the Canadian Imperial Bank of Commerce (CIBC), the Bank of Montreal (BMO), and the Bank of Nova Scotia (Scotiabank). From World War II until the 1970s, the automobile industry was dominated by three large firms: General Motors (GM), Chrysler, and Ford.

## Interdependence

All markets and all firms are, in a sense, interdependent. When a few large firms dominate an industry, they become strategically dependent on each others' actions. **Strategic dependence** is a situation in which one firm's actions with respect to price, quality, advertising, and related changes may be strategically countered by the reactions of one or more other firms in the industry. Such dependence can exist only when there are a limited number of major firms in an industry. The firms must recognize that they are interdependent. Any action on the part of one firm with respect to output, price, quality, or product differentiation will cause a reaction on the part of other firms. A model

**Strategic dependence** A situation in which one firm's actions with respect to price, quality, advertising, and related changes may be strategically countered by the reactions of one or more other firms in the industry.

of such mutual interdependence is difficult to build, but examples are not hard to find in the real world. Oligopolists in the supermarket industry, for example, are constantly reacting to each other.

Recall that in the model of perfect competition, each firm ignores the reactions of other firms because each is able to sell all that it wants at the going market price. At the other extreme, the pure monopolist does not have to worry about the reaction of current rivals because there are none. In an oligopolistic market structure, the managers of firms are like generals in a war: They must attempt to predict the reaction of rival firms. It is a strategic game.

## Barriers to Entry

Why are some industries dominated by a few large firms? Since new businesses are formed on a daily basis, some type of barrier to entry must be preventing these new firms from entering oligopoly industries.

**ECONOMIES OF SCALE.** In some industries, economies of scale prevent the entry of new firms. Recall that, when economies of scale exist, the firm's long-run average total cost declines as the firm increases its size of operation. Consequently, larger firms have a cost advantage over smaller firms. Given a limited total market demand, this cost disadvantage may prevent smaller new firms from entering the industry. Due to the high fixed costs related to acquiring and maintaining airplanes, as well as expensive reservation systems, economies of scale have been a factor in explaining why we have oligopoly (and, in some cases, monopoly) situations in the provision of domestic flights to Canadian cities.

**LEGAL BARRIERS.** Legal barriers to entry such as patents and government regulation may explain why a few firms dominate a market. In Canada, many new prescription drugs are protected by patents. In these cases, the company owning the patent may permit other competitors to sell similar substitutes of the new drug in return for payment of royalties, resulting in an oligopoly situation. The Canadian Radio-television and Telecommunications Commission (CRTC) is the regulatory agency of the federal government, in charge of licensing certain industries, including television and radio broadcasting, cable distribution, and Direct-to-Home. For many years, the commission's licensing practices have helped maintain oligopolies in such industries as cable TV distribution and national television network broadcasting.

**FIRM-CREATED BARRIERS.** The existing firms in an oligopoly industry frequently engage in behaviours that serve as barriers to entry for potential new firms. In some cases, existing oligopoly firms significantly lower the prices of their products, which makes it difficult for potential firms to earn a profit if they decide to enter the industry. Many oligopoly firms engage heavily in product differentiation, advertising, and brand proliferation, making it very costly for new entrants to gain a foothold in the market. In yet other oligopoly situations, the existing firms may practise exclusionary tactics that make it difficult for consumers to switch to the products that new firms offer. These firm-created barriers to entry will be discussed in more depth in later sections of this chapter.

Primarily, we have been talking about oligopoly in theoretical terms. It is time to look at the actual picture of oligopolies in Canada.

## Measuring Industry Concentration

As we have stated, oligopoly is a situation where a few interdependent firms control a large part of the total output in an industry. In an attempt to identify the prevalence of oligopoly in Canadian industries, economists compute the **concentration ratio**—the percentage of total industry sales contributed by the four largest firms—for each industry.

**Concentration ratio** The percentage of total industry sales contributed by the four largest firms.

Table 11–1 provides four-firm domestic concentration ratios for selected Canadian industries. In this table, you will notice that the concentration ratio for the beer industry is 90 percent. This means that the four largest Canadian breweries account for 90 percent of all annual Canadian beer sales. When an industry has a high concentration ratio, we refer to this industry as a highly concentrated industry.

**TABLE 11–1**

**Four-Firm Domestic Concentration Ratios for Selected Canadian Industries**

| | Percentage of Value of Total Domestic Shipments Accounted for by the Top Four Firms |
|---|---|
| Tobacco products | 99 |
| Beer | 90 |
| Petroleum and coal products | 75 |
| Storage | 72 |
| Nonalcoholic beverages | 69 |
| Transportation equipment | 68 |
| Communications | 65 |
| Primary metals | 63 |
| Metal mining | 59 |

Source: Adapted from Statistics Canada.

In general, for a given industry, the higher the level of concentration, the lower the level of industry competition. However, one must realize in computing concentration ratios that competing firms are identified assuming national market boundaries. In some cases, this may not accurately reflect the true state of competition in an industry. As an example, for a number of years the "Big Three" North American automakers—GM, Chrysler, and Ford—were the dominant firms actually manufacturing vehicles on Canadian soil. This situation would result in a relatively high domestic concentration ratio, suggesting a high level of concentration and a very low level of competition in the Canadian auto industry. However, to the extent that Canadian consumers were purchasing cars produced in other countries, then the industry definition used to compute the concentration ratio is inaccurate. In fact, if we expand the size of the industry to include foreign automakers, the level of concentration would be reduced.

What industries in Canada are oligopolistic in nature? If we recognize that some industries are local in nature while others can be defined at the national or international level, we can identify quite a few oligopoly industries. Some examples include motor vehicles, petroleum-refining products, tobacco products, beer products, soft drinks, pet foods, cereals, airline services, banking services, long-distance service, TV distribution services, credit card services, car rentals in airports, daily newspapers in a city, cement manufacturers in a city, and computer manufacturers.

# 11.5 Price Behaviour in Oligopoly

At this point, we should be able to show oligopoly price and output determination in the way we showed it for perfect competition, pure monopoly, and monopolistic competition, but we cannot. Whenever there are relatively few firms competing in an industry, each can and does react to the price, quantity, quality, and product innovations that the others undertake. The manner in which each firm reacts to its rival is called the oligopolist's **best response function.** Oligopolistic competitors are interdependent. Consequently, the decision makers in such firms must employ strategies. And we must be able to model their strategic behaviour if we wish to predict how prices and outputs are determined in oligopolistic market structures. In general, we can think of the reactions of other firms to one firm's actions as part of a game that is played by all firms in the industry. Not surprisingly, economists have developed *game theory* models to describe firms' rational interactions. **Game theory** is the analytical framework in which two or more individuals, companies, or nations compete for certain payoffs that depend on the strategy that the others employ.

**Best response function** The manner in which one oligopolist reacts to a change in price, output, or quality made by another competitor in the industry.

**Game theory** The analytical framework in which two or more individuals, companies, or nations compete for certain payoffs that depend on the strategy that the others employ.

## Some Basic Notions about Game Theory

Games can be either cooperative or noncooperative. If firms get together to collude or fix prices, that is considered a **cooperative game.** Whenever it is too costly for firms to negotiate such collusive agreements and to enforce them, they are in a **noncooperative game** situation. Most strategic behaviour in the marketplace would be described as a noncooperative game.

**Cooperative game** A game in which firms get together to collude or fix prices.

**Noncooperative game** A game in which it is too costly for firms to negotiate collusive agreements and to enforce them.

**Zero-sum game** A game in which one player's losses are offset by another player's gains; at any time, sum totals are zero.

**Negative-sum game** A game in which players as a group lose at the end of the game.

**Positive-sum game** A game in which players as a group end up better off.

Games can be classified by whether the payoffs are negative, zero, or positive. A **zero-sum game** is one in which one player's losses are offset by another player's gains; at any time, sum totals are zero. If two retailers have an absolutely fixed total number of customers, the customers that one retailer wins over are exactly equal to the customers that the other retailer loses. A **negative-sum game** is one in which players as a group lose at the end of the game (although one perhaps by more than the other, and it's possible for one or more players to win). A **positive-sum game** is one in which players as a group end up better off. Some economists describe all voluntary exchanges as positive-sum games. After an exchange, both the buyer and the seller are better off than they were prior to the exchange.

## Noncooperative Price Behaviour

**Strategy** A rule used to make a choice.

**Dominant strategies** Strategies that are generally successful no matter what actions competitors take.

Because oligopoly firms are mutually interdependent, each competitor (decision maker) has to devise a **strategy**, which is defined as a rule used to make a choice. The goal of the decision maker is, of course, to devise a strategy that is more successful than alternative strategies. Whenever a firm's decision makers can come up with certain strategies that are generally successful no matter what actions competitors take, these are called **dominant strategies.** The dominant strategy always yields the unique best action for the decision maker no matter what action the other "players" undertake. To better understand a noncooperative game and the notion of a dominant strategy, consider Example 11–2, "The Prisoners' Dilemma."

### EXAMPLE 11–2 The Prisoners' Dilemma

One real-world example of simple game theory involves what happens when two people, both involved in a bank robbery, are later caught. What should they do when questioned by police? The result has been called the prisoners' dilemma. The two suspects, Sam and Carol, are interrogated separately and confronted with alternative potential periods of imprisonment. The interrogator indirectly indicates to Sam and Carol the following:

1. If both confess to the bank robbery, they will both go to jail for five years.
2. If neither confesses, they will each be given a sentence of two years on a lesser charge.
3. If one prisoner confesses, that prisoner goes free and the other one, who did not confess, will serve 10 years on bank robbery charges.

**Payoff matrix** A matrix of outcomes, or consequences, of the strategies available to the players in a game.

You can see the prisoners' alternatives in the **payoff matrix**—a matrix of outcomes, or consequences, of the strategies available to the players in a game—in Figure 11–3.

The two options for each prisoner are "confess" and "don't confess." There are four possibilities:

**FIGURE 11–3**

**The Prisoners' Dilemma Payoff Matrix**

Regardless of what the other prisoner does, each person is better off if he or she confesses. So, confessing is the dominant strategy and each ends up behind bars for five years.

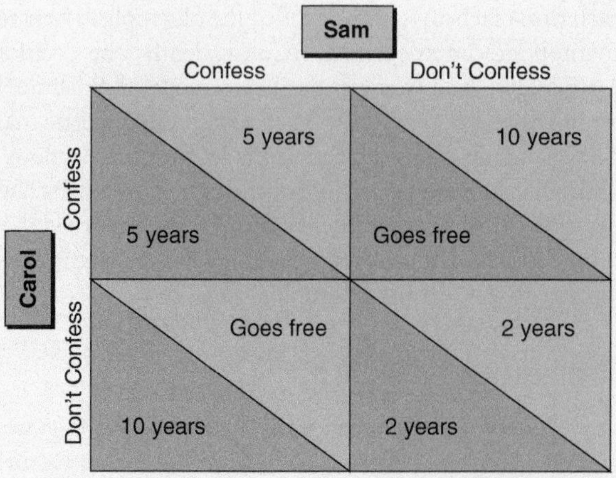


*continued*

1. Both confess.
2. Neither confesses.
3. Sam confesses, but Carol does not.
4. Carol confesses, but Sam does not.

In Figure 11–3, all of Sam's possible outcomes are shown on the upper half of each rectangle, and all of Carol's possible outcomes are shown on the lower half.

By looking at the payoff matrix, you can see that if Carol confesses, Sam's best strategy is to confess also—he will get only five years instead of 10. Conversely, if Sam confesses, Carol's best strategy is also to confess—she will get five years instead of 10. Now let us say that Sam is being interrogated and Carol does not confess. Sam's best strategy is still to confess because then he goes free instead of serving two years. Conversely, if Carol is being interrogated, her best strategy is still to confess even if Sam does not. She will go free instead of serving 2 years. To confess is a dominant strategy for Sam. To confess is also a dominant strategy for Carol. The situation is exactly symmetrical. So, this is the **prisoners' dilemma**—the strategic game in which two prisoners have a choice between confessing and not confessing to a crime; the game is used to understand why oligopoly firms may decide to engage in noncooperative pricing behaviour, even though it results in a negative-sum game. The prisoners know that both prisoners will be better off if neither confesses. Yet, it is in each individual prisoner's interest to confess, even though the collective outcome of each prisoner's pursuing his or her own interest is inferior for both.

**Prisoners' dilemma** The strategic game in which two prisoners have a choice between confessing and not confessing to a crime.

**For critical analysis:** Can you apply the prisoners' dilemma to the firms in a two-firm industry that agree to split the market by charging the same (high) price? (*Hint*: Think about the payoff to cheating on the market-splitting agreement.) Is there a dominant strategy?

Consider an oligopoly consisting of two firms with identical cost and demand curves. It can be shown that if each of these firms cooperates with the other to collectively produce the monopoly output and charges the *same* monopoly price, these two firms will maximize their joint profits. In Figure 11–4, this situation is displayed in the upper left hand portion of the payoff matrix, with both firms charging a *high* price resulting in each firm earning a profit of \$6 million. The joint profit of \$12 million is maximized with this cooperative pricing strategy.

The upper right (or lower left) portion of the payoff table shows that if one of the firms decides not to cooperate and, instead, lowers its price slightly below its competitor's, it is able to sell a larger quantity and earn a higher individual profit equal to \$8 million. While this firm has increased its profit, the joint profit of the two firms will now have been reduced to \$10 million. The firm charging the higher monopoly price will clearly be the loser, selling a much lower quantity and earning a mere \$2 million in profit. If both firms decide to lower their price, each of their profits will be \$4 million, as shown on the lower right portion of the payoff table.

Given the payoff matrix in Figure 11–4, what would be the dominant strategy for Firm 2? If Firm 1 were to charge the high monopoly price, the best thing for Firm 2 to do is to charge the low price and earn a profit of \$8 million. If, instead, Firm 1 were to charge the low price, the best action for Firm 2 is to also charge the low price and earn a profit of \$4 million. You can see that the dominant strategy for Firm 2 is to charge the low price. Using similar reasoning, you will conclude that the dominant strategy for Firm 1 is also to charge a low price.

If the game described in Figure 11–4 is played once, we can see that it is in each firm's individual self-interest to engage in noncooperative price behaviour and charge the low price even though, collectively, the firms would be better off if they charged the high price and earned a profit of \$6 million each. Noncooperative pricing constitutes a negative sum game. As with the prisoners' dilemma, oligopoly firms face a dilemma between cooperating to maximize joint profits and competing to maximize individual profit.

**REPEATED GAMES.** Let us expand our game theory analysis to more realistic situations where the same pricing game is repeated over a period of years. If we examine Figure 11–4 more closely, we can see that both Firm 1 and Firm 2 would increase their annual profits

**FIGURE 11–4**

**Game Theory and Pricing Strategies**

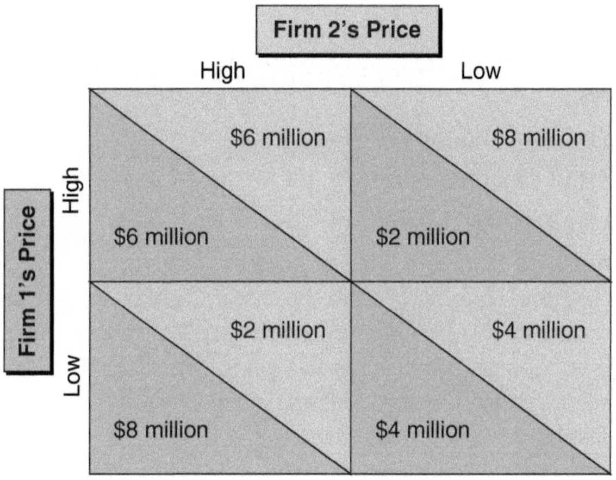


This payoff matrix shows that if both oligopolists choose a high price, each makes $6 million. If they both choose a low price, each makes $4 million. If one chooses a low price and the other does not, the low-priced firm will make $8 million. Unless they collude, however, they will end up at the low-priced solution.

from $4 million to $6 million if they colluded and decided to each charge the high price—the upper left portion of the payoff matrix in Figure 11–4. When competing firms collude, this is classed as a form of cooperative pricing behaviour.

Let us assume that Firm 1 and Firm 2 decide to collude and keep prices high, repeatedly, over a period of years. Again, if we refer to Figure 11–4, we can see that there is a strong incentive for one of the two firms, say, Firm 1, to eventually "cheat" and lower the price, hoping that the other firm, Firm 2, continues to keep the price high. If this occurs the cheating firm will increase profit from $6 million to $8 million per year! This type of cheating is referred to as **opportunistic behaviour** as it focuses solely on short-run gains and ignores the benefits of cooperation in the long run.

Opportunistic behaviour Actions that focus solely on short-run gains and ignore the benefits of cooperation in the long run.

As you might expect, if Firm 1 engages in opportunistic behaviour in one year, the competing firm, Firm 2, is likely to respond by punishing the cheater. One common oligopoly response to cheating is called the **tit-for-tat strategy**, in which a firm cheats in the current period if the rival firm cheated in the previous period but cooperates in the current period if the rival firm cooperated in the previous period. If both firms follow the tit-for-tat strategy, Firm 2 will respond to Firm 1's cheating by lowering the price in the next year, while Firm 1 goes back to raising the price. Figure 11–4 indicates that this will lower Firm 1's profits to $2 million, the worst possible result for Firm 1. Over the two-year period, Firm 1 achieves an average annual profit of $(8 + 2) \div 2 =$ $5 million. This is lower than the annual $6 million profit resulting from the cooperative pricing situation.

Tit-for-tat strategy A strategy in which a firm cheats in the current period if the rival firm cheated in the previous period but cooperates in the current period if the rival firm cooperated in the previous period.

Where does the tit-for-tat strategy lead in the long run? Suppose that both Firm 1 and Firm 2 pursue the tit-for-tat strategy, over a 10-year period. Assuming that the payoff matrix in Figure 11–4 applies to each of these 10 years, the average profit per year achieved by each firm will be $5 million (the simple average of the worst and best profits). Alternatively, if each firm had cooperated for each of the 10 years, the average yearly profit would be $6 million, a larger amount. In the long run, firms who experience the tit-for-tat strategy will likely see the benefits of pursuing some form of cooperative strategy. In other words, cooperative pricing is a positive-sum game.

## Cooperative Price Behaviour

In the previous section, we noted that the largest industry payoffs accrue to oligopoly firms in cases where the competitors collude or pursue cooperative price behaviour. Cooperative price behaviour can take many forms. One example would be a formal price-fixing agreement among the oligopoly firms operating in the same industry.

**PRICE FIXING.** The most lucrative price-fixing situation would be where the oligopoly firms agree to raise the price of the product to the level where a monopolist would maximize profits. If all the firms agree to raise prices, the consumers have little choice but to buy the product at the higher price. From the oligopoly firms' viewpoint, this would be an example of a positive-sum game, where all the firms as a group end up achieving higher total profits. In Canada, formal agreements to fix prices are frequently deemed to be illegal, as the following Policy Example 11–1 illustrates.

### POLICY EXAMPLE 11–1 Sweet Deal Between Canadian Chocolate Bar Makers?

On June 13, 2013, the Canadian Competition Bureau laid criminal charges against three companies and three company individuals accused of conspiracy under Canada's *Competition Act* for their role in fixing the price of chocolate bar products in Canada. The three companies charged were Nestlé Canada Inc. (Nestlé); Mars Canada Inc. (Mars); and ITWAL Limited (ITWAL), a national network of independent wholesale distributors. While it is alleged that both Cadbury Adams and Hershey were also party to the conspiracy, these companies avoided these latest criminal charges by cooperating with the authorities and by paying multimillion dollar settlements.

Since the charges were applied under the previous provisions of the *Competition Act*, maximum penalties include fines up to $10 million and five-year jail sentences. Under new provisions of the Act, this type of offence could result in fines up to $25 million and up to 14 years of imprisonment in Canada.

Canada's Competition Bureau asserts that a price-fixing conspiracy among the major chocolate manufacturers artificially inflated the price of chocolate bars such as Twix, Mars, Oh Henry, Dairy Milk, Crispy Crunch, Aero, and Smarties between 2001 and 2008. It is alleged that representatives of the large chocolate manufacturers held secret meetings to discuss prices. The Bureau contends that retail stores that attempted to undercut the retail prices suggested by the manufacturers would be penalized by having their supply of the popular chocolate bars restricted.

In September 2013, Canada's four largest candy bar makers—Nestlé Canada Inc., Hershey Canada Inc., Mars Canada Inc., and Cadbury Adams Canada Inc.—agreed to pay $23.2 million to settle a class-action lawsuit over the price-fixing of chocolate bars in the Canadian market. After an eight year investigation, all charges against the four candy bar makers were dropped. The Crown did not offer a reason or explanation of it's decision.

**For critical analysis:**

1. According to this example, is the alleged price-fixing agreement an example of a zero-sum, negative-sum, or positive-sum game?
2. Based on the allegations in the lawsuit, how does the agreement among the chocolate manufacturers attempt to keep chocolate bar prices inflated at the retail level?

Sources: "Chocolate price-fixing costs candy makers $23M." Business. CBC News. September 17, 2013. http://www.cbc.ca/news/business/chocolate-price-fixing-costs-candy-makers-23m-1.1857642 (Accessed April 5, 2014); "Charges Laid in a Price-fixing Cartel in the Chocolate Industry." Media Centre. Competition Bureau. June 6, 2013. http://www.competitionbureau.gc.ca/eic/site/cb-bc.nsf/eng/03569.html (Accessed April 5, 2014). Dana Flavelle. "Chocolate price-fixing probe ends." Business. The Star. Novevmber 18, 2015. https://www.thestar.com/business/2015/11/18/hersheys-only-firm-convicted-in-chocolate-price-fixing-probe.html (Accessed February 13, 2017).

**CARTEL.** Perhaps the most comprehensive form of cooperative pricing occurs when the oligopoly firms in an industry join a cartel. A **cartel** is an association of suppliers in an industry that agree to set common prices and output quotas to prevent competition. The purpose of a cartel is to raise prices to monopoly levels in order to increase the total profits received by cartel members. Since cartels engage in a form of price fixing, they are generally illegal in Canada.

**Cartel** An association of suppliers in an industry that agree to set common prices and output quotas to prevent competition.

One of the most successful international cartels ever is the Organization of Petroleum Exporting Countries (OPEC), an association of the world's largest oil-producing countries. It is estimated that the eleven OPEC members, in total, possess about 78 percent of the world's total proven crude oil reserves. All of the members of OPEC meet regularly to establish daily production quotas. The long-term strategy of OPEC has been to restrict the daily production of oil in order to keep the price of oil significantly above competitive levels, as Example 11–3 describes.

### EXAMPLE 11–3 OPEC Continues to Rule the World Oil Market?

On November 1, 2006, the Organization of Petroleum Exporting Countries (OPEC) announced that they would cooperatively reduce their combined daily crude oil production by 1.2 million

*continued*

barrels. Just a few months later, in February 2007, OPEC announced another production cut of 500 000 barrels per day, bringing total OPEC production to a level of just over 30 million barrels per day in March 2007. In order to ensure this daily production target, each OPEC member has been allocated a daily production quota (in barrels), as follows: Saudi Arabia, 8 510 000; Iran, 3 740 000; Venezuela, 2 411 000; United Arab Emirates, 2 466 000; Nigeria, 2 170 000; Iraq, 2 054 000; Kuwait, 2 400 000; Libya, 1 683 000; Angola, 1 602 000; Indonesia, 855 000; Algeria, 1 340 000; and Qatar, 795 000.

The OPEC production cut took place despite the fact that oil prices have quadrupled since November 2001, reaching $78.65 per barrel in August 2006.

Why did OPEC cut production when oil prices are already high? Industry analysts contend that Saudi Arabia enforced the decrease in quotas in response to the falling U.S. dollar, as oil is priced globally in U.S. dollars. The decline in the value of the U.S. dollar has the effect of reducing the real income of the OPEC nations, as oil is their key trading commodity.

Oil prices continued to increase to record levels, peaking at over $140 per barrel in July 2008. Then, the great global recession caused oil prices to plummet to just over $30 per barrel in December 2008. Effective January 2009, OPEC implemented a record quota reduction totalling 4.2 million barrels per day.

Did all OPEC nations abide by the decreased production quotas, given the incentive to cheat in the midst of a global recession? As of March 2009, there was 80 percent compliance to the quota cuts, and industry observers expected to see more producers comply in the following months, in light of the strategic behaviour taken by Saudi Arabia in the past. Repeatedly, Saudi Arabia has effectively said to other members of OPEC, "If you stick to your agreed-on production limits, so shall we; but if you expand production beyond those limits, so shall we."

OPEC members have seen Saudi Arabia follow through on its threats of retaliation. In the 1980s, when Iran and Iraq were selling in excess of their quotas to finance their war, Saudi Arabia responded by significantly increasing its oil production. Oil prices collapsed. In just one year (1985 to 1986), crude oil prices plunged from US$24.10 to US$12.50 per barrel.

OPEC failed to reach an agreement on production quotas in 2014 and oil prices plummeted from over $100 in 2014 a barrel to below $30 per barrel in early 2016.

OPEC latest attempt to cut production will allow Iran to continue in increasing their production after sanctions were lifted.

**For critical analysis:** What game theory strategy is being employed by the OPEC cartel? Why is Saudi Arabia so effective in enforcing this strategy?

Sources: Javier Blas, "Falling US dollar puts pressure on the buying power of OPEC nations. Financial Times, London, UK, July 24, 2007, p. 1; OPEC Monthly Oil Market Report. April 2007, p. 31. http://www.opec.org/home/Monthly%20Oil%20Market%20Reports/2007/pdf/mr042007.pdf; Stanley Reed. "OPEC sees good reasons to maintain production." Bloomberg Business Week. March 15, 2009. http://www.businessweek.com/globalbiz/content/mar2009/gb20090315_745055.htm?campaign_id=rss_daily; Leaky barrels. The Economist. February 22, 2014. http://www.economist.com/news/finance-and-economics/21596986-higher-production-elsewhere-undermining-cartel-leaky-barrels (Accessed April 6, 2014). Kim Hjelmgaard and Nathan Bomey, "OPEC agrees to oil production cuts." USA Today, November 30, 2016. http://www.usatoday.com/story/money/business/2016/11/30/oil-production-opec-meeting-vienna-saudi-arabia-iran/94652618/ (Accessed February 20, 2017).

**PRICE LEADERSHIP.** What if oligopolists do not actually collude to raise prices and share markets but do so implicitly? There are no formal cartel arrangements and no formal meetings. Nonetheless, there is tacit collusion. One example of this is the model of **price leadership**—a practice in many oligopolistic industries, in which the largest firm publishes its price list ahead of its competitors, which then match those announced prices.

**Price leadership** A practice in many oligopolistic industries in which the largest firm publishes its price list ahead of its competitors, who then match those announced prices. Also called parallel pricing.

In this model, the basic assumption is that the dominant firm, usually the biggest, sets the price and allows other firms to sell all they can at that price. The dominant firm then sells the rest. The dominant firm always makes the first move in a price leadership model. By definition, price leadership requires that one firm be the leader. Because of laws against collusion, firms in an industry cannot communicate this directly. That is why it is often natural for the largest firm to become the price leader. In the automobile industry, during the period of GM's dominance (until the 1980s), that company was traditionally the price leader. At various times in the breakfast-food industry, Kellogg was the price leader. In the banking industry, the Bank of Montreal has been the price leader in announcing changes in its prime rate, the interest rate charged on loans offered to the best credit risks. Typically, five or six hours after the Bank of Montreal would increase or decrease its prime rate, the other major banks would announce the same change in their prime rates.

## Factors Conducive to Cooperative Price Behaviour

What factors are likely to prompt cooperative price behaviour, as opposed to noncooperative price behaviour, in oligopoly? Economic research does point to various industry characteristics as being important in determining whether cooperation or competition will ensue in an oligopoly situation.

There will be a greater tendency for cooperation the *smaller the number of firms* in the industry. In this situation, if one firm attempts to cheat, it can expect significant retaliation, as this cheating will have a very large negative effect on the remaining competitors. Moreover, it is easier to identify a cheater with just a few large firms in the industry.

Cooperative price behaviour is more likely to be sustained in a *growing industry* than in a shrinking market. When demand is increasing, firms can easily increase sales without resorting to noncooperative pricing practices that steal customers away from their rivals. Conversely, in recessions, price agreements frequently break down as firms facing declining sales react in desperation by cutting prices.

The tendency toward joint pricing behaviour is greater for oligopoly firms supplying *identical* products as opposed to differentiated products. As an example, one would expect to see a greater degree of price cooperation in such industries as oil and steel refining, where competitors' products are relatively homogeneous. In these cases, rival firms can quickly and easily punish a cheating firm through reciprocal price cuts.

Forms of cooperative pricing, such as price fixing and cartels, are more likely to occur in countries where *legal sanctions preventing this activity are largely absent*. It has already been noted that in such countries as Canada and the United States, many types of cooperative pricing strategies are deemed to be illegal and can result in significant fines being imposed.

Example 11–4 describes how DeBeers, the dominant supplier of the world's rough diamonds, has made recent moves away from price cooperation, partly due to industry trends and partly due to its desire to sell more finished diamond products in the United States.

### EXAMPLE 11–4 De Beers Diamond Cartel: A Thing of The Past?

"Diamonds Are Forever." For decades, that expression has applied not just to diamonds but also to South Africa's De Beers diamond cartel. At the centre of the cartel's operations is De Beers' marketing subsidiary, the Central Selling Organization (CSO). By restricting diamond sales each year, the CSO has aimed to maximize profits earned by De Beers and other members of a global cartel of diamond producers.

The CSO attempted to purchase most of the world's rough diamonds, even those that were not produced by the cartel firms. Using this strategy, the CSO controlled the diamond supply to the ultimate consumers. Each year, the CSO withheld from the marketplace stockpiles of $4 billion to $5 billion in uncut diamonds. Between 1986 and 1998, diamond prices increased by 50 percent!



What type for oligopoly pricing behaviour is typical of the diamond industry?

Since 1998, things have not been going so smoothly for the cartel. Russia, Canada, and Australia have emerged as significant diamond producers, gradually loosening the De Beers cartel's grip on global diamond supply and pricing. Better techniques for making artificial diamonds have also played a role in bringing new competition to the industry.

De Beers has recently pledged to relinquish some of its practices intended to control the supply of rough diamonds. With diamond prices declining at the wholesale level, De Beers is making efforts to establish premium brand-name jewellery products at the retail level. Based on unresolved charges of price fixing, De Beers has been banned from competing in the lucrative U.S. retail diamond jewellery industry. In 2004, the South African company was reportedly in secret negotiations to end its exile from the United States. In July 2005, De Beers pleaded guilty in a U.S. court to fixing prices of industrial diamonds and agreed to a US$10 million fine.

Several class-action lawsuits were filed against De Beers asking for money damages on behalf of diamond purchasers. The lawsuits claim that De Beers monopolized diamond supplies

*continued*

and conspired to fix and inflate diamond prices, violating antitrust and consumer-protection laws. On May 27, 2008, a U.S. court approved a settlement whereby De Beers would pay $295 million to the various diamond purchasers that claimed damages in the class-action suits.

In the spring of 2010, the $295 million settlement was appealed. In July 2010, the Third Circuit overturned the original settlement. In December 2011, the Court of Appeals of the Third Circuit reinstated the original settlement. On July 2013, De Beers began distributing the US$295 million settlement. Anyone who purchased diamonds from January 1994 to March 2006 was eligible for compensation. However, claimants were generally not happy with the amounts received from the settlement.

**For critical analysis:** What factors help to explain why there has been a tendency away from the practice of cooperative pricing in the rough diamond industry?

Sources: David Finlayson. "Return of De Beers may boost industry: Guilty plea to price fixing will open U.S. market." *Edmonton Journal.* March 3, 2004. Pg. G3; Eric Onstad. "De Beers quits chasing carats; Diamond giant likely to drop Russia's Alrosa." *Calgary Herald.* July 21, 2007. Final edition. Pg. C10; Matthew Craze and David Voreacos. "De Beers to pay US$250M to settle U.S. lawsuits: Price fixing alleged." *National Post.* December 1, 2005. National edition. Pg. FP5; "Commonly asked questions and answers." Diamond Class Action Settlement website. https://diamondsclassaction.com/FAQ.htm#14; De Beers Antitrust Payouts May Face Further Delays. Rob Bates, Senior Editor. JCK Online. March 6, 2012. http://www.jckonline.com/2012/03/06/de-beers-antitrust-payouts-may-face-further-delays (Accessed April 6, 2014). Diamond Class Action Settlement. July 26, 2013. https://diamondsclassaction.com/ (Accessed February 20, 2017).

## Pricing to Deter Entry into an Industry

Some economists believe that all decision making by existing firms in a stable industry involves some type of game playing. As noted above, one important part of game playing has to do with how existing competitors might react to a decision by other existing rivals. Another type of strategic decision making requires that existing firms in an oligopoly industry come up with strategies to deter entry of new competitors. An example would be when existing firms(s) adopt pricing and investment tactics to deter entry.

**Predatory pricing** A strategy where existing firms cut the prices of their products below costs in order to discourage the entry of new firms.

**PREDATORY PRICING.** New companies are more likely deterred from entering an oligopoly industry if they expect economic losses over a protracted period of time. Existing oligopoly firms can create this expectation by engaging in predatory pricing behaviour. **Predatory pricing** is a strategy in which existing firms cut the prices of their products below costs in order to discourage the entry of new firms. To enhance the effectiveness of predatory pricing, the existing firm(s) might invest in excess capacity so that they can expand output for a prolonged period of time.

For example, an existing supermarket might build a mega-store with lots of excess capacity in a brand new subdivision. If a new rival food retailer announces future plans to enter this subdivision, the existing supermarket may engage in predatory pricing over a protracted period of time due its excess capacity. The new potential rival, faced with having to meet the low prices for an extended period of time, may be scared off by the prospect of prolonged economic losses.

Policy Example 11–2 explains how investigations conducted by the Competition Bureau (the federal government agency in charge of maintaining fair competition in Canada) support the view that Air Canada has engaged in predatory pricing strategies at the expense of smaller regional airlines.

### POLICY EXAMPLE 11–2 Turbulence in the Canadian Airline Industry

For many years, Canada was served by two national airlines—Air Canada and Canadian Airlines International. In January 2000, Air Canada purchased the financially plagued Canadian Airlines International, making Air Canada the dominant firm in the Canadian airline industry.

*continued*

After Air Canada, a number of regional airlines, such as WestJet and CanJet, have attempted to expand their services on a broader national scale. Both regional airlines have filed complaints with the Canadian government's Competition Bureau, claiming that Air Canada has been pursuing anti-competitive practices aimed at deterring entry into Eastern Canadian markets.

In March 2001, the Competition Bureau completed an investigation of Air Canada's response to the entry of WestJet Airlines and CanJet Airlines into seven Eastern Canadian routes—Halifax–Montreal, Halifax–Ottawa, Halifax–St. John's, Toronto–Moncton, Toronto–Saint John, Toronto–Fredericton, and Toronto–Charlottetown. The Bureau concluded that in these seven markets, Air Canada was engaged in entry-deterring predatory behaviour that included adding capacity and pricing below "avoidable cost." If these anti-competitive practices were to continue, they could cause WestJet and CanJet to abandon these routes, which would lead to higher airfares in the long run.

The Competition Bureau asked the federal government's Competition Tribunal for a legal court order prohibiting Air Canada from engaging in various entry deterrence strategies. At one point in 2003, Air Canada was offering one-way fares between Toronto and Ottawa for $12! In July 2003, the Competition Tribunal filed a preliminary report that concluded that Air Canada did engage in predatory pricing behaviour in at least two of the seven routes investigated. Air Canada subsequently appealed the findings of this report.

In January 2009, the Competition Bureau clarified its enforcement approach related to anti-competitive acts such as predatory pricing. In essence, for a dominant firm (such as Air Canada) to be found guilty, the investigation would have to show that the dominant airline was reducing prices below its avoidable costs and that this conduct was likely to result in a substantial lessening or prevention of competition.

No enforcement action has been taken against Air Canada (to date), perhaps because the competition from WestJet has been increasing, not lessening. In 2000, Air Canada commanded a 77 percent share of the Canadian market, while WestJet held 7 percent. As of 2015, Air Canada's market share had declined to 42 percent, and WestJet's share had increased to 13 percent. The lowest price for airline fuel since the 2008 recession has resulted in record level profits for Canada's two largest airlines.

**For critical analysis:** Using this example, identify and explain two entry-deterring strategies likely pursued by Air Canada.

Sources: Competition Bureau. "Competition bureau seeks order against anti-competitive practices by Air Canada." March 5, 2001. http://strategis.ic.gc.ca/epic/internet/incb-bc.nsf/en/ct02136e.html; The Canadian Press. "Airline flew for less than cost, tribunal decides." *Daily News*. Halifax, N.S., July 23, 2003, p. 23; Nicolas Van Praet. "Beddoe says Air Canada pursuing 'scorched earth policy' price war." *Edmonton Journal*. October 21, 2003. Pg. F3; Competition Bureau. "Competition bureau clarifies enforcement approach in the airline industry." September 23, 2004. http://www.competitionbureau.gc.ca/internet/index.cfm?itemID=247&lg=e; Brent Jang. "WestJet closing gap with Air Canada" *The Globe and Mail*. February 18, 2010. Pg. B9; WestJet sets sights on Air Canada's title. Brent Jang. Report on Business. The Globe and Mail. Jan. 01, 2012. http://www.theglobeandmail.com/report-on-business/westjet-sets-sights-on-air-canadas-title/article1358801/ (Accessed April 6, 2014). IBISWorld. Scheduled Air Transportation in Canada. http://clients1.ibisworld.ca/reports/ca/industry/majorcompanies.aspx?indid=1125 (Accessed February 20, 2017).

This chapter's Issues and Applications describes how game theory can be used in explaining entry-deterring behaviour (or the lack of it) in Canada's oligopolic brewing industry. As the Issues and Applications explains, strategic behaviour by the existing breweries can help explain the growth of the smaller microbreweries.

## Price Wars

Sporadic price wars frequently break out in oligopoly situations. A **price war** is a situation where competing firms respond to a rival's price cut with even larger price cuts. Many of us have witnessed price wars involving closely located supermarkets or gas price wars among gas retailers in a Canadian city. While most wars last for only a few days, some can drag into months and possibly even years.

**Price war** A situation where competing firms respond to a rival's price out with even larger price cuts.

Price wars are characteristic of oligopolies, due to the presence of interdependence, where one firm's price cut can significantly reduce the market share of a rival firm.

A price war can be caused by a variety of factors. It may be due to competing firms responding to opportunistic behaviour (cheating) on the part of one rival attempting to steal market share. Or this practice may be part of an overall strategy to deter new firms from successfully entering the oligopoly industry, as Example 11–5 suggests.

### EXAMPLE 11–5 Wind Blows Down Canadian Wireless Prices

In Canada, what is likely to happen to cellphone prices? Why?

According to a recent study conducted by the OECD, Canada's cellphone market is one of the most expensive among the developed nations. Of the 30 developed nations surveyed, Canada ranked twenty-eighth in terms of affordability. Many attribute Canada's high cellphone plan prices to the lack of competition in the wireless carrier market, which is dominated by the "Big Three" oligopoly firms: Telus, Bell, and Rogers.

In 2008 the Canadian government began to encourage competition in the Canadian wireless market by auctioning wireless services spectrum to new firms other than the "Big Three" which included Wind Mobile, Public Mobile, Mobilicity, Eastlink, and Videotron. Wind Mobile was permitted to enter the Canadian wireless industry despite being foreign owned. In the latter part of 2009, a price war emerged. It started with each of the Big Three firms dropping prices to the point of offering stripped-down, no-frills plans, including talk and text packages for as little as $15 per month. Telus's Koodo, Rogers's Fido, and Bell's Solo Mobile have been used to front this price war. These three firms were hoping to lock down as many customers as possible ahead of Wind Mobile's entry into the market. In December 2009, Wind Mobile and the other new entrants countered the Big Three's price cuts by offering stripped-down cellphone plans for as low as $10 per month.

At the end of 2013 the CRTC implemented new policies aimed at enhancing competition in the Canadian wireless industry that included: cancelling a phone contract after two years without penalty; imposing maximum limits on roaming charges; allowing consumers more freedom in having their phone unlocked.

In 2016, Shaw Communications purchased the struggling wireless carrier Wind Mobile. This adds a fourth competitor to the wireless industry. Roaming rates have been declining because of consumer dissatisfaction and the industry's hope to attract new customers. Increased competition would cause the roaming rates to decline further.

**For critical analysis:** According to this Example, what two tactics aimed at deterring entry have been employed by the Big Three? Explain.

Sources: Grant Robertson. "Globalive wades into wireless price battle." Report on Business. *The Globe and Mail*. December 13, 2009. http://www.theglobeandmail.com/report-on-business/globalive-wades-into-wireless-price-battle/article1398967/; Rick Eglinton. "Wind launches with cheaper phone rates." *Toronto Star*. December 16, 2009. http://www.thestar.com/business/article/739543—wind-launches-with-cheaper-cellphone-rates; Checklist: Do You Know Your Rights as a Wireless Consumer? The CRTC Wireless Code. Canadian Radio-television Telecommunications Commission. http://www.crtc.gc.ca/eng/info_sht/t13.htm (Accessed April 6, 2014); Canada's wireless policy has lacked ambition. April 4, 2014. Words by Nowak. http://wordsbynowak.com/2014/04/04/government-wireless/ (Accessed April 6, 2014). Martin Masse and Paul Beaudry. The State of Competition in Canada's Telecommunication Industry. MEI. May 5, 2016. http://www.iedm.org/60433-the-state-of-competition-in-canada-s-telecommunications-industry-2016 (Accessed Februrary 20, 2017).

## 11.6 Nonprice Forms of Competition in Oligopoly

Since price wars are costly and collusion can be illegal, many oligopoly firms have channeled their competitive energies into nonprice forms of competition. We will examine the following forms of nonprice competition: product differentiation, mergers, exclusive dealing, increasing switching costs, exploiting network effects, and innovation.

There are several reasons why oligopoly firms prefer nonprice forms of competition over price competition. Successful forms of nonprice competition cannot be duplicated as quickly and easily by rival firms as price reductions. For example, compared with price-cutting opportunistic behaviour, successful product differentiation or product improvements can often achieve more permanent gains in market share. In addition, nonprice competition can often increase total industry sales and so can be viewed by the firms as positive-sum games.

## Product Differentiation

Recall that product differentiation refers to the distinguishing of products by physical attributes, bundling of services, location and accessibility, sales promotion and advertising, and other qualities, real or imagined.

To appreciate the degree of product differentiation that can exist in oligopoly, consider the motor vehicle manufacturing industry and the "Big Three"—GM, Chrysler, and Ford. For each type of motor vehicle product line, there are many differences in styling features, options, financing plans, sales promotion and advertising campaigns, warranties, sponsorship of entertainment and sporting events, and so on.

**ADVERTISING.** Perhaps the most socially contentious form of product differentiation is advertising. Those critical of the advertising activities undertaken by large oligopoly firms have frequently put forth the following arguments. While advertising adds to the cost of the product(s) to consumers, much of the advertising conveys little or no valuable information. Does a TV commercial featuring a new Jeep in the middle of the desert or on the top of a cliff really convey valuable consumer information?

When oligopoly firms engage in expensive advertising campaigns, this can serve as a barrier to entry to entrepreneurs considering the prospect of entering the industry. If a new firm were to consider entering the national beer industry in Canada, the extensive amount of advertising and sales promotion that would be required to keep up with Molson and Labatt may well be a discouraging factor.

To the extent that a firm's advertising efforts are successful in establishing substantial brand-name loyalty, the consumer faces disadvantages similar to monopolized markets. The price charged on the brand name product might significantly exceed marginal and average total cost, thus resulting in allocative inefficiency and excess profits.

Finally, some advertisements and sales promotions deliberately mislead consumers. One of the most common violations of the *Canadian Competition Act* relates to firms' misrepresenting the regular or ordinary price of a product or service in an advertised sale or in-store sales promotion. In recent years, national Canadian retailers have been fined hundreds of thousands of dollars for tagging merchandise with percentage discounts off a misleading regular price. In other words, the original price indicated on the tagged merchandise did not represent the regular price, since the sale item was never sold for this amount. In some cases, the articles of merchandise were already tagged "Special" before even entering the store.

What are the social benefits of advertising? To the extent that media advertisements contain objective information about product characteristics and prices, the consumer can make a rational purchase decision without having to spend several days visiting competing stores. One way new firms can make consumers aware of their new products is through advertising.

Individual companies can use advertising to engage in signalling behaviour that can benefit consumers. By establishing a strong brand name or trademark, a firm is sending a signal to consumers that it plans to stay in business for a long time. Moreover, the strong brand name is used to indicate that the firm undertakes to provide a consistently high level of product quality. This type of signalling behaviour is especially important to those consumers who prefer to buy products through the Internet.

Example 11–6 suggests that, in some cases, advertising can actually lower per-unit costs and thereby promote productive efficiency.

### EXAMPLE 11–6 Can Advertising Lead to Efficiency?

Advertising budgets by major retailers may just seem like an added expense, not a step on the road to economic efficiency. According to research by economists Kyle Bagwell and Garey Ramey, just the opposite is true. When retailers advertise heavily, they increase the number of shoppers that come to their store. Such increased traffic allows retailers to offer a wider selection of goods, to invest in cost-reduction technology (such as computerized inventory and satellite communications),

*continued*

and to exploit manufacturers' quantity discounts. Such cost reductions can help explain the success of Walmart, Canadian Tire, and Home Depot. Consequently, Bagwell and Ramey conclude that advertising can help promote efficiency. Advertising that provides price information signals to consumers where they can find big-company, low-priced, high-variety stores.

**For critical analysis:** Which is true: "We are bigger because we are better," or "We are better because we are bigger"?

## Mergers

**Merger** The joining of two or more firms under single ownership or control.

**Horizontal merger** The joining of firms that are producing or selling a similar product.

**Vertical merger** The joining of a firm with another to which it sells an output or from which it buys an input.

**Conglomerate merger** The joining of two firms from unrelated industries.

One way an oligopoly firm can significantly increase its share of industry sales is through a merger. A **merger** is the joining of two or more firms under single ownership or control. There are three types of mergers: horizontal, vertical, and conglomerate. A **horizontal merger** involves the joining of firms that are producing or selling a similar product. If two daily newspapers in the same city merge, this is a horizontal merger. A horizontal merger reduces competition and so increases the level of concentration in an industry.

A **vertical merger** is the joining of a firm with another to which it sells an output or from which it buys an input. When an oil refining company, such as Shell, purchases retail gas stations, this is a vertical merger. A **conglomerate merger** is the joining of two firms from unrelated industries. If an automobile manufacturer purchases a chain of restaurants, this is a conglomerate merger. In situations where mergers result in a few large, dominant corporations operating in one market, other firms, faced with the prospect of raising large amounts of capital to compete successfully, are deterred from entering the industry.

## Exclusive Dealing

**Exclusive Dealing** A situation where the firm supplies its product to a customer on condition that the customer not buy similar products from rival firms supplying a similar product.

**Exclusive dealing** refers to a situation where a firm supplies its product to a customer on condition that the customer not buy similar products from rival firms supplying a similar product. Typically, the customer is another firm that plans to re-sell the product. If an oligopoly petroleum-refining company agreed to sell its gasoline to a Canadian gas retailer only if the gas station owner promised not to buy any gasoline from a rival refiner, this would be an example of an exclusive dealing agreement. This practice reduces price competition in that it prevents the gas retailer from contacting competing refiners to secure a lower price per litre. In turn, this makes the demand for each refiner's gasoline more inelastic so that refiners can charge higher prices.

It should be noted that in many countries, the practice of exclusive dealing is an illegal act and can result in a very large penalty, as Example 11–7 illustrates.

### EXAMPLE 11–7 Intel Bags Record Fine

On May 12, 2009, the European Union fined Intel Corporation a record EUR1.06 billion (US$1.45 billion) and ordered the world's biggest maker of computer chips to stop exclusive dealing practices that severely restrained the chip sales of its major rival, Advanced Micro Devices (AMD), for a five-year period. The EU charged Intel with giving rebates to computer manufacturers such as Acer Inc., Dell Inc., Hewlett-Packard, Lenovo Group and NEC Corp. for buying all or most of their chips for their new computers from Intel. As well, EU claimed that Intel paid computer manufacturers to stop or delay the launch of new computers based on AMD chips.

At the time the record fine was assessed, the computer chip industry was dominated by the two firms—Intel and AMD—and that Intel supplied about 80 percent of the world's computer chips. In July 2012, Intel appealed to Europe's second highest level court to have the EUR 1.06 billion fine overturned. Intel argued that in rendering the original fine, the European Union regulators mistakenly judged Intel's actions as illegal without checking if they actually shut AMD out of the market and had "immediate, substantial, direct and foreseeable effects" on sales to European customers. As of October 2016, Intel Corporation vs the European Commission has not been resolved.

*continued*

**For critical analysis:** Based on this example, who else has likely been significantly harmed by the exclusive practices of Intel, besides its rival chip makers?

Sources: Roger Parloff. "Intel settles with AMD. What's next?" *Fortune Magazine*. November 13, 2009. http://money.cnn.com/2009/11/13/technology/intel_amd_settlement.fortune/index.htm; Aoife White. "EU fines Intel $1.45 billion for sales tactics." *Daily Gleaner* (Fredericton, N.B.). May 14, 2009. Pg. D1; Intel fights $1.3 billion EU antitrust fine in court. Foo Yun Chee. Reuters Edition U.S. Jul 3, 2012. http://www.reuters.com/article/2012/07/03/us-intel-eu-appeal-idUSBRE8620OE20120703 (Accessed April 6, 2014). Stephanie Bodoni and Aoife White."Intel Wins Latest Round in Battle Over $1.17 Billion EU Fine". Bloomberg Technology. October 20, 2016. https://www.bloomberg.com/news/articles/2016-10-20/intel-should-win-fight-over-1-16-billion-fine-court-aide-says (Accessed February 20, 2017).

## Raising Customers' Switching Costs

If an existing firm can make it more costly for customers to switch from its product or service to a competitor's, the existing firm can better insulate itself from price competition as well as deter the entry of new firms. In other words, the oligopolistic firm can make the demand for its product or service more inelastic and by doing so can command a higher price.

There are a host of ways in which existing firms can raise customers' switching costs. In the past, makers of computer equipment produced operating systems and software that would not run on competitors' computers. Any customer wanting to change from one computer system to another faced a high switching cost. In the oligopolistic cellphone industry, customers who lock into cellphone contracts face increased switching costs in the form of cancellation penalties.

The Canadian banking industry provides a good illustration of high switching costs, as shown below in Example 11–8

### EXAMPLE 11–8 High Switching Costs in the Credit World

One way banks keep their customers is by raising the cost of switching to a different bank. RBC offers RBC Rewards to its Visa credit card holders. This incentive enables its Visa users to accumulate reward points on all credit card purchases. Once sufficient reward points have accumulated, the credit card user can redeem these points for free travel services or free merchandise. A Royal Bank Visa holder who has accumulated a significant number of reward points will be reluctant to switch to another credit card, as this would entail a switching cost equal to the loss in reward points.

Similarly, CIBC offers mortgages that enable customers to accumulate Aeroplan Miles for every dollar of mortgage interest paid. If a CIBC customer decides to renew a mortgage with CIBC, the customer receives a significant number of bonus Aeroplan Miles. Due to these incentives, a CIBC customer faces switching costs if he or she decides to renew a mortgage with another bank.

**For critical analysis:** Can you think of switching cost examples in other oligopolistic industries, besides banking?

## Network Effects

A common source of switching costs is a shared understanding among consumers about how to use a particular product, service, or brand. Such a shared understanding can sometimes generate **network effects**—situations where a customer's willingness to use an item depends on how other people use it. Common examples are telephones and fax machines. Ownership of a phone or fax machine is not very useful if no one else has one; but once a number of people own a phone or fax machine, the benefits that others gain from consuming these devices increases.

**Network effect** A situation where a customer's willingness to use an item depends on how many others use it.

In some industries, a few firms can reap most of the benefits of the network effect. Suppose that firms in an industry sell differentiated products or services that are subject to network effects. If the products or services of one, two, or a few firms catch on, these firms will capture the bulk of industry sales, and an oligopoly, or possibly even a near monopoly, will emerge.

People who tend to work on joint projects within a network of fellow employees, consultants, clients, suppliers, students, or professors naturally find it useful to share computer files. Trading computer files is much easier if all use the same word processing, spreadsheet, database, and presentation software. Clearly, the network effect has contributed to Microsoft's dominance in these office productivity software products. Any individual who contemplates switching to use a word processor other than MS Word is aware that he or she faces significant switching costs in terms of the time that will be required to convert files sent in Word to the rival word processor.

In the market for online auction services, an individual is more likely to use the services of an auction site if there is a significant likelihood that many other potential buyers or sellers also trade items on that site. Hence there is a network effect in the online auction industry so that eBay, Amazon, and Yahoo! account for more than 80 percent of total sales.

Online social networking has become one of the fastest-growing industries worldwide, with over 100 online social networking websites available in 2016. Each social networking site provides a multitude of ways for its users to interact, such as chats, messaging, e-mail, photos, videos, voice chats, file sharing, blogging, wikis, discussion groups, and social applications. As Example 11–9 illustrates, the network effect is quickly changing the Internet social networking industry into an oligopoly situation that is particularly attractive to advertisers worldwide.

### EXAMPLE 11–9 Facebook Frenzy

Because of the network effect, the online social networking industry is quickly becoming dominated by a few large websites. As of the first quarter of 2010, the major sites listed according to registered members were as follows: Facebook (400 000 000), Qzone (200 000 000) MySpace (180 000 000), Habbo (162 000 000), Windows Live Spaces (120 000 000), and orkut (100 000 000). It is interesting to note how fast a company can grow due to the network effect. Facebook added 370 000 000 new members in a period of less than three years! Indeed, Barack Obama benefited from this growth by using Facebook to gain voter support in the 2008 U.S. presidential election.

Facebook provides free membership to any individual who provides an e-mail address. Once a new member logs into the site, he or she typically fills out a personal profile, which can consist of personal demographics, interests, beliefs, and activities. Facebook provides simple navigation tools that allow individuals to easily join and interact with friends, family, colleagues, classmates, employees, and customers in a variety of networks and groups, based on their personal profiles. One key way that Facebook encourages the network effect is through its "Facebook Platform," which invites any software developer to create social networking applications that can be launched within Facebook. As more applications are developed, more users are attracted, which in turn attracts even more software applications.

In order for a Facebook user to gain permission to launch and use these applications, he or she may be asked to disclose additional personal information, such as his or her name, profile picture, gender, birthday, hometown, current residence, political views, activities, interests, musical preferences, favourite television shows, movie preferences, book preferences, favourite quotes, relationship status, dating interests, relationship interests, summer plans, Facebook user-network affiliations, education history, work history, course information, photo albums, and so on.

Advertisers are keenly interested in sites such as Facebook because they provide the opportunity to efficiently promote specific products and services to their target markets, based on the rich array of personal information that individual users provide in their profiles, interactions, and through the download of applications. It is estimated that in 2009, Facebook's annual revenue was approximately $800 million based on brand ads, ad deals with Microsoft, self service ads, and virtual goods.

On May 26, 2010, Facebook responded to world-wide privacy concerns by announcing plans to allow its individual users to more easily adjust privacy settings that limit access to users' personal information. At this time, the default settings still favour sharing of personal information.

In 2013 Facebook introduced a new Graph Search application that allows users to quickly search and retrieve information within Facebook in a structured, Google-like way. The information in Facebook that can be searched and retrieved include: people, photos, places, interests, status updates, photo captions, check-ins, and comments. As of 2016, no Facebook account is truly private. The ability to stop anyone from finding an account by searching has been removed. Once again Facebook users are concerned that their privacy is being seriously threatened.

*continued*

**For critical analysis:** Explain why the network effect applies to the online social networking industry.

Sources: "List of social networking sites." Wikipedia. http://en.wikipedia.org/wiki/List_of_social_networking_websites. (Accessed June 14, 2010.); Nicholas Carlson. "Everything you wanted to know about Facebook's revenue but didn't know who to ask. July 2, 2009. *Business Insider*. SAI. http://www.businessinsider.com/breaking-down-facebooks-revenues-2009-7; Matt Hartley. "Has Facebook finally got privacy right?" May 26, 2010. *Financial Post*. http://www.financialpost.com/story.html?id=3074979; ONLINE PRIVACY: 7 ways to control privacy on Facebook despite Graph Search. Technology and Science. CBC News. Oct 2, 2013. http://www.cbc.ca/news/technology/7-ways-to-control-privacy-on-facebook-despite-graph-search-1.1876092 (Accessed April 6, 2014). Thomas Fox-Brewster."Facebook is Playing Games With Your Privacy And There's Nothing You Can Do About It." June 29, 2016. http://www.forbes.com/sites/thomasbrewster/2016/06/29/facebook-location-tracking-friend-games/#48c7208d3348 (Accessed February 20, 2017).

## Innovation

Oligopoly firms can promote their own self-interest as well as public interest by engaging in the innovative activities of research and development that result in the adoption of more efficient methods of production or the creation of new and improved products. A number of theoretical arguments can be put forth to suggest that an oligopoly market structure can be conducive to technological innovation. The large size of many oligopoly firms enables them to undertake expensive research and development activities. As well, due to barriers to entry and the lure of long-run excess profits, oligopoly firms have the incentive to innovate. Finally, interdependent oligopoly firms may prefer to channel their competitive energies into constructive product innovation as opposed to destructive price competition.

According to the evidence, what type of firms and industries tend to account for most of the innovative activity in North America? Data presented by the OECD in 2009 indicated that the majority of research and development is conducted by large firms, rather than small and medium-sized businesses. The percentage of business innovation activity undertaken by large companies, many of which operate in high concentration industries, is 85 percent in the U.S. and 64 percent in Canada.

High technology industries conduct the majority of research and development in the manufacturing sector in both the U.S. (67 percent) and Canada (59 percent). The high tech industries supply the following types products and services: computer hardware and software; communications; audio, video and television; and medical and pharmaceuticals. Canadian examples of innovative high tech companies include Nortel (computer networks) and Research In Motion (the BlackBerry).

Apple Inc. is a good example of how an oligopoly firm can use innovation, as well as other forms of nonprice competition already discussed, to effectively compete in high technology industries, as illustrated in Example 11–10.

### EXAMPLE 11–10 Apple's iMania

On May 26, 2010, the $222.12 billion market value of Apple Inc. surpassed that of Microsoft Corporation ($219.18 billion) to make Apple the second most valued corporation in North America. This is a remarkable feat considering that just over a decade ago the chief technology officer of Microsoft declared Apple to be an "already dead" corporation. From a relatively broad viewpoint, one can attribute Apple's rapid growth to its focus on high-quality product innovation in high growth and high technology industries.

Apple's creation of the iPod in conjunction with its innovative iTunes software allowed it to challenge Sony and gain a prominent position in the music media and music distribution industries.

In the first quarter of 2010, Apple sold 8.75 million iPhones, double the number sold in the same period a year before. With this rapid growth in sales, the iPhone now ranks third in the global smartphone market, with a 14 percent share, behind the products of Nokia Corporation (47 percent) and Research In Motion (20 percent). In June 2010, the iPhone 4 was released,

*continued*

offering yet another set of innovative features, including video calling. By November 2012, Apple's share of the smartphone market had climbed to 53.3 percent.

In 2010, Apple also created the iPad, a unique tablet computer that has the potential to create a new category of computers. The iPad provides its user with new ways to interact with the web, photos, music, videos, podcasts, HD movies, eBooks, TV shows, and thousands of software applications made especially for the device. As of 2016 the iPad had the largest share of the global tablet market at 24.7 percent, with Samsung in second place at 15.1 percent.

As consumers build their lives around the iPhone and its 200, 000 software applications, they're potentially locked into buying newer versions of the iPhone as well as other Apple devices. The smartphones supplied by competitors cannot connect to iTunes, which manages iPhone owners' music, video, photos, and other files. Nor can rival phones run the vast array of iPhone software applications that its users have become dependent on. As more and more apps are developed for the iPhone, more consumers are encouraged to switch to the iPhone, which attracts even more software applications. Apple requires its third-party software developers to use only Apple's programming tools, excluding all programming tools provided by competitors such as Adobe.

**For critical analysis:** Identify and explain three nonprice forms of competition effectively used by Apple.

Sources: Jessica Mintz. "iPhone's sales outshine more advanced phones." Waterloo Region Record (Kitchener, Ont.). May 22, 2010. Pg. D14; Jenna Wortham. "Apple places new limits on app developers. New York Times. April 12, 2010. http://www.nytimes.com/2010/04/13/technology/companies/13apple.html?_r=1&scp=1&sq=apple%20places%20new%20limits%20on%20app%20developers&st=Search; Miguel Helft and Ashlee Vance. "Apple passes Microsoft as no. 1 in technology." New York Times. May 26, 2010. http://www.nytimes.com/2010/05/27/technology/27apple.html; Apple's iPhone Share Will Probably Take A Bigger Hit As iPhone 6 Speculation Ramps. Chuck Jones. Tech. Forbes. January 4, 2014. http://www.forbes.com/sites/chuckjones/2014/04/01/apples-iphone-share-will-probably-take-a-bigger-hit-as-iphone-6-speculation-ramps/ (Accessed April 6, 2014); Apple Is About To Blow It In Tablets Too. Steve Kovach. Tech. Business Insider. Feb 10, 2014. http://www.businessinsider.com/samsung-tablets-will-overtake-ipad-2014-1 (Accessed April 6, 2014). Statista. Global tablet market share by tablet vendors. https://www.statista.com/statistics/276635/market-share-held-by-tablet-vendors/ (Accessed February 20, 2017).

As the OECD study indicates, Canadian businesses spend less on research and development as a percentage of their economy (1.5 percent) than the average OECD nation (2.4 percent). Economists attribute this relatively low level of innovative activity to two major factors. First, the high tech industries that typically focus on research and development activities are not as important in the resource-driven Canadian economy as in other developed nations. In addition, a significant number of large firms operating in Canada are owned by global multinational corporations where the research and development activities are conducted in the head offices located in other countries.

## 11.7 Social Evaluation of Oligopoly

Since in oligopoly just a few major firms supply a similar product, there is a danger that the lack of competitive pressure, coupled with the tendency to employ resources in unproductive types of nonprice competition, can result in productive inefficiency. Moreover, due to barriers to entry, the existing oligopolistic firms can continue to enjoy excess profits in the long run. To the extent that an oligopolistic industry engages in cooperative behaviour and acts like a monopoly, the industry will tend to restrict output and drive up the price compared with a competitive industry.

Depending on the specific situation, an oligopolistic market structure may be socially preferred over a more competitive environment. If significant economies of scale exist, cost efficiencies may be realized with just a few firms supplying the product or service. As well, there are both theoretical arguments as well as empirical evidence to suggest that an oligopolistic market structure can be conducive to innovation. The challenge lies in ensuring that the positive aspects of an oligopolistic market structure end up benefiting the consumer and not just the shareholders and executives of large corporations.

ISSUES AND APPLICATIONS

# Game Theory: Opening Up the Brewing Industry

**Concepts Applied: Game Theory, Strategic Behaviour, Entry Deterrence**

Craft beers with exotic names like Warthog Cream Ale or Blanche de Chambly are slowly gaining a share of the beer market. The Labatt and Molson beer companies have found it more profitable not to fight their entry.

In total, $9 billion worth of beer was sold in Canada during 2015, an increase of 3.1 percent from the previous year. Beer remains the most popular alcoholic beverage in Canada, comprising 42 percent of the alcoholic beverage market, followed by wine at 31.4 percent. Together, Molson Coors and Labatt (Labatt is now part of Anheuser-Busch InBev) produce the lion's share of Canadian beer—70 percent of it. However, premium imports and small microbreweries have grown from virtually no sales in 1985 to capturing 30 percent of the Canadian beer market in 2015. There are now over 500 microbreweries in Canada, producing craft beers with exotic names like Warthog Cream Ale, Moosehead Premium Dry, Blanche de Chambly, Brewmasters Black Lager, Rig Pig Pale Ale, Clancy's Amber Ale, Heroica Oatmeal Stout, Razzykat Raspberry Ale, and Black Oak Pale Ale. Part of the reason for the success of microbreweries is that many of these brands are unpasteurized specialty beers brewed without preservatives. As Canadians have aged, they have begun to drink less and discriminate more, turning from the old standards—Labatt Blue and Molson Canadian—to the high-quality craft beers.

Industry analysts suggest that a 1 percent share of the beer market is worth about $16 million in profits. So, why have Molson and Labatt not fought the entry into the industry by the microbreweries and the import beers? We can use game theory to help us answer this question.

## Constructing the Game

The two players in this game are: (1) Molson and Labatt, which currently dominate the market for beer; and (2) a representative microbrewery that wants to enter the market. Molson and Labatt can fight its entry or acquiesce. Fighting entry would cost each firm $1 million. The microbrewery's strategies are to enter the industry—which requires a $1 million fixed cost investment—or to stay out. If the firm successfully enters the market, it will capture a 1 percent market share worth $16 million. If it encounters a fight from the major breweries, however, it will lose the $1 million earmarked for setup costs.

## The Solution

Molson and Labatt know that if the microbrewery wants to enter the market, fighting will cost them $18 million, while acquiescing will cost $16 million in lost profits. If the microbrewery decides to stay out of the market, then fighting will cost them $2 million, while acquiescing will cost nothing. In either case, the two breweries choose to acquiesce.

The microbrewery knows that if Labatt and Molson want to fight entry, it is better off staying out of the market and not losing its $1 million. If, however, Labatt and Molson want to acquiesce, the microbrewery is better off entering. Since Molson and Labatt's dominant strategy is to acquiesce, the microbrewery enters the market.

## No Symmetrical Solution

This game is not symmetrical, since the microbrewery has no dominant strategy. If the major brewers decided to fight, the microbrewery would not enter the market. Nevertheless, Molson and Labatt choose not to fight, since fighting is an expensive undertaking. By behaving strategically, Molson and Labatt face increasing competition from small, high-quality brands.

## The Payoffs

Figure 11–5 shows the payoff matrix for this game. If Molson and Labatt fight entry but are unsuccessful, they spend $2 million on the fight and lose $16 million in profits to the successful microbrewery, so they lose $18 million in total. If they fight and win, they spend $2 million fighting but retain the market share. If Molson and Labatt acquiesce, they lose a 1 percent market share to the microbrewery, for a payoff of negative $16 million. If they acquiesce and the microbrewery stays out, they spend nothing and lose nothing.

If the microbrewery chooses to enter the market and the major breweries fight, the firm spends $1 million on fighting off the two companies. If the microbrewery enters but Molson and Labatt acquiesce, the microbrewery earns a $16 million profit less the $1 million setup costs. If the microbrewery stays out, there are no profits and no costs involved.

### For critical analysis:

1. Is this game a positive-sum, zero-sum, or negative-sum game? How do you know?
2. What strategies, besides fighting, could Labatt and Molson use to deter entry by the microbreweries?

Source: Control and sale of alcoholic beverages, for the year ending March 31, 2012. The Daily. April 11, 2013. Statistics Canada. http://www.statcan.gc.ca/daily-quotidien/130411/dq130411a-eng.htm (Accessed February 22, 2017); 2013 Annual Report. Page 4. Investors. Molson Coors. http://ph"x.corporate-ir.net/phoenix.zhtml?c=101929&p=irol-reports annual (Accessed April 13, 2014); Bringing People Together Anheuser-Busch InBev / 2013 Annual Report. Page 16. http://www.ab-inbev.com/pdf/AR13/ABI_AR13_EN_Narrative.pdf (Accessed April 13, 2014). Terry Reith and Briar Stewart."Microbreweries not a pint-sized industy anymore". CBC News. http://www.cbc.ca/news/canada/edmonton/microbreweries-not-a-pint-sized-industry-anymore-1.3114370 (Accessed February 22, 2017).

**FIGURE 11–5**
**Payoff Matrix**

This payoff matrix shows that if the microbrewery enters the market, the best strategy for Molson and Labatt is to acquiesce. By acquiescing, the two dominant brewers lose $16 million, which is $2 million better than the $18 million loss that would occur if Molson and Labatt had fought the entry. If the microbrewery decides to stay out of the market, the best strategy of Molson and Labatt is also to acquiesce, as they would lose $0 compared to $2 million if they had fought the entry. Therefore the dominant strategy for Molson and Labatt is to acquiesce. Once Molson and Labatt decide to acquiesce, the best strategy for the microbrewery is to enter the market and earn $15 million in profit.

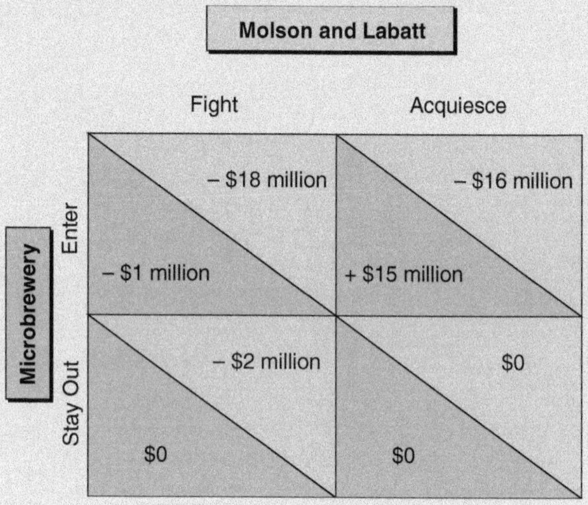


# SUMMARY

Here is what you should know after reading this chapter. MyEconLab will help you identify what you know, and where to go when you need to practise. We suggest that as soon as you review one of the Learning Objective sections below, you then proceed to go through the related section in MyEconLab.

| LEARNING OBJECTIVES | KEY TERMS | MYECONLAB PRACTICE |
|---|---|---|
| **11.1 The Characteristics of Monopolistic Competition.** Monopolistic competition, a market structure that lies between pure monopoly and perfect competition, has the following features: (1) a large number of sellers, (2) differentiated products, and (3) easy entry of firms in the long run. Each firm acts independently, as collusion is virtually impossible with a large number of competitors. | monopolistic competition, 280<br>product differentiation, 281 | • **MyEconLab** Study Plan 11.1 |

myeconlab

| LEARNING OBJECTIVES | KEY TERMS | MYECONLAB PRACTICE |
|---|---|---|
| **11.2 Short-Run Price, Output, and Profit in Monopolistic Competition.** Due to product differentiation, the demand curve for a firm in monopolistic competition is downward sloping, with marginal revenue below price. The firm chooses the profit-maximizing price-output combination—the output at which marginal revenue equals marginal cost, and the highest price possible at this output level, as determined by the demand curve. Total maximum profit equals the firm's maximum profit quantity level multiplied by the difference between the firm's price and average total cost, at the maximum profit quantity level. In the short run, the firm can be making a positive, negative, or zero economic profit. | | • **MyEconLab** Study Plan 11.2 |
| **11.3 Long-Run Equilibrium in Monopolistic Competition.** Similar to perfect competition, a monopolistically competitive firm will make a normal profit in the long run. The monopolistically competitive firm will operate at "excess capacity," which is at a quantity level that is less than the productively efficient, perfectly competitive, quantity level in the long run. Chamberlin argued that the difference between the average cost of production for a monopolistically competitive firm and a perfectly competitive firm is the cost of "differentness." | excess capacity, 284 | • **MyEconLab** Study Plan 11.3 |
| **11.4 The Characteristics of Oligopoly.** An oligopoly is a market situation dominated by a few interdependent sellers. An oligopoly market structure can exist for a homogeneous or a differentiated product. Oligopolies develop in the long run due to some type of barrier to entry such as economies of scale, legal restrictions, or firm-created barriers. Oligopoly industries exhibit high concentration ratios, which means that the top four or top eight firms account for a high percentage of industry sales. | oligopoly, 285<br>strategic dependence, 286<br>concentration ratio, 287 | • **MyEconLab** Study Plan 11.4 |

myeconlab

| LEARNING OBJECTIVES | KEY TERMS | MYECONLAB PRACTICE |
|---|---|---|
| **11.5 Pricing Behaviour in Oligopoly.** Since rival oligopoly firms are very interdependent, each firm must engage in strategic behaviour when determining its pricing strategy. One way to model this behaviour is to use game theory. The prisoners' dilemma game can be used to explain how an oligopoly firm, acting in its own individual self-interest, might engage in *noncooperative pricing behaviour*, even though this can reduce the joint profits of all the firms in the industry. In repeated games, the tit-for-tat strategy can result in *cooperative pricing behaviour.* Cooperative pricing strategies can include overt collusion tactics such as price fixing and cartels, or forms of tacit collusion such as price leadership. To the extent that oligopoly firms can cooperate and charge the monopoly price, joint profits will be maximized. There will be a greater tendency toward price cooperation (1) the smaller the number of rival firms, (2) in a growing industry situation, (3) the more identical the product supplied by all rivals, and (4) the lower the legal penalty attached to cooperative pricing behaviour. In some oligopoly situations the existing firms might engage in *price wars* or in order to deter new firms from entering the industry. | best response function, 287<br>game theory, 288<br>cooperative game, 288<br>noncooperative game, 288<br>zero-sum game, 288<br>negative-sum game, 288<br>positive-sum game, 288<br>strategy, 288<br>dominant strategies, 288<br>payoff matrix, 288<br>prisoners' dilemma, 289<br>opportunistic behaviour, 290<br>tit-for-tat strategy, 290<br>cartel, 292<br>price leadership, 293<br>predatory pricing, 294<br>price war, 296 | • **MyEconLab** Study Plan 11.5 |
| **11.6 The Nonprice Forms of Competition in Oligopoly.** Oligopoly firms often engage in nonprice forms of competition, including product differentiation, mergers, exclusive dealing, increasing switching costs, exploiting network effects, and innovation.<br>Types of product differentiation include differences in product features, consumer incentives, financing options, sales promotions, and advertising. These nonprice forms of competition can achieve more permanent gains in market share, when compared to price-cutting, opportunistic behaviour. Advertising creates some social disadvantages: (1) it can increase the cost of production without adding valuable consumer information; (2) it can act as a barrier to entry; (3) it can result in greater monopoly power; and (4) it can seriously mislead the | merger, 298<br>horizontal merger, 298<br>vertical merger, 298<br>conglomerate merger, 298<br>exclusive dealing, 298<br>network effects, 299 | • **MyEconLab** Study Plan 11.6 |

| LEARNING OBJECTIVES | KEY TERMS | MYECONLAB PRACTICE |
|---|---|---|
| consumer. Advertising also creates some social benefits: (1) it can provide valuable technical and price information about a product; (2) it can serve as a valuable signalling device; and (3) it can promote productive efficiency in cases where it increases the sales volume so that economies of scale can be achieved.<br>Oligopoly firms can increase market share quickly through horizontal mergers. Exclusive dealing refers to a situation where the firm supplies its product to a customer on condition that the customer not buy similar products from rival firms supplying a similar product. By increasing switching costs, an existing oligopoly firm can better insulate itself from price competition as well as deter the entry of new firms. If an oligopoly firm can exploit the network effect, it can gain market share very quickly, as Facebook had found.<br>Theoretical arguments suggest that an oligopoly market structure can be conducive to technological innovation. The large size of many oligopoly firms enables them to undertake expensive research and development activities. As well, due to barriers to entry and the lure of long-run excess profits, oligopoly firms have the incentive to innovate. Finally, interdependent oligopoly firms may prefer to channel their competitive energies in constructive product innovation as opposed to destructive price competition. | | |
| **11.7 Social Evaluation of Oligopoly.** The social cost of oligopoly can include productive inefficiency, allocative inefficiency, and excess profits. Oligopoly can benefit society if it results from economies of scale or if it contributes to innovation. | | • **MyEconLab** Study Plan 11.7 |

# PROBLEMS

(Answers to the odd-numbered problems appear at the back of the book.)

**LO 11.1 Identify and explain the characteristics of monopolistic competition.**

1. Local night clubs in a large city typically operate under what type of market structure? Explain.
2. Compare and contrast the characteristics of monopolistic competition with perfect competition.
3. Explain why it is not rational for a perfectly competitive firm to incur significant advertising expenditures.
4. Referring to Example 11-1, "A Canadian Retail Success: Twenty-Seven Years Running," identify the various ways that Running Room has engaged in product differentiation.

**LO 11.2 Using revenue and cost information, determine the price, output, and profit for a firm in monopolistic competition in the short run.**

5. Sue Willows, a preschool teacher, created and now sells a mail-order kids' basic interactive math game in a CD format that features a popular cartoon character. She competes with numerous other similar games that are sold in a hard copy book format or as board games sold by toy retailers as well as children's online math games that can be downloaded from the Internet for a fee. Sue promotes this game regularly on commercials that run on a popular children's TV channel. The accompanying graph describes the per-unit price, revenue, and cost data associated with selling the CD.

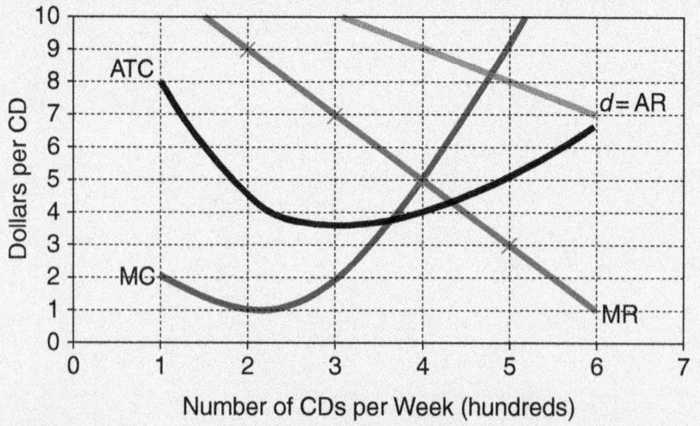


Based on this graph, complete the following.

a. Find the weekly profit-maximizing quantity.
b. Find the profit-maximizing price.
c. Find the total maximum weekly profit.
d. Which industry model best applies to Sue's game CD—perfect competition or monopolistic competition? Explain.

6. Tommy Soprano runs a take-out pizza outlet called The Healthy Alternative, which is located in a strip mall where there is a lot of parking available. Tommy sells only one type of pizza—a Loaded Vegetarian Pizza. The monthly fixed costs related to making and selling this pizza are: advertising $500; space and machine rental $1500; and salary and other costs $2000.

The variable costs involved in making and selling each pizza is $4 per pizza, regardless of the monthly quantity produced or sold.

Tommy directly competes with a children's pizza place, a meat lover's pizza parlour, as well as other takeout businesses selling hamburgers, subs, and Chinese food, all located within a three-block radius. Based on past experience, Tommy estimates the monthly demand for the Loaded Vegetarian Pizza as follows, depending on the pizza price.

| Price per Pizza (*P*) | Pizzas Sold Per Month (*Q*) | Total Revenue (TR) | Marginal Revenue (MR) | Marginal Cost (MC) |
|---|---|---|---|---|
| $18 | 3200 | ______ | ______ | ______ |
| 17 | 3600 | ______ | ______ | ______ |
| 16 | 4000 | ______ | ______ | ______ |
| 15 | 4400 | ______ | ______ | ______ |
| 14 | 4800 | ______ | ______ | ______ |

a. Fill in the blanks in the table. Note: To find marginal revenue, use the formula:

$$MR = (\text{Change in TR}) / (\text{Change in } Q)$$

b. Find the profit-maximizing quantity.
c. Find the profit-maximizing price.
d. Find the total maximum monthly profit.
e. Which industry model best suits Tommy's pizza firm—perfect competition or monopolistic competition? Explain.

**LO 11.3 Describe long-run equilibrium in monopolistic competition.**

7. The table at the top of the next page describes the price, revenue, and cost information for a small motel firm that rents rooms on a daily basis under monopolistic competition. Note that the quantity level refers to the number of rooms rented per night. The price refers to the nightly rental rate charged per room. Recall that marginal revenue is the extra revenue per room received, or the change in total revenue divided by the change in quantity.

a. Fill in the blanks in the table.
b. How many rooms must be rented per night in order to maximize profits?
c. What is the profit-maximizing price?
d. What is the amount of the total maximum profit?
e. Can this motel firm expect to earn these profits in the long run? Explain.
f. Identify the different ways motels and hotels can differentiate their "product."

| Quantity (# rooms) | Price (per room) | Total Revenue | Marginal Revenue | Marginal Cost | Average Total Cost |
|---|---|---|---|---|---|
| 0 | $95 | $____ | | | |
| 4 | 90 | ____ | $____ | $36 | $86.00 |
| 8 | 85 | ____ | ____ | 34 | 60.00 |
| 12 | 80 | ____ | ____ | 33 | 51.00 |
| 16 | 75 | ____ | ____ | 34 | 46.75 |
| 20 | 70 | ____ | ____ | 36 | 44.60 |
| 24 | 65 | ____ | ____ | 39 | 43.67 |
| 28 | 60 | ____ | ____ | 43 | 43.57 |
| 32 | 55 | ____ | ____ | 48 | 44.13 |

8. The graph below depicts long-run equilibrium for a monopolistic competitor.
   a. Which output rate represents equilibrium?
   b. Which price represents equilibrium?
   c. Which labelled point indicates that economic profits are zero?
   d. Which labelled point indicates minimum ATC?
   e. Is ATC at the equilibrium output rate above or at minimum ATC?
   f. Is the equilibrium price greater than, less than, or equal to the marginal cost of producing at the equilibrium output rate?
   g. At what quantity would a perfectly competitive firm operate in the long run? Explain. What would be the perfectly competitive firm's level of economic profit in the long run?

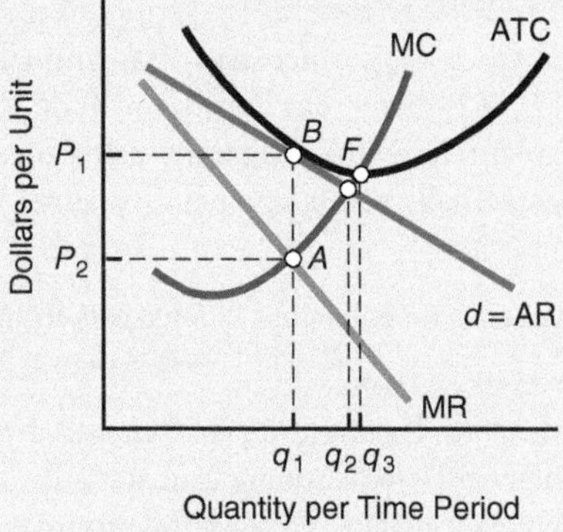


9. The following table depicts the hourly quantity sold, prices, and costs for a popular used bookstore located close to a university campus. This store competes with numerous rival used bookstores but capitalizes on its location and the word-of-mouth reputation of the coffee it serves to its customers.

| Quantity Sold (# Books) | Price ($) | Marginal Cost ($) | Average Total Cost ($) |
|---|---|---|---|
| 0 | 6.00 | | |
| 1 | 5.75 | 3.25 | 5.25 |
| 2 | 5.5 | 2.25 | 3.75 |
| 3 | 5.25 | 2.10 | 3.20 |
| 4 | 5.00 | 2.50 | 3.03 |
| 5 | 4.75 | 3.70 | 3.16 |
| 6 | 4.50 | 4.20 | 3.33 |
| 7 | 4.00 | 4.75 | 3.54 |

   a. Why would this bookstore be classed as a firm in monopolistic competition?
   b. In the short run, what would be the profit-maximizing hourly quantity, price, and total profit?
   c. Suppose that after long-run equilibrium were achieved, the bookstore ended up selling two books per hour. What would be the long-run price and economic profit?
   d. If this bookstore were operating in a perfectly competitive market, what would be the approximate price and economic profit, in the long run?

**LO 11.4 Identify and explain the characteristics of oligopoly.**

10. The following table indicates some information for industry A.

| Firm | Annual Sales ($ millions) |
|---|---|
| 1 | 200 |
| 2 | 150 |
| 3 | 100 |
| 4 | 75 |
| 5–30 | 300 |

   a. What is the four-firm concentration ratio for this industry (with just 30 firms)?
   b. Assume that industry A is the steel industry. What would happen to the concentration index if we redefined industry A as the cold rolled-steel industry? As the metals industry?

11. Classify each of the following as either a homogeneous product oligopoly or a differentiated product oligopoly.
   a. Cement manufacturing
   b. Auto manufacturing
   c. Oil refining
   d. Fast-food industry
   e. Soft drink manufacturing

12. Identify three types of barriers to entry characteristic of oligopoly.

**LO 11.5 Identify and explain the types of pricing behaviour that can occur in oligopoly.**

13. Suppose there are only two equal-sized firms—Firm A and Firm B—competing in an oligopoly industry. Each firm can decide either to raise or to lower the price of

the product. Each firm knows that the following outcomes will occur for each pricing decision, depending on how its rival reacts.

i. If both firms raise the price, each firm earns $5 million in annual profit.
ii. If both firms lower the price, each firm earns $3 million in annual profit.
iii. If one of the firms lowers the price while its rival raises the price, the firm with the low price will earn $7 million per year while the high-price firm will earn $1 million per year.

a. Construct a payoff matrix for these two oligopoly firms for all possible price decisions.
b. Assuming no collusion, what would be the dominant pricing strategy for each firm?
c. Suppose, in year 1, each firm decides to pursue cooperative pricing through collusion. What will be Firm A's annual profit?
d. Suppose, in year 2, Firm A decides to pursue opportunistic behaviour, while Firm B pursues a tit-for-tat strategy. What will be Firm A's profit in year 2?
e. If in year 3 both firms pursue a tit-for-tat strategy, what profit will Firm A earn in year 3?
f. In the long run, what would be the most profitable pricing strategy for each of these two firms?

14. Suppose two identical-sized oil refining firms, Apex and Petro, supply all the gasoline to a large city. If each firm agrees to limit its daily quantity to 20 000 litres per day, they will maximize their joint economic profits, with each firm earning $50 000 per day. If one of the firms increases its quantity to 40 000 litres, while the other firm supplies 20 000 litres, the economic profit earned by the firm with the larger quantity will increase to $75 000 per day, but the rival firm will be faced with an economic loss of $10 000 per day. If both companies increase their quantity so that each firm supplies 40 000 litres per day, zero economic profit will be earned by each competitor.
    a. Construct a payoff matrix.
    b. Assuming no collusion, in the short run, what would be the dominant quantity strategy for each firm?
    c. If the tit-for-tat strategy is repeatedly used, in the long run, what quantity strategy would each firm employ?

15. Explain whether each of the following will increase or decrease the tendency toward cooperative pricing in an oligopoly.
    a. The number of firms competing in the industry increases.
    b. All the firms produce an identical product.
    c. The industry sales are declining due to an economy wide recession.

16. On the basis of the information provided in Example 11–3, "OPEC Continues to Rule the World Oil Market," explain why Saudi Arabia is the key oil supplier responsible for the cooperative pricing behaviour displayed in OPEC.

17. Referring to Example 11–4, "De Beers Diamond Cartel: A Thing of the Past?", explain why diamonds are an attractive product to supply under a cartel arrangement.

**LO 11.6 Identify, explain, and evaluate the various nonprice forms of competition in oligopoly.**

18. Identify and explain three reasons why oligopolistic firms would favour nonprice competition over price competition.

19. According to Example 11–8, "Facebook Frenzy," social networking sites do not charge membership fees. Critically evaluate the idea that these online social networking sites are "free" to their members.

20. Identify and explain two arguments why an oligopoly industry environment might be very conducive to innovation.

21. When Coca-Cola increases its annual advertising expenses, it is likely that PepsiCo will do the same. Can you explain how this apparent self-cancelling behaviour can actually result in a positive-sum game for both companies?

**LO 11.7 Evaluate the behaviour in oligopoly from a social viewpoint.**

22. According to Example 11–6, "Can Advertising Lead to Efficiency?", advertising can actually contribute to productive efficiency. Explain the argument used in this example.

# BUSINESS APPLICATION

**LO 11.6 Identify, explain, and evaluate the various nonprice forms of competition in oligopoly.**

## Marketing: The Marketing Mix: The Four Ps

In order to enhance revenue and profit, firms operating under monopolistic competition and oligopoly may engage in product differentiation as well as price competition. In marketing terms, these firms attempt to create an effective *marketing mix* based on the needs and wants of their target market(s).

The *marketing mix* refers to the development of appropriate strategies for each of the "Four Ps"—*product*, *place*, *promotion*, and *price*. *Product* focuses on attributes such as design features, quality, types of services offered, guarantees, warranties, packaging, and style. *Place* refers to the selection and management of marketing channels and the physical distribution of products. In short, *place* is concerned with getting the product or service to the customer conveniently. *Promotion* refers to the methods the firm uses to enhance the target market's awareness and knowledge of the product or service being offered. These methods can include advertising, sales promotion, personal selling, and public relations. *Price* not only refers to the regular price of the product or service but also includes discounts, allowances, credit terms, and methods of payment accepted.

## Business Application Problem

Steve Boyd has just started a business called InfoMutual that will provide monthly Canadian mutual fund information to sophisticated investors and to firms that sell mutual funds such as brokers, banks, and other financial advisors. Indicate which one of the Four Ps best relates to each of the following.

a. After considering other alternatives such as mail and fax, Steve decides to distribute his mutual fund information through a website.

b. In addition to providing the latest information relating to each Canadian mutual fund's performance, Steve plans to conduct sophisticated statistical analysis measuring the risk related to each type of fund. His analysis will also relate each mutual fund's performance with other mutual funds and with economywide factors.

c. In order to make his service known to prospective customers, Steve decides to register InfoMutual with major Internet search engines such as Google and Bing, as well as Facebook.

d. Steve rejects the idea of charging a monthly fee. Instead, customers can access his monthly information by paying a six-month or a one-year subscription fee.

e. Every quarter, Steve plans to provide detailed research reports to paid subscribers. These reports will profile a specific family of funds.

f. Steve plans to offer a cheaper educational subscription rate for business schools in colleges and universities that purchase a "site licence" for his services.

g. InfoMutual will regularly participate in popular investor blog and wiki discussions on the Internet in order to increase consumer awareness of the new company.

h. In order to make it convenient to pay for InfoMutual's subscription fee, each new customer will be provided with a free one-month temporary password. This free month of full service should provide ample time for the customer to arrange for the secure payment of the subscription fee.

i. Steve plans to have animated ads for InfoMutual appear on popular news and sports websites.

# 12

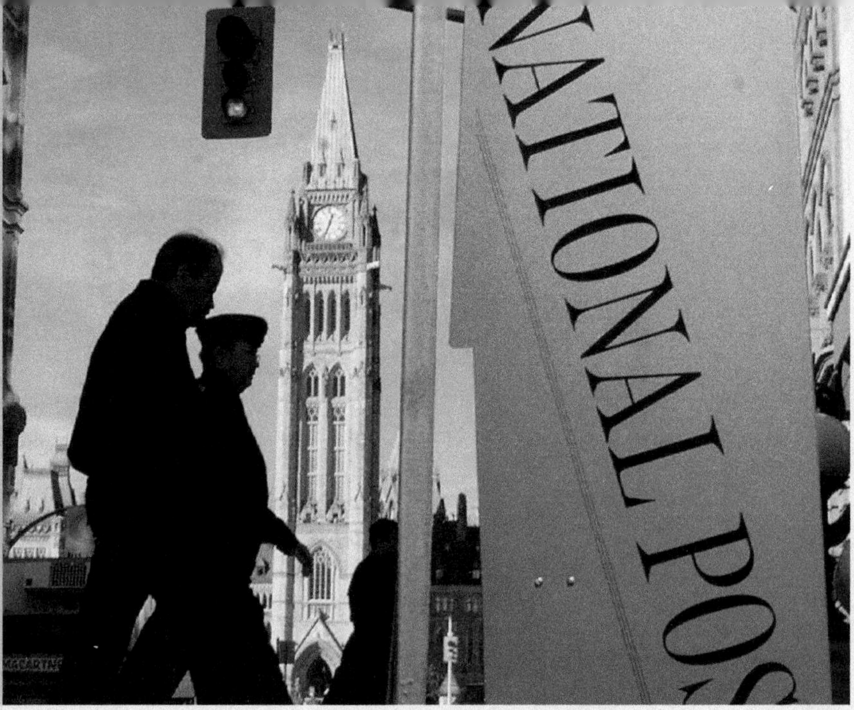

## LEARNING OBJECTIVES

After reading this chapter, you should be able to:

**12.1** Explain and evaluate the two broad types of government regulation of business.

**12.2** Identify and contrast the various theories used to explain the behaviour of regulators.

**12.3** Explain the short-run and long-run economic effects of deregulation.

**12.4** Describe the various ways in which Canada's *Competition Act* benefits consumers.

myeconlab

MyEconLab helps you master each objective and study more efficiently. See end of chapter for details

# Regulation and Competition Policy

On March 25, 2015 the Canadian Competition Bureau gave the green light to Postmedia Corporation's $316-million bid to buy Sun Media's English-language newspapers and digital properties from Quebecor Inc. Based on a five month review, , the Bureau has issued a No Action Letter confirming that it will not challenge the proposed transaction before the Competition Tribunal under the merger provisions of the Competition Act. As a result of the merger, there will be only one owner of daily paid circulation newspapers in a number of Canadian cities including Vancouver, Calgary, Edmonton, and Ottawa.

Less than 2 years before the Post Media merger, the Canadian regulator, Canadian Radio-television and Telecommunications Commission (CRTC), approved of a blockbuster merger, where Bell Media purchased Astral Media for $3.38 billion, resulting in just three major Canadian corporations – BCE (Bell), Rogers, and Shaw- owning and distributing the lion's share of English speaking Canadian radio and television channels and networks.

Is the concentration of ownership in Canadian media industries a social concern? To understand this issue, you need to know more about government regulation and competition policy.

Sources: "Bell's bid for Astral approved." Report on Business. Globe and Mail. June 27, 2013. http://www.theglobeandmail.com/report-on-business/bell-astral/article12861071/ (Accessed February 2, 2017). "Postmedia gets approval to buy Sun Media newspapers." By MADHAVI ACHARYA-TOM YEW. Wed March 25, 2015.Business. thestar.com. https://www.thestar.com/business/2015/03/25/postmedia-gets-ok-from-competition-bureau-to-buy-sun-media-newspapers.html (Accessed February 5, 2017).

# DID YOU KNOW THAT...?

Each year, thousands of pages of new or modified federal regulations are published. These regulations, found in the *Canada Gazette,* cover virtually every aspect of the way business can be conducted, products can be built, and services can be offered. In addition, every province and municipality publishes regulations relating to worker safety, restaurant cleanliness, and the number of lights needed in each room in a day-care centre. There is no question about it: Canadian business activities are highly regulated. Consequently, how regulators should act to promote the public's interest, and how they actually act are important topics for understanding today's economy.

Besides regulation, the Canadian government has an additional tool it uses to encourage businesses to better serve consumers. It is called competition policy, and it is the subject of the latter part of this chapter.

# 12.1 Types of Government Regulation

The federal government began regulating economic and social activity early in Canadian history, but the amount of government regulation significantly increased during the 20th century. There are two broad types of government regulation of Canadian business—economic regulation and social regulation.

## Economic Regulation

**Economic regulation** is intended to control the prices that regulated enterprises are allowed to charge. Various public utility commissions across the country regulate the rates (prices) of electricity and natural gas utilities and telephone operating companies. This is often referred to as *rate regulation.* The goal of rate regulation has, in principle, been to prevent monopoly firms from operating at inefficient levels of output and charging excessive prices.

**Economic regulation** Regulation that controls the prices that firms are allowed to charge.

Figure 12–1 describes a natural monopoly situation, where the long-run average total cost continues to decline over the relevant quantity levels of production. What type of price, quantity, and profit behaviour can we expect from the monopoly firm in Figure 12–1, if it is unregulated? As part (a) of Figure 12–1 describes, the unregulated monopolist will tend to restrict its supply to 5000 units of output and charge a relatively high price of $8 per unit, where marginal revenue equals marginal cost. At this output level, the monopoly firm earns an excess (economic) profit, as price exceeds average total cost. Since at 5000 units of output, the price, or marginal benefit, exceeds marginal cost, the monopolist is underallocating resources to the provision of this product or service. In other words, the monopolist is operating in an allocatively inefficient manner.

Do regulations help industries or hurt them?

Would it be in the public's best interests to have government pursue a strategy of encouraging more firms to enter the industry described in Figure 12–1? Not necessarily, as in a natural monopoly situation the one existing firm can operate at a lower cost per unit than would be the case if a number of firms supplied this product or service. What, then, should government do?

One solution is to maintain the monopoly situation but have government regulate the rate (price) and quantity that the monopoly firm can establish. Ideally, in order to fully achieve allocative efficiency, government should encourage marginal cost pricing where the price is set at a level equal to the marginal cost of production. In Figure 12–1 part (b), this would imply setting the price and quantity at $4 per unit and 9000 units, respectively. However, at 9000 units of output, price is below average total cost, so the firm would incur an economic loss. If the government were to enforce the $4 price over a long period of time, the firm would go out of business!

**COST OF SERVICE REGULATION.** In order to maintain the viability of the natural monopolist, rate regulation policies have typically involved cost-of-service regulation and rate-of-return regulation. A regulatory commission using **cost-of-service regulation** allows the regulated companies to charge prices that reflect the actual average cost of providing the services, with a normal profit included in the assessment of these costs. In terms of Figure 12–1 part (b), cost-of-service regulation would result in the monopoly firm establishing a price and quantity level of $6 per unit and 7000 units, respectively, where price just equals average total cost. Cost-of-service regulation is socially preferred over an unregulated monopoly situation in that the consumer enjoys a larger quantity at a lower price, and the monopolist just earns a normal profit.

**Cost-of-service regulation** Regulation that allows the regulated companies to charge prices that reflect the actual average cost of providing the services, with a normal profit included in the assessment of these costs.

**FIGURE 12–1**

**Profit Maximization and Regulation**

The unregulated profit-maximizing monopolist will produce at the point in part (a) where marginal revenue equals marginal cost, which means production of 5000 units of output. The price charged would be $8 and the firm would be making excess or positive economic profit as price exceeds long-run average total cost (LATC). Referring to part (b), if the regulatory commission enforced marginal cost pricing, production would take place at the point where the demand curve just equals the marginal cost curve, which results in a price and quantity level of $4 and 9000 units, respectively. At the 9000 quantity level, the price of $4 is less than the long-run average total cost, and so the firm will incur an economic loss. If, instead, the regulatory commission pursued cost-of-service or rate-of-return regulation, the firm would set a price of $6 and a quantity level of 7000 units, where the demand curve just equals the long-run average total cost curve.

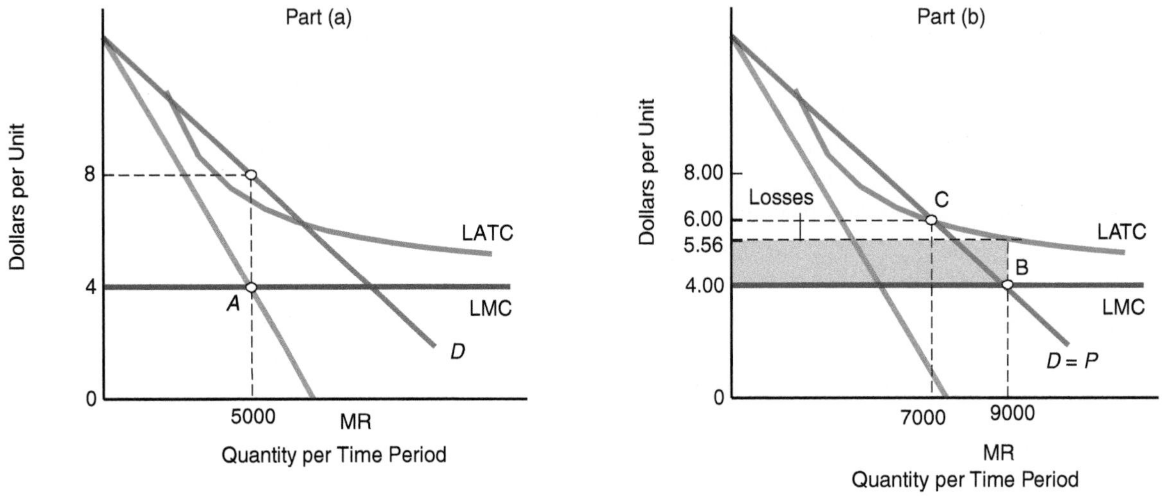


**Rate-of-return regulation**
Regulation that allows regulated companies to set prices that ensure a normal, or competitive, rate of return on the investment in the business.

**RATE OF RETURN REGULATION.** From a practical point of view, cost-of-service regulation is difficult and expensive to administer. If you think of the large-scale operations related to electricity, natural gas, and phone companies, you can imagine that an army of government accountants would be required to constantly monitor the movement of thousands of service and cost items, in order to compute an accurate average cost of production for each service provided. To efficiently regulate these large monopolies, governments typically use the **rate-of-return regulation** method, which allows regulated companies to set prices that ensure a normal, or competitive, rate of return on the investment in the business. In terms of Figure 12–1 part (b), the rate-of-return method of regulation will, in theory, result in a price–quantity combination of $6 per unit and 7000 units, where price equals average total cost, similar to cost-of-service regulation.

Critics of the rate-of-return method suggest that this form of regulation encourages regulated firms to "pad expenses" and therefore breeds inefficiency. For example, suppose that the regulator allows the monopoly firm to set its prices so that the firm achieves a 10 percent rate of return on its capital investment. Since the regulated company knows that it will be guaranteed a 10 percent rate of return, it can earn a larger dollar profit by overpurchasing capital equipment. What this suggests is that regulated firms have no incentive to keep costs at a minimum under the rate-of-return method of regulation.

Another problem common to both cost-of-service and rate-of-return regulation concerns the quality of the service or product provided. Consider the many facets of telephone service: getting a dial tone, hearing other voices clearly, getting the operator to answer quickly, having out-of-order telephone lines repaired rapidly, putting through a long-distance call quickly and efficiently—the list goes on and on. But regulation of a telephone company usually deals with the prices charged for telephone service. Of course, regulators are concerned with the quality of service, but how could that be measured? Indeed, it cannot be measured very easily. Therefore, it is extremely difficult for any type of regulation to be successful in regulating the *price per constant-quality unit.* Certainly, it is possible to regulate the price per unit, but we do not really know that the quality remains unchanged when the price is not allowed to rise "enough." Thus, if regulation does not allow prices to rise, quality of service may be lowered, thereby raising the price per constant-quality unit.

**NATURAL MONOPOLIES NO MORE?** For years, the electricity, natural gas, and telecommunications industries were subject to economic regulation because they were viewed as natural monopolies.

More recently, regulators decided the function of producing electricity or natural gas could be separated from the delivery of the product. This could be done because the significant economies of scale were in the distribution networks—pipelines and wire. The distribution networks are still regulated as natural monopolies, but in many jurisdictions the various producers of natural gas and electricity now compete in an unregulated environment.

In the telephone markets, both local and long distance, the traditional land-line phone companies in the larger urban areas are no longer natural monopolies, as they now face competition from cellphone services, Internet-VOIP, and cable companies. As Example 12–1 indicates, the regulators of Canada's telephone industries have started deregulating the various phone markets where there is no longer a natural monopoly situation.

## EXAMPLE 12–1 Deregulation Hits Canadian Phone Markets

On April 30, 2007, the CRTC, which regulates the traditional land-line phone companies, gave Bell Canada Enterprises (BCE Inc.), Telus Corporation, and other former monopolies more freedom to set local phone rates, letting them charge more in rural areas and vary rates among different sets of customers.

Under the old rules, BCE and Telus had to apply to the CRTC to change the rates they charged their customers until they could show that they had lost a 25 percent share of a given market to cable, cellular, and/or Internet phone competitors. This application could take two or three years to process and get approved. On the other hand, the rivals of the large land-line phone companies, such as the cable companies or the cellular companies, did not have to get CRTC approval to change their prices.

To level the playing field among all competitors, the federal Conservative government directed the CRTC to institute a new policy in the direction of deregulation. Under the new rules, the large, traditional phone providers such as BCE and Telus only have to show that they face three rival phone companies in a specific residential market or two rivals in a business market. The rivals could be cellular, Internet, or cable phone companies. After receiving the application to change phone rates, the CRTC must review and process the application within a 120-day period. Once approved, the large telecoms are free to lower prices, but if they raise prices on basic phone service, they are subject to a price ceiling set by CRTC. However, the new policy has scrapped price caps or limits in cases where prices are increased on optional services such as call waiting or voice mail. Overall, the deregulation policy will provide greater flexibility for the large phone companies to bundle telephone services with their other services such as Internet and television.

On June 3, 2013, the CRTC passed a new wireless code aimed at increasing competition in the deregulated telecom industry. For new cell phone contracts that start on or after Dec 2, 2013, customers can terminate these contracts after two years, without paying cancellation fees. As of June 3, 2015, additional pro-competitive practices become available to cell phone customers under the CRTC wireless code. First, the code will now apply to all existing mobile phone contracts in operation, and not jut new contracts. Cell phone customers can walk away from their contracts with no penalty, after two years have passed in their existing contract. Consumers who wish to switch carriers at any time before the two year period can do so by paying a reasonable fee constricted by the CRTC. A cap has been paid on monthly roaming charges to prevent "bill shock." Customers are afforded a trial period of 15 days, after signing the contract, to cancel without penalty. Consumers can get their cellphones unlocked after 90 days, or immediately if they paid for the device in full.

**For critical analysis:** Under the new policy of local phone deregulation, predict the different ways that the large telephone companies might practise price discrimination between its various customer groups and/or different services in order to enhance profits. Recall that price discrimination refers to the practice of charging different prices based on differences in willingness to pay (elasticity, etc.) and not on cost differences.

Source: Peter Nowak. "Phone firms gain freedom; Deregulation could result in price wars." *National Post*. National edition. April 5, 2007. Pg. A1; Ottawa cites more competition behind moves to regulate telecom industry. LuAnn LaSalle. Canadian Press. Dec 29, 2013. http://o.canada.com/business/2013-telecom-regulation-competition/

Should the cellphone industry in Canada be regulated?

(Accessed Feb 22, 2014); Canadians can cancel their wireless contracts after two years under new CRTC wireless code. News Releases 2013. Media. Canadian Radio-television and Telecommunications Commission. http://www.crtc.gc.ca/eng/com100/2013/r130603.htm (Accessed February 23, 2014). "New cellphone contract rules: What you need to know." CTVnews.ca staff. Business. CTVnews. June 3, 2015. http://www.ctvnews.ca/business/new-cellphone-contract-rules-what-you-need-to-know-1.2404459 (Accessed February 8, 2017).

## Social Regulation

**Social regulation** Regulation that reflects concern for public welfare across all industries.

**Social regulation** reflects concern for public welfare across all industries. In other words, regulation is focused on the impact of production on the environment and society, the working conditions under which goods and services are produced, and sometimes the physical attributes of goods. The aim is a better quality of life for all through a less polluted environment, better working conditions, and safer and better products, and through the promotion of other valued social goals. For example, Health Canada attempts to protect consumers against impure and unsafe foods, drugs, cosmetics, and other potentially hazardous products; the Atomic Energy Control Board (AECB) controls the use and disposal of all radioactive materials to ensure the health, safety, and security of the public and the preservation of the environment; the Workers' Compensation Board attempts to protect workers against work-related injuries and illnesses; and the Canadian Human Rights Commission seeks to ensure fair access for all to jobs.

In this chapter's Issues and Applications, it is noted that the CRTC has approved a number of company acquisitions that have significantly increased the concentration of economic power in Canada's media industries. For example, in 2000, the CRTC allowed BCE to buy the CTV network, a decision that created Canada's largest communications company. Similarly, in 2001, the CRTC let Quebecor purchase the TVA television network, making it a dominant firm in the Quebec television broadcasting market. This purchase was allowed, even though Quebecor already owned Videotron, Quebec's largest cable company, and Sun Media, the second-largest newspaper group in Canada. The CRTC approved these acquisitions on the condition that Bell and Quebecor undertake to create a significant amount of new Canadian television programming. These policy decisions are examples of social regulation where the policy goals include the encouragement of indigenous Canadian cultural activities and the promotion of jobs for Canadian artists, writers, and producers.

Table 12–1 lists some major federal regulatory agencies and their areas of concern. Although most people agree with the idea behind such social regulation, many disagree on whether we have too much regulation—whether it costs us more than the benefits we receive. Some contend that the costs that firms incur in abiding by regulations run into billions of dollars per year. The result is higher production costs, which are then passed on to consumers. Also, the resources invested in complying with regulatory measures could be invested in other uses. Furthermore, extensive regulation may have an anti-competitive effect because it may represent a relatively greater burden for smaller firms than for larger ones.

**TABLE 12–1**

**Some Federal Regulatory Agencies**

| Agency | Jurisdiction | Date Formed | Major Regulatory Functions |
|---|---|---|---|
| Canadian Dairy Commission | Product Markets | 1967 | Sets support prices for milk used in making dairy products for the domestic market. |
| CRTC | Product Markets | 1976 | Regulates broadcasting to balance interests of consumers, the creative community, and distribution industries. |
| Canada Industrial Relations Board | Labour Markets | 1948 | Enforces the *Canada Labour Code* where workers are direct employees of the federal government, or the employers fall within the authority of Parliament. |
| Bank of Canada | Financial Markets | 1934 | Regulates credit and currency and ensures the soundness of Canadian financial institutions. |
| Atomic Energy Control Board | Energy and Environment | 1946 | Enforces health, safety, security, and environmental standards for the use of nuclear energy, and licenses users of radioactive material. |
| Canadian Food Inspection Agency | Health and Safety | 1997 | Sets and enforces standards for food quality and food delivery systems. |
| Transport Canada | Health and Safety | 1936 | Establishes and enforces regulations necessary for safety in civil aviation, marine transport, and rail transport. |

But the *potential* benefits of more social regulation are many. For example, the water we drink in some cities is known to be contaminated with cancer-causing chemicals, and air pollution from emissions and toxic wastes from production processes cause many illnesses. Some contaminated areas have been cleaned up, but many other problem areas remain. Social regulation can address problems such as these.

The benefits of social regulation may not be easy to measure and may accrue to society over a long time. Furthermore, it is difficult to put a dollar value on safer working conditions and a cleaner environment. In any case, the debate goes on. However, it should be pointed out that the controversy is generally not about whether we should have social regulation, but about when and how it is being done and whether we take *all* of the costs and benefits into account. For example, is regulation best carried out by federal, provincial, or local authorities? Is a specific regulation economically justified through a complete cost–benefit analysis?

Policy Example 12–1 points to yet another potential problem with social regulation. It may not be very effective in attaining its stated goals in situations where foreign firms operate in Canadian markets and provide services to Canadian consumers.

### POLICY EXAMPLE 12–1 Can the CRTC Effectively Regulate Cable TV?

One function of the CRTC is to ensure that Canadian-made programs have a chance to be broadcast in Canada. The CRTC accomplishes this through its power to grant and renew broadcasting licences. The current standard is that Canadian broadcasters must include in their programming 60 percent Canadian content measured over a day, with at least 50 percent Canadian content in the evening hours. The CBC faces even greater content quotas.

Is the CRTC really ensuring that Canadians view Canadian-made programming? Not really. The spread of satellite dishes and pay-TV, for example, make American TV stations—such as WSBK in Boston, WGN in Chicago, and KTLA in Los Angeles—as accessible as Canadian stations. And the CRTC has no regulatory powers over those American broadcasters.

Over the past few years, companies such as Netflix, that stream movies and TV shows online, have experienced explosive growth in Canada. In April, 2016, forty-six percent per cent of Canadians said they used Netflix to stream a full-length movie or TV show in the past month. In 2011, that percentage stood at eleven per cent. In the one year period, June 2015 to June 2016, it is estimated that Netflix added more than one million new Canadian subscribers. Currently the CRTC does not require that the providers of these online streaming services meet Canadian content rules.

In 2015, the CRTC loosened the Canadian content rules imposed on traditional Canadian TV broadcasters and networks. While local and specialty stations will still have to devote half their prime-time schedule to Canadian content, the quota for daytime TV drops to zero from 55 per cent. The intent is to allow the traditional Canadian TV broadcasters and networks to better compete with online streaming services and foreign TV stations.

In August 2016, the CRTC reduced the number of points needed for a production to be deemed Canadian, effectively weakening the Canadian content rules.

**For critical analysis:** Is there any way the CRTC could ensure that the American channels carry Canadian content?

Source: "Netflix now has more than 5.2 million customers in Canada, report suggests."June 15, 2016. Business. News. CBCnews. http://www.cbc.ca/news/business/netflix-streaming-cord-cutting-1.3636305 (Accessed February 9, 2016); "Canadian screenwriters see red after recent CRTC funding rule changes."FRANCOIS MARCHAND. September 12, 2016. Local Arts. Arts and Life. Vancouver Sun (Accessed February 9, 2016).

## Creative Response and Feedback Effects: Results of Regulation

Regulated firms commonly try to avoid the effects of regulation whenever they can. In other words, the firms engage in **creative response**, which is a response that conforms to the letter of the law but undermines its spirit. Take federal laws requiring male–female pay equity: The wages of women must be on a par with those paid to men who are performing

**Creative response** A response that conforms to the letter of the law but undermines its spirit.

the same tasks. Employers that pay the same wages to both men and women are clearly not in violation of the law. However, wages are only one component of total employee compensation. Another component is fringe benefits, such as on-the-job training. Because on-the-job training is difficult to observe from outside the firm, employers could offer less on-the-job training to women and still not be in technical violation of pay-equity laws. This unobservable difference would mean that men were able to acquire skills that could raise their future income even though current wages among men and women were equal, in compliance with the law.

Individuals have a type of creative response that has been labelled the *feedback effect.* Regulation may alter individuals' behaviour after the regulation has been put into effect. If regulation requires fluoridated water, then parents know that their children's teeth have significant protection against tooth decay. Consequently, the feedback effect on parents' behaviour is that they may be less concerned about how many sweets their children eat. Example 12–2 shows that in the case of auto safety, the feedback effect may not always work to the consumer's advantage.

### EXAMPLE 12–2 The Effectiveness of Auto Safety Regulation

A good example of the feedback effect has to do with automotive safety regulation. For many years, the federal government has required automobile manufacturers to make cars increasingly safer. Some of the earlier requirements involved nonprotruding door handles, collapsible steering columns, shatterproof glass, daytime running lights, better seat belts, and airbags. The desired result was fewer injuries and deaths for drivers involved in accidents. According to economist Sam Peltzman, however, due to the feedback effect, drivers have gradually started driving more recklessly. Automobiles with more safety features have been involved in a disproportionate number of accidents.

More recent debates regarding the feedback effect and automobile safety relate to the introduction of red light cameras and backup cameras.

**For critical analysis:** The feedback effect has also been called the law of unintended consequences. Why?

# 12.2 Explaining Regulators' Behaviour

Regulation has usually been defended by contending that government regulatory agencies are needed to correct market imperfections. We are dealing with a nonmarket situation because regulators are paid by the government and their decisions are not determined or constrained by the market. A number of theories have been put forward to describe the behaviour of regulators. These theories can help us understand how regulation has often harmed consumers through higher prices and less choice and benefited producers through higher profits and fewer competitive forces. Two of the best-known theories of regulatory behaviour are the *capture hypothesis* and the *share-the-gains, share-the-pains theory.*

## The Capture Hypothesis

**Capture hypothesis** A theory of regulatory behaviour that predicts that the regulators will eventually be captured by the special interests of the industry being regulated.

It has been observed that with the passage of time, regulators often end up adopting the views of the regulated. According to the **capture hypothesis**[1]—a theory of regulatory behaviour that predicts that the regulators will eventually be captured by the special interests of the industry being regulated—no matter what the reason for a regulatory agency's having been set up, it will eventually be captured by the special interests of the industry that is being regulated. Consider the reasons.

Who knows best about the industry that is being regulated? The people already in the industry. Who, then, will be asked to regulate the industry? Again, people who have been in the industry. And people who used to be in the industry have allegiances and friendships with others in the industry.

[1] See George Stigler. *The Citizen and the State: Essays on Regulation.* Chicago: University of Chicago Press, 1975.

Also consider that whenever regulatory hearings are held, the affected consumer groups will have much less information about the industry than the people already in the industry, the producers. Additionally, the cost to any one consumer to show up at a regulatory hearing to express concern about a change in the rate structure will certainly exceed any perceived benefit that consumer could obtain from going to the rate-making hearing.

Because they have little incentive to do so, consumers and taxpayers will not be well organized, nor will they be greatly concerned with regulatory actions. But the special interests of the industry are going to be well organized and well defined. Political entrepreneurs within the regulatory agency see little payoff in supporting the views of consumers and taxpayers anyway. After all, few consumers understand the benefits deriving from regulatory agency actions. Moreover, how much could a consumer directly benefit someone who works in an agency? Regulators have the most incentive to support the position of a well-organized special-interest group within the industry that is being regulated.

## Share the Gains, Share the Pains

A somewhat different view of regulators' behaviour is given in the **share-the-gains, share-the-pains theory**[2], a theory of regulatory behaviour in which the regulators must take account of the demands of three groups: legislators, who established and who oversee the regulatory agency; members of the regulated industry; and consumers of the regulated industry's products or services. This theory looks at the specific aims of the regulators. It argues that a regulator simply wants to continue in the job.

**Share-the-gains, share-the-pains theory** A theory of regulatory behaviour in which the regulators must take account of the demands of three groups: legislators, members of the regulated industry, and consumers of the regulated industry's products or services.

Under the capture hypothesis, only the special interests of the industry being regulated had to be taken into account by the regulators. The share-the-gains, share-the-pains model contends that such a position is too risky because customers who are really hurt by improper regulation will complain to legislators, who might fire the regulators. Thus, each regulator has to attach some weight to these three separate groups. What happens if there is an abrupt increase in fuel costs for electrical utilities? The capture theory would predict that regulators would relatively quickly allow for a rate increase in order to maintain the profits of the industry. The share-the-gains, share-the-pains theory, however, would predict that there will be an adjustment in rates, but not as quickly or as completely as the capture theory would predict. The regulatory agency is not completely captured by the industry; it has to take account of legislators and consumers.

## Deregulation

In recent years, the cost of government regulation in Canada has been growing. In a study published by the Fraser Institute in 2001, it was found that between 1975 and 1999 over 117 000 new federal and provincial regulations were enacted, an average of 4700 per year. Over this 24-year period, federal and provincial governments published over 505 000 pages of regulations contained in volumes that measure 10 stories high. But actual direct costs to taxpayers are only a small part of the overall cost of regulation. Pharmaceutical manufacturing safety standards raise the prices of drugs. Automobile safety standards raise the prices of cars. Environmental controls on manufacturing raise the prices of manufactured goods. All of these increased prices add to the cost of regulation. Studies suggest that the cost of administering federal regulations is about $50 billion per year. When you add the cost of enforcing regulations at the municipal and provincial levels, the total rises to $86 billion, or about 12 percent of each year's GDP!

Despite the fact that all levels of government devote a significant amount of our limited resources to the regulation of businesses, it is not clear to what extent these government policies effectively achieve their stated goals. As we have just seen, rate-of-return regulation can encourage natural monopolies to be inefficient. Due to behaviour consistent with the capture hypothesis and creative response, the regulated firms may continue to operate to the detriment of public interest. Not surprisingly, the increasing cost of regulation on occasion has brought about cries for **deregulation**, the elimination of regulations on economic activity.

**Deregulation** The elimination of regulations on economic activity.

[2] See Sam Peltzman. "Towards a More General Theory of Regulation." *Journal of Law and Economics*, 19 (1976), pp. 211–40.

# 12.3 Short-Run versus Long-Run Effects of Deregulation

The short-run effects and the long-run effects of deregulation are quite different. In the short run, a regulated industry that becomes deregulated may experience numerous temporary adjustments. One is the inevitable shakeout of higher-cost producers with the accompanying removal of excess monopoly profits. Another is the sometimes dramatic displacement of workers who have laboured long and hard in the formerly regulated industry. The level of service for some consumers may fall; for example, after the deregulation of the Canadian National Railway (CNR), service to many small communities was eliminated, as the CNR off-loaded over 2000 kilometres of track. The power of unions in the formerly regulated industry may decrease. And bankruptcies may cause disruptions, particularly in the local economy where the headquarters of the formerly regulated firm are located.

Those who support deregulation, or at least less regulation, contend that there are long-run, permanent benefits. These include lower prices that are closer to marginal cost. Furthermore, lower monopoly profits are made in the deregulated industry. Such proponents argue that deregulation has positive *net* benefits.

Policy Example 12–2 describes how the Ontario government pursued a policy of electricity deregulation in order to bring about a more secure supply of power, lower electricity rates, and a reduced level of provincial government debt. Unfortunately, the short-run response to deregulation has caused the provincial government to pursue policies that work against the successful implementation of this type of deregulation in the long run.

### POLICY EXAMPLE 12–2 Ontario's Feeble Attempt at Energy Deregulation

The *Energy Competition Act* was passed by the Ontario government in November 1998, beginning the process of deregulating Ontario's electricity industry. Under this Act, the former Ontario Hydro monopoly was replaced by two separate commercial operations—Ontario Power Generation (OPG) and Hydro One Inc. OPG was to focus on the generation of electricity in Ontario, while Hydro One was responsible for the transmission and distribution of electricity in the province. Deregulation was to apply to the firms generating the electricity, thanks to small-turbine technology and the power grid. The distribution and transmission of electricity in Ontario was to continue as a regulated monopoly situation.

Why energy deregulation in Ontario? Prior to deregulation, all of the province's electricity was generated by one large government-owned monopoly firm, Ontario Hydro. By the late 1990s, Ontario Hydro had accumulated a massive debt of approximately $38.1 billion, which was about a third of the total provincial government debt. Ontario Hydro's financial woes were largely due to major cost overruns in the construction of large-scale nuclear generation facilities, many of which are currently out of operation. Moreover, despite the growing Ontario Hydro debt, industry analysts were projecting serious power shortages for the province within the next 10 to 15 years.

With the advent of new technology conducive to small-scale electricity generation, it seemed appropriate for the Ontario government to slowly get out of the electricity generation business. Private competitors would ultimately take over the responsibility for producing electricity in the province. In the long run, deregulation would yield the benefits of a more secure energy supply, lower energy prices, and a reduced provincial debt.

The Ontario electricity deregulation policy was not actually implemented until May 1, 2002. When the market opened up to competition, the average wholesale price was 3.01 cents per kilowatt-hour (kWh). By July 2002, the wholesale price had risen to 6.2 cents per kilowatt-hour. In September 2002, the price peaked at $1.03 per kilowatt-hour. In response to public outrage over escalating electricity bills, the Ontario government lowered and froze the retail price of electricity for low-volume consumers (residential users) at 4.3 cents per kilowatt-hour, the price that existed before deregulation. The freeze covered about half of all electricity consumed in the province. In March 2003, the provincial government extended the price freeze to consumers purchasing up to 250 000 kWh of electricity per year.

Can wind farms survive without subsidies?

On June 13, 2006, in order to quell mounting fears of future power shortages, the Ontario Liberal government announced a $46 billion energy plan that included the building and refurbishing of nuclear power plants in the province. In 2009, Ontario enacted the *Green Energy Act*. Ontario hopes to close down its coal-fired generating plants and replace them with highly subsidized wind power.

In 2013 the Ontario government published a new Long-Term Energy Plan (LTEP) containing five key principles: cost-effectiveness, reliability, clean energy, community engagement, and an emphasis on conservation and demand management before building new generation capacity. The Ontario Ministry of Energy is expected to release an updated LTEP early in 2017, based on massive studies and consultations in prior years. It is anticipated that the updated LTEP will include the use of nuclear energy as the base-load primary source of electricity generation, supplemented by hydro, wind, natural gas, and biofuel. As of February 2017, the major sources of electricity generation in Ontario were as follows: nuclear (56.3%), hydro (23.3%), wind (17.5%); followed by natural gas and biofuel.

**For critical analysis:** Explain how the actions of the Ontario government tended to work against the successful implementation of electricity deregulation in Ontario.

Sources: Michael Trebilcock and Roy Hrab. "What will keep the lights on in Ontario." C.D. Howe Institute Commentary. No. 191. December 2003. ISSN 0824-8001. pp. 1–6. http://www.cdhowe.org/pdf/commentary_191.pdf; April Lindgren "Energy plan to cost Ontario consumers $46 billion." National Post. All but Toronto edition. June 14, 2006. Pg. A6; Ontario Releases Long-Term Energy Plan. News Release. Ontario Ministry of Energy. http://www.energy.gov.on.ca/en/ltep/#.UwpOHu-Yboa (Accessed February 23, 2014). "Electricity Generated in Ontario Feb 10 2017." Canadian Nuclear Society. https://www.cns-snc.ca/media/ontarioelectricity/ontarioelectricity.html (Accessed February 10, 2017); "Ontario's Long-Term Energy Plan." Mark Fisher. December 20, 2016. Council of the Great Lakes Region. https://councilgreatlakesregion.org/ontarios-long-term-energy-plan/ (Accessed February 10, 2017).

## Deregulation and Contestable Markets

A major argument in favour of deregulation is that when government-imposed barriers to entry are removed, competition will cause firms to enter markets that previously had only a few firms with market power due to those entry barriers. Potential competitors will become actual competitors, and prices will fall toward a competitive level. Recently, this argument has been bolstered by a relatively new model of efficient firm behaviour that predicts competitive prices in spite of a lack of a large number of firms. This model is called the *theory of contestable markets*. Under the **theory of contestable markets**, most of the outcomes predicted by the theory of perfect competition will occur in certain industries with relatively few firms. Specifically, where the theory of contestable markets is applicable, the few firms may still produce the output at which price equals marginal cost in both the short run and the long run. These firms will receive zero economic profits in the long run.

**Theory of contestable markets** A hypothesis that most of the outcomes predicted by the theory of perfect competition will occur in certain industries with relatively few firms, due to easy entry.

**UNCONSTRAINED AND RELATIVELY COSTLESS ENTRY AND EXIT.** For a market to be perfectly contestable, firms must be able to enter and leave the industry easily. Freedom of entry and exit implies an absence of nonprice constraints and of serious fixed costs associated with a potential competitor's decision to enter a contestable market. Such an absence of important fixed costs results if the firm need buy no specific durable inputs in order to enter, if it uses up all such inputs it does purchase, or if all of its specific durable inputs are saleable upon exit without any losses beyond those normally incurred from depreciation. The important issue is whether potential entrants can easily get their investment out at any time in the future.

The mathematical model of perfect contestability is complex, but the underlying logic is straightforward. As long as conditions for free entry prevail, any excess profits or any inefficiencies on the part of incumbent firms will serve as an inducement for potential entrants. By entering, new firms can temporarily profit at no risk to themselves from the less-than-competitive situation in the industry. Once competitive conditions are again restored, these firms will leave the industry just as quickly.

**BENEFITS OF CONTESTABLE MARKETS.** Contestable markets have several desirable characteristics. One has to do with profits. Profits that exceed the opportunity cost of capital will not exist in the long run because of freedom of entry, just as in a perfectly competitive industry. The elimination of "excess" profits can occur even with only a couple of firms in an industry. The threat of entry will cause them to expand output to eliminate excess profit.

Also, firms that have cost curves that are higher than those of the most efficient firms will find that they cannot compete. These firms will be replaced by entrants whose cost curves are consistent with the most efficient technology. In other words, in contestable markets, there will be no cost inefficiencies in the long run.

## Rethinking Regulation Using Cost–Benefit Analysis

Rather than considering deregulation as the only solution to "too much" regulation, some economists argue that regulation should simply be put to a cost–benefit test, as demonstrated in Example 12–3. Specifically, the cost of existing and proposed regulations should be compared with the benefits. Unless it can be demonstrated that regulations generate net positive benefits (benefits greater than costs), such regulations should not be in effect.

### EXAMPLE 12–3 Cutting through the Red Tape

In a study published by the Canadian Federation of Independent Business in 2005, 7300 Canadian businesses were surveyed. These Canadian businesses estimated that the costs to business related to regulation—red tape, paperwork, and compliance costs—amount to $33 billion annually. Paperwork and government regulation was reported to be the second-most cost-related issue to Canadian business. In many cases, provincial regulations overlap federal regulations, leaving businesses with mounds of red tape to cut through each year. Governments in Canada have recognized the need to simplify regulatory procedures, and many of them are working on it now.

The federal government has adopted a cost–benefit approach to reviews of current regulations. Every federal regulatory agency must use a software-based business impact test to measure the effect on the private sector of proposed changes to its regulations.

On October 1, 2012, the government of Canada published the Red Tape Reduction Action Plan report. This plan consists of the following themes:

1. Reducing the regulatory burden on businesses by requiring each government department to abide by the "One for One" rule. According to this rule, when a new regulation increases the administrative burden cost on business, regulations with an equal or greater amount of administrative burden cost must be removed.
2. Making it easier to do business with regulators. All departments and agencies should have a published policy setting out how they interpret their regulatory requirements.
3. Improving service and predictability by having all government departments meet stated service standards, including time frames for regulatory approvals.

Canada's Red Tape Report published in 2015 by the Canadian Federation of Independent Business, estimates that there continue to be very large business costs related to federal and provincial government regulations. According to the report, in 2014, it cost Canadian businesses $37.1 billion to comply with regulations from all levels of government. It is estimated that the total average time spent on paperwork and compliance per business is 105 business days each year. In businesses with fewer than five employees, each employee spent, on average, 185 hours per year dealing with regulation and red tape in Canada, compared to 130 hours in the U.S. The cost of regulatory burden to a business in Canada with four employees would be $28,792 per year. By comparison, the regulatory cost is cut by almost half for a similar business in the U.S. at $16,960.

**For critical analysis:** What costs are attached to reviewing and revising regulations?

Sources: News Release. Research Reports. Canadian Federation of Independent Business. http://www.cfib.ca/research/reports/default.asp; Danielle Smith. "Business says province hasn't cut red tape." Calgary Herald. Final edition. June 5, 2004. Pg. A19; Reducing Red Tape. Initiatives. Canada's Economic Action Plan 2014. Government of Canada. http://actionplan.gc.ca/en/initiative/reducing-red-tape (Accessed February 23, 2014). "Canada's Red Tape Report 2015." Pages, 6–9. Canadian Federation of Independent Business 2015.

# 12.4 How Competition Policy Benefits the Consumer

It is the express aim of our government to foster efficiency and competition in the economy. To this end, numerous attempts have been made to legislate against business practices that seemingly destroy the competitive nature of the system. This is the general idea behind **anticombines legislation**: If the courts can prevent collusion among sellers of a product, monopoly prices will not result; there will be no restriction of output if the members of an industry are not allowed to join together in restraint of trade. Remember that the competitive solution to the price–quantity problem is one in which the price of the item produced is equal to its marginal social opportunity cost. Also, no *economic* profits are made in the long run.

**Anticombines legislation** Laws that make illegal certain economic activies that might restrain trade.

## The History of Anticombines Legislation

Anticombines legislation has a long history in Canada. *An Act for the Protection and Suppression of Combinations in Restraint of Trade* was passed by the federal government in 1889 and amended in 1892 to become Section 502 of the *Criminal Code*. This new law made it a criminal offence to act to unduly restrict competition in the marketplace. Over the next 100 years, the Act was amended many more times.

**THE ANTICOMBINES ACT OF 1910.** The *Anticombines Act* of 1910 expanded and clarified the powers bestowed under the 1889 Act. It set out procedures for initiating and investigating complaints of restrictive trade practice. On petition from any six persons, a judge could now order investigation of an alleged crime.

In 1915, the government established a board whose duties included regulating prices and preventing persons or firms from hoarding necessities in order to drive up price and increase profits. The courts, however, declared in 1922 that this board was unconstitutional under the terms of the *British North America Act*. Accordingly, in 1923, the government again amended the *Anticombines Act* to allow for a constitutional investigative body.

**EVOLUTION OF ANTICOMBINES LAW.** Over the first half of the twentieth century, the interpretation of anticombines law evolved to apply to three main offences: price fixing that unduly restricted competition; mergers or monopolies acting contrary to the public interest; and unfair trade practices. Convictions under the anticombines legislation were difficult to obtain, however, because of the *Criminal Code* requirement of proof beyond a reasonable doubt. Thus, in 1960, government passed an amendment to the *Combines Investigation Act* making offences under the Act civil, rather than criminal, matters. By applying the less restrictive burden of proof required in civil cases, the Restrictive Trade Practices Commission won many more convictions of offending companies.

The federal government added to the scope and power of the *Combines Investigation Act* in 1976. The Act was extended to cover service industries that had hitherto been exempt, and sections were added dealing with misleading advertising. The Restrictive Trade Practices Commission was given power to protect consumers by keeping suppliers from refusing to supply without good reason and from restricting the way in which a good is sold.

**THE *COMPETITION ACT* OF 1986.** In June 1986, the government repealed the *Combines Investigation Act* and replaced it with the *Competition Act* and the *Competition Tribunal Act*. The purpose of this new legislation was to "maintain and encourage competition in Canada in order to promote the efficiency and adaptability of the Canadian economy." The Competition Bureau provides the administrative and enforcement support necessary to carry out the provisions of the Act. The Commissioner of Competition heads the Competition Bureau.

The new Act contains both criminal and noncriminal provisions. Criminal offences include conspiracy, bid rigging, discriminatory and predatory pricing, price maintenance, and deceptive marketing practices. Where the Commissioner believes a criminal offence has occurred, the matter is referred to the Attorney General for prosecution before criminal courts. The courts may impose fines, order imprisonment, issue prohibition orders and interim injunctions or any combination of these remedies.

Mergers, abuse of dominant position, exclusive dealing, and tied selling (discussed below) are practices that relate to the noncriminal provisions, which are called "reviewable matters." To address these matters, the Commissioner of Competition can apply to the Competition Tribunal for an interim order or final order to stop the undesirable activities. Under this new legislation, Canada's anticombines legislation now applies to all economic activities except collective bargaining, amateur sports, securities underwriting, and government-regulated industries.

**BILL C-20: AN ACT TO AMEND THE *COMPETITION ACT*.** On March 11, 1999, the Canadian parliament assented to Bill C-20, an act to amend the *Competition Act*. Under the new act, the Competition Bureau can apply for civil court orders to halt misleading advertising and deceptive marketing practices quickly, rather than seek conviction in the criminal courts (which can be a lengthy process). For effective enforcement, the new law provides such tools as judicially authorized interception (through wiretap without consent) of private communications to deal with deceptive telemarketing practices. As well, deceptive telemarketing now becomes a criminal offence.

Bill C-20 gives the courts more scope and flexibility in the use of prohibition orders issued against persons convicted or suspected of engaging in criminal misconduct, such as bid rigging, conspiracy to fix prices or share markets, and misleading advertising with intent. Provisions of the new bill will improve and speed up the merger review process. Finally, the amendments to the *Competition Act* protect the identity of persons who report criminal offences under the Act to the Competition Bureau.

**BILL C-23: AN ACT TO AMEND THE *COMPETITION ACT* AND *THE COMPETITION TRIBUNAL ACT*.** On June 4, 2002, the Canadian parliament passed Bill C-23: *An Act to Amend the Competition Act* and the *Competition Tribunal Act*. The amendments include new provisions that facilitate greater cooperation with foreign competition authorities, prohibit deceptive notices of winning prizes, streamline the Competition Tribunal processes, and broaden the scope of the Competition Tribunal.

In an increasingly global economy, it is very important that competition agencies around the globe have the means to share information to gather evidence. Cooperation agreements between Canadian and foreign competition agencies will have the effect of strengthening Canada's *Competition Act*.

The creation of a new offence prohibiting deceptive notices of a prize is aimed at eliminating scam artists who send notices through the mail and the Internet. These notices deceive people into believing that they have won a prize when, in fact, there is some cost attached.

The new provisions designed to streamline Competition Tribunal processes will enhance the tribunal's ability to expeditiously resolve disputes. The amendments will allow some disputes to be settled without the need for a full hearing. Cost awards will enable the Tribunal to penalize a party that brings forth proceedings in order to delay the resolution of a dispute.

**BILL C-19: AN ACT TO AMEND THE *COMPETITION ACT*.** On November 2, 2004, the federal government introduced Bill C-19, consisting of proposed amendments to the *Competition Act*. The proposed changes strengthen Canada's competition framework in a global economy to benefit both consumers and businesses.

The amendments benefit consumers and businesses by providing authority for the Commissioner of Competition to seek restitution for consumer loss resulting from false or misleading representations; introducing a general administrative monetary penalty provision for abuse of dominance in any industry; removing the airline-specific provisions from the Act to return it to a law of general application; increasing the level of administrative monetary penalties for deceptive marketing practices; and decriminalizing the pricing provisions.

On October 27, 2005, the Government of Canada introduced amendments to Bill C-19. The amendments increased the fine level under the conspiracy provisions of the Act (section 45) from a maximum of $10 million to a maximum of $25 million, and increased the maximum prison time from 5 years to 14 years. This serves as a deterrent to illegal cartel-like conduct. In addition, other forms of anti-competitive competitor collaborations will be open to civil review and assessed to determine if they severely restrict competition. This bill also provides the Competition Bureau with the power to assess the state of competition, which will enable the Bureau to gather comprehensive data, including data not in the public domain, to conduct in-depth analysis of various industry sectors.

**AMENDMENTS ENACTED IN 2009 AND 2010.** Sweeping changes to Canada's *Competition Act* were implemented in 2009 and 2010. Key amendments are summarized below.

**CONSPIRACY (CARTELS).** A two-track policy has been enacted, with "*per se*" criminal offences under Section 45 for three types of "hard core" cartel agreements between actual or potential competitors (price-fixing, market allocation, and output restriction agreements) along with a second civil track for other types of non-hard core anti-competitive agreements that may prevent or lessen competition substantially. Removing the former competitive effects test relating to "undueness" will make it easier for private plaintiffs to commence civil actions and for the Competition Bureau to prove criminal conspiracy offences under section 45.

**CONSPIRACY PENALTIES.** Penalties for criminal conspiracy offences have been significantly enhanced, with fines of up to $25 million (per count) and/or imprisonment for up to 14 years.

**MISLEADING ADVERTISING.** The maximum fines for misleading advertising were increased to $750,000 for individuals and $10 million for corporations.

**BID-RIGGING.** A new bid-rigging offence has been implemented, making it a criminal offence to agree to withdraw a bid already made.

**CRIMINAL PRICING PROVISIONS.** The predatory pricing and price discrimination practices have been removed as criminal provisions, but still can be challenged under the abuse of dominance provisions of the *Competition Act* (sections 78 and 79).

**PRICE MAINTENANCE.** The price maintenance practice has been removed as a criminal provision, but still can be challenged by a market effects test, which requires that an "adverse effect on competition" be shown in addition to the other required elements under the new civil section 76.

**ABUSE OF DOMINANCE.** Significant civil fines of $10 million ($15 million for subsequent orders) have been introduced for abuse of dominance in Canada.

**MERGERS.** A new two-stage merger notification and review regime has been introduced. Competition Bureau powers have been expanded in terms of requesting additional information from merging parties. The period in which the Bureau may challenge completed mergers has been reduced from three years to one year. On December 9, 2014, the Canadian government released Bill C-49, the Price Transparency Act, to amend the Competition Act so as to authorize the Competition Bureau to, investigate and expose price discrimination practices undertaken by multinational corporations selling in Canadian markets. This Bill was motivated by previous studies concluding that Canadian consumers pay an average of 10 percent more than Americans for identical goods sold by the same multinational company.

On September 28, 2016, the Canadian liberal federal government introduced Bill C-25, which essentially replaced Bill C-49.

Source: Our Legislation. The Competition Bureau. http://www.competitionbureau.gc.ca/eic/site/cb-bc.nsf/eng/h_00148.html. (Accessed March 9, 2014.) "Federal Government Proposes to Prohibit "Unjustified" Canada-US Price Discrimination." April 2014. International Trade Bulletin. James B. Musgrove. mcmillan. http://www.mcmillan.ca/Federal-Government-Proposes-to-Prohibit-Unjustified-Canada-US-Price-Discrimination (Accessed February 11, 2017); "Bill C-25 broadens the Competition Act affiliation rules."POSTED ON OCTOBER 26, 2016.William Wu. Competition. The Competitor. http://www.thecompetitor.ca/2016/10/articles/competition/bill-c25-broadens-the-competition-act-affiliation-rules/ (Accessed February 11, 2017).

## Anti-Competitive Behaviour Prohibited by Competition Policy

Canada's current *Competition Act* prohibits a variety of business practices on the basis that they significantly reduce competition. Some of the business practices that are potentially illegal under Canada's *Competition Act* are abuse of dominant position, mergers detrimental to the public interest, anti-competitive conspiracies, price discrimination, resale price maintenance and refusal to supply, exclusive dealing and tied selling, and deceptive marketing practices. We will briefly explain each of these restrictive practices below.

**ABUSE OF DOMINANT POSITION.** Under the *Competition Act*, it is illegal for a dominant firm in an industry to pursue strategies that are aimed at reducing competition substantially in the market. These strategies might include selling a product or service at unreasonably low prices; using fighting brands introduced on a temporary basis in order to restrain or eliminate a competitor; squeezing, by a vertically integrated dominant supplier, of the margin available to an unintegrated customer who competes with the supplier; requiring a supplier to sell primarily to certain customers, or to refrain from selling to a competitor; and purchasing a supplier firm or customer firm in order to restrict competition in either the customer's market or the supplier's market.

In a previous chapter, we noted that in 2001, the Competition Bureau had asked the Competition Tribunal for an order prohibiting Air Canada from abusing its dominant position in the Canadian airlines market. It was the Bureau's view that Air Canada was charging unreasonably low prices—air fares below avoidable or variable costs—in an attempt to restrict competition from WestJet and CanJet on various routes in Eastern Canada. The Competition Tribunal did find that Air Canada engaged in predatory pricing.

**MERGERS DETRIMENTAL TO THE PUBLIC INTEREST.** Mergers that significantly reduce competition in a market may be illegal under the *Competition Act*. It should be noted, however, that the Competition Tribunal might allow a merger to take place even if it causes the industry's concentration ratio to substantially increase. That is, before prohibiting a proposed merger, the Tribunal would look at such factors as the extent to which foreign suppliers are likely to provide effective competition to the businesses of the parties to the merger; the extent to which good substitutes for products supplied by the parties to the merger are likely to be available; and the extent to which the merger results in significant gains in efficiency that will be passed on to consumers.

**ANTI-COMPETITIVE CONSPIRACIES.** Hard core cartel-like agreements between actual or potential competitors such as price-fixing, market allocation, and output restriction agreements are considered to be "per se" criminal offences. Other types of non-hard core anti-competitive agreements that may prevent or lessen competition substantially are challenged as civil offences.

**PRICE DISCRIMINATION.** It is potentially illegal for a firm to charge different prices to its different customers where the rationale is to substantially lessen competition or eliminate a competitor. For example, suppose a large computer manufacturer sells the same computer model to a number of different computer retail firms. The largest retailer, due to its sheer size and bargaining power, is able to buy the computer model at a lower price than its competitors, and this lower price is not justified by cost saving due to the larger volume purchased. To the extent that this practice constitutes an abuse of dominant position, this would be deemed to be a violation of the *Competition Act*.

**RESALE PRICE MAINTENANCE AND REFUSAL TO SUPPLY.** The *Competition Act* prohibits the manufacturer or supplier of a product from attempting to control the resale price of its product at the wholesale or retail level, to the extent that the practice is deemed to adversely affect competition. For example, it is illegal for a jeans manufacturer to put pressure on a jeans retailer to resell its jeans at a set price. This set price hurts consumers, as it prevents the retailer from offering discounts to its customers. It is also an offence, under the *Competition Act*, for the jeans manufacturer to threaten to refuse to continue supplying its jeans to a retailer, should the retailer decide to discount these jeans at the retail level.

**EXCLUSIVE DEALING AND TIED SELLING.** Exclusive dealing refers to a situation where a firm supplies its product to a customer on condition that the customer not buy similar products from competitive suppliers. If a petroleum refining company agreed to sell its gas to a gas station only if the gas station promised not to buy gas from other refiners, this would be an example of exclusive dealing. This practice reduces competition as it prevents gas retailers from contacting competing refiners in order to secure a lower cost price. This exclusionary tactic can further restrict competition, to the extent that it prevents other retailers from securing an adequate supply of the product.

As Example 12–4 illustrates, exclusive dealing must substantially lessen competition in order to be considered illegal under Canada's *Competition Act.*

### EXAMPLE 12–4 HMV Boycotts Rolling Stones Products

In October 2003, HMV Canada removed all Rolling Stones merchandise from its store shelves to protest an exclusive agreement that allowed only Best Buy stores to carry the Rolling Stones' *Four Flicks* DVD box set between October 2003 and March 2004. One month later, HMV filed a complaint with the Competition Bureau, arguing that the exclusive agreement between Best Buy and TGA Entertainment Ltd., the company responsible for the distribution of the Rolling Stones DVD, contravened Canada's *Competition Act*. HMV claimed that by preventing other retailers from reselling the *Four Flicks* DVD set, the exclusive agreement had the effect of reducing competition at the retail DVD level.

The Competition Bureau subsequently examined whether the exclusive agreement violated a number of provisions of the *Competition Act*, including exclusive dealing, refusal to supply, and abuse of dominance. After completing its investigation, the Bureau concluded that the agreement in question did not contravene the *Competition Act*, for reasons explained below.

To be considered illegal, exclusive dealing must substantially lessen competition. In the *Four Flicks* DVD example, the exclusive agreement covered only one DVD set released by just a single artist over a very limited period of time. As a result, the Bureau concluded that the agreement between Best Buy and TGA did not significantly reduce competition in the DVD music retail industry.

The Competition Bureau also investigated whether the exclusionary agreement constituted an offence under the refusal to supply provision of the *Competition Act*. For this to be the case, the firm being refused the supply (HMV) would have to prove that it was substantially negatively affected or that it was precluded from carrying on business as a result of the exclusionary arrangement. Since the agreement covered just one DVD from a single artist, the Bureau concluded that the refusal to supply provision was not violated.

Finally, the Bureau examined whether the exclusionary agreement could be viewed as an abuse of dominance situation under the Act. Under this provision, it must be shown that a dominant supplier is engaging in practices that are substantially reducing competition at the distribution or retail industry level. Since there are a multitude of producers, distributors, and retailers of DVD music products, the Competition Bureau ruled that neither Best Buy nor TGA was in a position to control the markets in which it competes. Since neither party to the agreement was in a dominant position, the abuse of dominance provision was considered to be irrelevant to the exclusionary agreement.

In response to thousands of customer complaints, HMV lifted its ban on Rolling Stones products in March 2004. While it was unsuccessful in bringing legal action against Best Buy and TGA, HMV felt that it was successful in sending a message to those considering similar exclusionary agreements in the future.

**For critical analysis:** On the basis of the information provided in this example, when would an exclusive agreement made between a specific manufacturer and a specific retailer likely contravene the *Competition Act*?

Sources: "Examination of the distribution agreement for the Rolling Stones Four Flicks DVD set." Backgrounders. Competition Bureau. December 18, 2003. http://competition.ic.gc.ca/epic/internet/incb-bc.nsf/en/ct02780e.html. (Accessed May 22, 2004.); Peter Brieger. "HMV Canada lifts its ban on Rolling Stones products." *National Post.* March 4, 2004. Pg. FP.07.

*Tied selling* refers to the practice of supplying a product only if the purchaser agrees to buy other products from the same supplier. For example, if a petroleum refinery agreed to supply its gas to a gas station on the condition that the gas station bought all of its petroleum products from the same refiner, this would constitute tied selling.

**DECEPTIVE MARKETING PRACTICES.** We will describe only a few of the deceptive marketing practices considered illegal under the *Competition Act*. Perhaps the most common offence is for a supplier to misrepresent the original price of an article, when the article is sold at a discounted rate. If a shoe retailer offered a brand of shoes at a discounted price of $90 and advertised the offer as being "50 percent off," the implied regular price is $180. However, the "50 percent off" advertisement would be considered to be illegal if the shoe retailer never sold the shoes at the $180 price. As Example 12–5 illustrates, the merchandise that is being promoted in a discounted price advertisement must have sold, at one time, at the implied regular price in significant quantities over a reasonable period of time.

### EXAMPLE 12–5 Suzy Shier Pays $1 Million to Settle Misleading Advertising Dispute

When is a bargain not a bargain? When it is always a bargain. Suzy Shier learned this lesson the hard way. On June 13, 2003, Suzy Shier reached a $1 million settlement with the Competition Bureau to resolve concerns over the company's discount pricing practices.

After completing an investigation, the Bureau charged that Suzy Shier placed discount price tags on garments that suggested misleading regular prices, as the advertised merchandise never sold at the implied regular prices in any significant quantity for any reasonable time period. According to the Bureau, Suzy Shier inflated the true regular prices of the garments, thereby overstating the savings realized by consumers who purchased the merchandise at the "discounted prices."

In addition to paying the $1 million, Suzy Shier filed a civil Consent Agreement that commits the company to ensure that all future price representations comply with the Ordinary Selling Price provisions of the *Competition Act* over the next 10 years. In a public statement, La Senza Corporation, which owned Suzy Shier, suggested that it did not act contrary to the *Competition Act* but nevertheless agreed to the fine. Hours after the settlement was announced, La Senza sold the Suzy Shier chain to YM Inc., the Toronto company that owned Stitches.

**For critical analysis:** Visit the website that displays the Deceptive Marketing Practices section of Canada's *Competition Act*. After visiting this site, explain the Ordinary Price provisions, as they pertain to a supplier's own product. In your description, make sure that you explain the conditions under which a representation pertaining to a regular price is considered a reviewable offence.

Sources: "Competition Bureau Investigation Leads to a $1-Million Settlement with Suzy Shier Inc." News Releases. Competition Bureau. June 13, 2003. http://competition.ic.gc.ca/epic/internet/incb-bc.nsf/en/ct02578e.html. (Accessed May 22, 2004.); Susan Lazaruk. "Suzy Shier fined $1-million for misleading sales." *The Province.* (Vancouver, B.C.) June 15, 2003. Pg. A19. (Accessed May 22, 2004.)

*Bait-and-switch selling*, another deceptive marketing practice, is where a supplier advertises a product at a bargain price but does not supply the discounted product in reasonable quantities, having regard to the nature of the market. The intent of this deceptive practice is to lure customers to the store so that the supplier can promote its higher-priced products.

ISSUES AND APPLICATIONS

# Media Concentration in Canada: A Public Concern?

**Concepts Applied: Regulation, Competition Policy, Media Concentration and the Public Interest**

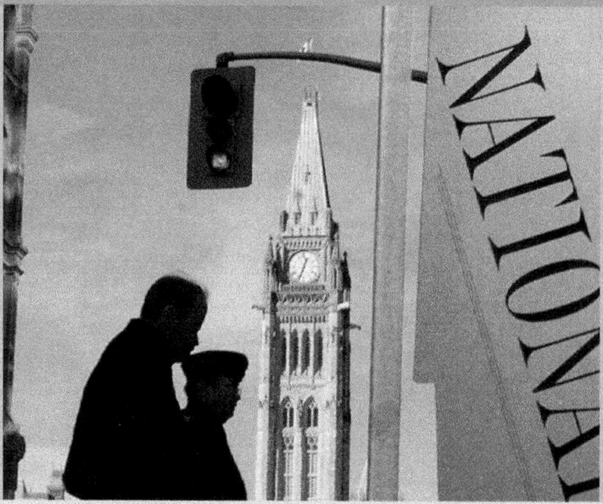


CanWest Global's newspaper, the *National Post*, competes with Canada's only other major national newspaper, *The Globe and Mail*, owned by BCE. CanWest and BCE have substantial media holdings in Canada. Does media concentration threaten editorial diversity?

## A Decade of Mega-Takeovers and Mergers

Over the past decade, Canada has experienced a significant increase in concentration in its various media industries, as noted below.

In mid 1996, Conrad Black, publisher of almost 650 newspapers worldwide, approached the Competition Bureau for approval of his plan to acquire 50.7 percent of Southam Incorporated, publisher of 32 Canadian daily papers. After the Bureau gave its consent, Mr. Black's company, Hollinger Inc., became the largest newspaper publisher in Canada. Subsequent to the acquisition, Hollinger owned 59 of the 105 daily newspapers in Canada, including all the dailies in Saskatchewan, Prince Edward Island, and Newfoundland. Shortly after, Mr. Black purchased the *Financial Post* and incorporated it in his new national newspaper, the *National Post*, which debuted on October 27, 1998.

On November 3, 2000, The Competition Bureau announced that it would not challenge the $3.2 billion acquisition by CanWest Global of the majority of Hollinger's Canadian media interests. As a result, on November 15, 2000, CanWest became the largest daily newspaper publisher in Canada and one of the country's leading international multimedia news, information, and entertainment providers. Immediately after its Hollinger purchase, CanWest owned 14 English language metropolitan daily newspapers in Canada, as well as 120 daily and weekly newspapers and shoppers in smaller communities all across Canada. Newspapers operated by CanWest Global just after the acquisition included the *National Post*, *Montreal Gazette*, *Ottawa Citizen*, *Windsor Star*, *Regina Leader-Post*, *Saskatoon Star Phoenix*, *Calgary Herald*, *Edmonton Journal*, *Vancouver Sun*, *Vancouver Province*, and *Victoria Times-Colonist*.

In addition to its newspaper holdings, CanWest Global owns Canada's Global Television Network, which broadcasts over the air via 11 television stations, licensed in eight provinces, and reaches 94 percent of English-speaking Canada. CanWest also owns Canada.com, which is one of Canada's largest Internet news sites.

In December 2000, the CRTC allowed BCE to buy the CTV network, a decision that created Canada's largest communications company—Bell Globemedia, later known as CTV Globemedia (CTVgm). The CTV purchase closely followed BCE's acquisition of *The Globe and Mail*. In securing the ownership of CTV, BCE promised the CRTC that it would pump over $200 million into Canadian broadcasting during the next seven years. The CRTC has stipulated that $140 million of these monies should go into drama and documentary production created by independent Canadian writers and producers.

On July 5, 2001, the CRTC approved Quebecor Inc.'s purchase of the TVA television network, the dominant firm in the Quebec television broadcasting market. Prior to the CRTC decision, Quebecor had already accumulated significant Canadian media assets including Videotron, the largest cable TV producer in Quebec, and Sun Media, the second-largest newspaper group in Canada, with eight metropolitan dailies, eight community dailies, and 175 local weeklies and specialty publications. As in the BCE decision, the CRTC made the Quebecor acquisition conditional on commitments by TVA to create additional independent Canadian productions. Quebecor has since applied for an all-news station that will compete with CTV and CBC.

On April 12, 2007, Astral Media Inc. agreed to pay $1.08 billion to take over 52 radio stations owned by Standard Radio Inc., located in five provinces, making Astral the largest radio broadcaster in Canada, with a total of 81 stations under its control.

On June 8, 2007, the CRTC approved CTV Globemedia's $1.7 billion bid to purchase CHUM Ltd. In this deal. CTV acquired the following assets: 34 radio stations across Canada, including CHUM FM in Toronto; 21 specialty television channels including Bravo, Cable Pulse 24 (80 percent), MuchMore Music, MuchMusic, Space, Star!, Book Television, Fashion Television, Razer,

CourtTV, Drive-In Classics, MuchLoud, MuchMore Retro, MuchVibe, PunchMuch, and TV Land; and the A Channel Network, which has seven stations, one in Victoria and six in Ontario.

In 2010, Shaw Communications struck a deal to take over the TV assets of Canwest Global. This will give Shaw 11 local Global TV stations and ownership of some specialty channels. It also gives Shaw, primarily a cable company, a larger broadcast ability. Shaw is also planning to enter into the wireless market in the future.

On June 27, 2013, the CRTC approved BCE (Bell Globemedia or CTV Globemedia) Inc.'s $3.4-billion takeover of the media giant Astral Media Inc. with the following conditions attached. Bell must sell off eleven television channels and ten radio stations.

The CRTC is requiring that BCE invest $246.9 million into creating original Canadian TV and radio programming.

Under the approved takeover, Bell will control 22.6 percent of the French-language television market and 35.8 percent of the English-language market, with a much stronger hold on the specialty pay television market.

On March 25, 2015 the Canadian Competition Bureau gave the green light to Postmedia Corporation's $316-million bid to buy Sun Media's English-language newspapers and digital properties from Quebecor Inc. Based on a five month review, the Bureau has issued a No Action Letter confirming that it will not challenge the proposed transaction before the Competition Tribunal under the merger provisions of the Competition Act. As a result of the merger, there will be only one owner of daily paid circulation newspapers in a number of Canadian cities including Vancouver, Calgary, Edmonton, and Ottawa.

## The Canadian Government Response: The Competition Bureau and the CRTC

Typically, both the Competition Bureau and the CRTC have to approve the type of mega-takeovers and mergers that have taken place in Canada's media industries. In general, the Competition Bureau focuses on whether competition in particular markets is substantially lessened due to the takeovers or mergers. Even if a takeover causes the industry's concentration ratio to substantially increase, it still may be allowed if foreign companies are likely to provide effective competition; good substitutes for products supplied by the parties to the merger are likely to be available; and/or the merger results in significant gains in efficiency that will be passed on to consumers. In the case of the media takeovers noted above, the Competition Bureau concluded that the takeovers did not significantly lessen the competition available to the advertisers who use the various forms of Canadian media.

After the Competition Bureau reviews a takeover, the CRTC assesses the same media business transaction in terms of its primary concerns, which is that the Canadian media industries stay under Canadian ownership and control; foster the creation and production of Canadian programming, music, and news; report regional and local news and events; and distribute a certain proportion of Canadian programming.

## The Issue of Editorial Diversity

The concentration of all forms of Canadian media, including newspaper, radio, television, and the Internet, in the hands of a few large corporations such as CanWest Global, BCE, and Quebecor, has brought forth concerns regarding the maintenance and encouragement of freedom of expression, freedom of speech, and editorial diversity in Canada. The ultimate fear is that Canadian news, views, music, programs, and Internet activities that run contrary to the interests of the large media corporations and their friends will not be aired or distributed to the Canadian public.

As an example, on June 16, 2002, Russell Mills, former publisher of the *Ottawa Citizen*, was fired by the newspaper's owner, CanWest Global. Mills claimed that his dismissal was for, among other things, not asking the owners of CanWest Global for their approval of the publication of an editorial calling for the resignation of Prime Minister Jean Chretien.

In preparation for the 2004 federal election, a top member of Bell Globemedia's editorial team took a leave of absence to help mastermind the Liberal Party's multi-million-dollar election advertising campaign. The campaign included ads that depict the leader of the opposition party as one who lacks Canadian values. This particular leave of absence has brought forth the criticism that the BCE media giant was prone to side with the incumbent Liberal Party throughout their media coverage of the 2004 federal election. As one can see, the issues relating to media concentration include the very preservation of values and behaviour consistent with a democratic society.

**For critical analysis:**

1. As this Issues and Applications explains, the CRTC has approved of significant Canadian media acquisitions involving CanWest, BCE, and Quebecor. Are these policy decisions examples of economic regulation or social regulation?
2. Explain how increased media concentration can operate against the interests of the Canadian public.

Sources: CRTC. "CRTC approves Quebecor acquisition of TVA on the condition it sell TQS, renews TVA's licence for another seven years." News Release. CRTC. July 5, 2001. http://www.crtc.gc.ca/eng/news/releases/2001/R010705.htm. (Accessed May 29, 2004.); CRTC. "CRTC Approves Acquisition Of CTV By BCE." News Release. CRTC. December 7, 2000. http://www.crtc.gc.ca/eng/news/releases/2000/R001207.htm. (Accessed May 29, 2004.); "Fired publisher settles with Canwest Global." Edmonton Journal. Edmonton, Alberta. December 14, 2002. Pg. A8; Gillian Cosgrove. "Bell Globemedia under Liberal thumb? ROBTV chief takes leave to run Liberal ad campaign." *National Post.* May 14, 2004, Pg. A10; Competition Bureau. "Competition bureau and Canwest resolve concerns about ROBTV." News Releases. November 3, 2000. Media Room. http://competition.ic.gc.ca/epic/internet/incb-bc.nsf/en/ct02067e.html. (Accessed May 29, 2004.); "Network takeover dials in new era; Astral Media goes coast-to-coast with $1.08B purchase of Standard Radio." *Edmonton Journal.* Final Edition. April 13, 2007. Pg. F3; Grant Robertson. "Regulator orders CTV to sell City-TV network." *Globe and Mail.* June 9, 2007. Pg. B6; Paul Vieira. "CRTC to focus on control in Canwest Deal; Alliance Atlantis; Canwest Global Communications Corp." *National Post.* National Edition. July 7, 2007. Pg. FP6; "CRTC approves Bell-Astral merger." Business. CBC News. June 27, 2014. http://www.cbc.ca/news/business/crtc-approves-bell-astral-merger-1.1367433 (Accessed March 9, 2014).

# SUMMARY

Here is what you should know after reading this chapter. MyEconLab will help you identify what you know, and where to go when you need to practise. We suggest that as soon as you review one of the Learning Objective sections below, you then proceed to go through the related section in MyEconLab.

| LEARNING OBJECTIVES | KEY TERMS | MYECONLAB PRACTICE |
| --- | --- | --- |
| **12.1 Types of Government Regulation.** The two broad types of regulation are economic and social regulation. In economic regulation, the government controls the prices that regulated enterprises can charge. This prevents monopoly firms from restricting output and charging excessive prices. In natural monopoly situations, consumers can be better served by a regulated monopoly as opposed to an unregulated competitive situation, where per-units costs could be greater. Two common types of economic regulation are cost-of-service and rate-of-return regulation. Cost-of-service regulation can be expensive to administer in large-scale companies. Rate-of-return regulation can encourage regulated companies to overcapitalize and pad their costs. A problem common to both types of regulation is that it is very difficult to regulate the price per constant quality unit. Social regulation seeks to promote public welfare across all industries.<br>The aim of social regulation is a better quality of life through a less-polluted environment, better working conditions, less discrimination, better quality and safer products, and the promotion of valued social goals. A major concern with social regulation focuses on whether governments conduct appropriate cost-benefit analyses when creating their various regulations.<br>Regulation can have undesirable consequences. Regulated firms may engage in creative responses and individuals may elicit a feedback effect due to regulation. | economic regulation, 313<br>cost-of-service regulation, 313<br>rate-of-return regulation, 314<br>social regulation, 316<br>creative response, 317 | • **MyEconLab** Study Plan 12.1 |

| LEARNING OBJECTIVES | KEY TERMS | MYECONLAB PRACTICE |
|---|---|---|
| **12.2 Explaining Regulators' Behaviour.** The capture hypothesis holds that regulatory agencies will eventually be captured by special interests of the industry. This is because consumers are a diffuse group who individually are not affected greatly by regulation, whereas industry groups are well focused and know that large amounts of potential profits depend on the outcome of regulatory proceedings. In the share-the-gains, share-the-pains theory of regulation, regulators must take account of the interests of three groups: the industry, legislators, and consumers. | capture hypothesis, 318<br>share-the-gains, share-the-pains theory, 319<br>deregulation, 319 | • **MyEconLab** Study Plan 12.2 |
| **12.3 Short-Run versus Long-Run Effects of Deregulation.** The short-run effects of deregulation often include bankruptcy and disrupted service. The long-run results in deregulated industries can include better service, more variety, and lower costs. One argument in favour of deregulation involves the theory of contestable markets—if entry and exit are relatively costless, the number of firms in an industry is irrelevant in terms of determining whether consumers pay competitive prices. | theory of contestable markets, 321 | • **MyEconLab** Study Plan 12.3 |
| **12.4 How Competition Policy Benefits the Consumer.** The purpose of Canada's *Competition Act* is to maintain and encourage competition in Canadian industries. The increased competition serves Canadian consumers by promoting allocative and productive efficiency. Some of the anti-competitive business practices that are potentially illegal under Canada's *Competition Act* are: abuse of dominant position; mergers detrimental to the public interest; anti-competitive conspiracies; price discrimination; resale price maintenance and refusal to supply; exclusive dealing and tied selling; and deceptive marketing practices. | anticombines legislation, 323 | • **MyEconLab** Study Plan 12.4 |

# PROBLEMS

(Answers to the odd-numbered problems appear at the back of the book.)

**LO 12.1 Explain and evaluate the two broad types of government regulation of business.**

1. Under what conditions would a regulated monopoly bring about lower costs and prices, when compared to the alternative of establishing a competitive industry?
2. Compare and contrast cost-of-service regulation and rate-of-return regulation.
3. The following table depicts the cost and demand structure a natural monopoly faces.

| Quantity | Price | Long-Run Total Cost |
|---|---|---|
| 0 | $ 100 | $ 0 |
| 1 | 95 | 92 |
| 2 | 90 | 177 |
| 3 | 85 | 255 |
| 4 | 80 | 331 |
| 5 | 75 | 406 |
| 6 | 70 | 480 |

   a. If the government pursued economic regulation in the form of marginal cost pricing, what would be the price and quantity level? What problem would arise, if the government enforced this type of regulation in the long term? Explain.
   b. If the government imposed rate-of-return regulation on this monopoly firm, what would be the price and quantity level? What would be the amount of economic profit?
   c. Critics suggest that rate-of-return regulation can breed inefficiency. Explain their argument.
4. Contrast the major objectives of economic regulation and social regulation.
5. State whether the following type of government regulation is best classed as economic regulation or social regulation. Recall that the CRTC refers to the Canadian Radio-television and Telecommunications Commission (CRTC).
   a. The CRTC regulates the phone rates that some local phone companies charge their customers.
   b. The CRTC restricts the degree to which foreigners can own Canadian media companies.
6. Referring to Example 12–1, "Deregulation Hits Canadian Phone Markets," what economics-related reasons explain why the CRTC has recently been deregulating some of the local phone markets in Canada.

**LO 12.2 Identify and contrast the various theories used to explain the behaviour of regulators.**

7. In 2003, the American government banned the importation of Canadian beef products into the United States, on the basis of fears related to "mad cow disease." Assuming that the scientific evidence suggested that there was no significant health risk related to human consumption of Canadian beef, what theory of regulatory behaviour best explains this situation?

**LO 12.3 Explain the short-run and long-run economic effects of deregulation.**

8. Referring to Policy Example 12–2, "Ontario's Feeble Attempt at Energy Deregulation," explain why the Ontario government was eager to deregulate its electricity generation industry. What economic reason explains why the government continued to operate the electricity distribution industry as a regulated monopoly?
9. Why is the right of free entry insufficient to prevent sustained economic profits in a deregulated natural monopoly situation?
10. "Philosophically, I am vehemently opposed to government interference in the marketplace. As the owner of a neighbourhood pub, however, I can tell you that deregulation will be bad for the citizenry. You would not want a neighbourhood pub on every corner, would you?" Why would you predict that a neighbourhood pub owner would defend regulation of the liquor industry in this way?

**LO 12.4 Describe the various ways in which Canada's *Competition Act* benefits consumers.**

11. What anti-competitive business practice, as defined under Canada's *Competition Act*, best relates to each of the following?
   a. A manufacturer will supply its popular leather jackets to a clothing retailer, only under the condition that the retailer sells the jackets at the manufacturer's suggested list price.
   b. In order to maintain its monopoly position in a large subdivision, a supermarket chain lowers the prices of its products below each item's average variable cost. These low prices deter the entry of rival supermarket stores.
   c. In order to be able to sell a manufacturer's line of computers, a computer retailer agrees to purchase all of its computer accessories from the same computer manufacturer.
   d. A large golf equipment retailer advertises a popular brand of clubs at 50 percent off, available only during its Canada Day sale. After the first 30 minutes of the sale, the retailer sold out all units of this brand of golf clubs.
   e. A leading soft drink manufacturer will allow large supermarkets to resell its cola products, only under the condition that the supermarkets refrain from selling the cola products produced by rival manufacturers.

12. Explain why Canada's *Competition Act* might approve of a merger that significantly increased an already high industry concentration ratio.
13. According to Example 12–4, "HMV Boycotts Rolling Stones Products," the Competition Bureau investigated whether the exclusive agreement between Best Buy and TGA Entertainment violated at least one of three provisions of the *Competition Act*. What three provisions were examined? Why did the Bureau rule that the exclusive agreement did not violate the *Competition Act*?

# BUSINESS APPLICATION

**LO 12.4 Describe the various ways in which Canada's *Competition Act* benefits consumers.**

## Marketing: Restrictive Trade Practices

In Canada, the federal *Competition Act* is an important aspect of the legal climate to consider in developing the marketing mix. Some of the restrictive trade practices listed below are prohibited under the *Competition Act*.

- Price fixing
- Bid rigging
- Price discrimination
- Predatory pricing
- Resale price maintenance
- False or misleading representations or claims (in a material respect)
- Exclusive dealing
- Tied selling
- Referral selling
- Bait-and-switch selling (non-availability of advertised specials)
- Pyramid selling (multi-level marketing practice)

## Business Application Problem

Visit the Competition Bureau website at http://www.competitionbureau.gc.ca. Search for three recent Canadian cases that each relate to a different prohibited practice listed above. (Alternatively, use a search engine to find the three cases.) Write a one-paragraph summary of each case. Properly reference the cases chosen.

PART 4 PRODUCTIVE FACTORS, POVERTY, THE ENVIRONMENT, AND THE PUBLIC SECTOR

# 13

## LEARNING OBJECTIVES

After reading this chapter, you should be able to:

**13.1** Explain the demand for labour, using the marginal physical product, marginal revenue product, and price elasticity of demand concepts.

**13.2** Analyze the supply of labour and shifts in labour demand and supply.

**13.3** Discuss the three main union goals and the five benefits of labour unions.

**13.4** Determine the impact on pricing and employment under various market conditions.

# Labour Demand and Supply

On February 10, 2016 a group of Manitoba and Saskatchewan farmers unanimously passed a resolution calling for the return of an organization similar to the Canadian Wheat Board with a single desk monopoly marketing system. The resolution states that the demise of the Canadian Wheat Board in 2012 has resulted in an increasingly ineffective rail grain handling system, lower prices to Canadian grain farmers, reduced grain quality guarantees to customers, and an overall loss of $6.5 billion to farmers' income over two years.

The farmers are essentially calling for a single buyer and single seller of wheat and barley in western Canada. In this chapter we will study how organizations such as the Canadian Wheat Board operate to affect prices and incomes.

Source: "Swan River meeting calls for return of CWB." Crops. Local News. February 22, 2016. Manitoba Co-operator. http://www.manitobacooperator.ca/crops/swan-river-meeting-calls-for-return-of-cwb/#_ga=1.148834039.1366153800.1486133036 (Accessed February 3, 2017).

myeconlab

MyEconLab helps you master each objective and study more efficiently. See end of chapter for details

# DID YOU KNOW THAT...?

On January 3, 2017, the Canadian Centre for Policy Alternatives reported that the 100 highest paid corporate chief executive officers (CEOs) received an average annual income of over $9.5 million. This average CEO income ends up being about 193 times more than the $49,510 average annual income earned by all Canadian workers. Alternately stated, by lunch-time on the first day back at work in January in a new year, the high paid CEO makes the same amount as what an average Canadian worker will make working full-time for that entire year. Besides the question of whether the CEO is worth it, to understand why firms pay different workers different wages requires an understanding of the demand for and supply of labour.

A firm's demand for inputs can be studied in much the same manner as we studied the demand for output in different market situations. Again, various market situations will be examined. Our analysis will always end with the same common-sense conclusion: A firm will hire employees up to the point beyond which it is not profitable to hire any more. It will hire employees to the point at which the marginal benefit of hiring a worker will just equal the marginal cost. Basically, in every profit-maximizing situation, it is most profitable to carry out an activity up to the point at which the marginal benefit equals the marginal cost. Remembering that guideline will help you in analyzing decision making at the firm level. We will start our analysis under the assumption that the market for input factors is perfectly competitive. We will further assume that the output market is perfectly competitive. This provides a benchmark against which to compare other situations in which labour markets or product markets are not perfectly competitive.

"CEO pay sets new record: study." News Releases. Newsroom. Canadian Centre for Policy Alternatives. January 3, 2017. https://www.policyalternatives.ca/newsroom/news-releases/ceo-pay-sets-new-record-study (Accessed February 3, 2017).

## 13.1 Demand for Labour

Thinking back to previous chapter concepts, you will remember that the four factors of production are land, capital, entrepreneurship, and labour. Land, capital, and labour prices are determined by demand and supply, like any other good or service. In this chapter, we will look at the labour market.

Should top executives be able to demand top wages?

### Competition in the Product Market

Let us take as our example a DVD-manufacturing firm that is in competition with many companies selling the same kind of product. Assume that the labourers hired by our DVD maker do not need any special skills. This firm sells its product in a perfectly competitive market. A DVD manufacturer also buys labour (its variable input) in a perfectly competitive market. A firm that hires labour under perfectly competitive conditions hires only a tiny proportion of all the workers who are potentially available. By "potentially available," we mean all the workers in a given geographical area who possess the skills demanded by our perfect competitor. In such a market, it is always possible for the individual firm to pick up extra workers without having to offer a higher wage. Thus, the supply of labour to the firm is perfectly elastic—that is, represented by a horizontal line at the going wage rate established by the forces of supply and demand in the entire labour market. The firm is a price taker in the labour market.

### Marginal Physical Product

Look at part (a) of Figure 13–1. In column 1, we show the number of workers per week that the firm can hire. In column 2, we show total physical product (TPP) per week, the total *physical* production that different quantities of the labour input (in combination with a fixed amount of other inputs) will generate in a week's time. In column 3, we show the additional output gained when a DVD maker adds workers to its existing manufacturing facility. This column, the **marginal physical product (MPP) of labour**, represents the change in output resulting from the addition of one more worker. If this firm adds a seventh worker, the MPP is 118. The law of diminishing marginal returns predicts that

**Marginal physical product (MPP) of labour** The change in output resulting from the addition of one more worker.

additional units of a variable factor will, after some point, cause the MPP to decline, other things being held constant.

## Why the Decline in MPP?

We are assuming all other nonlabour factors of production are held constant. So, if our DVD maker wants to add one more worker to its production line, it has to crowd all the existing workers a little closer together because it does not increase its capital stock (the production equipment). Therefore, as we add more workers, each one has a smaller and smaller fraction of the available capital stock with which to work. If one worker uses one machine, adding another worker usually will not double the output because the machine can run only so fast and for so many hours per day. In other words, MPP declines because of the law of diminishing marginal returns.

## Marginal Revenue Product

**Marginal revenue product (MRP)** The marginal physical product (MPP) times marginal revenue.

We now need to translate into a dollar value the physical product that results from hiring an additional worker. This is done by multiplying the marginal physical product by the marginal revenue of the firm. Because our DVD firm is selling its product in a perfectly competitive market, marginal revenue is equal to the price of the product. If the seventh worker's MPP is 118 and the marginal revenue is \$6 per DVD, the **marginal revenue product (MRP)**—the marginal physical product (MPP) times marginal revenue—is \$708 (118 × \$6). The MRP is shown in column 4 of part (a) of Figure 13–1. *The marginal revenue product represents the worker's contribution to the firm's total revenues.*

When a firm operates in a competitive product market, the marginal physical product times the product price is also sometimes referred to as the *value of marginal product (VMP).* Because price and marginal revenue are the same for a perfectly competitive firm, the VMP is also the MRP.

**Marginal factor cost (MFC)** The cost of using an additional unit of an input.

In column 5 of part (a) of Figure 13–1, we show the wage rate, or *marginal factor cost,* of each worker. The marginal cost of workers is the extra cost of using an additional unit of an input. We call that cost the **marginal factor cost (MFC)**—the cost of using an additional unit of an input. Otherwise stated,

$$\text{Marginal factor cost} = \frac{\text{Change in total cost}}{\text{Change in amount of resource used}}$$

Because each worker is paid the same competitively determined wage of \$498 per week, the MFC is the same for all workers. And because the firm is buying labour in a perfectly competitive labour market, the wage rate of \$498 per week really represents the firm's supply curve of labour. That curve is perfectly elastic because the firm can purchase all labour at the same wage rate, considering that it is a minuscule part of the entire labour-purchasing market. (Recall the definition of perfect competition.) We show this perfectly elastic supply curve as *s* in part (b) of Figure 13–1.

## General Rule for Hiring

Virtually every optimizing rule in economics involves comparing marginal benefits with marginal cost. The general rule, therefore, for the hiring decision of a firm is this:

> **The firm hires workers up to the point at which the additional cost associated with hiring the last worker is equal to the additional revenue generated by that worker.**

In a perfectly competitive situation, this is the point at which the wage rate just equals the marginal revenue product. If the firm hired more workers, the additional wages would not be covered by additional increases in total revenue. If the firm hired fewer workers, it would be forfeiting the contributions that those workers could make to total profits.

Therefore, referring to columns 4 and 5 in part (a) of Figure 13–1, we see that this firm would certainly employ the seventh worker because the MRP is \$708, while the MFC is

**FIGURE 13–1**

## Marginal Revenue Product

In part (a), column 4 shows marginal revenue product (MRP), which is the amount of additional revenue the firm receives for the sale of additional output produced by one worker. Marginal revenue product is simply the amount of money the additional worker brings in—the combination of that worker's contribution to production and the revenue that production will bring to the firm. For this perfectly competitive firm, marginal revenue is equal to the price of the product, or $6 per unit. At a weekly wage of $498, the profit-maximizing employer will pay for only 12 workers because then the marginal revenue product is just equal to the wage rate or weekly salary.

In part (b), we find the number of workers the firm will want to hire by observing the wage rate that is established by the forces of supply and demand in the entire labour market. We show that this employer is hiring labour in a perfectly competitive labour market and therefore faces a perfectly elastic supply curve represented by *s* at $498 per week. As in all other situations, we basically have a supply and demand model; in this example, the demand curve is represented by MRP, and the supply curve is *s*. Equilibrium occurs at their intersection.

Part (a)

| (1) Labour Input (workers per week) | (2) Total Physical Product (TPP) DVD per Week | (3) Marginal Physical Product (MPP) DVD per Week | (4) Marginal Revenue (MR = *P* = $6 net) x MPP = Marginal Revenue Product (MRP) ($ per additional worker) | (5) Wage Rate ($ per week) = Marginal Factor Cost (MFC) = Change in Total Costs / Change in Labour |
|---|---|---|---|---|
| 6 | 882 | | | |
| 7 | 1000 | 118 | 708 | 498 |
| 8 | 1111 | 111 | 666 | 498 |
| 9 | 1215 | 104 | 624 | 498 |
| 10 | 1312 | 97 | 582 | 498 |
| 11 | 1402 | 90 | 540 | 498 |
| 12 | 1485 | 83 | 498 | 498 |
| 13 | 1561 | 76 | 456 | 498 |

Part (b)

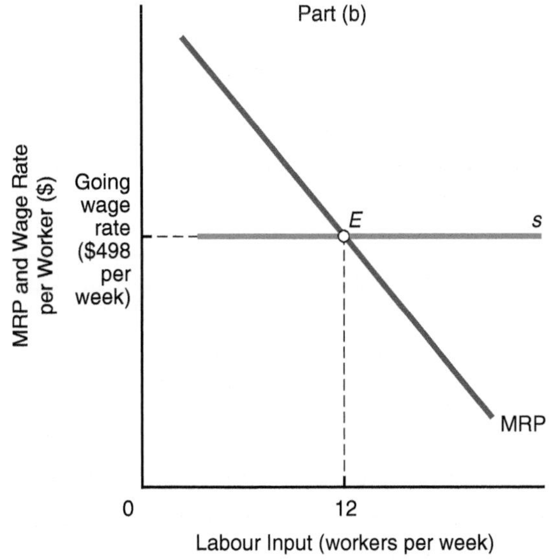

only \$498. The firm would continue to employ workers up to the point at which MFC = MRP because as workers are added, they contribute more to revenue than to cost.

## The MRP Curve: Demand for Labour

We can also use part (b) of Figure 13–1 to find how many workers our firm should hire. First, we draw a straight line across from the going wage rate, which is determined by demand and supply in the labour market. The straight line is labelled *s* to indicate that it is the supply curve of labour for the *individual* firm purchasing labour in a perfectly competitive labour market. That firm can purchase all the labour it wants of equal quality at \$498 per worker. This perfectly elastic supply curve, *s*, intersects the marginal revenue product curve at 12 workers per week. At the intersection, *E*, the wage rate is equal to the marginal revenue product. Equilibrium for the firm is obtained when the firm's demand curve for labour, which turns out to be its MRP curve, intersects the firm's supply curve for labour, shown as *s*. The firm in our example would not hire the 13th worker, who will add only \$456 to revenue but \$498 to cost. If the price of labour should fall to, say, \$456 per worker, it would become profitable for the firm to hire an additional worker; there is an increase in the quantity of labour demanded as the wage decreases.

## Derived Demand

**Derived demand** Input factor demand derived from demand for the final product being produced.

We have identified an individual firm's demand for labour curve as its MRP curve. Under conditions of perfect competition in both product and labour markets, MRP is determined by multiplying MPP times the product's price. This suggests that the demand for labour is a **derived demand.** That is to say that our CD firm does not want to purchase the services of labour just for the services themselves. Factors of production are rented or purchased not because they give any intrinsic satisfaction to the firms' owners but because they can be used to manufacture output that is expected to be sold for profit.

We know that an increase in the market demand for a given product raises the product's price (all other things held constant), which, in turn, increases the marginal revenue product, or demand for the resource. Figure 13–2 illustrates the effective role played by changes in product demand in a perfectly competitive product market. The MRP curve shifts whenever there is a change in the price of the final product that the workers are making. If, for example, the market price of DVDs goes down, the MRP curve will shift downward to the left from $MRP_0$ to $MRP_1$. We know that MRP = MPP × MR. If marginal revenue (here the output price) falls, so, too, does the demand for labour; at the same going wage rate, the firm will hire fewer workers. This is because at various levels of labour use, the marginal revenue product of labour falls so that at the initial equilibrium, the price of labour (here the MFC) becomes

**FIGURE 13–2**

**Demand for Labour, a Derived Demand**

The demand for labour is derived from the demand for the final product being produced. Therefore, the marginal revenue product curve will shift whenever the price of the product changes. If we start with the marginal revenue product curve MRP at the going wage rate of \$498 per week, 12 workers will be hired. If the price of DVDs goes down, the marginal product curve will shift to $MRP_1$, and the number of workers hired will fall to 10. If the price of DVDs goes up, the marginal revenue product curve will shift to $MRP_2$, and the number of workers hired will increase to 15.

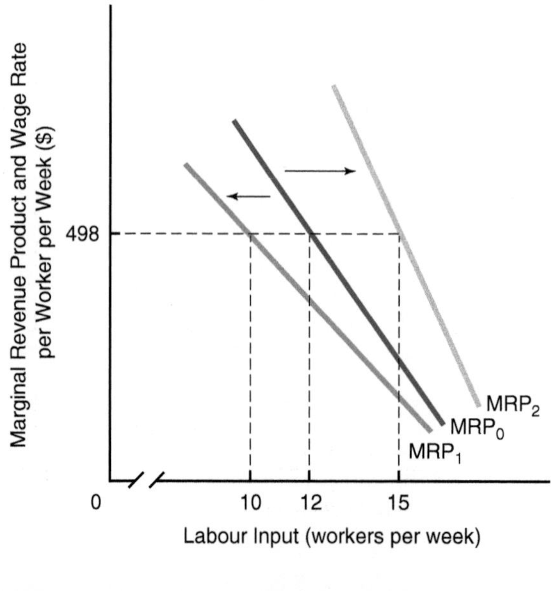

greater than MRP. Thus, the firm would reduce the number of workers hired. Conversely, if the marginal revenue (output price) rises, the demand for labour will also rise, and the firm will want to hire more workers at each and every possible wage rate.

We just pointed out that MRP = MPP × MR. Clearly, then, a change in marginal productivity, or in the marginal physical product of labour, will shift the MRP curve. If the marginal productivity of labour decreases, the MRP curve, or demand curve for labour will shift inward to the left. Again, this is because at every quantity of labour used, the MRP will be lower. A lower quantity of labour will be demanded at every possible wage rate.

## The Market Demand for Labour

The downward-sloping portion of each individual firm's marginal revenue product curve is also its demand curve for the one variable factor of production—in our example, labour. When we go to the entire market for a particular type of labour in a particular industry, we find that quantity of labour demanded will vary as the wage rate changes. Given that the market demand curve for labour is made up of the individual firms' demand curves for labour, we can safely assume that the market demand curve for labour will look like *D* in part (b) of Figure 13–3; it will slope downward. That market demand curve for labour in the DVD industry shows the quantities of labour demanded by all of the firms in the industry at various wage rates.

It is important to note that the market demand curve for labour is not a simple horizontal summation of the labour demand curves of all individual firms. Remember that the demand for labour is a derived demand. Even if we hold labour productivity constant, the demand for labour still depends on both the wage rate and the price of the final output. Assume that we start at a wage rate of $20 per hour and employment level 10 in part (a) of Figure 13–3. If we sum all such employment levels—point *a* in part (a)—across firms, we get a market quantity demanded of 2000—point *A* in part (b)—at the wage rate of $20. A decrease in the wage rate to $10 per hour induces individual firms' employment levels to increase toward a quantity demanded of 22. As all firms simultaneously increase employment, however, there is a shift in the product supply curve such that output increases. Hence, the price of the product must fall. The fall in the output price, in turn, causes a downward shift of each firm's MRP curve ($d_0$) to $MRP_1$ ($d_1$) in part (a). Thus, each firm's employment of labour increases to 15, rather than

**FIGURE 13–3**

**Derivation of the Market Demand Curve for Labour**

The market demand curve for labour is not simply the horizontal summation of all individual firms' demand curves for labour. If wage rates fall from $20 to $10, all firms will increase employment and therefore output, causing the price of the product to fall. This causes the marginal revenue product curve of each firm to shift inward, as from $d_0$ to $d_1$ in part (a). The resulting market demand curve, *D*, in part (b) is therefore less elastic than it would be if output price remained constant.

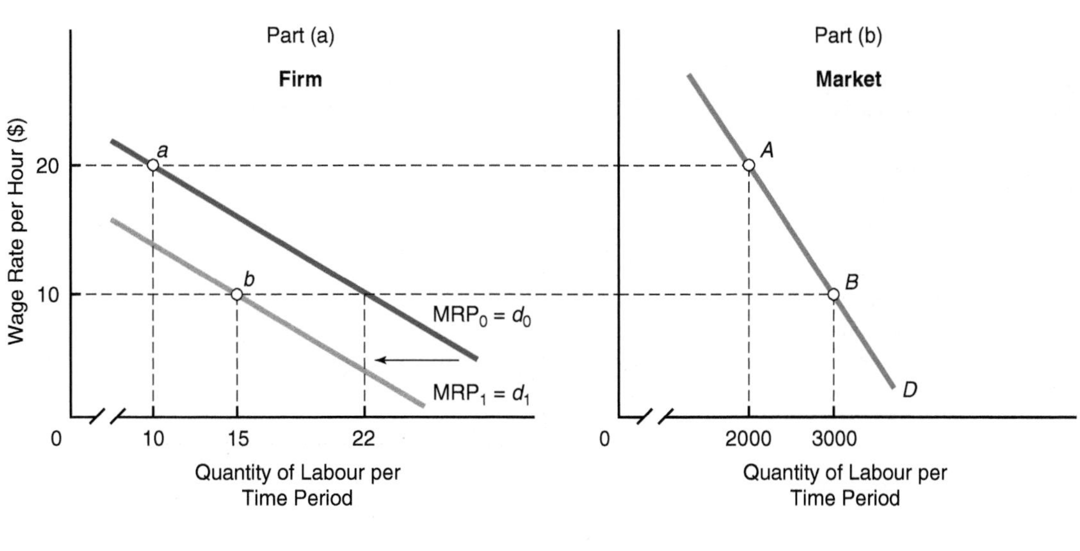

to 22, at the wage rate of $10 per hour. A summation of all such employment levels gives us 3000—point *B*—in part (b).

## Reasons for Labour Demand Curve Shifts

Many factors can cause the demand curve for labour to shift. We have already discussed a number of them. Clearly, because the demand for labour or any other variable input is a derived demand, the labour demand curve will shift if there is a shift in the demand for the final product. There are two other important determinants of the position of the demand curve for labour: changes in labour's productivity and changes in the price of related factors of production (substitutes and complements).

**CHANGES IN DEMAND FOR FINAL PRODUCT.** The demand for labour or any other variable input is derived from the demand for the final product. The marginal revenue product is equal to marginal physical product times marginal revenue. Therefore, any change in the price of the final product will change MRP. This happened when we derived the market demand for labour. The general rule of thumb is as follows:

> **A change in the demand for the final product that labour (or any other variable input) is producing will shift the market demand curve for labour in the same direction.**

**CHANGES IN LABOUR PRODUCTIVITY.** The second part of the MRP equation is MPP, which relates to labour productivity. We can surmise, then, that, other things being equal,

> **A change in labour productivity will shift the market labour demand curve in the same direction.**

Labour productivity can increase because labour has more capital or land to work with, because of technological improvements, or because labour's quality has improved. Such considerations explain why the real standard of living of workers in Canada is higher than in most countries. Canadian workers generally work with a larger capital stock, have more natural resources, are in better physical condition, and are better trained than workers in many countries. Hence, the demand for labour in Canada is, other things held constant, greater. Conversely, labour is relatively scarcer in Canada than it is in many other countries. One result of relatively greater demand and relatively smaller supply is a relatively higher wage rate. See Example 13–1 for further discussion.

Is there a payoff to increasing your skill level?

**Labour market signalling** The theory that even if higher education does not change productivity, it acts as an effective signal of greater individual abilities.

### EXAMPLE 13–1 Does It Pay to Study?

One way to increase labour productivity is to increase skill level. One way to do that, of course, is to go to college or university. Is there a big payoff? According to a recent study of identical twins carried out by economists Orley Ashenfelter and Alan Krueger, the answer is a resounding yes. They studied the earning patterns of more than 250 identical twins. In this manner, they were able to hold constant heredity, early home life, and so on. They focused on differences in the number of years of schooling. They discovered that each additional year of schooling increased wages almost 16 percent. Four years of post-secondary education yielded a 67 percent increase in monthly wages compared with none at all.

Some economists believe that a university degree is part of *labour market signalling*. Employers do not have much information about the future productivity of job applicants. Typically, the only way to find out is to observe someone working. Employers attempt to reduce the number of bad choices that they might make by using a job applicant's amount of higher education as a signal. According to the **labour market signalling** theory, even if higher education does not change productivity, it acts as an effective signal of greater individual abilities.

**For critical analysis:** Why does studying identical twins' earnings hold constant many of the factors that can determine differences in wages?

**CHANGE IN THE PRICE OF RELATED FACTORS.** Labour is not the only resource used. Some resources are substitutes and some are complements. If we hold output constant, we have the following general rule:

**A change in the price of a substitute input will cause the demand for labour to change in the same direction. This is typically called the substitution effect.**

Note, however, that if the cost of production falls sufficiently, the firm will find it more profitable to produce and sell a larger output. If this output effect is great enough, it will override the substitution effect just mentioned, and the firm will end up employing not only more of the relatively cheaper variable input but also more labour. This is exactly what happened for many years in the Canadian automobile industry. Car makers used more machinery (capital), but employment continued to increase in spite of rising wage rates. The reason: markets were expanding, and the marginal physical productivity of labour was rising faster than its wage rate.

With respect to complements, we are referring to inputs that must be used jointly. Assume now that capital and labour are complementary. In general, we predict the following:

**A change in the price of a complementary input will cause the demand for labour to change in the opposite direction.**

If the cost of machines goes up but they must be used with labour, fewer machines will be purchased and therefore fewer workers will be used.

## Determinants of Demand Elasticity for Inputs

Just as we were able to discuss the price elasticity of demand for different commodities, we can discuss the price elasticity of demand for inputs. The price elasticity of demand for labour is defined in a manner similar to the price elasticity of demand for goods: the percentage change in quantity demanded divided by the percentage change in the price of labour. When the numerical value of this ratio is less than 1, it is inelastic; when it is 1, it is unit-elastic; and when it is greater than 1, it is elastic.

There are four principal determinants of the price elasticity of demand for an input. The price elasticity of demand for a variable input will be greater:

1. The greater the price elasticity of demand for the final product
2. The easier it is for a particular variable input to be substituted for by other inputs
3. The larger the proportion of total costs accounted for by a particular variable input
4. The longer the time period being considered

Consider some examples. An individual radish farmer faces an extremely elastic demand for radishes, given the existence of many competing radish growers. If the farmer's labourers tried to obtain a significant wage increase, the farmer would not be able to pass on the resultant higher costs to radish buyers. So, any wage increase to the individual radish farmer would lead to a large reduction in the quantity of labour demanded.

Clearly, the easier it is for a producer to switch to using another factor of production, the more responsive that producer will be to an increase in an input's price. If plastic and aluminum can easily be substituted in the production of, say, car bumpers, then a price rise in aluminum will cause car makers to greatly reduce their quantity of aluminum demanded.

When a particular input's costs account for a very large share of total costs, any increase in that input's price will affect total costs relatively more. If labour costs are 80 percent of total costs, a company will cut back on employment more aggressively than if labour costs were only 8 percent of total costs, for any given wage increase.

Finally, over longer periods, firms have more time to figure out ways to economize on the use of inputs whose prices have gone up. Furthermore, over time, technological change will allow for easier substitution in favour of relatively cheaper inputs and against inputs whose prices went up. At first, a pay raise obtained by a strong telephone company union may not result in many layoffs, but over time, the telephone company will use new technology to replace many of the now more expensive workers.

# 13.2 Supply of Labour and Equilibrium

## Supply of Labour

Most people work to earn an income, so wages are a key factor in determining the amount of labour a person is willing to supply. At a wage rate of $5, an individual might not be willing to work at all; at a rate of $30, they would probably be willing to work 40 hours per week; pay higher than that and an individual might be happy working fewer hours so as to have more free time. The supply of labour would be influenced by other factors such as population, skills or training needed, mobility of the workforce, and the cost of living.

Having developed the demand curve for labour (and all other variable inputs) in a particular industry, let us turn to the labour supply curve. By adding supply to the analysis, we can come up with the equilibrium wage rate that workers earn in an industry. We can think in terms of a supply curve for labour that slopes upward in a particular industry, as illustrated in part (b) of Figure 13–4. At higher wage rates, more workers will want to enter that particular industry. The individual firm, however, does not face the entire *market* supply curve. Rather, in a perfectly competitive case, the individual firm is such a small part of the market that it can hire all the workers that it wants at the going wage rate as illustrated in part (a) of Figure 13–4. We say, therefore, that the industry faces an upward-sloping supply curve but that the individual *firm* faces a perfectly elastic supply curve for labour.

## Determinants of the Supply of Labour

There are a number of reasons why labour supply curves will shift in a particular industry. For example, if wage rates for factory workers in the DVD industry remain constant while wages for factory workers in the computer industry go up dramatically, the supply curve of factory workers in the DVD industry will shift inward to the left as these workers move to the computer industry.

Changes in working conditions in an industry can also affect its labour supply curve. If employers in the DVD industry discover a new production technique that makes working conditions much more pleasant, the supply curve of labour to the DVD industry will shift outward to the right.

Job flexibility also determines the position of the labour supply curve. For example, in an industry in which workers are allowed more flexibility, such as the ability to work at home via computer, the workers are likely to work more hours. That is to say, their supply curve will shift outward to the right. Some industries in which firms offer job sharing, par-

**FIGURE 13–4**

**Supply of Labour**

The individual firm faces a perfectly elastic supply curve for labour as illustrated in part (a).

The industry faces an upward-sloping supply curve as illustrated in part (b).

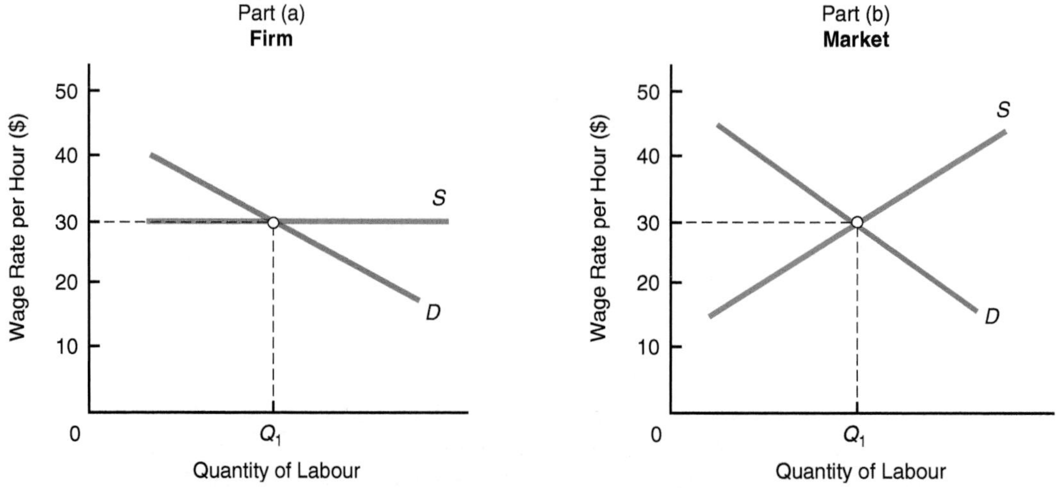

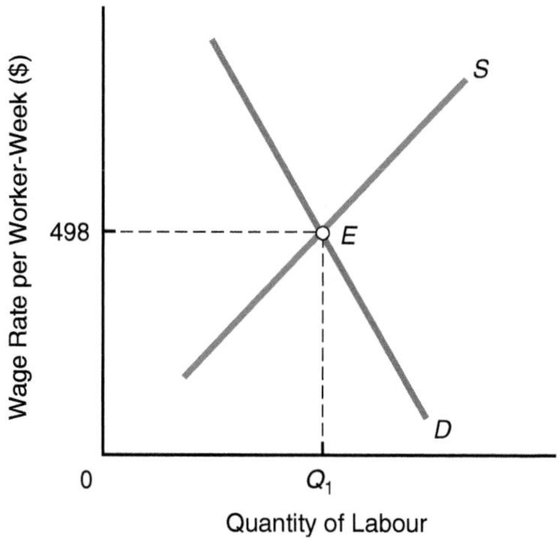


**FIGURE 13–5**

**The Equilibrium Wage Rate and the DVD Industry**

The industry demand curve for labour is *D*. We put in a hypothetical upward-sloping labour supply curve for the DVD industry, *S*. The intersection is at point *E*, giving an equilibrium wage rate of $498 per week and an equilibrium quantity of labour demanded of $Q_1$. At a price above $498 per week, there will be an excess quantity of workers supplied. At a price below $498 per week, there will be an excess quantity of workers demanded.

ticularly to people raising families, have found that the supply curve of labour has shifted outward to the right.

The demand curve for labour in the DVD industry is D in Figure 13–5, and the supply curve of labour is *S*. The equilibrium wage rate of $498 a week is established at the intersection of the two curves. The quantity of workers both supplied and demanded at that rate is $Q_1$. If for some reason the wage rate fell to $400 a week, in our hypothetical example, there would be an excess number of workers demanded at that wage rate. Conversely, if the wage rate rose to $600 a week, there would be an excess quantity of workers supplied at that wage rate.

We have just found the equilibrium wage rate for the entire DVD industry. The individual firm must take that equilibrium wage rate as given in the competitive model used here because the individual firm is a very small part of the total demand for labour. Thus, each firm purchasing labour in a perfectly competitive market can purchase all of the input it wants at the going market wage. See Policy Example 13–1 for more discussion on the minimum wage.

## POLICY EXAMPLE 13–1 Should the Minimum Wage Be Raised to Help Young People?

The equilibrium wage rate model shown in Figure 13–5 does not apply when the government sets a minimum wage rate below which employers are not allowed to pay workers and workers are not allowed to offer their services. Recall that, in general, a minimum wage (if set above equilibrium) creates an excess quantity of labour supplied (a surplus) at that legal minimum. Thus, young people probably would not be helped by an increase in minimum wages. Look at Figure 13–6. There, you see the unemployment rate for people aged 15 to 24. As minimum wages across the country rose during the 1990s, so did the rate of unemployment for young people. It started falling again only around 1993. Why? In part because what is important is the real, inflation-corrected minimum wage rate. In real terms, the minimum wage fell until about 1989. Then, it rose until 1993 and started falling again, exactly coincident with the reduction in the unemployment rate for young people.

A Statistics Canada study released in July 2014, noted that during the period 2005 to 2010, Canadian real minimum wage rates significantly increased relative to average Canadian wage rates. During this same period Canadian youth unemployment rates increased by almost 4 full percentage points.

So, to answer the policy question, raising the minimum wage probably would not help young people as a group, although it might help some young people who retain their jobs at the higher wage rate.

**For critical analysis:** Why are young people most affected by changes in the minimum wage? (Hint: Which workers produce the lowest MRP?)

Sources:"The ups and downs of minimum wage." by Diane Galarneau and Eric Fecteau. Catalogue no. 75-006-X. Statistics Canada. July 2014. http://www.statcan.gc.ca/pub/75-006-x/2014001/article/14035-eng.pdf (Accessed February 4, 2017); "Canada Youth Unemployment Rate 1976-2017." Trading Economics. Canada Youth Unemployment Rate 1976-2017 (Accessed February 4, 2017).

**FIGURE 13–6**

**Teenage Unemployment and the Real Minimum Wage**

Although the minimum wage has risen over the past 30 years, the real minimum wage has fallen since 1993, leading to a decrease in the rate of youth unemployment since then.

Source: Adapted from Statistics Canada data: http://www.statcan.gc.ca/pub/82-221-x/00502/t/th/4149286-eng.htm.

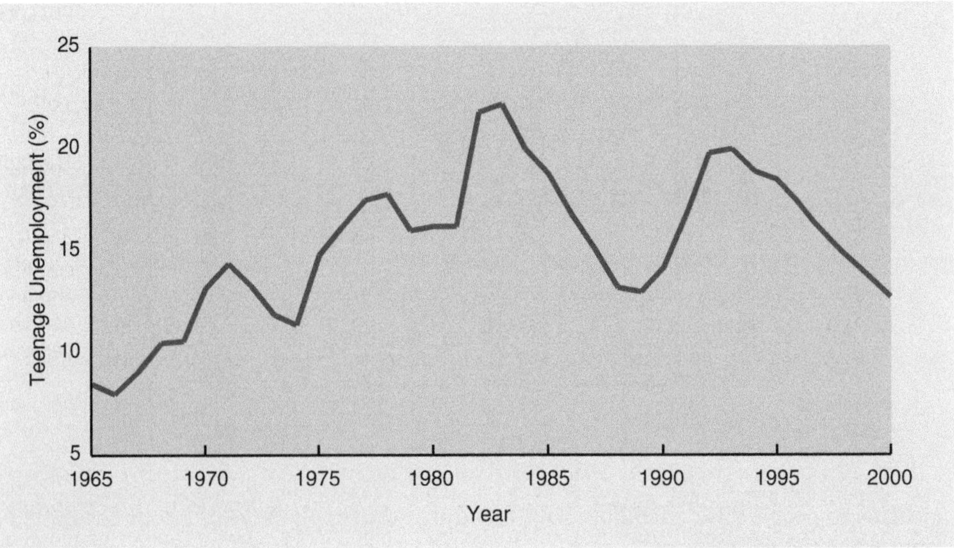


# 13.3 Union Goals and Labour Unions

## The Current Status of Labour Unions

Union membership grew quite rapidly from the 1940s to the late 1950s. Since 1967, union membership has been fairly stable, and is currently hovering around 30 percent of the civilian labour force. If you remove labour unions in the public sector—federal, provincial, and municipal government workers—private-sector union membership in Canada is about 16 percent of the civilian labour force.

As you can see from Figure 13–7, unionization increased in only three of the 16 major industry groups from 2012 to 2016. In the early stages of the Canadian union movement, unions were predominately male workers in factories, mines, and other blue collar trades. Today, a union member is more likely to be a woman, and working in an office, government, school, college , university, or hospital.

**FIGURE 13–7**

**Unionization Rates in Various Industries**

Source: Labour Force Survey estimates (LFS), employees by union status, North American Industry Classification System (NAICS) and sex, Canada. Table 282-0223. Labour Force Survey – 3701. Cansim. Statistics Canada: 2012–2016. http://www5.statcan.gc.ca/cansim/a47 (Accessed February 4, 2017).

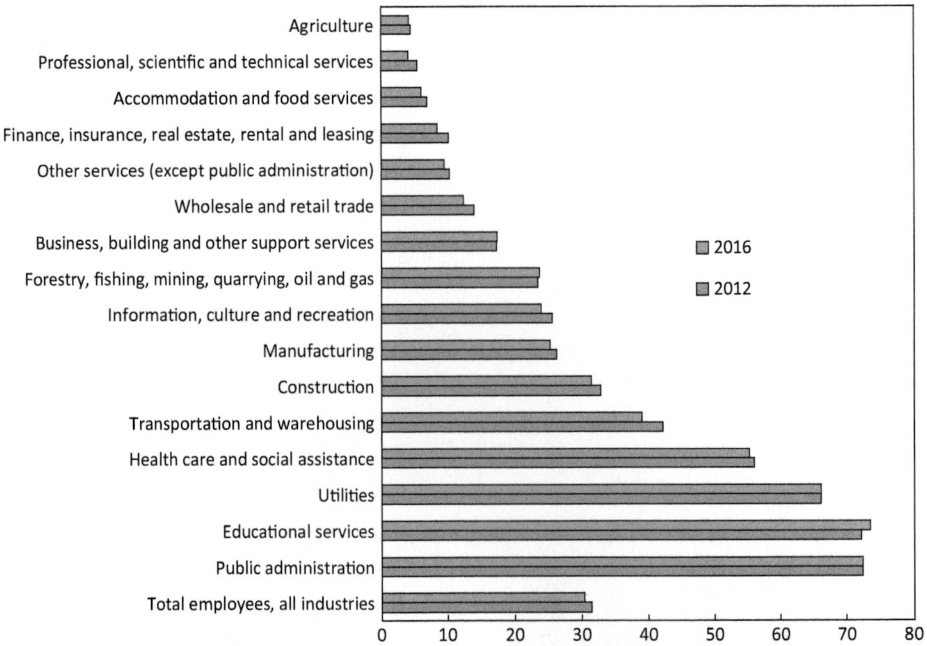

## Unions and Collective Bargaining Contracts

Unions can be regarded as setters of minimum wages. Through collective bargaining, unions establish minimum wages below which no workers can offer their services. Each year, collective bargaining contracts covering wages as well as working conditions and fringe benefits for about 2 million workers are negotiated. Union negotiators act as agents for all members of the bargaining unit. They bargain with management about the provisions of a labour contract.

Once union representatives believe that they have an acceptable collective contract, they will submit it to a vote of the union members. If approved by the members, the contract sets wage rates, maximum workdays, working conditions, fringe benefits, and other matters, usually for the next two or three years. Typically, collective bargaining contracts between management and the union apply also to nonunion members who are employed by the firm or the industry.

## Strike: The Ultimate Bargaining Tool

Whenever union–management negotiations break down, union negotiators may turn to their ultimate bargaining tool—the threat, or the reality, of a strike. The first recorded strike in Canadian history occurred in 1671, when shipyard workers in Quebec conducted a slowdown to secure better wages and working conditions. Strikes make headlines, but in only 4 percent of all labour–management disputes does a strike occur before the contract is signed. In the other 96 percent of cases, contracts are signed without much public fanfare.

The purpose of a strike is to impose costs on stubborn management to force its acceptance of the union's proposed contract terms. Strikes disrupt production and interfere with a company's or an industry's ability to sell goods and services. The strike works both ways, though. Workers draw no wages while on strike (they may be partly compensated out of union strike funds) and are not eligible to claim Employment Insurance benefits. Effects of this are illustrated in Example 13–2.

### EXAMPLE 13–2 Strike Activity in Canada

Although unionization rates have been fairly stable in Canada, the number of strikes and lockouts has decreased. As you can see from Figure 13–8, the highest number of strikes took place in the early 1980s, and the numbers peaked again in the mid-1980s. Strike activity has declined sharply since then and levelled off in 2003, 2004, and 2005 to around 300 strikes per year. More recently, between 2007 and 2016, the average annual number of strikes in Canada averaged only 126 strikes per year, indicating a continuing significant decline in work stoppages.

Typically, in a strike situation, the workers will lose wages, while companies' costs will increase. A gain for one union is likely to cause losses for other unions. Some economists even feel that the best wage-setting arrangement might be the automatic adjustments of wages to firm profitability.

Why has the number of strikes been declining?

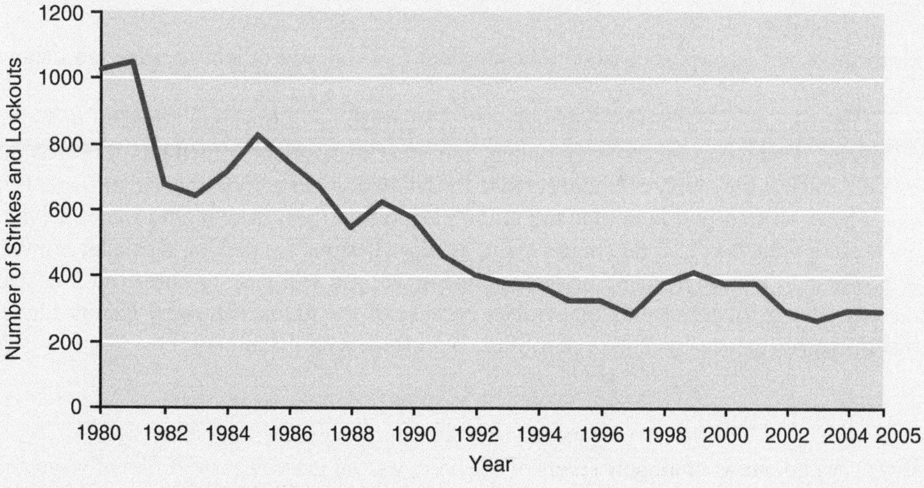


**FIGURE 13–8**

**The Declining Number of Strikes**

Source: Statistics Canada. Major wage settlements, inflation and labour disputes. *Perspectives on Labour and Income—Unionization.* http://www.statcan.ca/english/studies/75-001/comm/Fact-2.htm.

**For critical analysis:** In what way might a strike help organized labour? Could a rise in profit-sharing have caused the declines in strikes that we see in Figure 13–8? How?

The impact of a strike is closely related to the ability of striking unions to prevent nonstriking (and perhaps nonunion) employees from continuing to work for the targeted company or industry. Therefore, steps are usually taken to prevent others from working for the employer. **Strikebreakers** (temporary or permanent workers hired by a company to replace union members who are on strike) can effectively destroy whatever bargaining power rests behind a strike. Numerous methods—including violence on the picket lines—have been used to deter strikebreakers.

**Strikebreakers** Temporary or permanent workers hired by a company to replace union members who are on strike.

## Union Goals

We have already pointed out that one of the goals of unions is to set minimum wages. In many situations, any wage rate set higher than a competitive market clearing wage rate will reduce total employment in that market. This can be seen in Figure 13–9. We have a competitive market for labour. The market demand curve is *D*, and the market supply curve is *S*. The market clearing wage rate will be $W_e$; the equilibrium quantity of labour will be $Q_e$. If the union establishes by collective bargaining a minimum wage rate that exceeds $W_e$, an excess quantity of labour will be supplied (assuming no change in the labour demand schedule). If the minimum wage established by union collective bargaining is $W_U$, the quantity supplied would be $Q_S$; the quantity demanded would be $Q_D$. The difference is the excess quantity supplied, or surplus. Hence, the following point becomes clear:

**One of the major roles of a union that establishes a wage rate above the market clearing wage rate is to ration available jobs among the excess number of workers who wish to work in unionized industries.**

**FIGURE 13–9**

**Unions Must Ration Jobs**

If the union succeeds in obtaining wage rate $W_U$, the quantity of labour demanded will be $Q_D$, but the quantity of labour supplied will be $Q_S$. The union must ration a limited number of jobs to a greater number of workers; the surplus of labour is equivalent to a shortage of jobs at that wage rate.

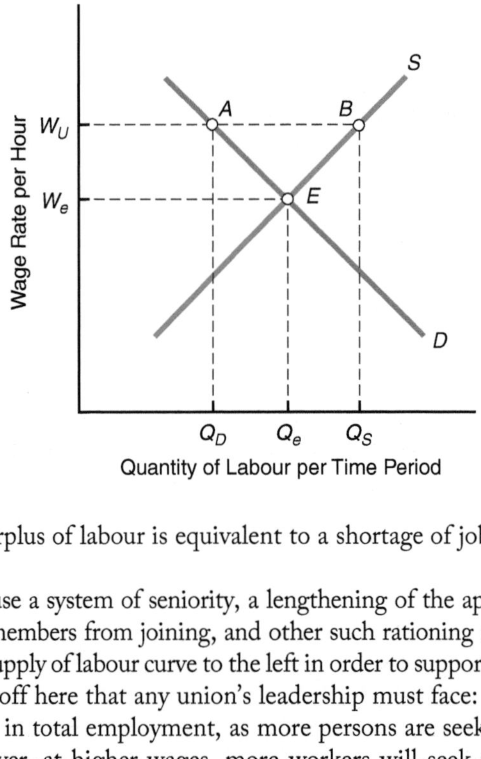


Note also that the surplus of labour is equivalent to a shortage of jobs at wage rates above equilibrium.

The union may use a system of seniority, a lengthening of the apprenticeship period to discourage potential members from joining, and other such rationing methods. This has the effect of shifting the supply of labour curve to the left in order to support the higher wage, $W_U$.

There is a trade-off here that any union's leadership must face: higher wages inevitably mean a reduction in total employment, as more persons are seeking a smaller number of positions. (Moreover, at higher wages, more workers will seek to enter the industry, thereby adding to the surplus that occurs because of the union contract.) Facing higher wages, management may replace part of the workforce with machinery.

## Union Strategies

If we view unions as monopoly sellers of a service, we can identify three different wage and employment strategies that they use: ensuring employment for all members of the union, maximizing aggregate income for all workers, and maximizing wage rates for some workers.

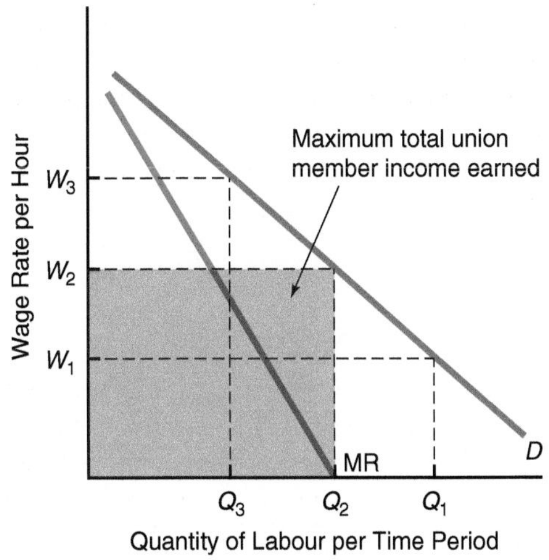


**FIGURE 13–10**

**What Do Unions Maximize?**

Assume that the union wants to employ all its $Q_1$ members. It will attempt to get wage rate $W_1$. If the union wants to maximize total wage receipts (income), it will do so at wage rate $W_2$, where the elasticity of the demand for labour is equal to 1. (The shaded area represents the maximum total income that the union would earn at $W_2$.) If the union wants to maximize the wage rate for a given number of workers, say, $Q_3$, it will set the wage rate at $W_3$.

**EMPLOYING ALL MEMBERS IN THE UNION.** Assume that the union has $Q_1$ workers. If it faces a labour demand curve such as *D* in Figure 13–10, the only way it can "sell" all of those workers' services is to accept a wage rate of $W_1$. This is similar to any other demand curve. The demand curve tells the maximum price that can be charged to sell any particular quantity of a good or service. Here, the service happens to be labour.

**MAXIMIZING MEMBER INCOME.** If the union is interested in maximizing the gross income of its members, it will normally want a smaller membership than $Q_1$—namely, $Q_2$ workers, all employed and paid a wage rate of $W_2$. The aggregate income to all members of the union is represented by the wages of only the ones who work. Total income earned by union members is maximized where the price elasticity of demand is numerically equal to 1. That occurs where marginal revenue equals zero. In Figure 13–10, marginal revenue equals zero at a quantity of labour $Q_2$. So, we know that if the union obtains a wage rate equal to $W_2$, and therefore $Q_2$ workers are demanded, the total income to the union membership will be maximized. In other words, $Q_2 \times W_2$ (the shaded area) will be greater than any other combination of wage rates and quantities of union workers demanded. It is, for example, greater than $Q_1 \times W_1$. Note that in this situation, if the union started out with $Q_1$ members, there would be $Q_1 - Q_2$ members out of *union* work at the wage rate $W_2$. (Those out of union work either remain unemployed or go to other industries, which has a depressing effect on wages in nonunion industries due to the increase in supply of nonunion workers there.)

**MAXIMIZING WAGE RATES FOR CERTAIN WORKERS.** Assume that the union wants to maximize the wage rates for some of its workers—perhaps those with the most seniority. If it wanted to keep a quantity of $Q_3$ workers employed, it would seek to obtain a wage rate of $W_3$. This would require deciding which workers should be unemployed and which should work, as well as for how long each week or each year they should be employed.

## Limiting Entry over Time

One way to raise wage rates without specifically setting wages is for unions to limit the size of their membership to the extent of their employed workforce when the union was first organized. No workers are put out of work at the time the union is formed. Over time, as the demand for labour in the industry increases, there is no net increase in union membership, and so larger wage increases are obtained than would otherwise be the case. We see this in Figure 13–11. Union members freeze entry into their union, thereby obtaining a wage rate of \$16 per hour instead of allowing a wage rate of \$15 per hour with no restriction on labour supply.

## Altering the Demand for Union Labour

Another way in which unions can increase wages is to shift the demand curve for labour outward to the right. This approach compares favourably with the supply restriction approach because it increases both wage rates and employment level. The demand for

**FIGURE 13–11**

**Restricting Supply over Time**

When the union was formed, it did not affect wage rates or employment, which remained at $14 and $Q_1$ (the equilibrium wage rate and quantity). However, as demand increased—that is, as the demand schedule shifted outward to $D_2$ from $D_1$—the union restricted membership to its original level of $Q_1$. The new supply curve is $S_2$, which intersects $D_2$ at $E_2$, or at a wage rate of $16. Without the union, equilibrium would be at $E_3$ with a wage rate of $15 and employment of $Q_2$.

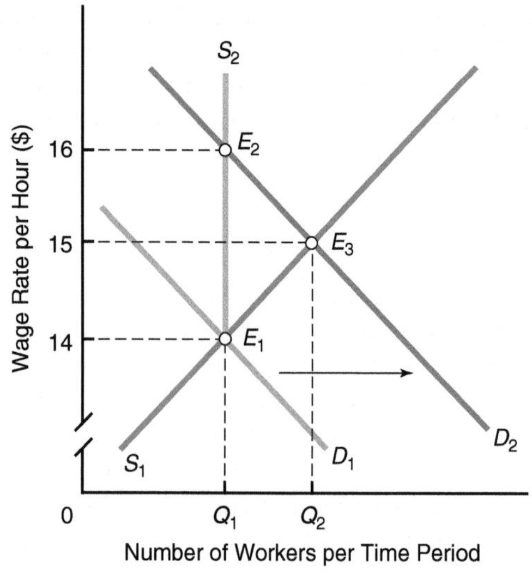


union labour can be increased by increasing worker productivity, increasing the demand for union-made goods, and decreasing the demand for nonunion-made goods.

**INCREASING WORKER PRODUCTIVITY.** Supporters of unions have argued that unions provide a good system of industrial jurisprudence. The presence of unions may induce workers to feel that they are working in fair and just circumstances. If so, they work harder, increasing labour productivity. Productivity is also increased when unions resolve differences and reduce conflicts between workers and management, thereby providing a smoother administrative environment.

**INCREASING DEMAND FOR UNION-MADE GOODS.** Because the demand for labour is a derived demand, a rise in the demand for products produced by union labour will increase the demand for union labour itself. One way in which unions attempt to increase the demand for union labour–produced products is by advertising "Look for the union label."

**DECREASING THE DEMAND FOR NONUNION-MADE GOODS.** When the demand for goods that are competing with (or are substitutes for) union-made goods is reduced, consumers shift to union-made goods, increasing the demand. A good example is when various unions campaign against imports. The result is greater demand for goods "made in Canada," which, in turn, presumably increases the demand for Canadian union (and nonunion) labour.

## Have Unions Raised Wages?

We have seen that unions are able to raise the wages of their members if they are successful at limiting the supply of labour in a particular industry. They are also able to raise wages above what wages would otherwise be to the extent that they can shift the demand for union labour outward to the right. This can be done using the methods we have just discussed, including collective bargaining agreements that require specified workers for any given job—for example, by requiring a pilot, a co-pilot, and an engineer in the cockpit of a jet airplane, even if an engineer is not really needed on short flights.

Economists have done extensive research to determine the actual increase in union wages relative to nonunion wages. They have found that in certain industries, such as construction, and in certain occupations, such as commercial airline pilot, the union wage differential can be 50 percent or more. That is to say, unions have been able in some industries and occupations to raise wage rates 50 percent or more above what they would be in the absence of unions.

In addition, the union wage differential appears to increase during recessions. This is because unions often, through collective bargaining, have longer-term contracts than nonunion workers so that they do not have to renegotiate wage rates, even when overall demand in the economy falls.

On average, unions appear to be able to raise the wage rates of their members relative to nonunion members by 10 to 20 percent. Note, though, that when unions increase wages beyond what productivity increases would permit, some union members will be laid off. A redistribution of income from low- to high-seniority union workers is not equivalent to higher wages for *all* union members.

## Can Unions Increase Productivity?

A traditional view of union behaviour is that unions decrease productivity by artificially shifting the demand curve for union labour outward through excessive staffing and make-work requirements. For example, some economists have traditionally felt that unions tend to bargain for excessive use of workers—referred to as **featherbedding**—as when requiring an engineer on all flights. Many painters' unions, for example, resisted the use of paint sprayers and required that their members use only brushes. They even specified the maximum width of the brush. Moreover, whenever a union strikes, productivity drops, and this reduction in productivity in one sector of the economy can spill over into other sectors.

**Featherbedding** Unions' tendency to bargain for excessive use of workers.

This view of unions has recently been countered by one that unions can actually increase productivity. The new labour economists argue that unions act as a collective voice for their members. In the absence of a collective voice, any dissatisfied worker either simply remains at a job and works in a disgruntled manner or quits. But unions, as a collective voice, can listen to worker grievances on an individual basis and then apply pressure on the employer to change working conditions and other things. The individual worker does not run the risk of being singled out by the employer and harassed. Also, the individual worker does not have to spend time trying to convince the employer that some change in the working arrangement should be made. Given that unions provide this collective voice, worker turnover in unionized industries should be less, and this should contribute to productivity. Indeed, there is strong evidence that worker turnover is reduced when unions are present. Of course, this evidence may also be consistent with the fact that wage rates are so attractive to union members that they will not quit unless working conditions become truly intolerable.

## The Benefits of Labour Unions

It should, by now, be clear that there are two opposing views about unions. One portrays them as monopolies whose main effect is to raise the wage rate of high-seniority members at the expense of low-seniority members. The other contends that they can increase labour productivity through a variety of means. Economists Richard B. Freeman and James L. Medoff argue that the truth lies somewhere in between. They came up with the following conclusions:

1. Unionism probably raises social efficiency, thereby contradicting the traditional monopoly interpretation of what unions do. Even though unionism reduces employment in the unionized sector, it does permit labour to develop and implement workplace practices that are more valuable to workers. In some settings, unionism is associated with increased productivity.
2. Unions appear to reduce wage inequality.
3. Unions seem to reduce profits.
4. Internally, unions provide a political voice for all workers, and unions have been effective in promoting general social legislation.
5. Unions tend to increase the stability of the workforce by providing such services as arbitration proceedings and grievance procedures.

Freeman and Medoff take a positive view of unionism. But critics of the two economists point out they may have overlooked the fact that many of the benefits that unions provide do not require that unions engage in restrictive labour practices, such as refusing to allow nonmembers to work in any particular company. Unions could still do positive things for workers without restricting the labour market.

# 13.4 Pricing and Employment in Various Market Conditions

## Monopsony: A Buyer's Monopoly

Let us assume that a firm is a perfect competitor in the product market. The firm cannot alter the price of the product it sells, and it faces a perfectly elastic demand curve for its product. We also assume that the firm is the only buyer of a particular input. Although this situation may not occur often, it is useful to consider. Let us think in terms of a factory town, like those dominated by textile mills or in the mining industry. One company not only hires the workers but also owns the businesses in the community, owns the apartments that workers live in, and hires the clerks, waiters, and all other personnel. This buyer of labour is called a **monopsonist**, the single buyer of a factor of production.

**Monopsonist** The single buyer of a factor of production.

What does an upward-sloping supply curve mean to a monopsonist in terms of the costs of hiring extra workers? It means that if the monopsonist wants to hire more workers, it has to offer higher wages. Our monopsonist firm cannot hire all the labour it wants at the going wage rate. If it wants to hire more workers, it has to raise wage rates, including the wage of all its current workers (assuming a non–wage-discriminating monopsonist). It therefore has to take account of these increased costs when deciding how many more workers to hire. See why cheating by colleges and universities would occur as a result of monopsony in Example 13–3.

### EXAMPLE 13–3 Monopsony in College Sports

How many times have you read stories about American colleges and universities violating National Collegiate Athletic Association (NCAA) rules? If you keep up with the sports press, you know that these stories about alleged violations occur every year. About 600 four-year colleges and universities in the United States belong to the NCAA, which controls more than 20 sports. In effect, the NCAA operates an intercollegiate cartel that is dominated by universities that operate large athletic programs. It operates as a cartel with monopsony (and monopoly) power in four ways:

1. It regulates the number of student athletes that universities can recruit.
2. It often fixes the prices that the university charges for tickets to important intercollegiate sporting events.
3. It sets the prices (wages) and the conditions under which the universities can recruit these student athletes.
4. It enforces its regulations and rules with sanctions and penalties.

The NCAA rules and regulations expressly prohibit bidding for college athletes in an overt manner. Rather, the NCAA requires that all athletes be paid the same for tuition, fees, room, board, and books. Moreover, the NCAA limits the number of athletic scholarships that can be given by a particular university. These rules are ostensibly to prevent the richest universities from "hiring" the best student athletes.

Not surprisingly, from the very beginning of the NCAA, individual universities and colleges have attempted to cheat on the rules in order to attract better athletes. The original agreement among the colleges was to pay no wages. Almost immediately after this agreement was put into effect, colleges switched to offering athletic scholarships, jobs, free room and board, travel expenses, and other enticements. It was not unusual for athletes to be paid $10 an hour to rake leaves when the going wage rate for such work was only $5 an hour. Finally, the NCAA had to agree to permit wages up to a certain amount per year.

If all American universities had to offer exactly the same money wages and fringe benefits, the less academically distinguished colleges in urban areas (with a large potential number of ticket-buying fans) would have the most incentive to violate the NCAA agreements (to compensate for the lower market value of their degrees). They would figure out all sorts of techniques to get the best student athletes. Indeed, such schools have, in fact, cheated more than other universities and colleges, and their violations have been detected and punished with a relatively greater frequency than those of other colleges and universities.

*continued*

**For critical analysis:** American college and university administrators argue that the NCAA rules are necessary to "keep business out of higher education." How can one argue that college athletics is related to academics?

## Marginal Factor Cost

The monopsonist faces an upward-sloping supply curve of the input in question because as the only buyer, it faces the entire market supply curve. Each time the monopsonist buyer of labour, for example, wishes to hire more workers, it must raise wage rates. Thus, the marginal cost of another unit of labour is rising. In fact, the marginal cost of increasing its workforce will always be greater than the wage rate. This is because in the situation in which the monopsonist pays the same wage rate to everyone in order to obtain another unit of labour, the higher wage rate has to be offered not only to the last worker but also to all its other workers. We call the additional cost to the monopsonist of hiring one more worker the marginal factor cost (MFC).

The marginal factor cost for the last worker is therefore that individual's wages plus the increase in the wages of all other existing workers. As we pointed out, marginal factor cost is equal to the change in total variable cost due to a one-unit change in the one variable factor of production—in this case, labour. For a competitive firm in the labour market, marginal factor cost was simply the competitive wage rate because the employer could hire all workers at the same wage rate.

## Derivation of a Marginal Factor Cost Curve

Part (a) of Figure 13–12 shows the quantity of labour purchased, the wage rate per hour, the total cost of the quantity of labour purchased per hour, and the marginal factor cost per hour for the additional labour bought.

We translate the columns from part (a) to the graph in part (b) of the figure. We show the supply curve as *S*, which is taken from columns 1 and 2. (Note that this is the same as the *average* factor cost curve; hence you can view Figure 13–12 as showing the relationship between average factor cost and marginal factor cost.) The marginal factor cost curve is taken from columns 1 and 4. The MFC curve must be above the supply curve whenever the supply curve is upward sloping. If the supply curve is upward sloping, the firm must pay a higher wage rate in order to attract a larger amount of labour. This higher wage rate must be paid to all workers; thus the increase in total costs due to an increase in the labour input will exceed the wage rate. Note that in a perfectly competitive input market, the supply curve is perfectly elastic and the marginal factor cost curve is identical to the supply curve.

## Employment and Wages under Monopsony

To determine the number of workers that a monopsonist desires to hire, we compare the marginal benefit with the marginal cost of each hiring decision. The marginal cost is the marginal factor cost curve, and the marginal benefit is the marginal revenue product curve. In Figure 13–13 on page 355 we assume competition in the output market and monopsony in the input market. A monopsonist finds its profit-maximizing quantity of labour demanded at *E*, where the marginal revenue product is just equal to the marginal factor cost.

How much is the firm going to pay these workers? In a nonmonopsonistic situation, it would face a given wage rate in the labour market, but because it is a monopsonist, it faces the entire supply curve, *S*.

A monopsonist faces an *upward-sloping* supply curve for labour. Firms do not usually face the market supply curve; most firms can hire all the workers they want at the going wage rate and thus usually face a perfectly elastic supply curve for each factor of production. The market supply curve, however, slopes upward.

The monopsonist therefore sets the wage rate so that it will get exactly the quantity, $Q_m$, supplied to it by its "captive" labour force. We find that wage rate is $W_m$. There is no reason to pay the workers any more than $W_m$ because at that wage rate, the firm can get exactly the quantity it wants. The actual quantity used is established at the intersection of

FIGURE 13–12

## Derivation of a Marginal Factor Cost Curve

The supply curve, *S*, in part (b) is taken from columns 1 and 2 of part (a). The marginal factor cost curve (MFC) is taken from columns 1 and 4. It is the increase in the total wage bill resulting from a one-unit increase in labour input.

Part (a)

| (1) Quantity of Labour Supplied to Management | (2) Required Hourly Wage Rate | (3) Total Wage Bill (3) = (1) x (2) | (4) Marginal Factor Cost (MFC) = $\frac{\text{Change in (3)}}{\text{Change in (1)}}$ |
|---|---|---|---|
| 0 | | | |
| 1 | $1.00 | $ 1.00 | $1.00 |
| 2 | 2.00 | 4.00 | 3.00 |
| 3 | 2.40 | 7.20 | 3.20 |
| 4 | 2.80 | 11.20 | 4.00 |
| 5 | 3.60 | 18.00 | 6.80 |
| 6 | 4.20 | 25.20 | 7.20 |

Part (b)

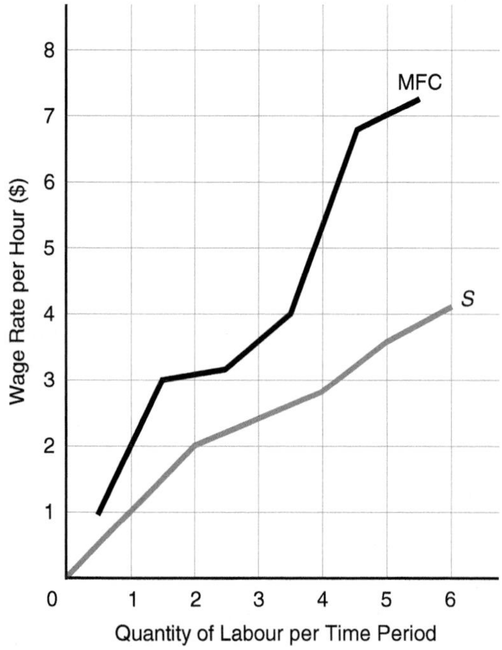


the marginal factor cost curve and the marginal revenue product curve for labour—that is, at the point at which the marginal revenue from expanding employment just equals the marginal cost of doing so.

Note that the profit-maximizing wage rate paid to workers ($W_m$) is lower than the marginal revenue product. That is, workers are paid a wage that is less than their contribution to the monopsonist's revenues. This is sometimes referred to as **monopsonistic exploitation** of labour—the difference between marginal revenue product and the wage rate. The monopsonist is able to do this because each individual worker has little power in bargaining for a higher wage. The organization of workers into a union, though, creates a monopoly supplier of labour, which gives the union some power to bargain for higher wages.

**Monopsonistic exploitation** Monopsonistic exploitation is the difference between marginal revenue product and the wage rate.

What happens when a monopsonist meets a union? This is the situation called **bilateral monopoly**, defined as a market structure in which a single buyer faces a single seller. An example is a provincial ministry of education facing a single teachers' union in the labour market. Another example is a professional players' union facing an organized group of team owners. Such bilateral monopoly situations have, indeed, occurred in professional baseball

**Bilateral monopoly** A market structure in which a single buyer faces a single seller.

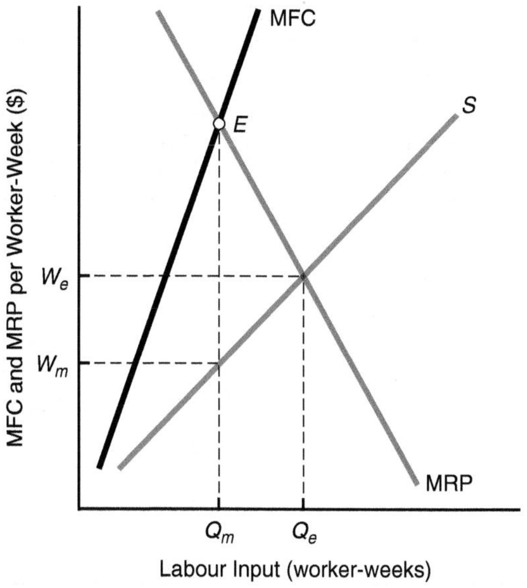


**FIGURE 13–13**

**Marginal Factor Cost Curve for a Monopsonist**

The monopsonist firm looks at a marginal cost curve, MFC, that slopes upward and is above its labour supply curve, *S*. The marginal benefit of hiring additional workers is given by the firm's MRP curve. The intersection of MFC with MRP, at point *E*, determines the number of workers hired. The firm hires $Q_m$ workers but has to pay them only $W_m$ in order to attract them. Compare this with the competitive solution, in which the wage rate would have to be $W_e$ and the quantity of labour would be $Q_e$.

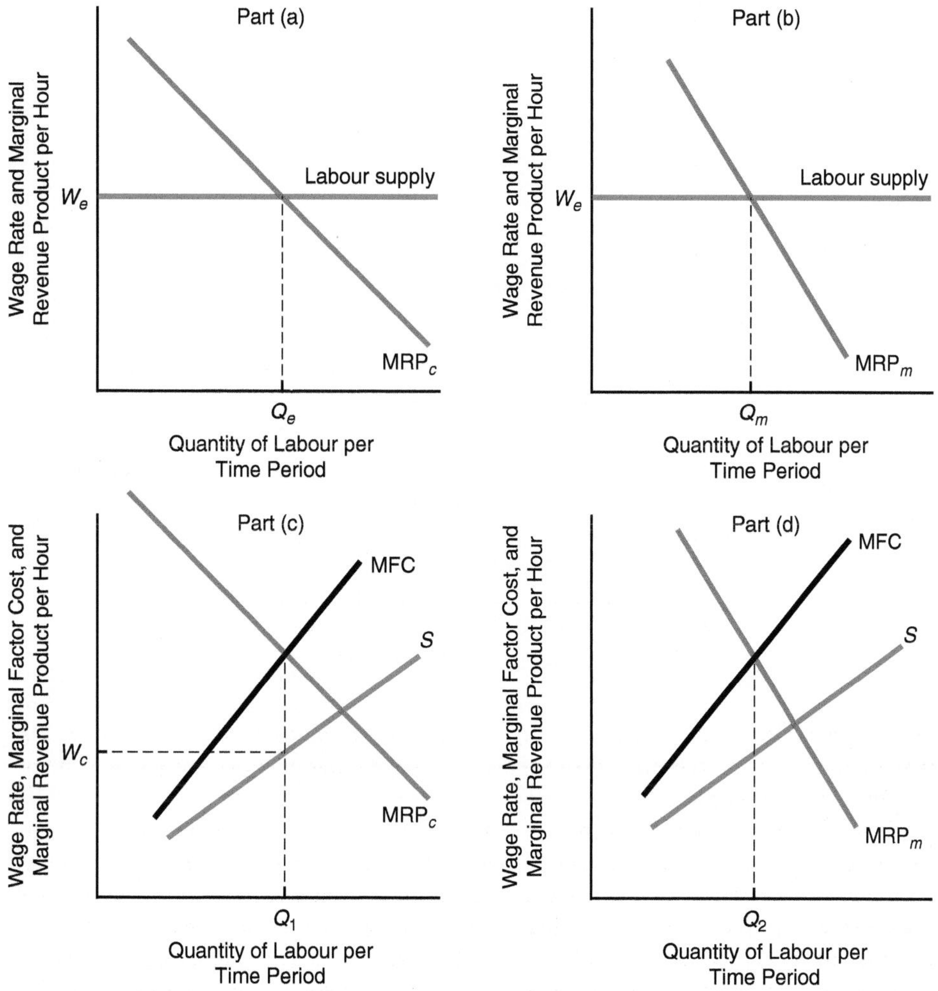


**FIGURE 13–14**

**Summary of Pricing and Employment under Various Market Conditions**

In part (a), the firm operates in perfect competition in both input and output markets. It purchases labour up to the point where the going rate $W_e$ is equal to $MRP_c$. It hires quantity $Q_e$ of labour. In part (b), the firm is a perfect competitor in the input market but has a monopoly in the output market. It purchases labour up to the point where $W_e$ is equal to $MRP_m$. It hires a smaller quantity of labour, $Q_m$, than in part (a). In part (c), the firm is a monopsonist in the input market and a perfect competitor in the output market. It hires labour up to the point where MFC = $MRP_c$. It will hire quantity $Q_1$ and pay wage rate $W_c$. Part (d) shows bilateral monopoly. The wage outcome is indeterminate.

and hockey. To analyze bilateral monopoly, we would have to look at the interaction of both sides, buyer and seller. The price outcome turns out to be indeterminate.

We have studied the pricing of labour in various situations, including perfect competition in both the output and input markets and monopoly in both the output and input markets. Figure 13–14 shows four possible situations graphically.

ISSUES AND APPLICATIONS

# Canadian Wheat Board: Monopoly or Monopsony

**Concepts Applied: Monopoly, Monopsony, Bilateral Monopoly, Monopolistic Exploitation**

Western Canadian farmers are discontented with the monopsony status of the G3 Canada LTD.

The Canadian Wheat Board (CWB) was formed in 1935 to act as the sole buyer and seller of wheat and barley produced by western Canadian farmers. One major reason for the establishment of the CWB was to equip the individual farmers with enhanced bargaining power when negotiating grain prices with a few large grain handling companies/railways.

## The Monopsony Power of the CWB

The CWB is not a true monopoly because, by definition, a monopoly is a single supplier of a good or service for which there is no close substitute. Grain prices are set by the world market, so the CWB is not the only seller; as a matter of fact, it provides less than 20 percent of world wheat exports.

Most people call the CWB a monopoly because western farmers must sell their wheat and barley to the CWB. Probably a better description of the CWB would be monopsony, the only buyer in a market.

The CWB faces the entire supply curve for western Canadian wheat and barley crops. So, when it alters the price it pays for wheat, the price received by all western wheat farmers changes. The CWB insists that it gets farmers premium prices, but individual farmers disputed this claim.

## Next Step: Bilateral Monopoly

A bilateral monopoly is defined as a market structure in which a single buyer faces a single seller. Should farmers form a union and, in effect, become a single seller? About 75 percent of Canadian grain is produced by a quarter of the growers. These are large growers who tend to be younger, better educated, and more competent managers. What would happen if those farmers banded together? Each individual farmer has little power in bargaining for a higher grain price, so the CWB can practise monopsonistic exploitation; farmers are paid less for their wheat than their contribution to the CWB's revenues. Farmers getting together would give them some bargaining power. In effect, the farmers could withhold their grain from the CWB to force better prices. The problem that farmers face is that they would all have to stop shipping to the CWB, and grain is a perishable commodity. In theory, the CWB is the farmers' union; in actuality, it is a government-controlled board that does not allow western farmers the same choice as eastern farmers, who can sell to any buyer they want.

## Taxpayers' Dollars, Too

Most taxpayers know little about the CWB, or that only western farmers are bound by the CWB. Some western farmers have even been thrown in jail for selling their wheat across the border. The CWB is fighting hard against dual desk marketing, stating that it is not a government agency. The federal government owns its assets and is responsible for its liabilities. In the past, the federal government has covered $1.5 billion in shortfalls arising from miscalculation and mismanagement of the CWB.

## The Demise of the CWB

In August 2012, the conservative Federal government abolished the single desk buyer/seller feature of the CWB, meaning that farmers would decide individually whether to sell their grain to CWB or, alternatively, sell directly to private grain buyers. This is called a dual marketing system.

On April 15, 2015, a majority stake in the CWB was purchased by a private consortium of large foreign companies and the CWB was renamed G3 Canada Limited. In effect the CWB was privatized.

On February 10, 2016 a group of Manitoba and Saskatchewan farmers unanimously passed a resolution calling for the return of an organization similar to the Canadian Wheat Board with a single desk monopoly marketing system. The resolution states that the demise of the Canadian Wheat Board in 2012 has resulted in an increasingly ineffective rail grain handling system, lower prices to Canadian grain farmers, reduced grain quality guarantees to customers, and an overall loss of $6.5 billion to farmers' income over two years.

**For critical analysis:**

1. Distinguish between a monopoly, a monopsony, and a bilateral monopoly.
2. What arguments can the CWB make to maintain their monopsony status?

Source: "Swan River meeting calls for return of CWB." Crops. Local News. February 22, 2016. Manitoba Co-operator. http://www.manitobacooperator.ca/crops/swan-river-meeting-calls-for-return-of-cwb/#_ga=1.148834039.1366153800.1486133036 (accessed February 3, 2017); "Canadian Wheat Board." The Great Depression. http://www.canadahistoryproject.ca/1930s/1930s-13-cwb.html (Accessed February 5, 2017).

# SUMMARY

Here is what you should know after reading this chapter. MyEconLab will help you identify what you know, and where to go when you need to practise. We suggest that as soon as you review one of the Learning Objective sections below, you then proceed to go through the related section in MyEconLab.

| LEARNING OBJECTIVES | KEY TERMS | MYECONLAB PRACTICE |
|---|---|---|
| **13.1 Demand for Labour.** In a competitive situation in which the firm is a very small part of the entire product and labour market, the firm will want to hire workers up to the point at which the marginal revenue product just equals the going wage rate. The marginal revenue product curve for the individual competitive firm is the input demand curve. The competitive firm hires up to the point at which the wage rate equals the MRP.<br>The summation of all the MRP curves does not equal the market demand curve for labour. The market demand curve for labour is less elastic than the sum of the MRP curves because as more workers are hired, output is increased and the price of the product must fall, lowering the MRP.<br>The demand for labour is derived from the demand for the product produced.<br>The elasticity of demand for an input is a function of several determinants, including the elasticity of demand for the final product. Moreover, the price elasticity of demand for a variable input will usually be larger in the long run than it is in the short run because there is time for adjustment. | marginal physical product (MPP) of labour, 337<br>marginal revenue product (MRP), 338<br>marginal factor cost (MFC), 338<br>derived demand, 340<br>labour market signalling, 342 | • **MyEconLab** Study Plan 13.1 |
| **13.2 Supply of Labour and Equilibrium.** The firm buying labour in a perfectly competitive labour market faces a perfectly elastic supply curve at the going wage rate because the firm can hire all it wants at that wage rate. The industry supply curve of labour slopes upward.<br>The demand curve for labour will shift if (a) the demand for final product shifts, (b) labour productivity changes, or (c) the price of a substitute or a complementary factor of production changes. | | • **MyEconLab** Study Plan 13.2 |

myeconlab

| LEARNING OBJECTIVES | KEY TERMS | MYECONLAB PRACTICE |
|---|---|---|
| **13.3 Union Goals and Labour Unions.** Unions raise union wage rates relative to nonunion wages. The union wage differential increases during recessions because of the longer-term nature of union collective bargaining contracts.<br>Because unions act as a collective voice for individual employees, they may increase productivity by reducing the time that employees spend trying to alter unproductive working arrangements. Unions may also increase productivity by reducing turnover. | strikebreakers, 348<br>featherbedding, 351 | • **MyEconLab** Study Plan 13.3 |
| **13.4 Pricing and Employment in Various Market Conditions.** Monopsony is a situation in which there is only one buyer of a particular input. The single buyer faces an upward-sloping supply curve and must therefore pay higher wage rates to attract additional workers. The single buyer faces a marginal factor cost curve that is upward-sloping and above the supply curve. The buyer hires workers up to the point at which the marginal revenue product equals the marginal factor cost. Then the labour buyer will find out how low a wage rate can be paid to get that many workers.<br>When a single buyer faces a single seller, a situation of bilateral monopsony exists. | monopsonist, 352<br>monopsonistic exploitation, 354<br>bilateral monopoly, 354 | • **MyEconLab** Study Plan 13.4 |

# PROBLEMS

(Answers to the odd-numbered problems appear at the back of the book.)

**LO 13.1 Explain the demand for labour using the marginal physical product, marginal revenue product, and price elasticity of demand concepts.**

1. Assume that the product in the table is sold by a perfectly competitive firm for $2 per unit.
   a. Use the information in the table to derive a demand schedule for labour.
   b. What is the most that this firm would be willing to pay each worker if five workers were hired?
   c. If the going salary for this quality of labour is $200 per week, how many workers will be hired?

| Quantity of Labour | Total Physical Product per Week | Marginal Physical Product (MPP) | Marginal Revenu Product (MRP) |
|---|---|---|---|
| 1 | 250 | ______ | ______ |
| 2 | 450 | ______ | ______ |
| 3 | 600 | ______ | ______ |
| 4 | 700 | ______ | ______ |
| 5 | 750 | ______ | ______ |
| 6 | 750 | ______ | ______ |

2. The table below presents some production function data for a firm in which the only variable input is capital; the labour input is fixed. First fill in the other columns. What quantity of capital will the firm use if the price of capital is $90 per machine-week? If the price of capital is $300 per machine-week, what quantity of capital will the firm use? Explain.

| Quantity of Capital (machine-weeks) | Total Physical Product (TPP) per Week | Marginal Physical Product (MPP) of Capital per Week | Marginal Revenue (product price) per Unit | Marginal Revenue Product (MRP) per Week |
|---|---|---|---|---|
| 0 | 0 | | $10 | |
| 1 | 25 | ______ | 10 | $______ |
| 2 | 45 | ______ | 10 | ______ |
| 3 | 60 | ______ | 10 | ______ |
| 4 | 70 | ______ | 10 | ______ |
| 5 | 75 | ______ | 10 | ______ |

**LO 13.2 Analyze the supply of labour and shifts in labour demand and supply.**

3. The accompanying graph indicates labour supply and demand in the construction industry.

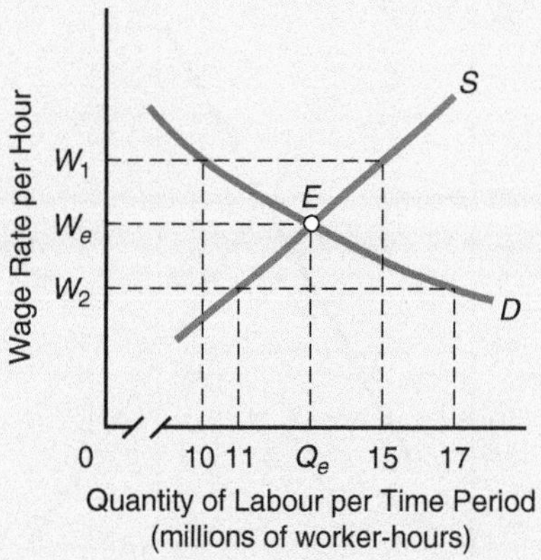


   a. When wage rates are $W_1$ per hour, how many worker-hours do workers intend to offer per unit?
   b. How much do businesses intend to buy at this wage rate?
   c. Which group can realize its intentions, and which cannot?
   d. What forces will be set in motion at wage rate $W_1$, given a free market for labour?

4. Using the graph in Problem 3, answer the following questions:
   a. At wage rate $W_2$, how many worker-hours do workers intend to offer?
   b. At $W_2$, how many worker-hours do businesses intend to purchase?
   c. Which group can realize its intentions, and which cannot?
   d. What forces will be set in motion at $W_2$ if a free market for labour exists in this industry?
   e. What will the equilibrium wage rate be?

5. The price elasticity of demand for the final output product directly affects the elasticity of demand for the input factor. Why?

6. Suppose that you are seeking to maximize output for a given outlay. If the marginal physical product of input $x$ is 10 and that of input $y$ is 20, and the prices of the two inputs are $3 and $7, respectively, how should you alter your input mix in order to increase output and profit?

**LO 13.3 Discuss the three main union goals and the five benefits of labour unions.**

7. What are the three union goals?
8. What are the five benefits of labour unions?
9. Example 13–2, "Strike Activity in Canada," shows that the number of strikes has been decreasing in Canada. Explain why this might be happening.

**LO 13.4 Determine the impact on pricing and employment under various market conditions.**

10. The accompanying graph indicates a monopsonistic firm that is also a perfect competitor in the product market.

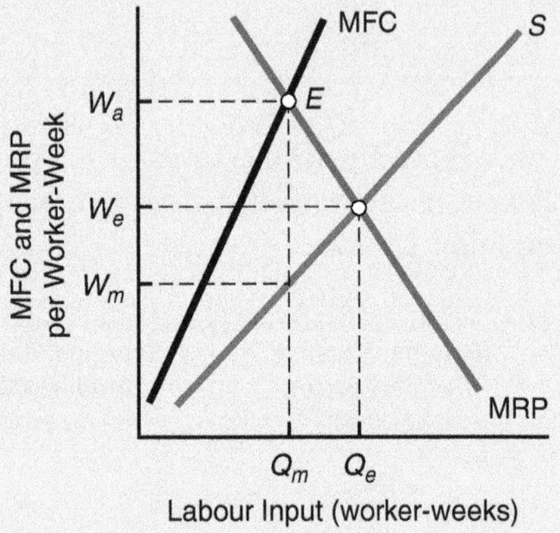


a. What does MRP stand for?
b. Which is the supply of labour curve?
c. How many labourers will this firm voluntarily hire?
d. Given the profit-maximizing employment rate, what is the lowest wage rate that this firm can offer to get this quantity of labour?

11. Imagine yourself managing a plant that is a monopsony buyer of its sole input and is also the monopoly seller of its output. You are currently employing 30 people, producing 20 units of output per day, and selling them for \$100 apiece. Your current wage rate is \$60 per day. You estimate that you would have to raise your wage scale for all workers to \$61 per day in order to attract one more person to your firm. The 31 employees would be able to produce 21 units of output per day, which you would be able to sell at \$99.50 apiece. Should you hire the thirty-first employee?
12. A firm finds that the price of its product changes with the rate of output. In addition, the wage it pays its workers varies with the amount of labour it employs. The price and wage structure that the firm faces is depicted in the following table:

| Labour Supplied | Total Physical Product | Required Hourly Wage Rate | Product Price |
|---|---|---|---|
| 10 | 100 | \$5 | \$3.11 |
| 11 | 109 | 6 | 3.00 |
| 12 | 116 | 7 | 2.95 |
| 13 | 121 | 8 | 2.92 |
| 14 | 124 | 9 | 2.90 |
| 15 | 125 | 10 | 2.89 |

This firm maximizes profits. How many units of labour will it hire? What wage will it pay?

13. In the short run, a tool manufacturer has a fixed amount of capital. Labour is a variable input. The cost and output structure that the firm faces is depicted in the following table:

| Labour Supplied | Total Physical Product | Hourly Wage Rate |
|---|---|---|
| 10 | 100 | \$ 5 |
| 11 | 109 | 6 |
| 12 | 116 | 7 |
| 13 | 121 | 8 |
| 14 | 124 | 9 |
| 15 | 125 | 10 |

Derive, at each level of labour supplied, the firm's total wage costs and marginal factor cost.

14. A single firm is the only employer in a labour market. The marginal revenue product, labour supply, and marginal factor cost curves that it faces are displayed in the diagram below. Use this information to answer the following questions.
    a. How many units of labour will this firm employ in order to maximize its economic profits?
    b. What hourly wage rate will this firm pay its workers?
    c. What is the total amount of wage payments that this firm will make to its workers each hour?

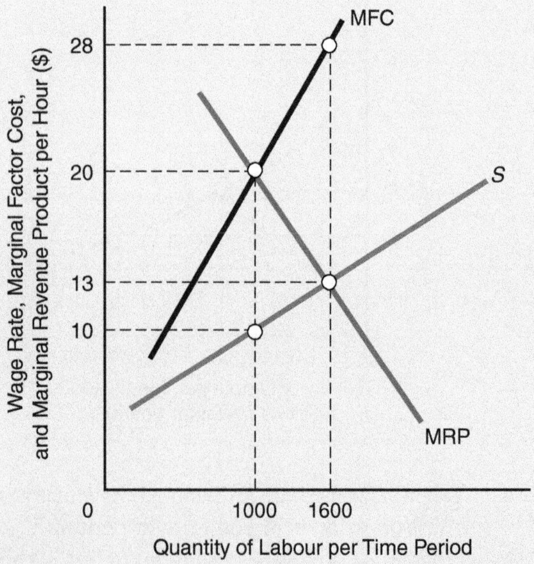

# BUSINESS APPLICATION

**LO 13.1 and 13.4 Explain the demand for labour using the marginal physical product, marginal revenue product, and price elasticity of demand concepts; determine the impact on pricing and employment under various market conditions.**

## Human Resources Management: Supply and Demand Factors and Negotiated Settlements

The typical textbook in economics tends to focus on the importance of market factors in the determination of hourly wage rates in the private sector. The following problem illustrates how supply and demand factors can affect the outcome of public sector negotiations between a professional association and the government.

## Business Application Problem

A provincial medical association representing Canadian doctors is in the process of negotiating the physicians' fee structure with the provincial government. In order to apply the theory in this chapter, consider the government as the employer and the doctors as labour. Predict whether each of the following events will tend to increase or decrease the demand or supply of labour (Canadian doctors). Also predict how each event will affect the overall level of medical fees that will be negotiated.

a. The population is aging.
b. The provincial government makes it easier for more immigrant doctors to practice in the province.
c. Private health maintenance organizations in the U.S. launch a campaign to aggressively hire Canadian doctors by offering higher salaries in the U.S.
d. Each doctor in the province agrees not to fill prescriptions over the phone with the patient's pharmacist. Instead, each patient wanting a new prescription must schedule an appointment with the doctor.
e. Due to extremely heavy workloads, a significant number of doctors opt for early retirement.
f. The government passes legislation that allows para-professionals (midwives, naturalists, psychologists) to perform services traditionally done exclusively by doctors, at lower cost.

# 14

## LEARNING OBJECTIVES

After reading this chapter, you should be able to:

**14.1** Explain why the distribution of wealth is different from the distribution of income.

**14.2** Discuss the four main determinants of income differences and two ways that income should be distributed.

**14.3** Define poverty and the four major federal income support programs.

# Income and Poverty

By some measures, Canada is one of the richest nations in the world, not only in terms of total annual national income, but also in terms of average annual income per person. Despite such riches, almost 1.3 million Canadian children under the age of 18 live in poverty. Over 40 percent of people who use food banks are children. In fact, Canada ranks second among the industrialized countries, behind only the United States, for the highest rate of child poverty. Can something be done to eradicate child poverty? To answer this question, you need to know more about the distribution of income and the facts about poverty in this country.

myeconlab

MyEconLab helps you master each objective and study more efficiently. See end of chapter for details

# DID YOU KNOW THAT...?

Over 300 000 Canadians earn more than $200 000 per year. That constitutes 1 percent of the Canadian population. When you go farther up the income ladder, there are only about 3,600 who earn more than $1 million per year. At the same time, over 5 million Canadians live in poverty. Why is the **distribution of income**, the way income is allocated among the population, the way it is? Economists have devised various theories to explain this distribution. We present some of these theories in this chapter. We also present some of the more obvious institutional reasons why income is not distributed equally in Canada.

## 14.1 The Distribution of Wealth and Income

**Distribution of income** The way income is allocated among the population.

### Income

Income provides each of us with the means of consuming and saving. Income can be derived from a payment for labour services or a payment for ownership of one of the other factors of production besides labour—land, physical capital, human capital, and entrepreneurship. In addition, individuals obtain spendable income from gifts and government transfers. (Some individuals also obtain income by stealing, but we will not discuss that here.) Right now, let us examine how money income is distributed across classes of income earners within Canada.

Should wealthy families pay more tax?

### Measuring Income Distribution: The Lorenz Curve

The **Lorenz curve**, named after American-born statistician Max Otto Lorenz who proposed it in 1905, is a geometric representation of the distribution of income. The Lorenz curve shows what portion of total money income is accounted for by different proportions of the country's households. Look at Figure 14–1. On the horizontal axis, we measure the *cumulative* percentage of households, lowest-income households first. Starting at the left corner, there are zero households; at the right corner, we have 100 percent of households; and in the middle, we have 50 percent of households. The vertical axis represents the cumulative percentage of money income. The 45-degree line represents complete equality: 50 percent of the households obtain 50 percent of total income, 60 percent of the households obtain 60 percent of total income, and so on. Of course, in no real-world situation is there such complete equality of income; no actual Lorenz curve would be a straight line. Rather, it would be some curved line, like the one labelled "Actual money income distribution" in Figure 14–1. For example, the bottom 50 percent of households in Canada

**Lorenz curve** A geometric representation of the distribution of income.

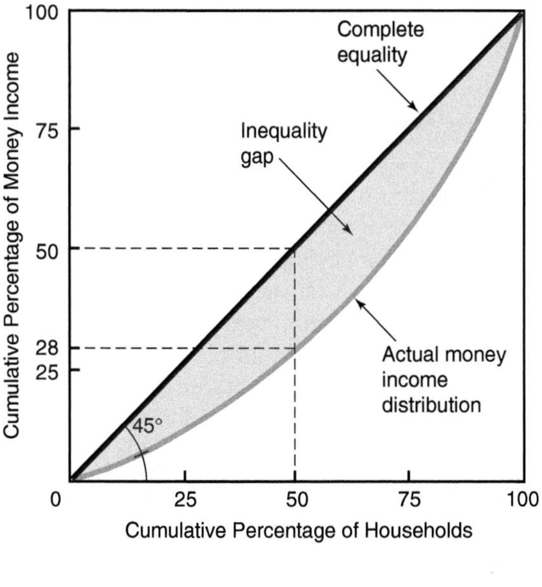


**FIGURE 14–1**
**The Lorenz Curve**

The horizontal axis measures the cumulative percentage of households from 0 to 100 percent. The vertical axis measures the cumulative percentage of money income from 0 to 100 percent. A straight line at a 45-degree angle cuts the box in half and represents a line of complete income equality, along which 25 percent of the families get 25 percent of the money income, 50 percent get 50 percent, and so on. The Lorenz curve, showing actual money income distribution, is not a straight line but rather a curved line as shown. The difference between complete money income equality and the Lorenz curve is the inequality gap.

**FIGURE 14–2**

**Family After-Tax Income Distribution, by Cumulative Income Shares, 1989 and 2004**

Sources: Statistics Canada, *Survey of Consumer Finances and Survey of Labour and Income Dynamics*; Andrew Heisz. "Income inequality and redistribution in Canada: 1976 to 2004." p. 37. Statistics Canada, Analytical Studies Branch Research Paper Series, No. 298. May 11, 2007. Catalogue no. 11F0019MIE2007298. http://www.statcan.ca/english/research/11F0019M1E/11F0019M1E2007298.pdf.

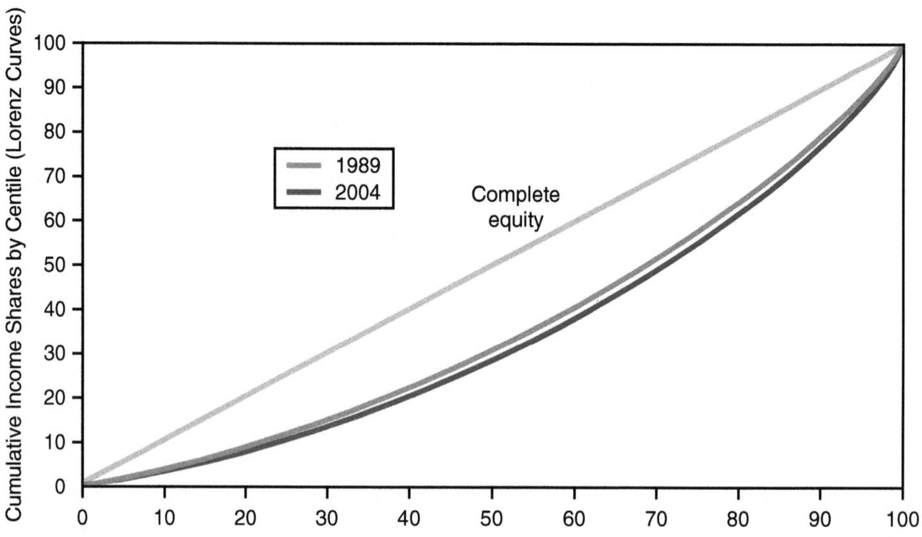


receive about 28 percent of total money income. In Figure 14–2, we show the actual money income distribution Lorenz curve for 1989 and 2004.

**CRITICISMS OF THE LORENZ CURVE.** In recent years, economists have placed less and less emphasis on the shape of the Lorenz curve as an indication of the degree of income inequality in a country. There are five basic reasons the Lorenz curve has been criticized:

**Income in kind** Income received in the form of goods and services.

1. The Lorenz curve is typically presented in terms of the distribution of *money* income only. It does not include **income in kind**, income received in the form of goods and services, such as health care, public school education, and goods or services produced and consumed in the home or on the farm.
2. The Lorenz curve does not account for differences in the size of households or the number of wage earners they contain.
3. It does not account for age differences. Even if all families in Canada had exactly the same *lifetime* incomes, chances are that young families would have lower incomes, middle-aged families would have relatively high incomes, and retired families would have low incomes. Because the Lorenz curve is drawn at a moment in time, it could never tell us anything about the inequality of *lifetime* income.
4. The Lorenz curve ordinarily reflects money income *before* taxes.
5. It does not measure unreported income from the underground economy, a substantial source of income for some individuals.

## Income Distribution in Canada

We could talk about the percentage of income earners within specific income classes—those earning between \$20 001 and \$30 000 per year, those earning between \$30 001 and \$40 000 per year, and so on. The problem with this type of analysis is that we live in a growing economy. Income, with some exceptions, is going up all the time. If we wish to make comparisons of the relative share of total income going to different income classes, we cannot look at specific amounts of money income. Instead, we talk about a distribution of income over five groups. Then, we can talk about how much the bottom fifth (or quintile) makes compared with the top fifth, and so on. In Figure 14–3, we see the median wealth of families. The figure ranks family units into five groups, from the lowest net worth to the highest. Each group represents 20 percent, or one-fifth, of all families. From 1999 and 2012, the lowest quintile shows that adjusted after-tax income stayed virtually unchanged, while the net worth of the highest quintile increased from around \$60 000 to \$80 000. One of the main reasons why the gap widened in the top quintile is

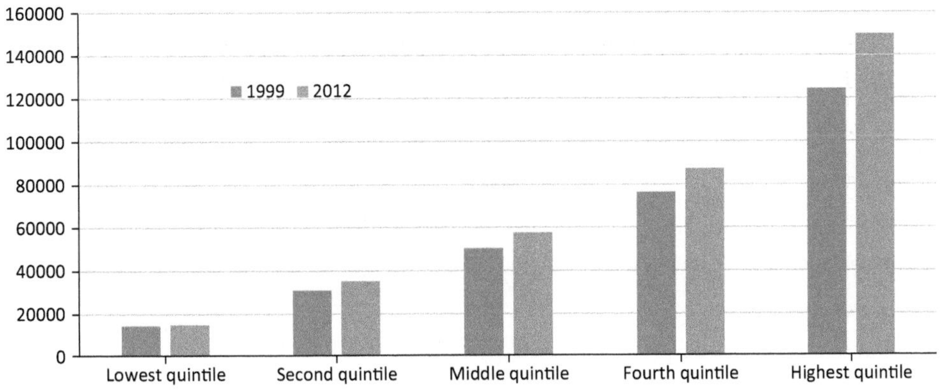


**FIGURE 14–3**

Source: Statistics Canada. Income in Canada: Analysis. http://www.statcan.gc.ca/pub/75-202-x/2007000/ct051-eng.htm Statistics Canada. Changes in wealth across the income distribution 1999 to 2012. http://www.statcan.gc.ca/pub/75-202-x/2010000/analysis-analyses-eng.htm

that more people in that quintile owned homes. Other factors impact income inequality as well. Look at Example 14–1 to see how having two spouses working can change income inequality.

### EXAMPLE 14–1 Increasing Income Inequality and Working Spouses

Income inequality is measured with respect to households. No distinction is made between one- and two-earner households. If two $80 000-a-year lawyers form a household, their household income is now $160 000, and they have moved into a higher income group. Not surprisingly, most single tax returns show smaller earnings than joint returns. In 1972, some 22 percent of working-age married couples had two earners; today, that figure is around 60 percent. Consequently, part of the reported increase in income inequality in Canada is simply due to an increase in the number of working spouses.

**For critical analysis:** Are households with two working spouses necessarily better off?

# The Distribution of Wealth

We have been referring to the distribution of income in Canada. We must realize that income (a flow) can be viewed as a return on wealth (both human and nonhuman), or as a capital stock. A discussion of the distribution of income in Canada is not the same thing as a discussion of the distribution of wealth. A complete concept of wealth would include tangible objects, such as buildings, machinery, land, cars, and houses—nonhuman wealth—as well as people who have skills, knowledge, initiative, talents, and so on—human wealth. The total of human and nonhuman wealth in Canada makes up our country's capital stock. (Note that the terms *wealth* and *capital* are often used only with reference to nonhuman wealth.) The capital stock consists of anything that can generate utility to individuals in the future. A fresh, ripe tomato is not part of our capital stock. It has to be eaten before it turns rotten, and once it has been eaten, it can no longer generate satisfaction.

Figure 14–4 shows the breakdown of people in the low-income group for 2010, 2012 and 2014. At 44.9 percent, female lone-parent families under 18 years are the biggest group, with persons 18 to 64 years old at 12.6 percent. These statistics are probably not news to any of us. What is clear is that the percent of people at the low income level has remained relatively

**FIGURE 14–4**
**Comparison of People in Low Income Bracket, 2010, 2012, 2014**

Source: From Statistics Canada. Low income statistics by age sex and economic family type. http://www5.statcan.gc.ca/cansim/a26?lang=eng&id=2060041 (Accessed February 22, 2017).

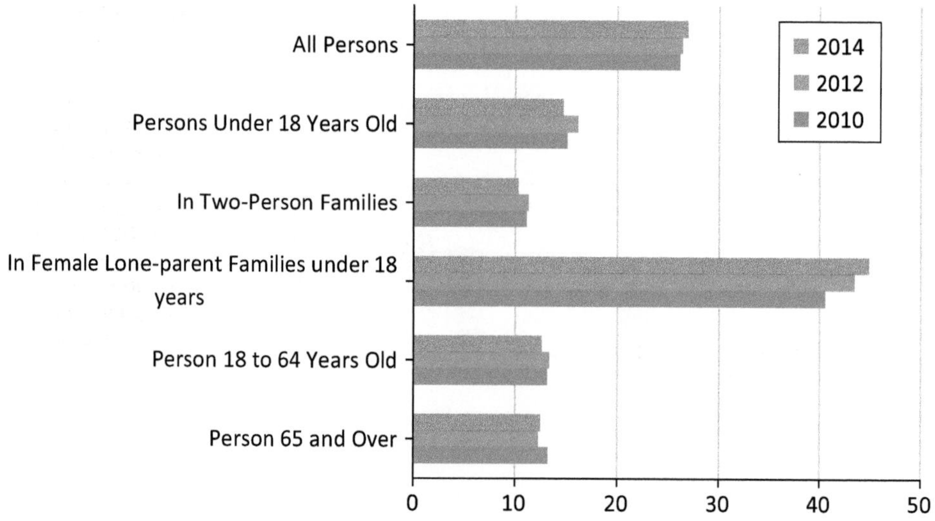


the same. In 2014, only 10.3 percent of two-parent families were in the low-income group, so why do many Canadians not feel like they are getting ahead? Example 14–2 might explain part of the reason.

**EXAMPLE 14–2 Are We Running to Stay in Place?**

There are a lot of statistics to show that the typical working person in Canada has not experienced an increase in standard of living for the last 20 years. If we correct take-home wages for inflation, that is an accurate statement. Indeed, Statistics Canada has frequently shown that real wages have actually fallen since 1980. There are at least two problems with such statements, though. The first concerns total compensation. Compensation of workers does not consist solely of wages. Whereas in 1971, nonsalary benefits (Workers' Compensation, Employment Insurance, pension payments, and so on) amounted to 8.5 percent of wages, they now come to around 30 percent. Second, even if after-tax real wages have not increased, the typical Canadian household is at least 20 percent better off than in 1971. Why? Because more households have a second breadwinner. Furthermore, fewer babies are being born, and so expenses per household are lower.

One other piece of data is telling: virtually every measure of consumption per capita is growing, year in and year out. Consequently, the majority of Canadians continue to experience increases in their standard of living as measured by their actual purchases of goods and services.

**For critical analysis:** Why might an individual be most concerned about total compensation?

# 14.2 Determinants of Income Differences

We know that there are income differences—that is not in dispute. An important question is why these differences in income occur, for if we know why they do, perhaps we can change public policy, particularly with respect to helping people in the lowest income classes climb the income ladder. What is more, if we know the reasons for income differences, we can ascertain whether any of these determinants have changed over time. We will look at four income difference determinants: age, marginal productivity, inheritance, and discrimination.

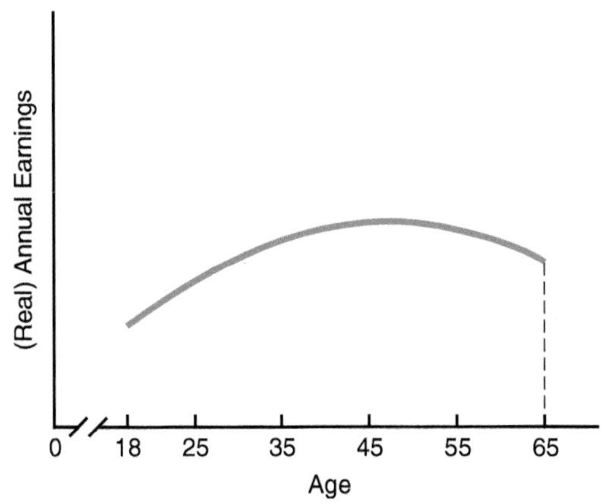


**FIGURE 14–5**

**Typical Age–Earnings Profile**

Within every class of income earners there is usually a typical age–earnings profile. Earnings are lowest when starting work at around age 18, reach their peak at around age 50, and then taper off until retirement at around age 65, when they become zero for most people. The rise in earnings up to age 50 is usually due to increased experience, longer working hours, and better training and schooling. (We abstract from economywide productivity changes that would shift the entire curve upward.)

## Age

Age turns out to be a determinant of income because with age comes, usually, more education, more training, and more experience. It is not surprising that within every class of income earners, there seem to be regular cycles of earning behaviour. Most individuals earn more when they are middle-aged than when they are younger or older. We call this the **age–earnings cycle**, the regular earnings profile of an individual throughout that person's lifetime.

**Age–earnings cycle** The regular earnings profile of an individual throughout that person's lifetime.

**THE AGE–EARNINGS CYCLE.** Every occupation has its own age–earnings cycle, and every individual will probably experience some variation from the average. Nonetheless, we can characterize the typical age–earnings cycle graphically, as shown in Figure 14–5. Here, we see that at age 18, income is relatively low. Income gradually rises until it peaks at about age 50. Then it falls until retirement, when it becomes zero (that is, currently earned income becomes zero, although retirement payments may then commence). The reason for such a regular cycle in earnings is fairly straightforward. When individuals start working at a young age, they typically have no work-related experience. Their ability to produce is less than that of more seasoned workers—that is, their productivity is lower. As they become older, they obtain more training and accumulate more experience. Their productivity rises, and they are therefore paid more. They also generally start to work longer hours. As the age of 50 approaches, the productivity of individual workers usually peaks. So, too, do the number of hours per week that are worked. After this peak in the age–earnings cycle, the detrimental effects of aging—decreases in stamina, strength, reaction time, and the like—usually outweigh any increases in training or experience. Also, hours worked usually start to fall for older people. Finally, as a person reaches retirement, both productivity and hours worked diminish rather drastically.

Do earnings increase with age?

Note that general increases in overall productivity for the entire workforce will result in an upward shift in the typical age–earnings profile given in Figure 14–5. Thus, even at the end of the age–earnings cycle, when just about to retire, the worker would not receive a really low wage compared with the starting wage 45 years earlier. The wage would be higher due to factors that contribute to rising real wages for everyone, regardless of the stage in the age–earnings cycle.

Now we have some idea why specific individuals earn different incomes at different times in their lives, but we have yet to explain why different people are paid different amounts of money for their labour. One way to explain this is to recall the marginal productivity theory.

## Marginal Productivity

When trying to determine how many workers a firm would hire, we had to construct a marginal revenue product curve. We found that as more workers were hired, the marginal revenue product fell due to diminishing marginal returns. If the forces of demand and supply established a certain wage rate, workers would be hired until their marginal physical product times marginal revenue was equal to the going wage rate. Then the hiring would stop. This analysis suggests what workers can expect to be paid in the labour market: they can each expect to be paid their marginal revenue product (assuming that there are low-cost information flows and that the labour and product markets are competitive).

In a competitive situation, with mobility of labour resources (at least on the margin), workers who are being paid less than their marginal revenue product will be bid away to better employment opportunities. Either they will seek better employment themselves, or other employers will offer them a slightly higher wage rate. This process will continue until each worker is being paid that individual's marginal revenue product.

You may balk at the suggestion that people are paid their marginal revenue product because you may personally know individuals whose MRP is more or less than what they are being paid. Such a situation may, in fact, exist because we do not live in a world of perfect information or in a world with perfectly competitive input and output markets. Employers cannot always seek out the most productive employees available. It takes resources to research the past records of potential employees, their training, their education, and their abilities. Nonetheless, competition creates a tendency toward equality of wages and MRP.

**DETERMINANTS OF MARGINAL PRODUCTIVITY.** If we accept marginal revenue product theory, we have a way of finding out how people can earn higher incomes. If they can increase the value of their marginal physical product, they can expect to be paid more. Some of the determinants of marginal physical product are talent, education, experience, and training. Most of these are means by which marginal physical product can be increased. Let us examine them in greater detail.

**TALENT.** This factor is the easiest to explain but difficult to acquire if you do not have it. Innate abilities and attributes can be very strong, if not overwhelming, determinants of a person's potential productivity. Strength, coordination, and mental alertness are facets of nonacquired human capital and thus have some bearing on the ability to earn income. Someone who is extremely tall has a better chance of being a basketball player than someone who is short. A person born with a superior talent for abstract thinking has a better chance of making a relatively higher income as a mathematician or a physicist than someone who is not born with that talent.

**EXPERIENCE.** Additional experience at particular tasks is another way of increasing productivity. Experience can be linked to the well-known *learning curve* that applies when the same task is done over and over. The worker repeating a task becomes more efficient: The worker can do the same task in less time or in the same amount of time but better. Take an example of a person going to work on an automobile assembly line. At first, the individual is able to fasten only three bolts every two minutes. Then, the worker becomes more adept and can fasten four bolts in the same time plus insert a rubber guard on the bumper. After a few more weeks, another task can be added. Experience allows this individual to improve productivity. The more effectively people learn to do something, the more quickly they can do it and the more efficient they are. Hence, we would expect experience to lead to higher productivity. And we would expect people with more experience to be paid more than those with less experience. More experience, however, does not guarantee a higher wage rate. The *demand* for a person's services must also exist. Spending a long time to become a first-rate archer in modern society would probably add very little to a person's income. Experience has value only if the output is demanded by society. Look at Example 14–3 to see the impact of age on productivity.

### EXAMPLE 14–3 Economics, Aging, and Productivity

Do the actions of professional economists fit the model that predicts a decrease in productivity after some workers peak at around age 50? Yes, according to economist Daniel Hamermesh. One measure of productivity of economics professors is the number of articles they publish in professional journals. The over-50 economists constitute 30 percent of the profession, but they contribute a mere 6 percent of the articles published in leading economics journals. Of economists between ages 36 and 50, 56 percent submit articles on a regular basis, while only 14 percent of economists over 50 do so.

**For critical analysis:** Why should we predict that an economist closer to retirement will submit fewer professional journal articles than a younger economist? (*Hint*: Normally, professors who have tenure cannot be fired.)

**TRAINING.** Training is similar to experience but is more formal. Much of a person's increased productivity is due to on-the-job training. Many companies have training programs for new workers. On-the-job training is perhaps responsible for as much of an increase in productivity as is formal education beyond high school.

**INVESTMENT IN HUMAN CAPITAL.** Investment in human capital is just like investment in any other thing. If you invest in yourself by going to college or university, rather than going to work after high school and earning more current income, you will presumably be rewarded in the future with a higher income or a more interesting job (or both). This is exactly the motivation that underlies the decision of many students to obtain a formal higher education. Undoubtedly, there would be students going to school even if the rate of return on formal education were zero or negative. But we do expect that the higher the rate of return on investing in ourselves, the more such investment there will be. Statistics Canada data demonstrate conclusively that on average, high school graduates make more than elementary-school graduates and that university graduates make more than high-school graduates. The estimated annual income of a full-time worker with four years of university in the mid-1990s was about $50 000. That person's high school counterpart was estimated to earn only $30 000, which gives a "university premium" of about 67 percent. Generally, the rate of return on investment in human capital is on a par with the rate of return on investment in other areas.

To figure out the rate of return on an investment in a university education, we first have to figure out the marginal costs of going to school. The main cost is not what you have to pay for books, fees, and tuition, but rather the income you forgo. *The main cost of education is the income forgone—the opportunity cost of not working.* In addition, the direct expenses of going to university must be paid. Not all students forgo all income during their university years. Many work part-time. Taking account of those who work part-time and those who are supported by grants and other scholarships, the average rate of return on going to university is somewhere between 8 and 12 percent. This is not a bad rate. Of course, this type of computation does leave out all the consumption benefits you get from going to university. Also omitted from the calculations is the change in personality after going to university. You undoubtedly come out a different person. Most people who go through university feel that they have improved themselves both culturally and intellectually in addition to having increased their potential marginal revenue product so that they can make more income. How do we measure the benefit from expanding our horizons and our desire to experience different things in life? This is not easy to measure, and such nonmoney benefits from investing in human capital are not included in normal calculations.

## Inheritance

It is not unusual to inherit cash, jewellery, shares, bonds, and homes or other real estate. Yet, only about 8 percent of income inequality in Canada can be traced to differences in wealth that was inherited. If, for some reason, government confiscated all property that had been inherited, there would be very little measured change in the distribution of income in Canada.

## Discrimination

Economic discrimination occurs whenever workers with the same marginal revenue product receive unequal pay due to some noneconomic factor, such as their race, gender, or age. Alternatively, it occurs when there is unequal access to labour markets. It is possible—and, indeed, quite obvious—that discrimination affects the distribution of income. Certain groups in our society are not paid wages at rates comparable with those received by other groups, even when we correct for productivity and education. Differences in income remain between people of different ethnicities and between men and women. For example, the median wage for Aboriginal men is about 80 percent that of white men. The median wage rate of women is about 73 percent that of men. What we need to do is discover why differences in income between groups exist and then determine if factors other than discrimination in the labour market can explain them. Then the unexplained part of income differences can rightfully be considered the result of discrimination.

**THE DOCTRINE OF COMPARABLE WORTH.** Discrimination can occur because of barriers to entry in higher-paying occupations and because of discrimination in the acquisition of human capital. Consider the distribution of highest-paying and lowest-paying occupations. The lowest-paying jobs are dominated by females of all ethnicities. For example, the proportion of women in secretarial, clerical, janitorial, and food service jobs ranges from 60 percent (food and beverage service) to 80 percent (clerical). Proponents of the **comparable-worth doctrine**—the belief that women should receive the same wages as men if the levels of skill and responsibility in their jobs are equivalent—feel that female secretaries, janitors, and food service workers should be making salaries comparable to those of male truck drivers or construction workers, assuming that the levels of skill and responsibility in these jobs are comparable. These advocates also believe that a comparable-worth policy would benefit the economy overall. They contend that adjusting the wages of workers in female-dominated jobs upward would create a move toward more efficient and less discriminatory labour markets.

**Comparable-worth doctrine**
The belief that women should receive the same wages as men if the levels of skill and responsibility in their jobs are equivalent.

## Theories of Desired Income Distribution

We have talked about the factors affecting the distribution of income, but we have not yet mentioned the normative issue of how income *ought* to be distributed. This, of course, requires a value judgment. We are talking about the problem of economic justice. We can never completely resolve this problem because there are always going to be conflicting values. It is impossible to give every individual what he or she thinks is just. Nonetheless, two particular normative standards for the distribution of income have been popular with economists. These are income distribution based on productivity and income distribution based on equality.

## Productivity

The *productivity standard* for the distribution of income can be stated simply as "To each according to what he or she produces." This is also called the *contributive standard* because it is based on the principle of rewarding according to the contribution to society's total output. It is also sometimes referred to as the *merit standard* and is one of the oldest concepts of justice. People are rewarded according to merit, and merit is judged by one's ability to produce what is considered useful by society.

However, just as any standard is a value judgment, so is the productivity standard. It is rooted in the capitalist ethic and has been attacked vigorously by some economists and philosophers, including Karl Marx, who felt that people should be rewarded according to need and not according to productivity.

We measure a person's productive contribution in a capitalist system by the market value of that person's output. We have already referred to this as the marginal revenue product theory of wage determination.

Do not immediately jump to the conclusion that in a world of income distribution determined by productivity, society will necessarily allow the aged, the infirm, and the physically or mentally challenged to die of starvation because they are unproductive. In Canada today, the productivity standard is mixed with a standard based on people's "needs" so that the aged, the physically and mentally challenged, the involuntarily unemployed, the very young, and other unproductive (in the market sense of the word) members of the economy are provided for through private and public transfers.

## Equality

The *egalitarian principle* of income distribution is simply "To each exactly the same." Everyone would have exactly the same amount of income. This criterion of income distribution has been debated as far back as biblical times. This system of income distribution has been considered equitable, meaning that presumably everybody is dealt with fairly and equally. There are problems, however, with an income distribution that is completely equal.

Some jobs are more unpleasant or more dangerous than others. Should the people undertaking these jobs be paid exactly the same as everyone else? Indeed, under an equal distribution of income, what incentive would there be for individuals to take risky, hazardous, or unpleasant jobs at all? What about overtime? Who would be willing to work overtime without additional pay? There is another problem: If everyone earned the same income, what incentive would there be for individuals to invest in their own human capital—a costly and time-consuming process?

Just consider the incentive structure within a corporation. Much of the pay differential between, say, the CEO and all of the vice-presidents is meant to create competition among the vice-presidents for the CEO's job. The result is higher productivity. If all incomes were the same, much of this competition would disappear, and productivity would fall.

There is some evidence that differences in income lead to higher rates of economic growth. Future generations are therefore made better off. Elimination of income differences may reduce the rate of economic growth and cause future generations to be poorer than they otherwise might have been.

# 14.3 Poverty and Federal Income Support Programs

Throughout the history of the world, mass poverty has been accepted as inevitable. However, this country and others, particularly in the Western world, have sustained enough economic growth in the past several hundred years so that *mass* poverty can no longer be said to be a problem for these fortunate countries. As a matter of fact, the residual poverty in Canada strikes us as bizarre, an anomaly. How can there still be so much poverty in a country of such abundance? Having talked about the determinants of the distribution of income, we now have at least some ideas of why some people are destined to remain low-income earners throughout their lives.

There are methods of transferring income from the relatively well-to-do to the relatively poor, and as a country, we Canadians have been using them for a long time. Today, we have a vast array of income support programs set up for the purpose of redistributing income. However, we know that these programs have not been entirely successful. Are there alternatives to our current income support system? Is there a better method of helping the poor? Before we answer these questions, let us look at the concept of poverty in more detail and at the characteristics of the poor. See Example 14–4 to see if other countries are more successful.

### EXAMPLE 14–4 Poverty Rates in the European Union

For years, politicians throughout much of the European Union have proclaimed their unwillingness to adopt the more laissez-faire, "let the chips fall where they may," economic model that prevails in the United States. They are convinced that the result is too much poverty. But they were shocked to discover in an article published in the newspaper *Le Monde* in 1997 that the poverty rate for the European Union was more than 17 percent—fully 57 million people out of a population of 330 million. Whereas the poverty rate in the United States has hovered between 13 and 15 percent of the population since the 1970s, the rate in Europe has increased over the same period from 10 percent to 17 percent. One-third of the officially poor in the European Union work, one-third are retired, and one-third are unemployed.

**For critical analysis:** What problems might there be in comparing poverty rates across nations?

## Defining Poverty

There is no official poverty line announced each year in Canada. However, Statistics Canada releases income thresholds, which it calls low-income cut-offs (LICOs), below which families and individuals are said to be living in "straitened circumstances." The LICO is widely used by both government and nongovernment agencies as a poverty line.

Statistics Canada first defined the LICO in 1959 as 70 percent of the average family income. It reasoned that the average family required one-half of its income to pay for necessities—food, shelter, and clothing. Thus, any family that needed 20 percent more than the average for necessities would have insufficient income left for transportation, health care, recreation, and so on. (The choice of 20 percent was arbitrary.) Over time, the LICO has changed as incomes have grown, from 70 percent of average family income in 1959 to 62 percent in 1962, 58.5 percent in 1980, and 56.2 percent in 1986; and in 2006 it was set at 50 percent of the average family income.

The LICO has also been expanded to apply to both families and single persons living in urban and rural areas. In 2014, the after-tax LICO for an individual living in a large city was $20160, and for an urban family of seven it was $52869. For rural areas, the LICO for a single person was $13188 and $34585 for a large family.

## Transfer Payments as Income

**Transfer payments.** Payments made to individuals for which no services or goods are concurrently rendered in return.

The LICO is based on pretax income, including wages, net income from self-employment, government **transfer payments**—such as Employment Insurance and Canada Pension Plan benefits—scholarships, and alimony payments. Excluded from the income calculation are winnings from gambling, inheritances, and income in kind, such as food produced on the farm for domestic use. If we correct the LICO for government transfers, the percentage of the population that is below the poverty line drops dramatically. Some of the people living below the poverty line partake in the informal, or underground, sectors of the economy without reporting their income from these sources. And some of the poor obtain benefits from owning their own homes.

## Attacks on Poverty: Major Federal Income

There are a variety of federal income support programs designed to help the poor. We examine a few of them here.

**OLD AGE SECURITY.** The current Old Age Security Plan came into force in 1952. It provides for income supplements for seniors aged 65 and over, and has three components: old age security (OAS), guaranteed income supplement (GIS) and spouse's allowance (SPA).

The amount of the OAS component payment is dependent on the recipient's length of residence in Canada, with longer residence earning a higher payment. This payment comes out of the federal government's general revenue; it is indexed to the Consumer Price Index (CPI) and is raised four times each year.

The GIS is paid to OAS recipients who have little or no additional income. This supplement is not taxable and its size is dependent on the marital status of the recipient. While the single rate exceeds the married rate, the combined married rate (i.e., a married couple in which both parties receive GIS) exceeds the single rate. The SPA is paid to the spouse of an OAS and GIS recipient when those pension payments constitute the only income for the family. This benefit is dependent on the spouse passing an income test.

**CANADA PENSION PLAN.** The Canada Pension Plan (CPP) and its counterpart Quebec Pension Plan (QPP) enroll virtually all employed and self-employed workers between the ages of 18 and 70 years. Both employees and employers must contribute a percentage of the employee's earnings to the plan, which provides insurance against retirement, disability, and death. (A self-employed person must contribute both shares.) No part of the pension payments comes from general government revenues; the CPP is a "pay-as-you-go" plan funded entirely by premiums and investment earnings.

The CPP came into force in 1966; it is fully indexed to the CPI and is adjusted each January. With the increase in the Canadian population, the contribution rates have risen; in 1986, employees and employers paid a combined 3.6 percent of eligible earnings into the plan; by 1997, they paid 5.85 percent. Beginning in 1998, in anticipation of the retirement of our "baby boomers" and the estimated 75 percent increase in the over-65 population, the premium rates were increased significantly to the year 2003, when they were capped at 9.9 percent. It is estimated that the CPP fund will grow to over $100 billion, sufficient to pay out the necessary pensions.

Benefit payments from the CPP redistribute income to some degree. However, benefit payments are not based on recipient need. Participants' contributions give them the right to benefits even if they would be financially secure without them. Thus, the CPP is not an insurance program because people are not guaranteed that the benefits they receive will be in line with the contributions they have made. It is not a personal savings account either. The benefits are legislated by government. In the future, government may not be as sympathetic toward older people as it is today. It could (and probably will have to) legislate for lower real levels of benefits instead of higher ones.

**EMPLOYMENT INSURANCE.** Employment Insurance (EI) is designed to provide income for the unemployed while they are looking for work. Like the CPP, it is funded by compulsory employee and employer contributions. Unlike the CPP, however, the premiums and benefit payments are part of the federal government's general revenues and expenditures. In 1997, there was a substantial surplus in the EI account, which helped government achieve the budget surplus that year.

The EI program replaced the Unemployment Insurance (UI) plan in 1996. While UI was designed to provide income support to contributors who became unemployed, EI is designed to help the unemployed find work as well. Re-employment benefits, such as retraining funds, act as incentives for the unemployed to find jobs in other fields. Automated job market information and federally funded job search services assist recipients in their quest for work.

**CANADA CHILD BENEFIT.** The federal government's primary program for helping families with children is the Canada Child Benefit (CCB). The CCB replaced the Canada child tax benefit (CCTB) and the universal child care benefit (UCCB) as of July 2016. Based on the 2015 tax year, the basic Canada child benefit for children under 6 amounted to $6400 per year and for children aged 6 to 17 $5400 for families with an annual net income below

With all our wealth, why is there still child poverty in Canada?

$30 000. The benefit is reduced if you family income is more then $30 000. Benefit payments are calculated every year based on your income tax return from the previous year.

## Reduction in Poverty Rates

The poverty rate in Canada has been declining but can the same be said for the child poverty rate? We attempt to shed some light on this question in the Issues and Applications section on child poverty, below.

ISSUES AND APPLICATIONS

# Eradicating Child Poverty

**Concepts Applied: Incentives, Marginal Tax Rate**

Food banks provide essential nourishment for millions of children who live in poverty. In spite of a federal government resolution to eradicate child poverty by the year 2000, rates are still on the rise.

In 1989, the House of Commons passed a resolution to "seek to achieve the goal of eliminating poverty among Canadian children by the year 2000." However, child poverty rates had climbed until 1995, as Figure 14–7 shows. One of the reasons for continuing child poverty is that many of the programs designed to help low-income families apply only to families on welfare. The working poor—those with low-paying jobs—do not qualify and so remain below the poverty line.

## Work versus Welfare

In most provinces, families receiving social assistance also receive other benefits for their children. These include free health and dental care and optometric services. Thus, finding employment brings with it a penalty: not only does the family lose its welfare payments, but it also loses the subsidized services. The working income tax benefit (WITB) was created to address this problem. The WITB is calculated based on numerous information such as: martial status, province, income etc. Nevertheless, the working poor still lag behind families on social assistance in combined federal and provincial child benefits.

## An Integrated Plan

The federal and provincial governments have been working on an integrated child benefit plan to assist all poor families, whether working or receiving social assistance. For its part, the federal government will provide a child tax credit, thereby raising a family's after-tax income. To create an incentive for families on welfare to find employment, the provinces will cut welfare payments by a part of the additional disposable income. The working poor, however, will be able to keep all of

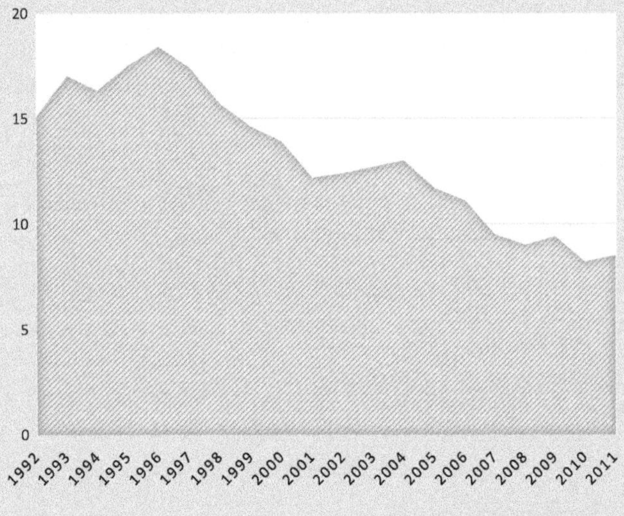


**FIGURE 14–7**

**Child Poverty Rate**

Since 1992, the child poverty rate in Canada has increased from 15.1 percent to 18.4 percent in 1996 and dropped to 8.5 in 2011.

Source: Statistics Canada. Persons in low income after tax (under 18 years of age). http://www.statcan.gc.ca/tables-tableaux/sum-som/l01/cst01/famil19a-eng.htm (Accessed February 24, 2017).

the increase. A further condition of this proposal is that the provincial governments redirect the savings on welfare payments to other programs to aid poor children: school lunch programs and health and dental services, for example.

Several of the provinces have already reformed their welfare systems to dovetail with the proposed federal plan, and to create incentives for families on social assistance to find employment. In British Columbia, for example, the B.C. Family Bonus program provides benefits to both working and nonworking families. A maximum bonus of $111 per month per child is paid to families with annual incomes of $18 000 or less. The bonus decreases as family income rises, finally disappearing at an annual income of $42 000 for a family with three children. Thus, the bonus acts to soften the effect of increasing marginal tax rates as the family works toward self-sufficiency. A recent study found that in B.C. the poverty gap for the working poor in general had been reduced by 19 percent and by 26 percent for single parents. (The poverty gap is that amount of income required to lift families below the poverty line out of poverty.)

## Support Payments or Job Creation?

Critics of improved social assistance plans argue that the money put into supporting the poor would be better spent improving economic conditions, which would, in turn, lead to more jobs for the unemployed. They also suggest that falling welfare cheques act as a better incentive than child tax benefits to induce welfare families to look for work. And once the families are working, child poverty would be reduced.

**For critical analysis:**

1. Do you think that the new integrated child benefit plan will end child poverty in Canada? Why or why not?
2. If the critics of improved social assistance plans succeeded in having money put into supporting the poor allocated instead to improving economic conditions, would this end child poverty?

# SUMMARY

Here is what you should know after reading this chapter. MyEconLab will help you identify what you know, and where to go when you need to practise. We suggest that as soon as you review one of the Learning Objective sections below, you then proceed to go through the related section in MyEconLab.

myeconlab

| LEARNING OBJECTIVES | KEY TERMS | MYECONLAB PRACTICE |
|---|---|---|
| **14.1 The Distribution of Wealth and Income.** We can represent the distribution of income graphically with a Lorenz curve. The extent to which the line is bowed from a straight line shows how unequal the distribution of income is. | distribution of income, 361<br>Lorenz curve, 361<br>income in kind, 362 | • **MyEconLab** Study Plan 14.1 |

| LEARNING OBJECTIVES | KEY TERMS | MYECONLAB PRACTICE |
|---|---|---|
| The distribution of pretax money income in Canada has remained fairly steady for the last 25 years. The lowest fifth of income earners still receive only about 5 percent of total pretax money income, while the top fifth of income earners receive over 40 percent.<br>The distribution of wealth is not the same as the distribution of income. Wealth includes such assets as houses, shares, and bonds. Though the apparent distribution of wealth seems to be more concentrated at the top, the data used are not very accurate, nor do most summary statistics take account of workers' claims on private and public pensions. | | |
| **14.2 Determinants of Income Differences.** Most individuals face a particular age–earnings cycle. Earnings are lowest when starting out to work at age 18 to 24. They gradually rise and peak at about age 50, then fall until retirement age. They go up usually because of increased experience, increased training, and longer working hours.<br>The marginal productivity theory of the distribution of income indicates that workers can expect to be paid their marginal revenue product. The marginal physical product is determined largely by talent, education, experience, and training.<br>Discrimination is usually defined as a situation in which a certain group is paid a lower wage than other groups for the same work.<br>One way to invest in your own human capital is to go to university or college. The investment usually pays off; the rate of return is somewhere between 8 and 12 percent. | age–earnings cycle, 367<br>comparable-worth doctrine, 370 | • **MyEconLab** Study Plan 14.2 |
| **14.3 Poverty and Federal Income Support Programs.** A definition of poverty made in relative terms means that there will always be poor in ur society because the distribution of income will never be exactly equal. The major federal income support programs are Old Age Security (OAS), Canada Pension Plan (CPP), and Employment Insurance (EI). | transfer payments, 372 | • **MyEconLab** Study Plan 14.3 |

# PROBLEMS

(Answers to the odd-numbered problems appear at the back of the book.)

**LO 14.1 Explain why the distribution of wealth is different from the distribution of income.**

1. It is often observed that women, on average, earn less than men in Canada. What are some possible reasons for these differences?
2. The accompanying graph shows Lorenz curves for two countries.

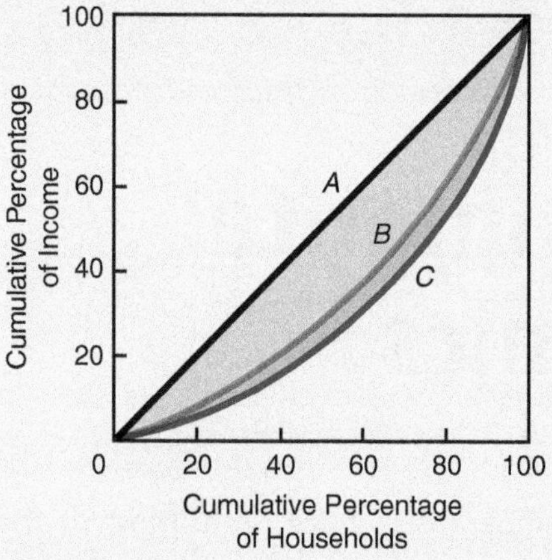


   a. Which line indicates complete equality of income?
   b. Which line indicates the most income inequality?
   c. One country's "income inequality" is described by line *B*. Suppose that this country's income is to be adjusted for age and other variables such that income on the *y*-axis reflects lifetime income instead of income in a given year. Would the new, adjusted Lorenz curve move inward toward *A* or outward toward *C*?
3. Example 14–1, "Increasing Income Inequality and Working Spouses," shows that income measures have flaws. What are some of the issues in the measurement of incomes?
4. Figure 14–4 shows 9.5 percent of people under 18 years old as low income (in 2007). What are some reasons for this?

**LO 14.2 Discuss the four main determinants of income differences and two ways that income should be distributed.**

5. What are the four main determinants of income differences?
6. What are two ways that income ought to be distributed?

**LO 14.3 Define poverty and the four major federal income support programs.**

7. What are the four major income support programs?
8. There is no real standard measurement for poverty. Should Canada update its low-income cut-offs (LICOs)?
9. This chapter's Issues and Applications feature talks about poverty in Canada. What are some of the programs that will help the working poor?

# BUSINESS APPLICATION

**LOs 14.1, 14.2, and 14.3 Explain why the distribution of wealth is different from the distribution of income; discuss the four main determinants of income differences and two ways that income should be distributed; define poverty and the four major federal income support programs.**

## Poverty and Wealth

If Canada has no real defined "poverty line," how can we distinguish who is poor and who is wealthy? Does the poverty line increase in Canada as wages increase?

Make a budget for yourself. List all the items that you spend money on every month. As a student, you might be considered to be living below the "poverty line." But what is poverty? Do you have enough food? As a student, is poverty not being able to afford to go out on Friday night? Is that true poverty?

Look at your budget. Is there anything you can cut from the budget to give you more spending money? Can you take public transit instead of driving your car? Do you really need to buy a coffee first thing in the morning?

Poverty is very hard to define. How about wealth? How much do you want to make to feel wealthy? Is wealth as hard to define as poverty? Developing countries have many people living in poverty, and relatively few who are very wealthy, often through unsavoury means. Can we, through legislation, distribute wealth equally?

15

# Environmental Economics

## LEARNING OBJECTIVES

After reading this chapter, you should be able to:

**15.1** Explain the difference between private and social costs and how externalities can occur.

**15.2** Discuss the marginal benefits and costs of pollution.

**15.3** Describe how common property impacts the environment.

**15.4** Explain how recycling is changing the way we look at our environment.

Since 1880, global temperatures have risen. Most of the warming occurred in the past 35 years, with 15 of the 16 warmest years on record occurring since 2001. The year 2015 was the first time the global average temperatures were 1 degree Celsius or more above the 1880-1899 average. Global sea level rose about 17 centimeters in the last century. The rate in the last decade, however, is nearly double that of the last century. Both the extent and thickness of Arctic sea ice has declined rapidly over the last several decades. The amount of spring snow cover in the Northern Hemisphere has decreased over the past five decades with the snow melting earlier. Nations across the globe are experiencing more frequent and more extreme weather events in the form of droughts, intense flooding, hurricanes, and tornadoes. Scientists, worldwide, attribute all of these ominous environmental trends to the phenomena called "global warming."

In this chapter we examine the various roles that economics can play in understanding some of the causes of environmental problems, as well as in devising possible solutions.

Source: "Climate change: How do we know?" Intergovernmental Panel on Climate Change.Evidence. Nasa Gobal Climate Change. http://climate.nasa.gov/evidence/.

myeconlab

EconLab helps you master each objective and study more efficiently. See end of chapter for details

## DID YOU KNOW THAT...?

The biggest oil spill disaster in history occurred in 2010 in the Gulf of Mexico. British Petroleum (BP), the owner of the oil rig that exploded and spilled oil into the gulf, is responsible for the cleanup, which could take decades. The costs associated with this disaster are not just monetary. Much of the wildlife and plants in the area will be affected. The shellfish and tourist industries will also suffer, leading to unemployment among people working in those industries.

The value of BP shares has decreased since the spill, and money that would have been dividends for investors will now most likely go toward the cost of the cleanup. That means that investors worldwide will lose money. Many retirees rely on those dividend cheques as part of their income, so their standard of living will decrease. The more the shares drop, the less the dividend cheques will be. In 2016 the movie "Deep Water Horizon" was released, which honours the men and women whose heroism would save many on board the oil rig, and change everyone's lives forever.

The oil spill is an environmental disaster, and its impact will be felt worldwide. Other oil companies are distancing themselves from BP in the hope that their own safety records will convince lawmakers not to punish them by stopping off-shore oil drilling. When a disaster like this happens, we look at the cleanup costs associated with the disaster. Society has to weigh those costs against the benefits derived from the use of oil, such as heat for our homes, cars for transportation, and other benefits that improve our standard of living.

# 15.1 Private versus Social Costs

Human actions often give rise to unwanted side effects—the destruction of our environment is one. Human actions generate pollutants that go into the air and the water. The question that is often asked is, "Why can individuals and businesses continue to create pollution without necessarily paying directly for the negative consequences?"

Will the oil spill in the Gulf of Mexico affect the cost of gas?

Until now, we have been dealing with situations in which the costs of an individual's actions are borne directly by the individual. When a business has to pay wages to workers, it knows exactly what its labour costs are. When it has to buy materials or build a plant, it knows quite well what these will cost. An individual who has to pay for car repairs or a theatre ticket knows exactly what the cost will be. These costs are what we term *private costs.* **Private costs** are borne solely by the individuals who incur them. They are *internal* in the sense that the firm or household must explicitly take account of them.

What about a situation in which a business dumps the waste products from its production process into a nearby river or one in which an individual litters a public park or beach? Obviously, a cost is involved in these actions. When the firm pollutes the water, people downstream suffer the consequences. They may not want to swim in or drink the polluted water. They may also be unable to catch as many fish as before because of the pollution. In the case of littering, the people who come along after our litterer has cluttered the park or the beach are the ones who bear the costs. The cost of these actions is borne by people other than those who commit the actions. The creator of the cost is not the sole bearer. The costs are not internalized by the individual or firm; they are external. When we add *external* costs to *internal,* or private, costs, we get **social costs**, the full costs borne by society whenever a resource use occurs. Pollution problems—indeed, all problems pertaining to the environment—may be viewed as situations in which social costs exceed private costs. Because some economic participants do not pay the full social costs of their actions but, rather, only the smaller private costs, their actions are socially unacceptable. In such situations, in which there is a divergence between social and private costs, we therefore see "too much" steel production, automobile driving, and beach littering, to pick only a few of the many possible examples.

**Private costs** Costs borne solely by the individuals who incur them; also called *internal costs.*

**Social costs** The full costs borne by society whenever a resource use occurs.

## The Costs of Polluted Air

Why is the air in cities so polluted from automobile exhaust fumes? When automobile drivers step into their cars, they bear only the private costs of driving. That is, they must pay for the gas, maintenance, depreciation, and insurance on their automobiles. However, they cause an additional cost, that of air pollution, which they are not forced to take account of when they make the decision to drive. Air pollution is a cost because it causes harm to individuals—burning eyes, respiratory ailments, and dirtier clothes, cars, and buildings. The air pollution created by automobile exhaust is a cost that individual operators of automobiles do not bear directly. The social cost of driving includes all the private costs plus at least the cost of air pollution, which society bears. Decisions made only on the basis of private costs lead to too much automobile driving or to too little money spent on the reduction of automobile pollution for a given amount of driving. Clean air is a scarce resource used by automobile drivers free of charge. They will use more of it than they would if they had to pay the full social costs.

## Externalities

**Externality** A situation in which a private cost diverges from a social cost; a situation in which the costs of an action are not fully borne by the two parties engaged in exchange.

When a private cost differs from a social cost, we say that there is an *externality* because individual decision makers are not paying (internalizing) all the costs. **Externality** is a situation in which a private cost diverges from a social cost and the costs of an action are not fully borne by the two parties engaged in exchange. Some of these costs remain external to the decision-making process. Remember that the full cost of using a scarce resource is borne one way or another by all who live in the society. That is, society must pay the full opportunity cost of any activity that uses scarce resources. The individual decision maker is the firm or the customer, and external costs and benefits will not enter into that individual's or firm's decision-making processes.

We might want to view the problem as it is presented in Figure 15–1. Here, we have the market demand curve, $D$, for the product X and the supply curve, $S_1$, for product X. The supply curve, $S_1$, includes only internal, or private, costs. The intersection of the demand and supply curves as drawn will be at price $P_1$ and quantity $Q_1$ (at $E_1$). However, we will assume that the production of good X involves externalities that the private firms did not take into account. Those externalities could be air pollution, water pollution, scenery destruction, or anything of that nature.

We know that the social costs of producing product X exceed the private costs. We show this by drawing curve $S_2$. It is above the original supply curve $S_1$ because it includes the full social costs of producing the product. If firms could be made to bear these costs, the price would be $P_2$ and the quantity $Q_2$ (at $E_2$). The inclusion of external costs in the decision-making process leads to a higher-priced product and a decline in quantity produced. Thus, we see that when social costs are not being fully borne by the creators of those costs, the quantity produced is "excessive," because the price is too low.

## Correcting for Externalities

We can see here an easy method for reducing pollution and environmental degradation. Somehow the signals in the economy must be changed so that decision makers will take

**FIGURE 15–1**

**Reckoning with Full Social Costs**

The supply curve, $S_1$, is equal to the horizontal summation of the individual marginal cost curves above the respective minimum average variable costs of all the firms producing good X. These individual marginal cost curves include only internal, or private, costs. If the external costs were included and added to the private costs, we would have social costs. The supply curve would shift upward to $S_2$. In the uncorrected situation, the equilibrium price would be $P_1$, and the equilibrium quantity would be $Q_1$. In the corrected situation, the equilibrium price would rise to $P_2$, and the equilibrium quantity would fall to $Q_2$.

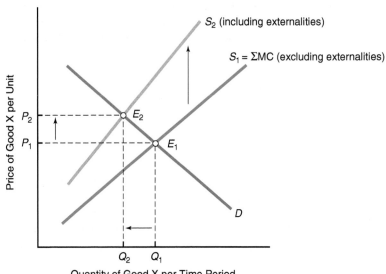

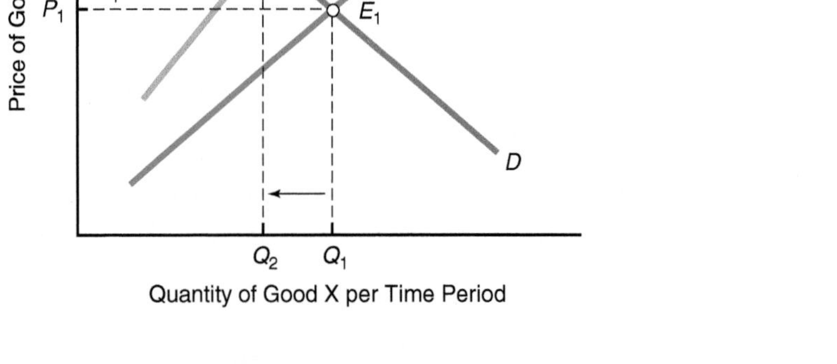

into account *all* the costs of their actions. In the case of automobile pollution, we might want to devise some method by which motorists are taxed according to the amount of pollution they cause.

We have all heard that it should be the polluter who pays. We immediately think of the firm that is spewing toxins into the air, or coal and mining operations, but the environment is something that concerns all people, globally. Often we expect governments to deal with negative externalities by using market-based incentives or disincentives. Some of the most common are taxes, tax credits, emissions fees, or carbon offsets.

## The 4 Rs—Reduce, Reuse, Recycle, and Recover

The social costs of pollution need to be addressed by all people, but it does not mean that your standard of living has to change; your response can be as simple as picking up that candy wrapper off the grass, or putting in a new energy-efficient furnace in your home. *Reduce* by buying products with no or minimal packaging, *reuse* shopping bags and jars, *recycle* using the guidelines of your municipality, try composting, and *recover* rain water and reuse it. Do you want to fly to Europe but not leave a carbon footprint? Buy carbon credits or offsets.

## Market Incentives

Market incentives are usually government-sponsored programs aimed at assisting industry to reduce the pollution created by producing goods. Governments can use a variety of incentives, such as emissions caps, to limit the total amount of pollution that can be emitted. Allowances are a permit to emit a fixed amount of a pollutant. To be compliant, the industry should own as many allowances as the amount of pollutants it emits for the compliance period. Firms have found that a "cap and trade" system allows them to purchase allowances to make up for any shortfall they might be encountering.

One of the best known "cap and trade" policies is the European Union Emissions Trading System (EU ETS) which is also referred to as a carbon trading system. Started in 2005, in response to the Kyoto Accord, the first phase of the EU ETS imposed national government caps on annual allowable CO2 emissions emitted by power generators and energy intensive industries. At the start of each year each company receives or purchases its annual allowable emission in the form of "allowances" (often called "carbon offsets"). At the end of each year each company must surrender enough allowances to cover all of its annual emissions. If a company was able to emit less than its annual allotment, it could keep its "spare allowance" to cover its emissions in future periods or the company could sell its "spare allowance" to other companies that were not able to meet its annual allowable emissions.

In subsequent years, the plan is for the governments to steadily reduce the annual allowable emission levels (and the allowances that relate to these declining levels). An attractive feature of the "cap and trade" system is that it helps to ensure that the reductions in emissions is undertaken by the companies who can do this in the most efficient manner, therefore economizing on limited resources. Example 15-1 highlights some of the problems that were encountered in the early stages of the EU ETS.

Source: "The EU Emissions Trading System." Climate Action. European Commission. https://ec.europa.eu/clima/policies/ets_en (Accessed on February 15, 2017).

### EXAMPLE 15-1 Carbon Offset Projects: Real or Just Hot Air?

The global carbon trading market tripled in one year, but the World Bank warned that unregulated carbon offset projects could reduce the effectiveness of the carbon market in combating climate change. The EU's emission trading scheme came under fire when carbon credit prices fell because the allowances in the initial stage were too generous. Allocations for the 2008 to 2012 phase have been tightened, but some investors are paying for emissions reductions that do not take place.

A *Financial Times* investigation "found widespread instances of people and organizations buying worthless credits that did not yield any reductions in carbon emissions," and "brokers providing services of questionable or no value." It pointed out that "Some companies are benefiting by asking 'green' consumers to pay them for cleaning up their own [company's] pollution."

In the period 2013 to 2020, a new phase of the EU ETS has been approved, which consists of the following changes. A single, EU-wide cap on emissions applies in place of the previous system of national caps. Auctioning is the default method for allocating allowances (instead of free allocation), and harmonized allocation rules apply to the allowances still given away for free.

More sectors and gases are included in the system.

**For critical analysis:** Is the carbon trading market viable, or are unregulated carbon offset programs harming the carbon market? Is the carbon trading market reducing actual pollution. or is it just an investment scheme to transfer money?

Source: "Global carbon trading market triples to 15Bn." The Guardian. May 3, 2007. http://www.guardian.co.uk/environment/2007/may/03/business.climatechange; "Industry caught in carbon 'smokescreen'." Financial Times. April 25, 2007. http://search.ft.com/ftArticle?queryText=industry+caughtin+carbon+%27smokescreen%27&y=8&aje=true&x=13&id=070425011309. "The EU Emissions Trading System." Climate Action. European Commission. https://ec.europa.eu/clima/policies/ets_en (Accessed on February 15, 2017).

Governments can also use regulatory requirements that create incentives for firms to find cheaper and better control techniques. An example of a regulatory requirement would be emissions standards for automobiles, or a requirement for 5 percent ethanol in motor vehicle fuel. These regulatory requirements can force firms to improve the products they offer to consumers.

Incentives can force firms to be more innovative and do more research and development to keep up with their competitors. Firms are becoming more environmentally aware because capital investors are requiring more information on a firm's environmental intentions.

Governments can also correct for positive externalities, such as the existence of vaccines against dangerous diseases, by financing the production of the needed drugs. Subsidies can be used by governments; for example, a student attending a university or college can be subsidized by as much as 80 percent of the total cost. Regulations such as the mandatory vaccination of all school children can also be used by governments.

Governments can also impose taxes such as a carbon tax. If government were to impose a pollution tax or effluent fee on the firm according to the amount of pollution it creates, the firm might be induced to install pollution abatement equipment or otherwise change production techniques so as to reduce the amount of pollution. This can be very costly for the firm, and even extra taxes or fines might not be enough to induce the firm to change its ways.

## Is a Uniform Tax Appropriate?

It may not be appropriate to levy a *uniform* tax according to physical quantities of pollution. After all, we are talking about social costs. Such costs are not necessarily the same everywhere in Canada for the same action.

Essentially, we must establish the amount of the *economic damages,* rather than the amount of the physical pollution. A polluting electrical plant in Toronto will cause much more damage than the same plant in Carstairs, Alberta. There are already innumerable demands on the air in Toronto, and so the pollution from smokestacks will not be cleansed naturally. Millions of people will breathe the polluted air and thereby incur such costs as sore throats, sickness, emphysema, and even early death. Buildings will become dirtier faster because of the pollution, as will cars and clothes. A given quantity of pollution will cause more harm in concentrated urban environments than it will in less dense rural environments. If we were to establish some form of taxation to align private costs with social costs and to force people to internalize externalities, we would somehow have to come up with a measure of *economic* costs instead of *physical* quantities. But the tax, in any event, would fall on the private sector and modify private-sector economic agents' behaviour. Therefore, because the economic cost for the same physical quantity of pollution would be different in different locations according to population density, the natural formation of mountains and rivers, and so forth, these optimal taxes on pollution would vary from location to location. (Nonetheless, a uniform tax might make sense when administrative costs, particularly the cost of ascertaining the actual economic costs, are relatively high.)

# 15.2 Pollution

The term *pollution* is used quite loosely and can refer to a variety of by-products of any activity. Industrial pollution involves mainly air and water but can also include noise and such concepts as aesthetic pollution, as when a landscape is altered in a negative way. For the most part, we will be analyzing the most common forms, air and water pollution.

Is society willing to absorb the costs of cleaning up the pollution it creates?

When asked how much pollution there should be in the economy, many people will respond, "None." But, again, if we ask those same people how much starvation or deprivation of consumer products should exist in the economy, many will say, "None at all." Growing and distributing food or producing consumer products creates pollution, however. In effect, therefore, there is no correct answer to how much pollution should be allowed in an economy because when we ask how much pollution there *should* be, we are entering the realm of normative economics. We are asking people to express values. There is no way to disprove somebody's value system scientifically. One way we can approach a discussion of the "correct" amount of pollution would be to set up the same type of marginal analysis we used in our discussion of a firm's employment and output decisions. That is to say, we should pursue measures to reduce pollution only up to the point at which the marginal benefit from further reduction equals the marginal cost of further reduction.

Look at Figure 15–2. On the horizontal axis, we show the degree of cleanliness of the air. A vertical line is drawn at 100 percent cleanliness—the air cannot become any cleaner.

Consider the benefits of obtaining a greater degree of air cleanliness. These benefits are represented by the marginal benefit curve, which slopes downward because of the law of diminishing marginal utility. When the air is very dirty, the marginal benefit from air that is a little cleaner appears to be relatively high, as shown on the vertical axis. As the air becomes cleaner and cleaner, however, the marginal benefit of a little bit more air cleanliness falls.

Consider the marginal cost of pollution abatement—that is, the marginal cost of obtaining cleaner air. In the 1960s, automobiles had no pollution abatement devices. Eliminating only 20 percent of the pollutants emitted by internal-combustion engines entailed a relatively small cost per unit of pollution removed. The cost of eliminating the next 20 percent rose, though. Finally, as we now get to the upper limits of removal of pollutants from the emissions of internal-combustion engines, we find that the elimination of one more percentage point of the amount of pollutants becomes astronomically expensive. To go from 97 percent cleanliness to 98 percent cleanliness involves a marginal cost that is many times greater than going from 10 percent cleanliness to 11 percent cleanliness.

It is realistic, therefore, to draw the marginal cost of pollution abatement as an upward-sloping curve, as shown in Figure 15–2. (The marginal cost curve slopes up because of the law of diminishing returns.)

## The Optimal Quantity of Pollution

The **optimal quantity of pollution** is defined as the level of pollution at which the marginal benefit equals the marginal cost of obtaining clean air. This occurs at the intersection of the marginal benefit curve and the marginal cost curve in Figure 15–2, at point *E*, which is analytically exactly the same as for every other economic activity. If we increased pollution control by one more unit greater than $Q_0$, the marginal cost of that small increase in the degree of air cleanliness would be greater than the marginal benefit to society.

**Optimal quantity of pollution** The level of pollution at which the marginal benefit equals the marginal cost of obtaining clean air.

**FIGURE 15–2**

## The Optimal Quantity of Air Pollution

As we attempt to get a greater degree of air cleanliness, the marginal cost rises until even the slightest attempt at increasing air cleanliness leads to a very high marginal cost, as can be seen at the upper right of the graph. Conversely, the marginal benefit curve slopes downward: the more pure air we have, the less we value an additional unit of pure air. Marginal cost and marginal benefit intersect at point *E*. The optimal degree of air cleanliness is something less than 100 percent at $Q_0$. The price that we should pay for the last unit of air cleanup is no greater than $P_0$, for that is where marginal cost equals marginal benefit.

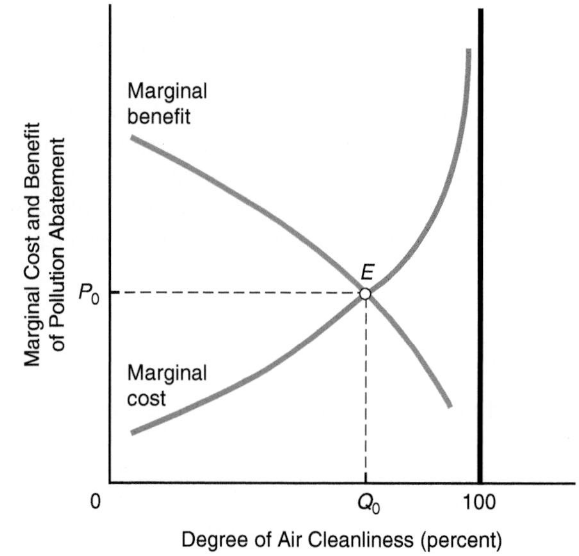


As is usually the case in economic analysis, the optimal quantity of just about anything occurs when marginal cost equals marginal benefit. That is, the optimal quantity of pollution occurs at the point at which the marginal cost of reducing (or abating) pollution is just equal to the marginal benefit of doing so. The marginal cost of pollution abatement rises as more and more abatement is achieved (as the environment becomes cleaner and cleaner, the *extra* cost of cleansing rises). The state of technology is such that early units of pollution abatement are easily achieved (at low cost), but attaining higher and higher levels of environmental quality becomes progressively more difficult (as the extra cost rises to prohibitive levels). At the same time, the marginal benefit of a cleaner and cleaner environment falls; the marginal benefit of pollution abatement declines as the concept of a cleaner and cleaner environment moves from human life-support requirements to recreation to beauty to a perfectly pure environment. The point at which the increasing marginal cost of pollution abatement equals the decreasing marginal benefit of pollution abatement defines the (theoretical) optimal quantity of pollution.

Recognizing that the optimal quantity of pollution is not zero becomes easier when we realize that it takes scarce resources to reduce pollution. It follows that a trade-off exists between producing a cleaner environment and producing other goods and services. In that sense, nature's ability to cleanse itself is a resource that can be analyzed like any other resource, and a cleaner environment must take its place with other societal wants.

Why is Canada facing a potentially very high marginal cost of trying to keep its anti-pollution promises? See Policy Example 15–1 and this chapter's Issues and Applications.

### POLICY EXAMPLE 15–1 Canada Confronts a High Marginal Cost of Pollution Abatement

Under the 1997 international pollution abatement treaty called the Kyoto Protocol, Canada promised that by 2012, it would reduce emissions of global-warming gases to a level 6 percent below its total 1990 emissions. Nevertheless, since 1997 Canada's emissions have actually *increased* by 1.5 percent per year. One activity that has helped fuel this growth in gas emissions has been Canadian oil production. As world oil prices increased during the 2000s, Canadian oil firms ramped up production from the nation's oil sands—vast deposits of sticky, black grit that constitute the largest single known source of oil outside Saudi Arabia. Extracting and transporting all this oil requires burning fossil fuels that create greenhouse gas emissions.

After failing to meet the Kyoto targets, Canada signed on to the Copenhagen Agreement in 2009. As a party to this agreement, the Conservative Canadian government committed to a 2020 target of reducing greenhouse gas (GHG) emissions to 17 percent below 2005 GHG levels. In subsequent years, the conservatives focused on reducing GHG emissions in two Canadian sectors. In 2010, Canada agreed to harmonized automobile emission standards with the U.S. As well, new regulations for reducing greenhouse gas (GHG) emissions from coal-fired electricity generation were formulated and implemented in 2015.

The Conservative government was heavily criticized for failing to impose GHG emission regulations on the oil and gas sectors in Canada. The critics were of the view that reducing carbon emissions resulting from oil and gas production is necessary to meet the GHG emission reductions promised as a party to the Copenhagen Agreement. By most estimates, though, keeping this promise would require the nation's oil industry to incur hundreds of millions of dollars in costs to reduce emissions. One predicted result would be a significant reduction in Canadian oil production, requiring Canada to forgo billions of dollars in export revenues. All told, the estimated explicit and opportunity costs to the entire Canadian economy of achieving any reductions would be at least $30 billion per year.

**For critical analysis:** If Canada's marginal benefit from reducing gas emissions was determined to be $25 billion, would the nation be better off if it engaged in more or less pollution abatement?

Sources: "Canada's auto emission goals integrated with the United States." April 5, 2010. The Council of Canadians Acting for Social Justice. http://canadians.org/node/5480. (Accessed February 19, 2017); "Harper Government Moves Forward on Tough Rules for Coal-Fired Electricity Sector." Sept. 5, 2012. News Releases. CNW a Cison Company. http://www.newswire.ca/news-releases/harper-government-moves-forward-on-tough-rules-for-coal-fired-electricity-sector-510687241.html. (Accessed February 19, 2017). "Canada falling far short on emission goals, Environment Canada reports." SHAWN MCCARTHY. October 24, 2013. Politics. News. The Globe and Mail. http://www.theglobeandmail.com/news/politics/canada-well-short-of-cutting-greenhouse-gas-emissions-by-2020-environment-canada-says/article15056716/ (Accessed February 19, 2017).

## 15.3 Common Property

In most cases, you do not have **private property rights**—exclusive rights of ownership—to the air surrounding you, nor does anyone else. Air is a **common property** resource—nonexclusive property that is owned by everyone and therefore by no one. Therein lies the crux of the problem. When no one owns a particular resource, no one has any incentive (conscience aside) to consider misuse of that resource. If one person decides not to pollute the air, there normally will be no significant effect on the total level of pollution. If one person decides not to pollute the ocean, there will still be approximately the same amount of ocean pollution—provided, of course, that the individual was previously responsible for only a small part of the total amount of ocean pollution. See Example 15–2.

**Private property rights** Exclusive rights of ownership.

**Common property** Nonexclusive property that is owned by everyone and therefore by no one.

### EXAMPLE 15–2 Wind as a Renewable Resource

Air is considered common property, owned by everyone. Some companies and governments are now starting to harness wind to create energy. Nova Scotia Power has a green power choice that allows individuals to purchase green power—power generated from wind—for their homes. Between 2011 and 2016, more wind energy has been built in Canada than any other form of electricity generation. Installed capacity is growing by an average of 18 per cent per year. As a result, in 2016 Canada ranks as the seventh largest market for new wind energy development in the world.

**For critical analysis:** Why would people be willing to pay more for green energy, when air, or wind, is owned by everyone?

source: "National." Wind Markets. Canadian Wind Energy Association. http://canwea.ca/wind-energy/national/ (Accessed February 20, 2017).

Basically, pollution occurs where we have poorly defined private property rights, as in the case of air and common bodies of water. We do not, for example, have a visual pollution problem when it comes to people's attics. That is their own property, which they choose to keep as clean as they want, given their preferences for cleanliness as weighed against the costs of keeping the attic neat and tidy.

Where private property rights exist, individuals have legal recourse to any damages sustained through the misuse of their property. When private property rights are well defined, the use of property—that is, the use of resources—will generally involve contracting between the owners of those resources. If you own land, you might contract with another person who wants to use your land for raising cows. The contract would most likely be written in the form of a lease agreement.

## Voluntary Agreements and Transactions Costs

Is it possible for externalities to be internalized via voluntary agreement? Take a simple example. You live in a house with a nice view of a lake. The family living below you plants a tree. The tree grows so tall that it eventually starts to cut off your view. In most cities, no one has property rights to views; therefore, you cannot normally go to court to obtain relief. You do have the option of contracting with your neighbour, however.

**VOLUNTARY AGREEMENTS: CONTRACTING.** You have the option of paying your neighbours (contracting) to trim the tree. You could start out with an offer of a small amount and keep going up until your neighbours agree or until you reach your limit. Your limit will equal the value you place on having an unobstructed view of the lake. Your neighbours will be willing if the payment is at least equal to the reduction in the intrinsic value of their property due to a stunted tree. Your offering the payment makes your neighbours aware of the social cost of their actions. The social cost here is equal to the care of the tree plus the cost suffered by you due to an impeded view of the lake.

In essence, then, your offer of money income to your neighbours indicates to them that there is an opportunity cost to their actions. If they do not comply, they forfeit the money that you are offering them. The point here is that *opportunity cost always exists, whoever has property rights.* Therefore, we would expect under some circumstances that voluntary contracting will occur to internalize externalities.[1] The question is, when will voluntary agreements occur?

**Transaction costs** All costs associated with making and enforcing agreements.

**TRANSACTION COSTS.** One major condition for the outcome just outlined above is that the **transaction costs**—all costs associated with making and enforcing agreements—must be low relative to the expected benefits of reaching an agreement. If we expand our example to a much larger one such as air pollution, the transaction costs of numerous homeowners trying to reach agreements with the individuals and companies that create the pollution are relatively high. Consequently, we do not expect voluntary contracting to be an effective way to internalize the externality of air pollution.

[1]This analysis is known as the *Coase theorem*, named after its originator, Ronald Coase, who demonstrated that negative or positive externalities do not necessarily require government intervention in situations in which property rights are defined and enforceable and transaction costs are relatively low.

## Changing Property Rights

In considering the problem of property rights, we can approach it by assuming that initially, many property rights and many resources in a society are not defined. But this situation does not cause a problem so long as no one cares to use the resources for which there are no property rights, or so long as enough of these resources are available that people can have as much as they want at a zero price. Only when and if a use is found for a resource, or the supply of a resource is inadequate at a zero price, does a problem develop. The problem requires that something be done about deciding property rights. If not, the resource will be wasted and possibly even destroyed. Property rights can be assigned to individuals who will then assert control; or they may be assigned to government, which can maintain and preserve the resource, charge for its use, or implement some other rationing device. What we have seen with common property, such as air and water, is that governments have indeed attempted to take over the control of those resources so that they cannot be wasted or destroyed.

Another way of viewing the pollution problem is to argue that property rights are "sacred" and that there are property rights in every resource that exists. We can then say that each individual does not have the right to act on anything that is not that person's property. Hence, no individual has the right to pollute because that amounts to using property that the individual does not specifically own.

Clearly, we must fill the gap between private costs and true social costs in situations in which we have to make up somehow for the fact that property rights are not well defined or assigned. There are three ways to fill this gap: taxation, subsidization, and regulation. Government is involved in all three. Unfortunately, government does not have perfect information and may not pick the appropriate tax, subsidy, or type of regulation. We also have to consider cases in which taxes are hard to enforce or subsidies are difficult to give out to "worthy" recipients. In such cases, outright prohibition of the polluting activity may be the optimal solution to a particular pollution problem. For example, if it is difficult to monitor the level of a particular type of pollution that even in small quantities can cause severe environmental damage, outright prohibition of such pollution may be the only alternative. Consider Example 15–3 and this chapter's Issues and Applications.

### EXAMPLE 15–3 Not In My Backyard (NIMBY)!

When the price of oil used to heat homes and power electrical generators rose during the 2000s, many energy-producing companies began moving away from oil in favour of nuclear power as an energy source. Environmentalists prefer wind or solar power, but the technology will not yet support a huge shift away from oil. Nuclear power generators can take up to 10 years to build, and waste disposal is still a problem. Wind turbines are appearing in most provinces, but they take up huge tracts of land and some people feel they are eye pollution. Power lines are being placed near towns and populated areas, and not everyone is happy with that. Everyone wants cheaper, cleaner energy, but *not in my backyard*!

**For critical analysis:** Should property rights, if the individual had them, allow individuals to stop environmental initiatives from occurring in their "backyards"?

Are alternative energy sources viable today?

## Are There Alternatives to Pollution-Causing Resource Use?

Some people cannot understand why, if pollution is bad, we still use pollution-causing resources, such as coal and oil, to generate any electricity at all. Why don't we forgo the use of such polluting resources and opt for one that apparently is pollution-free, such as solar energy? The plain fact is that in the short run, the cost of generating solar power in most circumstances is much higher than generating that same power through conventional means. We do not yet have the technology that allows us all the luxury of driving solar-powered cars—though such cars do exist. Moreover, with current technology, the solar parts necessary to generate the electricity for the average town would cover massive sections of the countryside, and the manufacturing of those solar parts would itself generate pollution.

## Wild Species, Common Property, and Trade-Offs

One of the most distressing common property problems concerns endangered species, usually in the wild. No one is too concerned about the quantity of dogs, cats, cattle, sheep, and horses. The reason is that virtually all of those species are private property. Peregrine falcons, swift foxes, piping plovers, and the like are typically common property. No one has a vested interest in making sure that they perpetuate in good health.

The federal government's *Canadian Endangered Species Protection Act* was proclaimed into law on March 31, 2000, in an attempt to protect certain species from extinction. As well, most provincial governments have similar legislation to protect dwindling stocks of wildlife. In the mid-1990s in British Columbia, for example, logging was cut back in two forestry districts when only 30 pairs of nesting spotted owls could be located. Up to 100 jobs in forestry were lost, and the process of generating a plan to save the spotted owl cost taxpayers $1 000 000, or about $17 000 per bird. The issues are not straightforward. Today, Earth has only .02 percent of all of the species that have ever lived. Every year, 1000 to 3000 new species are discovered and classified. Estimates of how many species are actually dying out vary from a high of 50 000 per year to a low of one every four years. Are trading quotas the answer? See Example 15–4.

### EXAMPLE 15–4 **Preventing Overfishing by Trading Quotas**

Under the European Union's Common Fisheries Policy, countries are allocated quotas for the amounts of different kinds of fish that their fishers can catch in various areas of the sea. In most European nations, governments control the allocation of fishing rights under these quotas. When fishers retire or die, their quotas go into a pool to be reallocated. In the United Kingdom, however, fishers can buy, sell, or lease their quotas. It turns out that this has had beneficial side effects for fish conservation.

The reason is that because many fishers would like to catch more fish than their quotas permit, there is always a temptation to exceed quota limits. If a British fisher thinks that he is more efficient at hauling in fish than another fisher, he can buy or lease the other fisher's quota. If he is right, he earns higher profits than he would by overfishing and trying to sell his excess catch (which the fishers call "black fish") illegally in the black market.

Indeed, many British fishers might be pleased if the European Union were to cut quotas in a further effort to repopulate stocks of fish. Their current incomes would fall, but the market value of their quotas would rise. The values of quotas are already relatively high. When a tragic accident recently led to the sinking of a fishing boat off the coast of Scotland, the deceased owner's quotas for herring, mackerel, and other fish sold for about $10 million.

During the December 2016 annual meeting of EU fisheries ministers, it is expected that much of the meeting will be devoted to the pursuit of two policies. First, the degree to which the 2017 annual fishing quotas exceed scientific advice should be reduced from the gap in 2016. Second, a greater portion of the fishing quotas should be given to the small, under 10-metre, boats that constitute the largest part of the fleet, fish more sustainably, employ more fishermen, and provide real benefits for their local communities.

**For critical analysis:** How does the existence of a market for quotas help keep the stocks of fish off the shores of Europe from dwindling?

source: "Reduce EU quotas to stop overfishing." John Stansfield. December 11, 2016. Fishing. the guardian. https://www.theguardian.com/environment/2016/dec/11/reduce-eu-quotas-to-stop-overfishing. (Accessed February 20, 2017.)

# 15.4 Recycling

As part of the overall ecology movement, there has been a major push to save scarce resources via recycling. **Recycling** involves the reuse of raw materials derived from manufactured products, such as paper products, plastics, glass, and metals, rather than putting them into solid waste dumps. Many cities have instituted curbside pickup recycling programs. See Example 15–5 for more discussion.

**Recycling** The reuse of raw materials derived from manufactured products.

The benefits of recycling are straightforward. Fewer *natural* resources are used. But some economists argue that recycling does not necessarily save *total* resources.

### EXAMPLE 15–5 Reducing Waste by Recycling

Recycling has come a long way from those first years when hardly anything could be recycled. Now cities are recycling everything from paper to computer products. In Toronto, residents can place organic materials into a green box, and in Edmonton, you can get rid of unwanted items at garbage fairs. Computers and their components are becoming a huge problem as more and more people are upgrading every one to two years, and the old computers have little or no resale value. A company in Toronto, Logic Box, hires artists to change old computer components into earrings and bracelets, and plans to sell these creations on eBay. Recycling has been proven to work as long as the people believe they are benefiting from it. Due to strong participation in the Green Bin Program and the plan to expand this organics collection program to more users, the city of Toronto implemented a new organic waste Green Bin Program in 2016. This program consists of new bins going out to households on daytime curbside collection service. This new service is designed for automated pickup, which adds to capacity and ease of use. The new bins consist of an animal resistant latch, which will encourage more households to participate in the program. The organic waste that is collected is transformed into compost, that is used on park-lands and gardens instead of being sent to landfill. In 2017 it is estimated that 37% of all garbage in Toronto consists of organic waste.

**For critical analysis:** What are some of the benefits of recycling?

Source: "Garbage and recycling." City of Toronto. http://www1.toronto.ca/wps/portal/contentonly?vgnextoid=a2c8b47620805510VgnVCM10000071d60f89RCRD (Accessed February 21, 2017).

## Recycling's Invisible Costs

The recycling of paper can also pollute. Used paper has ink on it that has to be removed during the recycling process. According to the National Wildlife Federation, the production of 98 tonnes of de-inked (bleached) fibre generates approximately 39 tonnes of sludge. This sludge has to be disposed of, usually in a landfill. A lot of recycled paper companies, however, are beginning to produce unbleached paper. In general, recycling does create waste that has to be disposed of.

There is also an issue involved in the use of resources. Recycling requires human effort. The labour resources involved in recycling are often many times more costly than the potential savings in scarce resources not used. That means that net resource use, counting all resources, may sometimes be greater with recycling than without it.

## Landfills

One of the arguments in favour of recycling is to avoid a solid waste "crisis." Some people believe that we are running out of solid waste dump sites in Canada. This is perhaps true in and near major cities, and indeed, the most populated areas of the country might ultimately benefit from recycling programs. In the rest of the country, however, the data do not seem to indicate that we are running out of solid waste landfill sites.

Throughout urban Canada, the disposal price per tonne of city garbage is rising rapidly. Prices vary, of course, for the 20 million tonnes of garbage generated each year. Toronto ended its reliance on the Michigan landfill in 2010.

Currently, municipalities burn about 16 percent of their solid waste and recycle a bit more. In all likelihood, partly because of increased recycling efforts, the amount of solid waste disposal will continue to drop as municipalities restrict the number of landfill sites in response to pressure from community groups that believe landfills are unsafe. If the number of landfill sites is being reduced, is it possible that we are running out of everything? See Example 15–6.

### EXAMPLE 15–6 Are We Running Out of Everything?

It is going to be a world with no more oil, natural gas, copper, or zinc. At least that is the impression one gets these days from the media. In reality, as economists have discovered, the real (inflation-corrected) prices for most nonrenewable resources have fallen over the past 125 years. Real energy prices have dropped an average of 1.6 percent per year, major mineral prices have dropped 1.3 to 2.9 percent a year, and even the price of land has dropped 0.8 percent per year. Unless supply and demand analysis is no longer valid, those numbers indicate that the supply of nonrenewable resources is increasing faster than the demand.

**For critical analysis:** Why would we *not* switch to using renewable resources?

## Should We Save Scarce Resources?

Periodically, the call for recycling focuses on the necessity of saving scarce resources because "we are running out." There is little economic evidence to back up this claim, because virtually every natural resource has fallen in price (corrected for inflation) over the past several decades, as described in Example 15-6. In 1980, economist Julian Simon made a $1000 bet with well-known environmentalist Paul Erlich. Simon bet $200 per resource that any five natural resources that Erlich picked would decline in price (corrected for inflation) by the end of the 1980s. Simon won. (When Simon asked Erlich to renew the bet for $20 000 for the 1990s, Erlich declined.) During the 1980s, the price of virtually every natural resource fell (corrected for inflation), and so did the price of every agricultural commodity. The same was true for every forest product. Though few people remember the dire predictions of the 1970s, many non-economists throughout the world argued at that time that the world's oil reserves were vanishing. If this were true, the pretax, inflation-corrected price of gasoline would not be the same today as it was in the late 1940s (which it is).

In spite of predictions in the early 1980s by World Watch Institute president Lester Brown, real food prices did not rise. Indeed, the real price of food fell by more than 30 percent for the major agricultural commodities during the 1980s. A casual knowledge of supply and demand tells you that since demand for food did not decrease, supply must have increased faster than demand.

## ISSUES AND APPLICATIONS

# Climate Change: What Can Canada Do?

### Concepts Applied: Externalities, Market Incentives, Pollution, Common Property

Pollution is a concern of all nations.

**For critical analysis:**

1. Will firms just move their plants to other countries in an attempt to comply with government regulations and targets?
2. If air is common property, is it only industries that are responsible for GHGs?

In 1997 the first major international pollution abatement treaty was formed called the Kyoto Protocol. In this global agreement, Canada promised that by 2012, it would reduce emissions of global-warming gases to a level 6 percent below its total 1990 emissions. Nevertheless, since 1997 Canada's emissions have actually increased by 1.5 percent per year, since signing the treaty. In failing to make progress to meet its Kyoto Accord, Canada signed on to the Copenhagen Agreement in 2009. As a party to this agreement, the Conservative Canadian government committed to a 2020 target of reducing greenhouse gas (GHG) emissions to 17 percent below 2005 GHG levels. In subsequent years, the conservatives focused on reducing GHG emissions in two Canadian sectors. In 2010, Canada agreed to harmonized automobile emission standards with the U.S. As well, new regulations for reducing greenhouse gas (GHG) emissions from coal-fired electricity generation were formulated and implemented in 2015.

The Conservative government was heavily criticized for failing to impose GHG emission regulations on the oil and gas sectors in Canada.

On December 12, 2015, the Canadian government joined the governments of 194 other countries to sign on to a new climate deal called the Paris Agreement. In this accord, each country committed to keeping the rise in global temperatures below two degrees, a level beyond which scientists think there could be catastrophic consequences. As part of this agreement,

Canada has promised to cut its emissions by 30 per cent between 2005 and 2030. While the emission targets are not legally binding on nations, the monitoring and reporting of emissions are. Countries are to meet every five years to review progress.

On October 3, 2016 Prime Minister Trudeau announced that the federal government plans to ensure that carbon pollution will cost $10 a tonne in 2018, rising to $50 a tonne by 2022. The current plan specifies that the provinces and territories will decide how they implement the carbon pricing, whether it's through a cap-and-trade system or by imposing the cost directly on polluters (i.e. such as a carbon tax). If the provinces refuse to impose these minimum carbon prices, the federal government will then intervene to ensure these pollution costs are levied.

In addition to federal government environment protection policies, some Canadian provinces have been quite pro-active in combatting climate change. B.C. has pursued a package of policies to reduce pollution that were implemented in 2007 through 2009. The province started by cancelling two planned coal-fired power plants and followed that with a requirement that new electricity supply be met through improved energy efficiency and renewable energy. During the same time period BC implemented a carbon tax as well as a low carbon fuel standard. The province met its own 2012 interim target to reduce carbon pollution.

In 2007, the Ontario government released its Climate Change Action Plan that set out a series of actions that include: closing all of Ontario's coal-fired electricity-generating stations; increased use of renewable energy resources in the production of electricity, and smart growth planning. Ontario was successful in reducing province's greenhouse gas emissions by six% below 1990 levels by 2014. In 2016 additional provisions to the Climate Change Action Plan were proposed that include: joining the carbon cap and trade system developed by Quebec and California; reducing the use of natural gas in home heating; increase the use of electric vehicles; increase the use of low carbon trucks and buses; Collaborate with Indigenous communities to transition to non-fossil fuel energy. It should be noted that the province of Ontario is anticipating that the revenues generated by the cap and trade system will help to finance the various provisions of the Climate Change Action Plan, as well as keep the costs of utility bills at reasonable levels.

The Government of Québec views the fight against climate change as a fundamental and top priority issue for Québec's future. Quebec's 2013-2020 Climate Change Action Plan consists of numerous programs led by 12 Government of Québec ministries and other bodies. These programs aim to: reduce fossil fuel consumption and improve the energy efficiency of buildings, industrial processes and vehicle fleets; provide greater support for the development of mass and active transit; accelerate the electrification of transport and the creation of new companies in this field; broaden the use of renewable energy sources in all activity sectors; encourage research and development in the field of clean technology. These programs receive funding from Quebec's Green Fund, which is supported by revenues of a carbon cap and trade program linked with other North America jurisdictions, such as Ontario and California.

On November 22, 2015, the Alberta NDP government unveiled the province's Climate Leadership Plan. Key elements of the plan include: starting a carbon tax levy on pollution emitters in 2017; ending coal generated electricity by 2030; capping oil sands emissions to 100 mega tonnes per year; reducing methane emissions by 45% by 2025; developing more renewable energy sources (i.e. wind and solar). All of the revenue generated from the carbon levy will be re-spent in the economy to fund: green initiatives; development of renewable energy projects; research and innovation; and rebates to offset increased costs (due to the tax) born by lower income groups.

On January 20, 2017, Donald Trump started his first term as president of the U.S. During his election campaign he vowed to reduce environment and climate change regulations and other barriers to the further development and production of energy based on fossil fuels. If Trump follows through with his election promises, this will reduce energy costs in the U.S. compared to Canada. This will, in turn, make Canadian products more expensive than their U.S. substitutes, causing an imbalance of Canadian trade and unemployment. As well, it will be much more attractive for investors to expand fossil fuel energy projects in the U.S. and cutback these type of projects in Canada, causing further unemployment.

Sources: "What Canada agreed to in Paris." CHRIS HANNAY. Ottawa. The Globe and Mail. Dec. 14, 2015.Politics. News. The Globe and Mail. http://www.theglobeandmail.com/news/politics/what-canada-agreed-to-in-paris/article27742735/ (Accessed February 22, 2017); "Alberta, Saskatchewan, Nova Scotia push back on Ottawa's climate change plans."The Canadian Press. October 3, 2016.Canada. News. thestar.com. https://www.thestar.com/news/canada/2016/10/03/alberta-wont-support-ottawas-climate-change-plans-without-a-pipeline-notley.html (Accessed February 22, 2017); "How B.C. does climate policy right." By Matt Horn. Dec. 11, 2014. Op-Eds. Media Room. Pembina Institute. http://www.pembina.org/op-ed/how-bc-does-climate-policy-right. (Accessed February 22, 2017); "2013-2020 Climate Change Action Plan/ Green Fund." Climate Change. Ministère du Développement durable, de l'Environnement et de la Lutte contre les changements climatiques. http://www.mddelcc.gouv.qc.ca/changementsclimatiques/index-en.htm. (Accessed February 22, 2017); "Climate Change Action Plan and Ontario's Energy Utilities: 6 Key Initiatives."; Zoë Thoms. June 10, 2016. Energy insider. http://energyinsider.ca/index.php/climate-change-action-plan-and-ontarios-energy-utilities-6-key-initiatives/ (Accessed February 22, 2017); "Climate change strategy." Ontario Government. https://www.ontario.ca/page/climate-change-strategy (Accessed February 22, 2017); "Climate Leadership Plan." Climate Change. Environment and Natural Resources. Alberta Government. https://www.alberta.ca/climate-leadership-plan.aspx (Accessed February 22, 2017).

# SUMMARY

**Here is what you should know after reading this chapter. MyEconLab will help you identify what you know, and where to go when you need to practise. We suggest that as soon as you review one of the Learning Objectives sections below, you then proceed to go through the related section in MyEconLab.**

| LEARNING OBJECTIVES | KEY TERMS | MYECONLAB PRACTICE |
|---|---|---|
| **15.1 Private versus Social Costs.** In some situations, there are social costs that do not equal private costs—that is, there are costs to society that exceed the cost to the individual. These costs may include air and water pollution, for which private individuals do not have to pay. Society, however, does bear the costs of these externalities. Few individuals or firms voluntarily consider social costs. | private costs, 379<br>social costs, 379<br>externality, 380 | • **MyEconLab** Study Plan 15.1 |

| LEARNING OBJECTIVES | KEY TERMS | MYECONLAB PRACTICE |
|---|---|---|
| **15.2 Pollution.** One way to analyze the problem of pollution is to look at it as an externality. Individual decision makers do not take into account the negative externalities they impose on the rest of society. In such a situation, they produce "too much" pollution and "too many" polluting goods.<br>It might be possible to ameliorate the situation by imposing a tax on polluters. The tax, however, should be dependent on the extent of the economic damages created, rather than on the physical quantity of pollution. This tax will therefore be different for the same level of physical pollution in different parts of the country because the economic damage differs, depending on location, population density, and other factors.<br>The optimal quantity of pollution is the quantity at which the marginal cost of cleanup equals the marginal benefit of cleanup. Pollution abatement is a trade-off. We trade off goods and services for cleaner air and water, and vice versa. | optimal quantity of pollution, 383 | • **MyEconLab** Study Plan 15.2 |
| **15.3 Common Property.** Another way of looking at the externality problem is to realize that it involves the lack of definite property rights. No one owns common property resources, such as air and water, and therefore no one takes into account the long-run pernicious effects of excessive pollution.<br>There are alternatives to pollution-causing resource use—for example, solar energy. We do not use solar energy because it is too expensive relative to conventional alternatives and because the creation of solar parts would itself generate pollution. | private property rights, 385<br>common property, 385<br>transaction costs, 386 | • **MyEconLab** Study Plan 15.3 |
| **15.4 Recycling.** Recycling involves reusing paper, glass, and other materials, rather than putting them into solid waste dumps. Recycling does have a cost, both in the resources used for recycling and in the pollution created during recycling. Landfills are an alternative to recycling. In rural Canada, these solid waste disposal sites are being expanded faster than the demand for them.<br>Resources may not be getting scarcer. The inflation-corrected price of most resources has been falling for decades. | recycling, 389 | • **MyEconLab** Study Plan 15.4 |

# PROBLEMS

(Answers to the odd-numbered problems appear at the back of the book.)

**LO 15.1 Explain the difference between private and social costs and how externalities can occur.**

1. Construct a typical supply-and-demand graph. Show the initial equilibrium price and quantity. Assume that the good causes negative externalities to third parties (persons not involved in the transactions). Revise the graph to compensate for that fact. How does the revised situation compare with the original?
2. Construct a second supply-and-demand graph for any product. Show the equilibrium price and quantity. Assuming that the good generates external benefits, modify the diagram to allow for them. Show the new equilibrium price and quantity. How does the revised situation compare with the original?
3. Why has the free market not developed contractual arrangements to eliminate excess air pollution in major Canadian cities?

**LO 15.2 Discuss the marginal benefits and costs of pollution.**

4. Examine the following marginal costs and marginal benefits associated with water cleanliness in a given locale.

| Quantity of Clean Water (%) | Marginal Cost ($) | Marginal Benefit ($) |
|---|---|---|
| 0 | 3 000 | 200 000 |
| 20 | 15 000 | 120 000 |
| 40 | 50 000 | 90 000 |
| 60 | 85 000 | 85 000 |
| 80 | 100 000 | 40 000 |
| 100 | Infinite | 0 |

   a. What is the optimal degree of water cleanliness?
   b. What is the optimal degree of water pollution?
   c. Suppose that a company creates a food additive that offsets most of the harmful effects of drinking polluted water. As a result, the marginal benefit of water cleanliness declines by $40 000 at each degree of water cleanliness at or less than 80 percent. What is the optimal degree of water cleanliness after this change?

5. Examine the following marginal costs and marginal benefits associated with air cleanliness in a given locale:

| Quantity of Clean Air (%) | Marginal Cost ($) | Marginal Benefit ($) |
|---|---|---|
| 0 | 50 000 | 600 000 |
| 20 | 150 000 | 360 000 |
| 40 | 200 000 | 200 000 |
| 60 | 300 000 | 150 000 |
| 80 | 400 000 | 120 000 |
| 100 | Infinite | 0 |

   a. What is the optimal degree of air cleanliness?
   b. What is the optimal degree of air pollution?
   c. Suppose that a state provides subsidies for a company to build plants that contribute to air pollution. Cleaning up this pollution causes the marginal cost of air cleanliness to rise by $210 000 at each degree of air cleanliness. What is the optimal degree of air cleanliness after this change?

6. The following table displays hypothetical annual total costs and total benefits of conserving wild tigers at several possible worldwide tiger population levels.

| Population of Wild Tigers | Total Cost ($ million) | Total Benefit ($ million) |
|---|---|---|
| 0 | 0 | 40 |
| 2 000 | 5 | 90 |
| 4 000 | 15 | 130 |
| 6 000 | 30 | 160 |
| 8 000 | 55 | 185 |
| 10 000 | 90 | 205 |
| 12 000 | 140 | 215 |

   a. Calculate the marginal costs and benefits.
   b. Given the data, what is the socially optimal world population of wild tigers?
   c. Suppose that tiger farming is legalized and that this has the effect of reducing the marginal cost of tiger conservation by $15 million for each 2000-tiger population increment in the table. What is the new socially optimal population of wild tigers?

7. When a government charges firms for the privilege of polluting, a typical result is a rise in the market price of the good or service produced by those firms. Consequently, consumers of the good or service usually have to pay a higher price to obtain it. Why might this be socially desirable?

**LO 15.3 Describe how common property impacts the environment.**

8. What is the problem with common property resources?
9. Suppose that polluters are to be charged by government agencies for the privilege of polluting.
   a. How should the price be set?
   b. Which firms will treat waste, and which will pay to pollute?
   c. Is it possible that some firms will be forced to close down because they now have to pay to pollute? Why might this result be good?
   d. If producers are charged to pollute, they will pass this cost on to buyers in the form of higher prices. Why might this be good?

**LO 15.4 Explain how recycling is changing the way we look at our environment.**

10. In Example 15–2, "Wind as a Renewable Resource," companies are offering people the choice to use renewable resources. Why would companies be willing to switch technologies at a great cost to them?
11. In Example 15–5, "Reducing Waste by Recycling," recycling is now considered something that everyone should participate in. How can people who are not recycling be forced to participate without a huge cost to governments?
12. This chapter's Issues and Applications talked about industries and government, but what can you do to reduce your costs of polluting?

# BUSINESS APPLICATION

**LO 15.2 Discuss the marginal benefits and costs of pollution.**

## Should You Convert Your House to Solar Power?

First, you need to price out the cost of solar power. How does it compare with conventional power?

Go on the Internet and price out the cost difference between solar power and conventional power. Is it worth spending extra money for solar? Would wind or thermal power make more economic sense?

Make up a balance sheet for each energy option you would consider for your house. Which option is best?

16

# The Public Sector

## LEARNING OBJECTIVES

After reading this chapter, you should be able to:

**16.1** Explain the four economic functions of government.

**16.2** Describe the two main political functions of government and how decision making differs depending on whether the individual is in the public or private sector.

**16.3** Distinguish between average and marginal tax rates and explain the Canadian tax system.

In Canada, over the course of a year, thousands of tax lawyers and accountants labour alone or with clients to help those clients reduce their tax liabilities and fill out their tax returns. Canadian taxpayers are each estimated to spend approximately 20 hours per year preparing their taxes. The opportunity cost exceeds $4 billion per year. And that is not the end of the story—many individuals spend a lot of valuable time figuring out ways to change their lifestyle so as to reduce the taxes they owe. Although there is never any way to avoid the cost of a tax system completely, there are ways to reduce compliance costs to society. One way is to switch to a more simplified tax system. To understand this issue, you need to know more about government and the public sector.

myeconlab

EconLab helps you master each objective and study more efficiently. See end of chapter for details

# DID YOU KNOW THAT...?

The average Canadian works from January 1 through June 10 each year to pay for all municipal, provincial, and federal taxes. The average B.C. resident works approximately two weeks longer to pay for all of the taxes owed each year when compared with the typical Quebec resident. Looked at another way, the average Canadian in a typical eight-hour day works about three hours and 36 minutes to pay for government at all levels. The average household with two or more people spends about $34 154 a year in taxes of all kinds. The total amount paid exceeds $295 billion. It would take more than 295 000 millionaires to have as much money as is spent each year by government. So, we cannot ignore the presence of government in our society. Government exists, at a minimum, to take care of what the price system does not do well.

## 16.1 Economic Functions of Government

Government performs many functions that affect the way in which exchange is carried out in the economy. Let us look at four economic functions of government.

**PROVIDING A LEGAL SYSTEM.** The courts and the police may not at first seem like economic functions of government (although judges and police personnel must be paid). Their activities, nonetheless, have important consequences on the economic activities in any country. You and I enter into contracts constantly, whether they be oral or written, express or implied. When we believe that we have been wronged, we seek redress of our grievances within our legal institutions. Moreover, consider the legal system that is necessary for the smooth functioning of our society. Our society has defined quite explicitly the legal status of businesses, the rights of private ownership, and a method for the enforcement of contracts. All relationships among consumers and businesses are governed by the legal rules of the game. We might consider government in its judicial function and then as the referee when there are disputes in the economic arena.

Much of our legal system is involved with defining and protecting *property rights*. **Property rights** are the rights of an owner to use and to exchange that property. One might say that property rights are really the rules of our economic game. When property rights are well defined, owners of property have an incentive to use the property efficiently. Any mistakes in their decision about the use of property have negative consequences that the owners suffer. Furthermore, when property rights are well defined, owners of property have an incentive to maintain that property so that if those owners ever desire to sell it, it will fetch a better price.

Establishing and maintaining a well-functioning legal system is not a costless activity, as you can see in Policy Example 16–1.

Tax freedom day has been coming earlier every year. What does this mean to the average household?

**Property rights** The rights of an owner to use and to exchange that property.

### POLICY EXAMPLE 16–1 Who Should Pay the High Cost of a Legal System?

When a huge multinational corporation gets into a lengthy and expensive "shouting match" with its detractors, the public ends up footing part of the legal bill. McDonald's operates worldwide, with annual sales of about $50 billion. It has property rights in the goodwill associated with its name. When two unemployed British social activists published a pamphlet with such chapter headings as "McDollar, McGreedy, McCancer, McMurder, McRipoff, McTorture, and McGarbage," McDonald's was not pleased. The pamphlet accused the American company of torturing animals, corrupting children, and exploiting the developing world. So, McDonald's went to court in London. When the case began, there were 26 preliminary hearings spread over a four-year time period, and when it went to trial, 180 witnesses were called. McDonald's itself will end up spending many millions of dollars, but British taxpayers will foot the entire bill for the use of the court system. According to the Lord Chancellor's Department, British taxpayers paid at least £2.5 million (well over $5.5 million).

*continued*

Should taxpayers continue to pay for all of the court system? No, according to policy makers in Britain. They have a plan to make litigants pay the full cost of court services, specifically judges' salaries. Such a system that forces litigants to pay for the full opportunity cost of the legal system has yet to be instituted in Canada or elsewhere.

**For critical analysis:** What other costs, besides judges' salaries, do citizens implicitly pay for in their legal system?

**PROMOTING COMPETITION.** Many people believe that the only way to attain economic efficiency is through competition. One of the roles of government is to serve as the protector of a competitive economic system. The federal and provincial governments have passed anticombines legislation, which makes illegal certain (but not all) economic activities that might, in legal terms, restrain trade—that is, prevent free competition among actual and potential rival firms in the marketplace. The avowed aim of anticombines legislation is to reduce the power of **monopolies**—firms that have great control over the price of the goods they sell. A number of laws have been passed that prohibit specific anti-competitive business behaviour. The Competition Bureau, which is part of Industry Canada, attempts to enforce these anticombines laws. Various provincial judicial agencies also expend efforts at maintaining competition.

**Monopoly.** A firm that has great control over the price of a good it sells.

**PROVIDING PUBLIC GOODS.** The goods used in our examples up to this point have been **private goods**—goods that can be consumed by only one individual at a time. When I eat a cheeseburger, you cannot eat the same one. So, you and I are rivals for that cheeseburger, just as much as rivals for the title of world champion are. When I use a DVD player, you cannot use the same player. When I use the services of an auto mechanic, that person cannot work at the same time for you. That is the distinguishing feature of private goods—their use is exclusive to the people who purchase or rent them. The **principle of rival consumption** is that one person's consumption reduces the amount of private goods available for others to consume. Rival consumption is easy to understand. With private goods, either you use them or I use them.

**Private goods** Goods and services that are both excludable and rivalrous.

**Principle of rival consumption** The principle that one person's consumption reduces the amount of private goods available for others to consume.

There is an entire class of goods that are not private goods. These are called **public goods**—these can be consumed jointly by many individuals simultaneously at no additional cost and with no reduction in quality or quantity. Military defence, police protection, and the legal system, for example, are public goods. If you partake of them, you do not necessarily take away from anyone else's share of those goods.

**Public goods** Goods that are neither excludable nor rivalrous. They can be consumed jointly by many individuals simultaneously at no additional cost and with no reduction in quality or quantity.

**CHARACTERISTICS OF PUBLIC GOODS.** Several distinguishing characteristics of public goods set them apart from all other goods.[1]

1. Public goods are indivisible. You cannot buy or sell $5 worth of a park. Public goods cannot usually be produced or sold very easily in small units.
2. Public goods can be used by more and more people at no additional cost. Once money has been spent for the park, the opportunity cost to you is zero.
3. Additional users of public goods do not deprive others of any of the services of the goods. If you use the park, it does not prevent someone else from also using it.
4. It is difficult to design a collection system for a public good on the basis of how much individuals use it. It is nearly impossible to determine how much any person uses or values parks. No one can be denied the benefits of the park for failing to pay for that public good. This is often called the **exclusion principle.**

**Exclusion principle** The principle that no one can be denied the benefits of a public good for failing to pay for it.

If we think about our park, we can determine the total marginal benefit of the park. Sam and Susan both would like some parks in their area. Each puts a different value on the park, as illustrated by Figure 16–1. Part (a) shows Susan's marginal benefit is $80 for

[1]Sometimes the distinction is made between pure public goods, which have all the characteristics we have described here, and quasi- or near-public goods, which do not. The major feature of near-public goods is that they are jointly consumed, even though nonpaying customers can be, and often are, excluded—for example, movies, football games, and concerts.

**FIGURE 16–1**

## Total Marginal Benefit of a Public Good

The total marginal benefit of a park is derived by adding the marginal benefits of all individuals.

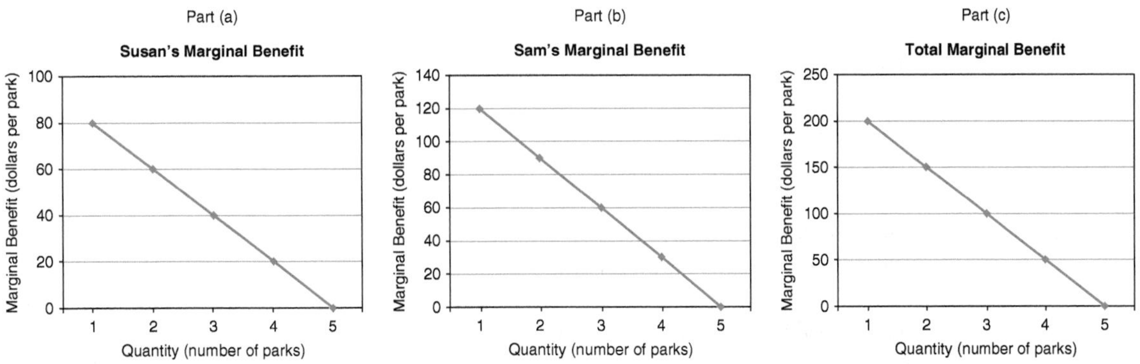


the first park, part (b) shows Sam's marginal benefit is \$120 for the first park, and part (c) shows the total benefit of the first park is \$200. The marginal cost of a public good is determined the same way you would derive the marginal cost for a private good.

One of the problems of public goods is that the private sector has a difficult, if not impossible, time in providing them. There is little or no incentive for individuals in the private sector to offer public goods because it is so difficult to make a profit in so doing. Consequently, a true public good must necessarily be provided by government. Read Example 16–1 for further discussion.

### EXAMPLE 16–1 Are Lighthouses a Public Good?

One of the most common examples of a public good is a lighthouse. In one instance, however, a lighthouse was not a public good in that a collection system was devised and enforced on the basis of how much individuals used it. In the thirteenth century, in the city of Aigues-Mortes, a port in Southern France, a tower called the King's Tower was erected to assert the will and power of Louis IX (Saint Louis). The 32-metre-high tower served as a lighthouse for ships. More importantly, it served as a lookout so that ships sailing on the open sea, but in its view, did not escape paying for use of the lighthouse. Those payments were then used for the construction of the city walls.

**For critical analysis:** Explain how a lighthouse satisfies the characteristics of public goods described in points 1, 2, and 3 on the previous page.

Are lighthouses a public good?

**FREE RIDERS.** The nature of public goods leads to the **free-rider problem**, a situation in which some individuals take advantage of the fact that others will shoulder the burden of paying for public goods, such as defence. Free riders will argue that they receive no value from such government services as defence and therefore really should not have to pay for them. Suppose that citizens were taxed directly in proportion to how much they told an interviewer that they valued military protection. Some people would probably say that they are unwilling to pay for it because they do not want any—it is of no value to them. Many of us may end up being free riders when we assume that others will pay for the desired public good. We may all want to be free riders if we believe that someone else will provide the commodity in question that we actually value.

**Free-rider problem** A situation in which some individuals take advantage of the fact that others will shoulder the burden of paying for public goods.

The free-rider problem is a definite issue among nations with respect to the international burden of defence and how it should be shared. A country may choose to belong to a multilateral defence organization, such as the North Atlantic Treaty Organization (NATO) but then consistently attempt not to contribute funds to the organization.

The nation knows it would be defended by others in NATO if it were attacked but would rather not pay for such defence. In short, it seeks a "free ride."

**ENSURING ECONOMYWIDE STABILITY.** Government attempts to stabilize the economy by smoothing out the ups and downs in overall business activity. Our economy sometimes faces the problems of unemployment and oscillating prices. Government, especially the federal government, has made an attempt to solve these problems by trying to stabilize the economy. The notion that the federal government should undertake actions to stabilize business activity is a relatively new idea in Canada, encouraged by high unemployment rates during the Great Depression of the 1930s and subsequent theories about possible ways by which government could reduce unemployment. In 1945, government formally assumed responsibility for economic performance. It established three goals for government accountability: full employment, price stability, and economic growth. These goals have provided the justification for many government economic programs during the post–World War II period.

# 16.2 The Political Functions of Government

At least two areas of government are in the realm of political—or normative—functions, rather than that of the economic ones discussed in the first part of this chapter. These two areas are (1) the regulation and/or provision of merit and demerit goods, and (2) income redistribution.

## Merit and Demerit Goods

**Merit good** Any good that the political process has deemed socially desirable.

Certain goods are considered to have special merit. A **merit good** is defined as any good that the political process has deemed socially desirable. (Note that nothing inherent in any particular good makes it a merit good. It is a matter of who chooses it.) Some examples of merit goods in our society are museums, ballets, sports stadiums (see Policy Example 16–2), and concerts. In these areas, government's role is the provision of merit goods to the people in society who would not otherwise purchase them at market clearing prices or who would not purchase an amount of them judged to be sufficient. This provision may take the form of government production and distribution of merit goods. It can also take the form of reimbursement for payment on merit goods or subsidies to producers or consumers for part of the cost of merit goods. Governments do, indeed, subsidize such merit goods as concerts, ballets, and museums. In most cases, such merit goods would rarely be so numerous without subsidization.

### POLICY EXAMPLE 16–2 Do Government-Funded Sports Stadiums Have a Net Positive Effect on Local Economies?

Probably not, even though in recent years many cities have decided that new football and baseball stadiums are merit goods worthy of public funding. Their rationale is that there is no collective mechanism besides government to ensure the construction of the stadiums that will draw big crowds. A local government, goes the argument, can regard a stadium as an investment because the crowds it draws benefit the local economy. Spending by the crowds can also generate tax revenues that help government recoup its expenses. According to economist Andrew Zimbalist, however, "there has not been an independent study by an economist over the last 30 years that suggests you can anticipate a positive economic impact" from government investments in sports facilities.

**For critical analysis:** In theory, explain how a sports stadium might result in positive externalities for the local economy.

Source: Noll, Roger G. & Andrew Zimbalist, Editors. *Sports, Jobs, and Taxes: The Economic Impact of Sports Teams and Stadiums.* Brookings Institution. 1997.

**Demerit goods** are the opposite of merit goods—they are goods that the political process has deemed socially undesirable. Cigarettes, gambling, and illegal drugs are examples. Government exercises its role in the area of demerit goods by taxing, regulating, or prohibiting their manufacture, sale, and use. Governments justify the relatively high taxes on alcohol and tobacco by declaring them demerit goods. The best-known example of governmental exercise of power in this area is the stance against certain psychoactive drugs. Most psychoactives (except nicotine, caffeine, and alcohol) are either expressly prohibited, as is the case for heroin, cocaine, and opium, or heavily regulated, as in the case of prescription psychoactives.

**Demerit good** Any good that the political process has deemed socially undesirable.

## Income Redistribution

Another relatively recent political function of government has been the explicit redistribution of income. This redistribution uses two systems: the progressive income tax (described later in this chapter) and transfer payments. **Transfer payments** are payments made to individuals for which no services or goods are concurrently rendered in return. The three key money transfer payments in our system are welfare, old age security payments, and employment insurance benefits. Income redistribution also includes a large amount of income **transfers in kind**—payments that are in the form of actual goods and services for which no goods or services are rendered concurrently in return. Two income transfers in kind are health care and low-cost public housing.

**Transfer payments.** Payments made to individuals for which no services or goods are concurrently rendered in return.

**Transfers in kind** Payments that are in the form of actual goods and services for which no goods or services are rendered concurrently in return.

Government has also engaged in other activities as a form of redistribution of income. For example, the provision of child-care spaces is, at least in part, an attempt to redistribute income by making sure that the very poor have access to child-care (see Example 16–2).

## Collective Decision Making: The Theory of Public Choice

The public sector has a vast influence on the Canadian economy. Yet, the economic model used until now has applied only to the behaviour of the private sector—firms and households. Such a model does not adequately explain the behaviour of the public sector. We shall attempt to do so now.

Governments consist of individuals. No government actually thinks and acts; rather, government actions are the result of decision making by individuals in their roles as elected representatives, appointed officials, and salaried bureaucrats. Therefore, to understand how government works, we must examine the incentives for the people in government as well as those who would like to be in government—avowed candidates or would-be candidates for elected or appointed positions—and special-interest lobbyists attempting to get government to do something. At issue is the analysis of *collective decision making*. **Collective decision making** involves how voters, politicians, and other interested parties act and how these actions influence nonmarket decisions. The analysis of collective decision making is usually called the **theory of public choice**. It has been given this name because it involves hypotheses about how choices are made in the public sector, as opposed to the private sector. The foundation of public-choice theory is the assumption that individuals will act within the political process to maximize their individual (not collective) well being. In that sense, the theory is similar to our analysis of the market economy, in which we also assume that individuals are motivated by self-interest.

**Collective decision making** How voters, politicians, and other interested parties act and how these actions influence nonmarket decisions.

**Theory of public choice** The analysis of collective decision making.

To understand public-choice theory, it is necessary to point out other similarities between the private market sector and the public, or government, sector; then, we will look at the differences.

## Similarities in Market and Public-Sector Decision Making

In addition to the similar assumption of self-interest being the motivating force in both sectors, there are other similarities.

**SCARCITY.** At any given moment, the amount of resources is fixed. This means that for the private and the public sectors combined, there is a scarcity constraint. Everything that is spent by all levels of government, plus everything that is spent by the private sector, must add up to the total income available at any point in time. Hence, every government action has an opportunity cost, just as in the market sector.

**COMPETITION.** Although we typically think of competition as a private market phenomenon, it is also present in collective action. Given the scarcity constraint government also faces, bureaucrats, appointed officials, and elected representatives will always be in competition for available government funds. Furthermore, the individuals within any government agency or institution will act as individuals do in the private sector: they will try to obtain higher wages, better working conditions, and higher job-level classifications. They will compete and act in their own, not society's, interests.

**SIMILARITY OF INDIVIDUALS.** Contrary to popular belief, there are not two types of workers, those who work in the private sector and those who work in the public sector; rather, individuals working in similar positions can be considered similar. The difference, as we shall see, is that the individuals in government face a different **incentive structure**, the system of rewards and punishments individuals face with respect to their own actions, from that in the private sector. For example, the costs and benefits of being efficient or inefficient differ when one goes from the private sector to the public sector.

**Incentive structure** The system of rewards and punishments individuals face with respect to their own actions.

One approach to predicting government bureaucratic behaviour is to ask what incentives bureaucrats face. Take Canada Post as an example. The bureaucrats running that Crown corporation are human beings with qualities similar to those possessed by workers in comparable positions at, say, Nortel or Air Canada. Yet, the post office does not function like either of these companies. The difference can be explained, at least in part, in terms of the incentives provided for the managers in the two types of institutions. When the bureaucratic managers and workers at Nortel make incorrect decisions, work slowly, produce shoddy products, and are generally "inefficient," the profitability of the company declines. The owners—millions of shareholders—express their displeasure by selling some of their shares of the company. The market value, as tracked on the stock exchange, falls. But what about Canada Post? If a manager, a worker, or a bureaucrat in the post office provides shoddy service, there is no straightforward mechanism by which the organization's owners—the taxpayers—can express their dissatisfaction. Despite the post office's status as a "government corporation," taxpayers as shareholders do not really own the organization's shares that they can sell.

The key, then, to understanding purported inefficiency in the government bureaucracy is not found in an examination of people and personalities but, rather, in an examination of incentives and institutional arrangements.

## Differences between Market and Collective Decision Making

There are probably more dissimilarities between the market sector and the public sector than there are similarities.

**GOVERNMENT GOODS AT ZERO PRICE.** The majority of goods that governments produce are furnished to the ultimate consumers without direct money charge. **Government, or political, goods** (and services) are goods and services provided by the public sector; they can be either private or public goods. The fact that they are furnished to the ultimate consumer free of charge does not mean that the cost to society of those goods is zero, however; it only means that the price charged is zero. The full opportunity cost to society is the value of the resources used in the production of goods produced and provided by government.

**Government, or political, goods** Goods (and services) provided by the public sector; they can be either private or public goods.

For example, none of us pays directly for each unit of consumption of most highways nor for police protection. Rather, we pay for all these things indirectly through the taxes that support our governments—federal, provincial, and municipal. This special feature of government can be looked at in a different way. There is no longer a one-to-one relationship between the consumption of a government-provided good and the payment for that good. Consumers who pay taxes collectively pay for every political good, but the individual consumer may not be able to see the relationship between the taxes paid and the consumption of the good. Indeed, most taxpayers will find that their tax bill is the same whether or not they consume, or even like, government-provided goods.

**USE OF FORCE.** All governments are able to engage in the legal use of force in their regulation of economic affairs. For example, governments can exercise the use of expropriation, which means that if you refuse to pay your taxes, your bank account and other assets may be seized by the Canada Revenue Agency. In fact, you have no choice in the matter of paying taxes to governments. Collectively, we decide the total size of government through the political process, but individually we cannot determine how much service we pay for just for ourselves during any one year.

**VOTING VERSUS SPENDING.** In the private market sector, a dollar voting system is in effect. This dollar voting system is not equivalent to the voting system in the public sector. There are, at minimum, three differences:

1. In a political system, one person gets one vote, whereas in the market system, the dollars one spends count as votes.
2. The political system is run by **majority rule**, a collective decision-making system in which group decisions are made on the basis of 50.1 percent of the vote, whereas the market system is run by **proportional rule**, a decision-making system in which actions are based on the proportion of the "votes" cast and are in proportion to them.
3. The spending of dollars can indicate intensity of want, whereas because of the all-or-nothing nature of political voting, a vote cannot.

**Majority rule** A collective decision-making system in which group decisions are made on the basis of 50.1 percent of the vote.

**Proportional rule** A decision-making system in which actions are based on the proportion of the "votes" cast and are in proportion to them.

Ultimately, the main distinction between political votes and dollar votes here is that political outcomes may differ from economic outcomes. Remember that economic efficiency is a situation in which, given the prevailing distribution of income, consumers get the economic goods they want. There is no corresponding situation using political voting. Thus, we can never assume that a political voting process will lead to the same decisions that a dollar voting process will lead to in the marketplace.

Indeed, consider the dilemma every voter faces. Usually, a voter is not asked to decide on a single issue (although this happens); rather, a voter is asked to choose among candidates who present a large number of issues and state a position on each of them. Just consider the average member of parliament who has to vote on hundreds of different issues during a five-year term. When you vote for that representative, you are voting for a person who must make hundreds of decisions during the next five years.

## The Role of Bureaucrats

Government programs require people to deliver them. This is manifested today in the form of well-established bureaucracies, in which **bureaucrats** (nonelected government officials) work. A **bureaucracy** is an administrative system run by a large staff following rules and procedures set down by government. Bureaucracies can exert great influence on matters concerning themselves—the amount of funding granted them and the activities in which they engage. In the political marketplace, well-organized bureaucracies can even influence the expression of public demand itself. In many cases, they organize the clientele (interest groups), coach that clientele on what is appropriate, and stick up for the "rights" of the clientele.

**Bureaucrats** Nonelected government officials.

**Bureaucracy** An administrative system run by a large staff following rules and procedures set down by government.

## Gauging Bureaucratic Performance

It is tempting, but incorrect, to think of bureaucrats as mere "technocrats," executors of orders and channels of information, in this process. They have at least two incentives to make government programs larger and more resistant to attack than we might otherwise expect. First, society has decided that in general, government should not be run on a profit-making basis. Measures of performance other than bottom-line profits must be devised. In the private market, successful firms typically expand to serve more customers; although this growth is often incidental to the underlying profitability, the two frequently go hand in hand. In parallel, performance in government is often measured by the number of clients served, and rewards are distributed accordingly. As a result, bureaucrats have an incentive to expand the size of their clientele—not because it is more profitable (beneficial) to society but because that is how bureaucrats' rewards are structured.

In general, performance measures that are not based on long-run profitability are less effective at gauging true performance. This makes it potentially easier for the government bureaucrat to appear to perform well, collect rewards for measured performance, and then leave for greener pastures. To avoid this, a much larger proportion of the rewards given to bureaucrats are valuable only as long as they continue being bureaucrats—large staffs, expensive offices, generous pensions, and the like. Instead of getting large current salaries (which can be saved for a rainy day), they get rewards that disappear if their jobs disappear. Naturally, this increases the incentives of bureaucrats to make sure that their jobs do not disappear.

## Rational Ignorance

At this point, you may well be wondering why this system still goes on. The answer lies in rational ignorance on the part of voters, ignorance that is carefully cultivated by the members of special interest groups.

On most issues, there is little incentive for the individual voter to expend resources to determine how to vote. Moreover, the ordinary course of living provides most of us with enough knowledge to decide whether we should invest in learning more about a given issue. For example, suppose that Canadian voters were asked to decide if the sign marking the entrance to an obscure national park should be enlarged. Most voters would decide that the potential costs and benefits of this decision are negligible. The new sign is unlikely to be the size of Prince Edward Island, and anybody who has even heard of the national park in question probably already has a pretty good idea of its location. Thus, most voters would choose to remain rationally ignorant about the exact costs and benefits of enlarging the sign, implying that (1) many will choose not to vote at all, and (2) those who do vote will simply flip a coin or cast their ballot on the basis of some other, perhaps ideological, grounds.

**WHY BE RATIONALLY IGNORANT?** For most political decisions, majority rule prevails. Only a coalition of voters representing slightly more than 50 percent of those who vote is needed. Whenever a vote is taken, the result is going to involve costs and benefits. Voters, then, must evaluate their share of the costs and benefits of any budgetary expenditure. Voters, however, are not perfectly informed. That is one of the crucial characteristics of the real world—information is a resource that is costly to obtain. Rational voters will, in fact, decide to remain at some level of ignorance about government programs because the benefits from obtaining more information may not be worth the cost, given each individual voter's extremely limited impact on the outcome of an election. For the same reason, voters will fail to inform themselves about taxes or other revenue sources to pay for proposed expenditures because they know that for any specific expenditure program, the cost to them individually will be small. At this point, it might be useful to contrast this situation with what exists in the nonpolitical private market sector of the economy. In the private market sector, the individual chooses a mix of purchases and bears fully the direct and indirect consequences of this selection (ignoring for the moment the problem of externalities).

# 16.3 Tax Rates and the Canadian Tax System

Jean-Baptiste Colbert, the seventeenth-century French finance minister, said the art of taxation was in "plucking the goose so as to obtain the largest amount of feathers with the least possible amount of hissing." In Canada, governments have designed a variety of methods of plucking the private-sector goose. To analyze any tax system, we must first understand the distinction between marginal tax rates and average tax rates.

## Marginal and Average Tax Rates

If somebody says, "I pay 28 percent in taxes," you cannot really tell what that person means unless you know whether the individual is referring to average taxes paid or the tax rate on the last dollar earned. The latter concept has to do with the **marginal tax rate.**[2]

The marginal tax rate is expressed as follows:

$$\text{Marginal tax rate} = \frac{\text{Change in taxes due}}{\text{Change in taxable income}}$$

**Marginal tax rate** The change in taxes due divided by the change in taxable income.

It is important to understand that the marginal tax rate applies only to the income in the highest tax bracket reached, where a **tax bracket** is defined as a specified level of taxable income to which a specific and unique marginal tax rate is applied.

The **average tax rate** is not the same thing as the marginal tax rate; it is defined as follows:

$$\text{Average tax rate} = \frac{\text{Total taxes due}}{\text{Total taxable income}}$$

**Tax bracket** A specified level of taxable income to which a specific and unique marginal tax rate is applied.

**Average tax rate** The total taxes due divided by total taxable income.

## Taxation Systems

No matter how governments raise revenues—from income taxes, sales taxes, or other taxes—all of those taxes can fit into one of three types of taxation systems—proportional, progressive, and regressive, expressing a relationship between the percentage tax (or tax rate) paid and income. To determine whether a tax system is proportional, progressive, or regressive, we simply ask the question: "What is the relationship between the average tax rate and the marginal tax rate?"

**PROPORTIONAL TAXATION. Proportional taxation** means that regardless of an individual's income, the taxes comprise exactly the same proportion, also called a flat-rate tax. In terms of marginal versus average tax rates, in a proportional taxation system, the marginal tax rate is always equal to the average tax rate. If every dollar is taxed at 20 percent, then the average tax rate is 20 percent, as is the marginal tax rate.

As mentioned earlier, a proportional tax system is also called a flat-rate tax. Taxpayers at all income levels end up paying the same percentage of their income in taxes. If the proportional tax rate were 20 percent, an individual with an income of $10 000 would pay $2000 in taxes, while an individual making $100 000 would pay $20 000, the identical 20 percent rate being levied on both. See this chapter's Issues and Applications for a more in-depth look at the flat tax issue.

**Proportional taxation** A tax system in which regardless of an individual's income, the tax bill comprises exactly the same proportion. Also called a flat-rate tax.

**PROGRESSIVE TAXATION.** Under **progressive taxation**, as a person's taxable income increases, the percentage of income paid in taxes also increases. In terms of marginal versus average tax rates, in a progressive system, the marginal tax rate is above the average tax rate. If you are taxed 5 percent on the first $10 000 you make, 10 percent on the next $10 000 you make, and 30 percent on the last $10 000 you make, you face a progressive income tax system. Your marginal tax rate is always above your average tax rate. Read Policy Example 16–3 to see how Canada compares with other countries.

**Progressive taxation** As taxable income increases, the percentage of income paid in taxes also increases.

**REGRESSIVE TAXATION.** With **regressive taxation**, a smaller percentage of taxable income is taken in taxes as taxable income increases. The marginal rate is below the average rate. As income increases, the marginal tax rate falls, and so does the average tax rate. The Goods and Services Tax (GST) is regressive. Someone earning $10 000 per year pays the same sales tax on a tube of toothpaste as someone earning $100 000 per year. But the tube of toothpaste takes up a much larger proportion of the low-income earner's budget, and so the marginal tax rate for that person is higher. The federal government tries to address this inequity by giving GST rebates to low-income earners who apply for them on their income tax returns each year.

**Regressive taxation** A smaller percentage of taxable income is taken in taxes as taxable income increases.

[2]The word *marginal* means "incremental" (or "decremental") here.

### POLICY EXAMPLE 16–3 Tax Freedom Day around the World

One of the measures that is getting a lot of attention from people is tax freedom day. Tax freedom day is the day people stop working to pay taxes to various governments and start working to pay themselves. It is easier for the average person to understand than a discussion on marginal and average tax rates. Canadians frequently complain that we pay too much tax, so the tax freedom day gives a quick, understandable measure of how we are doing against other nations.

**TABLE 16–1**

| Country | Day of Year | % Burden | Date of Year |
|---|---|---|---|
| India | 74 | 20% | 14-Mar |
| Albania | 84 | 23% | 25-Mar |
| Australia | 99 | 27% | 10-Apr |
| United States | 114 | 31% | 24-Apr |
| Estonia | 114 | 31% | 24-Apr |
| Switzerland | 121 | 33% | 1-May |
| Bulgaria | 121 | 33% | 2-May |
| Lithuania | 128 | 35% | 15-May |
| Belarus | 135 | 37% | 15-May |
| Slovenia | 164 | 37% | 13-Jun |
| Hungary | 140 | 38% | 20-May |
| Uruguay | 133 | 39% | 13-May |
| New Zealand | 141 | 39% | 21-May |
| South Africa | 141 | 39% | 22-May |
| Brazil | 151 | 41% | 31-May |
| United Kingdom | 154 | 42% | 3-Jun |
| Slovakia | 152 | 42% | 1-Jun |
| Canada | 157 | 43% | 6-Jun |
| Croatia | 161 | 44% | 10-Jun |
| Czech Republic | 161 | 44% | 11-Jun |
| Greece | 169 | 46% | 19-Jun |
| Poland | 173 | 47% | 22-Jun |
| Spain | 181 | 50% | 30-Jun |
| Germany | 192 | 52% | 11-Jul |
| Turkey | 194 | 53% | 14-Jul |
| Israel | 197 | 54% | 14-Jul |
| Norway | 210 | 57% | 29-Jul |
| France | 210 | 57% | 29-Jul |
| Belgium | 218 | 60% | 6-Aug |

Source: "Tax freedom day." Wikipedia. https://en.wikipedia.org/wiki/Tax_Freedom_Day. (Accessed March 13, 2017)

**For critical analysis:** Looking at all of the tax freedom days from around the world, how is Canada doing in comparison?

## The Most Important Federal Taxes

The federal government imposes income taxes on both individuals and corporations, and collects sales taxes as well as a variety of other taxes.

## The Federal Personal Income Tax

The most important tax in the Canadian economy is the federal personal income tax, which accounts for about 48 percent of all federal revenues. All Canadian citizens, non-residents, and most others who earn income in Canada are required to pay federal income tax on all taxable income. The tax rates depend on the amount of taxable income earned, as can be seen in Table 16–2. Marginal income tax rates at the federal level have varied from as low as 4 percent after the passage of the *Income Tax Act* in 1917, to as high as 98 percent during World War II.

Advocates of a more progressive income tax system in Canada argue that such a system redistributes income from the rich to the poor, taxes people according to their ability to pay, and taxes people according to the benefits they receive from government. Although there is much controversy over the "redistributional" nature of our progressive tax system, there is no strong evidence that, in fact, the tax system has ever done much income redistribution in this country. Currently, about 80 percent of all Canadians, rich or poor, pay roughly the same proportion of their income in federal income tax.

**TABLE 16–2**

**Federal Tax Rates (as of 2017)**

- 15% **on the first** $45,916 of taxable income, +
- 20.5% **on the next** $45,915 of taxable income (on the portion of taxable income over $45,916 up to $91,831), +
- 26% **on the next** $50,522 of taxable income (on the portion of taxable income over $91,831 up to $142,353), +
- 29% **on the next** $60,447 of taxable income (on the portion of taxable income over $142,353 up to $202,800), +
- 33% of taxable income **over** $202,800.

Source: http://www.cra-arc.gc.ca/tx/ndvdls/fq/txrts-eng.html.

## The Treatment of Capital Gains

The positive difference between the buying and selling prices of an asset, such as a share of stock or a plot of land, is called a **capital gain**, and the negative difference between the purchase price and the sale price of an asset is called a **capital loss**. Capital gains are taxed at ordinary income marginal tax rates. The taxable part of a capital gain is 50 percent of the net amount of your capital gains minus 50 percent of your capital losses for the year.

**Capital gain** The positive difference between the buying and selling prices of an asset.

**Capital loss** The negative difference between the purchase price and the sale price of an asset.

Capital gains are not always real. In Canada, gains on principal are not taxed, but if in one year you pay $100 000 for a house you plan to rent and sell it at a 50 percent higher price 10 years later, your nominal capital gain is $50 000. But what if, during those 10 years, there had been such inflation that average prices had also gone up by 50 percent? Your real capital gain would be zero. But you still have to pay taxes on that $50 000. To counter this problem, many economists have argued that capital gains should be indexed to the rate of inflation.

## The Corporate Income Tax

Corporate income taxes account for about 14 percent of all federal taxes collected, and 3.4 percent of all provincial taxes collected. Corporations are generally taxed at a flat rate of 28 percent on the difference between their total revenues (or receipts) and their expenses.

**DOUBLE TAXATION.** Because individual shareholders must pay taxes on the dividends they receive, paid out of after-tax profits by the corporation, corporate profits are taxed twice. If you receive $1000 in dividends, you have to declare it as income, and you must pay taxes at your marginal tax rate. Before the corporation was able to pay you those dividends, it had to pay taxes on all its profits, including any that it put back into the company or did not distribute in the form of dividends. Eventually, the new investment made possible by those **retained earnings**—profits not given out to shareholders—along with borrowed funds will be reflected in the increased value of the shares in that company. When you sell your shares in that company, you will have to pay taxes on the difference between what you paid for them and what you sold them for. In both cases, dividends and retained earnings (corporate profits) are taxed twice.

**Retained earnings** Profits not given out to shareholders.

**WHO REALLY PAYS THE CORPORATE INCOME TAX?** Corporations can exist only as long as employees make their goods, consumers buy their products, shareholders (owners) buy their shares, and bondholders buy their bonds. Corporations *per se* do not do

**Tax incidence** The distribution of tax burdens among various groups in society.

anything. We must ask, then, who really pays the tax on corporate income. This is a question of **tax incidence**, the distribution of tax burdens among various groups in society. (The question of tax incidence applies to all taxes, including sales and payroll taxes.) There remains considerable debate about the incidence of corporate taxation. Some economists say that corporations pass their tax burdens on to consumers by charging higher prices. Other economists believe that it is the shareholders who bear most of the tax. Still others believe that employees pay at least part of the tax by receiving lower wages than they would otherwise. Because the debate is not yet settled, we will not hazard a guess here as to what the correct conclusion should be. Suffice it to say that you should be cautious when you advocate increasing corporate income taxes. You may be the one who ends up paying the increase, at least in part, if you own shares in a corporation, buy its products, or work for it.

## Unemployment and Pension Taxes

An increasing percentage of federal revenues is accounted for each year by taxes (other than income taxes) levied on payroll. These payroll taxes are for Canada Pension Plan (CPP) benefits and employment insurance (EI).

Employment insurance is a compulsory federal program that provides income assistance in the event of unemployment. EI premiums are paid by employees and matched by employers. (The employer's contribution is really paid, at least in part, in the form of a reduced wage paid to employees, as explained in Example 16–2.) The maximum employee premium for the year 2017 was $836.19. EI premiums become part of government's general revenues; as of 1999, there was a large surplus in the EI account, which helped the federal government balance the budget for the 1999–2000 fiscal year.

### EXAMPLE 16–2 Employment Insurance

Countless articles have been written about the problem with the EI system in Canada. They all make reference to the employer and employee "contributions" to the EI fund. One gets the impression that EI premiums paid by employees go into a special government account and that employees do not pay for their employers' "contribution" to this account. Both concepts are not only flawed but grossly misleading as well. EI premiums are mixed in with the rest of government taxes collected and spent every year. The "contributions" are not contributions at all; they are merely taxes paid to the federal government. The so-called employer contribution, which matches the employee payments, is not, in fact, paid for by employers but rather by employees because of the lower wages that they are paid. Anybody who quits a job and becomes self-employed finds this out when the time comes to pay one's self-employment taxes (employment insurance "contributions"), which effectively double the payments previously being made as an employee.

**For critical analysis:** Should EI premiums go into a special account?

In 2017, the Canada Pension Plan (CPP) premium payable on eligible earnings to $55,300 was 4.95 percent, with employers contributing an equal share on behalf of the employee. CPP premiums do not form part of government's general revenue but are managed separately from the government budget. The CPP is a system in which current workers subsidize already retired workers. With the coming retirement of the postwar "baby boomers," the number of retired people will grow much more rapidly than the number of current workers. In anticipation of increased outlays in pension plan benefits, the combined (employer–employee) premium has risen to 9.9 percent of eligible earnings.

## The Goods and Services Tax

The Goods and Services Tax (GST) is a sales tax that makes up about 11 percent of federal government revenues. Consumers pay a 5 percent tax on virtually all goods and services they purchase in addition to any applicable provincial sales taxes. Prior to January 2008, the GST was 6 percent, having been reduced from 7 percent in 2006. The GST is a regressive tax, since it taxes consumption at the same rate for both the rich and the poor. The federal government tries to mitigate this, however, by giving a rebate of up to $76 four times a year to low-income earners. While consumers must pay GST on imports, Canadian exports are exempt.

Some economists argue that in spite of the regressive nature of sales taxes, such a tax as the GST is preferable to an income tax. Income taxes tax all income, whether it is spent or saved. Therefore, they argue, saving is discouraged. However, a sales tax taxes only income that is consumed, and so saving is encouraged. This chapter's Issues and Applications section revisits the pros and cons of this topic.

## Spending, Government Size, and Tax Receipts

The size of the public sector can be measured in many different ways. One way is to count the number of public employees. Another is to look at government outlays. Government outlays include all of the government expenditures on goods and services as well as all transfer payments. Transfer payments include employment insurance benefits, welfare, and old age security. In Figure 16–2, you can see that total government outlays (as a percentage of GDP) peaked in 2009 at about 44 percent and have since declined to 41 percent.

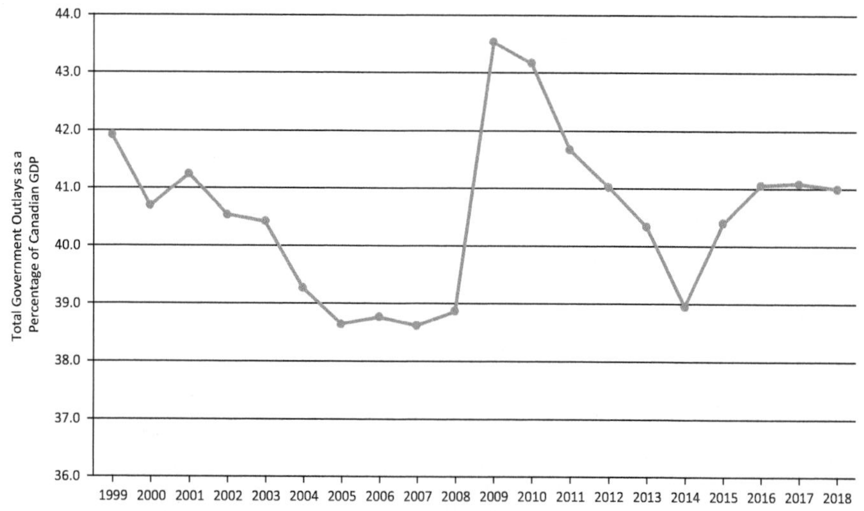


**FIGURE 16–2**
**Government Total Outlays over Time**

Total government outlays (as a percentage of GDP).

Source: "OECD Economic Outlook Annex Table 29". March 2017. http://www.oecd.org/eco/outlook/economic-outlook-annex-tables.htm.

## Government Receipts

The main revenue raiser for all levels of government is taxes. We show in the two pie diagrams in Figure 16–3 the percentage of receipts from various taxes obtained by the federal government and by the provincial and municipal governments.

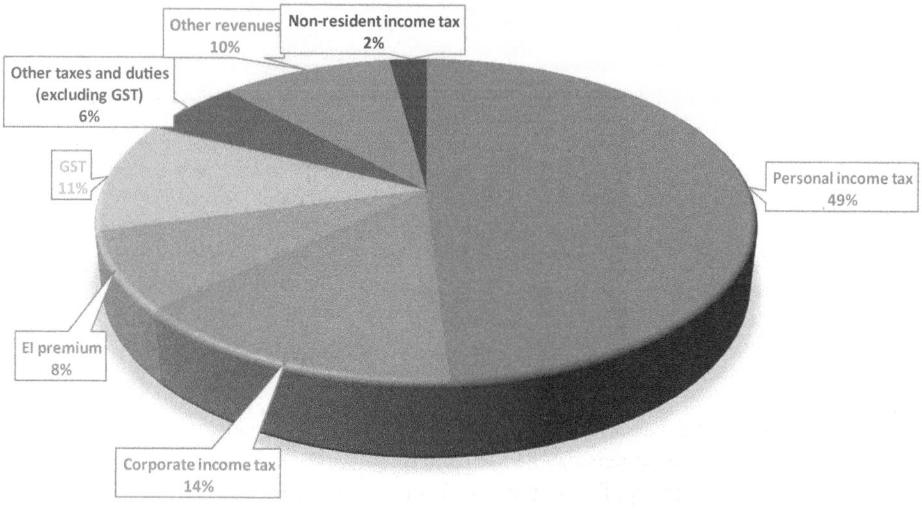


**FIGURE 16–3**
**Federal Revenues 2015–16**

Source: "Composition of revenues for 2015–16." Annual Financial Report of the Government of Canada Fiscal Year 2015–2016. Department of Finance Canada.https://www.fin.gc.ca/afr-rfa/2016/report-rapport-eng.asp#_Toc463249478.

**FIGURE 16–4**

**Federal Expenditures 2015–16**

Source: "Composition of expenses for 2015–16." Annual Financial Report of the Government of Canada Fiscal Year 2015–2016. Department of Finance Canada.https://www.fin.gc.ca/afr-rfa/2016/report-rapport-eng.asp#_Toc463249478.

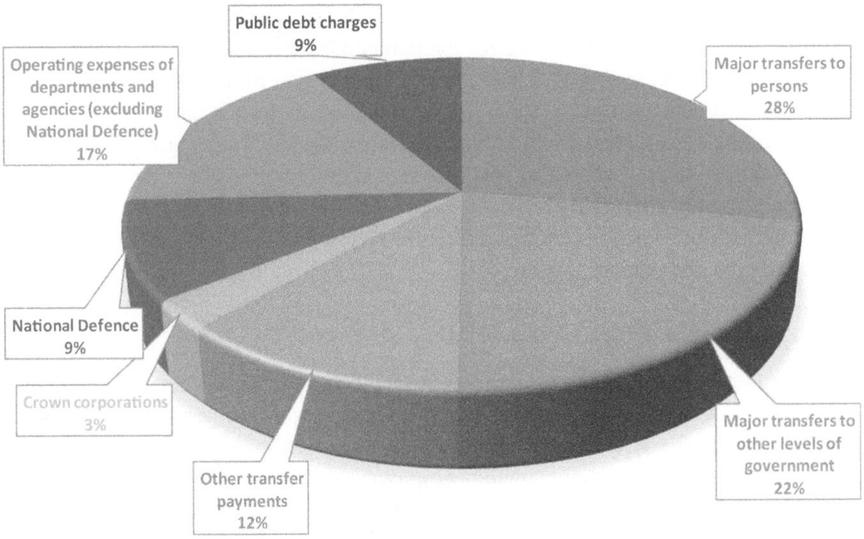


**THE FEDERAL GOVERNMENT.** The largest source of receipts for the federal government is the individual income tax. In 2006–7, individual income taxes accounted for 66 percent of all federal revenues. In 2008–9, they accounted for only 49.8 percent, a decrease of 16 percent, and they have held steady at about 49 percent since.

**COMPARING FEDERAL SPENDING WITH PROVINCIAL AND MUNICIPAL SPENDING.** A typical federal government budget is given in Figure 16–4. The categories of most importance in the federal budget are transfers to persons and governments, which make up over 50 percent.

## ISSUES AND APPLICATIONS

# Should We Switch to a Flat Tax?

### Concepts Applied: Average versus Marginal Tax Rates, Opportunity Cost, Progressive Income Tax System

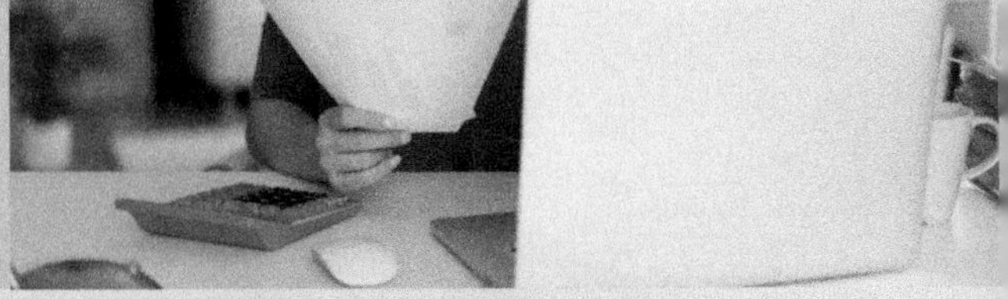

Each year, Canadian taxpayers spend numerous hours preparing their taxes or hire accountants to do so for them. Switching to a national sales tax, one alternative to our current system, would lead to the downsizing of the Canada Revenue Agency and all of the expenses associated with that organization.

Since the introduction of federal income tax, Canadians have faced a progressive system of taxation. The top marginal tax rate soared to 98 percent in 1943, dropped to 80 percent in 1948, dropped again to 60 percent in 1968, and settled at 47 percent starting in 1971. Government reduced the top marginal tax rate to 34 percent in 1983; today, it stands at 29 percent. The idea behind a progressive tax system is that the "rich" should pay more. In actuality, what happens is quite a different story. In Figure 16–5, you see that regardless of what the top tax rate is, the federal government obtains around 45 percent of its annual income as tax revenues.

Why? Because people respond to incentives. At high marginal tax rates, the following occurs: (1) Rich people hire more tax lawyers and accountants to help them figure out loopholes in the tax system to avoid high marginal tax rates; (2) Some people change their investments to take advantage of loopholes that allow them to pay lower marginal tax rates; (3) Some people drop out of the labour force, particularly secondary income earners, such as lower-paid working women; and (4) More people engage in off-the-books "underground" activities for cash on which no income taxes are paid.

## An Alternative: The Flat Tax

For decades, many economists have argued in favour of scrapping our progressive income tax system and replacing it with a so-called flat tax. The idea behind a flat tax is simple. To calculate what you owe, simply subtract the appropriate exemption from your income and multiply the rest by the flat tax rate, say, 20 percent. For example, a family of four might be able to earn as much as $25 000 or $35 000 a year before it paid any income tax. The major benefits of such a system, according to its advocates, would be the following: (1) fewer resources devoted to figuring out one's taxes; (2) fewer tax lawyers and accountants, who could then be engaged in more productive activities; (3) higher savings and investment; and (4) more economic growth. Opponents of a flat tax argue that (1) federal revenues will fall and a federal budget deficit will occur; and (2) the rich will pay less tax.

## Another Alternative: A National Sales Tax

Alternatively, we could apply some form of a value-added tax (VAT) in place of the current income tax. VAT is common throughout Europe. VAT is assessed on the value added by a firm at each stage of production. It is a tax on the value of products that a firm sells minus the value of the materials that it bought and used to produce the products. Such a tax is collected by all businesses and remitted directly to the federal government. One of the major benefits of VAT is that it would significantly downsize the Canada Revenue Agency and the expenses associated with that government department. A VAT of, say, 15 to 20 percent in lieu of a federal income tax would be quite similar to a consumption tax.

## A Consumption Tax

With a consumption tax, taxpayers pay taxes only on what they consume (spend) out of their incomes, not on all of what they earn. One way to determine such consumption in any year is simply to subtract what is saved from what is earned. The difference is consumption, and that is the base to which a consumption tax would apply. (A consumption tax is actually equivalent to the GST on all goods and services purchased.) In essence, a consumption tax provides an unlimited deduction for saving. As such, it encourages more saving. The less people choose to consume today, the faster the production possibilities curve will shift outward to the right, leading to more economic growth.

## What about Fairness?

Every time a new tax system is discussed, the issue of fairness arises. Is it fair, as with a flat federal income tax, that everybody pays the same marginal tax rate, no matter how much each individual earns? Stephen Entin of the Institute for Research on the Economics of Taxation thinks it is: "It is hard to find a definition of 'fairness' more compelling than the idea that every citizen is treated equally." What about a consumption tax, which might be regressive because the poor spend a larger portion of their income than the rich? Is that a "fair" system? For most economists, these are difficult questions because they are in the realm of the normative, the value-laden. We can point out that an examination of the evidence shows what reality is. Simply stated, when marginal income tax rates are high, the rich do

**FIGURE 16–5**

### Changing Maximum Marginal Income Tax Rates and Revenues Collected

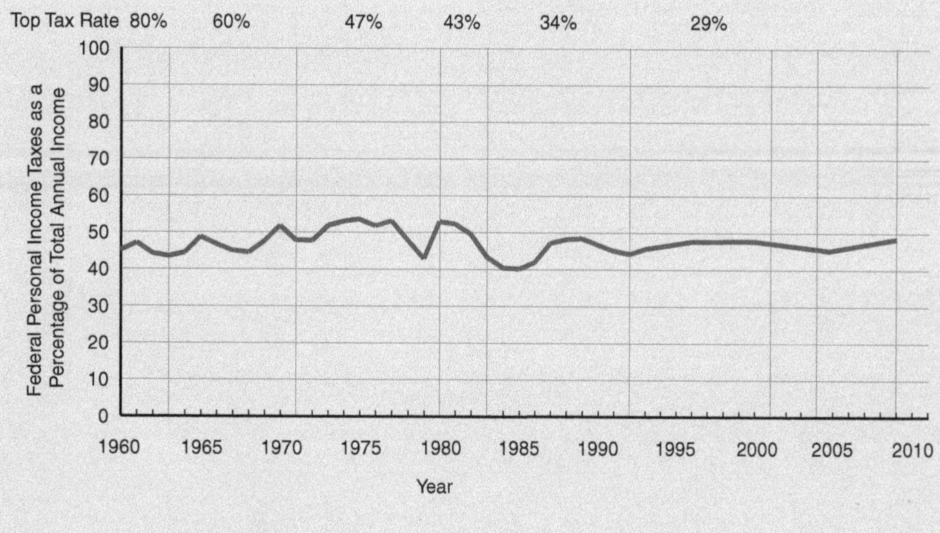


At the top of the diagram, you can see listed the top marginal tax rates from 1960 to 2010. On the side is the percentage of total annual income collected by the federal government from the income tax system. No matter how high the marginal income tax rate has been, government has collected about the same percentage of national income in taxes.

Source: W. Irwin Gillespie, *Tax, Borrow & Spend: Financing Federal Spending In Canada 1867–1990*. Ottawa: Carleton University Press, 1991.

not, in fact, pay a higher average tax rate than when marginal tax rates are lower. It behooves the rich to find methods to reduce tax liabilities and to expend resources to influence politicians to insert an increasing number of loopholes in the *Income Tax Act* in order to reduce effective marginal tax rates on those who earn a lot.

**For critical analysis:**

1. Do you think employees at the Canada Revenue Agency would be for or against the flat-tax system? Explain your choice.
2. Why is a flat-tax system more efficient than a progressive income tax system?

# SUMMARY

Here is what you should know after reading this chapter. MyEconLab will help you identify what you know, and where to go when you need to practise. We suggest that as soon as you review one of the Learning Objective sections below, you then proceed to go through the related section in MyEconLab.

| LEARNING OBJECTIVES | KEY TERMS | MYECONLAB PRACTICE |
| --- | --- | --- |
| **16.1 Economic Functions of Government.** Government provides a legal system in which the rights of private ownership, the enforcement of contracts, and the legal status of businesses are provided. In other words, government sets the legal rules of the game and enforces them.<br>Public goods, once produced, can be consumed jointly by additional individuals at zero opportunity cost. If users of public goods know that they will be taxed on the basis of their expressed valuation of those public goods, their expressed valuation will be low. They expect to get a free ride. | property rights, 397<br>monopoly, 398<br>private goods, 398<br>principle of rival consumption, 398<br>public goods, 398<br>exclusion principle, 398<br>free-rider problem, 399 | • **MyEconLab** Study Plan 16.1 |

| LEARNING OBJECTIVES | KEY TERMS | MYECONLAB PRACTICE |
|---|---|---|
| **16.2 The Political Functions of Government.** Merit goods (chosen as such, collectively, through the political process) may not be purchased at all or not in sufficient quantities at market-clearing prices. Therefore, government subsidizes or provides such merit goods at a subsidized or zero price to specified classes of consumers.<br>When it is collectively decided that something is a demerit good, government taxes, regulates, or prohibits the manufacture, sale, and use of that good.<br>The market sector and the public sector both face scarcity, feature competition, and contain similar individuals. They differ in that many government, or political, goods are provided at zero price. Collective action may involve the use of force, and political voting can lead to different results from that of dollar voting.<br>Bureaucrats often exert great influence on the course of policy because they are in charge of the day-to-day operation of current policy and provide much of the information needed to formulate future policy. Bureaucracies often organize their clientele, coach clients on what is appropriate, and stick up for their rights. | merit good, 400<br>demerit good, 401<br>transfers in kind, 401<br>collective decision making, 401<br>theory of public choice, 401<br>incentive structure, 402<br>government, or political, goods, 402<br>majority rule, 403<br>proportional rule, 403<br>bureaucrats, 403<br>bureaucracy, 403 | • **MyEconLab** Study Plan 16.2 |
| **16.3 Tax Rates and the Canadian Tax System.** Marginal tax rates are those paid on the last dollar of income, whereas average tax rates are determined by the proportion of income paid in income taxes.<br>With a proportional income tax system, marginal rates are constant. With a regressive system, they go down as income rises, and with a progressive system, they go up as income rises.<br>Government spending at the federal level is different from that at the provincial and municipal levels. Interest on the debt, elderly benefits, and transfers to the provinces account for almost 60 percent of the federal budget. Health care and education constitute over 40 percent of provincial government expenditures. | marginal tax rate, 405<br>tax bracket, 405<br>average tax rate, 405<br>proportional taxation, 405<br>progressive taxation, 405<br>regressive taxation, 405<br>capital gain, 407<br>capital loss, 407<br>retained earnings, 407<br>tax incidence, 408 | • **MyEconLab** Study Plan 16.3 |

## PROBLEMS

(Answers to the odd-numbered problems appear at the back of the book.)

**LO 16.1** Explain the four economic functions of government.

1. TV signals have characteristics of public goods, yet TV stations and commercial networks are private businesses. Analyze this situation.
2. Assume that you live in a relatively small suburban neighbourhood called Parkwood. The Parkwood Homeowners' Association collects money from homeowners to pay for upkeep of the surrounding stone wall, lighting at the entrances to Parkwood, and mowing the lawn around the perimeter of the area. Each year you are asked to donate $50. No one forces you to do it. There are 100 homeowners in Parkwood.
   a. What percentage of the total yearly revenue of the homeowners' association will you account for?
   b. At what level of participation will the absence of your $50 contribution make a difference?
   c. If you do not contribute your $50, are you really receiving a totally free ride?

**LO 16.2** Describe the two main political functions of government and how decision making differs depending on whether the individual is in the public or private sector.

3. A favourite political campaign theme in recent years has been to reduce the size, complexity, and bureaucratic nature of the federal government. Nonetheless, the size of the federal government, however measured, continues to increase. Use the theory of public choice to explain why.
4. Your small town would like to showcase all of the history of the town in a museum. What type of good would that be, and would government be likely to subsidize the museum or not? Why?
5. According to Policy Example 16–3, "Tax Freedom Day around the World," Canada's tax freedom day is June 19, while the U.S. tax freedom day is April 30. What does that imply about Canada's level of taxation?

**LO 16.3** Distinguish between average and marginal tax rates and explain the Canadian tax system.

6. Consider the following system of taxation, which has been labelled *degressive*. The first $5000 of income is not taxed. After that, all income is assessed at 20 percent (a proportional system). What is the marginal tax rate on $3000 of taxable income? $10 000? $100 000? What is the average tax rate on $3000? $10 000? $100 000? What is the maximum average tax rate?
7. You are offered two possible bonds to buy as part of your investment program. One is a corporate bond yielding 9 percent. The other is a tax-exempt municipal bond yielding only 6 percent. Assuming that you are certain you will be paid your interest and principal on these two bonds, what marginal tax bracket must you be in to decide in favour of the tax-exempt bond?
8. Consider the following tax structure:
   Mr. Smith has an income of $2500 per annum. Calculate his tax bill for the year. What is his average tax rate? His highest marginal tax rate?

| Income Bracket | Marginal Tax Rate |
|---|---|
| $0–$1500 | 0% |
| $1501–$2000 | 14% |
| $2001–$3000 | 20% |

9. In 2010, Canada Pension Plan premiums were 4.95 percent on wages up to $47 200. No further CPP premiums are paid on earnings above this figure. Calculate the average CPP tax rate for annual wages of (a) $4000, (b) $51 300, (c) $56 000, (d) $100 000. Is the CPP system a progressive, proportional, or regressive tax structure?

# BUSINESS APPLICATION

**LO 16.3 Distinguish between average and marginal tax rates and explain the Canadian tax system.**

## Small Business: Income Tax Planning Strategies

A sole proprietor of a business pays personal income tax on the profit earned by the business (not the corporate profit tax). For the following problems, refer to the tax table and the formulae displayed below.

The *marginal tax rate (MTR)* relating to the highest tax bracket of a sole-proprietor tax payer is frequently used to determine the tax savings that can be achieved using legal tax planning strategies. The following two formulae are frequently used:

*Formula 1: Extra Dollar Tax Payable = MTR × Extra Income Earned*

*Formula 2: Extra Dollar Tax Savings = MTR × Extra Deductions Claimed*

The table below compares the top marginal tax rates that apply to a sole proprietor earning an annual taxable income of $50 000 in the different Canadian provinces in 1998. The marginal tax rates shown combine the federal and provincial personal income tax rates for each province. (Source: *EY/Personal RRSP Calculator 1998, Ernst* and Young, June 22, 1998. Online. Internet. July 26, 1998. Available at http://www.eycan.com/tax/taxtools/98taxcalc/all.htm)

| | Top Marginal Tax Rates (in Percent) | | |
|---|---|---|---|
| **Province** | **Dividends** | **Capital Gains** | **Other Income** |
| British Columbia | 24.78 | 30.52 | 40.69 |
| Alberta | 24.93 | 30.31 | 40.42 |
| Saskatchewan | 29.61 | 34.49 | 45.99 |
| Manitoba | 29.86 | 33.61 | 44.82 |
| Ontario | 23.55 | 29.01 | 38.68 |
| Quebec | 31.89 | 34.76 | 46.34 |
| New Brunswick | 26.44 | 32.57 | 43.42 |
| Nova Scotia | 25.89 | 31.88 | 42.51 |
| P.E.I. | 27.15 | 33.43 | 44.58 |
| Newfoundland | 27.71 | 34.13 | 45.50 |

The Other Income category in the table applies to the net profit earned by sole-proprietor businesses. According to formula 1 and the table above, if a sole proprietor in B.C. earns an extra $1000 of profit, his or her extra tax payable would be $1000 × .4069 = $406.90

Some of the common tax planning strategies used to minimize a sole proprietor's personal income tax payable are described below. Of course, it is important to consult the *General Tax Guide* and the Canada Revenue Agency before applying any of these strategies.

### Strategy 1: Deducting home expenses related to a home business

1. Jane Doan uses about one-third of her home to run a small daycare business, as the sole proprietor, in New Brunswick. On her 1998 tax return, Jane claimed one-third of the following home expenses: utilities, mortgage interest, property taxes, insurance, telephone, maintenance and repairs, and depreciation on the home computer. In total, she claimed $9000 for just these home-related expenses. Calculate her extra tax savings.

### Strategy 2: Income splitting

2. Jody Coliger operates a sole-proprietor business writing and self-publishing college textbooks in Newfoundland. Until she hired her husband to help her with the business, she was earning $75 000 of taxable profit per year and was paying a 37.9 percent average tax rate. In order to reduce her tax payable, she hired her unemployed husband and paid him a salary of $25 000 in 1998 to operate the publishing side of the business. He pays an average tax rate of 21.5 percent on this salary. With her husband in the business, Jody now claims only $50 000 of taxable profit and so only pays a 31.6 percent average tax rate.
3. a. Calculate Jody's total tax payable when she was working alone in her business.
   b. Calculate the combined total tax payable incurred by Jody and her husband when they both worked in the business.
   c. How much total tax did this family save through this practice of income splitting?
   d. Would income splitting reduce tax payable if Canada adopted a flat-rate income tax system?

# Answers to Odd-Numbered Problems

## Chapter 1: The Nature of Economics

1. a. human capital
   b. land
   c. entrepreneurship
   d. physical capital
   e. labour
3. a. Macroeconomic, as the unemployment rate is national or economywide.
   b. Microeconomic, as wage increases of specific occupations, such as nurses and doctors, relate to specific parts of the economy.
   c. Microeconomic, as prices of a specific part of the economy—cigarettes—are being studied.
   d. Macroeconomic, as the inflation rate tracks the average price of all goods, which is an economywide measure.
   e. Macroeconomic, as the nation's total annual production is an economywide measure.
   f. Microeconomic, as an individual firm's situation, such as Eaton's bankruptcy, focuses on a specific part of the economy.
5. Jon's marginal cost of enrolling in the two-month computer course equals the cost of tuition, books, and fees plus the two months of earnings he sacrifices. This amounts to: $4500 + (2 × $3000) = $10 500
7. No, your cash withdrawals are not free as there is an opportunity cost equal to the interest sacrificed by not putting your $5000 in an account (or another investment) giving you a higher rate of interest.
9. The decision based on availability of funds is not a rational one. In order to allocate resources in a manner that maximizes the satisfaction of the city's wants, the mayor should compare the marginal (extra) benefit of constructing the city hall with the marginal (extra) cost, including alternatives sacrificed. If the extra benefit to the city of constructing the city hall is less than the value of some other alternative that has to be sacrificed, such as paving of city roads, the mayor's decision is not rational.
11. a. We should observe younger drivers to be more frequently involved in traffic accidents than older persons.
    b. Slower monetary expansion should be associated with lower inflation.
    c. Professional basketball players receiving smaller salaries should be observed to have done less well in their high-school studies.
    d. Employees being promoted rapidly should have lower rates of absenteeism than those being promoted more slowly.
13. a. Positive, for it is a statement that can be tested by the facts.
    b. Normative, involving a value judgment about what should be.
    c. Normative, involving a value judgment about what should be.
    d. Positive, for it is a statement that can be tested by the facts.

## Appendix A: Reading and Working with Graphs

A-1. a. Price is independent, number of notebooks is dependent.
     b. Work-study hours is independent, credit hours is dependent.
     c. Hours studied is independent, and grade is dependent.

A-3.

| x | y |
|---|---|
| 4 | 12 |
| 3 | 9 |
| 2 | 6 |
| 1 | 3 |
| 0 | 0 |
| –1 | –3 |
| –2 | –6 |
| –3 | –9 |
| –4 | –12 |

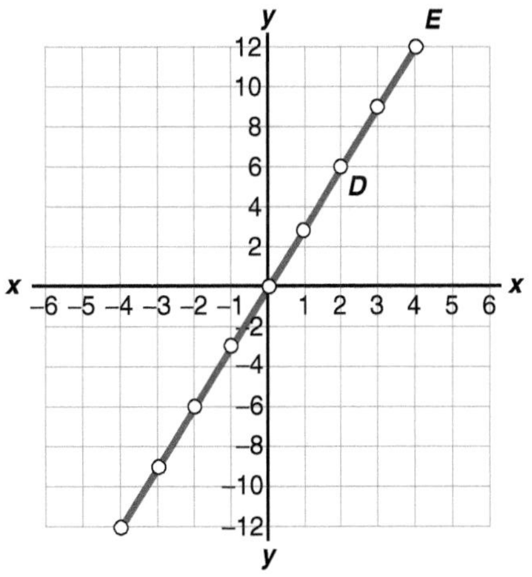

A-5. If you move along the line in Problem A-3 from point $D$ to point $E$, the slope equals the change in the $y$-values divided by the change in the $x$-values, which is:

$$(12 - 6)/(4 - 2) = 6/2 = 3.$$

A-7. For the ordered pair (4, 16) the tangent line is upward sloping, slope is positive.

For the ordered pair (0, 0) the tangent line is horizontal, slope is zero.

For the ordered pair (−4, 16) the tangent line is downward sloping, slope is negative.

## Chapter 2: Production Possibilities and Economic Systems

1. a. The maximum amount of factories will be 2000 as shown by the production possibilities curve.
   b. The maximum number of factories would be 5000, as shown by combination $A$.
   c. A fixed amount of resources and technology prevents Epica from being able to produce combination $J$ in 2017.
   d. If Epica is at point $I$, this could conflict with the goals of productive efficiency and full employment.
   e. i. The opportunity cost of an additional factory when moving from point $E$ to $D$ would be 2 yachts.
      ii. The opportunity cost of an additional factory when moving from point $C$ to $B$ would be 4 yachts.
   f. i. The opportunity cost of an additional yacht when moving from point $A$ to $B$ would be $1/5$ of a factory.
      ii. The opportunity cost of an additional yacht when moving from point $E$ to $F$ would be 1 factory.
   g. The Law of Increasing Relative Cost
   h. This situation conflicts with allocative efficiency.
   i. Economic growth will shift the production possibilities curve outward.

3. The plot of the product possibilities curve is displayed in the graph below.

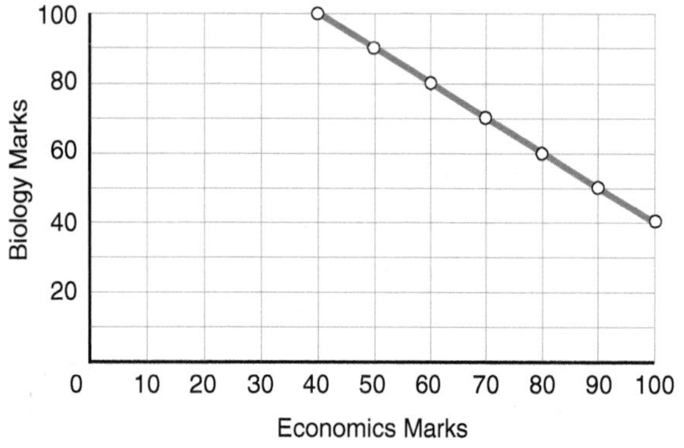


The PPC exhibits constant opportunity costs. That is, the cost of earning an additional mark in economics is always the same, in terms of additional biology marks sacrificed. In this case, the PPC is a straight line with the opportunity cost of earning an additional mark in economics always being 1 mark in biology.

5.

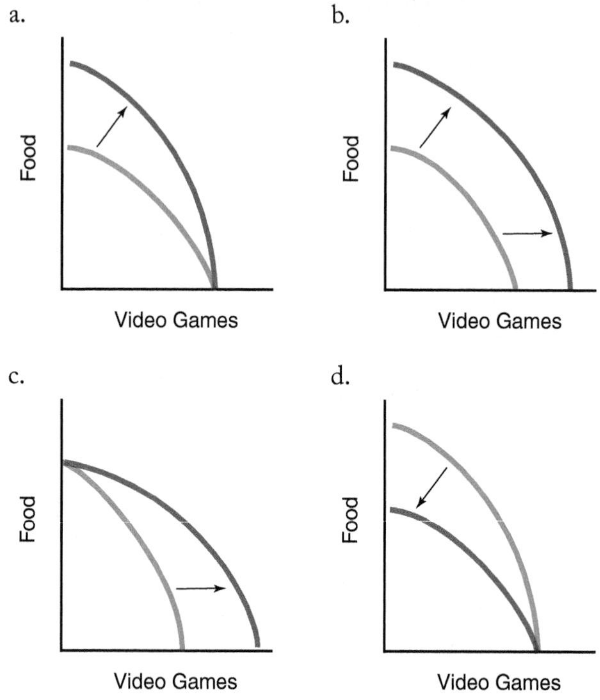


7. If we assume that a two-year college diploma consists of four 15-week semesters, this amounts to committing 60 weeks to college studies. The opportunity cost is: 60 wks × 35 h × \$7 = \$14 700. The incentive for incurring this cost is that, upon graduating, you will be earning an amount significantly in excess of \$7 per hour. You are sacrificing current consumption to obtain a greater amount of future consumption.

9. Yes, you and your roommate should specialize. Since your opportunity cost of completing a basket of laundry (two meals) is lower than your roommate's (three meals), you should specialize in the laundry completion, while your roommate should specialize in the meal preparation. As an example, if you complete an extra basket of laundry, you give up only two meals. However, you free up an additional three hours of your roommate's time, which allows your roommate to produce an additional three meals. Overall, one extra meal is gained.

11. a. Toby has the absolute advantage in pizzas.
    b. Tony has the lower opportunity cost in producing one lasagne supreme (gives up one pizza versus two pizzas for Toby) so Tony has a comparative advantage in lasagne.
    c. Toby has the comparative advantage in pizza and Tony in lasagne. For each hour of specializing in

the area of comparative advantage, there is a net gain of five pizzas (Toby: +10 pizzas and 5 lasagne; Tony +5 lasagne and −5 pizzas).

13. The invisible hand of self-interest and competition help to ensure that firms serve the consumer, without the heavy hand of government.

15. a. In the market system, the techniques that yield the highest (positive) profits will be used.

b. Profit equals total revenue minus total cost. Because revenue from 100 units is fixed (at $100), if the firm wishes to maximize profit, this is equivalent to minimizing costs. To find total costs, simply multiply the price of each input by the amount of the input that must be used for each technique.

Costs of $A$ = ($10)(6) + ($8)(5) = $100

Costs of $B$ = ($10)(5) + ($8)(6) = $98

Costs of $C$ = ($10)(4) + ($8)(7) = $96

Because technique $C$ has the lowest costs, it also yields the highest profits ($100 − $96 = $4).

c. Following the same methods yields these costs: $A$ = $98, $B$ = $100, and $C$ = $102. Technique $A$ will be used because it is the most profitable.

d. The profits from using technique $A$ to produce 100 units of $X$ are $100 $98 = $2.

## Appendix B: The Production Possibilities Curve and Comparative Advantage

B-1 a. The Richard family has the absolute advantage in each product, assuming that both families use the same amount of labour input, each day.

b. For the Martin family the opportunity cost of one litre of beer is one litre of wine. For the Richard family the opportunity cost of one litre of beer is three litres of wine.

c. The Martin family has the comparative advantage (lower opportunity cost) in beer and the Richard family has the comparative advantage in wine.

d. Total combined beer production increases from three litres to four litres per day, a gain of one litre. Total combined wine production increases from 17 litres to 18 litres per day, a gain of one litre.

e. For both families to share the gains from specialization, one litre of beer should trade for somewhere between one and three litres of wine (between each family's opportunity cost for beer).

## Chapter 3: Demand and Supply

1. The absolute prices of heating oil and natural gas have both increased. The relative price of heating oil decreased as it went from $1.00/$0.80 = 1.25 to $2.00/$3.20 = 0.63. This implies that the relative price of natural gas increased. Yes, consumers will increase their purchases of heating oil relative to natural gas, as heating oil's relative price has declined. This assumes that the prices shown in the table are per constant-quality unit.

3. a. Since the price of a substitute decreases, there will be a decrease in demand for Canadian beef and the demand curve will shift leftward.

b. An increase in demand will occur, where the demand curve shifts rightward.

c. An increase in quantity demanded will occur, which can be described as a movement along (down) the same demand curve.

d. A decrease in demand will occur, where the demand curve will shift leftward.

e. A decrease in quantity demanded will occur, which can be described as a movement along (up) the same demand curve.

5. a. $P_e$ = $11 and $Q_e$ = 80 million CDs.

b. At a price of $13, there would be a surplus equal to (120 − 60) = 60 million CDs. The surplus will drive down the price.

c. At a price of $10, there would be a shortage equal to (90 − 60) = 30 million CDs. The shortage will drive up the price.

7. The graph below illustrates a shift to the right in the demand curve, which indicates an *increase in demand*. The new equilibrium price and quantity are $12 and 100 million CDs. A change in any factor other than the price of CDs will cause an increase in demand, such as an increase in income or an increase in the popularity of rock music.

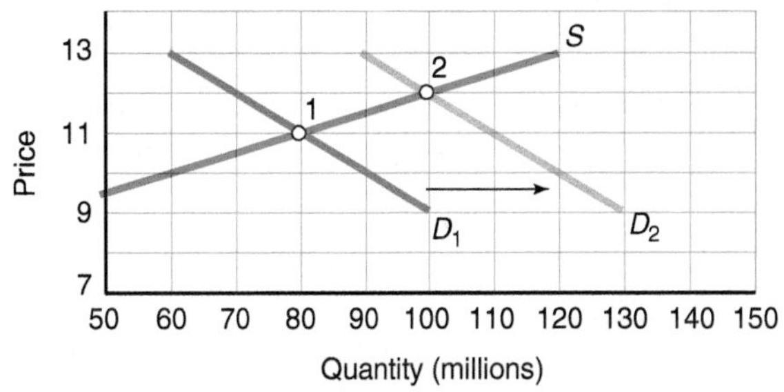


9. a. Increase in quantity demanded $Pe\downarrow$, $Qe\uparrow$ as a result of an increase in supply.

b. Increase in demand $Pe\uparrow$, $Qe\uparrow$

c. Increase in demand $Pe\uparrow$, $Qe\uparrow$

d. Increase in demand $Pe\uparrow$, $Qe\uparrow$

e. Decrease in demand $Pe\downarrow$, $Qe\downarrow$

11. a. At a price of $1.40, there would be a surplus equal to (5 − 3) or 2000 dozen eggs. This will drive down the price.

b. At a price of \$0.80, there would be a shortage equal to (6 − 2) or 4000 dozen eggs. This will drive up the price.

c. The equilibrium price and quantity is \$1.20 and 4000 dozen eggs.

d. i. Increase in demand, $Pe \uparrow$, $Qe \uparrow$

ii. Decrease in supply, $Pe \uparrow$, $Qe \downarrow$

iii. Decrease in demand, $Pe \downarrow$, $Qe \downarrow$

iv. Increase in supply, $Pe \downarrow$, $Qe \uparrow$

13. a. The equilibrium rent and quantity are \$400 and 4000 units per month.

b. There will be a shortage equal to (6 − 2) or 4000 units per month.

c. In the short run, by keeping the price of a substitute (one-bedroom units) lower, there will be a decrease in demand for two-bedroom units, causing a decrease in equilibrium rent and quantity of two-bedroom units. In the longer run, due to the shortage of one-bedroom units, there will be an increase in demand for two-bedroom units, causing equilibrium price and quantity to increase.

15. a. Increase in demand and increase in supply. While the equilibrium quantity will increase, the combined effect on equilibrium price is indeterminate.

b. Decrease in supply and increase in demand. While the equilibrium price will increase, the combined effect on equilibrium quantity is indeterminate.

c. Increase in supply and decrease in demand. While the equilibrium price will decrease, the combined effect on equilibrium quantity is indeterminate.

## Chapter 4: Elasticity

1. a.

| Quantity Demanded per Week (kilograms) | Price per Kilogram | Elasticity |
|---|---|---|
| 1000 | \$ 5 | |
| | | $\frac{1}{3}$, or 0.33 |
| 800 | 10 | |
| | | $\frac{5}{7}$, or 0.714 |
| 600 | 15 | |
| | | $\frac{7}{5}$, or 1.4 |
| 400 | 20 | |
| | | $\frac{9}{3}$, or 3 |
| 200 | 25 | |

b. This would depend on a person's preferences, one of the determinants of demand.

c. A person's preferences and income would determine whether tea is a luxury or necessity.

3. The problem is with the denominator, in calculating the percentage change in *P*. Because the initial price was zero, any increase in price is of infinite percentage. However, if we take the average elasticity over a segment, there will be no problem. *P* will become the average of $P_1$ (= 0) and $P_2$ (= 10), or $(P_1 + P_2)/2 = 5$.

5. a. The price elasticity of demand for cars is elastic.

b. The dealer's total revenue will increase.

7. a. Salt has few substitutes but is a very small portion of the total budget, and so it would be more inelastic.

b. There are many suppliers of ski boats, and so you would probably shop around for the best deal, so it would be more elastic.

c. A guitar pick takes up a very small portion of the total budget for a major rock band, and so it would be very inelastic.

7. No demand curve can possibly be perfectly inelastic, regardless of the price, because perfect inelasticity means absolutely no price responsiveness, no matter what the price, the quantity demanded remains unchanged.

9.

$$\frac{(2000 - 1000)/1500}{(20\,000 - 15\,000)/17\,500} = 0.67/0.286 = 2.34$$

a. The demand is elastic; as people's income increases, the demand for DVDs also increases.

b. Because the number is positive this would be considered a normal or luxury good.

11. a. (525 − 600)/(525 + 600)/ 2/(15 − 17)/ (15 + 17)/2 = 1200/1125 = 1.07

b. The supply of salt is price elastic, the elasticity coefficient of supply is greater than 1.

## Chapter 5: Market Efficiency and Market Failure

1. a. The maximum that consumers are willing to pay for the thousandth litre of PowerPlus is the height of the demand curve at $Q = 1000$ litres, which is \$3.

b. The marginal benefit of the two thousandth litre of PowerPlus is equal to the height of the demand curve at $Q = 2000$ litres, which is \$2.50.

c. The consumer surplus derived from consuming the two thousandth litre of PowerPlus at a price of \$2 equals marginal beneft − price at *Q* equal to 2000, which equals \$2.50 − \$2.00 = \$.50.

d. The minimum that sellers of PowerPlus must receive in order to supply the thousandth litre of PowerPlus is equal to the height of the supply curve at $Q = 1000$, which is \$1.

e. The marginal cost of the two thousandth litre of PowerPlus is equal to the height of the supply curve at $Q = 2000$ litres, which is \$1.50.

f. The producer surplus derived from supplying the thousandth unit of PowerPlus at a price of \$2 equals price − marginal cost at $Q$ equal to 1000 = \$2 − \$1 = \$1.

g. The allocatively efficient quantity level would be at market equilibrium at 3000 litres per week where demand (marginal benefit) equals supply (marginal cost).

h. The maximum total amount of producer and consumer surplus occurs at the market equilibrium quantity level of 3000 litres and equals the total of consumer and producer surplus at this quantity level. This equals the combined area of triangles $ABC$ and $BCD$ = [(1.5 × 3)/2] + [(1.5 × 3)/2] = \$4.5(1000) or \$4500.

i. If the government fixed the weekly quantity level at 2000 litres per week, the total amount of deadweight loss would equal the combined loss of consumer and producer surplus compared to the efficient quantity at 3000 litres. This equals the area between the demand and supply curves between $Q$ = 2000 and 3000 litres = .5 × (1 × 1) = \$.5(1000) = \$500.

3. a. This diagram relates to an external benefit situation, as the social marginal benefit curve ($D_2$) is higher than the private marginal benefit curve ($D_1$) at each quantity.

b. Under a free market, laissez-faire situation, 600 units per month will be produced, where the private demand curve, $D_1$, intersects the supply curve, $S$.

c. The socially optimum (allocatively efficient) quantity level = 800 units per month, where the social marginal benefit curve intersects the supply curve.

d. If the market produced the laissez-faire quantity identified in part b above, the deadweight loss = area between the demand ($D_2$) and supply curves between $Q$ = 600 and 800 litres =.5 × (2 × 200) = \$200.

5. a. Moral hazard is the type of market failure encouraged by the sickness/disability plan. When the individual is covered by the plan, she is able to shift the marginal costs related to living a less healthy lifestyle to the insurance company.

b. Since the sickness/disability plan reduces the individual's private marginal cost of changing to a less healthy lifestyle, the plan tends to overallocate resources to less healthy lifestyles. This can result in higher marginal social costs in the form of increased health costs when individuals get sick and use limited health care resources. If this is a private insurance plan this extra cost is shared by all policy holders, even the healthy ones, through increased insurance premiums.

c. The degree of allocative inefficiency can be reduced if the insurance company inserts terms in the policy that increases the annual premiums for those who claim for more than a stated number of sick days.

7. A common property resource situation will typically lead to the overproduction of a good or service as it is non-excludable but rivalrous. An example is commercial fishing in an ocean where it is difficult to exclude those who did not pay for a licence. The more one firm fishes, the less fish are available to another competing firm. This leads to overfishing.

## Chapter 6: Extensions of Demand, Supply, and Elasticity

1. Ticket scalpers are middlemen who ensure that the scarce tickets get sold to those consumers who value the tickets the most. In other words, scalpers use the price system to ensure an efficient allocation of tickets.

3. a. The equilibrium price and quantity of \$4 and 7 million crates would result.

b. A shortage of (8 − 4) or 4 million crates would occur. This is an example of a price ceiling policy.

c. The maximum black market price is that price associated with a quantity demanded of 4 million crates, which is \$6 per crate.

d. A surplus of (8 − 6) or 2 million crates would occur. This is an example of a price floor policy.

5. a. The equilibrium price and quantity of \$1 and 40 million litres would result.

b. At a maximum price of \$0.80, a shortage of (50 − 30) or 20 million litres will result. This would be called a price ceiling policy.

c. The black market price would be \$1.20.

d. At a minimum price of \$1.40, a surplus of (60 − 20) or 40 million litres will result. This would be called a price floor policy.

7. a. Total revenue received is \$4 per crate × 7 million crates = \$28 million.

b. A surplus of (8 − 6) or 2 million crates would occur. Total revenue received is \$5 × 8 million crates = \$40 million. The total taxpayer cost would be (Support price × Surplus) or (\$5 × 2 million) or \$10 million.

c. At a restricted quantity of 6 million crates, the quantity demanded schedule indicates that consumers would pay a price of \$5. With the marketing board, the total revenue would be (\$5 × 6 million) or 30 million. When the price is increased from the equilibrium price of \$4 to the marketing board price of \$5, the total revenue increases from \$28 million to \$30 million. This implies that the demand is inelastic.

9. a. Total revenue received is \$1 per litre 40 million litres, or \$40 million.

b. An Offer to Purchase price policy of \$1.20 would result in a surplus equal to (50 − 30) or 20 million litres. Total revenue received is \$1.20 × 50 million litres or \$60 million. The total taxpayer cost equals (\$1.20 × 20 million) or \$24 million.

c. If a marketing board restricts the quantity sold to 30 million litres, the price would be \$1.20. The total revenue would be \$1.20 × 30 = \$36 million. When the price is increased from \$1 to \$1.20 the total revenue decreases from \$40 million to \$36 million, indicating that demand is elastic—the marketing board policy does not support the farmer!

11. As illustrated in problem 10, the import quota would increase the price of California wines to Canadian consumers. If demand is inelastic, the higher price will result in Canadians spending a greater total revenue on California wines.

13. a. At the price of \$0.70 per litre, the gas suppliers will receive \$0.50 per litre in their pockets, after paying the \$0.20 per litre tax to the government. According to the before-tax supply table, if the firms receive \$0.50 per litre in their pockets, they will supply 60 million litres per day. Therefore, the after-tax market quantity supplied is 60 million litres when the price is \$0.70 per litre. The other market supplies (in millions of litres) starting with a price of \$0.60 per litre are: 50, 40, 30, 20, 10.

b. The after-tax equilibrium price and quantity is \$0.50 per litre and 40 million litres per day, respectively.

c. Since the equilibrium price went up from \$0.40 per litre to \$0.50 per litre, the buyer's portion of the tax burden equals \$0.10 per litre, which is the price increase. The seller's portion of the tax burden is the tax minus the buyer's portion, which is \$0.20 − \$0.10 = \$0.10 per litre.

d. The total tax revenue equals the tax per unit multiplied by the after-tax equilibrium quantity, which equals \$0.20 per litre × 40 million litres = \$8 million per day.

e. The daily tax revenue will increase when demand becomes less elastic.

f. The tax will more effectively reduce gas consumption when the demand becomes more elastic.

15. a. The before-tax equilibrium price and quantity are \$0.60 per CD and 50 million CDs per month.

b. The excise tax equals \$0.20 per CD, which is the vertical distance between the $S_1$ and $S_2$ supply curves.

c. The after-tax equilibrium price and quantity are \$0.70 per CD and 40 million CDs.

d. The buyers' portion of the tax burden equals the increase in equilibrium price, which is \$0.10 per CD. The seller's portion is equal to the tax per CD minus the buyer's tax burden, which is \$0.20 − \$0.10 = \$0.10 per CD.

e. The total monthly tax revenue equals the after-tax equilibrium quantity multiplied by the per-unit tax, which equals 40 million CDs × \$0.20 per CD equals \$8 million.

f. The tax revenue will increase when supply becomes less elastic.

g. The excise tax will more effectively discourage the use of CDs when supply becomes more elastic.

## APPENDIX C: THE DEADWEIGHT LOSS DUE TO GOVERNMENT PRICE CONTROLS

C-1 a. Under a laissez-faire policy, the equilibrium price of \$1.20 per litre and equilibrium quantity of 3 million litres will prevail. The consumer surplus that relates to a quantity of 3 million litres equals to the area under the demand curve but over the price line. This area equals (.5 × base × height) = (.5 × 3 million × \$.80 per litre) = \$1.2 million. The producer surplus that relates to a quantity of 3 million litres equals to the area over the supply curve but under the price line. This area equals (.5 × base × height) = (.5 × 3 million × \$1.20 per litre) = \$1.8 million. The sum of the consumer and producer surplus equals \$1.2 + \$1.8 = \$ 3 million.

b. Under a price ceiling of \$90 per litre, the quantity supplied will decrease from 3 million litres to 2 million litres per week. This will reduce the consumer surplus by (.5 × base × height) = .5 × 1 million × \$.40 = \$.2 million. The producer surplus will be reduced by (.5 × base × height) = .5 × 1 million × \$.30 = \$.15 million. The total allocative efficiency loss would be \$.2 + \$.15 = \$.35 million. Since this policy reduces the sum of consumer and producer surplus, this causes an allocatively inefficient situation.

c. The price ceiling policy results in an under production of gasoline as the marginal benefit of the last litre consumed (\$1.60) exceeds its marginal cost (\$.90).

## Chapter 7: Consumer Choice

1. For you, the marginal utility of the fifth kilogram of oranges is equal to the marginal utility of the third ear of corn. Apparently, your friend's tastes differ from yours—for her, the marginal utilities are not equal. For her, corn's marginal utility is too low, while that of oranges is too high—that's why she wants you to get rid of some of the corn (raising its marginal utility). She would have you do this until marginal utilities, for her, were equal. If you follow her suggestions, you will end up with a

market basket that maximizes her utility subject to the constraint of your income. Is it any wonder that shopping from someone else's list is a frustrating task?

3. Her marginal utility is 100 at $1. It is 200 at 50 cents, and 50 at $2. To calculate marginal utility per dollar, divide marginal utility by price per unit.

5. The utility-maximizing combination of cheeseburgers and french fries would be two cheeseburgers at 36 total utils and two french fries at 18 total utils, adding up to 54 total utils.

7. A fall in the price of the goods leads to more of that good being consumed, meaning that the satisfaction level has not been reached or diminishing marginal utility has not set in.

9. All that can be known for certain is that marginal utility is positive.

11.

| Number of Cheeseburgers | Total Utility of Cheeseburgers | Marginal Utility of Cheeseburgers | Boxes of French Fries | Total Utility of French Fries | Marginal Utility of French Fries |
|---|---|---|---|---|---|
| 0 | 0 | 0 | 0 | 0 | 0 |
| 1 | 20 | 20 | 1 | 8 | 8 |
| 2 | 36 | 16 | 2 | 14 | 6 |
| 3 | 48 | 12 | 3 | 18 | 4 |
| 4 | 56 | 8 | 4 | 20 | 2 |
| 5 | 60 | 4 | 5 | 20 | 0 |

13. If there was no diminishing marginal utility of potatoes, people would take all the potatoes they could, and leave no money. They would be unable to sell those potatoes because people can buy them directly from the farmers.

## Appendix D: More Advanced Consumer Choice Theory

D-1. The problem here is that such preferences are inconsistent (*intransitive* is the word that economists use). If this consumer's tastes really are this way, then when confronted with a choice among *A*, *B*, and *C*, she will be horribly confused because *A* is preferred to *B*, Which is preferred to *C*, which is preferred to *A*, which is preferred to *B*, which is preferred to *C*, and so on forever. Economists generally assume that preferences are consistent (or *transitive*): If *A* is preferred to *C*. Regardless of what people may say about their preferences, the assumption of transitivity seems to do quite well in predicting what people actually do.

D-3. With an income of $100 and the original prices, you could have consumed *either* 50 kilograms of beef *or* 5 units of shelter or any linear combination shown by the budget line labelled "Original" on the graph below. With the same income but the new prices, you can now consume 25 kilograms of beef or 10 units of shelter or any linear combination shown by the line labelled "New budget." Without information about your preferences, there is no way to tell whether you are better off or worse off. Draw a few indifference curves on the diagram. You will find that if you are a "shelter lover" (your indifference curves are relatively steep), the decline in the relative price of shelter will tend to make you better off. Conversely, if you are a beef lover (your indifference curves are relatively flat), the rise in the relative price of beef will make you worse off.

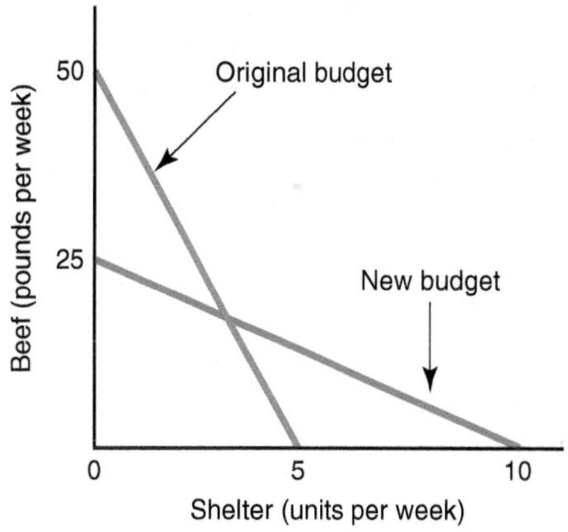


D-5. The first burrito is substituted at a rate of 10 servings of yogurt per burrito; the second burrito is substituted at a rate of 4:1; the third at a rate of 3:1; and the fourth at a rate of 2:1.

D-7. a. This person is simply indifferent between going or staying, an attitude that is perfectly consistent with our assumptions about consumer preferences.

b. This statement denies the law of substitution and so is inconsistent with our assumptions about preferences.

c. If we interpret "if I had my way" to mean "if I had an unlimited budget," this statement simply says that there is nonsatiation for these goods for this consumer—which is perfectly consistent with our assumptions about preferences.

## Chapter 8: The Firm: Cost and Output Determination

1. Explicit costs = \$12 000 + \$1000 + \$20 000 + \$4000 = \$37 000

   Implicit costs = \$40 000 + (5000 × 5%) = \$40 250

3. Accounting profit = \$200 000 − \$20 000 − (\$30 000 × 2) − \$12 000 − \$40 000 = \$68 000

   Economic profit = \$200 000 − \$20 000 (\$30 000 × 2) − \$12 000 − \$40 000 − \$40 000 − \$1000 = \$27 000

5.

| Input of Labour | Total Output | Marginal Physical Product |
|---|---|---|
| 0 | 0 | ---- |
| 1 | 25 | 25 |
| 2 | 60 | 35 |
| 3 | 85 | 25 |
| 4 | 105 | 20 |
| 5 | 115 | 10 |
| 6 | 120 | 5 |

7. a. Marginal performance was 5 out of 10, or 0.5.
   b. Since marginal performance was below average performance, average performance fell.
   c. Marginal performance would rise from 0.5 to 0.6, but average performance would still fall because 0.6 is less than the average, which was 0.8.

9. Total variable costs are equal to total costs of \$5 million, less total fixed costs of \$2 million, which equals \$3 million. Average variable costs are equal to total variable costs divided by the number of units produced. Average variable costs, therefore, equal \$3 million divided by 10 000, or \$300.

11. Average total costs will fall until marginal costs are equal to the average total costs.

13. a. $Q_3$ c. $Q_2$ e. $Q_4$
    b. $Q_4$ d. $Q_3$

15. a. Experiencing economies of scale, costs are still decreasing.
    b. Plant Size E.

## Chapter 9: Perfect Competition

1. a. Since there is one firm that can affect the market price, this is not perfect competition.
   b. This is not perfect competition, as each firm's product is not identical (not homogeneous) due to the differences in quality.
   c. Since government restricts entry through licensing, the easy-entry feature of perfect competition is violated.

3. a.

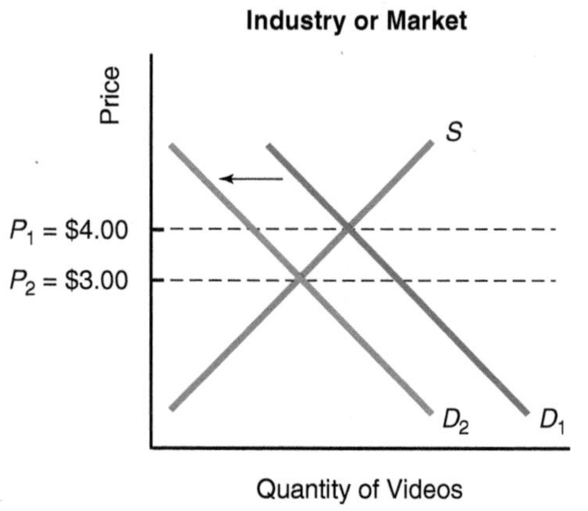


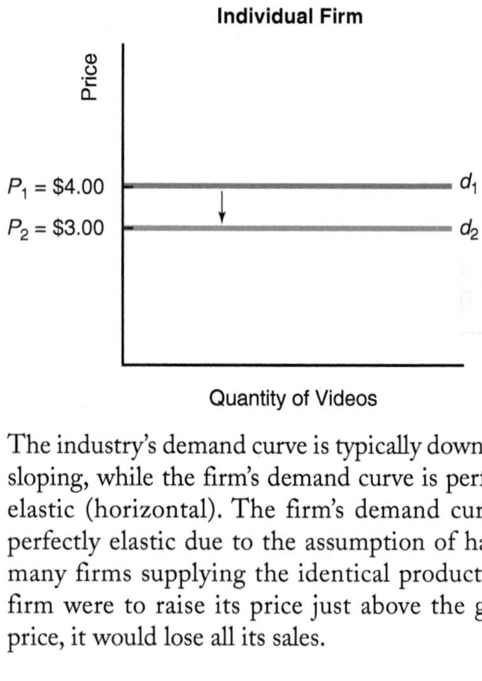


   b. The industry's demand curve is typically downward sloping, while the firm's demand curve is perfectly elastic (horizontal). The firm's demand curve is perfectly elastic due to the assumption of having many firms supplying the identical product. If a firm were to raise its price just above the going price, it would lose all its sales.

5. In the table below, Total Profit is calculated by the formula:

   Total Revenue − Total Cost:

| Hourly Quantity (# of pizzas) | 0 | 1 | 2 | 3 | 4 | 5 | 6 | 7 | 8 | 9 | 10 |
|---|---|---|---|---|---|---|---|---|---|---|---|
| Total Profit (Price = \$10) | −3 | 1 | 9 | 18 | 26 | 32 | 36 | 38 | 37 | 33 | 26 |
| Total Profit (Price = \$3) | −3 | −6 | −5 | −3 | −2 | −3 | −6 | −11 | −19 | −30 | −44 |
| Total Profit (Price = \$2) | −3 | −7 | −7 | −6 | −6 | −8 | −12 | −18 | −27 | −39 | −54 |

a. The profit at a price of \$10 is based on the total revenue formula: TR = 10 × *Q*. The profit-maximizing quantity is seven pizzas per hour with a total positive economic profit of \$38 per hour.

b. The profit at a price of \$3 is based on the total revenue formula: TR = 3 × *Q*. The loss-minimizing quantity is four pizzas per hour with a total negative economic profit (loss)of \$2 per hour. Note that by operating at four pizzas per hour, the firm minimizes its losses to be \$2. If it shuts down, its total losses would be its total fixed cost of \$3. The reason it should operate at four pizzas is that its total revenue of \$12 exceeds its total variable cost of \$11. By operating, it is able to contribute \$1 toward covering its total fixed costs.

c. The profit at a price of \$2 is based on the total revenue formula: TR = 2 × *Q*. The loss-minimizing quantity is zero pizzas per hour with a total negative economic profit (loss) of \$3 per hour, equal to total fixed cost. Since, at all quantities, total revenue is less than total variable cost, the firm should shut down.

7.

| Output (units per hour) | Average Fixed Cost (AFC) | Average Variable Cost (AVC) | Average Total Cost (ATC) | Marginal Cost (MC) |
|---|---|---|---|---|
| 1 | \$102.00 | \$40 | \$142.00 | |
| 2 | 51.00 | 35 | 86.00 | \$30 |
| 3 | 34.00 | 40 | 74.00 | 50 |
| 4 | 25.50 | 45 | 70.50 | 60 |
| 5 | 20.40 | 50 | 70.40 | 70 |
| 6 | 17.00 | 55 | 72.00 | 80 |
| 7 | 14.57 | 60 | 74.57 | 90 |

a. At a price of \$81, the profit-maximizing quantity is where marginal revenue (price) approximately equals marginal cost, at six units per day.

The total profit equals (Price − ATC) × Quantity = (81 − 72) × 6 = \$54 per hour.

b. At a price of \$61, the profit-maximizing quantity is where marginal revenue (price) approximately equals marginal cost, at four units per day. The total profit equals (Price − ATC) × Quantity = (61 − 70.50) × 4 = −\$38 per hour (minimum loss). No, if the firm were to shut down, it would face a larger loss equal to its total fixed cost of \$102 per hour.

c. At a price of \$31, the price is below minimum average variable cost, which is approximately \$35, and so the firm should shut down. Its minimum loss equals its total fixed cost of \$102.

d. The short-run breakeven point occurs at minimum average total cost, which is approximately \$70.40 per unit.

e. The short-run shutdown point occurs at minimum average variable cost, which is just below \$35.

9. a. At the price of \$50, firm J will sell 81 units, where price or marginal revenue equals marginal cost.

b. Total profit equals (*P* − ATC) × *Q* = (\$50 − \$43) × 81 = \$567.

c. Firm J will shut down when the price drops just below \$20, which is minimum average variable cost.

d. Long-run price = \$42 = minimum ATC

11. a. At \$5 per chair, the profit-maximizing quantity would be 400 chairs per day, where Price = MC. The daily maximum profit would be:

(Price − ATC) × Q = (\$5 − \$4) × 400 = \$400 per day

b. At \$3, at best, the firm would be making negative economic profits as the price will be below ATC.

c. At a price of \$3 per chair, the firm should NOT shut down as the price can exceed AVC.

d. At a price of \$1 per chair, the firm should shut down as the price cannot exceed AVC.

13.

| Price per Unit | Individual Quantity Supplied | Industry Supply (1000 firms) | Industry Demand |
|---|---|---|---|
| \$91 | 7 | 7000 | 5000 |
| 81 | 6 | 6000 | 6000 |
| 51 | 3 | 3000 | 8000 |
| 31 | 0 | 0 | 9000 |

a. The short-run equilibrium price will be \$81 per unit.

b. Short-run equilibrium is at six units, where marginal revenue (price) equals marginal cost. The total profit equals (Price − ATC) × Quantity = (81 − 72) × 6 = \$54 per hour.

15. a. No, \$81 will not be the long-run equilibrium price, as each firm is making a positive economic profit of \$54 per hour. In the long run, new firms will enter the industry, attracted by the positive profits. As new firms enter, the industry price will fall below \$81 and will keep falling until no more economic profit is being earned.

b. The long-run equilibrium price will just equal minimum long-run average total cost, which is approximately \$70.40. At this price, each firm will earn zero economic profit so that there will be no incentive for new firms to continue to enter the industry.

17. a. Since per-unit costs increase as the industry expands, this is an increasing-cost industry with an upward-sloping long-run supply curve.

b. Since per-unit costs decrease as the industry expands, this is a decreasing-cost industry with a downward-sloping long-run supply curve.

19. a. Since this competitive industry is producing a product that entails external benefits, it will under-allocate resources to its product.

b. Since this competitive industry is producing a product that entails external costs, it will over-allocate resources to its product.

## Chapter 10: Monopoly

1. a. Predatory behaviour

b. Legal restriction

c. Economies of scale

3. The perfectly competitive firm faces a perfectly elastic (horizontal) demand curve—it is a price-taker. This is because it competes with many firms in supplying the identical product. If the competitive firm were to increase its price just above the going price, it would lose all of its sales. The monopoly firm faces a downward-sloping demand curve, where the elasticity is neither perfectly elastic nor perfectly inelastic—it is a price-searcher. This is because the firm is the industry, and, as industry sales increase significantly, the price will decline.

5. a. The rectangle that shows total costs under $ATC_1$ is *0WCQ*. Total revenue is shown by *0XBQ*. This monopolist is in an economic profit situation. MC = MR is the output at which profit—the difference between total cost and total revenue—is maximized.

b. With $ATC_2$, the rectangle showing total costs is *0XBQ*. The same rectangle, *0XBQ*, gives total revenue. This monopolist is breaking even. MC = MR shows the only quantity that does not cause losses.

c. Under $ATC_3$, total costs are represented by rectangle *0YAQ*, total revenue by *0XBQ*. Here the monopolist is operating at an economic loss, which is minimized by producing where MC = MR.

7. a. The filled-in table should look as follows:

| Price | Quantity Demanded | Total Revenue | Marginal Revenue | Average Total Cost | Marginal Cost |
|---|---|---|---|---|---|
| $20 | 0 | $ 0 | $ – | – | – |
| 16 | 1 | 16 | 16 | $ 8.00 | $ 5.00 |
| 12 | 2 | 24 | 8 | 7.50 | 7.00 |
| 10 | 3 | 30 | 6 | 8.00 | 9.00 |
| 7 | 4 | 28 | –2 | 9.25 | 13.00 |
| 4 | 5 | 20 | –8 | 11.00 | 18.00 |
| 0 | 6 | 0 | –20 | 13.16 | 24.00 |

b. The maximum profit output would be 2 units where marginal revenue is close to, but exceeds, marginal cost.

c. The profit-maximizing price would be $12.00.

d. The amount of maximum profit would be

$(P - ATC) \times Q$ or $(12 - 7.5) \times 2$ or $9.00.

9. a. The profit-maximizing output is 200, where MR equals MC.

b. The profit-maximizing price is $14.00, derived from the demand curve.

c. The amount of maximum profit is equal to $(P - ATC) \times Q$ or $(14 - 12) \times 200$ or $400.00.

11. a. The loss-minimizing level is 1 million bottles per month, where MR = MC.

b. At 1 million bottles per month, losses will be minimized at: $(P - ATC)(Q) = (30 - 33)$(1 million bottles) = –$3 million per month

13. If the monopolist charges a single price for all suits cleaned, it will earn a maximum profit of $14 per day (where MR = MC). If the monopolist practises perfect price discrimination, it will clean eight suits per day (where $P$ = MC) and earn a maximum profit of $23. Therefore, it will increase profits by $9 per day.

15. a. Under perfect price discrimination, the marginal revenue column would be the same as the price column.

b. The maximum profit output would be where price approximately equals marginal cost or at three units.

c. The maximum profit is calculated by taking total revenue minus total cost or $(16 + 12 + 10)$ minus $(3 \times 8)$, which equals $(38 - 24) =$ $14 profit.

17. a. The business people's demand for hotels would be more inelastic than the leisured people's demand for the same hotel. Therefore, the monopolist could enhance its profit by charging a higher price for those who use the hotel for business purposes. That is why you often see lower hotel rates offered on weekends than during the week.

b. Business people do not have time to shop around for their fast-food meal, while retired people do have the time. Also, business people are likely to have a greater amount of income than retired people. These considerations would make the business people's demand for fast food more inelastic than the retired people's demand. The monopolist could increase profit by charging higher fast food prices to business people.

c. The cost of a movie for a family of four is a larger part of the family budget than for a couple only. The family's demand for movies will be more elastic than the couple's demand. The monopolist can increase profit by charging the family less, per person. This is often done by charging children a lower admission fee than adults.

19. a. A natural monopoly can promote productive efficiency. That is, because of economies of scale, one large monopoly firm could produce the product at

a lower average total cost than a smaller competitive firm.

b. A perfectly discriminating monopoly can promote allocative efficiency to the extent that it produces at a quantity level where price (marginal benefit) just equals marginal cost.

21. The daily total revenue and marginal revenue are shown below.

| Quantity | Price | TR | MR | ATC | MC |
|---|---|---|---|---|---|
| 1 | $500 | $ 500 | $ 500 | $500 | – |
| 2 | 450 | 900 | 400 | 350 | $200 |
| 3 | 395 | 1185 | 285 | 300 | 200 |
| 4 | 350 | 1400 | 215 | 275 | 200 |
| 5 | 300 | 1500 | 100 | 260 | 200 |
| 6 | 250 | 1500 | 0 | 250 | 200 |
| 7 | 200 | 1400 | (100) | 243 | 200 |

a. The maximum profit quantity (MR = MC) is 4 dishes per day, with a price of $350 and a daily profit of $300.00.

b. Under marginal cost pricing ($P$ = MC), the daily quantity would be 7 dishes per day, with a price of $200 and a daily profit of −$301.

c. Under average cost pricing ($P$ = ATC), the daily quantity would be 6 dishes per day, with a price of $250 and a daily profit of $0 or normal profit.

d. An unregulated monopolist tends to restrict output in order to drive up the price so as to make excess profits. Average cost pricing regulation provides a higher daily quantity at a lower price. The profit earned by the company is no more than a normal profit.

## Appendix E: The Deadweight Loss Due to Monopoly

E-1 a. Use the table in part (a) of Figure 10–4 to compute the consumer surplus assuming that the monopoly firm maximizes profit and produces at nine units of output and charges $5.75 per unit. As shown in the table below, you can add up the surplus derived by the consumers for each of the nine units of output produced. The total consumer surplus is $9. (See Table E-1a.)

b. Use the table in part (a) of Figure 10–4 to compute the producer surplus assuming that the monopoly firm maximizes profit and produces at nine units of output and charges $5.75 per unit. As shown in the table below, you can add up the surplus derived by the producer for each of the nine units of output produced. The total producer surplus is $22.50. (See Table E-1b.)

c. No, the monopoly firm is not maximizing the sum of consumer and producer surpluses. Both surpluses would be maximized where price equals marginal cost (allocative efficiency level) at approximately 11 units of output, with price being close to $5.25.

**Table E-1A**

| Quantity | 1 | 2 | 3 | 4 | 5 | 6 | 7 | 8 | 9 | Total Surplus |
|---|---|---|---|---|---|---|---|---|---|---|
| Maximum willing to pay (see price column) | $7.75 | $7.50 | $7.25 | $7.00 | $6.75 | $6.50 | $6.25 | $6.00 | $5.75 | |
| Price actually paid | 5.75 | 5.75 | 5.75 | 5.75 | 5.75 | 5.75 | 5.75 | 5.75 | 5.75 | |
| Surplus | $2.00 | $1.75 | $1.50 | $1.25 | $1.00 | $0.75 | $0.50 | $0.25 | $0.00 | $9.00 |

**Table E-1B**

| Quantity | 1 | 2 | 3 | 4 | 5 | 6 | 7 | 8 | 9 | Total Surplus |
|---|---|---|---|---|---|---|---|---|---|---|
| Minimum prepared to accept (see marginal cost table) | $4.00 | $3.50 | $3.25 | $3.05 | $2.90 | $2.80 | $2.90 | $3.15 | $3.70 | |
| Price actually received | 5.75 | 5.75 | 5.75 | 5.75 | 5.75 | 5.75 | 5.75 | 5.75 | 5.75 | |
| Surplus | $1.75 | $2.25 | $2.50 | $2.70 | $2.85 | $2.95 | $2.85 | $2.60 | $2.05 | $22.50 |

E-3 a. Under perfect competition, the price and quantity would be $4 and 3000 bagels, respectively, where demand equals supply. The total consumer surplus would be the area under the demand curve and above the price line, which would be (½) ($3 × 3000 bagels) = $4500. The total producer surplus would be the area under the price line and above the supply curve, which would be (½) ($3 × 3000 bagels) = $4500. The sum of both surpluses would be $9000.

b. Under monopoly, the price and quantity would be $5 and 2000 bagels respectively. The loss due to allocative inefficiency would be the deadweight loss equal to: (½)($2 × 1000 bagels) = $1000.

## Chapter 11: Monopolistic Competition and Oligopoly

1. Local night clubs would be classed as monopolistically competitive firms. This is because each night club sells a differentiated product in terms of the physical facilities and decor; the type of music played; the type of entertainment and food offered; and, finally, the type of clientele that regularly visits the establishment. Note that there are typically numerous night clubs competing with each other and that entry into this type of business is relatively easy.

3. It is not rational for a perfectly competitive firm to advertise, as it can sell all it wants at the given price (perfectly elastic demand).

5. a. The profit-maximizing quantity is 400 CDs per week, where MR = MC.
   b. The profit-maximizing quantity is $9 per CD, which is the vertical distance up to the demand curve, at a quantity of 400 CDs
   c. Maximum weekly profit = (Price − ATC) × 400 CDs = ($9 − $4) × 400 = $2000 per week.
   d. Monopolistic competition best applies to Sue's CD game for the following reasons. Since the firm's demand curve is downward sloping, this indicates that Sue has some control over the price per CD. There is product differentiation in the form of advertising and physical differences (CD, online, hard copy, board games) in the products available to teach kids math. Finally, entry into this industry is relatively easy, if one has the skills to create an interactive math game on a CD or online.

7. a. The filled-in table should look as follows:

| Quantity (# rooms) | Price (per room) | Total Revenue | Marginal Revenue | Marginal Cost | Average Total Cost |
|---|---|---|---|---|---|
| 0 | $95 | $ 0 | | | |
| 4 | 90 | 360 | $90 | $36 | $86.00 |
| 8 | 85 | 680 | 80 | 34 | 60.00 |
| 12 | 80 | 960 | 70 | 33 | 51.00 |
| 16 | 75 | 1200 | 60 | 34 | 46.75 |
| 20 | 70 | 1400 | 50 | 36 | 44.60 |
| 24 | 65 | 1560 | 40 | 39 | 43.67 |
| 28 | 60 | 1680 | 30 | 43 | 43.57 |
| 32 | 55 | 1760 | 20 | 48 | 44.13 |

   b. The maximum profit output is 24 rooms per night.
   c. The profit-maximizing price is $65 per room per night.
   d. The total amount of maximum profit is ($P$ − ATC) × $Q$ or ($65 − $43.67) × 24 or $511.92.
   e. No, due to easy entry the long-run profit will decline to zero economic profits.
   f. Product differentiation may include: spa facilities, pool, good food, different style of rooms, free parking, computer facilities, good entertainment, in-room movies, continental breakfast.

9. a. This bookstore operates in monopolistic competition. It competes with numerous rivals, it differentiates its product in terms of location and its coffee, it sells books that will differ from its competitors', and, finally, it is relatively easy to enter this type of business.
   b. The profit-maximizing quantity is at five books per hour, where the marginal revenue of $3.75 is approximately equal to the marginal cost of $3.70. The profit-maximizing price is $4.75 and the total profit is ($4.75 − $3.16) × 5 = $7.95 per hour.
   c. At a quantity of two books per hour, the long-run equilibrium price will be $3.75, which just equals average total cost so that zero economic profits are earned.
   d. If this were a perfectly competitive firm, it would have its price just equal minimum average total cost, which is somewhere between $3.03 and $3.16. At this price, zero economic profits would be earned.

11. a. Homogeneous oligopoly
    b. Differentiated oligopoly
    c. Homogeneous oligopoly
    d. Differentiated oligopoly.
    e. Differentiated oligopoly

13. a. The payoff matrix is described below. Firm A's payoffs are in the shaded areas.

| Firm A \ Firm B | Lower price | Raise price |
|---|---|---|
| Lower price | B: $3 million; A: $3 million | B: $1 million; A: $7 million |
| Raise price | B: $7 million; A: $1 million | B: $5 million; A: $5 million |

    b. The dominant strategy is for each firm to lower the price.
    c. Firm A's annual profit would be $5 million.
    d. Firm A's annual profit would be $7 million.
    e. Firm A's annual profit would be $1 million.
    f. The most profitable long-run strategy would be for each firm to raise the price, where the long-run average annual profit would be $5 million.

15. a. Decrease
    b. Increase
    c. Decrease

17. Diamonds are a great candidate for the cartel strategy of restricting quantity produced and sold, as that simply adds to the "rarity" or "scarcity" of this stone, enhancing its appeal to the consumer (especially the richer customers). Put another way, the price elasticity of demand for diamonds is inelastic, so that when quantity is restricted, total revenue increases, enhancing profits of the cartel firms, such as De Beer.

19. One could reasonably argue that social networking sites such as Facebook are far from being "free" from the members' viewpoint. To the extent that advertisers pay out monies to promote through Facebook, this adds costs to the products being sold, and at least some of these promotional costs will be passed on to consumers through increased product prices. As well, to the extent that members' personal information gets into the hands of third parties, this can cost various members in different ways. As an example, if in Facebook a member discloses specific information regarding his or her health problems, this information could be used by insurance companies to reject future applications for insurance coverage. Alternatively, dishonest individuals could use the personal information received through Facebook to commit various forms of identity theft.

21. When Pepsi quickly responds to Coke's ads, this can result in a positive-sum game for both firms in a number of ways. First, the heavy advertising can help both firms build significant barriers to entry and therefore prevent other firms from competing in a major way. Second, heavy advertising by both firms may cause the industry demand for their types of products (soft drinks, bottled water, and so on) to increase, thus benefiting all the firms in the industry.

## Chapter 12: Regulation and Competition Policy

1. Under a natural monopoly situation, per-unit costs are lower with just one firm supplying the product or service compared with a competitive situation. To the extent that, through economic regulation, the government can force the monopolist to charge a price that reflects these lower costs, consumers will enjoy lower prices under the monopoly situation.

3. a. Under marginal cost pricing, the government would enforce a price of $75 at a quantity level of five units. Since at five units of output the price of $75 is less than the average total cost of $81.20, the firm would incur economic losses. If this situation persisted in the long term, the firm would go out of business.

   b. Under rate-of-return regulation, the price is set to equal average total cost. This would occur if the price were set at $85 at a quantity level of three units. The economic profit is zero.

   c. Critics argue that rate-of-return regulation will encourage the monopoly firm to overpurchase capital equipment, which inflates the average total cost of production. This breeds productive inefficiency.

5. a. When the CRTC regulates the phone rates that some local phone companies charge their customers, this is an example of economic regulation.

   b. When the CRTC restricts the degree to which foreigners can own Canadian media companies, this is an example of social regulation. Here, the government wants to foster our own independent Canadian identity and culture.

7. The capture hypothesis best explains this situation. The American government is serving the interests of the American beef producers. The ban on Canadian beef significantly increased the price that American producers received for their beef. American beef producers benefit from this regulation, at the expense of American consumers.

9. In a natural monopoly, even under the conditions of free entry, only one company will survive in the industry due to economies of scale. This one surviving monopoly firm will likely earn positive economic profits under deregulation.

11. a Resale price maintenance
    b. Abuse of dominant position
    c. Tied selling
    d. Bait-and-switch selling
    e. Exclusive dealing

13. The three provisions that were examined were exclusive dealing, refusal to supply, and abuse of a dominant position. Exclusive dealing was not violated as competition was not substantially lessened due to the agreement, as only one DVD set from one artist was excluded for a limited period of time. Refusal to supply was ruled out as HMV was not significantly negatively impacted by the agreement. Finally, there was no abuse of a dominant position situation, as no dominant firm seemed to exist.

## Chapter 13: Labour Demand and Supply

1.

| Total Quantity of Labour | Product per Week | MPP | MRP |
|---|---|---|---|
| 1 | 250 | 250 | $500 |
| 2 | 450 | 200 | 400 |
| 3 | 600 | 150 | 300 |
| 4 | 700 | 100 | 200 |
| 5 | 750 | 50 | 100 |
| 6 | 750 | 0 | 0 |

a. Demand schedule for labour:

| Weekly Wage | Labourers Demanded per Week |
|---|---|
| $500 | 1 |
| 400 | 2 |
| 300 | 3 |
| 200 | 4 |
| 100 | 5 |

b. $100 each

c. Four

3. a. 15 million worker-hours per time period

b. 10 million per time period

c. Buyers can get all the labour they want at $W_1$; labourers cannot sell all they want to sell at $W_1$.

d. Because a surplus of labour exists, the unemployed will offer to work for less, and industry wage rates will fall toward $W_e$.

5. Suppose that the demand for the output product is highly elastic. Even a relatively small increase in the price of the input factor, which correspondingly raises the price of the output product, will cause a large decrease in the quantity of output demanded and therefore in the employment of the input.

7. The three union goals are
   - to employ all members in the union,
   - to maximize total income of workers, and
   - to maximize wages.

9. The state of the economy can have an impact on wages and, therefore, the number of strikes.

11. No, you should not. The MRP when you employ 31 people is $89.50 ($99.50 in revenue from selling the twenty-first unit, less $10 forgone in selling the first 20 units for 50 cents less than originally). The MFC is $91 ($61 to attract the twenty-first employee to your firm, plus the additional $1 per day to each of the original 30 employees). Because MFC exceeds MRP, you should not expand output.

13.

| Quantity of Labour Supplied | Total Physical Product | Required Hourly Wage Rate (per unit of hour) | Total Wage Bill | Marginal Factor Cost (per unit of labour) |
|---|---|---|---|---|
| 10 | 100 | $ 5 | $ 50 | – |
| 11 | 109 | 6 | 66 | $16 |
| 12 | 116 | 7 | 84 | 18 |
| 13 | 121 | 8 | 104 | 20 |
| 14 | 124 | 9 | 126 | 22 |
| 15 | 125 | 10 | 150 | 24 |

## Chapter 14: Income and Poverty

1. Men might invest more in human capital; women might receive less and a lower-quality education and/or training; women in the workforce may take periods out of the workforce in order to raise children and thus accumulate less experience than men; discrimination may exist.

3. Some of the issues are what exactly should be included as income and the fact that self-employed individuals can claim expenses that reduce their income for income tax purposes. What about full-time employment versus part-time employment?

5. The four main determinants of income differences are: talent, experience, training, and investment.

7. The four income support programs are: Old Age Security, Canada Pension Plan, Employment Insurance, and Child Tax Benefit.

9. Some of the programs for the working poor are: a child tax credit, school lunch programs, health and dental programs, and various provincial bonuses.

## Chapter 15: Environmental Economics

1. When the external costs are added to the supply curve (which is itself the sum of marginal costs of the industry), the total (private plus public) marginal costs of production are above the private supply schedule. At quantity $Q_1$ in the following graph, marginal costs to society are greater than the value attached to the marginal unit. The private supply curve is below the social supply curve. To bring marginal cost and marginal benefit back into line, thus promoting an economically efficient allocation of resources, quantity would have to be reduced to $Q_2$ and price raised to $P_2$.

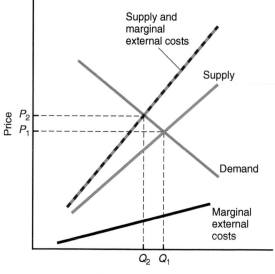

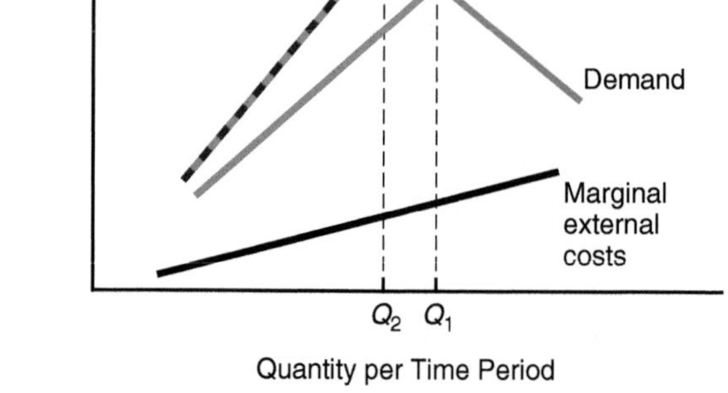

3. The free-market costs would increase, and therefore, their profits would decrease.
5. a. The optimal degree of air cleanliness is 40 percent.
   b. The optimal degree of air pollution is 40 percent.
   c. The optimal degree of air cleanliness now becomes 20 percent, taking into account that the optimal point occurs where the marginal cost equals the marginal benefit.
7. At the previous lower market price, consumers failed to pay an amount that reflected the social costs (including those relating to pollution) of resources that the firms used to produce the good or service.
9. a. The price should be set using various methods, depending on the industry.
   b. Depending on the industry, voluntary agreements, carbon credits, and other methods could be used.
   c. Some firms could be forced to close down, depending on the industry. The reduction in pollution might counter the jobs lost.
   d. If buyers have to pay more, they will reduce their purchases of the pollutant.
11. A user fee could be applied to the people who do not recycle. This could encourage people to dump their garbage in someone else's trash bin, so this might not be the best method. Awareness campaigns could be used effectively to encourage people to recycle.

## Chapter 16: The Public Sector

1. TV stations are private businesses given licences to operate by the CRTC. If they do not operate according to the rules outlined by the CRTC, they can lose their licences.
3. The theory of public choice is about collective decision making; the individual will act to maximize his or her individual well-being. This often forces governments to provide more services rather than less so that the government can continue to get the votes of the people.
5. This implies that Canadians are taxed at a higher rate than Americans. Americans are free from tax much earlier than Canadians, but it might be due to the fact that Canadians get more universal programs such as health care.
7. In order for the tax-exempt bond to be more attractive, you would have to be in a marginal tax bracket where you are paying more than the 6 percent yield.
9. a. \$4000 4.95% = \$198; \$198/\$4000 = 4.95%
   b. \$42 100 4.95% = \$2083.95; \$2083.95/\$51 300 = 4.06%
   c. \$42 100 4.95% = \$2083.95; \$2083.95/\$56 000 = 3.72%
   d. \$42 100 4.95% = \$2083.95; \$2083.95/\$100 000 = 2.08%

   Thus the CPP system is an example of a regressive tax system.

# Answers to Business Applications

## Chapter 1: The Nature of Economics

a. i. Macroeconomic event, as the decline in the Canadian dollar is a broad national trend.

ii. Increase the stock price, as Timber Corp's sales will increase, resulting in an increased profit.

b. i. Microeconomic event, as the tax focuses on a specific industry: cigarette manufacturing.

ii. Decrease the price of the stock. A tax increase will raise the costs of production and reduce the annual profit.

c. i. Macroeconomic event, as the inflation is a broad global factor.

ii. Increase the stock price. When inflation is out of control, investors often purchase gold, as it has historically been popular in times of economic crisis. As gold prices rise, the profits of gold mines increase.

d. i. Microeconomic event, as this is a factor that affects the specific firm in question.

ii. Increase the stock price. When sales stay the same but operating costs decrease, the annual profit will increase.

e. i. Macroeconomic event, as interest rate trends tend to be a nationwide phenomenon.

ii. Decrease the stock price. Since investors are selling stocks across all industries, this reduces stock prices, which, in turn, reduces the profit of Morgan Mutual Fund.

## Chapter 2: Production Possibilities and Economics Systems

a. A Bachelor of Commerce Degree is a capital good from an individual's view, to the extent that it increases the individual's future earning power. It is therefore better suited to deficit financing.

b. A civic convention center would be considered to be a capital item from a city's viewpoint, and therefore better suited to deficit financing. One of the primary uses of this type of government resource is to generate revenues for the city in future years by bringing in visitors or convention delegates who will spend money on the city's hotels, restaurants, shops, and entertainment venues. Also, new business can be generated for firms in the cities who showcase their products and services through events such as trade shows.

c. The exercise gym can be viewed as a capital item from the employer's view, to the extent that it contributes towards healthier, more productive employees with better work attendance. It is therefore better suited to deficit financing.

d. The season's pass would more likely be a capital good for the insurance salesman to the extent that he meets potential clients on the golf course. It is therefore better suited to deficit financing.

e. From a city's view, it would seem that a sports team would more likely enhance future revenues as opposed to a city hall. The sports team would bring in players and fans from outside the city. As a result, more money would be spent in the city's hotels, restaurants, shops, and entertainment spots. The sports team is therefore better suited to deficit financing.

## Chapter 3: Demand and Supply

a. Decrease in demand for tennis, increase in demand for golf (because it is less strenuous)

b. Increase in demand for Diet Coke (healthier), decrease in demand for Pepsi (because it appeals to a younger generation)

c. Increase in demand for urban condominiums, decrease in demand for suburban homes (for accessibility)

d. Decrease in demand for minivans, increase in demand for recreational vehicles (for retirement)

e. Decrease in demand for red meat, increase in demand for chicken (for health reasons)

## Chapter 4: Elasticity

The demand for pharmaceutical drugs is very inelastic for at least two reasons. The consumer (patient) perceives pharmaceutical drugs to be necessity items. As well, many of the prescription drugs sold by a pharmaceutical company are sold in a monopoly environment, protected by patents. If the demand is very inelastic, the company will tend to charge high prices relative to the cost of producing the products, resulting in high profit margins. Based on the notion of fundamental stock analysis, the higher profit margins can account for higher stock price performance.

## Chapter 5: Market Efficiency and Market Failure

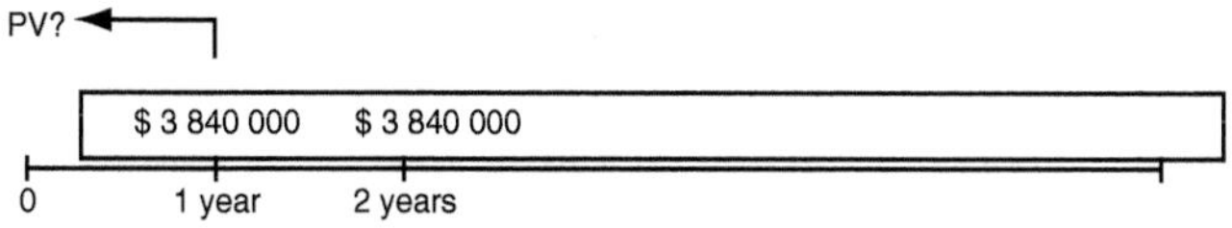


The present value of an annuity formula is as follows:

$$PV = \$R\left(\frac{1 - (1 + i)^{-n}}{i}\right) = \$3\ 840\ 000$$

$$\times \left(\frac{1 - (1 + .10)^{-10}}{.10}\right) = \$23\ 595\ 138$$

Based on the above calculation, the maximum amount of financial assistance that Ridaway can expect to get from the government is \$23 595 138.

## Chapter 6: Extensions of Demand, Supply, and Elasticity

1. a. Decrease in demand, fee will decrease
   b. Decrease in demand, fee will decrease
   c. Decrease in demand, fee will decrease
   d. Decrease in demand, fee will decrease
   e. Increase in supply, fee will decrease
2. Negative outlook, as all the events are putting downward pressure on the fees that dentists can charge. In turn, this will translate into decreased profit.
3. a. Decrease in supply, fee will increase
   b. Decrease in supply, fee will increase
   c. Increase in demand, fee will increase
   d. Increase in demand, fee will increase
   e. Increase in demand, fee will increase
4. a. Equilibrium price = \$600 per crown, where market demand equals market supply
   b. Total revenue = $P_e \times Q_e$ = \$600 × 12 000 = \$7200.
   c. With the marketing board policy, there is a new vertical supply curve fixed at 11 000 crowns per year. This new supply curve intersects the demand curve at \$800 per crown. The annual total revenue equals \$800 × 11 000 = \$8 800 000.
   d. The demand is inelastic, since as we have just seen, when the price increases from \$600 to \$800, total revenue increased. In general, when the price increases and total revenue increases, demand is inelastic.

## Chapter 7: Consumer Choice

Yes. If just \$1 is re-allocated away from hiring a beat police officer in order to spend an extra dollar on fighting crime with a vehicle, there would be an extra \$4 contribution towards reducing theft. This extra contribution would be achieved without increasing the total budgetary expense!

## Chapter 8: The Firm: Cost and Output Determination

a. Average fuel cost = 1074.60 ÷ 18 000 = \$.0597 per km; total gas cost = \$.0597 × 500 km = \$29.85

b. Average variable cost = 1728 ÷ 18 000 = \$.096 per km; total variable cost = \$.096 × 500 = \$48

c. Average total cost = 7469.61 ÷ 18 000 = \$.41497 per km; total cost = \$.41497 × 500 = \$207.49

d. Average variable cost, as this includes all additional costs attributable to the business trip.

## Chapter 9: Perfect Competition

a. AVC: 124, 120, 125, 135, 150, 170
   MC: 124, 116, 135, 165, 210, 270
   ATC: 374.00, 245.00, 208.33, 197.50, 200.00, 211.67

b. Profit maximizing quantity = 5000 tonnes per month; total profit = \$150 000 per month.

c. Loss minimizing quantity = 3000 tonnes per month; total loss = \$204 990 per month.

d. Loss minimizing quantity = 0 tonnes per month (shutdown); total loss = \$250 000 per month.

e. No. As the example above shows, as prices change in the short run, profit maximization criteria will dictate varying optimal production levels. As an example, in part b above, the profit maximizing level is at q = 5000 tonnes. The minimum cost per unit occurs at q = 4000 tonnes.

f. No. As part c above illustrates, if Monique's operates at 3000 tonnes per month, the loss per month is \$204 990, compared to a loss of \$250 000 per month if the firm shut down. In this case, staying in operation creates a savings of \$45 010.

## Chapter 10: Monopoly

1.

| | | | | | |
|---|---|---|---|---|---|
| TR: | 0 | 720 | 1320 | 1740 | 2000 |
| | 2100 | 2040 | 1820 | 1440 | |
| MR: | 720 | 600 | 420 | 260 | 100 |
| | (60) | (220) | (380) | | |

2. a. $Q$ = 3; b. Total maximum profit = \$840
3. a. $Q$ = 5; b. Economic profit = 0, so the doctor just earns a normal profit.
4. a. $Q$ = 4; b. Total maximum profit = \$1060

## Chapter 11: Monopolistic Competition and Oligopoly

a. place

b. product

c. promotion
d. price
e. product
f. price
g. promotion
h. price
i. promotion

## Chapter 12: Regulation and Competition Policy

Student answers will vary.

## Chapter 13: Labour Demand and Supply

a. Increase the demand; increase the fees
b. Increase the supply; decrease the fees
c. Decrease the supply; increase the fees
d. Increase the demand; increase the fees
e. Decrease the supply; increase the fees
f. Decrease the demand; decrease the fees

## Chapter 14: Income and Poverty

Student answers will vary.

## Chapter 15: Environmental Economics

Student answers will vary.

## Chapter 16: The Public Sector

1. Extra savings = \$9000 × .4342 = \$3907.80
2. a. Total tax payable = 75 000 × .379 = \$28 425
   b. Combined total tax payable = (\$25 000 × .215) + (\$50 000 × .316) = \$5375 + \$15 800 = \$21 175
   c. Savings through income splitting = \$28 425 − \$21 175 = \$7250
   d. No, income splitting reduces tax payable when the tax system is progressive. Under a flat-rate tax, Jody and her husband would be subject to the same average tax rate.

# Answers to "For Critical Analysis" Questions

## Chapter 1: The Nature of Economics

### Example 1–1: The Economics of Web Page Design

The web designer of a frequently visited web page, such as Yahoo!'s home page, has "unlimited wants" that include such goals as: provide maximum exposure to all of Yahoo!'s own products and services; maximize revenue from selling advertising space to other companies; present high-quality images and animations; and prevent the web page from becoming too cluttered. The "limited resources" include a limited screen space size (that one views without scrolling) and limited time to hold the web surfer's attention.

### Example 1–2: Is the Opportunity Cost of Finding a Mate Lower on the Internet?

There is a smaller selection of available people who match very specific characteristics. Therefore, the desire by persons to find people with very specific characteristics will involve higher search costs, in terms of the time spent dating, than would be the case with less picky requirements. In other words, the opportunity cost of dating in person is higher, which implies that people would be willing to pay more to avoid this by using the Internet alternative. This example shows how understanding opportunity cost can help the Internet firm decide on the appropriate price to charge for its different matching services.

### Example 1–3: What Does a Year at College Really Cost?

Jane did not correctly determine the cost related to the decision to enroll in college full-time for eight months. She should add only the *extra* or *marginal* costs, which would be the tuition, books, college fees, and the income she sacrifices from not working full-time for eight months. This implies that the total costs of going to college would be \$3600 + (8 months) × (\$2000 per month) = \$19 600 for the eight months spent at college. The other expenses, such as rent, food, transportation, personal care, and entertainment, can be viewed as unavoidable expenses she decided to incur before making any education decision that we would class as sunk costs. Sunk costs should not be included in computing the marginal or extra cost relating to her education decision. In order to make a rational decision, the marginal cost should be compared to the marginal benefit of enrolling in the business college program.

### Policy Example 1–1: International Smuggling and Counterfeiting

Policies aimed at increasing the marginal cost of smuggling and counterfeiting include increasing the level of enforcement to increase the chances that criminals get caught (e.g., employing 50 000 special agents) as well as increasing the level of fines and other penalties for those criminals found guilty of crimes. Policies aimed at lowering the marginal benefits related to smuggling and counterfeiting include the lowering of taxes on the legal sale of cigarettes. This lowers the price of legal cigarettes relative to illegal cigarettes, and lowers the potential profits earned from smuggling and counterfeiting.

### Example 1–4: Nice Guys Can Finish First

The findings of the study in this Example suggest that if a person engages in generous behaviour, he or she will be rewarded in terms of being attractive to the opposite sex, especially for long-term relationships.

### Example 1–5: The Science Behind COLD-fX

The study examines the relationship between COLD-fX medication and the frequency of contracting colds and their duration and severity. The study attempts to apply the *ceteris paribus* assumption by holding constant other factors that might affect the frequency, duration, and severity, such as having just had a flu vaccination, taking other cold medication at the same time, the placebo effect, researcher's bias in favour of finding that COLD-fX is effective, and the general health of the subjects in the study.

### Example 1–6: An Economic Model of Crime

An increase in the unemployment rate reduces the opportunity cost related to the time spent planning and committing the crime and the time spent evading being caught or, if caught, time spent in jail. This reduces the marginal cost of engaging in a criminal act so we would predict that an increase in the unemployment rate would increase the crime rate. A decrease in conviction rates reduces the expected punishment costs related to committing a crime. In turn, this reduces the marginal cost of engaging in a criminal act so we would predict that this would increase the crime rate.

### Issues and Applications: Bottled Water: The Hummer of Beverages?

1. Scarcity brings home the point that resources are limited in the face of unlimited wants. Knowing this

makes one concerned about whether the $100 billion bottled water industry is effectively allocating our limited resources, as there are many other wants yet to be satisfied. Opportunity cost refers to the value of the best alternative that must be given up because a choice was made. By allocating $100 billion of resources to the bottled water industry we give up the opportunity to satisfy other wants such as promoting a pollution-free environment and increasing global access to safe water. Economics is the social science that is concerned with how our limited resources are being allocated to satisfy unlimited wants. The fact that the bottled water industry uses up a significant amount of limited resources makes it an economic issue.

2. Since this issue focuses on one industry or product area, the bottled water industry, it entails a microeconomic focus. A macroeconomic focus would relate to the level or growth of production or consumption in all Canadian industries.
3. In order to create the incentives necessary to reduce the amount of resources used to produce bottled water, the government would have to reduce the marginal benefit that firms derive from supplying bottled water. One way to do this would be to ban all exclusivity agreements, which would increase competition and reduce the prices that Coca-Cola and PepsiCo could charge for bottled water.

   Another way of reducing the marginal benefit would be to mount a major educational campaign that publicized the opportunity costs related to bottled water. If the campaign could get people to reduce their demand for bottled water, it would reduce the marginal benefit derived from supplying this product.
4. Policy analysis refers to the important process of relating a proposed policy to various socio-economic goals. In this example, the Toronto City Council's proposed policy of levying a tax on the sale of bottled water was related to equity and employment. That is, the beverage companies, in arguing against the tax, noted that it would be unfair to single out just one commodity, especially a healthier product, for taxation. Also, the beverage companies projected that if the tax was implemented it would cause people to buy less bottled water (and possibly other groceries) in Toronto, which could conflict with the employment goal. On a broader level, one could look at leaving the bottled water industry alone (status quo) as another possible policy. As this issue suggests, this status quo policy can conflict with other goals such as a cleaner, healthier environment, less global warming, and providing aid to poorer nations.

## Chapter 2: Production Possibilities and Economic Systems

### Example 2–1: Beware of "Free" Lecture Podcasts

1. The example notes that if you skip class, you give up the opportunity to ask questions during the lecture, as well as to interact with other class members. You may also end up scoring low on class participation marks. Other costs that you might incur include the cost of having to take the full responsibility of pacing yourself appropriately through all the course material in all your courses. It becomes too easy to postpone viewing the online lectures, so that you eventually get far behind in your course studies. By not getting to know your instructor, you might incur the cost of not being able to use your instructor as a reference for a future job opportunity.
2. Students who do attend class bear some of the opportunity cost of your absenteeism, as they have may not be able to complete the work that requires teamwork or group discussion. If there is a peer evaluation portion of a group mark, you would likely score low on this.

### Example 2–2: One Laptop per Child

One Laptop per Child promotes productive efficiency in that it seeks to deliver education to poorer nations at a much lower cost than traditional bricks-and-mortar education. As noted in the example, traditional bricks-and-mortar education is simply too expensive (thousands of dollars per student) for poorer nations to afford. With One Laptop per Child, the major education cost is the $100 laptop per student.

### Policy Example 2–1: The Multibillion Dollar Park

Production Possibilities Curve: Wilderness Area Goods and Oil and Gas Goods

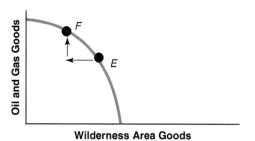

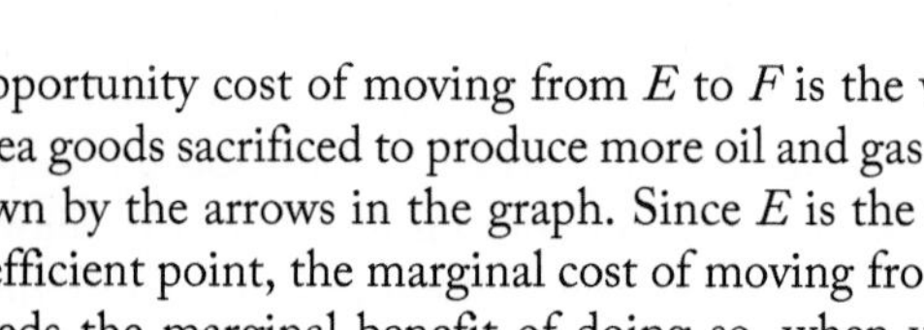


The opportunity cost of moving from $E$ to $F$ is the wilderness area goods sacrificed to produce more oil and gas goods, as shown by the arrows in the graph. Since $E$ is the allocatively efficient point, the marginal cost of moving from $E$ to $F$ exceeds the marginal benefit of doing so, when viewing this from society's viewpoint.

**Example 2–3:** Canadian Post-secondary Education Pays Off Big Time!

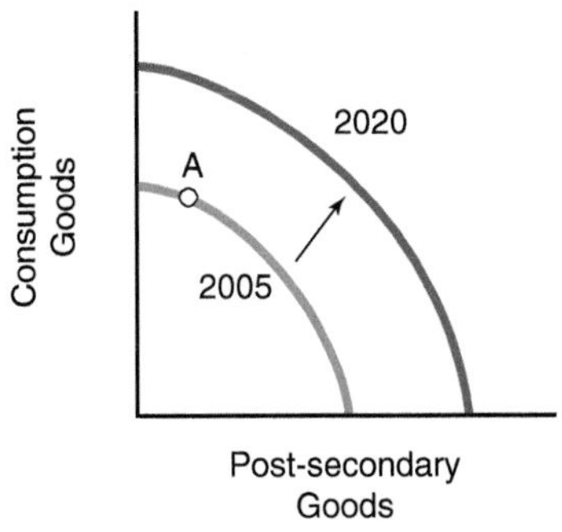


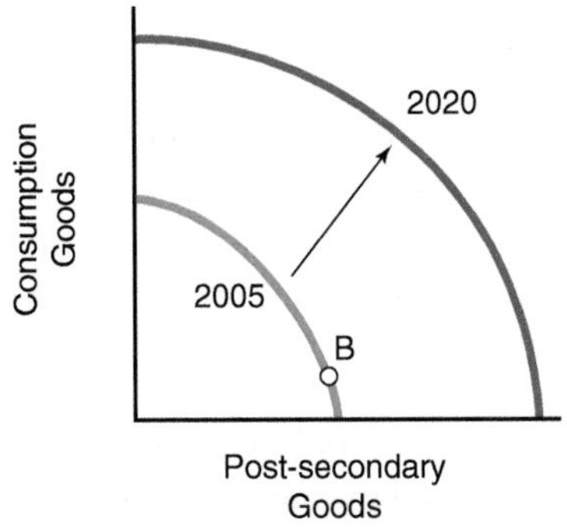


**Example 2–4:** Specializing in Providing Baggage-Free Business Trips

1. The new company FlyLite allows Steve Zilinek (the owner) to specialize in baggage handling, where he has a comparative advantage. At the same time, the business traveller can specialize in his or her business (as opposed to spending time on packing, baggage handling, etc.). Both of these people will make more money by spending more time on activities where they have a comparative advantage. This is a "win-win" situation.
2. If the trend is to take more time handling personal baggage at airports, this increases the opportunity cost related to the business traveller doing this activity as opposed to spending more time on his or her business. In turn, this will cause more business travellers to use FlyLite's services.

**Policy Example 2–2:** Canadian Politics: Right, Left, and Centre

Policy A: Waiting time for surgeries is reduced through the expansion of government-funded surgical units located in government-run hospitals. This is more consistent with the New Democrats as this involves providing more services through the government. Policy B: Waiting time for surgeries is reduced through the provision of new surgical services through privately owned health-care clinics. This is more consistent with the Conservatives as this involves providing more services through the private sector.

**Example 2–5:** India Has More Cellphones Than Toilets

In this Example, the way in which India has answered its "for whom" question is to create a very inequitable or uneven distribution of income: a small proportion of the population is very rich and own lots of cellphones, and a significant proportion is very poor and cannot afford toilet facilities. In other words, the uneven distribution of income affects "what and how much will be produced" in that more cellphones are produced than toilets.

One policy would be to more heavily tax the rich and use these tax dollars to produce more toilets. This will pay off in the long run with reduced government spending on health and support for those living in poverty.

**Issues and Applications:** Private or Public Auto Insurance: What Is Best for Canada?

1. Due to its no-fault feature, the pure command system does not have to employ the expensive legal and court-related resources to establish fault and the amount of damages experienced by injured parties. Since the government is the sole insurance provider in the province, it does not have to employ resources to market its services to the customer. Moreover, a government monopoly is able to avoid the duplication in administrative resources that typically occurs when numerous private car insurance companies compete with each other in the same province. Because the public system can offer the same insurance coverage with minimal use of resources, it is productively efficient.
2. By charging higher premiums for those individuals falling into high-risk classes, such as younger males, the private system helps to keep the riskier drivers off the road. Also, the fault system can provide an incentive to be more careful and avoid accidents. In a fault system, the injured party's right to sue for damages helps to ensure that the dollar value of the compensation resulting from an accident claim (marginal benefit) is sufficient to cover the full marginal cost related to the individual injuries and losses sustained from the accident. In this way, a fault system allocates the claim benefits (marginal benefits) in a way that matches the marginal accident costs of each individual, promoting allocative efficiency.

3. When a pure command system does not charge higher premiums based on age and gender, an equity trade-off may occur. On the one hand, equity is promoted when younger drivers with clean driving records pay lower premiums than older people who have accident histories. On the other hand, equity is compromised if the "no discrimination" practice increases collisions by encouraging riskier drivers to take to the road. In this case, older, female, safe drivers end up in more accidents caused by the riskier drivers and end up paying higher premiums.
4. With a rate freeze, the revenue from premiums stays the same but the expenses for paying out claims could increase with inflation, causing financial losses. In this situation, the private insurance companies may refuse to provide insurance in the province operating this type of mixed system. As a result, the only option would be for the government to provide the insurance.

## Chapter 3: Demand and Supply

### Example 3–1: Why RFID Tags are Catching On Fast

The law of demand explains the increased use of RFID tags. As this example explains, the price of RFID tags has been declining at a significant rate. As well the cost savings that companies achieve also amount to a reduced price of using the RFID technology.

### Example 3–2: A Recession Tale of Two Macs

1. In the recession, as incomes decreased, the demand for Mac computers also decreased. Since there is a direct relation between income and demand, Mac computers is a normal good.

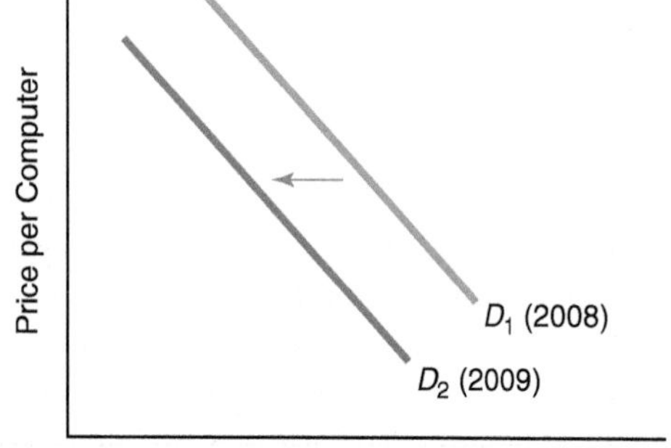


2. In the recession, as incomes decreased, the demand for McDonald's meals increased. Since there is an inverse relation between income and demand, McDonald's meals is an inferior good.

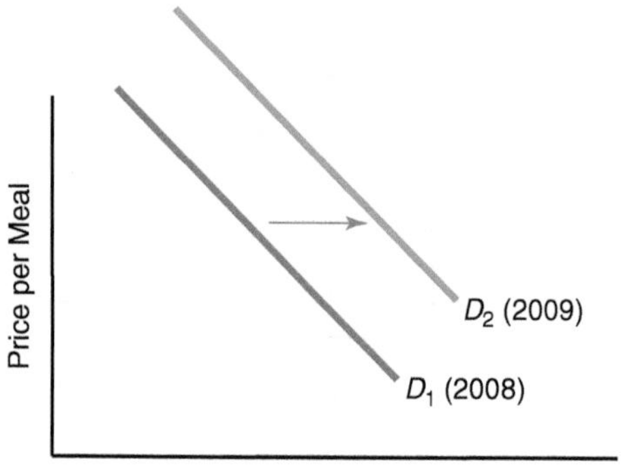


### Example 3–3: Brunettes Now Have More Fun

Taste-related factors have increased the demand for brunette hair dyes. Graphically, this is reflected in a rightward shift in the demand curve for brunette hair dyes as shown below. The specific taste-related factors include: prominent female movie stars who are brunette; ethnic groups that are becoming more prominent in Canada have natural brunette hair shades; an aging population that prefers to use brunette hair dyes to cover gray hair.

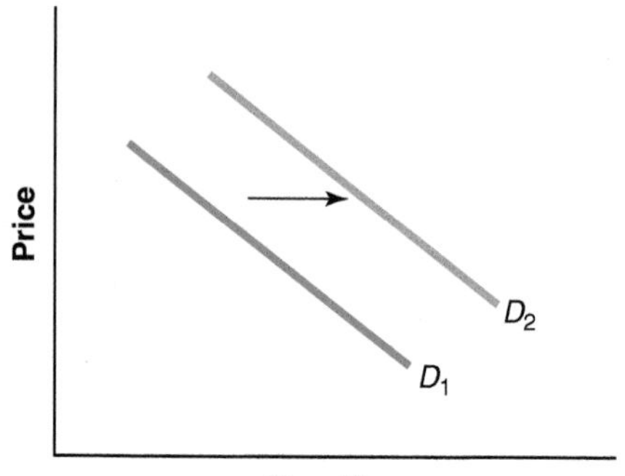


### Example 3–4: Garth Brooks, Used CDs, and the Law of Demand

According to this example, a used-CD market lowers the net price of a CD from $15 to $10, which would result in "an increase in quantity demanded" and a movement along the demand curve from point *A* to point *B*. At the same time, used CDs serve as a cheaper substitute for new music CDs. This second effect will decrease the demand for new music CDs and shift the demand curve to the left. If this decrease in demand exceeds the increase in quantity demanded, as shown in the accompanying diagram, Garth Brooks' fear of the used-CD market is justified.

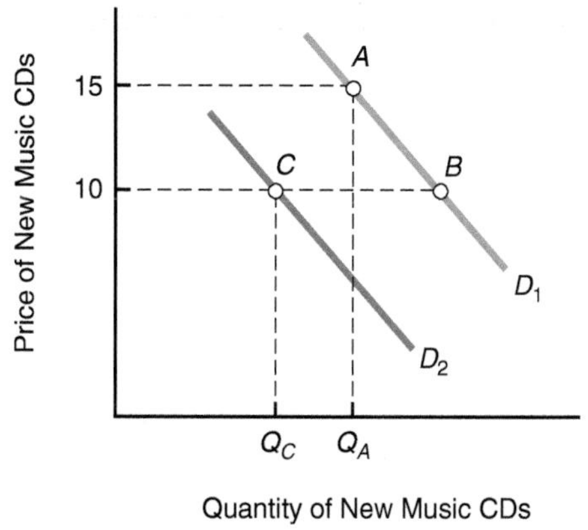


## Example 3–5: Surge in Electronics Sales Follow Dramatic Drop in LCD Prices

The market supply for LCD flat screen TVs has been increasing or shifting to the right, as indicated by the accompanying diagram. The determinants responsible for this shift in supply include falling prices (costs) of a key input—LCD panels, and increased technology devoted to LCD flat screen TVs.

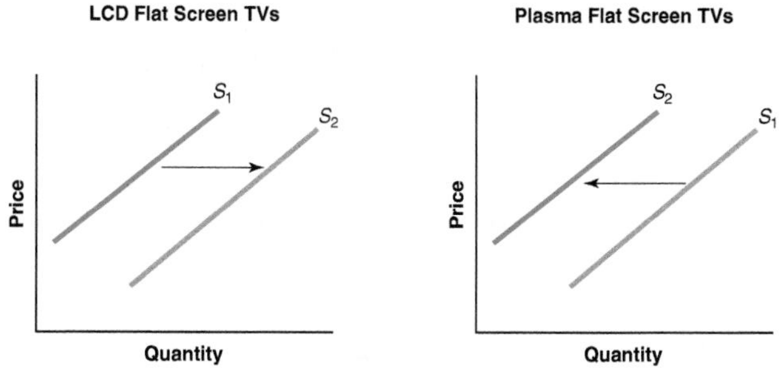


The example predicts that, in the future, the market supply for plasma TVs will start to decline or shift left, as described in the diagrams above.

## Example 3–6: Chocoholics Beware

1. Factors that are causing an increase in demand and thus an increase in equilibrium price of chocolate bars include an increase in average household income in China and India and the perceived cancer-fighting antioxidant health benefits of eating dark chocolate. Graphically, there will be a rightward shift in the demand curve for chocolate bars, causing an increase in equilibrium price.
2. Factors that are causing a decrease in supply and thus an increase in equilibrium price of chocolate bars include persistence of very dry weather conditions; social tensions; a reduction in government fertilizer and pest control subsidies; and an export tax put on cocoa by the government of Indonesia, which reduces the supply of cocoa for the use of making chocolate bars. Graphically, there will be a leftward shift in the supply curve for chocolate bars, causing an increase in equilibrium price.

## Example 3–7: Shale Natural Gas: A Game Changer for Alberta?

The factors causing a steep decline in natural gas prices include:

1. Global recession causing a decrease in demand
2. Warm winter causing a decrease in demand
3. New, cost-efficient source of natural gas in the U.S. causing an increase in supply

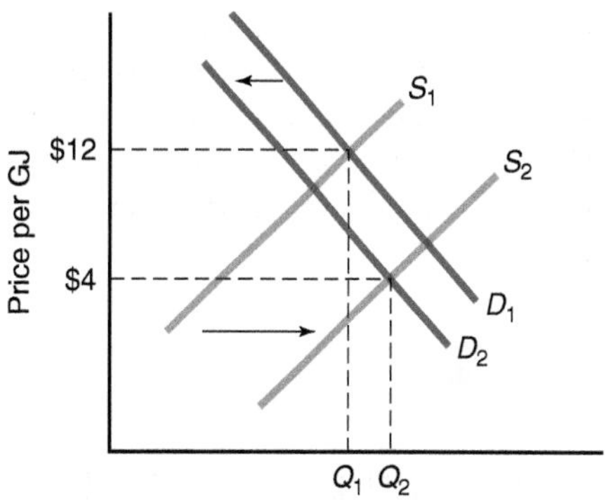


## Issues and Applications: A Canadian Housing Bubble?

1. The one key factor increasing the demand to own Canadian homes is the low mortgage interest rates.

   The effects of the decrease in demand are shown in the following graph:

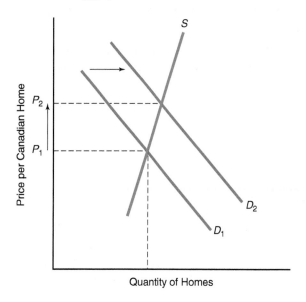

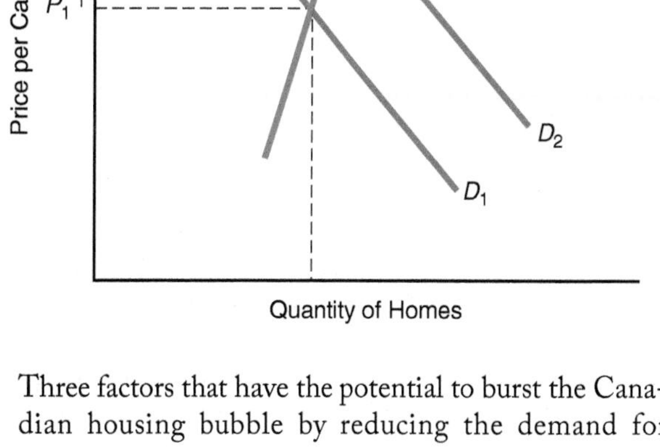


2. Three factors that have the potential to burst the Canadian housing bubble by reducing the demand for

Canadian owner-occupied homes include higher unemployment rates, high debt-to-asset and debt-to-income ratios, an aging population, and implementation of tighter lending rules.

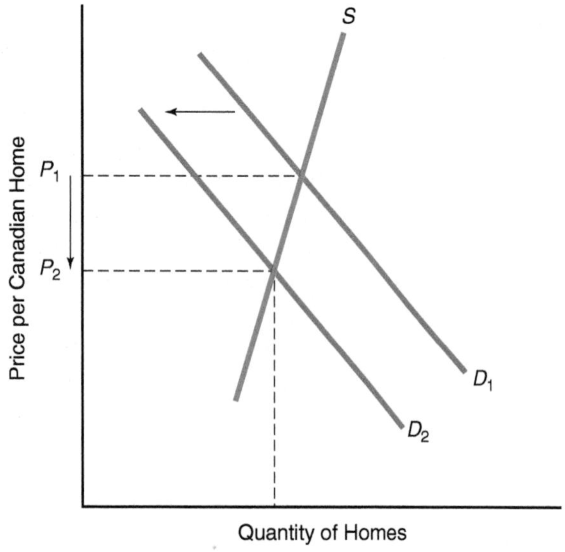


3. One can rationally purchase a home even if it turns out to be a bad investment based on the consumption benefits one derives from the home purchase: privacy; pride of ownership; tenure of home ownership—nobody can ask you to leave once your home is paid for; freedom to have pets; and freedom to renovate and landscape to suit your own preferences. Owning your own home can also enhance the enjoyment you derive from shopping for home-related items such as home furnishings, tools, and art.

## Chapter 4: Elasticity

### Example 4–1: "If They Doubled the Price, We'd Still Drink Coffee"

As we have all experienced, when the price of gas rises, because there are few substitutes, we usually do not change the amount we drive. Some will perhaps take the bus or start to carpool, but most will go on as before.

### Example 4–2: The Price Elasticity of Demand for a Tablet Device

If we had not used the average-values formula, we would not have taken into account the change over a range. It makes a difference where we start the analysis when we deal with a range.

### Policy Example 4–1: Who Pays Higher Cigarette Taxes?

As stated in the example, the price elasticity of demand for cigarettes is relatively low, between 0.2 to 0.4, so an increase in excise taxes of 10 percent would lead to a decline in cigarette purchases of 2 percent to 4 percent.

### Example 4–3: What Do Real-World Price Elasticities of Demand Look Like?

In the short run, only minor adjustments to buying habits can be made; in the long run, major adjustments can be made.

### Policy Example 4–2: Do People Substitute Wireless Phone Services for Wired Services?

As younger people switch more toward cellphones, the use of land-line phones will decrease.

### Example 4–4: Frequent Flyer Miles as Income

The demand for travel will decrease because people will not perceive the flights as "free" anymore.

### Issues and Applications: To Combat Cigarette Consumption, Should the Government Raise Taxes on Beer?

1. Cigarette consumers pay the bulk of the taxes imposed on cigarettes.
2. Cigarette consumers would need a large price change before they changed their habits, while beer drinkers could substitute some other alcoholic beverage for beer, so the beer producers would be more likely to see a decrease in their total revenues.

## Chapter 5: Market Efficiency and Market Failure

### Example 5–1: Price Discrimination: Do All Discounts Benefit the Consumer?

Last minute discounts are often found in perishable products or services where the value of the item is about to expire and the extra cost of providing an additional unit of is item is very small. As an example, if there are empty seats in an airplane just minutes before takeoff, the airline may be willing to offer deep discount "standby" airfares to last minute customers. While most of the seats were sold at the regular fare, the last empty seats are filled by offering deep discounts. Another example would a hotel that has empty rooms to rent out late at night. Just like the airline, the owner of the hotel may offer a deep discount at the last minute in order to rent out all the rooms.

**Example 5–2:** What's Wrong with Alberta's Oil Sands?

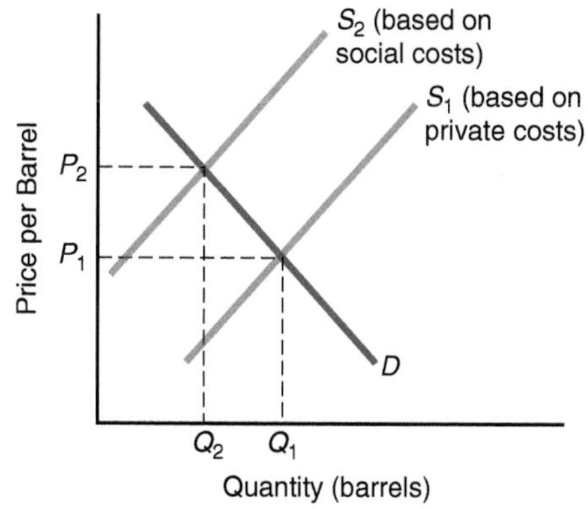


Under a laissez-faire policy, the oil sands company incurs the private costs of producing crude oil, reflected in $S_1$, so $Q_1$ barrels of oil is produced. As this example indicates, there are external costs in the form of air and water pollution, global warming, and destruction of boreal forests, which are all harmful to the health of humans and wildlife. These external costs cause the social costs to exceed the private costs, so that the supply curve that reflects social costs is $S_2$ and the allocatively efficient quantity is $Q_2$. Under a laissez-faire policy, the oil sands company overproduces crude oil.

**Policy Example 5–1:** Why Should the Public Financially Support Higher Education?

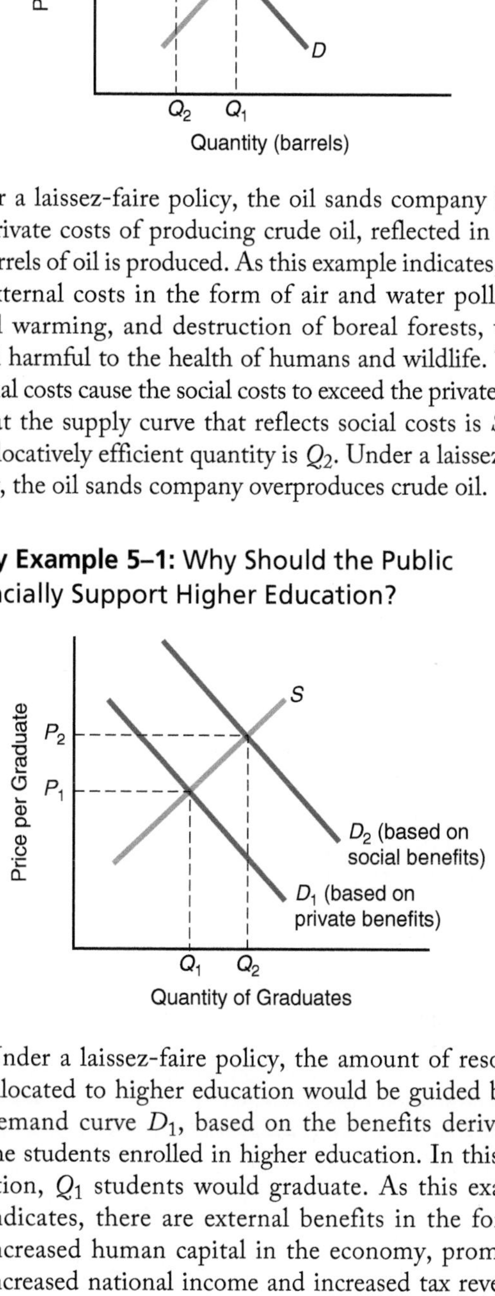


1. Under a laissez-faire policy, the amount of resources allocated to higher education would be guided by the demand curve $D_1$, based on the benefits derived by the students enrolled in higher education. In this situation, $Q_1$ students would graduate. As this example indicates, there are external benefits in the form of increased human capital in the economy, promoting increased national income and increased tax revenues; a reduction in smoking and alcohol abuse; a reduction in unemployment and welfare and unemployment benefit payments; and a reduction in crime. These external benefits cause the social benefits to exceed the private costs, so that the demand curve that reflects social benefits is $D_2$ and the allocatively efficient quantity is $Q_2$. Under a laissez-faire policy, the economy will underproduce college and university graduates.
2. A zero tuition policy—free higher education—will likely cause productive inefficiency in the production of higher education graduates. This would happen to the extent that this policy causes many students to enroll in higher education (because of zero tuition) who are not serious students and who end up dropping out before graduating. In other words the limited resources devoted to higher education will produce less graduates (output of higher education) causing productive inefficiency.

**Policy Example 5–2:** Should Our Tax Dollars Pay for Own the Podium?

1. The example suggests that the ability to produce athletes that win Olympic medals is a public good situation. To this extent, a laissez-faire policy will underproduce these types of elite athletes, from society's viewpoint, causing market failure. One way to increase the production of these elite athletes to a level more closely aligned with society's desires is to use tax dollars to subsidize programs such as Own the Podium. This would promote allocative efficiency.
2. Even if we all agree that producing award-winning elite athletes is a public good, we should still recognize that there is an opportunity cost of allocating tax dollars to programs such as Own the Podium. As an example, there may be other, more serious market failures in the economy, such as underfunding of health care or education. Funding programs such as Own the Podium with tax payer dollars would *not* promote allocative efficiency if it is at the expense of resources being allocated to education or health care.

**Policy Example 5–3:** Global Trade Ban on the Porsche of the Oceans?

1. The Bluefin Tuna situation is a common property resource where the tuna catch is non-excludable but is rivalrous. That is, it is very difficult to control access to this type of fishing, yet the more tuna that is caught, the less that is available for others. Indeed, this tuna is facing the danger of extinction. The European governments

have made the extinction threat worse by subsidizing bluefin tuna fishers, which increases the rate of catch.

2. Since 80 percent of the tuna is exported (traded) to Japan, a trade ban would overwhelmingly reduce the demand for this tuna and this in turn will significantly reduce the profit incentive to catch this type of fish.

### **Issues and Applications:** The Great Global Recession of 2009

1. The U.S. housing bubble refers to the significant increase in housing demand between 2000 and 2006. In terms of the supply and demand graph below, this is reflected in a large rightward shift in the market demand for U.S. homes.

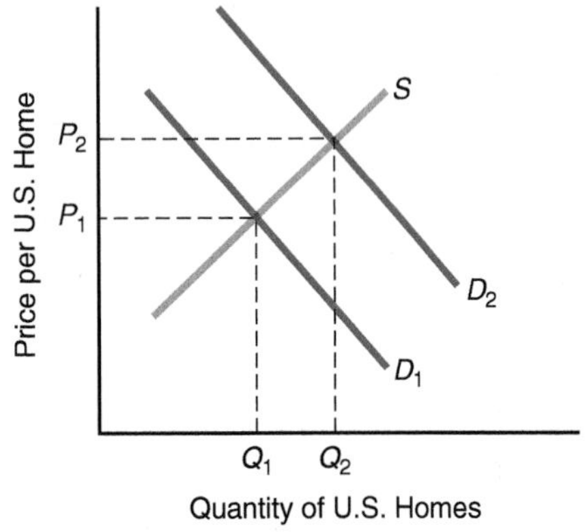


Factors that caused a rightward shift in demand include the following:

- Low stock market returns encouraged investors to switch to housing as an investment item.
- Low interest rates made the cost of buying a home much less.
- Sub-prime mortgage lending allowed potential homeowners to easily access borrowed funds to buy homes.

2. Moral hazard has resulted in allocative inefficiency in the mortgage lending market preceding and during the great recession. That is, under the sub-prime mortgage model, banks were relatively lax in lending to many homeowners who could not afford these mortgage loans, as the banks could pass the risks to third parties due to the securitization of mortgage loans. Therefore, too many mortgage loans were created. That is, too much of global savings went to U.S. homeowners to the point where many of them could not afford to pay back these loans.

3. Regarding the statement that "the financial crisis is a result of irrational behaviour," one can argue quite the contrary. That is, rational behaviour in terms of pursuing one's self-interest played a large role in causing the great recession due to misguided incentives. Banks created sub-prime mortgage loans because they could make greater profits from them—they could pass the risks to other parties, including holders of MBSs. Mortgage brokers would pressure people to buy homes even if they could not afford to because the brokers earned more commissions following this practice. Executives of the shadow (investment) banks earned handsome bonuses based on the volume of mortgage backed securities the firms initially created and sold regardless of how these investments ultimately performed.

   It is important to know that rational behaviour in terms of responding to misguided incentives did play a role in causing the great recession. This gives us hope that if the incentives are changed so as to reward more responsible behaviour and long-term profitability (versus short term gains), we can get the economy back on track.

4. The billions of dollars that national governments have spent bailing out both financial and non-financial corporations can have the unintended result of making these companies even more unprofitable in the longer run due to moral hazard. As an example, if we continue to bail out the north American auto companies—GM and Chrysler—then these companies can engage in risky and unprofitable behaviour as they may feel that they can always pass the risk of making bad decisions onto the taxpayers, who will continually bail them out.

## **Chapter 6:** Extensions of Demand, Supply, and Elasticity

### **Example 6–1:** Booking Your Airline Flight—An Agent or the Web?

As the Example notes, studies over the past five years suggest that it is cheaper, on average, to book flights through professional agents. As well, since intermediaries are independent of the airlines, travel agents can reduce the transaction costs of finding the lowest-cost carrier(s) for customers to reach and return from a given destination. Online services do indeed allow airline customers the advantage of making their own reservations for relatively uncomplicated flights to their destinations. The cost of time spent searching for the best deal for more complicated routes could be quite high for someone who only occasionally flies and is thus unlikely to be familiar with the timetables, or for someone who has a high opportunity cost of time. Travel agents would be valuable to such persons. Using an agent can really help in cases where travel plans fail to materialize as planned. If problems should occur during your trip, help is a phone call away. It is up to your travel agent to provide a solution. If you purchase a ticket online, you are on your own. Most web fares are nonrefundable and nonchangeable; many have restrictions that travellers may be unaware of. A professional travel agent can frequently work behind the scenes on the traveller's behalf. Finally, since there are often a lot of alternative forms of lodging, each with quite different bundles of services and amenities, a consumer can derive a significant benefit by dealing with a knowledgeable agent who specializes in the destination region. In the end, the peace of mind travellers get when booking through professional travel agents is priceless.

### **Example 6–2:** Is Ticketmaster in Cahoots with Scalpers?

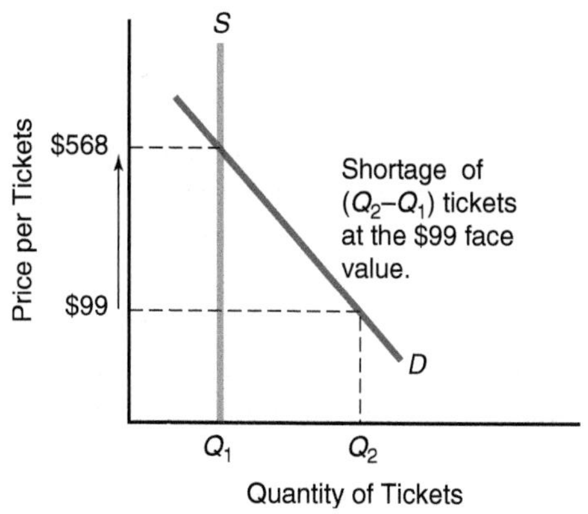


### **Policy Example 6–1:** Assisted Human Reproduction Not for Sale in Canada?

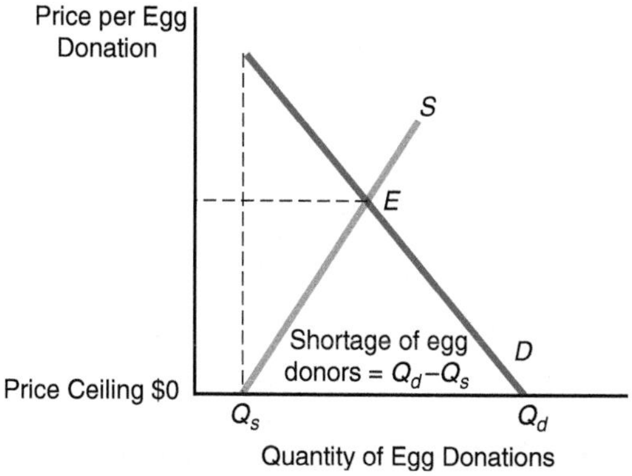


### **Policy Example 6–2:** Do Minimum Wage Rates Benefit Canadian Workers?

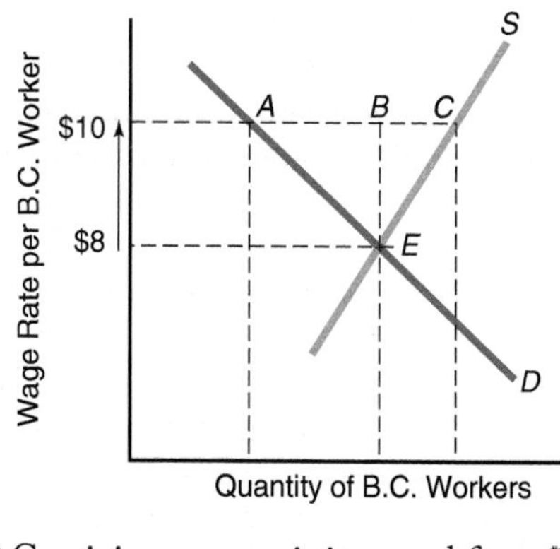


If the B.C. minimum wage is increased from $8 to $10, the quantity of workers demanded by B.C. firms will decrease from *B* to *A*, while the quantity of workers who want to supply their labour increases from *B* to *C*. Overall, this policy will cause surplus of labour (unemployment) equal to distance *AC*. The study estimates this unemployment to be between 10 898 and 52 200 jobs lost.

### **Policy Example 6–3:** The Beginning of the End for the Canadian Wheat Board?

In the accompanying demand and supply diagram, $P_m$ stands for the marketing board price. Assuming that the wheat board is effective in negotiating a higher price for barley farmers, the price of barley would be at $P_m$ if all sales are through the wheat board. As more and more farmers bypass the wheat board, the price will move toward equilibrium at $P_e$. If demand is inelastic, this would cause the farmers' total revenue to decline.

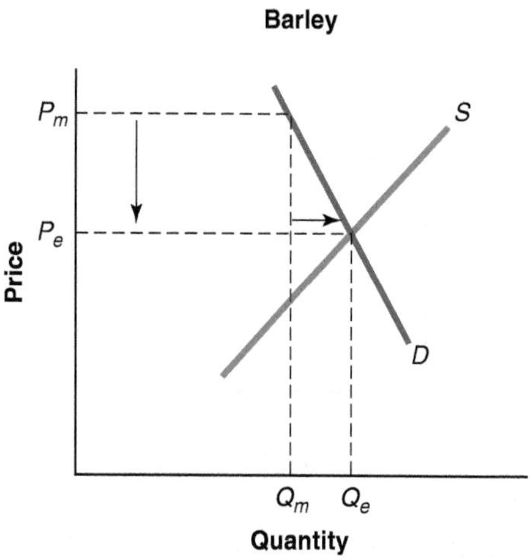


### **Policy Example 6–4:** Could Legalizing Marijuana Reduce Mexican Drug Violence?

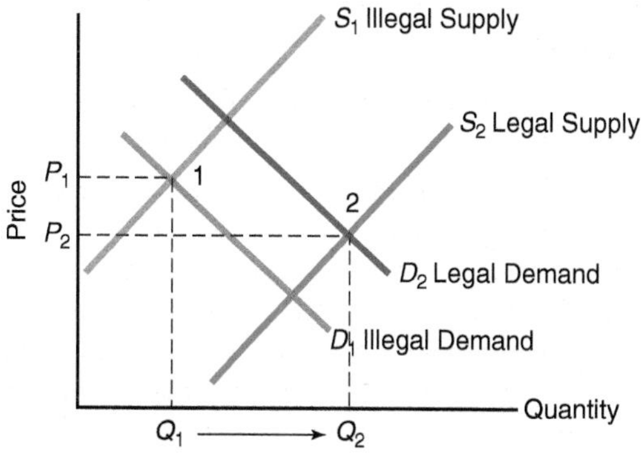


With an outright ban on marijuana, the supply is relatively small (far left) at $S_1$ due to the higher costs related to the risks of getting caught and convicted of supplying the banned drug. Also, $D_1$ reflects a lower demand at each price due to the consumers' risks of getting caught and convicted for possession. If marijuana is legalized, both the demand and supply will increase (shift right) to $D_2$ and $S_2$ due to the elimination of the risks. While the equilibrium quantity will increase, the effect on equilibrium price is indeterminate. If the increase in supply exceeds the increase in demand, as shown in the graph, the price will decrease under legalization.

### **Policy Example 6–5:** An Excise Tax on Music Piracy?

The more inelastic the demand for or supply of blank media, the greater are the proceeds collected from the private copying levies. These levies will be relatively effective in discouraging the copying of music, the more elastic the demand and/or supply. Consumers who use blank media, such as CDs, to back up noncopyrighted material unfairly pay the private copying levies.

### **Issues and Applications:** For-Profit Health Care in Canada?

1. Medicare's zero price ceiling policy for visits to the doctors and the hospitals prevents prices from efficiently allocating the limited health-care resources. Since the Canadian patient does not pay an additional charge for each additional hospital or doctor's visit, there is the danger that the limited health-care resources do not get allocated to the highest-value uses. Inefficient nonprice forms of rationing health-care resources, such as queuing, result from this price ceiling policy.
2. a. Features of the American system, such as insurance co-payments (user fees) and experience ratings serve as allocatively efficient forms of price rationing. In other words, only the patients who value the medical visits the most will be willing to pay the additional user fees or experience rating premiums. These user fees will discourage frivolous use of the limited health-care resources.

   b. The private for-profit health maintenance organizations are faced with incentives to provide a given level of health care with minimal use of resources and thus promote productive efficiency. These incentives include the profit motive and competition from other private health corporations.
3. User fees paid by the patients will not promote allocative efficiency, as consumers (patients) do not possess the expertise necessary to judge the true value of a contemplated visit to the doctor or hospital due to a health problem. Also, in many cases, the doctors act on behalf of the patient in decisions relating to the additional consumption of health-care resources.
4. User fees will reduce the access that poorer consumers have to health-care resources. In addition, the chronically ill are the ones who will pay the most out of their pockets, with user fees. The chronically ill end up paying twice—once because they are ill and a second time when they pay the user fee.
5. In the United States, there are a number of private for-profit corporations (HMOs) providing health insurance and hospital services. As a result, a much larger portion of every dollar spent on health care in the United States is spent on activities not directly related to patient health care, such as administration, marketing, and earning corporate profits. In other words, it costs more for the United States to provide the same patient care, which is productively inefficient.

## Chapter 7: Consumer Choice

### **Example 7–1:** Newspaper Vending Machines versus Candy Vending Machines

There are certain events that would make people want more than one paper, such as disasters, sports (winning the Stanley Cup), major celebrations, and so on.

### **Example 7–2:** The Price of Water in Saudi Arabia

Some of the effects on human behaviour would be: fewer baths/showers, less waste of water, and the purchase of more perfume.

### **Issues and Applications:** Contingent Valuation: Pricing the "Priceless"

1. Opinion polls ask people to value something they are not purchasing. It is easy for an individual to put a $500 value on the use of a park; it is unlikely that this same individual would pay $500 to use it. Demand curves show real willingness to pay for a quantity of a specific good or service.
2. Individuals normally express their perceived level of satisfaction by purchasing or not purchasing the good or service in question. If the individual values a product more than the price, that individual will purchase the product.

## Chapter 8: The Firm: Cost and Output Determination

### **Policy Example 8–1:** Nonprofit Firms Join in the Quest for Profits

A normal rate of return is the amount that must be paid to an investor to induce investment in a business, and so nonprofit organizations still need some way to entice people to contribute to their organization.

### **Example 8–1:** China's Increasing Labour Costs

Labour is one of the most important costs that a company has to consider when trying to determine where to build a factory. But other costs are also relevant, such as business taxes, raw material availability, cost of land, and even stability of the country's present government.

### **Example 8–2:** The Cost of Driving a Car

Variable costs are the per-kilometre costs, while the fixed costs are the annual costs. The average total costs are the

\$0.42 per kilometer, and the marginal costs are dependent on the kilometers driven.

### Example 8–3: Economies of Scale at Dell

Dell's short-run average cost curves have decreased, making Dell more cost-efficient.

### Issues and Applications: Business Look toward Costs to Determine Viability

Student answers will vary.

## Chapter 9: Perfect Competition

### Example 9–1: When Blogging Becomes a Competitive Business

Entry into the blogging business is not entirely free, as there are costs involved in setting up this business. The biggest cost is the opportunity cost of the blogger's time used in the business. Other costs would include the monthly cost of the Internet service provider.

### Policy Example 9–1: Quelling Fears of "Mad Cow Disease" in Asia

According to this Example, the marginal revenue of selling an additional cow carcass to Europe is \$200. On the basis of marginal analysis, beef producers would be willing to incur a marginal cost of up to \$200 to test all animals destined for Asian consumption.

### Example 9–2: High Sunk Costs Can Mean Deep Discounts

Moments before take-off, virtually all the costs related to filling an additional seat on the flight are fixed. These fixed costs would include the expenses related to the capital costs of the plane, airport landing fees, making the reservations and issuing tickets for this flight, hiring the flight's pilot and crew, and paying for the fuel for the flight. Since the marginal cost of filling an additional seat is very close to zero, the airline would be getting a contribution toward its fixed costs, as long as the standby fee were a positive amount (deep discount).

### Example 9–3: U.S. Recession Takes Its Toll on Canadian Lumber Firms

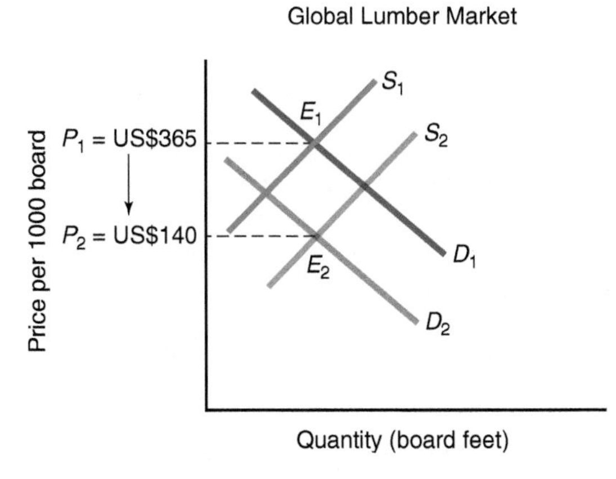


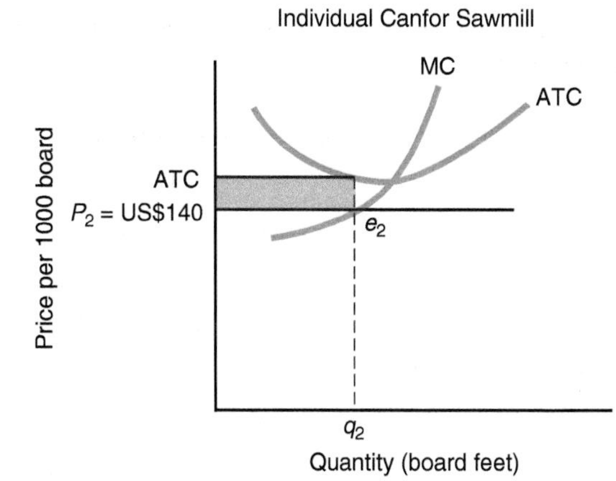


In the global lumber market, there has been both a decrease in demand and increase in supply, causing the equilibrium price to fall to US\$140 per 1000 board feet. In the Canfor sawmill diagram, we see how the price of US\$140 is below average total cost, causing economic losses. In fact, the price is also below average variable cost, causing the sawmill to shut down in the short run. The shaded area represents Canfor's total economic losses.

### Example 9–4: The Big Rush to Provide Digital Snaps in a Snap

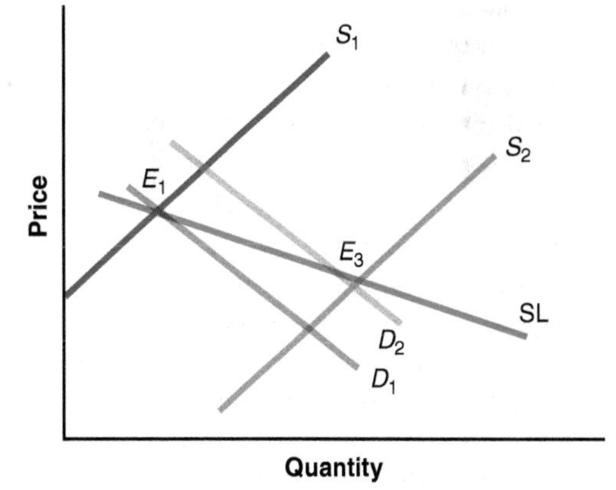


The long-run supply, SL, is formed by joining the points $E_1$ and $E_2$. As you can see, SL is downward sloping, indicating a decreasing-cost industry. As the industry expands, each firm's average total costs curve is shifting down (per-unit costs are declining).

### Issues and Applications: Does Your Local Video Store Have a Future?

1. The new-release and best-seller home-video movie industry in Canada possesses a number of characteristics that conform to perfect competition. In a typical Canadian city, such as Toronto, there are a large number of buyers and sellers for the rental services relating to new-release and best-seller video movies. The large number of sellers include the many bricks-and-mortar stores renting videos in the same market area, as well as competition

from close substitutes, including online video rentals, and purchases of videos from mass retailers. Each of the video rental firms competing with each other rents a homogeneous or identical service—the same new-release videos and best-sellers. There is easy entry in the video movie rental industry. That is evident from the fact that there are numerous small independent firms competing in this industry. As well, new close substitutes have entered the industry, such as renting videos online and buying DVDs supplied by mass retailers.

2. According to the theory covered in this chapter, the selling of a DVD at a price below average total cost could still contribute to fixed costs and possibly profit from other operations, as long as the price exceeds the average variable cost of selling the DVD—the shutdown price. If we assume that the average variable cost of each DVD is equal to the cost of goods sold of $25 per DVD, then, as long as the price exceeds $25, the DVD sale will contribute to fixed costs and possibly profit from the sale of other company products. Also, it was noted in this Issues and Applications that selling DVDs at low prices can attract additional customer traffic to the store. Once more customers enter the store, there is a greater chance that some of these customers will purchase other items, besides DVDs.
3. The typical firm renting new-release and best-seller video movies operates in an industry that new firms can easily enter. This being the case, new firms will continue to enter until zero economic profit, or a normal profit, will be earned.
4. The home-video movie industry's long-run supply curve will be downward sloping, as it is a decreasing-cost industry. As the home-video movie industry has expanded over time, new technology has lowered (and will continue to lower) the cost that the supplier will pay for video movies. The technological change to DVDs (versus VHS) has significantly lowered the cost of goods sold to the video retailer. In the future, when movies are typically downloaded over the Internet, the cost of distributing each DVD will be significantly lower (no shipping costs etc.).

## Chapter 10: Monopoly

### Example 10–1: Microsoft's Abuse of Monopoly

According to this example, Microsoft engaged in predatory behaviour in a number of ways. It significantly eliminated competition in the browser market by giving Internet Explorer away, by integrating Explorer into its operating system, and by entering into agreements with computer manufacturers and Internet providers that restricted the distribution of competing software, such as Netscape Navigator. Similarly, by closely bundling Microsoft Media Player with its Windows operating system, it puts its rivals, such as RealNetworks, at an unfair disadvantage.

### Policy Example 10–1: Should Canada Post Remain a Monopoly—Or Does It Matter?

1. The price elasticity of demand for Canada Post's letter mail service has become more elastic due to the increased competition from faxes and e-mail. Similarly, the price elasticity of demand for Canada Post's parcel delivery service has become more elastic due to the increased competition from large private courier companies. Since the emerging e-commerce industries involve the delivery of goods to one's home by courier, Canada Post could increase its presence in e-commerce and the package courier service.
2. If Canada Post loses its legal monopoly it will have to lower prices on the postal service it provides on the lucrative high population routes. This means that it will likely not have the profit from these routes to subsidize postal service on the remote rural routes. Either these routes will lose postal service or pay very high rates for postal delivery.

### Policy Example 10–2: Forcing Individuals to Reveal How Much They Are Willing to Pay

1. By auctioning off each licence plate to the highest bidder, the maximum price that consumers are willing to pay for each licence plate is extracted. As an example, the first plate may go for $4000, the second plate for $3998, etc. This is a good approximation of perfect price discrimination under a monopoly situation. One reason the government pursues this practice is to maximize profit from the sale of licence plates.
2. By restricting the distribution of licence plates, the government is encouraging the citizens to use public transit, which reduces pollution and traffic congestion.

### Example 10–2: Pricing Internet Service to Maximize Profit

1. Market 1 is the business market as it has relatively inelastic demand.
2. Reasons why the demand for Internet services is more inelastic for business users compared to personal users include: the Internet is more of a necessity to business users, and business users can write off Internet expenses as a tax deduction. Therefore, business users are willing to pay more for the same service.
3. The Internet service provider can enhance its profits by charging a higher price in the inelastic market, which increases total revenue. By lowering the price in the

elastic market (personal user market) this will also increase total revenue. Another way to explain this is to set the price where marginal revenue equals marginal cost in each graph. You will see that this implies having the price set higher in Market 1, the business market, as shown in the graph below.

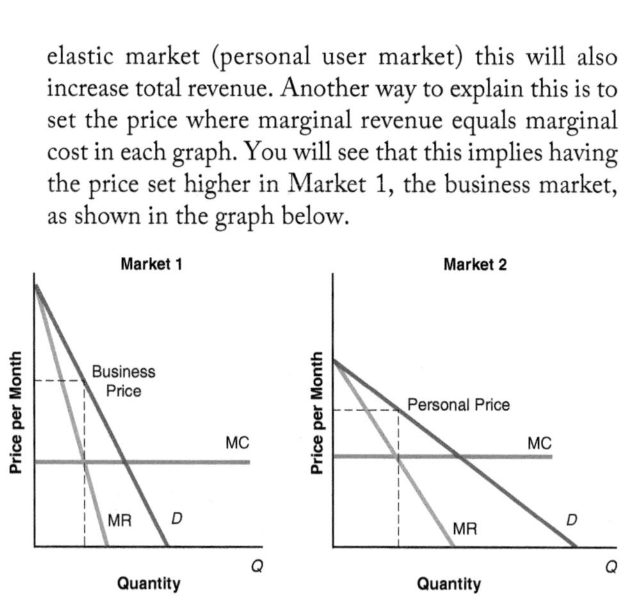


### Example 10–3: The High Cost of Staying Alive

This Example suggests that Celgene, the monopoly supplier of thalidomide, charges an extremely high price, restricts the availability of the drug, and makes an above-normal profit, all of which are consistent with monopoly behaviour. Since thalidomide is now being used to prevent the return of a life threatening cancer, the demand for the drug would be extremely inelastic, thus allowing Celgene to charge exorbitant prices.

### Policy Example 10–3: Monopolies are Milking Canadian Food Consumers

According to this Example, the social costs of farm marketing boards (monopolies) include the following. Like any typical monopoly, the boards restrict output and raise the price (relative to competitive levels), causing allocative inefficiency. The boards typically earn excess or above-normal profits in the long run. The boards conflict with productive efficiency by unnecessarily raising costs due to lobbying activities and resources being spent on enforcing trade barriers. Finally, the boards conflict with economic growth by slowing down the process of developing and expanding new food product areas and by preventing opportunities to expand trade with the fast-growing Asian and Pacific Rim markets.

### Policy Example 10–4: Swapping Songs on the Internet: Is it Really Free?

There are many individuals and companies that "pay" for the actions of those who freely download music files over the Internet. Because of the infringement of copyright, the music artists and recording companies suffer a loss of income due to the decline in legitimate music sales noted in the example. Other parties that lose out include the industries that distribute music legally, such as the manufacturers of music CDs, the companies that supply music downloads over the Internet for a fee, and the bricks-and-mortar music stores. Users who are successfully sued for their practice of freely downloading music files will also pay a price. Finally, we all lose out when copyright is infringed, to the extent that artists and recording companies lose the incentive to create high-quality musical productions that contribute to the enrichment and diversity of our culture and our freedom of expression.

### Issues and Applications: Is It Fair to Practise Price Discrimination in Higher Education?

1. According to this Issue and Applications, universities charge a higher tuition fee in inelastic markets and lower fees in elastic markets. This is consistent with the practice of price discrimination under a monopoly (or near-monopoly) situation, which we know increases total tuition revenue and profit collected from tuitions. This can be shown graphically as follows below, where "profit maximization at MR = MC" implies a higher tuition fee in the inelastic market—international students and medical students.
2. For very prestigious universities, there is a very strong monopoly situation, which means that for those who can afford to attend the university, the demand is very inelastic. This would have the effect of leading to very high tuition fees for those student groups in the inelastic market. Often these prestigious universities have a large amount of money for student financial aid, so that poorer students can get access at a very low cost. In other words, charging rich students very high tuition fees provides the funds for financial aid to poorer students.

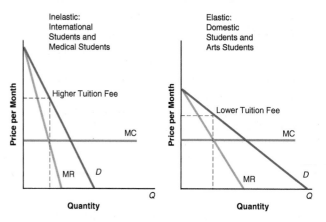

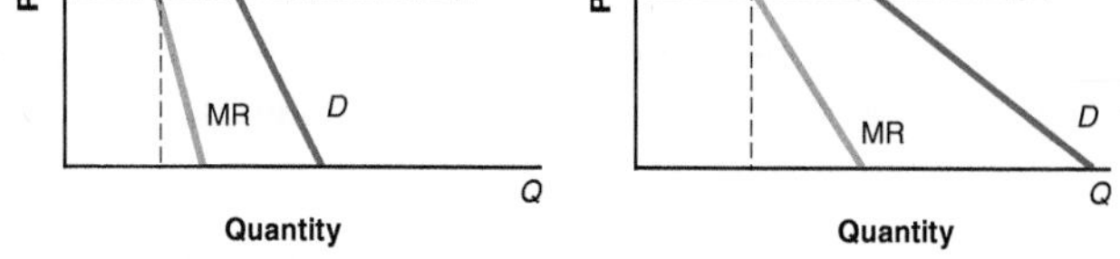


3. The advantages are:
   1. Tuition fees would no longer serve a barrier for low-income students to enroll in the university. This may help ensure that poor individuals who have a high level of ability are able to get the appropriate university education to reach their potential.

In this way, society will get the best doctors, lawyers, engineers, and business people.

2. The "free" university price will increase the enrollments at the universities and, to the extent that this results in increased graduates, this can enhance economic growth.

The disadvantages are:

1. If access to university is "free," students may not value their education, and so this policy attracts a lot of registrations but much fewer graduates. This would lead to a very inefficient use of educational resources. The quality of education would decline due to the entry of students who are not very serious about their studies.
2. When there are no tuition fees, this reduces the revenue available to the university to hire resources including paying high salaries to attract top notch professors and researchers. This may impede economic growth in the future.

## Chapter 11: Monopolistic Competition and Oligopoly

### Example 11–1: A Canadian Retail Success: Thirty Years Running

The Canadian retail footwear industry would be classed as monopolistic competition. There are many firms competing in the same market area, and there is product differentiation. The Example indicates there can be physical differences in the product sold by different suppliers, such as western footwear, children's shoes, or quality running shoes. As Running Room illustrates, firms can compete on the basis of complementary services provided, such as running clinics; running clubs; and the sponsorship of running, walking and charity events. Also, different retail firms can offer different price levels, which conflicts with perfect competition where only one standardized price is charged.

### Example 11–2: The Prisoners' Dilemma

Yes. Assume that two firms, A and B, agree to share the market and charge a high monopoly profit-maximizing price. Assume that there are now four possibilities:

(1) Both stick to the price agreement and each makes \$100 in profits; (2) both ignore the agreement and charge lower prices, and each makes \$40 in profits; (3) A sticks to the agreement, while B ignores and lowers the price. A makes a profit of \$30 and B makes a profit of \$120; and (4) B sticks to the agreement, while A ignores and lowers the price. B makes a profit of \$30 and A makes a profit of \$120. The dominant strategy is for neither to stick to the agreement, if it cannot be enforced.

### Policy Example 11–1: Sweet Deal between Canadian Chocolate Bar Makers?

a. The price fixing agreement alleged that the major chocolate manufacturers secretly met to agree to artificially inflate prices from 2001 to 2008. This alleged behaviour is consistent with a positive-sum cooperative pricing model, where all parties to the agreement, as a group, are better off compared to a non-cooperative pricing situation.

b. The manufacturers are alleged to have sold the bars to the various retailers with the understanding that all the retailers would make sure that they maintained the retail prices at levels suggested by the manufacturers. If the retailers undercut the suggested retail prices, they would face the possibility of not being able to purchase the popular bars from the manufacturers.

### Example 11–3: OPEC Continues to Rule the World Oil Market?

Saudi Arabia, as the largest oil producer, can have the largest impact on oil production and prices. Since all OPEC members know this, they will be less likely to cheat when it is clear that Saudi Arabia will practise a tit-for-tat strategy and flood the market for oil if it finds one or more members of the cartel cheating.

### Example 11–4: De Beers Diamond Cartel: A Thing of the Past?

The increased competition due to the greater presence of Russia, Canada, and Australia and due to better quality artificial diamonds moves the industry away from cooperative pricing tactics, such as cartels.

### Policy Example 11–2: Turbulence in the Canadian Airline Industry

According to this example, Air Canada is being charged with two entry-deterring strategies—excess capacity and pricing below "avoidable costs," which we would call variable costs. The excess capacity allows Air Canada to add flights to any route that is challenged by WestJet or CanJet. Even without the excess capacity, a strategy of pricing below average variable cost would deter entry by WestJet or CanJet.

### Example 11–5: Wind Blows Down Canadian Wireless Prices

The Big Three wireless firms—Telus, Bell, and Rogers—employed two tactics to prevent the successful entry of Wind Mobile. First, they dropped the prices of their plans. This meant that Wind Mobile had to enter the industry charging quite low plan prices, thus reducing the profits earned by Wind Mobile (or increasing its losses). Second, the Big Three sold plans that had lock-in clauses, where a penalty would have to be paid by any consumer wanting to switch to Wind Mobile's plans.

### **Example 11–6:** Can Advertising Lead to Efficiency?

According to this example, both can be true. "We are better because we are bigger" is really the theme of this example, in that advertising allows a firm to get bigger, and this, in turn, can make the firm more efficient. To the extent that the firm gets more efficient, it can get even bigger (as it steals market share from rivals), so the phrase "We are bigger because we are better" can also hold true.

### **Example 11–7:** Intel Bags Record Fine

Consumers who have purchased new computers worldwide have likely been harmed by the exclusive sales practices of Intel. That is because these practice result in less competition in the computer chip market and higher computer chip prices, which translate to higher computer prices. That is why there were about 80 consumer class-action lawsuits filed against Intel at the time that Intel offered to settle with AMD.

### **Example 11–8:** High Switching Costs in the Credit World

In the auto industry, such firms as General Motors offer customers GM credit cards that accumulate reward points toward a discount for the purchase of a new vehicle, if purchased from General Motors. Gas stations, such as Petro-Canada, offer cards (i.e., Petro Points) that accumulate gas discounts based on volume usage.

### **Example 11–9:** Facebook Frenzy

To explain how the network effect applies to the online social networking industry, let us first review the definition of "networking effect," which is a situation where a customer's willingness to use an item depends on how many others use it. In the case of social networking sites, a potential member is more likely to choose a site with a larger membership. The potential user is more likely to connect with long-lost friends or friends from other geographical regions if the user joins a large social network membership site. Other potential users (such as people running for political office) are more likely to join a site where they can more easily pick up large blocks of supporters, which would be the larger website. Also, advertisers are more likely to pay advertising dollars to larger websites as each advertising dollar will more likely reach a larger target audience.

### **Example 11–10:** Apple's iMania

The forms of nonprice competition used by Apple include the following. Apple has effectively focused on innovation as a way to increase its market share. Examples include the novel hardware and software related to the iPod, iPhone, and iPad. Apple engages in exclusive dealing when it only allows software developers to develop applications for its "i-products" if the developers use Apple's programming tools and not competitors' tools. Apple has created significant "switching costs" in that iPod, or iPhone or iPad users would have to abandon their existing set of music and video playlists, photo albums, and software applications if they were to switch to a competitor's phone. Finally, Apple has effectively encouraged the network effect by encouraging third-party developers to develop apps that exclusively work with the iPhone. As well, iPhone 4's new video calling feature will encourage the network effect.

### **Issues and Applications:** Game Theory: Opening Up the Brewing Industry

1. This game is a negative-sum game. Although the microbrewery gains $15 million, Labatt and Molson together lose $16 million.
2. Labatt and Molson could use other entry-deterring strategies. They could substantially increase their already high annual advertising expenditures as a barrier to entry. They could also reduce the price of their beer to average total cost. They would not earn economic profits, but the competing breweries would no longer have an incentive to enter the industry. Labatt and Molson could also introduce switching costs. For example, they could offer frequent flyer miles so that customers have a vested interest in staying with one company. In fact, Molson has offered Air Miles with the purchase of 15-can cases of its Canadian brand.

## Chapter 12: Regulation and Competition Policy

### **Example 12–1:** Deregulation Hits Canadian Phone Markets

The different ways that the large phone companies are likely to practise price discrimination include the following. In rural phone markets where there is less competition, demand will be inelastic, so the large phone companies will raise rates to increase total revenue. It should be noted that under the new rules, the phone companies can raise rates in rural areas for basic phone service only by the inflation rate or 5 percent per year, whichever is less. In the urban areas, where there is a lot of competition, demand is elastic, so the large phone companies will lower phone rates to increase total revenue. A large phone company might also price discriminate between potential new customers (more elastic) and existing customers (more inelastic) so that the former get a lower promotional price for a few months if they switch to the large phone company. Finally, once a customer makes a decision to buy basic phone service from a large phone company, the customer's demand for the optional services may tend to be relatively inelastic. If this is the case, one would expect to see significant hikes in the price of optional services.

### **Policy Example 12–1:** Can the CRTC Effectively Regulate Cable TV?

The CRTC would have to be able to block transmission of the American channels if it were to enforce Canadian content regulations. Given the increasing effectiveness and decreasing cost of satellite dishes, it is unlikely the CRTC would be successful. The CRTC has established rules that are meant to apply to approved cable TV and satellite TV providers. These rules ensure that the "basic" cable and satellite packages consist of specified Canadian channels and that "optional" packages are designed to ensure that Canadians receive a majority of Canadian programming. There will always be some nonapproved satellite providers operating in Canada who do not abide by these Canadian content rules.

### **Example 12–2:** The Effectiveness of Auto Safety Regulations

The purpose of the safety regulations was to make automobile accidents less dangerous and to reduce the number of injuries and deaths by eliminating certain hazardous features and by adding safety devices to cars. The regulators did not consider that *ceteris paribus* conditions would not continue as a result of the regulations. The unintended effect of having safer cars has been an increase in reckless driving and more accidents, which has increased, at least not reduced, the number of injuries. Regulation to achieve a certain goal does not take into account that people's likely response can have effects that were unforeseen and not intended.

### **Policy Example 12–2:** Ontario's Feeble Attempt at Energy Deregulation

First of all, the Ontario government dragged its feet in implementing deregulation, with the Act being passed in 1998 and the actual implementation taking place in 2002. This created a lot of uncertainty, which hindered private-sector investment in new electricity capacity. Second, the price freeze will have the effect of reducing private-sector investment in additional electricity generating capacity. If the government had stayed out of the electricity market, the higher prices would have served as an incentive to increase the private-sector supply of electricity. As well, the higher prices would have encouraged energy conservation and thereby would have reduced the shortage situation. Finally, the fact that the Liberal government subsequently talked about the possibility of the government's investing public funds in new electricity capacity would likely have had the effect of stifling additional private sector investment in new electricity facilities.

### **Example 12–3:** Cutting through the Red Tape

Government costs attached to reviewing and revising regulations are mainly the opportunity costs of labour. Civil servants must research the effects of the regulation and then devise improvements. This is a time-consuming task. In addition, every time regulations change, businesses must spend valuable time reviewing these changes so as to abide by the new regulations. In many cases, businesses will have to incur legal and accounting costs in order to keep abreast of, and abide by, changes in regulations.

### **Example 12–4:** HMV Boycotts Rolling Stones Products

The Example clearly illustrates that not all exclusive agreements contravene the *Competition Act*. For a violation to take place, competition must be substantially lessened at the industry level or one competitor must be significantly negatively impacted, if not precluded from carrying on its business.

### **Example 12–5:** Suzy Shier Pays $1 Million to Settle Misleading Advertising Dispute

According to Canada's *Competition Act*, a representation pertaining to an article's regular (ordinary) price constitutes a reviewable matter when the article did not sell at this stated regular price in significant quantities over a reasonable period of time.

### **Issues and Applications:** Media Concentration in Canada: A Public Concern?

1. The CRTC's approval of media acquisitions is an example of social regulation, not economic regulation. In economic regulation, the goal is typically to reduce the rates or prices that would be charged by the companies being regulated. In the media examples, the acquisitions being approved have the effect of increasing media concentration, which, if anything, will lead to an increase in the rates charged by the media providers. The CRTC has approved the media acquisitions on the basis of the social goal of fostering new Canadian television productions that contribute to our cultural identity.
2. Increased media concentration can operate to the detriment of the Canadian public in a number of ways. By lessening competition, it can result in higher rates being charged for the services being provided by the Canadian media companies. In addition, as more and more of the Canadian media are concentrated in fewer and fewer hands, there is a danger that editorial diversity will be reduced. In other words, the media companies will produce and distribute news that is biased to serve narrow corporate interests. This may include news that is biased toward governments and political parties that support the media corporations.

## Chapter 13: Labour Demand and Supply

### Example 13–1: Does It Pay to Study?

Identical twins have exactly the same genetic make-up. Therefore, they have the same physical appearance and abilities. They will normally have the same childhood influences from family. They may also have the same (or nearly the same) IQ. Thus, any innate abilities and familial influences should be the same. The only real differences between them that would determine wage differences would be education, training, and experience, or all of those factors that determine human capital differences.

### Policy Example 13–1: Should the Minimum Wage Be Raised to Help Young People?

Young workers are most affected by changes in the minimum wage because they are the most likely to be in positions where they are earning only the minimum wage. They are also the most likely to be laid off if the minimum wage increases.

### Example 13–2: Strike Activity in Canada

A strike can help increase the wages of workers in the long run. Yes, an increase in profit sharing would make workers less likely to strike and lose those profits.

### Example 13–3: Monopsony in College Sports

College athletics can increase the visibility of a college, thereby attracting more students in all fields.

### Issues and Applications: Canadian Wheat Board: Monopoly or Monopsony

1. Monopoly—a firm that has great control over the price of a good it sells. Monopsony—a single buyer of a factor of production. Bilateral monopoly—a market structure in which a single buyer faces a single seller.
2. The CWB can argue that it gets the best price because of its ability to speak for all western wheat farmers. It can also use the fact that it has all the infrastructure that farmers need to get their grain to the market.

## Chapter 14: Income and Poverty

### Example 14–1: Increasing Income Inequality and Working Spouses

No, households with two incomes have other expenses that must be considered, such as child care, two vehicles needed, and so on.

### Example 14–2: Are We Running to Stay in Place?

The "perks" of a job can have an impact on an individual's living standard. For example, if you get a company car to drive, you do not need to purchase one of your own and gas is paid by the company, saving hundreds of dollars.

### Example 14–3: Economics, Aging, and Productivity

An economist close to retirement has already made his or her name and is not fighting for a permanent position at a college. A lot of colleges require that their professors publish articles as a condition of employment.

### Example 14–4: Poverty Rates in the European Union

Every nation collects income information differently, so in order to have an equal basis for comparison, all countries would have to agree to collect the information in the same manner. They would also need to agree on a definition of poverty.

### Issues and Applications: Eradicating Child Poverty

1. The new integrated child benefits plan will probably not end child poverty in Canada although it will likely improve the material conditions of many poor children. There are too few resources to be allocated to this plan to bring all children above the poverty level. Since poverty is measured on a relative scale, some children will always be at the low end of the scale and will be classified as poor.
2. There are two main reasons implementing the critics' plan might be unsuccessful. First, putting money into improving economic conditions might not work. The money could be misplaced, it could provide a one-time improvement that doesn't continue over the long run, or it could be insufficient to make noticeable improvements in the economy. Second, people who are currently on social assistance may not necessarily get the jobs created by economic improvement. A physically challenged unemployed person may not qualify for the job. The jobs created may not be close to a centre of poverty, so those who need the jobs would not be able to get to work.

## Chapter 15: Environmental Economics

### Example 15–1: Carbon Offset Projects: Real or Just Hot Air?

The carbon trading market is viable if regulated. Unregulated carbon offset programs tend to attract profiteers who do nothing to reduce actual pollution. Some carbon trading projects actually do reduce pollution, but most are just a transfer of money from developed countries to undeveloped countries.

### **Policy Example 15–1:** Canada Confronts a High Marginal Cost of Pollution Abatement

Canada would be better off if it engaged in less pollution abatement because the marginal cost of achieving the promised emission reduction is at least $30 billion per year, while the marginal benefit is only $25 billion in total.

### **Example 15–2:** Wind as a Renewable Resource

In the short run, it might cost more to switch to alternative methods of using energy, but in the long run, the costs should be reduced.

### **Example 15–3:** Not in My Backyard (NIMBY)!

If an individual owns the property, they should be allowed to decide what development they want on their property. This can usually be accomplished by negotiation and compensation by the interested parties. Canada does not have property rights enshrined in the Constitution, so the different levels of government can force an individual to give up their rights by offering a "fair market price."

### **Example 15–4:** Preventing Overfishing by Trading Quotas

The quotas themselves become valuable only if the fishers do not exceed the quotas. If they exceed their quotas, then the value of having a quota decreases and the fishers lose.

### **Example 15–5:** Reducing Waste by Recycling

The benefits of recycling are less pollution, reuse of materials, and conservation of expensive landfill resources.

### **Example 15–6:** Are We Running out of Everything?

Switching to using renewable resources is often more expensive than using nonrenewable resources.

### **Issues and Applications:** Climate Change: What Can Canada Do?

1. Firms might move their operations to countries that do not have as many regulations and targets if the regulations are too stringent. This depends on whether the raw materials the firm uses are easily transferred or acquired in the undeveloped country. The Alberta oil sands are impossible to move to another country.
2. Industries account for about 50 percent of the GHGs. Consumers have a responsibility to use nonrenewable resources wisely. Climate change is a problem for not only industry, but for governments and individuals.

## Chapter 16: The Public Sector

### **Policy Example 16–1:** Who Should Pay the High Cost of a Legal System?

Some of the implicit costs that you could list would be time, buildings and their maintenance, court clerks, and public officers who must appear before the court.

### **Example 16–1:** Are Lighthouses a Public Good?

In point 1, it would be difficult to sell a lighthouse to one individual. In point 2, the cost of the lighthouse does not increase if more people make use of its services, and in point 3, because one person makes use of the lighthouse, it does not mean that others cannot use it as well.

### **Policy Example 16–2:** Do Government-Funded Sports Stadiums Have a Net Positive Effect on Local Economies?

A sports stadium will increase employment and spending within the economy. It is often seen that facilities built for the Olympics are then used by the cities for years after the event. This improves the image of the cities, as they can offer first-class facilities and attract other events, boosting their economies.

### **Policy Example 16–3:** Tax Freedom Day around the World

The longer you have to wait for tax freedom day, the higher your level of taxation. Swedes have to wait until August 8th for their tax freedom day, while U.S. citizens get to celebrate on April 30th. The lucky winners (on March 14th) are residents of India.

### **Example 16–2:** Employment Insurance

Canada Pension Plan payments are not part of government's general revenue, and it might be reassuring to workers to know that EI premiums are handled the same way. If there is a surplus in the account, government should not be able to use it to balance its budget.

### **Issues and Applications:** Should We Switch to a Flat Tax?

1. Employees at the Canada Revenue Agency (CRA) might well be against a flat-tax system. Advocates of a flat tax claim that one of the benefits would be a significantly downsized CRA, implying that many CRA employees might lose their jobs. We know from Chapter 1 that the rationality assumption tells us that people usually do not make decisions that reduce their well being. It is likely that CRA employees would want to keep their

jobs to maintain their well being and would thus oppose a flat-tax system.

2. A flat-tax system is more efficient than a progressive tax system because the method of calculation of tax owing is much simpler: There is only one calculation to make, rather than the many calculations required in a progressive system. There would be efficiencies realized by taxpayers who could complete their tax returns easily, and by CRA employees who could check the calculation equally simply. The opportunity cost of the yearly tax return would fall, leaving resources free to pursue more productive activities.

# Glossary

**Absolute advantage** The ability to perform a task using the fewest number of labour hours.

**Accounting profit** Total revenue minus total explicit costs.

**Age–earnings cycle** The regular earnings profile of an individual throughout that person's lifetime.

**Aggregates** Economywide measures.

**Allocative efficiency** Producing the mix of goods and services most valued by consumers.

**Anticombines legislation** Laws that make illegal certain economic activies that might restrain trade.

**Asymmetric information** Exchange situations where one party directly participating in the market possesses special knowledge that is not available to the other party.

**Average cost pricing** Pricing that occurs when the monopoly firm is forced to set price equal to average total cost.

**Average fixed costs** Total fixed costs divided by the number of units produced.

**Average physical product** The total product divided by the number of workers expressed in output per hour.

**Average tax rate** The total taxes due divided by total taxable income.

**Average total costs** Total costs divided by the number of units produced; sometimes called per-unit total costs.

**Average variable costs** Total variable costs divided by the number of units produced.

**Best response function** The manner in which one oligopolist reacts to a change in price, output, or quality made by another competitor in the industry.

**Bilateral monopoly** A market structure in which a single buyer faces a single seller.

**Black market** A market in which the price-controlled good is sold at an illegally high price through various under-the-table methods.

**Breakeven** The output that a firm must produce to reach the point where its profits are zero.

**Bureaucracy** An administrative system run by a large staff following rules and procedures set down by government.

**Bureaucrats** Nonelected government officials.

**Capital gain** The positive difference between the buying and selling prices of an asset.

**Capital loss** The negative difference between the purchase price and the sale price of an asset.

**Capture hypothesis** A theory of regulatory behaviour that predicts that the regulators will eventually be captured by the special interests of the industry being regulated.

**Cartel** An association of suppliers in an industry that agree to set common prices and output quotas to prevent competition.

**Ceteris paribus [KAY-ter-us PEAR-uh-bus] assumption** The assumption that nothing changes except the factor or factors being studied; "other things being constant," or "other things being equal."

**Collective decision making** How voters, politicians, and other interested parties act and how these actions influence nonmarket decisions.

**Common property** Nonexclusive property that is owned by everyone and therefore by no one.

**Common property resources** Goods or resources that are nonexcludable but are rivalrous.

**Comparable-worth doctrine** The belief that women should receive the same wages as men if the levels of skill and responsibility in their jobs are equivalent.

**Comparative advantage** The ability to perform an activity at the lowest opportunity cost.

**Complements** Two goods are complements if both are used together for consumption or enjoyment.

**Concentration ratio** The percentage of total industry sales contributed by the four largest firms.

**Conglomerate merger** The joining of two firms from unrelated industries.

**Constant returns to scale** No change in long-run average costs when output increases.

**Constant-cost industry** An industry that can increase its output in the long run, without affecting input prices.

**Consumer optimum** Reached when the consumer has attained an optimum consumption set of goods and services.

**Consumer surplus** The difference between the maximum amount that consumers are willing to pay and the actual amount paid for all units of a product consumed.

**Consumption** The use of goods and services for direct personal satisfaction.

**Cooperative game** A game in which firms get together to collude or fix prices.

**Cost-of-service regulation** Regulation that allows the regulated companies to charge prices that reflect the actual average cost of providing the services, with a normal profit included in the assessment of these costs.

**Creative response** A response that conforms to the letter of the law but undermines its spirit.

**Cross-elasticity of demand (*Exy*)** The percentage change in the quantity demanded of one good (holding its price constant) divided by the percentage change in the price of a related good.

**Deadweight loss** The decrease in consumer and producer surplus that results from a situation of allocative inefficiency.

**Decreasing-cost industry** A situation where input prices decrease as the industry expands in the long run.

**Demand** The quantities of a specific good or service that individuals are willing to purchase at various possible prices, other things being constant.

**Demand curve** A graphical representation of the law of demand.

**Demerit good** Any good that the political process has deemed socially undesirable.

**Dependent variable** A variable whose value changes according to changes in the value of one or more independent variables.

**Deregulation** The elimination of regulations on economic activity.

**Derived demand** Input factor demand derived from demand for the final product being produced.

**Diminishing marginal utility** The principle that as an individual consumes more of a particular commodity, the total level of utility, or satisfaction, derived from that consumption usually increases. Eventually, however, the rate at which it increases diminishes as more is consumed.

**Diseconomies of scale** Increases in long-run average costs that occur as output increases.

**Distribution of income** The way income is allocated among the population.

**Division of labour** Individuals specializing in a subset of tasks related to a specific product.

**Dominant strategies** Strategies that are generally successful no matter what actions competitors take.

**Economic profits** Total revenues minus total opportunity costs of all inputs used, or total revenues minus the total of all implicit and explicit costs.

**Economic regulation** Regulation that controls the prices that firms are allowed to charge.

**Economic system** The social arrangements or institutional means through which resources are used to satisfy human wants.

**Economic way of thinking** Assumes that the typical response to an economic problem of scarcity is rational behaviour.

**Economics** A social science that studies how people allocate their limited resources to satisfy their wants.

**Economies of scale** Decreases in long-run average costs resulting from increases in output.

**Elastic demand** A demand relationship in which a given percentage change in price will result in a larger percentage change in quantity demanded.

**Empirical** Using real-world data to test the usefulness of a model.

**Entrepreneurship** Human resources that perform the functions of risk taking, organizing, managing, and assembling other factors of production to make business ventures.

**Equilibrium** A point from which there tends to be no movement unless demand or supply changes.

**Excess capacity** A situation where the firm is operating at an output level below that required to achieve minimum average total cost.

**Excise tax** A tax imposed on a particular commodity or service.

**Exclusion principle** The principle that no one can be denied the benefits of a public good for failing to pay for it.

**Exclusive dealing** A situation where the firm supplies its product to a customer on condition that the customer not buy similar products from rival firms supplying a similar product.

**Explicit costs** Expenses that business managers must take account of because they must actually be paid out by the firm.

**External benefits** A situation where the marginal social benefits from producing a product exceed the marginal private benefits.

**External costs** Situations where the marginal social costs of producing a product exceed the marginal private costs of production.

**Externality** A situation in which a private cost diverges from a social cost; a situation in which the costs of an action are not fully borne by the two parties engaged in exchange.

**Featherbedding** Unions' tendency to bargain for excessive use of workers.

**Firm** An organization that brings together factors of production—labour, land, physical capital, human capital, and entrepreneurial skill—to produce a product or service that it hopes can be sold at a profit.

**Fixed costs** All costs that do not vary—that is, all costs that do not depend on the rate of production.

**Free-rider problem** A situation in which some individuals take advantage of the fact that others will shoulder the burden of paying for public goods.

**Game theory** The analytical framework in which two or more individuals, companies, or nations compete for certain payoffs that depend on the strategy that the others employ.

**Goods** The physical items that consumers are willing to pay for.

**Government, or political, goods** Goods (and services) provided by the public sector; they can be either private or public goods.

**Horizontal merger** The joining of firms that are producing or selling a similar product.

**Human capital** The education and training of workers.

**Implicit costs** Expenses that business managers do not have to pay out of pocket.

**Import quota** A supply restriction that prohibits the importation of more than a specified quantity of a particular good in a one-year period.

**Incentive** Inducement to take a particular action.

**Incentive structure** The system of rewards and punishments individuals face with respect to their own actions.

**Income elasticity of demand** A horizontal shift in the demand curve in response to changes in income.

**Income in kind** Income received in the form of goods and services.

**Increasing-cost industry** A situation where input prices increase as the industry expands in the long run.

**Independent variable** A variable whose value is determined independently of, or outside, the equation under study.

**Industry supply curve** The locus of points showing the minimum prices at which given quantities will be forthcoming from the industry; also called the market supply curve.

**Inelastic demand** A demand relationship in which a given percentage change in price will result in a less than proportionate percentage change in the quantity demanded.

**Inferior goods** Goods for which demand falls as income rises.

**Interest** Income earned by capital.

**Labour market signalling** The theory that even if higher education does not change productivity, it acts as an effective signal of greater individual abilities.

**Labour** Productive contributions made by individuals who work.

**Laissez-faire** French term for "leave it alone"; the government should leave it (the economy) alone or "let it be."

**Land** Nonhuman gifts of nature.

**Law of demand** The observation that there is an inverse relationship between the price of any good and its quantity demanded, holding other factors equal.

**Law of diminishing (marginal) returns** The observation that after some point, successive equal-sized increases in a variable factor of production, such as labour, added to fixed factors of production, will result in smaller increases in output.

**Law of increasing relative cost** When society takes more resources and applies them to the production of any specific good, the opportunity cost increases for each additional unit produced.

**Law of supply** The observation that there is a direct relationship between the price of any good and its quantity supplied, holding other factors constant.

**Long run** The period of time in which all inputs can be varied.

**Long-run average cost curve** The locus (path) of points representing the minimum unit cost of producing any given rate of output, given current technology and resource prices.

**Long-run industry supply curve** A market supply curve showing the relationship between quantities supplied by the entire industry and prices, after sufficient time has passed to allow firms to change plant sizes and enter or exit the industry.

**Lorenz curve** A geometric representation of the distribution of income.

**Macroeconomics** The study of the behaviour of the economy as a whole.

**Majority rule** A collective decision-making system in which group decisions are made on the basis of 50.1 percent of the vote.

**Marginal benefit** The maximum amount that consumers are willing to pay for a specified unit of quantity. It is the height of the demand curve at the specified unit of quantity.

**Marginal cost** The minimum amount that firms must receive in order to supply a specified unit of quantity. It is the height of the supply curve at the specified unit of quantity.

**Marginal costs** Costs that result from a one-unit change in the production rate.

**Marginal cost pricing** A system where the price charged to the consumer is equal to the opportunity cost to society of producing the last unit of the good in question.

**Marginal factor cost (MFC)** The cost of using an additional unit of an input.

**Marginal physical product** The change in output caused by a one-unit change in the labour input.

**Marginal physical product (MPP) of labour** The change in output resulting from the addition of one more worker.

**Marginal revenue** The change in total revenues attributable to changing production by one unit of the product in question.

**Marginal revenue product (MRP)** The marginal physical product (MPP) times marginal revenue.

**Marginal tax rate** The change in taxes due divided by the change in taxable income.

**Marginal utility** The change in total utility divided by the change in the number of units consumed.

**Market** All of the arrangements that individuals have for exchanging with one another.

**Market clearing price** or **equilibrium price** The price at which market quantity demanded equals market quantity supplied.

**Market demand** Determined by adding the individual demand at each price for all the consumers in the market.

**Market failure** A situation in which perfect competition either overallocates or underallocates resources to a good or service.

**Market structure** Characteristics of an industry—such as the number of sellers, the ease of entry of new firms, each firm's ability to set the price, and the degree to which each firm's product differs from its competitor's.

**Marketing boards** A policy that allows producers to band together to restrict total quantity supplied by using quotas.

**Merger** The joining of two or more firms under single ownership or control.

**Merit good** Any good that the political process has deemed socially desirable.

**Microeconomics** The study of decision making undertaken by individuals and by firms in specific parts of the economy.

**Minimum efficient scale (MES)** The output rate when economies of scale end and constant economies of scale start.

**Minimum wage** The lowest hourly wage rate that firms may legally pay their workers.

**Mixed economy** An economic system in which decisions about how resources are used are made partly by the private sector and partly by the public sector.

**Models or theories** Simplified representations of the real world used to understand and predict economic phenomena.

**Money price** The actual price that you pay in dollars and cents for any good or service at any point in time.

**Monopolist** A single supplier of a good or service for which there are no close substitutes.

**Monopolistic competition** A market structure in which there is a relatively large number of firms offering similar but differentiated products.

**Monopoly** A firm that has great control over the price of a good it sells.

**Monopsonist** The single buyer of a factor of production.

**Monopsonistic exploitation** Monopsonistic exploitation is the difference between marginal revenue product and the wage rate.

**Moral hazard** A situation where one party to a transaction has both the ability and incentive to shift costs to other parties.

**Natural monopoly** The firm that first takes advantage of economies of scale in order to establish a monopoly position.

**Negative-sum game** A game in which players as a group lose at the end of the game.

**Network effect** A situation where a customer's willingness to use an item depends on how many others use it.

**Noncooperative game** A game in which it is too costly for firms to negotiate collusive agreements and to enforce them.

**Nonprice-rationing devices** Methods used to ration scarce goods that are price controlled.

**Normal goods** Goods for which demand rises as income rises.

**Normal rate of return** The amount that must be paid to an investor to induce investment in a business.

**Normative economics** Analysis based on value judgments made about what ought to be.

**Offer-to-purchase policy** A price floor policy reinforced by the purchase of surplus output by the government.

**Oligopoly** A market situation that consists of a small number of interdependent sellers.

**Opportunistic behaviour** Actions that focus solely on short-run gains and ignore the benefits of cooperation in the long run.

**Opportunity cost** The value of the best alternative that must be given up because a choice was made.

**Opportunity cost of capital** The amount of income, or yield, that could have been earned by investing in the next-best alternative.

**Optimal quantity of pollution** The level of pollution at which the marginal benefit equals the marginal cost of obtaining clean air.

**Payoff matrix** A matrix of outcomes, or consequences, of the strategies available to the players in a game.

**Perfect competition** A market structure in which each firm is such a small part of the industry that it cannot affect the price of the product in question.

**Perfectly elastic demand** A demand that has the characteristic that even the slightest increase in price will lead to zero quantity demanded.

**Perfectly elastic supply** When the slightest reduction in price will cause quantity supplied to fall to zero.

**Perfectly inelastic demand** A demand that exhibits zero responsiveness to price changes.

**Perfectly inelastic supply** When no matter what the price, the quantity supplied remains the same.

**Physical capital** Factories and equipment used in production.

**Planning curve** The curve that represents the various average costs attainable at the planning stage of the firm's decision making.

**Planning horizon** The long run, during which all inputs are variable.

**Plant size** The physical size of the factories that a firm owns and operates to produce its output.

**Policies** Action plans designed to achieve goals.

**Positive economics** Analysis that can be tested by observing the facts.

**Positive-sum game** A game in which players as a group end up better off.

**Predatory pricing** A strategy where existing firms cut the prices of their products below costs in order to discourage the entry of new firms.

**Price ceiling** The maximum price that may be allowed in an exchange.

**Price controls** Government- mandated minimum or maximum prices that may be charged for goods and services.

**Price discrimination** The practice of charging different prices for units of the same product, not justified by cost differences.

**Price elasticity of demand (*E*p)** The relative amount by which the quantity demanded will change in response to a change in the price of a particular good.

**Price elasticity of supply (*Es*)** The responsiveness of the quantity supplied of a commodity to a change in its price.

**Price floor** A minimum price below which a good or service may not be sold.

**Price leadership** A practice in many oligopolistic industries in which the largest firm publishes its price list ahead of its competitors, who then match those announced prices. Also called parallel pricing.

**Price searcher** A firm that must determine the price–output combination that maximizes profit because it faces a downward-sloping demand curve.

**Price support policies** Policies that aim to help the farmers by enhancing the prices they receive for the farm products they supply.

**Price system** An economic system in which relative prices are constantly changing to reflect changes in supply and demand for different commodities.

**Price taker** A competitive firm that takes price as a given, something determined outside the individual firm.

**Price war** A situation where competing firms respond to a rival's price out with even larger price cuts.

**Principle of rival consumption** The principle that one person's consumption reduces the amount of private goods available for others to consume.

**Prisoners' dilemma** The strategic game in which two prisoners have a choice between confessing and not confessing to a crime.

**Private costs** Costs borne solely by the individuals who incur them; also called *internal costs.*

**Private goods** Goods and services that are both excludable and rivalrous.

**Private marginal benefits** The marginal benefits that accrue to the direct consumers of the product or service.

**Private marginal costs** The extra costs that the firms supplying the market must pay for.

**Private property rights** Exclusive rights of ownership.

**Producer surplus** The difference between the actual amount that producers receive for a product and the lowest amount that they would be prepared to accept for it.

**Product differentiation** The ways that the firm distinguishes its product, in a positive manner, from similar products or services offered by competitors.

**Production** Any activity that results in the conversion of resources into goods and services.

**Production function** The relationship between the amount of physical output the firm can produce and the quantity of capital and labour used to produce it.

**Production possibilities curve (PPC)** A curve that represents all possible production combinations of two goods that can be produced.

**Productive efficiency** Occurs when a given output level is produced at minimal cost.

**Productively inefficient point** Any point below the production possibilities curve, assuming resources are fully employed.

**Profit** Income earned by the entrepreneur.

**Profit-maximizing rate of production** The rate of production that maximizes total profits, or the difference between total revenues and total costs; also, the rate of production at which marginal revenue equals marginal cost.

**Progressive taxation** As taxable income increases, the percentage of income paid in taxes also increases.

**Property rights** The rights of an owner to use and to exchange that property.

**Proportional rule** A decision-making system in which actions are based on the proportion of the "votes" cast and are in proportion to them.

**Proportional taxation** A tax system in which regardless of an individual's income, the tax bill comprises exactly the same proportion. Also called a flat-rate tax.

**Public goods** Goods that are neither excludable nor rivalrous. They can be consumed jointly by many individuals simultaneously at no additional cost and with no reduction in quality or quantity.

**Pure capitalist economy** An economic system characterized by private ownership of all property resources.

**Pure command economy** An economic system characterized by public ownership of all property resources.

**Rate-of-return regulation** Regulation that allows regulated companies to set prices that ensure a normal, or competitive, rate of return on the investment in the business.

**Rationality assumption** An individual makes decisions based on maximizing his or her own self-interest.

**Recycling** The reuse of raw materials derived from manufactured products.

**Regressive taxation** A smaller percentage of taxable income is taken in taxes as taxable income increases.

**Relative price** Any commodity's price in terms of another commodity.

**Rent** Income earned by land.

**Rent control** The placement of a price ceiling or maximum price on rents.

**Retained earnings** Profits not given out to shareholders.

**Scarcity** The condition that arises because wants always exceed what can be produced with limited resources.

**Services** The tasks performed by others that consumers are willing to pay for.

**Share-the-gains, share-the-pains theory** A theory of regulatory behaviour in which the regulators must take account of the demands of three groups: legislators, members of the regulated industry, and consumers of the regulated industry's products or services.

**Shortage** A situation in which the quantity demanded exceeds the quantity supplied at a price below the market clearing price.

**Short run** Any time period that is so short that there is at least one input that the firm cannot alter.

**Short-run breakeven price** The price at which a firm's total revenues equal its total costs.

**Short-run shutdown price** The price that just equals minimum average variable cost.

**Shutdown** A short-run situation where the firm stays in business but temporarily produces at a zero quantity level.

**Social costs** The full costs borne by society whenever a resource use occurs.

**Social marginal benefits** Private marginal benefits plus external benefits.

**Social marginal costs** Private marginal costs plus external costs.

**Social regulation** Regulation that reflects concern for public welfare across all industries.

**Specialization** Working at a relatively well-defined, limited endeavour; individuals, regions, and nations producing a narrow range of products.

**Strategic dependence** A situation in which one firm's actions with respect to price, quality, advertising, and related changes may be strategically countered by the reactions of one or more other firms in the industry.

**Strategy** A rule used to make a choice.

**Strikebreakers** Temporary or permanent workers hired by a company to replace union members who are on strike.

**Substitutes** Two goods are substitutes when either one can be used to satisfy a similar want.

**Sunk costs** Irreversible costs incurred prior to your decision.

**Supply** The quantities of a specific good or service that firms are willing to sell at various possible prices, other things being constant.

**Supply curve** An upward-sloping curve that shows the typically direct relationship between price and quantity supplied.

**Surplus** A situation in which quantity supplied is greater than quantity demanded at a price above the market clearing price.

**Tariffs** Special taxes that are imposed on certain imported goods.

**Tax bracket** A specified level of taxable income to which a specific and unique marginal tax rate is applied.

**Tax incidence** The distribution of tax burdens among various groups in society.

**Technology** Society's pool of applied knowledge concerning how goods and services can be produced.

**Terms of exchange** The prices we pay for the desired items.

**Terms of trade** The amount of one product that must be traded in order to obtain an additional unit of another product.

**Theory of contestable markets** A hypothesis that most of the outcomes predicted by the theory of perfect competition will occur in certain industries with relatively few firms, due to easy entry.

**Theory of public choice** The analysis of collective decision making.

**Three Ps** Private property, Profits, and Prices inherent in capitalism.

**Tit-for-tat strategy** A strategy in which a firm cheats in the current period if the rival firm cheated in the previous period but cooperates in the current period if the rival firm cooperated in the previous period.

**Total costs** The sum of all costs incurred.

**Total revenues** The quantity sold multiplied by the price.

**Transaction costs** The costs associated with finding out exactly what is being exchanged as well as the cost of enforcing contracts.

**Transfer payments.** Payments made to individuals for which no services or goods are concurrently rendered in return.

**Transfers in kind** Payments that are in the form of actual goods and services for which no goods or services are rendered concurrently in return.

**Unit elasticity of demand** A demand relationship in which the quantity demanded changes exactly in proportion to the changes in price.

**Util** A representative unit by which utility is measured.

**Utility** The want-satisfying power of a good or service.

**Utility analysis** The analysis of consumer decision making based on utility maximization.

**Variable costs** Costs whose magnitude varies with the rate of production.

**Vertical merger** The joining of a firm with another to which it sells an output or from which it buys an input.

**Voluntary exchange** Acts of trading between individuals that make both parties to the trade subjectively better off.

**Wages** Income earned by labour.

***x*-axis** The horizontal axis in a graph.

***y*-axis** The vertical axis in a graph.

**Zero-sum game** A game in which one player's losses are offset by another player's gains; at any time, sum totals are zero.

# Index

Page numbers followed by italic *f* indicate figures, and those followed by italic *t* indicate tables.


## A

absolute advantage, 40
abuse of dominant position, 326
accounting
  cost accounting, 211, 243
  monopoly situations, 273
  short-run analysis, 243
accounting profits, 189, 190–191, 191*f*
*An Act for the Protection and Suppression of Combinations in Restraint of Trade*, 323
administrative burden, 323
Advanced Micro Devices (AMD), 298
advertising, 297, 328
affordability of homes, 85
age-earnings cycle, 367, 367*f*
aggregates, 4
aging, and productivity, 369
aging population, 85, 91
Air Canada, 134, 294–295
air pollution, 379–380, 383*f*
airline bookings, 134
airline industry, 294–295
Alberta, 82, 119
Algeria, 292
allocative efficiency
  defined, 34
  described, 34
  and government market intervention, 160, 160*f*
  and market equilibrium, 116–117, 117*f*
  and monopoly, 258–260, 259*f*, 276–277, 276*f*–277*f*
  and perfect competition, 233–234, 233*f*, 276, 276*f*
allocative inefficiency
  and monopoly, 276–277, 276*f*–277*f*
  price ceiling policies, 161–162, 161*f*, 162*f*
alternative energy resources, 386–387
altruistic behaviour, 9
American Cancer Society, 190
American International Group (AIG), 125
American Medical Association, 190
Angola, 292
annuity, 131
anti-competitive conspiracies, 326
*Anticombines Act*, 323–324
anticombines legislation, 323–325
Apple Inc., 67, 301–302
Armstrong, Heather, 214
Ashenfelter, Orley, 342
Asia, 218–219
assisted human reproduction, 140
*Assisted Human Reproduction Act*, 140
assumptions
  bounded rationality assumption, 173
  *ceteris paribus* assumption, 10–11, 62, 225
  models and theories, 10–11
  production possibilities curve (PPC), 30
  rationality assumption, 5, 173
Astral Media Inc., 312, 329
asymmetric information, 121–122
Atomic Energy Control Board, 316*t*
auto insurance, 29, 34, 47–50, 48*f*, 49*f*
auto safety regulation, 318, 320
average cost pricing, 265
average costs, 199–200
average fixed costs, 197
average tax rate, 405
average total costs, 197
average variable costs, 197

## B

baggage-free business trips, 41
bait-and-switch selling, 328
bank failures, 121–122
Bank of Canada, 316*t*
barriers to entry
  monopoly, 245–248
  oligopoly, 286–287
beer industry, 303–304
beer tax, 107
behavioural economics
  consumer choice, prediction of, 173–174
  *vs.* utility analysis, 173–174
Bell Canada Enterprises (BCE Inc.), 315, 316, 329–330
Bell Globemedia, 329–330
Bentham, Jeremy, 165–166
Best Buy, 327
best response function, 287
Betamax doctrine, 263
bilateral monopoly, 354
Bill C-19, 324
Bill C-20, 324
Bill C-23, 324
Black, Conrad, 312, 329
black market, 138, 146
blogging, 214
bluefin tuna trade ban, 123–124
Bottled Water Free Day, 1
bottled water industry, 15–16
bounded rationality assumption, 173
bovine spongiform encephalopathy (BSE), 219
breakeven, 203
brewing industry, 303–304
*British North America Act*, 324
British Petroleum (BP), 379
Brooks, Garth, 70
Brown, Lester, 389
budget, and price elasticity of demand, 100–101
budget constraint, 183–184, 183*f*
budget line, 183
bureaucracy, 404
bureaucrats, 404
business. *See* the firm

## C

cable television industry, 248, 317
Cadbury Adams Canada Inc., 291
Canada
  airline industry, 294–295
  annual national health expenditures, 153*t*
  auto insurance in, 47–50
  banks in, 126
  during global recession of 2009, 126–127
  health achievement levels, 153*t*
  health care, 151–154
  home sales, 61
  housing bubble, 83–86, 83*t*
  income distribution, 364–365, 364*f*
  as location for business, 213
  media concentration, 329–330
  phone markets, 315
  pollution abatement, 384

potato industry, 235–236
poverty in, 362, 372*f*
strike activity, 347, 347*f*
tax system. *See* taxes
wealth distribution, 365–366, 366*f*
wireless market, 296
Canada Beef Export Federation (CBEF), 218–219
Canada Child Tax Benefit (CCTB), 374
*Canada Gazette*, 313
Canada Industrial Relations Board, 316*t*
Canada Pension Plan (CPP), 373, 408, 409
Canada Post, 250, 402
*Canada Post Corporation Act*, 250
Canadian Airlines International, 294–295
Canadian College of Physicians and Surgeons, 248
Canadian Dairy Commission, 316*t*
Canadian Federation of Independent Business, 322
Canadian Food Inspection Agency, 316*t*
Canadian Radio-television and Telecommunications Commission (CRTC), 248, 286, 312, 315, 316, 316*t*, 317, 329–330
Canadian Recording Industry Association (CRIA), 263
Canadian Wheat Board, 145, 336, 356
candy vending machines, 168
Canfor Corporation, 227–228
CanJet, 294–295
CanWest Global Corporation, 312, 329, 330
capital
normal rate of return, 189
opportunity cost of, 189
owner-provided, opportunity cost of, 190
production function, 193–194, 194*f*
capital gains, 407
capital goods, 37–38, 38*f*
capital loss, 408
capitalism
competition, 45
consumer sovereignty, 44
features of, 44–45
laissez-faire, 45
limited government, 45
markets and prices, 44
private ownership of resources, 44
self-interest, 44
and three economic questions, 46–47
Three Ps, 45
capture hypothesis, 318
carbon offset projects, 381
cardinal utility analysis, 166
cars
auto insurance, 29, 34, 47–50, 48*f*, 49*f*
auto safety regulation, 318
driving, costs of, 200
reimbursement of employees, 211
cartel, 292
C.D. Howe Institute, 261–262
Celgene, 260
cellphone industry, 46–47, 296
Central Selling Organization (CSO), 293–294
*ceteris paribus* assumption, 10–11, 62, 225
Chamberlin, Edward, 280, 285
change in quantity demanded, 69–70
change in quantity supplied, 75
cheques, 379
child-care spaces, 401
child poverty, 374–375, 375*f*
China, 8, 193, 255
chocolate manufacturers, 79–80, 291
CHUM Ltd., 312, 330
cigarettes
beer tax, effect of, 107
smuggling and counterfeiting, 8
taxes on, 92, 96–97, 96*f*, 147–151
circular flow model, 44, 44*f*
climate change, 389–390
Coase theorem, 385
cocoa prices, 79–80
coffee, 94
Colbert, Jean-Baptiste, 405
COLD-fX, 11
collective bargaining contracts, 347
collective decision making, 402, 403–404
college costs, 7, 7*t*
college sports, 352–353
collusion, 280
*Combines Investigation Act*, 324
Commission on the Future of Health Care in Canada, 153
common property, 384–387
common property resources, 123–124
communism, 43
comparable-worth doctrine, 370
comparative advantage, 40–41, 42, 56–59
Comparative Advantage Principle, 57–58
competition
and capitalism, 45
kinds of. *See* market structure
and marginal revenue product, 368
promotion of, 398
and public sector, 402
and wages, 368
*Competition Act*, 324–325, 328, 334
Competition Bureau, 291, 294–295, 312, 327, 328, 330
competition policy
abuse of dominant position, 325–326
amendments, 324–325
anti-competitive conspiracies, 326–327
bait-and-switch selling, 328
deceptive marketing practices, 328
exclusive dealing, 298, 326, 327
history of anticombines legislation, 323–325
mergers detrimental to public interest, 326
misleading advertising, 328
price discrimination, 325, 326
prohibited behaviour, 326–328
refusal to supply, 327
resale price maintenance, 327
reviewable matters, 324
tied selling, 327
*Competition Tribunal Act*, 324–325
Competitive Alternatives 2014, 213
complements, 68–69
concentration ratio, 286, 287*t*
conglomerate merger, 298
Conservative Party, 45
conspiracies, 326
constant-cost industry, 230, 231*f*
constant returns to scale, 204, 205*f*
consumer choice
advanced consumer choice theory, 179–187
and behavioural economics, 173–174
budget constraint, 183–184, 183*f*
changes in income, effects of, 184–185, 185*f*
combinations yielding equal satisfaction levels, 179*f*
consumer optimum, 169–170, 170*t*, 171, 184, 184*f*
demand curve, deriving, 186, 186*f*
diminishing marginal utility, 168–174
income-consumption curve, 185, 185*f*
indifference curves, 179–181, 180*f*
indifference map, 182, 182*f*
marginal rate of substitution, 181–182, 182*t*
and monopolistic competition, 285
price-consumption curve, 185, 185*f*
and utility maximization, 173–174
utility theory, 165–168
consumer optimum, 169–170, 170*t*, 171, 184, 184*f*
consumer sovereignty, 44
consumer surplus, 113–115, 114*f*, 274–275, 274*f*–275*f*
consumer tastes and preferences, 68, 165

consumption
  consumer optimum, 169–170, 170*t*, 171, 184, 184*f*
  defined, 37
  forgoing current consumption, 37
  income-consumption curve, 185, 185*f*
  price-consumption curve, 185, 185*f*
  principle of rival consumption, 398
consumption goods, 37–39, 86
consumption possibilities curve, 183
consumption tax, 412
contestable markets, 322
contingent valuation, 174–175
contributive standard, 370–371
Convention on International Trade in Endangered Species (CITES), 123
cooperative game, 287
cooperative price behaviour, 290–294
copyright, 262
Copyright Board of Canada, 150
corporate income tax, 408
cost accounting, 211, 243
cost-benefit analysis, 322–323
cost curves
  contestable markets, 322
  and diminishing marginal returns, 201–203, 202*f*
  long-run average cost curve, 203–207
  marginal factor cost curve, 353, 354*f*, 355*f*
  monopolistic competition, 283
  natural monopoly, 246, 246*f*
  short-run average cost curves, 197
  short-run cost curves, 201
cost-of-service regulation, 313–314
costs
  alternative cost principle, 189
  average costs, 199–200
  average fixed costs, 197
  average total costs, 197
  average variable costs, 197
  China's labour costs, 193
  of driving a car, 200
  explicit costs, 189
  external costs, 118–119, 118*f*, 234
  fixed costs, 196
  higher education costs, 7, 7*t*, 121, 244, 266–267, 266*t*
  implicit costs, 189
  of inputs, 74
  of legal system, 397–398
  marginal cost. *See* marginal cost
  marginal factor cost (MFC), 338, 353
  and output, 202*f*
  of polluted air, 379–380
  private costs, 379–382
  private marginal costs, 118
  production costs, 198*f*
  of recycling, 388
  short-run costs, 196–200
  social costs, 379–382, 380*f*
  social marginal costs, 118
  sunk costs, 7, 221–222
  switching costs, 299
  total costs, 196
  transaction costs, 133, 385
  variable costs, 197, 199
  and viability, 207
counterfeiting, 8
creative response, 317
crime, economic model of, 12–13
*Criminal Code*, 323, 324
cross-elasticity of demand, 103
CTV Globemedia, 312, 329–330
CTV network, 316, 329

## D

De Beers diamond cartel, 293–294
deadweight loss
  defined, 117, 277
  government market intervention, 160–162
  monopoly, 274–277
debt
  household, 83
  to asset ratio, 85–86
deceptive marketing practices, 328
decreasing-cost industry, 230–231, 231*f*
deficit financing, 55
Dell Computer Corporation, 206
demand
  changes in, vs. changes in quantity demanded, 69–70
  decrease in demand, 79
  decrease in demand and decrease in supply, 81, 81*f*
  decrease in demand and increase in supply, 82
  defined, 62
  derived demand, 340–341, 340*f*
  determinants of demand, 66–70
  elastic demand, 95, 98
  and expectations, 69
  and income, 66–67
  increase in demand, 78
  increase in demand and decrease in supply, 81
  increase in demand and increase in supply, 80, 81*f*
  inelastic demand, 96, 98
  for labour. *See* labour demand
  market demand, 64
  perfectly elastic demand, 97
  perfectly inelastic demand, 97
  and population, 69
  price elasticity of demand. *See* price elasticity of demand (*Ep*)
  and prices of related goods, 68–69
  shifts in, 66–70
  shifts in, and equilibrium, 78–82, 78*f*
  for tablet devices, 95
  and tastes and preferences, 68
demand and supply, 76*f*
  demand and supply curves combined, 77
  demand and supply schedules combined, 76–77
  and excise taxes, 147–151
  marijuana, 146
  and price support policies, 143
  quantity restrictions, 158
  shortages, 77
  surpluses, 77
demand curve
  defined, 64
  different prices for different units of same product, 255
  diminishing marginal utility, 171–172
  indifference curve analysis, 186, 186*f*
  individual demand curve, 64*f*
  individual *vs.* market demand curves, 64
  and marginal benefit, 113–114
  market demand curve for labour, 341–343, 341*f*
  monopolistic competition, 283
  monopoly, 249*f*
  movement along, 70*f*, 104
  of perfect competitor, 215, 215*f*
  shift in, 67*f*, 104
  supply curve, combined with, 77
demand schedule, 63, 64*f*, 65*f*, 76–77
demerit goods, 401
dependent variable, 21
deregulation, 315, 320, 321, 322
derived demand, 340–341, 340*f*
desired income distribution theories, 370
diamond cartel, 293–294
diamond-water paradox, 172–173, 172*f*
digital photo printing industry, 231–232
diminishing marginal product. *See* law of diminishing (marginal) returns
diminishing marginal returns. *See* law of diminishing (marginal) returns
diminishing marginal utility
  consumer optimum, 169–170, 170*t*, 171
  defined, 168
  demand curve, 171–172
  described, 168–169
  diamond-water paradox, 172–173, 172*f*

example, 168
utility maximization rule, 170–171
direct relationship, 21
disasters, 174
discounts, 114–115, 115*f*, 221–222
discrimination, 370
diseconomies of scale, 204, 205*f*
distribution of income
age-earnings cycle, 367, 367f
in Canada, 364–365, 364*f*
comparable-worth doctrine, 370
defined, 363
desired income distribution theories, 370
determinants of income differences, 366–371
discrimination, 370
egalitarian principle, 371
government, and redistribution of income, 401
inheritance, 370
Lorenz curve, 363–364, 363*f*
marginal productivity, 368–369
measurement of, 363–364
productivity standard, 370–371
division of labour, 42
dominant strategies, 288
Dooce, 214
double taxation, 408
Dow Jones Industrial Average, 125
down payment, 83
driving a car, costs of, 200

## E

economic analysis, 4–5
economic crisis, 112, 125
economic discrimination, 370
economic functions of government, 397–400
economic growth, 14, 36, 36*f*
economic models. *See* models
economic policies. *See* policies
economic profits, 190–191, 191*f*
economic regulation, 313–315
economic systems
current debates, 47
defined, 42
mixed economies, 43
pure capitalist economy, 43
pure command economy, 43
economic theories. *See* theories
economic way of thinking, 5
economics
defined, 3–5
empirical science, 11
macroeconomics, 4
microeconomics, 4
normative economics, 13–14
positive economics, 13–14
rational decision making, 5–9
scientific method, 9–13
three basic economic questions. *See* three economic questions
*The Economics of Imperfect Competition* (Robinson), 280
economies of scale
defined, 204
dimensional factor, 205
and long-run average cost curve, 204–205, 205*f*
monopoly, 246, 262
oligopoly, 286
productive equipment, 205
and specialization, 205
editorial diversity, 330
education, 3, 369
efficiency
and advertising, 297
allocative efficiency. *See* allocative efficiency
allocative inefficiency, 161–162, 161*f*, 162*f*
consumer surplus, 113–115, 114*f*
and perfect competition, 233–234
as policy goal, 14
producer surplus, 115–116
and production possibilities curve (PPC), 33–34
productive efficiency. *See* productive efficiency
productively inefficient point, 33
and rent controls, 138–139
resource management, 178
egalitarian principle, 371
elastic demand, 95, 98
elasticities
cross-elasticity of demand, 103
income elasticity of demand, 104
price elasticity of demand. *See* price elasticity of demand (*Ep*)
price elasticity of supply. *See* price elasticity of supply (*Es*)
and price support policies, 143
electronics sales, 74–75
empirical science, 11
employment
under monopsony, 353–355
under various market conditions, 352–355, 355*f*
Employment Insurance (EI), 373–374
endangered species, 387
energy deregulation, 321
Entin, Stephen, 412
entrepreneurship, 3
entry
barriers to entry, 245–248, 286–287
contestable markets, 321–322
governmental restrictions on entry, 248
legal restrictions on entry, 248, 286
monopolistic competition, 281–283
monopoly, 245, 248
perfect competition, 214
pricing to deter entry, 294–296
environmental controls, 320
environmental economics
climate change, 389–390
externalities, 380–381
four Rs, 381
landfills, 388
market incentives, 381–382
nonrenewable resources, 35–36, 388–389
private *vs.* social costs, 379–382
recycling, 381, 387–389
solar power, 386
uniform tax, 382
wind power, 385, 386
equality, 371
equi-marginal principle, 178
equilibrium
and allocative efficiency, 116–117, 117*f*, 160, 160*f*
changes in, 78–82
defined, 77
equilibrium quantity, 226–227
in geometric form, 179
long run, in monopolistic competition, 282*f*, 284
long run, in perfect competition, 228–230, 229*f*
in monopolistic competition, 282*f*, 283–284
rationing function of prices, 134–137
shifts in both demand and supply, 80–82
shifts in demand or supply, 78–80, 78*f*
short run, in monopolistic competition, 282*f*, 283–284
short run, in perfect competition, 226–228
short-run industry equilibrium price, 226, 226*t*, 227*f*
wage rate, 344–345, 345*f*
equilibrium price, 76–77
equity, 14, 139
Erlich, Paul, 390
European Union, 247, 298, 372, 387
excess capacity, 106, 285
excise taxes, 147–151
exclusion principle, 398
exclusive dealing, 298, 326, 327

exit
contestable markets, 322
perfect competition, 213
expectations
and demand, 69
price expectations, 74
experience, 368
explicit costs, 189
external benefits, 120, 120*f*, 131, 235
external costs, 118–119, 118*f*, 234
externalities
correcting for, 380–381
defined, 118, 380
described, 380
external benefits, 120, 120*f*, 131
external costs, 118–119, 118*f*
transaction costs, 385
voluntary agreements, 385
*Exxon Valdez*, 174

F

Facebook, 300
factors of production, 2–3, 192, 352
featherbedding, 351
federal government revenues and expenditures, 410, 410*f*, 411*f*
federal income support programs, 373–374, 375
federal regulatory agencies, 316*t*
federal tax rates, 407*t*
file-sharing software, 263
finance
deficit financing, 55
fundamental stock investment analysis, 20
pharmaceutical companies, as profitable investments, 111
financial crisis, 112, 124–125
financial management, 131
financing a home purchase, 83–84
the firm
accounting profits *vs.* economic profits, 190–191
average physical product, 195
capital, opportunity cost of, 189
cost curves, 201–203
defined, 191
diseconomies of scale, 204, 205–206
economies of scale, 204–205, 205*f*
large-scale firms, 205
law of diminishing returns, 194–196, 201–203, 202*f*
long-run cost curves, 203–207
marginal physical product, 195
minimum efficient scale, 206–207, 206*f*
nonprofit firms, 190
number of firms, and market structure. *See* number of firms
output and inputs, 192–193
owner-provided labour and capital, 190
price taker, 214
production function, 193–194, 194*f*
profit maximization, as goal, 191
profits of, 189–191
short-run cost curves, 201
short-run costs, 196–200
short-run equilibrium, 226–228
short run *vs.* long run, 191–196
first-come, first-served, 135, 138
fishing quotas, 388
fixed costs, 196
flat-rate tax, 406, 411–412
flu shots, 120*f*
food sector, 143–145, 144*f*, 261–262
for-profit health care, 151–154
foreclosure, 125
"free" podcast lectures, 32
free-rider problem, 122, 399
*Freeing Up Food: The Ongoing Cost, and Potential Reform, of Supply Management*, 261
Freeman, Richard B., 351
frequent flyer points, 104
full employment, 14
fundamental stock investment analysis, 20

G

gains from trade, 58–59, 59*t*
game theory
basic notions, 287–288
beer industry, 303–304
cooperative game, 287
cooperative price behaviour, 290–294
defined, 287
negative-sum game, 288
noncooperative price behaviour, 288–290
noncooperative game, 287
payoff matrix, 288, 304*f*
positive-sum game, 288
and pricing strategies, 290*f*
Prisoners' Dilemma, 288–289, 288*f*
repeated games, 290
tit-for-tat strategy, 290
zero-sum game, 288
general rule for hiring, 338
generous behaviour, 9
global recession, 67, 124–127
Global Television Network, 329
*The Globe and Mail*, 329
goods
capital goods, 37–38, 38*f*
common property resources, 123–124
complements, 68–69
consumption goods, 37–39
defined, 2
demerit goods, 401
government goods, 403
inferior goods, 67
merit goods, 400
non-excludable goods and services, 122–124
normal goods, 67
political goods, 403
private goods, 122, 398
public goods, 122–123, 398–400, 399*f*
related goods, 68–69
rivalrous goods, 122
substitutes, 68
union-made goods, 350
Goods and Services Tax (GST), 405, 408–409
government
and capitalism, 45
cost-benefit analysis, 322–323
demerit goods, 401
economic functions of, 397–400
economic stability, 400
environmental incentives, 381–382
federal *vs.* provincial and municipal spending, 410
financial support, 131
free-rider problem, 122, 399
income redistribution, 401
market intervention, and deadweight loss, 160–162
merit goods, 400
political functions of, 400–405
public goods, 122–123, 398–400, 399*f*
regulation. *See* regulation
spending, 409–410, 410*f*, 411*f*
tax revenues, and elasticities of demand and supply, 150
government goods, 402
governmental restrictions on entry, 248
graphs
combining vertical and horizontal number lines, 22–23, 22*f*
construction of, 22–23
defined, 21
dependent variable, 21
direct relationship, 21
independent variable, 21
inverse relationship, 22
negative slope, 25–26, 25*f*
number line, 22
numbers in a table, 23, 23*t*, 23*f*
positive slope, 25–26, 25*f*
slope of a line, 24–27
slope of linear curve, 24–27
slope of nonlinear curve, 26–27, 26*f*
x-axis, 22, 22*f*–23*f*
y-axis, 22, 22*f*–23*f*

greenhouse gas, 119, 389
Grokster, 263
Gross Debt Service (GDS) ratio, 84
guaranteed income supplement (GIS), 373

H

hair colour, tastes in, 68
Health Canada, 316
Heritage Classic hockey event, 135–137, 136*f*
Hershey Canada Inc., 291
high-speed Internet market, 257–258, 257*f*, 257*t*
higher education costs, 121, 244, 266–267, 266*t*
HMV Canada, 327
Hollinger, Inc., 312, 329
home sales, 61
horizontal merger, 298
horizontal number lines, 22–23, 22*f*
household spending, 62
housing bubble, 83–86, 83*t*
housing starts, 85–86
human capital, 3
human capital investments, 369
human resources management, 361
Hydro One Inc., 321

I

illegal acts, 326–328
implicit costs, 189
import quota, 147
in vitro fertilization (IVF), 140
incentive structure, 402
incentives, 7–8, 381–382
income
  changes in, effect of, 184–185, 185*f*
  and demand, 66–67
  described, 363
  distribution of income, 363–366
  frequent flyer points, 104
  income-consumption curve, 185, 185*f*
  income in kind, 364
  income inequality, increasing, 365
  and quantity demanded, 104*t*
  from resources, 3
  transfer payments, 372
  working spouses, 365
income-consumption curve, 185, 185*f*
income distribution. *See* distribution of income
income elasticity of demand, 104
income in kind, 364
*Income Tax Act*, 407, 412
increased division of tasks or operations, 205
increasing-cost industry, 230, 231*f*
independence, 281
independent variable, 21
India, 46–47
indifference curve
  curvature, 180–181
  defined, 179
  demand curve, deriving, 186, 186*f*
  indifference map, 182, 182*f*
  properties of, 180–181
  slope, 180, 180*f*
  straight-line indifference curve, 180, 181*f*
indifference map, 182, 182*f*
Indonesia, 79, 292
industry supply curve
  defined, 225
  long-run industry supply curve, 230–232
  short-run industry supply curve, 224–225, 225*f*
inelastic demand, 96, 98
inferior goods, 67
infringement of copyright, 262
inheritance, 370
innovation, 235, 301–302
inputs
  cost of, 74
  and output, relationship between, 192–193
  price elasticity of demand, 343
Institute for Research on the Economics of Taxation, 412
Intel Corporation, 298
interdependence, 286
interest, 3
interest rates, and Canadian housing prices, 85
intermediaries, 134
international smuggling and counterfeiting, 8
international trade
  and comparative advantage, 41–42
  import quotas, 147
  quantity restrictions, 147
Internet
  airline bookings, 134
  copyright infringement, 263
  high-speed Internet service, pricing, 257–258, 257*f*, 257*t*
  Match.com, 6, 6*f*
  music file sharing, 263
  online auction industry, 300
  social networking, 300
  usage, 2, 3–4
interprovincial trade, 42
inverse relationship, 22
invisible hand, 45
Iran, 292
Iraq, 292
Issues and Applications
  bottled water industry, growth of, 15–16
  Canadian housing bubble, 83–86, 83*t*
  Canadian potato industry, 235–236
  Canadian Wheat Board, 356
  child poverty, eradicating, 374–375, 375*f*
  cigarette consumption, and beer tax, 107
  climate change, 389–390
  contingent valuation, 174–175
  costs, and viability, 207
  flat tax, 411–412
  for-profit health care in Canada, 151–154
  game theory, and beer industry, 303–304
  global recession of 2009, 124–127
  media concentration in Canada, 329–330
  price discrimination in higher education, 266–267
  private or public auto insurance, 47–50

J

John Labatt Ltd., 279

K

Kazaa, 263
Krueger, Alan, 342
Kuwait, 292
Kyoto Protocol, 384, 389–390

L

labour
  average physical product, 195
  costs, in China, 193
  defined, 3
  demand for. *See* labour demand
  as factor of production, 3
  marginal factor cost, 353
  marginal factor cost curve, 353, 354*f*, 355*f*
  marginal physical product, 195
  marginal productivity of labour, 195
  monopsony, 352–355
  owner-provided, opportunity cost of, 190
  production function, 193–194, 194*f*
  productivity, 342
  supply, 344–346, 344*f*, 345*f*
  unions. *See* labour unions
labour demand
  competition in product market, 337
  demand for final product, changes in, 342
  derived demand, 340–341, 340*f*

labour demand(*continued*)
determinants of demand elasticity for inputs, 343
general rule for hiring, 338
labour productivity, changes in, 342
marginal factor cost (MFC), 338, 353
marginal physical product (MPP) of labour, 337–339
marginal revenue product (MRP), 338, 339*f*, 368
marginal revenue product (MRP) curve, 340
market demand curve for labour, 341*f*
market demand for labour, 341–342
price of related factors, change in, 343
reasons for demand curve shifts, 342–343
labour market signalling, 342
labour supply, 344–346, 344*f*, 345*f*
labour unions
benefits of, 351
bilateral monopoly, 354
collective bargaining contracts, 347
current status of, 346
demand for union labour, 349–350
featherbedding, 351
limiting entry over time, 349, 350*f*
and productivity, 351
raising wages, 350–351
strikebreakers, 348
strikes, 347–348, 347*f*
union goals, 348, 348*f*
union strategies, 348–349, 349*f*
unionization rates, various industries, 346*f*
laissez-faire, 45
land, 3
land-line phone companies, 315
landfills, 388
large-scale firms, 205
law of demand
change in quantity demanded, 69–70
demand curve, 63–64, 64*f*
demand schedule, 63, 65*f*
described, 62
determinants of demand, 66–70
Garth Brooks, and used CDs, 70
shifts in demand, 66–70
law of diminishing (marginal) returns
application of concept, 195
and cost curves, 201–203, 202*f*
defined, 194
example, 196
hypothetical case, 194*f*
measurement of diminishing marginal returns, 195
point of saturation, 196
law of increasing relative cost, 34–35, 35*f*
law of supply
change in quantity supplied, 75
defined, 71
shifts in supply, 73–75
supply curve, 71, 72*f*
supply schedule, 71, 72*f*
LCD TVs, 74–75
learning curve, 368
legal restrictions on entry, 248, 286
legal system, 397, 398
legislation. *See* regulation
Liberal Party, 45, 330
Libya, 292
licences, 248
licence plate auctions, 255
lighthouses, 399
LimeWire, 263
linear curve, slope of, 24–27
Logic Box, 388
long run
defined, 192
equilibrium, in perfect competition, 228–230, 229*f*
management planning terms, 192
planning horizon, 203
regulation, effects of, 320–323
*vs.* short run, 191–196
long-run average cost curve
constant returns to scale, 204, 205*f*
defined, 204
diseconomies of scale, 204–206, 205*f*
economies of scale, 204–205, 205*f*
generally, 203
minimum efficient scale, 206–207, 206*f*
monopoly, 246, 246*f*
and preferable plant size, 204*f*
U-shape of, 204
long-run industry supply curve
constant-cost industry, 230, 231*f*
decreasing-cost industry, 230–231, 231*f*
defined, 230
increasing-cost industry, 230, 231*f*
long-run price elasticity of demand, 101*f* 102,
long-run price elasticity of supply, 105–106*f*
Long-Term Energy Plan, 321
Lorenz curve, 363–364, 363*f*
loss minimization, 220–221, 220*f*
lotteries, 135
low-income cut-offs (LICOs), 372
lumber industry, 227–228

## M

macroeconomics
defined, 4
*vs.* microeconomics, 4
mad cow disease, 218–219
majority rule, 403
management
equi-marginal principle, 178
reimbursement of employees' use of personal cars, 211
marginal analysis
profit-maximizing rate of production, 217
utility analysis, 166
marginal benefit
defined, 7, 113
and demand curve, 113–114
of home ownership, 85
private marginal benefits, 120
public good, 399*f*
social marginal benefits, 120
marginal cost
and average cost, relationship between, 199–200
defined, 7, 115, 199
of home ownership, 84–85
in monopoly, 251
pollution abatement, 384
private marginal costs, 118
short-run costs, 199
social marginal costs, 118
and supply curve, 115–116
and variable cost, relationship between, 199
marginal cost pricing, 233, 265
marginal factor cost curve, 353, 354*f*, 355*f*
marginal factor cost (MFC), 338, 353
marginal physical product (MPP) of labour, 337–339
marginal product, 194*f*
marginal productivity, 195, 368–369
marginal rate of substitution, 181–182, 182*t*
marginal revenue, 217, 248–249, 249*f*, 251
marginal revenue product (MRP), 338, 339*f*, 368
marginal revenue product (MRP) curve, 340
marginal tax rate, 405, 415
marginal utility, 166, 167–168, 167*f*, 171*f*, 172–173
marijuana, 146
market
capitalism and, 44
defined, 64
labour market. *See* labour
product market, 337
market clearing price, 76–77
market demand, 64

market demand schedule, 65*f*
market economy, 43
market efficiency. *See* efficiency
market equilibrium. *See* equilibrium
market failure
asymmetric information, 121–122
defined, 117, 234
externalities, 117–121
non-excludable goods and services, 122–124
and perfect competition, 234–235
market opportunities, 183
market-oriented health-care model, 152–153
market segmentation, 91
market structure
comparison of, 213*t*
defined, 213
monopolistic competition, 280–285
monopoly. *See* monopoly
oligopoly. *See* oligopoly
perfect competition. *See* perfect competition
market supply curve, 71–72, 73*f*
market supply schedule, 73f
market system. *See* price system
marketing
market segmentation, 91
marketing mix, 311
restrictive trade practices, 334
marketing boards, 143–145, 144*f*
Mars Canada Inc., 291
Match.com, 6, 6*f*
McDonald's Corp., 67, 397
media concentration, 329–330
medical practice, 248
Medicare, 151–154
Medoff, James L., 351
mega-takeovers, 329–330
mergers, 298, 326, 329–330
merit goods, 400
merit standard, 370–371
Mexican drug violence, 146
microeconomics
defined, 4
*vs.* macroeconomics, 4
Microsoft, 247
Microsoft Corporation, 301
Mills, Russell, 330
minimum cost points, 200
minimum efficient scale (MES), 206–207, 206*f*
minimum wage, 140–141, 141*f*, 345, 347
misleading advertising, 327–328
mixed economies, 43, 50
models
assumptions, 10–11
of behaviour, *vs.* thought processes, 12
of crime, 12–13
defined, 9
and realism, 10
testing models, 11–12
Molson Brewing Co. Ltd., 279
money price, 62–63, 63*t*
monopolist, 245
monopolistic competition
characteristics of, 280–284
and consumer choice, 285
cost curves, 283
defined, 280
demand curve, 283
easy entry, 281–283
example, 281–283
long-run equilibrium, 282*f*, 284
number of firms, 280–281
output, 283–284
*vs.* perfect competition, 284–285, 284*f*
price, 283–284
product differentiation, 281
productive efficiency, 285
profit, 283–284
short-run equilibrium, 282*f*, 283
short-run price, output, and profit, 283
monopoly
and allocative efficiency, 258–260, 259*f*, 276–277, 276*f*
barriers to entry, 245–248
bilateral monopoly, 354
Canada Post, 250
characteristics of, 245–250
competitive price *vs.* monopoly price, 260
deadweight loss, 274–277
demand curves, 249*f*
economies of scale, 246, 262
and elasticity, 249–250
elimination of, 262
examples of, 245
food sector, 261–262
high-speed Internet market, 257–258, 257*f*, 257*t*
legal or governmental restrictions, 248
long-run excess profit, 261–262
marginal revenue, 248–249, 249*f*
marginal revenue curve, 249*f*
marginal revenue-marginal cost approach, 251
natural monopoly, 246, 246*f*, 264–265, 315
no guarantee of profits, 254
output, determination of, 251–254
ownership of resources without close substitutes, 245–246
predatory behaviour, 247
price, determination of, 251–254
price and revenue behaviour, 248–249
price discrimination, 254–258
price searcher, 245
and productive efficiency, 261
profit, calculation of, 253–254, 253*f*
profit, determination of, 251–254
raising capital, problems in, 246
and regulation, 313
regulation of, 398
Shanghai's licence plate auctions, 255
single seller, 245
social evaluation of, 258–263
total revenues-total costs approach, 251, 252*f*
monopsonist, 352
monopsonistic exploitation, 354
monopsony, 352–355
moral hazard, 121–122, 126
Morpheus, 263
mortgage, 83–84, 85, 125
mortgage-backed securities (MBS), 125–126
municipal spending, 410
music file sharing, 263
music piracy, 150–151
Muskwa-Kechika land-use area, 35–36

## N

National Collegiate Athletic Association (NCAA), 352–353
National Geographic Society, 190
National Geographic Ventures, Inc., 190
*The National Post*, 329
National Wildlife Federation, 388
natural gas, 82
natural monopoly, 246, 246*f*, 264–265, 315
natural resources, 389
negative-sum game, 288
Nestlé, 15–16
Nestlé Canada, 291
Netflix, 317
network effects, 299–300
New Democratic Party, 35
*New England Journal of Medicine* (*NEJM*), 260
newspaper vending machines, 168
Nigeria, 292
Nokia Corporation, 301
noncooperative game, 287
noncooperative price behaviour, 288–290
non-excludable goods and services, 122–124
nonlinear curve, slope of, 26–27, 26*f*
nonprice forms of competition, 296–302

nonprice-rationing devices, 138
nonprofit firms, 190
non-recourse mortgage, 125
nonrenewable resources, 388–389
nonuse values, 174
normal goods, 67
normal rate of return, 189
normative analysis, 13–14
Nortel, 402–403
Northern Gateway pipeline project, 36
not in my backyard (NIMBY), 386
number line, 22
number of firms
  in industry, 74
  in monopolistic competition, 280–281
  monopoly, 245
  oligopoly, 285–286

O

offer-to-purchase policy, 143, 143*f*
oil sands, 119
oil spill, 379
Old Age Security, 373
oligopoly
  advertising, 297
  barriers to entry, 286–287
  best response function, 287
  cartel, 291
  characteristics of, 285–287
  cheating, response to, 290
  concentration ratio, 286, 287*t*
  cooperative price behaviour, 290–294
  defined, 285
  dominant strategies, 288
  economies of scale, 286
  exclusive dealing, 298
  firm-created barriers, 286–287, 294–296
  game theory, 288–296
  innovation, 301–302
  interdependence, 286
  legal barriers, 286
  mergers, 298
  network effects, 299–300
  noncooperative price behaviour, 288–290
  nonprice forms of competition, 296–302
  opportunistic behaviour, 290
  payoff matrix, 288
  predatory pricing, 294–295
  price behaviour, 287–296
  price fixing, 290–291
  price leadership, 292
  price war, 295–296
  pricing to deter entry, 294–296
  Prisoners' Dilemma, 288–289, 288*f*
  product differentiation, 296–297
  repeated games, 290
  small number of firms, 285
  social evaluation, 302
  strategic dependence, 285
  strategy, 288
  switching costs, raising, 299
  tit-for-tat strategy, 290
One for One rule, 323
One Laptop per Child (OLPC), 33
online auction industry, 300
Ontario, 321
Ontario Power Generation (OPG), 321
opinion data, 175
opportunistic behaviour, 290
opportunity cost
  of blogging, 214
  of capital, 189
  choices and, 5–6
  consumption goods, 37
  defined, 6
  education, 369
  example, 6*f*
  implicit costs, 189
  and production possibilities curve (PPC), 34–36
  and property rights, 384–385
optimal quantity of pollution, 383–384
ordinal measurement, 166
Organization of Petroleum Exporting Countries (OPEC), 291–292
"other things being equal," 10–11
output
  breakeven, 203
  and costs, 202*f*
  and inputs, relationship between, 192–193
  in monopolistic competition, 283–284
  in monopoly, 251–254
  natural monopoly, 264–265
  production function, 193–194, 194*f*
  short run, in perfect competition, 215–228
overproduction, 117
Own the Podium program, 123
own *vs.* rent, 84–85, 84*t*

P

Panasonic, 75
patent, 248, 262
payoff matrix, 288, 304*f*
payroll taxes, 408–409
Peltzman, Sam, 318, 320*n*
per-unit tax, 147, 148*f*
perfect competition
  and allocative efficiency, 233–234, 233*f*, 276, 276*f*
  characteristics of, 213–214
  defined, 213
  demand curve, 215, 215*f*
  entry and exit, ease of, 214
  homogeneous product, 214
  and innovation, 235
  large numbers, 214
  long-run adjustments to technological change, 232
  long-run equilibrium, 228–230, 229*f*
  long-run industry supply curves, 230–232
  loss minimization in short run, 220–221, 220*f*
  and market failure, 234–235
  market structure of, 213–214
  *vs.* monopolistic competition, 284–285, 284*f*
  and normal profit, 234
  perfect market information, 214
  possible shortcomings, 234–235
  price taker, 214
  and productive efficiency, 233
  profit-maximizing rate of production, 217
  short-run breakeven price, 222, 222*f*
  short-run equilibrium, 226–228
  short-run industry equilibrium price, 226, 226*t*, 227*f*
  short-run industry supply curve, 224–225, 225*f*
  short-run profit and output, 215–228, 219*f*
  short-run shutdown price, 222–223, 222*f*, 223*t*
  short-run supply, 224–225
  short-run supply curve, 224, 224*f*
  social evaluation of, 233–235
  total revenues, 216–217
  zero economic profits, 223–224
perfect market information, 214
perfectly elastic demand, 97
perfectly elastic supply, 105
perfectly inelastic demand, 97
perfectly inelastic supply, 105
personal income tax, 407–408
pharmaceutical companies, 111, 260, 320
phone markets, 315
physical capital, 3
physical force, 135
piracy, 263
planning curves, 203–204
planning horizon, 203
plant size, 192, 204*f*
point of saturation, 196

policies
  competition policy. *See* competition policy
  defined, 14
  goals of, 14
  price controls. *See* price controls
  price support policies, 142–145
  and theory, 14
policy examples
  assisted human reproduction, 140
  bluefin tuna trade ban, 123–124
  Canada Post as monopoly, 250
  Canadian airline industry, 294–295
  Canadian politics, 45
  Canadian Wheat Board, 145
  chocolate bar manufacturers, and price fixing, 291
  CRTC and cable television industry, 317
  energy deregulation, 321
  excise tax on music piracy, 150–151
  government-funded sports stadiums, 400
  international smuggling and counterfeiting, 8
  legal system, cost of, 397–398
  mad cow disease fears, 218–219
  marijuana, legalization of, 146
  minimum wages, 142, 345
  monopolies, and Canadian food consumers, 261–262
  multi-billion dollar park, 35–36
  nonprofit firms and profits, 190
  Own the Podium program, 123
  pollution abatement, 384
  public financial support for higher education, 121
  Shanghai's licence plate auctions, 255
  tax freedom day, 406–407, 406*t*
  wireless phone services, 103
political functions of government, 400–405
political goods, 402
political power, 135
pollution
  abatement, 384
  air pollution, 379–380, 383*f*
  alternative energy resources, 386–387
  carbon offset projects, 381
  changing property rights, 386
  and common property, 384–387
  generally, 382–384, 383*f*
  not in my backyard (NIMBY), 386
  optimal quantity of pollution, 383–384
  taxes, 386
pollution abatement, 384
population
  aging population, 85, 91
  and demand, 69
positive economics, 13
positive slope, 25–26, 25*f*
positive-sum game, 288
positively sloped curve, 25*f*
post-secondary education, 39, 39*f*
potato industry, 235–236
poverty
  in Canada, 362, 372*f*
  child poverty, 374–375, 375*f*
  defining poverty, 372
  in European Union, 372
  federal income support programs, 373–374, 375
  low-income cut-offs (LICOs), 372
  reduction in, 374
  transfer payments, 372
predatory behaviour, 247
predatory pricing, 247, 294–295
preferences, 68, 165
present value of an annuity, 131
price
  average cost pricing, 265
  and capitalism, 44
  change in, and quantity of good demanded, 69–70, 70*f*
  in competitive industry, 234
  and consumer optimum, 171
  to deter entry, 294–296
  equilibrium price, 76–77
  expectations, 74
  as indicator of relative scarcity, 134
  marginal cost pricing, 233, 265
  marginal revenue less than price, 248–249, 249*f*
  market clearing price, 76–77
  money price, 62–63, 63*t*
  in monopolistic competition, 283
  in monopoly, 248–249, 251–254
  natural monopoly, 264–265
  in oligopoly, 287–296
  per constant-quality unit, 63, 314
  predatory pricing, 247, 294–295
  price-consumption curve, 185, 185*f*
  of the priceless, 174–175
  rationing function of prices, 134–137
  of related goods or factors, 68–69, 343
  relative price, 62–63, 63*t*
  short-run breakeven price, 222, 222*f*
  short-run industry equilibrium price, 226, 226*t*, 227*f*
  short-run shutdown price, 222–223, 222*f*, 223*t*
  terms of exchange, 133
  under various market conditions, 352–355, 355*f*
  water in Saudi Arabia, 173
price ceiling, 137–140, 152*f*, 161, 161*f*
price controls
  and allocative inefficiency, 161–162, 161*f*, 162*f*
  and black market, 138
  defined, 137
  Medicare, 152*f*
  minimum wage, 140–141, 141*f*
  price ceiling, 137–140, 152*f*, 161, 161*f*
  price floor, 137, 140–141, 161–162, 161*f*, 162*f*
  rent controls, 137–139, 137*f*, 161–162, 161*f*, 162*f*
price discrimination
  additional profits from perfect price discrimination, 256*f*
  defined, 255
  different prices for different buyers of same product, 257–258
  different prices for different units of same product, 255
  and discounts, 114–115, 115*f*
  in higher education, 266–267, 266*t*
  necessary conditions for, 258
  as prohibited behaviour under competition policy, 326
price elasticity of demand (*Ep*)
  calculation of, 94–95
  defined, 93
  demand for tablet devices, 95
  determinants of, 100–102
  elastic demand, 95, 98
  and excise taxes, 147–151
  extreme elasticities, 97, 97*f*
  and government tax revenue, 150
  inelastic demand, 96, 98
  for inputs, 343
  labelling elasticity, 98–100
  long-run, 102, 101*f*
  and monopoly, 249–250
  movement along the demand curve, 104
  negative, 94
  perfectly elastic demand, 97
  perfectly inelastic demand, 97
  ranges, 95–100
  real-world price elasticities, 102, 102*t*
  relative quantities, 94
  and resource allocation, 149
  share of budget, 100–101
  short-run, 102, 101*f*
  substitutes, 100
  and tax incidence, 148–149, 150*f*
  time for adjustment, 101–102
  and total revenues, 97–98, 100*t*
  unit elasticity of demand, 95, 98
  zero elasticity, 97

price elasticity of supply (*Es*)
classification of, 105
defined, 105
determinants of, 105–106
and excise taxes, 147–151
and government tax revenue, 150
long-run, 105–106*f*
perfectly elastic supply, 105
perfectly inelastic supply, 105
and resource allocation, 149
short-run, 105–106*f*
and tax incidence, 148–149, 150*f*
unit-elastic supply, 105
price fixing, 280, 290–291
price floor, 137, 140–141, 161–162, 161*f*, 162*f*
price leadership, 292
price searcher, 245
price stability, 14
price support policies
defined, 143
marketing boards, 143–145, 144*f*
offer-to-purchase policy, 143, 143*f*
price system
defined, 43, 133
health-care model, 152–153
intermediary, role of, 134
rationing function of prices, 134–137
signalling aspect, 133
ticket scalping, 135–137
transaction costs, 133
voluntary exchange, 133
price taker, 214
price war, 295–296
principle of rival consumption, 398
Prisoners' Dilemma, 288–289, 288*f*
private costs, 379–382
private goods, 122, 398
private marginal benefits, 120
private marginal costs, 118
private ownership of resources, 44
private property rights, 384–385
producer surplus, 115–116, 275
product
average physical product, 195
homogeneous product, 214
marginal physical product, 195
marginal physical product (MPP) of labour, 337–339
marginal product, 194*f*
marginal revenue product (MRP), 338, 339*f*, 368
product differentiation, 281, 296–297
product market, 337
production
complexity of, 106
costs of, hypothetical case, 198*f*
defined, 2, 193
factors of production, 2–3
overproduction, 117
production function, 193–194, 194*f*
profit-maximizing rate of production, 217
underproduction, 117
production function, 193–194, 194*f*
production possibilities curve (PPC)
applications of, 31–36
assumptions, 30
and comparative advantage, 56–59
defined, 30
and economic growth, 36, 36*f*
and efficiency, 33–34
example, 30–31
and opportunity cost, 34–36
scarcity and trade-offs, 31–32
and unemployment, 32
productive efficiency
described, 33
monopolistic competition, 285
and monopoly, 261
and perfect competition, 233
productively inefficient point, 33
productivity
and aging, 369
and income distribution, 370–371
labour productivity, 342
marginal productivity, 368–369
marginal productivity of labour, 195
and specialization, 39–42
and supply, 74
and unions, 350, 351
profit
accounting profits, 189, 190–191, 191*f*
defined, 3
economic profits, 190–191, 191*f*
of firm, 189–191
long-run excess profit, in monopolies, 261–262
in monopolistic competition, 283–284
in monopoly, 251–254, 253*f*, 261–262
and nonprofit firms, 190
perfect competition, 234
and price discrimination, 254–258
profit maximization. *See* profit maximization
short run, in perfect competition, 215–228
zero economic profits, 223–224
profit maximization
described, 191
in monopoly, 251–254
natural monopoly, 264–265, 264*f*
perfect competition, 215
profit-maximizing rate of production, 217
and regulation, 314
short run, in perfect competition, 215–217, 216*f*, 219*f*
timing of maximization of profit, 218
total costs, 217
total revenues, 216–217
profit-maximizing rate of production, 217
progressive taxation, 405
prohibited behaviour, 326–328
property rights, 384–387, 397
proportional rule, 403
proportional taxation, 406
provincial spending, 410
public franchise, 248
public goods, 122–123, 398–400, 399*f*
public sector
bureaucrats, role of, 404
collective decision making, 402, 403–404
and competition, 402
government goods at zero price, 403
incentive structure, 402
influence on economy, 402
rational ignorance, 404–405
scarcity constraint, 402
similarities with market decision making, 402–403
size of, 409–410
use of force, 403
voting *vs.* spending, 403–404
public welfare, 316–317
pure capitalist economy, 43
pure command economy, 43, 49, 50

## Q

Qatar, 292
quantity restrictions, 146–147, 158
Quebec Pension Plan (QPP), 373
Quebecor Inc., 316, 329

## R

rate of return, 189
rate-of-return regulation, 314
rational decision making
incentives, 7–8
at the margin, 7
and opportunity cost, 5–6
rationality assumption, 5
self-interest, 9
rational ignorance, 404–405
rationality assumption, 5, 173
rationing by queues, 135
rationing function of prices, 134–137
raw materials, availability of, 106
resale listings, 86

real GDP, 125
recession, 67, 85, 125, 227–228
Recording Association of America (RIAA), 263
recover, 381
recycling, 381, 387–389
reduce, 381
refusal to supply, 326
regressive taxation, 406
regulation
  anticombines legislation, 323–325
  auto safety regulation, 318
  capture hypothesis, 318
  cost-benefit analysis, 322–323
  cost-of-service regulation, 313–314
  creative response, 317
  deregulation, 315, 320, 322
  economic regulation, 313–315
  explanations of regulators' behaviour, 318–320
  federal regulatory agencies, 316*t*
  feedback effects, 317
  and monopoly, 313
  natural monopolies, 315
  and profit maximization, 314
  rate-of-return regulation, 314
  results of regulation, 317
  share-the-gains, share-the-pains theory, 320
  short-run *vs.* long-run effects, 320–323
  social regulation, 316–317
  theory of contestable markets, 322
  types of government regulation, 313–318
relative price, 62–63, 63*t*
rent, 3
rent controls, 137–139, 137*f*, 161–162, 161*f*, 162*f*
rent *vs.* own, 84–85, 84*t*
repeated games, 290
reproductive technologies, 140
resale price maintenance, 327
Research in Motion, 301
resource allocation, 149
resource management, 178
restrictive trade practices, 334
retained earnings, 408
reuse, 381
revenue
  marginal revenue, 217
  under monopoly, 248–249
  tax revenues, 150
  total revenues. *See* total revenues
reviewable matters, 324
RFID tags, 64, 66
rivalrous goods, 122
Robinson, Joan, 280
Rolling Stones, 327
Romanow Report, 153
Running Room Canada Inc., 281–283

## S

Saudi Arabia, 173, 292
scarcity
  competition, 135
  defined, 2
  market and public-sector decision making, 402
  and price, 134
  production possibilities curve (PPC) and trade-offs, 31–32
  and resources, 2–3
  scarce resources, 389
  specialization and self-interest, 41
  three basic economic questions, 43
  and wants, 2
scientific method
  assumptions, 10–11
  behavioural models, *vs.* thought processes, 12
  crime, economic model of, 12–13
  models or theories, 9–10
  testing models, 11–12
self-interest, 9, 41, 44
services, 2
shale natural gas, 82
Shanghai, 255*f*
share-the-gains, share-the-pains theory, 320
Shaw Communications, 257, 330
short run
  costs. *See* short-run costs
  defined, 192
  equilibrium, in perfect competition, 226–228
  industry supply curve, 224–225, 225*f*
  *vs.* long run, 191–196
  loss minimization, 220–221, 220*f*
  management planning terms, 192
  output and profit, in perfect competition, 215–228
  regulation, effects of, 320–323
  supply, in perfect competition, 224–225
short-run analysis in accounting, 243
short-run average cost curves, 197
short-run breakeven price, 222, 222*f*
short-run cost curves, 201
short-run costs
  average and marginal costs, relationship between, 199–200
  average fixed costs, 197
  average total costs, 197
  average variable costs, 197
  fixed costs, 196
  marginal costs, 199
  minimum cost points, 200
  short-run average cost curves, 197
  total costs, 196
  variable costs, 197
short-run price elasticity of demand, 102, 101*f*
short-run price elasticity of supply, 105–106, 106*f*
short-run shutdown price, 222–223, 222*f*, 223*t*
shortage
  defined, 76
  and demand and supply, 77
shutdown, 221
signalling, 133
Simon, Julian, 390
slope
  budget constraint, 183–184, 183*f*
  different prices for different units of same product, 255
  indifference curve, 180–181, 180*f*, 181*f*
  of a line, 24–27
  linear curve, 24–27
  marginal cost curve, 201
  negative slope, 25–26, 25*f*
  nonlinear curve, 26–27, 26*f*
  positive slope, 25–26, 25*f*
small business income tax planning, 415
Smith, Adam, 5, 42
smoking, 92
smuggling, 8
social assistance programs, 373–374, 375
social costs, 379–382, 380*f*
social marginal benefits, 120
social marginal costs, 118
social networking, 300
social regulation, 316–317
socialism, 43
socioeconomic goals, 14
solar power, 386, 393
Southam Incorporated, 329
specialization
  absolute advantage, 40
  comparative advantage, 40–41, 42
  defined, 39
  division of labour, 42
  and economies of scale, 205
  gains from trade, 58–59, 59*t*
  and greater productivity, 39–42
  scarcity and self-interest, 41
sports stadiums, government-funded, 400
spouse's allowance, 373
standard of living, 366

Standard Radio Inc., 329
Stanton, John, 281–282
Statistics Canada, 366
Stigler, George, 318*n*
straight-line indifference curve, 180, 181*f*
strategic dependence, 285
StreamCast Networks, 263
strikebreakers, 348
strikes, 347–348, 347*f*
studying, 342
sub-prime mortgage securitization model, 125–126
subsidies, 74
substitutes, 68, 100
Sun Media, 312, 316, 329
sunk costs, 7, 221–222
supply
- ceteris paribus assumption, 225
- change in, *vs.* changes in quantity supplied, 75
- and cost of inputs, 74
- decrease in supply, 79
- decrease in supply and decrease in demand, 81, 81*f*
- decrease in supply and increase in demand, 81
- defined, 71
- determinants of, 73–75
- increase in supply, 79
- increase in supply and decrease in demand, 82
- increase in supply and increase in demand, 80, 81*f*
- labour supply, 344–346, 344*f*, 345*f*
- marketing board regulation of, 143–145
- and number of firms in industry, 74
- per-unit tax, effect of, 147, 148*f*
- perfectly elastic supply, 105
- perfectly inelastic supply, 105
- price elasticity of supply. *See* price elasticity of supply (*Es*)
- and price expectations, 74
- shifts in, 73–75
- shifts in, and equilibrium, 78–82, 78*f*
- short run, in perfect competition, 224–228
- taxes and subsidies, 74
- technology and productivity, 74
- unit-elastic supply, 105

supply curve
- defined, 71
- demand curve, combined with, 77
- extreme elasticities, 105*f*
- horizontal summation, 72*f*
- individual supply curve, 72*f*
- long-run industry supply curves, 230–232
- and marginal cost, 115–116
- market supply curve, 71–72, 73*f*
- movement along, 75
- shift in, 73*f*
- short run, in perfect competition, 224, 224*f*
- short-run industry supply curve, 224–225, 225*f*

supply schedule, 71, 72*f*, 76–77
surplus
- consumer surplus, 113–115, 114*f*, 274–275, 274*f*, 275*f*
- defined, 76
- and demand and supply, 77
- producer surplus, 115–116, 275

Suzy Shier, 328
switching costs, 299

## T

tablet devices, demand for, 95
talent, 368
tar sands, 119
tariffs, 248
tastes, 68, 165
tax bracket, 405
tax incidence, 148–150, 149*f*, 408
taxes
- average tax rate, 405
- on beer, and effect on cigarette smoking, 107
- capital gains and capital losses, 408
- cigarette taxes, 92, 96–97, 96*f*
- corporate income tax, 408
- double taxation, 408
- excise taxes, 147–151
- and fairness, 412
- federal tax rates, 407*t*
- flat-rate tax, 406, 411–412
- Goods and Services Tax (GST), 405, 408–409
- government tax revenues, 150
- income tax planning strategies, 415
- marginal tax rate, 405, 415
- national sales tax, 412
- payroll taxes, 408–409
- per-unit tax, 147, 148*f*
- personal income tax, 407–408
- and pollution, 386
- progressive taxation, 406
- proportional taxation, 406
- regressive taxation, 406
- as revenue raiser, 410
- and supply, 74
- tax freedom day, 406–407, 406*t*
- taxation systems, 406
- unemployment and pension taxes, 408–409

technology
- defined, 30
- innovation, 235, 301–302
- long-run adjustments to technological change, 232
- and perfect competition, 235
- reproductive technologies, 140
- and supply, 74

Telus Corporation, 315
terms of exchange, 133
terms of trade, 58–59
Terms of Trade Principle, 58–59
TGA Entertainment, 327
thalidomide, 260
theories
- assumptions, 10–11
- defined, 9
- and policy, 14

theory of contestable markets, 322
*The Theory of Monopolistic Competition* (Chamberlin), 280
three economic questions
- and capitalism, 46–47
- how it will be produced, 43
- scarcity, 43
- what and how much will be produced, 43
- for whom it will be produced, 43

Three Ps, 45
ticket scalping, 135–137
Ticketmaster, 136–137
tied selling, 327
tit-for-tat strategy, 290–291
toilets in India, 46–47
Topaz International, 134
total costs, 196, 251, 252*f*
Total Debt Service (TDS) ratio, 84
total revenues
- defined, 216
- and elasticity, 97–98, 100*t*
- in monopoly, 251, 252*f*

total utility, 166, 167*f*, 172–173, 172*f*
trade-offs
- automobiles and newsprint, 31*f*
- common property and endangered species, 387
- production possibilities curve (PPC) and scarcity, 31–32

training, 3, 369
transaction costs, 133, 385
transfer payments, 372, 401

transfers in kind, 401
Transport Canada, 316*t*
travel agents, 134
tuition fees. *See* higher education costs
TVA network, 316, 329

## U

underproduction, 117
unemployment, and production possibilities curve (PPC), 32
unemployment rates, 85
union-made goods, 350
unions. *See* labour unions
unit-elastic supply, 105
unit elasticity of demand, 95, 98
United Arab Emirates, 292
United States
  annual national health expenditures, 153*t*
  college sports, 352–353
  for-profit health maintenance organizations (HMOs), 153
  health achievement levels, 153*t*
  housing bubble, 126
  as location for business, 213
  in vitro fertilization (IVF), 140
Universal Child Care Benefit (UCCB), 374
university costs, 7, 7*t*, 244, 266–267, 266*t*
university degree, 342
university education, 39, 39*f*
use of force, 403
used CDs, 70
util, 165–166
utilitarianism, 165
utility
  analysis of. *See* utility analysis
  and consumer tastes and preferences, 165
  defined, 165
  diamond-water paradox, 172–173, 172*f*
  diminishing marginal utility, 168–174
  marginal utility, 166, 167–168, 171*f*, 172–173
  maximization of, 165
  measurement of, 165–166
  negative marginal utility, 168
  ordinal measurement, 166
  subjective concept, 165
  total utility, 166
  utility maximization rule, 170–171
utility analysis
  *vs.* behavioural economics, 173–174
  cardinal utility analysis, 166
  defined, 165
  graphic analysis, 166–167, 167*f*
  marginal analysis, 166
utility maximization rule, 170–171

## V

value-added tax (VAT), 411
value-free economics, 13
value of marginal product (VMP), 338
variable costs, 197, 199
variable factors of production, 192
variable inputs, 192
variables, 21
vending machines, 168
Venezuela, 292
vertical merger, 298
vertical number lines, 22–23, 22*f*
viability, and costs, 207
Videotron, 316, 329
voluntary agreements, 385
voluntary exchange, 133

## W

wages
  defined, 3
  equality of, 368
  minimum wage, 140–141, 141*f*
  under monopsony, 353–355
  and unions, 350–351
  wage rate, 344–345, 345*f*
Wanamaker, John, 280
wants, 2
water in Saudi Arabia, 173
wealth distribution, 365–366, 366*f*
*The Wealth of Nations* (Smith), 5, 42
web page design, economics of, 3–4
WestJet, 294–295
wind power, 385, 386
Windows operating system, 247
wireless phone services, 103, 296
working spouses, 365
World Bank, 381
World Watch Institute, 389

## X

x-axis, 22, 22*f*–23*f*

## Y

y-axis, 22, 22*f*–23*f*

## Z

zero economic profits, 223–224
zero elasticity, 97
zero-sum game, 288

# Photo Credits

**Chapter 1** Pages 1 and 15 Huguette Roe/Shutterstock; page 4 Comstock/Thinkstock; page 6 Sakala/Shutterstock; page 12 Monkey Business Images/Shutterstock; **Chapter 2** pages 29 and 47 Charlie Hutton/Shutterstock; page 32 Pixland/Thinkstock; page 33 iStockphoto/Thinkstock; page 46 Paul Prescott/Shutterstock; **Chapter 3** pages 61 and 83 Hemere/Thinkstock; page 69 AP Wideworld Photos; page 74 Yuri Arcurs/Shutterstock; page 79 R. Gino Santa Maria/ Shutterstock; **Chapter 4** pages 92 and 107 © Steve Manson/Getty Images; page 93 Jirka Bursik/ Shutterstock; page 101 Shutterstock; page 102 Shutterstock; **Chapter 5** pages 112 and 124 Hemera/Thinkstock; page 114 Digital Vision/Thinkstock; page 119 Kolaczan/Shutterstock; page 122 Sergei Bachlakov/Shutterstock; **Chapter 6** pages 132 and 151 CP/Ryan Remiorz; pages 135 aceshot1/Shutterstock; page 139 Hemera/Thinkstock; page 146 Desiree Walstra/ Shutterstock; **Chapter 7** pages 164 and 174 The Slide Farm/Al Harvey; page 165 Getty Images Entertainment; page 168 AP Wideworld Photos; page 173 Yuri Arcurs/Shutterstock; **Chapter 8** pages 188 and 207 Yuri Arcurs/Shutterstock; page 193 Christophe Testi/ Shutterstock; page 199 Shutterstock; **Chapter 9** pages 212 and 235 onepony/fotolia; page 214 Sean Buck/Shutterstock; page 221 iStockphoto/Thinkstock; page 228 Comstock/ Thinkstock; **Chapter 10** pages 244 and 266 CP/Tom Hanson; page 247 Photodisc/ Thinkstock; page 255 Brian Tan/Shutterstock; page 263 Pixland/Thinkstock; **Chapter 11** pages 279 and 303 Courtesy of Moosehead; page 282 Brendan Howard/Shutterstock; page 293 Boris 15/Shutterstock; page 296 Stockbyte/Thinkstock; **Chapter 12** pages 312 and 329 CP/ Tom Hanson; page 313 Picsfive/Shutterstock; page 315 Ronen/Shutterstock; page 320 irabel8/Shutterstock; **Chapter 13** pages 336 and 356 Noam Armonn/Shutterstock; page 337 DD Photography/Shutterstock; page 342 Lev Olkha/Shutterstock; page 347 Brad Collett/Shutterstock; **Chapter 14** pages 362 and 374 Courtesy of Monkey Business Images/Shutterstock; page 363 Evok20/Shutterstock; page 367 Monkey Business Images/Shutterstock; page 374 Suzanne Tucker/Shutterstock; pages 362 and 274 Courtesy of Monkey Business Images/Shutterstock; **Chapter 15** pages 378 and 391 Toronto Star/Dick Look/Canadian Press; page 379 Ten Denson/Shutterstock; page 383 Romanenkova/Shutterstock; page 387 BESTWEB/Shutterstock; **Chapter 16** pages 396 and 410 Courtesy of gpointstudio/Shutterstock; page 397 iofoto/Shutterstock; page 399 Norman Pogoson/Shutterstock; pages 396 and 410 Courtesy of gpointstudio/ Shutterstock.

# Appendix F

## ECON1110 Microeconomics Problems, Reviews, and Sample Exams

Provided by the faculty at NAIT

# ECON1110 Microeconomics

## Problems, Reviews and Sample Exams

**BUSINESS ADMINISTRATION - YEAR ONE**

NAIT

NAIT COURSE PACK

1601

JR SHAW
SCHOOL OF BUSINESS

NAIT COURSE PACK

# 1601

**Micro Formulas**

$$Ep = \frac{\text{change in Q}}{\text{sum of quantities/ 2}} \div \frac{\text{change in P}}{\text{Sum of prices /2}}$$

$$\text{Accounting profit} = \text{Total revenue} - \text{Explicit costs}$$

$$\text{Economic profit} = \text{Total revenues} - (\text{Explicit} + \text{Implicit costs})$$

$$\text{Total costs (TC)} = \text{Total fixed costs (TFC)} + \text{Total variable cost (TVC)}$$

$$\text{Average total costs (ATC)} = \frac{\text{Total costs (TC)}}{\text{Output (Q)}}$$

$$\text{Average total costs (ATC)} = \text{Average fixed costs (AFC)} + \text{Average variable costs(AVC)}$$

$$\text{Average variable costs (AVC)} = \frac{\text{Total variable costs (TVC)}}{\text{Output (Q)}}$$

$$\text{Average fixed costs (AFC)} = \frac{\text{Total fixed costs (TFC)}}{\text{Output (Q)}}$$

$$\text{Marginal costs (MC)} = \frac{\text{Change in total cost (TC)}}{\text{Change in output (Q)}}$$

$$\text{Breakeven quantity (BQ)} = \frac{\text{Total fixed cost (TFC)}}{\text{Selling price} - \text{Average variable costs (AVC)}}$$

$$\text{Target profit quantity} = \frac{\text{Total fixed cost (TFC)} + \text{Profit}}{\text{Selling price} - \text{Average variable costs (AVC)}}$$

$$\text{Total revenue (TR)} = \text{Price (P)} \times \text{Quantity (Q)}$$

$$\text{Total Profit} = [\text{Price (P)} - \text{Average Total Cost (ATC)}] \text{ x } \text{Quantity (Q)}$$

$$\text{Marginal revenue (MR)} = \frac{\text{Change in total revenue (TR)}}{\text{Change in output (Q)}}$$

$$\text{Marginal Tax Rate} = \frac{\text{Change in taxes due}}{\text{Change in taxable income}}$$

$$\text{Average Tax Rate} = \frac{\text{Total taxes due}}{\text{Total taxable income}}$$

## CHAPTER 1

## Problems

1. Help with Graphing

| | CASES OF BEER | |
|---|---|---|
| PRICE | DEMAND | SUPPLY |
| 16 | 2 | 8 |
| 12 | 3 | 6 |
| 8 | 4 | 4 |
| 4 | 5 | 2 |

a. Using the above data, construct the graph below.
Start with plotting price and demand for your demand curve, and then plot price and supply for your supply curve. Include an appropriate title, source, and appropriate labels.

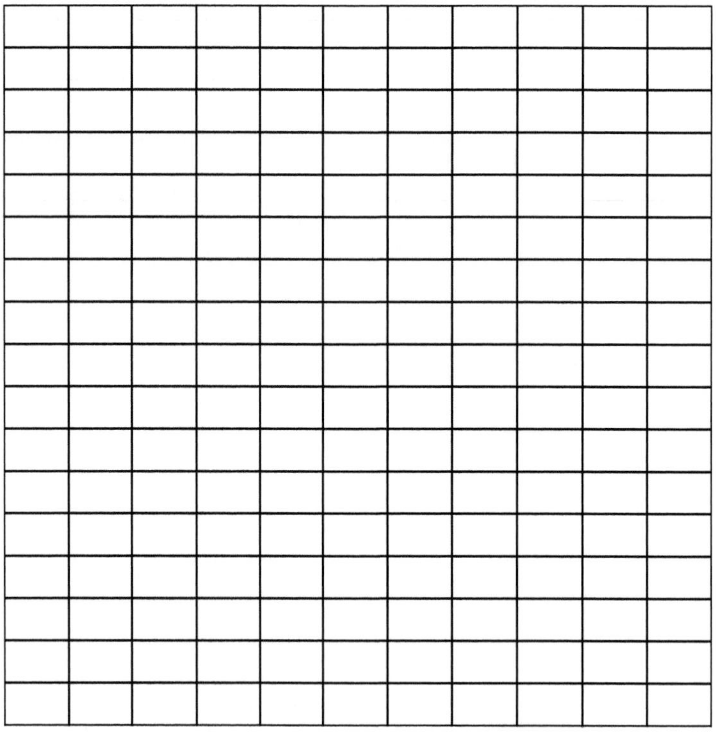

b. Which variable(s) is/are the independent variable(s)? Dependent variable(s)?

c. Which variables have a direct relationship?

d. Which variables have an inverse relationship?

e. What does the intersection of supply and demand indicate?

2. Factors of Production

Fill in the following table by listing each of the four types of factors of production. Then list the type of resource income earned by the resource when engaged in production.

| Type of Resource | Type of Resource Payment of Income |
|---|---|
| | |
| | |
| | |
| | |
| | |

**Solutions**

1. Help with Graphing

a. 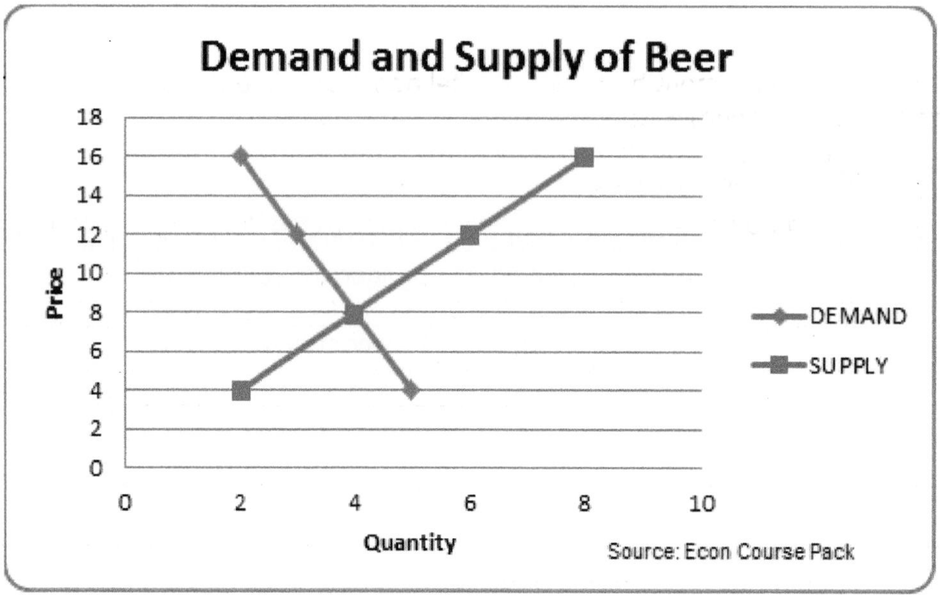


b. Independent is price, dependent are quantity demanded and quantity supplied

c. Price and supply

d. Price and demand

e. What the equilibrium price for beer should be so that demand will meet supply at a P=$8 and a Q=4

2. Factors of Production

| Type of Resource | Type of Resource Payment of Income |
|---|---|
| Land | Rent |
| Capital | Interest |
| Labour | Wages |
| Entrepreneurial | Profits/Loss |
| Human Capital | Additional wages |

## CHAPTER 2

### Problems

1. Create a Production Possibilities Curve

Assumptions:

- Country A produces more hammers (capital good) and Country B produces more pizza (consumer good) with all the resources in our world.
- During the analysis, technology does not change.
- All resources are fully employed (full production, full employment)
- The available resources can produce these goods in the following combinations only:

| Production Alternatives | Hammers (millions) | Pizza (millions) |
|---|---|---|
| A | 0 | 70 |
| B | 20 | 65 |
| C | 40 | 54 |
| D | 60 | 40 |
| E | 80 | 18 |
| F | 90 | 0 |

Use the table to create a Production Possibilities Curve below and label where country A and B will produce on the graph, Country A favours capital goods and Country B favours consumer goods.

a. Which country consumes more of its current output?

b. Which country invests more of its current output?

c. Which economy should we expect to grow faster?

d. What is the benefit (advantage) of this faster growth?

e. What is the cost of this faster growth?

f. Assume Country A had unemployment. On the graph above, mark with an X where its economy would likely be located.

g. Would Country A now be more or less efficient (productive) than before? Why?

h. Suppose Country B geologists then discovered a huge previously unknown oil deposit. Indicate on the graph above what you would expect to happen to the PPC.

2. Circular Flow Model

Answer the questions below, based on the following diagram often called the "**Circular Flow Model**." This model is often used to provide an overview of Pure Capitalism.

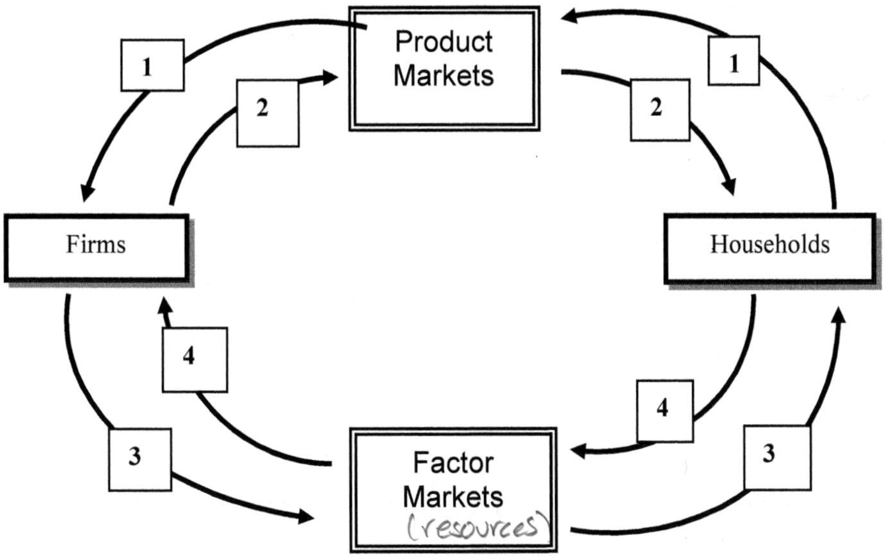


a. Match the following flow descriptions with the appropriate number.

| Flow Description | Flow Number? |
|---|---|
| Flow of Land, Labour, Capital, Entrepreneurship | 4 |
| Flow of Consumer Dollar Expenditures | 1 |
| Flow of Wages, Rent, Interest, Profit | 3 |
| Flow of Goods and Services | 2 |

b. Circle the appropriate terms presented below:

i. The (firm / household) supplies (resources / products) in the factor markets.

ii. The (firm / household) supplies (resources / products) in the product markets.

iii. The (firm / household) demands (resources / products) in the product markets.

**Solutions**

Create a production possibilities curve:

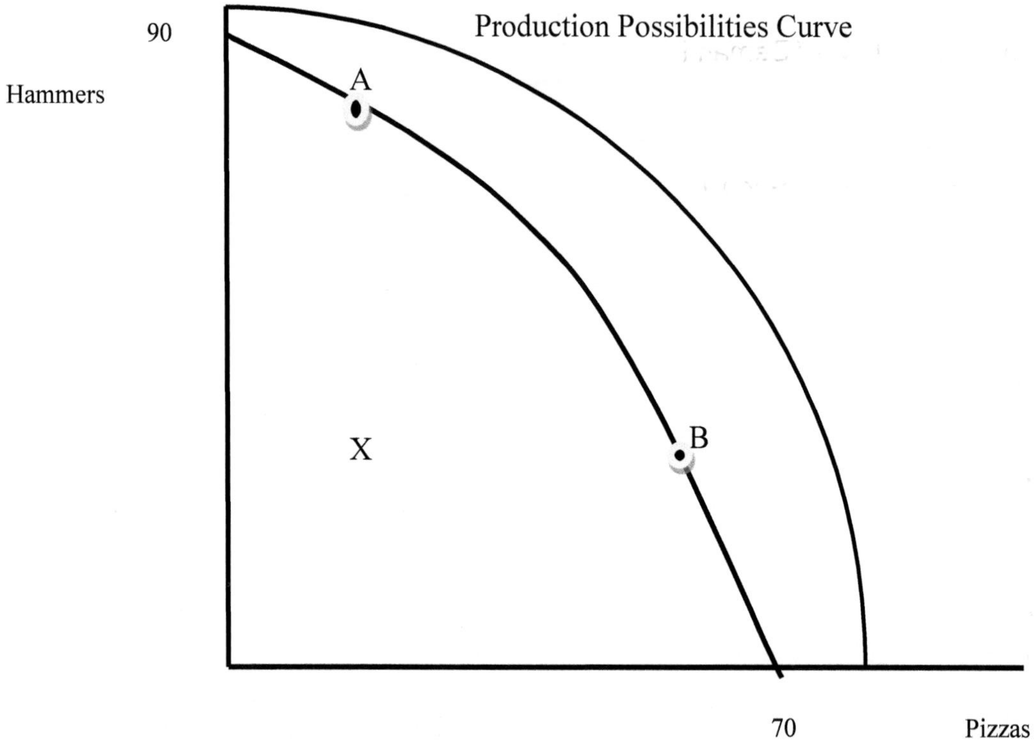


Source: Micro Course Pack

a. Country B – produces a consumer good
b. Country A – produces a capital good
c. Country A
d. Faster growth will allow more products to be produced with the resources
e. Growing too fast can lead to waste and the inefficient production of goods
f. See above diagram.
g. Country A would be producing fewer hammers.
h. See above diagram Country B will be able to produce more pizza and hammers only if there is a demand for oil.

Circular Flow:

a. 4, 1 ,3 ,2
b. i. Household, resources
   ii. Firm, products
   iii. Household, products

## CHAPTER 3

## Problems

1. Demand and Supply

a. Briefly explain the Law of Demand.

b. Briefly explain the Law of Supply.

c. On the graph below, draw and label a typical demand and supply curve.

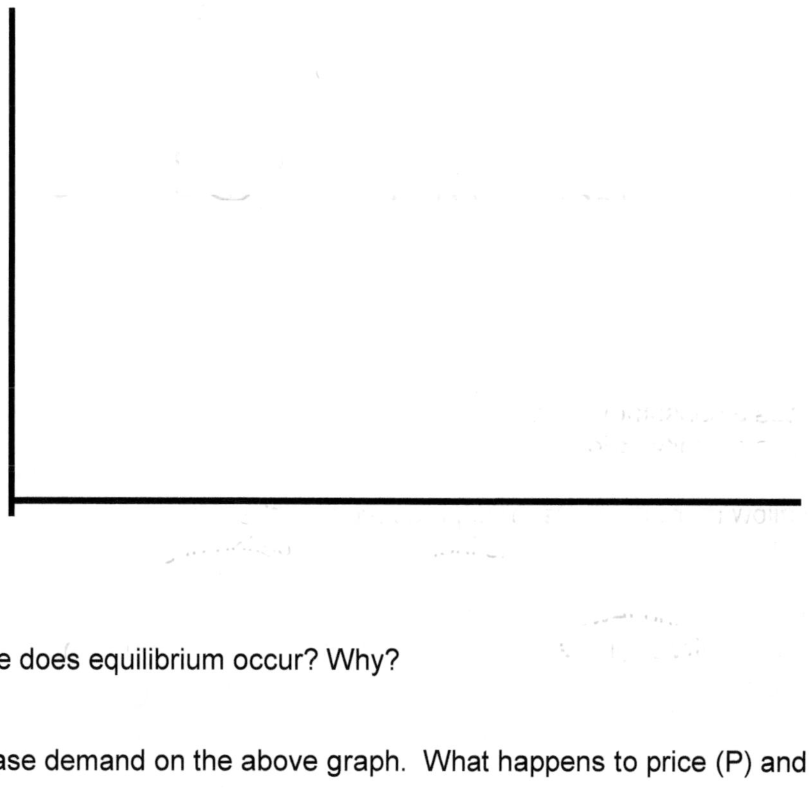

d. Where does equilibrium occur? Why?

e. Increase demand on the above graph. What happens to price (P) and quantity (Q)?

f. What typically tends to increase demand (D)?

g. Now increase supply on the above graph. What happens to P and Q?

h. What typically tends to increase supply?

i. If S > D, would buyers (consumers) be demanding all that producers (suppliers) were supplying to the market? Why? What situation would this cause?

j. In this case, what would have to happen to clear the market?

k. If D > S, a (shortage or surplus) would exist. What is needed to clear the market?

l. What role must P play to clear the market?

m. On the graph below, if P was $15, a (shortage or surplus) would exist. What should happen to price to solve this problem?

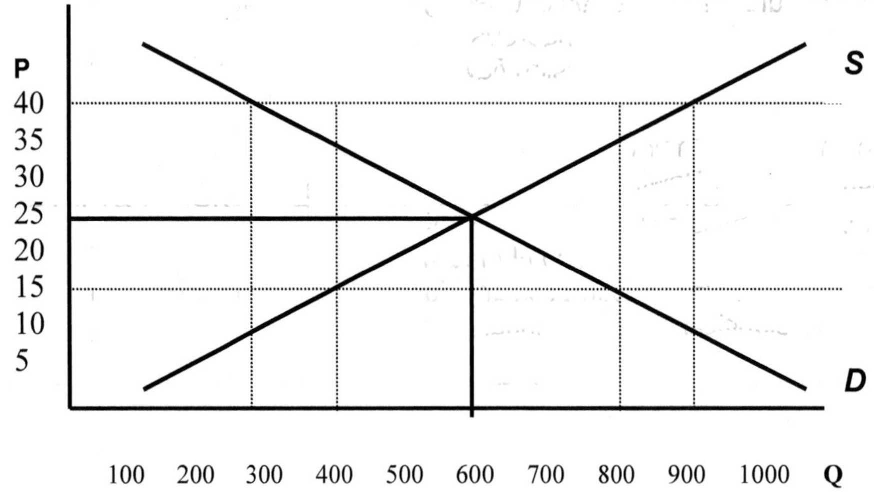


n. What if P was $40?

2. Lightning 123 Automobiles

Assume you have recently been hired into the strategic planning department of a large automobile manufacturer in rural Alberta. During your first week on the job you are assigned the task of determining the potential effect of the following independent items on prices for your new company's cars. Complete the following table supplied by your new boss (**note**: keeping your job and any future promotions depend upon your answers). An example is given for your reference.

**note:** the ceteris paribus assumption is in effect.

| ITEM | Area of Market Affected | Anticipated Effect on Price |
|---|---|---|
| Your company has just been awarded a lucrative military contract to build several thousand high-tech Killer-K battle tanks. | ↓S | ↑P |
| a. To keep your factory in rural Alberta open, the government has just announced a new subsidy program which will pay your firm $1,500 per car produced. | | |
| b. The militant unionised workers at your factory have been on strike for two weeks with no break-through anticipated for several more weeks. | | |
| c. An international auto magazine has criticised your firm's cars as some of the most dangerous on the road due to serious engineering design flaws. | D↓ | Price↓ |
| d. One of your competitors unveils a $10 million marketing campaign for their new sports coupe to kick off the upcoming Super Bowl. | D↓ | Price↓ |
| e. The insurance industry is about to announce that improved driver-training programs combined with anti-drinking campaigns have reduced accident claims, allowing them to significantly reduce insurance premiums. | D↑ | |

**Solutions**

1. Demand and Supply

a. An inverse relationship, as price increases, demand will fall
b. relationship, as price increases, supply will increase
c.

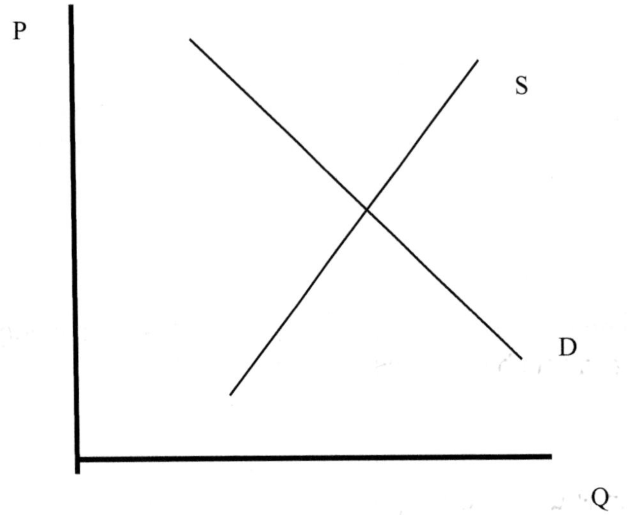


d. Intersection of S and D, price where consumers are able and willing to pay and where suppliers are willing to produce.
e. P increases, Q increases

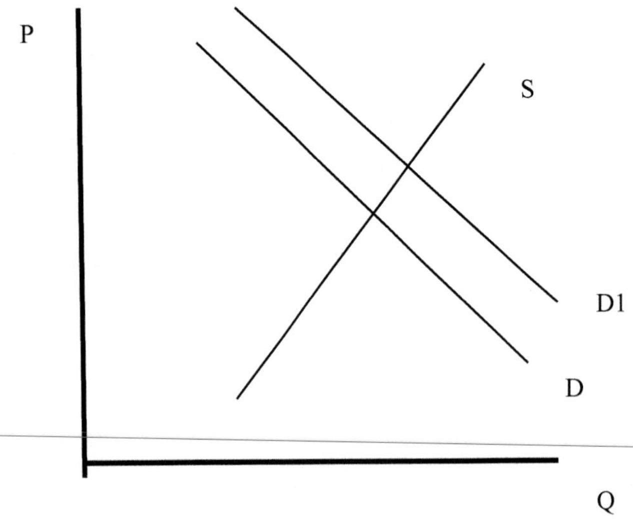


f. The main determinant of demand is price, other determinants are income, tastes and preferences, prices of related goods, expectations and population.

g. Pe decreases, Qe increases

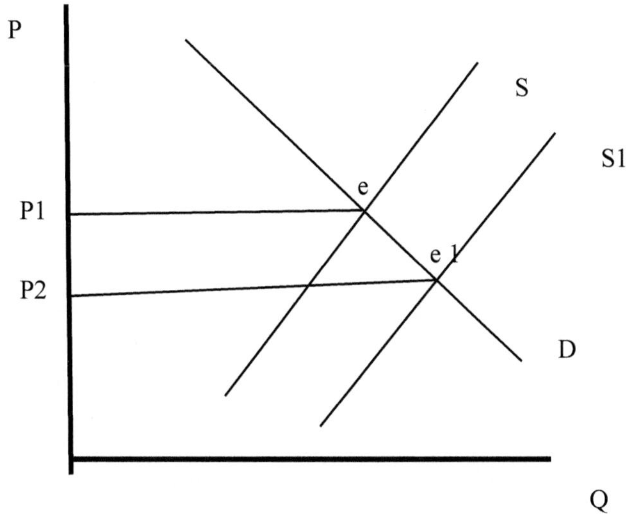


h. The main determinant of supply is price, other determinants are costs of inputs, technology, taxes and subsidies, price expectation, and number of firms in the industry.
i. No, P is too high so surplus exists
j. P has to decrease
k. Shortage, P would increase
l. P must adjust to equate Qd and Qs (rationing function of prices)
m. Shortage of 400 (P must increase)
n. Surplus of 600 (P must decrease)

2. Lightening 123 Autos

a. S increases, P decreases
b. S decreases, P increases
c. D decreases, P decreases
d. D decreases, P decreases
e. D increases, P increases

Price↑ Quantity↓

## CHAPTER 4

Key Formulae

$$Ep = \frac{\text{change in Q}}{\text{sum of quantities}/2} \div \frac{\text{change in P}}{\text{Sum of prices}/2}$$

### Problems

1. Vic's Vintage Videos

Victor Olshevski is a video buff who has just opened his own video store specialising in old movies and videos. He has had some problems determining the price to charge and has experimented with various prices for his videos. He is puzzled by the reaction of his customers to price changes he has made.

Knowing you are a NAIT business student he asks you for some help as you are renting the video "Revenge of the Killer Dandelions from Planet X". He gives you a computer printout showing the following historical data:

| Price per Video ($) | # Videos Rented per Week | Total Revenue | Elasticity of Demand | Elastic/ Inelastic |
|---|---|---|---|---|
| 1 | 4,000 | 4,000 | ---------- | ---------- |
| 2 | 2,000 | 4,000 | 1 | Unit elastic |
| 3 | 1,000 | 3,000 | 1.667 | |
| 4 | 200 | 800 | | |

a. What does elasticity of demand (Ep) measure?

Response between Price and Quantity Demand.

b. How is it related to total revenue?

c. Complete the table above.

d. What are three factors that can affect elasticity of demand?

| | |
|---|---|
| 1. | Subsitutes |
| 2. | Budget |
| 3. | time |

2. Dieter Ducklington Enterprises

Dieter Ducklington owns the Red Deer Ruffians, A professional rugby team. Each time the team plays in Ruffian Stadium it costs Dieter $150,000 for rent, staffing, field preparation, etc. Current ticket prices for a ruffian home game are $15 per ticket, and an average game draws 10,000 fans even though the Stadium can accommodate twice that number.

a. At current ticket prices, how much profit does Dieter make per game?

TR = 150,000

TC = 150,000

Profit = 0

Dieter has just had a marketing survey completed that indicated if prices were raised to $20 per ticket, average attendance would drop to 9,000 fans.

b. At a price of $20 per ticket what would Dieter's average profit be per game?

20 x 9000

180,000

30,000 = Profit

c. Calculate the elasticity of demand coefficient between these two price points.

$E_D = \frac{1000}{9,500} / \frac{5}{17.5}$

$ED = \frac{0.1052}{0.2857}$

0.368 = ED ✓

d. Between these price points, is Ep elastic or inelastic? How can you tell?

inelastic Because ED is less than 1

e. As price increases, what happens to Q and TR?

Q will go down and TR ingreases

The marketing study also indicated that if prices were dropped to $12 per ticket from the current $15, average attendance would increase to 12,000 fans.

f. Calculate Ep between the $12 and $15 price points.

$12 12,000

$15 10,000

$\frac{\Delta Q}{\text{ave } Q} / \frac{\Delta P}{\text{ave } P}$

$\frac{2,000}{11,000} / \frac{3}{13.5}$

$\frac{0.1818}{0.2222}$ 0.818 = ED

g. As price decreases, what happens to Q and TR?

Q goes up TR goes down

h. What would Dieter's average profit per game be at the $12 ticket price?

144,000 − 150,000

= −6,000 Loss No Profit

i. As an entrepreneur out to maximise his profits, and given the information in the marketing survey, what price should Dieter charge per home game ticket?

as much as possible without losing that much money.

j. Dieter is thinking about hiring Bo Sampson, a superstar from the Kiwi All Greys. Assume that Dieter has already made the decision to keep prices at $15 per ticket and the ruffians play ten home games per year. The marketing survey indicated that having Bo on the team would increase attendance by 4,000 fans per game. Bo has several offers already, but is still available. What is the maximum amount per year that Dieter should be willing to pay for Bo?

## Solutions

1. Vic's Vintage Videos

| P | Q | TR=P*Q | Ed | Type |
|---|---|---|---|---|
| $1 | 4,000 | $4,000 | -------- | -------- |
| $2 | 2,000 | 4,000 | 1.00 | unitary (Ep = 1.0) |
| $3 | 1,000 | $3,000 | 1.67 | elastic (Ep>1.0) |
| $4 | 200 | $800 | 4.67 | elastic (Ep>1.0) |

a. Sensitivity of consumers to a change in price (effect of change in P on Qd)

b. If Ep is elastic, as P increases, TR decreases (consumers are very sensitive to P)
   if Ep is inelastic, as P increases, TR increases (consumers are not very sensitive to P)

c. See table

d. Substitutability, proportion of income, time

2. Dieter Ducklington

a. TR = $150,000; TC= $150,000; profit = TR - TC = 0

b. TR = $180,000; TC = $150,000; profit = $30,000

c. Ep = .368 (inelastic)

d. Inelastic (Ep < 1.0) or as P increases, TR increases

e. As P increases, Q Decreases, TR increases

f. Ep = .818 (inelastic)

g. As P decreases, Q Increases, TR decreases (positive relationship if inelastic)

h. $6,000 loss

i. $20

j. 4,000 tickets * $15 per ticket * 10 games = $600,000

## CHAPTER 5

### Problems

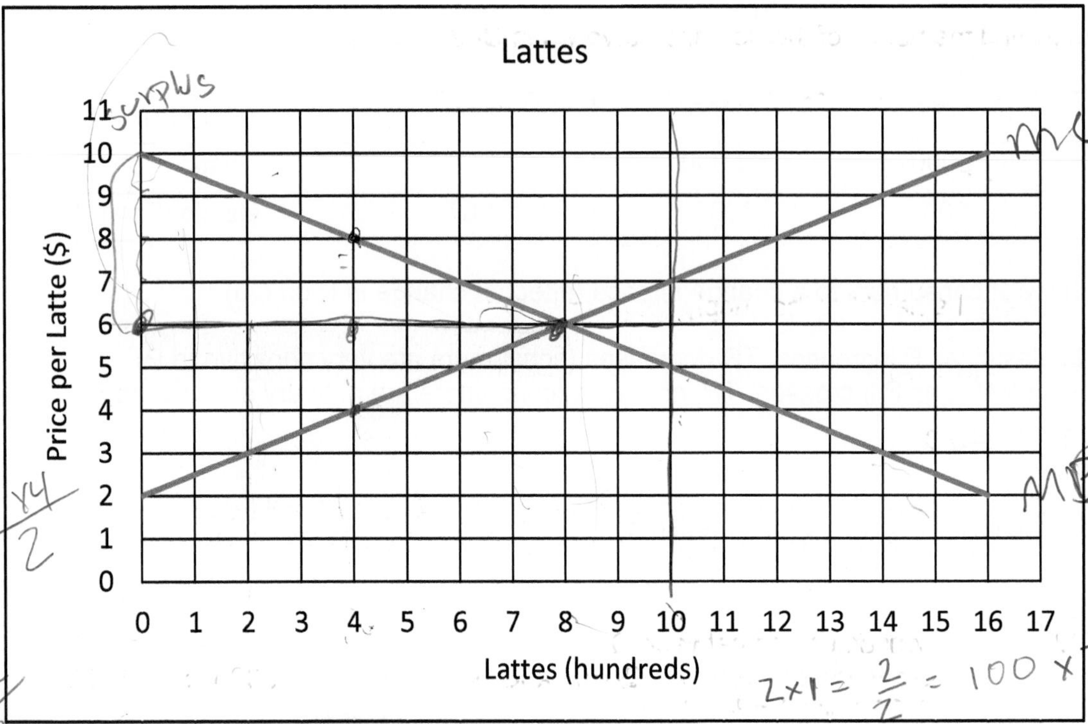


1. What is the maximum that consumers are willing to pay for the two hundredth latte?
   9.00$
2. What is the marginal benefit of the four hundredth latte?
   800$
3. What is the consumer surplus derived from consuming the four hundredth latte?
   2$ $8 - 6$ = 2$
4. What is the minimum amount the sellers of lattes must receive in order to supply the two hundredth latte?
   $6 - $3 = $3
5. What is the marginal cost of the four hundredth latte?
   $4
6. What is the producer surplus derived from supplying the four hundredth latte?
   $6 - 4$ = $2
7. What would be the allocatively efficient quantity level be (lattes per day)? Briefly explain.
   Q = 8 MB = MC at equilibrium
8. What would be the maximum total amount of producer and consumer surplus in the latte market?
   8×4/2 ×2 = 3200 Area of the 2 triangles
9. If the government fixed the weekly quantity level at 10,000 lattes per day, what would be the total amount of deadweight loss? ↳ area of the 2 smaller triangles when there is overproduction
   2×1/2 = 100 × 2 = 200$

## Solutions

1. \$9.00 find the height of the demand curve when Q=2

2. \$8.00 find the height of the demand curve when Q=4

3. \$2 MB-$P_e$ \$8-\$6

4. \$3 find the height of the supply curve when Q=2

5. \$4 find the height of the supply curve when Q=4

6. \$2 $P_e$- MC \$6-\$4

7. Q=8 MB=MC

8. \$3,200 consumer surplus at equilibrium (10-6) x 800 x 0.5 = \$1,600
   producer surplus at equilibrium (6-2) x 800 x 0.5 = \$1,600
   \$1,600 + \$1,600 = \$3,200

9. \$200 consumer loss between Q=800 and Q=10,000 (6-5) x 200 x 0.5 = \$100
   producer loss between Q=800 and Q=10,000 (7-6) x 200 x 0.5 = \$100
   \$100 + \$100 = \$200

## CHAPTER 6

**Problems**

1. Snake Oil
Below are the schedules relating to the weekly demand and supply of snake oil pills in Canada:

| Quantity Demanded (Qd) | Price ($) | Quantity Supplied (Qs) |
|---|---|---|
| 1,000 | 100 | 15,000 |
| 2,000 | 90 | 10,000 |
| * 2,500 | 80 | 7,000 |
| 3,000 | 70 | 4,500 |
| 3,100 | 60 | 3,100 |
| * 3,150 | 50 | 1,000 |

If a free market were allowed to operate

a. What would be the equilibrium price of snake oil?
60

b. What would be the equilibrium quantity?
3100

c. Would there be a shortage or surplus at this price?
neither its equal

Now suppose that the Canadian government decided to interfere in the snake oil market in an attempt to help lower income families purchase snake oil by passing a law stating that snake oil could not be sold for more than $50 per pill (price ceiling).

d. How much snake oil would be demanded by Canadians?
3150

e. How much snake oil would be produced by suppliers?
1,000

f. Would there be a shortage or surplus of snake oil? How much?
Shortage by 2150 Because Qd > Qs

Suppose that a new political party was elected, and they passed a new law to aid the snake oil producers who supported them in the election. The new law guaranteed them $80 per snake oil pill through a series of price supports (price floor).

g. How many snake oil pills would Canadian consumers demand?
2500

h. How many pills would snake oil producers supply?
7,000

i. Would there be a shortage or surplus? Of how much?
Surplus 4,500 Because Qd < Qs

j. In this case, who wins and who loses? How?
Producers because higher price and more quantity demanded
Loser Consumers higher price paid.

2. Rouge Vin

As a stockbroker, you have been asked to analyze the red wine market. Some of your best clients want to invest in corporations that primarily are involved in the production and distribution of red wine.

For each of the following events, your task is to predict:

i. whether the event will, in the first instance, lead to an "increase in demand" or "decrease in demand" or "increase in supply" or "decrease in supply" of red wine.

ii. in which direction the equilibrium price and equilibrium quantity will change, for red wine, as a result of the event in question.

Event 1: Recent research reports suggest that red wine reduces the risk of heart disease.

Predictions? Increase in demand ~~decrease in supply~~

ep will increase

eq will increase

Event 2: A shortage of grapes occurs due to severe worldwide weather conditions.

Predictions? decrease in Supply

ep will increase

eq will decrease

Event 3: The price of white wine decreases.

Predictions?

decrease in demand

ep will decrease

eq will decrease

Event 4: Chemists have come up with a new chemical reaction that significantly speeds up the process by which grapes are fermented into a fine red wine.

Predictions?

increase in Supply

ep will decrease

eq will increase

Event 5: The price of red meat, a complement product, significantly increases.

Predictions?

decrease in demand

ep will decrease

eq will decrease

**Solutions**

1. Snake Oil

a. $60
b. 3,100
c. neither
d. 3,150
e. 1,000
f. shortage of 2,150
g. 2,500
h. 7,000
i. surplus of 4,500
j. producers win (higher P and Q), consumers lose (higher P and taxes)

2. Rouge Vin

| | | |
|---|---|---|
| Event 1: | i. Demand increases | ii. Price increases and quantity increases |
| Event 2: | i. Supply decreases | ii. Price increases and quantity decreases |
| Event 3: | i. Demand decreases | ii. Price decreases and quantity decreases |
| Event 4: | i. Supply increases | ii. Price decreases and quantity increases |
| Event 5: | i. Demand decreases | ii. Price decreases and quantity decreases |

## CHAPTER 8

Key Formulae

$$\text{Accounting profit} = \text{Total revenue} - \text{Explicit costs}$$

$$\text{Economic profit} = \text{Total revenues} - (\text{Explicit} + \text{Implicit costs})$$

$$\text{Total costs (TC)} = \text{Total fixed costs (TFC)} + \text{Total variable cost (TVC)}$$

$$\text{Average total costs (ATC)} = \frac{\text{Total costs (TC)}}{\text{Output (Q)}}$$

$$\text{Average total costs (ATC)} = \text{Average fixed costs (AFC)} + \text{Average variable costs(AVC)}$$

$$\text{Average variable costs (AVC)} = \frac{\text{Total variable costs (TVC)}}{\text{Output (Q)}}$$

$$\text{Average fixed costs (AFC)} = \frac{\text{Total fixed costs (TFC)}}{\text{Output (Q)}}$$

$$\text{Marginal costs (MC)} = \frac{\text{Change in total cost (TC)}}{\text{Change in output (Q)}}$$

$$\text{Breakeven quantity (BQ)} = \frac{\text{Total fixed cost (TFC)}}{\text{Selling price} - \text{Average variable costs (AVC)}}$$

$$\text{Target profit quantity} = \frac{\text{Total fixed cost (TFC)} + \text{Profit}}{\text{Selling price} - \text{Average variable costs (AVC)}}$$

## Problems

**1.** Green Brutus Veggie Farm

After graduating from the NAIT Business program, you are hired as assistant manager at Yellow Flowers Fast Food Restaurant. Your salary is $15.00 per hour and you work 35 hours per week, with 2 weeks paid vacation per year. You have always wanted to be your own boss, but could never afford to start up or purchase your own company. Next week you will turn 25 and will gain access to your $150,000 trust fund which is currently invested at 12%.

Last week you attended a conference where you learned of a new fast food franchise that was opening in St. Albert. An email has arrived from the Green Brutus Veggie Farm Inc. in response to your inquiries. The email stated that the new Veggie Farm due to open next month in St. Albert was still available for $100,000, and if you acquire the franchise you will be expected to work 3,600 hours per year as "your own boss". A decision from you is needed by the end of the week.

The annual estimates for the first few years of operation supplied by Veggie Farms are:

| | | |
|---|---|---|
| Sales: | $260,000 | |
| Expenses: | | |
| Franchise Fee | 30,000 | explicit costs |
| Rent of Building | 50,000 | non-owners. |
| Product Costs | 80,000 | |
| Employee Salaries | 50,000 | |
| Business Taxes | 12,000 | |
| | 222000 | |

a. List the decision alternatives facing you.

Buy it or don't

b. What implicit costs are associated with owning the franchise?

Salary / Intrest

c. From an accounting viewpoint, should you purchase the franchise? Find the accounting profit or loss.

260,000 - 30,000 - 50,000 - 80,000 - 50,000 - 12,000 = 38,000 Buy it

d. From an economic viewpoint, should you purchase the franchise? Find the economic profit or loss.

38000 - 39,300 = (1,300)

Loss Don't Buy

2. Tom and Jerri

Tom Smith is considering purchasing a new car. The price of the car is $11,000, and Tom hopes to keep it four years and then sell it for $5,000. Based on past experience, Tom drives about 16,000 km per year and lives in a downtown apartment where he must pay a $20 per month parking fee.

Tom has budgeted the following automobile expense items for the next four years:

| ITEM | COST | FIXED/VARIABLE |
|---|---|---|
| 1. Gasoline (10 Litres/100 km @ $.55/Litre) | 3,520 | Variable |
| 2. License Fees | 120 | Fixed |
| 3. Insurance | 2,000 | Fixed |
| 4. Tune-ups/Maintenance | 420 | Variable |
| 5. Tires | 270 | Variable |
| 6. Storage ($20/month * 48 months) | 960 | Fixed |
| 7. Interest on car loan | 3,520 | Fixed |
| 8. Depreciation or Amortization | 6,000 | Fixed |

a. Classify the above items as either fixed costs (FC) or variable costs (VC). TFC =

b. Using your classification, calculate (for 4 years):

Total Fixed Costs (TFC) 12,600

Total Variable Costs (TVC) 4,210

Total Costs (TC) 16,810

Average Fixed Costs per km (AFC) ~~0.79 $/km~~ 0.197 km

Average Variable Costs per km (AVC) 0.066/km

Average Total Costs per km (ATC) 0.2621/km

c. Tom and his friend Jerri plan to drive his new car to Florida during spring break. The round trip is expected to be 1,000 km, and they plan to split the car costs 50-50. Calculate Jerri's share of the cost of the trip under the assumption that costs are split as follows.

i. Gas Only

0.55 • 10 • 10 = 55/2 = 27.50

27.50

ii. Variable Costs

4210/2

AVC • Q = TVC/2 = 33$

iii. Total Costs

331.5

ATC • Q = TC/2 = 131$

3. Klondike Daze

As an enterprising NAIT student needing cash to finance your education and active social life, you decided to sell sandwiches at the Klondike exhibition this year. You quickly discover that you cannot sell your sandwiches for more than $.60 each due to competition, and that each sandwich costs you $.40 to make. If you do not sell all your sandwiches by closing time you must store them until the next day. Each morning you make up enough sandwiches to start the day with 500 sandwiches in your refrigerator.

It is now noon on the last day of the exhibition, and you still have 150 sandwiches on hand. Since you will not be able to sell any leftover sandwiches once the exhibition is over, you are considering lowering the price to sell as many as possible, but you also want to maximize your profit. Your best estimate of sales per price are as follows:

| Price | Expected Sales (#sandwiches) | Total Revenue |
|---|---|---|
| $.70 | 30 | 21$ |
| .55 | 60 | 33$ |
| .40 | 90 | 36 |
| .20 | 120 | |
| .10 | 150 | |

a. Complete the table.

b. What are your marginal costs at noon on the final day of the exhibition?

c. Should you lower your price? If so, to what level?

4. Costs of Production Worksheet

ATC
58.4
49.2 .5
43.67 .6

a. Complete the following table.

| P | Q | TFC | AFC | TVC | AVC | TC | ATC | MC | TR |
|---|---|---|---|---|---|---|---|---|---|
| 12 | 0 | 100 | ------- | 0 | -------- | 100 | -------- | -------- | |
| 11 | 1 | 100 | 100 | 84 | 84 | 184 | 184 | 84 | |
| 10 | 2 | 100 | 50 | 108 | 54 | 208 | 104 | 24 | |
| 9 | 3 | 100 | 33.3 | 120 | 40 | 220 | 73.33 | 12 | |
| 8 | 4 | 100 | 25 | 132 | 33.00 | 232 | 58 | 12 | |
| 7 | 5 | 100 | 20 | 146 | 29.20 | 246 | 49.2 | 14 | |
| 6 | 6 | 100 | 16.67 | 162.02 | 27.00 | 262.02 | 43.67 | 16.02 | |
| 5 | 7 | 100 | 14.29 | 180 | 25.71 | 280 | 40 | 17.98 | |
| 4 | 8 | 100 | 12.5 | 201 | 25.13 | 301 | 37.63 | 21 | |
| 3 | 9 | 100 | 11.11 | 225 | 25 | 325 | 36.11 | 24 | |
| 2 | 10 | 100 | 10 | 252 | 25.20 | 352 | 35.20 | 42.07 | |
| 1 | 11 | 100 | 9.09 | 296.01 | 26.91 | 396.01 | 36.00 | 44.01 | |
| 0 | 12 | 100 | 8.33 | 344.04 | 28.67 | 444.04 | 37.00 | 48.03 | |

b. On the graph below, label AFC, AVC, ATC and MC.

***P***

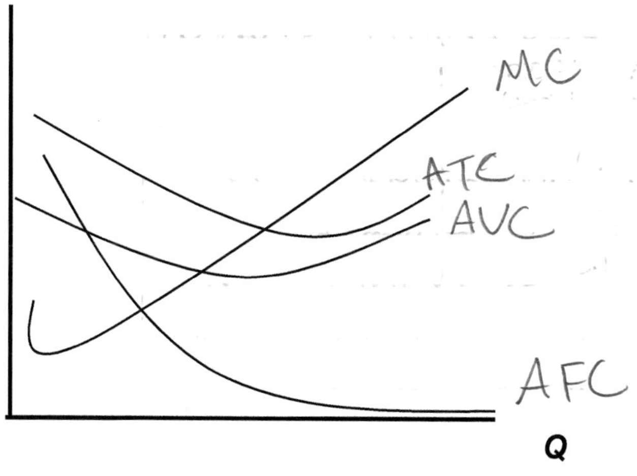


***Q***

c. Where does MC intersect AVC and ATC? Why?

at the minimums

5. The Eco186 Financial Calculator

Steve and Tillie have just returned from a trip to Japan where they discovered a calculator with built-in economic functions, graphs and formulae. This type of calculator (the Eco186) is not yet available in Canada, and Sam feels that there would be a great demand. Steve and Tillie are considering importing and selling them in the Edmonton area for $25 each. Tillie developed the following information in regards to their anticipated business venture.

| | | | |
|---|---|---|---|
| Fixed Costs | Advertising and promotion | $10,000 | TFC |
| | Rent | 5,000 | |
| | Salaries | 5,000 | |
| Variable Costs | Price of calculator | $10.00 | AVC |
| | Selling Commissions | 2.50 | |
| | Sales tax and duty | 2.50 | |

a. How many calculators would Steve and Tillie need to sell to breakeven (BE)?

b. List the two decision alternatives facing Steve and Tillie.

A1

A2

c. How can breakeven analysis help them?

6. Sticky Wickets

You have been offered the contract to sell jackets for the Sticky Wickets Cricket Team. You hope to make the $7,000 necessary to get you through your second year in Business Admin. at NAIT. Before signing on the dotted line you do some preliminary research and make the following costs and revenue estimates.

| | FC or VC |
|---|---|
| Stall rental for the duration of the cricket season is $4,000. | |
| A local wholesaler is willing to sell you the jackets for $38 each. | |
| Municipal business taxes for the season will be $200. | |
| At a price of $52 each you estimate you could sell 600 jackets. | |
| At a price of $45 each you estimate you could sell 800 jackets. | |

a. At a price of $45, what is your breakeven point?

b. How many jackets do you need to sell to pay for your second year expenses?

c. At $45, what is your expected profit?

d. At $52, what is your expected profit? How many jackets do you need to sell to meet your second year expenses?

e. What selling price would you choose for your jackets? Why?

## Solutions

**1.** Green Brutus Veggie Farm

a. Buy franchise or do not buy franchise

b. Salary foregone, interest foregone

c. 260,000 – (30,000 + 50,000 + 80,000 + 50,000 + 12,000) = 38,000

d. 260,000 – (30,000 + 50,000 + 80,000 + 50,000 + 12,000) = 38,000 – (27,300 + 12,000) = (1,300)

2. Tom and Jerri

a. 1. Variable
   2. Fixed
   3. Fixed
   4. Variable
   5. Variable
   6. Fixed
   7. Fixed
   8. Fixed, using straight line method of depreciation.

b. TFC = $12,600; TVC = $4,210; TC = $16,810
   AFC = $.197/km; AVC = $.066/km; ATC = $.263/km

c. i. $27.50
   ii. $33.00
   iii. $131.50

3. Klondike Daze

a.

| P | Qd(Sales) | TR |
|---|---|---|
| $.70 | 30 | 21 |
| .55 | 60 | 33 |
| .40 | 90 | 36 |
| .20 | 120 | 24 |
| .10 | 150 | 15 |

b. none (all costs are sunk)
c. yes, sell @ $.40 each to maximize profit @ $36

4. Cost of Production Worksheet

a.

| P | Q | TFC | AFC | TVC | AVC | TC | ATC | MC | TR |
|---|---|---|---|---|---|---|---|---|---|
| 12 | 0 | 100 | ------ | 0 | ------ | 100 | ------ | ------ | 0 |
| 11 | 1 | 100 | 100.0 | 84 | 84.0 | 184 | 184.0 | 84 | 11 |
| 10 | 2 | 100 | 50.00 | 108 | 54.0 | 208 | 104.0 | 24 | 20 |
| 9 | 3 | 100 | 33.33 | 120 | 40.0 | 220 | 73.33 | 12 | 27 |
| 8 | 4 | 100 | 25.00 | 132 | 33.0 | 232 | 58.00 | 12 | 32 |
| 7 | 5 | 100 | 20.00 | 146 | 29.2 | 246 | 49.20 | 14 | 35 |
| 6 | 6 | 100 | 16.67 | 162 | 27.0 | 262 | 43.67 | 16 | 36 |
| 5 | 7 | 100 | 14.29 | 180 | 25.7 | 280 | 40.00 | 18 | 35 |
| 4 | 8 | 100 | 12.50 | 201 | 25.1 | 301 | 37.62 | 21 | 32 |
| 3 | 9 | 100 | 11.11 | 225 | 25.0 | 325 | 36.11 | 24 | 27 |
| 2 | 10 | 100 | 10.00 | 252 | 25.2 | 352 | 35.20 | 27 | 20 |
| 1 | 11 | 100 | 9.09 | 296 | 26.9 | 396 | 36.00 | 44 | 11 |
| 0 | 12 | 100 | 8.33 | 344 | 28.6 | 444 | 37.00 | 48 | 0 |

b.

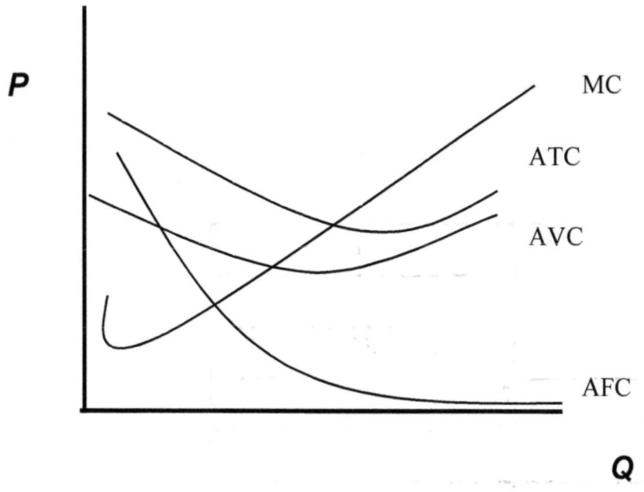


c. MC intersects AVC and ATC at the minimum point. When MC is below average cost, average cost falls.

5. Eco 186 Financial Calculator

a. BE = $20,000/(25-15) = 2,000 calculators
b. A1 = status quo (stay as is) A2 = import and sell calculators
c. Provides a target volume for BE

6. Sticky Wickets

| | FC or VC |
|---|---|
| Stall rental for the duration of the cricket season is $4,000. | F |
| A local wholesaler is willing to sell you the jackets for $38 each. | V |
| Municipal business taxes for the season will be $200. | F |
| At a price of $52 each you estimate you could sell 600 jackets. | - |
| At a price of $45 each you estimate you could sell 800 jackets. | - |

a. 600 jackets
b. 1,600 jackets
c. (800 * $45) - (800 * $38) - $4,200 = $1,400
d. (4,200 + 7,000) / (52 - 38) = 800 jackets (note: you can only expect to sell 600 jackets @ $52.)
e. $52 for profit of $4,200

JR SHAW
SCHOOL OF BUSINESS

Last Name:____________________

First Name:____________________

# ECON1110 Microeconomics – Version A

Midterm Examination
Time 1.5 hours
Value 30%

INSTRUCTIONS

- Please print your first and last name on this title page.
- Your Scantron must have the following information:
  - Name as it appears on your NAIT ID
  - TEST NO: fill in A, B, C or D depending on your version identified on this page
  - Write your Student ID number then fill in the corresponding circles
  - Fill in the VER above the Student ID depending on your version
  - Make sure the TEST NO and VER are the same

| | |
|---|---|
| Total Marks | / 75 |

## Micro Formulas

$$Ep = \frac{\text{change in Q}}{\text{sum of quantities/ 2}} \div \frac{\text{change in P}}{\text{Sum of prices /2}}$$

$$\text{Accounting profit} = \text{Total revenue} - \text{Explicit costs}$$

$$\text{Economic profit} = \text{Total revenues} - (\text{Explicit} + \text{Implicit costs})$$

$$\text{Total costs (TC)} = \text{Total fixed costs (TFC)} + \text{Total variable cost (TVC)}$$

$$\text{Average total costs (ATC)} = \frac{\text{Total costs (TC)}}{\text{Output (Q)}}$$

$$\text{Average total costs (ATC)} = \text{Average fixed costs (AFC)} + \text{Average variable costs(AVC)}$$

$$\text{Average variable costs (AVC)} = \frac{\text{Total variable costs (TVC)}}{\text{Output (Q)}}$$

$$\text{Average fixed costs (AFC)} = \frac{\text{Total fixed costs (TFC)}}{\text{Output (Q)}}$$

$$\text{Marginal costs (MC)} = \frac{\text{Change in total cost (TC)}}{\text{Change in output (Q)}}$$

$$\text{Breakeven quantity (BQ)} = \frac{\text{Total fixed cost (TFC)}}{\text{Selling price} - \text{Average variable costs (AVC)}}$$

$$\text{Target profit quantity} = \frac{\text{Total fixed cost (TFC)} + \text{Profit}}{\text{Selling price} - \text{Average variable costs (AVC)}}$$

$$\text{Total revenue (TR)} = \text{Price (P)} \times \text{Quantity (Q)}$$

$$\text{Total Profit} = [\text{Price (P)} - \text{Average Total Cost (ATC)}] \text{ x } \text{Quantity (Q)}$$

$$\text{Marginal revenue (MR)} = \frac{\text{Change in total revenue (TR)}}{\text{Change in output (Q)}}$$

$$\text{Marginal Tax Rate} = \frac{\text{Change in taxes due}}{\text{Change in taxable income}}$$

$$\text{Average Tax Rate} = \frac{\text{Total taxes due}}{\text{Total taxable income}}$$

Use your SCANTRON and choose the one alternative that best completes the statement or answers the question. Use a HB pencil to shade in your answer. [1 mark each]

1) Scarcity means
   A. not being able to satisfy all of everyone's limited needs.
   B. not being able to satisfy all of everyone's unlimited wants.
   C. the same thing as shortage.
   D. not having enough of a product to serve all customers who wish to buy it.

2) Production refers to
   A. any activity that results in the conversion of resources into goods and services that can be consumed.
   B. any activity carried on by a firm, whether a corporation, partnership, or sole proprietorship.
   C. any activity that causes a material conversion of an object.
   D. physically producing material goods only.

3) A person goes to college to become an engineer. This is an example of an
   A. investment in human capital.
   B. investment in physical capital.
   C. increase in entrepreneurship.
   D. increase in labour.

4) Opportunity cost is
   A. based on the intrinsic value of the good itself.
   B. the value of the best alternative that was given up.
   C. the combined value of all the alternatives not selected.
   D. the same thing as the money price of a good.

5) Production is allocatively efficient when
   A. the maximum output possible is produced given available resources and current technology.
   B. the mix of goods and services most desired by society is produced.
   C. it generates a point beyond the production possibility curve.
   D. technological change occurs.

6) The law of increasing relative cost states that
   A. the production possibilities curve will be a straight line.
   B. producing additional units of one good results in proportionately smaller reductions in output of the other good.
   C. producing additional units of one good results in increasing amounts of lost output of the other good.
   D. the economy will be producing on its production possibilities curve.

Fig. 1-1

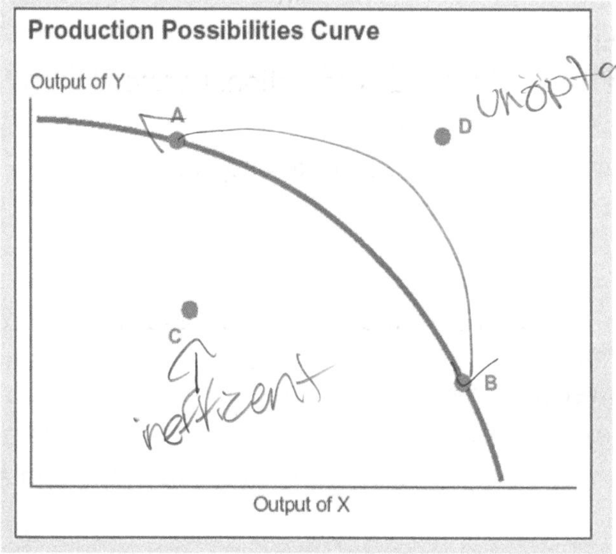


7) In Fig. 1-1 identify where productive efficiency occurs:
   A. point C.
   B. points C and D.
   C. points A and B.
   D. point D.

8) When a society forgoes current consumption to invest in the production of capital goods,
   A. the less the society can consume next year.
   B. the easier it will be for the society to consume less in the future because people will become accustomed to less.
   C. the more the society can consume in the future.
   D. the less capital the society can produce in the future.

9) Generally, specialization allows
   A. greater productivity.
   B. constant opportunity costs.
   C. greater self-reliance.
   D. the production of fewer capital goods.

10) Which of the following is NOT one of the three basic economic questions?
   A. What amounts of which goods and services will be produced?
   B. For whom will goods and services be produced?
   C. How will goods are services be produced?
   D. What prices will be charged for the goods and services produced?

11) An economic system in which individuals own productive resources, and those individuals can use the resources in whatever manner they choose, subject to common protective legal restrictions, is known as
   A. a command economy.
   B. capitalism.
   C. socialism.
   D. communism.

12) The law of demand states that, other things being equal,
   A. people demand less at lower prices and more at higher prices.
   B. the quantity of a good or service demanded is inversely related to its price.
   C. changes in price and changes in quantity demanded move in the same direction.
   D. the quantity of a good or service demanded is directly related to its price.

13) If macaroni and cheese is an inferior good and an increase in consumer income occurs, then which of the following statements is true?
   A. At a given price, more will be spent on the good.
   B. The demand curve for the macaroni and cheese will shift farther away from the origin.
   C. There will be an increase in demand for macaroni and cheese.
   D. There will be a decrease in the demand for macaroni and cheese.

14) If two goods are substitutes, then
   A. there is an inverse relationship between changes in the price of one good and changes in the demand for the other.
   B. changes in the quantity demanded of one good will not affect the demand for the other.
   C. an increase in the price of one causes the demand for the other to fall.
   D. if the price of one good falls, the demand for the other good falls also.

? Shift not price

15) Any improvement in overall production technology that permits more output to be produced with the same level of inputs causes
   A. no movement of the supply curve, but a fall in price and a decrease in quantity supplied.
   B. a movement up the supply curve resulting in both a higher equilibrium price and greater quantity.
   C. a rightward shift of the supply curve so that more is offered for sale at each price.
   D. a leftward shift of the supply curve so that less is offered for sale at each price.

Table 3-2

| Price per X | Quantity of X Demanded | Quantity of X Supplied |
|---|---|---|
| $10 | 0 | 150 |
| 8 | 20 | 120 |
| 6 | 40 | 90 |
| 4 | 60 | 60 |
| 2 | 80 | 30 |
| 0 | 100 | 0 |

16) In Table 3-2, at a price of $8 per unit,
   A. a shortage of 80 units will exist on the market.
   B. a surplus of 100 units will exist on the market.
   C. consumers will continue to bid prices upward.
   D. there will be no tendency for the market to approach a stable equilibrium.

17) In Table 3-2, if other influences remain constant and the market is free to adjust, a
stable equilibrium price will be established at
   A. $6
   B. $4
   C. $8
   D. $2

18) A shortage will occur when
   A. the price is above the market-clearing level.
   B. the price is below the market-clearing level.
   C. there is excess supply.
   D. the price equals the market-clearing level.

19) When demand decreases and supply increases

A. equilibrium quantity will rise.

B. equilibrium price will fall.

C. equilibrium price will rise.

D. equilibrium quantity will fall.

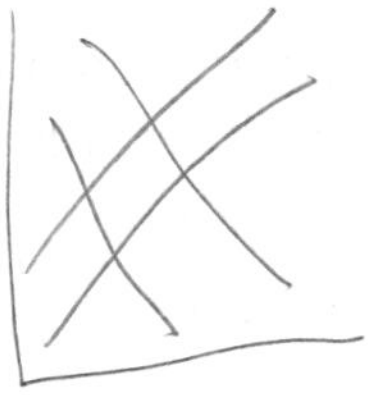

20) If the market were free to adjust, growth in demand for Canadian prescription drugs by U.S. consumers would be expected to

A. cause Canadian demand curves to shift toward the origin.

B. cause equilibrium Canadian drug prices to increase

C. cause equilibrium Canadian drug prices to decrease

D. cause Canadian drug company supply curves to shift outward.

21) The price elasticity of demand is a measure of

A. the demand for a product holding prices constant.

B. the horizontal shift in the demand curve when the price of a good changes.

C. the responsiveness of the quantity of a good demanded to changes in the price of the good.

D. the quantity demanded of a good at a given price.

22) When demand is perfectly inelastic, an increase in price will

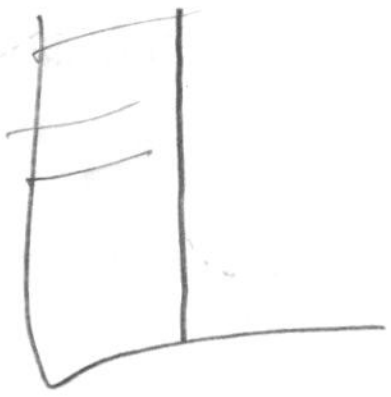

A. decrease total revenue.

B. leave total revenue unchanged.

C. increase total revenue.

D. either increase total revenue or decrease total revenue, but it is impossible to tell which.

23) Compared to the demand for necessities, demand for luxury goods tends to be

A. more elastic.

B. less price responsive.

C. more inelastic.

D. more predictable.

24) An important determinant of a good's price elasticity of demand is

A. the number of sellers in the market.

B. the profits of suppliers.

C. the ease with which consumers can substitute other goods for it.

D. the numbers of buyers in the market.

25) When two goods are complements for each other,

A. the selling price of one good has no effect on the other good.
B. an increase in the price of one good will increase the demand for the other.
C. an increase in the price of one good will decrease the demand of the other.
D. consumers will buy equal quantities of each good.

26) The free-rider problem is

A. the use of the public goods provided by a state by residents of another state.
B. the incentive people have to avoid paying for a good they cannot be excluded from consuming.
C. a concern for firms and their revenue.
D. that people cannot be forced to accept public goods.

27) Consumer surplus is defined as

A. the excess of quantity supplied over quantity demanded at market prices.
B. the difference between marginal revenue and marginal cost, summed over all units of output produced.
C. the excess of quantity demanded over quantity supplied at market prices below equilibrium.
D. the difference between the maximum amount consumers would be willing to pay and the actual amount paid for all units of a product consumed.

28) Which of the following is an example of an external cost? ⇒ additional cost ↳ outside of control

A. the cost of labour to a firm
B. automobile exhaust pollution
C. the cost of tires for your automobile
D. the opportunity cost of getting a college education

29) Suppose there are two factories on a river, and both need clean water for their production processes. The upstream factory takes in clean water and dumps dirty water back into the river. The downstream firm must clean up the water it gets from the river before using it. In this situation,

A. the private marginal costs of the downstream factory are more than the private marginal costs of the upstream factory, but for both, private marginal costs and social marginal costs are the same.
B. the social marginal costs are greater than the private marginal costs for the upstream firm, while the social marginal costs are less than the private marginal costs for the downstream firm.
C. the upstream factory's private marginal costs are less than its social marginal costs, and its external costs are borne by the downstream factory.
D. the internal costs of the upstream factory are externalized by the downstream factory, who then passes them on to its customers.

30) Moral Hazard occurs when

A. one party to a transaction has both the ability and incentive to shift costs to the other parties.
B. two parties involved in a transaction has both the ability and incentive to shift costs to the other parties.
C. three parties involved in a transaction has both the ability and incentive to shift costs to the other parties.
D. one party to a transaction has both the ability and incentive to shift utility to the other parties.

31) Prices in a market economy perform a rationing function because they reflect

A. the relative scarcity of the goods.
B. the strength of supply curve.
C. the extent to which the goods are necessities.
D. the demand of all buyers in the market.

32) When a government imposes price controls, the result is that

A. the price system operates more efficiently.
B. scarcity usually disappears.
C. all trades are as mutually beneficial to each party as possible.
D. the rationing function of prices is not allowed to function freely.

set prices

33) A policy that allows producers to band together to restrict total quantity supplied by using quotas is called a

A. marketing board.
B. import quota.
C. rent control.
D. minimum wage.

34) The difference between explicit costs and implicit costs is that

A. explicit costs are opportunity costs while implicit costs are not.
B. implicit costs involve resources that are purchased and explicit costs involve resources the firm already owns.
C. explicit costs are short-run costs and implicit costs are long-run costs.
D. implicit costs are opportunity costs while explicit costs are not.

35) Economic profits are

A. the same as accounting profits when firms do not own capital equipment.
B. Accounting profit minus opportunity costs and normal profit
C. equal to accounting profits plus the implicit costs of the firm.
D. always greater than accounting profits.

36) The period of time when plant size cannot be changed is called
A. the long run.
B. the planning horizon.
C. the short run.
D. the very long run.

37) The law of diminishing returns states that
A. after some point, successive equal-sized increases in labour, when added to fixed factors of production, will result in smaller increases of output.
B. output will continue to increase indefinitely if more variable factors of production are added to an existing stock of fixed factors.
C. a doubling of all inputs will double output.
D. variable costs tend to decrease with output.

38) Fixed costs are
A. not actually costs since they do not affect the decisions of a firm.
B. costs that a firm must pay when output is zero.
C. costs that increase at a constant rate when output increases.
D. costs that increase as revenue increases.

Figure 8-3

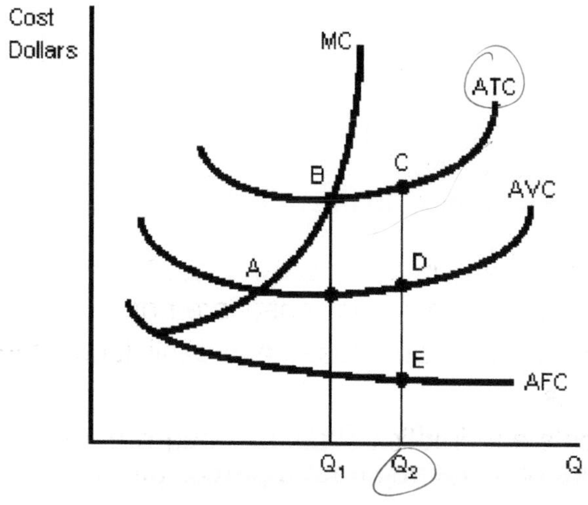


39) In Figure 8-3, the average total cost of producing Q2 is shown at point
A. A B. B C. C D. D

40) In Figure 8-3, average total costs are at a minimum at point
A. A B. B C. C D. D

41) If total costs are $50,000 when 1,000 units are produced, and total costs are $50,100 when 1,001 units are produced, we can conclude that at 1,001 units
   A. average fixed costs are $100.
   B. average total costs are $100.
   C. average variable costs are $100.
   D. marginal costs are $100.

42) The selling price of VIP luggage is $125 per case. The production cost are as follows: Total Fixed Costs = $18,000 and Average Variable Cost = $75. Calculate the Breakeven quantity to produce.
   A. 144
   B. 240
   C. 360
   D. 900

43) Any firm's short-run costs contain
   A. only variable costs.
   B. only fixed costs.
   C. both variable and fixed costs.
   D. only opportunity costs.

44) Economies of scale are said to exist when
   A. the long-run average cost curve is increasing.
   B. the long-run average cost curve is decreasing.
   C. the long-run average cost curve is tangent to the marginal cost curve.
   D. the long-run average cost curve is horizontal.

45) Minimum efficient scale
   A. occurs when the firm produces the maximum quantity of output.
   B. is the point at which economies of scale begin for a particular firm.
   C. is the lowest rate of output at which long-run average costs are minimized for a particular firm.
   D. is the point at which diseconomies of scale begin for a particular firm.

**Case 1: Opportunity Cost**

Upon graduating from NAIT, you open a franchise called the Bagel Bar. It is a successful business and eventually your managerial skills attract a job offer from a large hotel chain. They offer you $64,000 a year. In order to make your decision as to whether you sell the Bagel Bar, you consider the costs of $39,480 and revenues of $76,480. Remembering your microeconomics course you perform the following analysis to assist your decision:

46) Using case 1 data, the accounting profit for the Bagel Bar is:
   A. $64,000
   B. $39,480
   C. $37,000
   D. -$27,000

47) Using case 1 data, the economic profit for the Bagel Bar is:
   A. $64,000
   B. $39,480
   C. $37,000
   D. -$27,000

48) Using case 1 data, what are the implicit costs?
   A. $64,000
   B. $39,480
   C. $37,000
   D. -$27,000

49) Using case 1 data, what are the explicit costs?
   A. $64,000
   B. $39,480
   C. $37,000
   D. -$27,000

**<u>Case 2: Supply and Demand</u>** The following graph describes the milk market.

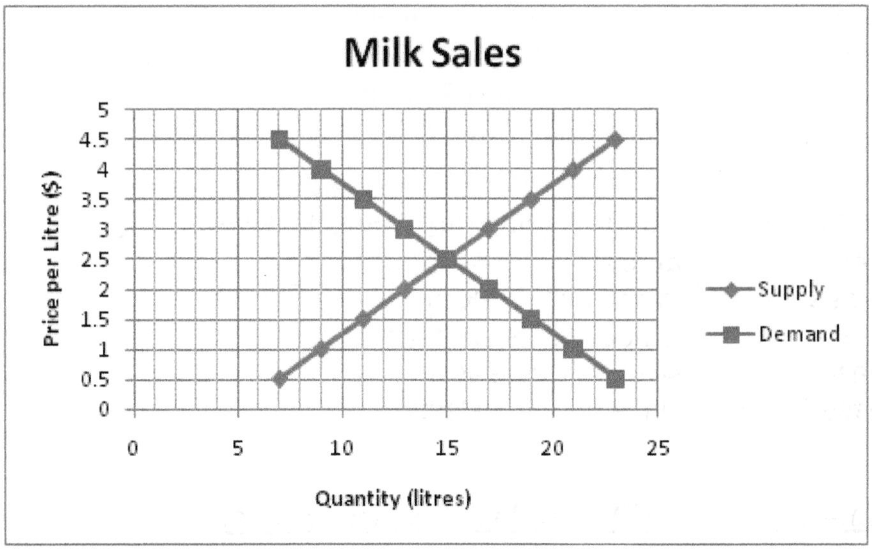


50) Using case 2 data, the equilibrium price is:
   A. $15.00
   B. $2.50
   C. $3.00
   D. $2.00

51) Using case 2 data, the equilibrium quantity is:
   A. 15
   B. 10
   C. 16
   D. 2

52) Using case 2 data, suppose the government fixes the milk price at $1 per litre, this would be:
   A. Price fixing.
   B. Price floor.
   C. Price ceiling.
   D. Government control policy.

53) Using case 2 data, this government-imposed fixed price policy will probably result in a:
   A. Shortage of 12 litres
   B. Surplus of 12 litres.
   C. Shortage of 10 litres.
   D. Surplus of 10 litres.

54) Using case 2 data, this price elasticity of demand in the range from $2.50 to $3.00 would be:

A. -0.0259
B. 0.7857
C. 1
D. 5.50

55) Using case 2 data and based on your elasticity calculation, if the milk retailers wish to increase their total revenue they should:

A. decrease the price since milk is elastic
B. decrease the price since milk is inelastic
C. increase the price since milk is elastic
D. increase the price since milk is inelastic

**Case 3: <u>Change in Supply/Demand for the Beer Market</u>**

Indicate what happens in relation to the beer market for the following events:

56) The price of wine (a substitute for beer) goes down:

A. Demand for beer increases
B. Supply of beer increases.
C. Demand for beer decreases.
D. Supply of beer decreases.

57) The price of pretzels (a complement for beer) goes down:

A. Demand for beer increases
B. Supply of beer increases.
C. Demand for beer decreases.
D. Supply of beer decreases.

58) Consumer incomes decrease (assume beer is an inferior good):

A. Price increases and quantity decreases
B. Price decreases and quantity decreases.
C. Price increases and quantity increases.
D. Price decreases and quantity increases.

59) The government subsidizes beer production:

A. Price increases and quantity decreases
B. Price decreases and quantity decreases.
C. Price increases and quantity increases.
D. Price decreases and quantity increases.

**Case 4: Cost Calculations for a Firm**

The following cost ($) information is for a computer manufacturing company in the short run.

| Q | TFC | TVC | TC | AFC | AVC | ATC | MC |
|---|---|---|---|---|---|---|---|
| **0** | | **0** | **82** | | | | |
| **1** | | **42** | | | | | |
| **2** | | | | | **33.50** | | |
| **3** | | | | | | **61.67** | |
| **4** | | | **231** | **20.50** | | | |
| **5** | | **218** | | | | | |

60) Using case 4, calculate the total fixed costs (TFC):
A. $42
B. $100
C. $0
D. $82

61) Using case 4, average fixed costs (AFC) at quantity 2 are:
A. $42
B. $41
C. $33.50
D. $82

62) Using case 4, total variable costs (TVC) at quantity 3 are:
A. $103
B. $41
C. $33.50
D. $61.67

63) Using case 4, average variable costs (AVC) at quantity 4 are:
A. $20.50
B. $37.25
C. $57.75
D. $82

64) Using case 4, the total costs (TC) at quantity 2 are:

A. $82
B. $67
C. $149
D. $41

65) Using case 4, the marginal cost (MC) at quantity 5 are:

A. $42
B. $46
C. $69
D. $0

**CASE 5: Breakeven Analysis**

You want to sell dog treats at the farmer's market. You research pricing and find that you can charge $5 for a 100 gram bag. Your fixed costs for the season are $4000 and your average variable costs of creating the dog treats are $1.50 per 100 gram bag.

66) Using case 5 data, what is your breakeven quantity?

A. 4,000
B. 1,143
C. 1,100
D. 616

67) Using case 5 data, what is your target profit quantity if you want to make $3000
this season?

A. 4,000
B. 1,143
C. 2,000
D. 1,077

68) Using case 5 data, what is your total revenue at your breakeven quantity?

A. $1,143
B. $2,000
C. $4,001
D. $5,715

**CASE 6: Graphing**

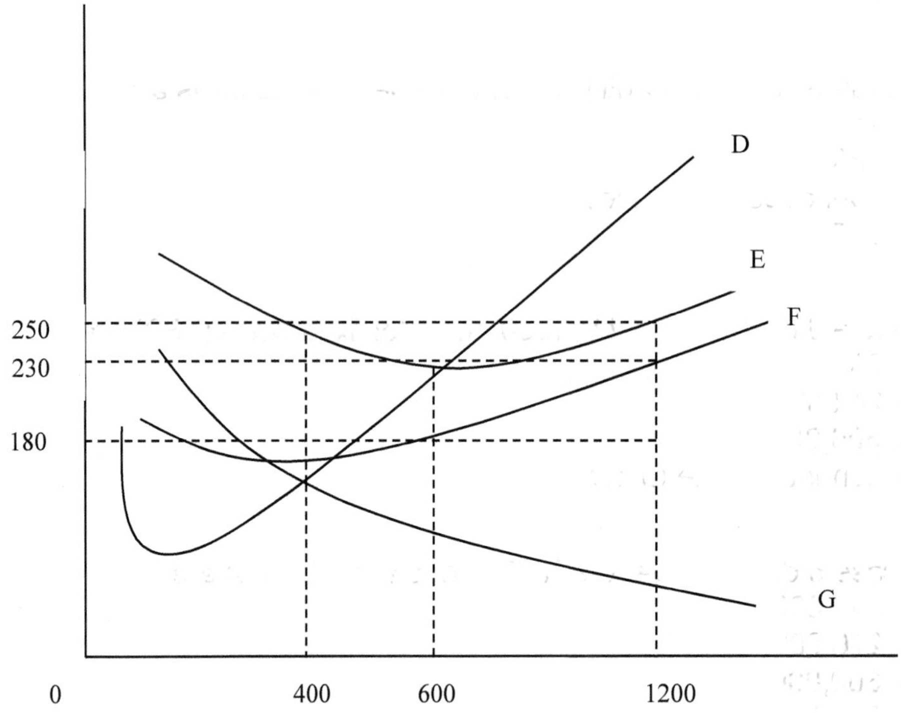


69) Using case 6 data, line D is
   A. marginal cost
   B. average fixed cost
   C. average variable cost
   D. average total cost

70) Using case 6 data, line E is
   A. average variable cost
   B. average total cost
   C. marginal cost
   D. average fixed cost

71) Using case 6 data, line G is
   A. average variable cost
   B. average fixed cost
   C. average total cost
   D. marginal cost

72) Using case 6 data, at quantity 1200, average total costs (ATC) are

A. 250
B. cannot be determined
C. 180
D. 230

73) Using case 6 data, at quantity 1200, average variable costs are

A. 250
B. 180
C. cannot be determined
D. 230

74) Using case 6 data, at quantity 1200, the total fixed costs (TFC) are

A. 20
B. 24,000
C. 300,000
D. cannot be determined

75) Using case 6 data, at quantity 1200, the total costs (TC) are

A. 340,000
B. 276,000
C. 300,000
D. 24,000

## Solutions Midterm Exam

1. B
2. A
3. A
4. B
5. B
6. C
7. C
8. C
9. A
10. D
11. B
12. B
13. D
14. D
15. C
16. B
17. B
18. B
19. B
20. B
21. C
22. C
23. A
24. C
25. C
26. B
27. D
28. B
29. C
30. A
31. A
32. D
33. A
34. D
35. B
36. C
37. A
38. B
39. C
40. B
41. D
42. C
43. C
44. B
45. C
46. C
47. D
48. A
49. B
50. B
51. A
52. C
53. A
54. B
55. D
56. C
57. A
58. C
59. D
60. D
61. B
62. A
63. B
64. C
65. C
66. B
67. C
68. D
69. A
70. B
71. B
72. A
73. D
74. B
75. C

## CHAPTER 9

Key Formulae

$$\text{Total revenue (TR)} = \text{Price (P)} \times \text{Quantity (Q)}$$

$$\text{Total Profit} = [\text{Price (P)} - \text{Average Total Cost (ATC)}] \times \text{Quantity (Q)}$$

$$\text{Marginal revenue (MR)} = \frac{\text{Change in total revenue (TR)}}{\text{Change in output (Q)}}$$

1. Perfect Competition – Finding Important Numbers from a Graph

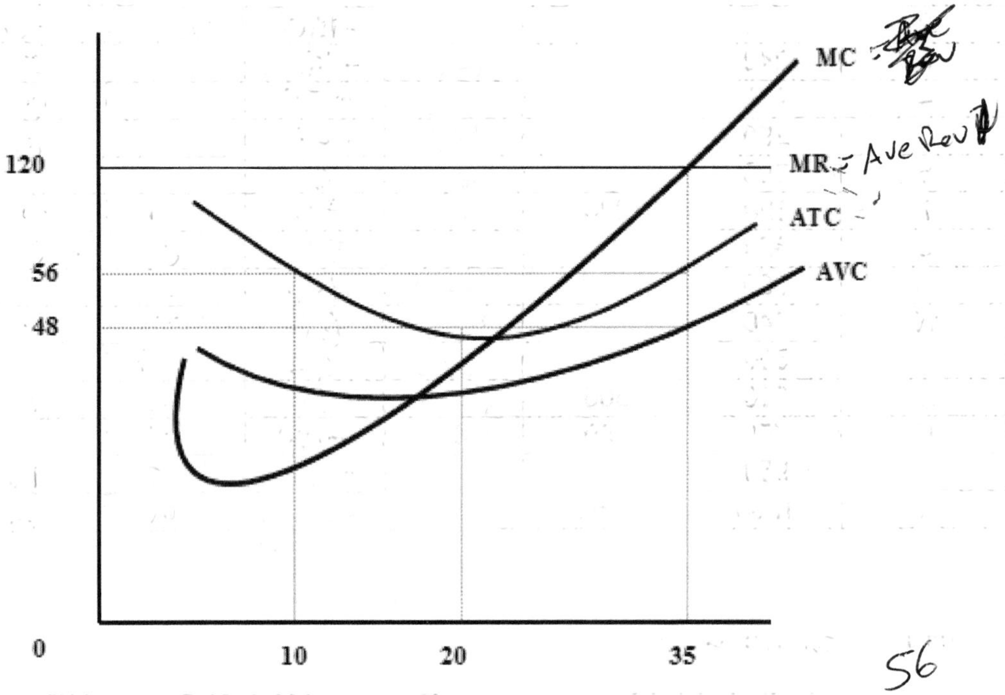


56
-48

a. At what quantity should this firm operate? 35

Using the quantity found in a, find the following:

| | | | |
|---|---|---|---|
| b. Average Variable Cost | = 48 | Total Variable Cost | = 1680 |
| c. Average Fixed Cost | = 8 | Total Fixed Cost | = 280 |
| d. Average Total Cost | = 56 | Total Cost | = 1960 |
| e. Average Revenue | = 120 | Total Revenue | = 4200 |
| f. Average Profit/Loss | = 64 | Total Profit/Loss | = 2240 |

2. The Relationship Between Costs: Total Revenue = Total Cost Approach

a. Fill in the table below.

| Total Fixed Costs = $100 | | | Price = $50 | | Price = $40 | | Price = $20 | |
|---|---|---|---|---|---|---|---|---|
| Unit of Output Q | Total Costs | Total Variable Costs | Total Revenue | Profit (Loss) | Total Revenue | Profit (Loss) | Total Revenue | Profit (Loss) |
| 0 | $100 | 0 | 0 | -100 | 0 | -100 | 0 | -100 |
| 1 | 150 | 50 | 50 | -100 | 40 | -110 | 20 | -130 |
| 2 | 200 | 100 | 100 | -100 | 80 | -120 | 40 | -160 |
| 3 | 240 | 140 | 150 | -90 | 120 | -120 | 60 | -180 |
| 4 | 270 | 170 | 200 | -70 | 160 | -110 | 80 | -190 |
| 5 | 290 | 190 | 250 | -40 | 200 | -90 | 100 | -190 |
| 6 | 300 | 200 | 300 | 0 | 240 | -60 | 120 | -180 |
| 7 | 320 | 220 | 350 | 30 | 280 | -40 | 140 | -180 |
| 8 | 350 | 250 | 400 | 50 | 320 | -30 | 160 | -190 |
| 9 | 390 | 290 | 450 | 60 | 360 | -30 | 180 | -210 |
| 10 | 440 | 340 | 500 | 60 | 400 | -40 | 200 | -240 |
| 11 | 500 | 400 | 550 | 50 | 440 | -60 | 220 | -280 |
| 12 | 600 | 500 | 600 | 0 | 480 | -120 | 240 | -360 |
| 13 | 750 | 650 | 650 | -100 | 520 | -230 | 260 | -490 |
| 14 | 950 | 850 | 700 | -250 | 560 | -390 | 280 | -670 |
| 15 | 1250 | 1150 | 750 | -500 | 600 | -650 | 300 | -950 |

b. Fill in the Table Below

| | Price | | |
|---|---|---|---|
| | $50 | $40 | $20 |
| 1. Produce? | Yes | Yes | NO |
| 2. How much? | 10 | 9 | 0 |
| 3. Profit (Loss)? | 60 | -30 | -100 |

Shut down Price P= min AVC

Q8 here

3. The Relationship Between Costs – Marginal Revenue: Marginal Cost Approach

a. Use the information below to fill in the table. TFC = 100
Note: Profit = (Price – ATC) * Q

| AFC | Unit Q | AVC | ATC | TC | MC | Price=$50 Profit | Price=$40 Profit | Price=$20 Profit |
|---|---|---|---|---|---|---|---|---|
| — | 0 | — | — | 100 | — | -100 | -100 | -100 |
| 100 | 1 | 50 | 150 | 150 | 50 | -100 | -110 | -130 |
| 50 | 2 | 50 | 100 | 200 | 50 | -100 | -120 | -160 |
| 33.3 | 3 | 46.67 | 80 | 240 | 40 | -90 | -120 | -180 |
| 25 | 4 | 42.5 | 67.5 | 270 | 30 | -70 | -110 | -190 |
| 20 | 5 | 38 | 58 | 290 | 20 | -40 | -90 | -190 |
| 16.67 | 6 | 33.33 | 50 | 300 | 10 | 0 | -60 | -180 |
| 14.29 | 7 | 31.43 | 45.71 | 320 | 20 | 30.03 | -39.97 | -179.97 |
| 12.5 | 8 | 31.25 | 43.75 | 350 | 30 | 50 | -30 | -190 |
| 11.11 | 9 | 32.22 | 43.33 | 390 | 40 | 60.03 | -29.97 | -209.97 |
| 10 | 10 | 34 | 44 | 440 | 50 | 60 | -40 | -240 |
| 9.09 | 11 | 36.36 | 45.45 | 500 | 60 | 50.05 | -59.95 | -279.95 |
| 8.33 | 12 | 41.67 | 50 | 600 | 100 | 0 | -120 | -360 |
| 7.69 | 13 | 50 | 57.69 | 750 | 150 | -99.97 | -229.97 | -489.97 |
| 7.14 | 14 | 60.71 | 67.86 | 950 | 206 | -250.04 | -390.04 | -670.04 |
| 6.67 | 15 | 76.67 | 83.33 | 1250 | 300 | -499.95 | -649.95 | -949.95 |

b. Fill in the table below

| | Price | | |
|---|---|---|---|
| | $50 | $40 | $20 |
| 1. Produce? | Yes | Yes | NO |
| 2. How much? | 9 | 9 | 0 |
| 3. Profit (Loss)? | 60.03 | -29.97 | -100 |

4. Hotel Hydeaway

The following graph relates to a perfectly competitive hotel firm with a total fixed cost of $10,800 per day. The quantity is the # of rooms rented per day.

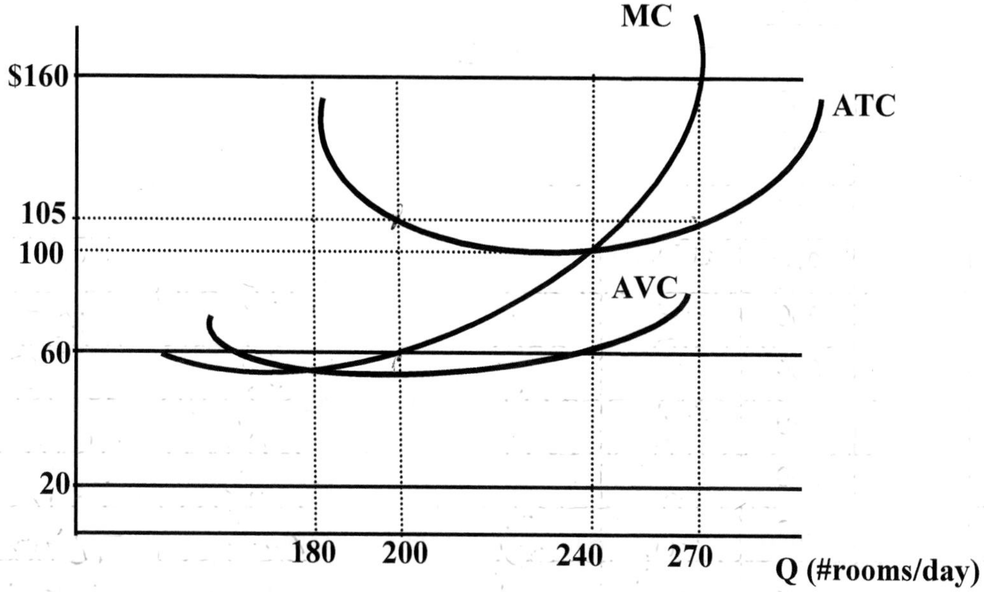


160 − 105
× 270

a. If the price in December is $160 per room:

I. The best quantity to rent out is 270.

II. The total $ profit is 14850.

(P − ATC) × Q

b. If the price in March drops to $60 per room:

I. The best quantity to rent out is 200.

II. The total $ profit would be Loss 9000.

60 − 105 × 200

c. If the price in May drops to $20 per room:

I. The best quantity to rent out would be 0.

II. The total $ profit would be Loss 10800 − the fixed costs.

20 −
20 − 80 VC

d. In the long run predict the long run Q = 240, long run P = 100,

long run profit = 0.

**Solutions**

1. Perfect Competition: Finding Important Numbers from a Graph

a. 35
b. 48, 1680
c. 8, 280
d. 56, 1960
e. 120, 4200
f. 64, 2240

2. The Relationship Between Costs: Total Revenue = Total Cost Approach

a.

| Total Fixed Costs = $100 | | | Price = $50 | | Price = $40 | | Price = $20 | |
|---|---|---|---|---|---|---|---|---|
| Unit of Output Q | Total Costs | Total Variable Costs | Total Revenue | Profit (Loss) | Total Revenue | Profit (Loss) | Total Revenue | Profit (Loss) |
| 0 | $100 | 0 | 0 | -100 | 0 | -100 | 0 | -100 |
| 1 | 150 | 50 | 50 | -100 | 40 | -110 | 20 | -130 |
| 2 | 200 | 100 | 100 | -100 | 80 | -120 | 40 | -160 |
| 3 | 240 | 140 | 150 | -90 | 120 | -120 | 60 | -180 |
| 4 | 270 | 170 | 200 | -70 | 160 | -110 | 80 | -190 |
| 5 | 290 | 190 | 250 | -40 | 200 | -90 | 100 | -190 |
| 6 | 300 | 200 | 300 | 0 | 240 | -60 | 120 | -180 |
| 7 | 320 | 220 | 350 | 30 | 280 | -40 | 140 | -180 |
| 8 | 350 | 250 | 400 | 50 | 320 | -30 | 160 | -190 |
| 9 | 390 | 290 | 450 | 60 | 360 | -30 | 180 | -210 |
| 10 | 440 | 340 | 500 | 60 | 400 | -40 | 200 | -240 |
| 11 | 500 | 400 | 550 | 50 | 440 | -60 | 220 | -280 |
| 12 | 600 | 500 | 600 | 0 | 480 | -120 | 240 | -360 |
| 13 | 750 | 650 | 650 | -100 | 520 | -230 | 260 | -490 |
| 14 | 950 | 850 | 700 | -250 | 560 | -390 | 280 | -670 |
| 15 | 1250 | 1150 | 750 | -500 | 600 | -650 | 300 | -950 |

b.

| | Price | | |
|---|---|---|---|
| | $50 | $40 | $20 |
| 1. Produce? | Yes | Yes | No |
| 2. How much? | 10 | 9 | 0 |
| 3. Profit (Loss)? | 60 | -30 | -100 |

3. The Relationship Between Costs: Marginal Revenue: Marginal Cost Approach

a.

| Unit Q | AVC | ATC | TC | MC | Price=$50 | Price=$40 | Price=$20 |
|---|---|---|---|---|---|---|---|
| | | | | | Profit | Profit | Profit |
| 0 | --- | --- | 100 | | -100 | -100 | -100 |
| 1 | 50 | 150 | 150 | 50 | -100 | -110 | -130 |
| 2 | 50 | 100 | 200 | 50 | -100 | -120 | -160 |
| 3 | 46.67 | 80 | 240 | 40 | -90 | -120 | -180 |
| 4 | 42.5 | 67.5 | 270 | 30 | -70 | -110 | -190 |
| 5 | 38 | 58 | 290 | 20 | -40 | -90 | -190 |
| 6 | 33.33 | 50 | 300 | 10 | 0 | -60 | -180 |
| 7 | 31.43 | 45.71 | 320 | 20 | 30.03 | -39.97 | -179.97 |
| 8 | 31.25 | 43.75 | 350 | 30 | 50 | -30 | -190 |
| 9 | 32.22 | 43.33 | 390 | 40 | 60.03 | -29.97 | -209.97 |
| 10 | 34 | 44 | 440 | 50 | 60 | -40 | -240 |
| 11 | 36.36 | 45.45 | 500 | 60 | 50.05 | -59.95 | -279.95 |
| 12 | 41.67 | 50 | 600 | 100 | 0 | -120 | -350 |
| 13 | 50 | 57.69 | 750 | 150 | -99.97 | -229.97 | -489.97 |
| 14 | 60.71 | 67.86 | 950 | 200 | -250.04 | -390.04 | -670.04 |
| 15 | 76.67 | 83.33 | 1250 | 300 | -499.95 | -649.95 | -949.95 |

b.

| | Price | | |
|---|---|---|---|
| | $50 | $40 | $20 |
| 1. Produce? | Yes | Yes | No |
| 2. How much? | 9 | 9 | 0 |
| 3. Profit (Loss)? | 60.03 | -29.97 | -100 |

4. Hotel Hydeaway

a. i. 270
   ii. (160-105) x 270 = 14,850
b. i. 200
   ii. (60 – 105) x 200 = -9,000
c. i. 0
   ii. –10,800
d. 240, 100, 0

## CHAPTER 10

### Problems

1. APEX Power and Light Company

As President and CEO of APEX Power and Light you are planning price strategy for next year. Your operations department has provided you with the following information.

| P (per million Kilowatts) | Q (millions of kilowatts) | TR | MR | TC | MC | ATC |
|---|---|---|---|---|---|---|
| 120,000 | 1 | 120,000 | -------- | 180,000 | -------- | 180,000 |
| 108,750 | 2 | 217,500 | 97,500 | 225,000 | 45,000 | 112,500 |
| 97,500 | 3 | 292,500 | 75,000 | 262,500 | 37,500 | 87500 |
| 86,250 | 4 | 345,000 | 52,500 | 315,000 | 52,500 | 78 750 |
| 75,000 | 5 | 375,000 | 30,000 | 375,000 | 60,000 | 75,000 |
| 63,750 | 6 | 382,500 | 7,500 | 438,750 | 63,750 | 73 125 |
| 52,500 | 7 | 367500 | (-15,000) | 504,000 | 65,250 | 72 000 |
| 41,250 | 8 | 330,000 | (-37,500) | 575,640 | 71,640 | 71 955 |
| 30,000 | 9 | 270,000 | (-60000) | 750,000 | 174 360 | 83,333.33 |

a. Complete the table above.

b. Using the table above, determine the profit maximizing P, Qs and profit given.

i. a non-discriminating profit maximizing monopoly:

Rule MR = MC P 86,250 Qs 4 Profit 30,000

ii. a perfect price discriminating monopoly: (one unit purchased at each price)

Rule P = MC P 63 750 Qs 6 Profit 112,500

iii. a marginal cost pricing policy: various

Rule P = MC P 63 750 Qs 6 Profit (-56,250)

iv. an average cost pricing policy:

Rule P = ATC P 75,000 Qs 5 Profit 0, Break even

2. Monopoly Phone Company

| Quantity: # Phones | Price per Phone | Total Revenue | Marginal Revenue | Average Total Cost | Marginal Cost |
|---|---|---|---|---|---|
| 1 | $240 | 240 | ---------- | $215 | ---------- |
| 2 | 220 | 440 | 200 | 137.5 | $60 |
| 3 | 200 | 600 | 160 | 118.33 | 80 |
| 4 | 180 | 720 | 120 | 117.75 | 116 |
| 5 | 160 | 800 | 80 | 126 | 160 |
| 6 | 140 | 840 | 40 | 140 | 210 |
| 7 | 120 | 840 | 0 | 158.57 | 270 |

a. If the firm in the table above is unregulated and does not discriminate: MC=MR

i. Find the profit maximizing quantity level 4?

ii. Find the profit maximizing price 180? 471

iii. Find the total dollar profit 249?

b. If the firm above faces average cost pricing regulation: P=ATC

i. Find the average cost quantity 6?

ii. Find the average cost price 140?

c. If the firm above faces marginal cost pricing regulation: P=MC

i. Find the marginal cost quantity 5?

ii. Find the marginal cost price 160?

d. If the firm above perfectly price discriminates: TR=

i. Find the total revenue at Q = 5 phones 1000?

ii. Find the total profit 370?

630

3. Monopoly: Graphic Example

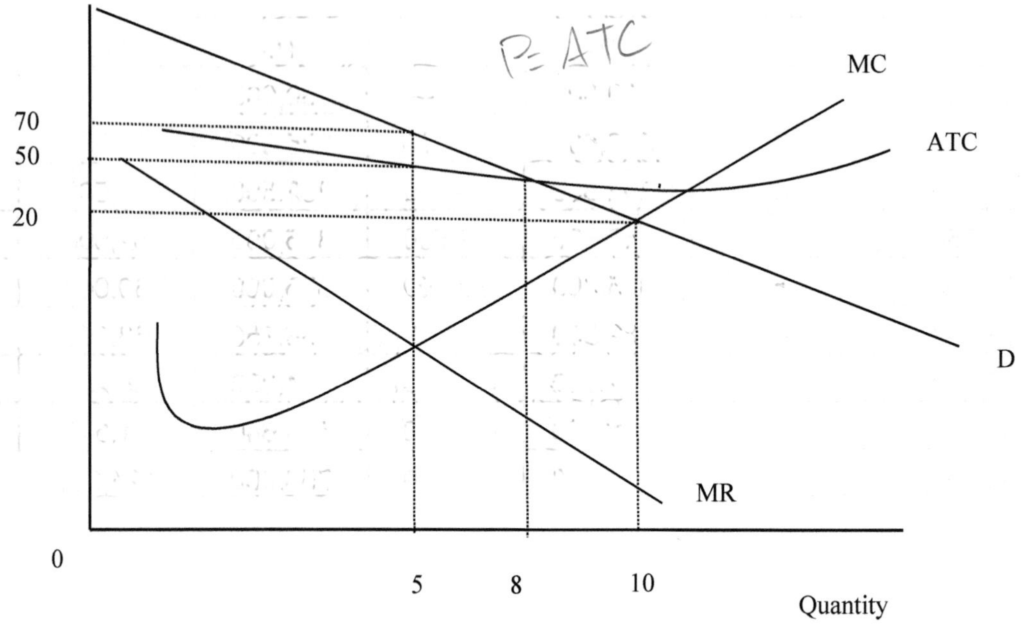


350
-250

a. If the firm above is unregulated and doesn't discriminate, find:

   i. Profit maximizing quantity ___5___?

   ii. Profit maximizing price ___70___?

   iii. Total profit ___100___?

b. If the firm above is subject to average cost pricing, find:

   i. Average cost quantity ___8___?

   ii. Average cost price ___/50___?

**Solutions**

1. APEX Power and Light Company

a.

| P | Q | TR | MR | TC | MC | ATC |
|---|---|---|---|---|---|---|
| 120,000 | 1 | 120,000 | -------- | 180,000 | -------- | 180,000 |
| 108,750 | 2 | 217,500 | 97,500 | 225,000 | 45,000 | 112,500 |
| 97,500 | 3 | 292,500 | 75,000 | 262,500 | 37,500 | 87,500 |
| 86,250 | 4 | 345,000 | 52,500 | 315,000 | 52,500 | 78,750 |
| 75,000 | 5 | 375,000 | 30,000 | 375,000 | 60,000 | 75,000 |
| 63,750 | 6 | 382,500 | 7,500 | 438,750 | 63,750 | 73,125 |
| 52,500 | 7 | 367,500 | (15,000) | 504,000 | 65,250 | 72,000 |
| 41,250 | 8 | 330,000 | (37,500) | 575,640 | 71,640 | 71,955 |
| 30,000 | 9 | 270,000 | (60,000) | 750,000 | 174,360 | 83,333 |

b.

| | Rule | P | Qs | Profit |
|---|---|---|---|---|
| i. | MR = MC | 86,250 | 4 | 345,000 – 315,000 = 30,000 |
| ii. | P = MC | Various | 6 | (120,000 + 108,750 + 97,500 + 86,250 + 75,000 + 63,750) – 438,750 = 112,500 |
| iii. | P = MC | 63,750 | 6 | 382,500 – 438,750 = (56,250) |
| iv. | P = ATC | 75,000 | 5 | 375,000 - 375,000 = 0 |

2. Monopoly Phone Company

| Quantity: # Phones | Price per Phone | Total Revenue | Marginal Revenue | Average Total Cost | Marginal Cost |
|---|---|---|---|---|---|
| 1 | $240 | 240 | ---------- | $215 | ---------- |
| 2 | 220 | 440 | 200 | 137.5 | $60 |
| 3 | 200 | 600 | 160 | 118.33 | 80 |
| 4 | 180 | 720 | 120 | 117.75 | 116 |
| 5 | 160 | 800 | 80 | 126 | 160 |
| 6 | 140 | 840 | 40 | 140 | 210 |
| 7 | 120 | 840 | 0 | 158.57 | 270 |

a. i. 4
   ii. 180
   iii. 249
b. i. 6
   ii. 140
c. i. 5
   ii. 160
d. i. 1000
   ii. 370

3. Monopoly: Graphic Example

a. i. 5
   ii. 70
   iii. 100
b. i. 8
   ii. 50

## CHAPTER 11

### Problems

1. Sid's Cycles Ltd.

You are the owner of Sid's Cycles Ltd., one of the several cycle shops selling a line of high quality Italian racing bicycles. Your costs are as follows:

| | |
|---|---|
| Advertising | $4,000 per year |
| Rent | 2,000 per month |
| Other Fixed Costs | 2,000 per year |

= 24,000/year

=30,000 fixed

Each bicycle you purchase from the supplier costs $200, and your salesperson works on a commission of $25 per bicycle sold.

225/unit

You have been selling these bicycles for $500 each and are planning to place next year's order soon. However, you are not satisfied with your profits, and are considering changing your prices for next year. After some checking, you estimate the volume of bikes sold next year as follows.

| Price per Bike | # Bikes Sold (Q) | TR | MR | TC | MC |
|---|---|---|---|---|---|
| 550 | 100 | 55,000 | – | 52,500 | — |
| 500 | 130 | 65,000 | 333.33 | 59,250 | 225 |
| 450 | 160 | 72,000 | 233.33 | 66,000 | 225 |
| 400 | 200 | 80,000 | 200 | 75,000 | 225 |

a. Complete the above table.

b. Find the profit-maximising P, Q, and profit

P=450 Q=160 Profit = 6,000

c. What type of industry is represented by Sid's Cycles? Explain.

monopolistic cometition

d. Identify two socio-economic benefits related to competition, in the long run.

Product differentiation and innovation

e. Identify two potential socio-economic costs related to monopolistic competition, in the long run.

no production efficiency
allocative
efficency

2. Monopolistic Competition

| Price | Output (Demand) | Total Revenue | Total Cost | Marginal Revenue | Marginal Cost | Profit (Loss) |
|---|---|---|---|---|---|---|
| $210 | 0 | 0 | 100 | | | |
| 200 | 1 | 200 | 150 | | | |
| 190 | 2 | 380 | 200 | | | |
| 180 | 3 | 540 | 240 | | | |
| 170 | 4 | 680 | 270 | | | |
| 160 | 5 | 800 | 290 | | | |
| 150 | 6 | 900 | 300 | | | |
| 140 | 7 | 980 | 320 | | | |
| 130 | 8 | 1040 | 350 | | | |
| 120 | 9 | 1080 | 390 | | | |
| 110 | 10 | 1100 | 440 | | | |
| 100 | 11 | 1100 | 500 | | | |
| 90 | 12 | 1080 | 600 | | | |
| 80 | 13 | 1040 | 750 | | | |
| 70 | 14 | 980 | 950 | | | |
| 60 | 15 | 900 | 1250 | | | |

a. Fill in the above table.

b. At what output level would the monopolistic competitor operate ________________?

c. At what price level ____________________?

d. What would be the profit/loss at this level ______________?

3. Oligopoly

Suppose there are three equal-sized firms—Microsoft (Xbox 360), Nintendo (Wii), Sony (playstation3) —competing in the video game consoles industry. Assuming there is no collusion, answer the following questions:

a. If Nintendo decides to raise their price, what will Microsoft and Sony do? What will happen to Nintendo's revenue?

If Nintendo does raise their price Microsoft and sony would not raise their price therefore revenue will go down.

b. If Nintendo decides to decrease their price, what will Microsoft and Sony do? Who benefits?

If Nintendo decreases there price Sony and microsoft will also lower there price and this benifits the consumer

c. How can Nintendo increase revenue?

Try to use non price options to promote company or collude

**Solutions**

1. Sid's Cycles Ltd.

a.

| P | Q | TR | MR | TC | MC |
|---|---|---|---|---|---|
| 550 | 100 | 55,000 | -------- | 52,500 | -------- |
| 500 | 130 | 65,000 | 333.33 | 59,250 | 225 |
| 450 | 160 | 72,000 | 233.33 | 66,000 | 225 |
| 400 | 200 | 80,000 | 200 | 75,000 | 225 |

b. Q = 160, P = \$450; thus TR = \$72,000; TC = \$30,000+(160)(\$225) = \$66,000; profit = \$6000

c. Monopolistic competition

d. More choice, more innovation

e. Less customer loyalty, less service

2. Monopolistic Competition

a.

| Price | Output (Demand) | Total Revenue | Total Cost | Marginal Revenue | Marginal Cost | Profit (Loss) |
|---|---|---|---|---|---|---|
| $210 | 0 | 0 | 100 | ------ | ------ | -100 |
| 200 | 1 | 200 | 150 | 200 | 50 | 50 |
| 190 | 2 | 380 | 200 | 180 | 50 | 180 |
| 180 | 3 | 540 | 240 | 160 | 40 | 300 |
| 170 | 4 | 680 | 270 | 140 | 30 | 410 |
| 160 | 5 | 800 | 290 | 120 | 20 | 510 |
| 150 | 6 | 900 | 300 | 100 | 10 | 600 |
| 140 | 7 | 980 | 320 | 80 | 20 | 660 |
| 130 | 8 | 1040 | 350 | 60 | 30 | 690 |
| 120 | 9 | 1080 | 390 | 40 | 40 | 690 |
| 110 | 10 | 1100 | 440 | 20 | 50 | 660 |
| 100 | 11 | 1100 | 500 | 0 | 60 | 600 |
| 90 | 12 | 1080 | 600 | -20 | 100 | 480 |
| 80 | 13 | 1040 | 750 | -40 | 150 | 290 |
| 70 | 14 | 980 | 950 | -60 | 200 | 30 |
| 60 | 15 | 900 | 1250 | -80 | 300 | -350 |

b. 8 or 9
c. 130 or 120
d. 690

3. Oligopoly

a. Microsoft and Sony will not raise their prices, so Nintendo's revenues will decrease.

b. Microsoft and Sony will lower their prices, and a price war could ensue. The consumer benefits from lower prices.

c. They can compete using advertising, modifications to the systems, or they could get together with the others and collude to raise prices.

CHAPTER 13

Problems

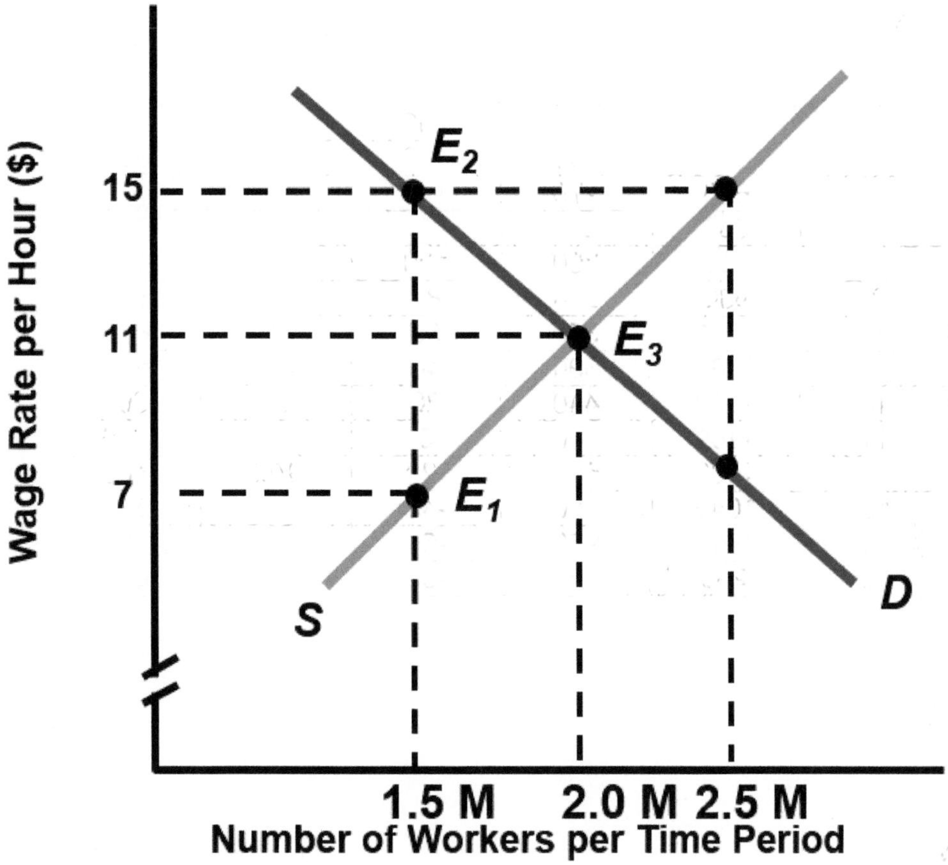


Assume that the minimum wage rate is $15.00 per hour.

a. What is the equilibrium wage rate in this market?

b. What is the quantity supplied of labour at the minimum wage rate?

c. What is the quantity demanded for labour at the minimum wage rate?

d. What market situation exists at the minimum wage rate?

e. How many workers were laid-off, due to the minimum wage rate?

f. How many workers entered the labour force, seeking a job, due to the minimum wage rate?

g. Are workers in this industry better off or worse off as a result of this minimum wage?

h. Which workers are more likely to be laid off?

**Solutions**

a. $11
b. 2.5 M
c. 1.5 M
d. Surplus, or excess quantity supplied of labour
e. 0.5 M
f. 0.5 M
g. Those who kept their jobs are better off; those who became unemployed are worse off.
h. Younger, lower income – lower productivity workers.

## CHAPTER 14

### Problems

The paper, by Brian Murphy, Xuelin Zhang and Claude Dionne of Statistics Canada's income statistics division, examines 34 years of low-income levels in Canada. It looks at what different measures of poverty show, and how trends changed between 1976 and 2009.

It comes as public debate over income inequality is heating up, in Canada and around the world, as evidence points to a growing polarization between the rich and the poor.

Here are some of the Statscan paper's findings:

- Low-income people have accounted for as much as 16 per cent of the population and as little as 9 per cent over the past 34 years, depending on the time period and low-income line used.
- Between 2000 and 2007, the low-income population in Canada fell by more than half a million people, using two measures: the low income cut-offs (or LICO) and the market basket measure (MBM). Under the low-income measure (LIM), it rose by half a million (the paper explains the reasons for the difference).
- Between 2007 and 2009, though, the downward trend in low income rates under the LICO and MBM began to reverse itself. Levels in 2008 and 2009 under those two measures are higher than in 2007, though they still represent the second-lowest annual rates of the past 34 years. The LICO, too, shows a slight upward trend in low-income in that time......

***Source:*** The changing face of poverty in Canada, Globe and Mail March 21, 2012

a. What are two of the determinants of why there is income inequality?
b. As the article states, the low income population in Canada has been falling. What income support programs does Canada have in place to help low income families?
c. Will poverty ever be zero? Why or why not?

### Solution

a. Age, marginal productivity, inheritance, discrimination.
b. Old age security, Canada pension plan, employment insurance, Canada child benefit
c. Poverty can be reduced as has been the case, but it can never be zero.

## CHAPTER 15

## Problems

1. Carbon Tax

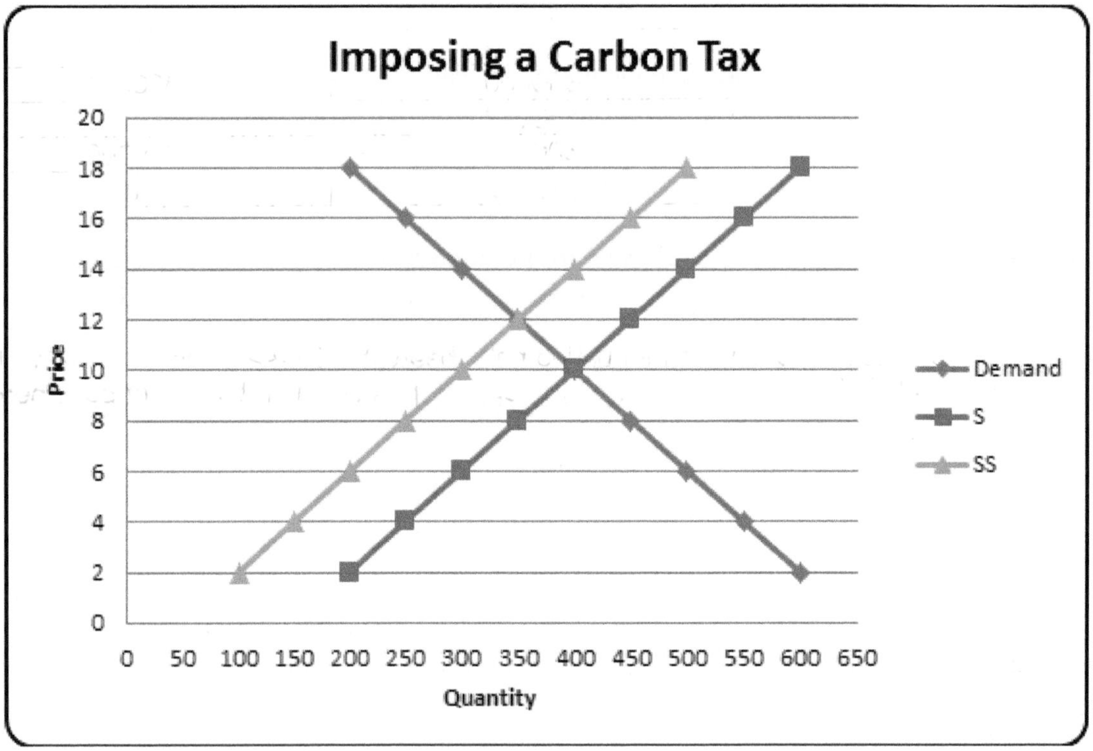


Use the graph to answer the following questions.

a. Which curve represents the marginal private costs of producing the good in question?

b. Which curve reflects the marginal social costs of producing this good?

c. Which curve represents both the marginal private benefits and the marginal social benefits of this good?

d. How many units of this good will be produced by the private sector?

e. An agency has determined that if production is limited to 350 tonnes per day, the impact on the environment will be minimal. The agency wants to impose a tax on the sector. What tax per unit of output is necessary to achieve the agency's goals?

f. Can we conclude that if the agency charges this tax, society is better off? Why or why not?

2. Marginal Benefits and Marginal Costs of Protecting Polar Bears

Polar bears are considered protected by the US Wildlife service. Look at the following marginal benefits and marginal costs associated with protecting them.

| Quantity of Polar Bears % | Marginal Costs | Marginal Benefits |
|---|---|---|
| 0 | 150000 | 700000 |
| 20 | 250000 | 450000 |
| 40 | 300000 | 300000 |
| 60 | 400000 | 250000 |
| 80 | 500000 | 220000 |
| 100 | infinite | 0 |

a. What is the optimal percent of protection for polar bears?

b. Suppose the state imposed fines for hunting polar bears that increase the marginal costs at all levels by 200,000, now what would be the optimal percent of protection for polar bears?

**Solutions**

1. Carbon Tax

a. S
b. SS
c. D
d. 400
e. $4
f. No, we have no information on how much society values less pollution, and we have no guarantee that pollution will be reduced by imposing a carbon tax.

2. Marginal Benefits and Marginal Costs of Protecting Polar Bears

a. 40
b. 20

| Quantity of Polar Bears % | Marginal Costs | Marginal Benefits |
|---|---|---|
| 0 | 350000 | 700000 |
| 20 | 450000 | 450000 |
| 40 | 500000 | 300000 |
| 60 | 600000 | 250000 |
| 80 | 700000 | 220000 |
| 100 | infinite | 0 |

## CHAPTER 16

Key Formulae

$$\text{Marginal Tax Rate} = \frac{\text{Change in taxes due}}{\text{Change in taxable income}}$$

$$\text{Average Tax Rate} = \frac{\text{Total taxes due}}{\text{Total taxable income}}$$

## Problems

> B.C. will drop the HST and return to an "improved" PST next year with all previous exemptions, Finance Minister Kevin Falcon announced on Monday in Victoria.
>
> "We've got a much improved PST. It's not like the old piece of whatever you want to call it which was in place before, which was enormously frustrating for a lot of our small business community in particular," Falcon said.
>
> "It is dramatically improved, simplified, administratively more clear."
>
> The legislation introduced Monday includes some significant changes to the old tax, but only a few basic exemptions — such as those food and fuel — were contained in the bill.
>
> Falcon promised those would be included in regulations to be introduced in the fall.
>
> "As promised, on April 1, 2013 consumers will only pay PST on those goods and services that were subject to PST before the implementation of the HST. All permanent PST exemptions will be re-implemented," said Falcon.
>
> "There will be no PST on purchases like food, restaurant meals, bicycles, gym memberships, movie tickets or for personal services like haircuts, just as it was previously."
>
> Source: B.C. to drop HST for 'improved' PST, CBC, May 14, 2012

a. What type of tax does the HST represent?
b. Why did BC residents want to go back to a provincial sales tax and the GST instead of the harmonized sales tax?
c. What is the reason for government taxation? What are governments roles in society?

## Solution

a. The HST is a harmonized sales tax that is an example of regressive taxation.
b. The harmonized sales tax impacted items that previously did not have a sales tax.
c. Providing a legal system, promoting competition, providing public goods, ensuring economy wide stability.

JR SHAW
SCHOOL OF BUSINESS

Last Name:________________________

First Name:________________________

# ECON1110 Microeconomics – Version A

Final Examination
Time 2 hours
Value 40%

INSTRUCTIONS

- Please print your first and last name on this title page.
- Your Scantron must have the following information:
    - Name as it appears on your NAIT ID
    - TEST NO: fill in A, B, C or D depending on your version identified on this page
    - Write your Student ID number then fill in the corresponding circles
    - Fill in the VER above the Student ID depending on your version
    - Make sure the TEST NO and VER are the same

| | |
|---|---|
| Total Marks | / 82 |

## Micro Formulas

$$Ep=\frac{\text{change in Q}}{\text{sum of quantities/ 2}} \div \frac{\text{change in P}}{\text{Sum of prices /2}}$$

$$\text{Accounting profit} = \text{Total revenue} - \text{Explicit costs}$$

$$\text{Economic profit} = \text{Total revenues} - (\text{Explicit} + \text{Implicit costs})$$

$$\text{Total costs (TC)} = \text{Total fixed costs (TFC)} + \text{Total variable cost (TVC)}$$

$$\text{Average total costs (ATC)} = \frac{\text{Total costs (TC)}}{\text{Output (Q)}}$$

$$\text{Average total costs (ATC)} = \text{Average fixed costs (AFC)} + \text{Average variable costs(AVC)}$$

$$\text{Average variable costs (AVC)} = \frac{\text{Total variable costs (TVC)}}{\text{Output (Q)}}$$

$$\text{Average fixed costs (AFC)} = \frac{\text{Total fixed costs (TFC)}}{\text{Output (Q)}}$$

$$\text{Marginal costs (MC)} = \frac{\text{Change in total cost (TC)}}{\text{Change in output (Q)}}$$

$$\text{Breakeven quantity (BQ)} = \frac{\text{Total fixed cost (TFC)}}{\text{Selling price} - \text{Average variable costs (AVC)}}$$

$$\text{Target profit quantity} = \frac{\text{Total fixed cost (TFC)} + \text{Profit}}{\text{Selling price} - \text{Average variable costs (AVC)}}$$

$$\text{Total revenue (TR)} = \text{Price (P)} \times \text{Quantity (Q)}$$

$$\text{Total Profit} = [\text{Price (P)} - \text{Average Total Cost (ATC)}] \text{ x } \text{Quantity (Q)}$$

$$\text{Marginal revenue (MR)} = \frac{\text{Change in total revenue (TR)}}{\text{Change in output (Q)}}$$

$$\text{Marginal Tax Rate} = \frac{\text{Change in taxes due}}{\text{Change in taxable income}}$$

$$\text{Average Tax Rate} = \frac{\text{Total taxes due}}{\text{Total taxable income}}$$

Use your SCANTRON and choose the one alternative that best completes the statement or answers the question. Use a pencil to shade in your answer. [1 mark each]

1) Which of the following is a characteristic of a perfectly competitive market?
   A) It is easy for a firm to enter or leave the market.
   B) Each firm is a price searcher.
   C) There are few buyers and sellers in the market.
   D) The products sold by the firms in the market are heterogeneous.

2) In a perfectly competitive industry, each firm's demand curve is
   A) always above the marginal revenue curve.
   B) vertical.
   C) downward sloping.
   D) the same as the marginal revenue curve.

3) Firms in a perfectly competitive industry all are
   A) price takers.
   B) price competitors.
   C) price makers.
   D) price searchers.

4) A perfectly competitive firm will maximize profits when
   A) marginal cost is greater than marginal revenue.
   B) marginal cost is equal to marginal revenue.
   C) average cost is equal to average revenue.
   D) average cost is greater than marginal revenue.

5) For a firm in perfect competition
   A) more output can be sold only if the firm lowers its selling price.
   B) marginal revenue and product price are equal at every level of output.
   C) the demand curve is unitary elastic throughout.
   D) the elasticity of demand is zero.

6) The short-run shut down price for the firm in perfect competition is where price equals
   A) MR    B) minimum AVC    C) minimum ATC    D) AR

7) For any firm, whether a price taker or a price setter, profit maximization occurs at the rate of output for which
   A) marginal revenue equals marginal cost.
   B) marginal revenue equals average total cost.
   C) marginal cost is equal to average total cost.
   D) average total cost is minimized.

8) For a perfect competitor, if price is $5, marginal cost is $5, average total cost is $3, and the quantity produced is 150 units, then
   A) the firm is not maximizing profit.
   B) the firm is earning $150 and not maximizing profit.
   C) the firm is earning $300 and maximizing profit.
   D) the firm is earning $2 and maximizing profit.

2

9) At the short-run break-even point, the competitive firm is
A) making zero economic profits.
B) making negative economic profits.
C) just covering its total variable costs.
D) making positive economic profits.

**Figure 9-2**

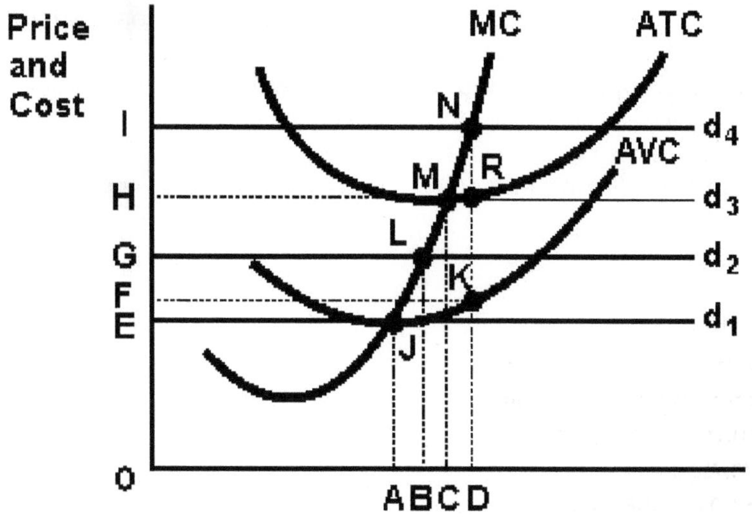


10) In Figure 9-2, the firm will shut down if price falls below
A) H. B) E. C) I. D) F.

11) The firm in Figure 9-2 breaks even when market price is
A) H. B) G. C) E. D) I.

12) The firm in Figure 9-2 will make positive economic profits when market price is
A) E.
B) G.
C) H.
D) I.

13) Which of the following is correct concerning perfectly competitive firms in the long run?
A) The opportunity cost of capital is zero.
B) Price equals minimum long-run average cost.
C) Economic profits are greater than zero.
D) Entrepreneurs earn more than the opportunity cost of their investment.

14) A monopolist is correctly defined as
A) a single supplier of a good or service for which there are no close substitutes.
B) a large firm, making substantial profits, that is able to make other firms do what it wants.
C) a firm with annual sales over $10 million.
D) a producer of a good or service that is expensive to produce, requiring large amounts of capital equipment.

15) The most significant difference between perfect competition and monopoly is
A) the monopoly always faces an inelastic demand curve and the perfect competitor always faces an elastic demand curve.
B) a monopoly does not respond to the market, while a perfect competitor does respond.
C) a monopoly is profitable in the short run and a perfect competitor is not.
D) the monopoly faces a downward sloping demand curve and the perfect competitor faces a horizontal demand curve.

16) In order for a firm to receive monopoly profits in the long run, there must be
A) homogeneous products.
B) barriers to market entry.
C) free entry and exit to the market.
D) mutual interdependence among firms.

17) Which of the following is a barrier to entry?
A) patents
B) Canadian competition legislation
C) low fixed costs
D) diseconomies of scale

18) The demand curve faced by the pure monopolist
A) is the same as its marginal revenue curve.
B) is the market demand curve.
C) is perfectly inelastic.
D) lies below the marginal revenue curve.

19) A monopolist will earn negative economic profit when
A) ATC is completely above the demand curve.
B) ATC is completely below the demand curve.
C) AVC is a minimum.
D) AFC is very high.

20) Which of the following is a necessary condition for a firm to price discriminate?
A) Buyers in different markets must have the same elasticities of demand.
B) Resale of the product must be preventable.
C) The firm's marginal cost curve must be declining.
D) The firm must be a price-taker.

21) A problem with monopoly regulation using average cost pricing is that
A) firms may have reduced incentives to be cost efficient.
B) average costs are more difficult to calculate than marginal costs.
C) it does not allow investors to make a fair rate of return on investment.
D) firms have a reduced incentive to purchase capital equipment.

22) Economists criticize monopolies because monopolies
A) sell the product for more than consumers are willing to pay.
B) restrict output compared to a competitive situation.
C) always price discriminate.
D) always make excessive profits.

23) Price discrimination would most likely happen when the firm is selling
A) groceries B) electricity C) topsoil D) gasoline

24) Monopolistic competitors advertise because
A) the demand curves they face are very inelastic compared to other firms in the industry.
B) they produce goods that can be differentiated from the goods of other firms in the industry.
C) they have perfectly elastic demand curves
D) they can prevent new entrants if they advertise.

25) In the short run within monopolistic competition, the firm will produce where
A) P = MC. B) MR = ATC. C) MR = MC. D) MC = ATC.

26) Under monopolistic competition, there will be
A) one firm and two slightly differentiated products.
B) one firm and one product.
C) many firms and a standard, undifferentiated product.
D) many firms and a differentiated product.

27) In the short run, a monopolistic competitor
A) can make positive, negative, or zero economic profits.
B) always makes positive accounting profits.
C) always makes positive economic profits.
D) never makes positive or zero economic profits.

28) When firms make short-run profits in monopolistic competition, we expect to see
A) new firms trying to enter the industry, but unable to do so because of barriers to entry.
B) new firms enter the industry. The combined effect is to cause all firms to make zero profits in the long run.
C) existing firms increasing prices to try to capture larger profits.
D) existing firms increasing quantity of output to make zero profits.

29) In the long run there will not usually be economic profit in monopolistic competition because
A) input prices will be bid up.
B) production will not be at minimum average cost.
C) average total cost will shift up to meet the demand curve.
D) new firms will enter the industry.

30) In the long run in monopolistic competition, price will be
A) greater than the minimum ATC.
B) equal to the minimum ATC.
C) equal to MC.
D) equal to MR.

31) An oligopoly is a market situation in which
A) there is a single firm producing several varieties of a product.
B) all the sellers act independently of the others.
C) there are many firms producing a differentiated product.
D) there are few sellers and they recognize their interdependence.

32) In general, horizontal mergers would be expected to
A) increase competition in an industry.
B) reduce economic profits in an industry.
C) decrease the number of firms in an industry.
D) increase the number of firms in an industry.

33) The concentration ratio for an industry describes
A) the average size of the firms in an industry expressed as a percentage.
B) the total sales of any four firms in an industry.
C) the percentage of total industry sales contributed by the four largest firms.
D) the sales of the four largest firms divided by the sales of the eight largest firms.

34) In a zero-sum game
A) both players are better off at the end of the game.
B) both players collude to make both of them better off.
C) one player's losses are exactly offset by another player's gains.
D) both players are worse off at the end of the game.

35) An association of producers that fix common prices and set output quotas is known as a
A) common selling organization.
B) joint-marketing arrangement.
C) cartel.
D) trade association.

36) In game theory, a strategy that always yields the highest benefit for the player using it no matter what choice a rival makes is called the
A) dominant strategy.
B) cooperative strategy.
C) matrix strategy.
D) prisoners' strategy.

37) Game theory would treat a cartel under the topic of
A) dominant-strategy games.
B) cooperative games.
C) noncooperative games.
D) zero-sum games.

38) To deter entry, firms in the industry must signal to potential entrants that the price after entry would be
A) unchanged.
B) above the competitive price.
C) below the competitive price.
D) below the price the entrant would need to make a profit.

need to make profit
But can't

39) As the wage rate rises, other things constant, firms will choose to employ
A) more workers.
B) less capital.
C) the same number of workers.
D) fewer workers.

40) Coal and iron ore are complementary inputs in the manufacture of steel. An increase in the price of coal would lead to
A) an increase in the demand for iron ore as producers substitute more iron ore for coal in the production process.
B) a decrease in the demand for iron ore as steel manufacturers reduce production of steel.
C) an increase in the supply of iron ore as iron ore producers see an opportunity to expand their markets.
D) no change in the demand for iron ore since the steel makers must use both iron ore and coal if they are to make steel.

41) Holding other things constant, an increase in the use of capital in production would be expected to
A) increase the marginal productivity of labour.
B) decrease, but not proportionately, the marginal productivity of labour.
C) not affect the marginal productivity of labour.
D) decrease proportionately the marginal productivity of labour.

42) Profit-maximizing firms will hire additional units of labour until
A) the cost of hiring an extra worker would exceed the additional revenue generated by that worker.
B) the additional cost of hiring the last worker equals the marginal factor cost of the worker.
C) the extra revenue from hiring the last worker equals the marginal physical product of labour.
D) the extra cost from hiring the next worker would be greater than the price of the product.

43) Higher wages for college graduates than for high school graduates can be explained, in part, by
A) the backward bending labour supply curve.
B) the income and substitution effects.
C) labour market signaling.
D) the increases in the number of college graduates.

44) Lorenz curves show graphically the

A) demand for jobs.
B) supply of jobs.
C) elasticity of jobs.
D) income distribution.

45) An earnings profile of an individual over his or her lifetime is known as

A) the Lorenz curve.
B) the age-earnings cycle.
C) the marginal productivity theory.
D) the comparable worth doctrine.

46) In the absence of discrimination, as an individual's human capital investments increase, wages will generally

A) decrease.
B) increase.
C) remain constant.
D) fluctuate randomly.

47) One express purpose of the Canadian Employment Insurance (EI) program is to

A) tax high-income earners.
B) provide an income supplement for low-income earners.
C) assist the unemployed to find jobs.
D) help the federal government achieve a budget surplus.

48) An external cost such as pollution by a coal-fired power generation plant, is

A) a cost paid by consumers of the product.
B) a cost paid by producers of the product.
C) not a true opportunity cost of production.
D) a cost paid by a third party or by society at large.

⇒ every ones pays

49) Which of the following involves a positive externality?

A) jobs created by expansion of a local business
B) lower crime rates in communities with more highly educated residents
C) playing a boom box loudly in a crowded park
D) rush hour traffic

50) Social costs are

A) private costs plus any external costs.
B) the same as external costs.
C) costs incurred when common property is used.
D) costs associated with reaching and enforcing agreements.

51) The most efficient way to get firms to reduce pollution in most cases would be to
- A) set uniform emission standards, require all firms to meet the standards, and impose jail terms on executives of firms violating the standards.
- B) make the worst polluters shut down and go out of business.
- C) make them pay for the production of pollution and let them decide how to respond to the higher costs.
- D) provide firms and consumers with the information about the effects of their actions and encourage them to behave responsibly.

52) When private property rights do not exist or are weak,
- A) there will be no production.
- B) resource misuse is likely because there are few or no incentives to care for common property.
- C) externalities will be internalized by voluntary arrangements among a small group of parties.
- D) society will produce beyond the production possibilities frontier.

53) The provision of a legal system is an important economic function of the government because
- A) lawyers and judges tend to be high-income people.
- B) people need to feel safe when they go to work.
- C) the legal system affects how exchange takes place through its enforcement of contracts.
- D) the legal system affects the distribution of income by awarding damages in accident claims.

54) The free-rider problem is encountered when
- A) all individuals are willing to pay for what they consume.
- B) someone benefits from the consumption of a good without paying his or her full share.
- C) all individuals who consume a public good pay for it.
- D) all goods consumed and produced are private goods.

55) Scholarships awarded to students with high Grade Point Averages are an example of
- A) transfers in kind.
- B) transfer payments.
- C) public goods.
- D) externalities.

56) The economic functions of government differ from the political functions of government in that

A) the economic functions are carried out by provincial and municipal governments, while the political functions are carried out by the federal government.
B) the economic functions involve things that affect the way exchange is carried out while the political functions include policies that are intended to affect income redistribution.
C) the economic functions are carried out by the federal government, while the political functions are carried out by provincial and municipal governments.
D) the economic functions include policies that affect income redistribution, while the political functions involve things that affect the way exchange is carried out.

57) The largest source of receipts for the Canadian federal government is

A) corporate income taxes.
B) personal income taxes.
C) capital gains taxes.
D) import duties.

58) An example of a regressive tax is the

A) personal income tax.
B) inheritance tax.
C) corporate income tax.
D) goods and services tax.

GST
no really targeting low income However affects everyone

**Case 1: Perfect Competition**

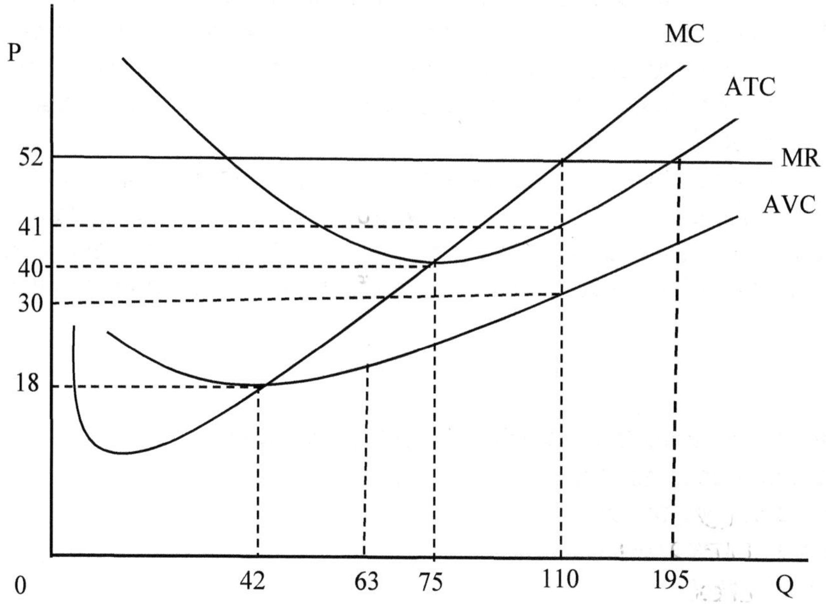


59) Using case 1 data, the profit-maximizing quantity of output for this firm is:
A) 42
B) 75
C) 110
D) 195

60) Using case 1 data, the selling price would be:
A) $42
B) $52
C) $30
D) $40

61) Using case 1 data, the average fixed cost (AFC) is:
A) $41
B) $10
C) $30
D) $11

62) Using case 1 data, the total cost (TC) is:
A) $4,510
B) $4,100
C) $4,400
D) $4,000

63) Using case 1 data, the total profit/loss is:
A) $2,420
B) $1,000
C) $1,100
D) $1,210

64) Using case 1 data, the shutdown point/price would be:

A) $41
B) $40
C) $30
D) $18

65) Using case 1 data, the breakeven point/price would be:

A) $41
B) $40
C) $30
D) $28

**Case 2: Monopoly**

| Q | P | TR | MR | TC | MC | ATC |
|---|---|---|---|---|---|---|
| 0 | | 0 | - | 200 | - | - |
| 10 | 120 | 1200 | 120 | 1000 | 80 | |
| 20 | 110 | 2200 | 100 | 1750 | 75 | |
| 30 | 100 | 3000 | 80 | 2450 | 70 | |
| 40 | 90 | 3600 | 60 | 3050 | 60 | |
| 50 | 80 | 4000 | 40 | 3700 | 65 | |
| 60 | 70 | 4200 | 20 | 4400 | 70 | |
| 70 | 60 | 4200 | 20 | 5400 | 100 | |

66) Using case 2 data, the profit-maximizing quantity for a monopolist is:

A) 30
B) 40
C) 50
D) 90

67) Using case 2 data, the profit-maximizing price for a monopolist is:

A) $40
B) $90
C) $100
D) $120

68) Using case 2 data, the profit for a monopolist is:

A) $0
B) $60
C) $550
D) $3600

69) Using case 2 data, the quantity for a price discriminating monopolist is:

A) 10
B) 40
C) 60
D) 70

70) Using case 2 data, the profit for a price discriminating monopolist is:

A) $-200
B) $0
C) $4,200
D) $13,800

71) Using case 2 data, the quantity for a regulated monopolist using marginal cost pricing is:

A) 10
B) 40
C) 60
D) 70

72) Using case 2 data, the price for a regulated monopolist using marginal cost pricing is:

A) $60
B) $70
C) $110
D) $120

73) Using case 2 data, the profit/loss for a regulated monopolist using marginal cost pricing is:

A) $-200
B) $0
C) $4,200
D) $13,800

74) The profit for a regulated monopolist using average cost pricing is:

A) always postive
B) cannot be determined
C) always negative
D) 0

**Case 3: Monopolistic Competition**

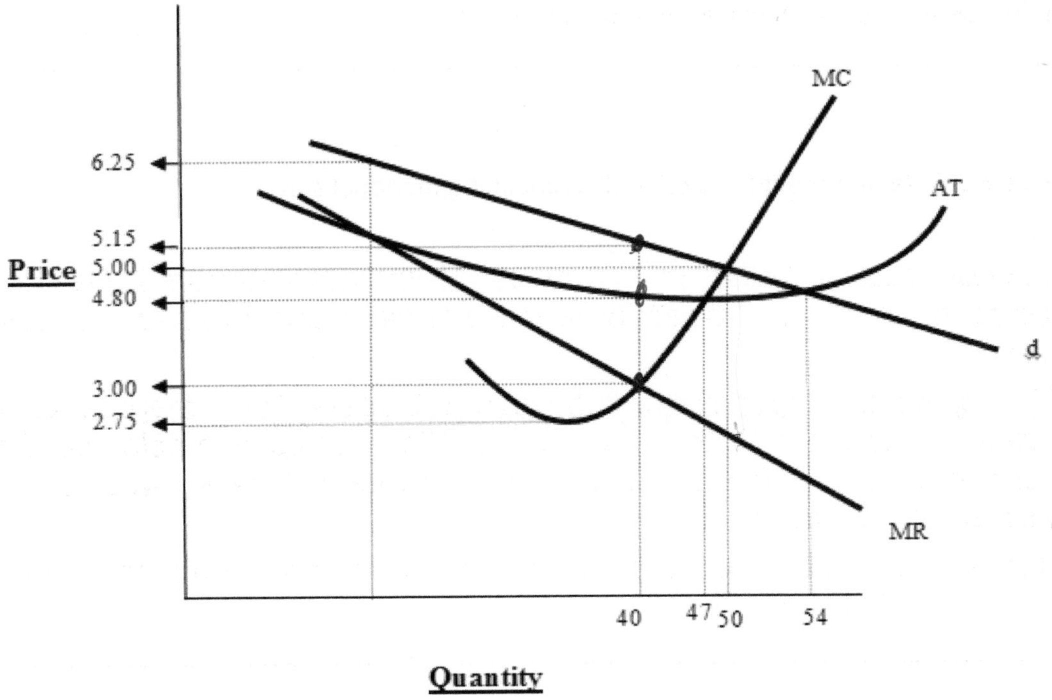


75) Using case 3 data, the profit-maximizing quantity for this monopolistically competitive firm is:
- A) 40
- B) 47
- C) 50
- D) 54

76) Using case 3 data, the profit-maximizing price for this monopolistically competitive firm is:
- A) $6.25
- B) $5.15
- C) $5.00
- D) $3.00

77) Using case 3 data, the average total cost for this monopolistically competitive firm is:
- A) $4.80
- B) $5.15
- C) $5.00
- D) $3.00

78) Using case 3 data, the total profit/loss for this monopolistically competitive firm is:
- A) $0
- B) $5.15
- C) $6
- D) $14

**Case 4: Market Structure**

Read the following article and answer the questions below:

> **Ottawa's wireless auction could cut cellphone rates**
>
> *CTV.ca News Staff - Updated: Wed. Nov. 28 2007 10:03 PM ET*
>
> Ottawa announced it will hold an auction of the wireless spectrum in May 2008, which could mean more competition and lower cellphone rates for Canadians next year.
>
> [...] 105 megahertz of spectrum will be sold to bidders. Forty megahertz will be set aside for newcomers to the industry. ...Companies who hold less than 10 per cent of revenues in Canada's wireless market will be allowed to bid for [that part of the spectrum.]
>
> The industry is currently dominated by three big players in Canada: Rogers Communication, Bell Mobility, and Telus.

79) Using case 4 data, the market structure is:
- A) perfect competition
- B) monopoly
- C) oligopoly
- D) monopolistic competition

80) Using case 4 data, if Rogers Communication lowers its cellphone rates, what will Bell and Telus do:
- A) increase their price.
- B) talk to each other and set as price.
- C) decrease their price.
- D) advertise more than Rogers.

81) Using case 4 data, if Rogers Communication raises its cellphone rates, what will Bell and Telus do:
- A) increase their price.
- B) talk to each other and set as price.
- C) decrease their price.
- D) keep their prices as they presently have them.

82) Using case 4 data, what does the government want to accomplish by forcing these 3 companies to share their wireless infrastructure?
- A) increase prices for everyone.
- B) get them to talk to each other and set a price (collude).
- C) increase the quantity provided by all 3 providers.
- D) increase their tax revenues because the price will increase.

**Solutions Final Exam**

1. A
2. D
3. A
4. B
5. B
6. B
7. A
8. C
9. A
10. B
11. A
12. D
13. B
14. A
15. D
16. B
17. A
18. B
19. A
20. B
21. A
22. B
23. B
24. B
25. C
26. D
27. A
28. B
29. D
30. B
31. D
32. C
33. C
34. C
35. C
36. A
37. B
38. D
39. D
40. B
41. A
42. A
43. C
44. D
45. B
46. B
47. C
48. D
49. B
50. A
51. C
52. B
53. C
54. B
55. B
56. B
57. B
58. D
59. C
60. B
61. D
62. A
63. D
64. D
65. B
66. B
67. B
68. C
69. C
70. D
71. C
72. B
73. A
74. D
75. A
76. B
77. A
78. D
79. C
80. C
81. D
82. C